Teacher's Annotated Edition

WORLD HISTORY
Perspectives on the Past

Larry S. Krieger

Social Studies Supervisor
Edison, New Jersey

Jim R. L. Coulon

Contributing Writer
San Diego, California

Published simultaneously in Canada

Printed in the United States of America

International Standard Book Number: 0-669-20190-1

1 2 3 4 5 6 7 8 9 0

D.C. Heath and Company

Lexington, Massachusetts
Toronto, Ontario

WORLD HISTORY

The one to COMPARE all others to . . .

WORLD HISTORY: PERSPECTIVES ON THE PAST surveys the panorama of human history from earliest times to the present. As you examine the text we invite you to:

COMPARE . . .

☐ **The readable style that brings the past to life**

The clear, lively writing style helps students follow the action and find the "story" in history. Each chapter opens with a dramatic event that relates to the chapter's theme. For example, the Athenian debate on how to meet a Persian attack (page 94) highlights democracy in ancient Greece. Joan of Arc's determination to raise the siege of Orleans (page 234) is linked to the development of nationalism in the late Middle Ages.

COMPARE . . .

☐ **The art program that enlivens as it teaches**

History is a written record of the past, but history has also been captured in paintings, sculptures, scrolls, photographs, and posters. WORLD HISTORY: PERSPECTIVES ON THE PAST makes full use of the rich visual sources of history. Students gain a broader understanding of the past through visual records of events such as the Battle of Hastings (page 221). At the same time, art conveys a vivid sense of family life (pages 126, 226, 276), sports (pages 99, 313, 570, 714), science (pages 180, 359, 564), religion (pages 73, 219, 357), and other aspects of human life. The world's artistic heritage is apparent in the landscapes and pottery of the Sung dynasty (page 266), in the powerful perspective skills of the Renaissance (page 330), in the vibrant colors of impressionism (page 569), and in the stark images of Picasso's "Guernica" (page 660).

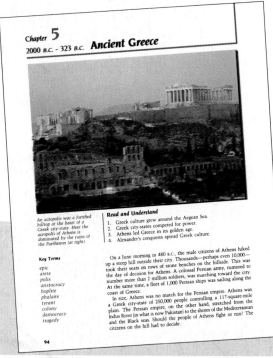

♦ "Comparing Pictures" uses photographs and captions to help students build higher level thinking skills. Here is an example of the Parthenon as it looks today, while an illustration shows it in the Age of Pericles.

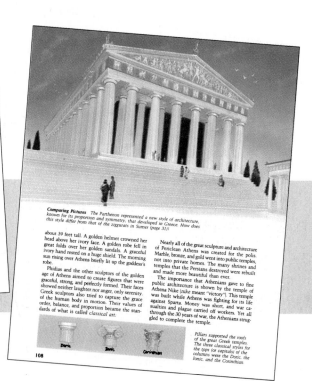

COMPARE . . .
☐ **The abundance of primary sources**

The past speaks for itself through the frequent quotations embedded in the narrative. Students will read the words of an anxious Sumerian schoolboy (page 26), the last plea of a Byzantine emperor (page 184), and the ringing speeches of Winston Churchill (page 669).

In addition, every chapter has a special feature called *Voice from the Past* that presents a longer extract from a historical source. These features are chosen from a variety of sources, including journals (page 308), letters (page 424), laws (page 443), poetry (page 239), and speeches (page 772). To help student comprehension, study questions accompany each *Voice from the Past* reading.

COMPARE . . .
☐ **Views of daily life that link past to present**

WORLD HISTORY: PERSPECTIVES ON THE PAST helps students make connections between life long ago and life today. The narrative is enriched by colorful accounts describing what people wore, what they ate, and how they made a living. Topics range from the exotic foods served at a Roman banquet (page 149) to occupations in Elizabethan London (pages 394–395).

In each chapter, a feature called *Daily Life* or *Economics in Daily Life* presents an invention, tool, or skill of the time. From tulips (page 374) to tunnels (page 714), from cosmetics (page 59) to canned food (page 462), students see how items from everyday life changed with the times.

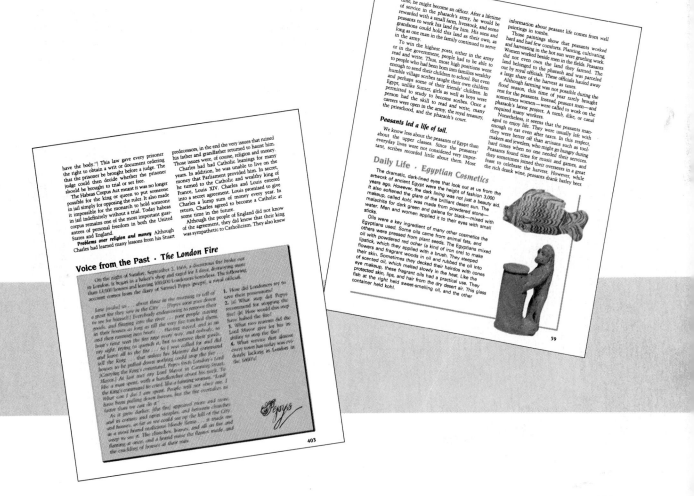

WORLD HISTORY

Gives students . . .

❏ A strong chronological framework

Students need to develop a sense of history's time scale. WORLD HISTORY: PERSPECTIVES ON THE PAST keeps chronology at the forefront. Besides the title of each chapter, dates identify the time span to be covered. Dates appear frequently in the text, not as isolated facts for memorization, but as aids to chronological understanding. At the beginning of each unit, a time line provides a summary of the key political/governmental, economic/technological, and sociological/cultural events of each time period studied.

❏ Maps for skill-building and reference

Just as students need to acquire a sense of chronology, they also need to develop an awareness of geography. More than 90 maps help students locate the cities, countries, and empires they are reading about. A Map Study question appears with every map to help students make use of geographic information.

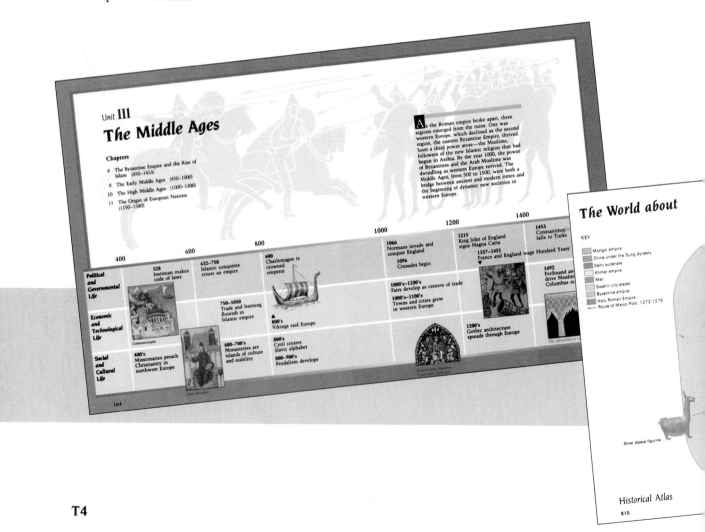

Unit III
The Middle Ages

Chapters

8 The Byzantine Empire and the Rise of Islam (450–1453)
9 The Early Middle Ages (450–1000)
10 The High Middle Ages (1000–1300)
11 The Origin of European Nations (1150–1580)

As the Roman empire broke apart, three regions emerged from the ruins. One was western Europe, which declined as the second region, the eastern Byzantine Empire, thrived. Soon a third power arose—the Muslims, followers of the new Islamic religion that had begun in Arabia. By the year 1000, the power of Byzantines and the Arab Muslims was dwindling as western Europe revived. The Middle Ages, from 500 to 1500, were both a bridge between ancient and modern times and the beginning of dynamic new societies in western Europe.

| | 400 | 600 | 800 | 1000 | 1200 | 1400 |

Political and Governmental Life
528 Justinian makes code of laws
632–750 Islamic conquests create an empire
800 Charlemagne is crowned emperor
1066 Normans invade and conquer England
1096 Crusades begin
1215 King John of England signs Magna Carta
1337–1451 France and England wage Hundred Years
1453 Constantinople falls to Turks
1492 Ferdinand and drive Muslim Columbus re

Constantinople

Economic and Technological Life
750–1050 Trade and learning flourish in Islamic empire
800's Vikings raid Europe
1000's–1200's Fairs develop as centers of trade
1000's–1100's Towns and cities grow in western Europe
1200's Gothic architecture spreads through Europe

The Alhambra at

Social and Cultural Life
400's Missionaries preach Christianity in northwest Europe
600–700's Monasteries are islands of culture and stability
800's Cyril creates Slavic alphabet
800–900's Feudalism develops

104

The World about

KEY

- Mongol empire
- China under the Sung dynasty
- Delhi sultanate
- Khmer empire
- Mali
- Swahili city-states
- Byzantine empire
- Holy Roman Empire
- → Route of Marco Polo, 1272-1275

Silver alpaca figurine

Historical Atlas

810

by D.C. Heath

a better perspective on time and place.

☐ **Geographic Themes in Every Unit Review**
Each Unit Review focuses on understanding one of the five geographic themes: location, place, interaction, movement, and regions. Students learn to apply these themes in a historical context. Map, chart, and graph visuals help illustrate these key geographic themes.

☐ **Handbook for Time and Place**
This handbook provides valuable background information for students on topics such as: the history of calendars, key terms for labeling time, using time lines, and understanding the five geographic themes. This teachable handbook includes section reviews to check students' comprehension.

◆ As a reference tool, *WORLD HISTORY: PERSPECTIVES ON THE PAST* offers a unique 16-page historical atlas. Each atlas page shows the world at a key period in history.

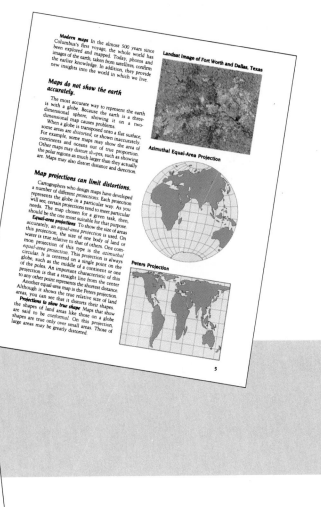

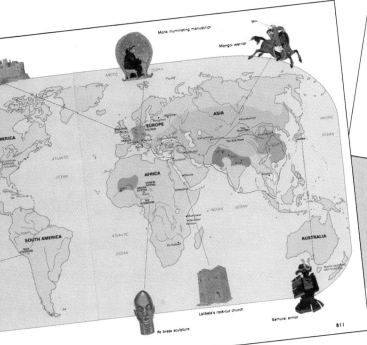

WORLD HISTORY

Gives students . . .

☐ **Chapters are introduced with**

♦ *Key Terms* highlighted to preview vocabulary from the chapter.

Chapter **12**
300 - 1650

Golden Ages in China and Japan

Emperor Yang-ti rides through the imperial gardens with some attendants, while others care for his water lilies.

Key Terms

gentry
steppe
khan
clan
samurai
shogun
daimyo

Read and Understand

1. Two great dynasties ruled China.
2. The Mongols conquered a vast empire.
3. China chose stability over change.
4. Japan developed a unique civilization.
5. Japan turned to isolation.

Day after day, the golden leaves of autumn fluttered lazily to the ground outside the palace of the Chinese emperor Yang-ti. Yet the trees in Yang-ti's garden remained as green as in the summertime. How could this be!

Watchful peasants were seated in the branches of every tree. Each peasant held a basket filled with artificial leaves made of green silk. Whenever a natural leaf fell, a peasant instantly replaced it with a silken leaf.

At the same time, on Yang-ti's huge artificial lake, other peasants paddled boats among the thousands of floating lotus flowers. Blossoms that had withered overnight were plucked off and replaced by delicate petals of white and pink silk. Thus did the ambitious Yang-ti, who

260

♦ *Read and Understand* guides students to better comprehension of chapter themes.

♦ A dramatic event related to the theme of the chapter.

♦ *Footnotes to History* offer interesting sidelights, including anecdotes, word origins, humor, and links to the present.

T6

♦ *City Tours* give students a closer look at cities important to world history.

fingernails long. (A two-inch fingernail showed clearly that its owner did no manual labor.) Finally, the scholar-official could use his special privileges to gain land and amass a fortune.

China continued to use the examination system for over 1,000 years. The system had its weaknesses. It did not weed out selfish or corrupt officials. Also, training in writing poetry and quoting Confucius was not always helpful in collecting taxes or supervising canal repairs.

With all its faults, however, the system gave China a remarkably intelligent governing class. No longer did a few ruling families control the country. Now talent was more important than high birth in winning power. As a result, many moderately wealthy families shared in China's government. Scholar-officials and their families formed a new class in Chinese society. This class is often described as the *gentry*, a large, well-to-do group of people who rank below nobles but above the common people.

Some scholars struggle with their exams, while others wait outside to learn if they passed.

Ch'ang-an was the T'ang capital.

The capital of T'ang China was Ch'ang-an, a city of about 2 million people. Ch'ang-an's layout showed the Chinese passion for order. Its walls, 18 feet high, formed a rectangle 6 miles long and 5 miles wide. The walls were carefully aligned with the cardinal points of the compass. In each wall were three evenly spaced gates. The streets within the city formed neat, rectangular blocks. The main avenue was almost 500 feet wide, about 5 times wider than New York's Fifth Avenue.

The imperial palace lay within a complex of palaces and beautifully landscaped parks. The stone-paved road that led to the main palace curved in the shape of a dragon's tail.

Booming drums regulated daily life in Ch'ang-an. At daybreak, the police who patrolled the streets beat on their drums to announce the opening of the city gates. At sunset, the markets closed and people scurried home to the beat of drums as the police locked the city gates. Anyone caught on the streets after the evening drums had sounded could be severely punished.

Within the city, more than 200 different trades and professions had their own sections. So did the various groups of foreigners—Jewish traders and shopkeepers, traders from India, musicians and dancers from Burma, Buddhist pilgrims from many lands, and caravan leaders from the deserts.

Shops in Ch'ang-an sold rugs from Persia, glassware from Syria, lapdogs from Samarkand (in central Asia), pine nuts from Korea, peacock feathers from Burma, and ivory and gems from Vietnam. Chinese women took up foreign fashions. Their silk gowns (tight bodice, plunging neckline, winglike shoulderpads) were modeled after Persian styles. Their hair was done up in the elaborate fashion begun by the princesses of Samarkand.

Once, China had been cut off from the rest of the world by oceans, mountains, and deserts. The T'ang emperors did not isolate themselves behind such barriers. Imperial armies guarded the Great Silk Road, which linked China to the west. Merchandise and travelers moved safely across it in both directions. Sea trade connected China to India and Southeast Asia. In fact, China was more open to foreign trade and influence during the T'ang years than at any other time in history.

263

Graceful lines and subtle colors were characteristic of Chinese landscape painting during the Sung dynasty. In pottery, colors were soft but rich, as in this bowl for narcissus bulbs.

comfort by unrolling a scroll to view the beauties of nature. When he had sat long enough with trees, waterfalls, and mountain mists, he rolled up the scroll and returned it to the cabinet.

Sung artists did not use brightly colored paints. Black ink was their favorite paint. Said one Sung artist, "Black is ten colors." Grace of line was at the heart of Sung art.

China led the world in technology.

During the years of the T'ang and the Sung dynasties, no other area of the world was China's equal in skilled workers, science, and technology. Three Chinese inventions—printing, gunpowder, and the compass—were destined to have a revolutionary impact on the rest of the world. All three originated during the T'ang dynasty and were fully developed during the Sung.

Printing The Chinese began to print books around the year 600. Printers first cut a block of wood the size of two book pages. Over the block they pasted a sheet of thin paper on which the text was written. Using the writing on the paper as a guide, they carved around the characters so that they stood out in relief. By brushing ink onto the carved block and pressing it onto blank sheets of paper, a printer could produce a copy

of the original page. In one day, an expert printer could make 2,000 copies.

Sometime in the Sung dynasty, probably in the 1040's, an inventor named Pi Sheng (bee shung) took the next logical step—movable type. He arranged the individual characters on an iron plate coated with sticky resin and tar to hold them in place. Thus, the same characters could be used over and over, instead of carving a new set for each page. (Europeans did not discover how to print books until 1450.)

Magnetic compass The Chinese also learned that a magnetized needle floating in a bowl of water always points north-south. They first used

Footnote to History

Beginning in Sung times, the Chinese considered it beautiful for women to have very tiny feet. Upper-class parents would wrap their daughter's feet in tight bandages when she was about five years old. As the child grew, the wrappings forced her foot to curl painfully until the toes and heel came together. Women whose feet had been bound could hobble only a few steps. For a man, having such a wife was a sign of wealth because she could do little household work.

266

by D.C. Heath

an organization that promotes learning

◆ Every map is accompanied by a Map Study exercise to help students gain proficiency in map skills.

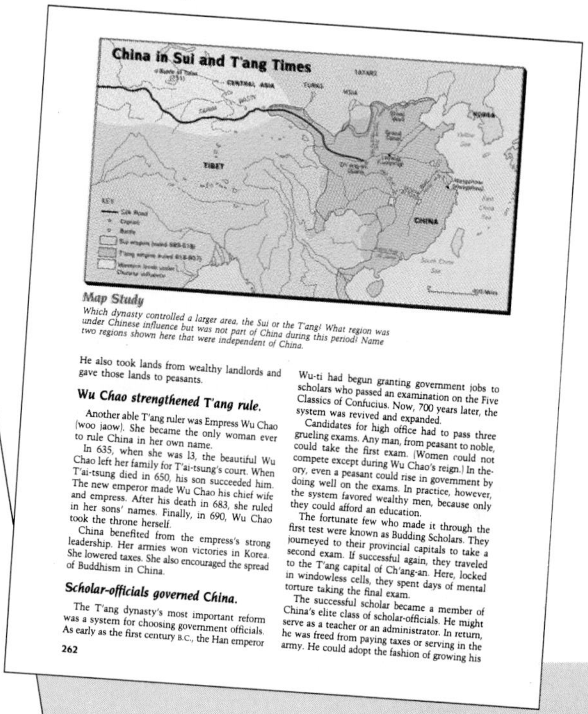

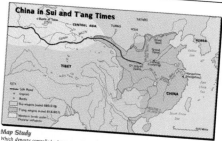

China in Sui and T'ang Times

Map Study

Which dynasty controlled a larger area, the Sui or the T'ang? What region was under Chinese influence but was not part of China during this period? Name two regions shown here that were independent of China.

[Reproduced textbook page spread: "A writing system developed."]

A writing system developed.

The earliest evidence of Chinese writing comes from Shang times. At Anyang and other Shang cities, archaeologists have found hundreds of animal bones and tortoise shells with written symbols scratched on them. These strange objects are known as oracle bones because priests used them to foretell the future. The writing on the oracle bones showed that people 3,500 years ago were part of the same cultural tradition that continues in China today. Some of the characters are very much like those in a modern Chinese newspaper.

In the Chinese method of writing, each character stands for an idea, not a sound. Recall that many of the Egyptian hieroglyphs stood for sounds in their spoken language. Sumerian cuneiform and the Phoenician alphabet also corresponded to spoken language. In contrast, there were practically no links between China's spoken language and its written language. One could read Chinese

without being able to speak a word of it. (This seems less strange when you think of our own number system. Both a French person and an American can understand the written equation 2 + 2 = 4, but an American may not understand the spoken statement, *"Deux et deux font quatre."*)

The Chinese system of writing had one great advantage. People in all parts of China could learn the same system of writing, even if their spoken languages were very different. Thus, the Chinese written language was very important in unifying a large and diverse land.

The disadvantage of the Chinese system was the enormous number of written characters to be memorized. To be barely literate, a person needed to know at least 1,000 characters. To be a true scholar, one needed to know between 5,000 and 10,000 characters. For centuries, this severely limited the number of literate, educated Chinese. As a general rule, a noble's children learned to write, but a peasant's children did not.

Economics in Daily Life · The Most Treasured Fabric

According to legend, silk was discovered by the 14-year-old empress Hsi Ling-shi, who lived around 2500 B.C. Hsi Ling-shi was walking one day among the mulberry trees near the palace. A few days earlier, the trees had been covered with caterpillars eating the mulberry leaves. Now the caterpillars hung from the branches in mummylike cocoons.

Curious about the cocoons, Hsi Ling-shi plucked one from a branch and took it home. She dropped it in a pot of water and watched it soften into a loose, tangled web. When she picked up the web, she found she could unravel it like a skein of yarn to form a single long thread of silk.

The legend may or may not be true. The process of making silk became China's best-kept secret for the next 3,000 years. Foreign gold and silver poured into China from the silk trade. To pass on the secret of silk-making to the outside world was treason, punishable by death.

Silk was one of the first items carried in long-distance trade. During the Han dynasty, caravans loaded with silk began to travel the Silk Road, the long route between China and the Mediterranean area. The Chinese monopoly on silk production lasted until about A.D. 550, when Europeans smuggled mulberry seeds and silkworm eggs out of China. Silk still remained important in trade with the East.

80

◆ *Economics in Daily Life* identifies and applies economic concepts in a historical context.

❑ **Thorough section reviews**

◆ Each section concludes with a Section Review.

◆ Students begin by defining key terms and identifying important people, places, and events.

◆ Review questions ask students to recall basic facts and main ideas.

◆ Each Section Review includes Critical Thinking questions that encourage students to go beyond the level of factual recall.

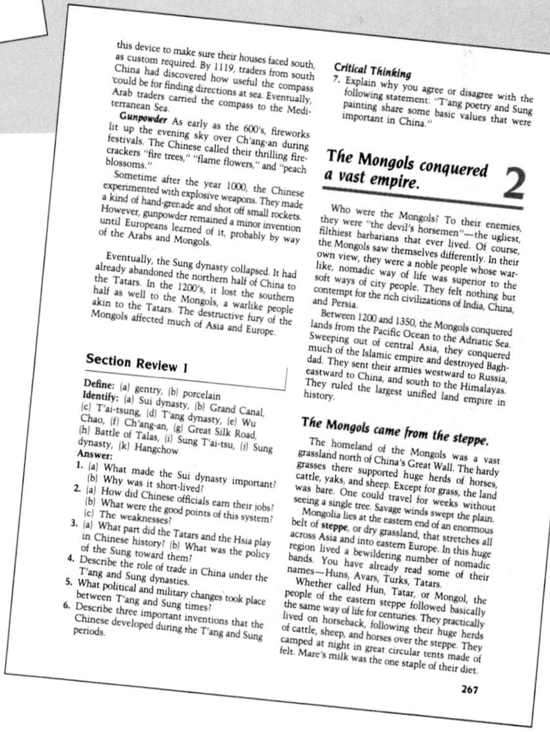

[Reproduced textbook page: page 262]

He also took lands from wealthy landlords and gave those lands to peasants.

Wu Chao strengthened T'ang rule.

Another able T'ang ruler was Empress Wu Chao (woo jaow). She became the only woman ever to rule China in her own name.

In 635, when she was 13, the beautiful Wu Chao left her family for T'ai-tsung's court. When T'ai-tsung died in 650, his son succeeded him. The new emperor made Wu Chao his chief wife and empress. After his death in 683, she ruled in her sons' names. Finally, in 690, Wu Chao took the throne herself.

China benefited from the empress's strong leadership. Her armies won victories in Korea. She lowered taxes. She also encouraged the spread of Buddhism in China.

Scholar-officials governed China.

The T'ang dynasty's most important reform was a system for choosing government officials. As early as the first century B.C., the Han emperor

Wu-ti had begun granting government jobs to scholars who passed an examination on the Five Classics of Confucius. Now, 700 years later, the system was revived and expanded.

Candidates for high office had to pass three grueling exams. Any man, from peasant to noble, could take the first exam. (Women could not compete except during Wu Chao's reign.) In theory, even a peasant could rise in government by doing well on the exams. In practice, however, the system favored wealthy men, because only they could afford an education.

The fortunate few who made it through the first test were known as Budding Scholars. They journeyed to their provincial capitals to take a second exam. If successful again, they traveled to the T'ang capital of Ch'ang-an. Here, locked in windowless cells, they spent days of mental torture taking the final exam.

The successful scholar became a member of China's elite class of scholar-officials. He might serve as a teacher or an administrator. In return, he was freed from paying taxes or serving in the army. He could adopt the fashion of growing his

262

[Reproduced textbook page: page 267]

this device to make sure their houses faced south, as custom required. By 1119, traders from south China had discovered how useful the compass could be for finding directions at sea. Eventually, Arab traders carried the compass to the Mediterranean Sea.

Gunpowder As early as the 600's, fireworks lit up the evening sky over Ch'ang-an during festivals. The Chinese called their thrilling firecrackers "fire trees," "flame flowers," and "peach blossoms."

Sometime after the year 1000, the Chinese experimented with explosive weapons. They made a kind of hand-grenade and shot off small rockets. However, gunpowder remained a minor invention until Europeans learned of it, probably by way of the Arabs and Mongols.

Eventually, the Sung dynasty collapsed. It had already abandoned the northern half of China to the Tatars. In the 1200's, it lost the southern half as well to the Mongols, a warlike people akin to the Tatars. The destructive fury of the Mongols affected much of Asia and Europe.

Section Review 1

Define: (a) gentry, (b) porcelain
Identify: (c) T'ai-tsung, (d) Grand Canal, (e) Sui dynasty, (f) Ch'ang-an, (g) Wu Chao, (h) T'ang dynasty, (i) Wu Chao, (h) Battle of Talas, (i) Sung T'ai-tsu, (j) Sung dynasty, (k) Hangchow
Answer:
1. (a) What made the Sui dynasty important? (b) Why was it short-lived?
2. (a) How did Chinese officials earn their jobs? (b) What were the good points of this system? (c) The weaknesses?
3. (a) What part did the Tatars and the Hsia play in Chinese history? (b) What was the policy of the Sung toward them?
4. Describe the role of trade in China under the T'ang and Sung dynasties.
5. What political and military changes took place between T'ang and Sung times?
6. Describe three important inventions that the Chinese developed during the T'ang and Sung periods.

Critical Thinking
7. Explain why you agree or disagree with the following statement. "T'ang poetry and Sung painting share some basic values that were important in China."

The Mongols conquered a vast empire. [2]

Who were the Mongols? To their enemies, they were "the devil's horsemen"—the ugliest, filthiest barbarians that ever lived. Of course, the Mongols saw themselves differently. In their own view, they were a noble people whose warlike, nomadic way of life was superior to the soft ways of city people. They felt nothing but contempt for the rich civilizations of India, China, and Persia.

Between 1200 and 1350, the Mongols conquered lands from the Pacific Ocean to the Adriatic Sea. Sweeping out of central Asia, they conquered much of the Islamic empire and destroyed Baghdad. They sent their armies westward to Russia, eastward to China, and south to the Himalayas. They ruled the largest unified land empire in history.

The Mongols came from the steppe.

The homeland of the Mongols was a vast grassland north of China's Great Wall. The hardy grasses there supported huge herds of horses, cattle, yaks, and sheep. Except for grass, the land was bare. One could travel for weeks without seeing a single tree. Savage winds swept the plain.

Mongolia lies at the eastern end of an enormous belt of **steppe**, or dry grassland, that stretches all across Asia and into eastern Europe. In this huge region lived a bewildering number of nomadic bands. You have already read some of their names—Huns, Avars, Turks, Tatars.

Whether called Hun, Tatar, or Mongol, the people of the eastern steppe followed basically the same way of life for centuries. They practically lived on horseback, following their huge herds of cattle, sheep, and horses over the steppe. They camped at night in great circular tents made of felt. Mare's milk was the one staple of their diet.

267

WORLD HISTORY

Gives students . . . extensive review opportunities.

☐ **Chapter reviews feature:**

◆ Summaries of each section;

◆ Reinforcement for names, dates, places and events;

◆ Timelines illustrating major events in the chapter.

☐ **Unit reviews feature:**

◆ Geographic Themes related to unit content;

◆ Suggestions for thinking, speaking and writing about history.

◆ Skills Practice in the research techniques used by historians.

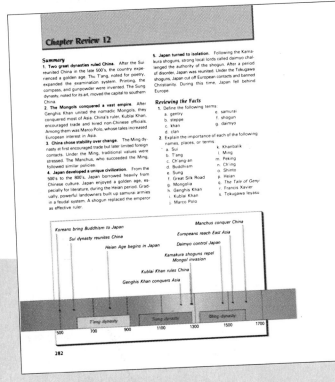

◆ Critical Thinking Skills to analyze, compare, and evaluate events;

◆ Research and Reporting Skills such as outlining, notetaking and preparing a research paper;

◆ and Basic Skills important to studying world history.

by D.C. Heath

Gives teachers . . . superior instructional support

☐ **An outstanding Lesson Planner,** found in the Teacher's Edition, assists teachers in developing lessons by providing background information to enrich the text, teaching strategies to encourage comprehension and critical thinking, and a lesson design in concert with your district's instructional goals.

The Lesson Planner features

◆ *Section Objectives,* tied to major chapter headings that guide teaching of key concepts and themes.

◆ *Teaching Strategies* that directly support objectives with in-depth suggestions for

- Discussing History
- Using Geographic Themes
- Teaching with Pictures
- Skill Building
- Integrating Geography in History
- Relating Past to Present
- Analyzing a Quote
- Transferring Ideas

◆ *Guided and Independent Practice* that correlates in-text and ancillary materials by section for optimum use.

◆ *Enrichment* that provides suggested activities to deepen and extend the learning, using primary sources and researching techniques.

◆ *Reteaching and Evaluation* that suggest means to review and evaluate concepts and skills presented in each chapter and unit of the text. This includes references to both the Teacher's Resource File and Computer Test Bank.

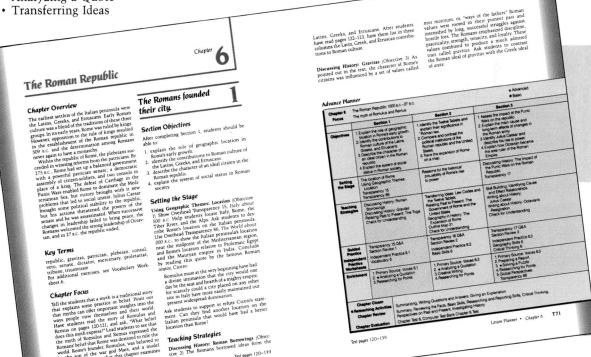

WORLD HISTORY

Gives teachers . . . superior instructional support

☐ **A comprehensive resource package**

♦ *Teacher's Annotated Edition* features the complete Lesson Planner, additional background information, and references to ancillary components.

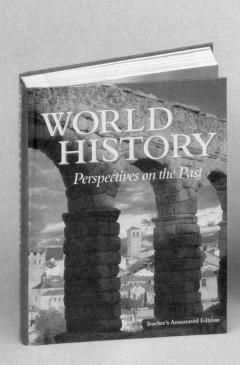

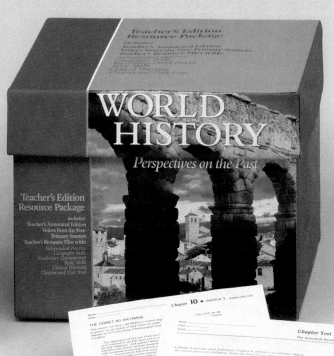

♦ *Teacher's Resource File* maximizes use of support and evaluation materials by organizing them as you do, by chapter. Each Resource File folder includes the following materials in copymaster format:

- Independent Practice
- Geography Skills
- Vocabulary Development
- Primary Sources (Voices from the Past)
- Basic Skills
- Critical Thinking
- Chapter and Unit Tests

In addition, you'll find Outline Maps and Sample Overhead Transparencies in the Resource File.

by D.C. Heath

◆ *Computer Test Bank*, with Teacher's Guide, allows you to customize tests to match topics emphasized in your course.

◆ *Voices from the Past* is a collection of primary-source readings with study questions in a pupil workbook format. A Teacher's Annotated Edition is available.

◆ *Overhead Transparencies* is a set of 96 full-color maps and diagrams ideal for full-group instruction. Activity suggestions accompany each transparency.

Alternative Content Approaches

WORLD HISTORY: PERSPECTIVES ON THE PAST offers a chronological survey of world history that covers all major regions. However, if your curriculum calls for a more specialized approach, you can base your course on selected chapters and sections of this text. The table below outlines five alternative approaches: Western Civilization, European History, Nonwestern Civilization, World History to 1500, and World History since 1500.

	Western Civilization	European History	Nonwestern Civilization	World History to 1500	World History since 1500
Suggested Chapter Sequence	1	5	1	1	15
	2	6	2	2	16
	3	7	3	3	17
	5	9	4	4	18
	6	10	8	5	19
	7	11	10 (5)	6	20
	9	15	11 (5)	7	21
	10	16	12	8	22
(Numbers in parentheses refer to sections within the chapter.)	11	17	13	9	23
	15	18	14	10	24
	16	19	15 (4)	11	25
	17	20	19 (2)	12	26
	18	21	23 (3)	13	27
	19	22	24 (1)	14	28
	20	23 (1, 2, 4)	25	15	29
	21	24 (1, 2, 3)	27		30
	22	25 (1)	28		31
	23	26	29		32
	24	27	31		33
	25 (1)	28	32 (3)		34
	26	30	34		35
	27	31	35		36
	28	32 (1, 2)	36		37
	30	33	37 (1, 2)		
	31				
	32 (1,2)				
	33				
	37				

World History: Perspectives on the Past by D.C. Heath

Program Goal

WORLD HISTORY: PERSPECTIVES ON THE PAST offers students and teachers a rich, exciting full year study of world history from prehistoric times to the present. The lively, narrative writing style is widely applauded by students. The Teacher's Edition, with its Lesson Planner and support components, allows teachers to create outstanding lessons that bring the people, places, and events of world history to life.

Student Edition

WORLD HISTORY: PERSPECTIVES ON THE PAST, by D.C. Heath, brings the study of the world to life. The text combines an action-filled narrative that explains the significance of events and themes with high-interest features to encourage students to read about, empathize with, and understand the people who have shaped world history. The text gives comprehensive coverage to the places, events, trends, ideas, and personalities of world history, telling the story of the development of the world civilizations in a concrete, vivid style that high school students will enjoy. Developments in the humanities and sciences are part of this story, as are themes from geography and economics. Following are features of the student text.

◆ **Handbook for Time and Place** starts the student text by establishing background knowledge on information such as the history of calendars, vocabulary used for labeling time, reading time lines, working with maps and map projections, and understanding the five geographic themes.

◆ **Units** open with a time line and period silhouette that introduce the key political, governmental, economic, technological, sociological, and cultural events of the period being studied. Photographs of people and places, as well as reproductions of art from the unit, are placed with the time line to stimulate students' interest and prepare students for the exciting journey on which their reading of the unit will lead them.

◆ **Chapters** begin with a dramatic event, story, or vignette from the time period that draws students into the chapter and invites them to read on. This opening story is enhanced by a large photograph or reproduction of a work of art and an identification of the chronological time period being studied. To aid students' comprehension and for pre-reading discussion, the chapter opener includes "Key Terms," vocabulary defined in the chapter and glossary, and "Read and Understand," a preview of the main themes covered in the chapter.

◆ **Sections** divide chapters into manageable, understandable lessons. Sections conclude with a review that asks students to define vocabulary; identify key people, places, and events; and think critically about what they have read.

◆ **Illustrations** contribute significantly to enlivening the text for students. Rich reproductions of paintings, sculptures, scrolls, photographs, and posters as well as a variety of charts, graphs, and diagrams add to the drama and to students' comprehension of key events and trends in world history. The illustrations help students visualize what life was like, understand the role of art and religion in daily life, and build a record of the events that shaped the world. Captions accompanying certain illustrations are called *Comparing Pictures*. These captions ask students to use critical thinking skills as they compare and contrast visuals in the text.

◆ **Primary Sources** and quotations are embedded throughout the text narrative. In addition, every chapter contains a special feature called "Voice from the Past." This feature draws on diaries, letters, speeches, poetry, and legal documents to give students a real sense of the times in an authentic voice. Questions accompany these primary source readings so students can monitor their comprehension. This feature can be enriched with additional readings, one for each section of the pupil text, found in the Voices from the Past Resource Book.

◆ **Maps** placed throughout the pupil text strengthen students' understanding of geography as well as map reading skills as they study history. Map Study questions accompany each map to help students focus on the relationship between time and place.

◆ **Daily Life** is presented in another feature appearing in every chapter. Here students gain a sense of the differences between life long ago and life today. The material in these features focuses on aspects of life that are of high interest to students.

◆ **Chapter Reviews** allow students to prepare for formalized testing and to further develop skills. A *Summary* recaps each section; *Reviewing the Facts* reinforces names, dates, places, and events; A *Time line* illustrates major events in the chapter; *Basic Skills* reviews important skills for studying world history; *Researching and Reporting Skills* helps students research, plan, and present oral and written research projects; *Critical Thinking* provides opportunities to analyze, compare, and evaluate events; *Perspectives on Past and Present* encourages the transfer of ideas from times long ago to the present; and *Investigating History* suggests special interest topics to curious, motivated students.

◆ **Unit Reviews** include instruction on the five *Geographic Themes*; *Understanding History* reviews details related to people, places, and events; *Critical Thinking* challenges students to use higher level thinking skills in relation to the unit; *Making Decisions* looks at the impact of critical decisions made by world leaders and everyday people on world history; *Continuity and Change* focuses on major historic themes to provide a transition from one unit to the next.

◆ A **Historical Atlas** is included in the reference section of the student text. It includes eight 2-page maps, each highlighting a key period of world history.

Teacher's Support Materials

Teacher's Annotated Edition

The Teacher's Edition of WORLD HISTORY: PERSPECTIVES ON THE PAST features a comprehensive Lesson Planner. Using research on effective teaching models, this unique tool helps teachers create high quality lessons that meet the needs of a wide variety of students. The Lesson Planner contains the elements that follow.

◆ **Chapter Overview** supplies background information, based on author research, to help the teacher present the chapter.

◆ **Advance Planner** is a chart that gives teachers a clear, graphic presentation of the objectives of each section, suggested teaching strategies, and a correlation of the ancillary materials that may be used to support those objectives.

◆ **Key Terms** identify the vocabulary students should know to fully comprehend the chapter.

◆ **Chapter Focus** is designed to help the teacher use the introductory materials, such as the art and dramatic events, to get lessons off to a successful start.

◆ **Section Objectives** are tied to major section headings that always teach a specific period of history.

◆ **Setting the Stage** also relates to section objectives and sets goals for instruction.

◆ **Teaching Strategies** are a bank of strategies teachers may draw upon to create dynamic, exciting lessons. The number and diversity of strategies enable teachers to accommodate their own teaching styles and interests. The Teaching Strategies are: *Discussing History, Using Geographic Themes, Teaching with Pictures, Skill Building, Geography in History,*

Economics in History, Relating Past to Present, Analyzing a Quotation, Transferring Ideas, and *Writing about History.*

◆ **Check for Understanding** allows teachers to monitor and adjust their teaching.

◆ **Practice** is designed for both guided and independent practice. This part of the Lesson Planner outlines support materials found in the Resource File.

◆ **Enrichment** challenges more able students with "Voices from the Past" primary source readings. **Enrichment** also suggests ways students can do outside research and writing on a topic pertinent to that section.

◆ **Chapter Closer** helps teachers bring lessons to a successful ending.

◆ Complete **Answers** to Section, Chapter, and Unit Reviews are found in the Lesson Planner.

◆ **On-page annotations** throughout the Teacher's Edition add useful background information for the teacher and answers to questions in captions for Map Study, Reading a Graph, Reading a Table, and Comparing Pictures.

Teacher's Resource File

The Teacher's Resource File for WORLD HISTORY: PERSPECTIVES ON THE PAST is a well-organized system that provides ancillary teaching support. A resource file folder for each chapter contains the resources teachers look for to meet the needs of a wide variety of students.

◆ **Basic Skills** provide students with additional practice on reading and interpreting graphs, tables, diagrams, cartoons, and maps.

◆ **Vocabulary Development** spotlights key vocabulary words from the text and provides exercises for students to develop a better understanding of these words, their meanings, and usage.

◆ **Geography Skills** support the map and globe skills students need to understand the important relationship between history and geography.

◆ **Critical Thinking Skills** move students beyond literal comprehension of events and times to higher-level reasoning about the meaning and significance of events and times. Worksheets focus on skills essential for decision making such as analyzing sources and evidence; recognizing point of view, bias, stereotypes, and generalizations; and asking effective questions as about history.

◆ **Primary Source** readings called "Voices from the Past" are provided to accompany every section of the text. These materials challenge able students to understand the lives and times of major figures in world history. The "Voices from the Past" primary sources are also available in a student workbook format.

◆ **Independent Practice** allows students to work on their own to review the content of each chapter. A variety of formats makes the exercises interesting and useful for chapter review and test preparation.

◆ **Testing** for chapters and units is also included in the resource file folders. Two-page tests for chapters and units ask students to respond to a variety of test items including multiple choice, matching, fill-in, short answer, and essay questions.

There are additional folders in the Resource File with Outline Maps, sample Overhead Transparencies, Research Skills Handbook, Answer Keys, Program Bibliography, and a Student Atlas.

Overhead Transparencies

Overhead transparencies are a set of 96 full-color transparencies of historical maps, charts, and diagrams. Each transparency is accompanied by suggested activities for basic and advanced groups.

Computer Test Bank

The Computer Test Bank, including a Teacher's Guide, program disks and back-up disks, allows teachers to customize the testing program to match the emphasis of their course. Test items are designed for varying ability levels and with different types of items.

Lesson Planner

Table of Contents

Handbook For Time and Place

Historians need ways to represent time.

I

Summary

Calendars allow historians to measure the passage of time, to place events in sequence, and to determine accurate dates. In this text, years are labeled B.C. ("before Christ") and A.D. ("anno domini"). The text also uses the terms *decade* (10 years), *century* (100 years), and *millenium* (1,000 years). Broad zones of time are called ages and eras.

Objectives

Students should be able to:

1. explain why historians need ways to represent time.
2. describe different calendars in use in the world today.
3. explain the difference between B.C. and A.D.
4. use and make time lines.

Setting the Stage

Discussing History: Ways to Represent Time (Objective 1) Write the following list of objects on the chalkboard: coins, newspapers, birth certificates, diplomas, receipts, and grave stones. Ask your students to examine this list and determine the one characteristic the objects have in common (each contains a date). Ask your students to list reasons why dates are important. For example, why does each listed item have a date? How would the absence of a date affect each item? Explain that historians use dates to determine when events occurred and to place events into a correct sequence. This section describes how modern historians measure time.

Teaching Strategies

Discussing History: Calendars (Objective 2) Explain that people throughout history have invented different systems for measuring time. For example, the Jewish calendar measures time from the year in which Jews believe God created

the world. In contrast, the Muslim calendar begins with the year in which Muhammad founded their religion. The ancient Greek geographer Eratosthenes invented a calendar based on the Olympic Games, called Olympiads, which occurred at regular four year intervals. Eratosthenes simply numbered the Olympiads from the first (held in 776 B.C.) to the most recent. If we were still using his system, 1988 would be the first year of Olympiad 692.

Discussing History: B.C. and A.D. (Objective 3) Explain that all calendars need some fixed point from which to count the passage of time. Modern historians use the birth of Jesus as a common fixed point. Use the information provided in the section, "Historians label time in various ways," to explain the distinction between B.C. and A.D.

Skill Building: Using Time Lines (Objective 4) Direct students' attention to the time line on page 3. Explain that this time line is a chart that measures time. Have students examine the time line to determine how much time each unit represents (100 years). Then ask them to find the dates that mark the beginning and end of this time line (400 B.C. and A.D. 2000). Explain that most time lines also include specific dates that mark important events. For example, the time line on page 3 locates the birth of Jesus in the year 1.

Practice

Lead a guided discussion of the questions on page 3. (Answers are below.)

Define:
(a) ten-year period (b) hundred-year period (c) thousand-year period (d) and (e) broad time zone in which people shared patterns of thought and life

Answer:

1. (a) Christian or Common Era system (b) It will be the 5,761st year since the creation of the world, according to Jewish teachings. (c) It will be that many years since the Muslim religion was founded.
2. (a) 736 B.C. (b) A.D. 12 (c) A.D. 1750
3. (a) 7th century B.C. (b) 21st century (c) 15th
4. century
   Starting, ending dates; important events
5. Change is gradual and reaches people in different places at different times.

6. (a) Students may take a variety of approaches, all of which should focus as much as possible on dominant trends. (Nuclear Age, Industrial Era, Computer Age, Age of Ecology, Age of Superpowers) (b) Few labels can account for the whole world, traditional and industrial societies alike. Exceptions: Age of Nuclear Threat, Age of Population Glut

Enrichment Activities

1. **Making a Bulletin Board** Divide your class into committees. Explain that during the course of the year, each committee will create a number of bulletin boards. Ask your first committee to create a display showing a number of dated objects.

2. **Making a Time Line** Ask your students to make a time line entitled, "My Life Thus Far." Their time lines should include specific units of time, particular dates, and several important events.

3. **Researching for Bonus Points** Award bonus points to students who can answer this question: Who invented A.D.? (A.D. was invented by a monk named Dionysius Exiguus ["the little"] in the year we call A.D. 525.)

Historians use maps to represent place. II

Summary

Historical events occur in physical settings. Historians use maps to depict these settings. The mapmakers' problem is in making an accurate map of a three-dimensional sphere on a flat two-dimensional surface without causing distortions of shape, distance, size, and directions. Mapmakers have designed a number of projections to help overcome these distortions; however, no single projection can eliminate all distortions.

Objectives

Students should be able to:

1. describe the contributions the ancient Greeks and early explorers made to geography.
2. explain the characteristics of equal-area, conformal, and equidistant projections.

Setting the Stage

Ask your students to recall the last time they used a map and list their answers on the chalkboard. Ask students to list some reasons why historians use maps. Compare and contrast the two lists. This section begins with an overview of the long history of mapmaking and then looks at how mapmakers deal with the problem of representing a round object on a flat surface.

Teaching Strategies

Discussing History: Mapmaking (Objective 1) Review the contributions made by Eratosthenes, Hipparchus, Ptolemy, and European sea captains. Your students might be interested to learn that Ptolemy worked in the famous library in Alexandria between A.D. 127 and A.D. 150. He wrote a famous eight-volume study entitled *A Guide to Geography* that remained an authoritative source for over 1,000 years. Unfortunately, Ptolemy's book included a number of errors. For example, he badly underestimated both the size of the Atlantic Ocean and the earth's circumference. Ptolemy's errors later encouraged Columbus in his attempt to reach the Indies by sailing west across the Atlantic Ocean.

Skill Building: Using Different Projections (Objective 2) Explain that an accurate flat map would have the following four properties: 1) Landforms would be depicted with their true shapes; 2) the scale of distance would be the same for all parts of the map; 3) landforms would be depicted with their correct sizes; and 4) directions would be the same for all points on the map. Emphasize that no world map can have all four of these properties. Review the advantages and disadvantages of each of the projections discussed in the text.

Practice

Lead a guided discussion of the questions on page 6. (Answers are below.)

Define:
(a) to show inaccurately; (b) a way of representing the globe on a flat surface; (c) a projection designed to accurately show the size of an area; (d) a projection designed to show the true shape of an area; (e) a circular projection centered on a single point on the globe; (f) projections that accurately maintain distances.

Identify:
(a) Greek geographer who conceived of the earth as a sphere; (b) Greek geographer who developed a

system of grids to locate places on the earth; **(c)** sea captain who drew careful maps of the lands he explored; **(d)** Dutch cartographer who invented one of the first conformal projections.

Answer:

1. The ancient Greeks made the first attempts to present the world in an accurate and systematic way.
2. They charted coastlines and extended the boundaries of the known world.
3. It is difficult to show a three-dimensional sphere on a two-dimensional map.
4. The most common distortions are size, shape, distance, and direction.
5. Equal-area projections show how the size of one body of land or water is true relative to that of others. The Mercator projection accurately shows the shapes of land in the low and middle latitudes. Equidistant projections accurately represent distances. The azimuthal equidistant projection accurately shows both direction and distance.
6. Accurate maps are vital in an age of global transportation and communication.

Enrichment Activities

1. **Preparing a Report** Geographers have invented a number of different projections. Ask each student to prepare a report and illustration of one of the following projections: Goode's Interrupted Equal-Area Projection, Polar Projection, Sinusoidal Projection, Robinson Projection, and the Gall-Peters Projection.

2. **Researching a Topic** Ask advanced students to prepare a report on the Landsat satellite program. Their report should include a description of the program's history, an explanation of the types of equipment used by the Landsat satellites, a summary of the program's major discoveries, and an assessment of the program's impact on modern cartography.

3. **Researching for Bonus Points** Award bonus points to students who can answer this question: How did Eratosthenes calculate the earth's circumference? (Eratosthenes began with two facts—he knew that the earth was a sphere and he also knew that a straight pole at Aswân casts no shadow on June 22nd, the date of the summer solstice. Eratosthenes began by measuring the angle of a shadow at Alexandria on June 22. The angle measured 7° 12′ or 1/50th of a circle. Eratosthenes correctly reasoned that the distance from Alexandria to Aswân must be 1/50th of the earth's circumference.)

Historians use ideas from geography. III

Summary

Place is important to both historians and geographers. These two groups share many ideas about the world, among which are five basic themes or topics: location, place, human-environment interacton, movement, and region. These five themes provide ways for thinking about the world of the past, as well as the world of the present.

Objectives

Students should be able to:

1. explain the distinction between absolute and relative location.
2. identify location, place, human-environment interaction, movement, and region as important geographic themes.

Setting the Stage

Write the following five questions on the chalkboard:

1. Where is a place located?
2. What are the place's physical and human characteristics?
3. How have people interacted with their environment in that place?
4. How do people, goods, and ideas move from place to place?
5. What qualities does a place have that it also shares with other places?

Ask students to explain why these questions are important to both geographers and historians. Explain that each of these questions is a major theme or topic studied by modern geographers. This section introduces these themes and explains how historians use them.

Teaching Strategies

Skill Building: Using Absolute and Relative Location (Objective 1) Emphasize the distinction between absolute and relative location. In order to reinforce these concepts, ask students to use a map to determine the absolute location of your state capital. Then ask them to describe your state capital's location relative to Washington, D.C.

Skill Building: Using The Five Themes (Objective 2) Use the text's discussion on the Rock of Gibraltar to illustrate each of the five themes. Then ask your students to identify the theme illustrated by each of the following five statements:

1. The Rock of Gibraltar is not "solid as a rock." It now contains over thirty miles of man-made tunnels. (interaction)
2. The Rock of Gibraltar is made out of limestone. (place)
3. During the mid-1960's, Spanish border authorities severely restricted the flow of traffic between Spain and Gibraltar. (movement)
4. The Spanish government insists that Gibraltar should be a part of Spain. (region)
5. The Rock of Gibraltar is near the entrance to the Mediterranean Sea. (location)

Practice

Lead a guided discussion of the questions on page 9. (Answers are below.)

Answer:
1. (a) Where a place exists; (b) by absolute and relative location; (c) answers will vary.
2. (a) Physical, human, and cultural characteristics; (b) landforms, population density, and religious beliefs.
3. (a) The physical character of a place affects the way people live; (b) people can change their environment by cutting down forests, planning grasslands, and building cities and roads.
4. People, goods, and ideas all spread from place to place.
5. (a) Physical or cultural; (b) answers will vary.
6. They provide historians with important tools for studying places and events.
7. (a) Time and place are the temporal and physical settings within which historical events occur. (b) Examples will vary.

Enrichment Activities

1. **Applying Concepts** Divide your class into five groups and assign each one of the five themes. Ask them to apply the theme to their hometown or city. Have each group report its findings to the class.

2. **Researching for Bonus Points** Award bonus points to students who can find the answer to this question: What is the absolute location of the Alamo in San Antonio, Texas? (29° 25′ 30″N, 98° 29′ 8″W)

To the Teacher

Purpose of the Lesson Planner

This Lesson Planner is designed to help teachers create outstanding lessons. The writers—Larry Krieger, a social studies supervisor and an author of *World History: Perspectives on the Past* pupil textbook, and Jim Coulon, a curriculum writer and high school history teacher—have given teachers fresh ideas aimed at bringing a sense of discovery and joy to their world history classes as well as clear plans to integrate the wealth of materials that make up the complete package of *World History: Perspectives on the Past.*

In writing strategies and other teaching suggestions for this Lesson Planner, the authors asked themselves, "How will this idea work in classrooms with today's students?" By focusing on this question, they developed a set of strategies for teaching *World History: Perspectives on the Past* that is at once forward-looking and practical. The strategies teachers have at their fingertips in this Lesson Planner have been used, tested, or scrutinized by active professionals in classrooms very much like your own.

Students and teachers alike will find *World History: Perspectives on the Past* rich in narrative content, reproductions of art and architecture, primary source excerpts and quotations, anecdotes, and good stories. The Lesson Planner enhances these abundant materials by providing teachers with background information, facts, and vivid details to share with their students. It will help teachers focus students' study and bring that study to life.

Every component of the program is correlated and supported in the Lesson Planner. To make the best use of these materials, teachers should read the description of the Lesson Planner that follows.

Creating Outstanding Lessons Lesson plans for each section of the pupil textbook form the core of the Lesson Planner. Lessons are developed using an effective teaching model. At the beginning of each chapter (in Chapter Focus) and each section (in Setting the Stage), there are suggestions for tapping prior knowledge, involving learners, and identifying for students the objectives of study. Ways for teachers to use the picture and vignette that introduce each text chapter are included in Chapter Focus.

For text sections, there are Teaching Strategies that develop each of the section objectives. Ten different strategies form a pool that will enable teachers whose styles or interests differ to find abundant support.

The Teaching Strategies suggest ways to

- engage in critical thinking about lesson content
- integrate study of geography and economics, the humanities, and scientific achievements into the study of world history
- reinforce instruction in the writing process
- use cooperative learning techniques

Finally, following the section strategies teachers will find suggestions for comprehension checks enabling them to monitor and adjust their teaching and at the end of each chapter suggestions for chapter closure.

Planning Successfully *World History: Perspectives on the Past* presents teachers with many options for many kinds of students and teaching situations. One purpose of the Lesson Planner is to give teachers the support necessary to optimize the use of program components. In the Lesson Planner teachers have an excellent guide providing easy access to all support materials and a convenient tool for planning how to use these materials.

At the beginning of each chapter teachers will find an Advance Planner. By using this chart, teachers will see, at a glance, which ancillary materials and which parts of the Lesson Planner to use to teach the objectives listed for each section of the pupil textbook.

In addition, all worksheets, outline maps, transparencies, tests, and Voices from the Past are referenced at point of use in the unit, chapter, and section materials. Teachers will also find answers to all text questions at point of use.

Meeting a Variety of Student Needs Materials for *World History: Perspectives on the Past* support students with differing learning styles and a wide range of ability levels. Teachers will want to assign Independent Practice Worksheets, Geography Skills Worksheets, Vocabulary Worksheets, Basic Skills Worksheets, and Critical Thinking Worksheets to almost all of their students.

Higher-ability students will profit especially from Voices from the Past and Critical Thinking Worksheets. Under the heading Enrichment Activities at the end of each section in the Lesson Planner there are suggestions for research, writing, and other projects that will work especially well with these students.

Students whose progress is slower will find Vocabulary Worksheets and Basic Skills Worksheets particularly helpful. Suggestions for altering teaching strategies to help these students with their study of key objectives are also found at the end of each chapter of the Lesson Planner under the heading Reteaching Activities.

The Beginnings of Civilization

Overview

This unit traces the development of civilization from prehistoric cultures to the mighty empires of Southwest Asia, Egypt, India, and China. This was a time of beginnings—of agriculture, languages, religions, governments, cities, and trade. Above all, it was the time when the first civilizations began in different parts of the world.

During the earliest and longest period of prehistory, the Paleolithic Age, nomadic hunters and gatherers learned to use fire, developed language, and became skilled toolmakers. In time, the nomadic life gave way to the farming, herding, and permanent settlements that marked the Neolithic Age.

Historians believe that the Sumerians, who lived in the Fertile Crescent of Southwest Asia, built the world's first civilization. Their complex culture was characterized by cities, specialized workers, a system of writing, advanced technology, and complex institutions such as religion and government. Each new group that invaded the Fertile Crescent adapted the basic ideas of Sumerian civilization to its specialized needs and made its own unique cultural contributions.

Egyptian civilization, which existed at the same time as the empires of Southwest Asia, survived through periods of strength and weakness for more than 3,000 years. Egypt was blessed by the Nile River, which flooded in a predictable pattern and provided a reliable transportation link between Upper and Lower Egypt.

At the same time, people in the Indus River Valley were building well-planned cities. That region was later conquered by Aryans from Central Asia, who fused their culture with Indian beliefs to produce Hinduism, a uniquely Indian religion reinforced by a structured social caste system.

Chinese civilization began in the valleys of the Yellow and Yangtze rivers and remained isolated from all other civilizations for hundreds of years. The first two millenia of China's history were marked by a succession of four dynasties. In times of turmoil, philosophers offered ways to reform society.

Resources

Several resources are designed to supplement the study of each unit.

1. The time line that forms the introduction to each unit shows the extent of time and the sequence of major events for that unit. The theme for the Unit I time line, shown on pages 10–11, is the foundations of civilization as represented by the people of Sumer going about their daily tasks.
2. The Geographic Theme page at the end of each unit develops a major geographic concept in relation to some aspect of the unit. For Unit I, the theme *Location* on page 90 deals with the growth of ancient cities. Because it focuses on the cities of the Fertile Crescent, you might want to use it in relation to Chapter 2.
3. The Reference Section contains a Historical Atlas of eight maps that provides a survey of world cultures at certain times in history. These maps are particularly useful for maintaining a global perspective. The map *The World about 1700 B.C.* is found on pages 804–805. The Global Perspectives activity for Unit 1 is based on Overhead Transparency 85, which appears in Chapter 2 of the Lesson Planner.
4. The Lesson Planner provides suggested answers to open-ended and interpretive questions that appear in the chapter and unit reviews.

Chapter Titles

1 Prehistoric Cultures 300,000 B.C.–3,500 B.C. (pages 12–25)
2 Civilizations and Empires in Southwest Asia 3500 B.C.–331 B.C. (pages 26–46)
3 Ancient Egypt 3100 B.C.–322 B.C. (pages 47–65)
4 Ancient India and China 2500 B.C.–A.D. 220 (pages 66–89)

Prehistoric Cultures

Chapter Overview

Because prehistory lacks written records, knowledge of prehistoric times depends on the information archaeologists deduce from the remains of ancient societies and from their methods of dating these material remains. Knowledge of the hunting-gathering culture of the Paleolithic people comes from their technology, art, and remains of their prehistoric campsites. We know that they lived in small groups, used fire, and developed some type of language.

The Neolithic Age, which began about 10,000 years ago, was a period of comparatively rapid change. Hunting and gathering gave way to farming and herding, a way of life that led to the formation of permanent settlements. New ways of living required new technologies, and an increase in the food supply resulted in an increase in world population. The changes that occurred in the Neolithic Age laid the basis for modern society.

Key Terms

archaeologist, prehistory, society, culture, nomads, technology
For additional exercises, see Vocabulary Worksheet 1.

Chapter Focus

Direct students' attention to the painting on page 12. Explain that the bison shown in this picture was painted on a cave wall about 15,000 years ago. Over the years, experts have carefully studied this and other paintings in the cave. Ask students to examine the painting and then have them identify each of the following statements as True, False, or Don't Know. Point out that you will compare their answers with those reached by experts.

1. The painting was created for enjoyment.
2. The bison is a sacred symbol designed to provide good luck in the next hunt.
3. The painting is part of an illustrated story about a successful hunt.
4. The painting was used as part of a secret ceremony during which young boys were initiated into their tribe.

After reading these statements, announce that "Don't Know" is the correct answer for all four. Have students read the chapter opening (pages 12–13) to explain why experts do not have answers for these statements. Help students understand that the painting on page 12 was created during a period of time before the beginning of written records. Historians call this time *prehistory*. Stress that without written records we can only guess what the artist had in mind when he or she painted the bison shown on page 12. Despite the absence of written records, prehistory is an important era in the human experience. Tell students that this chapter examines ways archaeologists study prehistory and the revolutionary advances that occurred during this period.

Prehistory lacks written records. 1

Section Objectives

After completing Section 1, students should be able to:

1. describe several methods that archaeologists use to determine the relative and absolute dates of the remains they find.
2. explain how archaeologists make deductions about prehistoric societies and cultures.

Setting the Stage

Remind students that time is one of the key dimensions historians use to describe the past. Time tells us when people lived and the events that occurred. Dates thus allow historians to place events in their correct sequence.

Ask students to explain why establishing accurate dates would be a particularly difficult problem during the prehistoric period. Students should note that prehistoric people did not keep a written record of their history. As a result, pinpointing dates that occurred thousands of years ago is very difficult. Despite these problems, archaeologists have developed techniques for determining prehistoric dates. Explain that this section discusses how archaeologists study the prehistoric period.

Teaching Strategies

Discussing Prehistory: Dating Prehistoric Objects

(Objective 1) Ask students what methods scientists use to determine dates (carbon 14, counting clay layers, counting tree rings). Explain that dating prehistoric objects requires knowledge, patience, and careful detective work. If possible, obtain the October 1988 issue of *National Geographic*. It contains a case example of how a professional archaeologist attempted to authenticate and date a carving thought to be a prehistoric

Advance Planner

Unit I **Theme**	The Beginnings of Civilization The development of civilization from prehistoric cultures to early empires		
Chapter 1 **Focus**	Prehistoric Cultures 300,000 B.C.–3500 B.C. Paleolithic cave art		★ Advanced ● Basic

	Section 1	**Section 2**	**Section 3**
Objectives	1. Describe several methods that archaeologists use to determine the relative and absolute dates of the remains they find. 2. Explain how archaeologists make deductions about prehistoric societies and cultures.	1. Describe the geography of regions that attracted Paleolithic hunters. 2. Explain how Paleolithic tools were made. 3. Describe Paleolithic life. 4. Recognize cause and effect relationships in Paleolithic society.	1. Explain why farming and the domestication of animals began. 2. Describe the geography of places that served as the sites of the first farming villages. 3. Identify the technological needs of Neolithic people. 4. Compare and contrast Paleolithic and Neolithic societies.
Setting the Stage	Unit I time line The importance of time	The Paleolithic Age	The transition from hunting and gathering to herding and farming
Teaching Strategies	Discussing Prehistory: Dating Prehistoric Objects Skill Building: Making Deductions about a Culture Check for Understanding	Using Geographic Themes: The Physical Characteristics of a Place Discussing Prehistory: Paleolithic Technology Discussing Prehistory: Mammoth-Bone Shelters Skill Building: Recognizing Cause and Effect Relationships Check for Understanding	Discussing Prehistory: The Origins of Farming Using Geographic Themes: The Physical Characteristics of a Place Discussing Prehistory: The Technological Needs of Neolithic People Skill Building: Comparing and Contrasting Societies Geography in History: Neolithic Settlements Check for Understanding
Guided Practice	Section Review 1	Section Review 2	Section Review 3
Independent Practice Worksheets	Independent Practice 1.1 Geography Skills 1 Vocabulary 1	Independent Practice 1.2 Basic Skills 1	Independent Practice 1.3 Critical Thinking 1
Enrichment	1. Primary Source: Voices 1.1 2. Researching for Points	1. Primary Source: Voices 1.2 2. Preparing a Report: Cave Paintings 3. ★ Researching Stone Age Beliefs 4. Researching for Points	1. Primary Source: Voices 1.3 2. Preparing a Report: Farming Villages 3. ★ Interpreting a Quotation 4. Researching for Points

Chapter Closer ● **Reteaching Activities**	Summarizing, Outlining, Listing
Chapter Review	Summary, Reviewing the Facts, Basic Skills, Researching and Reporting Skills, Critical Thinking, Perspectives on Past and Present, Investigating History
Chapter Evaluation	Chapter Test 1, Computer Test Bank Chapter 1 Test

object. Show students the carved head on the cover. Explain that a Czech family currently living in Australia brought the carving to Dr. Alexander Marschak, a well-known authority on prehistoric remains. They told Dr. Marschak that the carving had originally been discovered in the 1890's in a field near a Czech village where archaeologists have found a number of prehistoric works of art.

Ask students to place themselves in Dr. Marschak's position. What questions would they have asked about the carving? What techniques would they have used to date it? Dr. Marschak was immediately struck by the carving's realistic facial features. He knew that the only other realistic human head from the Ice Age is a carved female head (See the Voices from the Past Resource Book, 1.3.) excavated at a 26,000-year level at the same Czech village. Was this new head a 26,000-year-old portrait of an Ice Age hunter?

Dr. Marschak began his detective work with a microscopic analysis of the head. He determined that the ivory had indeed been carved with tools. Additional laboratory tests suggest that the object had been buried in the ground for a long time. But for how long? Dr. Marschak wanted to use carbon-14 dating to find out. However, he realized that while highly accurate, this procedure would have the unfortunate disadvantage of consuming a portion of the statuette. Experts at the Radiation Physics Lab at the University of Kansas suggested an alternative strategy. They performed an alpha-particle spectral analysis to locate radioactive elements that could be used to estimate the carving's age. They discovered unusually high quantities of uranium. Additional tests suggested that the carved ivory might be 26,000 years old.

Although excited, Dr. Marschak recognized that more study needed to be done. For example, he wanted to know more about the location where the carving was discovered. Nonetheless, he tentatively concluded "that the head may be the earliest known portrait of an Ice Age man."

Skill Building: Making Deductions about a Culture (Objective 2) Review the section, "Archaeologists make deductions about society and culture," to be sure students understand the distinction between society and culture. Divide the class into five or six groups and give each group an object that is part of our daily culture but the function of which is not necessarily obvious from its appearance. (Possible objects to consider include a telephone, credit card, bottle opener, umbrella, and paper clip.)

Ask students in each group to imagine themselves to be archaeologists who have just dis-

covered the object they have been given in the year A.D. 3000. Have each group make a careful list of the characteristics of their object. Then ask them to make deductions about how this object was used and what it tells us about the society and culture of the people who made it.

Check for Understanding Write the following terms on the chalkboard: prehistory, carbon 14, culture. Ask students to give a word or phrase relating each term to the lesson.

Practice

Guided Practice
Lead a guided discussion of the questions in Section Review 1. (Answers are below.)

Define:
(a) person who studies the remains of ancient societies (b) era of history before written records (c) designation of "older than" or "newer than" something else (d) define date expressed as a number, usually approximated through scientific tests (e) a network of people who interact with one another (f) way of life developed by a people and passed along to their children as a blueprint for living

Answer:
1. Prehistory lacks written records and uses material remains for historical evidence.
2. noting layer of soil where object was found, comparing objects from one site to items from another site, carbon dating, counting layers of clay or tree rings.
3. (a) technology and some aspects of daily life (b) thoughts, feelings, religious outlooks, values
4. (a) Cave paintings represent a more abstract level of intelligence and are clues to prehistoric beliefs, feelings, and traditions. (b) Answers may include preconceived ideas of scholars about cave dweller's lack of intelligence and artistic ability.

Independent Practice
Independent Practice 1.1
Geography Skills 1
Vocabulary 1

Enrichment Activities

1. **Reading a Primary Source** Assign Voices from the Past Resource Book 1.1.

2. **Researching for Bonus Points** Award bonus points to students who can answer these questions: When was carbon-14 dating discovered? Who discovered it? (Carbon 14 was discovered in 1947 by the U.S. chemist Frank Libby.)

Paleolithic people hunted and gathered. 2

Section Objectives

After completing Section 2, students should be able to:

1. describe the geographic characteristics of regions that attracted Paleolithic hunters.
2. explain how Paleolithic tools were made.
3. describe Paleolithic life.
4. recognize cause and effect relationships in Paleolithic society.

Setting the Stage

Begin by asking each student to make a list of the machines and tools that are currently shaping contemporary life. The list could include computers, televisions, and nuclear weapons. Then remind students that historians divide time into ages or eras when people shared certain patterns of life and thought. Have students use their lists of machines and tools to determine an appropriate name for our era.

After completing this activity, explain that historians call the earliest part of human prehistory the Old Stone Age. Scholars call this period the Old Stone Age because people in those years used stone to make many of their basic tools. Emphasize that like any other label, the Old Stone Age is an oversimplification. Historians now recognize that the Old Stone Age witnessed a number of significant achievements. Tell students that this section discusses the most important aspects of life in the Paleolithic Age.

Teaching Strategies

Using Geographic Themes: The Physical Characteristics of a Place (Objective 1) Point out that hunters typically chose to inhabit territories where different environments met. Ask your students to explain the advantages of this type of environment.

The Dordogne region in southwestern France provides an example of an environment that attracted Stone Age hunters. While you describe the region (as follows), have students think about the advantages of the environment: The Vezere River slowly wound its way through a valley lined with limestone cliffs. The river provided water

and a ready supply of fish. Hundreds of caves honeycombed the cliffs. Most of the caves faced south thus offering protection from cold winter winds. A plateau region east of the valley provided grazing land for herds of reindeer, horses, and bisons. Now, explain to students that small hunting bands occupied the caves in this region over a period of thousands of years. Thus far, archaeologists have discovered prehistoric cave paintings in about 200 of these caves.

Discussing Prehistory: The Paleolithic Tool Kit (Objective 2) As noted in the text, archaeologists have learned a great deal about Stone Age tools. By the end of the Paleolithic Age, toolmakers used stone, bone, antler, and ivory to create over 100 different tools. Explain that their "tool kit" included knives, scrapers, perforators, stone saws, spear points, and chisels. Two of the most important tools were the spear thrower and a cutter known as a burin. The spear thrower enabled hunters to hurl a seven-foot spear up to 150 yards, or twice as far as they could normally throw the spear. The burin enabled toolmakers to cut bone, antler, and ivory into sewing needles, harpoons, and spear throwers. Although Stone Age tools appear to be simple, very few people today can make them. (*Cro-Magnon Man* by Tom Prideaus contains a photo-essay [pages 83–91] in which a modern expert demonstrates how Stone Age tools were created.

Discussing Prehistory: Mammoth-Bone Shelters (Objective 3) Contrary to popular belief, Stone Age groups did not always live in caves. Archaeologists working on the Ukraine's flat plains have recently unearthed shelters built with mammoth bones. Explain that mammoths were gigantic wooly creatures that stood fourteen feet high and weighed five tons. A single mammoth tusk was nine feet long and weighed 100 pounds. Archaeologists believe that Stone Age hunting groups gathered mammoth bones and then used them to construct bone huts. They estimate that a hut required about 46,000 pounds of bones and took ten people five days to construct. Describe these facts to students and ask them to make inferences about Paleolithic life. Elicit that building the huts required group effort and linguistic skills.

Skill Building: Recognizing Cause and Effect Relationships (Objective 4) Have students give an effect for each of these causes:

1. A given area of land would support only so many people. (Paleolithic groups stayed small.)
2. Paleolithic hunters and gatherers learned to use fire. (Fire changed the way people lived by giving them heat, protection, and light)

3. The number of people in the world increased. (Less land became available for each group and there was a threat of hunger.)

Check for Understanding Have students write a paragraph describing life in Paleolithic times by explaining the technology (stone tools and use of fire), roles of men and women (women were plant specialists and men were hunters), and social developments (language, small group living) of this prehistoric society. Ask students to make two inferences about Paleolithic beliefs based on what they have read about cave paintings and burials. (People may have believed in magic and in an afterlife.)

Practice

Guided Practice
Lead a guided discussion of the questions in Section Review 2. (Answers are below.)

Define:
(a) person who traveled from place to place in search of food (b) tools and the skills needed to use them

Answers:
1. People in these old *(paleo)* times used stone *(liths)* to make many of their basic tools.
2. by hunting and gathering
3. (a) People lived in groups of 25 to 40 individuals, most of whom were probably blood relatives, they regarded one another as equals. (b) People may have believed that magic helped bring them luck in the hunt; they may have believed in an afterlife.
4. Competition for land and for food increased.
5. Possible answer: tools that give humans control over their environment; fire that provides light and warmth, scares off animals, and cooks food; language that enables people to work effectively together and transmit knowledge.

Independent Practice
Assign Independent Practice Worksheet 1.2
Assign Basic Skills Worksheet 1.

Enrichment Activities

1. **Reading a Primary Source** Assign Voices from the Past Resource Book 1.2.

2. **Preparing a Report** The cave paintings found in France and Spain are among the most vivid remains of prehistoric culture. Ask your students to prepare a report on prehistoric cave paintings. The October 1988 issue of *National Geographic* contains a vivid feature on the Lascaux Cave. (Chapter 4 in *Cro-Magnon Man* by Tom Prideaux provides a description of prehistoric art.)

3. **Researching Stone Age Beliefs** The Voice from the Past for this chapter (page 19) provides a reading on Alexander Marschak's theory that a Stone Age rock contains lunar notations. Ask advanced students to read Marschak's article "Exploring the Mind of Ice Age Man" (See *National Geographic,* January 1973.) Then have students prepare an oral report summarizing Marschak's key points.

4. **Researching for Bonus Points** The prehistoric people who lived from 40,000 B.C. to 10,000 B.C. are called Cro-Magnons. Award bonus points to students who can answer this question: How did the name Cro-Magnon originate? (The first Cro-Magnon bones were found in 1868 near a rock shelter in France called Cro-Magnon. The shelter was named after a local hermit called Magnou who lived there.)

Answers to Voice from the Past

1. The markings corresponded to the changing phases of the moon.
2. Their intelligence showed in their tools, paintings, and development of language.
3. It would help them keep track of seasonal migration of game animals, of fruit- or nut-bearing times for gathering, and possibly of tides.

Neolithic people learned to farm. 3

Section Objectives

After completing Section 3, students should be able to:

1. explain why farming and the domestication of animals began.
2. describe the geography of places that served as the sites for the first farming villages.
3. identify the technological needs of Neolithic people
4. compare and contrast Neolithic and Paleolithic societies.

Setting the Stage

Ask the students to consider the following problem: It is ten years from now and they are all married and raising families. Both spouses in each family are self-employed. The women have to work an average of only two hours a day while the men work a maximum of five hours a day. This labor is sufficient to provide for their basic needs of food, clothing, and shelter. All of their remaining time can be devoted to recreational, social, and religious affairs. Ask students if they would exchange this situation for jobs that would require at least ten hours of labor a day. Although the new jobs require more work, they have the potential to produce a higher standard of living.

After discussing student responses, explain that archaeologists now believe that Paleolithic hunter-gatherers did not have to work long hours to provide for their basic needs. Yet, about 10,000 years ago they began to abandon their life-style for a new pattern based on farming and herding. Explain that this was one of the most revolutionary changes in human history. Historians call the new era the New Stone Age or the Neolithic Age. Inform students that this section discusses the causes and consequences of this historic change.

Teaching Strategies

Discussing Prehistory: The Origins of Farming (Objective 1) To show students how farming changed the lives of hunters and gatherers, explain that the global population now exceeds five billion people. Then point out that 10,000 years ago only about ten million hunter-gatherers were spread over the entire globe. Ask students if they would describe the situation 10,000 years ago as a population crisis. Explain that by the standards of hunters and gatherers, the world was indeed becoming too crowded. At that time, hunters and gatherers needed about 250 square miles of land to feed a band of twenty-five people. As the world's population increased, supplies of wild food became scarcer.

As noted in the text, women may have been the first farmers. Over a period of time, their small fields became more and more important for a group's survival. Farming proved to be an efficient way of providing food for an expanding population. Point out that the early farming villages only needed six square miles of land to feed 150 people.

Using Geographic Themes: The Physical Characteristics of a Place (Objective 2) Explain that the first farming villages required special environ-

ments. Ask students to speculate on what the environment would need. For example, Jarmo was located on the hills of the Zagros Mountains along the bend of a small stream. The Zagros region had just enough rainfall to support wild wheat while also discouraging the growth of dense forests which would have hindered early farmers. Ask students how Jarmo met the needs of the first farmers.

Discussing Prehistory: Technological Needs of Neolithic People (Objective 3) Review the section, "People developed new skills." Emphasize that farming created new technological needs. This point can be illustrated by describing a simple experiment conducted by Jack Harlan, a professor of agronomy at the University of Oklahoma. Harlan wanted to find out what it was like to harvest wild wheat. He began by using his bare hands. This technique, however, produced painful blisters and only five and one-half pounds of grain per hour. Ask students what technological need this experiment revealed. Explain that early farmers invented a flint sickle to help them harvest grain more easily. When Harlan switched to a 9,000-year-old sickle he harvested six and one-quarter pounds of grain per hour—and his blisters healed!

Skill Building: Comparing and Contrasting Societies (Objective 4) Write the following sentence beginnings on the chalkboard. Have students compare and contrast Paleolithic and Neolithic societies by completing each sentence.
1. Paleolithic people gathered roots and berries for food, but Neolithic people (learned to farm).
2. Paleolithic people were nomads, while Neolithic people (settled in permanent homes).
3. Paleolithic toolmakers chipped or flaked pieces of stone to make a sharp edge, but Neolithic toolmakers (began to grind and polish pieces of stone to sharpen them).
4. In both Paleolithic and Neolithic societies, women had the role of (plant specialists).
5. The diet of Paleolithic hunters and gatherers was healthier than the diet of people in Jarmo, who ate (grains, peas, lentils, snails, and meat).

Geography in History: Neolithic Settlements Have students use a map of the Middle East to fill in the following labels on Outline Map 22: The Middle East–Iraq, Jarmo, Turkey, Çatal Hüyük, Anatolian Plateau, Zagros Mountains, Black Sea, Mediterranean Sea, Syrian Desert. Ask students to use the map to describe the geography of the Neolithic settlements. On what type of landform was Çatal Hüyük located? (plateau) Why was the soil of Jarmo fertile for farming? (Jarmo was located in Tigris Euphrates River valley.)

Check for Understanding Ask students to answer to the following questions: When and why did prehistoric people become farmers and herders? What were the consequences of this change?

Practice

Guided Practice
Lead a guided discussion of the questions in Section Review 3. (Answers are below.)

Define:
(a) period following Paleolithic, marked by introduction of agriculture and permanent settlements
(b) black glass formed naturally by volcanoes
(c) weight that helped a spindle turn

Identify:
(a) archaeological site of a Neolithic farming village in Southwest Asia (b) remains of large Neolithic town in what is now Turkey

Answer:
1. Experience gathering plants taught them about good growing places, use of seeds, and growing cycles, experience hunting animals helped them develop expertise about animals and the skill of domesticating certain animals for human use.
2. People no longer needed to travel in search of food.
3. It was much larger, more luxurious.
4. (a) pottery making, grinding tools (b) Pottery bowls protected food supplies from rodents, insects and dampness; grinding, people could make tools that would last much longer with which they could clear more land for farming.
5. Different kinds of wild plants grew in different environments around the world.
6. Population increased as never before.
7. Students might note the following changes:
   a. Because people could grow more food than they needed for survival, they could trade the surplus and possibly acquire wealth and status in the group.
   b. With wealth, material possessions would become more important and social structure more stratified.
   c. Certain people in the society would have more time to develop technologies, communicate ideas, and pursue artistic endeavors.

Independent Practice
Assign Independent Practice Worksheet 1.3
Assign Critical Thinking Worksheet 1.

Enrichment Activities

1. **Reading a Primary Source** Assign Voices from the Past Resource Book 1.3.

2. **Preparing a Report** Ask your students to prepare a report on one of the following farming villages: Jarmo, Jericho, Lepenski Vir, and Çatal Hüyük. (See *The World's Last Mysteries* by Readers Digest, pages 141–152.)

3. **Interpreting a Quotation** Ask your advanced students to interpret the following passage about the importance of agriculture: "When those early agriculturists began domesticating wild wheat and barley and the sheep and goats on the hillsides around them, they were, in a sense, also domesticating themselves."

4. **Researching for Bonus Points** Award bonus points to students who can answer these questions: What modern industry is still based on food-gathering? (Fishing and whaling industries still are strictly food-gathering enterprises.) What does a paleoethnobotanist study? (The plant remains of ancient cultures).

Answers to Voices from the Past

1. sorrowful, resentful, bitter, vengeful
2. to sing of their homeland and be pleasant
3. to remember Jerusalem always
4. It and its people will be destroyed

Concluding the Chapter

1. **Chapter Closer**
   Ask students to summarize the major prehistoric events. Challenge each student to choose the single most important item he or she feels changed the course of human development.

2. **Reteaching Activities**
   a. **Summarizing** Have students write a paragraph summarizing the ways archaeologists determine prehistoric dates.
   b. **Outlining** Have students use the section title, heads, and subheads to write an outline of Section 2.
   c. **Listing** Have students list five important changes that took place in the Neolithic Age.

3. **Chapter Review Activities**
   Assign Chapter Review 1 activities. The Chapter Review activities are designed to develop a wide range of basic skills, critical thinking skills, and individual or group activities.

Chapter Evaluation

Chapter Test 1 and Computer Test Bank Chapter 1 Test can be used to evaluate your students' understanding of this chapter.

Answers to Chapter Review 1

Reviewing the Facts
1. **(a)** person who studies remains of ancient societies **(b)** long period of distant past before written records **(c)** network of people who interact with one another **(d)** way of life a group of people develops and passes on to its children **(e)** person who moves often in search of food **(f)** tools and the skill to use them
2. **(a)** site of 1879 discovery of skilled prehistoric art **(b)** early Neolithic farming village **(c)** gave evidence that Neolithic people had developed luxuries, and advanced technology, and a system of religious beliefs **(d)** longest period in history; saw the development of language, stone tools, social organization, and the use of fire **(e)** marked the beginning of agriculture and permanent homes
3. **(a)** by noting layers in which objects are found or by comparing objects found at one site with objects found at another site **(b)** by using the carbon-14 method or by counting layers of clay
4. by studying remains of ancient societies, such as bones, tools, jewelry, campsites, ashes, soil
5. **(a)** to search for food **(b)** An area would support only so many people **(c)** They buried food and treasured objects with their dead.
6. They learned how to farm and herd.
7. Neolithic people developed technologies needed for an agricultural society.

Basic Skills
1. **(a)** 300,000 B.C., 3,500 B.C. **(b)** Intervals are reduced from 1,000,000 years to 1,500 years. **(c)** to indicate a change in scale.
2. **(a)** Paleolithic, almost 300,00 years; Neolithic, 4,500 **(b)** The Neolithic was a time of more rapid change.
3. **(a)** From tools and bones of animals archaeologists make deductions about the tools people made and the food they ate; from campsites or housing deductions about the way the people

lived together. **(b)** Food was plentiful and varied; so was leisure time.
4. **(a)** pottery making and grinding stone tools **(b)** Pottery was needed to store surplus food; stone tools to clear the land.

Critical Thinking
1. Both cultures had language, art, religion and hunting and gathering activity. In Neolithic times farming was introduced and family groups living as nomads gave way to larger groups settled in villages. New technologies such as pottery making, weaving and stone grinding appeared.
2. **(a)** Producing food caused an increase in population, the building of villages and cities, and the development of trade and industry. **(b)** Have students suggest and discuss what other events might be of similar importance.

Researching and Reporting Skills
1. **(a)** a long lasting pattern of organization in a society **(b)** *Civilization* includes cities, specialized workers, writing, advanced technology, and complex institutions. **(c)** skilled workers who make good by hand
2. **(a)** campsites, tools, bones, artwork **(b)** in addition to sources in **(a)**, constructions, writing, and pottery
3. Language made communication and the development of ideas possible. Toolmaking allowed people to make use of and control their environment Farming led to better supplies of food, population growth, the development of specialized work, trade, and the building of cities.
4. Permanent settlements allowed people to produce more food, to store surpluses, and support a larger population. People could think beyond survival and plan for the future, build lasting constructions, develop industries for their own use or for trading, and accumulate wealth.

Perspectives on Past and Present
1. Answers will vary.
2. Student might explain how Paleolithic leisure activities depended on imagination where ours today depend heavily on technology.
3. Help students think what some of these people's greatest needs were, then identify what in modern society might be most useful to them.

Investigating History
Students' research findings will vary.

Civilizations and Empires in Southwest Asia

Chapter Overview

Chapter 2 focuses on the civilizations and empires that flourished in and around the area known as the Fertile Crescent. Historians believe that the Sumerians built the world's first civilization because Sumer had five key traits that set it apart from the earlier societies: cities, specialized workers, writing, advanced technology, and complex institutions.

Sumer overcame geographic problems only to succumb to political ones. Constant warfare among Sumer's independent city-states from 3000 B.C. to 2000 B.C. left them too weakened to withstand attacks from foreign enemies. Each new group of conquerors adopted the Sumerians' way of life and contributed new ideas to civilization. The Babylonians' major achievement was the law code of King Hammurabi; the Phoenicians invented a simplified alphabet for writing; and the Jews developed a monotheistic religion.

Well-equipped with iron weapons and highly disciplined, the Assyrian army conquered Southwest Asia and parts of North Africa from 850 B.C. to 650 B.C. In 612 B.C., Assyria fell to the Chaldeans, and Babylon became the center of the last of the Mesopotamian empires. The next empire to rise in Southwest Asia was that of the Persians who, with tolerance and good government, established political order over a vast area.

Key Terms

civilization, artisan, cuneiform, institution, city-state, barter, polytheist, empire, literacy, monotheist, prophet
For additional exercises, see Vocabulary Worksheet 2.

Chapter Focus

Direct students' attention to the story about the Sumerian school boy on pages 26–27. Explain that the young boy's story was written about 4,000 years ago. Over the years, professional historians and their students have read and studied this story. Now examine the story to help students identify the following statements as True, False, or Don't Know. Point out that you will compare their answers with those reached by experts.

1. The young boy's mother prepared him a lunch to take to school.
2. School officials expected their students to arrive on time.
3. Students were expected to be respectful toward their teachers.
4. School officials punished students who broke school rules.

After reading these statements, announce that all of them are true. Experts did not know the answer to the four statements (see page 00 of the Lesson Planner) about the picture on page 12. Ask students to explain why both experts and beginning world history students can agree that the four statements about the young boy and his school are all true. Remind your students that the painting on page 12 was created *before* the beginning of written records. In contrast, the young boy's story was written *after* the development of written records. The boy, unlike the prehistoric painter, can speak to us across time. Explain that this exciting development enables us to begin our study of history. Point out to students that this chapter will discuss the history of the various people who lived in Southwest Asia between 3500 B.C. and 331 B.C.

Civilization arose in the Fertile Crescent. 1

Section Objectives

After completing Section 1, students should be able to:

1. locate the Fertile Crescent on a map.
2. list the five key traits of a civilization and explain how they apply to Sumer.
3. explain how Sumer's civilization was shaped by their ability to solve three geographic problems.
4. discuss the various aspects of daily life among the Sumerians.

Setting the Stage

Explain that the young school boy lived and studied in an ancient region called the Fertile Crescent. Remind students that regions are geographic units that share some quality. Ask students to examine the map on page 28. Ask, "What quality makes the Fertile Crescent a region?" Students should see that three rivers—the Jordan, Tigris, and Euphrates—provide this region with fertile soil and good supplies of water. Explain that this section examines the unique developments that occurred in the eastern end of the Fertile Crescent in a land known as Mesopotamia.

Geography in History: The Fertile Crescent (Objective 1) Show Transparency 1, *The Fertile Crescent about 2500 B.C.*, and distribute Outline Map 17, *The Fertile Crescent*. Have students locate and label the Mediterranean Sea, Persian Gulf, Tigris and Euphrates Rivers, and Mesopotamia, and also shade in the region of the Fertile Crescent.

Advance Planner

Chapter 2 Focus	Civilizations and Empires in Southwest Asia 3500 B.C.–331 B.C. A Sumerian student's day at school		★ Advanced ● Basic
	Section 1	**Section 2**	**Section 3**
Objectives	1. Locate the Fertile Crescent on a map. 2. List the five key traits of a civilization and explain how they apply to Sumer. 3. Explain how Sumer's civilization was shaped by their ability to solve three geographic problems. 4. Discuss various aspects of daily life among the Sumerians.	1. Explain the significance of Hammurabi's law code. 2. Describe some of the Phoenicians' achievements 3. Compare and contrast the religious beliefs of the Jews with those of the Sumerians.	1. Discuss the rise and fall of the Assyrian empire. 2. Describe aspects of everyday life in Babylon. 3. Explain how the Persians ruled their empire.
Setting the Stage	Geography in History: The Fertile Crescent Transparency 1 Outline Map 17	Babylonian methods for solving problems Transparency 2	Peoples of the "cuneiform world" Transparency 3
Teaching Strategies	Discussing History: The Key Traits of a Civilization Using Geographic Themes: Human-Environment Interaction Teaching with Pictures: Daily Life in Ancient Ur Check for Understanding	Discussing History: Hammurabi's Code Discussing History: The Phoenician Alphabet Skill Building: Comparing and Contrasting Religious Beliefs Check for Understanding	Discussing History: Assurbanipal's Question Discussing History: The Wonders of Babylon Skill Building: Creative Writing Transparency 4 Check for Understanding
Guided Practice	Transparency 1 Q&A Section Review 1	Transparency 2 Q&A Section Review 2	Transparency 3 Q&A Transparency 4 Q&A Section Review 3
Independent Practice Worksheets	Independent Practice 2.1 Geography Skills 2 Vocabulary 2	Independent Practice 2.2 Basic Skills 2	Independent Practice 2.3 Geography in History: The The Persian and Assyrian Empires Outline Map 17 Critical Thinking 2
Enrichment	1. Primary Source: Voices 2.1 2. Discussing Sumerian Proverbs 3. Researching for Points	1. Primary Source: Voices 2.2 2. ★ Solving a Puzzle 3. Preparing a Report 4. Researching for Points	1. Primary Source: Voices 2.3 2. Researching for Points 3. Global Perspectives Transparency 85

Chapter Closer	
● **Reteaching Activities**	Summarizing, Recalling Important Ideas, Recalling Important People
Chapter Review	Summary, Reviewing the Facts, Basic Skills, Researching and Reporting Skills, Critical Thinking, Perspectives on Past and Present, Investigating History
Chapter Evaluation	Chapter Test 2, Computer Test Bank Chapter 2 Test

Teaching Strategies

Discussing History: The Key Traits of a Civilization (Objective 2) Review the concept of culture (page 14). Explain that a civilization is a complex form of culture. Ask students to name traits they think would distinguish a civilization from the culture of Neolithic society and list their responses on the chalkboard. Next to the list, write the traits most scholars agree are essential for civilization. Have students read pages 27–30 and then cite examples of the five traits that made Sumer a civilization.

Using Geographic Themes: Human-Environment Interaction (Objective 3) The Sumerians' response to geographic problems provides a case example of the theme of human-environmental interactions. Begin your discussion by asking students to read, "Sumerians faced geographic problems" (page 30) and list the three geographic problems that confronted the Sumerians. Ask students to explain how the Sumerians solved these problems. (Students may be interested to learn that Arnold Toynbee, a famous historian, believed that all civilizations begin as a result of a successful response to the challenge of the physical environment.) Ask students to evaluate the way in which the Sumerians responded to their environmental challenge. Ask, "Would the Sumerians have been able to create a civilization without a geographic challenge?"

Teaching with Pictures: Daily Life in Ancient Ur (Objective 4) Have students read the sections on Sumerian life on pages 30–33 then direct their attention to the artistic recreation on page 31. Explain that the large building featured in this painting is a temple or ziggurat dedicated to the moon god Nanna and his wife Ningal. As pointed out in the text, *ziggurat* is a word meaning "mountain of god." Ziggurats were built high to represent a mountain where the gods could live and still be with their people. Note the priests climbing the ziggurat steps. Perhaps they were chanting hymns to praise Nanna and scare off Wicked Udugs! Now ask students to pretend that they are standing on top of this ziggurat. Their assignment is to write an imaginative paragraph describing the various sights that they can see in this painting. Encourage students to use concepts and ideas discussed in the chapter. For example, they can see merchants bartering goods in the shops outside the ziggurat.

Check for Understanding Have students give examples from Sumerian society of a specialized worker, complex institution, and religious belief.

Practice

Guided Practice
Lead a guided discussion of the questions in Overhead Transparency 1 and in Section Review 1. (Answers are below.)

Define:
(a) complex form of culture with the following key traits: cities, specialized workers, writing, advances technology, and complex institutions (b) professional writer (c) skilled worker who makes goods by hand (d) Sumerian writing (e) symbol that pictured the thing it stood for (f) symbol that stood for an abstract idea (g) long-lasting pattern of organization in community (h) system of bringing water to crops (i) self-governing, independent city and the surrounding countryside that it controlled (j) exchanging goods for other goods (k) tiered, towering temple (l) person who believes in many gods

Identify:
(a) fertile area between the Persian Gulf and the Mediterranean Sea (b) area at the eastern end of the Fertile Crescent between the Tigris and Euphrates rivers (c) city-states in southern Mesopotamia

Answers:
1. Answers should note larger population in city than in village; people farm in village, diversity of work is available in city; wealth and luxury as well as class distinctions apparent in city.
2. (a) Advantages: fertile land; ease of transportation; abundance of reeds. Disadvantages: no natural barriers for protection; no good supplies of stone, metal, and wood; irregular flooding pattern of the rivers. (b) Sumerians built city walls with mud bricks to protect settlements, used reeds to build boats and huts, and dug irrigation ditches to bring water to crop fields.
3. Possible answer: Priests manage grain storehouses or keep track of the calendar; merchants bargain; artisans shape clay into vessels; farmers plant crops, tend to the irrigation system; slaves perform household duties for a family.
4. Bronze was very important in the making of tools and weapons.
5. (a) Students may consider the pervasiveness of electronic media and attempt to identify a role within these media for print. (b) Students may speculate on a world without wheels, plows.

Independent Practice
Assign Independent Practice Worksheet 2.1.
Assign Geography Skills Worksheet 2.
Assign Vocabulary Worksheet 2.

Enrichment Activities

1. **Reading a Primary Source** Assign Voices from The Past Resource Book 2.1

2. **Discussing Sumerian Proverbs** The following is a list of Sumerian proverbs. Read them to the students and ask if the proverbs hold true today.

   • A sweet word is everybody's friend.
   • Tell a lie; then if you tell me truth, it will be deemed a lie.
   • A loving heart builds the home; a hating heart destroys the home.
   • Into an open mouth, a fly enters.
   • Friendship lasts a day; kinship lasts forever.

   Now ask students to make a list of modern proverbs.

3. **Researching for Bonus Points** Award bonus points to students who can find the answers to these questions: Who was the first person to decipher cuneiform? (Henry C. Rawlinson) What new river is formed by the meeting of the Tigris and Euphrates rivers? (The Shatt al-Arab)

Newcomers contributed to civilization.

2

Section Objectives

After completing Section 2, students should be able to:

1. explain the significance of Hammurabi's law code.
2. describe some of the Phoenicians' achievements.
3. compare and contrast the religious beliefs of the Jews with those of the Sumerians.

Setting the Stage

Describe the following problem: A builder built a house for a man. However, the builder failed to use sound construction techniques. As a result, the house collapsed causing the owner's death. What action, if any, should be taken against the builder? Briefly discuss your students answers. Then explain that this problem actually occurred 4,000 years ago in an ancient city called Babylon. Tell

students that in this section, they will see how a Babylonian king named Hammurabi solved this problem. Emphasize that Hammurabi and other people living in the Fertile Crescent faced many problems that concern all civilizations. As students will see, the people's solutions to these problems still influence us. Use Overhead Transparency 2, *Peoples of Southwest Asia 2000 B.C. –1000 B.C.*, to show students the general location of the Babylonian Empire, the Phoenicians, Canaan, and the Hittites.

Teaching Strategies

Discussing History: Hammurabi's Code (Objective 1) Ask students to discuss reasons why societies develop laws, and list their reasons on the chalkboard. Then ask students to read, "Babylonians wrote a code of laws" (pages 34–35). Explain that Hammurabi created his law code "to cause justice to prevail in the land, to destroy the wicked and the evil, to prevent the strong from oppressing the weak ... and to further the welfare of the people." Discuss how these reasons compare with the students' list. Direct students' attention to the five laws listed on page 34. Ask, "On what principle of justice are these laws based?" (Since justice requires balance, the punishment should fit the crime.) Based on this principle, what punishment did Hammurabi's code give to the builder who built the house that collapsed on its owner? (The builder was put to death.)

Discussing History: The Phoenician Alphabet (Objective 2) Have students read, "Phoenicians invented the alphabet," (pages 35–36). Explain that Phoenician merchants faced a practical problem: They could not afford to take expensive scribes along on every voyage to keep records with the cumbersome cuneiform. Because of the demands of trade, the Phoenicians discovered a way to keep their records by using only twenty-two symbols. (Later the ancient Greeks and Romans changed the shape of the twenty-two letters and added from others, making the alphabet we know today.) As noted in the text, the new alphabet helped expand trade and literacy. The Phoenician city of Byblos soon specialized in the manufacture of writing materials. The Greeks took their word for book, *biblion*, from Byblos. Our own words *Bible* and *bibliography* are in turn derived from *biblion*.

Skill Building: Comparing and Contrasting Religious Beliefs (Objective 3) Ask students to complete the following chart (answers in *italics*) contrasting the religious beliefs of the Sumerians with those of the Jews.

	Sumerians	Jews
Number of gods	(3,000 gods)	(one God)
Where god(s) lived	(temples, homes, water, clouds, and stars)	(not limited to any geographic location)
Characteristics of god(s)	(immortal, all-powerful but also with human characteristics)	(not arbitrary; God was ruler of universe)
What was expected of god(s)	(protection during life)	(protection in return for honoring the commandments)

Check for Understanding Ask students to describe how the Babylonians, Phoenicians, and Hebrews solved some of the problems they faced.

Practice

Guided Practice
Lead a guided discussion of the questions in Overhead Transparency 2 and in Section Review 2. (Answers are below.)

Define:
(a) recorded, unified, consistent body of law **(b)** state that has conquered other lands and rules them **(c)** ability to read and write **(d)** person who believes in one God **(e)** promise (between God and the Jews)

Identify:
(a) first conquerors of Sumer, from city of Babylon **(b)** Babylonian king and developer of law code **(c)** powerful traders and merchants around the Mediterranean in about 1100 B.C. **(d)** small group in Southwest Asia who became monotheists and who settled in Palestine **(e)** according to the Bible, the man who led Jewish people into Canaan around 2000 B.C. **(f)** strip of land near the Mediterranean, later called Palestine **(g)** man who led the Jews out of slavery in Egypt and who, according to the Bible, climbed Mount Sinai and received the Ten Commandments **(h)** Jewish kingdom in Canaan **(i)** capital of the kingdom of Israel **(j)** most powerful of Jewish kings

Answer:
1. The basic ideas of Sumerian civilization were adapted by the newcomers.
2. The laws were published for all who could read

to see; they also represented balance in the meting out of punishment.
3. It used many fewer symbols.
4. It stressed the worship of one God; it emphasized the ideas of justice, morality, and an individual relationship with God.
5. **(a)** Iron making is a more complicated process, requiring higher temperatures than are needed to make bronze. **(b)** It is harder, more common.
6. *writing:* facilitated the record-keeping necessary in the empire's administrative work; *law codes:* assured orderly treatment of different people.

Independent Practice
Assign Independent Practice Worksheet 2.2.
Assign Basic Skills Worksheet 2.

Enrichment Activities

1. **Reading a Primary Source** Assign Voices from The Past Resource Book 2.2.

2. **Solving a Puzzle** The people living in the Fertile Crescent enjoyed playing a complex board game. The board has survived but its rules have been lost. For a picture of the board, see *The Age of God-Kings* by the editors of Time-Life Books, pages 28–29. Ask your advanced students to try inventing rules for playing the game.

3. **Preparing a Report** The Torah is the most sacred object in the Jewish religion. Ask interested students to prepare a report describing the Torah's unique place in Judaism.

4. **Researching for Bonus Points** Award bonus points to students who can answer this question: What was the name of the snail which the Phoenicians gathered to make purple dye? (the murex snail)

Conquerors ruled even larger empires.   3

Section Objectives

After completing Section 3, students should be able to:

1. discuss the rise and fall of the Assyrian empire.
2. describe aspects of everyday life in Babylon.
3. explain how the Persians ruled their empire.

Setting the Stage

Ask students to recall the geographic characteristic shared by the lands within the Fertile Crescent. Then explain that over time, this region also developed a shared culture. As noted in the text, modern scholars refer to it as "the cuneiform world." Explain that farming, irrigation, city life, and cuneiform writing were used throughout this cultural region. Explain to students that this section examines three powerful peoples—the Assyrians, Chaldeans, and Persians—who conquered and united the entire region. Show students Overhead Transparency 3, *The Assyrian Empire*, and ask them to name some of the peoples of the cuneiform world about 650 B.C.

Teaching Strategies

Discussing History: Assurbanipal's Question (Objective 1) Have students read, "The Assyrian empire rose and fell" (page 40). Discuss the factors that caused Assyria's rise and fall. Conclude the discussion by explaining that Assurbanipal felt unappreciated. One of the tablets in his library bears this inscription: "I did well unto god and man, to dead and living. Why have sickness, ill-health, misery and misfortune befallen me? ... Disturbing scandals oppress me always. Misery of mind and of flesh bow me down; with cries of woe I bring my eyes to an end." Read this passage to your students and ask them how each of the following people might answered Assurbanipal's question: a Hebrew prophet, the Sumerian wise man Utnapishtim (see Voices from the Past Resource Book 2.1), and a modern psychologist.

Discussing History: The Wonders of Babylon (Objective 2) Have students read, "The Chaldeans rebuilt Babylon" (pages 40-42). Explain that Babylon was one of the greatest cities in the ancient world. A huge wall sixty-five feet high provided security against attack. Over 1,000 temples and shrines provided places to worship the city's many gods and goddesses. The most important temple of all belonged to Babylon's chief god, Marduk. Marduk demanded constant attention. At one annual festival, worshippers offered their god more than two tons of frankincense. Priests attended to Marduk's golden image. When the priests were away, they left behind statues of hairdressers, a butler, and even a baker to attend to Marduk's every whim.

Skill Building: Creative Writing (Objective 3) First review the section, "The Persians united a vast area." Show students Overhead Transparency 4, *The Persian Empire, 500 B.C.*, and ask them how the Royal Road helped unify the empire. Then have students pretend that they are Darius' royal governors or satraps. Their assignment is to write Darius a letter describing the conditions in their province. Each student should carefully examine the map on page 43 and then select a specific area. The letter could include a discussion of local roads, customs, conquered peoples, and geography.

Check for Understanding Read the following descriptions aloud and have students identify the people described.

1. believed stars determine human destiny; conquered the Jews; rebuilt Babylon (Chaldeans)
2. ruled a vast area with tolerance and good government; used standardized coinage (Persians)
3. had a highly disciplined army; uprooted and enslaved conquered peoples (Assyrians)

Practice

Guided Practice
Lead a guided discussion of the questions with Overhead Transparency 3 and Transparency 4 and Section Review 3. (Answers are below.)

Define:
(a) group of stars (b) study of the heavens (c) royal governor of each province of the Persian Empire

Identify:
(a) empire builders from northern Mesopotamia (b) mighty kings of Assyria (c) conquerors of the Assyrians who rebuilt Babylon (d) resplendent capital of Chaldean kingdom (e) king of Chaldeans (f) homeland of Persians (g) people from Iran who conquered all of the Fertile Crescent and Asia Minor (h) Persian king who began rise of Persia (i) later Persian king responsible for building Royal Road (j) Persian prophet

Answer:
1. with skillful fighting, discipline, and brute force
2. rebuilding and beautifying Babylon; developing astronomical and astrological information
3. They continued to worship their one God.
4. Cyrus was tolerant and did not interfere with local customs; the Assyrians built their empire on fear.
5. It included the notion of a heaven attainable by all who followed Ahura-Mazda.
6. Answers should consider the strengths and weaknesses of the two: Sumer—greater independence than Persian Empire but gloomier

outlook; warfare among city-states; Persia— improvements in daily life; more hopeful religious outlook; good government.

Independent Practice
Assign Independent Practice Worksheet 2.3.
Assign Critical Thinking Worksheet 2.

Enrichment Activities

1. **Reading a Primary Source** Assign Voices from the Past Resource Book 2.3.

2. **Researching for Bonus Points** Award bonus points to students who can solve this riddle: What Babylonian beast had the head of a horned viper, the forelegs of a lion, the hind legs of a bird of prey, and a tail tipped with a scorpion sting? (the scaly-coated mushhushshu, or dragon of Marduk)

3. **Global Perspectives** Using Transparency 85, *The World about 1700 B.C.* survey with students the various world cultures about 1700 B.C.

4. **Geography in History: The Persian and Assyrian Empire** Ask students to draw a key for Outline Map 17, indicating a symbol or color for the Assyrian empire and for the Persian empire. Then, referring to the maps on pages 39 and 43, have students use the map key to designate areas over which the Assyrians and Persians ruled. Ask, "What territories did the Persians rule that the Assyrians did not?" (lands east of the Fertile Crescent, most of Asia Minor, Egypt, and India)

Answers to Voice from the Past

1. sorrowful, resentful, bitter, vengeful
2. to sing of their homeland and be pleasant
3. to remember Jerusalem always
4. It and its people will be destroyed.

Concluding the Chapter

1. **Chapter Closer**
   Ask students to explain the significance of written records for reconstructing the story of the past. Have students refer to the written records described in this chapter and the information these records disclose about life in ancient Southwest Asia.

2. **Reteaching Activities**
   a. **Summarizing** Have students write five statements describing the key traits of the Sumerian civilization.

b. **Recalling Important Ideas** Have students identify the significance of each of the following: Hammurabi, Phoenicians, alphabet, Moses, Solomon, and the prophets.

c. **Recalling Important People** Have students write a sentence to explain the importance of each of the following people: Assurbanipal, Nebuchadnezzar, and Cyrus.

3. **Chapter Review Activities**
   Assign Chapter Review 2 activities.

Chapter Evaluation

Chapter Test 2 and Computer Test Bank Chapter 2 Test can be used to evaluate your students' understanding of this chapter.

Answers to Chapter Review 2

Reviewing the Facts

1. **(a)** complicated form of culture **(b)** skilled worker who makes goods by hand **(c)** way of writing that used wedge-shaped letters **(d)** long-lasting pattern of organization in a community **(e)** city and the surrounding countryside it controlled **(f)** exchanging goods for other goods **(g)** believer in many gods **(h)** state that has conquered other lands and now rules them **(i)** ability to read and write **(j)** believer in one god **(k)** religious teacher

2. **(a)** where first civilization developed **(b)** eastern end of Fertile Crescent between Tigris and Euphrates rivers **(c)** Period during which people learned to use bronze **(d)** period during which people shifted from using bronze to iron **(e)** where the first civilization developed **(f)** developed and made public a law code **(g)** developed a 22-symbol alphabet **(h)** believed in one God **(i)** led enslaved Jews out of Egypt and received from God ten commandments **(j)** most powerful of Jewish kings and builder of a temple in Jerusalem **(k)** home of group who established a large empire in southwestern Asia **(l)** captured Jerusalem and rebuilt Babylon **(m)** established vast empire built on tolerance and good government **(n)** established policy of generosity

toward conquered people **(o)** extended Persian empire and developed government of provinces ruled by satraps, an excellent road system, and standardized coinage **(p)** offered religious belief that people could control their fate by electing to follow path of goodness

3. **(a)** cities, specialized workers, writing, advanced technology, complex institutions **(b)** Sumer was organized into city-states; had many specialized workers; developed cuneiform writing; used new technology; had organized religion.

4. **(a)** alphabet **(b)** monotheism **(c)** observations that formed the basis for astronomy and astrology

Basic Skills

1. **(a)** About 1900 years, 2100 years, 1064 years **(b)** 238, 200

2. to the west, the Mediterranean Sea; to the north, the Taurus Mountains; to the east, the Zagros Mountains; to the South, the Syrian Desert and the Persian Gulf

3. Persian Government
   a. Darius divided empire into provinces.
      1. People kept their culture
      2. Satraps governed provinces
   b. Two important tools helped to unify the empire.
      1. An excellent road system
      2. Coins to facilitate trade

4. Possible examples: for *political history:* Sumerians created city-states, Babylonians wrote a code of law; for *economic history:* Sumerians had an irrigation system, Phoenicians traded dye and cedars for other goods; *social history:* in Sumerian society there were many classes, women could join the priesthood; *cultural history:* Jewish people adopted monotheism, Sumerians had a form of writing.

Researching and Reporting Skills
Students' answers will vary.

Critical Thinking

1. Surplus was used to pay taxes to support government, and to pay for specialized labor. Surplus food and manufactured goods became the object of trade. Accumulation of surplus created personal wealth. Social classes resulted from accumulation of wealth and specialization of work.

2. **(a)** Hammurabi's code was based on existing practices; the Ten Commandments were religious in origin, believed to have been given by God to Moses. **(b)** Hammurabi's code established a principle of equal retribution for harm done to one of equal status; the Ten Commandments established a system of morality that condemned wrongdoing for all.

3. **(a)** The Assyrians established a rule of terror, including uprooting people; the Persians, a rule of tolerance **(b)** Tolerance makes acceptance by the conquered people more likely.

4. **(a)** Sailing vessels helped to carry traded items to distant countries; writing helped to keep business records for increasingly complex trading activity. **(b)** Sailing vessels made long-distance sea trade possible. Writing aided both record keeping and long-distance communication.

5. Monotheism, the belief in one supreme being, is the basis for most of the major world religions today.

6. The statement is supported: nobles are seated, their servants are not (page 26); King Gudea is seated (page 32); both husband and wife are seated, indicating equality (page 33); the god of justice is seated and the king stands (page 35).

Perspectives on Past and Present
Answers will vary. Students should point out that today's standards support the idea that all people are equal before the law.

Investigating History
Students' answers will vary.

Ancient Egypt

Chapter Overview

The Nile River enabled Egyptian civilization to grow and prosper for more than 3,000 years. It provided a relatively predictable supply of fertile soil and an easy means of transportation. The Egyptians worshipped the Nile as a god who gave them life and who seldom turned against them. Deserts on either side of the Nile shielded Egypt from attack. Egyptian farming villages were united first into agricultural districts called *nomes* and then into two kingdoms, Upper and Lower Egypt. A strong king named Menes united the two kingdoms in about 3100 B.C.

Egypt's rulers, or pharaohs, were considered divine and immortal. They ruled Egypt during three periods of peace and prosperity known as the Old, Middle, and New Kingdoms. Two periods of invasion and turmoil disrupted the pharaohs' rule. Around 1200 B.C., waves of invasion led to a decline from which ancient Egypt never recovered.

Egyptian society retained the same basic form for 3,000 years. Nobles lived in luxury, peasants worked in the fields, and slaves served their masters. Egyptian religion emphasized *maat*, or justice. Those who lived according to maat could expect eternal life in the afterworld. The Egyptians' rich cultural achievements included a system of writing, methods for surveying land, a calendar, and sophisticated medical practices.

Key Terms

cataract, delta, dynasty, pharaohs, pyramid, maat, hieroglyphics
For additional exercises, see Vocabulary Worksheet 3.

Chapter Focus

Ask students to write down at least two thoughts that come to mind when they think of Ancient Egypt. Call on a number of students and list their answers on the chalkboard. Typical student answers include King Tut, gold, the Nile river, pharaohs, and the pyramids. Explain that this chapter discusses each of these famous people and places. In addition, they will also learn about the cultural achievements of one of history's oldest and longest civilizations.

Direct students to the chapter opener on the discovery of Tutankhamon's tomb (pages 46-47). Students might be interested to learn that Carter's workers removed more than 200,000 tons of dirt and rubble before finding the tomb. Carter later wrote, "never before in the whole history of excavation had such an amazing sight been seen as the light of our torch revealed to us."

Carter was not exaggerating. During the next five years, he carefully removed more than 3,000 items from Tutankhamon's tomb. This fabulous treasure included more than two tons of gold. The picture on page 47 shows Tutankhamon's gold burial mask. Ask students to examine the mask. Explain that the vulture and cobra represent the gods of Upper and Lower Egypt; Tutankhamon's beard likens him to an underworld god; and, finally, his eyes symbolize the sun and moon. Point out that Tutankhamon was an unimportant ruler. We can only imagine what wonders must have filled the tombs of ancient Egypt's greatest rulers.

The Nile River shaped Egyptian life. **1**

Section Objectives

After completing Section 1, students should be able to:

1. identify the physical characteristics of ancient Egypt.
2. explain how the Nile influenced the development of Egyptian culture.
3. compare and contrast the effects of environment on Egyptian and Sumerian ways of life.

Setting the Stage

Begin by asking students to name geographic features they believe would contribute to the growth and development of a successful civilization. List students' responses on the chalkboard. Possible answers include fertile soil, natural resources, natural barriers for protection, waterways, and access to an ocean or sea. Show students Overhead Transparency 5, *Ancient Egypt,* and ask them to name places that correspond with some of the geographic features identified in the list. Ask students to use the map on page 49 to determine which of the geographic features they listed were present in ancient Egypt. Would they predict that Egypt would produce a successful or an unsuccessful civilization? Explain that this section examines Egypt's unique geography.

Teaching Strategies

Using Geographic Themes: The Location and Physical Characteristics of a Place (Objective 1) Ask students to turn to the map "The World About 1700 B.C." in the Historical Atlas on pages 804–805, or use Overhead Transparency 85. Have students locate Egypt's position relative to Mesopotamia. Ask, "What was the closest nearby civilization at the time shown on this map?"

Advance Planner

Chapter 3 Focus	Ancient Egypt 3100 B.C.–332 B.C. The discovery of Tutankhamen's tomb		★ Advanced ● Basic
	Section 1	**Section 2**	**Section 3**
Objectives	1. Identify the location and physical characteristics of ancient Egypt. 2. Explain how the Nile influenced the development of Egyptian culture. 3. Compare and contrast the effects of environment on Egyptian and Sumerian ways of life.	1. Explain the role of the pharaohs. 2. Discuss how and why the pyramids were constructed. 3. Compare and contrast Egypt's three kingdoms. 4. Identify and locate the empire built by the pharaohs of the New Kingdom.	1. Compare and contrast the lives of nobles and peasants in Egyptian Society 2. Define the concept of maat and explain its significance in Egyptian religion 3. Identify Akhenaton and explain his religious reforms. 4. Describe some of the achievements of Egyptian culture.
Setting the Stage	Egypt's unique geography Transparency 5	Impressions of the pyramids	Traditional values and agents of change
Teaching Strategies	Using Geographic Themes: The Physical Characteristics of a Place Transparency 85 Using Geographic Themes: Human-Environment Interaction Skill Building: Studying Cause and Effect Check for Understanding	Discussing History: Who Built the Pyramids? Discussing History: How were the Pyramids Built? Skill Building: Comparing and Contrasting Egyptian Kingdoms Geography in History: Making a Map Outline Map 22 Check for Understanding	Discussing History: Egyptian Nobles and Peasants Discussing History: Analyzing Egyptian Religion Skill Building: Analyzing Effects Discussing History: Identifying Reasons for Egypt's Great Achievements Check for Understanding
Guided Practice	Transparency 5 Q&A Transparency 85 Q&A Section Review 1	Section Review 2	Section Review 3
Independent Practice Worksheets	Independent Practice 3.1 Geography Skills 3 Vocabulary 3	Independent Practice 3.2 Basic Skills 3	Independent Practice 3.3 Critical Thinking 3
Enrichment	1. Primary Source: Voices 3.1 2. Preparing a Report 3. ★ Researching the Aswan Dam 4. Researching for Points	1. Primary Source: Voices 3.2 2. Researching for Points	1. Primary Source: Voices 3.3 2. ★ Analyzing a Primary Source: Hymn to Aton 3. Researching for Points
Chapter Closer ● **Reteaching Activities**	Outlining, Summarizing, Organizing Information		
Chapter Review	Summary, Reviewing the Facts, Basic Skills, Researching and Reporting Skills, Critical Thinking, Perspectives on Past and Present, Investigating History		
Chapter Evaluation	Chapter Test 3, Computer Test Bank Chapter 3 Test		

(Babylonia) "What was the most distant civilization?" (China)

Now have students take another look at the map on page 49. Explain that ancient Egypt had a number of unusual physical characteristics. Note that about 95 percent of Egypt was (and still is) a desert. The remaining five percent are oases watered by the Nile River. Make sure that students understand that the Nile divides Egypt into two distinctive regions — the Nile Valley (or Upper Egypt) and the Nile Delta (or Lower Egypt). The Nile Valley is a very narrow strip of land in places not more than a mile wide on each bank. In contrast, the delta is about 130 miles across. It contains some of the world's most fertile soil. This rich layer of soil was provided by the Nile's annual 100-day flood. (For a picture of the Nile flood, see *National Geographic's Peoples and Places of The Past*, page 49.)

Using Geographic Themes: Human-Environment Interaction (Objective 2) Review the discussion of the theme of human-environment interaction (text page 9). Then write the following sentence on the chalkboard: Egypt was the "gift of the Nile," but every gift must be paid for. Ask students to interpret this thought in terms of the theme of human-environment interaction. Encourage them to name the environmental "gifts" (transportation, water, fertile soil) that the Nile provided. Then point out that these gifts had no value until shaped by human culture. For example, the Egyptians developed an intricate network of irrigation ditches to water their fields. In order to take full advantage of the Nile, they gave up their local rule and united under the leadership of a single ruler.

Skill Building: Studying Cause and Effect (Objective 3) Ask students to recall the geographic problems Sumerians faced and the solutions they found (text page 30). Ask students which of these problems were not concerns for the Egyptians and why. Students might note that the Nile was calm and predictable compared to the Tigris-Euphrates, that the Nile valley had natural defenses on its boundaries, and that Egyptians had greater local access to needed natural resources. Ask students how the different conditions created differences between the Sumerian and Egyptian ways of life. Students might note that Egyptian religion was more optimistic, daily life was more secure, and territory better protected from invasion. Egypt's geography encouraged the development of unified kingdoms, while Sumer's geography encouraged the development of city-states linked only by trade. Egypt's delta supported a much larger population and therefore a more complex social system and larger scale public works.

Check for Understanding Write the following terms on the chalkboard and have students tell the significance of each to Egypt: Nile, deserts, Menes, delta.

Practice

Guided Practice
Lead a guided discussion of the questions in Transparency 5, Transparency 85, and in Section Review 1. (Answers are below.)

Define:
(a) churning rapid (b) triangular region at the mouth of a river (c) system of supplying crops with water (d) agricultural district

Identify:
(a) archaeologist who discovered tomb of Tutankhamon (b) boy king who ruled Egypt 1347 B.C.–1338 B.C. (c) world's longest river; winds through Egypt (d) narrow strip of land extending south from the First Cataract (e) northern part of Egypt (f) king who united all of Egypt

Answer:
1. When the flood waters receded, they left behind a rich layer of soil.
2. The deserts forced Egyptians to stay near the river and shielded Egypt from invaders.
3. He united Upper and Lower Egypt.
4. The Nile gave them life and security.

Independent Practice
Assign Independent Practice Worksheet 3.1.
Assign Geography Skills Worksheet 3.
Assign Vocabulary Worksheet 3.

Enrichment Activities

1. **Reading a Primary Source** Assign Voices from the Past Resource Book 3.1.

2. **Preparing a Report** Have interested students research Carter's discovery of Tutankhamon's tomb. (See *Gods, Graves and Scholars* by C.W. Ceram, pages 201–237.)

3. **Researching the Aswan Dam** The Aswan Dam provides a dramatic example of how culture can affect the environment. Ask advanced students to prepare a report examining the advantages and disadvantages of the Aswan Dam.

4. **Researching for Bonus Points** Award bonus points to students who can find the answer to

this question: In which country does the Nile River originate? (On a hilltop in Burundi, four degrees south of the Equator.)

Answers to Voice from The Past

1. hunger, violence, lawlessness, unhappiness
2. **(a)** He was led by a dream vision to make an offering to a god and pray for the Nile's return. **(b)** One might look to other countries for relief and then build a system of dams.

Egypt's pharaohs ruled as gods. 2

Section Objectives

After completing Section 2, students should be able to:

1. explain the role of the pharaohs.
2. discuss how and why the pyramids were constructed.
3. compare and contrast Egypt's three kingdoms.
4. identify and locate the empire built by the pharaohs of the New Kingdom.

Setting the Stage

Direct students' attention to the picture of the pyramids on page 53. Ask students to pretend that they are standing near the base of the Great Pyramid (note the car and group of people on the left side of the picture). Their assignment is to write a few sentences describing their impressions of the pyramids. After the students have completed this task, explain that many famous writers have also written about their first impression of the pyramids. For example, Julian Huxley wrote of his "pride in the magnitude of the human achievement involved ... to produce an effect different from that of any other work of man." Now ask students to read their impressions. This section explains the purpose of the pyramids and how they were built.

Teaching Strategies

Discussing History: Who Built the Pyramids? (Objective 1) As noted in the text, the Egyptians were convinced that their pharaohs had a spiritual double, or *ka*, which could live forever. As a result, they believed that a pharaoh could influence life even after his death. It seemed natural to the Egyptians that if the soul of a man—like the seed of a plant—could be preserved through the human equivalent of a 'dry' season, he would be restored to life in another world when the time came for his "rebirth." (This observation was made by historian Joseph Strayer.) The pyramid thus functioned as a giant "safe-deposit vault" that protected the pharaoh's *ka*. Ask students to summarize the role of the pharaoh in Egyptian society.

Discussing History: How Were the Pyramids Built? (Objective 2) The pyramids are a remarkable engineering feat. The Great Pyramid is still the largest stone structure in the world. One engineer estimated that the energy required to build the Great Pyramid could power a 10,000 ton steamship for 70 voyages around the globe at a speed of 20 knots! Ask students to speculate on how the Egyptians moved such huge masses of stone without the use of wheels. (The National Geographic book *Ancient Egypt* provides a photo-essay showing how modern researchers believe the pyramids were constructed.)

Skill Building: Comparing and Contrasting Egyptian Kingdoms (Objective 3) Using their texts as a reference, have students complete a chart comparing and contrasting the Old, Middle, and New Kingdoms of Egypt. Suggested headings for the chart are: Dates, Pharaohs, Main Events, Cultural Achievements, and Causes of Decline.

Geography in History: Making a Map (Objective 4) Distribute Outline Map 22: The Middle East. Ask students to label Lower and Upper Egypt, the Nile River, the Mediterranean and Red Seas, Palestine, Syria, and the Sinai Peninsula. Have students use information in the text to determine the extent of the New Kingdom empire at its height, and to show that information on their maps.

Check for Understanding Write the following statements on the chalkboard:

1. The pyramids were public museums.
2. The history of ancient Egypt was marked by periods of prosperity and strong rulers, interspersed with periods of weakness.
3. The desert always protected Egypt from invasion.

Ask students to identify the sentence that is an accurate statement about Egypt (2) and to explain why the other statements are inaccurate.

Practice

Guided Practice
Lead a guided discussion of the questions in Section Review 2. (Answers are below.)

Define:
(a) succession of rulers from a single family (b) king of Egypt considered to be a god (c) pharaoh's eternal spirit (d) huge tomb built for a pharaoh

Identify:
(a) Asian invaders who ruled Egypt from 1640 B.C. to 1570 B.C. (b) queen who helped expel the Hyksos (c) pharaoh after Ahhotep; continued to fight the Hyksos (d) female pharaoh who supported trade (e) warlike pharaoh who extended Egyptian empire (f) Egypt's last great pharaoh (g) invaders who conquered Egypt.

Answer:
1. believed to be gods as well as temporal rulers
2. (a) resident of pharaohs after death (b) Pictures represented people and things he needed; jewels and fine clothes would supply luxuries
3. The bounty of the Nile dried up, resulting in "diseases" that made life in Egypt difficult.
4. They undertook public works projects.
5. (a) period of 70 years in which civil war left Egypt open to Hyksos invaders (b) A series of warlike Egyptian rulers drove the Hyksos out.
6. (a) through trade (b) through conquest
7. competing civilizations; wave of invasions in Mediterranean area
8. regular flooding of Nile; law-abiding behavior; freedom from invasion; proper worshiping of gods and pharaohs
9. Herodotus lived in a society with a large slave population and may not have understood the willingness of Egyptians to work for the glory of the pharaoh and their need to find work during the flood season.

Independent Practice
Assign Independent Practice Worksheet 3.2.
Assign Basic Skills Worksheet 3.

Enrichment Activities

1. **Reading a Primary Source** Assign Voices from The Past Resource Book 3.2.

2. **Researching for Bonus Points** Award bonus points to students who can find the answer to this question: How did the Sphinx receive its name? (The Greeks named it after the Sphinx, a monster that spoke in riddles.)

Egypt's way of life endured 3,000 years. 3

Section Objectives

After completing Section 3, students should be able to:

1. compare and contrast the lives of nobles and peasants in Egyptian society.
2. define the concept of maat and explain its significance in Egyptian religion.
3. identify Akhenaton and explain his religious reforms.
4. describe some of the achievements of Egyptian culture.

Setting the Stage

Ask students to react to the following statement: "Social change is questionable and should in general be avoided. It's best to maintain traditional ways as much as possible." Ask students to give their opinions concerning this statement. Point out that most Egyptians placed a high value in maintaining tradition. They believed that their gods created a beautifully balanced social system. Each generation had a responsibility to maintain the rituals and patterns of life that their parents had followed. Explain that this section examines various aspects of daily life in Ancient Egypt. It also examines one of Egypt's greatest agents of change—the pharaoh Akhenaton.

Teaching Strategies

Discussing History: Egyptian Nobles and Peasants (Objective 1) Review the text's discussion (pages 57-60) of the lifestyles of nobles and peasants. Point out that wealthy nobles built spacious villas in the country. A villa might include shady gardens and a pool. Nobles filled their homes with luxurious furniture made out of ebony and cedar. The wealthy took great pride in their beds—while the poor slept on the ground, the rich reclined on mattresses cushioned with layers of sheets. As noted in the text, most wealthy Egyptians were born as nobles; however, it was possible for peasants to earn high positions in the army or in the government.

Emphasize that most Egyptians were peasants. They plowed the fields, paid taxes, and mined the pharaoh's gold. The peasants normally endured their grueling work with few complaints; however, in about 1170 B.C., the government failed to pay a group of Theban workers for more than two months. The frustrated workers finally left their jobs, chanting: "We are hungry! We are hungry!" The government officials were forced to pay them, thus ending the first recorded strike in history.

Discussing History: Analyzing Egyptian Religion (Objective 2) Review the concept of maat (page 60). Emphasize that maat was an idea of goodness that included justice, right, truth, and order. The "negative confession" on page 60 provides a good example of maat. The following statements were also part of this confession: "I have not added weight to the scales; I have not held up the water in its season; I have not neglected offerings to the gods." Read these statements to students and ask them to explain why it was important for Egyptians to avoid these deeds.

Skill Building: Analyzing Effects (Objective 3) Ask students to recall Amonhotep's decision to elevate the god Aton above all other gods. List on the board students' answers to the question, "What were all the effects of Amonhotep's decision?" (See text pages 61-62.) Then ask students to study the list and distinguish immediate effects, short-term effects, and long-term effects. Immediate effects might include Amonhotep's name change to Akhenaton and his announcement to the priests and the people of the changes he wanted. Short-term effects might include relocation of the capital, discrimination against the worshippers of other gods and the closing of their temples, decline in the power of priests, and the driving of religious cults "underground." Point out that long-term effects were negligible and ask students to suggest why. Students should be able to note that all the changes ended with Akhenaton's death and made no lasting impression on Egyptian culture. Ask students to write, on the basis of this analysis, definitions of immediate, short-term, and long-term effects.

Discussing History: Identifying Reasons for Egypt's Great Achievements (Objective 4) On the board write, "Necessity is the mother of invention." Ask students to cite four examples from ancient Egyptian civilization that support this observation. (Out of a need for assessing and collecting taxes, Egyptians invented numbers; to survey and measure areas, geometry and surveying; to keep track of time between floods, a calendar; and to improve a crude writing system, hieroglyphics.)

Check for Understanding Ask students to give an oral true or false response to each statement below and to correct each false statement.

1. Egyptian religion gave little power to priests. (F — Egyptians believed that priests would influence the gods with magic.)
2. Egyptians needed a knowledge of reading and writing to rise to the highest posts. (T)
3. Egyptian peasants were the lowest social class. (F — Slaves were the lowest class.)

Practice

Guided Practice
Lead a guided discussion of the questions in Section Review 3. (Answers are below.)

Define:
(a) idea of justice, right, truth, order (b) Egyptian form of writing (c) paper-like material

Identify:
(a) Egyptian god of the dead (b) monotheistic pharaoh (c) sun-god worshipped by Akhenaton (d) Egyptian god of air, wind, and breath of life (e) boy king who restored polytheism (f) stone inscribed in three languages, used to decipher hieroglyphics (g) Frenchman who broke the code of the Rosetta Stone

Answer:
1. (a) serve as governor, tax collector, general, official, priest (b) farm and work on public projects
2. belief in maat; belief that a righteous life would lead to eternal life
3. by studying Rosetta Stone and comparing hieroglyphics with ancient Greek language
4. (a) assessing and collecting taxes (b) redrawing of boundaries each year after the Nile's flooding (c) keeping track of time between floods to determine planting and harvesting times
5. Answer should stress idea of maat and idea that pharaohs felt responsible for well-being of subjects.

Independent Practice
Assign Independent Practice Worksheet 3.3.
Assign Critical Thinking Worksheet 3.

Enrichment Activities

1. **Reading a Primary Source** Assign Voices from the Past Resource Book 3.3.

2. **Analyzing a Primary Source** Ask advanced students to prepare an analysis of Akhenaton's famous hymn to Aton. (See Will Durant's *Our Oriental Heritage*, pages 206–209.)

3. **Researching for Bonus Points** Award bonus points to students who can find the answers to these questions: What does the name Nefertiti mean? ("the beautiful one is come") Who was Tutankhamon's wife? (Ankhasenaman)

Concluding the Chapter

1. **Chapter Closer**
   Recall that the pyramids are the most commonly identified symbols of ancient Egypt. Ask students to write essays describing how the contents of pyramids reveal other important symbols of Egyptian civilization.

2. **Reteaching Activities**
   a. **Outlining** Have students use the headings to write a sentence outline of Section 1.
   b. **Summarizing** Have students write a paragraph summarizing the achievements of the Old Kingdom, the Middle Kingdom, and the New Kingdom.
   c. **Organizing Information** Have students compile three lists—one identifying the social classes in ancient Egypt, another identifying the characteristics of Egyptian religious beliefs, and the third identifying the cultural achievements of ancient Egypt.

3. **Chapter Review Activities**
   Assign Chapter Review 2 activities.

Chapter Evaluation

Chapter Test 3 and Computer Test Bank Chapter 3 Test can be used to evaluate your students' understanding of this chapter.

Answers to Chapter Review 3

Reviewing the Facts

1. **a.** rapids of a river **b.** region in which branches of a river fan out over a broad, marshy, triangular area of land **c.** series of rulers from a single family **d.** term for the ruler of Egypt **e.** immense structure built as a tomb for the pharaoh **f.** idea of justice, right, truth, and order **g.** form of writing
2. **a.** region of Egypt to the south of the First Cataract **b.** region of Egypt to the north, beginning one hundred miles before the Nile enters the Mediterranean **c.** made possible the growth of Egyptian civilization **d.** narrow corridor of land which invaders eventually crossed to reach Egypt **e.** united Egypt **f.** nomadic people who invaded and conquered Egypt **g.** female pharaoh who encouraged trade instead of war **h.** extended Egyptian empire to its greatest size **i.** Egypt's last great pharaoh **j.** invaders who broke Egypt's power forever **k.** Egyptian god of the dead **l.** pharaoh who tried to convert Egyptians to a monotheistic religion **m.** reestablished the religion of Amon **n.** broke the code of the hieroglyphics in 1822
3. The flood cycle of the Nile gave Egyptians rich farmlands and an optimistic attitude.
4. **a.** The pharaoh was regarded as a god with unlimited power. **b.** The Mesopotamian king was considered a representative of the gods.
5. **a.** pharaoh, nobles, artisans and shopkeepers, peasants, and slaves **b.** reading and writing, valor and service in pharaoh's army
6. belief in many gods, an afterlife for the just
7. system of numbers, geometry, surveying, calendar, medical knowledge and practice

Basic Skills

1. Possible answers: pyramids—Abu Rawash, Giza, Abusir, Saqqara, Maidum, el-Lahun, Thebes; temples—Karnak, Luxor, Abu Simbel; mines—copper and turquoise in Sinai, gold east of Thebes and south of Abu Simbel; quarry—east of Akhetaton; cataracts—three on the Nile south of Syene
2. **(a)** north **(b)** south, north, west
3.

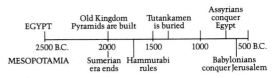

4. *Political:* the Nile Valley provided geographic unity to Egypt. *Religious:* Egyptians worshipped the Nile as a god that gave them life. *Economic:* irrigation and flooding from the Nile shaped agricultural activity.

Researching and Reporting Skills
Students' research findings will vary.

Critical Thinking
1. The cataracts formed a barrier to communication and travel.
2. Students may conclude that Egyptians thought makeup and jewelry beautified their appearance, or that they were vain.
3. **(a)** Students may use such words as stiff, stylized, flat, idealized. **(b)** Images of pharaohs

Advance Planner

Chapter 4	Ancient India and China 2500 B.C.–A.D. 220			★ Advanced
Focus	The teachings of Buddha in India and of Confucius in China			● Basic

	Section 1	Section 2	Section 3	Section 4
Objectives	1. Identify and locate the landforms of the Indian subcontinent. 2. Make inferences about Indus valley civilization from archaeological findings. 3. Identify and explain the basic ideas of Hinduism. 4. Explain the relationship between castes and the concepts of karma and dharma.	1. Describe the rise and spread of Buddhism 2. Compare and contrast Hindu and Buddhist religions. 3. Identify Ashoka and explain how he contributed to the growth of Buddhism.	1. Identify the geographic features that isolated ancient China from other civilizations. 2. Explain how the family and royal government held Chinese society together. 3. Describe the cultural achievements of the Shang dynasty. 4. Compare and contrast the teachings of Confucius, Lao Tzu, and the Legalists.	1. Describe the achievements of Emperor Shih Huang-ti. 2. Describe the achievements of Emperor Wu-ti. 3. Locate and compare the boundaries of the Ch'in and Han dynasties.
Setting the Stage	Geography of India Geography in History: Making a Map Key Transparency 6 Outline Map 20	Discussing History: The Rise and Spread of Buddhism.	Geography of China Geography in History: The Isolation of China Transparency 8 Outline Map 19	The Ch'in and Han dynasties Transparency 10
Teaching Strategies	Skill Building: Making Inferences About Indus Valley Civilization Discussing History: Hindu Beliefs Discussing History: Castes Check for Understanding	Discussing History: Comparing Buddhism and Hinduism Discussing History: Ashoka's Rule Transparency 7 Check for Understanding	Discussing History: The Son of Heaven Teaching with Pictures: Bronze Treasures Transparency 9 Discussing History: A Conversation in Time Check for Understanding	Teaching with Pictures: Shih Huang-ti's Burial City Using Geographic Themes: Movement Geography in History: The Ch'in and Han Empires Outline Map 19 Check for Understanding
Guided Practice	Transparency 6 Q&A Section Review 1	Transparency 7 Q&A Section Review 2	Transparency 8 Q&A Transparency 9 Q&A Section Review 3	Transparency 10 Q&A Section Review 4
Independent Practice Worksheets	Independent Practice 4.1 Vocabulary 4	Independent Practice 4.2 Geography Skills 4 Basic Skills 4	Independent Practice 4.3 Critical Thinking 4	Independent Practice 4.4
Enrichment	1. Primary Source: Voices 4.1 2. Preparing a Report: Monsoons 3. ★ Applying Hindu Concepts 4. Researching for Points	1. Primary Source: Voices 4.2 2. Preparing a Report 3. Comparing Leaders 4. Researching for Points	1. Primary Source: Voices 4.3 2. Creative Writing 3. ★ Understanding Confucius 4. Researching for Points	1. Primary Source: Voices 4.4 2. Creative Writing 3. Researching for Points

Chapter Closer	
● **Reteaching Activities**	Summarizing, Writing Identifications, Defending Opinions
Chapter Review	Summary, Reviewing the Facts, Basic Skills, Researching and Reporting Skills, Critical Thinking, Perspectives on Past and Present, Investigating History
Chapter Evaluation	Chapter Test 4, Computer Test Bank Chapter 4 Test

Unit I Review	
Geographic Theme:	Location: Where did ancient cities develop?
Unit Perspectives	Understanding History (Relating, Locating, Sequencing), Critical Thinking, Making Decisions, Continuity and Change
Unit Evaluation	Unit I Test

they can make from the following information uncovered by archaeologists:

1. Although Mohenjo-Daro and Harrapa were 350 miles apart, each was laid out with streets running north-south and east-west like a grid. (cities were formally planned; the two cities were in direct communication)
2. Each major city had huge warehouses for storing grain. (The cities produced surpluses for storage and central distribution.)
3. Small clay seals made in the Indus valley have been found in ancient Mesopotamia. (The two regions exchanged goods.)

Discussing History: Hindu Beliefs (Objective 3) Explain that Hinduism is the world's largest religion. Unlike Christianity or Islam, Hinduism has no central figure or single sacred book; nevertheless, the *Upanishads* (the name is derived from two Sanskrit words, *upa*, meaning "near" and *shad*, "to sit") and the Vedas discuss the central ideas of the Hindu faith. Review the four key ideas discussed on page 71. The relationship between Brahman (the World Soul) and Atman (the Self) is particularly important. The following parable explains this relationship:

"Fetch me a fruit from the banyan tree," said Svetaketu's father to his son.
"Here is a fruit, sir."
"Break it."
"I have broken it, sir."
"What do you see?"
"Very tiny seeds, sir."
"Break one."
"I have broken it, sir."
"Now what do you see?"
"Why, nothing sir."
"Dear son, what you do not see is the essence of the banyan tree. In that essence the mighty banyan tree exists. The essence, my dear, is the unseen spirit which pervades everywhere. It is the Self of all things. And you are that Self, Svetaketu."

Read this parable, "Svetaketu's Education," to your advanced students. Ask what lesson (that everyone is part of the universal spirit) the parable teaches.

Discussing History: Castes (Objective 4) Explain that a caste consisted of a group of people who shared the same or similar occupations, who ate together, and who intermarried. Membership was hereditary. (For a discussion of the privileges enjoyed by the Brahmans, see *Our Oriental Heritage* by Will Durant, pages 484–487.) Ask students how the caste system is tied to the ideas of rebirth, karma, and dharma. Students should be able to identify the belief that rebirth provided the only means of changing one's caste. Leading the best possible life while fulfilling one's dharma (duty) could positively influence one's karma (fate) with the result that one was reborn into a higher caste. Failing to observe the discipline of dharma could have the opposite effect. Ask students how this belief contrasts with traditional American beliefs about raising one's social status. Students might suggest the traditional view that people can be whatever they wish during their lifetimes if they work hard enough for it.

Check for Understanding Have students complete the following sentence fragments:

1. The region in which India is located is often called a subcontinent because _____ .
2. The Indus valley civilization was invaded by _____ .
3. Brahman is a _____ .
4. The social divisions within the Indian Society are called _____ .

Practice

Guided Practice
Lead a guided discussion of the questions in Overhead Transparency 6 and in Section Review 1. (Answers are below.)

Define:
(a) large part of a continent separated by some natural barrier from the rest of the continent (b) seasonal wind (c) passing of inner self from body to body (d) state of perfect understanding (e) "birth group" (f) outcast (g) ethical law of cause and effect (h) duties and obligations of each caste

Identify:
(a) mountains separating China and India (b) Its valley was the site of early civilizations. (c) largest ancient cities in the Indus valley (d) nomads from central Asia who arrived in the Indus valley around 1500 B.C. (e) set of beliefs and practices derived from the mingled traditions of the Indus valley dwellers and the Aryans (f) collections of Aryan hymns (g) essays seeking to explain the meaning of Vedic hymns (h) highest, priestly caste (i) second highest caste (j) third highest caste (k) fourth caste

Answer:
1. (a) regular pattern of city buildings (b) seals that merchants used to mark shipment of goods also found in ancient Mesopotamia (c) discovery of

kilns, vats for dyeing cloth (d) quality of building became poorer, signs of violence

2. Aryans were nomadic herders; Indus valley
people were farmers and city-dwellers with
trades. Aryans were illiterate; Indus valley
people had writing system.

3. (a) contain ancient, sacred hymns (b) contain
insights into India during the Vedic Age

4. (a) A Hindu goal is the attainment of *moksha*, a
merging of the self with *Brahman*, the universal spirit. Those not attaining this goal are
locked in a cycle of reincarnation. (b) By the
law of *karma*, proper behavior will guarantee
rebirth into a higher caste and immoral acts
will send a soul to a lower caste in the next
reincarnation.

Independent Practice
Assign Independent Practice Worksheet 4.1.
Assign Vocabulary Worksheet 4.

Enrichment Activities

1. **Reading a Primary Source** Assign Voices from
the Past Resource Book 4.1.

2. **Preparing a Report** Monsoon rains have been
called India's "breath of life." Predicting their
arrival is said to be the world's most important
weather forecast. Ask students to prepare a
report on the monsoons. Students might consult the December 1984 issue of *National
Geographic* for information on monsoons.

3. **Applying Hindu Concepts** The great Hindu
epic the *Mahabharata* contains a section
called the *Bhagavad Gita* ("Lord's Song"). It
tells the story of a prince named Arjuna who
was forced to fight a war against his deceitful
relatives. Before the battle, he turns to the god
Krishna and asks, "What victory can bring delight, what rich spoils could profit, what rule
recompense, what span of life itself seem sweet,
bought with such blood?" Read Arjuna's question to advanced students. Ask them to write a
reply using the key Hindu beliefs discussed in
Section 1. (Krishna reminds Arjuna that it is
his dharma or duty as a prince to fight. He also
explains that Arjuna will not actually kill his
relatives since their souls are eternal and will
be reincarnated.)

4. **Researching for Bonus Points** Award bonus
points to students who can find the answer to
this question: What is the name of the cape
where the Bay of Bengal meets the Arabian Sea?
(Cape Comorin)

Buddhism spread under Mauryan rulers. 2

Section Objectives

After completing Section 2, students should be
able to:

1. describe the rise and spread of Buddhism.
2. compare and contrast Hindu and Buddhist
religions.
3. identify Ashoka and explain how he contributed to the growth of Buddhism.

Setting the Stage

**Discussing History: The Rise and Spread of Bud-
dhism** (Objective 1) Have students imagine what
it would be like to be a prince living in India during the sixth century B.C. Everyone agrees that the
prince is handsome, athletic, and intelligent. He
lives in three palaces with a lovely wife and a
healthy son. Now ask your students if there is any
reason for the prince to be unhappy. Explain that a
young prince named Gautama Siddhartha enjoyed
all of these luxuries. He seemed to have everything until, one day, he awoke to the shocking fact
that he did not have wisdom. For the first time in
his life, he visited a city where people of lower
castes lived. He saw there a man who was terribly
sick, another who was old and feeble, and another
who was dead. Gautama decided then that life was
largely an endless sorrow and the only way to
escape it was by seeking wisdom. Explain that
this section examines the wisdom Gautama found
and taught. It also discusses a dynasty that united
India and helped spread a religion that became
known as Buddhism. Buddhism spread throughout India and into present-day Sri Lanka, Afghanistan, Tibet, China, Mongolia, Korea, and Japan.
Buddhism also spread southeast into Burma,
Southeast Asia, Malaysia, and Indonesia. Have students use the map on page 819 in the Historical
Atlas to trace this spread.

Teaching Strategies

**Discussing History: Comparing Buddhism and
Hinduism** (Objective 2) After students have read
"Buddhism taught nonviolence" (pages 73–74), discuss how it would feel to live in a society in which
there was no hope of improving one's status during
a lifetime. Point out that Hinduism teaches that

each person has to repeat the cycle of life, death, and rebirth many times before achieving *moksha*. Buddha agreed with the Hindu goal of escaping from the pain of this world; however, his method of escape differed. Review Buddha's Four Noble Truths. Emphasize that Buddha believed that anyone who understood these Truths and followed the Eightfold Path could achieve *nirvana*. As Buddha told his disciples, "Go into all lands and preach this gospel. Tell them that the poor and lowly, the rich and the high, are all one, and that all castes unite in this religion as do the rivers in the sea." At this time, you might direct your students' attention to the Voice from the Past on page 75, which presents several of Buddha's best-known ideas.

Discussing History: Ashoka's Rule (Objective 3) After reading "The Mauryan dynasty built an empire," have students compare and contrast the reigns of Chandragupta and Ashoka. Ask students if a ruler should strive to be loved or feared. Use Overhead Transparency 7 to show students the extent of the Mauryan Empire and the distribution of Ashoka's edicts. Emphasize that Ashoka played an important role in helping to spread Buddhism to the rest of Asia.

Check for Understanding Write the following names on your chalkboard: Ashoka, Chandragupta, and Buddha. Have students match each person with one of the following quotations:

1. "Government is the science of punishment" (Chandragupta)
2. "the Enlightened One" (Buddha)
3. "officials of righteousness" (Ashoka)

Practice

Guided Practice
Lead a guided discussion of the questions in Overhead Transparency 7 and in Section Review 2. (Answers are below.)

Define:
(a) release from pain and selfishness (b) ruling family (c) public announcement of policy

Identify:
(a) wisdom-seeker who came to be called Buddha (b) religion that teaches the Four Noble Truths and the Eightfold Path (c) cruel leader who united northern India and founded Mauryan dynasty (d) last strong ruler of Mauryan dynasty

Answer:
1. (a) by following the Eightfold Path one step at a

time (b) Buddhism required no rituals, recognized no castes or divisions of people.
2. 298 B.C. to 180 B.C.
3. (a) uniting India (b) spreading Buddhism
4. The suffering in Hinduism is a result of improper behavior (failure to respect *dharma*). In Buddhism, suffering is caused by self-centered cravings and can be avoided.

Independent Practice
Assign Independent Practice Worksheet 4.2.
Assign Geography Skills Worksheet 4.
Assign Basic Skills Worksheet 4.

Enrichment Activities

1. **Reading a Primary Source** Assign Voices from the Past Resource Book 4.2.

2. **Preparing a Report** Ask students to prepare a report on Buddha, Chandragupta, or Ashoka.

3. **Comparing Leaders** Ask advanced students to write an essay that compares and contrasts the reigns and reforms of Akhenaton and Ashoka.

4. **Researching for Bonus Points** Award bonus points to students who can find the answer to this question: What were the names of Buddha's wife and son? (Princess Yasodhara and Rahula)

Answers to Voice from The Past

1. The paired verses are making a basic contrast between a life of evil and a life of good—that is, a religious life.
2. Thou shalt not speak or act with an evil thought. Thou shalt not harbor thoughts of hatred. Thou shalt not let passion dominate thy mind. Thou shalt not fail to follow the law.
3. People should seek the qualities of pure thought, love for others, reflectiveness, lawfulness, true knowledge, and serenity of mind. The phrases are found in the second part of each verse.

Imperial government united China. 3

Section Objectives

After completing Section 3, students should be able to:

1. identify the geographic features that isolated ancient China from other civilizations.
2. explain how the family and royal government held Chinese society together.
3. describe cultural achievements of the Shang dynasty.
4. compare and contrast the teachings of Confucius, Lao Tzu, and the Legalists.

Setting the Stage

Geography in History: The Isolation of China (Objective 1) Begin by using Overhead Transparency 8, *Ancient China*, to help students identify major geographic features. Point out the location of the Yellow and Yangtze rivers. Explain that the Yellow River was the most important river in ancient China. As noted in the text, the river derives its name from yellow dust called *loess* deposited by northwest winds from the Gobi Desert. A layer of fertile loess up to 450 feet thick covers the North China Plain. As a result, this region became China's fertile heartland. The Chinese called this region the Middle Kingdom since they believed that it was situated at the center of the world. Geography encouraged the belief. Ask your students to name the geographic barriers that isolated the Middle Kingdom. Geographic isolation permitted China to develop a unique cultural tradition that this section examines.

Conclude by distributing Outline Map 19: China and Japan. Ask students to label the major rivers, mountains, and deserts. They should also locate the major countries that surround China and the major seas that border China.

Teaching Strategies

Discussing History: The Son of Heaven (Objective 2) Discuss the role the family played in Chinese society. Explain that the Chinese believed in an all-powerful force called Heaven that regulated the universe. Heaven granted the right to rule, or Mandate of Heaven, to a family demonstrating unusual virtue. Known as the Son of Heaven, the ruler formed a crucial link between the human world and the forces governing the universe. Point out that the Son of Heaven held a demanding job. As the head of state, he commanded vast armies. As the Middle Kingdom's moral teacher, he had the responsibility of living a virtuous life. Emphasize that rulers who failed to fulfill their duties lost the Mandate of Heaven and could expect natural calamities and ultimately a revolution. The Chinese called the rise and fall of ruling families the dynastic cycle.

Teaching with Pictures: Bronze Treasures (Objective 3) Ask students to read "Civilization emerged in Shang times" (pages 78–79). First show Overhead Transparency 9 to trace the extents of the Shang Empire and the succeeding Chou Empire. Then review the cultural contributions of Shang artisans. Direct students' attention to the pictures of bronze objects on page 79. Chinese bronzesmiths used bronze to make tools, weapons, and ornamental containers. Modern experts believe that the bronzesmiths created work of great skill and beauty. The ax blade on page 79 is fourteen inches long. Archaeologists found it on the entrance ramp of a large tomb. Forty-eight decapitated skeletons were found nearby. The ancient Chinese buried sacrificial victims inside their royal tombs, but some of the victims may have been sacrificed outside the tomb to serve as armed guards protecting it from evil spirits. Ask students what other craft developed during Shang times. (the spinning and weaving of silk)

Discussing History: A Conversation in Time (Objective 4) Explain that the unrest near the end of the Chou dynasty deeply disturbed many Chinese. Confucius, the Taoists, and the Legalists all offered solutions to restore social order. Carefully review each of these three schools of thought. Then divide students into teams of three. Each team should include a Confucian, a Taoist, and a Legalist. Each team member should discuss his or her views on how to restore social order. Allow some teams to present their arguments to the class.

Check for Understanding Write the five traits of a civilization on the chalkboard (cities, specialized workers, writing, advanced technology, complex institutions) and call on students to give examples of each trait in the ancient Chinese civilization.

Practice

Guided Practice
Lead a guided discussion of the questions in Overhead Transparencies 8 and 9, and in Section Review 3. (Answers are below.)

Define:
(a) China's name for itself (b) belief that royal authority came from heaven (c) pattern of strength, decline, and replacement that characterizes dynasties (d) fertile yellow soil carried by rivers

Identify:
(a) one of two rivers that water China's heartland (b) the other river (c) mountainous region west of China (d) region north of China, inhabited by

nomads **(e)** first historic family to rule China **(f)** dynasty that followed the Shang **(g)** scholar whose teachings later became basis for religion **(h)** Chinese thinker who stressed the natural order, or Tao

Answer:

1. **(a)** respect for and duties to the family and king or emperor **(b)** At the family level, religion revolved around the spirits of ancestors; at the government level, ancestral spirits authorized the power of a ruler.
2. **(a)** served in army and government **(b)** tilled the soil **(c)** created objects from bronze; wove silk
3. **(a)** People whose spoken languages were different could all read the written language. **(b)** The great number of characters in written Chinese required long years of study.
4. Nobles fought each other and chaos ruled.
5. **(a)** Social order can be maintained by upholding traditions. **(b)** Following the natural order is the way to achieve harmony. **(c)** A powerful leader can restore order by severely punishing misdeeds and greatly rewarding obedience.
6. **(a)** It suggests that virtuous behavior on the part of the ruler will spare him catastrophes. **(b)** Look for a discussion of specific contemporary leaders considered to be honorable and wise and those who are not.

Independent Practice

Assign Independent Practice Worksheet 4.3.
Assign Critical Thinking Worksheet 4.

Enrichment Activities

1. **Reading a Primary Source** Assign Voices from the Past Resource Book 4.3.

2. **Creative Writing** Ask students to pretend that they are Egyptian officials who have just returned to Thebes after visiting the Middle Kingdom. Their assignments are to write reports for the Pharaoh comparing and contrasting everyday life in ancient Egypt and China.

3. **Understanding Confucius** Ask advanced students to compile a list of five sayings of Confucius. The students should also prepare a brief explanation of what each saying means to them. *(Bartlett's Familiar Quotations* contains several of Confucius' most famous sayings.)

4. **Researching for Bonus Points** Award bonus points to students who can find the answer to this question: What was the ancient Chinese symbol for King and what do the different strokes mean? (The symbol was ‡ ˙ The three

horizontal strokes stand for heaven, earth, and humanity. The vertical stroke stands for the king who connects all three.)

Ch'in and Han emperors strengthened China. 4

Section Objectives

After completing Section 4, students should be able to:

1. describe the achievements of Emperor Shih Huang-ti.
2. describe the achievements of Emperor Wu-ti.
3. locate and compare the boundaries of the Ch'in and Han dynasties.

Setting the Stage

Ask students if any of them can answer these questions: Who built the Great Wall and why? What is inside the world's most incredible tomb? What was the Great Silk Road? Why would people have their bodies encased inside a jade suit? Then explain that they will learn the answers to these questions as they study Section 4, "Ch'in and Han emperors strengthened China." Use Overhead Transparency 10 to point out the locations of the Ch'in and Han empires, the Great Wall, and the Silk Road.

Teaching Strategies

Teaching With Pictures: Shih Huang-ti's "Buried City" (Objective 1) Identify Shih Huang-ti and review his achievements. Then direct students' attention to the picture on page 85. Explain that Shih Huang-ti feared death. In order to find immortality, he commanded over 700,000 workers to build him a huge underground burial city. Local farmers discovered the site in 1974. The picture on page 85 shows a small portion of an underground army that protected the eastern side of the burial city. Archaeologists have to date unearthed more than 7,000 life-sized warriors, 100 chariots, and 400 chariot horses. No two warriors are alike. (Researchers have identified twenty-four different styles of facial hair.) The site, or trench, is 700 feet long and 200 feet wide and is now a great indoor museum.

Tell students that even greater wonders await archaeologists. The clay army stands about one mile east of an earth mound that is thought to cover Shih Huang-ti's tomb. According to a Han historian, the First Emperor's tomb lies behind a magnificent jade door. A wooden dragon (symbolizing great fortune) carries a copper coffin across a topographic map of the Ch'in empire. The Yellow River and other bodies of water are represented by mercury. (The April 1978 issue of *National Geographic* has an artistic recreation of what this burial city might look like.) A recent geological survey suggests that there is a heavy concentration of mercury in the area covered by the earthen mound. As of this writing, archaeologists have not yet attempted to excavate Shih Huang-ti's tomb.

Using Geographic Themes: Movement (Objective 2) After students read, "Civilization flowered under the Han dynasty," review the achievements of Wu-ti. Then direct students' attention to the map of the Great Silk Road on page 86. Explain that before the Silk Road was opened, China's trade was mainly coastal to Japan, Southeast Asia, Indonesia, and India. Indian traders brought Chinese goods to Persia and Arabia. Chinese goods reached the Roman Empire through Arab traders. The Silk Road made it possible for western peoples to trade more directly for Chinese goods by land. The Chinese exported silk, cinnamon, and jade. In return, they received horses, gold, silver, and several new foods including pomegranates, broad beans, grapes, and clover. Emphasize that few, if any, caravans actually made the entire journey. Instead, the traders exchanged goods at established change-over points.

Geography in History: The Ch'in and Han Empires (Objective 3) Distribute Outline Map 19. Ask students to construct a key that includes symbols for the Ch'in and Han empires. Using the text and the map on page 86 as references, have students designate the lands controlled by the Ch'in and Han dynasties. Ask students to also draw the Great Wall and use the map scale to check that the wall they have drawn extends about 1,400 miles.

Check for Understanding Ask students to write three achievements of the Ch'in dynasty and three achievements of the Han dynasty.

Practice

Guided Practice
Lead a guided discussion of the questions in Overhead Transparency 10 and in Section Review 4.

(Answers are below.)

Define:
someone even greater than a king

Identify:
(a) dynasty that followed Chou (b) first emperor of China (c) protective wall that extended 1,400 miles (d) dynasty following Ch'in (e) most powerful Han emperor (f) greatest writings of Chou times, said to have been collected by Confucius (g) words of wisdom spoken by Confucius (h) trade route for silk

Answer:
1. (a) stopped internal wars, built wall, gave China lasting form of government (b) drew new boundary lines to take away nobles' power and set up administrative districts, burned books, used peasant labor
2. (a) founded university to teach the Five Classics (b) sent traders along Great Silk Road
3. contacts through trade; need for religious comfort in bitter times
4. *period of strength:* Wu-Ti's reign, including advancements in learning and trade; *period of decline:* civil war, rebellions, and decline in prosperity; *period of replacement:* collapse of Han dynasty

Independent Practice
Assign Independent Practice Worksheet 4.4.

Enrichment Activities

1. **Reading a Primary Source** Assign Voices from the Past Resource Book 4.4.

2. **Creative Writing** Ask students to write an eye-witness account of what they might have seen at one of the cross-over points on the Great Silk Road.

3. **Researching for Bonus Points** The picture on page 87 shows the jade burial suit made for Han prince Liu Sheng. Award bonus points to students who can find the answer to this question: Who was Liu Sheng's wife and how was she buried? (His princess, Lady Dou Wan, was also buried inside a jade burial suit.)

Concluding the Chapter

1. **Chapter Closer**
   Ask students to recall the chapter focus discussion on Buddha and Confucius. Have each student write a chapter summary explaining how Indian and Chinese achievements reflected the goals of Buddha and Confucius.

2. Reteaching Activities

a. Summarizing Have students write one paragraph describing four important features of India's first civilization and a second paragraph explaining four basic beliefs of Hinduism.

b. Summarizing Have students use the headings and subheadings in this chapter to summarize the teachings of Buddha and the contributions of the Mauryan dynasty.

c. Writing Identifications Have students write a sentence about each of the following traits of early Chinese civilization: the family, the view of government, crafts, the teachings of Confucius, and Chinese writing.

d. Defending Opinions Have students write a paragraph stating in which dynasty, Ch'in or Han, they would have preferred to live and why.

3. Chapter Review Activities

Assign Chapter Review 4 activities.

Chapter Evaluation

Chapter Test 4 and Computer Test Bank Chapter 4 Test can be used to evaluate your students' understanding of this chapter.

Answers to Chapter Review 4

Reviewing the Facts

1. **a.** large part of a continent separated from the rest of the continent by natural barriers **b.** passing of the inner self from body to body **c.** birth group in the Indian society, signifying social status **d.** announcement of a ruler's policies

2. **a.** mountain chain separating India from rest of Asia **b.** site of first Indian civilization **c.** one of two largest cities in India's first civilization **d.** nomadic people from central Asia whose culture blended with that of Indus valley people **e.** collections of Aryan hymns **f.** name for Sidhartha Gautama after he achieved enlightenment **g.** united northern India, founded Mauryan dynasty **h.** became an enlightened Buddhist ruler **i.** site of China's first civilization **j.** river in China flowing from Tibet **k.** first historic Chinese dynasty **l.** second historic Chinese dynasty **m.** third historic Chinese dynasty **n.** fourth historic Chinese dynasty **o.** Chinese teacher and philosopher who urged social harmony **p.** Chinese philosopher who believed in emulating order in nature **q.** founder of lasting form of government; responsible for building the Great Wall **r.** most powerful emperor of Han dynasty; responsible for beginning of silk trade

3. well-planned and regularly laid-out cities, public buildings, artifacts

4. **(a)** from the mingled beliefs of Aryans and Indus valley people **(b)** Hindu view supported caste system and defined role of each caste.

5. **(a)** Ashoka converted to Buddhism and made Buddhism the official religion of the kingdom. **(b)** People can attain enlightenment and *nirvana* by following the Eightfold Path. They had to treat all living things with loving kindness.

6. **(a)** united northern India and founded a strong dynasty **(b)** adopted Buddhism and sent missionaries to neighboring lands

7. respect for family and for government

8. Confucianism, Taoism, and Legalism.

9. restored internal order, built Great Wall

10. **(a)** a period of peace, unity, trade with new places **(b)** Buddhism spread through China.

Basic Skills

1. **(a)** Page 77, physical geography; page 86, political geography **(b)** The Ch'in empire occupied the plains formed by the Yangtse and Yellow rivers, surrounded by sea, mountains, and desert. The Han empire extended beyond these natural boundaries.

2. *Geographic Features:* both isolated by natural boundaries and centered on fertile river plains. *Social Patterns:* India—Hinduism promoted caste system, Buddhism, a concern for all individuals; China—social classes, peasant revolts; close family ties and obedience to elders; greater importance to group than to individual; absolute authority of ruler. *Major Achievements:* India—city planning, cotton weaving and dyeing, many crafts; China—cities, writing, producing and weaving silk, Great Wall, network of highways. *Philosophies of Life:* India—Hinduism, Buddhism; China—Confucianism, Taoism, Buddhism, Legalism.

3. Bronze Age

4. **(a)** approximately 700 miles **(b)** Located in a wide river plain, good for farming and supporting a growing population; on a waterway, and on major routes crossing the mountains between India and Asia Minor; good for trade.

(c) Entered India by Khyber and Bolan passes; would descend into the wide plain of the Indus past farmland, scattered villages, and cities; would then pass into the even broader, fertile valley of the Ganges, ending at the Bay of Bengal.

Researching and Reporting Skills
1. In Gupta period, Chinese monks came to India to study Buddhism; in Rajput period, Buddhism declined. Buddha was worshipped in Hindu temples. During Ming period, Chinese scholars turned to Confucianism, which later spread to Japan.
2. Answers will vary.
3. Primary sources: b, d and e: secondary sources: a and c

Critical Thinking
1. (a) *Indian caste system:* hereditary, based on religion and ritual purity; *Chinese social classes:* traditional, based on occupation (b) In India, people were locked in by the caste system. In China, individuals were limited to their class though revolts occurred and individuals occasionally improved their status.
2. (a) unfavorable (b) favorable (c) favorable in later period
3. *agreed:* in India, Chandragupta, Ashoka in the early period; in China, Legalists, Ch'in Shih Huang Ti and his son; *disagreed:* in India, Buddha, Ashoka in later period; in China, Confucius, Lao-Tzu, Wu-ti
4. The Vedas provided the basis for a caste system in India. Confucius promoted traditional values and good morals as standards of wise government in China.

Perspectives Past and Present
1. Have students use a world map of religions in an atlas such as Goode's *World Atlas* (Rand McNally).
2. Students should be aware of the official separation between church and state in many countries today. Yet many political issues involve religious or moral principles. Have students identify some of these issues.

Investigating History
Students' research findings will vary.

Unit I *Review Activities*

1. Assign Geographic Theme: Location.
2. Assign Unit Perspectives questions.

Unit I *Review Answers*

Geographic Theme: Location
1. Memphis: on Nile near start of Delta; Thebes: on Nile in central Egypt; Babylon: on Euphrates River in central Mesopotamia; Uruk: on Euphrates in southern Mesopotamia; Çatal Hüyük: at northern edge of Taurus Mountains in Anatolia; Jericho: on oasis west of Jordan River and on north-south trade route; Jarmo: in foothills of Zagros Mountains east of Tigris River; Jerusalem: north and west of Dead Sea.
2. A good supply of water, a protected site, valuable resources nearby.
3. Ninevah, capital of Assyria; Memphis, early capital of Egypt; Thebes, later capital of Egypt.

Unit *Perspectives*

Understanding History
1. **a.** Civilization is a complex form of culture, characterized in part by the use of advanced technology. **b.** Archaeologists study the artifacts from prehistory. **c.** Cuneiform was the writing system invented by the Sumerians, and hieroglyphics was a form of writing invented by the Egyptians. **d.** Pharaohs built pyramids as homes for their afterlife. **e.** Paleolithic and Neolithic are two prehistoric periods. **f.** A polytheist worships many gods. A monotheist worships only one God. **g.** An ideogram is a more advanced form of writing than is a pictograph.
2. **a.** archaeological site of tiny Neolithic settlement in Iraq **b.** large Neolithic settlement in Turkey **c.** area between the Tigris and Euphrates rivers where Sumerian civilization arose **d.** longest river in the world, around which ancient Egyptian civilization developed **e.** highest mountain range in the world; separated ancient Chinese civilization from Indian civilization. **f.** large city built along Indus River **g.** river on which China's civilization began
3. **a.** 3, 1, 2 **b.** 2, 3, 1 **c.** 2, 3, 1 **d.** 1, 3, 2

Critical Thinking
1. (a) Taoism stresses natural order; Confucianism, tradition and morals. (b) Prophets were messengers of God; pharaohs were gods. (c) Nebuchadnezzar conquered and ruled by violence; his palace was a place of pleasure. Buddha taught nonviolence and turning away from pursuit of pleasures.
2. Egypt—worship of the Nile, of the pharaohs;

power of priests through magic. Mesopotamia —priests all powerful, interceded with the gods, managed major industries, irrigation, timing of planting and harvesting. India—Hinduism structured Indian society into castes; Buddhism influenced some of India's rulers.

3. (a) presence of cities; also in China bronze work indicates specialized workers, in Mesopotamia code of law indicates complex government institutions, in Egypt Tutankhamon's head indicates empire, religion and specialized work. (b) No cities, so no civilization, but elaborate religious temple in England and figurine in clay illustrating preparation of food based on farming in Mexico

4. Conquest and trade were the two principal means of spreading culture. India received Hinduism from Aryan conquerors. Buddhism spread to China through trade. Egyptians learn spinning, weaving, making bronze, using chariots from their Hyksos conquerors. Sumerian civilization spread through the empire of their Babylonian conquerors.

Making Decisions

(a) unwise, likely to meet resistance of the people
(b) good, likely to make his rule acceptable

(c) worst, destroyed precious literature that was lost to posterity (d) very good, likely to get him support of people

Continuity and Change

1. (a) new discoveries of ancient centers of civilization, some perhaps older than those we know now, perhaps on new continents (b) new discoveries being made by current explorations; new scientific techniques making research more effective; enigmas such as that of Stonehenge and the "Peoples of the Sea" waiting to be answered.

2. (a) and (b) Influence spread; became the basis for world religions. (c) and (d) Power declined; overthrown by invasions.

3. Possible answers: (a) cities, armies (b) trade, ironwork (c) religion, language

Unit Evaluation

Unit I Test can be used to evaluate your students' understanding of this unit.

The Mediterranean World

Overview

This unit surveys the rise of new civilizations in the Mediterranean region. The civilizations that developed in ancient Greece and Rome became so great that they became known as the *classical civilizations*. To some extent, they helped to transmit the developments of earlier civilizations. Their greatest contributions, however, lay in the new knowledge and ideas they gave the Western world.

The Minoans on the island of Crete and the Mycenaeans on mainland Greece laid the foundations of Greek culture. After a brief Dark Age, the Greek city-states began to develop. In Sparta, a form of government evolved which emphasized military might above all else. In contrast, Athens turned to a democratic form of government which was unique in the ancient world. Athens prospered during its golden age, and the arts of drama, sculpture, poetry, and philosophy also flourished. Alexander the Great's conquest of the Greek city-states ended their independence but helped spread Greek culture as far east as Asia. Although the Greek city-states never recovered their former glory, they passed along a precious cultural legacy to the Romans and to the modern world as well.

The Romans experimented with two forms of government. The first government, a republic, blended ideas of monarchy, aristocracy, and democracy. As Roman territory expanded and political struggles between competing factions increased, the Romans turned from republican government to one-man rule. The Roman Empire's first and most successful emperor was Augustus. His wise policies began the Pax Romana which lasted for more than two hundred years. During this period of peace, the Romans continued Greek traditions in the arts and philosophy and extended Greek culture. The Romans also made original contributions in law, literature, engineering, and architecture.

During the period of Roman rule, Christianity began to gain followers. Christians were accepted at first but, by the end of the second century, were actively persecuted. The Roman emperor Constantine became a Christian, ended the persecution, and legalized the religion, facilitating its spread.

Constantine also moved the capital from Rome to Byzantium, in effect creating two Christian empires. Barbarians overran the western empire, and, after the sack of Rome in 476, Roman power disappeared. However, Greco-Roman cultural traditions were to influence western Europe for centuries.

Resources

The resources that supplement the study of this unit are:

1. The time line for Unit II, found on pages 92–93. The theme for this time line includes the ideals of wisdom, beauty, and citizenship that inspired Greek and Roman life.
2. The Geographic Theme, found on page 162. The theme *Region* deals here with Rome's success in unifying the Mediterranean world.
3. The Historical Atlas map on pages 806–807. It shows the world about 200 B.C., with Rome already dominating the Mediterranean area.
4. The Global Perspectives activity in Chapter 6 of the Lesson Planner, which is used with Overhead Transparency 86.

Chapter Titles

Ancient Greece

Chapter Overview

The ancient Greeks were not members of a united country. Instead, they belonged to many independent city-states. Geography and climate influenced the development of Greek society. Mountainous terrain promoted the development of city-states that cooperated in times of outside danger but could not work together once the threat of war had ended. After the defeat of the Persians, Athens assumed leadership of a group of city-states known as the Delian League. Under Pericles, Athens experienced a flowering of the arts—Greece's golden age. However, rivalry between Athens and Sparta culminated in a war that weakened them both and left them vulnerable to conquest. Through Alexander the Great's conquest and creation of a vast empire, Greek culture spread throughout the Mediterranean world.

Key Terms

epic, arete, polis, aristocracy, hoplite, phalanx, tyrant, colony, democracy, tragedy
For additional exercises, see Vocabulary Worksheet 5.

Chapter Focus

Begin by asking students to describe how Ramses II, Chandragupta, and Shih Huang-ti reached major decisions that affected their empires. Students should recall that these three leaders had the power to decide on all matters affecting their empires. Ask the class to read the introductory section (pages 94–95), and lead a discussion answering these three questions: What problem did the citizens of Athens face? What process did they use to solve this problem? How was this process different from the way decisions were reached in ancient Egypt, India, and China? Conclude by explaining that the Greeks were different from any other people they have previously studied. In Greece, civic decisions were made through open debate. No other ancient society had such a keen awareness of individual worth or such a strong belief in what free people could achieve. Explain that this chapter examines the origins and achievements of Greek civilization.

Greek culture grew up around the Aegean Sea. 1

Section Objectives

After completing Section 1, students should be able to:

1. map areas of Greek settlement.
2. describe the geography of Greece and explain its effects on the development of Greek civilization.
3. describe the Greek heroic ideal and contrast it with contemporary ideas of a hero.
4. discuss aspects of early Greek culture.

Setting the Stage

Geography in History: Greek Settlement (Objective 1) Duplicate and distribute Outline Map 18: Greece. Have students use the map on page 96 to help them label Athens, Sparta, Crete, Asia Minor, and the Aegean, Ionian, Mediterranean, and Black seas. Have students shade in the areas of Greek settlement in Asia Minor, make a key, and write titles for their maps.

Show Overhead Transparency 11, *Greece in the Bronze Age*, and ask students first to examine the area settled by the Greeks and then to compare it with the maps of the Fertile Crescent (page 28), Ancient Egypt (page 49), the Indus Valley (page 68), and Ancient China (page 77). Ask, "How did the areas settled by the Greeks differ from these four regions?" Students should note that Greece was divided by mountains, lacked a major river valley, and included a long coastline with many inlets and bays. Explain that this combination of physical features had an important influence on Greek character and history.

Teaching Strategies

Skill Building: Identifying Cause and Effect Relationships (Objective 2) Have students complete each statement below by writing an effect:

1. The Greek islands formed handy stepping

stones which encouraged the Greeks (to become sailors and trade with other lands).

2. Because the mountains made it difficult for the Greeks to unite their country under one government (the Greeks lived in a collection of small independent communities).

Advance Planner

Unit II Theme	The Mediterranean World			
	The rise of the classical civilizations of Greece and Rome			

Chapter 5 Focus	Ancient Greece 2000 B.C.–323 B.C.		★ Advanced	
	Decision making in Athens		● Basic	

	Section 1	Section 2	Section 3	Section 4
Objectives	1. Map areas of Greek settlement. 2. Describe the geography of Greece and explain its effects on the development of Greek civilization. 3. Describe the Greek heroic ideal and contrast it with contemporary ideas of a hero. 4. Discuss aspects of early Greek culture.	1. Describe a phalanx and its effect on the power of ordinary citizens. 2. Compare and contrast Athens and Sparta. 3. Identify reasons the Greeks were able to defeat the Persians.	1. Describe Athenian achievements during the golden age. 2. Discuss the causes and consequences of the Peloponnesian War. 3. Recall the contributions of Socrates, Plato, and Aristotle.	1. Explain how Philip of Macedon gained control over Greece. 2. Describe and evaluate the achievements of Alexander the Great. 3. Explain how Greek culture spread during the Hellenistic Age.
Setting the Stage	Unit II time line Geography in History: Greek Settlement Transparency 11 Outline Map 18	Characteristics of Greek city-states Transparency 12	The golden age of Athens	The goals of Alexander the Great
Teaching Strategies	Skill Building: Identifying Cause and Effect Relationships Relating Past to Present: The Ideal Hero Discussing History: Early Greek Culture Check for Understanding	Teaching with Pictures: The Phalanx Discussing History: Sparta and Athens Analyzing a Quotation: Herodotus Explains the Athenian Victory Transparency 13 Check for Understanding	Teaching with Pictures: The Parthenon Discussing History: Causes and Effects of the Peloponnesian War Analyzing Quotations: Wisdom of the Greek Philosophers Check for Understanding	Discussing History: Philip of Macedon Discussing History: What made Alexander "Great"? Transparency 14 Using Geographic Themes: Movement Check for Understanding
Guided Practice	Transparency 11 Q&A Section Review 1	Transparency 12 Q&A Transparency 13 Q&A Section Review 2	Section Review 3	Transparency 14 Q&A Section Review 4
Independent Practice Worksheets	Independent Practice 5.1 Vocabulary 5	Independent Practice 5.2 Geography Skills 5 Basic Skills 5	Independent Practice 5.3 Critical Thinking 5	Independent Practice 5.4
Enrichment	1. Primary Source: Voices 5.1 2. Creative Writing 3. ★ Preparing a Book Report 4. Researching for Points	1. Primary Source: Voices 5.2 2. Preparing a Report 3. Analyzing a Quotation: Herodotus 4. Researching for Points	1. Primary Source: Voices 5.3 2. Creative Writing 3. ★ The trial of Socrates Tragedy? 4. Researching for Points	1. Primary Source: Voices 5.4 2. ★ Solving a Puzzle 3. Preparing a Report 4. Researching for Points

Chapter Closer	
● Reteaching Activities	Identifying Important Ideas, Writing Questions and Answers, Summarizing, Recalling Main Ideas
Chapter Review	Summary, Reviewing the Facts, Basic Skills, Researching and Reporting Skills, Critical Thinking, Perspectives on Past and Present, Investigating History
Chapter Evaluation	Chapter Test 5, Computer Test Bank Chapter 5 Test

3. Because of the absence of a large river valley, the Greeks (had no need for large-scale irrigation controlled by powerful priests and kings).

Relating Past to Present: The Ideal Hero (Objective 3) Have students describe the qualities they associate with being heroic. Then have students provide a description of the Greek heroic ideal. Discuss how the Greek heroic ideal is similar to and different from the heroic ideal students have described. Have students construct a dialogue between Andromache and a modern-day Hector who has the traits of students' ideal hero. Would the reply to Andromache's plea (page 99) be the same as that of the ancient Trojan warrior?

Discussing History: Early Greek Culture (Objective 4) One important aspect of early Greek culture was the Olympic Games, held in honor of Zeus. As many as 45,000 spectators—all male—attended the five-day festival held at Olympia. The pictures on page 99 show two of the contests. The discus thrower is hurling a flat, circular bronze plate weighing about twelve pounds. The best throws are reported to have reached 100 feet. The chariot races began with a loud trumpet blast. As many as forty chariots skidded and collided in bone-breaking accidents as they fought for position in a nine-mile race. Although women could not compete, they could own chariot teams. Prizes were awarded to the owners rather than to the jockeys. On some occasions the winning horse received a statue.

Another aspect of early Greek culture was the practice of seeking predictions of the future at shrines. The most famous shrine of all was located at Delphi, at a place that was supposed to be the center of the earth. The Greeks believed that Apollo, the sun-god and patron of knowledge, spoke there through the voice of a priestess, or oracle, called the Pythia. The Pythia answered questions in a frenzied, incoherent babble. Special priests then translated her message into a deliberately vague prophecy. It was expected that mere mortals might easily misinterpret the message. Even so, the Greeks rarely made an important decision without consulting the Delphic Oracle.

Check for Understanding Ask students to explain the role that geography, Homer's epic poems, and religion played in shaping Greek civilization.

Practice

Guided Practice
Lead a guided discussion of the questions in Overhead Transparency 11 and in Section Review 1.

(Answers are below.)

Define:
(a) marketplace (b) wandering poet (c) long, heroic poem (d) heroic ideal (e) athletic contest (f) story about gods

Identify:
(a) sea east of Greece (b) sea west of Greece (c) sea east of Thrace (d) civilization on Crete (e) mainland Greece civilization of the Bronze Age (f) legendary basis of Homer's *Iliad* (g) great epic poet (h) Greeks who lived during Greece's Dark Ages (i) period in Greek history during which skill of writing was lost (j) Homer's epic about end of Trojan War (k) Homer's epic about adventures of Odysseus (l) athletic competitions begun in 776 B.C.

Answer:
1. (a) served as link (b) made travel difficult, helped develop self-reliance (c) encouraged outdoor gatherings, civic life
2. farming kingdoms; also carried on trade; characterized by splendor of rulers
3. brought on the Dark Ages
4. glorified the heroes of old, thus uniting Greeks, and set up ideal standards
5. no powerful priestly class; religion linked to government, civic pride
6. (a) It was lost during the Dark Ages, so it could not have been too widespread. (b) Sample answer: computer technology; its loss would send day-to-day operations back to slower, less efficient techniques.

Independent Practice
Assign Independent Practice Worksheet 5.1.
Assign Vocabulary Worksheet 5.

Enrichment Activities

1. **Reading a Primary Source** Assign Voices from the Past Resource Book 5.1.

2. **Creative Writing** Ask students to pretend that they are reporters assigned to cover the ancient Olympic Games. Have each student write an imaginative report describing events at the games. Encourage students to read background information about the Olympic Games before writing their reports.

3. **Preparing a Book Report** Ask advanced students to prepare a book report on *In Search of the Trojan War* by Michael Wood.

4. **Researching for Bonus Points** Award bonus points to students who can find the answers to

these questions: Who was Helen's Greek husband? (Menelaus) What two phrases were carved onto the temple at Delphi? ("Know Thyself" and "Nothing Too Much")

Greek city-states competed for power. 2

Section Objectives

After completing Section 2, students should be able to:

1. describe a phalanx and its effect on the power of ordinary citizens.
2. compare and contrast Sparta and Athens.
3. identify reasons the Greeks were able to defeat the Persians.

Setting the Stage

Ask students, "If you could live anywhere you wanted, would you prefer to live in a city, a suburban area, a small town, or on a farm? After tabulating responses explain that (according to the 1987 Gallup Youth Survey) 39 percent of a representative sample of sixteen- to seventeen-year-olds preferred to live in the suburbs. The remainder chose cities (29 percent), small towns (20 percent), and rural farms (29 percent). Then explain that if ancient Greek teenagers had been asked this question, the overwhelming majority would have preferred to live in a small city-state or polis.

The introductory section (page 100) provides a discussion of the characteristics of Greek city-states. Review these characteristics and then explain that the period after the Dark Ages was marked by the rise and development of the two most powerful city-states—Sparta and Athens. Use Overhead Transparency 12, *Greece and its Colonies*, to show the rise of other Greek city-states around the Mediterranean.

Teaching Strategies

Teaching with Pictures: The Phalanx (Objective 1) Direct students' attention to the painting of the phalanx (page 101). Explain that the phalanx was a disciplined body of heavily-armed foot-soldiers arranged in formations eight to sixteen men deep and up to 200 men wide. The citizen-soldiers, or hoplites, wore bronze helmets, breastplates, and leg protectors called *greaves*. They carried long spears eight to ten feet long. As shown in the picture, the spears formed hedges that broke up flights of enemy arrows. The soldiers sang hymns as they marched or even ran into battle. It is important to emphasize that the phalanx increased the power of its citizen-soldiers while reducing the need for an aristocratic cavalry.

Discussing History: Sparta and Athens (Objective 2) Begin by pointing out that Sparta was originally a center of Greek culture. Then discuss how Sparta responded to the problem of overpopulation by conquering and annexing Messinia. As a result of this conquest, Sparta controlled 3,200 square miles of territory and a rebellious subject-population of helots who outnumbered the Spartans eight to one. In order to maintain control, the Spartans adopted a severe code of laws. Ask students to discuss the advantages and disadvantages of Spartan life.

After students have read "Athens turned to democracy," have them identify the internal problem that confronted Athens during the sixth century (a power struggle between rich and poor). Review how the reforms of Solon and Cleisthenes solved this problem while also creating a democratic government. The Athenian Assembly voted each year to decide if any citizen had become dangerously powerful. If a citizen received more than 6,000 votes (scratched onto pieces of broken pottery called *ostraka*) he was ostracized and sent into exile for ten years. Conclude asking students to evaluate the strengths and weaknesses of Athenian democracy.

Analyzing a Quotation: Herodotus Explains the Athenian Victory (Objective 3) First review the story of how the Athenians repelled the Persian invasion. Use Overhead Transparency 13, *Greece in the Persian Wars*, to show the areas involved in the conflicts. Point out that the force led by Xerxes was the largest naval invasion of Europe until the Allied invasion of Sicily and Italy in 1943. Ask students to explain how the Greeks defeated this vast empire, and then to evaluate the following explanation offered by Herodotus:

Thus Athens went from strength to strength and proved, if proof were needed, how noble a thing freedom is, not in one respect only but in all: for while they were oppressed under a despotic government, they had no better success in war than any of their neighbors, yet, once the yoke was flung off, they proved the finest fighters in the world. This clearly shows that, so long as they were held down by authority, they deliberately shirked their duty in the field, as slaves shirk working for their masters: but when freedom was won, then every man amongst them longed to distinguish himself.

Check for Understanding Ask students to identify the importance of each of the following key terms, people, and events: phalanx, Lycurgus, Solon, battles of Marathon, and Xerxes.

Practice

Guided Practice
Lead a guided discussion of the questions in Overhead Transparencies 12 and 13 and in Section Review 2. (Answers are below.)

Define:
(a) city-state (b) fortified hilltop (c) government run by noble families (d) foot soldiers (e) formation of foot soldiers forming solid wall (f) ruler who came to power through rebellion (g) settlement abroad (h) peasant forced to stay on land (i) government in which all citizens take part

Identify:
(a) city-state in southern Greece, known for its army (b) neighboring land conquered by Sparta (c) Spartan lawgiver who supposedly starved himself (d) democratic city-state (e) economic and political reformer of Athens (f) made Athens a full democracy (g) Persian king set on defeating Athens (h) historian of the Persian Wars (i) site of victory in 490 B.C. for Athenians against Persians (j) citizen who convinced Athenians to give up their city but to fight Persians by sea (k) site of great Spartan bravery and sacrifice in Persian War (l) son and successor to Darius (m) site of Greek naval victory over Persians (n) site of Spartan victory over Persians (o) alliance of city-states, actually Athenian empire

Answer:
1. It was the central force in Greek life.
2. could now afford weapons and revolt
3. tended to favor interests of small farmers, artisans
4. (a) Helots greatly outnumbered Spartans. (b) They enforced harsh laws.
5. (a) There existed a power struggle between rich and poor. (b) Athenians turned to Solon to lead a reform.
6. It led to a golden age and formation of the Delian League with Athens as its leader.
7. Look for answers that show a need to make all classes more economically and politically equal.

8. Look for answers to stress the polis as the focus of Greek loyalty.

Independent Practice
Assign Independent Practice Worksheet 5.2.
Assign Geography Skills Worksheet 5.
Assign Basic Skills Worksheet 5.

Enrichment Activities

1. **Reading a Primary Source** Assign Voices from the Past Resource Book 5.2.

2. **Preparing a Report** While Athens is now the capital of Greece and a major tourist site, very few people visit modern Sparta. Ask students to prepare a report on what Sparta is like today.

3. **Analyzing a Quotation** Herodotus opened his history of the Persian War with this statement:

   These are the researches of Herodotus of Halicarnassus, which he publishes, in the hope of thereby preserving from decay the remembrance of what men have done, and of preventing the great and wonderful actions of the Greeks and the Barbarians from losing their due need of glory: and withal to put on record what were their grounds of feud.

   Read this passage to your class and then ask, "Why did Herodotus want to publish an account of the Persian Wars? How was Herodotus influenced by the value of arete?"

4. **Researching for Bonus Points** Award bonus points to students who can answer this question: How was the distance of a modern marathon determined? (The distance of a modern marathon was fixed at 26 miles, 385 yards during the 1924 London Olympics. The length represents the distance from Windsor Castle to the Royal Box in the Olympic stadium.)

Athens led Greece in its golden age. 3

Section Objectives

After completing Section 3, students should be able to:

1. describe Athenian achievements during the golden age.
2. discuss the causes and consequences of the Peloponnesian War.

3. Recall the contributions of Socrates, Plato, Aristotle.

Setting the Stage

Write the section title, "Athens led Greece in its golden age," on the chalkboard. Ask the class what the phrase "golden age" means. What types of achievements would help make a period in history a golden age? Then explain that during the fifth century B.C., Athens experienced the first and perhaps the most famous golden age in world history. This section examines the explosion of cultural creativity in this period.

Teaching Strategies

Teaching with Pictures: The Parthenon (Objective 1) Identify the three goals of Pericles as listed on page 107. One of these goals was to glorify Athens by building a new temple to honor Athena. After students have read, "Art flourished in Athens," direct their attention to the artistic recreation of the Parthenon (page 108).

Explain that constructing the Parthenon kept a small army of workers busy for fifteen years. First, the marble was cut in huge blocks from quarries and dragged ten miles to the foot of the Acropolis. Then it was hoisted along the sloping side of that great hill. Some 22,000 tons of marble were chiseled with such precision that no mortar was needed to hold the stones together.

As noted in the text, the Parthenon was designed in a traditional rectangular shape. The Parthenon's architects, however, breathed life into its stone structure by playing a few subtle tricks on the eye. The corner columns tilt slightly inward so that their tops are a few inches closer together than their bottoms. This barely visible tilt helps give the Parthenon its upward thrust. In addition, each column has a slight bulge in the middle bringing a sense of lightness to the whole building.

Once inside the temple, visitors could admire a band of carved stone, called a *frieze*, that told the story of the Great Panathenaic Festival the Athenians held every four years to honor Athena. Sculptors painted the background in rich colors to make the carved figures stand out.

As noted in the text, the Parthenon also housed a magnificent statue of Athena. (See *Classical Greece* by C.M. Bowra, page 115.) Visitors to the Parthenon today see only a shell of its former grandeur. Athena's statue was carried away to Constantinople in about A.D. 400 and later disappeared. The roof was blown off in A.D. 1687 by a gunpowder explosion. Sculptural masterpieces tumbled to the ground. The best preserved figures were purchased and removed by the British Ambassador Lord Elgin. Known as the Elgin Marbles, they are on display in the British Museum in London.

Discussing History: Causes and Effects of the Peloponnesian War (Objective 2) First review the section, "Sparta defeated Athens in war." Then explain that when the Athenians surrendered, many of their enemies urged the Spartans to burn the city. Although the Spartans did tear down the Long Walls, they ordered that Athens be allowed to stand. According to Thucydides, the Spartans spared Athens because they remembered the city's role in defeating the Persians. Recall that Spartans and Athenians fought side by side in battles against the Persians; yet, fifty years after the end of the Persian War, the Spartans invaded Athenian lands. Ask students to suggest a main cause of the Peloponnesian War. (political rivalry between two very different societies) Write students' responses to the question, "What were the effects of the war on the Athenians?" (loss of population to warfare and disease; loss of farmlands, fleet, Long Walls; loss of Athenian wealth, power, and prestige; loss of confidence in democracy) Have students distinguish between immediate effects and long-term effects. Point out that the Peloponnesian War left all the Greek city-states in decline and vulnerable to outside invasion.

Analyzing Quotations: Wisdom of the Greek Philosophers (Objective 3) Have students review "Philosophers Searched for Truth" (pages 112–114). Divide the class into three groups and assign each group one of the three philosophers—Socrates, Plato, Aristotle. First, ask each group to prepare a summary of the philosopher's contributions. Then assign the following quotations to the appropriate groups. Have each group discuss its quotations and prepare explanations of them and examples of present-day applications.

- There is only one good, knowledge, and one evil, ignorance. (Socrates)
- Bad men live that they may eat and drink, whereas good men eat and drink that they may live. (Socrates)
- The life which is unexamined is not worth living. (Plato)
- The direction in which education starts a man will determine his future life. (Plato)
- We make war that we may live in peace. (Aristotle)
- We should behave to our friends as we would wish our friends to behave to us. (Aristotle)

Check for Understanding Have students briefly identify the contributions of Pericles, Phidias, Aeschylus, and Socrates to the golden age.

Practice

Guided Practice
Lead a guided discussion of the questions in Section Review 3. (Answers are below.)

Define:
(a) style of art that includes standards of order, balance, and proportion (b) type of drama in which gods punish hero for sinning (c) one who loves wisdom (d) logically related statements

Identify:
(a) leading statesman of Athens during golden age (b) Greek temple (c) goddess of wisdom and protector of Athens (d) sculptor (e) wrote Greek tragedies during Age of Pericles (f) author of *Oedipus* (g) war between Sparta and Athens (h) historian of Peloponnesian War (i) Greek playwright who wrote comedies (j) Greek philosopher condemned to death (k) wrote *The Republic* (l) school started by Plato (m) Plato's vision of a perfect society (n) developer of syllogism

Answer:
1. He used money from the Delian League for a navy and for great works of art.
2. (a) reflected Greek standard of order, balance, proportion (b) form of public education that dealt with important issues
3. Women and girls were rarely seen outside the home, lived in separate quarters, and could not own or inherit land or vote.
4. (a) attack on Athens by Sparta, weakening of Athens by plague and defeat in Sicily, surrender of Athens (b) Athens lost self-confidence.
5. (a) democracy, patriotism, religion (b) led to charges of "corrupting the youth of Athens"
6. (a) The death of Socrates convinced him that average citizens of a democracy were unable to govern wisely. (b) He wanted to see a society led by a ruling class of people with a philosopher-king at its head.
7. He developed a system for organizing and testing ideas that was important for science.
8. (a) Look for *yes* answers to discuss artistic, political, and intellectual heights. Look for *no* answers to discuss inequality. (b) Answers may include political harmony, artistic greatness, social equality, intellectual stimulation.
9. They assumed that the universe was governed by absolute and unchanging laws people could understand through reason.

Independent Practice
Assign Independent Practice Worksheet 5.3.
Assign Critical Thinking Worksheet 5.

Enrichment Activities

1. **Reading a Primary Source** Assign Voices from the Past Resource Book 5.3.

2. **Creative Writing** Ask students to imagine that they have just spent a day in ancient Athens during the golden age. Their assignment is to write a diary entry summarizing their day.

3. **The Trial of Socrates** Recall the definition of tragedy in Greek drama (page 109). Explain that the Greeks believed that a tragedy had three recognizable elements. First, the hero was stricken by *ate*, a blindness sent by the gods; then the blindness led to *hubris*, a false pride that led to an unforgivable sin; and finally the gods punished the hero. The punishment was called *nemesis*. Ask advanced students to apply these concepts to the case of Socrates. Was Socrates an example of a Greek tragic hero? Explain why or why not.

4. **Researching for Bonus Points** Award bonus points to students who can answer this question: What gift did the Athenians present to Athena at the Panathenaic festival? (A new robe, or peplos, woven by the women of the city, represented the battle of the gods and giants.)

Answers to Voice from the Past

1. government favoring many over few
2. arts, business, politics
3. (a) "school" of Greece (b) Others copy Athens.

Alexander's conquests spread Greek Culture. 4

Section Objectives

After completing Section 4, students should be able to:

1. explain how Philip of Macedon gained control over Greece.
2. describe and evaluate the achievements of Alexander the Great.
3. explain how Greek culture spread during the Hellenistic Age.

Setting the Stage

Point out that most people have a personal goal or dream. Ask students to silently think of a personal goal. Then explain that this section examines the ambitious goals of a Macedonian ruler known as Alexander the Great. As a youth, Alexander dreamed of performing a "great and brilliant deed to show the world." The deed he had in mind was to conquer and then unite the known world.

Teaching Strategies

Discussing History: Philip of Macedon (Objective 1) After students have read "Philip built Macedon's power," ask them to explain why Philip was able to accomplish what the Persian emperors had failed to do—namely, to conquer the Greek city-states. Lead a discussion that emphasizes the following three factors: First, Philip developed a powerful new army featuring phalanxes sixteen men across and sixteen deep. The soldiers were equipped with a new weapon, the *sarissa*, an eighteen-foot lance, which was much longer than that used by the Greek soldiers. Second, Philip used skillful diplomacy, bribery, and flattery to divide and then conquer the city-states. Finally, Philip was a bold and determined leader. Conclude by asking students to react to this description of Philip by the Athenian orator Demosthenes: "For the sake of ruling and wielding power, he has had an eye knocked out, his shoulder smashed, his leg and hand mutilated; he jettisons whatever part of his body fate wants to take away, just so long as he can live in honor and glory with what is left."

Discussing History: What made Alexander "Great"? (Objective 2) Show students Overhead Transparency 14, *The Empire of Alexander the Great*, and review the text's discussion of Alexander's conquests. Point out that Alexander was called "The Great" because of his impressive victories. Ask students to suggest criteria for evaluating the greatness of a leader. What qualities other than military success might be considered? Recall the long-term effects of Alexander's conquests, and suggest that greatness is often attributed to individuals whose actions had lasting impact. Ask, "How does history judge a leader's greatness?"

Using Geographic Themes: Movement (Objective 3) The diffusion of Hellenistic culture illustrates the theme of movement. Ask students to list the various means by which Greek culture spread eastward. Students should note that Alexander founded a number of cities (sixteen of which were named Alexandria), that served as focal points of Greek culture. After Alexander's death, thousands of Greeks settled in these cities and throughout the conquered lands. They built gymnasiums, theaters, and council halls. In time, the Greeks came to speak a common Greek called Koine, the "common language." Interestingly, while Greek art, architecture, and language flowed eastward, Persian religious ideas and astrology flowed westward.

Check for Understanding Have students describe the achievements of Philip of Macedon, Alexander the Great, and Archimedes.

Practice

Guided Practice
Lead a guided discussion of the questions in Overhead Transparency 14 and in Section Review 4. (Answers are below.)

Define:
Greek-Persian culture

Identify:
(a) kingdom north of Greece (b) king of Macedon who conquered Greece (c) battle at which Philip defeated Athens and Thebes (d) Philip's son and successor (e) general who took control of Egypt (f) Alexander's general who took Asia Minor and the Fertile Crescent (g) Alexander's general who took Macedon

Answer:
1. (a) used war, diplomacy, bribery, trickery (b) respect
2. (a) Asia Minor and the eastern coast of Mediterranean to Egypt; from Egypt north and east to Persia, eastward to Indus River valley (b) broke apart
3. He hellenized them.
4. (a) logically organized Greek geometry into system used for centuries (b) applied system to real life
5. (a) breakup of empire, decline of Hellenism, eventual takeover by Romans (b) lasting influences of Hellenistic culture

Independent Practice
Assign Independent Practice Worksheet 5.4.

Enrichment Activities

1. **Reading a Primary Source** Assign Voices from the Past Resource Book 5.4.
2. **Solving a Puzzle** Philip's death remains an unsolved puzzle. Ask advanced students to

write a research report that attempts to explain who killed Philip and why.

3. **Preparing a Report** In 1977, archaeologists unearthed a spectacular Macedonian tomb in Vergina, Greece. Ask students to prepare a report on what archaeologists found and why they believe they located Philip's royal tomb. (One source is found in *National Geographic*, July 1978.)

4. **Researching for Bonus Points** Award bonus points to students who can find the answer to this question: What was the name of Alexander's famed horse? (Bucephalus)

Concluding the Chapter

1. **Chapter Closer**
Ask students to summarize what they have learned by supporting the opinion that the spirit and ideas of Greek civilization long outlived ancient Greece.

2. **Reteaching Activities**
   a. **Identifying Important Ideas** Ask students to write a sentence explaining the significance of each of the following: Bronze Age, Crete, Trojan War, Homer, and Olympic Games.
   b. **Writing Questions and Answers** Have students turn the headings in Section 2 into questions and then answer each question.
   c. **Summarizing** Have students write one paragraph summarizing the contributions of Pericles, Sophocles, Phidias, and Plato.
   d. **Recalling Main Ideas** Have students explain how each of the following individuals relates to the history of the Hellenistic Age: Philip of Macedon, Alexander the Great, Ptolemy, and Archimedes.

3. **Chapter Review Activities**
Assign Chapter Review 5 activities.

Chapter Evaluation

Chapter Test 5 and Computer Test Bank Chapter 5 Test can be used to evaluate your students' understanding of this chapter.

Answers to Chapter Review 5

Reviewing the Facts

1. **a.** long, heroic poem **b.** heroic idea of excellence **c.** city-state **d.** form of government run by noble families **e.** foot soldier **f.** formation of foot soldiers forming solid wall of fighters **g.** ruler who came to power through rebellion and usually stood for the rights of the small farmers and artisans **h.** settlement abroad with ties to a city-state back home **i.** form of government in which citizens took part **j.** type of drama in which men and women of strong character were led by their very strength to downfall.

2. **a.** island near Greece where the Minoan civilization developed during the Bronze Age **b.** leading city on mainland Greece; where the Mycenaen civilization developed in the Bronze Age **c.** last of the Bronze Age Greeks' triumphs before the Mycenaen civilization collapsed **d.** poet who glorified the old heroes of Mycenae and Troy in the *Iliad* and the *Odyssey* **e.** city-state that created a democracy through reforms and became cultural center of ancient Greece **f.** city-state with the most powerful army in Greece **g.** Athenian reformer who prevented civil war in Athens with his economic and political reforms **h.** Athenian leader who introduced a series of laws that made Athens a full democracy **i.** wrote *History of the Persian Wars* and was justly called the first true historian **j.** year Athenians defeated the Persians on Marathon plain, preventing the destruction of Athens **k.** 27-year war between Athens and Sparta that ruined Athens and weakened all of Greece **l.** Athenian ruler who strengthened Athenian democracy, enlarged wealth and power of Athens, and made Athens the cultural center of Greece **m.** the 27 years of war with Sparta, during which Athens lost its fleet, its empire, its power, and its wealth **n.** writer of classic tragedy who helped invent drama **o.** author of about 100 plays, including *Oedipus* **p.** Greek philosopher who taught that people must examine their ideas by standards of truth and reason **q.** philosopher who wrote *The Republic*, which explained his idea of a perfectly governed society **r.** philosopher who developed a set of logical statements known as a syllogism, which was important for developing rational and scientific thought **s.** Macedonian king who united Greece under his leadership **t.** king of Macedon who helped spread a common culture, Hellenism, throughout the many lands he conquered **u.** year when Alexander died and his empire broke apart into three sections—Egypt, Asia Minor and the Fertile Crescent, and Macedon

3. Major changes include:

- 1200 B.C.—Bronze Age dominated by warrior kings.
- 750–110 B.C.—kings lost power; rise of aristocracy.
- Citizen-soldiers revolted against the nobles; tyrants came to power.
- 750 B.C.—city-states, such as Sparta and Athens, developed.
- 600–371 B.C.—Sparta built military state.
- 594 B.C.—Athens adopted political and economic reforms to create a democratic government.

4. excellence, courage, fame, and honor
5. Solon's contributions: reformed Athenian laws so that every male citizen participated in political debate and decision-making; began legal system in which any citizen could bring charges against anyone who had committed a wrong. Cleisthenes's contributions: increased power of the Athenian assembly and created the Council of Five Hundred to propose laws and advise the assembly.
6. The arts of drama, sculpture, poetry, philosophy, architecture, and science reached new heights.
7. Philip used a combination of war, diplomacy, bribery, and trickery to defeat the Greek city-states one by one.
8. Everywhere Alexander conquered he established governments run by Greek administrators and had public buildings fashioned in the Greek style.

Basic Skills
1. Greek culture grew up around the Aegean Sea: the map shows Greek settlements clustered on the coastlines around the Aegean Sea.
2. *Title:* Greece in the Bronze Age; Greece and Its Colonies. *Historical period:* Bronze Age: 750–550 B.C. *Region included:* Greece and lands bordering the Aegean Sea; Europe, Asia Minor, North Africa. *Scale:* about 100 miles to an inch; about 400 miles to an inch.
3. Siege of Troy, Dark Ages, Solon's reforms, Persian Wars, Age of Pericles, death of Socrates, Alexander's conquests, Hellenistic Age.
4. Greek Philosophers
   A. Socrates
      1. questioned all accepted values.
      2. was condemned for his thinking.
   B. Plato
      1. founded a school.
      2. wrote *The Republic*.
   C. Aristotle
      1. studied with Plato.
      2. developed a system of logic.

Researching and Reporting Skills
Students' findings will vary.

Critical Thinking
1. For Sparta, students should mention the army, self-discipline, idealism, and endurance; for Athens, their democratic principles, powerful fleet, and achievements in the arts, philosophy, and science. Reasons should support the opinion given.
2. **(a)** Both had the same democratic ideas of equal opportunity and justice for all citizens. Athenians gave more importance to the political responsibility of individuals. **(b)** In Athens, any citizen could speak to the assembly. In the United States, citizens speak through representatives. Athenian "citizens" comprised only one fifth of the population. In the United States, citizenship and participation in the democratic process are open to all. **(c)** Answers will vary. The United States does not limit citizenship and participation. The "direct democracy" of the Athenians, however, permitted "one citizen, one vote," which is more strictly democratic than the electoral college system.
3. In Chinese society, the group was more important than the individual and obedience to authority was more important than self-expression. The result was an authoritarian society with dynastic rule. In Greece the rights of the individual were emphasized, resulting in a democratic society.

Perspective on Past and Present
1. Pericles would say that nonvoters are not true citizens. Have students discuss reasons for the lack of citizen participation in government in the United States today.
2. Answers will vary. Refer students to "The First Olympics" in *Smithsonian,* June 1984.

Investigating History
Students' findings will vary.

The Roman Republic

Chapter Overview

The earliest settlers of the Italian peninsula were the Latins, Greeks, and Etruscans. Early Roman culture was a blend of the traditions of these three groups. In its early years, Rome was ruled by kings. However, opposition to the rule of kings resulted in the establishment of the Roman republic in 509 B.C. and the determination among Romans never again to have a monarchy.

Within the republic of Rome, the plebeians succeeded in winning reforms from the patricians. By 275 B.C., Rome had set up a balanced government with a powerful patrician senate, a democratic assembly of citizen-soldiers, and two consuls in place of a king. The defeat of Carthage in the Punic Wars enabled Rome to dominate the Mediterranean Sea, but victory brought with it new problems that led to social unrest. Julius Caesar brought some political stability to the republic, but his actions threatened the powers of the senate and he was assassinated. When successive changes in leadership failed to bring peace, the Romans welcomed the strong leadership of Octavian, and in 27 B.C. the republic ended.

Key Terms

republic, gravitas, patrician, plebeian, consul, veto, senate, dictator, mercenary, proletariat, tribune, triumvirate
For additional exercises, see Vocabulary Worksheet 6.

Chapter Focus

Tell the students that a myth is a traditional story that explains some practice or belief. Point out that myths can offer important insights into the ways people view themselves and their world. Have students read the story of Romulus and Remus on pages 120-121, and ask, "What belief does this myth express?" Lead students to see that the myth of Romulus and Remus expressed the Romans' belief that Rome was destined to rule the world. Rome's founder, Romulus, was believed to be the son of the war god Mars, and a model Roman. Tell students that this chapter examines the rise of the Roman republic.

The Romans founded their city. 1

Section Objectives

After completing Section 1, students should be able to:

1. explain the role of geographic location in Rome's early growth.
2. identify the contributions to Roman culture of the Latins, Greeks, and Etruscans.
3. describe the character of an ideal citizen in the Roman republic.
4. explain the system of social status in Roman society.

Setting the Stage

Using Geographic Themes: Location (Objective 1) Show Overhead Transparency 15, *Italy about 500 B.C.* Help students locate Italy, Rome, the Tiber River, and the Alps. Ask students to describe Rome's location on the Italian peninsula. Use Overhead Transparency 86, *The World about 200 B.C.*, to show the Italian peninsula's location near the midpoint of the Mediterranean region, and Rome's location relative to Ptolemaic Egypt and the Mauryan empire in India. Conclude by reading this quote by the famous Roman orator, Cicero:

> Romulus must at the very beginning have had a divine intimation that the city would one day be the seat and hearth of a mighty empire, for scarcely could a city placed on any other site in Italy have more easily maintained our present widespread domination.

Ask students to support or refute Cicero's statement. Can they find another location on the Italian peninsula that would have had a better location than Rome?

Teaching Strategies

Discussing History: Roman Borrowings (Objective 2) The Romans borrowed ideas from the

Latins, Greeks, and Etruscans. After students have read pages 122–123, have them list in three columns the Latin, Greek, and Etruscan contributions to Roman culture.

Discussing History: Gravitas (Objective 3) As pointed out in the text, the character of Rome's citizens was influenced by a set of values called *mos maiorum*, or, "ways of the fathers." Roman values were rooted in their pioneer past and intensified by long, successful struggles against hostile foes. The Romans emphasized discipline, practicality, strength, tenacity, and loyalty. These values combined to produce a much admired trait called *gravitas*. Ask students to contrast the Roman ideal of *gravitas* with the Greek ideal of *arete*.

Advance Planner

Chapter 6	The Roman Republic 1000 B.C.–27 B.C.		★ Advanced
Focus	The myth of Romulus and Remus		● Basic

	Section 1	Section 2	Section 3
Objectives	1. Explain the role of geographic location in Rome's early growth. 2. Identify the contributions to Roman culture of the Latins, Greeks, and Etruscans. 3. Describe the character of an ideal citizen in the Roman republic. 4. Explain the system of social status in Roman society.	1. Identify the Twelve Tablets and explain their significance in Roman law. 2. Compare and contrast the political institutions of the Roman republic and the United States. 3. Trace the expansion of Rome on a map.	1. Assess the impact of the Punic Wars on the republic. 2. Explain the main cause and long-term effects of changes in the Roman army. 3. Identify Julius Caesar and describe his rise to power. 4. Explain how Octavian became the sole ruler of the Roman Empire.
Setting the Stage	The location of Rome Using Geographic Themes: Location Transparency 15 Transparency 86	Reasons for the historical probability of Rome's rise to power	Discussing History: The Impact of the Punic Wars on the Roman Republic Transparency 17
Teaching Strategies	Discussing History: Roman Borrowings Discussing History: *Gravitas* Relating Past to Present: The Toga Check for Understanding	Transferring Ideas: Law Codes and the Twelve Tablets Relating Past to Present: The Government of Rome and the United States Geography in History: The Expansion of Rome Outline Map 21 Check for Understanding	Skill Building: Identifying Cause and Effect Relationships Writing about History: Julius Caesar Writing about History: Octavian's Resignation Check for Understanding
Guided Practice **Independent Practice Worksheets**	Transparency 15 Q&A Section Review 1 Independent Practice 6.1 Vocabulary 6	Transparency 16 Q&A Section Review 2 Independent Practice 6.2 Basic Skills 6	Transparency 17 Q&A Section Review 3 Independent Practice 6.3 Geography Skills 6 Critical Thinking 6
Enrichment	1. Primary Source: Voices 6.1 2. ★ Analyzing a Quotation 3. Researching for Points	1. Primary Source: Voices 6.2 2. ★ Analyzing a Quotation 3. Creative Writing 4. Researching for Points	1. Primary Source: Voices 6.3 2. Preparing a Report 3. ★ Solving a Puzzle 4. Researching for Points 5. Global Perspectives: Transparency 86

Chapter Closer	
● **Reteaching Activities**	Summarizing, Writing Questions and Answers, Giving an Explanation
Chapter Review	Summary, Reviewing the Facts, Basic Skills, Researching and Reporting Skills, Critical Thinking, Perspectives on Past and Present, Investigating History
Chapter Evaluation	Chapter Test 6, Computer Test Bank Chapter 6 Test

Relating Past to Present: The Toga (Objective 4) Ask students to identify the Roman social classes and the grounds for membership in each. After the students have read the Daily Life feature, "The Roman Toga" (page 124), have them explain the significance of this famous Roman garment. Then ask, "In what ways do clothes indicate social status in American society today? How are the Roman and American class systems similar? How are they different?"

Check for Understanding Ask students to explain the significance of the following concepts: republic, gravitas, patrician, and plebeian.

Practice

Guided Practice
Lead a guided discussion of the questions in Overhead Transparency 15 and in Section Review 1. (Answers are below.)

Define:
(a) government in which citizens vote to choose their leaders (b) virtue of weightiness or seriousness (c) father of the family (d) worn draped around the body (e) member of Roman privileged family (f) common person (g) massive military unit (h) 1/60th of a legion

Identify:
(a) peninsula in Mediterranean (b) central city of Roman republic (c) mythical founder of Rome (d) hilltop center of Rome (e) mountain range separating Italy from rest of Europe (f) river flowing through Rome (g) mountain range running down length of Italy (h) group from across the Alps who settled near the Tiber River (i) civilized settlers who entered northern Italy between 1200 and 800 B.C. (j) public meeting place

Answer:
1. central position helped military and trade
2. (a) earliest settlers (b) introduced Greek culture and certain religious ideas (c) influence on Roman writing, architecture, trade, and religious ideas
3. "the ways of the fathers," which emphasized discipline, strength, loyalty
4. (a) *pater familias* was head of household with complete power over his family (b) in charge of daily running of household (c) were citizens, could own property and testify in court, could eat with and advise husband
5. All male citizens had to serve in the army; no one could hold public office until he served ten years.

6. Look for answers to include a discussion of social, political, and religious values.

Independent Practice
Assign Independent Practice Worksheet 6.1. Assign Vocabulary Worksheet 6.

Enrichment Activities

1. **Reading a Primary Source** Assign Voices from the Past Resource Book 6.1.

2. **Analyzing a Quotation** The modern historian Michael Grant wrote, "Italy's central position in the Mediterranean is a call to self-assertion, suggesting many promising opportunities if and when its population is capable of grasping them." Ask advanced students to evaluate this statement in relation to early Roman history.

3. **Researching for Bonus Points** Award bonus points to students who can find the answer to this question: The Romans changed the names of eleven of the twelve Greek Olympians. Which god retained the same name? (Apollo)

The Roman republic spread its power.

2

Section Objectives

After completing Section 2, students should be able to:

1. identify the Twelve Tablets and explain their significance in Roman law.
2. compare and contrast the political institutions of the Roman republic and the United States.
3. trace on a map the expansion of Rome.

Setting the Stage

Have the students suggest some strengths of the Roman republic, identified in the first section. Strengths might include Rome's central geographic location, stable political system, military power, and belief in a destiny to rule the world. Tell students that some historians have described Rome's rise to power as inevitable. Ask students what inevitability means. Help them to distinguish between the idea of inevitability and the concept of historical probability. Point out that patterns and trends in history can make some events more likely, but that historical developments are not necessarily inevitable. Explain that this section examines how the Romans unified the Mediterranean world.

Teaching Strategies

Transferring Ideas: Law Codes and the Twelve Tablets (Objective 1) Ask students why they think the plebeians wanted a written code of laws. Recall that Babylon had a written code of laws under Hammurabi and the Hebrews had the Ten Commandments. Have students compare and contrast the reasons for establishing the Babylonian, Hebrew, and Roman legal codes. Students should recognize that an important function of the Twelve Tablets was to establish the idea that all free citizens had the right to be protected by the law. Ask students what effect this code had on Rome's social system.

Relating Past to Present: The Governments of Rome and the United States (Objective 2) Ask students to describe the executive, legislative, and judicial branches of American government. Have students compare the office of consul with the office of the President. Ask "What might be some advantages and disadvantages of dividing the executive branch of government between two leaders?" Then have students compare the membership and functions of the Roman Senate and Assembly with those of the United States Congress. Ask, "What might be some advantages and disadvantages of dividing the legislative branch of government into two bodies?"

Geography in History: The Expansion of Rome (Objective 3) Distribute copies of Outline Map 21: The Roman Empire. Tell students that, for this activity, they will need to refer to the maps on pages 121, 129, and 130. Have students label the Mediterranean Sea, Italy, Gaul, Spain, Greece, Sicily, Macedon, Pergamum, Asia Minor, Africa, Egypt, and the cities of Rome and Carthage. Ask students to draw a map key and use the symbols in the key to show all areas controlled by the Etruscans or Latins in 500 B.C., the extent of Roman territory by 265 B.C., and the area controlled by Rome in 133 B.C. After students have completed their maps, have them write a map caption explaining how the Romans extended their power.

Check for Understanding Ask students to use the information presented in this section to answer this question: What factors contributed to the likelihood of Rome's rise to power?

Practice

Guided Practice

Lead a guided discussion of the questions in Overhead Transparency 16 and in Section Review 2. (Answers are below.)

Define:
(a) one of two rulers of Rome (b) power to overrule (c) aristocratic branch of Roman government (d) democratic side of Roman government (e) absolute ruler for six months (f) soldier who fights for pay

Identify:
(a) letters on Roman coins that stood for "the senate and the Roman people" (b) first written laws of Rome (c) dictator in 458 B.C. who represented the Roman ideal (d) people from Po valley who sacked Rome (e) Greek king and general who fought Romans, won every battle, but lost the war (f) trading center and former Phoenician colony (g) war between Rome and Carthage for control of Sicily and western Mediterranean (h) Carthaginian military leader who destroyed three Roman armies (i) site of Roman victory over Hannibal (j) Roman leader who defeated Hannibal (k) grandson of Scipio Africanus; led Roman army in destroying Carthage

Answer:
1. (a) They were barred from holding most important positions in government and were governed by severe laws. (b) by refusing to fight in the Roman army (c) won rights for plebeians to hold some political offices, avoid enslavement for debt, marry patricians, and share in political power
2. part monarchy, part aristocracy, part democracy
3. by granting certain citizenship rights and treating conquered people as partners
4. (a) It had three times the population of Rome, was a wealthy trading center, had a huge navy, and employed mercenaries. (b) It had half a million troops in reserve; citizen-fighters were more loyal than mercenaries; warfare was specialty.
5. It set the stage for Rome, not Carthage, to be the transmitter of culture down through the ages.
6. (a) The Romans had freed them from the rule of Philip V of Macedon. (b) Romans interfered in Greek politics and crushed all opposition.
7. (a) Answers should include the roles of consuls, senate, and the assembly and their powers and membership. (b) right of all citizens to participate in government

8. **(a)** destruction of Corinth and sack of Carthage **(b)** no citizenship and outright destruction outside Italy

Independent Practice
Assign Independent Practice Worksheet 6.2.
Assign Basic Skills Worksheet 6.

Enrichment Activities

1. **Reading a Primary Source** Assign Voices from the Past Resource Book 6.2.

2. **Analyzing a Quotation** The famed historian Charles Gibbon wrote that Rome was "sometimes vanquished in battle, always victorious in war." Ask advanced students to interpret and evaluate this statement, using facts to support their arguments.

3. **Creative Writing** Show students Overhead Transparency 16, *Rome and Carthage,* and have them trace the route of Hannibal's invasion of Rome. Ask students to imagine that they are accompanying Hannibal on his legendary march over the Alps. Their assignment is to write journal entries describing their experiences. (See the chapter, "Through The Alps to The Gates of Rome" in National Geographic's *Greece and Rome.*)

4. **Researching for Bonus Points** Award bonus points to students who can answer this question: Where did Hannibal die and what were his last words? (Hannibal died in his house in Libyssa in the kingdom of Bithynia, now a part of modern Turkey. His final words were: "It's time now to end the great anxiety of the Romans who have grown weary of waiting for the death of a hated old man.")

Republican government collapsed in Rome. 3

Section Objectives

After completing Section 3, students should be able to:

1. assess the impact of the Punic Wars on the republic.
2. explain the main cause and long-term effects of changes in the Roman army.

3. identify Julius Caesar and describe his rise to power.
4. explain how Octavian became the sole ruler of the Roman Empire.

Setting the Stage

Discussing History: The Impact of the Punic Wars on the Roman Republic (Objective 1) Use Overhead Transparency 17, *Roman Power in 133 B.C.,* to show students the extent of Rome's control after the Punic Wars. Ask students to speculate about the advantages for the Romans of conquering Carthage. List their ideas on the chalkboard. When the list is complete, point out that the text states, "Carthage was not the only loser of the Punic Wars. Rome was also hurt in many ways." Ask students why they think this was true. Tell students that in this section they will learn how the Punic Wars created conditions that led to the end of the Roman Republic.

Teaching Strategies

Skill Building: Identifying Cause and Effect Relationships (Objective 2) Ask students to identify the main cause and the long-term effects of Marius' decision to allow the Roman poor to enlist in the army. (Cause: Marius needed more soldiers to defend Rome, and there weren't enough landowners to fill the ranks of citizen-soldiers. Only landowners could serve in the army and the number of landowners had declined as farmers were forced to sell their lands. Effect: Marius' decision created armies of professional soldiers loyal to particular military leaders rather than to the republic. Military leaders could use their armies to advance their own political careers and, as a result, precipitate political instability and civil war.)

Writing about History: Julius Caesar (Objective 3) After students have read the sections on Julius Caesar (pages 134–136), tell them that the Greek historian Herodotus wrote, "Circumstances rule men; men do not rule circumstances." Ask students to interpret the quotation and apply it to Julius Caesar's career. Draw two columns on the board. Have students find facts supporting Herodotus' proposition, and list their responses in the first column. Then ask students to find facts supporting the view that Caesar rose above circumstances in forging his career, and list students' responses in the second column. Conclude by asking students to take a point of view and write a letter to Herodotus agreeing or disagreeing with his statement, and including three pieces of evidence to support their arguments.

Check for Understanding Have students explain the roles of the following individuals in the collapse of republican government in Rome: Tiberius Gracchus, Gaius Gracchus, Marius, Sulla, Julius Caesar, Crassus, Pompey, and Octavian.

Practice

Guided Practice
Lead a guided discussion of the questions in Overhead Transparency 17 and in Section Review 3. (Answers are below.)

Define:
(a) huge estates (b) urban, landless poor (c) person trained to fight for entertainment (d) official who spoke for the plebeians (e) rule of three

Identify:
(a) leader of a slave revolt who was crucified (b) brothers who attempted to reform Rome's government (c) army leader who saved Rome from Germanic invasion (d) foe of Marius who ruled as dictator in 82 B.C. (e) provincial governor who became dictator (f) Caesar, Crassus, Pompey (g) Egyptian queen who wooed Caesar and Antony (h) conspirator in death of Julius Caesar (i) Caesar's grandnephew and adopted son; ruled Rome for 41 years (j) Antony, Octavian, and Lepidus (k) Octavian's chief rival (l) senate's greatest orator, killed for having spoken out against absolute rule

Answer:
1. created proletariat and immense wealth; increased number of slaves
2. Slave revolt was always a threat.
3. land reforms to benefit the poor, weaken senate, and deal with unemployment
4. could pay for armies to win power
5. (a) game of Roman politics, including bribery (b) soldiers, poorer citizens (c) senators, republicans
6. (a) to destroy Caesar's enemies (b) Octavian defeated Lepidus and Antony.
7. Many students might choose Caesar's crossing of the Rubicon, giving the following reasons: it defied the senate's order and challenged Pompey; it led to Caesar's appointment as dictator.

Independent Practice
Assign Independent Practice Worksheet 6.3.
Assign Geography Skills Worksheet 6.
Assign Critical Thinking Worksheet 6.

Enrichment Activities

1. **Reading a Primary Source** Assign Voices from the Past Resource Book 6.3.

2. **Preparing a Report** Caesar is often ranked among history's greatest military commanders. Ask students to prepare a report on Caesar's conquest of Gaul and Britannia.

3. **Solving a Puzzle** Caesar received numerous warnings to avoid the Senate on the fateful day of his assassination. Ask advanced students to research Caesar's death and propose a hypothesis answering this question: Why did Caesar go unarmed to the Senate meeting?

4. **Researching for Bonus Points** Award bonus points to students who can answer this question: Who was the son of Caesar and Cleopatra and what happened to him? (Caesarion. Octavian had him killed.)

5. **Global Perspectives** Have students perform the activities in Overhead Transparency 86, *The World about 200 B.C.*

Answers to Voice from The Past

1. lavish in offerings to gods, thrifty at home, loyal to friends, bold in warfare, just in peace
2. lust for money, lust for power
3.

early Romans	*later Romans*
generous, religious, thrifty, kind, honest, understanding, just	greedy, godless, spendthrift, cruel, dishonest, insolent, ambitious

4. Look for an understanding of the temptations wealth and prosperity can bring.

Concluding the Chapter

1. **Chapter Closer**
Ask students to recall the myth of Romulus and Remus. Have students write evaluations of the extent to which Romulus' prophecy for Rome was fulfilled.

2. **Reteaching Activities**
   a. **Summarizing** Have students write a paragraph summarizing how geography and military organization helped Rome expand.
   b. **Writing Questions and Answers** Have students turn each of the headings in Section 2 into a question and then answer each question.
   c. **Giving an Explanation** Have students

explain how each of the following items contributed to the collapse of the Roman republic: the rise of the proletariat class; the formation of armies loyal to military leaders; and the failure of the triumvirates.

3. **Chapter Review Activities**
Assign Chapter Review 6 activities.

Chapter Evaluation

Chapter Test 6 and Computer Test Bank Chapter 6 Test can be used to evaluate your students' understanding of this chapter.

Answers to Chapter Review 6

Reviewing the Facts
1. (a) government in which citizens have right to vote to choose their leaders (b) weightiness or seriousness (c) member of privileged families who claimed descent from founders of Rome (d) person who was a free citizen but had less power than a patrician (e) one of two officials who took the place of king of Rome (f) power to overrule (g) aristocratic branch of Roman government (h) absolute ruler for six months chosen by consuls and elected by senate (i) soldier who fights in any country's army for pay (j) urban, landless poor (k) official who spoke on behalf of the plebeians (l) rule of three
2. (a) centrally located city where Roman republic began and from which it spread its power (b) peninsula near midpoint of Mediterranean (c) first settlers in Italy and Rome (d) third group of settlers in Rome who brought writing system and helped develop Rome's trade (e) when Roman republic was set up (f) father of the family, who had complete control (g) Rome's strongest enemy, located near midpoint of Mediterranean coast (h) first written Roman laws that established idea that all free citizens had a right to protection of the law (i) decided which city, Rome or Carthage, would control Sicily and the western Mediterranean (j) Carthaginian military genius who defeated Roman armies twice (k) ended second Punic War when Scipio defeated Hannibal (l) date Carthage was destroyed (m) brothers who attempted reforms of Rome's government

(n) consul of Rome, general, absolute ruler of Rome for ten years (o) date when Caesar defied senate's orders and marched against Pompey (p) date Caesar was murdered (q) Egypt's queen who married Caesar, wooed and won Antony, and caused third civil war in Rome (r) Caesar's friend who helped kill Caesar (s) Caesar's grandnephew and adopted son who became ruler of Rome for 41 years (t) Octavian's chief rival.
3. (a) Rome was a central point within a central peninsula, making it an ideal position from which to send out ships and armies in all directions. (b) Latin settlers were simple farmers and shepherds and had little influence on the growth of Rome. Greek settlers established prosperous and commercially active cities and brought them into closer contact with Greek civilization. Etruscan settlers had great cultural influence on Romans and developed Rome's trade. (c) There was constant conflict between patricians who had all the authority to make laws for Rome and its people and plebeians. (d) It forced both patrician and plebeian men in Rome to lead double lives as farmers and soldiers.
4. (a) Patricians controlled Rome's government, plebeians could be enslaved, and patricians and plebeians could not marry each other. (b) The Twelve Tables established the idea that all free citizens had a right to the protection of the law.
5. Consuls commanded Rome's army and directed its government, had power of life and death over citizens in wartime and great powers in peacetime as well; one consul could always veto others' decisions. Senate—members served for life; exercised enormous influence over both foreign and domestic policy. Assembly—democratic side of Roman government; little power in comparison to the consuls and the senate. Dictator—had absolute power to make laws and command the army, but power lasted for only six months.
6. Roman conquerors were willing to extend citizenship to people outside Rome itself.
7. (a) Rome took over Sicily, dominated and conquered the western and eastern halves of the Mediterranean Sea. At the end of the Third Punic War, Rome's Mediterranean empire stretched from Asia Minor to Spain. (b) Thousands of soldiers were killed and whole Roman armies destroyed, along with farms, homes, and villages.
8. They came to power through the use of their private armies.

Basic Skills

1. **(a)** about 200 miles **(b)** about 325 miles **(c)** Scale in the first map is about one inch to 100 miles; scale in the second map is about one inch to 300 miles, making areas seem smaller and distances seem shorter.

2.

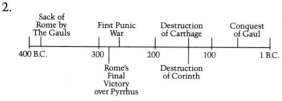

3. Located at the midpoint of the Italian peninsula; located at the center of the Mediterranean, ideal for sending out troops and ships; located on the Tiber on convenient trade routes.

4.

	Rome	Carthage
Population	83,500	250,000
Army	500,000 loyal reserves	mercenaries
Navy	no fleet	500 ships
Resources	little wealth; war experience	wealth from trade

5. **(a)** Expected outcome: Roman defeat **(b)** The Romans copied a captured Carthaginian ship and improved on its design. Their new fleet was superior to Carthage's.

6. **(a)** Scipio Africanus **(b)** Tiberius Gracchus **(c)** Sulla **(d)** Julius Caesar

Researching and Reporting Skills
Students' findings will vary.

Critical Thinking

1. **(a)** *Gravitas* emphasized discipline, strength and loyalty. *Arete* emphasized individual striving for excellence, courage, honor, and glory. **(b)** Roman civilization was concerned with strength, steadiness, duty to family and country, law, and the glory of Rome; Athenian society was concerned with individual achievement and self-expression.

2. **(a)** You might defeat your enemies and take control of the empire. **(b)** You will be a traitor and might be killed. **(c)** You would cross, because otherwise your army would be disbanded and you would be stripped of your power.

3. **(a)** The army gained needed manpower; members of the proletariat found needed employment; soldiers were better trained and more willing to fight. **(b)** Armies were no longer loyal to Rome and became instruments of individual rivalries and civil war.

4. **(a)** Rome gained control of the western Mediterranean and of Sicily with its supply of wheat, slaves, and loot. **(b)** Among the social and economic costs were the destruction of many farmlands in Italy; small farmers dispossessed of lands as grain from Sicily flooded the market; large farmers acquired land for raising cattle (latifundia); cheap slave labor deprived citizens of work; poverty and unemployment created proletariat and caused riots; spoils from conquest flooded the markets; the rich became spoiled with luxuries; the growth of slavery undermined traditional values.

Perspectives on Past and Present
Sallust's viewpoint is that power and wealth corrupt people's moral standards. Sallust was probably referring to the violence, bloodshed, and political rivalries that followed the victories of the Punic Wars and to the excessive disparity of wealth among citizens. In present day-application, students might agree or disagree that money is the root of all evil and that ambition and greed can cause a society's decline.

Investigating History
Students' arguments will vary.

The Roman Empire

Chapter Overview

The rule of Augustus ushered in Rome's greatest period of peace and prosperity—the Pax Romana. Augustus established economic programs and a stable government that allowed Rome to survive a series of untalented emperors; however, the succession problem was never permanently solved.

The Romans extended Greek ideals in art, literature, and philosophy, while making unique and enduring contributions in law, architecture, and engineering. Within the empire, great differences between classes developed. Jews and Christians challenged Roman traditions. Both groups were persecuted by many Roman emperors. Beginning in the third century, economic, military, and political problems weakened the empire, making possible the barbarian invasions that led to the empire's fall in A.D. 476.

Key Terms

civil service, satire, villa, bishop, pope, inflation
For additional exercises, see Vocabulary Worksheet 7.

Chapter Focus

Explain that a symbol is something that stands for or represents another thing. Point out that all famous buildings have some symbolic significance. For example, ask students to select a famous building (or monument) in the United States. Ask, "What does this building symbolize?" Then direct students' attention to the photograph of the Colosseum on page 140 and have them read pages 140–141. Ask, "Why is the Colosseum called a symbol of the Roman Empire? What political purposes did the gladiator contests serve?" The Colosseum is a symbol of the Roman Empire at the peak of its power. Tell students that this chapter explains how the Romans used their peace and prosperity to make advances in architecture, law, philosophy, and literature. Students will learn how the Romans responded to the challenges of internal conflict, changing economic and political conditions, and barbarian invasions.

Augustus' rule began the Pax Romana. 1

Section Objectives

After completing Section 1, students should be able to:

1. assess the political skills of Augustus.
2. describe Roman achievements in constructing public works such as roads and aqueducts.
3. show on a map the Roman Empire at its height.
4. define the problem of succession and explain its impact on Roman politics.

Setting the Stage

Discussing History: Octavian's Rule (Objective 1) Recall that in Chapter 6 students learned that Octavian (Augustus) ruled Rome for forty-one years. Ask students to identify characteristics they think a ruler might need to be an effective leader of the Roman Empire. Write the titles *Princeps*, *Augustus*, and *Imperator* on the chalkboard. Tell students that these titles mean respectively, "First citizen," "Revered and Exalted One," and "Commander." Augustus held all three titles but managed to avoid the senate jealousy that led to Julius Caesar's downfall. Although Octavian had absolute power, he gave the impression of working with the senate and avoided humiliating the senators. At the same time, he maintained firm control of government processes by setting up a civil service system. Ask, "What is a civil service system? In what way could a civil service system benefit the emperor?"

Teaching Strategies

Teaching with Pictures: Aqueducts (Objective 2) Have students read the sections on Roman roads and public buildings (pages 141–142). Then direct their attention to the picture of the aqueduct on page 142. Explain that this aqueduct still delivers water to Segovia by gravity from a mountain

Advance Planner

Chapter 7	The Roman Empire 29 B.C.–A.D. 476		★ Advanced
Focus	The Colosseum as a symbol of the Roman Empire		● Basic

	Section 1	Section 2	Section 3	Section 4
Objectives	1. Assess the political skills of Augustus. 2. Describe Roman achievements in constructing public works, such as roads and aqueducts. 3. Show on a map the Roman Empire at its height. 4. Define the problem of succession and explain its impact on Roman politics.	1. Identify and discuss the ideas of Roman philosophers and writers. 2. Describe the Roman Forum. 3. List important principles of Roman law. 4. Recognize realities of daily life that limited life expectancy in ancient Rome.	1. Explain the origins of Chanukah. 2. Discuss the main teachings of Jesus. 3. Describe how Christianity spread through the Roman Empire. 4. Explain why the Romans warred against the Jews and persecuted the Christians.	1. Identify problems that led to Rome's decline. 2. Evaluate the solutions offered by Diocletian and Constantine to solve Rome's problems. 3. Explain how the Germanic tribes overran and destroyed the western half of the empire.
Setting the Stage	Discussing History: Octavian's Rule	The diffusion of Greco-Roman culture	Sources of religious persecution	Multiple causes of the decline and fall of Rome
Teaching Strategies	Teaching with Pictures: Aqueducts Geography in History: The Roman Empire Outline Map 21 Transparency 18 Relating Past to Present: The Problem of Succession Check for Understanding	Identifying Quotations: Roman Philosophy and Literature Teaching with Pictures: The Roman Forum Discussing History: Roman Law Discussing History: Life Expectancy in the Roman Empire Check for Understanding	Discussing History: The Origins of Chanukah Analyzing a Quotation: The Sermon on the Mount Using Geographic Themes: Movement Transparency 19 Discussing History: Religious Persecution Check for Understanding	Discussing History: Why Did Rome Fall? Transparency 20 Skill Building: Identifying Cause and Effect Relationships Using Geographic Themes: Movement Transparency 21 Check for Understanding
Guided Practice	Transparency 18 Q&A Section Review 1	Section Review 2	Transparency 19 Q&A Section Review 3	Transparency 20 Q&A Transparency 21 Q&A Section Review 4
Independent Practice Worksheets	Independent Practice 7.1 Vocabulary 7	Independent Practice 7.2 Basic Skills 7	Independent Practice 7.3 Critical Thinking 7	Independent Practice 7.4 Geography Skills 7
Enrichment	1. Primary Source: Voices 7.1 2. ★ Answering Augustus' Last Question 3. Researching for Points	1. Primary Source: Voices 7.2 2. Preparing a Report: Nero's 3. ★ Analyzing a Quotation 4. Researching for Points	1. Primary Source: Voices 7.3 2. Preparing a Report: The Siege of Masada 3. Researching for Points	1. Primary Source: Voices 7.4 2. Creative Writing 3. Researching for Points

Chapter Closer	
● **Reteaching Activities**	Writing an Essay, Outlining, Explaining, Recalling Information
Chapter Review	Summary, Reviewing the Facts, Basic Skills, Researching and Reporting Skills, Critical Thinking, Perspectives on Past and Present, Investigating History
Chapter Evaluation	Chapter Test 7, Computer Test Bank Chapter 7 Test

Unit II Review	
Geographic Theme:	Region: How did Rome unify the Mediterranean world?
Unit Perspectives	Understanding History (Defining, Reading Maps, Sequencing Events), Critical Thinking, Making Decisions, Continuity and Change
Unit Evaluation	Unit II Test

spring ten miles away. The aqueduct is ninety-three feet high. Roman engineers used a block and tackle to raise granite blocks weighing up to six tons. Point out the use of arches. Discuss with students why a secure supply of water was essential to the growth of cities.

Now direct students' attention to the cover of the textbook. Ask them to speculate on why the Segovia aqueduct was chosen for the cover. Suggest that the aqueduct is a surviving symbol of the origins and achievements of a great civilization.

Geography in History: The Roman Empire (Objective 3) Distribute copies of Outline Map 21: The Roman Empire. Have students create a map comparing the Roman republic by 133 B.C. and the Roman Empire at its height. Ask students to use map symbols and a map key to show the comparison. (See the maps on pages 130 and 144 for reference, or use Overhead Transparency 18, *The Roman Empire at its Height.*)

Relating Past to Present: The Problem of Succession (Objective 4) Ask students to identify the various methods the Romans used to try to resolve the problem of succession. Then ask, "Why was the lack of a fixed rule for succession a serious problem? Why were Romans unable to agree on a particular method of succession?" Conclude by asking students to describe the procedures established by the United States Constitution to resolve the problem of succession. (You might wish to briefly review Article 2, Amendment 22, and Amendment 25.) Ask, "Does this procedure work? Why, or why not?"

Check for Understanding Have students cite evidence to support the following statement from page 143: "The system of government set up by Augustus proved to be more stable and effective than its individual leaders."

Practice

Guided Practice
Lead a guided discussion of the questions in Overhead Transparency 18 and in Section Review 1. (Answers are below.)

Define:
(a) salaried, experienced workers (b) order of taking over power

Identify:
(a) sports arena (b) 207 years of Roman peace between 27 B.C. and A.D. 180 (c) Roman emperor who built foundation for Pax Romana (d) descended from family of Julius Caesar (e) succeeded one another peacefully

Answer:
1. expanded trade and transportation, developed public building program, instituted civil service
2. (a) no method of succession (b) adopted or named their successors during their reigns
3. the spread of disease, defeat of Roman legions on the northern frontier by Germanic tribes
4. Necessary government work would continue no matter who the ruler was.

Independent Practice
Assign Independent Practice Worksheet 7.1.
Assign Vocabulary Worksheet 7.

Enrichment Activities

1. **Reading a Primary Source** Assign Voices from the Past Resource Book 7.1.

2. **Augustus' Last Question** Just before he died, Augustus asked family members gathered around him this question: "Have I played my part in the farce of life creditably enough?" Ask your advanced students to write an answer to Augustus' question.

3. **Researching for Bonus Points** Award bonus points to students who can find the answer to this question: When the gladiators marched into the Colosseum, what phrase did they use to salute the emperor? ("Hail, Caesar; we who are about to die salute you.")

Answers to Voice from the Past

1. (a) No, some are subjects. (b) those who are "more cultured, better born, and more influential"
2. no need to keep troops in distant cities
3. would probably be better informed about local issues and less resented
4. Answers should consider benefits and drawbacks to Rome and to the conquered.

Romans extended Greek culture. 2

Section Objectives

After completing Section 2, students should be able to:

1. identify and discuss the ideas of Roman philosophers and writers.
2. describe the Roman Forum.
3. list important principles of Roman law.
4. recognize realities of daily life that limited life expectancy in ancient Rome.

Setting the Stage

Explain that cultural diffusion occurs when ideas and goods spread from one culture to another. Ask students to identify examples of cultural diffusion that they have already studied. Students should recall that the Silk Road and the conquests of Alexander the Great helped to promote the spread of new ideas and goods. Now ask students to identify Roman achievements that would stimulate cultural diffusion. Students should note that the Pax Romana and the new system of roads helped to spread Greek and Roman achievements across the empire. The blend of these two cultures is called *Greco-Roman* culture. Explain that this section begins with a discussion of Greco-Roman philosophy and then examines Roman literature and law.

Teaching Strategies

Identifying Quotations: Roman Philosophy and Literature (Objective 1) First review the sections on philosophy and Latin literature. Then read or distribute each of the following quotations. Have students identify the philosopher or writer they would most associate with each. Ask students to explain the reasons for their choices.
• Pleasure is the beginning and the end of living happily. (Epicurus)
• Death is nothing to us, since when we are, death has not come, and when death has come, we are not. (Epicurus)
• One universe, made up of all that is; and one God in it all, and one principle of being, and one law, the reason, shared by all thinking creatures, and one truth. (Marcus Aurelius; the Stoics)
• All the doings of mankind, their wishes, fears, anger, pleasure, joys, and varied pursuits, form the motley subject of my book. (Juvenal)
• The great cycle of the ages is renewal. Now justice returns, returns the Golden Age; a new generation now descends from on high. (Virgil)

Teaching with Pictures: The Roman Forum (Objective 2) After students have read the section on Rome (pages 147–148), direct their attention to the artistic rendering of the Roman Forum on page 148. Ask them to pretend that they are part of the crowd standing in the foreground of the painting.

You are showing them the sights and wonders of one of the ancient world's most famous public squares. Begin by explaining that the Forum was the political, religious, and commercial center of the Empire. Triumphal processions, important trials, and political meetings all took place there. The column on the right was known as the Rostra. Great crowds often gathered around it to listen to well-trained orators give stirring speeches. (The word *rostrum* today refers to any platform for public speaking.) The Arch of Tiberius stands just behind the Rostra. Roman justices administered the law in the great Basilica Julia to the left. Temples to Saturn and Vespasian tower in the background. Although it cannot be seen, the Forum also contained a stone known as the Umbilicus (or "navel") from which all distances in the Roman Empire were counted. Statues of heroes, gods, and goddesses decorate all of the buildings. Proud Romans boasted that their city was "the home of gods." Conclude by asking students to write postcards home describing the sights they have just seen.

Discussing History: Roman Law (Objective 3) Explain that a great Roman jurist named Ulpian defined justice as "a constant and perpetual will to give every man his due." Have students explain this definition in their own words. Then review the basic principles of Roman law on page 149. Ask students to explain how these principles illustrate Ulpian's definition of justice.

Discussing History: Life Expectancy in the Roman Empire (Objective 4) Ask students to read the section on Roman society (pages 149–150). Then explain that many historians have described the Pax Romana as one of history's greatest golden ages. Many modern researchers, however, challenge this view. They point out that newborn Romans had a life expectancy of only 23 to 25 years. The population was vulnerable to smallpox, measles, malaria, pneumonia, and other diseases. In addition, many people suffered from poor nutrition because of the difficulty of transporting food overland from prosperous farms to famine-stricken cities. The high death rate and low life expectancy led many women to marry at a young age. Historians now estimate that about 50 percent of all Roman women married by the age of 15. Ask students to clarify the concept of a golden age in light of this information.

Check for Understanding Have students cite examples of Greek influence on Roman culture and give examples of distinctly Roman cultural achievements.

Practice

Guided Practice
Lead a guided discussion of the questions in Section Review 2. (Answers are below)

Define:
(a) belief that the way to happiness was to free body from pain and mind from fear (b) philosophy espousing virtues of duty, reason, and courage under Universal Law (c) writing that mocks society (d) country estate

Identify:
(a) Greek philosopher whose ideas about happiness influenced Romans (b) Greek philosopher who developed Stoicism (c) journal kept by Marcus Aurelius (d) patriotic historian (e) author of *Aeneid* (f) Virgil's epic poem about Roman origins (g) writer of satire (h) historian who criticized Roman government (i) domed building dedicated to all the gods

Answer:
1. (a) upheld the traditional Roman virtues (b) stressed human laws should be reasonable and just
2. Criticism, satire replaced patriotism, praise.
3. (a) rich: fancy houses, costly foods, leisurely, indulgent life; poor; inadequate food, crowded tenements, unemployment (b) Roman government provided food and housing.
4. (a) answers should include ideas of innocent until proved guilty, rights of the accused, and unjust laws. (b) part of Western legal system

Independent Practice
Assign Independent Practice Worksheet 7.2.
Assign Basic Skills Worksheet 7.

Enrichment Activities

1. **Reading a Primary Source** Assign Voices from the Past Resource Book 7.2.
2. **Preparing a Report: Nero** Roman historians denounced Nero as one of their worst emperors. Ask students to prepare a report agreeing or disagreeing with this assessment.
3. **Analyzing a Quotation** The famed historian Edward Gibbon wrote, "If a man were called upon to fix the period in the history of the world during which the condition of the human race was most happy and prosperous, he would without hesitation name that which elapsed from the accession of Nerva to the death of Aurelius." Ask advanced students to cite evidence supporting or refuting this statement.

4. **Researching for Bonus Points** Award bonus points to students who can answer this question: What name did Romans give to the cold water room in their baths? (the frigidarium)

Christianity spread through the empire. 3

Section Objectives

After completing Section 3, students should be able to:

1. explain the origins of Chanukah.
2. discuss the main teachings of Jesus.
3. describe how Christianity spread through the Roman Empire.
4. explain why the Romans warred against the Jews and persecuted the Christians.

Setting the Stage

Ask students to recall the definitions of polytheism and monotheism. Ask them why a polytheist might tolerate a monotheist, but a monotheist might not tolerate a polytheist. What conditions might lead to the persecution of religious minorities? Explain that this section describes the struggle between Romans and Jews. It also discusses the teachings of Jesus and the growth of a new monotheistic religion— Christianity.

Teaching Strategies

Discussing History: The Origins of Chanukah (Objective 1) Point out that the eight-day Chanukah celebration, also known as the "Festival of Lights," dates to events described in this section. After students have read, "Jews came under Roman rule" (page 151), tell them that the holiday of Chanukah commemorates the struggle of Jews led by Judas Maccabee to recapture the Jewish temple in Jerusalem. The Hebrew word *Chanukah* means "rededication" and refers to the purification of the temple in 165 B.C. When the temple was rededicated, only enough oil was found to burn for one day. Miraculously, the sacramental oil lasted for eight days. In present-day practice, on each of the eight nights of Chanukah, Jews light a candle to commemorate a miracle associated with the purification of the temple.

Analyzing a Quotation: The Sermon on the Mount
(Objective 2) Jesus won many followers because he taught that God's kingdom was open to everyone and that God is love. One of Jesus' most famous sermons is known as the Sermon on the Mount. In this sermon Jesus gave eight blessings known as beatitudes. Ask students to identify the qualities Jesus emphasized and to contrast them with qualities admired by the Romans.

> Blessed are the poor in spirit: for theirs is the kingdom of heaven.
> Blessed are they that mourn: for they shall be comforted.
> Blessed are the meek: for they shall inherit the earth.
> Blessed are they which do hunger and thirst after righteousness: for they shall be filled.
> Blessed are the merciful: for they shall obtain mercy.
> Blessed are the pure in heart: for they shall see God.
> Blessed are the peacemakers: for they shall be called the children of God.
> Blessed are they which are persecuted for righteousness' sake: for theirs is the kingdom of heaven.

Using Geographic Themes: Movement (Objective 3) First, review the section, "Apostles spread Jesus' teachings." Then display Overhead Transparency 19, *The Spread of Christianity in Roman Times.* Have students identify the regions to which Christianity had spread by A.D. 300. Point out Paul's role in spreading the new faith to key cities in the eastern half of the Roman Empire. Use the map transparency to show Christianity's rapid expansion between A.D. 300 and A.D. 450. Ask students by what date Christianity had spread beyond the boundaries of the Roman Empire. (A.D. 450)

Discussing History: Religious Persecution (Objective 4) Begin by explaining that a scapegoat is a person or group blamed for the errors of others or for bad times. The Roman emperors found it convenient to use the Christians as scapegoats. As the third century Christian writer Tertullian explained, the Romans "take the Christians to be the cause of every disaster to the state, of every misfortune to the people. If the Tiber reaches the wall ... if there is a famine, or if there is a plague, the cry is at once, 'the Christians to the lions.'" Suggest that the persecutions of the Christians showed the empire's growing weakness.

Check for Understanding Have students explain why the Romans persecuted the Jews and the Christians. How did these persecutions affect both religions?

Practice

Guided Practice
Lead a guided discussion of the questions in Overhead Transparency 19 and in Section Review 3. (Answers are below.)

Define:
(a) follower (b) savior (c) disciple who spread the word of Jesus (d) person who sacrifices his or her life for the sake of a cause or belief (e) church official (f) father of the Christian Church

Identify:
(a) the town where the Jewish temple was located and where Jesus was sentenced to death (b) a ruler who was a romanized Jew (c) founder of Christianity (d) books of the New Testament that tell the story of Jesus' life (e) Roman governor who sentenced Jesus to death (f) Jew who dedicated his life to spreading the teachings of Jesus (g) Jewish revolutionaries who tried to overthrow Roman rule (h) Jewish fortress near the Dead Sea (i) doctrine that Roman bishops outranked others

Answer:
1. (a) tolerant (b) Followers were monotheistic, did not worship other (Roman) gods.
2. kingdom of God in which all who accepted Jesus as their savior would find eternal life; love
3. spread Christianity throughout the Roman empire and wrote a large part of the New Testament
4. (a) Peace and cultural unity provided an ideal opportunity for the spread of Christianity. (b) Christians were persecuted, tried, and executed.
5. Students may see the attempt to create a scapegoat or distraction in these actions.

Independent Practice
Assign Independent Practice Worksheet 7.3.
Assign Critical Thinking Worksheet 7.

Enrichment Activities

1. **Reading a Primary Source** Assign Voices from the Past Resource Book 7.3.

2. **Preparing a Report** Ask interested students to prepare a report on the siege of Masada. Their reports should include a discussion of why Masada has become an important symbol for modern Israel.

3. **Researching for Bonus Points** Award bonus points to students who can answer this question: What was the name of the apostle who replaced Judas? (Matthias)

Rome's empire declined and fell. 4

Section Objectives

After reading Section 4, students should be able to:

1. identify problems that led to Rome's decline.
2. evaluate the solutions offered by Diocletian and Constantine to solve Rome's problems.
3. explain how the Germanic tribes overran and destroyed the western half of the empire.

Setting the Stage

Ask students to recall a "contest or game" in which the side they were rooting for lost. Have students list reasons why their side lost. Ask, "How many listed only one reason? How many listed two or more reasons?" Emphasize that events can rarely be explained by one cause. Historians always look for multiple causes to help explain why an event occurred. This section examines one of the most famous events in history—the fall of the Roman Empire. Point out that no single factor caused Rome's decline and fall. Historians have identified a number of forces that worked together over an extended period of time.

Teaching Strategies

Discussing History: Why Did Rome Fall? (Objective 1) Begin by having students list Rome's problems. Students should recall the problem of succession, the gap between the rich and the poor, the rise of competing professional armies, the declining faith in the old gods and the struggles against the Jews and the Christians. Explain that these problems worsened during the third century. Have students read the section, "Crises weakened the Empire," and give example's of Rome's economic, military, and political decay. Ask, "Which problem do you think posed the gravest threat to Rome's security? Why?" Use Overhead Transparency 20, *Trade in the Roman Empire*, to link Rome's economic problems with its networks of trade.

Skill Building: Identifying Cause and Effect Relationships (Objective 2) Explain that the Romans tried to solve their problems. Have students read the sections on the reforms of Diocletian and Constantine. Then draw a three-column chart on the chalkboard. Label the columns "Problems,"

"Solutions," and "Consequences." In the first column, have students list problems that plagued the empire during the crises of the third century. Then ask the class to review the reforms initiated by Diocletian and Constantine and to link each reform with one or more of the problems on the chart. Enter this information in the "Solutions" column. Have students complete the chart by assessing the success or failure of each reform and entering this information in the "Consequences" column.

Using Geographic Themes: Movement (Objective 3) The Germanic invasions illustrate the theme of movement. Have students read the sections on how the Germanic tribes overran the western half of the empire. Then use Overhead Transparency 21, *The Barbarian Invasions*, to trace the movement of each tribe.

Check for Understanding Have students identify three main causes of the decline of the Roman Empire.

Practice

Guided Practice
Lead a guided discussion of the questions in Overhead Transparencies 20 and 21 and the questions in Section Review 4. (Answers are below.)

Define:
increase in prices as a result of devaluing money

Identify:
(a) weak emperor whose rule began the decline of Rome (b) emperor who instituted reforms to restore order and build economic stability (c) emperor who brought an end to Christian persecution and moved capital to Byzantium (d) part of Roman empire that included the Greek-speaking east (e) part of Roman empire that included Italy, Gaul, Britannia, and Spain (f) where Constantine won the victory that made him emperor of western empire (g) law that changed Christianity from outlawed sect to approved religion (h) name for Byzantium (i) semibarbaric people who spoke Germanic languages (j) nomadic people from central Asia (k) king of Visigoths who sacked Rome (l) Vandal king who led a second attack on Rome (m) Hun chieftain who led raids against much of Roman empire (n) first powerful pope of Rome (o) last Roman emperor, a 14-year-old boy (p) barbarian general who overthrew Romulus Augustus

Answer:
1. disruption of trade routes, inflation, agricultural crisis

2. repeatedly defeated; soldiers fought strictly for money
3. (a) He enacted edict of Milan, which gave Christianity legal status. (b) He moved the center of the Roman empire to Byzantium.
4. (a) because of pressure from the attacking Huns (b) too disorganized
5. (a) Possible answers: secured Rome's boundaries, stabilized economy and rule, restored faith in Roman gods and prestige of the emperor (b) Possible answers: Gains in almost all areas were only temporary; persecution of Christians may have made "problem" worse; dividing empire contributed to the fall of Rome.

Independent Practice
Assign Independent Practice Worksheet 7.4.
Assign Geography Skills Worksheet 7.

Enrichment Activities

1. **Reading a Primary Source** Assign Voices from the Past Resource Book 7.4.

2. **Creative Writing** The fall of Rome might seem the inevitable result of crisis and decline; however, this was not necessarily the perception of the Romans, who proudly recalled their tradition of overcoming adversity. Divide students into groups representing members of a family living in Rome. Assign family statuses (patrician, plebeian, slave). Have each group write a family diary containing entries for each of the following years: 192, 260, 290, 313, 330, 410, 452, and 476. Entries should describe key events in those years and their impact on family life.

3. **Researching for Bonus Points** Award bonus points to students who can answer this question: What were the names of Constantine's three sons? (Constantius, Constantinus, and Constans)

Concluding the Chapter

1. **Chapter Closer**
   Recall that the Colosseum is a symbol of Roman power. Challenge students to use the information and pictures in this chapter to choose and explain another symbol of Rome's greatness and a symbol of Rome's decline.

2. **Reteaching Activities**
   a. **Writing an Essay** Have students write a short essay supporting the following statement: "Without the rule of Augustus, there would not have been a Pax Romana."

   b. **Outlining** Ask students to use the headings in Section 2 to construct an outline of the section content.
   c. **Explaining** Ask students to explain how early Christianity became organized as the Christian Church.
   d. **Recalling Information** Ask students to explain how Alaric, Attila, and Odoacer contributed to the fall of Rome.

3. **Chapter Review Activities**
   Assign Chapter Review 7 activities.

Chapter Evaluation

Chapter Test 7 and Computer Test Bank Chapter 7 Test can be used to evaluate your students' understanding of this chapter.

Answers to Chapter Review 7

Reviewing the Facts
1. **a.** salaried people of all ranks who performed work to run the empire **b.** writing that mocked society for its foolishness and wickedness **c.** country estate owned by wealthy city dweller, used as an escape from city life **d.** church official who set moral standards and supervised finances of several local churches **e.** father and leading bishop of Christian Church **f.** increase in prices
2. **a.** 207 years of Roman peace between 27 B.C. and A.D. 180 **b.** Roman emperor who built foundation for Pax Romana **c.** Roman emperor who wrote *Meditations*; Pax Romana ended with his death **d.** year Pax Romana ended **e.** Greek philosopher whose ideas about happiness influenced Romans **f.** Greek philosopher who developed Stoicism **g.** patriotic historian whose works were sponsored by Augustus **h.** epic poet and author of *Aeneid* **i.** founder of Christianity **j.** apostle who dedicated his life to spreading teachings of Jesus **k.** disciple of Jesus who was Rome's first bishop **l.** Jewish revolutionaries who tried to overthrow Roman rule **m.** emperor who tried to restore order in the empire and increase its strength **n.** emperor who ended Christian persecution and moved capital from Rome to Byzantium **o.** new name for Byzantium **p.** law that changed Christianity from an outlawed sect to a religion approved

by emperor **q.** year when last Roman emperor was overthrown

3. The Roman empire was largely free of war. Trade and transportation were improved. Public building program was initiated. Civil service began. Roman law developed.

4. **(a)** kingdom of God for believers; people should follow a "golden rule" **(b)** With the exception of Nero, emperors during the first century did not actively persecute Christians. Toward the end of the second century, Christians were cruelly persecuted. In the third century, Constantine gave state approval to Christianity.

5. **(a)** Trade was disrupted on both land and sea; Rome's gold and silver were drained away to buy luxuries from other lands; harvests became increasingly meager. **(b)** At one time, Romans were willing to sacrifice their lives for their republic. In later centuries, citizens were not actively disloyal but were indifferent. It was no longer considered an honor to hold political office. Recruitment of barbarians into the army made the loyalty of troops suspect. **(c)** Germanic invasions destroyed the western half of the Roman empire.

Basic Skills

1. **(a)** 1,000 years; 600 years **(b)** 100 B.C. to 1 B.C. **(c)** about 100 years to one-half inch; about 100 years to one inch **(d)** the Pax Romana

2.

	Europe	Africa	Asia
Minerals	lead, gold, tin, copper, iron, silver	copper	silver
Foods	wine, olive oil, dried fish	grain, olive oil, spices, palm oil	spices, pepper, wine
Building Materials		marble	marble, timber
Clothing	wool, furs		silks, wool
Jewelry	amber	ivory, tortoise-shell	jade, pearls, ivory
Manufactured goods	glass, pottery, bronzeware	glass, incense, papyrus	glass, incense
Other	slaves, horses, hunting dogs	slaves	purple dye

3. Summaries should include governing ability; encouragement of trade through coinage, elimination of border taxes, and building of roads; glorification of Rome through a public building program using concrete and marble; efficient civil service made up of salaried, experienced workers.

Researching and Reporting Skills

1. Group projects will vary.
2. Primary sources: St. Paul's Epistle, Constantine's triumphal arch, Marcus Aurelius's *Meditations*. These were works of contemporaries of the period. Secondary sources: Livy's description of the early heroes of Rome. Livy was a historian writing about the past.

Critical Thinking

1. **(a)** During the Republic only Romans could be citizens. Citizenship gave males the right to participate in the assembly and equal access to public office (287 B.C.). Citizenship was later extended to non-Romans and conquered peoples. In Greece citizenship was not extended to foreigners, women, or slaves. In Rome, Athens, and Sparta citizens had military and political duties to the state. **(b)** In the United States citizenship extends to all persons born in United States territory or to an American parent, and to naturalized immigrants.
2. Buddhism also appealed to the poor. Both religions taught concern for all human beings and belief in a merciful God.
3. Students should provide examples from Roman history proving or disproving the characteristics listed in the quotation.
4. **(a)** Students might note that Roman law is practiced in many countries today. **(b)** Students might mention Roman roads, architecture, and political institutions as enduring achievements.
5. **(a)** a general increase in prices **(b)** too many expensive luxuries imported from abroad; little to export in exchange; paid for imports with large quantities of silver and gold; as these were in short supply, the Roman government minted coins with less and less silver content; these coins lost their value and more were needed to pay for goods, thus increasing prices dramatically. **(c)** All people were poorer since their money was worth less. The poor in particular suffered greatly from the high prices for necessities. Imports became unaffordable and trade slowed down.

Perspectives on Past and Present

1. Students might point out the use of Roman columns and arches in monumental architecture.

2. Answers will vary, but students should point out that Rome had no established procedure for the transition of power. As a result, such times often caused crises. In the United States, the president is elected every four years. In the U.S.S.R., there is no established procedure; often there is a period of shared power with a struggle between leaders until one takes control. In many countries, constitutional monarchies are hereditary, with power held by a parliament. In countries with dictatorships, there may also be a president; often the army controls or decides the outcome of elections. Succession also may occur by a coup, or abrupt seizure of power often involving military action.

Investigating History
Students' findings will vary.

Unit II Review Activities

1. Assign Geographic Theme: Region
2. Assign Unit Perspective Questions

Unit II Review Answers

Geographic Theme: Location
1. Rome's location was a major factor in its political expansion. Its central location in the Italian peninsula permitted expansion both northward and southward. Its central location in the Mediterranean region permitted expansion both eastward and westward.
2. (a) By 133 B.C. Rome had expanded to include Italy, Spain, Carthage, Greece, Macedon, and Pergamum. Between 133 B.C. and A.D. 117, Rome added Numidia, Mauretania, Gaul, Britain, Dacia, Thrace, Phrygia, Asia Minor, Syria, Judea, Egypt, and Libya. (b) The pattern in the first stage was to take over lands bordering the north shore of the Mediterranean and Carthage on the south shore. The second stage pattern was to expand farther into Mediterranean coastal regions and then to move inland, even crossing the Channel to Britain.
3. In order to expand into distant coastal areas Rome had to control the Mediterranean Sea. Carthage stood in the way.

4. Roman political expansion resulted in the spread of Roman law, ideas of government, economic life, construction, and cultural characteristics to the whole Mediterranean area.

Unit Perspectives Questions

Understanding History
1. (a) government in which all citizens participate as in Athens (b) government in which citizens who have the right to vote choose their leaders as in Rome (c) form of government where rule is in the hands of a small group of noble families as in Greece during Dark Ages (d) leader who came to power through citizen rebellion and helped farmers, artisans (e) consuls took place of Roman king (f) aristocratic branch of Roman government (g) democratic side of Roman government (h) power to overrule one consul had over other (i) in Rome, chosen and given absolute power for a six-month period during war (j) salaried, experienced workers who do the everyday tasks of running a government; set up by Augustus in Rome
2. (a) both (b) both (c) Roman (d) both (e) empire of Alexander (f) empire of Alexander (g) Roman (h) Roman
3. (a) Persian Wars (b) Diocletian divides the empire. (c) Roman takeover of Judea (d) Roman conquest of Italy (e) Rise of Julius Caesar (f) Peloponnesian War

Critical Thinking
1. (a) Short term, loss of the city; long term, Athens defeated the Persians and became head of the Delian League; a new city was built. (b) Short term, destroyed what was left from the sacking by the Visigoths; long term, signaled the end of the Roman Empire.
2. Possible answers include: (a) *similarity*—the side with the least resources won a major naval battle; *difference*—Athens, the victorious city, was burnt down; Carthage, the losing city, was destroyed. (b) *similarity*—bodies of foot soldiers; *difference*—legion broken up into smaller groups, more flexible. (c) *similarity*—citizens and non-citizens; *difference*—in Greece citizens equal, in Rome patricians and plebeians (d) *similarity*—Rome adopted many features of Greek architecture; *difference*—Greeks used marble and tall columns, Romans used concrete and built domes.
3. (a) approve heartily (b) overall approve except for Greeks' sense of duty to the city
4. Approved. (Sallust) "justice, integrity";

(Pericles) "... laws offer equal justice ... high position does not depend on wealth"; (Sallust) "... good morals ... watched over themselves and their country ..."; (Pericles) "... citizens see to their own livelihoods but capable of making political decisions ..."; "... man who does not take part in public life ... useless"; (Sallust) "... boldness in warfare ..."; (Pericles) "... Athens for which these men nobly fought and died."

5. **(a)** Sparta's victory marked the end of Athenian glory and the decline of Greece as a whole; Sparta itself came out strong. **(b)** Caesar took power by force, used popular support against the senate. **(c)** Patricians were members of noble families exercising great political power.

Making Decisions

1. **(a)** inherited this ideal from his father; wished for revenge against the Persians; successful in destroying the threat from Persia, establishing an enormous empire, and spreading Greek culture, but empire was politically and militarily very shaky and fell apart at his death; Alexander met his goals but overreached himself in pushing too far east. **(b)** Better located for trade, better defenses, eastern half more prosperous and Christian; weakened the already weaker western half of the empire, leaving it prey to barbarian invasions; new center was economic and cultural center of the times, but move hastened fall of the west into barbarian hands.

Continuity and Change

1. Philip of Macedon took control of Greece. Alexander conquered Persia and Egypt. After his death, his generals divided the empire into three kingdoms. In Greece cities formed leagues and fought among themselves. Roman Empire gained control of Greece, Asia Minor, and Egypt.
2. Farming villages in North and Central America; Kingdom of Kush; Roman civilization spread through Italy; Mauryan empire in India; Chinese empire under Han dynasty; more cities; Great Wall of China; Parthian empire, Seleucid empire, Ptolemaic Egypt

---

Unit Evaluation

Unit II Test can be used to evaluate your students' understanding of this unit.

The Middle Ages

Unit Overview

This unit explores the changes that came about following the collapse of Rome and during the reintegration of society in Europe. The Middle Ages were more than a period of transition. They were also years of faith, accomplishment, and triumph over adversity.

After the fall of Rome, the center of power and civilization shifted to Constantinople. This city was the capital of the Byzantine empire, a place of great wealth, and a hub of trade. Under the rule of emperor Justinian, the Byzantines tried to restore the Roman empire to its former glories. Although that effort failed, Justinian left a heritage of a massive compilation of Roman law.

During the seventh century, a new religion, Islam, arose on the Arabian peninsula. Within 100 years, converts to Islam had conquered an empire that extended from Spain in the west to the Indus River in the east.

Internal dissension weakened both the Byzantine and Islamic empires. By the fifteenth century, both had fallen to Turkish invaders.

While the Byzantine and Islamic empires were flourishing in the Middle East, western Europe was slowly recovering from the fall of Roman civilization. The period between the fall of Rome and the beginning of the modern world (500–1500) is known as the Middle Ages. In the early Middle Ages, Germanic leaders and customs replaced Roman government and law. The Church functioned as the preserver of learning and order. From the Germanic kingdom of the Franks, Charlemagne created an empire. After his death, Europe suffered a new series of invasions, including those of the Vikings. Western Europe sought security and stability in the political and economic institution of feudalism.

The High Middle Ages brought the revival of towns, trade, and interest in learning. In England and France, strong central governments began to emerge. Germany remained a group of feudal kingdoms. The year 1095 marked the start of the Crusades. The first Crusade captured Jerusalem, but later Crusades accomplished little.

In the later years of the Middle Ages, England, France, and Spain began to build nation-states. The Great Schism weakened the authority of the Church, and plague and the Hundred Years' War weakened feudalism. New monarchs replaced feudal kings in western Europe, and a new empire arose in Russia.

Resources

The resources that supplement the study of this unit are:

1. The time line for Unit III, found on pages 164–165. The themes for this time line include feudalism, chivalry, and the Crusades.
2. The Geographic Theme, found on page 256. The theme *Interaction* deals with the emergence of new economic activity and new routes for trade in the later Middle Ages.
3. The Historical Atlas maps on pages 808–809 and 810–811. These show the world in about 800 and in about 1250, with Europe still mainly contained within its continental limits. The Global Perspectives enrichment activities in Chapters 9 and 11 refer to these maps, which also appear in overhead transparencies.

Chapter Titles

8 The Byzantine Empire and the Rise of Islam 450–1453 (pages 166–186)
9 The Early Middle Ages 450–1000 (pages 187–208)
10 The High Middle Ages 1000–1300 (pages 209–233)
11 The Origin of European Nations 1150–1580 (pages 234–255)

The Byzantine Empire and the Rise of Islam

Chapter Overview

Chapter 8 discusses the growth of both the Byzantine and the Islamic empires, their spread from Southwest Asia into North Africa and Europe, and their final decline. The Byzantine emperor Justinian, who reigned between A.D. 527 to A.D. 565, tried to reconquer Roman lands to the west, oversaw codification laws, and undertook a building program in Constantinople. In 1054 (with the separation of the Roman Catholic Church and the Eastern Orthodox Church), the political break between the eastern and western parts of the old Roman empire became a religious break as well.

In the Arabian Peninsula, Muhammad attracted followers to a new monotheistic religion, which became known as Islam. Between A.D. 630 and A.D. 732, Islam expanded to the east and west. The building of an empire changed Islamic society by bringing non-Muslims under Muslim rule. Meanwhile, religious differences divided Islam.

By the eleventh century, both the Islamic and the Byzantine empires were troubled by invasions, problems of internal disunity, and political instability. The Seljuk and Ottoman Turks helped bring an end to both empires.

Key Terms

excommunicate, heretic, patriarch, jihad, caliph, sultan.
For additional exercises, see Vocabulary Worksheet 8.

Chapter Focus

Write *sacred* on the chalkboard. Ask students to suggest possible definitions. Emphasize that sacred, or holy, places are dedicated to religious use. Now have the class read the chapter opener (pages 166–167) and study the photograph on page 166. Ask students to name the three religious groups mentioned in this section and to explain why Jerusalem is sacred to each. Students should note that Jerusalem is sacred to Jews as the site of the Western Wall (the last remnant of Solomon's Temple) and to Christians as the site of Christ's ministry and death. Point out that Jerusalem is also a sacred city of Muslims. The Dome of the

Rock shown on page 166 encloses the sacred stone of Mount Moriah. Muslims believe that this stone marks the spot from which the prophet Muhammad ascended to heaven. They also believe that on Judgment Day scales will be hung from arches outside the Dome of the Rock to weigh souls. The conflicting claims to Jerusalem today can be traced in part to the strong attachment the followers of three major faiths have to the sacred places in this ancient city. This chapter begins with the first confrontation between Christians and Muslims over Jerusalem and then discusses the growth and continued rivalry of the Byzantine empire and the Islamic empire.

Constantinople ruled an eastern empire. 1

Section Objectives

After completing Section 1, students should be able to:

1. explain the geographic advantages of Constantinople's location.
2. identify the boundaries of the Byzantine empire.
3. identify evidence to support main ideas about the Byzantine empire.
4. discuss Constantinople's role as the religious center of the first Christian empire.

Setting the Stage

Using Geographic Themes: Location and Place (Objective 1) Show the map of Constantinople on Overhead Transparency 22. First explain that Constantinople is located on a peninsula bordered by the Golden Horn, Bosporus Strait, and the Sea of Marmara. The Golden Horn provides Constantinople with a spacious harbor. The peninsula's land side is only five miles long and could easily be fortified with a wall. Now explain that a traveler once said that Constantinople's location provided a key that could unlock two worlds and two seas. Ask students to examine Overhead Transparency 22 and to explain what the traveler meant. Point out that Constantinople is located at a point where the land routes from Asia and Eastern Europe meet. It is the only city in the world that straddles two continents. In addition, Constantinople also dominates the north-south sea route linking the Black Sea to the Mediterranean Sea. This section examines how a ruler named Justinian used Constantinople's natural defenses and commercial advantages to turn the city into the capital of a powerful Christian empire.

Advance Planner

Unit III	The Middle Ages		
Theme	The Middle Ages was a period of reintegration of European societies after the fall of Rome.		
Chapter 8	The Byzantine Empire and the Rise of Islam 450–1453		★ Advanced
Focus	The sacred places of Christians, Jews, and Muslims		● Basic

	Section 1	Section 2	Section 3
Objectives	1. Explain the geographic advantages of Constantinople's location. 2. Identify the boundaries of the Byzantine empire. 3. Identify evidence to support main ideas about the Byzantine empire. 4. Discuss Constantinople's role as the religious center of the first Christian empire.	1. Describe the career of the prophet Muhammad. 2. Identify the Five Pillars of Islam, and explain the significance of the Kaaba. 3. Trace the spread of Islam. 4. Discuss aspects of Arab art and architecture during the Islamic golden age.	1. Describe how the Slavs became Christians. 2. Make a time line of the decline and fall of the Islamic and Byzantine empires. 3. Describe the last siege of Constantinople.
Setting the Stage	Unit III time line Geography of the Byzantine empire Using Geographic Themes: Location and Place Transparency 22	The rise and spread of Islam	The diffusion of Islam to Slavs and Turks Transparency 24 Transparency 25
Teaching Strategies	Geography in History: Byzantine Empire Outline Map 21 Skill Building: Supporting Main Ideas Discussing History: A City Tour Check for Understanding	Discussing History: The Prophet Muhammad Teaching with Pictures: The Kaaba Geography in History: The Spread of Islam Transparency 23 Transparency 87 Teaching with Pictures: Islamic Art and Architecture Check for Understanding	Discussing History: The Slavs Become Christians Skill Building: Making a Time Line Discussing History: The Fall of Constantinople Check for Understanding
Guided Practice	Transparency 22 Q&A Section Review 1	Transparency 23 Q&A Section Review 2	Transparency 24 Q&A Transparency 25 Q&A Section Review 3
Independent Practice Worksheets	Independent Practice 8.1 Geography Skills 8 Vocabulary 8	Independent Practice 8.2 Basic Skills 8	Independent Practice 8.3 Critical Thinking 8
Enrichment	1. Primary Source: Voices 8.1 2. Researching for Points	1. Primary Source: Voices 8.2 2. Preparing a Report: Pilgrimage to Mecca 3. Researching for Points	1. Primary Source: Voices 8.3 2. Preparing a Report 3. Creative Writing 4. Researching for Points

Chapter Closer	
● **Reteaching Activities**	Summarizing, Answering Questions, Outlining
Chapter Review	Summary, Reviewing the Facts, Basic Skills, Researching and Reporting Skills, Critical Thinking, Perspectives on Past and Present, Investigating History
Chapter Evaluation	Chapter Test 8, Computer Test Bank Chapter 8 Test

Teaching Strategies

Geography in History: Byzantine Empire (Objective 2) Explain that Justinian considered himself the rightful heir to the lands once controlled by the Roman empire. As discussed in the text, he commanded Belisarius to reconquer these lands. Distribute Outline Map 21: Roman Empire. Using the map on page 169 as a guide, have students use one color to shade in the area showing the Byzantine empire before Justinian and another color to show the area conquered by Justinian. Students should label North Africa, Italy, Greece, Spain, Asia Minor, Egypt, and Palestine; the Mediterranean Sea, Black Sea, Red Sea, and Atlantic Ocean. Remind students to provide keys and titles.

Skill Building: Supporting Main Ideas (Objective 3) Write the following statements on the chalkboard. Have students write two facts to support each statement.
1. Legal reforms were Justinian's most important contribution. (He ordered the codification of all Roman laws and legal opinions of the preceding 400 years. Justinian's Code became the basis of Byzantine law for the next 900 years and later of western European laws.)
2. Constantinople was a well-protected city. (Sea walls guarded it from hostile navies. To the west, a moat and three walls blocked the only land route to the city.)
3. Differences developed between Byzantine Christians and Christians of western Europe. (Byzantine priests conducted services in local languages, while western European priests used Latin. Byzantine priests could marry, while Roman priests could not. The pope in Rome claimed independence from emperors and leadership of all Christians, but the Byzantine patriarchs accepted the authority of their emperor and refused to accept the pope in Rome as their superior.)

Discussing History: A City Tour (Objective 4) Emphasize to students that Constantinople was the first Christian capital of the first Christian empire. Pilgrims journeyed great distances to see such holy relics as the Crown of Thorns, parts of the True Cross, and the Virgin Mary's robe. However, all of these relics were over-shadowed by the immense presence of Hagia Sophia—the Church of the Holy Wisdom. When the first church of Hagia Sophia burned down, Justinian immediately commissioned a new one. More than 10,000 workers labored for almost six years. When he first saw the completed church, Justinian extended his arms towards heaven and cried: "Glory to God, who deemed me worthy of fulfilling such a work. O Solomon, I have surpassed thee!" (See *Hagia Sophia* by Lord Kinross.) Point out that Hagia Sophia, like the Parthenon and the Colosseum, was a symbol of the civilization that created it. Noting that the church was illuminated each night by thousands of candles, one Byzantine described Hagia Sophia as a "sacred light" that guided sailors into the city's safe harbor. The church thus symbolized a spiritual lighthouse for the world's first Christian capital.

Check for Understanding Have students explain the importance of Bosporus, Code of Justinian, Hagia Sophia, Patriarch of Constantinople.

Practice

Guided Practice
Lead a guided discussion of the questions in Overhead Transparency 22 and in Section Review 1. (Answers are below.)

Define:
(a) compilation of laws in which contradictions are resolved (b) small art objects that depict Christian figures (c) icon smasher (d) to place outside the church (e) person whose ideas are incorrect in the opinion of a church (f) bishop of Constantinople

Identify:
(a) Rome's first Christian emperor and founder of Constantinople (b) eastern capital of Roman empire built at Byzantium (c) gateway between Sea of Marmara and the Black Sea (d) Roman emperor who codified laws and undertook a massive building program in Constantinople (e) court historian under Justinian (f) general who temporarily recaptured Roman lands (g) wife of Justinian (h) cathedral in Constantinople (i) where Greece and Macedon are located (j) eastern branch of Christian Church (k) western branch of Christian Church

Answer:
1. (a) horn because of its shape; golden because of the wealthy cargoes that floated on its waters (b) Merchants' tables lined it on both sides.
2. political powers of Roman ruler and religious power as new apostles of Jesus
3. (a) reconquer Roman lands to the west (b) only temporarily, because after his death lands were soon lost again to barbarians
4. (a) codified laws and settled contradictions; basis of Byzantine law for 900 years (b) Western Europe came to know again benefits of Roman law.

5. (a) disagreements over use of icons, language in which services were conducted, behavior of priests, superiority of pope (b) East and west split into two hostile branches.
6. geographic: favorable location for trade; historic; shift from west gave opportunity for new vitality; cultural: blending of Greek and Roman traditions with the added feature of Christianity
7. Answers should include consideration of his immediate achievements as well as his long-term impact.

Independent Practice

Assign Independent Practice Worksheet 8.1.
Assign Geography Skills Worksheet 8.
Assign Vocabulary Worksheet 8.

Enrichment Activities

1. **Reading a Primary Source** Assign Voices from the Past Resource Book 8.1.

2. **Researching for Bonus Points** Award bonus points to students who can find the answer to this question: What happened to the Holy Table inside Hagia Sophia? (It was stolen by the Venetians in 1204; however, the ship carrying it sank and the Holy Table is now on the bottom of the Sea of Marmara.)

Answers to Voice from the Past

1. to remain or flee in ships
2. (a) usually not considered appropriate, but under the circumstances, not worth debating (b) not highly valued
3. (a) to stay and fight back (b) It is preferable to becoming a fugitive. (c) He might want to trade his safety as a fugitive for death.
4. To die while defending the empire is reward enough to suffer the pain of death.

A new faith spread from Arabia.　2

Section Objectives

After completing Section 2, students should be able to:

1. describe the career of the prophet Muhammad.
2. identify the Five Pillars of Islam, and explain the significance of the Kaaba.
3. trace the spread of Islam.
4. discuss aspects of Arab art and architecture during the Islamic golden age.

Setting the Stage

Ask students to pretend that it is A.D. 600. As military advisers to the Byzantine emperor, their duty is to report on any threats to the empire's borders. Have students examine the map on page 169 and make a list of the peoples who surrounded the Byzantine Empire. Their list should include the Persians, Huns, Slavs, Gepids, Lombards, Franks, Visigoths, Berbers, and Arabs. Ask, "Which groups might pose a threat to Constantinople?" Point out that the Byzantine military advisers recognized the Persian Empire and the Germanic tribes as powerful long-term rivals. They did not give much thought to the scattered Arab tribes then living in the Arabian desert. However, within thirty years a new religion called Islam burst forth from the Arabian desert and its followers conquered a huge new empire stretching from Spain to the Indus River. This section introduces the prophet Muhammad and explains the basic beliefs of Islam. It also discusses the cultural achievements of the Islamic golden age.

Teaching Strategies

Discussing History: The Prophet Muhammad (Objective 1) Have the class list the problems Muhammad faced when he first announced that he was Allah's prophet. Students should note that Muhammad faced a formidable challenge—he was an illiterate merchant living in a polytheistic society. Explain that Muhammad successfully overcame these disadvantages. Illiteracy was not a severe handicap in the desert culture of Arabia. The Bedouins admired the spoken word and believed that particularly eloquent speakers were possessed by a supernatural force. Gabriel's visits filled Muhammad with confidence and his passionate sermons convinced people that he was indeed Allah's prophet. Muhammad's experience with his wife's caravan business also proved to be an advantage. On his journeys, he met Byzantine Christians and Jews who told him about their monotheistic religions. Muhammad's message about a stern but compassionate god called Allah, his emphasis on charity to the poor, and his promise of an eternal reward for the faithful soon won many converts.

Teaching with Pictures: The Kaaba (Objective 2) Have students read the section on the Five Pillars of Islam (page 176) and direct students' attention to the picture of the Kaaba on page 175. Explain that more than two million Muslim pilgrims visit the Kaaba each year. Men and women, rich and poor, dress in plain white clothes, symbolizing the idea that all Muslims are equal in the eyes of Allah. The Kaaba is fifty feet high. Muslims believe that it was originally built by Abraham and his son Ishmael. The eastern corner of the Kaaba contains a black meteor encased in silver. Muslims believe that the Black Stone represents the right hand of Allah. Pilgrims circle the Kaaba seven times hoping to touch or kiss the Black Stone. The Kaaba itself is empty. It is covered with an embroidered black cloth called a *kiswa*. More than 100 artisans work full time to produce a new kiswa each year. The finished kiswa contains 2,500 square feet of cloth and weighs two tons.

Geography in History: The Spread of Islam (Objective 3) Have students read the section, "Islam expanded east and west" (pages 176–178). Then show Overhead Transparency 23, *The Spread of Islam*. Point out that the Muslim armies successfully conquered more territory than the Romans — all in one century. Have students locate Mecca and trace the boundaries of eastward and westward Islamic expansion. Note that the Muslim armies were finally stopped by the Franks at the battle of Tours and by the Byzantine navy outside the gates of Constantinople. Conclude by showing Overhead Transparency 87, *The World about 800*. Have students identify the three empires that bordered the Islamic empire. Note Baghdad's central location in the Eurasian world.

Teaching with Pictures: Islamic Art and Architecture (Objective 4) Review the achievements of the Islamic golden age. Then direct students' attention to the picture of the Dome of the Rock. Point out that this mosque is widely admired as one of the great works of Islamic art and architecture. Standing underneath its dome, visitors are awed by the golden arabesques swirling around in a pattern that has no beginning and no end. To Muslims, this design represents the splendor of Allah, the radiance of paradise, and the endlessness of infinity. Circling around the rim of the golden dome are bands inscribed with a swirling, golden script. Calligraphy is considered the highest form of Islamic decorative art. Like other Muslim mosques, the Dome of the Rock does not contain a picture of Muhammad or any other human or animal form. Such pictures are thought to be an offense to Allah, who alone can create a living creature.

Check for Understanding Have students define or identify the following items: Bedouin, Muhammad, Koran, Kaaba, Hegira, Mecca, and Baghdad.

Practice

Guided Practice
Lead a guided discussion of the questions in Overhead Transparency 23 and in Section Review 2. (Answers are below.)

Define:
(a) religious journey (b) holy war (c) leader after Muhammad (d) person who tried to turn ordinary metals into gold (e) device used to chart the positions of a star

Identify:
(a) peninsula along the Red Sea (b) desert nomads (c) capital of Islam (d) shrine housing the Black Stone (e) prophet and founder of Islam (f) Muslims' name for God (g) wife of Muhammad (h) city in which Muhammad first began to attract many converts (i) followers of Muhammad (j) name of religion founded by Muhammad (k) holy book of Islam (l) Muhammad's escape to Medina (m) Muslim holy month

Answer:
1. During a life of meditation, Muhammad had a vision that the angel Gabriel revealed that he was the chosen prophet of God.
2. marked the turning point for Muhammad
3. strict guidelines for Muslims to follow in matters of faith, prayer, alms, fasting, pilgrimage
4. (a) Spain and Portugal, North Africa, Egypt, Palestine, Mesopotamia, Persia, northwest India, and Arabia (b) passionate faith, overpopulation on Arabian peninsula, weak resistance
5. orthodox caliphate: period of wars of conquest and assassinations; Umayyad caliphate: time of able rules who conquered many lands but were brought down by revenge for Husayn's death; Abbasid caliphate: period marked by split among Muslims and conflicts with Shi'ites
6. Shi'ites believed Husayn had been the rightful caliph and split from the Sunni Muslims.
7. Byzantine emperors claimed they held the political powers of a Roman ruler and ruled in Jesus' name as new apostles. Islamic empires used ties with Muhammad as their authority.

Independent Practice
Assign Independent Practice Worksheet 8.2.
Assign Basic Skills Worksheet 8.

Enrichment Activities

1. **Reading a Primary Source** Assign Voices from the Past Resource Book 8.2.

2. **Preparing a Report** Ask interested students to prepare a report on the rituals associated with a pilgrimage to Mecca. (See *National Geographic*, November 1978.)

3. **Researching for Bonus Points** Award bonus points to students who can answer this question: What does the phrase, "La ilaha illa Allah, Muhammad rasul Allah," mean? ("There is no god but Allah, and Muhammad is His Prophet.")

The empires influenced Slavs and Turks. 3

Section Objectives

After completing Section 3, students should be able to:

1. describe how the Slavs became Christians.
2. make a time line of the decline and fall of the Islamic and Byzantine empires.
3. describe the last siege of Constantinople.

Setting the Stage

Recall the definition of *cultural diffusion*. Remind students that cultural diffusion is a process in which ideas and goods are transmitted from one society to another. Explain that this section describes how Byzantine culture influenced the early Russians. Use Overhead Transparency 24 to introduce the geography of Russia. This section also discusses how the Turks converted to Islam following their contact with the Islamic empire. The chapter concludes with the dramatic story of how Constantinople fell to the Ottoman Turks. Use Overhead Transparency 25 to trace the decline of the Byzantine Empire.

Teaching Strategies

Discussing History: The Slavs Became Christians (Objective 1) To help students realize the significance of eastern culture for the Slavs, ask "What was the importance of the Cyrillic alphabet?"

(separated Slavs from peoples using Roman alphabet) For what reasons did the early Russians convert to Byzantine rather than to Roman Christianity, and why was this a significant decision? (beauty of Hagia Sophia; decision isolated Russia from western ideas)

Skill Building: Making a Time Line (Objective 2) Ask each student to use the information in this section to prepare a time line that shows the events leading to the breakup of the Islamic and Byzantine empires. The time line should cover the years 750–1453.

Discussing History: The Fall of Constantinople (Objective 3) Point out that Constantinople was a military prize that eluded Muslim conquerors for more than 750 years. Muhammad II, the 21-year-old Ottoman Sultan, inherited this centuries-old dream along with his crown in 1451. Muhammad spent the first two years of his reign assembling an army of 100,000 men and building a fleet of 125 ships. On the morning of April 5, 1453, the Turks assumed their positions around Constantinople. The city's power had already declined. Its forces were reduced to an army of 7,000 men and a navy of twenty-five ships. Nevertheless, the city, led by Constantine XI, and was protected by fourteen miles of walls that had withstood every attempt to take them for more than 1,000 years.

The great siege began on April 6, 1453. For the next two weeks, fighting raged on both land and sea. While the Ottoman cannons hammered away at the city's ancient walls, waves of Turks attempted to scale them. Fighting against overwhelming odds, the city's defenders hurled back every attack. Meanwhile, the Ottoman navy was unsuccessful in its attempt to break through a strong chain boom that protected the Golden Horn.

Explain that Muhammad devised an ingenious strategy enabling him to seize control of the Golden Horn. The Sultan's plan called for the construction of a timber causeway connecting the Bosporus with the Golden Horn, thus bypassing the protective chain. Muhammad's plan worked. With their city effectively blockaded, the Byzantines recognized that they had little hope of surviving. Finally, on May 28, the citizens of Constantinople gathered together for a final mass inside Hagia Sophia. The next day, the Ottomans broke through a small gate and stormed the city.

Check for Understanding Have students write a paragraph explaining the influence of Byzantine culture on the Slavs, and a paragraph explaining the influence of Islamic civilization on the Seljuk Turks.

Practice

Guided Practice
Lead a guided discussion of the questions in Overhead Transparencies 24 and 25 and in Section Review 3. (Answers are below.)

Define:
Persian ruler who ended the caliph's political power

Identify:
(a) nomads who migrated into eastern Europe (b) monk who invented Slavic alphabet (c) hunters from Scandinavia, the first Russians (d) second capital of early Russia (e) ruler of Kiev, an early Russian Christian (f) nomadic peoples from central Asia

Answer:
1. Slavs could read the Bible in their own language.
2. Slavs invited the Rus to be their rulers in 862.
3. Russia kept ties with the east and was cut off from western Europe.
4. (a) Baghdad, all of Asia Minor (b) all the rest of the Byzantine empire, including Constantinople
5. (a) They had nothing to lose; they were mobile, could strike anywhere. (b) money, weapons (c) internal weakness and division in empire

Independent Practice
Assign Independent Practice Worksheet 8.3.
Assign Critical Thinking Worksheet 8.

Enrichment Activities

1. **Reading a Primary Source** Assign Voices from the Past Resource Book 8.3.

2. **Preparing a Report** Have students prepare a report on the role the Greek Orthodox Church plays in the Soviet Union today.

3. **Creative Writing** The fall of Constantinople shocked both Muslims and Christians. Ask some students to take a Muslim point of view and other students to assume the point of view of a Christian. The assignment is to write a newspaper article describing the fall of Constantinople. Compare and contrast the two sets of reports.

4. **Researching for Bonus Points** Award bonus points to students who can answer this question: What did the Ottomans call Constantinople? (They called it *eis ten Polin*—Greek for "to the city." Istanbul did not become the city's official name until after World War I.)

Concluding the Chapter

1. **Chapter Closer**
   Have students relate present-day conflicting claims to the Holy Land to the events described in this chapter.

2. **Reteaching Activities**
   a. **Summarizing** Ask students to name the three major projects undertaken by Justinian and to tell the outcome of each.
   b. **Answering Questions** Have students turn each of the headings in Section 2 into a question and to write the answer to the question.
   c. **Outlining** Have students use the headings in Section 3 to write a sentence outline.

3. **Chapter Review Activities**
   Assign Chapter Review 8 activities.

Chapter Evaluation

Chapter Test 8 and Computer Test Bank Chapter 8 Test can be used to evaluate your students' understanding of this chapter.

Answers to Chapter Review 8

Reviewing the Facts
1. (a) to place outside the church, cut off from Christians (b) person whose ideas are incorrect in the opinion of a church (c) bishop of Constantinople (d) holy war (e) leader with religious power (f) Persian ruler with political power
2. (a) eastern capital of the Roman empire (b) Byzantine emperor who codified law and built splendid buildings in Constantinople (c) served as basis for Byzantine law for 900 years and guide to western Europe for legal questions (d) desert nomads in Arabia (e) important religious center, birthplace of Muhammad (f) founder of Islam (g) year of Hegira (h) holy book of Islam (i) center of Muslim civilization during its golden age (j) nomads who migrated into Eastern Europe from plains of Asia (k) second capital of early Russia (l) ruler of Kiev who set Russia on path of Eastern Orthodox religion (m) year when the break between Roman and Byzantine churches became final (n) nomads from Central Asia who conquered Baghdad, all of Asia Minor (o) conquered the rest of the Byzantine empire (p) year when

Constantinople fell to the Ottoman Turks

3. disagreements over use of icons, language in which services were conducted, behavior of priests, superiority of the pope

4. (a) marked first year of Islamic era (b) Islam's holy book that helped spread Arabic language in Middle East and North Africa (c) set out the duties for believers (d) group that split from the orthodox Muslims

5. (a) Umayyads considered Persians second-class citizens; Abbasids promised to return to Islamic idea of equality among believers (b) Umayyad: conquered North Africa and Spain, pushed the borders of the empire to the Indus River valley; were able rulers and administrators. Abbasid: built the city of Baghdad, which became the center of Muslim civilization where arts and sciences flourished during its golden age.

6. (a) converted to Christianity; imitated Byzantine art and architecture (b) converted to Islam

Basic Skills

1. The conflict between the Byzantine Empire and Islam was not only military but also religious.

2. This time of crisis justifies a woman's speaking up. Ordinary men might flee, but an emperor cannot endure without his empire.

3. Notes will vary. For example *People* might include population size, language, religion, and occupations.

4. Spain, North Africa, Palestine, Sicily, Corsica, Crete, Sardina, parts of Asia Minor and Persia

5. Slavic invasions began (700); Seljuk Turk invasions began (1050); Battle of Manzikert (1071); Ottoman Turk invasions began (1300); sieges of Constantinople (1397, 1422, 1453)

6. It took about 130 years from Hegira to height of empire.

Researching and Reporting Skills
Students' research findings will vary.

Critical Thinking

1. *Similarities:* Both were believed to have been received by prophets as the word of God; affirmed belief in one God; established customs, moral laws, special days of worship, rules against worship of idols. *Differences:* The Ten Commandments and the Koran specify different moral duties and religious practices. For example the Koran mentions the requirements of daily prayer, alms, fasting, and pilgrimage.

2. (a) Students' opinions will vary. (b) Under Augustus, a Gaul—if a citizen—would have the same rights as the Romans, including access to public office. The protection of Roman law would follow him wherever he went. There would be no limitations to trading activity throughout the empire. Under the Abbasids, a Greek would be considered a second class citizen, would have to convert to Islam or pay taxes; would be free to trade or do business; would benefit from the advanced state of Islamic arts and sciences.

3. Arts, sciences, and trade flourish; public building programs beautify the cities; education is encouraged; government is efficient and stable.

4. *Political:* Islam's rule spread more widely than Byzantium's; Justinian's Code established a common system of law in his empire. Islam was weakened by political divisions. *Economic:* Constantinople controlled major land and sea routes between Mediterranean and Asia. Baghdad controlled caravan routes to India and China; its harbor on the Tigris was visited by ships from India and Arabia; set up first banks with "saak" (checks) to facilitate trade. *Religious:* Eastern Orthodox religion spread to Byzantine empire and was adopted by Russia. Islam spread through military conquests to Africa, Spain, and many other lands; became one of the world's major religions. *Cultural:* Constantinople and Baghdad were rivals in splendor, Hagia Sophia rivaled in beauty with the Dome of the Rock in Jerusalem. The University of Constantinople kept alive the works of ancient writers. Greek was the language of scholarship. In Islam, Arabic was the language used by scholars throughout the empire; ancient Greek manuscripts were translated into Arabic; literature, medicine, mathematics, and science flourished. Baghdad, the Abbasid capital, had great works of architecture and was a center of learning.

Perspectives on Past and Present

1. The writings preserved Greek and Roman culture, Roman law, the histories and philosophies of the ancient world, and Islamic literature and science.

2. Countries of today that were part of the Islamic empire in 755 include Iran, Iraq, Syria, eastern Turkey, Lebanon, Israel, Jordan, Egypt, Saudi Arabia, the Yemen Arab Republic, the People's Democratic Republic of Yemen, Oman, Kuwait, Bahrain, Qatar, and United Arab Emirates.

Investigating History
Students' findings will vary.

The Early Middle Ages

Chapter Overview

With the end of the Roman empire, life in western Europe changed in many ways. Towns declined, trade collapsed, and people returned to a rural way of life. The Roman Catholic Church acted as the strongest civilizing force in western Europe. Monasteries remained the only institution upholding learning and an orderly way of life.

Under the leadership of Charlemagne, the Franks created an empire. During his rule, Charlemagne spread Christianity and encouraged learning. However, after the death of Charlemagne's son, the unified empire was greatly weakened by its division among his three grandsons.

From the ninth to the eleventh centuries, Viking, Slav, and Magyar invaders further disrupted life in the monasteries and towns of western Europe. Between A.D. 850 and A.D. 950, the system of feudalism developed in response to the disorder and political instability of the times. Under this system, lords and vassals provided land and protection for the people who served them, and peasants on manors supplied the goods and services needed to survive.

Key Terms

monastery, knight, count, feudalism, lord, vassal, investiture, fief, aid, manor, serf
For additional exercises, see Vocabulary Worksheet 9.

Chapter Focus

Review the principles of Roman law. Then have students read pages 187–188. Ask them to describe how a Roman legal expert might have reacted to the trial. Emphasize that Roman law was based on the application of reason and human justice. Thus, people accused of crimes had a right to face their accusers and to defend themselves before a judge. If there were doubt about a person's guilt, he or she would be judged innocent. In contrast, the trial by ordeal was based on an appeal to divine justice. Point out that the Germanic peoples believed that God would protect the innocent and expose the guilty. He would therefore heal a burned hand, if the hand was innocent. Lake water, blessed by a priest, would "accept" an innocent

soul by allowing it to sink, but "reject" a guilty soul by forcing it to float. In trial by combat, God would always cause the innocent party to prevail.

The trial by ordeal provides a vivid example of the decline of civilization following the fall of the Roman empire. Tell students that this chapter examines a new period of history known as the Early Middle Ages.

New ways of life developed in Europe.

1

Section Objectives

After completing Section 1, students should be able to:

1. describe how civilization changed following the collapse of the Roman empire.
2. identify St. Benedict and explain the importance of the Benedictine rule.
3. identify Gregory I and discuss his achievements.

Setting the Stage

Transferring Ideas: The Decline of Civilization (Objective 1) Review the five key characteristics of civilization (pages 27–30). Then have students read "Roman civilization collapsed" and "Personal ties replaced citizenship" (pages 188–190). Have students describe the various ways in which civilization changed. Use Overhead Transparency 26, *The Barbarian Kingdoms about 500*, to locate areas occupied by Germanic tribes. Now ask, "Which institution best survived the fall of Rome?" Students should identify the Church as the strongest remaining civilizing force in western Europe. Explain that this section describes the contributions Church leaders made in rebuilding a new way of life in Europe.

Teaching Strategies

Discussing History: The Rule of St. Benedict (Objective 2) Point out that monasteries were self-sufficient communities. Both men and women

Advance Planner

			★ Advanced
Chapter 9	The Early Middle Ages		
Focus	The contrast between Roman laws and the Germanic trial by ordeal		● Basic

	Section 1	Section 2	Section 3	Section 4
Objectives	1. Describe how civilization declined following the collapse of the Roman empire. 2. Identify St. Benedict and explain the importance of the Benedictine rule. 3. Identify Gregory I and discuss his achievements.	1. Explain the importance of the Battle of Tours for western Europe. 2. Describe the relationship between the Frankish kings and the Roman popes during the Early Middle Ages. 3. Explain how Charlemagne expanded the Frankish empire and revived learning. 4. Explain how central authority broke down after Charlemagne's death.	1. Describe a Viking ship and explain its importance. 2. Trace Viking routes on a map. 3. Explain why the Viking age ended.	1. State reasons for the development of feudalism. 2. Support general statements about feudalism. 3. Contrast the feudal economic system and the economic system of a modern industrial society. 4. Chart the duties and benefits of nobles, vassals, knights, peasants, and serfs.
Setting the Stage	Transferring Ideas: The Decline of Civilization Transparency 26	Discussing History: The Battle of Tours	The Viking invaders of Europe	Discussing History: Feudalism
Teaching Strategies	Discussing History: The Rule of St. Benedict Discussing History: Gregory I Check for Understanding	Skill Building: Identifying Cause and Effect Relationships Discussing History: The Revival of Learning Transparency 27 Transferring Ideas: The Problem of Succession Transparency 28 Check for Understanding	Teaching with Pictures: A Viking Ship Using Geographic Themes: Movement Transparency 29 Outline Map 9 Discussing History: The End of the Viking Age Check for Understanding	Skill Building: Supporting Generalizations Economics and History: Contrasting Medieval and Modern Economic Systems Transparency 93 Discussing History: Analyzing the Feudal System Check for Understanding
Guided Practice	Transparency 26 Q&A Section Review 1	Transparency 27 Q&A Transparency 28 Q&A Section Review 2	Transparency 29 Q&A Section Review 3	Transparency 93 Q&A Section Review 4
Independent Practice Worksheets	Independent Practice 9.1 Geography Skills 9 Vocabulary 9	Independent Practice 9.2 Basic Skills 9	Independent Practice 9.3 Critical Thinking 9	Independent Practice 9.4
Enrichment	1. Primary Source: Voices 9.1 2. Solving a Puzzle 3. ★Analyzing a Quotation 4. Researching for Points	1. Primary Source: Voices 9.2 2. Preparing a Report: Life of Charlemagne 3. Researching for Points 4. Global Perspectives: Transparency 87	1. Primary Source: Voices 9.3 2. Preparing a Report: Viking Life 3. ★Creative Writing 4. Researching for Points	1. Primary Source: Voices 9.4 2. Creative Writing: Manor Life 3. Researching for Points

Chapter Closer	
● **Reteaching Activities**	Supporting a Generalization, Explaining Political Changes, Answering Questions, Explaining Key Phrases
Chapter Review	Summary, Reviewing the Facts, Basic Skills, Researching and Reporting Skills, Critical Thinking, Perspectives on Past and Present, Investigating History
Chapter Evaluation	Chapter Test 9, Computer Test Bank Chapter 9 Test

were expected to follow the threefold rule of poverty, chastity, and obedience. Benedict's rules created a disciplined schedule that enabled monks and nuns to serve God and perform charitable services. Read the following rules aloud and ask students to discuss why Benedict included them:

- Let him (the Abbot) make no distinction of persons in the monastery. Let not one be loved more than another, save such as be found to excel in obedience or good works.
- Whenever any weighty matters have to be transacted in the monastery, let the abbot call together all the community and himself propose the matter for discussion. After hearing the advice of the brethren let him consider it in his own mind and then do what he shall judge most expedient.
- All guests who come shall be received as though they were Christ.

Discussing History: Gregory I (Objective 3) Point out that Gregory's reputation for greatness rests on four accomplishments. First, he made the papacy an office of both spiritual and political power. Second, he helped bring Christianity to England. Third, he wrote popular books that trained bishops and inspired common people. Finally, he captured the Church's imagination with his vision of Christendom as a spiritual kingdom. Gregory's successors canonized him, and admiring historians called him Gregory the Great. Ask students to identify the measures Gregory took to strengthen the papacy. What effect did Gregory's actions have on the history of the Middle Ages?

Check for Understanding Have students name two examples to support each of these statements:

(a) Civilization in western Europe declined after the fall of Rome. **(b)** The Roman Catholic Church became increasingly powerful.

Practice

Guided Practice
Lead a guided discussion of the questions in Overhead Transparency 26 and in Section Review 1. (Answers are below.)

Define:
(a) task to determine guilt or innocence **(b)** belonging to the Middle Ages **(c)** ability to read and write **(d)** community of Christians who lived simple lives **(e)** man who lived in monastery **(f)** monastic leader **(g)** woman who lived in convent

Identify:
(a) established Christianity in Ireland **(b)** Frankish king who converted to Roman Catholicism

(c) branch of Christianity followed by Germanic groups **(e)** Benedict's sister and head of a convent **(f)** pope who established idea of Christendom **(g)** fierce Germanic people who invaded northern Italy **(h)** spiritual kingdom

Answer:
1. classical Roman heritage, beliefs of the Roman Catholic Church, customs of Germanic tribes
2. collapse of trade and towns, loss of literacy
3. **(a)** through missionaries and conversion **(b)** Clovis could help against other Germanic peoples.
4. **(a)** life of poverty, chastity, and prayer **(b)** established rules for monastic life **(c)** operated schools, maintained libraries, and copied books
5. wrote books, sent out missionaries, established Rome as spiritual center of Christendom
6. **(a)** Family ties and personal loyalty bound Germanic society. Public government and law bound Romans. **(b)** Roman ideas are closer. Citizens are loyal to nation and bound by public laws.
7. Look for answers to recognize the unifying influence of both with the distinction that Christianity was concerned only with the spiritual.

Independent Practice
Assign Independent Practice Worksheet 9.1.
Assign Geography Skills Worksheet 9.
Assign Vocabulary Worksheet 9.

Enrichment Activities

1. **Reading a Primary Source** Assign Voices from the Past Resource Book 9.1.

2. **Solving a Puzzle** In 1939, archaeologists discovered an Anglo-Saxon ship buried on the northeast English coast at a site now known as Sutton Hoo. The ship contained a fortune in gold, silver, and jewelry, but no human remains. Ask students to prepare a report speculating on what king, if any, was buried at Sutton Hoo. (See *The Barbarian Kings* by Lionel Casson.)

3. **Analyzing a Quotation** The historian Will Duran wrote that Gregory the Great "dominated the end of the sixth century as Justinian had dominated its beginning: and his effect on religion was exceeded in this epoch only by that of Muhammad." Ask advanced students to give evidence supporting or contradicting this statement.

4. **Researching for Bonus Points** Benedictine monks pray eight times a day. Award bonus

points to students who can answer this question: What are the names of the eight canonical hours? (nocturns, matins or lauds, prime, tierce, sext, none, vespers, and at bedtime, compline—the completion.)

Charlemagne revived the idea of empire. 2

Section Objectives

After completing Section 2, students should be able to:

1. explain the importance of the Battle of Tours.
2. describe the relationship between the Frankish kings and the Roman popes.
3. explain how Charlemagne expanded the Frankish empire.
4. explain how central authority broke down in the years following Charlemagne's death.

Setting the Stage

Discussing History: The Battle of Tours (Objective 1) Ask students to find information in Chapter 8 about the Battle of Tours (pages 176–178). Then ask, "Why was this battle significant for western Europe?" Point out that if the Muslims had won, western Europe might have become a part of the Islamic empire. The loss of these lands would have diminished the power of the Roman Catholic Church. Explain that Martel's dramatic victory at the Battle of Tours stopped the Muslim invasion and made Charles a Christian hero. Explain that this section describes how Martel's descendants extended the power of the Franks and created a new Christian empire in western Europe.

Skill Building: Identifying Cause and Effect Relationships (Objective 2) Explain that the conversion of Clovis to the Roman Catholic Church marked the beginning of a special relationship between the Frankish kings and the Catholic Church. To help illustrate the causes and consequences of this relationship draw a cause and effect chart on the board. Label the main elements "Problems," "Solutions," and "Consequences," with arrows indicating causal links from one label to the next. Then, subdivide "Problems" as follows: "Of Kings," "Of Popes." Help students use the dia-

gram to analyze the relationship between Mayor of the Palace Pepin and Pope Stephen II. Pepin's problem was that he had power but lacked authority. Pope Stephen's problem was that he needed protection from the Lombards. The pope solved Pepin's problem by anointing Pepin's head with holy oil and declaring him "king by the grace of God." Pepin solved Stephen's problem by defeating the Lombards and creating the Papal States. These actions gave the Frankish kings political and spiritual authority. The popes became the political rulers of the Papal States. Use this chart and the same procedure to analyze the relationship between Charlemagne and Pope Leo III. Ask students to make generalizations and to predict future problems that might arise from the new relationship between popes and kings.

Discussing History: The Revival of Learning (Objective 3) Show students Overhead Transparency 27, *The Empire of Charlemagne in 814.* Explain that Charlemagne's conquests carved out an impressive but short-lived empire. In contrast, his role in the revival of learning had significant long-term consequences. Ask students to identify these consequences. As noted in the text, Charlemagne made his palace a center for the revival of learning. This brief but significant burst of scholarly activity is known as the Carolingian Renaissance. Alcuin and his fellow monks labored to make handwritten copies of rare Latin manuscripts. To save time, the monks invented a new style of lettering known as Carolingian minuscule. Point out that it still took three to four months to finish copying a manuscript of average length. Even so, ninth century monks did a thorough job of preserving the ancient Roman classics. Many Roman poems and histories had been lost before Charlemagne's reign—but none were lost there after.

Transferring Ideas: The Problem of Succession (Objective 4) Ask students to recall how the problem of succession contributed to the fall of Rome. Then explain that the Carolingian rulers also had a serious problem of succession. Frankish law and custom required the ruler to divide his empire among all of his sons. Have students explain what problems this system created. Then direct students' attention to "Charlemagne's heirs ruled weakly" (pages 197–198). Point out that Louis the Pious divided his empire into three parts as shown in the map on page 197. Louis' three sons promptly fought a bitter civil war that finally ended with the Treaty of Verdun. The provisions of this treaty are shown on Overhead Transparency 28, *The Division of the Carolingian Empire, 843.* After the

Treaty of Verdun, Carolingian kings became almost as feeble as the Merovingian "do-nothing" kings. Once again, central authority broke down. Kings' nicknames in this period—Louis the Stammerer, Louis the Sluggard, and Charles the Simple—suggest the low level of leadership.

Check for Understanding Have students explain why Charlemagne is an important historical figure in French history.

Practice

Guided Practice

Lead a guided discussion of the questions in Overhead Transparencies 27 and 28 and in Section Review 2. (Answers are below.)

Define:

(a) armored horseman (b) landowner who ruled a county (c) agents sent to see that counts governed justly (d) lettering developed in monasteries

Identify:

(a) inhabitants of Europe's strongest kingdom (b) Clovis and his successors (c) real power behind the Merovingian throne (d) defeated Muslims at Battle of Tours (e) son of Charles Martel who was anointed by pope (f) Italian lands over which pope had political rule (g) Pepin's son who extended Frankish empire (h) Charlemagne's descendants (i) divided Charlemagne's empire

Answer:

1. (a) letting the surviving sons divide the kingdom at the death of the king (b) the major domo's
2. (a) King needed credibility afforded by pope; pope needed military protection for Roman lands. (b) by being crowned by the pope (c) Pepin defeated the Lombards and gave the pope control of the Papal States.
3. (a) with the use of counts and *missi dominici* (b) supported royal court and government
4. recruited scholars, opened school at palace, ordered monasteries to open schools
5. (a) emperor of Rome (b) widened split between eastern and western Catholics
6. divided it into three kingdoms and weakened it
7. Muslims, Magyars, Vikings
8. Answers might stress the revival of learning, the spread of Christianity, his political and military achievements, or reviving the idea of empire.

Independent Practice

Assign Independent Practice Worksheet 9.2.
Assign Basic Skills Worksheet 9.

Enrichment Activities

1. **Reading a Primary Source** Assign Voices from the Past Resource Book 9.2.
2. **Preparing a Book Report** Einhard's *Life of Charlemagne* provides interesting insights into the life of this remarkable ruler. Ask interested students to prepare a report on this book.
3. **Researching for Bonus Points** Charlemagne and other members of the official family at Aachen sometimes addressed each other by classical or Biblical names. Award bonus points to students who can answer this question: What name was Charlemagne called? (David)
4. **Global Perspectives** Have students study Overhead Transparency 87, *The World about 800*, which also appears on pages 808–809 in the Historical Atlas. Ask students to relate Charlemagne's empire to contemporary developments in other parts of the world.

Vikings terrorized Europe. 3

Section Objectives

After completing Section 3, students should be able to:

1. describe a Viking ship and explain its importance.
2. trace Viking routes on a map.
3. explain why the Viking age ended.

Setting the Stage

Ask students to recall previous examples of how barbarian peoples invaded civilized areas. Then have students read the introduction (page 198), which describes one of the first Viking raids on Charlemagne's empire. To capture the impact of this raid, have students suggest news headlines that might have appeared in the "Norse News" and in the "Lindisfarne Ledger." Emphasize that the sudden Viking raids stunned the peoples of western Europe. One Frankish monk wrote that, "They overthrow, they destroy, they ravage; sinister cohort, fatal phalanx, cruel host!" Explain that this section introduces the Vikings, describes their raids on Europe, and traces their voyages of exploration.

Teaching Strategies

Teaching with Pictures: A Viking Ship (Objective 1) Point out that it is inaccurate to stereotype the Vikings as ferocious brutes. Their minds were as keen as their sharp-edged swords. The ships (or "steeds of the waves") that carried them on journeys of piracy and commerce were the technological marvel of their age. The ship illustrated on page 199 is an example of the type of vessel that raided Lindisfarne. Archaeologists discovered the ship in a trench near Oseberg, Norway, in 1904. A blue clay covered the ship and helped preserve its thousands of fragments. Archaeologists painstakingly marked and numbered each fragment before reconstructing the ship. The reassembled vessel is seventy-one feet long. Its prow rises sixteen feet above the deck. The ship contained the skeleton of a ninth century Norwegian queen, Asa. Students might be interested to learn that Asa had ruled alone after having her husband, Gudrod the Magnificent, killed. The ship also contained the skeleton of a servant as well as a carved cat and several sledges. (See *Fury of Northmen* by the Editors of Time-Life Books.)

Using Geographic Themes: Movement (Objective 2) The Vikings were more than frightening raiders. They were also wily traders and brave explorers. Use Overhead Transparency 29, *The Age of Invasions, 800–1000*, to show the range of Viking explorations. Explain that the Viking world stretched from the edge of North America to the banks of the Dnieper River in Russia. Now distribute Outline Map 9: Physical Europe. Have students label the following places: Scandinavia, England, Normandy, Ireland, Spain, Iceland; and the North Sea, Baltic Sea, Atlantic Ocean, Mediterranean Sea and Black Sea. Using the map on page 200 as a reference, ask students to draw the routes the Vikings followed to England, Ireland, Iceland, Spain, and Russia.

Discussing History: The End of the Viking Age (Objective 3) First have students read, "The Viking Age ended about 1000" (page 201). Discuss the three reasons listed in the text explaining why the Viking raids ended. Conclude by pointing out that although the Viking terror disappeared, the Viking influence remained. For example, English-speaking people use Viking names for the days of the week: Wednesday, Thursday, and Friday. On the Old English calendar, each of these days honored a different Norse god. Wednesday was originally Odin's (Woden's) Day; Thursday was Thor's day; and Friday was Frey's day.

Check for Understanding Have students name three achievements of the Vikings and explain their significance in the history of Europe.

Practice

Guided Practice
Lead a guided discussion of the questions in Overhead Transparency 29 and in Section Review 3. (Answers are below.)

Identify:
(a) sea-faring raiders from Scandinavia (b) today Norway, Sweden, and Denmark (c) Arctic island settled by Vikings in 900's (d) Viking who sailed to Greenland (e) island discovered and misnamed by Eric the Red (f) Eric's son who sailed to what is now Newfoundland (g) island Vikings discovered

Answer:
1. (a) Scandinavia (b) They came in ships and were still pagan.
2. Greenland and Newfoundland (the Americas)
3. better defenses on part of Europeans, conversion of Vikings to Christianity, warmer climate
4. Kings had little power and few resources. The Vikings raided with such swiftness that the Europeans did not have time to muster troops.

Independent Practice
Assign Independent Practice Worksheet 9.3.
Assign Critical Thinking Worksheet 9.

Enrichment Activities

1. **Reading a Primary Source** Assign Voices from the Past Resource Book 9.3.

2. **Preparing a Report** Have students prepare a report on one aspect of Viking life. Possible topics include Viking religion, Viking traders in Russia (see *National Geographic*, March 1985), and the construction of Viking warships.

3. **Creative Writing** Viking poets called *skalds* recorded the heroic deeds of their warrior leaders. Ask advanced students to assume the role of a skald. Their assignment is to research a Viking adventure and then write a poem or story commemorating it.

4. **Researching for Bonus Points** Award bonus points to students who can find the answer to this question: At what site in North America did archaeologists confirm Viking settlement? (L'Anse aux Meadows in Newfoundland)

Feudalism became the basis for government. 4

Section Objectives

After completing Section 4, students should be able to:

1. state reasons for the development of feudalism.
2. support general statements about feudalism.
3. contrast the feudal economic system and the economic system of a modern industrial society.
4. chart the duties and benefits of nobles, vassals, knights, peasants, and serfs in the feudal system.

Setting the Stage

Discussing History: Feudalism (Objective 1) Have students read the introduction on page 201. Then ask them to suggest why there was a need for new political and military arrangements in western Europe. Recall that, in the years following the collapse of the Roman empire, personal loyalties replaced the Roman sense of civic responsibility toward the state. Ask students how they think this shift toward personal loyalties might have related to the increasing emphasis on local government and local self-sufficiency. Tell the class that this section explains how personal loyalties contributed to a new political system known as *feudalism*. Ask students to identify the most important goal of feudalism. (to acquire land)

Teaching Strategies

Skill Building: Supporting Generalizations (Objective 2) Write the following statements on the chalkboard. Have students cite details to support each. Details supporting these generalizations appear on pages 201–204.

1. The control of land was the key to feudalism.
2. Feudalism was a system in which public power became private power.
3. Feudalism provided a system of local defense.
4. In theory, feudal society was a pyramid.

Economics and History: Contrasting Economic Systems (Objective 3) Use Overhead Transparency 93 *The Medieval Manor* to show a typical medieval manor. Ask students how the basic needs for food, clothing, and shelter were met under the manorial system and how these needs are met in a

modern industrial society. Discuss with students the advantages of economic self-sufficiency in the Early Middle Ages. Ask students to name factors that discouraged economic interdependence in the Middle Ages. Point out that poor roads, outlaws, and frequent warfare made transportation and trade perilous. Ask students whether they think feudalism could work in an industrialized nation; have them give reasons for their answers.

Discussing History: Analyzing the Feudal System (Objective 4) Work with students to draw a five-column chart on the chalkboard. The chart should describe the duties and benefits of feudalism from the perspective of lords, vassals, knights, peasants, and serfs. Ask, "Who received the greatest benefits from this system? Who had the greatest responsibilities?" Ask students why peasants may have felt that the right to stay on the manor was more important than the freedom to leave.

Check for Understanding Have students explain the economic role of the manor in feudal society.

Practice

Guided Practice
Lead a guided discussion of the questions in Overhead Transparency 93 and in Section Review 4. (Answers are below.)

Define:
(a) political and military system based on holding of land (b) person who transfers control of a fief (c) person who receives land from lord (d) symbolic gesture representing the granting of the land (e) piece of land given to a vassal (f) grant of money lord could ask from his vassals (g) small estate from which a lord's family gained its livelihood (h) peasant who was bound to the land

Answer:
1. (a) oath of loyalty (b) fief (c) by dividing his fief and giving parts away to warriors who agreed to be his vassals
2. (a) 40 days of fighting, good equipment, good fighting skill (b) handling matters of justice, tax collection
3. (a) through inheritance or in the name of a young son (b) same as others
4. (a) 2–3 days farming labor per week; paying tax on grain ground in lord's mill (b) Hard times might force trade of freedom for food and shelter.
5. (a) Except for salt, iron, and a few other items, everything was produced on the manor. (b) With decline of cities and public law, goods were

not available in markets and trade routes were unsafe.

Independent Practice
Assign Independent Practice Worksheet 9.4.

Enrichment Activities

1. **Reading a Primary Source** Assign Voices from the Past Resource Book 9.4.

2. **Creative Writing** Using Overhead Transparency 93, ask students to imagine that they live as peasants in the manor shown on this transparency. Their assignment is to write a report describing daily life on the manor.

3. **Researching for Bonus Points** Award bonus points to students who can find the answer to this question: What privilege gave a lord the right to travel to one of his vassal's fiefs and be entertained for several days? (the right of purveyance)

Answers to Voice from the Past

1. all of them
2. right to marry as they please
3. (a) landholdings of her husband (b) inheritance of husband's land
4. to inherit half of her grandfather's lands and to marry as she pleases

Concluding the Chapter

1. **Chapter Closer**
   Ask students to give three examples of how Roman and Germanic cultures blended to create a new civilization in the Early Middle Ages.

2. **Reteaching Activities**
   a. **Supporting a Generalization** Write the following statement on the chalkboard: "Throughout the Early Middle Ages, the Church acted as the strongest civilizing force in western Europe." Have students explain this statement and give evidence from the text to support it.
   b. **Explaining Political Changes** Have students write a paragraph explaining the decline of the Merovingian dynasty and a paragraph describing the contributions to the Carolingian empire of Charles Martel, Pepin the Short, and Charlemagne.
   c. **Answering Questions** Have students rewrite each heading in this section as a question and answer the question.

d. **Explaining Key Phrases** Have students explain how each of the following phrases relates to feudalism: military system, political system, and landholding system.

3. **Chapter Review Activities**
   Assign Chapter Review 9 activities.

Chapter Evaluation

Chapter Test 9 and Computer Test Bank Chapter 9 Test can be used to evaluate your students' understanding of this chapter.

Answers to Chapter Review 9

Reviewing the Facts

1. (a) community in which Christians live in poverty and worship God (b) armored horseman (c) powerful landowner who ruled a county (d) political and military system based on holding of land (e) person who could transfer control of a piece of land (f) person who received land from a lord (g) symbolic gesture representing granting of land (h) piece of land given to a vassal (i) grant of money lord could ask from his vassals (j) small estate from which a lord's family gained its livelihood (k) peasants who were bound to the land on which they were born

2. (a) established Christianity in Ireland (b) Frankish king who converted to Christianity (c) set of rules for monastic life (d) pope who established idea of Christendom (e) spiritual kingdom on earth (f) Clovis and his successors (g) father of Charlemagne who seized the Frankish throne with pope's blessing (h) Frankish king who expanded empire (i) royal agents sent out to see that counts governed justly (j) Charlemagne's capital (k) year Charlemagne was crowned emperor by pope (l) Charlemagne's descendants (m) divided Charlemagne's empire among his three grandsons (n) sea-faring raiders from Scandinavia (o) Viking explorer who sailed to what is now Newfoundland

3. (a) recruited scholars, opened schools at palace, and ordered monasteries to open schools (b) trained future monks and priests, maintained libraries, developed a readable style of lettering

4. Christian missionaries traveled among the Germanic and Celtic groups to spread their beliefs.

Pagan kings, such as Clovis, converted and helped the church to fight other Germanic groups who in turn were converted.

5. Kingdom was divided into counties, each ruled in the king's name by a count; counts administered justice and raised armies; king sent out royal agents to see that counts governed justly.

6. In return for an oath of loyalty, the lord transferred a piece of land called a fief to his vassal with a symbolic gesture (investiture). In turn, the vassal subdivided the land and gave to warriors smaller fiefs in return for support of armies. In cases of financial emergencies, lords could ask for aid, grants of money, from their vassals.

7. **(a)** emperor of the Romans and pope **(b)** The pope gained a protector and power because he named the emperor. The emperor became the protector of all Christendom, with spiritual and political authority.

8. **(a)** basic economic unit of feudalism **(b)** cleared for growing grain, as pasture, forest

9. **(a)** two or three days' labor every week on lord's land; giving a certain portion of the grain grown on the serf's own land to the lord; paying taxes **(b)** food and protection

Basic Skills

1. **(a)** Charlemagne was crowned emperor **(b)** Leif Ericson's voyage to America

2.

Spain	France	Germany	Britain
Basques	Franks	Franks	Picts
Suevi	Bretons	Saxons	Celts
Visigoths	Burgundians	Thuringians	British
	Visigoths	Frisians	Angles
			Saxons
			Jutes

3. The diagram would link the third white knight with both Richard and William. The knight's shield might reflect the alliances by being divided in half, one part white and the other part blue.

4. Charlemagne maintained a centralized government by personally supervising the counts as well as sending out his emissaries, the *missi dominici*. His successors did not keep such close control over the counts.

5. The church was the only institution to survive the fall of the Roman empire. Its monasteries were centers of order, stability and learning; their libraries copied and preserved ancient manuscripts. Monasteries and cathedrals opened schools. Monks were the educators, secretaries, biographers of kings. Missionaries spread Christianity to the barbarians, converting and educating some of their leaders.

Pope Gregory I became the spiritual and political leader of Rome. He promoted a vision of a united Christendom in western Europe.

Researching and Reporting Skills

1. "Feudalism in Western Europe," "The Life of Charlemagne" too broad; "Lindisfarne Island during the Roman Empire" too narrow.

2. Students' research findings will vary.

3. The ceremony should convey the transferring of land use in exchange for oath of loyalty.

Critical Thinking

1. **(a)** Warfare brought an end to trade and a return to the land. The end of the empire also meant less need of administrative centers. **(b)** The decay of cities meant the end of specialized work activity, of government institutions, and of many cultural activities.

2. **(a)** Each feudal lord had a loyal following ready to take up his cause against other feudal lords or even against the king. It meant endless "feuds." **(b)** Negative. Constant warfare; people had no recourse against their lord; had no higher system of justice to defend them.

3. **(a)** Both events implied that the Pope was legitimizing the king or emperor's political authority, as well as giving him spiritual authority over his subjects. It implied an alliance between these rulers and the Pope, whose spiritual and temporal authority they now defended. The crowning of Charlemagne also revived the idea of a western Christian empire. **(b)** Likely to lead to confusion of temporal and spiritual powers; set the scene for future conflicts between popes and temporal rulers, who will try to control church matters and to limit the power of the pope in their territories. Since royal authority is legitimated by the Church, popes will claim some control over kings. Popes will also become dependent on the support of the Frankish kings or Holy Roman Emperor for their authority.

Perspectives on Past and Present

(a) Political and religious authority overlapped. **(b)** The pope ruled over the papal estates and crowned kings. The kings fought the enemies of the church, imposed their religious beliefs on their subjects, and appointed bishops. **(c)** In the United States, the Bill of Rights forbids Congress to make laws on the establishing a religious practice or preventing the exercise of religious freedom. It thereby affirms the principle of separation between Church and state.

Investigating History

Students' findings will vary.

The High Middle Ages

Chapter Overview

In the High Middle Ages, improvements in farming technology and increased food production stimulated population growth, which led to a revival of town life. Merchant and craft guilds formed to control trade, and a growing middle class won new liberties. The power and prestige of the Roman Catholic Church also increased during the High Middle Ages and royal governments in England and in France grew stronger.

By the late 1100's, a revival of learning had begun. The first universities were established in western Europe and scholars took a new interest in the works of the ancient Greeks. As the ideals of society changed, a code of chivalry developed.

The High Middle Ages were also the Age of Faith. In 1095, Pope Urban II appealed to that faith and called on all knights in Christendom to rescue Jerusalem from the Muslim Turks. Thus began the first of the eight Crusades.

Key Terms

burghers, bourgeoisie, guild, apprentice, journeyman, cardinals, interdict, canon law, friars, common law, chivalry, crusaders
For additional exercises, see Vocabulary Worksheet 10.

Chapter Focus

Begin by asking students to read the chapter opener (page 209–210). Then direct their attention to the question asked by the abbot on page 210. Ask, "Why did powerful princes and nobles help workers pull huge stones to the construction site in Chartres?" Explain that the people of Chartres (and indeed all of Christendom) believed that the Virgin Mary had chosen Chartres as her special residence on earth. This belief was based on the fact that Chartres Cathedral possessed a sacred relic—the red tunic (or Virgin's Veil)—which Mary was said to have worn at the birth of Christ. The tunic was given to Charlemagne while he was in Rome. His grandson, Charles the Bald, then gave it to Chartres in A.D. 876. Point out that when the tunic miraculously survived a fire in

1194, the townspeople interpreted this as a sign that Mary required a new and even grander church.

The cathedral at Chartres is more than a home for the Virgin's Veil. Emphasize that like other great monuments, Chartres is an expression of the civilization that created it. The imagination, energy, and faith needed to construct Chartres reflect a revival of Europe's spirit after the long Dark Ages. Though they still hauled stones in crude wooden carts, the people who built Chartres Cathedral were at the same time building a vigorous new civilization.

Section Objectives

After completing Section 1, students should be able to:

1. explain how new ways of farming helped to revive European agriculture.
2. compare and contrast life in the towns with life on the manor.

Setting the Stage

Remind students that the collapse of the Carolingian empire was followed by a period of destructive Viking raids. In addition, most Europeans lived as impoverished serfs on feudal manors. Survival was a daily worry. Then something unexpected happened. European society started to show signs of strength. By the twelfth century, the society was capable of erecting monumental works like Chartres Cathedral. Ask students to speculate on the causes of this surprising burst of energy. Point out that they have studied the negative forces that cause civilizations to decline and fall. This section discusses the positive forces that enabled medieval Europe to grow strong.

Teaching Strategies

Economics and History: Technology and the Revival of Agriculture (Objective 1) Have students read, "New ways of farming increased food." Then ask them to list three new techniques that improved farming in the Middle Ages, and to explain why they represented improvements. Point out that heavier plows enabled farmers to take advantage of the rich, deep soil found in Europe's many river valleys. As a result of the new harness, medieval horses could pull four to ten times more weight than Roman horses could. The three-field system further increased agricultural productivity.

Emphasize that these new agricultural techniques helped medieval farmers produce a surplus. Greater amounts of food meant greater numbers of people. As the population increased, pioneers gradually cut down the dense forests that covered four-fifths of Europe. Point out that wood to burn was the only source of fuel. This "great age of clearing" further stimulated agricultural production. As surpluses rose, more people could leave the countryside to settle in towns. Conclude by pointing out that changes in agricultural practices continue to play an important role in modern economies. For example, pesticides, machinery, and hybrid seeds enable a small number of farmers to feed a large population.

Discussing History: Comparing Towns and Manors (Objective 2) Have students read the sections on guilds and towns (pages 213–214) and the Voice from the Past (page 214). Emphasize that town life was strikingly different from life on the manor. Note these fundamental differences in outlook:

• For the merchant, wealth was based on the possession of money. For the lord, wealth was based on the possession of land.
• For the merchant, a person's status in society was achieved by labor and bargaining. For the noble lord, a person's status was inherited as a fact of birth. In a nobleman's eyes, an industrious merchant—no matter how successful—could never climb higher than even the poorest knight.

As a result of these differences, feudal barons frequently treated burghers with contempt. Fortunately for the towns, a burgher's money could be very persuasive. In exchange for a bag of money, lords grudgingly consented to grant the town a written charter similar to the one on page 214. Towns became more independent and attracted people seeking greater personal freedom.

Check for Understanding Have students complete the following equation: $x + y + z =$ growth of towns. Variables should include increased farm production, population growth, and increase in trade.

Practice

Guided Practice
Lead a guided discussion of the questions in Section Review 1. (Answers are below.)

Define:
(a) unplanted (b) one field was fallow while other was planted (c) two out of three fields were planted while one lay fallow (d) town dweller (e) burgh dwellers (f) gathering at which goods were traded

Advance Planner

	Section 1
Objectives	1. Explain how new ways of farming helped to revive European agriculture. 2. Compare and contrast life in the towns with life on the manor.
Setting the Stage	Signs of strength in medieval society
Teaching Strategies	Economics and History: Technology and the Revival of Agriculture Discussing History: Comparing Towns and Manors Check for Understanding
Guided Practice	Section Review 1
Independent Practice Worksheets	Independent Practice 10.1 Geography Skills 10 Vocabulary 10
Enrichment	1. Primary Source: Voices 10.1 2. ★ Preparing a Report 3. Researching for Points

(g) association of people who worked at the same occupation (h)worker in training (i) worker who completed training but is not yet a master

Identify:
(a) town southwest of Paris (b) years 1000–1300

Answer:
1. (a) heavier plow, use of horsepower, three-field system (b) plow: opened up new lands to plant; horsepower: speeded up plowing; three-field system: allowed more land to be sown each year
2. (a) They did not fit into the traditional groups. (b) business managers, lenders, bankers, traders
3. (a) Trade increased. (b) bought at fairs (c) at great fairs
4. (a) Merchant guilds – traders; craft guilds – skilled artisans (b) set and enforced standards, prices
5. fought or bought charters with money
6. Example: Increased food production supported a larger population. A larger population led to settlement of towns. Towns became centers of trade.

Independent Practice
Assign Independent Practice Worksheet 10.1.
Assign Geography Skills Worksheet 10.
Assign Vocabulary Worksheet 10.

Chapter 10	The High Middle Ages 1000–1300		★ Advanced
Focus	The Cathedral of Chartres as a symbol of the High Middle Ages		● Basic

Section 2	Section 3	Section 4	Section 5
1. Identify three abuses of power that Church reformers wanted to end. 2. Describe the powers held by medieval popes. 3. Describe gothic architecture and explain its significance.	1. Discuss the consequences of the Norman conquest of England. 2. Compare the efforts of the German, French, and English rulers to build royal power. 3. Draw a map of Europe in 1160.	1. Describe aspects of student life in medieval universities. 2. Describe aspects of the life of medieval nobles. 3. Compare the status of medieval women with that of women in ancient Egypt, Greece, and Rome.	1. Describe aspects of warfare in the Holy Land. 2. List and evaluate the consequences of the Crusades.
The role of reformers	European monarchs	The importance of literacy	Pope Urban II's speech at Clermont calling for a crusade
Discussing History: Reforming the Church Discussing History: Excommunication Teaching with Pictures: Gothic Cathedrals Transparency 94 Check for Understanding	Discussing History: The Norman Conquest Skill Building: Making Comparisons Geography in History: Making a Map Transparency 30 Outline Map 9 Check for Understanding	Discussing History: Medieval Students Teaching with Pictures: Life in a Castle Skill Building: Comparing and Contrasting Women's Status Check for Understanding	Teaching with Pictures: The Mighty Krak Transparency 31 Discussing History: Consequences of the Crusades Check for Understanding
Transparency 94 Q&A Section Review 2 Independent Practice 10.2	Transparency 30 Q&A Section Review 3 Independent Practice 10.3	Section Review 4 Independent Practice 10.4 Basic Skills 10	Transparency 31 Q&A Section Review 5 Independent Practice 10.5 Critical Thinking 10
1. Primary Source: Voices 10.2 2. Preparing a Report 3. Researching for Points	1. Primary Source: Voices 10.3 2. Researching for Points	1. Primary Source: Voices 10.4 2. ★ Preparing a Report 3. Researching for Points	1. Primary Source: Voices 10.5 2. Researching for Points

Chapter Closer	
● Reteaching Activities	Recalling Main Events, Organizing Information
Chapter Review	Summary, Reviewing the Facts, Basic Skills, Researching and Reporting Skills, Critical Thinking, Perspectives on Past and Present, Investigating History
Chapter Evaluation	Chapter Test 10, Computer Test Bank Chapter 10 Test

Enrichment Activities

1. **Reading a Primary Source** Assign Voices from the Past Resource Book 10.1.

2. **Preparing a Report** Ask advanced students to prepare a report comparing the role of a medieval guild with the role of a modern workers' union.

3. **Researching for Bonus Points** Award bonus points to students who can answer this question: Where were the four Champagne Fairs held? (at Troyes, Bar, Lagny, and Provins)

Answers to Voice from the Past

1. formalized agreement between king and townspeople
2. refers to people of town, who are party to the agreement
3. feudal relationships based on personal loyalty; citizenship based on membership in community
4. phrase applies to newcomers who have left feudal lands and ties to live in town

Religious leaders wielded great power. 2

Section Objectives

After completing Section 2, students should be able to:

1. identify three abuses of power that Church reformers wanted to end.
2. explain the causes and consequences of the Investiture Contest between Pope Gregory VII and Henry IV.
3. describe the powers held by medieval popes.
4. describe Gothic architecture and explain its significance.

Setting the Stage

Ask students to define *reformer*. Explain that reformers want to improve society by correcting a problem or abuse. Ask students to recall reformers whom they have already studied. Students might identify the Hebrew prophets, Confucius, Solon, and the Gracchi as examples of reformers. Then explain that the troubles that plagued Europe during the Early Middle Ages also affected the

Church. Explain that this section begins with a description of the problems facing the Church in the High Middle Ages. It then explains how reformers solved these problems and in the process contributed to European renewal.

Teaching Strategies

Discussing History: Reforming the Church (Objective 1) Have students identify the three practices church reformers wanted to correct. Explain that reformers wanted to end clerical marriages because they believed that a priest could not act as a spiritual father and a worldly father at the same time. Reformers also wanted to stop simony—the buying and selling of Church offices. (For example, one wealthy family in southern France purchased the position of archbishop for their ten-year-old son.) Finally, reformers wanted to abolish the practice of lay investiture. Explain that lay investiture was the appointment and the installation of Church officials by feudal lords and kings. Ask students to explain why reformers saw this practice as a major threat to the Church. Point out that during the eleventh century, German emperors frequently selected popes who cared more about wealth than about serving the Church.

Discussing History: Excommunication (Objective 2) Explain that medieval popes possessed enormous power. As explained in the text, they led a well-organized kingdom that included the papal curia, legates, bishops, and priests. The Church could also collect taxes, enforce canon law, and punish heresy. The pope's most formidable weapon, however, was a spiritual penalty known as excommunication. Point out that excommunication was like a spiritual death sentence. A priest first pronounced the name of an excommunicated sinner. A bell then tolled as at a person's funeral. Next, a Bible was slammed shut. Finally, the light of a candle was snuffed out. Thus, "by bell, book, and candle," a person was expelled from Christian society and deprived of the holy sacraments. An excommunicated person could not act as a judge, juror, or witness, and could not enter into a legal contract.

Teaching with Pictures: Gothic Cathedrals (Objective 3) Use Overhead Transparency 94, *The Gothic Cathedral*, to help illustrate pointed arches, flying buttresses, and ribbed vaults. Point out that these techniques enabled Gothic architects to achieve height and light. Now direct students' attention to the picture of Bourges Cathedral (page 219). Ask students to describe how they would feel if they were standing inside this cathedral. Emphasize that the cathedral's pointed arches created a feeling of soaring height designed to lift the worshipper's spirit upward to another world. Now direct students' attention to the picture of the rose window from Chartres Cathedral. Explain that stained-glass windows used symbols to illustrate stories from the Bible. For example, the outer ring of this window shows twelve minor prophets. The next ring contains twelve *fleur-des-lis*, the symbols of the French royal family. A circle of twelve kings of Judah follows. Then comes an inner ring containing four doves, four angels, and four horses. Finally, all eyes focus upon the image of a crowned Mary, the Queen of Heaven, holding the Christ Child.

Check for Understanding Have students explain the roles of Pope Gregory VII, Francis of Assisi, and Abbot Suger in Church reforms of the High Middle Ages.

Practice

Guided Practice

Lead a guided discussion of the questions in Overhead Transparency 94 and in Section Review 2. (Answers are below.)

Define:
(a) leading bishop (b) buying and selling of church offices (c) practice in which feudal lord or king granted Church offices (d) papal punishment (e) pope's diplomat (f) Church law (g) dissenter from Church doctrine (h) wandering monk

Identify:
(a) site of monastery (b) monastic order (c) clashed with Gregory VII (d) church reformer who became pope (e) Italian town where Henry IV met with Gregory VII (f) compromise reached by Church and emperor regarding investiture (g) pope's advisors (h) Church experts delegated to find heretics (i) founded Dominicans (j) founded Franciscans (k) abbot of Saint Denis (l) architecture characterized by round arches, thick pillars (m) architecture characterized by flying buttresses and pointed arches

Answer:
1. abolish marriage of priests, simony, and lay investiture
2. (a) It gave him power. (b) Henry challenged the pope's ban; the pope excommunicated Henry; Henry was forgiven by Gregory.
3. governed by single ruler, had system of law, collected taxes, performed social services
4. (a) to find and judge heretics (b) to win heretics back

5. more height and more light
6. Both emperor and pope retained powers.
7. Examples: church as center of town, wandering friars, presence of monks and nuns, inquisitors questioning people

Independent Practice
Assign Independent Practice Worksheet 10.2.

Enrichment Activities

1. **Reading a Primary Source** Assign Voices from the Past Resource Book 10.2.

2. **Preparing a Report** Ask interested students to prepare a report on the life and teachings of Francis of Assisi.

3. **Researching for Bonus Points** Award bonus points to students who can find the answer to these questions: What was Gregory VII's name before he became pope? (Hildebrand) What were the names of the architects who designed Chartres Cathedral? (Their names are unknown. Chartres was designed to glorify God and not individuals.)

Royal governments grew stronger. 3

Section Objectives

After completing Section 3, students should be able to:

1. discuss the consequences of the Norman conquest of England.
2. compare the efforts of the German, French, and English rulers to build royal power.
3. draw a map of Europe in 1160.

Setting the Stage

Ask students to write three qualities that they feel a present-day national leader should possess. List these qualities on the chalkboard. Then explain that the leadership of kings played an important role in the political revival of Europe. Explain that this section examines the achievements of several early kings of England, France, and Germany. Each king demonstrated different leadership qualities, but all played an important role in shaping the development of their kingdoms.

Teaching Strategies

Discussing History: The Norman Conquest (Objective 1) Have students read the sections on the Norman conquest and William the Conqueror. Ask students to suggest three significant consequences of the Norman conquest. Point out that England emerged as the first centralized feudal kingdom in Europe. In addition, some 200,000 Normans settled in England by 1087. The Norman ruling class brought with them their French language and culture. As a result, about one fourth of the words in modern English are of French origin. Finally, explain that the Duke of Normandy became both the King of England and the vassal of the French king. Ask students to explain why this could have been a source of conflict. Lead students to see that William's successful conquest of England created a fierce rivalry between the kings of England and France.

Skill Building: Making Comparisons (Objective 2) To help students compare the successes of English, French, and German rulers in increasing royal power, draw a chart on the chalkboard for students to complete. Include the names of rulers, developments that increased power, and developments that decreased power. After the chart has been completed, ask students to state a generalization they have derived from the information in their charts. (Possible generalization: Invasions of foreign countries did not help rulers to increase power at home.)

Geography in History: Making a Map (Objective 3) Explain to students that the consolidation of territory is one result of centralized power. Show students Overhead Transparency 30, *The Kingdoms of Europe in 1160*, and have them locate the territories held by the Norman kings (England), Capetian kings (France), and the German emperors (Holy Roman Empire). Then distribute copies of Outline Map 9: Physical Europe. Using the map on page 222 as a guide, have students label the Mediterranean Sea, Atlantic Ocean, and North Sea. Have students use three different symbols to distinguish the kingdoms of England, France, and the Holy Roman Empire. Then have them compare their work to a map of present-day Europe.

Check for Understanding Have students explain why the English kings were most successful and the German kings least successful in building royal power.

Practice

Guided Practice
Lead a guided discussion of the questions in Over-

head Transparency 30 and in Section Review 3. (Answers are below.)

Define:
(a) local people who answered questions about a case (b) body of law common to the whole kingdom

Identify:
(a) Norman who became king of England (b) English king defeated by William (c) battle at which Normans defeated English (d) strong ruler of England (e) founder of Capetian dynasty (f) strongest ruler of medieval Germany (g) lands controlled by Barbarossa (h) Holy Roman Emperor (i) battle at which Italian foot soldiers defeated Frederick's knights

Answer:
1. gave some land to Norman lords, kept one fifth
2. The royal courts settled all disputes.
3. Twelve peers would tell what they believed to be true and a judge would decide the outcome.

Independent Practice
Assign Independent Practice Worksheet 10.3.

Enrichment Activities

1. **Reading a Primary Source** Assign Voices from the Past Resource Book 10.3.

2. **Researching for Bonus Points** Harold and William were two of the three contenders for Edward's throne. Award bonus points to students who can answer this question: Who was the third contender for Edward's throne? (The Norwegian king Harold Hardrada. He was defeated in battle by Harold Godwinson.)

Learning revived and spread.   4

Section Objectives

After completing Section 4, students should be able to:

1. describe aspects of student life in medieval universities.
2. describe aspects of the life of medieval nobles.
3. compare the status of medieval women with that of women in ancient Egypt, Greece, and Rome.

Setting the Stage

Have students discuss the importance of literacy and education in today's world. Ask, "What does an education give someone in our society—power, money, prestige, happiness?" Explain that literacy gave the medieval clergy great influence. Only the literate could read contracts, laws, and the most important document of the time—the Bible. Tell students that this section examines how the spread of learning had a lasting effect on Western civilization. Help students to transfer knowledge from Section 3 by connecting the concept of learning to the need of the new monarchies for officials who could read and write.

Teaching Strategies

Discussing History: Medieval Students (Objective 1) Have students read the section, "Scholars gathered at universities" (page 224). Explain that medieval students could be any age. There were some female students, usually from well-to-do families. The most famous schools were Paris (theology), Oxford (theology), Bologna (law), and Salerno (medicine). There were about 80 universities in medieval Europe. No one is certain how large the universities were, but scholars believe that the larger ones had 6,000 to 10,000 students. As noted in the text, a bachelor's degree required three to five years of study. However, students were given a "long vacation" from June to September because of the need for their labor in the fields at harvest time. Students might be interested to learn that student life was not all work. As today, many students preferred fun to study. As one medieval student-poet wrote: "Let's away with study, Folly's sweet. Treasure all the pleasure of our youth."

Teaching with Pictures: Life in a Castle (Objective 2) Have students read the section, "Knights lived by a code of chivalry." Review the steps in a knight's education and explain that most of this training took place in and around a castle. Then direct students' attention to the picture on page 226. Point out that minstrels were a favorite form of medieval entertainment. This painting shows a wedding banquet. Normally, the biggest meal of the day was dinner. It was typically served at about 10:00 A.M. Table manners were primitive. Knights were known to butter bread with their thumbs and toss bones across the table. The guests at this banquet are seated around long tables. Most castles had few pieces of furniture. The lord of the castle was usually the only one who had a chair—

the origin of the name "chairman" for the person who presides at a meeting. Finally, point out that most medieval castles were not comfortable. Castles usually used open slits in the walls instead of elegant windows shown in the picture. As a result, flies, mosquitoes, and cold winds were a constant problem.

Skill Building: Comparing and Contrasting Women's Status (Objective 3) Ask students to compare and contrast the social status of Egyptian women (page 57), Greek women (pages 103–104), Roman women (page 123), and medieval European women (page 203). Ask, "In which societies did women enjoy higher status and more rights?" Ask advanced students to assess the effects of the code of chivalry on the perception and treatment of women during the Middle Ages. What was the role of noblewomen in the feudal political system? How did women's arts, such as tapestries, reflect the realities of daily life for ladies of the castle? Have any elements of women's history carried over from medieval times to the present?

Check for Understanding Ask students to write a paragraph describing the lifestyles of medieval students, nobles, and women.

Practice

Guided Practice
Lead a guided discussion of the questions in Section Review 4. (Answers are below.)

Define:
(a) group of scholars (b) code of behavior governing knights (c) served a lord (d) rank above page (e) mock battle (f) poet who sang

Identify:
(a) Christian scholar who linked faith and reason (b) Aquinas's great work (c) heroic *chanson de geste* (d) mother of Richard the Lionheart

Answer:
1. few books, uncomfortable classrooms, long duration of study
2. (a) through Muslim libraries (b) They were written by pagans. (c) It fused classical reasoning with Christian faith.
3. as page, learned manners; as squire, served a knight
4. increasingly limited to the home and convent
5. diverted energy from war

Independent Practice
Assign Independent Practice Worksheet 10.4.
Assign Basic Skills Worksheet 10.

Enrichment Activities

1. **Reading a Primary Source** Assign Voices from the Past Resource Book 10.4.

2. **Preparing a Report** Ask advanced students to prepare a report on the great debate between Abelhard and St. Bernard. (See *The Age of Faith* by Will Durant.)

3. **Researching for Bonus Points** Award bonus points to students who can recite Roland's last words as he lay dying on the field of battle. (O God the Father who has never lied, who called the holy Lazarus back to life, and Daniel from the lion's jaws preserved, Protect my soul, and pardon all my sins.")

Crusaders marched against Islam.   5

Section Objectives

After completing Section 5, students should be able to:

1. describe aspects of warfare in the Holy Land.
2. list and evaluate the consequences of the Crusades.

Setting the Stage

Begin by locating Clermont on the map on page 229. Then ask students to imagine that they are standing in a field outside Clermont on a cold November day in the year 1095. Like thousands of others, they have come to hear their fellow Frenchman, Pope Urban II. Urban implores them to free the Holy Land from the Muslims. Now read the following excerpts from Urban's speech, and ask students to write a brief reaction to each:

1. "On whom, then, rests the labor of avenging these wrongs, and of recovering this territory, if not upon you — you upon whom, above all others, God has conferred remarkable glory in arms, great bravery, and strength to humble the heads of those who resist you?"

2. "Jerusalem is a land fruitful above all others, a paradise of delights. That royal city, situated at the center of the earth, implores you to come to her aid. Undertake this journey eagerly for the remission of your sins, and be assured of the reward of imperishable glory in the Kingdom of Heaven."

Sample students' reactions. Then explain that after hearing the Pope's speech, the excited crowd roared, "God wills it!" Within minutes, nobles, knights, monks, and serfs pledged to go on a crusade to free the holy land. This section examines the causes and consequences of the Crusade.

Teaching Strategies

Teaching with Pictures: The Mighty Krak (Objective 1) Review the sections on the Crusades. Have students trace the routes of the Crusades on Overhead Transparency 31 and locate Syria on the map. Tell students that the crusaders defended their conquests in the Holy Land by building great castles, such as Krak des Chevaliers ("Castle of the Knights") in Syria. Direct students' attention to the picture of Krak on page 230. Explain that construction of Krak began in 1110. Because the castle was built into a hillside, its massive walls were in some places 80 feet thick. The walls protected garrisons that included 2,000 knights and 400 horses. Huge storage rooms and cisterns held a five-year supply of food and water. The Muslims were never able to successfully storm the might Krak. Instead, a clever Sultan used a forged surrender order to trick a small garrison of knights into surrendering. The might Krak fell in 1271.

Discussing History: Consequences of the Crusades (Objective 2) Have students relate the goals of the Crusades with the actual results. Explain that although the Crusades failed to regain the Holy Land, they had a number of other consequences that were not expected. First, they stimulated trade with Asia, thus strengthening the merchant class. Second, they enhanced the status of noble women, who managed the castles and manors while their husbands were away at war. Third, the Crusades weakened the nobility because many knights and lords were killed, captured, or lost. Finally, western Europe acquired the inventions of Asia, such as gunpowder, the crossbow, the compass, and Arabic numerals. The failure of the Crusades also contributed to the decline of Church power.

Check for Understanding Have students write short paragraphs explaining why the Crusades were a "sign of the times" in the High Middle Ages. Ask them to explain how the crusades reflected the growing importance of the Church and expressed the concepts of knighthood and chivalry.

Practice

Guided Practice

Lead a guided discussion of the questions in Overhead Transparency 31 and Section Review 5. (Answers are below.)

Define:
someone who fights on behalf of a religious cause

Identify:
(a) pope who summoned fighters for the First Crusade (b) holy city won from the Muslims in First Crusade (c) land in which Jerusalem is located (d) eastern Christian empire centered at Constantinople (e) Muslim leader with whom Richard the Lionheart reached agreement in 1192 (f) king of England who took part in Third Crusade (g) capital of Byzantine empire (h) Holy Roman emperor who led Sixth Crusade (i) pope who called for the Fourth Crusade

Answer:
1. wars fought to regain Holy Land
2. (a) to show the pope's power, reunite Byzantine and Roman Christians (b) religious zeal, plunder and glory (c) to win control of key trade routes
3. First Crusade
4. (a) Three of Europe's most powerful kings took part. (b) Muslims were chivalrous.
5. Crusaders took Zara, sacked Constantinople.
6. They became commonplace; people expected their kings to rule wisely at home; loyalty to idea of Christendom lessened.
7. religious zeal, prejudice, hardships suffered

Independent Practice
Assign Independent Practice Worksheet 10.5.
Assign Critical Thinking Worksheet 10.

Enrichment Activities

1. **Reading a Primary Source** Assign Voices from the Past Resource Book 10.5.

2. **Analyzing a Quotation** The modern historian Will Durant wrote: "All medieval development, all the expansion of commerce and Christendom, all the fervor of religious belief, all the power of feudalism and glamour of chivalry came to a climax in a Two Hundred Years' War for the soul of man and the profits of trade." Ask advanced students to interpret and evaluate this statement.

3. **Researching for Bonus Points** Award bonus points to students who can answer this question: What happened to Richard the Lionheart as he traveled across Europe on his way home from the Third Crusade? (He was captured and held for ransom.)

Concluding the Chapter

1. **Chapter Closer**
   Have students explain how cathedral building symbolized the spirit of the High Middle Ages.

2. **Reteaching Activities**
   a. **Recalling Main Ideas** Remind students how the Chartres cathedral represented the faith and optimism of the High Middle Ages. Challenge students to describe other achievements of the period that reflect this faith and optimism.
   b. **Organizing Information** Have students design a concept map for this chapter. With "The High Middle Ages" at the center, students draw and label radiating lines, naming events that taken together characterize the High Middle Ages.
   c. **Summarizing** Ask students to summarize the main points of this chapter by describing visits to the following places: a medieval fair, the monastery at Cluny, a royal court in England, a medieval university, and Jerusalem during the first crusade.

3. **Chapter Review Activities**
   Assign Chapter Review 10 activities.

Chapter Evaluation

Chapter Test 10 and Computer Test Bank Chapter 10 Test can be used to evaluate your students' understanding of this chapter.

Answers to Chapter Review 10

Reviewing the Facts
1. a. town dwellers b. collective name for burgh dwellers c. gathering at which goods were traded d. association of people who worked at the same occupation e. worker in training f. worker who had completed training but was not yet a master g. leading bishop h. punishment by which no Church ceremonies could be performed in an offending ruler's lands i. law of the Church j. wandering monk who lived by begging k. twelve people who answered facts about a case for a royal judge l. rulings of England's royal judges that formed a unified body of law m. code of behavior governing knights n. someone who fought to regain the Holy Land

2. **a.** system in which two out of three fields were planted while one lay fallow **b.** site of monastery that led way in Church reforms **c.** Italian town to which Henry IV traveled in the snow to beg forgiveness from Gregory VII and thereby save his throne **d.** agreement that settled disputes about investiture **e.** experts sent by the Church to find and judge heretics **f.** architectural style emphasizing light and height **g.** defeated Harold at Battle of Hastings **h.** the year of Battle of Hastings **i.** William's great-grandson and strong ruler of England **j.** founder of Capetian dynasty **k.** strongest ruler of medieval Germany **l.** first ruler to call his lands the Holy Roman Empire **m.** lands under the control of Frederick Barbarossa **n.** great Christian scholar who linked faith and reason **o.** capital of Byzantine empire, which was sacked in 1204, ending the Fourth Crusade **p.** holy city won from Muslims in First Crusade **q.** Muslim leader with whom Richard the Lionheart reached agreement in 1192
3. resulted in better harvests and, subsequently, a population increase, increased trade, revival of towns and increased trade
4. enforced standards of quality, fixed the price of goods, provided insurance for members and their families, arranged business details, trained new workers
5. Bishops were powerful nobles and kings wanted to control them. Popes believed that bishops should not be controlled by a king.
6. Unlike England and France, Germany did not become a united country.
7. **(a)** built ribs from the roof to the columns to help support the roof's weight **(b)** allowed walls to become frames for huge stained-glass windows
8. **(a)** Jewish scholars working in Muslim libraries translated Arabic copies of Greek writers into Latin. **(b)** Byzantine scholars made Latin translations of Justinian's code. **(c)** Monks copied the writings.
9. **(a)** The Crusades won wide support in Europe at first because of the pope's promise of forgiveness of sins; increasingly the prospects of glory, adventure, and increased trade replaced religious fervor. **(b)** little.

Basic Skills
1. **(a)** masons, stonecutters, bricklayers, farmers, shepherds, shoemakers, shopkeepers **(b)** picks, cement mixing, trowels, T-squares, horse-drawn plough, earthenware, pewter or silver-smithing, boot making, jewelry making, woven goods

2. Students should mention the growing power of popes and of kings, the development of rule by law, the Crusades, the rise of independent towns, improvements in food production, the role of trade fairs and of guilds, the revival of learning, rise of chivalry, and changing roles of women.
3. First: from Lyons and Ratisbon by land and sea to Constantinople, then to Syria and Jerusalem; Second: from Metz to Constantinople, then by land and sea to Antioch and Palestine; Third: from northern France and Paris to Marseilles by land and sea, then by sea to Palestine; also from Raisbon to Constantinople; Fourth: from Venice to Constantinople

Researching and Reporting Skills
1. Students' advertisements or posters will vary.
2. (b), (d), (f) These sources pertain to the topic and refer to the correct time period.

Critical Thinking
1. **(a)** Chivalry helped regulate feudal relationships, and expressed Christian ideals. **(b)** Chivalry affected the conduct of warfare and the status of women, and found expression in romantic love, literature, and song.
2. Noblewomen inherited fiefs and managed estates. Townswomen worked in craft guilds and in trade. Mostly, women were confined to home or convent, lacked political rights, and had little say in choosing marriage partners.
3. Although German kings headed the Holy Roman Empire, they failed to consolidate their power. Most land remained in the hands of powerful princes who elected the king.
4. Students might suggest that **(a)** guilds often supported the king against the nobles; **(b)** guilds often obtained town charters, winning independence from the feudal system.
5. **(a)** The Church governed from a central capital through curia and legates. Its bishops operated courts of law. It collected taxes. **(b)** absolving allegiances to the king, excommunicating the king, using the interdict.

Perspectives on Past and Present
1. Burghers' sons studied for jobs in government or in the Church; no women were allowed; classrooms and books had to be rented; exams were oral and in Latin.
2. Students' responses to movies will vary.

Investigating History
Students' findings on medieval cities, trade leagues, and romantic literature will vary.

The Origin of European Nations

Chapter Overview

Chapter 11 traces the growth of nation-states in England, France, Spain, and Russia. In France, royal power increased when the king won control of land held by English kings. In England, King John's need for funds to defend English lands in France enabled the barons to force him to sign the Magna Carta, the historic document that limited royal power. Under Edward I, Parliament became part of English government. In France, central government was strengthened during the reign of Louis IX.

As feudal loyalties were being replaced by national loyalties, the church was weakened by the Great Schism. Plague reduced the population, and the scarcity of workers doomed the manorial economy. New weapons and wars dealt a death blow to feudal warfare.

New monarchs—Louis IX, Henry Tudor, and Isabella and Ferdinand—replaced feudal kings. To the northeast, the Russian empire began its rise to power. By the 1400's, Moscow was the strongest of Russian states under Mongol control. Later, the czars freed Moscow from Mongol rule and increased Russian territory.

Key Terms

nation-state, nationalism, boyars
For additional exercises, see Vocabulary Worksheet 11.

Chapter Focus

Have students read the chapter introduction on pages 234–235. Call attention to the words Joan of Arc spoke to the English. Explain to students that the French believed strongly in both Christianity and in the French monarchy, and that Joan of Arc embodied these two beliefs. She believed she had divine inspiration to fight for her country. This blend of religion and patriotism was a new phenomenon.

Tell students this chapter examines the rise of nation-states and the concept of nationalism. Help students define nationalism, which relates to the concepts of loyalty to country, patriotism, homeland, and allegiance. Ask students to find examples of these concepts as they read. Point out that nationalism was a new phenomenon that paralleled the development of nation-states and governments. This chapter examines the origins of political ideas and institutions that exist today.

England and France developed as nations.

1

Section Objectives

After completing Section 1, students should be able to:

1. identify events that contributed to the political development of France and England.
2. analyze the purposes and results of the Model Parliament and of the Estates General.

Setting the Stage

Explain to students that Section 1 examines how France and England developed into nation-states. Point out that the political boundaries and forms of government shaped during the thirteenth century formed the basis for modern England and France. Ask students to recall the strategies for increasing royal power discussed in Chapter 10 (pages 220–223). Challenge them to remember why the German kings had less power than the kings in England and France. Point out that the key to centralizing power was gaining control over the nobles and acquiring territory. Norman kings of England accomplished this, for example, by holding lands in England and France and by establishing royal courts of justice. Ask students to determine, as the read, if similar strategies contributed to the rise of nation-states in England and France.

Teaching Strategies

Writing about History: The Conflict between France and England (Objective 1) After students have read the section, explain that the conflict

Identify:
(a) king of England from 1154 to 1179 (b) signed Magna Carta (c) king of France (d) English document limiting royal power (e) king of England 1271–1307 (f) first gathering of lords and commoners (g) wrote *The Canterbury Tales* (h) French king 1226–1270 (i) called Estates General (j) parliamentary meeting in France

Answer:
1. feudal ties between French and English
2. (a) military weaknesses (b) His barons forced him to sign the Magna Carta.
3. (a) no taxation without representation; due process of law (b) limited it
4. (a) included commoners (b) House of Lords was made up of nobles and bishops; House of Commons was made up of burgesses and knights.
5. (a) gave France a strong central government (b) created Supreme Court for France (c) extended political power to middle class
6. It established the idea of a supreme law binding on everyone and guaranteed basic civil rights.
7. They were included in the ruling bodies.
8. elevated English to the status of literary language; set concerns of English-speaking people apart from those of French

Independent Practice
Assign Independent Practice Worksheet 11.1.
Assign Vocabulary Worksheet 11.

Enrichment Activities

1. **Reading a Primary Source** Assign Voices from the Past Resource Book 11.1.

2. **Preparing a Report** Ask advanced students to read "Saint Joan" by George Bernard Shaw. Have them compare what they have learned about the historic role played by Joan of Arc to the treatment the story is given by this early modern playwright.

3. **Researching for Bonus Points** Award bonus points to students who can answer this question: What were Henry II's final words? (Shame, shame, on a conquered king.")

Answers to Voice from the Past

1. A king's greatest duty was to govern justly and well.
2. Louis made himself accessible to people seeking justice. He also commanded officials to see that justice was done.
3. He would strengthen the popularity of the monarchy.

The Church faced a crisis in the 1300's.

2

Section Objectives

After completing Section 2, students should be able to:

1. analyze changes in the relationship between the church and secular governments.
2. identify the main effect of the Great Schism on the power of the Church.

Setting the Stage

Point out to students that after the King of France made Pope Boniface VII a captive, there was little reaction from the French people. They did not protest or express public outrage, but accepted the king's actions. Tell students that this section, examines how people's attitudes towards the Church changed. Help students understand this development and review the growing influence of the Church as discussed in Chapter 10 (pages 215–218). Recall that the powers of the Church included taxation and courts of canon law. Ask students how the development of the English and French monarchies might conflict with the power of the Church. Tell students that Section 2 examines such a conflict between a determined king, Phillip IV, and an equally determined pope. Ask students to anticipate, as they read, the outcome of this conflict.

Teaching Strategies

Discussing History: Thomas Becket (Objective 1) Share with students the dramatic story of the relationship between Henry II and Thomas Becket to illustrate the bitter conflict between the Church and the king. Before he was made Archbishop of Canterbury, Becket showed no traits of the single-minded, austere, almost fanatical clergyman he eventually became. As Henry's chancellor and friend, he enjoyed the sumptuous royal lifestyle to which his position gave him access. Despite Becket's warnings, Henry appointed his friend Archbishop of Canterbury. The king reasoned that his ally would serve him well in this sensitive and powerful post. Imagine Henry's surprise when the new archbishop, and former ally, began a life of devoted service—not to his king, but to the Church. Becket pursued his new career with determined forthrightness. He abandoned his former lifestyle for the austere trappings of a medieval monk. Henry's attempts to consolidate royal power often violated church jurisdictions now staunchly defended by his old friend. Tensions mounted as former companions became enemies. In a fit of rage, Henry uttered words that he would later regret: "What cowards have I about me that no one will deliver me from this low born priest?" In their eagerness to please their king, loyal knights carried out his inadvertent command and killed Becket in his own church.

Thomas Becket proved to be even more powerful in death. Perhaps both to assuage his own feelings of guilt and to placate negative public opinion, Henry journeyed to Canterbury. There, in the cathedral of his slain friend, Henry knelt down before a long row of monks who obeyed the king's orders to beat him across his bare back.

Discuss how this episode illustrates the difficulty of resolving the growing rivalry between the Church and developing monarchies. Challenge students to recall an earlier struggle between a monarch and a churchman. Ask them to think of Canossa in 1077 when the German emperor Henry IV was humbled by Pope Gregory VII.

Skill Building: Drawing Conclusions (Objective 2) Before analyzing the Great Schism, ask students to comment on the importance of stability for any institution. Ask: "What is the effect of instability? How does instability weaken an organization?" Explain that the Avignon papacy and the resulting Church Schism are important for what they show us about the declining power of the Church. Ask students to comment on the difficulties the schism must have caused for the peoples of Europe as well. To help them understand the chaotic nature of this crisis, have students write sentences about the papacy and the Church in 1380 from the points of view of a French cardinal, an Italian bishop, and a commoner married by a recently excommunicated priest.

Check for Understanding Refer students to the Daily Feature on chess (page 241). Ask students to compare the struggle between the Church and governments to a game of strategy such as chess, a popular pastime for nobles in the Middle Ages. Ask, "Based on what you have read in this section, who was winning the game of strategy? How had the balance of power changed?"

Practice

Guided Practice
Lead students in a guided discussion of the questions in Section Review 2. (Answers are below.)

Define:
(a) official statement made by the pope (b) split (c) cast out of the Church (d) person whose religious beliefs differed from those of the Church

Identify:
(a) pope taken captive at Anagni (b) French king against whom Boniface issued his *Unam Sanctam* (c) pope who moved to Avignon (d) home of the popes during the "Babylonian captivity" (e) Italian pope chosen after death of Gregory XI (f) split in the Church over rightful pope (g) wrote that the pope had more power than was his due (h) Bohemian who spoke for religious reform (i) meeting that ended Great Schism

Answer:
1. (a) that kings must obey popes (b) sent army to kidnap pope
2. Church was held captive at Avignon, just as the Jews had been held captive in Babylon.
3. (a) Philip the Fair persuaded cardinals to elect a French pope who moved papacy to Avignon. (b) divided the Church (c) with resignation of three popes and election of one
4. Jesus was the true head of the Church; clergy should be poor; Bible was the final authority.
5. (a) preached in Czech rather than in Latin (b) tried as a heretic and burned at the stake
6. The Great Schism undermined confidence in the authority of the pope; conflicting opinions gained wider support; increasing nationalism weakened ties to Rome.

Independent Practice
Assign Independent Practice Worksheet 11.2.

Enrichment Activities

1. **Reading a Primary Source** Assign Voices from the Past Resource Book 11.2.

2. **Researching for Bonus Points** Award bonus points to students who can determine in what country Avignon was located in 1305. (Avignon was in the Holy Roman Empire.)

The 1300's brought plague and war. 3

Section Objectives

After completing Section 3, students should be able to:

1. explain the social and physical effects of the plague.
2. analyze the warfare between France and England and its effects on nationalism.

Setting the Stage

Explain how plague compounded the instability and disorder already being felt by the peoples of western Europe. Suggest to students that besides the great loss of life, the Black Death had emotional and economic repercussions as well. Demoralized by the fear of death, people lost interest in their careers and ambitions. As farms went untended, livestock wandered aimlessly through once productive fields. Towns disappeared as inhabitants fled the ravages of the frightening and mysterious Black Death. Explain that Section 3 examines how the plague and warfare lead to a general disintegration of medieval life. Remind students that the struggles between the Church and the emerging national governments (discussed in Section 2) had already created an atmosphere of apprehension and instability. Ask students to follow these themes as they read.

Teaching Strategies

Writing about History: The Plague (Objective 1) Ask students to write about the plague from the viewpoint of a survivor in a town that has been ravaged by the disease. Before they begin writing, brainstorm on the following subjects:

• What are some of the ramifications of the possibility that half of the townpeoples have died or moved away?
• What is the emotional impact of the likelihood that everyone has lost family members and friends?
• How might the plague have affected the economy?
• How might the plague change one's lifestyle and one's expectations about the future?

Have students write a first-person account from the perspective of a young person their age. Encourage them to be creative, but to use their knowledge of this period in history to make their stories accurate.

Discussing History: The War between France and England (Objective 2) Before reading the section on warfare, review with students the technology and tactics of medieval warfare. Explain that new developments in weaponry changed the face of battle.

After students have read about the Hundred Years' War, point out that the war added to the

European misery. New weapons resulted in a staggering loss of life. For example, at the battle of Agincourt, where about 10,000 Frenchmen were slain, archaeologists uncovered a single trench that contained an estimated 6,000 bodies. Explain that archery had become the national sport in England. This gave young men practice with the longbow, which could pierce armor at 100 yards. Until this time, the use of cannons was limited. Previously they were too dangerous and unreliable, as likely to destroy the person firing them as the intended target. Ask students to explain how the longbow and cannon redefined military strategy and further diminished the role of traditional medieval knights. Show students Overhead Transparency 32, *France in the Hundred Years' War*, and have them locate the great battle sites of the conflict. Conclude your discussion by asking students how the battles of Agincourt and Orleans contributed to the development of a spirit of nationalism in France and in England.

Check for Understanding Ask students how the Black Death, new weapons, and feelings of nationalism helped end feudalism.

Practice

Guided Practice
Lead students in a guided discussion of the questions in Overhead Transparency 32 and in Section Review 2. (Answers are below.)

Define:
(a) feeling of loyalty to one's own land and people
(b) eldest son of a French king

Identify:
(a) great plague in 1347 (b) war over English king's claims to land in France (c) forced Charles VI to sign away his kingdom (d) battle at which English defeated French (e) French warrior-saint (f) French city saved by Joan of Arc (g) French prince whom Joan of Arc helped restore to the throne

Answer:
1. (a) terrible plague (b) carried along trade routes from Italy to elsewhere in Europe (c) depleted population thereby helping end serfdom and manorial system
2. English king's claims to land in France
3. (a) to drive the English out of France and give the French crown to Charles the Dauphin (b) the above (c) She was condemned by the English as a witch and heretic and burned at the stake.
4. (a) longbow and cannon (b) longbow: lessened

effectiveness of knights in armor; cannon: battered down castle walls

5. The smaller population created a demand for workers and gave serfs new bargaining power.
6. It changed feudal warfare, making knights and castles obsolete.
7. (a) shouts of English during Battle of Agincourt for "Merrie England" (b) People from many sections of France united behind her.

Independent Practice

Assign Independent Practice Worksheet 11.3.
Assign Basic Skills Worksheet 11.

Enrichment Activities

1. **Reading a Primary Source** Assign Voices from the Past Resource Book 11.3.

2. **Researching for Bonus Points** Award bonus points to students who can answer the following question: What was the average weight of the cannons used in the 1300's? (6,000 to 8,000 pounds)

New Monarchs ruled in Western Europe. 4

Section Objectives

After completing Section 4, students should be able to:

1. explain the phrase *new monarchies.*
2. explain characteristics of Henry VII's reign.

Setting the Stage

Ask students to recall the title of this chapter (The Origin of European Nations). Have students name the attributes of a *nation-state* and write responses on the board. Then ask students to list the traits of the feudal system. Have students compare the lists, and suggest why the feudal system was unworkable in the emerging nation-states of western Europe. Explain to students that Section 4 explores changes in government and society that further eroded the old medieval order.

Teaching Strategies

Discussing History: The New Monarchs (Objective 1) On the board list the three new sources of power available to the new monarchs: broad taxing power, a professional army, and professional officials. Students might be interested to know that one reason Charles VII needed a professional army was to combat a growing number of bandits and outlaws, who were terrorizing the general population. Because the king's soldiers came from all classes and were paid from general taxes, the middle classes felt closer to their monarch. They no longer depended on the nobles for protection. Ask students to explain how the new monarchies were different from feudal kingdoms.

Writing about History: The Reign of Henry VII (Objective 2) *Pre-writing* Discuss with students the importance of stability in politics. Point out that after the War of the Roses, the desire for peace and order among the English middle classes was very strong. They were tired of war and also of squabbling barons. Explain that the reign of Henry VII was a response to the desire for stability. Have students design a concept map to organize their writing. Students write *stability* and list reasons it was needed. Next, they draw lines from this central idea to statements describing the actions of Henry VII that contributed to stability.

Writing Have students use their concept maps to write analyses of Henry's reign. Encourage them to include their own opinions about Henry's methods of governing. Students might also response to this statement from the text: "It is probably fair to say that Henry was respected but not loved."

Check for Understanding Ask students to explain how Louis XI, Henry Tudor, and Isabella and Ferdinand were *new monarchs.*

Practice

Guided Practice

Lead a guided discussion of the questions in Overhead Transparency 33 and in Section Review 4. (Answers are below.)

Define:
(a) ruler who did not base his power on feudalism (b) source of funds for feudal kings (c) tax on land (d) tax on salt (e) tax on imported goods

Identify:
(a) French king who set monarchy on road to recovery (b) the "Spider King" (c) civil war in England between two branches of the royal family (d) new monarch who ruled a prosperous and peaceful England (e) drive to move the Muslims out of Span (f) heir to Aragon; became king of Spain (g) heiress to Castile; became queen of Spain

Answer:

1. imposed taxes; set up professional armies, hired professional officials
2. set up a royal council and first permanent royal army, drove English out of France
3. **(a)** He used trickery. **(b)** could raise money from two well established taxes whereas English needed to call Parliament to raise money
4. **(a)** served as chief ministers, justices of the peace **(b)** the Court of Star Chamber and having Parliament outlaw private armies
5. **(a)** heiress of Castile joined with heir of Aragon **(b)** Jews and Muslims were expelled.
6. **(a)** medieval rulers: land, plunder; new monarchs: taxes **(b)** medieval rulers: feudal system; new monarchs: paid soldiers from any class **(c)** medieval rulers: nobles; new monarchs: nobles plus middle-class townspeople

Independent Practice

Assign Independent Practice worksheet 14.4.
Assign Critical Thinking Worksheet 14.

Enrichment Activities

1. **Reading a Primary Source** Assign Voices from the Past Resource Book 11.4.

2. **Researching for Bonus Points** Award bonus points to students who can answer the following question: Which religious order was responsible for implementing the Spanish Inquisition. (the Dominicans)

A *new empire arose* in Russia.

5

Section Objectives

After completing Section 5, the students should be able to:

1. explain the influence of Mongol rule on the development of the Russian empire.
2. describe the geography of Russia and its effects on Russian's development as a nation-state.
3. compare the relationship between czars and boyars with that between the kings and barons of western Europe.

Setting the Stage

Point out that as feudalism was declining in Western Europe, this economic and social system was just developing in the Eurasian region that became Russia. The peoples there paid tribute to foreign invaders, the Mongols. Tell students that in the thirteenth century the Mongols conquered a vast territory in Asia, including all of China. The Mongols were people of the steppes and followed the steppes into Europe in the course of their conquests. The trading cities of Kiev and Moscow were at the western extent of the Mongol empire. The centralization of power leading to the unification of Russia began during Mongol rule. Explain that this section examines the events that led to the emergence of the nation-state known as Russia.

Teaching Strategies

Discussing History: The Influence of the Mongols (Objective 1) Ask students how the Mongols governed Russia. Students should recognize that the Mongols did not govern, but were content to collect revenues. Otherwise, princes were allowed to independently rule their principalities. Ask how this arrangement led to Moscow's emergence as a major principality. What were the Russian princes' sources of power? Point out that Moscow became the center of the Eastern Orthodox Church, and that the princes ruled through terror, as had their Mongol overlords.

Geography in History: Russia (Objective 2) Ask what roles rivers played in Russian history. Show students Overhead Transparency 34, *Russia and Eastern Europe in 1480*. Point out that Russia's location has been characterized as "isolated." Have students describe Russia's geographical location in relation to the idea of isolation. Ask students to hypothesize why Moscow became the place from which the Russian empire expanded.

Check for Understanding Have students suggest reasons Russia did not develop as a nation-state to the same extent as France and England.

Practice

Guided Practice

Lead a guided discussion of the questions in Section Review 5. (Answers are below.)

Define:

(a) Russian word for caesar or emperor **(b)** Russian nobles **(c)** Ivan IV's police force

Identify:

(a) divide Europe from Asia **(b)** migrants from Asia who settled in eastern Europe **(c)** trade center in early Russia **(d)** prince of Moscow under Mongols **(e)** walled citadel in Moscow **(f)** Ivan the Terrible

Answer:
1. Refer students to page 251.
2. **(a)** mid 1200's **(b)** united Russia under Mongol rule but allowed Russian princes local rule
3. **(a)** location in northern forests and nearness to rivers **(b)** trade, rise of Ivan I
4. expulsion of the Mongols, tripling of territory
5. **(a)** victories against Mongols; development of code of laws; expanded trade **(b)** turned against boyars, carried on a reign of terror
6. **(a)** conflict with nobles **(b)** no council like Parliament or Estates General to check power

Independent Practice
Assign Independent Practice Worksheet 11.5.

Enrichment Activities

1. **Reading a Primary Source** Assign Voices from the Past Resource Book 11.5.

2. **Researching for Bonus Points** Tell students that architecture in Moscow in the 1400's reflected Russian traditions and goals. Give bonus points to students who can identify the designers of the Kremlin in the late 1400's and the goal this choice was intended to fulfill. (In the Muscovites' rush to claim international stature and to become the "third Rome," Italian architects were employed.)

3. **Global Perspectives** Have students study Overhead Transparency 88, *The World about 1250,* which also appears on pages 810–811 in the Historical Atlas.

Concluding the Chapter

1. **Chapter Closer**
   Ask students to explain why "The Origin of European Nations" is an appropriate title for this chapter.

2. **Reteaching Activities**
   a. **Outlining** Have students write a sentence outline of Sections 1 and 2, using the headings from the sections.
   b. **Making a Time Line** Have students prepare a time line covering events that took place between 1150–1580.

3. **Chapter Review Activities**
   Assign Chapter Review 11 activities.

Chapter Evaluation

Chapter Test 11 and Computer Test Bank Chapter 11 Test can be used to evaluate your students' understanding of this chapter.

Answers to Chapter Review 11

Reviewing the Facts
1. **a.** people with definite territory, united under one government **b.** feeling of loyalty to one's own land and people **c.** Russian word for emperor **d.** minor prince in Russia
2. **a.** year Magna Carta was signed **b.** gathering called by Edward I including commoners and lords; **c.** meeting of First, Second, and Third Estates **d.** period when papacy was in Avignon **e.** period when there were two popes **f.** council that resolved Great Schism **g.** plague during 1300's that weakened feudalism **h.** war between France and England over English land in France **i.** French heroine who defeated English at Battle of Orleans **j.** English civil war between Houses of York and Lancaster **k.** first Tudor king **l.** French king who set French monarchy on road to recovery **m.** Spanish king under whose rule Spain reached its modern borders **n.** with Ferdinand, revived Inquisition, expelled Jews and Muslims **o.** drive to expel Muslims out of Spain **p.** year Columbus sailed on first voyage of discovery **q.** capital of Russian empire **r.** first czar of united Russian nation
3. **(a)** Conflicts in France over English lands, John's need to raise taxes, and the barons' demands. **(b)** guarantees no taxation without representation and due process of law; limits power of monarchy
4. **(a)** included commoners as well as knights, bishops, and lords **(b)** 1295
5. **(a)** won back all King John's land in France **(b)** established Parlement of Paris which could overturn decisions of local courts **(c)** drove English out of France except for Calais; set up a royal council; set up the first permanent royal army **(d)** added dukedom of Burgundy to French state; ruled without needing to call Estates General
6. **(a)** People concluded that Avignon popes were hirelings of the French court; were shocked at extravagance of Avignon papacy. **(b)** Great Schism caused Christians to question the source of true religious authority: the pope — or which of several popes, a church council, or the Bible.
7. crop failures — caused famine; plague — killed millions of people; war — killed both French and English soldiers
8. Englishmen rejoiced at the news of their king's victories in France; Joan of Arc changed a

prince into a king, led the French army to victory, awakened national spirit; in both countries, king was seen as a national leader fighting for glory of nation-state.

9. used new sources of power—control of taxes, a professional army, and officials.

10. Mongols began work of uniting Russia; by the 1400's, Moscow was strongest Russian state. Ivan III, first czar, freed Moscow from Mongols and made it capital of a true empire.

Basic Skills

1.

| 1337 | 1357 | 1377 | 1397 | 1417 | 1437 | 1457 |

- 1356 Battle of Portiers
- 1346 Battle of Crécy
- 1429 Victory of Orleans
- 1415 Battle of Agincourt
- 1431 Joan's death at the stake

2. **(a)**

	England	France
Taxes	Magna Carta: limited king's power to tax (1215); Edward I taxed towns	King's bailiffs collected taxes
Parliament/ Estates General	Burgesses part of Model Parliament (1295); powers over taxation	Third Estate part of General Estates (1302); no powers over taxation
Royal Courts	Right to jury trial (1215); Edward I strengthened royal courts	Bailiffs presided over king's courts; Louis IX created Parlement of Paris

(b) changes reflect growing importance of middle class and extension of civil rights.

3. All three countries neared present-day political boundaries. France acquired English territory within France. Spain and Portugal conquered Muslim territory. Italian, Polish, and Hungarian kingdoms acquired territory from the Holy Roman Empire.

4. Monarchs relied less on vassals for help; tax base and military enrollment broadened to all classes, with less dependence on feudal aid and on noble knights; administrative tasks given to new educated middle class.

Researching and Reporting

1. Students' interviews will vary.
2. Students' surveys will vary.

3. Picture on page 234 is primary source for Middle Ages, but not for Joan of Arc, because the portrait was not painted during her lifetime. Pictures of Magna Carta (page 237) and St. Basil's Cathedral (page 253) are primary sources because they show physical remains. Other pictures give valuable information about life in the Middle Ages, but might be primary or secondary sources depending on the dates they were produced. Primary source quotations appear on pages 235, 244, and 246.

Critical Thinking

1. **(a)** The statement is more like an opinion than a fact; it is a reasoned judgment based on evidence. **(b)** losses of French territory helped English identify with England and limit royal power.

2. Middle classes, prosperous from trade, bought freedom from the feudal system. King sought their political and financial support against nobles, which gave them power over the king. **(b)** In England middle class limited power of king. In France Third Estate took part in government but had less power.

3. Spain was left without tradespeople for thriving cities and healthy economy; without intellectuals to lead Spain into the modern era.

Perspectives on Past and Present

1. Examples include the Bill of Rights and the Nixon impeachment.
2. The existence of various denominations provides for wider range of beliefs. Principle of religious toleration gives acceptance to different beliefs. Within a given religious group, tolerance of dissent varies.

Investigating History

Students' answers will vary.

Unit III Review Activities

1. Assign Geographic Theme: Interaction
2. Assign Unit Perspectives Questions

Unit III Review Answers

Geographic Theme: Interaction

1. Italy: Venice, Florence, Genoa, Milan, Rome, Naples; northwestern Europe: Bruges, Amsterdam, Cologne, Paris, Lubeck, Hamburg,

Bremen; Baltic area: Stockholm, Danzig, Copenhagen

2. Flanders and northern France: fish, salt, flax, wine, wheat, paper, iron, textiles, manufactured goods; Spain: cork, cotton, fruit and foodstuffs, olives, wool, iron, copper, paper, metalware, leather; England: tin, lead, iron, fish, textiles, manufacturing; Baltic region: grain, fish, flax, copper, hemp, wax, furs, honey. The Italian and Flemish cities had textiles and other manufacturing; already had industry; other regions were mainly producers of food and raw materials. England did have some textiles and other manufacturing.

3. Answers will vary, but main changes are expansion of trade and manufacturing within Europe and extension of trade to Americas and Asia.

Unit Perspectives

Understanding History

1. **a.** Roman Catholicism; traveled preaching the Church's ideas **b.** Eastern Orthodoxy; capital of Byzantine empire **c.** Islam; book of Muhammad's words **d.** Eastern Orthodoxy; bishop of Constantinople **e.** Roman Catholicism; law of the Church **f.** Roman Catholicism; leading bishop **g.** Roman Catholicism; pope whose ideas of Christendom and papal power became a central part of the Middle Ages **h.** Islam; capital of Muslim empire **i.** Roman Catholicism; compromise between Church and German emperor over investiture **j.** Islam; leader who followed Muhammad **k.** Eastern Orthodoxy; cathedral in Constantinople **l.** Roman Catholicism; split in the Church when there were two popes

2. **a.** 1453 **b.** 793 **c.** 570 **d.** 732 **e.** 843 **f.** 1180 **g.** 800 **h.** 1066 **i.** 1215 **j.** 1455–1485

3. **a.** ended Byzantine empire **b.** threatened much of Europe **c.** Muhammad founded religion of Islam. **d.** Muslims were defeated. **e.** divided Charlemagne's empire **f.** led to development of universities **g.** marked growing split between eastern and western branches of Christian church **h.** made England most centralized feudal kingdom in Europe **i.** limited rights of monarch **j.** marked real end to feudal warfare

Critical Thinking

1. Possible answers: **(a)** *similar*—holy wars; *different*—purpose to rescue Jerusalem from the Muslims; to spread Islamic faith **(b)** *similar*—incited rulers to take a brave stand against their enemies; *different*—to defend Constantinople; to go to Rheims to be crowned **(c)** *similar*—Christian churches; *different*—Byzantine; gothic **(d)** *similar*—introduced judicial reforms; *different*—use of jury; Court of Star Chamber

2. **(a)** split between Shi'ite and Sunni Muslims as result of killing of Husayn **(b)** took a man's role **(c)** nationalism replaced feudal loyalties.

3. **(a)** Possible answers: *destructive*—Hundred Years' War, Black Death, Viking raids, Great Schism, Inquisition; *constructive*—monasteries, growth of towns and trade, Justinian's code of law, gothic art, Magna Carta; **(b)** Answers will vary.

4. **(a)** growth of cities and guilds with independent charters; participation of Commoners in Parliament and the Estates General **(b)** Persecution of Spanish Jews and Muslims harmed trade and banking; German kings sought conquest rather than middle class support.

Making Decisions

1. **(a)** prestige and power of church enhanced **(b)** church gave support to Frankish kings **(c)** reinforced papal authority **(d)** blended religion and nationalism, used power of state to enforce religion

2. **(a)** permanently limited royal power, gave nobles a voice; **(b)** further limited royal power by including commons and by consulting Parliament on taxes; **(c)** extended power of central government and of the monarch

Continuity and Change

1. **(a)** monastic orders, guilds, parliaments, fairs, etc. **(b)** Answers will vary.

2. Monks preserved Roman writings; Justinian's code of law updated Roman law; Constantinople and the Arabs preserved Greek texts of philosophy and science. Arabs translated and advanced Greek scientific knowledge. Aquinas sought to reconcile Aristotle's thought with Christian faith. Art and architecture of the period survive today.

Unit Evaluation

Unit III Test can be used to evaluate your students' understanding of this unit.

An Age of Empires

Unit Overview

This unit surveys more than a thousand years of political, economic, social, and cultural developments in China, Japan, India, Southeast Asia, Africa, and the Americas. In more than a millennium of change, myriad kingdoms, empires, and dynasties rose and fell, and all the world regions saw golden ages.

Between periods of chaos and Mongol invasion, the T'ang, Sung, and Ming dynasties brought prosperity, political stability, and cultural glory to China. Influenced by Chinese ways, Japan then expressed its own cultural development in the elegant Heian Age and developed a feudal society. India enjoyed a golden age in art, science, and literature during the Gupta dynasty. Centuries of conflict between Hindus and conquering Muslims left India vulnerable to civil strife. Influenced by Indian ways, Southeast Asia saw successions of local kingdoms and the rise of the Khmer and Thai empires. China dominated Vietnam. Hinduism, Buddhism, and Islam all became part of Southeast Asian life.

In Africa, culturally rich kingdoms based on kinship emerged. Trade led to the growth of great empires in the west, such as Ghana, Mali, and Songhai, and to prosperous city-states in the east. Complex civilizations appeared in the Western Hemisphere. The Mayas built great cities. The Aztecs and Incas established vast empires in Mexico and in Peru. In 1500, the Aztec and Inca empires were at their height.

Until around 1500, the different world regions developed in comparative isolation. While trade linked Europe, Asia, and Africa, each region maintained its own cultural distinctiveness and integrity. Cultural developments in North and South America were entirely separate. Around 1500, European ships began to reach ports in Africa, Asia, and the Americas. Their coming heralded a new age of discovery and exploration, cultural contact and migration, and global networks of trade.

Resources

The resources that supplement the study of this unit include:

1. The time line for Unit IV, found on pages 528–529. The theme for this time line is the emergence of great civilizations in comparative isolation on different continents.
2. The Geographic Theme, found on page 318. The theme, *Place,* refers to great cities of the age of empires, such as Kublai Khan's Khanbalik, described by Marco Polo, and the Malian city of Watala, described by Ibn Battuta. The theme's focus is the Aztec capital of Tenochtitlán. The environment, layout, and architectural details of this great city were described by the Spanish observer Bernal Diaz, an eyewitness to Cortés' conquest of the Aztecs.
3. The Historical Atlas map on pages 812–813. This map of the world about A.D. 1500 shows the development of civilizations in Asia, Africa, and the Americas in relation to European history at the beginning of the age of exploration.
4. The introduction to research skills, a series of special skill-building activities beginning in Chapter 12 and culminating in students' writing formal research papers in Unit VII. The special research skill activities appear in chapter reviews under the heading Researching and Reporting Skills. The skill sequence in Unit IV begins in Chapter 12 with Formulating a Research Question, and continues in Chapter 13 with Forming a Hypothesis.

Chapter Titles

12 Golden Ages in China and Japan—A.D. 300–A.D. 1650 (pages 260–283)
13 Civilizations of India and Southeast Asia—A.D. 300–A.D. 1700 (pages 284–297)
14 Africa and the Americas—1200 B.C.–A.D. 1500 (pages 298–317)

Golden Ages in China and Japan

Chapter Overview

China's civilization developed under a series of strong dynasties with occasional periods of weakened control between the dynasties. Until about 1450, China was the world's greatest naval power. After that time, China abandoned its navy, lost interest in exploration, and turned inward. Beginning in 1513, when the Portuguese arrived, China limited its foreign contacts.

The Japanese were greatly influenced by Chinese ideas and customs. Buddhism reached Japan from China and, from about A.D. 600 to A.D. 800, Japanese scholars went to China to study its civilization.

Clans dominated early Japan. Between 1000 and 1200, Japan developed a feudal system with warriors called *samurai*. A powerful warlord called a *shogun* became the dominant power, ruling in the name of the emperor. After the decline of the shoguns, the most powerful feudal lords became nearly independent; warfare and disorder ruled the country until the sixteenth century.

The first European ships were welcomed in Japan in 1543, but by 1638 most European merchants had been banned, and Japan remained closed to Europeans for 200 years.

Key Terms

gentry, steppe, khan, clan, samurai, shogun, daimyo
For additional exercises, see Vocabulary Worksheet 12.

Chapter Focus

Begin by having students read the chapter opener (pages 260–261). Then ask students to speculate why Chapter 12 begins with a description of Yang-ti's garden and artificial lake. Explain that the emperor's wealth is a symbol of the political unity won by rulers of China's Sui dynasty. Now show Overhead Transparency 87, *The World about 800*. Point out that previous chapters discussed the Byzantine, Islamic, and Carolingian empires. Tell students that this chapter covers 1,300 years in the history of China and Japan.

Two great dynasties ruled China.

1

Section Objectives

After completing Section 1, students should be able to:

1. identify the Grand Canal and explain how it helped unify China.
2. describe how the Chinese used examinations to help choose government officials.
3. draw a map of the T'ang and Sung empires.
4. identify and discuss China's major technological inventions.

Setting the Stage

Ask students to recall what the phrase "golden age" means. Emphasize that a golden age refers to a period of peace, prosperity, and cultural creativity. Have students list golden ages that they have already studied. Then explain that this section describes how the T'ang and Sung dynasties ruled China during two famous golden ages.

Teaching Strategies

Economics and History: The Grand Canal (Objective 1) Have students read, "The Sui dynasty reunited China" (page 261). Explain that the Grand Canal played a vital role in unifying China. More than three million men and women toiled for five years to dig a canal twenty feet deep, sixty feet wide, and 1,000 miles long. Yang-ti celebrated the Grand Canal's opening with a pleasure cruise on his royal barge—the Imperial Dragon Junk. This dragon-shaped riverboat stretched 200 feet from mouth to tail. Four decks were stacked one atop the other to a height of fifty feet. Yang-ti sat on his gilded Dragon Throne on the highest deck.

Tell students that the Grand Canal served as more than a waterway for the Imperial Dragon Junk. Both the Yangtze and the Yellow rivers flow west to east. Use the map on page 262, or Overhead Transparency 35, *China in Sui and T'ang Times*, to show students how the Grand Canal provided a north-south artery linking the rice fields of the Yangtze delta to the northern provinces. A huge trading fleet of 40,000 ships carried rice and other supplies to the armies defending China's northern frontiers. In addition to helping the north, the canal also stimulated the development of the Yangtze region.

Relating Past to Present: Examinations (Objective 2) Ask students to describe how they feel before and after taking an important test. Then have them read, "Scholar-officials governed China" (pages 262–263). Explain that thousands of Chinese students took a civil service examination given each year. Fewer than 10 percent of the candidates passed. Read or distribute the following poem that describes the joy a Chinese student felt when he learned he had passed the exam:

I met someone who told me I had passed;
I was bowled over by this thunderclap of joy
    and surprise,
I thought it was a mistake, thought it was
    only a dream;
I was in a sorry state of doubt and dread ...
Parents, however much they love a child,
Have not the power to place him among the
    chosen few.
Only the examiner can bring the youth to
    notice,
And out of darkness carry them to heaven.

Recall the definition of civil service. Note that many government jobs in the present-day United States require qualifying exams. Ask students how civil service examinations might affect the quality of government.

Geography in History: Making a Map (Objective 3) Show students Overhead Transparency 36, *China in Sung Times*. Ask students how China's boundaries changed between the times of the Sui and the T'ang dynasties. Distribute Outline Map 19: China and Japan. Have students refer to the maps on pages 262 and 265, draw a map key, use map symbols to show the boundaries of each of the three dynasties, and label the three capitals. Tell students to save their maps to use again in Sections 3 and 4.

Discussing History: Printing (Objective 4) Have students read, "China led the world in technology" (pages 266–267). Explain that the stimulus for discovering a means of producing multiple copies of a document may have been provided by Buddhists who wanted to make copies of their sacred writ-

ings. The earliest printed book that we can still read is a Buddhist text called the *Diamond Sutra*.

Advance Planner

	Section 1
Objectives	1. Identify the Grand Canal and explain how it helped unify China. 2. Describe how the Chinese used examinations to help choose government officials. 3. Draw a map of the T'ang and Sung empires. 4. Identify and discuss China's major technological inventions.
Setting the Stage	The concept of a Golden Age Unit IV Time Line Transparency 87
Teaching Strategies	Economics and History: The Grand Canal Transparency 35 Relating Past to Present: Examinations Geography in History: Making a Map Transparency 36 Outline Map 19 Discussing History: Printing Check for Understanding
Guided Practice	Transparency 35 Q&A Transparency 36 Q&A Transparency 87 Q&A Section Review 1
Independent Practice Worksheets	Independent Practice 12.1 Geography Skills 12 Vocabulary 12
Enrichment	1. Primary Source: Voices 12.1 2. Preparing a Report 3. Creative Writing 4. Researching for Points

It consists of six sheets of text and was published in A.D. 868. Point out that the concept of block printing did not reach Europe until the fourteenth century. Ask students to suggest factors that

Unit IV	An Age of Empires
Theme	Golden ages and the rise and fall of kingdoms in 1300 years of change in China, Japan, India, Southeast Asia, Africa, and the Americas.

Chapter 12	Golden Ages in China and Japan 300–1650	★ Advanced
Focus	Emperor Yang-ti's garden as a symbol of China's political unity under Sui rulers	● Basic

Section 2	Section 3	Section 4	Section 5
1. Identify the Eurasian Steppe as a geographic region. 2. Identify Genghis Khan and list reasons the Mongols were successful conquerors. 3. Locate on a map the boundaries of the Mongol empire. 4. Discuss the consequences of the Mongol conquests.	1. Locate the boundaries of the Ming Empire. 2. Identify and describe the Forbidden City. 3. Relate causes and effects in China's isolation.	1. Describe Japan's geography and explain its influence on Japanese culture. 2. Explain how the Japanese adapted Chinese ideas. 3. Discuss aspects of daily life during the Heian Age. 4. Identify the samurai and explain the code of bushido.	1. Describe the impact of the Portuguese on Japan. 2. Identify Oda Nobunaga, Toyotomi Hideyoshi, and Tokugawa Ieyasu and explain how they unified Japan. 3. Define Zen Buddhism and give examples of its influence on Japanese culture.
Using Geographic Themes: Region	Mongol leaders lose the Mandate of Heaven.	Using Geographic Themes: Human-Environment Interactions Transparency 39	Causes of the collapse of the Kamakura shogunate and the Age of the Country at War
Discussing History: The Mongol Success Transparency 37 Geography in History: Mongol Conquests Outline Map 12 Skill Building: Identifying Effects Check for Understanding	Geography in History: Using Map Symbols Transparency 38 Outline Map 19 Teaching with Pictures: The Forbidden City Skill Building: Recognizing Cause and Effect	Using Geographic Themes: Movement Discussing History: Life in Heian Discussing History: The Samurai Warrior Check for Understanding	Using Geographic Themes: Movement Discussing History: The Three Unifiers Teaching with Pictures: Zen Gardens Check for Understanding
Transparency 37 Q&A Section Review 2	Transparency 38 Q&A Section Review 3	Transparency 39 Q&A Section Review 4	Section Review 5
Independent Practice 12.2	Independent Practice 12.3. Critical Thinking 12	Independent Practice 12.4	Independent Practice 12.5 Basic Skills 12
1. Primary Source: Voices 12.2 2. Relating Past to Present: Present-Day Mongols 3. Researching for Points	1. Primary Source: Voices 12.3 2. ★ Creative Writing 3. Researching for Points	1. Primary Source: Voices 12.4 2. Preparing a Report 3. Researching for Points	1. Primary Source: Voices 12.5 2. Preparing a Report 3. Researching for Points

Chapter Closer	
● Reteaching Activities	Making a Chart, Making a Time Line, Identifying Historical Figures
Chapter Review	Summary, Reviewing the Facts, Basic Skills, Researching and Reporting Skills, Critical Thinking, Perspectives on Past and Present, Investigating History
Chapter Evaluation	Chapter Test 12, Computer Test Bank Chapter 12 Test

might affect the rate of exchange of new ideas and new technology between different cultures.

Check for Understanding List the four dynasties on the chalkboard and ask students to describe one significant development that occurred in each.

Practice

Guided Practice
Lead a guided discussion of the questions in Overhead Transparencies 35, 36, and 87 and in Section Review 1. (Answers are below.)

Define:
(a) large group of well-to-do people who rank below nobles but above common people (b) fine, bone-hard substance used to make china

Identify:
(a) dynasty that reunited China under strong central government in the late 500's (b) canal built by Yang-ti to connect Yellow River in the north and Yangtze River in the south (c) founder of T'ang dynasty (d) dynasty in power during China's golden age (618–907) (e) only woman to rule China in her own name (f) capital of T'ang China (g) trading route between China and the west (h) battle at which Arabs defeated Chinese (i) army leader who founded the Sung dynasty (j) dynasty that marked beginning of military decline (k) market city in China

Answer:
1. (a) It reunited China and laid the foundation for the golden age that followed. (b) It overtaxed and overworked the people, who revolted.
2. (a) by examination (b) gave China an intelligent ruling class, created gentry (c) did not weed out corruption or guarantee workers skilled in government or administration
3. (a) took control of China's northern lands and eventually captured Sung capital (b) paid bribes to appease them
4. T'ang—trade reached heights never matched again; Sung—busy trade centered on Hangchow
5. decline in military power and defeats by Arabs; decline in trade
6. printing, magnetic compass, gunpowder
7. Answers are likely to stress the similarities, particularly the emphasis on nature and simplicity.

Independent Practice
Assign Independent Practice Worksheet 12.1.
Assign Geography Skills Worksheet 12.
Assign Vocabulary Worksheet 12.

Enrichment Activities

1. **Reading a Primary Source** Assign Voices from the Past Resource Book 12.1.

2. **Preparing a Report** Have students prepare a report on one of the following topics: the Grand Canal, T'ai-tsung, Empress Wu, Ch'ang-an, Tu Fu, Li Po, Sung porcelain, the magnetic compass, the invention of gunpowder.

3. **Creative Writing** Ask students to select any picture of a landscape. Their assignment is to write a poem about the picture using the three characteristics of T'ang poetry as discussed in the text.

4. **Researching for Bonus Points** Award bonus points to students who can find the answer to this question: What was the name of the main avenue in Ch'ang-an? (Street of the Vermilion Sparrow)

The Mongols conquered a vast empire. 2

Section Objectives

After completing Section 2, students should be able to:

1. identify the Eurasian steppe as a geographic region.
2. identify Genghis Khan and list reasons the Mongols were successful conquerors.
3. locate on a map the boundaries of the Mongol empire.
4. discuss the consequences of the Mongol conquests.

Setting the Stage

Using Geographic Themes: Region (Objective 1) Have students recall the definition of a geographic region. Remind students that a region is an area that shares common characteristics. Now ask students to read the section, "The Mongols came from the steppe," and to identify the geographic characteristics that made the steppe a region. Explain that the Mongols were nomads who lived on the grassy steppes north of the Great Wall. Tell students that this section describes how Genghis Khan and his successors conquered and ruled a huge Mongol empire that stretched from the Pacific Ocean to the Black Sea.

Discussing History: The Mongol Success (Objective 2) First direct students' attention to the map of the Mongol Empire on page 269, or use Overhead Transparency 37. Then ask, "How could groups of nomadic horsemen conquer such a huge empire?" Point out that Genghis Khan is regarded as a military genius and a brilliant organizer. As noted in the text, his army was carefully organized into platoons, companies, and brigades. The Mongol cavalry included tireless horsemen who could travel as far as ninety miles a day on their hardy ponies. Genghis Khan and his successors used terror to spread fear, while also making skillful use of spies to find out enemy weaknesses.

Geography in History: Mongol Conquests (Objective 3) Distribute Outline Map 12: Asia. Have students refer to the map on page 269 and then fill in the areas of the Mongol conquests. Ask, "What areas in addition to China did the Mongols conquer?" Point out that the Mongols achieved the only successful winter invasion of Russia in history. They invaded Russia in the winter so that their cavalry could use the frozen rivers as highways. Then have students add labels to their maps naming the regions on the frontiers of the Mongol Empire.

Skill Building: Identifying Effects (Objective 4) Explain that the Mongols did not create an enduring civilization during their brief rule. Nevertheless, the Mongol conquests did have important consequences. Ask students to find information in the text identifying the consequences, and list students' responses on the board. The Mongols made the caravan routes across Central Asia safe for trade and travel. As a result, knowledge of gunpowder and reports about the wealth of Asia slowly spread westward. Tell students that the Mongol conquests also marked the end of an era. The Mongols were the last of many generations of nomadic invaders who burst out of the steppes to threaten civilization.

Check for Understanding Ask students to explain the significance of Genghis Khan, Kublai Khan, and Marco Polo to historical developments in China and Europe.

Practice

Guided Practice
Lead a guided discussion of the questions in Overhead Transparency 37 and in Section Review 2. (Answers follow.)

Define:
(a) person who travels from place to place rather than living in one location (b) dry grassland (c) Mongol leader (d) "divine wind"

Identify:
(a) ruled the largest unified land empire in history (b) leader who united Mongols (c) grandson of Genghis Khan and conqueror of Sung China (d) name of Kublai Khan's dynasty (e) served as an official in the court of Kublai Khan and spread information about China

Answer:
1. (a) nomadic (b) experienced in using bows while on horseback
2. organizational skill, shrewdness, cruelty
3. (a) most of Asia (b) Persia, Baghdad, Kievan Russia, eastern Europe, China (c) central steppes of Turkestan, Persia, Russia, and China
4. made the caravan routes across Asia safe
5. burning of coal, gift of 100,000 white horses, postal service on paved roads
6. (a) Kublai Khan spent nearly his whole life in China and adopted many of its ways. (b) Kublai Khan's highest officials were foreigners.

Independent Practice
Assign Independent Practice Worksheet 12.2.

Enrichment Activities

1. **Reading a Primary Source** Assign Voices form the Past Resource Book 12.12.

2. **Relating Past to Present: Present-Day Mongolia** Ask interested students to prepare a report on life in modern Mongolia. (See *National Geographic*, February 1985.)

3. **Researching for Bonus Points** Award bonus points to students who can answer this question: What was the name of Genghis Khan's capital and what is its only monumental remain? (Karakorum—a large stone tortoise)

Answers to Voice from the Past

1. square design, gates, street plan
2. Crowds and number of houses are greater than the mind can grasp and suburbs have even more people than cities.
3. Things that are rare and valuable in the world find their way to Khanbalik; number of pack-horses arriving; many merchants
4. laid out in squares, about the same size, same street plan; night curfew; both cities important trading centers

China chose stability over change.

3

Section Objectives

After completing Section 3, students should be able to:

1. locate the boundaries of the Ming Empire.
2. identify and describe the Forbidden City.
3. relate causes and effects in China's isolation during the Ming dynasty.

Setting the Stage

Begin by having students read the introduction (page 271). Ask students to recall the Mandate of Heaven and the dynastic cycle (discussed on page 78). Then ask students to assume the point of view of Chinese officials of about 1300. Ask, "How would you interpret the troubles experienced by the Mongol rulers?" Lead students to understand that from the Chinese point of view the Mongol leaders following Kublai Khan had clearly lost the Mandate of Heaven. Under such circumstances, the people had a right to rebel and to follow virtuous leaders who would establish a new dynasty. Tell students that this section describes how the Chinese overthrew the Mongols and established a new period of recovery and stability under the Ming dynasty.

Geography in History: Using Map Symbols (Objective 1) Have students refer to the map on page 271, or show Overhead Transparency 38, *China in Ming Times*. Have students add a symbol to their map keys on Outline Map 19 and use the symbol to show China during the Ming dynasty. Ask, "In which empire—Sui, T'ang, or Ming—did China have the largest land area?"

Teaching with Pictures: The Forbidden City (Objective 2) First, have students read the section, "The Ming dynasty brought peace" (pages 271–272). Then direct students' attention to the artistic recreation on page 272 of a courtyard in the Forbidden City. Explain that the Forbidden City was located in the heart of Peking (Beijing). It was the emperor's official residence and the Chinese saw it as the true center of their empire and of the world. The painting on page 272 shows one of the Forbidden City's three great throne halls. Its yellow-tiled roof symbolizes both the sun and the

emperor. The reddish-purple walls symbolize the North Star—the fixed point around which the heavens revolve. The Emperor's Honor Guard is shown standing at attention, waiting for the emperor to enter his royal litter and be carried to another part of the Forbidden City. Hundreds and sometimes thousands of attendants were required anytime the emperor moved from place to place. Ask students how the Chinese view of their place in the world might affect their relations with other civilizations.

Skill Building: Recognizing Cause and Effect (Objective 3) Point out that the Grand Fleet was the world's largest naval armada. It included over 100 ships manned by 27,000 sailors. The Grand Fleet vividly symbolized the power and potential of the Ming dynasty. However, the Ming emperors deliberately chose to abandon their naval program. Ask students to suggest possible reasons for this decision. Explain that the Chinese ruling classes were convinced of their cultural superiority, distrustful of foreign "barbarians," and satisfied to receive tribute and to exchange luxury goods. In addition, China's scholar-landlords opposed the naval program as a waste of resources. In the Chinese social system, merchants had low status. Ask students what events in contact with Europeans were contributing causes of China's growing isolation. Point out that the introduction of Christianity threatened the traditional culture and that Portuguese ships threatened China's ports.

Check for Understanding Ask students to identify the main causes of the rise and fall of the Ming dynasty.

Practice

Guided Practice
Lead a guided discussion of the questions in Overhead Transparency 38 and in Section Review 3. (Answers are below.)

Define:
ability to read and write

Identify:
(a) freed China from the Mongols and became first Ming emperor (b) dynasty that followed Mongol rule (c) capital of Ming T'ai-tsu, on the Yangtze River (d) Yung-lo's northern capital (e) walled city inside Imperial City (f) commander of China's Grand Fleet (g) Portuguese trading base in China (h) Italian missionary who studied and worked in Peking (i) land to the north and east of China (j) name of Manchu dynasty

Answer:

1. **(a)** Ming T'ai-tsu's son, Yung-lo, wanted to rule from the north and chose Khanbalik, which he renamed. **(b)** Forbidden City was a walled city inside the Imperial City.
2. establishment of elementary schools, publishing of an encyclopedia
3. **(a)** abandonment of Grand Fleet **(b)** He learned Chinese, dressed like a scholar-official, and impressed with his knowledge of astronomy.
4. corrupt officials, lack of money, high taxes, hunger, peasant revolt, Manchu invasion
5. to be associated with splendor, to administer a huge domain

Independent Practice

Assign Independent Practice Worksheet 12.3.
Assign Critical Thinking Worksheet 12.

Enrichment Activities

1. **Reading a Primary Source** Assign Voices from the Past Resource Book 12.3.
2. **Creative Writing** Ask advanced students to write essays hypothesizing how history might have changed if China had not abandoned its Grand Fleet.
3. **Researching for Bonus Points** Award bonus points to students who can find the answer to this question: How did court officials and guests show proper respect to the emperor? (They "kowtowed" by kneeling and touching the ground with their foreheads.)

Japan developed a unique civilization.   4

Section Objectives

After completing Section 4, students should be able to:

1. describe Japan's geography and explain its influence on Japanese culture.
2. explain how the Japanese adapted Chinese ideas.
3. discuss aspects of daily life during the Heian age.
4. identify the samurai and explain the code of bushido.

Setting the Stage

Using Geographic Themes: Human-Environment Interactions (Objective 1) Introduce this section by showing Overhead Transparency 39, *Japan, 1200–1600.* Point out that Japan is an archipelago that includes about 3,000 volcanic islands. Most Japanese have always lived on the four largest islands: Hokkaido, Honshu, Shikoku, and Kyushu. Now distribute Outline Map 19, and have students label these four islands.

Ask students how the island geography of Japan might have affected Japanese life. Suggest that the mountainous, volcanic islands were barriers to Japan's political unification. In addition, the small size of areas suitable for farming meant that the Japanese had to be very efficient in their use of land resources, and to use to the fullest all the food resources in the surrounding seas. With no other land to expand to as their population grew, Japanese communities developed ways of living together without feeling over-crowded. These ways included close family ties and the use of formal politeness. Tell students that the Japanese worshipped the beauty of their land. Landscape artists painted the mountains and volcanos, the birds and flowering trees, fishermen with their nets and boats, and the sea in all its moods. Tell students that this chapter describes the development of Japanese culture and the rise of feudalism in Japan.

Teaching Strategies

Using Geographic Themes: Movement (Objective 2) Ask students, "If you could send America's most valuable cultural gift to another people, what would you give?" List students' suggestions on the board and ask them to explain the reasons for their selections. Then explain that in A.D. 552 a Korean ruler sent ambassadors to Japan carrying his peoples' most valuable cultural gift—books of Buddhist doctrine and a gold and copper image of the Buddha. The introduction of Buddhism awakened Japan's interest in Chinese civilization. During the next 200 years, the Japanese sent many scholars to study Chinese ways. As noted in the text, the Japanese adopted Chinese styles of architecture, painting, and writing. Point out that the Japanese are the first people we know about in history who deliberately transformed their own culture. Ask students to relate this aspect of Japan's history to other examples of cultural diffusion they have read about.

Discussing History: Life in Heian (Objective 3) Have students read, "Court Society developed at Heian" (pages 276–277). The nobles at Heian enjoyed lives of luxury and elegance. Ask students what they think of the idea that one had to write poetry to be accepted. Explain that court poetry expressed a sentiment expressed by the words *mono no aware* — a sadness at the transience of things. For example, men and women wrote poems about the reflection of a cherry blossom in a pond's surface, or the setting of a pale moon in a garden thick with mist. Point out that these examples illustrate the love of nature and romantic search for beauty that characterized Heian culture. Conclude by asking students to write examples of beautiful or inspiring fleeting moments in nature that they have noticed.

Discussing History: The Samurai Warrior (Objective 4) Samurai warriors were the heroes of Japan's feudal age. Unlike the poets of Heian, the samurai lived according to a harsh code called *bushido* that stressed the ideals of strength, courage, and physical hardship. Explain that dying an honorable death was deemed more important than living a long life. When news was brought of a husband's death, women of the warrior class were expected to rejoice.

Ask students to compare and contrast the Samurai and the knights of medieval Europe. Students should recognize that bushido and chivalry had similar elements as formal codes of conduct suitable to feudal relationships. Point out that these codes represented law and order in societies lacking a central authority.

Check for Understanding Ask students to explain the roles of clans, nobles, samurai, and shoguns in Japan's history.

Practice

Guided Practice
Lead a guided discussion of the questions in Overhead Transparency 39 and in Section Review 4. (Answers are below.)

Define:
(a) group of people who believed they were descended from the same ancestor (b) nature god (c) simple script used by Japanese women writers (d) warriors who fought for feudal lords (e) "the way of the warrior" (f) military dictator

Identify:
(a) leading clan of early Japan (b) chief religion of

early Japan (c) convert to Buddhism, largely responsible for spreading Chinese influence in Japan (d) Japanese capital from 710 to 784 (e) old name for Kyoto; name of Japan's golden age (f) modern city, formerly Heian (g) author of *The Tale of Genji* (h) name of clan whose leader was first to be named shogun (i) site of shogun's military headquarters

Answer:
1. (a) 500 miles east of China (b) mountainous islands with land area size of California; temperate climate; forests; only one fifth of land suitable for farming
2. (a) writing system, landscape painting, architecture, arts of everyday living, government (b) tried to introduce examination system and build a strong central government
3. (a) golden age when Heian was capital of Japan (b) Nobles lived an elegant life, outdoors as much as possible. They dressed in colorful clothes, used cosmetics heavily, and wrote poetry.
4. (a) Each lord had bodyguard of loyal warriors. Lesser lords fought for greater lords in exchange for protection. (b) lived by harsh code of honor, courage, and loyalty
5. (a) powers of a military dictator (b) Early shogunates built upon feudal system.
6. (a) Both were nominally ruled by an emperor. (b) Differences: In Japan, the emperor had little real power; Japan was a country where noble birth was necessary to winning power and only a few great families held power; Japan had long periods of rule by military dictators called shoguns.

Independent Practice
Assign Independent Practice Worksheet 12.4.

Enrichment Activities

1. **Reading a Primary Source** Assign Voices from the Past Resource Book 12.4.

2. **Preparing a Report** Have students prepare a report on one of the following topics: the training and equipment of samurai warriors, the art of women of the Heian Court, Shintoism, and the imperial cities of Nara and Kyoto.

3. **Researching for Bonus Points** Award bonus points to students who can find the answer to this question: Who was the legendary founder of the Japanese imperial family? (Emperor Jimmu)

Japan turned to isolation.   5

Section Objectives

After completing Section 5, students should be able to:

1. describe the impact of the Portuguese on Japan.
2. identify Oda Nobunaga, Toyotomi Hideyoshi, and Tokugawa Ieyasu and explain how they unified Japan.
3. define Zen Buddhism and give examples of its influence on Japanese culture.

Setting the Stage

Ask students to recall that conditions in the Roman Empire after Rome's victory over Carthage led to the collapse of the republic and to an era of civil wars. Then ask students to find an example in this section of a similar situation. Students should note that the Japanese victory over the Mongols also led to conditions that caused the collapse of government and civil war. Point out that the long struggle against the Mongols drained the Japanese economy and led to the collapse of the Kamakura shogunate. During the ensuing Age of the Country at War, more than sixty independent rulers struggled for power. Tell students that this section describes how a series of strong leaders restored order. It also discusses the effects of contact with Portuguese merchants and missionaries and Japan's decision to isolate itself from European culture.

Teaching Strategies

Using Geographic Themes: Movement (Objective 1) Have students read the sections, "Europeans reached Japan" and "Japan's door slammed shut." Explain that the Portuguese contact with Japan provides an example of the movement of cultural ideas and products. The Portuguese introduced the Japanese to Arabian ponies, clocks, playing cards, pantaloons, spectacles, Christianity, and guns. Point out that a series of ruthless daimyos used the new firearms to help them restore order and unify Japan. Ask students what goods the Portuguese merchants sought in Japan. Point out that wealthy Europeans wanted silks, spices, porcelains, and other luxury goods. Ask students why the Japanese were not particularly impressed with

the Portuguese. Conclude by having students discuss why Tokugawa Ieyasu banned Christianity.

Discussing History: The Three Unifiers (Objective 2) Have students read the section, "Strong leaders restored order" (page 279). Ask students to make a chart on the chalkboard comparing the contributions of Nobunaga, Hideyoshi, and Ieyasu in unifying Japan. Students should note that Nobunaga's use of firearms enabled him to gain control over about one-third of Japan. Hideyoshi successfully united Japan, but failed to establish a new ruling dynasty. That accomplishment was left to Tokugawa Ieyasu. The last of Japan's great unifiers, Ieyasu defeated his remaining rivals, assumed the title of Shogun, and moved Japan's capital to the then small village of Edo. Conclude by asking students to explain how Ieyasu protected his power.

Teaching with Pictures: Zen Gardens (Objective 3) Explain that Zen enlightenment did not require one to spend long hours studying Buddhist scriptures. Instead, Zen Buddhists sought spiritual enlightenment through self-discipline and meditation. Have students read the sections, "Zen Buddhism stressed meditation" and "Art suggested nature." Ask, "How did Zen influence Japanese culture?" Point out that the Zen emphasis on meditation strongly influenced painting, the tea ceremony, and gardening. Direct students' attention to the picture of a Zen garden (page 281). Ask students how the garden's design might promote a meditative calm. In addition to order and simplicity, Zen gardens have elements that are intended to be interpreted symbolically. Thus, the sand might represent water, and the rocks, mountains. (For a photo-essay on Zen gardens see, *The Lords of Japan* by Henry Wiencek.)

Check for Understanding Ask students to explain the significance of each of the following in Japan's history from 1300 to 1600: Francis Xavier, daimyos, Toyotomi Hideyoshi, and Zen Buddhism.

Practice

Guided Practice

Lead a guided discussion of the questions in Section Review 5. (Answers are below.)

Define:
(a) feudal lord who became a nearly independent ruler (b) Japanese name for Portuguese sailors

Identify:
(a) leader of first Christian mission to Japan (b) ruthless daimyo who began the process of uniting Japan (c) successor to Nobunaga, regarded

as greatest of Japan's founders (d) last of Japan's unifiers (e) meditation (f) Zen monk and artist

Answer:
1. Rival armies attacked and burned the capital; disorder spread through the country.
2. (a) 1543 (b) with amusement and courtesy
3. (a) conquered and ruled area around and including Kyoto (b) conquered daimyos who defied him, set up strict divisions between social classes (c) completed unification
4. (a) required them to spend half their time in Edo to keep them from rebelling (b) banned Christianity and merchants except Dutch
5. (a) isolation from European countries (b) Japan had a long period of peace but fell behind Europe in science, technology, and military power.
6. (a) In early days, policy allowed Christians to travel about and make converts; later, policy banned Christianity. (b) feared Christians might side with Europeans in case of invasion, influence of missionaries

Independent Practice
Assign Independent Practice Worksheet 12.5.
Assign Basic Skills Worksheet 12.

Enrichment Activities

1. **Reading a Primary Source** Assign Voices from the Past Resource Book 12.5.

2. **Preparing a Report** Have interested students prepare reports on Japanese castles. A photo-essay on a castle known as the White Heron is found in *Early Japan* by Jonathan Leonard. Other topics for reports might include Zen gardens, the art of bonsai, and Japanese floral arrangements.

3. **Researching for Bonus Points** Award bonus points to students who can answer this question: What was Toyotomi Hideyoshi's nickname? (Monkey-Face)

Concluding the Chapter

1. **Chapter Closer**
   Have students compare the development of China and Japan between the years 300 and 1650. Students should identify main similarities and differences.

2. **Reteaching Activities**
   a. **Making a Chart** Ask students to make a chart on the Chinese dynasties studied in this chapter. The chart should include these

headings: Name of dynasty, Period of rule, Major contributions, and Causes of decline.
   b. **Making a Time Line** Have students make a time line showing the key events in Japanese history discussed in this chapter.
   c. **Identifying Historical Figures** List the following names on the chalkboard and ask students to identify each: T'ai-tsung, Empress Wu, Genghis Khan, Marco Polo, T'ai-tsu, Cheng Ho, Prince Shotoku, Lady Murasaki, Francis Xavier, and Tokugawa Ieyasu.

3. **Chapter Review Activities**
   Assign Chapter Review 12 activities.

Chapter Evaluation

Chapter Test 12 and Computer Test Bank Chapter 12 Test can be used to evaluate your students' understanding of this chapter.

Answers to Chapter Review 12

Reviewing the Facts
1. **a.** large group of well-to-do people who rank below nobles but above common people **b.** dry grassland region **c.** Mongol leader **d.** group of people who believed they were descended from the same ancestor **e.** warriors who fought for lords **f.** military dictator **g.** strong feudal lord
2. **a.** dynasty that united China in the late 500's **b.** dynasty in power during China's golden age (618–907) **c.** capital of T'ang China **d.** Chinese religion brought by Koreans to Japan **e.** dynasty that marked beginning of Chinese military decline **f.** trading route between China and Europe **g.** homeland of the Mongols **h.** leader who united Mongols **i.** conqueror of Sung China **j.** Venetian official in the court of Kublai Khan **k.** capital city of Kublai Khan **l.** dynasty that followed Mongol rule **m.** Yung-lo's northern capital, formerly Khanbalik **n.** name of Manchu dynasty **o.** chief religion of early Japan **p.** old name for Kyoto and name of Japan's golden age **q.** written by Lady Murasaki Shikibu; has been called the world's first novel **r.** leader of first Christian mission to Japan **s.** shogun who moved government to Edo (Tokyo)

3. **(a)** by passing 3 exams **(b)** freedom from paying taxes, serving in the army, performing manual labor; also, could gain land and fortune
4. printing, magnetic compass, gunpowder
5. **(a)** organizational skill, shrewdness, and cruelty **(b)** central steppes of Turkestan, Persia, Russia, China
6. **(a)** welcoming **(b)** isolation

Basic Skills

1. Approximate answers: **(a)** 4400 and 1800 miles; **(b)** 2000 and 600 miles; **(c)** 8,800,000 and 1,080,000 square miles; Mongol empire approximately 8 times the size of Alexander's empire

2.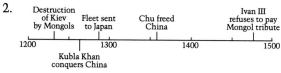

3. *Political*—T'ang: vast empire, scholar officials, capital Chang'an; Sung: smaller empire mostly in south, capital Hangchow; Ming: united China, capital Nanking in south, moved to Peking in north which enclosed Imperial City and Forbidden City, scholar officials. *Economic* —T'ang: lowered taxes, gave land to poor, expanded trade by land and sea; Sung: paid Tatars for peace with silk, silver and tea, had paper money, traded silk and porcelain; Ming: traded with Africa, abandoned Grand Fleet and sea trade, closed harbors to Europeans, opened trading post at Macao. *Cultural*—T'ang: drums regulate city, poetry, Confucianism, interest in foreign culture; Sung: gunpowder, printing, compass, poetry, golden age of painting; Ming: emphasis on education, elementary schools, high literacy, revival of Confucianism, encyclopedia, rejection of foreign influence.

Researching and Reporting Skills

1. Students' research findings will vary.
2. Answers will vary. Students might select the T'ang for their scholarship, political and economic achievements, the Sung for their poetry and painting, or the Ming for their peace and prosperity, literacy and preservation of the past.
3. Examples of research questions: How did Buddhism influence art or customs in China? In Japan? In what ways did the Japanese modify Buddhism?

Critical Thinking

1. Feudalism in both Europe and Japan was built on complex networks of personal loyalties among nobles—the king, vassals, and knights in Europe, and the emperor, shogun, daimyos and samurai in Japan. The objects of relationships were land, power, protection, and prestige. The labor of peasants supported both feudal systems. Feudalism arose in Europe through the lack of strong, centralized governing authorities, and declined as kings consolidated their power and as an independent, urban middle class emerged. Feudalism arose in Japan through competition between landowners and governing authorities and ended in civil war among the daimyos, leading to absolute rule by the victorious daimyo.
2. **(a)** as barbarians **(b)** despised them and their civilization **(c)** Students might say Mongols were great for their military skills, endurance, but cruel, destructive, and lacking in civilized ways.
3. **(a)** Patterns include growing internal problems, such as peasant rebellions due to excessive taxes and the decline of trade; **(b)** Advice might include: treat your peasants well, keep trade flourishing, be prepared to defend your frontiers.
4. **(a)** simplicity of line, appreciation for beauty of the moment, of nature, landscapes, pagodas with winglike roofs **(b)** influence of China on Japan in early times: influence of Buddhism, Taoism, and Zen.

Perspectives on Past and Present

1. China—loss of interest in exploration and trade, horror of European "ocean devils;" Japan —fear of influence of missionaries, invasion. Today, Japan limits imports. Advantages: protects Japanese goods from outside competition; prevents or lessens foreign debt. Disadvantage: isolates from new ideas and goods.
2. Long fingernails were a sign that a man did not perform manual labor. Women whose feet had been bound could do little household work. Modern status symbols are usually a display of expensive items, such as home, car, or jewelry.

Investigating History

Students' reports will vary.

Civilizations of India and Southeast Asia

Chapter Overview

After the Mauryan dynasty fell in 180 B.C., India was beset by 500 years of invasions until the Gupta dynasty ushered in a golden age in northern India. Science, learning, and the arts thrived during the Gupta period. Under constant attack by the Huns, the dynasty disappeared during the 600's and six centuries of turmoil ensued. First, Rajput warrior-kings ruled in northern India. They became Hindu converts and built kingdoms and great temples. In the 700's, wars between Hindus and Muslims ended in Muslim rule by the Delhi sultans. Tamerlane, a Turkish-Mongol conqueror from central Asia, destroyed Delhi in 1398 but failed to build an empire that outlasted his life. Turkish sultans ruled from a rebuilt Delhi, but none was able to dominate India. In 1526, Babur, another Turkish-Mongol conqueror, ended the Delhi sultanate and established the Mughal dynasty. The Mughals were Muslim, although early Mughal rulers tolerated other religions. However, later Mughal rulers oppressed non-Muslims and left a heritage of bitter religious conflict. Europeans reached India in 1498 and began setting up strong bases along the major Asian sea lanes.

Except in Vietnam, where China's influence was strong, Indian culture was the main influence in Southeast Asia, the area that includes the modern countries of Burma, Laos, Kampuchea, Thailand, Vietnam, Malaysia, and Indonesia. In this region of diverse languages and cultures, control of harbors and trade routes was the key to power. The Khmers built the longest-lasting empire in this region where many kingdoms rose and fell. Between the 1200's and 1400's, Muslim traders introduced the religion of Islam, which soon became important in the area along with Hinduism and Buddhism.

Key Term

purdah
For additional exercises, see Vocabulary Worksheet 13.

Chapter Focus

Ask students to name the most beautiful building they have ever seen. Then direct their attention to the picture of the Taj Mahal (page 284). Ask, "How does the Taj Mahal compare with your building?" Explain that the Taj Mahal was built by a husband to honor his wife's last request. Just before she died, Mumtaz Mahal asked Shah Jahan to build a monument that expressed "the eternal wonder of the power of love and the inevitability of its passing with death." Have students read the description of the Taj Mahal on pages 284–285. Explain that the Taj Mahal is more than an expression of love. It is also a symbol of the two religions—Hindu and Muslim—that together shaped Indian history from 300 to 1700. Tell students that this chapter begins with a discussion of a dynasty of Hindu rulers who created a golden age of Indian culture. It then describes how the Muslims conquered India and produced a golden age of their own. The chapter concludes with a discussion of the kingdoms that arose in Southeast Asia.

India flourished under the Guptas. 1

Section Objectives

After completing Section 1, students should be able to:

1. identify scientific advances made by Gupta scholars.
2. describe the Ajanta temples.
3. explain how the Hindus and Muslims became fierce rivals.

Setting the Stage

Show students Overhead Transparency 7, *India under the Mauryan Dynasty*. Ask, "Who can identify the Mauryans?" Explain that 500 years of disunity followed the end of the Mauryan dynasty. Now show Overhead Transparency 40, *The Gupta Empire*. Describe how the Gupta dynasty conquered a mighty empire that ruled northern India during the fourth and fifth centuries. Tell students that this section describes the achievements of the Gupta dynasty.

Teaching Strategies

Discussing History: The Achievements of Indian Science (Objective 1) Begin by writing "XXIV + LIX = ?" and "34 + 59 = ?" on the chalkboard. Ask students which equation is easier to solve. Have students suggest advantages of Arabic numerals. (place value system, use of zero as a place holder) Explain that Europeans called the concepts zero to nine Arabic numerals because Arabs brought the symbols and the number system to Europe. Point out that, during the Gupta period, Hindu mathematicians were actually the first to use a system of numbers based on ten. Have students read the section, "Science and learning advanced" (page 286) to find out what other intellectual advances were made during the Gupta dynasty. Students might be interested to learn that Indians discovered the process for twisting cotton fibers into a fine thread. Arabs called the lightweight Indian fabric *quittan*—hence our word *cotton*. The fabrics we call cashmere, calico, chintz, and dungaree were also first worn in India.

Teaching with Pictures: The Ajanta Caves (Objective 2) Direct students' attention to the picture of

Advance Planner

Chapter 13 Focus	Civilizations of India and Southeast Asia 300–1700 The Taj Majal as a symbol of forces that shaped Indian history		★ Advanced ● Basic
	Section 1	**Section 2**	**Section 3**
Objectives	1. Identify scientific advances made by Gupta scholars. 2. Describe the Ajanta temples. 3. Explain how the Hindus and Muslims became fierce rivals.	1. Identify Akbar and describe his achievements. 2. Compare and contrast the extremes of wealth and poverty in the Mughal empire. 3. Locate strategic bases in the Indian Ocean trade and explain their significance to the Portuguese.	1. Label the major rivers, bodies of water, and countries of Southeast Asia. 2. Identify and describe Angkor Wat. 3. Describe the impact of Chinese influence on the Vietnamese.
Setting the Stage	Comparing the Mauryan and Gupta empires Transparency 7 Transparency 40	India as a land of contrasts	Stereotypes of Vietnam
Teaching Strategies	Discussing History: The Achievements of Indian Science Teaching with Pictures: The Ajanta Caves Relating Past and Present: Conflict between Hindus and Muslims Check for Understanding	Discussing History: Akbar, the "Very Great" Mughal Skill Building: Comparing and Contrasting Using Geographic Themes: Location Check for Understanding	Geography in History: Strategic Waterways of Southeast Asia Transparency 41 Outline Map 24 Teaching with Pictures: Angkor Wat Discussing History: China and Vietnam Check for Understanding
Guided Practice	Transparency 40 Q&A Section Review 1	Section Review 2	Transparency 41 Q&A Section Review 3
Independent Practice Worksheets	Independent Practice 13.1 Vocabulary 13	Independent Practice 13.2 Basic Skills 13 Critical Thinking 13	Independent Practice 13.3
Enrichment	1. Primary Source: Voices 13.1 2. Reading a Play 3. Researching for Points	1. Primary Source: Voices 13.2 2. Preparing a Report 3. ★Solving a Riddle 4. Researching for Points	1. Primary Source: Voices 13.3 2. Preparing a Report 3. Researching for Points
Chapter Closer ● **Reteaching Activities**	Summarizing, Making a Time Line, Finding Main Ideas		
Chapter Review	Summary, Reviewing the Facts, Basic Skills, Researching and Reporting Skills, Critical Thinking, Perspectives on Past and Present, Investigating History		
Chapter Evaluation	Chapter Test 13, Computer Test Bank Chapter 13 Test		

the Ajanta caves (page 287). Explain that the caves are actually twenty-nine tunnels cut at regular intervals into a granite cliff. Each tunnel penetrates the rock to a depth of about sixty-five feet. The caves contain well-preserved murals illustrating Buddha's life and incarnations. Colonies of Buddhist monks once slept on stone pillows that lined a series of small chambers. Everything in the cave—statues, columns, living quarters—was chiselled from the cliff wall. Tell students that the last caves were created in the seventh century, just as India's golden age was coming to an end. The abandoned caves were not rediscovered until the nineteenth century.

Relating Past and Present: Conflict between Hindus and Muslims (Objective 3) Have students examine the map of modern South Asia (page 739). Explain that Pakistan and Bangladesh are Muslim nations while India is a Hindu nation. Point out that this modern division has its roots in the conflict between Hindus and Muslims that began during the 700's. Have students read the sections, "Hindus and Muslims met in war" and "Muslim sultans ruled from Delhi" (pages 287–288). Ask, "Why did Muslims and Hindus develop such a bitter conflict?" Explain that religious differences were at the center of the conflict. Muslim conquerors such as Mahmud of Ghazni plundered Indian temples and destroyed centuries worth of work.

Check for Understanding Have students explain the significance of each of the following for Indian history: the Gupta dynasty, Kalidasa, the Ajanta caves, the Rajputs, and Mahmud of Ghazni.

Practice

Guided Practice
Lead a guided discussion of the questions in Overhead Transparency 40 and in Section Review 1. (Answers are below.)

Define:
(a) oral accounts of Indian history (b) social grouping in Indian society (c) injection to prevent disease (d) one of eight pure emotions that formed the basis of Indian drama (e) rite in which faithful Hindu wife dies honorably on her husband's funeral pyre (f) Turkish Muslim leader

Identify:
(a) builder of the Taj Mahal (b) wife in whose memory Taj Mahal was built (c) India's greatest monument (d) first of Gupta dynasty (e) rulers who brought golden age to India (f) number system based on ten, first used by Hindu mathematicians (g) great Indian poet and dramatist (h) warlike

tribes from Asia who attacked and destroyed Gupta empire (i) warrior-kings who ruled small kingdoms in northern India in the 800's and 900's (j) Muslims from Afghanistan who conquered India and set up the Delhi sultanate

Answer:
1. (a) united the region and led it into a golden age (b) inoculation, surgery, number system based on ten, great dramatic works
2. invasion of the Huns
3. (a) honor and bravery (b) devotion to her husband
4. rising importance of three Hindu gods—Brahman, Shiva, and Vishnu; decline of Buddhism as a separate religion
5. (a) rule of northern India by Turkish sultans in Delhi (b) Muhammad Ghuri conquered city after city, destroying much of northern India. (c) Hindus treated as conquered peoples.
6. (a) religion of people conquered by Turks, blended with Buddhism (b) almost ceased to exist as a separate faith (c) religion of Turkish rulers

Independent Practice
Assign Independent Practice Worksheet 13.1.
Assign Vocabulary Worksheet 13.

Enrichment Activities

1. **Reading a Primary Source** Assign Voices from the Past Resource Book 13.1.

2. **Reading a Play** Encourage interested students to read *Shakuntala* by Kalidasa. One source is *Masterpieces of the Orient*, edited by G.L. Anderson. Have students prepare an oral presentation for the class giving a synopsis of the plot and excerpts that reflect the love of nature characteristic of both Hinduism and Buddhism.

3. **Researching for Bonus Points** Award bonus points to students who can find the answer to this question: How does the play *Shakuntala* end? (The king finds a magic ring that he had given to Shakuntala. He then recovers his memory and the pair are reunited.)

Answers to Voice from the Past

1. (a) espionage (b) impoverishment
2. (a) Muslim (b) the Koran
3. reduction to poverty to make obedient, submissive
4. to prevent rebellion in which many would die.

Mughals ruled India in splendor.

2

Section Objectives

After completing Section 2, students should be able to:

1. identify Akbar and describe his achievements.
2. compare and contrast the extremes of wealth and poverty in the Mughal empire.
3. locate strategic bases in the Indian Ocean trade and explain their significance to the Portuguese.

Setting the Stage

Explain that many historians have described India as a land of contrasts. Ask students to give examples justifying this claim. Students should identify the contrast between Muslims and Hindus, studied in Section 1. Explain that this section describes the contrast between the incredible wealth of India's Mughal rulers and the desperate poverty of India's people. It also introduces the first Europeans to reach India's coast and contrasts their rising strength with India's declining power.

Teaching Strategies

Discussing History: Akbar, the "Very Great" Mughal (Objective 1) Ask students to list Akbar's achievements. Explain that Akbar was a successful commander who extended the Mughal empire to include almost all of northern India and much of the Deccan. Akbar was also an inventor who designed a crude machine gun that fired fourteen rifles at once. He also created a huge cannon and built a portable war tent with two bedrooms. Finally, Akbar was a religious philosopher who created a new religion. Ask students to identify Akbar's strategies for securing power.

Skill Building: Comparing and Contrasting (Objective 2) Direct students' attention to the painting of the Red Fort (page 291). Explain that the Red Fort was one of three royal residences. Shah Jahan's apartments gleamed with ruby-encrusted ornaments and ceilings of solid gold. As the emperor strode from room to room, he could listen to music performed by musicians stationed throughout the Red Fort. While Shah Jahan performed state duties, a team of kitchen slaves kept fifteen complete meals ready to be served at a moment's notice.

Tell students that Shah Jahan's incredible wealth dazzled European visitors, but the same travelers were also shocked by the poverty and misery they saw throughout the Mughal empire. Have students read the two descriptions of poverty on pages 290–292. Ask them to identify the causes of this difference between wealth and poverty.

Using Geographic Themes: Location (Objective 3) Explain that some geographic locations are more strategic or advantageous than others. Ask students to recall why the locations of Rome and Constantinople were strategic. Then have the class read the section, "Europeans reached India's coast." Ask, "Which four bases did the Portuguese use to dominate trade in the Indian Ocean?" Use the map on page 813 to locate these bases. Have students explain why these locations had such great strategic value.

Check for Understanding Ask students to explain the significance of Mughal and Portuguese influence on Indian history.

Practice

Guided Practice
Lead a guided discussion of the questions in Section Review 2. (Answers are below.)

Define:
(a) Muslim practice of keeping women in seclusion (b) religious teacher

Identify:
(a) conqueror of Delhi (b) Turkish-Mongol conqueror from central Asia who set up Mughal empire (c) empire established by Babur (d) Babur's grandson who greatly expanded Mughal empire (e) son of Shah Jahan who tried to make empire an Islamic state (f) followers of Nanak who tried to blend Islam and Hinduism (g) Portuguese captain who reached India by sailing around Africa

Answer:
1. (a) gravely weakened (b) undone entirely
2. greatly expanded Mughal empire; treated Hindus with respect and invited them to help rule
3. royal: ornate, elaborate, splendid palaces such as the Taj Mahal; poor: mud-thatched roofs, little furniture, few bedclothes for warmth
4. clothing style, veiled women's faces, purdah
5. (a) Control of sea lanes around India passed to outsiders. (b) set up strong bases at strategic points all along the major Asian sea lanes
6. (a) Hindus were polytheists, Muslims were

monotheists; Hinduism accepted castes, Islam treated all believers equally. **(b)** Akbar eased tension by bringing Hindus into government and society; Aurangzeb and Shah Jahan increased tension by being cruel to Hindus, destroying Hindu temples, and taxing non-Muslims heavily.

Independent Practice
Assign Independent Practice Worksheet 13.2.
Assign Geography Skills Worksheet 13.
Assign Basic Skills Worksheet 13.
Assign Critical Thinking Worksheet 13.

Enrichment Activities

1. **Reading a Primary Source** Assign Voices from the Past Resource Book 13.2.

2. **Preparing a Report** The six Mughal rulers from Babur to Aurangzeb are known as the "Great Mughals." Ask students to prepare a report on one of these rulers. (See *National Geographic*, April 1985, and *The Taj Mahal* by David Carroll.)

3. **Solving a Riddle** Ask advanced students to prepare a report on Akbar's new religion, *Din Ilahi*. The report should also attempt to explain why the new religion failed to attract many followers. (See *The Taj Mahal* by David Carroll and *Our Oriental Heritage* by Will Durant.)

4. **Researching for Bonus Points** Award bonus points to students who can find the answer to this question: What inscription was carved on the ceiling of the emperor's throne room at the Red Fort? ("If anywhere on Earth there is paradise, It is Here! It is Here! It is Here!)

Kingdoms arose in Southeast Asia. 3

Section Objectives

After completing Section 3, students should be able to:

1. label the major rivers, bodies of water, and countries of Southeast Asia.
2. identify and describe Angkor Wat.
3. describe the impact of Chinese influence on the Vietnamese.

Setting the Stage

Introduce this section by writing "Southeast Asia" on the chalkboard. Then ask students to write down the first thought that comes to mind when they think of Southeast Asia. Call on a number of students and list their answers on the chalkboard. Many students will associate Southeast Asia with the Vietnam War. Explain that the Vietnam War had a significant impact on the recent history of this region. Tell students that this section describes the major civilizations and cultural influences that shaped Southeast Asia between 500 and 1500.

Teaching Strategies

Geography in History: Strategic Waterways of Southeast Asia (Objective 1) Distribute Outline Map 24, Southeast Asia. Using the text, or Overhead Transparency 41, *The Kingdoms of Southeast Asia*, have students label the major rivers (Irrawaddy, Salween, Chao Phraya, Mekong, Red) and the bodies of water into which the rivers flow (Irrawaddy and Salween: Andaman Sea; Chao Phraya: Gulf of Siam; Mekong and Red: South China Sea). Then have students locate and label the Strait of Malacca, Sunda Strait, and Java Sea. Ask, "Why are these waterways considered strategic?" (These narrow straits pass through an area with few sea routes. As a result, they control most sea traffic between the Indian and Pacific oceans.) Conclude this map activity by having students refer to the map on page 819 to help them label the present-day countries in Southeast Asia.

Teaching with Pictures: Angkor Wat (Objective 2) Have students locate Angkor on the map on page 293. Explain that the city of Angkor covered seventy-five square miles—an area more than twice as large as Manhattan. Then refer them to the picture of Angkor Wat (page 295). Point out that Angkor Wat is actually one of seventy-two major stone temples and monuments that stood inside Angkor. Angkor Wat was built by Suryavarman II to honor the Hindu god Vishnu. The moat symbolizes the oceans while the outer wall stands for the mountains at the end of the world. The five central towers represent the peaks of Mount Meru, the Hindu home of the gods and the celestial center of the universe. The temple was damaged during the Cambodian civil war. However, restoration was resumed in 1987.

Discussing History: China and Vietnam (Objective 3) Ask students to explain the consequences of the Chinese conquest of Vietnam. Point out

that the Chinese built dikes and introduced Buddhism. While the Vietnamese were willing to
learn from the Chinese, they resented outside rulers. Vietnamese soldiers used hit-and-run tactics
to drive out the larger Chinese armies. Emphasize
that the determination to be independent is an
important theme in Vietnamese history.

Check for Understanding Ask students to name
the two major influences on the cultures of Southeast Asia and to give examples of each influence.

Practice

Guided Practice
Lead a guided discussion of the questions in Over-
head Transparency 41 and in Section Review 3.
(Answers are below.)

Identify:
(a) body of water separating India and Southeast
Asia (b) area including modern-day countries of
Burma, Thailand, Laos, Kampuchea, Vietnam,
Malaysia, and Indonesia (c) peninsula off mainland whose gold attracted Indian traders (d) people
in Southeast Asia who built the longest-lasting
empire in the region (e) capital city of Khmer kingdom and name given to empire's greatest period

Answer:
1. (a) east of India across Bay of Bengal (b) islands
   separated by sea and straits, mountainous
   peninsula with many rivers
2. Indian traders and merchants and Buddhist
   missionaries helped to spread Indian culture.
3. (a) the area that is today Kampuchea (b) late
   500's; height 850–1250 (c) threats by Mongols,
   capture of Angkor War in 1430 by Thais
4. through Muslim traders from India and Arabia
5. dominated the culture of Vietnam
6. (a) Key to political power was control of trade
   routes and harbors; kings who protected
   merchants from pirates became powerful.
   (b) allowed Vietnam to fall under China's rule
   and influence; parts of region more easily accessible from India became subject to Indian influences; resources attracted foreign traders and
   explorers

Independent Practice
Assign Independent Practice Worksheet 13.3.

Enrichment Activities

1. **Reading a Primary Source** Assign Voices from
   the Past Resource Book 13.3.

2. **Preparing a Report** Ask interested students to
   prepare a report on Angkor Wat. (See *National
   Geographic*, April 1960 and May 1982.)

3. **Researching for Bonus Points** Award bonus
   points to students who can find the answer to
   this question: What is a wat? (A wat is a Buddhist monastery.)

Concluding the Chapter

1. **Chapter Closer**
   Have students identify three significant shifts
   in power in India's history and their consequences.

2. **Reteaching Activities**
   a. **Summarizing** Have students write a para-
      graph summarizing the scientific and cul-
      tural achievements of the Gupta period.
   b. **Making a Time Line** Have students prepare
      time lines showing key people and events in
      Indian history from Tamurlane to the arrival
      of the Portuguese.
   c. **Finding Main Ideas** Ask students to turn
      each subheading in Section 3 into a ques-
      tion and then write two answers for each
      question.

3. **Chapter Review Activities**
   Assign Chapter Review 13 Activities.

Chapter Evaluation

Chapter Test 13 and Computer Test Bank Chapter
13 Test can be used to evaluate your students'
understanding of this chapter.

Answers to Chapter Review 13

Reviewing the Facts
1. Muslim practice of keeping women in seclusion
2. a. brought golden age to India b. first of Gupta
   dynasty c. great Indian poet and dramatist
   d. destroyed Gupta empire e. warrior-kings
   who ruled small kingdoms in northern India
   f. important Hindu gods g. Muslims who conquered India h. city from which northern India

was ruled by Turkish sultans **i.** conqueror of Delhi **j.** empire established by Babur **k.** greatly expanded Mughal empire **l.** India's greatest monument **m.** followers of Nanak **n.** Portuguese reached India by sailing around Africa **o.** built longest-lasting empire of the region **p.** Khmer temple to Vishnu

3. union of northern India under one ruler; inoculation, surgery, number system based on ten, great dramatic works

4. **(a)** Rajputs converted to Hinduism, built temples. **(b)** almost ceased to exist as separate faith **(c)** beginning of hatred between Muslims and Hindus

5. ruled fairly and expanded empire

6. **(a)** Indian jewels, spices, and cloth sold for high prices in Europe. **(b)** They set up bases along major Asian sea lanes.

7. The presence of many islands, rivers, hills, and mountains limited travel, communication, and the development of unity.

8. India, China, and, later, European countries

Basic Skills

1. **(a)** during Khmer Empire: first Muslim invasion of India, rise of Rajput kingdoms, building of Angkor Wat **(b)** 603 years

2. **(a)** Chandra Gupta, Samudra Gupta, Chandra Gupta II, Rajput warrior kings, Mahmud of Ghazni, Muhammad Ghuri, Turkish sultans, Tamerlane, Babur, Akbar, Nur Jahan, Shah Jahan, Aurangzeb ordered destruction of Hindu temples. **(b)** Comments on each leader will vary.

3. Summary should mention location, splendor of Angkor period, Angkor Wat, aristocrats' life style, women's status, influence of Muslim traders, fall of empire.

4. Notes should mention conquest of Indus valley (712); Mahmud's troops' sacking Indian cities, taking Hindus into slavery (917); Muhammad Ghuri's revenge and destruction of Nalanda (1191); Delhi sultans' treatment of Hindus; Akbar's tolerance and cooperation with Hindus (1156); his successors' intolerance and persecution of Hindus and Sikhs.

Researching and Reporting Skills
Students' findings will vary.

Critical Thinking
1. China: considered foreigners "ocean devils," limited trading to Macao; Japan: welcomed by some daimyos, considered amusing "southern barbarians," traded silk for guns; India: Mughals showed little interest, allowed spice trade to develop, and Portuguese to set up trading bases.

2. **(a)** Rajputs: women respected, had property rights; highest virtue was devotion to husband demonstrated by suttee; Mughals: Hindu as well as Muslim women adopted purdah and veiled their faces. **(b)** In Southeast Asia women had higher status; lower class women could trade; women could be royal judges; all royal guards and servants were women.

3. **(a)** Similarities might include: onion domes in St. Basil, Taj Mahal and Red Fort; pointed dome in Dome of the Rock; pointed arches in Dome of the Rock, Taj Mahal, Red Fort; ornate decorations with geometric patterns in stone work or mosaic in all four. **(b)** possible hypothesis: Mughal architecture was influenced by Russian, Byzantine, and Islamic styles of architecture as a result of Turkish conquests. **(c)** further research: trace styles found in Mughal architecture back to other examples of Byzantine and Islamic architecture along the routes of conquest by the Turks.

4. Possible answers include: **(a)** An all-inclusive religion might help unify Indians but might antagonize people from different faiths. **(b)** Students might adopt a policy of tolerance for all religions to foster respect, openness and understanding.

5. Situated on sea routes linking Europe, India, and Africa with China and Japan; many ethnic groups with different languages passed through and settled; meeting place of Indian and Chinese culture, and of three major religions.

Perspectives on Past and Present
Students might refer to the long history of extremes of wealth and poverty in India, institutionalized in the caste system and the Hindu belief in Karma.

Investigating History
Students' answers will vary, but should include the information that the Ganges is sacred to Hindus. All three rivers are important as sources of water for irrigation. All are also prone to flooding because of seasonal rains and deforestation.

Africa and the Americans

Chapter Overview

Geographically, Africa is divided into four regions —the northern and southern coasts, the deserts, the savannas, and the rain forest. Historically, the Sahara has been a dividing line in Africa. People south of the Sahara often traded with North Africa, but their cultures were very different. Among the great societies south of the Sahara were those of Meroe (the Kushite capital), Axum, and the Swahili city-states Malindi, Mombasa, and Zanzibar—all in the east. In the 1500's, the Portuguese conquered the Swahili cities along Africa's east coast. Between A.D. 300 and 1600 three empires, Ghana, Mali, and Songhai, rose in western Africa. All the African empires were important trading centers.

In North America, there were many Indian cultures and language groups. Two groups known to archaeologists are the Hopewell of the eastern woodlands and the Hohokam of the southwestern desert. In Mexico and Central and South America, three mighty empires developed. They were the Maya in Guatemala and southern Mexico, the Aztec in central Mexico, and the Inca in Peru. The earlier Olmecs influenced later civilizations.

Key Terms

oasis, savanna, lineage
For additional exercises, see Vocabulary Worksheet 14.

Chapter Focus

Begin by directing students' attention to the world map on page 819. Ask, "Can you locate a country where a major historic event could occur without the rest of the world finding out about it?" Point out that modern communications make it virtually impossible for any country to exist in complete isolation from the rest of the world. Have students read the chapter introduction (pages 298–299). Ask, "Which three continents had civilizations that were isolated from the rest of the world until the late 1400's?" Point out that the people living in sub-Saharan Africa, North America, and South America were isolated from each other and from the rest of the world. This chapter traces the rise and fall of the major civilizations that developed on the three continents. It also explains why they were isolated from civilizations in Europe and Asia.

Early Civilizations arose in Africa. 1

Section Objectives

After completing Section 1, students should be able to:

1. identify and describe the major climate regions in Africa.
2. locate on a map the major geographic regions of Africa.

Setting the Stage

Using Geographic Themes: Place and Location (Objective 1) Direct students' attention to the map of Africa (page 300). Point out that northern Africa is close to southern Europe and to the centers of civilization in the Fertile Crescent. Ask, "What geographic factors limited Africa's contact with Europe and Asia?" Explain that the Sahara Desert discouraged contact between Europe and sub-Saharan Africa. Then point out that Africa's long coastlines lack natural harbors and easily navigable rivers. Rivers fall steeply from the central African plateau. In addition, the prevailing winds on Africa's Atlantic coast blow from north to south. European ships could therefore travel down the coast but found it harder to return against the wind. Tell students that this section presents additional information on African geography and discusses Africa's unique cultural traditions.

Teaching Strategies

Using Geographic Themes: Desert Regions (Objective 2) Have students read "Africa has four major regions" (pages 299–300). Then direct their attention to the map showing the Sahara Desert on page 300, or use Overhead Transparency 42, *Regions of Africa*. Point out that the Sahara is as large as the United States and contains half of the world's desert surface. Ask students what natural factors cause desert regions. Explain that the Sahara's dryness originates in the rainy tropics at the Equator. As the hot equatorial air rises it loses its moisture and cools. The cooled air then falls and is warmed up again (between 15° and 30° north latitude), but over the desert the air is too dry for clouds and rain to form. Point out that the Sahara's size and extent have changed many times. Ask students what factors in human-environment interaction contribute to the spread of deserts. Tell students that a combination of drought, deforestation, and overgrazing is currently causing the Sahara to expand at an alarming rate. During the past half century over 400,000 square miles of once productive land on the southern edge of the Sahara has become desert.

Distribute Outline Map 13: Africa. Have students design a map key to illustrate the geographic regions of Africa. Then have them label the major rivers.

Check for Understanding Have students write a paragraph describing Africa's four regions and identifying three widespread cultural traditions in African societies.

Practice

Guided Practice
Lead a guided discussion of the questions in Overhead Transparency 42 and in Section Review 1. (Answers are below.)

Define:
(a) place in desert where underground water comes to the surface (b) grassy plain with scattered trees (c) group in which all members believe they are descended from a common ancestor (d) belief in one supreme God (e) belief in many gods (f) village member trained in communicating with spirits (g) record keeper who memorized and passed down history orally

Identify:
(a) largest desert in the world (b) Africa's second longest river

Answer:
1. northern and southern coasts, deserts, savannas, and rain forest
2. (a) farming and herding (b) fishing and growing of root crops
3. took the place of kings or other rulers; served

religious functions
4. Most African groups honored many gods and spirits, but they believed in a principal creator.
5. orally, through griots
6. The spirits of departed ancestors were the guardians of traditions, values, and laws. To bring good fortune, families believed they had to honor the traditions of lineage ancestors

Independent Practice
Assign Independent Practice Worksheet 14.1.
Assign Vocabulary Worksheet 14.
Assign Basic Skills Worksheet 14.

Enrichment Activities

1. **Reading a Primary Source** Assign Voices from the Past Resource Book 14.1.

2. **Preparing a Report** Have students prepare a report on African sculpture. (See *The African Kings* by Mary Cable and *African Kingdoms* by Basil Davidson.) Alternatively, interested students might prepare a report on the impact of the expansion of desert on present-day Africa.

3. **Researching for Bonus Points** Award bonus points to students who can find the answer to this question: What are the names of four of the deserts located in Africa? (Sahara, Namib, Nubian, and Kalahari.)

African empires thrived on trade. 2

Section Objectives

After completing Section 2, students should be able to:

1. describe the economic importance of eastern Africa's Indian Ocean trade.
2. explain the economic significance of West African gold–salt trade.
3. identify the Kingdom of Axum and describe the rock churches of Lalibela.
4. compare and contrast the Ghana, Mali, and Songhai empires.

Setting the Stage

Ask students to answer this question, "What role does trade play in the growth of cities?" Explain that the exchange of goods and services creates

Advance Planner

Chapter 14	Africa and the Americas 1200 B.C.–A.D. 1500			★ Advanced
Focus	The rise and fall of isolated civilizations on three continents			● Basic

	Section 1	**Section 2**	**Section 3**	**Section 4**
Objectives	1. Identify and describe the major climate regions in Africa. 2. Locate on a map the major geographic regions of Africa.	1. Describe the economic importance of eastern Africa's Indian Ocean trade. 2. Explain the economic significance of the West African gold–salt trade. 3. Identify the kingdom of Axum and describe the rock churches of Lalibela. 4. Compare and contrast the Ghana, Mali, and Songhai empires.	1. Explain how people first came to North America. 2. Explain how the discovery of agriculture changed life in the Americas. 3. Describe aspects of life among the Hopewell.	1. Describe and use the Mayan number system. 2. Explain why the Aztecs made human sacrifices to their gods. 3. Describe the Inca empire and its rulers.
Setting the Stage	Using Geographic Themes: Place and Location	The role of trade in the growth of cities Transparency 43	Asian hunters as the true discoverers of America	Civilizations without the wheel
Teaching Strategies	Using Geographic Themes: Desert Regions Transparency 42 Outline Map 13 Check for Understanding	Economics and History: Africa's Indian Ocean Trade Economics and History: The Gold–Salt Trade Teaching with Pictures: The Rock Churches of Lalibela Transparency 43 Skill Building: Comparing and Contrasting African Kingdoms Transparency 44 Check for Understanding	Using Geographic Themes: Movement Transparency 45 Transferring Ideas: The Discovery of Agriculture Discussing History: The Hopewells Transparency 46 Check for Understanding	Discussing History: Mayan Math Discussing History: The "Son of the Sun" Check for Understanding
Guided Practice	Transparency 42 Q&A Section Review 1	Transparency 43 Q&A Transparency 44 Q&A Section Review 2	Transparency 45 Q&A Transparency 46 Q&A Section Review 3	Section Review 4
Independent Practice Worksheets	Independent Practice 14.1 Vocabulary 14 Basic Skills 14	Independent Practice 14.2 Geography Skills 14 Critical Thinking 14	Independent Practice 14.3	Independent Practice 14.4
Enrichment	1. Primary Source: Voices 14.1 2. Preparing a Report: African Sculpture 3. Researching for Points	1. Primary Source: Voices 14.2 2. Role Playing 3. Preparing a Report 4. Researching for Points	1. Primary Source: Voices 14.3 2. Preparing a Report 3. ★ Solving a Riddle 4. Researching for Points	1. Primary Source: Voices 14.4 2. Creative Writing 3. Researching for Points

Chapter Closer ● **Reteaching Activities**	Making a Time Line, Making a Chart
Chapter Review	Summary, Reviewing the Facts, Basic Skills, Researching and Reporting Skills, Critical Thinking, Perspectives on Past and Present, Investigating History
Chapter Evaluation	Chapter Test 14, Computer Test Bank Chapter 14 Test

Unit IV Review **Geographic Theme:**	Place: What are the characteristics of three cities of the past?
Unit Perspectives	Understanding History, Critical Thinking (Comparing, Analyzing, Identifying Viewpoints, Identifying Causes and Consequences, Forming a Hypothesis), Continuity and Change, Making Decisions
Unit Evaluation	Unit IV Test

jobs, promotes urban development, stimulates cultural interaction, and produces the wealth that supports artistic expression. Tell students that this section describes how trade routes promoted the growth of cities and empires in sub-Saharan Africa.

Teaching Strategies

Economics and History: Africa's Indian Ocean Trade (Objective 1) Have students read, "Coastal cities traded with Asia" (pages 303–304). Then direct their attention to the map on page 305. Explain that between the twelfth and fifteenth centuries, a complex system of trade transformed the lands bordering the Indian Ocean into one of the wealthiest trading areas in the world. Point out that the commerce in this region was based on the exchange of highly prized luxury goods. East African city-states provided India and China with elephant tusks, tortoise shells, and rhinoceros horns. The fifty-pound ivory tusks were carved into chess pieces and hilts for swords and daggers. Skilled craftsmen used tortoise shells to make combs. The rhinoceros horns were ground into a powder and sold to wealthy Chinese as a life-giving, magical drug. In return, the East Africans received cotton cloth, beads and jewels from India, and porcelain and stoneware from China. These luxuries filled warehouses and shops that lined busy streets of coastal trading cities.

Economics and History: The Gold–Salt Trade (Objective 2) Ask students if they would exchange gold for salt. Explain that this unlikely exchange was the driving force behind the great trans-Saharan trade that brought enormous wealth to Ghana, Mali, and Songhai. Tell students that miners working near the headwaters of the Niger and Senegal rivers extracted about 3,500 tons of gold from shafts up to 100 feet deep.

The miners exchanged their treasure for horses, daggers, silks, jewelry, and fine clothing from North Africa. However, the product that they needed the most was salt. Explain that salt is an essential ingredient in the human diet and in the preservation of food. Because salt was scarce in West Africa, the people of these regions were said to have developed a craving for it. In contrast, salt could be found in such great abundance in the western Sahara village of Taghaza that great blocks of it were used to construct the walls of houses.

Arab traders, eager to obtain West African gold, formed caravans loaded with huge quantities of salt. The land near the bend of the Niger River formed an ideal meeting point for the exchange of gold and salt. This commerce stimulated the emergence of thriving commercial cities that became the centers of three great empires.

Teaching with Pictures: The Rock Churches of Lalibela (Objective 3) Show students Overhead Transparency 43, *The Kingdoms of Kush and Axum*. Point out the Kingdom of Axum and explain that it became rich and powerful by controlling trade between the African interior and the Red Sea. Now ask students to locate the city of Lalibela. Explain that a devout thirteenth century king named Lalibela ordered his architects to construct an unusual group of ten churches near this town. Direct students' attention to the picture of the Church of St. George (page 303). Ask, "Why is this church unusual?" Explain that workers first dug a trench forty feet deep into a hillside of volcanic rock. Skilled craftsmen then carved the huge block of stone into a Greek cross. The interior of St. George contains beautiful mosaics and finely decorated columns. According to legend, King Lalibela constructed this church when St. George galloped into town and demanded to know why no church had yet been built in his honor. Local residents still show visitors a rock that contains a curious hooflike mark.

Skill Building: Comparing and Contrasting African Kingdoms (Objective 4) Draw a chart with four columns and three rows on the chalkboard. Label the columns "Location," "Source of Wealth," "Achievements," and "Reasons for Collapse." Label the rows "Ghana," "Mali," and "Songhai." Show Overhead Transparency 44, *African Kingdoms, 1000–1500*. Have students name the capital cities of these empires. Review pages 306–308 and the map on page 305. Then have students fill in the chart as a class activity. When the class chart has been completed, use it as the basis of a discussion of the following questions: 1. What role did trade play in the development of West African empires? 2. What were the most significant achievements of these empires? 3. What general statement can you make about the reasons these empires fell?

Check for Understanding Ask students to explain the role that trade played in stimulating growth of city-states and empires in Africa.

Practice

Guided Practice
Lead a guided discussion of the questions in Overhead Transparencies 43 and 44 and in Section Review 2. (Answers follow.)

Identify:

(a) eastern African kingdom whose economy was based on iron (b) early Christian kingdom (c) culture resulting from the intermarriage of Bantu and Arab (d) Soninke title for king and name of region he ruled (e) Sundiata's empire that controlled gold trade (f) group that replaced Mandingo as controllers of gold trade (g) people of the Ghana empire (h) people of the Mali empire (i) founder of Mali empire (j) Muslim king of Mali (k) ruthless Songhai king

Answer:

1. from conquered to conquerors
2. (a) by controlling trade between the African interior and the Red Sea (b) its Christianity
3. Arab middlemen brought Asian luxuries to Africa and African luxuries to Asia.
4. They conquered the trading cities but ruined trade with their heavy taxes and wars with Arabs.
5. They all controlled and taxed the gold–salt trade.
6. lack of cannon and gunpowder
7. Kushites—made wide use of iron-working technology for economic gain; Portuguese and Moroccans—made use of cannon for military gain
8. introduced Christianity, Islam, Arab language, and cannon to Africa

Independent Practice

Assign Independent Practice Worksheet 14.2.
Assign Geography Skills Worksheet 14.
Assign Critical Thinking Skills Worksheet 14.

Enrichment Activities

1. **Reading a Primary Source** Assign Voices from the Past Resource Book 14.2.

2. **Preparing a Report** Have students prepare a report on one of the city-states identified on the map on page 305.

3. **Researching for Bonus Points** Award bonus points to students who can find the answer to this question: What was the name of the Christian king Europeans hoped to find in Ethiopia? (Prester John)

Answers to Voice from the Past

1. women treated with more respect than men
2. (a) People of Walata study the Koran carefully, pray regularly; people of Mali hate injustice, maintain security and order. (b) He admired it.

3. They lived apart from men, wore veils, and were not treated as equals to men.

Indians developed many ways of life. 3

Section Objectives

After completing Section 3, students should be able to:

1. explain how the first people came to North America.
2. explain how the discovery of agriculture changed life in the Americas.
3. describe aspects of life among the Hopewell.

Setting the Stage

Begin by asking, "Who discovered America?" List responses on the chalkboard. Then explain that historians believe nomadic hunters from Asia were the true discoverers of America. Tell students that this section describes how the hunters are believed to have reached the Americas. It also explains how the discovery of agriculture changed life in the Americas.

Teaching Strategies

Using Geographic Themes: Movement (Objective 1) Show Overhead Transparency 45, *Early Migrations to the Americas.* Tell students that about 20,000 years ago towering glaciers up to two miles thick covered up to one-third of the earth's surface. Explain that the glaciers absorbed huge quantities of water that normally would have gone into the oceans. As the glaciers expanded, the level of the world's oceans dropped by about 400 feet. As a result, land was exposed that had once been at the bottom of the sea. Falling sea levels uncovered a land bridge 55 miles long and 1000 miles wide that connected Asia with North America. Bands of wandering hunters crossed the land bridge and unknowingly became the first Americans. Have students read, "The Americas have many environments" (page 309). Ask them to describe the different environments the Paleolithic hunters encountered as they migrated across the Americas.

Transferring Ideas: The Discovery of Agriculture (Objective 2) Ask students to recall the Neolithic revolution and describe its importance. Then explain that by about 5000 B.C. people living near present-day Mexico City had learned to grow corn. In four months a family of three could grow and harvest enough corn to feed themselves for a year. The domestication of corn enabled the early Americans to make the transition from food gathering to settled agricultural communities.

Discussing History: The Hopewells (Objective 3) Ask students to locate the Ohio River on the map on page 311, or show Overhead Transparency 46, *Some Early Cultures of the Americas.* Then ask, "How could the Ohio River provide a central route for trade?" Explain that the Hopewell used their central location on the Ohio River to obtain mica from the Appalachians, shells from the Gulf of Mexico, grizzly-bear teeth from the Rockies, and copper nuggets from the area around Lake Superior. Point out that the Hopewells were skilled craftsmen as well as clever traders. Sculptors carved stone into pipes shaped like falcons, beavers, and wildcats. Other artists hammered sheets of copper into eagles and sliced mica into bird claws. The Hopewells buried many of their finest products inside thousands of earthen mounds. For example, a mound near present-day Cillicothe, Ohio, contained bear-teeth necklaces, a 38-pound copper axe, and a number of beautifully carved pipes.

Check for Understanding Ask students to contrast the ways of life of the Hopewell and the Hohokam.

Practice

Guided Practice
Lead a guided discussion of the questions in Overhead Transparencies 45 and 46 and in Section Review 3. (Answers are below.)

Define:
(a) frozen, treeless land (b) narrow strip of land connecting two land masses

Identify:
(a) site of earliest farms in America (b) name for earliest Americans (c) Indians of the eastern woodlands (d) Indians of the southwest

Answer:
1. by crossing land bridge between Asia and North America
2. in the Tehuacán Valley about 5000 B.C.
3. (a) large houses made of bent saplings covered with bark, skins, or mats (b) Society was organized with strong leaders and many specialized workers.

4. farming with irrigation
5. permanent settlements; well-organized, co-operative societies

Independent Practice
Assign Independent Practice Worksheet 14.3.

Enrichment Activities

1. **Reading a Primary Source** Assign Voices from the Past Resource Book 14.3.

2. **Preparing a Report** Have students prepare a report on one of the following topics: the Hohokam, the Anasazi, the Hopewell, and the Mississippians. (See *The First Americans* by Robert Claiborne.)

3. **Solving a Riddle** Explain that there is still a lively debate among scholars as to when the first nomadic hunters reached America. Some scientists believe that there is no evidence of humans in the Western Hemisphere earlier than 12,000 years ago. Others argue that the first people reached the New World over 30,000 years ago. Ask advanced students to prepare a report on this topic. (See *National Geographic,* September 1979 and *The First Americans,* by Brian Fagan.)

4. **Researching for Bonus Points** Award bonus points to students who can find the answer to this question: What is the name scientists have given to the land bridge that once connected Asia and North America? (Beringia)

Empires flourished in the Americas. 4

Section Objectives

After completing Section 4, students should be able to:

1. describe and use the Mayan number system.
2. explain why the Aztecs made human sacrifices to their gods.
3. describe the Inca empire and its rulers.

Setting the Stage

Introduce this section by asking students to discuss the advantages of wheeled vehicles pulled by beasts of burden, such as horses and oxen. Then point out that all of the civilizations they have studied thus far had wheeled vehicles. Ask, "Is it possible for a civilization to develop without this advantage?" Tell students that this section discusses how the Mayas, Aztecs, and Incas built impressive civilizations without the wheel.

Teaching Strategies

Discussing History: Mayan Math (Objective 1) Have students read, "The Mayas built great cities" (page 313–314). Point out that the Mayas were skilled mathematicians who created an advanced system of numbers that used only three symbols— a dot, a bar, and a shell shape. Explain that each dot stood for the numeral 1, each bar stood for the numeral 5, and the shell shape represented zero. As illustrated below, all numerals up to 19 were expressed by a combination of these three symbols.

0	1	2	3	4
5	6	7	8	9
10	11	12	13	14
15	16	17	18	19

Remind students that our number system is based on 10's, with the number on the right representing units, the next figure 10's, and so on. In contrast, the Mayas counted in 20's and wrote large numerals in columns. In this system the bottom row stood for numerals between 0 and 19, the second row stood for multiples of 20, the third row for multiples of 400, the fourth row for multiples of 8,000 and so on. For purposes of illustration, the numbers 267 and 2,953 are explained below.

(13 sets of 20, or 260)
(1 bar and 2 dots, or 7)} = 267

(7 sets of 400, or 2,800)
(7 sets of 20, or 140)
(2 bars and 3 dots, or 13)} = 2,953

After the students have mastered this system, divide the class into groups and assign each group three numbers. Ask the groups to translate their numbers into Mayan symbols as rapidly and accurately as possible.

Discussing History: The "Son of the Sun" (Objective 2) Tell students that the Inca rulers established their capital in Cuzco. Its most splendid building, the famous Temple of the Sun, was dedicated to the sun god. Sheets of polished gold covered the temple's walls and reflected the sun's rays. An inner courtyard contained a garden with ears of corn made out of solid gold.

Explain that Inca emperors claimed to be descendants of the sun god. As the living "Son of the Sun," they enjoyed great wealth. Royal tailors wove robes made of bat fur and hummingbird feathers. The emperor also wore golden ear plugs to symbolize his absolute power. Conclude by asking students to recall other examples of royal status symbols they have previously studied. For example, Roman emperors wore purple robes.

Check for Understanding Call on students to identify the Olmecs, Tikal, Tenochtitlán, and the Incas.

Practice

Guided Practice
Lead a guided discussion of the questions in Section Review 4. (Answers are below.)

Define:
(a) political division (b) Inca system of keeping records

Identify:
(a) creators of the first major American civilization (b) people of the southern Gulf Coast region and present-day Guatemala, whose brilliant civilization lasted from about 500 B.C. to A.D. 900 (c) barbarians who invaded Valley of Mexico and developed a mighty empire (d) Aztec capital (e) Indians who built empire in Peru

Answer:
1. Mexico's Gulf Coast
2. (a) into city-states (b) calendar, concept of zero
3. invaded and conquered existing civilizations
4. through skilled administration and good roads
5. Mayas: great pyramids; Aztecs: city of Tenochtitlán, canals, palace; Incas: stone fortresses that still stand, stone highways; all cultures: great stonework without iron tools
6. lack of written records that were deciphered

Independent Practice
Assign Independent Practice Worksheet 14.4.

Enrichment Activities

1. **Reading a Primary Source** Assign Voices from the Past Resource Book 14.4.

2. **Creative Writing** Ask students to pretend that they have been transported back in time to one of these three cities: Tikal, Tenochtitlán, or Cuzco. Have them write journal entries describing an aspect of daily life in one of these cities. (See *National Geographic*, December 1973, December 1975, and December 1980.)

3. **Researching for Bonus Points** Award bonus points to students who can find the answer to this question: What was the name of the Aztec Sun god? (Huitzilopochtili)

Concluding the Chapter

1. **Chapter Closer**
   Discuss the achievements of the African and American cultures. Ask students how ways of life in these areas were different from those of European civilizations.

2. **Reteaching Activities**
   a. **Making a Time Line** Have students create a time line to show the rise and fall of Ghana, Mali, and Songhai.
   b. **Making a Chart** Have students prepare a chart with three columns labeled "Maya," "Aztec," and "Inca." For each culture, have them give the dates when the empire flourished, where it was located, the name of its major city, and at least two achievements of the culture.

3. **Chapter Review Activities**
   Assign Chapter Review 14 activities.

Chapter Evaluation

Chapter Test 14 and Computer Test Bank Chapter 14 Test can be used to evaluate your students' understanding of this chapter.

Answers to Chapter Review 14

Reviewing the Facts

1. **a.** place in desert where underground water comes to the surface in a spring or well **b.** grassy plain with a few scattered trees **c.** group in which all members believe they are descended from a common ancestor

2. **a.** largest desert in the world **b.** group of people known for their bronze sculptures **c.** record keepers who memorized and passed on a community's history and laws **d.** first group of people to build cities in sub-Saharan Africa **e.** early Christian kingdom **f.** Soninke title for king and name of region he ruled **g.** Sundiata's empire **h.** people who replaced Mandingo as controllers of gold trade **i.** Muslim king of Mali **j.** site of earliest farms in America, about 150 miles southeast of modern Mexico City **k.** North American Indians of the eastern woodlands who built mounds **l.** North American Indians of the southwest who used irrigation for farming **m.** creators of first major American civilization **n.** people of the southern Mexican Gulf Coast region and present-day Guatemala, whose brilliant civilization lasted from about 500 B.C. to A.D. 900 **o.** barbarians who invaded Valley of Mexico and developed a mighty empire **p.** Aztec capital and island city **q.** Indians who built an empire in Peru

3. northern and southern coasts—fertile land, moderate rainfall, warm temperatures, hot and dry summers; deserts—hot, dry, and with oases; savannas—grassy plains with a few scattered trees; rain forests—almost daily rainfall, towering mahogany and teak trees, nearly bare ground

4. **(a)** In addition to living family members, a lineage included past generations (spirits) and future generations. **(b)** took the place of kings or other rulers; acted as a support group

5. The Hopewell lived in the well-watered woodlands, farming, hunting, fishing, and gathering wild foods. They made cone-shaped burial mounds and were skilled potters and jewelers. Family groups lived together in large, rectangular houses made of bent saplings covered with bark, skins, or grass mats. The Hohokam triumphed over their harsh desert environment by building dams and digging irrigation canals; they grew corn and cotton. They made pottery, wove cloth, and made jewelry. A Hohokam house was made of branches and brush raised over a pit.

Basic Skills

1. All events occurred over a period of time.
2. **(a)** T'ang and Sung dynasties in China, Heian Age in Japan, first Muslim invasion and rise of Rajput kingdoms in India **(b)** Ming dynasty in China, Daimyo control in Japan, Delhi sultanate and De Gama's arrival in India
3. Examples of main ideas: **(a)** Kush civilization was heavily influenced by Egypt. **(b)** Christianity has been the religion of Axum and Ethiopia

through the centuries. (c) In the coastal cities, a blending of races, religion, and languages resulted from trade and immigration. (d) Ghana flourished through control of the salt–gold trade. (e) In Mali, Muslim influence grew. (f) In Songhai, Timbuktu became a famous center of learning.

4.

	Aztecs	Incas
Location	Island on lake	High in mountains
Political organization	Empire taking tribute from conquered people	Empire taking tribute, strong administration
Religion	sun worship	sun worship
Achievements	splendid city, canals, causeways, fountains, baths, zoo	stone masonry, highway network, messenger service, quipu, cities

Researching and Reporting Skills

1. Possible answers include: a. Egyptian writings, b. inscriptions at Meroë, c. Portuguese travellers' accounts, d. Arab geographer al-Bakri, e. Ibn Battuta's accounts and reports of Mansa Musa's pilgrimage to Mecca, f. report of visitors to Timbuktu, g. burial mounds, h. village sites, i. ruins of cities
2. Official writings and inscriptions, likely to be informative and objective about historical and political events; travelers' accounts, contemporary reports very informative about social and cultural aspects, but may be biased or exaggerated; burials, ruins, artifacts, informative but subject to interpretation.
3. Students' references will vary.
4. Students' titles will vary.

Critical Thinking

1. a. location on trade routes; mineral resources, b. western kingdoms depended on trade in salt and gold; eastern kingdoms on iron and on trade from interior to the coast
2. a. gold, salt, ivory, skins, iron, tortoise shells, iron, b. jewelry, glass, cloth, porcelain, silk and other luxuries form India, Arabia and China
3. Location on upper Nile and on land routes to Red Sea.
4. Answers will vary, but as examples: The east-coast cities of Africa became places for the exchange of goods from the interior for goods from Asia. In North America, people of the Hopewell culture lived by hunting and fishing in their forest environment.

5. Maya—surmounted by temple, used as place of worship; Egyptian—peaked, used as tombs of pharaohs
6. a. *Maya:* cities, pyramids, calendar, concept of zero; *Aztec:* Tenochtitlán, architecture, city planning, political organization; *Inca:* agricultural, highways, stone-walled fortresses, political organization; b. Answers will vary, but the Mayas—for their early time, created a very sophisticated civilization.

Perspectives on Past and Present
Students' findings will vary.

Investigating History
Students' projects will vary.

Unit IV Review Activities

1. Assign Geographic Theme: Place.
2. Assign Unit Perspectives questions

Unit IV Review Answers

Geographic Theme: Place
1. Diaz thought Tenochtitlán was a great city and that it compared favorably with Constantinople and Rome in terms of layout, size, and orderliness.
2. Tenochtitlán was situated on an island in a lake, with bridges connecting it to the mainland. The lake provided protection.
3. Answers will vary. However, Marco Polo's description of Khanbalik is the most precise in detail.
4. Marco Polo's description shows a very orderly city, with great wealth and trade. The presence of the nighttime guards suggests that the city is orderly—perhaps in an autocratic way. Ibn Battuta's description is mainly about the role of women. The culture of Walata is strongly influenced by Islam. The people of Mali believe strongly in justice and security from crime. Diaz emphasized the size and beauty of Tenochtitlán and the planning shown by the aqueduct as evidence of culture. The orderliness among great crowds of people suggests a stable and disciplined society.

Unit Perspectives

Understanding History

1. **a.** Mongol empire, ruler of Yuan dynasty **b.** Tokugawa shogunate in Japan, unifier of Japan **c.** Japan, Zen monk and artist **d.** India, first of Gupta dynasty **e.** Mughal empire in India, expanded empire and ruled with fairness **f.** Axum, triumphed over Kushites **g.** Mali, undertook dramatic pilgrimage to Mecca
2. **a.** 2 **b.** 1 **c.** 5 **d.** 3 **e.** 4
3. **a.** northern China; contained Imperial City **b.** Japan; Japan's golden age known as the Heian age **c.** China; capital of T'ang China **d.** Ethiopia; trade center **e.** western Africa; trade center **f.** eastern Africa; where Swahili lived **g.** Guatemala; largest Mayan city **h.** Valley of Mexico; Aztec capital

Critical Thinking

1. Possible answers: **(a)** *similar*—travelers reporting on civilizations little known in their country of origin; visited China; *different*—Polo, a European, reported on China; Ibn Battuta, an Arab, on Africa. **(b)** *similar*—both wealthy Muslim kings; *different*—in India; in Africa. **(c)** *similar*—observed the Koran; *different*—Africans practiced religious tolerance, did not require purdah. **(d)** *similar*—famous universities; *different*—Nalanda offered science and Hindu philosophy; Timbuktu attracted Muslim scholars. **(e)** *similar*—highly efficient, used stone highways; *different*—Incas used runners; Chinese used horses.
2. Possible answers: **(1)** Kushite's development of iron led to prosperity and trade. **(2)** Aztecs' choice of island for building their city involved building of aqueducts, canals, causeways. **(3)** Olmecs' clearing of the rain forest to farm the land.
3. Possible answers: **(a)** despised Hinduism for its many gods; **(b)** amazed to find Christian worship in fine churches; **(c)** revered tradition and ancient wisdom; **(d)** perceived mathematics as useful for keeping calendar and predicting events.
4. **(a)** cause: Ming empire's focus on Chinese tradition; effect: greater isolation; Portuguese control of sea trade. **(b)** cause: search for new hunting grounds; effect: human settlements throughout the Americas; **(c)** cause: ambitions of Islamic and Turkish rulers; religious differences; effect: spread of Islam to India.
5. Possible answer: Muslims in India were conquerors of the Hindus; in Africa, merchants interested in trade. In India, Muslim conquest was bloody; Delhi sultans treated Hindus as conquered people. In Africa, Muslims came to trade with savanna kingdoms and with Swahili coastal towns; they were immigrants who intermarried with local populations.
6. **(a)** They lived by a code of honor and bravery. **(b)** Hindu gods rose to new importance, great temples were built, and Buddhism almost ceased to exist as a separate faith.
7. **(a)** For thousands of years, many groups of people passed through Southeast Asia on routes linking Asia and the Pacific islands. As a result, the region has a great variety of languages and cultures. **(b)** Burma, Laos, Kampuchea, Thailand, Vietnam, Malaysia, and Indonesia
8. The city-states of East Africa were centers of overseas trade with other countries around the Indian Ocean. The savanna kingdoms of western Africa were the centers of land trade based on the exchange of gold from the south and salt from the north.

Making Decisions

(a) What the Grand Canal would cost, how long it would take, how many people were needed, what it would do for his empire; **(b)** whether this would enable him to retain his throne; whether he could afford to pay the tribute; whether Mongolia would honor their agreement; **(c)** whether he could trust Marco Polo; whether Marco would be a good official; **(d)** what he would lose and gain by moving his capital.

Continuity and Change

1. **(a)** Aztecs, Incas, Russia, Ottoman empire, Mughal empire, Ming dynasty **(b)** Mali, Mongols, Delhi Sultanate, Khmer, Swahili cities, Sung dynasty **(c)** China, India
2. Answers will vary, but students may conclude that the center of civilization has shifted from Europe to other continents where the civilizations owed nothing to Greece and Rome. Also, new civilizations were emerging in some places.

Unit Evaluation

Unit Test IV can be used to evaluate your students' understanding of this unit.

The Spread of New Ideas

Unit Overview

Unit V focuses on a period in European history characterized by reform, revolution, and exploration. It was a period when long-held beliefs were challenged, startling discoveries made, and vast empires acquired.

About 1300, in the urban centers of northern Italy, a region dominated by wealthy merchants concerned with individual achievement and encouragement of the arts, the painter Giotto and writers Dante and Petrarch explored new art forms, bridging the gap between the Middle Ages and the golden age known as the Renaissance. Scholars revived the classical texts of Greece and Rome, which influenced painting, sculpture, and architecture. In the 1400's Florence, under control of the Medici family, was the center of Renaissance activity. Such artists as Ghiberti, Brunelleschi, Donatello, and Masaccio beautified the city with their works. The 1500's, known as the High Renaissance, was dominated by three artistic giants: Michelangelo, Leonardo, and Raphael.

The Renaissance was the most important of several forces weakening the power of the Catholic Church. Demands for reform culminated in Martin Luther's 95 theses. The spread of Luther's ideas, made possible by the invention of the printing press, gained him many followers in Germany and northern Europe. To combat Protestantism, two reforming popes led a counter, or Catholic, Reformation affirming basic Catholic doctrines agreed to at the Council of Trent in 1545. Catholic beliefs were also challenged by new observations of scientists such as Copernicus, Kepler, and Galileo. This period of scientific inquiry is known as the Scientific Revolution.

Politically, the 1500's and 1600's were a time of conquest and violent conflict over religion. The exploits of conquistadors enabled Spain to amass a huge empire in the Americas. However, Spain's newly acquired wealth was not sufficient to enable Spain's Catholic King Philip II to overthrow Protestant rulers throughout Europe. Spain's power declined in the 1600's, and the Dutch, who had won independence from Spain, became the commercial leaders of Europe.

While the Netherlands flourished, France was wracked by civil and religious strife. Eventually, France gained some stability, first under Henry IV and then under the virtual rule of Cardinal Richelieu.

In 1618 the religious conflict between Catholics and Protestants culminated in a war that was to last thirty years. The war led to the destruction of German unity, the decline of Hapsburg Spain and Austria, and the emergence of France as the strongest state in Europe.

Resources

The resources that supplement the study of this unit include:

1. The time line for Unit V, found on pages 320–321. The themes for this time line include the changes in European life brought about by the Renaissance, the Age of Exploration, the Reformation, the Scientific Revolution, and nation-building in the sixteenth and seventeenth centuries. The focus is a fleet of caravels representing overseas exploration and trade.
2. The Geographic Theme, found on page 384. The theme *Movement* explores the spread of European civilization throughout the world. Students use a map of the world showing major European overseas empires in about 1700 to trace trade routes.
3. The Historical Atlas map on pages 812–813. This map shows the world in about 1500, relating Europe's Renaissance and Reformation to contemporary historical developments in other parts of the world. This map also appears as Overhead Transparency 89. A global perspectives activity based on this transparency appears in Chapter 15.
4. The Researching and Reporting Skills activities in the chapter reviews. Students continue developing their writing skills in preparation for writing a formal research paper in Unit VII.

Chapter Titles

The Renaissance and Exploration

Chapter Overview

The Renaissance, a period of intellectual and artistic creativity, began about 1300 in northern Italy. It was a time of intellectual and artistic creativity. Three of its earliest geniuses were the writers Dante and Petrarch and the artist Giotto. The 1400's saw the golden age of Florence in which artists such as Donatello, Ghiberti, Brunelleschi, and Masaccio flourished under the patronage of the powerful Medici family. As the golden age gave way to years of war and political upheaval, Machiavelli wrote *The Prince,* a book of advice to rulers. In Rome during the High Renaissance of the early 1500's, da Vinci, Raphael, and Michelangelo lifted Renaissance art to new brilliance.

The Renaissance was also a period of exploration and discovery. Encouraged by the need for new trade routes and by the development of technologies making long voyages possible, Spain and Portugal led in voyages of discovery. The explorations of Vasco da Gama, Columbus, and Magellan hastened the colonization of Africa and the Americas, and the growth of the slave trade.

Key Terms

vernacular, humanists, caravel
For additional exercises, see Vocabulary Worksheet 15.

Chapter Focus

After students have read the chapter introduction, ask them to define "genius." List responses on the chalkboard. Challenge students to support da Vinci's claim to genius. Tell students that da Vinci's philosophy of art set him apart from other artists. Da Vinci was not content to imitate the classics. Above all, he valued originality and scoffed at imitators of antique art. To him, nature, not the ancient Greeks, presented the perfect study. Students might be interested to know that da Vinci's obsession with innovation resulted in the loss of many of his works. This was due to his constant experimentation with new pigments and dyes that caused paintings to deteriorate prematurely. Tell students that the intensity of da Vinci's work and his views about art are a symbol of the Renaissance spirit.

The Renaissance began in Northern Italy. 1

Section Objectives

After completing Section 1, students should be able to:

1. analyze the economic, social, and political conditions that gave rise to the Renaissance.
2. describe how the works of Giotto, Dante, and Petrarch differed from the art of the Middle Ages.
3. identify Renaissance values and ideals.

Setting the Stage

Explain to students that *renaissance* means rebirth and ask them to define this concept. Write students' responses on the chalkboard. Direct students' attention to the pictures throughout Chapter 15. Explain that Renaissance art was characterized by the themes of individualism, originality, and discovery. Suggest that the Renaissance was more than a rebirth because Renaissance artists created works that were innovative and original. Tell students that Section 1 examines the social, economic, and political conditions in northern Italy that helped artists such as Leonardo da Vinci to produce their work. Challenge students to define the characteristics that made cities in northern Italy different from those in other parts of Europe.

Skill Building: Classifying Information (Objective 1) Ask students to identify the conditions in northern Italy that supported a Renaissance. Write "Economic," "Political," and "Social" on the chalkboard and have students classify information from the text in terms of the categories. Economic conditions included prosperity through trade and a powerful merchant class. Political conditions included well-defended, well-funded, independent city-states. Social conditions included secular, urban lifestyles, and competition among newly rich merchants to achieve and to become sponsors of the arts.

Explain that Northern Italy was more urbanized

than any other part of Europe. For example, in England only 10 percent of the population lived in cities, while in Tuscany nearly 26 percent were city dwellers. Show Overhead Transparency 47, *Renaissance Italy*, and have students identify and locate the three cities that had populations of more than 100,000 (Venice, Genoa, Florence). Tell students that the open, competitive nature of

Advance Planner

Unit V	The Spread of New Ideas			
Theme	The European Renaissance, Reformation, and Rise of Colonial Powers			

Chapter 15	The Renaissance and Exploration 1300–1600		★ Advanced	
Focus	Leonardo di Vinci's claim to genius		● Basic	

	Section 1	Section 2	Section 3	Section 4
Objectives	1. Analyze the economic, political, and social conditions that gave rise to the Renaissance. 2. Describe how the works of Giotto, Dante, and Petrarch differed from the art of the Middle Ages. 3. Identify Renaissance values and ideals and their relationship to Renaissance art.	1. Explain the role of the Medici family in Florentine society. 2. Identify Florentine artists and describe their contributions. 3. Analyze the political philosophy of Machiavelli.	1. Define the period known as the High Renaissance. 2. Describe the art of Michelangelo, Raphael, and Leonardo da Vinci. 3. Evaluate the qualities that distinguish great art.	1. Outline the causes and effects of the age of exploration. 2. Trace the routes of Spanish and Portuguese explorers on a map. 3. Identify characteristics of the slave trade in the 1500's.
Setting the Stage	The meaning of Renaissance	How the story of Ghiberti's doors reveals Renaissance priorities	Michelangelo's impact on his contemporaries	Voyages of discovery carried out the spirit of the Renaissance
Teaching Strategies	Skill Building: Classifying Information Transparency 47 Writing about History: Comparing Medieval and Early Renaissance Thought Discussing History: Renaissance Ideals Check for Understanding	Relating Past to Present: The Medicis and the Arts Writing About History: Florentine Artists Discussing History: Machiavelli's Views Check for Understanding	Discussing History: The High Renaissance Teaching with Pictures: High Renaissance Works of Art Skill Building: Making Reasoned Judgments Check for Understanding	Skill Building: Relating Cause and Effect Using Geographic Themes: Movement Transparency 48 Outline Map 2 Discussing History: The Slave Trade Check for Understanding
Guided Practice	Transparency 47 Q&A Section Review 1	Section Review 2	Sections Review 3	Section Review 4 Transparency 48 Q&A
Independent Practice Worksheets	Independent Practice 15.1 Vocabulary Skills 15 Basic Skills 15	Independent Practice 15.2	Independent Practice 15.3 Critical Thinking 15	Independent Practice 15.4 Geography Skills 15
Enrichment	1. Primary Source: Voices 15.1 2. Writing a Report 3. Researching for Points	1. Primary Source: Voices 15.2 2. ★ Creative Writing 3. Researching for Points	1. Primary Source: Voices 15.3 2. ★ Preparing a Report 3. Learning Through Pictures 4. Researching for Points	1. Primary Source: Voices 15.4 2. Preparing a Report 3. Researching for Points 4. Global Perspective Transparency 89

Chapter Closer ● **Reteaching Activities**	Explaining, Identifying Main Ideas, Recalling Information, Outlining
Chapter Review	Summary, Reviewing the Facts, Basic Skills, Researching and Reporting Skills, Critical Thinking, Perspectives on Past and Present, Investigating History
Chapter Evaluation	Chapter Test 15, Computer Test Bank Chapter 15 Test

these cities was an advantage for Renaissance artists. The cities were vibrant and colorful trade centers. Artists as well as merchants moved from city to city as opportunities arose. The merchant class gave the cities an independent spirit. Unlike nobility, members of the merchant class owed their position to talent, not to inherited status. Leonardo da Vinci and other artists were comfortable among these people and admired their self-reliance and competitiveness. Ask students to suggest reasons the economic, political, and social climate of northern Italian cities was favorable to artists.

Writing about History: Comparing Medieval and Early Renaissance Thought (Objective 2) *Prewriting* Discuss the medieval influences in Renaissance art, including Giotto's religious subjects; Dante's emphasis on religious faith, romantic love, and Roman poetry; and Petrarch's spiritual muse, use of Latin, and love of classical writing. Renaissance developments might include Giotto's portrayal of depth and of real people in real situations, Dante's use of the vernacular and his portrayal of real people in true adventures, and Petrarch's striving for classical simplicity. *Writing* Ask student to write essays supporting the idea that the works of Giotto, Dante, and Petrarch represented a transition from medieval to Renaissance thought. Ask students to explain how the works changed medieval styles and views.

Discussing History: Renaissance Ideals and Values (Objective 3) Ask students to identify Renaissance values (pages 325–326). Explain that today the terms "renaissance man" and "renaissance woman" describe people who have many skills and interests or who are well-versed in many fields of knowledge. Invite students to evaluate Castiglione's descriptions of the ideal man and ideal woman. Ask, "What do the descriptions reveal about the status of women in Renaissance society?" Invite students to try to develop similar definitions for the ideal man and ideal woman in present-day American society.

Explain that Renaissance values were not universally accepted. Some religious leaders found the emphasis on worldly pleasures to be immoral. In Italy, a Dominican monk named Girolamo Savonarola was a powerful critic of the Renaissance lifestyle. His dramatic oratory often moved audiences to burn wigs, makeup, and other trappings of Renaissance society in bonfires of protest.

Check for Understanding Have students explain how the pictures in this section illustrate Renaissance ideals and values.

Practice

Guided Practice
Lead a guided discussion of the questions in Overhead Transparency 47 and in Section Review 1. (Answers are below.)

Define:
(a) period of rebirth of cultural and artistic creativity beginning in about 1300 (b) painting done on wet plaster (c) everyday language of one's homeland (d) scholar who studied classical texts

Identify:
(a) artist, engineer, architect of Renaissance period (b) painter who began revolution in art by painting realistic people (c) poet who wrote in the vernacular (d) Dante's masterpiece (e) poet and letter writer whose work reflected a modern, simple style (f) book by Castiglione outlining ideal accomplishments and behavior for men and women (g) outstanding Renaissance woman in northern Italy

Answer:
1. bustling urban centers dependent on trade, a merchant class that fostered a belief in individual achievement
2. painted lifelike figures and created an illusion of depth
3. (a) hell, purgatory, and paradise (b) included real people and political events, wrote in vernacular
4. imitated style of Cicero, used Latin in poems
5. portrait painting and autobiography
6. celebration of individual, love of classical learning, enjoyment of worldly pleasures
7. (a) well-educated in Greek and Latin classics, charming and witty; able to dance, write poetry, sing, play music, wrestle, ride horses, be a swordsman (b) well-educated in classics; could write well, paint, make music, dance, be charming, inspire poetry and art
8. Artists needed support of wealthy patrons.
9. Possible answer: the emphasis on humans rather than God as "the measure of all things"

Independent Practice
Assign Independent Practice Worksheet 15.1.
Assign Vocabulary Worksheet 15.
Assign Basic Skills Worksheet 15.

Enrichment Activities

1. **Reading a Primary Source** Assign Voices from the Past Resource Book 15.1.

2. **Writing a Report** Have students read excerpts from *The Courtier*. Ask students to report on

Castiglione's observations at the court of the Duke of Urbino and how these observations related to his ideas on Renaissance values.

3. **Researching for Bonus Points** Award bonus points to students who can answer the following questions: Which Renaissance writer wrote, "Abandon all hope, ye who enter here?" (Dante Alighieri) To what do these words refer? ("the inferno")

Florence led the way in arts.

2

Section Objectives

After completing Section 2, students should be able to:

1. explain the role of the Medici family in Florentine society.
2. identify Florentine artists and describe their contributions.
3. analyze the political philosophy of Machiavelli.

Setting the Stage

After students have read the section on Ghiberti's doors, tell them that when Ghiberti heard he had won he exclaimed, "I have surpassed everyone!" Ghiberti included two self-portraits in the doors, an example of the Renaissance individualism. Ask students what Renaissance priorities this story reflects. (open competition, pride in achievement, individuality, and creativity) Explain to students that the creative use of perspective, realism, and detail is typical of the bold direction taken by Renaissance artists. Tell students to look for these traits as they read.

Relating Past to Present: The Medicis and the Arts (Objective 1) Explain to students that as head of a banking and trading empire stretching from Cairo to London, the Medici could afford impressive displays of art. People today are the beneficiaries of the Medici goal to beautify Florence with impressive architecture and art. Ask students how artists earn a living in the United States today. Point out that patrons of the arts still play an important role. Patrons include private collectors, philanthropists, and corporations; the government also sponsors artists. Artists may compete for commissions and for grants from federal, state, and local funds. Artists also sell their work directly or from art galleries to museums or other buyers. Have students comment on the suggestion that the prosperity and greatness of a society is reflected in how well it supports its artist communities.

Writing about History: Florentine Artists (Objective 2) *Prewriting* Use a clustering exercise (diagram concepts on chalkboard) to discuss the innovations of Florentine artists. List the following names on the chalkboard: Ghiberti, Brunelleschi, Donatello, and Masaccio. Refer students to the text to identify the innovations these Florentine artists developed. Diagram students' responses to the headings on the chalkboard (Massaccio/perspective, etc.) *Writing* Have students use the listed phrases to write essays on the topic, "The innovations of Florentine artists." Essays should include references to specific artists presented in this section.

Discussing History: Machiavelli's Views (Objective 3) Tell students that Machiavelli studied the political motivations and actions of people in power. He studied how rulers acquired power and their methods of keeping it. Explain that Florentines emphasized diplomatic skills. Surrounded by enemies, they worked to avoid any disruptions by skillfully using diplomacy. Machiavelli based his writings on observations of the underlying realities of Florentine political life.

Write the following quotations on the chalkboard:

"The end justifies the means."

"a prince ... must if necessary be prepared to do evil."

"From this arises the question whether it is better to be loved rather than feared, or feared rather than loved. It might perhaps be answered that we should wish to be both: but since love and fear can hardly exist together, if we must choose between them, it is far safer to be feared than loved."

Have students explain the political factors in northern Italy that led Machiavelli to these conclusions. Ask, "Can Machiavelli's analysis be applied to present-day situations?" Have students discuss each quotation, agree or disagree, and offer evidence to support their judgments.

Check for Understanding Ask students to explain the significance of Florentine politics and of the Medici family in the development of Renaissance art and architecture.

Practice

Guided Practice
Lead a guided discussion of the questions in Section Review 2. (Answers are below.)

Define:
the 1400's

Identify:
(a) wealthy ruler of Florence for 30 years (b) Cosimo's grandson and leader of Florence (c) created bronze doors for Baptistry in Florence (d) architect who built dome on Cathedral of Florence (e) sculptor of lifelike statues (f) developed concept of perspective (g) author of treatise *The Prince*

Answer:
1. textiles and banking
2. (a) republican in name, allowing only about 3 percent of population to vote (b) as a virtual dictator, power behind the scenes
3. (a) wanted figures to seem real and alive (b) created free-standing figures
4. developed principles of perspective
5. (a) innately selfish, fickle, and corrupt (b) Hold power in whatever way you can in the interest of the state.
6. conflict between Spain and France, French and Spanish invasions of Italy
7. Florentine merchants and bankers embarked on a civic beautification program that led to the creation of brilliant works of art.

Independent Practice
Assign Independent Practice Worksheet 15.2.

Enrichment Activities

1. **Reading a Primary Source** Assign Voices from the Past Resource Book 15.2.

2. **Creative Writing** Have advanced students write a rebuttal to Machiavelli's conclusion that the end justifies the means. Students should use examples to support their views.

3. **Researching for Bonus Points** Award bonus points to students who can answer the following question: Who was the real-life model for Machiavelli's description in *The Prince?* (Cesare Borgia, Roman politician)

Answers to Voice from the Past

1. (a) to win the prince's favor (b) They would prevent him from knowing the truth.
2. by heeding the advice of wise men he has been given liberty to speak the truth

3. because counselors may speak only on matters the prince asks about
4. might prefer flattery to truth or be unable to distinguish between the two

---

Three artistic giants led the Renaissance. 3

Section Objectives

After completing Section 3, students should be able to:

1. define the period known as the High Renaissance.
2. describe the art of Michelangelo, Raphael, and Leonard da Vinci.
3. evaluate the qualities that distinguish great art.

Setting the Stage

Set the tone by sharing with students the spirit and intensity of Michelangelo's work and personality. In biographies written by his contemporaries, it is apparent that Michelangelo inspired and awed people around him. Like da Vinci, he felt that imitations of the works of ancient Greece and Rome did not express Renaissance values. He used classical styles and subjects but portrayed the personalities and struggles of people of his own time. Tell students that Michelangelo and others worked in a period known as the High Renaissance. Section 3 explains how this period got its name.

Discussing History: The High Renaissance (Objective 1) Tell students that months before the unveiling of Michelangelo's work in the Sistine Chapel, Florence was abuzz with anticipation. The citizens of Florence were not disappointed. Michelangelo's work challenged people's ideas about life and art and was a highlight in the High Renaissance. After students have read Section 3, have them identify the characteristics that distinguish the High Renaissance. Ask, "How was it different from the Early Renaissance? What role did Popes play in High Renaissance art?" Then ask students to give examples of High Renaissance art and of the works commissioned by Popes to beautify Rome. List student responses on the chalkboard. Ask students why these works are so admired.

Teaching with Pictures: High Renaissance Works of Art (Objective 2) Direct students' attention to the works of Raphael (page 326), Michelangelo (pages 332–333), and Leonardo da Vinci (page 334). Ask, "How does Raphael's painting show perspective? What does Michelangelo's 'Pieta' convey concerning Christ's death?" Tell students this sculpture was commissioned by a cardinal. Michelangelo had a contract reading, "...it shall be the finest work in marble which Rome today can show." Michelangelo's work surpassed earlier sculpture and made him, at age 24, immediately famous. Earlier representations of Christ's death stressed the brutal aspects. Michelangelo, however, presented a vision of serenity, sad beauty, and peace. Explain that *pieta* in Italian means "pity." Ask students to speculate on Michelangelo's interpretation of Christ's death; then tell students that Michelango believed the body should reflect what is in the soul. Ask, "How do his sculptures express his belief?"

Writing about History: Evaluating High Renaissance Art (Objective 3) *Prewriting* Before students write, ask them what distinguishes great art. Write their responses on the chalkboard. Students should recognize that there are many standards and values used in evaluating works of art. Ask students what they admire in certain works of past or present-day art. Tell students that works that are referred to as "great" usually show technical skills and originality, but also portray great themes or communicate great ideas to viewers. *Writing* Have students apply discussion ideas by selecting an artwork described in this section and then writing an essay using the following outline:

a. Opening paragraph: description of qualities of great art, including student's own views.
b. Main body: evaluation of an artwork of the High Renaissance in relation to the concept of great art.
c. Concluding paragraph: relationship between artwork and student's views on qualities for great art.

Practice

Guided Practice
Lead a guided discussion of the questions in Section Review 3. (Answers are below.)

Identify:
(a) great painter whose paintings transformed the library of Julius II into a kind of Renaissance hall of fame (b) painter of Sistine chapel ceiling and creator of powerful sculpture (c) Pope who undertook beautification of Rome

Answer:
1. (a) disrepair (b) Julius II
2. "Pieta": moving depiction of Mary grieving over body of crucified son; "David": statue of the Biblical king which radiates strength and dignity; Sistine Chapel: many scenes including God reaching out to infuse spirit into Adam
3. to show unity between Christian and classical works
4. first psychological portrait
5. to glorify themselves and their power
6. Look for reasons that suggest qualities of genius and innovations in artistic style.

Independent Practice
Assign Independent Practice Worksheet 15.3.
Assign Critical Thinking Worksheet 15.

Enrichment Activities

1. **Reading a Primary Source** Assign Voices from the Past Resource Book 15.3.

2. **Preparing a Report** Students have read about the stormy relationship between Michelangelo and Julius II. Have them research this relationship further to determine whether Michelangelo was helped or hindered by this powerful pope. Challenge students to determine whether his commission to paint the Sistine Chapel ceiling was intended as a punishment for the temperamental artist.

3. **Teaching with Pictures** Ask interested students to prepare scrapbooks or collages of Renaissance art and architecture and to share them with class. Students should caption or explain each selection.

4. **Researching for Bonus Points** Award bonus points to students who can identify Michelangelo's first works in stone. (*Madonna of the Stars* and *Battle of the Centaurs*)

Explorers opened new sea routes.   4

Section Objectives

After completing Section 4, students should be able to:

1. outline causes and effects of the age of exploration.

2. trace on a map the routes of Spanish and Portuguese explorers and list some effects of contact between Europeans and Indians.
3. describe characteristics of the slave trade in the 1500's.

Setting the Stage

Tell students that the explorers embodied the same spirit of individualism and originality as characterized the artists of the Renaissance. The renewed interest in ancient writings that inspired Renaissance artists also gave the explorers new knowledge about mathematics, astronomy, and geography. Point out that these voyages of discovery were also a psychological feat for the new navigators. Europeans believed that boiling seas filled with monsters and a fiery sun that burned the skin awaited sailors who were bold enough to explore uncharted waters. Tell students that Section 4 discusses the courageous discoveries of these sailors.

Skill Building: Relating Cause and Effect (Objective 1) Have students work in pairs and assume the role of advisors to Queen Isabella, giving advice on the wisdom of Columbus' trip to the New World. One advisor argues for the trip and the other argues against it. Students should include economic, geographic, and technological (navigation, ship requirements) facts to support their arguments. Next ask, "What conditions and events led to exploration?" (page 335) Write students' responses on the chalkboard. Conclude by having each pair of students compare the advice they gave and agree on a recommendation to the Queen. Record groups' decisions on the chalkboard to determine a final recommendation.

Using Geographic Themes: Movement (Objective 2) Show students Overhead Transparency 48, *Voyages of Discovery*. Then distribute Outline Map 2: The World. Have students use the information in Section 4 and the map on page 336 to label areas discovered by the Spanish and by the Portuguese. Have students select four explorers, design a map symbol for each, and use the symbols to draw the routes of the four explorers on their outline maps. Ask, "What areas of the world were claimed by Spain and by Portugal?"

Tell students that historians use the term "Columbian exchange" to describe the mingling of cultures initiated by Columbus. Ask students to explain how the blending of cultures had both positive and negative effects. Students should note the effects of disease epidemics on Indian populations. Point out that the peoples of Europe benefited from the new foods they found in the Americas and that Indians benefited from the introduction of horses, pigs, and cattle. These animals changed both the American landscape and the Indians' way of life.

Discussing History: The Slave Trade (Objective 3) Tell students that the slave trade was part of a triangular route that began in a seaport in western Europe. Carrying rum, gunpowder, and trinkets, traders sailed to the "Slave Coast" in Africa. Slaves were transported to this coast by African slave hunters who ruthlessly raided rival kingdoms to capture their victims. The prisoners were then sold to the Europeans. The slaves' voyage to the New World is called the "Middle Passage." Have students explain why so many slaves died during this trip. Ask, "Why was the slave trade important to the European colonization of the Americas?"

Check for Understanding Have students "solve" in writing the following equation: x + y + z = voyages of exploration. (Answers should refer to economic factors and new technology, knowledge, and ideas.)

Practice

Guided Practice

Lead a guided discussion of the questions in Overhead Transparency 48 and in Section Review 4. (Answers are below.)

Define:
new sailing vessel designed for ocean travel

Identify:
(a) explorer who reached the Americas by crossing Atlantic in 1492 (b) patron of explorers and king of Portugal (c) Portuguese captain who sailed to the southernmost tip of Africa (d) Portuguese captain who reached India by sailing around the Cape of Good Hope (e) Florentine merchant who described Brazilian coastline (f) explorer who discovered Pacific Ocean (g) line dividing newly found lands between Spain and Portugal (h) explorer whose expedition rounded the globe.

Answer:
1. Columbus read Marco Polo's book.
2. (a) overland from Asia through Antioch and Alexandria to Italy for distribution throughout Europe (b) to avoid extra charges imposed by Italian middlemen
3. caravel, compass, astrolabe

4. (a) to find a route around Africa to Asia (b) Vasco da Gama
5. (a) to reach Asia by going west (b) never found the civilization described by Marco Polo
6. Pope Alexander's ruling of Line of Demarcation and Cabral's exploration of Amazon River
7. proved Americas were separate continents and world was larger than previously thought
8. (a) gained political mastery of two huge continents and won control of the seas (b) spread of epidemics decimated native American population; growth of slave trade provided labor
9. (a) with the selling of twelve slaves to a Portuguese sea captain (b) Workers became scarce as the native population was wiped out in epidemics.
10. felt that the world was his to conquer

Independent Practice
Assign Independent Practice Worksheet 15.4.
Assign Geography Skills Worksheet 15.

Enrichment Activities

1. **Reading a Primary Source** Assign Voices from the Past Resource Book 15.4.
2. **Preparing a Report** Have students report on the slave trade in the 1500's. Ask students to include information on slave ships, how slaves were captured, and how they were sold.
3. **Researching for Bonus Points** Award bonus points to students who can answer the following question: What Venetian explorer, sailing for Henry VII of England, explored the coast of Newfoundland in 1497? (John Cabot)
4. **Global Perspectives** Assign students the activities in Overhead Transparency 89, *The World about 1500.*

Concluding the Chapter

1. **Chapter Closer**
   Have students give four reasons why "Renaissance" is an apt name for the period described in this chapter.

2. **Reteaching Activities**
   a. **Explaining** Have students explain the significance of Northern Italian city-states and of the Medici in Europe's Renaissance.
   b. **Summarizing Main Ideas** Have students write statements summarizing the main ideas of Machiavelli, Petrarch, and Dante.

c. **Recalling Information** Have students explain how each of the following artists contributed to the Renaissance: Leonardo da Vinci, Michelangelo, and Raphael.
d. **Outlining** Have students use the headings in Section 4 to outline the information about voyages of exploration.

3. **Chapter Review Activities**
   Assign Chapter Review 15 activities.

Chapter Evaluation

Chapter Test 15 and Computer Test Bank Chapter 15 Test can be used to evaluate your students' understanding of this chapter.

Answers to Chapter Review 15

Reviewing the Facts
1. **a.** everyday language of one's homeland **b.** scholar who studied classical texts **c.** sailing vessel designed for ocean travel
2. **a.** Renaissance artist, engineer, architect **b.** painter who revolutionized art by painting life-like figures **c.** early Renaissance poet who wrote *The Divine Comedy* **d.** poet whose writings reflected classical virtues of simplicity and purity **e.** book by Castiglione that described ideal man and woman **f.** most honored woman of the Renaissance in northern Italy **g.** 15th century (1400's) **h.** northern Italian city that led the way in the arts **i.** wealthy ruler of Florence for 30 years who beautified the city **j.** Cosimo's grandson and leader of Florence who continued tradition of beautifying the city **k.** sculptor whose free-standing statues seemed real and alive **l.** painter who developed principles of perspective **m.** book by Machiavelli that gave advice to rulers about political power **n.** Michelangelo painted its ceiling with more than 300 massive human figures **o.** famous artist who painted walls of Julius II's library **p.** prince of Portugal and patron of explorers **q.** year when Dias reached southernmost tip of Africa **r.** year of Columbus's first Atlantic crossing, when he reached the Bahamas **s.** Florentine merchant-explorer who described newly discovered continent and for

whom America was named **t.** line drawn by pope to divide newly found lands between Spain and Portugal **u.** Portuguese explorer whose expedition rounded the globe **v.** Portuguese explorer who discovered Brazil

3. **(a)** golden age of creative and intellectual activity that began around 1300 **(b)** in northern Italy
4. **(a)** Portrait painting and autobiography developed because wealthy merchants wanted to be remembered beyond their lifetimes. **(b)** Artists and writers wanted to be known as individuals, and fame became the final reward for superior talent. **(c)** Explorers were confident, ambitious, and eager for individual glory.
5. **(a)** They wanted a share of the profitable Asian trade and routes they could control. **(b)** The Portuguese reached India by sailing around Africa, and Columbus reached the Americas while trying to sail to Asia across the Atlantic Ocean.
6. **(a)** introduction of new food crops **(b)** introduction of new food crops and diseases **(c)** development of the slave trade to the Americas

Basic Skills
1. *Portugal* — Da Gama: Africa, India; Dias: Africa; Cabral: South America, Africa, India. *Spain* — Columbus: West Indies, Central America; Balboa: Central America; Magellan: South America, Spice Islands, East Indies, Africa; Vespucci: South America, West Indies.
2. A. New values shaped the Renaissance.
     1. Celebration of the individual
        a. portrait painting
        b. autobiography
     2. Love of classical learning
        a. Greek and Roman art
        b. Greek and Roman writings
        c. rise of humanism
     3. Enjoyment of worldly pleasures
        a. display of fashion
        b. interest in earthly matters

Researching and Reporting Skills
1. Students' reports will vary.
2. Students' headlines will vary.

Critical Thinking
1. **(a)** Middle Ages: little interest in the individual; religious focus to most activities, asceticism, learning of theology; code of chivalry; women to inspire love and art, but to remain wives or nuns. Renaissance: individual achievement and glory; admiration for the ancient classics and their standards of beauty; competence

in many fields; appreciation of worldly pleasures; women to be educated, to inspire and patronize the arts. **(b)** Examples in *art* — medieval: anonymity of artists; subjects relating to religion or daily life; portrayal of religious or anonymous figures; Renaissance: artist often portrays self in picture; classical themes and codes of beauty; realistic portraits of individuals; *architecture* — medieval: Gothic reaching up to heaven in pointed arches and spires; Renaissance: classical columns, domes, rounded or horizontal lines; *literature* — medieval: anonymity of author: heroes religious, fictitious, or legendary; Renaissance: autobiographies, features real people.
2. Thesis: **(a)** The values and ideals of the Renaissance inspired the explorers. **(b)** Explorers showed the confidence and the love of glory and achievement that was the Renaissance ideal; used ancient Greeks such as Ptolemy as a source of knowledge about the world.
3. **(a)** more interested in worldly matters, political and cultural, than in religion. **(b)** Yes; Dante is referred to as bridging medieval and Renaissance values, Petrarch as having crossed that bridge and standing fully in the Renaissance.
4. **(a)** Economic prosperity provides a favorable climate for artistic activity. **(b)** Prosperity helped Pericles, Augustus, and Justinian beautify their cities. In the Sung empire, prosperity encouraged appreciation of beauty in the arts.
5. **(a)** In both, women were expected to inspire the arts, act as good hostesses, but not to take an active role themselves. Their influence or power was often through others or the result of belonging to a powerful family, not based on their own merit or competence. **(b)** Answers will vary but should include information about the era chosen.

Perspectives on Past and Present
Students should mention the shared ideal of achievement, personal glory, or fame. In the Renaissance this is expressed as "Man can do anything he will." This ideal excluded women, and it took no account of individual differences. In the United States, individual achievement is a goal for both men and women. Society recognizes the need to compensate for economic and social limitations so that everyone has an opportunity.

Investigating History
Students' findings will vary.

The Reformation and the Scientific Revolution

Chapter **16**

Advance Planner

Chapter 16 Focus	The Reformation and the Scientific Revolution 1450–1650 Conflicts caused by new ideas			★ Advanced ● Basic
	Section 1	**Section 2**	**Section 3**	**Section 4**
Objectives	1. Describe the conditions that led to a religious revolt. 2. Explain the main teachings of Martin Luther. 3. Assess the reactions to Luther's teachings and trace their spread.	1. Explain the effects of the Reformation in England. 2. Discuss significant traits of Calvinism. 3. Trace the distribution of religions in Europe in the 1500's.	1. Identify the goals of the Jesuits. 2. Describe reactions of the Church to Protestantism. 3. Explain how the Reformation contributed to disunity in the Holy Roman Empire.	1. Explain why the ideas of Copernicus and Galileo threatened the Church. 2. Explain the scientific method and describe scientific achievements of the sixteenth and seventeenth centuries. 3. Discuss why new ideas often cause conflict.
Setting the Stage	Luther's courage	Henry VIII's reactions to Luther's teachings	The concept of "Counter-Reformation"	Copernicus' conclusion
Teaching Strategies	Discussing History: Causes of the Reformation Discussing History: The 95 Theses of Martin Luther Skill Building: Analyzing Effects Transparency 49 Check for Understanding	Discussing History: The Reformation in England Discussing History: Calvinism Geography in History: Protestant and Catholic Europe in the 1500's Transparency 50 Check for Understanding	Discussing History: The Jesuits Skill Building: Supporting Conclusions Skill Building: Comparing and Contrasting Reformation Monarchs Check for Understanding	Discussing History: Copernicus and Galileo Skill Building: Making Inferences Relating Past to Present: Problems of Change Check for Understanding
Guided Practice	Transparency 49 Q&A Section Review 1	Transparency 50 Q&A Section Review 2	Section Review 3	Section Review 4
Independent Practice Worksheets	Independent Practice 16.1 Vocabulary 16 Geography Skills 16	Independent Practice 16.2 Basic Skills 16	Independent Practice 16.3 Critical Thinking 16	Independent Practice 16.4
Enrichment	1. Primary Source: Voices 16.1 2. Researching for Points	1. Primary Source: Voices 16.2 2. Preparing a Report: Women in the Reformation 3. Researching for Points	1. Primary Source: Voices 16.3 2. Preparing a Report 3. Researching for Points	1. Primary Source: Voices 16.4 2. Researching for Points
Chapter Closer ● **Reteaching Activities**	Summarizing, Outlining			
Chapter Review	Summary, Reviewing the Facts, Basic Skills, Researching and Reporting Skills, Critical Thinking, Perspectives on Past and Present, Investigating History			
Chapter Evaluation	Chapter Test 16, Computer Test Bank Chapter 16 Test			

Chapter Overview

The power and authority of the Catholic Church began to weaken by 1500. The invention of the printing press made the works of Christian humanists and reformer Martin Luther available to those who could read. Luther's teachings spread within Germany, and his followers became known as Lutherans. The movement of Christians who turned away from the Catholic Church became known as the Protestant Reformation.

Protestantism spread to England when King Henry VIII broke with the Catholic Church after the pope would not set aside the king's first marriage. In Geneva, John Calvin systematized the Protestant philosophy and introduced the ideas of predestination and theocracy. To stop the spread of Protestantism, the Catholic Church initiated reforms to strengthen and purify itself.

Meanwhile, a scientific revolution had been developing more slowly and quietly than the religious one. Scholars such as Copernicus, Kepler, and Galileo challenged ancient scientific theories, while others developed tools that aided in making precise observations. Some of the new ideas were in direct conflict with the teachings of the Catholic Church.

Key Terms

predestination, theocracy
For additional exercises, see Vocabulary Worksheet 16.

Chapter Focus

Begin by asking students if they have ever kept an idea to themselves because they were afraid their friends or family members would ridicule them. Discuss with students the difficulties of presenting new ideas and of challenging old ones. Tell them that this chapter examines the conflicts caused by new ideas, notably the ideas of the Protestant Reformation. Ask students to recall religious revolts studied previously, for example the Great Schism and the reforms of Cluny. Explain that Luther never meant to break away from the Church, only to reform it. Ask students as they read, to identify conditions that led to a climate of reform. For example the invention of the printing press and widespread dissatisfaction with the Church helped spread Luther's teachings. Tell students this chapter also describes another challenge to established teachings during the sixteenth century—the discovery of the scientific method.

Martin Luther began a religious revolt. 1

Section Objectives

After completing Section 1, students should be able to:

1. describe the conditions that led to a religious revolt.
2. explain the main teachings of Martin Luther.
3. assess the reactions to Luther's teachings and trace their spread.

Setting the Stage

Begin by asking students to imagine Luther's thoughts as he stood before the Imperial Diet. Tell them that Luther knew how John Huss had been executed one hundred years earlier in a similar confrontation before the Council of Constance. Have students recall the main ideas of John Huss and John Wycliffe from Chapter 11 (page 242). Remind students that young Huss was burned at the stake after the Holy Roman Emperor withdrew his guarantees of safe conduct. These thoughts must have occurred to Luther as he stood before the Emperor. Ask students to consider the courage having strength of conviction requires. Section 1 explains why Martin Luther felt compelled to speak out, and how his actions started the Protestant movement.

Teaching Strategies

Discussing History: Causes of the Reformation (Objective 1) Share with students this phrase by Tetzel: "So soon as coin in coffer rings, the soul from purgatory springs." Tell students that Johann Tetzel was a Dominican monk who opposed Luther. Tetzel's ability to raise large sums for the Church was well known. This slogan was used to raise money for St. Peter's Cathedral in Rome. However, Luther knew that money Tetzel raised was diverted to local bishops and banks. Explain that Martin Luther objected to Church corruption and to the sale of indulgences. Luther called monks like Tetzel, "pardon merchants." Ask students what other complaints people had about the Church and list students' responses on the chalkboard.

Challenge students to explain how humanist writers helped change public opinion. Point out that critics of the Church such as Savonarola,

Erasmus, and Thomas More felt that the Church was indifferent to Christ's teachings about humility, poverty, and piety. Their views reflected a new emphasis among Europeans on religious piety.

Discussing History: The 95 Theses of Martin Luther (Objective 2) Select a student to read the main ideas of Martin Luther (page 349). Ask students to explain Luther's ideas concerning "good works." Ask, "How was Luther taking power away from priests? Why were these ideas threatening to the authority of the Catholic Church?" Ask students to speculate on how the Catholic Church would react to Luther's ideas. Explain that Section 3 examines the Church's reaction.

Skill Building: Analyzing Effects (Objective 3) Write the following headings on the board: "Immediate Effects," "Short-Term Effects," and "Long-Term Effects." Have students supply information for each column on the effects of Luther's actions. Students should note that Luther was excommunicated by Pope Leo X and that Charles V issued the Edict of Worms, which branded Luther as an outlaw and a heretic. Short-term effects included the peasant revolt of 1524–1525 and conflict between princes of the Holy Roman Empire. Use Overhead Transparency 49, *Lands Ruled by Charles V* to show the areas of conflict. Students should note that long-term effects (changes in language and clergy, rise of Lutheranism and Protestantism) continued to the present day, far outweighing immediate and short-term effects.

Check for Understanding Have students explain how the following people and events influenced the Protestant movement: need for Church reforms, humanist writers, teaching of Martin Luther, and the printing press.

Practice

Guided Practice
Lead a guided discussion of questions in Overhead Transparency 49 and in Section Review 1. (Answers are below.)

Define:
(a) person whose beliefs contradict those of the Church (b) separate from the Church (c) pardon from the Church (d) Protestant name given to priests

Identify:
(a) German monk who challenged the Church and started Protestant Reformation (b) assembly at which Luther and his ideas were on trial (c) Italian friar who called for reform (d) Christian humanist

who wrote *In Praise of Folly* (e) Christian humanist who wrote *Utopia* (f) book about a nearly perfect society (g) German printer who used movable type to print Bible (h) Holy Roman emperor who condemned Luther as heretic (i) powerful Austrian family from which most Holy Roman emperors were chosen.

Answer:
1. lived too extravagantly, were poorly educated, did not keep their vows of chastity
2. Printing press gave critics of popes a vehicle for spreading their views, encouraged popular piety, made Bible available to all Christians who could read, and helped new ideas spread quickly.
3. (a) Tetzel's selling of indulgences (b) Faith alone is key to salvation; Bible is only authority for Christian life; all believers have a relationship with God and do not need priests to interpret the Bible.
4. (a) order issued by Charles V declaring Luther an outlaw and heretic (b) size of empire and German nationalism
5. (a) princes who supported Luther (b) any Christian who turned away from Catholic Church
6. (a) It was too big an empire to govern effectively and suppress spread of Lutheranism. (b) Nationalistic Germans resented sending their money to Rome. (c) Princes saw an economic advantage—the seizure of Church lands—in Lutheranism.
7. Answers should include discussion of Luther's break with tradition, defiance of authority, and role as catalyst in launching a new era.

Independent Practice
Assign Independent Practice Worksheet 16.1.
Assign Vocabulary Worksheet 16.
Assign Geography Skills Worksheet 16.

Enrichment Activities

1. **Reading a Primary Source** Assign Voices from the Past Resource Book 16.1.

2. **Researching for Bonus Points** Award bonus points to students who can answer this question: What was Thomas More's official title before he was beheaded? (Chancellor of England)

Answers to Voice from the Past

1. Iron is more useful.
2. by using gold and silver for common, everyday items, minimizing their rarity, associating them with criminals.

3. the prizing of material possessions, especially those considered rare

Protestantism spread in northern Europe. 2

Section Objectives

After completing Section 2, students should be able to:

1. explain the effects of the Reformation in England.
2. identify the main traits of Calvinism.
3. trace the distribution of religions in Europe in the 1500's.

Setting the Stage

Before students read Section 2, share this quotation: (Explain that it is Henry VIII's criticism of Martin Luther.)

> What serpent so venomous as he who calls the pope's authority tyrannous? ... the whole Church is subject not only to Christ but ... to Christ's only vicar, the pope of Rome.

Tell students that Section 2 examines how Henry himself rejected the pope's authority, although he never changed his mind about Martin Luther. Tell students that Henry repudiated the authority of Rome and dismantled the Catholic Church in England, but did not embrace the teachings of Martin Luther. One result of Henry's actions was the spread of Protestantism. Ask students to try to find out Henry's motives as they read Section 2.

Teaching Strategies

Discussing History: The Reformation in England (Objective 1) Ask students how England's monarchs responded to Protestantism. After they read about Henry VIII's break with Rome tell them the king decided to strike directly at the Church's main source of power: the monasteries and their wealth. Recall that the Catholic Church controlled one-third of the land in England. Explain that besides property, the clergy controlled 10 percent of England's wealth. By closing the monasteries and selling the property, Henry greatly increased his wealth. The king's actions were carried out by royal agents—ominously known as "visitors"—who compiled itemized lists of the clerical treasures. Later they returned to take everything. Besides taking treasure, the king's agents destroyed relics that had been venerated for centuries. In all, nine tons of jewels and precious metal was taken from the ransacked monasteries. Discuss with students the impact Henry's actions had on the Catholic Church. Ask students what they can infer about support for the Catholic Church in light of Henry's ability to close and sell the monasteries. Conclude by asking if Henry's children continued his policies (page 353).

Writing about History: Calvinism (Objective 2) *Prewriting* Ask students to identify the traits of Calvinism (page 354). Ask students why the Calvinists' belief in predestination emphasized religious and moral behavior. Have students recall Renaissance values (pages 325–326). Explain that many Protestants were rebelling against these values. In Geneva, the followers of John Calvin founded a city based on their religious beliefs (theocracy). *Writing* Ask students to compare Calvinism to Renaissance values by writing a first-person narrative from the perspective of a Florentine citizen visiting Geneva. Narratives should include comparisons of religious beliefs, lifestyles, and politics. Encourage creativity by having students contrast Florence and Geneva.

Geography in History: Protestant and Catholic Europe in the 1500's (Objective 3) Show students Overhead Transparency 50, *Protestantism and Catholicism in the 1500's*. Distribute Outline Map 10: Europe. Ask, "In what areas of Europe was Protestantism the strongest? What countries had strong Calvinist movements?" Have them use the map on page 355 as a reference while they label the countries of Europe, draw a map key, and use symbols in the key to designate areas of Europe that were Catholic or Protestant in the 1500's.

Practice

Guided Practice

Lead a guided discussion of the questions in Overhead Transparency 50 and in Section Review 2. (Answers are below.)

Define:

(a) according to Calvin, the few people who will be saved from sin by God's grace (b) Calvin's doctrine holding that God has known from the beginning of time who will be saved (c) government controlled by church leaders (d) laymen who governed community churches in Scotland

Identify:
(a) Tudor king of England who began Church of England (b) first wife of Henry VIII (c) second wife of Henry (d) parliament that met at the king's summons from 1529–1536 (e) Henry's son and successor; staunch Protestant (f) Edward's half-sister and successor; Catholic who returned English Church to rule of pope (g) Queen of England who restored Protestantism (h) French religious reformer (i) preacher who spread Calvinism to Scotland

Answer:
1. feared his wife would not give birth to a boy and that there would be succession problems
2. superseded papal supremacy and greatly strengthened powers of king
3. (a) closed monasteries, seized their wealth, and sold their land (b) Edward VI—gave Protestants power; Mary—returned kingdom to Catholicism, Elizabeth—brought back Protestantism
4. (a) Elect are the few people who are chosen by the grace of God to be saved form sin and whose duty it is to rule society so as to glorify God. (b) Luther preached obedience to earthly rulers, but Calvin wanted a theocracy.
5. Knox and Protestant nobles overthrew Mary Stuart, put her infant son on throne, retained power themselves, and made Calvinism official religion.
6. Sweden, Norway, and Denmark
7. (a) duty to God greater than to king (b) Often rulers turned away from Catholicism and demanded that their subjects do the same or face punishment.

Independent Practice
Assign Independent Practice Worksheet 16.2.
Assign Basic Skill Worksheet 16.

Enrichment Activities

1. **Reading a Primary Source** Assign Voices from the Past Resource Book 16.2.

2. **Preparing a Report: Women in the Reformation** Have students prepare a report on Marguerite of Navarre, Margaret More, or Catherine Parr. Ask students to explain how these women influenced the Protestant Reformation. Interested students might wish to examine why opportunities for women were greater at the beginning of the Reformation, and how these opportunities later diminished.

3. **Researching for Bonus Points** Award bonus points to students who can answer this question: What was the name of the Archibishop of Canterbury who annulled Henry VIII's marriage to Catherine of Aragon? (Thomas Cranmer)

The Catholic Church made reforms. 3

Section Objectives

After completing Section 3, students should be able to:

1. identify the goals of the Jesuits.
2. describe reactions of the Church to Protestantism.
3. explain how the Reformation contributed to disunity in the Holy Roman Empire.

Setting the Stage

Discussing History: Jesuits (Objective 1) Explain to students that one result to the Protestant Reformation was a counter-reform movement by the Catholic Church. This counter-reformation was spearheaded by the Jesuits. Tell students that the Jesuits had no prescribed attire: each dressed according to his job as a teacher, priest, missionary, or Church envoy. Yet, the Jesuits had a uniform purpose and mission. Have students identify the Jesuits' goals. Explain that the Jesuits took a special vow to serve the pope and were trained to perform the most difficult and dangerous missions for the Church. These missions included venturing into Protestant countries where their beliefs could be considered traitorous. To gain spiritual strength the Jesuits performed rigorous mental tests. One test was to concentrate intensely on the horrors of hell in order to reinforce dedication. The success of the Jesuits can be attributed to their strong mental discipline and the single-mindedness of their faith. As they read, ask students to think about why the Jesuits were so valuable to the Catholic counter-reformation.

Teaching Strategies

Skill Building: Supporting Conclusions (Objective 2) Tell students to imagine that they are leaders of the Catholic Church during the Reformation. Have them explain the difficulties the Reformation posed for Church leaders. List students' responses on the chalkboard. Next, direct students' attention to the doctrines of the Council of Trent (page 356). Have students explain the four measures taken by the Church to counteract the Reformation. Ask how Pope Paul IV carried out the council's decrees. Discuss with students the effect of the Protestant Reformation on the Catholic Church. Ask, "In light of these reforms, did the Protestant Reformation strengthen or weaken the Catholic Church?" Have students use facts to support their conclusions.

Skill Building: Comparing and Contrasting Reformation Monarchs (Objective 3) Ask students whether the Peace of Augsburg was a success or a failure for Charles V. Point out that it weakened the Holy Roman emperor's central rule. Have students recall the characteristics of the governments of England and of the Holy Roman Empire (See Chapter 10 and Chapter 11). Explain that Charles V's inability to unite his kingdom represented a continuation of historical trends in the Holy Roman Empire. Unlike Henry VIII in England, Charles had no unifying Parliament to legitimize his efforts to impose a state religion. Ask students to explain how parliament helped Henry become head of the Anglican church, in contrast to Charles' difficulties with the German princes.

Check for Understanding Have students complete the following sentence: As a response to the Protestant Reformation, the Catholic Church took the following actions: _____ .

Practice

Guided Practice
Lead students in a guided discussion of the questions in Section Review 3. (Answers are below.)

Identify:
(a) founder of Jesuits (b) monastic order founded by Loyola (c) meeting at which Catholic leaders drew up doctrines reforming the Church (d) list of books Pope Paul IV considered dangerous to the Catholic faith (e) agreement allowing each German prince to choose Catholicism or Lutheranism

Answer:
1. (a) monastic order started by Ignatius Loyola (b) founding good schools, converting non-Christians to Catholicism, and preventing Protestantism from spreading
2. (a) directed investigation of abuses in Church practices, approved Jesuit order, called a council of Church leaders (b) carried out council's decrees, drew up *Index of Forbidden Books*
3. Pope's word was final; good works as well as

faith were necessary for salvation, the Bible and the Church were equal authorities for Christian conduct; indulgences, pilgrimages, venerations of holy relics were acceptable religious practices.
4. led to religious division
5. (a) Counter-Reformation; Catholic Reformation (b) Counter — suggests that it is a defensive movement with a goal of preventing Protestantism from spreading, Catholic — stresses the desire of Catholics to end abuses and purify their own religion. (c) Writings of historians reflect their prejudices.

Independent Practice
Assign Independent Practice Worksheet 16.3.
Assign Critical Thinking Worksheet 16.

Enrichment Activities

1. **Reading a Primary Source** Assign Voices from the Past Resource Book 16.3.

2. **Preparing a Report** Have students write a report on the Jesuit Order. Reports should include information on the present-day work of the Jesuits. Students might wish to focus on Jesuit schools.

3. **Researching for Bonus Points** What did the vow taken by the Jesuits require? Hint: Ignatius Loyola called it, "the cause and principal foundation" of his society. (obedience to the pope)

Scientists challenged old assumptions. 4

Section Objectives

After completing Section 4, students should be able to:

1. explain why the ideas of Copernicus and Galileo threatened the Church.
2. explain the scientific method and describe scientific achievements of the sixteenth and seventeenth centuries.
3. discuss why new ideas often cause conflict.

Setting the Stage

Tell students that social scientists in the present-day United States have found that an average of fifteen years elapses between a discovery and its widespread acceptance. Ask students if they think future historians might identify television, computers, and medical technology as part of a scientific revolution. Ask them, how these scientific advances have changed our world. Tell students to observe the effect of scientific discoveries as they read Section 4.

Teaching Strategies

Discussing History: Copernicus and Galileo (Objective 1) Ask students why Copernicus' discoveries might be referred to as the "Copernican Revolution." Then ask students to imagine Galileo's excitement over his observations with the telescope. Explain that he expected the heavenly bodies to be perfectly smooth spheres. Instead, he observed craters on the moon, rings around Saturn, and spots on the Sun. Galileo was using a scientific method perfected by Renaissance artists: observation. Remind students how Renaissance artists studied nature to understand anatomy. Like the findings of Leonardo da Vinci and Michelangelo, Galileo's discoveries led him to challenge learning that was based on ancient writings. Like Martin Luther, Galileo professed ideas that threatened the Catholic Church. Discuss with students Galileo's decision to recant his beliefs. Ask students how Galileo and Copernicus changed the way people viewed their physical and spiritual worlds.

Skill Building: Making Inferences (Objective 2) Remind students that a conclusion is the last step in the process of inductive reasoning, the basis of the scientific method. In inductive reasoning, conclusions are based on an accumulation of specific facts that are gathered through experiments and observations. This was the method used by Galileo and Kepler. Tell students that medieval scholars, such as Ptolemy, did not base their work on observation or experiments, but on mathematical rules formulated by ancient Greek mathematicians. Facts were deduced based on application of the rules. Ask students why the telescope, microscope, thermometer, and barometer are tools for inductive researchers. Ask, "How might the inductive method be better than the deductive method for scientific research?" (Facts can be verified; rules and principles might be wrong.)

Relating Past to Present: Problems of Change (Objective 3) Discuss with students the statement from the text: "Rarely are new ideas accepted right away. In fact, they are more likely to be treated at first with deep suspicion." Ask students if they

believe present-day cultures regard new discoveries with suspicion. Ask them to speculate if the rapid pace of scientific discoveries in the twentieth century has made our culture more accustomed to changes. Have students relate their observations to the changes caused by the Scientific Revolution of the sixteenth and seventeenth centuries. Explain that Galileo challenged ideas on which Church doctrine was based. With the Protestant Reformation gaining ground, the Church did not want another challenge to its teachings.

Check for Understanding Ask students to explain how perceptions about the universe were changed by scientific discoveries in the 1500's.

Practice

Guided Practice
Lead students in a guided discussion of the questions in Section Review 4. (Answers are below.)

Define:
changes in scientific thought in 1500's challenging the ideas of the ancient thinkers

Identify:
(a) ancient astronomer who wrote that Earth was the center of the universe (b) Polish scholar who theorized that Earth and other planets moved around the sun (c) German astronomer who confirmed Copernicus' ideas of planetary motion (d) Italian scientist who observed surface of the moon through a telescope and conducted experiments in physics (e) Dutch scientist who used microscope to observe bacteria (f) German physicist who made the first mercury thermometer (g) Swedish astronomer who created another scale for mercury thermometer (h) student of Galileo who developed barometer

Answer:
1. (a) center (b) Earth revolved around sun. (c) Copernicus' theory
2. Moon had mountains and plains on its surface; sun had many dark spots.
3. telescope to enlarge far-off objects; microscope to enlarge minute objects; thermometer to measure temperatures; barometer to measure atmospheric pressure
4. (a) by writing a book that appeared to support Copernican theory (b) He was forced to recant and was kept under house arrest until his death.
5. (a) through observation and the study of data (b) Medieval thinkers drew conclusions without testing by relying on classics and Bible as authorities. (c) Possible answer: Scientific

method would try to study past patterns of earthquake occurrence and other geological data to explain reasons for earthquakes; medieval method would rely on past authorities who wrote about earthquakes or on biblical passages to explain earthquakes.

Independent Practice
Assign Independent Practice Worksheet 16.4.

Enrichment Activities

1. **Reading a Primary Source** Assign Voices from the Past Resource Book 16.4.

2. **Researching for Bonus Points** Award bonus points to students who can determine the magnifying power of Galileo's first telescope. (power of 32)

Concluding the Chapter

1. **Chapter Closer**
   Ask students to choose two events described in this chapter that they think had the greatest impact on European history. Students should give evidence to support their choices.

2. **Reteaching Activities**
   a. **Summarizing** Ask students to summarize the teachings of Martin Luther and John Calvin.
   b. **Outlining** Have students use the headings in Section 1 to write a sentence outline.

3. **Chapter Review Activities**
   Assign Chapter Review 16 activities.

Chapter Evaluation

Chapter Test 16 and Computer Test Bank Chapter 16 Test can be used to evaluate your students' understanding of this chapter.

Answers to Chapter Review 16

Reviewing the Facts
1. **a.** government controlled by church leaders **b.** Calvin's doctrine stating that God has known from the beginning of time who will be saved
2. **a.** Italian friar who called for Church reform **b.** Christian humanist who wrote *In Praise of Folly* **c.** Christian humanist who wrote *Utopia*

d. More's book that describes a nearly perfect society **e.** German printer who printed a Bible, the first full-size book with movable type **f.** German artist whose drawings of biblical figures stirred religious feelings **g.** German monk who challenged the Church and began Protestant Reformation **h.** Holy Roman emperor who issued Edict of Worms declaring Luther heretic **i.** meeting of German princes and bishops for trial of Luther **j.** king of England who broke with pope **k.** first wife of Henry VIII **l.** parliament that approved the Act of Supremacy **m.** returned English Church to the rule of the pope **n.** set forth systematic Protestant philosophy that taught predestination **o.** according to Calvin, the few people who will be saved by God's grace **p.** Swiss city which became Calvinistic **q.** brought Calvinism to Scotland **r.** founder of Jesuits **s.** list of books considered dangerous to the Catholic faith **t.** agreement allowing German princes to choose either Catholicism or Lutheranism as official state religion and outlawing Calvinism and other forms of Protestantism **u.** challenged Ptolemaic ideas with theory that Earth and other planets moved around the sun **v.** confirmed Copernicus' ideas of planetary motion **w.** observed surface of the moon through a telescope and was condemned by the Church for supporting Copernicus

3. **(a)** Bands of angry German peasants demanding an end to economic and political bondage went about the countryside raiding monasteries, pillaging, and burning. **(b)** Luther wanted only peaceful reform and he urged the German princes to crush the revolt. The lower classes felt betrayed by Luther.

4. **(a)** The Act made the English king, not the Roman pope, the official head of England's Church. **(b)** He closed all monasteries, seized their wealth and lands, and sold much of the land to nobles and members of the middle class, giving them reason to support Protestantism **(c)** Edward VI was a staunch Protestant; Mary, a Catholic; and Elizabeth I, a Protestant.

5. **(a)** God has predestined who will be saved. **(b)** protestant nobles led by John Knox overthrew the Catholic queen of Scotland, created a national church, and made Calvinism Scotland's official religion

Basic Skills
1. **(a)** Calvinists, Lutherans **(b)** Calvinism: Geneva, Netherlands, Scotland; Lutheranism: Brandenburg, Saxony, Denmark, Norway, Sweden
2. 1509, *In Praise of Folly*; 1516, *Utopia*; 1521,

Diet of Worms; 1534, Act of Supremacy; 1555, Peace of Augsburg; 1559, *Index of Forbidden Books*

3. Role in Reformation: Luther sparked the Reformation by accusing Pope and Church of straying from the Bible; attacked "pardon merchants"; Calvin gave order to the new faith. Doctrine: Luther, salvation by faith alone, Bible the only authority, priesthood of all believers; Calvin, human nature sinful, only the elect will be saved, predestination. Political Ideas: Luther had support of peasants, then sided with princes against peasants; believed in obedience to earthly rulers, preached revolt against ungodly rulers. Calvin promoted ideal of theocracy; led a theocracy in Geneva. Writings—Luther: 95 Theses, translation of Bible into German; pamphlets, sermons. Calvin: *Institutes of the Christian Religion.*

Researching and Reporting Skills

1. Reaction against Renaissance: Reformation condemned luxuries, worldliness, immoral life, search for pleasure; preached sobriety and piety and return to virtues of the Bible. Reformation as result of humanistic thought: encouraged challenge of established ideas and authority; critical of uneducated priesthood; favored individualism by encouraging reading and personal interpretation of the Bible; asserted the priesthood of all believers, rejected Pope's authority.
2. Pamphlet might make the following points: (1) Dangers of heresy; need to preach Christianity to the heathens; need for more educated clergy who will observe obedience and chastity. (2) Spiritual army is the answer. (3) Describes the Society of Jesus and its goals, showing how it is the answer. (4) Calls upon the reader to join.

Critical Thinking

1. Immediate causes: Henry VIII's wish to remarry and the pope's refusal to annul his marriage. Henry's hunger for church wealth; Luther's denouncing the selling of indulgences; Calvin's leadership. Remote causes: nationalism conflicted with papal supremacy; people were indignant at luxurious living of Church authorities and at low moral and educational standards of priests; humanistic ideas challenged established thinking and encouraged individualism; printing gave people the opportunity for individuals to read the Bible and helped to spread reformers' ideas.
2. Luther opposed certain teachings of the Church, role of priests, selling of indulgences; wanted salvation by faith, not good works, with Bible as the only authority, and a direct relation of individuals to God.

3. (a) Eliminating abuses and improving moral, religious, and educational standards of clergy; fighting Protestantism by reaffirming authority of the church and of tradition, and the doctrine that faith without good works will not save. (b) Coming to an agreement about the status of Protestantism in Germany in view of the failure of Charles V's efforts to crush the Protestant princes.

4. (a) Church lands that constituted one third of English lands were seized by Henry VIII and sold to nobles or wealthy middle class people. Luther's ideas resulted in peasant revolts against serfdom which Luther encouraged the princes to put down ruthlessly. German princes used the Reformation as a pretext to seize Church lands. (b) Landowners in possession of Church lands became staunch supporters of the Reformation in both England and Germany. Luther lost the support of the peasants and gained that of the princes.

5. (a) ideas of Aristotle and Ptolemy that the earth was center of the universe and that sun and stars circled round the earth; that earth was made of impure matter, whereas sun, moon and stars were made of pure, eternal substances, smooth and perfect. (b) The earth is not center of the universe. It circles round the sun and rotates on itself. Neither sun nor moon are made of pure substance of heavenly light. The telescope showed mountains on the moon, and dark spots on the sun. (c) Religious authorities were outraged, particularly if they took the Bible literally. It took science many years to develop the implications of these discoveries.

6. (a) Both were questioning authority and challenging established ideas. (b) The Reformation, because issues and conflicts of religion touched the daily lives of all people. The findings of the Scientific Revolution were condemned by the Church so that it took many years for them to have their full impact.

Perspectives on Past and Present

Evaluations will differ. Students should realize what printing and the availability of books meant for the spreading of ideas and the growth of knowledge. They should then compare what television and computers have meant in terms of communication and processing of ideas.

Investigating History

Students' reports will vary.

The Spanish Empire and Shifts in European Power

Chapter Overview

The 1500's and 1600's saw a major power struggle in Europe. Spain gained an enormous empire in the Americas. In 1581, the northern part of the Netherlands won independence from Spain. The Dutch developed a capitalist economic system and soon replaced the Italians as bankers.

During Germany's Thirty Years' War, in which Protestants fought Catholics, France entered on the side of the Protestants. When the war ended, Germany's political unity was destroyed, and its economy was in shambles. France was the strongest state in Europe.

The 1500's and 1600's were also a time of creativity. The paintings of El Greco and Velázquez in Spain and those of Rembrandt and Hals in Amsterdam reflected the values of their times. In France, the writings of Rabelais, Montaigne, and Descartes marked a sharp break with the ideas of the Middle Ages.

Key Terms

conquistadors, capitalism
For additional exercises, see Vocabulary Worksheet 17.

Chapter Focus

Tell students that understanding how different cultures interact is a part of studying the past. Cultural differences are potential sources of conflict. Note that many present-day conflicts center on divergent beliefs about economics and religion, like the conflicts this chapter examines. Direct students' attention to the picture on page 363. Ask, "What cultural contact does the picture show? What were some cultural differences between the Aztecs and the Europeans?" Explain that the Spanish voyages of exploration (Chapter 15) became voyages of conquest. The wealth that flowed to Spain as a result of the conquests in the Americas enabled Spain to pursue its religious and political goals. Tell students this chapter discusses the consequences of the meeting between Cortés and Montezuma.

Advance Planner

	Section 1
Objectives	1. Contrast the Spanish and Aztec cultures. 2. Identify Spanish motivations for conquests in the Americas. 3. Compare and contrast Spaniards' goals and explain their consequences for the Indians.
Setting the Stage	Spain's need for Indian wealth and labor
Teaching Strategies	Writing about History: Montezuma and Cortés Transferring Ideas: Crusading Conquistadors Skill Building: Comparing and Contrasting Goals of Conquest Check for Understanding
Guided Practice	Transparency 51 Q&A Section Review 1
Independent Practice Worksheets	Independent Practice 17.1 Basic Skills 17 Geography Skills 17 Vocabulary 17
Enrichment	1. Primary Source: Voices 17.1 2. ★ Analyzing a Quotation 3. Researching for Points

Spain built an overseas empire.

1

1. contrast the Spanish and Aztec cultures.
2. identify Spanish motivations for conquests in the Americas.
3. compare and contrast Spaniards' goals and explain their consequences for the Indians.

Section Objectives

After completing Section 1, students should be able to:

Setting the Stage

Ask students to imagine the anxiety of Spanish officials as they waited in the Seville harbor for

| Chapter 17 | The Spanish Empire and Shifts in European Power 1500–1650 | ★ Advanced |
| Focus | The consequences of the meeting between Cortés and Montezuma | ● Basic |

Section 2	Section 3	Section 4	Section 5
1. Describe the political goals and leadership style of Philip II. 2. Explain why Cervantes' work is regarded as the first modern European novel. 3. Identify reasons for Spain's economic decline after 1600.	1. Contrast the economies of Spain and the Netherlands. 2. Explain the role of human-environment interaction in Amsterdam's development. 3. Describe elements of Rembrandt's art.	1. Explain the methods of Henry IV in uniting France and strengthening the monarchy. 2. Describe the political views and tactics of Cardinal Richelieu.	1. Identify the causes of the Thirty Years' War. 2. Describe the alliances and main events of the Thirty Years' War. 3. Explain how the provisions of the Treaty of Westphalia affected the nations of Europe.
Spain's economic decline	The importance of a leader's ability to communicate	Effects of religion and politics on nation-building	Discussing History: Causes of the Thirty Years' War
Discussing History: The Escorial and Philip II Skill Building: Analyzing a Quotation Economics and History: Inflation Check for Understanding	Economics and History: Capitalism Using Geographic Themes: Human-Environment Interaction Teaching with Pictures: Nightwatch Check for Understanding	Writing about History: Henry IV Discussing History: Cardinal Richelieu Check for Understanding	Discussing History: Alliances in the Thirty Years' War Skill Building: Recognizing Main Ideas Check for Understanding
Section Review 2 Independent Practice 17.2 Critical Thinking 17	Section Review 3 Independent Practice 17.3	Section Review 4 Independent Practice 17.4	Section Review 5 Independent Practice 17.5
1. Primary Source: Voices 17.2 2. ★ Creative Writing 3. Researching for Points	1. Primary Source: Voices 17.3 2. Creative Writing 3. Researching for Points	1. Primary Source: Voices 17.4 2. ★ Analyzing a Quotation 3. Researching for Points	1. Primary Source: Voices 17.5 2. Preparing a Time Line 3. Researching for Points

Chapter Closer ● Reteaching Activities	Summarizing, Identifying Main Ideas, Recalling Information
Chapter Review	Summary, Reviewing the Facts, Basic Skills, Researching and Reporting Skills, Critical Thinking, Perspectives on Past and Present, Investigating History
Chapter Evaluation	Chapter Test 17, Computer Test Bank Chapter 17 Test

Unit V Review Geographic Theme:	Movement: How did European civilization spread around the globe?
Unit Perspectives:	Understanding History (Classifying, Identifying, Relating), Critical Thinking, Making Decisions, Continuity and Change
Unit Evaluation	Unit V Test

the gold and silver shipment from America. Tell students that in 1545 the Spanish discovered rich gold and silver mines in Mexico and in Peru. The precious metals were transported to Spain once a year in large convoys that were protected from pirates by warships. Spain relied on these shipments to maintain its vast empire and to finance the religious wars of Philip II.

Tell students that many Aztecs died from overwork and harsh treatment while mining gold and silver for their Spanish overlords. Despite their disregard for the rights of Indians, many Spaniards regarded the Aztec and Inca civilizations as highly advanced. They expressed astonishment that a non-Christian empire could be so well organized. Have students recall Spain's need for Indian wealth and labor.

Teaching Strategies

Writing about History: Montezuma and Cortés (Objective 1) *Prewriting* Tell students that Cortés was thirty-four years old when he met the forty-year-old Montezuma. Cortés was ambitious and determined to bring gold and glory to Spain and to himself. (Explain that Cortés had written a number of letters to the Emperor, describing the incredible wonders he saw and the reasons for his decision.) Equally ambitious, Montezuma had ruled a large empire successfully for seventeen years, although he had been troubled by bad omens. *Writing* Divide students into pairs. Have one student in each pair portray Montezuma, and the other, Cortés. Direct students to write from the point of view of Montezuma or Cortés, as follows: Montezuma's Diary—Have students write journal entries, interpreting the unfolding events of Spanish contact from Montezuma's point of view. Cortés' Letter—Have students write a letter from Cortés to Charles V. Conclude by having pairs of students write and role play a dialogue between Cortés and Montezuma. What differences between Aztec and Spanish cultures do the dialogues reveal?

Transferring Ideas: Crusading Conquistadors (Objective 2) Explain that Spanish expeditions included priests whose job was to convert the Indians to Catholicism. The conquistadors were motivated by an intense Catholic faith as well as a desire for treasure. Ask students how the Spaniards' belief in the superiority of Christianity was demonstrated in their attitudes toward the Aztecs and the Incas. Recall the motives of the crusaders (page 228). Ask, "What two motivations did both the crusaders and the conquistadors share?" (religion and profit)

Skill Building: Comparing and Contrasting Goals of Conquest (Objective 3) Explain to students that the Indians in New Spain were controlled by three competing groups—Spanish settlers, Catholic priests, and the government in Spain. Ask students to identify the different interests of each group. Tell students that many friars wanted the Indians to be treated as Christians and as Spanish citizens. Ask, "How would such treatment contradict the needs of the *encomienda* system?" (The system depended on forced labor.) Ask, "Why were Spanish settlers unwilling to treat Indians as equals?" (Settlers wanted Indian lands.) Next have students explain the role of the viceroy, who represented the government in Madrid. Discuss with students the relationship among the three groups and the effects of each group on Indian life.

Check for Understanding Call on students to identify the main economic and cultural effects of the Spanish conquests on the following groups: conquistadors, Indians, Spanish government.

Practice

Guided Practice
Lead a guided discussion of the questions in Overhead Transparency 51 and in Section Review 1. (Answers are below.)

Define:
(a) Spanish fortune hunter (b) Spanish nobleman who acted as royal agent (c) privilege granted to certain settlers

Identify:
(a) emperor of Aztecs (b) capital city of the Aztecs (c) conqueror of Aztecs (d) Indian woman who helped Cortés (e) Spain's overseas territories (f) conqueror of Incas (g) Inca ruler killed by Pizarro (h) Spaniard who claimed the Mississippi River for Spain (i) Spaniard who explored as far north as Kansas (j) helped extend Spain's conquests in the Andes (k) woman who helped conquer Chile for Spain

Answer:
1. (a) Quetzalcoatl was the light-skinned god who had once ruled the land around Lake Texcoco and had vowed to return to reclaim his kingdom. (b) The Aztecs thought that Cortés was this god and let him enter the capital.
2. used an army of Aztec-hating Indians
3. There was no one to lead the Inca army.
4. (a) by which the Council of the Indies met in Spain and sent its laws to viceroys in Mexico City and Lima (b) being born in Spain
5. (a) farming and mining (b) Indian slave labor

6. Look for answers that consider such things as superior weapons, superstitious fear over Quetzalcoatl's return, Doña Marina's role as translator, the inherent trust of the natives, fate, the role of Indians who hated the Aztecs, disease.

Independent Practice

Assign Independent Practice Worksheet 17.1.
Assign Geography Skills Worksheet 17.
Assign Vocabulary Worksheet 17.

Enrichment Activities

1. **Reading a Primary Source** Assign Voices from the Past Resource Book 17.1.

2. **Analyzing a Quotation** Hernando Cortés wrote to Charles V: "It seems most credible that our Lord God has purposefully allowed these lands [Mexico] to be discovered ... so that Your Majesties may be fruitful and deserving in His sight by causing these barbaric tribes to be enlightened and brought to the faith by Your Hand." Have advanced students analyze this quotation and explain its significance for understanding the Spanish conquests in the Americas.

3. **Researching for Bonus Points** Award bonus points to students who can answer this question. Who discovered the lost Inca city of Machu Picchu in 1911. (Hiram Bingham)

Answers to Voice from the Past

1. A battle has destroyed houses and people and the inhabitants are grieving.
2. had to eat twigs, grasses, lizards, rats, worms
3. **(a)** despair and destruction **(b)** adobe walls, quetzal feathers

Spain was a Catholic bulwark.　2

Section Objectives

After completing Section 2 students should be able to:

1. describe the political goals and leadership style of Philip II.
2. explain why Cervantes' work is regarded as the first modern European novel.

3. identify reasons for Spain's economic decline after 1600.

Setting the Stage

Ask students to recall the definition of *empire* and the problems faced by rulers of the Roman and Byzantine empires. Ask, "What makes ruling a large empire difficult?" List students' responses on the chalkboard. Select a student to read the first paragraph of Section 2 (page 368). Then tell students that fifty years later, Spain was nearly bankrupt. Ask students to predict how a country with access to unlimited wealth could go bankrupt. Explain that Section 2 examines the causes of Spain's economic decline.

Teaching Strategies

Discussing History: The Escorial and Philip II (Objective 1) After students have read Section 2, suggest that the Escorial reflected Philip's dedication to the Church. Students should recall that the Escorial was a monastery, as well as the seat of government and that Philip surrounded himself with priests rather than with courtiers. Tell students that Philip did not live in the grand chambers of the Escorial, but in small, unadorned rooms. From these chambers he ruled over half of Christendom in a style that some observers called plodding, slow, and meticulous—but always determined. Philip's style of governing reflected his general distrust. How did Philip's actions against the Turks and the Dutch reflect his religious commitment?

Skill Building: Analyzing a Quotation (Objective 2) Read and discuss the excerpt from *Don Quixote* (page 371). Ask students why many critics regard *Don Quixote* as the first "modern" European novel. (It is a satire of medieval values.) Define a *satire* as a literary work that pokes fun at or mocks the manners and morals of a society. Satires include *irony*—using words to mean something different from what they usually mean. When Sancho Panza says "there are ... maybe only one and a half" [of us], he is suggesting that Don Quixote is "not all there." This is an example of irony. Have students find information in the text supporting the idea that Cervantes satirized the manners and morals of the Middle Ages. Students might also give examples of satire and irony in present-day contexts. Conclude by asking students to speculate why *Don Quixote* is still widely read.

Economics and History: Inflation (Objective 3) Ask students to define *inflation* and to explain why it is an economic crisis. Point out that the conditions that ruined Spain's economy in the 1650's have caused economic problems in many countries throughout history. Explain that inflation is a sharp and continuing rise in prices for goods and services. The rise in prices is caused by an oversupply of money in relation to the supply of goods. As a result, the value of the money decreases and has less "buying power." That is, a given amount of money buys less than it did before. Ask students what caused Spain's inflation in the 1650's. (an oversupply of silver and gold from Spain's American colonies)

Check for Understanding Have students list three reasons for Spain's rise to power and three reasons for Spain's economic decline.

Practice

Guided Practice
Lead a guided discussion of the questions in Section Review 2. (Answers are below.)

Define:
upward spiral of prices

Identify:
(a) king of Spain from 1556 to 1598, who ruled an empire that circled the globe (b) Philip's palace (c) sea battle resulting in major victory for Christendom against the Muslims (d) Spanish fleet sent by Philip II to defeat Protestant England (e) Greek-born artist whose major works were painted in Spain (f) painter of Spain's royal family (g) Spanish author of *Don Quixote de la Mancha* (h) character in Cervantes' book

Answer:
1. (a) Spain, its American colonies, duchy of Milan, kingdom of Naples, Franche-Comté, and the Netherlands (b) Portugal and its strongholds in Africa, India, and the East Indies
2. Philip demanded many reports from his advisors, agonized over decisions, and trusted no one to help him.
3. to strengthen Catholic Church and his monarchy
4. (a) helped crush the Ottoman Turks in the Battle of Lepanto (b) the Netherlands and England
5. Gold and silver flooded Spain, causing the value of these metals to drop and prices to rise.
6. Philip would have approved of the contributions El Greco and Velázquez made to the strengthening of both the Catholic Church and the monarchy and probably would have disapproved of Cervantes' satire.

Independent Practice
Assign Independent Practice Worksheet 17.2.
Assign Critical Thinking Worksheet 17.

Enrichment Activities

1. **Reading a Primary Source** Assign Voices from the Past Resource Book 17.3.

2. **Creative Writing** Have advanced students read excerpts from *Don Quixote* and write essays relating episodes from the novel to the present day. Share students' work with the class.

3. **Researching for Bonus Points** Award bonus points to students who can answer this question: To what saint is the Escorial dedicated? (Saint Lawrence)

The Netherlands won independence. 3

Section Objectives

After completing Section 3, students should be able to:

1. contrast the economies of Spain and the Netherlands.
2. explain the role of human-environment interaction in Amsterdam's development.
3. describe elements of Rembrandt's art.

Setting the Stage

Ask students what problems might arise if the President of the United States did not speak English and was not familiar with American customs. Discuss the importance of communication and rapport between a leader and his or her country. Tell students that the Spanish king Philip II did not share the same language, religion, political values or economic policies as his Dutch subjects. The Netherlands had embraced the new ideas of the Renaissance and the Reformation, while Spain clung to medieval traditions. Ask students to trace these differences as they read.

Teaching Strategies

Economics and History: Capitalism (Objective 1) Have students compare the economies of Spain and the Netherlands. Ask, "How was Dutch capitalism different from Spanish mercantilism?"

Point out that Spain's mercantilism depended on wealth from the American colonies. Clarify the definition of capitalism as the buying and selling of goods and services through the use of money and for the purpose of making a profit. Ask, "How did the business class in Holland use trade and banking to earn profits?" Have students write paragraphs summarizing how the Dutch East Indies Company practiced capitalism.

Using Geographic Themes: Human-Environment Interaction (Objective 2) Tell students that Amsterdam's population rapidly increased as the Dutch economy grew strong. The city planners built a system of canals to give Amsterdam's merchants easy access to waterways. The canals were dug by hand and extended to seacoast ports. Explain that the land on which Amsterdam was built lies twelve feet below sea level. To keep the city from being flooded at high tides, the Dutch built an intricate system of dikes and locks to control water levels. Two hundred bridges spanned the canals, facilitating transportation and trade within the city. Ask students to explain how the Dutch used their unique environment to strengthen their economy. Tell students that most of the canals built in the 1600's are still in use.

Teaching with Pictures: *Nightwatch* (Objective 3) Tell students that the group portrait was a Dutch innovation and was perfected by Dutch and Flemish artists. Direct students' attention to the picture of Rembrandt's *Nightwatch* (page 375). This painting was commissioned by a military captain and seventeen of his guardsmen. Each of the guardsmen had paid an equal amount of money for the painting. Ask students why some guardsmen might have felt slighted. Explain that Rembrandt is renowned for his ability to combine light, shadow, color, and movement. Ask how this picture utilizes these four elements. Have students suggest how the painting portrays liveliness and motion. Explain that in the *Nightwatch*, Rembrandt experimented with the concept of group portraiture by including children, dogs, and other elements not directly related to his main subjects. Art historians say that Rembrandt's unconventionality and mischievousness are reflected in his work. Ask students to recall Renaissance artists, such as Leonardo da Vinci, who had a similar temperament.

Check for Understanding Ask students to explain the economic and religious differences between Spain and the Netherlands, and how these differences led to Dutch independence.

Practice

Guided Practice
Lead a guided discussion of the questions in Section Review 3. (Answers are below.)

Define:
(a) elective system of government (b) economic system the goal of which is to make profits (c) money invested in business ventures (d) money remaining after all costs of a business are paid (e) economic changes toward capitalism

Identify:
(a) name given low marshland region between northern Germany and northern France (b) angry Calvinists who rampaged through Catholic churches (c) Dutch leader of the revolt against Spain (d) elected governor of a province (e) trading firm with all the powers of a sovereign state (f) financial and commercial center of Europe by 1650 (g) greatest Dutch painter during the 1600's

Answer:
1. (a) It had many Protestant congregations, did not hold to the feudal and guild systems, and took the lead in new ways of doing business. (b) It had been part of the Holy Roman Empire and was given to Philip II by Charles V.
2. (a) policies aimed at stamping out Protestantism and raising taxes (b) antagonized many Dutch; led to rampages on Catholic churches.
3. (a) to free the Netherlands from Spain (b) to establish a country where both Protestantism and Catholicism were tolerated (c) Seven provinces declared independence and became United Provinces of Netherlands in 1581; idea of religious toleration gradually took root.
4. by opening the floodgates
5. (a) 7 provinces (b) remained under Spanish control
6. (a) republic with each province having an elected governor (b) organized to make profits, reinvest profits
7. (a) to break Portugal's hold on the Indian Ocean spice trade; capital needed too much for investor (b) power to make war, coin money, and rule colonies
8. United Provinces was not a kingdom but a republic, and it permitted religious tolerance.

Independent Practice
Assign Independent Practice Worksheet 17.3.

Enrichment Activities

1. **Reading a Primary Source** Assign Voices from the Past Resource Book 17.3.

2. **Creative Writing** Ask students to imagine they are journalists during the Dutch revolt. Have them write news accounts of the measures the Dutch took to drive out the Spanish.

3. **Researching for Bonus Points** Award bonus points to students who answer this question: What was the formal name of Rembrandt's painting, *Nightwatch? (The company of Captain Frans Banning Cocq and Lieutenant Willem van Ruytenburch)*

France's crown changed hands.

4

Section Objectives

After completing Section 4, students should be able to:

1. explain the methods of Henry IV in uniting France and strengthening the monarchy.
2. describe the political views and tactics of Cardinal Richelieu.

Setting the Stage

Ask students why they think the framers of the United States Constitution separated religion from government. Why might religious struggles be more harmful to a country than strictly political conflicts? Have students recall how divergent religious beliefs embittered the Spanish and the Dutch. Ask students if they think compromise is an effective tactic in solving religious disputes. Tell them that Section 4 discusses the efforts of a French king and a French cardinal to resolve conflicts between Protestants and Catholics in France.

Teaching Strategies

Writing about History: Henry IV (Objective 1) *Prewriting* Ask students why Henry IV decided to become a Catholic. Students should recognize that Henry needed the support of France's Catholic majority. He also knew that to rule France successfully he would need the support of the Huguenots. Recall the events during Catherine de Medici's rule that had alienated the Huguenots. Ask students how Henry solved his dilemma through compromise (Edict of Nantes). Explain that the Edict of Nantes marked the first official recognition of the idea that two religions can co-

exist in the same nation. *Writing* Have students write short essays contrasting the policies of Henry IV of France with those of Philip II of Spain in resolving religious conflicts and strengthening their monarchies.

Discussing History: Cardinal Richelieu (Objective 2) Have students recall Machiavelli's ideas about politics (page 331). Ask, "According to Machiavelli, what qualities did a political leader need to be successful?" Tell students that Richelieu's political career reflected his belief in Machiavellian principles of winning and maintaining power. Richelieu believed that his goal of making France a secure and unified nation necessitated severe governance, not kindness. Critics and admirers alike acknowledged that Richelieu was an outstanding statesman. By strengthening the French monarchy he accomplished what many had failed to do. Ask students to explain how Richelieu's *intendants* helped to weaken enemies of the monarchy. Then have students explain the significance of Richelieu's actions at La Rochelle (page 379). Tell students that Section 5 examines Richelieu's role in weakening the Hapsburgs while strengthening France.

Check for Understanding Have students explain the roles of the following people in the unification of France: Huguenots, Catherine de Medici, Henry IV, and Cardinal Richelieu.

Practice

Guided Practice
Lead a guided discussion of the questions in Section Review 4. (Answers are below.)

Define:
(a) French Catholic leaders who wanted peace and worked for strong monarchy and religious toleration (b) French government agents (c) short written work on a single topic

Identify:
(a) family that ruled France from 1328 to about 1590 (b) power behind the throne of her sons (c) French followers of Calvinism (d) first Bourbon king of France (e) declaration of religious tolerance (f) virtual ruler of France during reign of Louis XIII (g) French monk, author of satires (h) French thinker who introduced the essay (i) founder of modern philosophy

Answer:
1. (a) wars with Spain for control of Italy, death of king (b) Hatred between Huguenots and Catholics led to violence.

2. (a) Bourbon and Guise (b) Protestant, Catholic
3. (a) She arranged for Coligny, a Protestant advisor to her son, to be killed in order to protect her position as power behind the throne. (b) Charles IX agreed to Coligny's assassination only if Huguenots would also be killed; Catherine approved of massacre.
4. religious toleration and a strong monarchy
5. (a) for the sake of his war-weary country (b) declared in the Edict of Nantes that Huguenots could worship in peace; set up at least one house of worship in every district except Paris
6. (a) increase the power of the Bourbon monarchy and make France the strongest state in Europe (b) Huguenots had right to fortify their cities, and a walled city could defy the king. (c) ordered many to take down their fortified castles and strengthened the powers of intendants to collect taxes and administer justice
7. Henry did not state that he believed in one specific religion.
8. He wanted peace for France and a strong monarchy and was nationalistic more than religious.

Independent Practice
Assign Independent Practice Worksheet 17.4.

Enrichment Activities

1. **Reading a Primary Source** Assign Voices from the Past Resource Book 17.4.

2. **Analyzing a Quotation** Have advanced students explain Descarte's claim, "I think, therefore I am." How did Descarte's philosophy reflect his faith in science and reason?

3. **Researching for Bonus Points** Award bonus points to students who can answer this question: Who was the founder of the French Academy? (Richelieu)

Religious wars split Germany. 5

Section Objectives

After completing Section 5 students should be able to:

1. identify the causes of the Thirty Years' War.
2. describe the alliances and main events of the Thirty Years' War.

3. explain how the provisions of the Treaty of Westphalia affected the nations of Europe.

Setting the Stage

Discussing History: Causes of the Thirty Years' War (Objective 1) Ask students to recall why the Peace of Augsburg was partly a failure for Charles V (page 357). Explain that the Thirty Years' War was a result of Charles' inability to unite his kingdom and to relieve tension between Protestant and Catholic princes. Tell students that religious disputes in the Holy Roman Empire were compounded by the intervention of France and Spain, and that the war left the Holy Roman Empire weak and destitute. Have students trace the effects of the war on the Holy Roman Empire as they read.

Teaching Strategies

Discussing History: Alliances in the Thirty Years' War (Objective 2) Have students identify the participants in the war and their alliances. Explain that even though Swedish armies beat Wallenstein in one of the final battles of the Thirty Years' War, the forces of Gustavus Adolphus did not rejoice. The Swedish general, killed in battle, had been loved and respected by his troops for his courage and justness. Ask students why the Swedes entered the Thirty Years' War. Explain that aside from defending Protestantism, Sweden hoped to establish defensive bases in Northern Germany. Then have students describe Wallenstein's style of leadership. Ask, "How did Wallenstein pay his troops? How did this method contribute to Germany's ruin?" Explain that when citizens ran out of booty, soldiers resorted to torture and murder. Tell students that the Austrian king, Ferdinand, admired Wallenstein's military ability, but worried that Wallenstein would gain too much political power. Ask students to explain the role of France in bringing the Thirty Years' War to an end.

Skill Building: Recognizing Main Ideas (Objective 3) Tell students that the peace negotiations for the Thirty Years' War were difficult and acrimonious. For example, the Protestant Swedish delegation refused to sit in the same room with Papal representatives. Papal delegates refused to sit with the "heretics," and Pope Innocent X refused to sign the treaty. Furthermore, the French ambassador refused to negotiate unless negotiators addressed him as "your highness." Have students list the major provisions of the Treaty of Westphalia. Ask, "Why was France the major winner of the Thirty

Years' War? How did the treaty weaken the Hapsburgs? How was Sweden rewarded in the treaty? Why were Spain and Rome unhappy with the treaty?" Conclude by asking if the Treaty of Westphalia solved the problem of religious disputes in the Holy Roman Empire.

Check for Understanding Ask students to explain how the Treaty of Westphalia attempted to resolve the political and religious conflicts that had caused the Thirty Years' War.

Practice

Guided Practice
Lead a guided discussion of the questions in Section Review 5. (Answers are below.)

Identify:
(a) German-speaking Austrian Catholic king of Bohemia (b) Czech kingdom (c) religious war lasting almost 30 years (d) soldier of fortune hired to fight for the Catholics in Thirty Years' War (e) Swedish king who drove Hapsburg armies out of northern Germany (f) ended the Thirty Years' War

Answer:
1. (a) They were angry because their king was both a foreigner and an ardent Catholic. (b) Several German Protestant princes took this chance to challenge their Catholic emperor.
2. 1630, when the Swedish king, Gustavus Adolphus, landed on the north coast of Germany
3. Richelieu, the power behind the French throne, loved France and feared the Hapsburgs.
4. (a) War left Germany ravaged, its economy in shambles. The population dropped from 20 million to 13.5 million. (b) Germany lost what little unity it had.
5. (a) Alsace (b) parts of northern Germany (c) recognition as an independent state (d) equal privileges with Lutherans and Catholics
6. (a) Hapsburg states of Austria and Spain (b) France
7. Example: Richelieu, though Catholic, entered the war on the side of the Protestants.

Independent Practice
Assign Independent Practice Worksheet 17.5.

Enrichment Activities

1. **Reading a Primary Source** Assign Voices from the Past Resource Book 17.5.
2. **Preparing a Time Line** Have students prepare a time line covering events that took place in the Holy Roman Empire between 1618 and 1648.

3. **Researching for Bonus Points** Award bonus points to students who can recite Gustavus Adolphus' last words. ("I am the King of Sweden, who do seal the religion and liberty of the German nation with my blood.")

Concluding the Chapter

1. **Chapter Closer**
   Have students write essays on the shift in power in Europe between 1500 and 1650. Encourage students to include the social, religious, and political changes that they feel were most significant in changing the balance of power in Europe.

2. **Reteaching Activities**
   a. **Summarizing** Have students identify reasons the Spanish economy was bankrupt in 1650.
   b. **Identifying Main Ideas** Have students discuss the ways in which Henry IV and Richelieu strengthened the French monarchy.
   c. **Recalling Information** Have students list the participants in the Thirty Years' War and the effects of the Treaty of Westphalia on each.

3. **Chapter Review Activities**
   Assign Chapter Review 17 activities.

Chapter Evaluation

Chapter Test 17 and Computer Test Bank Chapter 17 Test can be used to evaluate your students' understanding of this chapter.

Answers to Chapter Review 17

Reviewing the Facts
1. a. Spanish fortune hunter b. Spanish noble who acted as royal agent in Americas c. upward spiral of prices d. economic system the goal of which is to make enough money to pay all the costs of a business venture plus profit
2. a. Spanish conquistador who conquered the Aztec empire in Mexico b. Spanish adventurer who conquered the Incas in Peru c. privilege granted to certain settlers to become master of a particular area d. king of Spain from 1556 to 1598 who built an empire that circled the globe e. Greek seaport where, in 1571, Christendom

triumphed over Muslim Ottoman Turks **f.** fleet assembled by Philip II in attempt to defeat Protestant England **g.** Spanish writer, author of *Don Quixote de la Mancha*, the first modern European novel **h.** Greek artist whose major works were painted in Spain **i.** Dutch leader of revolt against Spain who hated foreigners ruling his country **j.** greatest Dutch painter of the 1600's **k.** French follower of Calvinism **l.** power behind the throne of Catholic rulers of France, wife of Henry II **m.** French Catholic leader who worked for peace, a strong monarchy, and religious toleration **n.** first Bourbon king; brought peace and religious toleration to France **o.** declaration of religious tolerance **p.** Catholic cardinal and virtual ruler of France during reign of Louis XIII **q.** French government agent who collected taxes and administered justice **r.** French monk, author of satires *Gargantua* and *Pantagruel* **s.** French thinker who used a new form of literature, the essay, to write his thoughts **t.** French mathematician and founder of modern philosophy **u.** dates of the Thirty Years' War **v.** royal German family **w.** treaty that ended the Thirty Years' War

3. **(a)** defeat of the Ottoman navy, triumph of Christendom over Muslims **(b)** defeated by skilled English sea captains **(c)** Dutch revolt and declaration of seven provinces as independent from Spain

4. capitalistic approach to trade and business and other economic changes of the late 1500's to 1600's

5. **(a)** In 1618, Ferdinand II sent an army into Bohemia to put down a Protestant revolt. Several German Protestant princes took this chance to challenge their Catholic emperor. **(b)** It left Germany ravaged and led to the decline of Hapsburg Spain and Austria.

Basic Skills

1. **(a)** silver $623.8 million; gold 292.8 million **(b)** costly wars against Netherlands in revolt, against England (the Armada); costly imports of needed manufactured goods

2. **(a)** Value of gold dropped, prices went up. **(b)** Because Spain was heavily dependent on imports, gold and silver flooded Europe, and their value fell. Spain continued to import goods, rather than developing its own industries; inflation raised prices for goods Spain needed.

3. **(a)** parts of Indonesia; Ceylon; southwest tip of Africa near Capetown **(b)** Indonesia gave them access to the spice trade; Capetown was an important stopping point on the trade route to India and the East Indies.

Researching and Reporting Skills

1. Editorials will vary. English editorial should reflect pride in English victory and skill of English seamen, together with admiration for Drake and relief that the Netherlands, England's ally, was saved from a Spanish invasion. A Spanish editorial should reflect dismay at loss of Spanish fleet, anger at England and the Netherlands, and sorrow for the loss of Spanish ships and sailors.

2. Cortés probably aroused his men's enthusiasm for conquest by promises of riches to be gained, opportunities to become landowners, and the chance to share in the new Spanish empire they would help to create.

Critical Thinking

1. **(a)** Philip II of Spain used wealth from Spain's colonies to build up his army and navy and to strengthen Catholicism and weaken Protestantism wherever possible—for example, in the Netherlands. Henry IV established religious toleration in France and sought to build up France's economy. **(b)** Philip II did not succeed; his Armada was destroyed and the Netherlands remained Catholic. Henry IV did succeed: France became prosperous, and religious toleration contributed to peace within France. **(c)** Philip left a legacy of a nation in debt and an economy weakened by lack of investment in industry and trade.

2. **(a)** Although Spaniards claimed they were conquering new lands for Christendom, the true motive was acquiring gold and other wealth. **(b)** The description is accurate. Spaniards showed no concern for teaching Christian values, love or human respect for the conquered. They exploited the conquered people without mercy and caused the destruction of their civilization.

3. **a.** One hypothesis might deal with location, another with centralized government, and a third with competition with the Italian city-states. **b.** For location, both Spain and Portugal have coasts and seaports on the Atlantic; therefore, it was natural for them to venture out on that ocean for exploration and trade. Both countries became unified nation-states relatively early and could organize their resources to support exploration and trade. Because the Italian city-states had a monopoly of trade with the eastern Mediterranean, Spain and Portugal were excluded and therefore sought other routes to the source of goods from the East.

4. **(a)** Capitalism was based on the idea of investing money for profit. This profit could be

income from capital invested or interest on money lent over a period of time. **(b)** Medieval church was opposed to charging more than a "just price," thus prohibiting profit. It also opposed the idea that money could produce wealth; this was considered usury.

5. **a.** *Causes:* The German princes electors were divided into opposing two groups, the Protestant's Union and the Catholic League. In 1618, a riot in Prague touched off a war between the two groups. Also, the Protestant Czechs hated their king, who was Austrian and Catholic. *Outcomes:* The war caused great destruction of property and loss of life in Germany. The was ended in defeat for the Hapsburgs. **b.** Answers will vary, but the war actually changed little in terms of religious questions involved; therefore, it was relatively futile. **c.** *Old Problems solved:* German princes almost independent of Holy Roman Empire, Calvinism was recognized, and the independence of the Netherlands was recognized. *New problems created:* France obtained Alsace, and Sweden gained lands in Northern Germany. France emerged as Europe's strongest nation.

Perspectives on Past and Present
(a) The treachery by which the Spanish defeated the Aztecs and Incas was accepted; so was enslavement of the Indians through the system of encomiendas which was approved by Spain. The Indians were despised as heathens and treated as less than human. **(b)** Would be considered violations of human rights and officially condemned. **(c)** Genocide implies intentional killing of a whole race. Answers may vary, but students should recognize that, although Spain did little to protect the Indians from extermination, disease was responsible for more deaths than the cruelty and hardships imposed by the Spaniards.

Investigating History
Students' answers will vary.

Unit V Review Activities

1. Assign Geographic Theme: Movement.
2. Assign Unit Perspectives questions.

Unit V Review Answers

Geographic Theme: Movement
1. *Portugal:* Brazil, Mozambique, Zanzibar, Macao, Cape Verde, Gold Coast, Angola; *Spain:* Mexico, Cuba, Santo Domingo, Puerto Rico, Venezuela, Columbia, Peru, Chile, Philippines; *Netherlands:* Dutch Guiana, Cape of Good Hope, East Indies; *England:* Newfoundland, Atlantic Colonies, Hudson Bay, Jamaica, Bombay, Madras, Calicut, Calcutta; *France:* New France, Louisiana, Haiti, French Guiana
2. Brazil, Mozambique, Tanzania, India, Senegal, Ghana, Angola; Mexico, Cuba, Santo Domingo, Puerto Rico, Venezuela, Columbia, Peru, Bolivia, Chile, Argentina, Philippines; Suriname, Union of South Africa, Indonesia; Newfoundland, United States, Canada, Jamaica, India; Canada, United States, Haiti, French Guiana.
3. European civilization spread to all areas of the globe during the seventeenth century. Where Europeans held only trading posts, as in East Africa, India, and the Spice Islands, there was little cultural impact; where Europeans settled, as in Canada and the 13 colonies, the cultural impact was greater.
4. through oral and written traditions, arts and crafts, religion and festivals, and family life.

Unit Perspectives

Understanding History
1. **a.** Age of exploration; viceroy—a royal agent who ruled Spain's American territories from Mexico City or Lima; conquistador—Spanish fortune hunter **b.** Reformation; theocracy—government controlled by church leaders; predestination—Calvin's doctrine that God has known since the beginning of time who will be saved **c.** Renaissance; vernacular—everyday language of one's homeland; humanist—scholar who studied classical texts **d.** Age of Exploration; capitalism—economic system that is set up to make enough money to pay all the costs of a business venture plus profit; Commercial Revolution—economic changes that were important to the future of Europe
2. **a.** Renaissance artist who painted the portrait "Mona Lisa" **b.** religious leader who challenged Catholic Church and, with followers, formed separate religious group **c.** religious leader who

founded monastic order called Society of Jesus **d.** religious leader who wrote systematized Protestant philosophy, including predestination and ideas about the "elect;" set up theocracy in Geneva **e.** explorer who conquered the Aztecs **f.** explorer whose expedition was first to sail around the world **g.** Renaissance artist who painted the wall of Pope Julius II's private library **h.** religious leader who brought Calvinism to Scotland **i.** Renaissance artist who painted the ceiling of Sistine Chapel **j.** Spanish explorer who conquered the Incas **k.** Spanish writer who wrote *Don Quixote de la Mancha* **l.** Florentine merchant-explorer who correctly identified the lands Columbus had explored as a newly discovered continent and was honored by having continent named for him.

3. **a.** Act of Supremacy made the English king, not the Roman pope, the official head of England's church **b.** Council of Trent established four doctrines: pope's interpretation of Bible was final; Christians were saved by both faith and good works; the Bible and Church tradition shared equal authority for guiding a Christian's life; indulgences, pilgrimages, and venerations of holy relics were all valid expressions of Christian piety. **c.** Peace of Augsburg stated that each German prince could choose Lutheranism or Catholicism for his state. Calvinism and other forms of Protestantism were outlawed. **d.** Edict of Nantes declared that the Huguenots could worship in peace. **e.** Treaty of Westphalia gave Calvinism equal privileges with Lutheranism and Catholicism.

Critical Thinking

1. Possible answers include: **(a)** *similarity* — accepted Protestantism; *difference* — Augsburg banned Calvinism, resulted in further disunity and war; Nantes accepted Calvinism, resulted in period of peace and prosperity. **(b)** *similarity* — end justifies the means; *difference* — Unlike Machiavelli's Prince, Richelieu was not selfish and corrupt; he worked loyally for good of king and state. **(c)** *similarity* — wanted Church reform; *difference* — Calvinists sought reform outside the Church and opposed the pope; Jesuits fought for reform within the Church and supported the pope. **(d)** *similarity* — great painters from wealthy cities; *difference* — Italian, influenced by classical ideals of beauty; subjects drawn from antiquity, Bible, and heroic individuals. Dutch, influenced by Reformation; mastery of light and shadow; subjects drawn from Dutch society, group portraits or activity. **(e)** *similarity* — scientists studied optics and astronomy; *difference* — Italian, developed science of dynamics; French, developed analytical geometry and applied scientific method to philosophy.

2. **(a)** and **(b)** Major characteristics of the Renaissance included an interest in secular and worldly matters (shown in desire for wealth and fame), focus on vernacular language *(The Divine Comedy* written in Italian), new style in art based on perspective and lifelike representation (Giotto's frescoes), humanism and focus on the individual (portrait painting and autobiography), and the recovery of classical learning (shown in art and architecture)

3. **(a)** Geographic discovery related to pursuit of classical ideas, pursuit of new information, curiosity about the world, and secular interests rather than spiritual. **(b)** The desire for precious metals, trade, and colonies encouraged exploration.

4. Italian: Ideals of beauty and subjects inspired by antiquity; focus on the individual; Spain: piety, drama, Spanish pride, and court society; Dutch: interest in activities of daily life, group portraits, civic activities.

5. **(a)** England: Henry VIII broke with the Catholic Church and made himself head of the Church of England. Approved by Parliament in the Act of Supremacy in 1534. France: Remained mainly Catholic; Protestant Huguenots were a minority that won toleration in the Edict of Nantes in 1598. Holy Roman Empire: Became divided between Catholic and Protestant lands by the Peace of Augsburg in 1556. **(b)** England: strengthened the monarchy; France: strengthened the monarchy; Holy Roman Empire: weakened the position of the emperor and strengthened the princes, who could determine the religion in their lands.

6. Merchants in the sixteenth and seventeenth centuries accepted the concepts of profit and interest that had been forbidden by the medieval Church. Merchants used money (capital) as an investment in enterprises that were intended to earn a profit.

7. **(a)** Valid: Copernicus was the first to challenge Ptolemy's theories; **(b)** not valid: Italian Renaissance art peaked with Michelangelo, but did not end there; Renaissance expanded to other countries and to other fields than art; **(c)** valid: defeat of Hapsburgs in Thirty Years' War left France more powerful than before.

Making Decisions

Decisions chosen will vary. Sample answers follow. **(a)** Decision: to protest publicly against "pardon merchants"; option: could have kept quiet; wise decision: led to his condemnation at Diet of Worms, but made his ideas known, so that he became a leader of the Reformation. **(b)** Decision: to try Luther and condemn him; option: could have avoided matters of religion; poor decision, because Charles did not have power to enforce the verdict and Luther became an asset to his political opponents. **(c)** Decision: helped Protestant side in Thirty Years' War; option: could have remained neutral or sided with Catholic Hapsburgs; right decision, achieved his goal of weakening Hapsburgs at relatively little cost to France. **(d)** Decision: wrote book presenting ideas of both Ptolemy and Copernicus; option: could have ordered that his book not be published until after his death; poor decision, caused his trial in Rome and condemnation.

Continuity and Change

1. **(a)** Different continents became linked by exploration, conquest, and cultural exchange. **(b)** New ideas, technology, and ideals led to change. **(c)** The Americas, Africa, and Asia would become increasingly important in the history of other continents; rivalries would develop for access to riches of new continents discovered.
2. **(a)** Factors contributing to the growth of national power included the growing sense of nationalism, strengthening of the monarchy, rise of a middle class, greater freedom from influence of the Church; acquisition of land overseas, and wealth from trade. **(b)** That power would lead to national rivalries within Europe and overseas.

Unit Evaluation

Unit V Test can be used to evaluate your students' understanding of this unit.

The Transition to Modern Times

Unit Overview

This unit covers the period between 1558, when Elizabeth I ascended the English throne, and 1815, when Napoleon's empire collapsed. Elizabeth's reign was marked by religious conflicts, political plots, financial burdens of war, and a golden age of culture. Under the succeeding Stuart kings, unresolved problems between the monarch and Parliament led to a civil war. Following a Puritan victory, Oliver Cromwell established a harsh military dictatorship. Upon Cromwell's death, the monarchy was restored. However, fear of Catholicism led to a Glorious Revolution in which William and Mary assumed the British throne and signed the Bill of Rights recognizing Parliament as a leading partner in ruling England.

At the same time that Parliament was gaining power in England, Louis XIV ruled as an absolute monarch in France. The expenses of his grandiose court and unsuccessful wars left France politically and economically weakened. In Russia, Peter the Great turned his backward, isolated country into a westernized nation, gained a Baltic port, and built a new capital, St. Petersburg. Austria, under Hapsburg rule, and Prussia, under the Hohenzollerns, clashed over land and political dominance and realigned the balance of power in Europe.

The eighteenth century ushered in an age of reason. Enlightened thinkers advocated political and economic theories based on the ideas of individual freedom, happiness, and progress. Enlightened despots such as Frederick II of Prussia and Catherine the Great of Russia ostensibly used their power for the benefit of their people. In Great Britain, the development of the cabinet system moved that nation closer to democracy.

Enlightenment thinkers greatly influenced leaders in the American colonies. The Declaration of Independence was a clear statement of enlightened ideals. Within a decade of the American war for independence, a Paris mob stormed the Bastille. During the first stage of the French Revolution, leaders wrote a constitution and a bill of human rights. The second stage was a Reign of Terror, led by Robespierre. The radicals were overthrown by a moderate Directory, which was, in turn, overthrown by Napoleon, who made himself emperor. Under Napoleon's leadership, France soon controlled most of Europe. A series of disastrous misjudgments, culminating in an invasion of Russia, eventually toppled Napoleon's empire.

Resources

The resources that supplement the study of this unit are:

1. The time line for Unit VI, found on pages 386 –387. The themes for this time line focus on political ideas from the emergence of absolutism to the rise of Enlightenment thought and its effects on political developments in the Americas and in France.
2. The Geographic Theme, found on page 468. The theme, *Place*, compares the layouts of Paris and Versailles and focuses on the effects of planning on the growth of cities.
3. The Historical Atlas map on pages 814–815, or Overhead Transparency 90, *The World about 1800.* The Global Perspectives activity in Chapter 21 is based on this map.
4. This Unit continues the development of Researching and Reporting Skills leading to students' completion of a formal research paper in Unit VII.

In Chapter 18, students do a group research project on the English Civil War. Specific skills practiced in this activity include finding primary and secondary sources, compiling a bibliography, listing supporting arguments, and debating viewpoints. In Chapters 19, 20, and 21, students write historical essays, following specific steps. Steps in Chapter 19 include choosing a topic and developing a working thesis. Steps in Chapter 20 include consulting sources and refining the thesis. In Chapter 21, students complete their essays.

Chapter Titles

England: Tudor Queen and Stuart Kings

Chapter Overview

Elizabeth I, the last and greatest of the Tudor dynasty, ruled England from 1558 to 1603. She faced many challenges: conflicts with Parliament over religious issues and monetary problems; a plot to overthrow her rule; and threats from Philip II of Spain. Despite political problems, Elizabethan England during the late 1500's was a golden age.

Elizabeth's successor, James I, inherited many of her unresolved problems. His belief in the divine right of kings led to heightened conflict with Parliament. However, James's reign was also marked by two notable achievements—the creation of the King James Bible and the settlement of the first English colonies in North America. James' son, Charles I, faced even more serious problems with Parliament, leading to civil war.

In 1660, at the request of Parliament, Charles II restored the monarchy. During the Restoration, theater and the arts flourished, the Habeas Corpus Act was passed, and political parties took shape. The throne passed to James II, whose beliefs excited the fears of English Protestants and led to the Glorious Revolution. James lost his throne and Parliament invited James' Protestant daughter, Mary, and Dutch husband, William, to rule England. During their joint rule, Parliament asserted its authority and passed the Bill of Rights.

Key Terms

joint-stock company, divine right
For additional exercises, see Vocabulary Worksheet 18.

Chapter Focus

Ask students to imagine that they are the rulers of a country that faces imminent invasion by a powerful nation. Explain that a mixture of facts and rumors are pouring into the royal palace. Some reports suggest that the enemy fleet has been badly damaged. At the same time, their commanders are urgently requesting more supplies of gunpowder and cannon balls. Their advisers want them to leave the palace for a safer castle farther inland. Others say stay and fight. Ask students what they would do. How does Elizabeth's decision to personally defend England (pages 388–389) compare with the decisions reached by students? Ask students how they would have reacted to Elizabeth's speech. Explain that her speech electrified her tense army. Although the defiant Queen and her inspired army were not forced to defend their homeland, the speech marked a moment of supreme triumph for Elizabeth. Victorious, England was free to begin a period of extraordinary national development. Tell students that this chapter describes Elizabeth's golden age and examines the great contest between Parliament and the Stuart kings.

Elizabeth I faced many challenges. 1

Section Objectives

After completing Section 1, students should be able to:

1. explain how Elizabeth settled England's religious problems.
2. identify the Spanish Armada and explain how England defeated it.
3. explain the advantages of a joint-stock company.

Setting the Stage

Have students read the introductory section about Elizabeth (page 389). Then ask students to pretend that they are writers for the *London Times*. Their assignment is to write an article assessing the new queen's strengths and weaknesses and predicting how she will handle England's religious conflicts, financial difficulties, and the threats posed by Mary Stuart and Philip II. Have several students read their articles to the class. Then tell students that this section describes how Elizabeth solved the problems that confronted England.

Teaching Strategies

Discussing History: The Art of Compromise (Objective 1) Begin by having students recall the

Text pages 388–407

extraordinary religious changes that had occurred in England after the reign of Henry VIII. Recall that Henry VIII created a new Anglican Church. However, his son, Edward VI, allowed the Anglican Church to adopt many Protestant ideas and practices. Edward's half-sister, Queen Mary, suddenly reversed this trend when she reinstated the Catholic Church.

Point out that Elizabeth inherited a difficult and dangerous problem. About two-thirds of the people supported the restored Catholic Church. However, the Protestant minority demanded that Elizabeth adopt Protestant ideas. Ask students to define *compromise*. Emphasize that in a compromise both sides have to give up something in order to reach an agreement. Ask students to explain how Elizabeth used compromise to resolve the religious issues that divided England. What were some strengths and weaknesses of this settlement?

Advance Planner

Unit VI	The Transition to Modern Times			
Theme	Conflicts between European monarchs and their subjects led to rebellion and an Age of Enlightenment.			
Chapter 18	England: Tudor Queen and Stuart Kings, 1558–1688		★Advanced	
Focus	Queen Elizabeth's decision to participate in England's defense against the Spanish Armada		● Basic	

	Section 1	**Section 2**	**Section 3**	**Section 4**
Objectives	1. Explain how Elizabeth settled England's religious problems. 2. Identify the Spanish Armada and explain how England defeated it. 3. Explain the advantages of a joint-stock company.	1. Identify William Shakespeare and explain why he is considered a great playwright. 2. Describe the Globe Theater.	1. Explain the theory of the divine right of kings. 2. Describe how the civil war and Cromwell's rule affected England.	1. Explain why James II lost his throne. 2. Identify the Bill of Rights and explain its importance. 3. Compare and contrast the view of Thomas Hobbes and John Locke on the purpose of government.
Setting the Stage	Unit VI time line Elizabeth's strengths and weaknesses as Queen of England	The Elizabethan golden age	Conflict between the Stuart kings and Parliament	The Restoration
Teaching Strategies	Discussing History: The Art of Compromise Teaching with Pictures: The Spanish Armada Economics and History: The Joint-Stock Company Check for Understanding	Analyzing a Quotation: Shakespeare Teaching with Pictures: The Globe Theater Check for Understanding	Analyzing a Quotation: Divine Right of Kings Writing about History: The Civil War and Protectorate Check for Understanding	Discussing History: Why James II Lost His Throne Transferring Ideas: Limiting the King's Power Skill Building: Comparing Views on Government Check for Understanding
Guided Practice	Section Review 1	Section Review 2	Section Review 3	Section Review 4
Independent Practice Worksheets	Independent Practice 18.1 Vocabulary 18 Basic Skills 18	Independent Practice 18.2 Critical Thinking 18	Independent Practice 18.3 Geography Skills 18	Independent Practice 18.4
Enrichment	1. Primary Source: Voices 18.1 2. Researching for Points	1. Primary Source: Voices 18.2 2. ★Preparing a Report 3. Researching for Points	1. Primary Source: Voices 18.3 2. Researching for Points	1. Primary Source: Voices 18.4 2. ★Creative Writing 3. Researching for Points

Chapter Closer	
● **Reteaching Activities**	Outlining, Recalling Information
Chapter Review	Summary, Reviewing the Facts, Basic Skills, Researching and Reporting Skills, Critical Thinking, Perspectives on Past and Present, Investigating History
Chapter Evaluation	Chapter Test 18, Computer Test Bank Chapter 18 Test

Teaching with Pictures: The Spanish Armada (Objective 2) Explain that the Spanish fleet maintained a tight crescent formation as it slowly sailed up the English Channel. Although faster and more agile, the English fleet could not penetrate the Spanish formation. The two fleets fired more than 100,000 cannonballs at each other with little effect. Direct students' attention to the painting on page 392. Point out the fireships and ask students to explain why the English used them. The fireships scattered the Armada, making it vulnerable to the English guns. The Spaniards had heavy losses, while the English did not loose a single vessel.

Economics and History: The Joint-Stock Company (Objective 3) Explain that the Portuguese and the Spanish dominated East Indian trade throughout the sixteenth century. English merchants recognized that small partnerships could not raise enough capital to finance the expensive fleets needed to compete with Spain and Portugal. The English solved this problem by forming an association of investors known as a joint-stock company. Emphasize that anyone could invest in a joint-stock company. Individuals bought shares and then shared in the profits (and losses) in proportion to their investments. Ask students to pretend that they are organizers for the East India Company. Their assignment is to write a brief advertisement urging people to invest in the company's first venture. Tell students that the East India Company's first fleet returned with one million pounds of pepper, the sale of which earned a 95 percent profit. Point out that there were risks. For example, the first fleet lost one ship and more than 25 percent of its original crew of 480 men.

Check for Understanding Have students explain how Elizabeth solved each of the four problems discussed in this section.

Practice

Guided Practice
Lead a guided discussion of the questions in Section Review 1. (Answers are below.)

Define:
organization set up to attract capital

Identify:
(a) last and greatest Tudor ruler (b) religious law that established a national church in England (c) law declaring Elizabeth Supreme Governor of England's church and state (d) Elizabeth's Catholic cousin who was beheaded for plotting to become England's queen (e) king of Spain who sent Armada to attack England (f) sailed around the world (g) Spanish fleet defeated by English in 1588 (h) area in North America named in honor of Virgin Queen (i) most successful of England's joint-stock companies (j) person who wanted to purify Church of England

Answer:
1. (a) Henry had broken with pope and declared himself head of Church of England. (b) decided to establish state church that moderates from both religions would accept
2. (a) She schemed to overthrow and murder Elizabeth. (b) Elizabeth ordered Mary beheaded.
3. (a) Elizabeth encouraged sea dogs to attack Spanish treasure ships. (b) Elizabeth aided Dutch Protestants in their revolt against Catholic Spain. (c) Elizabeth executed Mary Stuart, a Catholic, provoking Philip to wage war against England.
4. formation of joint-stock companies
5. (a) Puritan members demanded changes in the Church of England. (b) claimed that the ritual and organization of the Church were her business, not that of Parliament
6. Possible answer: By remaining unmarried, Elizabeth was least likely to alienate factions and most likely to win diplomatic advantages.

Independent Practice
Assign Independent Practice Worksheet 18.1.
Assign Basic Skills Worksheet 18.
Assign Vocabulary Worksheet 18.

Enrichment Activities

1. **Reading a Primary Source** Assign Voices from the Past Resource Book 18.1.

2. **Researching for Bonus Points** Award bonus points to students who can answer this question: Who was the commander of the Spanish Armada? (Don Alonzo Perez De Guzman VII, Duke of Medina Sidonia.)

The Elizabethan era was a golden age.   2

Section Objectives

After completing Section 2, students should be able to:

1. identify William Shakespeare and explain why he is considered a great playwright.
2. describe the Globe Theater.

Setting the Stage

England's victory over the Spanish Armada released a surge of national confidence and energy. Ask students to identify other events that contributed to the "good times" that allowed England to flourish. Tell students that this section describes life in London during the Elizabethan golden age.

Teaching Strategies

Analyzing a Quotation: Shakespeare (Objective 1) Ask why Shakespeare is considered a great poet and playwright. Can students name some of his plays? Students might mention *Hamlet, Romeo and Juliet, Merchant of Venice, Othello, Macbeth, A Midsummer Night's Dream, Henry IV, Twelfth Night,* or others. Explain that Shakespeare was a skilled observer of human nature and a master of the English language. Write the following passage from *As You Like It* on the chalkboard:

All the world's a stage,
And all the men and women merely players.
They have their exits and their entrances,
And one man in his time plays many parts.

Ask students to interpret this passage in their own words.

Teaching with Pictures: The Globe Theater (Objective 2) Direct students' attention to the drawing of the Globe Theater (page 397). As Shakespeare noted, the Globe was octagonal, shaped like a "wooden O." It probably had an outside diameter of eighty-six feet and a height of thirty-three feet. Have students contrast the Globe with modern theaters. Note that elaborate props were not used and all the actors were men. Elizabethan audiences were expected to use their imagination. Modern scholars estimate that about one-tenth of London's population attended a play each week.

Check for Understanding Have students describe places they could visit or events they could attend in Elizabethan London.

Practice

Guided Practice

Lead a guided discussion of the questions in Section Review 2. (Answers are below.)

Identify:
(a) England's commercial and cultural center (b) poet and dramatist (c) actor who built first permanent theater (d) theater in which Shakespeare's plays were first performed

Answer:
1. (a) reflected transportation via Thames (b) reflected lack of plumbing (c) reflected necessity to keep idle workers from rioting (d) reflected concern with personal appearance (e) reflected lack of trades available (f) reflected crime
2. insight into human nature and skill with words
3. no fixed stage; audience sat around a central yard open to the sky
4. Answers should consider which of Shakespeare's qualities would have been traits of a genius in any age or culture.

Independent Practice
Assign Independent Practice Worksheet 18.2.
Assign Critical Thinking Worksheet 18.

Enrichment Activities

1. **Reading a Primary Source** Assign Voices from the Past Resource Book 18.2.

2. **Preparing a Report** Ask advanced students to find and interpret three excerpts from Shakespeare's writings. *Bartlett's Familiar Quotations* contains a number of famous quotations.

3. **Researching for Bonus Points** Award bonus points to students who can answer this question: What role did Shakespeare perform in his play, *Hamlet?* (Hamlet's father's ghost)

England had a civil war. 3

Section Objectives

After completing Section 3, students should be able to:

1. explain the theory of the divine right of kings.
2. describe how the civil war and Cromwell's rule affected England.

Setting the Stage

Explain that James I and Charles I—the two kings who followed Elizabeth—were constantly in debt. For example, in 1617 James I owed 726,000 pounds, which was a huge sum at that time. Ask students to recall from whom the two kings had to request money. The class should recall that English kings had to ask Parliament for additional funds. Tell students that this section discusses the growing conflict between the Stuart kings and the Parliament over money and religion. This conflict led to a bloody civil war.

Teaching Strategies

Analyzing a Quotation: Divine Right of Kings (Objective 1) Have students explain the theory of divine right of kings. Then read or distribute the following excerpt from a speech given by James I to Parliament in 1610:

> The state of monarchy is the supremest thing upon earth: for kings are not only God's lieutenants upon earth, and sit upon God's throne, but even by God himself they are called gods. God has power to create or destroy, make or unmake, at his pleasure to give life or send death, to judge all and to be judged. And the like power have kings: they make and unmake their subjects, they have power of raising, and casting down; of life, and of death.

After students have read this passage, ask, "According to James I, what was the relationship between a king and God? How were kings and God alike? If you had been a member of Parliament, how would you have felt about the king's speech?"

Writing about History: The Civil War and Protectorate (Objective 2) Ask students to write diary entries from the point of view of a Royalist (Cavalier) or a Roundhead. Diaries should refer to the following events: Charles' flight to the north in 1642, his capture in 1648, his execution, and the rise and fall of Oliver Cromwell. Have students share their writings and summarize the differences in views between the Cavaliers and the Roundheads.

Check for Understanding Have students describe the events leading to Cromwell's rule.

Practice

Guided Practice
Lead a guided discussion of the questions in Section Review 3. (Answers are below.)

Define:
belief that royal power comes from God

Identify:
(a) first Stuart king (b) version of Bible commissioned by James I (c) Virginia community named to honor James I (d) son of and successor to James (e) document signed by Charles I listing concessions to royal power (f) archbishop determined to force Presbyterian Scots to follow style of Church of England (g) person who remained loyal to King Charles (h) Puritan townsperson and merchant who supported Parliament (i) Roundhead leader, later Lord Protector of England (j) Cromwell's military machine

Answer:
1. (a) over how much say Parliament would have in governing England (b) King James Bible, founding of first permanent English colonies in North America
2. (a) for same reasons as James and mainly over money (b) Parliament refused to grant Charles any money unless he signed the document.
3. (a) Laud decided to force Presbyterian Scots to follow style of Church of England (b) Charles's flight from London to north to raise army
4. (a) Cavaliers and Roundheads (b) whether people would be governed by an absolute monarch or a democratic system
5. (a) Cromwell (b) Merrymaking and amusement became illegal in England. In Ireland, the English seized Drogheda, killed priests and friars, and drove people from their homes and land.
6. Answers should note that the execution of Charles was revolutionary and represented a great threat to other monarchs. Most students will probably advise rulers to be more conciliatory.

Independent Practice
Assign Independent Practice Worksheet 18.3.
Assign Geography Skills Worksheet 18.

Enrichment Activities

1. **Reading a Primary Source** Assign Voices from the Past Resource Book 18.3.
2. **Researching for Bonus Points** Award bonus points to students who can answer this question: Who was Praise-God Barebones? (A Puritan leader in the Barebones Parliament. Cromwell dissolved this Parliament and then was proclaimed Lord Protector.)

Parliament won political power.

4

Section Objectives

After completing Section 4, students should be able to:

1. explain why James II lost his throne.
2. identify the Bill of Rights and explain its importance.
3. compare and contrast the views of Thomas Hobbes and John Locke on the purpose of government.

Setting the Stage

Ask students to review the problems that led to the conflict between Charles I and Parliament. What advice would students give to Charles II for dealing with Parliament, obtaining money, settling religious issues, and restoring entertainment? Tell students that this section describes how Charles II restored the monarchy and acted on each of these issues. It also explains how James II lost his throne, and how the English people won a bill of rights.

Teaching Strategies

Discussing History: Why James II Lost His Throne (Objective 1) After students have read about James II, write this statement on the chalkboard: James II had none of the Stuarts' virtues and all of their vices. Ask students to agree or disagree with this statement, and identify Stuart "virtues" and "vices." Point out that James II was both a practicing Catholic and a strong believer in the divine right of kings. He lacked his father's tact in dealing with political and religious opponents. For example, he openly violated the Test Acts passed by Parliament, which prohibited a Catholic from holding any public office. Ask students how debate over James' succession led to the rise of political parties. Point out that while Whigs and Tories disagreed about the extent to which the monarchy ought to be limited, they agreed that the king would not be above the law. Ask students what groups were threatened by the birth of a male Catholic heir. Explain that while England's various Protestant sects disagreed with one another about doctrine, they were united against Roman Catholicism. Both Whigs and Tories there-

fore invited William and Mary to overthrow James II for the sake of Protestantism.

Transferring Ideas: Limiting the King's Power (Objective 2) Point out that the idea of placing limits on the monarch's power began with the Magna Carta. Have students recall the effects of the Magna Carta, Petition of Right, and Habeas Corpus Act in limiting the king's power. Ask students to explain the purpose of each provision in the Bill of Rights (page 405). Emphasize that the Bill of Rights marked a turning point in the history of democracy. It protected the principle of representative government while ensuring that citizens would be secure from arbitrary authority. Have students compare the English Bill of Rights with the First Amendment of the United States Constitution.

Skill Building: Comparing Views on Government (Objective 3) Point out that the rebellions against Charles I and James II raised troubling questions about the relationship between a people and their government. Was it lawful for subjects to overthrow their monarch? Were people capable of governing themselves? Tell students that the answer depended on one's view of human nature. Have students compare the views of the English philosophers Thomas Hobbes and John Locke. Allow students to debate the underlying philosophical question of whether people are by nature good or bad. Students should see that these opposing beliefs would naturally lead to different ideas about proper government.

Check for Understanding Have students explain the significance of the following concepts: divine right, habeas corpus, bill of rights.

Practice

Guided Practice
Lead a guided discussion of the questions in Section Review 4. (Answers are below.)

Identify:
(a) invited by Parliament to restore the monarchy after the death of Cromwell (b) period of rule under Charles II (c) greatest writer of the Restoration (d) forbids holding a prisoner indefinitely without a trial (e) member of Parliament who opposed James's succession (f) member of Parliament who defended both the king and his Catholic brother (g) successor to Charles II who was overthrown for the sake of Protestantism (h) Protestant daughter of James and Protestant prince of Netherlands who agreed to rule England (i) bloodless overthrow of James II in which William and

Mary came to power (**j**) document listing restrictions on ruler's power (**k**) English philosopher and author of *Leviathan* (**l**) English philosopher who asserted that governments are formed to protect life, liberty, and property

Answer:
1. theater, sporting events, dancing
2. (**a**) He did not restore divine right and, in religion, he tried to steer a middle course. (**b**) Charles turned to Louis XIV, wealthy Catholic king of France, for funds. People feared Charles's Catholic leanings and the fact that his successor would be his Catholic brother.
3. Parliament fiercely debated James II's succession.
4. (**a**) for the sake of Protestantism (**b**) It prohibited the sovereign from keeping a standing army in peacetime, levying taxes without a specific grant from Parliament, and suspending laws.
5. The fact that one could not be held indefinitely without being charged and tried limited the imprisonment of the ruler's opponents.
6. Events leading to Charles II's beheading convinced Hobbes that humans were naturally wicked. Influenced by the fact that James II was overthrown without bloodshed, Locke had a more positive view.

Independent Practice
Assign Independent Practice Worksheet 18.4.

Enrichment Activities

1. **Reading a Primary Source** Assign Voices from the Past Resource Book 18.4.
2. **Creative Writing** Plague and the Great Fire of London occurred during the mid-1660's. Ask advanced students to write a diary describing what it was like to live in London during this time. Encourage students to refer to Pepys' diary.
3. **Researching for Bonus Points** Award bonus points to students who can answer this question: What was the name of the treaty that contained the secret agreement between Charles II and Louis XIV? (Treaty of Dover)

Answers to Voice from the Past

1. by carrying their goods to the river
2. (**a**) that houses be pulled down (**b**) by providing no material to fuel the flames
3. Either people wouldn't obey him or the fire overtook them faster than they could work.
4. an equipped, on-call fire department

Concluding the Chapter

1. **Chapter Closer**
   Ask students to describe three characteristics of the Elizabethan golden age.
2. **Reteaching Activities**
   a. **Outlining** Have students write a sentence outline of Section 1 and Section 2, using section headings and subheadings.
   b. **Recalling Information** Have students identify reasons that both James I and Charles I were unpopular with Parliament.
3. **Chapter Review Activities**
   Assign Chapter Review 18 activities.

Chapter Evaluation

Chapter Test 18 and Computer Test Bank Chapter 18 Test can be used to evaluate your students' understanding of this chapter.

Answers to Chapter Review 18

Reviewing the Facts
1. **a.** organization set up to attract capital **b.** belief that royal power comes from God
2. **a.** last and greatest ruler of the Tudor dynasty **b.** person who wished to purify Church of England **c.** Catholic queen of Scotland who plotted to overthrow Elizabeth **d.** king of Spain who sent Armada to attack England **e.** greatest English sea dog **f.** fleet assembled by Philip II of Spain to invade England **g.** great poet and dramatist **h.** responsible for creating a new Bible and founding first permanent English colonies in North America **i.** ruler whose policies led to civil war **j.** document signed by Charles I granting concessions to Parliament **k.** person loyal to the king during the English civil war **l.** Puritan who supported Parliament **m.** dictator after civil war **n.** restored the monarchy after the death of Cromwell **o.** member of group that opposed James II **p.** member of group that supported James II
3. (**a**) London was a bustling, heavily populated, commercial, culturally advanced city. (**b**) Shakespeare's writings reveal human nature in all its forms.
4. Cromwell's protectorate—all merrymaking and amusement illegal; Restoration—restored

5. (a) He believed that governments protected people from their naturally evil ways. (b) He believed that rebellion was justified if governments abused rights.

Basic Skills

1. (a) 1626 Parliament dismissed; Charles demanded forced loans, quartered troops in private homes. 1628 Parliament presented Charles with Petition of Right; Charles dissolved Parliament. 1639 Archbishop Laud sought to impose Church of England on Scots. Needing money, Charles called Parliament. 1641 Parliament passed laws to limit king's power. 1642 Charles entered Parliament with armed men. Mob reaction forced Charles to leave London; raised army. Civil war began. 1646 Cromwell defeated king's forces, dismissed Parliament. 1648 king taken prisoner. 1649 tried for treason and executed. (b) 1685 James, a Catholic, asserted divine right to rule without Parliament's consent. Alienated Tory support by appointing Catholics to high office. When Parliament protested, James dismissed Parliament. 1687 King announced that Catholics could have government posts; stationed soldiers outside London. When son (heir) was born to James, Parliament planned to overthrow James; invited William and Mary to rule. (c) Similarities: Both kings tried to rule without Parliament; religious policies a major concern. Use or threat of armed force against Parliament and London brought resistance. Differences: Charles, Church of England; James, Catholic. Charles' quarrel with Parliament about taxes led to civil war, bloodshed, trial, and execution. James tried to rule without Parliament; led to peaceful revolution and new monarch.
2. established state church acceptable to moderate Catholic and Protestant groups; had Mary Stuart executed; delayed question of marrying Philip II, aided Dutch protestants, aided defeated Spanish Armada; encouraged Joint-Stock company, obtained treasure from Spain.

Researching and Reporting Skills

Students' answers will vary according to their research and the viewpoints assumed.

Critical Thinking

1. (a) treacherous enemy, cruel, heretic; (b) good sport; winks at us when we raid Spanish ships; (c) flirts with papist religion; loves luxury and power; disregards our concerns.
2. Fact: "I am come amongst you … to live or die amongst you … think foul scorn." Opinion: "My loving people … I have placed my chiefest strength and safeguard in the loyal hearts and good will of my subjects … I know I have the body of a weak and feeble woman, but I have the heart … of a king."
3. Joint-stock companies helped to launch England into the Commercial Revolution and to expand its political and economic power
4. (a) Precedents included Magna Carta and Model Parliament, both limiting power of king. (b) Tudors mostly cooperated with Parliament, at least in appearance; found means of income without raising taxes. (c) Henry VIII sought Parliamentary support for Act of Supremacy; Elizabeth, for Act of Uniformity; she disagreed with Parliament but did not dissolve it.
5. (a) James I declared that he was not answerable to people or Parliament, only to God. Charles I and James II both acted as if they were above the law. (b) Habeas Corpus limited monarch's power to jail or keep individuals in jail without trial. Bill of Rights affirmed limits to monarch's power, the authority of Parliament, and freedom of individuals; also forbade standing army in time of peace.
6. Elizabethan era a time of new ideas, great literature, a taste for adventure, a reaching out to the world.

Perspectives on Past and Present

(a) Freedom of speech and petition, no excessive bail; (b) United States Bill of Rights includes freedom of religion and assembly, which were not included in English Bill of Rights. Neither religious tolerance nor separation of Church and state were practiced in England at that time.

Investigating History

Students' answers will vary but should reflect knowledge of events and the ideas and actions of Cromwell.

Europe in the Age of the Absolute Monarchs

Chapter Overview

Because Louis XIV was only five years old when he came to the French throne, the real power of the country remained with Cardinal Jules Mazarin, whose policies led to a series of revolts called the *Fronde*. After Mazarin died, Louis's minister of finance, Jean Baptiste Colbert, strengthened France's economy and industry following a policy of mercantilism. Unfortunately, Louis undid much of Colbert's work by persecuting the Huguenots, many of whom were skilled workers and business leaders.

Peter the Great of Russia was also an absolute monarch. When he became czar in 1682, Russia was an isolated and backward country. He gained access to a warm-water port, "modernized" Russian customs and institutions, and built a new capital city.

Austria, the most powerful state in the Holy Roman Empire, was ruled by the Hapsburgs. Prussia was created by the Hohenzollern rulers of Brandenburg. In 1740, Frederick the Great of Prussia invaded Silesia, an iron-rich territory held by the Austrian Hapsburgs. Maria Theresa, Austria's queen, opposed the Prussian attack. Other European countries, trying to keep the balance of power, became involved as well. As a result of the War of the Austrian Succession (1740–48) and the Seven Years' War (1756–1763), alliances shifted in Europe.

Key Terms

absolute monarch, mercantilism, balance of trade, tariff, balance of power.
For additional exercises, see Vocabulary Worksheet 19.

Chapter Focus

Have students read the opening section (pages 408–409). Point out that complex rules of etiquette regulated every detail of life at Versailles. Ask, "Why do you think Louis enforced these rules?" List student responses. Then explain that Louis once cautioned, "Those who imagine that these rules are merely matters of ceremony are gravely mistaken. The people over whom we reign, being unable to apprehend the basic reality of things, usually derive their opinions from what they see with their eyes." Ask students to describe how Louis would evaluate the answers listed on the chalkboard. Emphasize that in France, "the basic reality of things" was that Louis XIV ruled as an absolute monarch by divine right. Unlike the kings and queens of England, Louis exercised an undisputed monopoly over all the power of the French state. As a ruler with absolute or unchallenged power, Louis formulated foreign policy, commanded the army, regulated the economy, headed the church, and was the final judge of manners, fashion, and art.

The daily rituals at Versailles were thus a visual display of the power and grandeur of the French king. Tell students that this chapter is about Louis XIV and the other absolute monarchs who dominated European history between 1648 and 1763.

The Sun King ruled France.   1

Section Objectives

After completing Section 1, students should be able to:

1. define mercantilism and explain how Colbert improved France's economy.
2. explain the concept of balance of power.

Setting the Stage

Have students write three adjectives or phrases that describe the sun. List student answers on the chalkboard. Possible choices include "brilliant," "dazzling," "center of attention," and "powerful." Ask students how they would feel if they were the sun. Discuss their responses. Now explain that the people of Europe called Louis XIV the "Sun King." Like the sun, Louis dazzled all who looked at him. And like the sun, Louis moved majestically and predictably through his day. Tell students that this section describes the Sun King, and discusses the achievements and failures of his long reign.

Teaching Strategies

Economics and History: Colbert and Mercantilism (Objective 1) Point out that Jean-Baptiste Colbert, the king's finance minister, faced a number of serious economic problems. France's domestic economy was disorganized. For example, a merchant attempting to transport goods from Paris to Calais had to pay tolls at sixteen points. These tolls raised the price of French goods, making them less competitive in Europe's markets. As a result, France had an annual trade deficit of between eight and sixteen million dollars.

Explain that Colbert's approach to solving these problems was guided by his belief in the goals of an economic doctrine known as *mercantilism*. According to this doctrine, gold and silver constituted the most important form of national wealth. Because France lacked gold and silver mines, the country could obtain a surplus of these minerals only by achieving a favorable balance of trade.

Tell students that Colbert worked tirelessly to strengthen the French economy. He recruited skilled weavers from Flanders, metal-workers from Germany, and mirror-workers from Venice to help develop new industries. (Competition for these workers was fierce. Italian agents poisoned the first two mirror-workers who left Venice.) At

Advance Planner

Chapter 19 Focus	Europe in the Age of the Absolute Monarchs Louis XIV's Versailles as a symbol of the power and grandeur of European monarchs		★ Advanced ● Basic
	Section 1	**Section 2**	**Section 3**
Objectives	1. Define mercantilism and explain how Colbert improved France's economy. 2. Explain the concept of balance of power.	1. Explain why Russia was isolated from western Europe. 2. Describe how Peter the Great modernized Russia.	1. Locate Hapsburg and Hohenzollern lands on a map. 2. Explain why Prussia and Austria fought over Silesia. 3. Describe the alliances that formed during the War of the Austrian Succession and during the Seven Years' War.
Setting the Stage	Louis XIV, the "Sun King"	Peter the Great's achievements	Competition between Austria and Prussia for control of eastern Europe
Teaching Strategies	Economics and History: Colbert and Mercantilism Teaching with Pictures: The Versailles Palace Writing about History: Balance of Power Check for Understanding	Using Geographic Themes: Movement Transparency 53 Discussing History: Westernizing Russia Geography in History: St. Petersburg Check for Understanding	Geography in History: Hapsburg and Hohenzollern lands Transparency 52 Outline Map 9 Discussing History: The Importance of Silesia Discussing History: Shifting Alliances Check for Understanding
Guided Practice	Section Review 1	Transparency 53 Q&A Section Review 2	Transparency 52 Q&A Section Review 3
Independent Practice Worksheets	Independent Practice 19.1 Vocabulary 19 Basic Skills 19 Critical Thinking 19	Independent Practice 19.2 Geography Skills 19	Independent Practice 19.3
Enrichment	1. Primary Source: Voices 19.1 2. Researching for Points	1. Primary Source: Voices 19.2 2. ★ Analyzing a Quotation 3. Researching for Points	1. Primary Source: Voices 19.3 2. Creative Writing 3. Researching for Points
Chapter Closer ● **Reteaching Activities** **Chapter Review** **Chapter Evaluation**	Summarizing, Identifying Main Ideas, Outlining Summary, Reviewing the Facts, Basic Skills, Researching and Reporting Skills, Critical Thinking, Perspectives on Past and Present, Investigating History Chapter Test 19, Computer Test Bank Chapter 19 Test		

the same time, Colbert doubled the tariff on foreign imports.

These measurers were only the beginning. Colbert eliminated many of the internal tolls. A new 162-mile Languedoc Canal promoted trade by connecting the Mediterranean Sea with the Bay of Biscay. Colbert and Louis chartered companies to trade with India, Morocco, and the East Indies. Finally, all able-bodied men were put to work. French workers toiled twelve hours for about thirty cents a day. Workers received only ninety days of rest a year.

Conclude your discussion by asking students to describe how Colbert might view America's current trade and budget deficits. What measures do they think Colbert would recommend to solve these problems?

Writing about History: Balance of Power (Objective 2) Have students read, "Louis fought costly wars" (pages 413–414). Explain the concept of balance of power. Reinforce this concept by having students write an imaginary dialogue among the rulers of England, Austria, the Dutch republic, and Portugal after they learn about Charles' decision to bequeath the Spanish throne to Louis' grandson. The dialogues should incorporate the political leaders' concern over maintaining a balance of power. Ask several students to read their dialogues to the class.

Check for Understanding Have students define and give examples of absolute monarchy, mercantilism, and balance of power.

Practice

Guided Practice
Lead a guided discussion of the questions in Section Review 1. (Answers are below.)

Define:
(a) ruler with unlimited power (b) policy of favoring exports over imports (c) ratio of imports to exports (d) tax on goods arriving in a country (e) defensive strategy in which weaker nations combine to equal or exceed power of stronger

Identify:
(a) absolute monarch of France from 1643 to 1715 (b) power behind the throne during Louis XIV's childhood (c) minister of finance under Louis XIV (d) royal country house of Louis XIV (e) comic actor and playwright (f) French dramatist whose specialty was tragedy (g) French dramatist who modeled his works on the ancient Greek playwrights

Answer:
1. (a) revolt led by nobles (b) led to hatred of Paris and its mobs (c) It was better than the alternative, rebellion.
2. Louis was the center of France's government.
3. (a) encouraged skilled workers from abroad to settle in France (b) Louis revoked the Edict of Nantes.
4. (a) by sponsoring opera, drama, and the fine arts (b) glorifying the king
5. (a) a costly war fought when Spain's King Charles II bequeathed his throne to Louis XIV's grandson, Philip (b) Philip V was allowed to remain King of Spain as long as France and Spain were not united; France kept Alsace; Great Britain gained Gibraltar from Spain and colonies in North America from France; Austrian Hapsburgs gained Netherlands, Sardinia, Naples, and Milan.
6. Look for answers to include the idea that other countries admired French styles and art but that admiration did not carry over into a willingness to accept political domination.

Independent Practice
Assign Independent Practice Worksheet 19.1.
Assign Basic Skills Worksheet 19.
Assign Critical Thinking Worksheet 19.
Assign Vocabulary Worksheet 19.

Enrichment Activities

1. **Reading a Primary Source** Assign Voices from the Past Resource Book 19.1.

2. **Researching for Bonus Points** Award bonus points to students who can answer this question: Louis rewarded one lucky noble at the end of each day by allowing him to hold a certain object. What was the object? (a candlestick)

Peter the Great changed Russia. 2

Section Objectives

After completing Section 2, students should be able to:

1. explain why Russia was isolated from western Europe.
2. describe how Peter the Great modernized Russia.

Setting the Stage

Introduce this section by asking, "Which rulers that you have studied have had the greatest impact on their countries?" List students' responses on the chalkboard. Then explain that this section describes the achievements of an extraordinary Russian czar—Peter the Great. Tell students that the section examines how Peter successfully ended Russia's isolation from Europe, made the czar's power absolute, and built a new capital that gave Russia an outlet to the sea.

Teaching Strategies

Using Geographic Themes: Movement (Objective 1) Ask students to describe factors or conditions that promote the movement of goods and ideas. Students should recall the role of trade routes, military invasions, voyages of exploration, and new inventions such as the printing press in spreading ideas. Then explain that while the nations of Europe were benefiting from an unprecedented age of discovery and movement, Russia remained isolated from these developments.

Ask students to recall factors that they have previously studied that help explain Russia's isolation from western Europe. Point out that geographic barriers kept Russia closed in on itself. Travel by land was slow and expensive, and Russia's only seaport at Archangel was choked with ice much of the year. In addition, the Mongol conquest cut Russia off from the ideas of the Renaissance, Scientific Revolution, and Age of Exploration. While the Russians did expand eastward into Siberia, they lacked foreign colonies and thus did not benefit from the trade with the New World. Tell students that religious differences also widened the gap between western Europeans and Russians. Recall that the Russians adopted the Byzantine, or Eastern Orthodox, branch of Christianity. Russians thus shunned Roman Catholics and Protestants as heretics. Show Overhead Transparency 53, *The Growth of Russia.* Ask students how the acquisition of land by Peter the Great made Russia less isolated.

Discussing History: Westernizing Russia (Objective 2) Explain that Peter was determined to end Russia's isolation from western Europe. During his dramatic eighteen-month tour he visited Prussia, Hanover, Holland, England, Austria, and Poland. Peter's trip created a sensation throughout Europe. The czar worked in shipyards, visited workshops, studied microscopy with Leeuwenhoek, and even learned to pull teeth and to cobble

shoes. Peter returned to Moscow with more than 700 European technicians, including naval captains, doctors, and mining engineers. He also brought back cases packed with guns, sail cloth, compasses, and anchors.

Most importantly, Peter brought back a desire to modernize Russia. Review the list of reforms (pages 416–417) and encourage students to explain their importance. In addition to these changes, Peter also reformed the Russian alphabet, opened mints to coin money, and built libraries, vocational schools, and a naval academy.

Stress that Peter's reforms marked a watershed in Russian history. They strengthened the czar's power while also ending Russia's isolation from Europe. From that time on, Russia began to play a leading role in European affairs. As noted by Will Durant, "Russia had discovered Europe, and Europe had discovered Russia."

Check for Understanding Ask students to cite three ways in which Peter the Great changed Russia.

Practice

Guided Practice
Lead a guided discussion of the questions in Overhead Transparency 53 and in Section Review 2. (Answers are below.)

Define:
(a) noble landowning family (b) worker who was almost a slave

Identify:
(a) czar who made Russia a major European power (b) Byzantine or Eastern Orthodox branch of Christianity (c) proclaimed capital by Peter

Answer:
1. (a) in 1613 (b) dominated by boyars; lands worked by serfs; isolated from western Europe
2. (a) religious differences, geographic barriers (b) to make it a modern nation
3. (a) westernized the calendar, strengthened the economy, introduced new crops, aided iron industry, started newspaper (b) abolished the office of patriarch in favor of the Holy Synod of which he was the head, promoted able men from lower ranking families to positions of power, and developed and trained a standing army
4. (a) for a piece of the Baltic coast (b) gave Russia a broad belt of land on the Baltic Sea
5. (a) ignorance of western Europe, feeling that western Europeans were heretics (b) While political and military changes can usually be

forced or imposed on a people, social changes are adaptive and evolve.

Independent Practice
Assign Independent Practice Worksheet 19.2.
Assign Geography Skills Worksheet 19.

Enrichment Activities

1. **Reading a Primary Source** Assign Voices from the Past Resource Book 19.2.

2. **Analyzing a Quotation** In his book, *The Rulers of Russia*, the historian Peter Andrews wrote that, "Peter's contemporary Louis XIV of France may have shone more brightly than any monarch in Europe, but it was Peter who cast the longer shadow." Ask advanced students to evaluate this statement.

3. **Researching for Bonus Points** Award bonus points to students who can answer this question: What assumed name did Peter the Great use while he worked in a Dutch shipyard? (Peter Mikhailov)

Austria and Prussia rose to power. 3

Section Objectives

After completing Section 3, students should be able to:

1. locate Hapsburg and Hohenzollern lands on a map.
2. explain why Prussia and Austria fought over Silesia.
3. describe the alliances that formed during the War of the Austrian Succession and during the Seven Years' War.

Setting the Stage

Begin by writing the word *vacuum* on the chalkboard. Explain that a vacuum is a space with nothing in it. Ask, "What happens when a vacuum is exposed to air?" Point out that the air will rush in to fill the vacuum. Then write the words *power vacuum* on the chalkboard. Ask students to recall that in politics a power vacuum occurs when a government lacks enough strength to defend its territorial boundaries. Explain that powerful nations have historically attempted to take advantage of

power vacuums to control or conquer other countries. Tell students that by the end of the seventeenth century eastern Europe's power vacuum provided opportunities for aggressive new states. This section explains how Austria and Prussia competed to dominate eastern Europe.

Teaching Strategies

Geography in History: Hapsburg and Hohenzollern Lands (Objective 1) Distribute Outline Map 9: Europe. Ask students to locate and label the lands ruled by the Austrian Hapsburgs and those ruled by the Hohenzollerns. Show Overhead Transparency 52, *Europe in 1715*. Ask, "Which part of Prussia was not within the Holy Roman Empire?" Have students identify who controlled Berlin and Vienna.

Discussing History: The Importance of Silesia (Objective 2) Ask students to find Silesia on the map of Europe (page 420). Explain that Silesia had great strategic importance for both Prussia and Austria. It contained valuable iron and coal deposits that made it the most industrially advanced region in eastern Europe. Frederick the Great recognized that the conquest of Silesia would almost double Prussia's population while more than doubling its resources. With Silesia, Prussia could become a great power; without it, Prussia would remain a small vulnerable state. Point out that the Austrian queen Maria Theresa recognized Silesia's strategic value and was determined to prevent Prussia from conquering it. Then tell students that one historian called Silesia the "keystone of Germany." Ask students to explain why this description was true.

Discussing History: Shifting Alliances (Objective 3) The War of the Austrian Succession and the Seven Years' War can be confusing. Use the following list of basic facts to help students sort out who fought whom in which war and for what reason:

• In both wars, Prussia fought Austria for possession of Silesia.
• In both wars, England fought France for possession of trading bases in India and colonial empires in North America.
• In the War of the Austrian Succession, Austria had England for an ally, while Prussia was supported by France.
• In the Seven Years' War, England and France remained enemies, but switched allies. Prussia became England's ally and Austria became France's.

Check for Understanding Ask students to explain why Prussia and Austria became bitter rivals.

Practice

Guided Practice
Lead a guided discussion of the questions in Overhead Transparency 52 and in Section Review 3. (Answers are below.)

Define:
member of Prussia's landowning nobility

Identify:
(a) empire of about 300 geographically scattered holdings in eastern Europe (b) Austrian ruling family (c) Prussian ruling family (d) agreement in which all participating countries agreed to recognize Maria Theresa as rightful heir to all Hapsburg territories (e) Hohenzollern prince (f) first Hohenzollern king (g) unstable Hohenzollern king (h) Hohenzollern king who invaded and occupied Silesia (i) daughter of Charles VI; ruler of Hapsburg lands

Answer:
1. (a) rolling plains (b) Absence of natural frontiers left area vulnerable to being conquered.
2. (a) dukedom of Austria, kingdom of Bohemia, kingdom of Hungary (b) by persuading other European rulers to sign the Pragmatic Sanction
3. by building a strong standing army
4. (a) first to call himself a king (b) grouped together under the name Prussia
5. (a) to claim Silesia's iron-rich land for Frederick II, king of Prussia (b) Prussia replaced France as Austria's chief foe; Austria, France, and Russia became allied against Britain and Prussia.
6. (a) because Prussia's Frederick II, with powerful enemies on three sides, decided to strike first (b) France (c) Great Britain
7. Answers should consider economic, cultural, and philosophical effects of militarism on a society.
8. The size of the Hapsburg empire diminished its strength. It was a patchwork geographically and culturally, hard to unite or defend.

Independent Practice
Assign Independent Practice Worksheet 19.3.

Enrichment Activities

1. **Reading a Primary Source** Assign Voices from the Past Resource Book 19.3.
2. **Creative Writing** Ask students to choose an event discussed in this section that they would like to have witnessed. Then ask them to write a paper entitled, "I Wish I'd Been There," explaining why they chose this event and what they wish to learn about it.

3. **Researching for Bonus Points** Award bonus points to students who can answer this question: What was unusual about Frederick William's famed Potsdam Regiment? (All of the men were between six and seven feet tall.)

Answers to Voice from the Past

1. ruled by Hapsburgs
2. (a) to stake everything on saving Bohemia (b) to give up Bohemia and concentrate on defending Austria and Hungary
3. (a) Both show determination to defend their realms and both stress resolve to be amidst those in battle. (b) initiative, courage, and leadership

Concluding the Chapter

1. **Chapter Closer**
   Have students explain how powerful leaders influenced events in France, Austria, Russia, and Prussia. Ask students why "Europe in the Age of the Absolute Monarchs" is an appropriate title for this chapter.

2. **Reteaching Activities**
   a. **Summarizing** Have students list three positive aspects and three negative aspects of Louis XIV's reign.
   b. **Identifying Main Ideas** Have students discuss how Peter the Great changed each of the following in Russia: role of women, economy, army, calendar, capital, and boundaries.
   c. **Outlining** have students use the heads and subheads to write an outline of Section 3.

3. **Chapter Review Activities**
   Assign Chapter Review 19 Activities.

Chapter Evaluation

Chapter Test 19 and Computer Test Bank Chapter 19 Test can be used to evaluate your students' understanding of this chapter.

Answers to Chapter Review 19

Reviewing the Facts
1. **a.** ruler with unlimited power **b.** policy of favoring exports over imports **c.** tax on goods arriving in a country **d.** ratio of imports to exports

e. defensive strategy in which no one country or group of countries can dominate others

2. **a.** absolute monarch known as Sun King **b.** prime minister whose harsh policies led to riots **c.** Louis' minister of finance who used mercantile policy to build France's economy **d.** comic actor and playwright **e.** ruler who modernized Russia **f.** Swedish king whom Peter fought in the Great Northern War. **g.** ruling family of Prussia **h.** Austrian ruling family **i.** Hapsburg monarch who succeeded to the throne according to the terms of the Pragmatic Sanction **j.** new state that rose to power in late 1600's

3. **(a)** backward society that knew little about western Europe **(b)** to modernize Russia; to acquire a warm-water port **(c)** To modernize Russia, he traveled to western Europe to learn western European customs. To gain a warm-water port, he modernized the army and won a large area of land on the Baltic Sea.

4. **(a)** Hapsburgs ruled over many lands; much territory had been won in the War of Spanish Succession. **(b)** The lands under the Hapsburg rule were widely scattered.

5. **(a)** Frederick William developed a strong standing army whose services he offered to any power that granted him territory. **(b)** Hohenzollern formula for success: build a good army and strike bargains for land and power.

Basic Skills

1701–1713 War of Spanish Succession: cause—Louis XIV's grandson taking the throne of Spain; countries involved—France and Spain against England, Austria, Netherlands, Denmark, Portugal, several German states, Savoy; outcome—Louis' grandson remained king but thrones of France and Spain could never be united; France kept Alsace; Britain got Gibraltar, Nova Scotia, Newfoundland, Hudson Bay Territory; Austria got Belgium and Spain's Italian lands of Sardinia, Naples, Milan; Prussia and Savoy were recognized as kingdoms. 1740–1748 War of Austrian Succession: cause—Prussian invasion of Silesia; countries involved—Prussia, France, Spain, Bavaria, against Austria, Britain, Russia, Netherlands; outcome—Austria lost Silesia to Prussia. 1756–1763 Seven Years' War: cause—Austria's effort to regain Silesia; countries involved—Prussia, Britain, against Austria, France, Russia; outcome—Silesia remained with Prussia, France surrendered Canada to Britain.

Researching and Reporting Skills

Students' choices of topics and development of these will vary.

Critical Thinking

1. **a.** Possible answers: in France, etiquette of Versailles, building of Versailles, control over nobility, Edict of Nantes, decisions to make war, economic tariffs, patronizing of the arts. **b.** Louis managed to rule without the Estates General; did not need their approval to levy taxes. In England, Parliament had already established the principle of representation and used this power to gain further limitations on royal authority.

2. **a.** Aimed to have favorable balance of trade by increasing production and exports and limiting imports. This reduced debt and built country's wealth, particularly its gold supply. **b.** Subsidized industry, established tariffs on imports, encouraged skilled workers to come to France, built navy to protect trade, built canals and roads to facilitate trade.

3. The Huguenots in France and the Jews and Muslims in Spain were the leaders in business and trade, representing the middle class. In both cases, religious unity was achieved but at considerable economic cost, although the cost was higher for Spain.

4. Russia was geographically cut off from trade by sea. Peter fought to gain harbors on the Baltic and Black seas. The winter cold of Russia helped Peter defeat the Swedes.

5. Both built up their armies. Hohenzollerns used army and diplomacy to gain power and new lands. Peter the Great used social and economic reforms to modernize and strengthen Russia and make it a European power. He fought to obtain for Russia a window on the sea to improve trade and communication with Europe.

Perspectives on Past and Present

(a) Answers will vary. Consensus probably would be that France still leads in fashion but that cultural leadership is dispersed among many countries. **(b)** Profitable; prestige lent to the nation's products makes them highly desirable.

Investigating History

Students' reports will vary.

Enlightenment in Europe, Revolution in America

Chapter Overview

The Age of Enlightenment in Europe brought together the ideas of the Renaissance and the Scientific Revolution. *Reason* and *freedom* were the watchwords of the time.

In practice, the age of Enlightenment represented an inconsistent application of philosophical and intellectual ideals. Despite their pronouncements and intentions, Frederick II of Prussia and Catherine II of Russia paid only lip service to freedom and tolerance. Britain's government, a limited democracy, won the admiration of Enlightenment thinkers. The citizens of the American colonies, however, believed that the policies of the British government, far from being enlightened, violated their natural rights. They revolted, won their independence, and established a republic.

Key Terms

philosophes, executive, legislative, judicial, separation of powers, enlightened despots, constitutional monarchy, cabinet, prime minister, federal For additional exercises, see Vocabulary Worksheet 20.

Chapter Focus

Ask students to recall how it feels to be accused of something they didn't do. Note that unfair treatment and violations of rights are examples of injustice. Tell students that the introduction (pages 427–428) describes a case of injustice that occurred in France in 1761. After students have read the introduction ask them why Jean Calas was treated unjustly. Explain that French law discriminated against Huguenots by forbidding them to hold public office or to attend Protestant services. The people of Toulouse believed that since Calas practiced an "evil" religion, he would also act in evil ways. They therefore ignored the facts and demanded that Calas be tortured and executed.

Jean Calas' other son, Donat, escaped and sought Voltaire's help. Ask, "Why was Voltaire sympathetic to Donat and what help did Voltaire give?" Explain that Voltaire was a famous writer who had fought injustice, prejudice, and intolerance. He wrote letters to arouse the conscience of Europe. The Queen of England, the Empress of

Russia, and the King of Poland contributed to a legal defense fund. A special council reviewed the case and ruled that Jean Calas was innocent.

Conclude by asking, "According to Voltaire, why did the Calas case win?" Emphasize that Voltaire believed reason had triumphed over ignorance. Tell students that this chapter discusses Voltaire and other thinkers of the eighteenth century. It explains how they hoped to reform society and to create a new Age of Enlightenment in Europe and in the English colonies of North America.

European thinkers expressed new ideas. 1

Section Objectives

After completing Section 1, students should be able to:

1. identify Isaac Newton and explain the impact of his ideas on the Enlightenment.
2. identify the philosophes and discuss five of their main ideas.
3. identify Denis Diderot and explain the significance of the *Encyclopedia*.
4. describe how scientific knowledge advanced during the 1700's.

Setting the Stage

Ask students if they have ever seen two streams merge into one river. Point out that currents of thought can also merge to form a new and more powerful way of viewing human affairs. Identify the Renaissance and the Scientific Revolution as two streams of ideas that students have previously studied. Stress that the Renaissance produced a new confidence in human intelligence and a curiosity about the world. The Scientific Revolution produced a new method of studying the physical world based on observation and experiment. Tell students that this section explains how the writers of the Enlightenment attempted to combine Renaissance curiosity with the scientific method in order to study and improve society.

Teaching Strategies

Discussing History: Sir Isaac Newton (Objective 1) Have students read, "Newton discovered the law of gravity" (pages 428–429). Explain that Newton's use of the scientific method to discover the law of gravity had a profound impact on the leading thinkers of the eighteenth century. They believed that the next logical step was to apply the scientific method to the study of the political, economic, and religious problems that plagued their society. They thought they could then formulate laws of human behavior enabling them to suggest reforms to help eliminate tyranny, ignorance, and intolerance.

Relating Past to Present: Progress (Objective 2) Begin by asking, "Is it possible to create better societies and better people?" Challenge students to explain their answers. What examples can they cite to show how Americans strive to improve their society? Then explain that Enlightened thinkers, or *philosophes*, believed that progress was both possible and desirable. Point out that belief in progress was one of five main ideas of the Enlightenment.

Have students read the discussion on the leading ideas of the Enlightenment (page 429). Ask, "Which ideas gave the philosophes confidence that progress was possible?" Explain that the philosophes believed that people could use reason to discover both natural and social laws. Conclude by asking, "What benefits did the philosophes expect to gain from social progress?" Stress that the philosophes believed that progress would lead to greater liberty and human happiness. Point out that the idea of progress is a cornerstone of American history. Ask students to discuss the concept of progress in the United States today. How is progress defined? What benefits might progress bring? Are there any limits to progress?

Relating Past to Present: Encyclopedias (Objective 3) Ask students to name encyclopedias that they have used. Then ask, "What is the purpose of an encyclopedia?" Explain that a philosophe named Denis Diderot first proposed to compile a comprehensive collection of alphabetically arranged articles on all important fields of knowledge. His purpose was to inform and "to change the general ways of thinking" by providing knowledge that could be utilized for social reform. In order to create this vast project, Diderot solicited and edited articles from about 200 writers. The finished work included clear step-by-step drawings on how to do things, such as making Auvergne cheese and preparing wigs. The *Encyclopedia* also

included articles that argued for greater liberty and for freedom of the press. (See *The Age of Enlightenment* by Peter Gay.)

Discussing History: Scientific Advances (Objective 4) Explain that the German philosophe Immanuel Kant urged his readers, "Dare to know! Have the courage to use your own intelligence." Point out that many eighteenth century scientists followed Kant's advice. As students read "Scien-

Advance Planner

	Section 1
Objectives	1. Identify Isaac Newton and explain the impact of his ideas on the Enlightenment. 2. Identify the philosophes and discuss five of their main ideas. 3. Identify Denis Diderot and explain the significance of the *Encyclopedia*. 4. Describe how scientific knowledge advanced during the 1700's.
Setting the Stage	The roles of the Renaissance and the Scientific Revolution in the Age of Enlightenment
Teaching Strategies	Discussing History: Sir Isaac Newton Relating Past to Present: Progress Relating Past to Present: Encyclopedias Discussing History: Scientific Advances Check for Understanding
Guided Practice	Section Review 1
Independent Practice Worksheets	Independent Practice 20.1 Vocabulary 20 Critical Thinking 20
Enrichment	1. Primary Source: Voices 20.1 2. ★Comparing Buddhists and Philosophes 3. Researching for Points

tific knowledge advanced" (pages 431–432), have them list the Enlightenment's scientific discoveries. Other notable advances include Linnaeus' system of classifying plants and animals and Herschel's discovery of Uranus.

Check for Understanding Have students use the five key ideas of the Enlightenment to complete this sentence: Discover by (reason) and experience the (natural laws) that should operate in any situation; remove obstacles to their operation, and the result will be (progress) toward (happiness) and (freedom).

Practice

Guided Practice
Lead a guided discussion of the questions in Section Review 1. (Answers are below.)

Chapter 20	Enlightenment in Europe, Revolution in America		★ Advanced
Focus	Voltaire's case against injustice and the origins of the Age of Enlightenment		● Basic

Section 2	Section 3	Section 4	Section 5
1. Identify Adam Smith and discuss his three laws of economics. 2. Identify Baron de Montesquieu and explain the concept of separation of powers.	1. Compare and contrast Frederick II and Catherine the Great as enlightened despots. 2. Describe how Catherine the Great changed the political geography of eastern Europe.	1. Compare and contrast the role of the cabinet in the British and the American systems of government. 2. Identify and locate on a map parts of Britain's North American empire in 1763. 3. Explain the economic importance of the sugar trade. 4. Explain the causes and effects of the Stamp Act.	1. Explain why the American colonists declared their independence from Great Britain. 2. List reasons the Americans defeated the British. 3. Explain how the ideas of the Enlightenment influenced the United States Constitution.
Contributions of the philosophes to ideals of good government	The characteristics of an enlightened ruler	Britain's constitutional monarchy	Are people ever justified in using force to change their government?
Economics and History: Adam Smith Relating Past to Present: Separation of Powers Check for Understanding	Skill Building: Comparing and Contrasting Enlightenment Rulers Geography in History: The Partition of Poland Transparency 53 Check for Understanding	Skill Building: Comparing and Contrasting Systems of Government Geography in History: Britain's American Colonies Transparency 54 Outline Map 3 Economics and History: The Sugar Trade Economics and History: The Stamp Act Check for Understanding	Analyzing a Quotation: Why Did the Colonists Rebel? Discussing History: The French Alliance Transferring Ideas: The United States Constitution Check for Understanding
Section Review 2 Independent Practice 20.2	Transparency 53 Q&A Section Review 3 Independent Practice 20.3	Transparency 54 Q&A Section Review 4 Independent Practice 20.4 Basic Skills 20	Section Review 5 Independent Practice 20.5 Geography Skills 20
1. Primary Source: Voices 20.2 2. Creative Writing 3. Researching for Points	1. Primary Source: Voices 20.3 2. Analyzing a Quotation 3. Researching for Points	1. Primary Source: Voices 20.4 2. Creative Writing 3. Researching for Points	1. Primary Source: Voices 20.5 2. ★ Creative Writing 3. Researching for Points

Chapter Closer ● **Reteaching Activities**	Writing a Paragraph, Identifying Main Ideas, Applying Main Ideas
Chapter Review	Summary, Reviewing the Facts, Basic Skills, Researching and Reporting Skills, Critical Thinking, Perspectives on Past and Present, Investigating History
Chapter Evaluation	Chapter Test 20, Computer Test Bank Chapter 20 Test

Define:
(a) thinker who subscribed to the notion that reason could be applied to all aspects of life (b) place for refined conversation

Identify:
(a) mid-1700's during which ideas of liberty and reason were central (b) discoverer of laws of gravity (c) French writer and enlightened thinker (d) most influential salon hostess (e) author of *Encyclopedia* (f) compilation of most current and enlightened thinking (g) English scientist who separated oxygen from air (h) scientist who named oxygen (i) American printer who discovered lightning's connection with electricity (j) English navigator and mapmaker who explored the South Pacific (k) term first used for ornate music (l) one of the two great baroque composers (m) one of the two great baroque composers (n) "Father of the Symphony" (o) child prodigy and composer of brilliant operas (p) considered by many to be greatest European composer

Answer:
1. reason, or the absence of intolerance, bigotry, and prejudice; nature, including natural laws governing economics and politics; happiness, or well-being on Earth; progress, or the notion that human beings and society could be perfected; liberty, to be obtained through reason
2. (a) Guests read a poem or played a piece of music, and other guests commented and engaged in refined conversation. (b) drama and music critics
3. (a) to bring together all most current and enlightened thinking (b) *Encyclopedia Britannica*
4. (a) discovery of oxygen, use of inoculation, understanding of electricity (b) baroque — ornate music stressing counterpoint and fugue; classical — style stressing unity, clarity, balance
5. Look for answers to include Copernicus, Kepler, Galileo, and Descartes among the giants and to consider that discovery leads to further questions for investigation.

Independent Practice
Assign Independent Practice Worksheet 20.1.
Assign Vocabulary Worksheet 20.
Assign Critical Thinking Worksheet 20.

Enrichment Activities

1. **Reading a Primary Source** Assign Voices from the Past Resource Book 20.1.
2. **Comparing Buddhists and Philosophes** Ask advanced students to prepare a report that compares and contrasts Buddhists' and philosophes' views on enlightenment.
3. **Researching for Bonus Points** Award bonus points to students who can answer this question: What famous scientist died the same year that Newton was born? (Galileo)

Writers advocated liberty and reason. 2

Section Objectives

After completing Section 2, students should be able to:
1. identify Adam Smith and discuss his three laws of economics.
2. identify Baron de Montesquieu and explain the concept of separation of powers.
3. compare and contrast the views of Jean Jacques Rousseau and John Locke.

Setting the Stage

Introduce this section by asking, "What are the responsibilities of a good citizen?" List students' responses on the chalkboard. Then call attention to Diderot's definition of a good citizen (page 433). Explain that Diderot and other philosophes shared a concern for the welfare of society, the freedom of the individual, and the happiness of humanity. Tell students that the philosophes believed that these ideals could be achieved in a society that allowed economic and political liberty. This section introduces three enlightened thinkers — Adam Smith, Baron de Montesquieu, and Jean Jacques Rousseau — whose writings advocated economic and political liberty.

Teaching Strategies

Economics and History: Adam Smith (Objective 1) Ask students to recall the definition of mercantilism and its relationship to a favorable balance of trade. Students should recall Jean Colbert's economic advice to Louis XIV (pages 410–411). Ask students what advice Adam Smith would have given. Then divide the class into groups representing the interests of a monarchy, followers of Adam Smith, and followers of Jean Colbert. Suggest that the monarch impose a high tariff on foreign imports, and have students argue the point according to their group roles. Ask the group representing the monarchy's interests to announce a decision and explain the reasons for their choice. Have students evaluate Smith's three natural laws of economics and give examples of self-interest, competition, and supply and demand in the present-day American economy.

Relating Past to Present: Separation of Powers (Objective 2) Ask students to name the three branches of government outlined in the United States Constitution. Then ask, "Why did the writers of the Constitution choose to divide the government into three separate branches?" Explain that Montesquieu first discussed the concept of the separation of powers in his influential book: *On The Spirit of Laws*. Like other philosophes, Montesquieu opposed tyranny and promoted liberty. He believed that a separation of powers would prevent the concentration of authority in one person. Emphasize that his ideas had a significant influence on the writers of the United States Constitution.

Check for Understanding Ask students to match each of the following names with the statement that best describes that individual's philosophy: (a) Rousseau; (b) Smith; (c) Montesquieu.

- Competition forces people to make a better product. **(b)**
- When the legislative and executive powers are united in the same person, there can be no liberty. **(c)**
- The only legitimate government is one that rules with the consent of its people. **(a)**

Practice

Guided Practice
Lead a guided discussion of the questions in Section Review 2. (Answers are below.)

Define:
(a) carrying out laws (b) law-making (c) interpreting laws (d) division of power into three branches

Identify:
(a) French economic theorist who believed that government regulations interfered with the production of wealth (b) French for "leave alone" (c) author of *The Wealth of Nations* (d) French noble who believed political liberty hinged on separation of powers (e) author of *The Social Contract*

Answer:
1. **(a)** believed people could be happy only in

society that allowed freedom in these areas **(b)** Adam Smith **(c)** Montesquieu and Rousseau
2. self-interest, competition, supply and demand
3. **(a)** the loss of political liberties **(b)** separation of powers
4. **(a)** Legitimate government ruled with consent of people. **(b)** Rousseau believed in a broader democracy than did Locke.
5. **(a)** Each branch of government would limit the power of the other branches, and thus no branch could become a threat to liberty. **(b)** Enlightened ideas held that happiness was possible on Earth and that political liberties were crucial to it.

Independent Practice
Assign Independent Practice Worksheet 20.2.

Enrichment Activities

1. **Reading a Primary Source** Assign Voices from the Past Resource Book 20.2.
2. **Creative Writing** Ask students to suppose that they can travel in time. Which philosophe discussed in Section 1 and Section 2 would they choose to meet? Have students write papers explaining the reasons for their choices and proposing three questions they would ask during their visits.
3. **Researching for Bonus Points** In *Wealth of Nations*, Adam Smith used the production of pins as an example of the advantages of the division of labor. Award bonus points to students who can answer this question: How many pins could one person make in a day? How many pins could 10 people make? (1; 48,000)

Enlightened despots sought progress.   3

Section Objectives

After completing Section 3, students should be able to:

1. compare and contrast Frederick II and Catherine the Great as enlightened despots.
2. describe how Catherine the Great changed the political geography of eastern Europe.

Setting the Stage

Write the term *enlightened despot* on the chalkboard. Tell students that both Frederick II, king of Prussia, and Catherine the Great of Russia thought of themselves as enlightened rulers. Ask students what actions a ruler might take to demonstrate his or her enlightenment. Explain that the philosophes were willing to consider a ruler enlightened if he or she favored religious tolerance, made economic and legal reforms, and enacted policies that were useful to society. Tell students that this section discusses the monarchies of Frederick and Catherine in relation to the philosophes' criteria for enlightened rulers.

Teaching Strategies

Skill Building: Comparing and Contrasting Enlightenment Rulers (Objective 1) Draw on the chalkboard a chart with two columns and four rows. Label the columns "Frederick II" and "Catherine the Great." Label the rows "religious tolerance," "economic reforms," "legal reforms," and "usefulness to society." As a class activity, ask students to use information in the text to fill in the chart. Use the class chart as the basis of discussion: (a) What were the strengths and weaknesses of Frederick and Catherine as Enlightenment rulers? (b) Were Frederick and Catherine enlightened despots?

Geography in History: The Partition of Poland (Objective 2) Show students Overhead Transparency 53, *The Growth of Russia, 1505–1796.* Have students locate and describe Poland's boundaries before the First Partition in 1772. Explain that before 1772, Poland was the largest European state west of Russia. Point out that its territory stretched more than 800 miles across the northern European plain. Have students use the map scale to calculate the distance from Moscow to the Polish frontier (more than 200 miles).

Ask students to recall the concept of a power vacuum. Point out that Poland's weak government represented a power vacuum. Between 1772 and 1795, Russia, Prussia, and Austria divided the entire Polish state among themselves. Have students explain how the partitions of Poland contributed to Catherine's goals for enlarging Russia. What other territory was added before the end of Catherine's reign? Conclude by asking students how the partitions were supposed to affect the balance of power among Austria, Prussia, and Russia.

Check for Understanding Have students define *enlightened despot* and name two enlightened rulers and the countries they ruled.

Practice

Lead a guided discussion of the questions in Overhead Transparency 53 and in Section Review 3. (Answers are below.)

Define:
absolute ruler who used power for good of people and embraced enlightenment ideas

Identify:
(a) Prussian king who called himself "the first servant of the state" (b) Russian monarch who claimed to rule by enlightened principles

Answer:
1. favor religious tolerance, make economic and legal reforms, justify his or her reign by its usefulness to society rather than by divine right
2. (a) Frederick III of Prussia and Catherine the Great of Russia (b) practiced some religious tolerance, reduced the use of torture, and accepted various enlightened ideas (c) Neither improved life of peasants.
3. (a) by waging war (b) threatened balance of power in eastern Europe (c) dividing Polish lands among Austria, Prussia, and Russia
4. His primary role was one of service to the people.
5. Answers should focus on the importance of liberty as an ideal of the Enlightenment and on the partitioning of Poland as counter to this ideal.

Independent Practice
Assign Independent Practice Worksheet 20.3.

Enrichment Activities

1. **Reading a Primary Source** Assign Voices from the Past Resource Book 20.3.
2. **Analyzing a Quotation** The philosophe Denis Diderot visited Catherine in 1773. Catherine agreed with his theories but disagreed with his suggestions for specific political reforms. Years later she summarized their conversations by writing:

   If I had believed him everything would have been turned upside down in my kingdom; legislation, administration, finance—all would have been turned topsy-turvy to make room for impractical theories.... Then, speaking openly to him, I said: Monsieur Diderot, I have listened with the greatest pleasure to all that your brilliant intellect has inspired. With all your high principles one would make fine books, but very bad business.... You work only upon paper, which endures all things; ... but I, poor Empress as I am, work on the human skin, which is irritable and ticklish to a different degree.

Read or distribute this passage and ask students these questions:

- What does Catherine believe would happen if she tried to implement Diderot's ideas?
- What did Catherine mean when she said, "but, I, poor Empress as I am, work on the human skin, which is irritable and ticklish to a different degree?" Ask students what ideas of Diderot Catherine might have found impractical.

3. **Researching for Bonus Points** Award bonus points to students who can answer this question: What gift did Count Orlov give Catherine in an unsuccessful attempt to win her love? (The 193-carat Orlov Diamond—the fourth largest in the world.)

Britain developed new forms of leadership. 4

Section Objectives

After completing Section 4, students should be able to:

1. compare and contrast the role of the cabinet in the British and the American systems of government.
2. identify and locate on a map parts of Britain's North American empire in 1763.
3. explain the economic importance of the sugar trade.
4. explain the causes and effects of the Stamp Act.

Setting the Stage

Point out that Britain, unlike Prussia and Russia, was never ruled by an enlightened despot. Ask, "What made English politics different from the politics of the other major states of Europe?" Students should recall that the powers of the English monarchs were limited by law. Explain that historians call this type of government a *constitutional monarchy*. Tell students that this section describes how the British government developed during the eighteenth century. It also discusses how the power of Britain spread to North America.

Teaching Strategies

Skill Building: Comparing and Contrasting Systems of Government (Objective 1) Ask, "How are the British and the American systems of choosing leaders different?" Students should recognize that Americans have an elected president (not a hereditary monarch), who appoints members of the cabinet. Point out that a British cabinet is more powerful than an American cabinet because its members, including the prime minister, hold seats in the legislature—Parliament. So long as their party commands majority support, British cabinet ministers control both the legislative power of Parliament and the executive power of the king. In contrast, neither an American president nor any of his cabinet members can vote in the United States Congress. Ask students to assess the advantages and disadvantages of the two systems in preserving democracy.

Geography in History: Britain's American Colonies (Objective 2) Distribute Outline Map 3: North America. Show Overhead Transparency 54, *British North America, 1763*, or have students use the map on page 441 to shade in and label the areas in North America that were part of the British empire by 1763. Ask, "What were the names of Britain's colonies in the Caribbean?" (Jamaica, Hispaniola, Puerto Rico, Cuba)

Economics and History: The Sugar Trade (Objective 3) Explain that the West Indies sugar trade played a vital role in the British economy. Between 1713 and 1792, Great Britain imported sugar from the West Indies valued at more than $800 million. During the same period, British imports from all of India and China were valued at only $500 million. The sugar sold readily in Europe and was a major reason for British prosperity. Point out that the sugar trade also had unintended consequences. Demand for sugar encouraged the development of the plantation system, which increased the slave trade. For example, between 1700 and 1786, Jamaican planters imported 610,000 African slaves. One modern historian estimates that by 1800 more Africans than Europeans had made the voyage to the "New World."

Economics and History: The Stamp Act (Objective 4) Tell students that Britain's national debt doubled to $700 million during the Seven Years' War. The British calculated that about half of their debt had been incurred defending the colonies during the French and Indian War. They also claimed that the average American taxpayer paid less than one twenty-fifth as much in taxes as the average English taxpayer. It therefore seemed fair to ask the colonists to pay for part of the cost of maintaining British soldiers in the colonies. Explain that the Stamp Act was designed to raise revenue. For example, the act required a one-shilling (about 25 cents) stamp on newspapers, a three-shilling stamp on legal documents, and a two-pound (about 10 dollars) stamp on college diplomas. The American colonists reacted with outrage. They pointed out that none of Britain's 558 members of Parliament were from the colonies. Claiming, "No taxation without representation," the colonists intimidated British tax collectors and boycotted British goods. The protests became so fierce that Parliament repealed the Stamp Act in 1766. Nevertheless, a basic question remained unanswered: What was the economic and political relationship between the thirteen colonies and Great Britain?

Check for Understanding Have students explain the role of the prime minister in the British government.

Practice

Guided Practice
Lead a guided discussion of the questions in Overhead Transparency 54 and in Section Review 4. (Answers are below.)

Define:
(a) monarchy in which the power of the ruler is limited by law (b) executive committee which acts in ruler's name but represents majority party in House of Commons (c) leader of the majority party in Parliament

Identify:
(a) first Hanoverian king of Great Britain (b) first person to act as modern prime minister (c) British king at time American colonies declared independence (d) restrictions limiting colonists (e) law requiring colonists to pay a tax

Answer:
1. power of ruler limited by law
2. (a) Each had to have the consent of the other. (b) cabinet system
3. king's cabinet dominated by a prime minister as center of power and policymaking
4. (a) winning and controlling colonies (b) because economic strength was derived from colonies and because a mercantilist policy catered to the interests of wealthy merchants and aristocrats
5. (a) worldwide, including territories in Asia and North America (b) imposed Navigation Acts and the Stamp Act
6. (a) Because the colonies had benefited from Britain's victory, the king and cabinet expected colonists to help pay costs of war. (b) with outrage and riots
7. (a) Did the colonies exist to enrich Britain, or were they entitled to trade for their own profit? (b) ideas of Adam Smith, physiocrats, and John Locke
8. Good answers would consider such factors as the natural rights of the governed, imposition by Britain of laws it was at a disadvantage to enforce, and the concepts of taxation without representation and of equality.
9. Monarch's power is limited by law.

Independent Practice
Assign Independent Practice Worksheet 20.4.
Assign Basic Skills Worksheet 20.

Enrichment Activities

1. **Reading a Primary Source** Assign Voices from the Past Resource Book 20.4.

2. **Creative Writing** Ask students to write a paper predicting what might have happened if the British had allowed the colonists to send representatives to Parliament. Tell students that the colonists would have been entitled to 112 representatives out of a total of 670.

3. **Researching for Bonus Points** Award bonus points to students who can answer this question: How many colonies did the British have in North America and the Caribbean in 1775? (32)

Americans created a republic. 5

Section Objectives

After completing Section 5, students should be able to:

1. explain why the American colonists declared their independence from Great Britain.
2. list reasons the Americans defeated the British.
3. explain how the ideas of the Enlightenment influenced the United States Constitution.

Setting the Stage

Explain that after the Stamp Act, many Americans began to question their relationship with Great Britain. Ask, "Are people ever justified in using force to change their government?" Discuss student answers. Then ask, "How did John Locke answer this question?" Tell students that this section describes why the American colonists declared their independence from Great Britain. It also explains how the Americans won their independence and then wrote a new constitution.

Teaching Strategies

Analyzing a Quotation: Why Did the Colonists Rebel? (Objective 1) Ask, "What do you think was the most important reason the colonists declared their independence from Great Britain?" Explain that after the revolution, a prominent Massachusetts lawyer, Mellen Chamberlain, asked this question to Captain Levi Preston, a veteran of the battle of Concord.

Chamberlain: My histories tell me that you men of the Revolution took up arms against intolerable oppressions: What were they?

Preston: Oppressions? I didn't feel them.

Chamberlain: Why, were you not oppressed by the Stamp Act?

Preston: I never saw one of these stamps ... I am certain I never paid a penny for one of them.

Chamberlain: Well, what then about the tea tax?

Preston: Tea tax! I never drank a drop of the stuff; the boys threw it all overboard.

Chamberlain: Well, then what was the matter? And what did you mean in going to the fight?

Preston: Young man, what we meant in going for the redcoats was this: We always had governed ourselves, and we always meant to. They didn't mean we should."

Read or distribute this passage and ask students these questions:

• How did the Stamp Act and the Tea Party affect Captain Preston?
• According to Captain Preston, why did the colonists declare their independence from Great Britain?
• Would Thomas Jefferson have agreed with the reason given by Captain Preston?

Discussing History: The French Alliance (Objective 2) Review the five factors that help to explain why the Americans were able to defeat the British. Explain that French aid played a decisive role in the American victory. Ask, "Why would the

French king support a democratic revolution?" Explain that while Louis XVI did not sympathize with America's democratic goals, he did want to get back at Britain for defeating France. During the two years of the Revolutionary War, France secretly sent money, trained engineers, and gunpowder. For example, France supplied 90 percent of the guns and gunpowder used by the Patriots at Saratoga. George Washington's army recognized the vital importance of the French alliance. When Washington announced the news that France had formally recognized American independence, his soldiers cheered, "Huzza! Long live the King of France!" The usually grave General joined in the cheering.

Transferring Ideas: The United States Constitution (Objective 3) Have students review the key ideas of the Enlightenment (page 429) and the theories of Montesquieu (pages 434–435). Ask, "Which Enlightenment ideas are expressed in the preamble to the Constitution?" Explain that the preamble expresses a commitment to reason and to a belief in liberty and human progress. Then ask, "How did the political theories of Montesquieu influence the Constitution?" Students should note that the Constitution divides the United States government into three separate branches. In addition, each branch can check the power of the other branches.

Check for Understanding Have students explain how the ideas of the Enlightenment contributed to American independence and to the formation of the United States government.

Practice

Guided Practice
Lead a guided discussion of the questions in Section Review 5. (Answers are below.)

Define:
form of government in which power is divided between national government and state governments

Identify:
(a) document justifying the American Revolution (b) prime author of the Declaration of Independence (c) raid in Boston harbor (d) gathering of representatives of all colonies except Georgia to protest treatment of Boston (e) commander of American army and first president of the United States (f) document that established U.S. government

Answer:
1. (a) They were committing treason. (b) justified in rebelling

2. Boston Tea Party; First Continental Congress' demands being little heeded by George III; open confrontation in Lexington
3. (a) superior motivation in defending homeland; use of hit-and-run tactics; British difficulty of fighting a long-distance war; relative mediocrity of British generals; alliance of France, Spain, and several German states against Britain (b) persuaded France to enter the war
4. divided the government into branches to provide balance of power and ensure that laws of Congress would reflect "the consent of the governed"
5. by making a commitment to reason, liberty, and a belief in human progress

Independent Practice
Assign Independent Practice Worksheet 20.5.
Assign Geography Skills Worksheet 20.

Enrichment Activities

1. **Reading a Primary Source** Assign Voices from the Past Resource Book 20.5.
2. **Creative Writing** Explain that Voltaire died in 1778, nine years before the United States Constitution was written. However, what if Voltaire had lived to read the Constitution? Ask advanced students to write a letter from Voltaire to George Washington, reacting to the Constitution and giving Washington advice about his new job as President.
3. **Researching for Bonus Points** Award bonus points to students who can answer this question: What song did Cornwallis' band play as he surrendered? ("The World Turn'd Upside Down")

Answers to Voice from the Past

1. unrestricted freedom in matters of religion
2. (a) They reflect the ideas of reason as the absence of intolerance or prejudice and of liberty as the absence of religious restriction. (b) Such religious freedom had never before been granted.

Concluding the Chapter

1. **Chapter Closer**
   Discuss with students how Enlightenment thinkers attempted to improve society. Have them explain how the ideas of the Enlightenment affected events in England, Prussia and the United States in the eighteenth century.

2. **Reteaching the Chapter**
   a. **Writing a Paragraph** Have students write a short paragraph explaining how Newton and Voltaire personified the thinking and accomplishments of the Enlightenment.
   b. **Identifying Main Ideas** Have students write statements explaining the ideas of Adam Smith, Montesquieu, and Rousseau.
   c. **Applying Main Ideas** Have students explain how the ideas of the Enlightenment influenced the American revolution.

3. **Chapter Review Activities**
   Assign Chapter Review 20 activities.

Chapter Evaluation

Chapter Test 20 and Computer Test Bank Chapter 20 Test can be used to evaluate your students' understanding of this chapter.

Answers to Chapter Review 20

Reviewing the Facts
1. **a.** French thinker who believed in reason **b.** power to carry out the laws **c.** power to make laws **d.** power to interpret laws **e.** division of power into executive, legislative, and judicial branches **f.** absolute ruler who embraced some Enlightenment ideas **g.** monarchy in which ruler is limited by law **h.** executive committee that represented majority party of House of Commons **i.** leader of majority party in Parliament **j.** government in which power is divided between national and state governments
2. **a.** discovered law of gravity **b.** exemplified Enlightenment thinking **c.** editor of *Encyclopedia* **d.** discovered lightning's connection with electricity **e.** first European to explore South Pacific **f.** argued in favor of a free economy **g.** believed political liberty hinged on separation of powers **h.** argued that only legitimate government was one that ruled with consent of governed
3. (a) reason—divine force that applied to all aspects of life; nature—all that was good and reasonable; happiness—existed for all who lived by nature's laws; progress—used to perfect society; liberty—belief that society could be set free of restrictions (b) Salons publicized

and spread Enlightenment ideas. (c) It brought together the most current thinking.

4. (a) Services are provided for the selfish motive of making money. (b) forces people to make a better product (c) insures right amount of goods at lowest possible prices

Basic Skills
Political authority: absolute monarch held power by divine right; enlightened despot, by working for the good of the state. Both absolute in that they controlled all powers of government. Religion: absolute monarch wanted religious unity; enlightened despot, religious tolerance. Role of individual: absolute monarch oppressed individuals to control power; enlightened despot believed in granting legal rights and freedom to individuals. Cultural activities: absolute monarch patronized arts at his court; enlightened despot believed in progress based on education and scientific discovery, and supported learning.

Researching and Reporting Skills
Students' experiences with writing will vary.

Critical Thinking
1. Renaissance focused thinking on worldly matters, interest in science; Reformation questioned authority, encouraged individual critical thinking, though focused on religious matters; Scientific Revolution developed belief in methods of natural science but did not perceive them in conflict with religion. Enlightenment integrated these different trends and took them a step further — to belief in scientific method, in ability to understand all aspects of life, including religion, laws of society, and principles of government.

2. Answers may include separation of executive, legislative and judicial branches; in economics, laissez faire; sovereignty of the people; religious tolerance; education of the people as liberation, and *laissez faire* in economics.

3. To kings who considered themselves the ultimate authority, the idea of questioning authority and applying reason to it were very threatening. However, the hostility of political authority increased the determination of Voltaire and Diderot to make their ideas known.

4. A free market means that competition will determine what goods are produced and establish the lowest price for goods sold. This provides what people want and eliminates those who produce inefficiently and cannot compete. In these ways, the public good is served.

Perspectives on Past and Present
(a) Cabinet ministers are official advisers chosen by the prime minister and who share the executive power with him/her. They also represent the majority party in the legislature. The prime minister is usually the head of the majority party. (b) In the United States, the president is head of the executive branch. The cabinet consists of advisers chosen by the present and having no involvement with Congress (the legislature).

Investigating History
The executive power rests with the president, assisted by his advisers, and is separate from the legislative. In constitutional monarchies, the two overlap.

The French Revolution and Napoleon

Chapter Overview

In 1789, the bourgeoisie, workers, and peasants who made up France's Third Estate rebelled against the feudal and monarchical institutions of the Old Regime. The creation of a National Assembly was the first act of revolution, followed shortly by the fall of the Bastille. Over the next two years, the National Assembly created a new constitution for France, made sweeping religious and administrative changes, and created a constitutional monarchy. King Louis XVI discredited the plan for constitutional monarchy and increased the power of the radicals. It was not until 1795 that moderates again gained control and drafted a new constitution.

In 1800, Napoleon seized control, eventually crowning himself emperor. He restored order and created Europe's greatest empire since Roman times. Eventually, Napoleon made some fatal errors culminating in a disastrous invasion of Russia. The weakened French empire crumbled under the attack of the Grand Alliance.

Key Terms

estate, bourgeoisie, coalition, coup, plebiscite, guerrilla
For additional exercises, see Vocabulary Worksheet 21.

Chapter Focus

Point out that July 4th marks the signing of the American Declaration of Independence and is celebrated as a national holiday. Ask students what July 14th marks. List students' responses on the chalkboard. Then have students read the introduction (pages 448–449). Explain that July 14th marks the fall of the Bastille and is celebrated as the French Independence Day. Tell students that the storming of the Bastille became a great symbolic event in a historic upheaval known as the French Revolution. This chapter describes the causes and the consequences of the French Revolution.

The French monarchy faced a crisis.

1

Section Objectives

After completing Section 1, students should be able to:

1. identify the three estates and explain why the Third Estate hated the Old Regime.
2. describe the financial crisis that forced Louis XVI to call a meeting of the Estates General.
3. identify the National Assembly and explain how it took power.

Setting the Stage

Explain that major upheavals such as the Reformation or the French Revolution have many causes. A number of reasons have been offered to explain why the French people suddenly revolted against institutions that their ancestors had accepted for hundreds of years. Ask students to identify conditions that might lead to a revolution. Students might mention a tyrannical king who refused to make needed reforms, the poverty or economic backwardness of a country, or the jailing of writers and leaders who opposed the king's policies. These conditions were not factors in the French Revolution. However, Louis XVI prohibited the use of torture in obtaining confessions, freed the French Protestants, and liberated the few remaining serfs. France had a booming economy that supported an increasingly prosperous middle class. The Bastille contained only seven prisoners on July 14, 1789. This section describes the social and economic conditions that led to the French Revolution.

Teaching Strategies

Analyzing a Quotation: Resentments of the Third Estate (Objective 1) Discuss the terms *Old Regime*, *estates*, and *bourgeoisie*. Then ask, "Why did the bourgeoisie, the sans-culottes, and the peasants all have reasons to hate the Old Regime?" Emphasize that the members of the Third Estate resented the unfair privileges of the French Church and the nobles. The French writer Beaumarchais voiced this resentment through a fictional character named Figaro. Outraged by Count Almaviva's pursuit of his bride-to-be, Figaro denounces the abuses of aristocratic society:

Advance Planner

Chapter 21 Focus	The French Revolution and Napoleon 1789–1815 Independence Day in France			★ Advanced ● Basic
	Section 1	**Section 2**	**Section 3**	**Section 4**
Objectives	1. Identify the three estates and explain why the Third Estate hated the Old Regime. 2. Describe the financial crisis that forced Louis XVI to call a meeting of the Estates General. 3. Identify the National Assembly and explain how it took power.	1. Describe the government created by the National Assembly and explain how it used the ideas of the philosophes. 2. Explain why the National Convention voted to execute Louis XVI.	1. List the reasons for Napoleon's victories. 2. Explain how Napoleon restored order to France.	1. Explain why the Spanish revolted against Napoleon. 2. Describe Napoleon's losses in the invasion of Russia. 3. Evaluate Napoleon's achievements and failures.
Setting the Stage	Causes of the French Revolution	Goals and achievements of the National Assembly	How Napoleon seized power	The roles of Great Britain, Spain, and Russia in Napoleon's downfall
Teaching Strategies	Analyzing a Quotation: Resentments of the Third Estate Economics and History: The French Financial Crisis Teaching with Pictures: The Tennis Court Oath Check for Understanding	Transferring Ideas: The Rights of Man Writing about History: Sentencing Louis XVI Check for Understanding	Discussing History: "The Little Corporal" Relating Past to Present: Napoleon's Enduring Reforms Check for Understanding	Teaching with Pictures: The Spanish Revolt Discussing History: The Invasion of Russia Transparency 95 Writing about History: Napoleon's Place in History Check for Understanding
Guided Practice	Section Review 1	Section Review 2	Transparency 55 Q&A Section Review 3	Transparency 95 Q&A Section Review 4
Independent Practice Worksheets	Independent Practice 21.1 Vocabulary Skills 21 Basic Skills 21	Independent Practice 21.2 Geography Skills 21 Critical Thinking 21	Independent Practice 21.3	Independent Practice 21.4
Enrichment	1. Primary Source: Voices 21.1 2. Researching for Points	1. Primary Source: Voices 21.2 2. Creative Writing 3. Researching for Points	1. Primary Source: Voices 21.3 2. Researching for Points	1. Primary Source: Voices 21.4 2. ★ Solving a Mystery: Napoleon's Death 3. Researching for Points 4. Global Perspectives Transparency 90

Chapter Closer ● **Reteaching Activities**	Preparing a Time Line, Summarizing, Identifying Main Ideas
Chapter Review	Summary, Reviewing the Facts, Basic Skills, Researching and Reporting Skills, Critical Thinking, Perspectives on Past and Present, Investigating History
Chapter Evaluation	Chapter Test 21, Computer Test Bank Chapter 21 Test

Unit VI Review **Geographic Theme:**	Place: How did planning change the growth of cities?
Unit Perspectives	Understanding History (Relating, Matching, Defining, Explaining), Critical Thinking, Making Decisions, Continuity and Change
Unit Evaluation	Unit VI Test

No, my Lord Count, you shan't have her, you shall not have her! Because you are a great nobleman you think you are a great genius.... Nobility, fortune, rank, position! How proud they make a man feel! What have you done to deserve such advantages? Put yourself to the trouble of being born—nothing more! For the rest—a very ordinary man! Whereas I, lost among the obscure crowd, have had to deploy more knowledge, more calculation and skill merely to survive than has sufficed to rule all the provinces of Spain for a century! Yet you would measure yourself against me.

Read or distribute this passage to your class and ask them to answer these questions:

• According to Figaro, what has Count Almaviva done to deserve his advantages?
• What does Figaro mean when he says, "Whereas I ... have had to deploy more knowledge, more calculation and skill merely to survive than has sufficed to rule all the provinces of Spain for a century!"
• Why do you think Louis XVI forbade the presentation of these lines in the play, *The Barber of Seville?*

Economics and History: The French Financial Crisis (Objective 2) Explain that although France itself was prosperous, the French government faced a grave financial crisis. The government debt tripled between 1774 and 1789. French support for the American Revolution caused about half of this debt. Much of the remaining debt came from the cost of maintaining the royal family at Versailles. For example, Marie Antoinette spent 100,000 livres a year on clothing at a time when 50,000 livres would support a lavish lifestyle, and the average peasant earned 500 to 700 livres a year. By 1789, the government used 50 percent of its budget to pay interest on its debt and 13 percent to support the royal family's household staff of 15,000 people. Point out that Louis' ministers hoped to avoid bankruptcy by taxing the nobles. The nobles, however, refused to pay taxes unless the king called a meeting of the Estates General.

Teaching with Pictures: The Tennis Court Oath (Objective 3) Explain that Louis tried to stop the National Assembly by ordering royal troops to ban the deputies from their chamber. However, the deputies refused to give up and instead met in a nearby indoor tennis court. Direct students' attention to the painting on page 451. It shows the president of the Assembly, Jean Sylvain Bailly, reading a motion known as the Tennis Court Oath. As the crowd outside shouted *"Vive l'Assembleé,"* the deputies pledged, "never to separate but to meet in any place that circumstances may require, until the constitution of the kingdom is laid and established on firm foundations." Ask students to describe the three men embracing in the front of the painting. Explain that the artist Jacques Louis David attempted to symbolize the historic union of the three estates. David also used the painting to portray several famous Revolutionary leaders. For example, the Abbé Sieyès is seated to the right of Bailly while Mirabeau strikes a dramatic pose in the right foreground.

Check for Understanding Have students explain how Louis XVI, the National Assembly, Abbé Sieyès, and the fall of the Bastille helped to bring about the French Revolution.

Practice

Guided Practice
Lead a guided discussion of the questions in Section Review 1. (Answers are below.)

Define:
(a) French social classes (b) city-dwelling middle class (c) urban workers of Third Estate (d) form of tax paid with work

Identify:
(a) date of fall of Bastille (b) fortress used in the 1700's as a jail for political prisoners (c) king of France at the time of the French Revolution (d) monarchy and feudalism (e) lawmaking body (f) King Louis XVI's wife (g) assembly that passed laws and reforms in the name of the French people (h) wave of panic

Answer:
1. (a) First—clergy; Second—nobles; Third—bourgeoisie, urban lower classes, and peasant farmers (b) First—held 10 percent of land; Second—held high offices in church, army, government, and courts; Third—supplied labor
2. (a) bourgeoisie, some of whom were well-educated professionals and prosperous merchants; manual laborers (b) Some of the bourgeoisie were as rich as nobles, yet the law treated them as peasants; poor people could not depend on a steady diet; and peasants had to pay high taxes.
3. Louis allowed matters to drift; Marie Antoinette bought expensive items.
4. The nobles refused to pay taxes unless he did.
5. (a) Each estate had one vote. (b) wanted the votes of all members to count equally and individually (c) He ordered the estates to follow the old rules. (d) creation of the National Assembly

6. (a) forced Louis to give up his plans of bringing foreign troops into the city (b) reduced king's power and saved the National Assembly (c) became a symbol of the revolution
7. Peasants banded together, broke into nobles' manor homes, tore legal papers binding them to pay feudal dues, and burned the houses.
8. Revolt suggests a short-term disruption; revolution suggests permanent change.

Independent Practice

Assign Independent Practice Worksheet 21.1.
Assign Vocabulary Worksheet 21.
Assign Basic Skills Worksheet 21.

Enrichment Activities

1. **Reading a Primary Source** Assign Voices from the Past Resource Book 21.1.

2. **Researching for Bonus Points** Award bonus points to students who can answer this question: Where are the keys to the Bastille located today? (In George Washington's home at Mount Vernon.)

Revolution brought reform and terror. 2

Section Objectives

After completing Section 2, students should be able to:

1. describe the government created by the National Assembly and explain how it used the ideas of the philosophes.
2. explain why the National Convention voted to execute Louis XVI.
3. describe the causes and effects of the Terror.

Setting the Stage

Have each student write a paragraph summarizing the goals and achievements of the National Assembly. Emphasize that the National Assembly had successfully defied the king and had pledged to enact constitutional reforms. Remind students that serious problems still remained, such as the financial crisis and the Third Estate's demand for reforms. Tell students that this section explains how the revolutionary leaders brought both reform and terror to France.

Teaching Strategies

Transferring Ideas: The Rights of Man (Objective 1) Have students read, "The Assembly adopted many reforms" (pages 453–454). Ask, "What Enlightenment ideas were contained in the *Declaration of the Rights of Man and of the Citizen?*" Stress that the word *man* was used to designate all human beings. The Declaration used the philosophes' ideas of equality and natural law to justify the destruction of an unjust government based on absolutism and privilege. Instead, the new social order would be based on people's natural rights to "liberty, property, security, and resistance to oppression." Now ask, "How did the new government reflect the ideas of Montesquieu?" Point out that the National Assembly created a limited constitutional monarchy that divided power between the king and an elected assembly. Explain that despite the new government, many difficult problems still remained.

Writing about History: Sentencing Louis XVI (Objective 2) The deputies to the National Convention unanimously agreed that Louis was guilty of treason. Then they had to decide on his sentence. Tell students that each deputy had to stand and explain his decision. Ask students to pretend that they are deputies to the National Convention. Their assignment is to write a statement explaining their decision on sentencing Louis. Compare students' decisions with these statements made by actual deputies:

Lacaze: Citizens, Louis has spilt much blood; but will not this war which he has brought upon us shed much more? Should we not use Louis' life to prevent it? From the depths of my conscience I vote for imprisonment until there is peace, and until such time as the foreign powers have recognized the republic; and then for exile.

Dartigoeyte: As a judge, I must avenge the blood of citizens spilt by the orders of the tyrant; as a statesman, I must do what seems in the best interests of the republic: I myself fear the return of tyranny if Louis lives. I vote for his immediate death.

Danton: One must never compromise with tyrants. One can only strike at kings through the head; nothing can be expected from European kings except by force of arms. I vote for the death of the tyrant.

Check for Understanding Have students explain the significance of the *Declaration of the Rights* *of Man and of the Citizen*, Robespierre, the Reign of Terror, and the Directory.

Practice

Guided Practice
Lead a guided discussion of the questions in Section Review 2. (Answers are below.)

Define:
(a) nobles who had fled during the peasant uprising (b) machine used for beheading (c) temporary alliance between groups usually on different sides

Identify:
(a) document espousing liberty and other human rights (b) elective group that succeeded the National Assembly (c) radical city council (d) radical political club (e) leader of Paris Commune (f) prominent radical leader (g) leader who brought about Reign of Terror (h) committee that judged who was an enemy of the people (i) Robespierre's period of rule (j) executive body of five men

Answer:
1. liberty, property, security, and resistance to oppression
2. (a) created limited monarchy, created departments (b) took away church's lands and political independence
3. discredited royal family and plan for constitutional monarchy
4. (a) conservatives, radicals, and moderates (b) Even today radicals are seen as "on the left;" moderates "in the middle;" and conservatives "on the right."
5. (a) under threat of Parisian radicals (b) beheaded
6. It was a people's army of loyal patriots.
7. (a) period in which Robespierre had almost dictatorial powers, executing many (b) with members of the National Convention turning on Robespierre, sending him to the guillotine
8. moderate
9. (a) Robespierre, Marat, and many other revolutionary leaders were eventually executed in the name of revolution. (b) Answers should consider such characteristics of revolution as violence, a general climate of discontent and disorder, and the need for new leaders to take a more extreme position than the preceding.

Independent Practice
Assign Independent Practice Worksheet 21.2.
Assign Geography Skills Worksheet 21.
Assign Critical Thinking Worksheet 21.

Enrichment Activities

1. **Reading a Primary Source** Assign Voices from the Past Resource Book 21.2.
2. **Creative Writing** Ask students to prepare a class newspaper on the events discussed in this section.
3. **Researching for Bonus Points** Both Louis XVI and Marie Antoinette were executed in the Place de la Revolution. Award bonus points to students who can find the answer to this question: What was the original name of the square, and what is its name today? (Place Louis XV and Place de la Concord)

Answers to Voice from the Past

1. same rights as those granted to men
2. all those suited to a particular woman's talents
3. (a) the "right" to be executed (b) the right to a voice in government

Napoleon conquered much of Europe.   3

Section Objectives

After completing Section 3, students should be able to:

1. list the reasons for Napoleon's military victories.
2. explain how Napoleon restored order to France.
3. identify and locate the lands and kingdoms Napoleon dominated.

Setting the Stage

Explain that the early disorders of the French Revolution left a power vacuum ready to be filled. Ask students to identify some of the disorders. Then write on the chalkboard, "In the weakness of authority ... the person who really commands the army is your master." Ask students to interpret the statement and to recall military leaders who took over their countries during periods of disorder. Point out that the power of Julius Caesar and Yoritomo was based on their control over the Roman and Japanese armies. Tell students that this section describes how Napoleon Bonaparte seized power in France and then dominated most of Europe.

Teaching Strategies

Discussing History: "The Little Corporal" (Objective 1) Explain that a number of factors contributed to Napoleon's victories. He often worked 20-hour days preparing for a battle. He poured over huge maps, carefully measuring distances and studying the terrain for the best places to locate his artillery. While his opponents rested, Napoleon boldly marched at night and attacked an enemy in the rain or on a Sunday. In battle, Napoleon concentrated his forces and shrewdly waited for the enemy to make a mistake. Finally, Napoleon won the loyalty of his soldiers by sometimes fighting alongside them. His battle-hardened troops nicknamed Napoleon "the little corporal" because generals rarely fought with their armies.

Relating Past to Present: Napoleon's Enduring Reform (Objective 2) List Napoleon's reforms on the chalkboard. Then explain that many of his changes continue to influence France today. For example, at least half of the 2,300 articles in the Napoleonic Code are still in effect. The Bank of France remains France's most important financial institution. Finally, France still has a highly centralized government. As one author noted, "To this day a city cannot build a road or a bridge without approval from Paris."

Check for Understanding Have students list three of Napoleon's achievements.

Practice

Guided Practice
Lead a guided discussion of the questions in Overhead Transparency 55 and Section Review 3. (Answers are below.)

Define:
(a) swift, unexpected seizure of power (b) election in which all citizens vote yes or no (c) agreement

Identify:
(a) military genius, emperor of France (b) code of laws (c) victory of Napoleon's forces over Russian and Austrian troops (d) commander of the British fleet who defeated Napoleon (e) sea battle that forced Napoleon to give up plans to invade Britain

Answer:
1. He defended the palace where National Convention was meeting; the Directory appointed him commander of the French army.
2. by ordering his troops to occupy one chamber of the national legislature; the second chamber then voted to turn its power over to three consuls, one of whom was Napoleon

3. by proposing laws that the people readily passed
4. (a) welcomed them as long as they behaved politically (b) his system of merit promotions (c) concordat, recognizing Catholicism as the faith of "the great majority of Frenchmen"
5. (a) by abolishing the three estates and granting equal rights (b) by censoring newspapers, abolishing right of women to hold property, and restoring slavery in the colonies
6. Austria, Prussia, and Russia
7. annexed—Dutch republic and some Italian states; independent but controlled by Napoleon—Spain, Grand Duchy of Warsaw, and some German-speaking kingdoms in central Europe; allied—Russia, Prussia, and Austria
8. (a) held elections (b) True base of power was army.

Independent Practice
Assign Independent Practice Worksheet 21.3.

Enrichment Activities

1. **Reading a Primary Source** Assign Voices from the Past Resource Book 21.3.

2. **Researching for Bonus Points** Award bonus points to students who can answer this question: Who was Napoleon's second wife? (Marie Louise, the daughter of the emperor of Austria)

Napoleon's empire collapsed. 4

Section Objectives

After completing Section 4, students should be able to:

1. explain why the Spanish revolted against Napoleon.
2. describe Napoleon's losses in the invasion of Russia.
3. evaluate Napoleon's achievements and failures.

Setting the Stage

Refer to the map on page 461, *The Empire of Napoleon*. Explain that three of the countries shown in this map played a leading role in causing Napoleon's downfall. Ask students to predict the identities of the three countries and to explain why these countries might have caused Napoleon trouble. Tell students that this section describes how Napoleon made disastrous mistakes with Great Britain, Spain, and Russia, which caused his empire's collapse. The section then describes Napoleon's dramatic attempt to regain power and evaluates his long career.

Teaching Strategies

Teaching with Pictures: The Spanish Revolt (Objective 1) Explain that Napoleon planned to remove the Spanish royal family and make his brother Joseph king of Spain. On May 2, 1808, a large crowd gathered in Madrid to watch as French troops escorted the Spanish royal family out of Spain. The angry crowd suddenly attacked and massacred the French guard. The French commander promptly proclaimed martial law and ordered savage reprisals. Direct students' attention to Goya's painting (page 463) showing French troops executing Spanish rebels. Explain that the violence on May 2 sparked a nationwide uprising against Napoleon. The long struggle drained his strength and ended the myth of his invulnerability.

Discussing History: The Invasion of Russia (Objective 2) Have students read, "Napoleon invaded Russia" (pages 463–464). Show Overhead Transparency 95, *Napoleon's Losses in the Invasion of Russia.* Tell students that the Grand Army had 422,000 troops when it crossed the Niemen River into Russia. Ask, "How many troops did Napoleon have when he entered Moscow three months later?" Explain that Napoleon lost about 40,000 troops in battle. Epidemics and desertion claimed more than 250,000 men. Ask, "How many soldiers did Napoleon have when the Grand Army returned to the Niemen River?" Explain that bitter cold and repeated Russian attacks caused the loss of about 90,000 more men. The situation became so desperate that Napoleon asked for a vial of poison in case he was captured. When Napoleon finally reached the Niemen, only about 10,000 exhausted survivors of the once proud Grand Army remained.

Writing about History: Napoleon's Place in History (Objective 3) Explain that historians still debate Napoleon's achievements and failures. Divide the class into four groups and assign each one of the following roles: middle-class leaders who supported the goals of the French Revolution, veterans of Napoleon's army, wealthy British aristocrats, and modern historians. Ask each group to write a brief report evaluating Napoleon's achievements and failures. Compare and contrast the different viewpoints.

Check for Understanding Call on students to identify the Continental System, Alexander I, Waterloo, and the Duke of Wellington.

Practice

Guided Practice
Lead a guided discussion of the questions in Overhead Transparency 95 and in Section Review 4. (Answers are below.)

Define:
ordinary person who wages unconventional warfare

Identify:
(a) Napoleon's policy intended to destroy British economy (b) French war fought with Spain (c) destroying possible provisions (d) Britain, Russia, Austria, and Sweden (e) Napoleon's last bid for power after exile to Elba (f) where Napoleon was defeated

Answer:
1. trying to cut off trade with Britain; planning to make his brother king of Spain; invading Russia
2. (a) by imposing a blockade (b) weakened economies of own lands
3. wasted money and men
4. Refer students to page 464.
5. His enemies joined forces.
6. (a) Thousands welcomed him. (b) gathering of armies
7. (a) by the British and Prussians at Waterloo (b) exiled to St. Helena where he died
8. Look for answers to consider the extent to which Napoleon replaced one form of tyranny with another, Napoleon's administrative skills, and the lasting achievements of his rule.

Independent Practice
Assign Independent Practice Worksheet 21.4.

Enrichment Activities

1. **Reading a Primary Source** Assign Voices from the Past Resource Book 21.4.

2. **Solving a Mystery** Ask advanced students to prepare a report answering these questions: How did Napoleon die? Was his death a murder? (For two sources see *Smithsonian* [April 1982] and *The Murder of Napoleon* by Ben Weider and David Hapgood.)

3. **Researching for Bonus Points** Award bonus points to students who can answer this question: Where are Napoleon's remains now buried? (at the Invalides in Paris)

4. Global Perspectives Have students perform the activities in Overhead Transparency 90, *The World about 1800.*

Concluding the Chapter

1. **Chapter Closer**
   Have students outline the four phases of the French revolution by identifying each phase and listing three significant events for each.

2. **Reteaching the Chapter**
   a. Preparing a Time Line Have students prepare a time line covering the main events between 1789 and 1815.
   b. Summarizing Have students write paragraphs summarizing Napoleon's rise to power and his acquisition of an empire.
   c. Identifying Main Ideas Have students identify Napoleon's three disastrous misjudgments.

3. **Chapter Review Activities**
   Assign Chapter Review 21 activities.

Chapter Evaluation

Chapter Test 21 and Computer Test Bank Chapter 21 Test can be used to evaluate your students' understanding of this chapter.

Answers to Chapter Review 21

Reviewing the Facts

1. **a.** city-dwelling middle class **b.** temporary alliance between groups **c.** seizure of power **d.** yes/no election **e.** ordinary person fighting unconventional war
2. **a.** fall of Bastille **b.** overthrown by the revolution **c.** monarchy and feudalism **d.** social classes **e.** urban workers **f.** wife of Louis XVI **g.** panic that swept France **h.** nobles who fled France **i.** most radical of the political clubs **j.** machine to behead people **k.** governed France **l.** Robespierre's period of power **m.** French military genius who became emperor of France **n.** unsuccessful blockade of British ships **o.** where Napoleon's last battle was fought
3. **(a)** moderate stage (1789–1792) **(b)** radical stage (1793–1794) **(c)** period of reaction (1794–1799) **(d)** final stage (1799–1815)

4. Clergy formed the First Estate; nobles, the Second Estate; and commoners, the Third Estate.
5. **(a)** The nobles refused to pay taxes unless the king called a meeting. **(b)** Third Estate demanded that all three estates meet together.
6. limited, constitutional monarchy
7. **(a)** The Legislative Assembly was split into three general groups, and the most radical had leaders who were successful in having the king removed. **(b)** republic **(c)** Robespierre ruled as dictator and Committee of Public Safety executed many.
8. Bonaparte ordered his troops to occupy one chamber of the national legislature and drive out its elected members. The chamber turned over power to three officials known as consuls, and Bonaparte assumed dictatorial powers.

Basic Skills

1. Summary should include: were 98% of population. Composed of three groups: bourgeoisie, made up of professionals and business people; wealthy and well educated yet with no political power; urban lower classes, made up of manual workers, tradespeople, and servants, all of whom were very poor. Peasants—the largest group—crushed by taxes from the king, the church, and the nobility, and by the corvée.
2. **a.** Belgium, Netherlands, northern and western Italy, Illyrian provinces **b.** Spain, Confederation of the Rhine, Grand Duchy of Warsaw, eastern and southern Italy. These had only puppet governments, three of them headed by Napoleon's brothers; were very unpopular. Spain responded with guerrilla warfare. In Germany and Italy the people also turned against the French. **c.** Norway, Denmark, Prussia, Austria, Russia were very unwilling allies, ready to change sides at the first opportunity.
3. Storming of Bastille: reduced king's power, saved National Assembly; Parisians led Revolution. Republic: National Convention abolished monarchy, declared a republic. First Coalition: Britain, Spain, Portugal, Prussia, and Austria formed alliance against France; threatened revolution in France. Reign of Terror: radical period in which Robespierre led destruction of aristocracy and many common people. Directory: end of Reign of Terror; shift to conservative right and period of order. Napoleon: start of conservative, military strong-man rule. Napoleon becomes emperor: agreed to by people, end of representative government; Napoleon above law. France invades Russia: high point of French

conquests under Napoleon. Waterloo: final defeat of Napoleon after the Hundred Days.

Researching and Reporting Skills
Students' writing of historical essays will vary; should follow sequence given.

Critical Thinking
1. National Assembly marked entry of Third Estate into French government, start of representative government, beginning of revolutionary change.
2. **a.** bewilderment, anger, fear, sense of injury; **b.** mistrust of other revolutionary leaders, determination to destroy enemies of the Republic; **c.** fearful, feeling of having sacrificed nobly by giving up privileges, angry at extremes such as loss of lands and clergy appointed by election **d.** angry, determined, wanting change in hopes of obtaining food.
3. National debt leading to heavy taxes; taxes not equally shared but burdening heavily the Third Estate; poor harvests pushing up the price of bread.
4. **a.** Many revolutionary events were identified as being done for France, for its people, for the Republic. The fall of the Bastille was the taking over of power by the French people. The king, married to a foreign queen, defended by Swiss guards, supported by foreign powers, soon became identified with the foreign armies threatening the French. The people formed a citizen-army to defend their country. **b.** This increased the sense of pride and loyalty to Napoleon. When Napoleon provided leadership, his ideal of the greatness of France was eagerly adopted and followed by the people.
5. Answers will vary. Students may criticize Napoleon's opinion as exaggerating the good and ignoring the harm done during his reign. Students may agree with the concluding paragraph or criticize it for being too harsh on Napoleon. Personal conclusions will vary.

Perspectives on Past and Present
a. During the reign of Peter the Great, the Swedes had been defeated by the winter cold of Russia. Hitler's armies in World War II encountered a purposely devastated countryside as well as the cold of winter. **b.** In all three cases, the invading armies were greatly weakened or destroyed, leading to the victory of Russia and the breaking of the invaders' strength.

Investigating History
Students' reports will vary.

Unit VI Review Activities

1. Assign Geographic Theme: Place
2. Assign Unit Perspectives questions

Unit VI Review Answers

Geographic Theme: Place
1. Paris located on Seine River, Versailles in swampy area. Paris layout not precise; Versailles planned in regular layout of streets and avenues.
2. Paris developed during Middle Ages when religion was central to peoples' lives. Versailles was built to glorify the king.
3. Versailles was a secular center, representing worldliness, and its planned streets and layout accommodated expansion. Also recognized the need for planning.

Unit Perspectives

Understanding History
1. **a.** Elizabeth I reigned in England from 1588 to 1603. During this time, Philip II, a Catholic, was in power in Spain. In 1588, England defeated Philip's Spanish Armada. **b.** Charles I's reign began in 1625. His difficulties with Parliament led to civil war in which Puritans led by Oliver Cromwell took over the king's forces and Parliament. **c.** James II reigned from 1685 to 1688 when William of Orange, a Protestant, took over the British throne. **d.** Cardinal Jules Mazarin was Prime minister when Louis XIV became king at age 5, in 1643. **e.** Peter, czar of Russia, and Charles XII, king of Sweden, fought each other in the Great Northern War from 1700 to 1721. **f.** Maria Theresa came to power in Austria in 1740, the same year Frederick II became king of Prussia. During their reigns, the War of the Austrian Succession and the Seven Years' War were fought. **g.** Catherine II was crowned ruler of Russia in 1762. Voltaire was a French Enlightenment thinker with whom Catherine corresponded. **h.** In 1776, Thomas Jefferson was the primary author of the Declaration of Independence, which severed ties between the colonies and Britain ruled by George III. **i.** Robespierre called for the execution of Louis XVI, who was overthrown during the French Revolution of 1789.

2. **1.** h **2.** g **3.** a **4.** f **5.** i **6.** d **7.** e **8.** c **9.** b **10.** j
3. **a.** Balance of power is a defensive strategy in which no one country or group of countries can dominate others. Balance of trade is the ratio of a country's imports to exports. **b.** Divine right of kings is the theory that royal power comes from God. Constitutional monarchy is a government ruled by a monarch whose power is limited by law. **c.** Roundheads opposed Charles I in the civil war and supported Parliament. Cavaliers remained loyal to the king. **d.** Radicals hated the king and wanted to set up a republic. Conservatives trusted the king and upheld the idea of limited monarchy.
4. **a.** He thought governments were created to protect people from their own selfishness. **b.** He believed governments were formed to protect basic human rights. **c.** He advocated separation of powers. **d.** He argued that the only legitimate government was one that ruled with the consent of the people.

Critical Thinking
1. **(a)** A system of alliances in which one group of countries cooperated against another so that one side would not dominate the other. **(b)** The balance of power was always delicate and was tested repeatedly by war. **(c)** It did not prevent war but did prevent overwhelming defeat or takeover of one country by another.
2. **(a)** Louis XIV considered that he represented France. His power as a monarch was absolute. **(b)** Prejudice, superstition, and intolerance were in Voltaire's view the worst enemies of reason. **(c)** Peter the Great was determined to secure a window on the sea both to further trade and to foster better communication with western Europe. **(d)** *Laissez-faire* was the policy advocated by the French physiocrats, who believed that government interference by tariffs in world trade hindered production of wealth, whereas letting trade take its course would result in the greatest prosperity for all.
3. **(a)** Renaissance ideas reflected in the ideas of the philosophes included a secular outlook, concern for society and individuals, and interest in new ideas and those of the classical age. **(b)** Ideas from the Scientific Revolution developed further in the 1700's included Newton, who built on the ideas of Galileo and Kepler; Priestly and Franklin who continued the use of scientific method begun by Galileo and Kepler; and Cook, who extended the geographic knowledge introduced by Columbus, Magellan, and others.

4. Both refused to come to recognize the growing power of Parliament/Estates General and to come to terms with them. Both tried to threaten these elected bodies with military force.

Making Decisions
Answers will vary but should reflect knowledge of facts. Philip II's decision to attack England was understandable in view of his hatred for Protestant England, England's help to the Netherlands, and Spain's rivalry with England. The outcome—the loss of most of the Armada—was an economic and political disaster for Spain. Louis XIV's decision to reek control of Spain was consistent with his ambitions in general. However, Louis should have realized that this was unacceptable to other nations, at least without some limits. The war of the Spanish Succession was a disaster for both France and Spain. Louis' war brought economic ruin to France. Napoleon's decision to invade Russia was consistent with his ambition but foolish in terms of military logistics; he could not hope to supply, and he did not reckon with the Russian winter. Therefore, this decision led to a disaster for Napoleon.

Continuity and Change
1. **(a)** Between 1500 and 1800, the main political philosophy prevailing in Europe was that of monarchy, leading to the concept of absolute monarchy, as with Louis XIV, and then to enlightened despotism as with Frederick II in Prussia. The exception to this was England, where Parliament limited the power of the monarch. **(b)** The success of the Glorious Revolution in England, together with the new political ideas introduced by Locke, Montesquieu, and Rousseau, prepared the way for representative government, new forms of government such as the United States republic, and greater acceptance of the power of the people in government.
2. One obvious change from 1500 and 1800 was that non-European areas of the globe became involved with events in Europe; a global political scene had emerged. In addition, China and Russia expanded greatly. Finally, new nations had appeared—for example, the United States and the Netherlands.

Unit Evaluation

Unit Test VI can be used to evaluate your students' understanding of this unit.

The Age of European Dominance

Unit Overview

The focus of Unit VII is the nineteenth century — a time of great economic and social changes brought about by the Industrial Revolution and the building of railroads. Problems arose as industrial cities grew and the gap between the rich and the poor widened.

In 1815, the Congress of Vienna tried to restore Europe to the political conditions that existed before the Napoleonic wars. Yet, at the same time, nationalist movements were developing in Latin America, in Greece, in Italy and Germany, and in many parts of the Austrian and Ottoman empires. In the arts, romanticism, which rejected the rationality of the Enlightenment, echoed much of the spirit of the time.

A global economy developed as faster, more efficient methods of transportation and communication became available. One response to the global economy was the rise of imperialism, as nations competed to acquire colonies for raw materials and markets. Africa and Asia were divided up, as were the islands in the Pacific. Japan was the only non-Western country to join the race for colonies.

The wealth and privileges many industrialized nations enjoyed were distributed unequally. Middle and lower classes began to gain better working conditions and the right to vote. Socialists offered their solutions as well. Women, however, were still excluded from sharing citizens' rights, and, before the end of the century, they too began demanding suffrage and other rights.

Throughout the nineteenth century, the wave of inventions and discoveries continued, changing the ways people lived. More leisure time brought about the development of mass culture, and movies and sports became popular forms of entertainment. New ideas in science and changes in health care substantially raised the standard of living. Darwin's theory of evolution caused an upheaval in science that had economic and political repercussions. Meanwhile, unrest continued among national groups in eastern Europe, shaking Europe's fragile peace and balance of power.

Resources

1. The time line for Unit VII, which appears on pages 470–471. The theme for this time line is the Industrial Revolution.
2. The Geographic Theme on page 578. The theme *Movement* traces the origins of a global economy to nineteenth century industrialization.
3. The Historical Atlas map on pages 816–817. This map shows the world about 1900. Students can visualize events that occurred at the turn of the century. This map also appears as Overhead Transparency 91. A Global Perspectives enrichment strategy using this transparency appears in Chapter 26.
4. The Researching and Reporting Skills activities in Chapter Reviews. In Unit VII, students write formal research papers and give oral presentations.

Chapter Titles

The Industrial Revolution

Chapter Overview

Chapter 22 traces the growth of the Industrial Revolution, especially in Great Britain in the 1700's and early 1800's. The Industrial Revolution began with the agricultural revolution and the enclosure of farmland. A rising population and new inventions that increased industrial output made the revolution possible. Industrialization brought changes in transportation, including the beginning of the Railway Age. In the early nineteenth century, the Industrial Revolution reached other parts of Europe and the United States. While some people became wealthier, others faced increasing misery because of dangerous working conditions and factory abuses. Industrial growth brought with it social problems as new cities mushroomed with little or no planning for housing, sanitation, or education. Unions and new laws were two methods of coping with the miserable conditions of the working poor.

Key Terms

enclosure, crop rotation, factory, entrepreneur, union
For additional exercises, see Vocabulary Worksheet 22.

Chapter Focus

Ask students if they would call Sam Adams, Thomas Jefferson, Danton, and Robespierre revolutionary leaders. Ask the class to read the introduction (pages 472–473). Would students call Joseph Pease a revolutionary leader? Explain that Pease would probably not have considered himself a leader in a historic revolution. Yet, he was part of an important revolutionary change in human history — the substitution of power-driven machine tools for hand tools and animal power. Explain that historians have traditionally labeled this change the "Industrial Revolution." This chapter describes how the Industrial Revolution began in England and then transformed the production and distribution of goods, created new social classes, and redefined the relationship between employers and workers.

Text pages 472–489

Many factors aided industrial growth.

1

Section Objectives

After completing Section 1, students should be able to:

1. list the geographic advantages that helped Great Britain become the world's first industrialized nation.
2. identify the enclosure movement and explain its importance.
3. explain how a good banking system gave Britain an important economic advantage.

Setting the Stage

Geography in History: Great Britain's Resources (Objective 1) Show Overhead Transparency 56, *The Industrial Revolution in Great Britain.* Explain that Britain had geographic advantages that enabled it to become the world's first industrialized nation. Point out that Britain is an island nation with many fine harbors — no place is more than ninety miles from the sea. The country also possesses many fast-flowing streams. Flowing water was the energy resource for powering mills and factories. Also, Great Britain had accessible deposits of iron ore, coal, and limestone — materials that were essential for building and operating steam-powered machinery. By 1850, networks of canals and railways carried materials to cities, factories, and ports. Ask students to think of factors needed to begin an industrial revolution other than geographic advantages. This section identifies social and economic conditions that helped Britain become an industrialized nation.

Teaching Strategies

Discussing History: The Enclosure Movement (Objective 2) Explain that the enclosure movement enabled landowners to consolidate small farms into large, efficient units. By the 1850's about 500 families controlled half of the land in Great Britain. Another 1,300 families owned most of the remaining land. Point out that the consolidation of farm lands permitted large landowners such as Charles Townshend to try new agricultural techniques. Stress that the enclosure movement enabled Britain to produce more food. It also forced many small farmers off the land, which caused the rapid growth of cities and created a large supply of workers for the new industries.

Economics and History: British Banks (Objective 3) Explain that Britain had the most highly developed banking system in Europe. The Bank of England, founded in 1694, was the world's first modern bank. It accepted deposits and made loans on a national scale. In addition, it also printed bank notes that were widely accepted as convenient substitutes for gold and silver. Between 1780 and 1815 the number of banks increased from 300 to more than 700. As a result of Britain's commercial prosperity, the banks held large enough deposits of money to make loans at low interest rates. Explain that interest is a fee or charge for using money, and that interest rates go down as the supply of money increases. Ask students how low interest rates for bank loans might stimulate an industrial revolution. Explain that during the eighteenth century, the interest rate on loans dropped from 10 to 3 percent. These low rates encouraged businesses to borrow more money to buy machinery, to build factories, and to expand operations. Inexpensive loans also enabled entrepreneurs to start new business enterprises.

Check for Understanding Have students explain how geography, the enclosure movement, and the banking system established a foundation for Britain's industrial growth.

Practice

Guided Practice
Lead a guided discussion of the questions in Overhead Transparency 56 and in Section Review 1. (Answers are below.)

Define:
(a) process by which landowners bought up farm land and rented fields to tenant farmers; new owners often fenced in their land (b) process of keeping a field fertile by planting different crops each year

Identify:
(a) invented seed drill (b) allowed farmers to sow seeds in well-spaced rows at specific depths (c) found that crop rotation restored the soil (d) improved livestock by allowing only the best animals to breed (e) London club for the exchange of scientific ideas

Answer:
1. (a) series of dramatic changes in way work was done (b) middle 1700's (c) an economic, not political, revolution
2. (a) A landowner with a large estate was free to experiment with scientific farming methods. (b) forced small farmers off the land (c) supplied extra workers and created a demand for goods
3. abundant natural resources, especially water-power and coal; favorable geography, an island nation with many harbors; favorable climate for new ideas; good banking system, with loans available at reasonable rates; political stability, with no wars on British soil
4. transformed from a sleepy farming village into a bustling seaport
5. Answers should consider scientific farming as necessary to feed the rapidly growing population and as a cause of the displacement of small farmers who became part of the industrial labor force.

Independent Practice
Assign Independent Practice Worksheet 22.1.
Assign Vocabulary Worksheet 22.

Enrichment Activities

1. **Reading a Primary Source** Assign Voices from the Past Resource Book 22.1.
2. **Researching for Bonus Points** Award bonus points to students who can find the answer to this question: What was the Norfolk rotation? (the crop rotation invented by Charles Townshend to improve harvests on his Norfolk estate, which called for the successive planting of wheat, turnips, barley, and clover)

Britain led in the rise of industry. 2

Section Objectives

After completing Section 2, students should be able to:

1. identify the inventors and inventions that revolutionized the textile industry.
2. identify cause and effect relationships among technological developments.

Setting the Stage

Explain that in the textile industry short fibers are spun into lengths of thread, which are then woven into cloth. The British textile industry produced only woolen cloth prior to the eighteenth century. Wool was important in British life. However, imported cotton from India steadily grew in popularity. Cotton offered a number of advantages. It was

Advance Planner

Unit VII	The Age of European Dominance			
Theme	Economic and political changes in Europe between 1700 and 1914			

Chapter 22	The Industrial Revolution 1700–1850		★ Advanced	
Focus	The concept of a technological revolution		● Basic	

	Section 1	Section 2	Section 3	Section 4
Objectives	1. List the geographic advantages that helped Great Britain become the world's first industrialized nation. 2. Identify the enclosure movement and explain its importance. 3. Explain how a good banking system gave Britain an important economic advantage.	1. Identify the inventors and inventions that revolutionized the textile industry. 2. Identify cause and effect relationships among technological developments.	1. Describe how Britain's railroad age began. 2. Assess the impact of railroads on life in Great Britain. 3. Identify factors that slowed the spread of industrialization to America and Europe.	1. Link industrialization with urbanization. 2. Describe the living and working conditions of British factory workers during the early 1800's. 3. Support opinions about *laissez-faire* economic policy.
Setting the Stage	Unit VII time line Geography in History: Great Britain's Resources Transparency 56	Britain's textile industry	The impact of canals and railroads on Britain's industrial development	Manchester's transformation to an industrial city
Teaching Strategies	Discussing History: The Enclosure Movement Economics and History: British Banks Check for Understanding	Skill Building: Making a Chart Skill Building: Relating Cause and Effect Check for Understanding	Economics and History: The Liverpool-Manchester Railway Writing about History: The Impact of the Railroads Transparency 96 Geography in History: The Spread of Industrialization Outline Map 9 Check for Understanding	Writing about History: Problems of Urbanization Economics and History: A Manchester Family's Weekly Budget Skill Building: Supporting Opinions Check for Understanding
Guided Practice	Transparency 56 Q&A Section Review 1	Section Review 2	Transparency 96 Q&A Section Review 3	Section Review 4
Independent Practice Worksheets	Independent Practice 22.1 Vocabulary 22	Independent Practice 22.2	Independent Practice 22.3 Basic Skills 22	Independent Practice 22.4 Geography Skills 22 Critical Thinking 22
Enrichment	1. Primary Source: Voices 22.1 2. Researching for Points	1. Primary Source: Voices 22.2 2. Preparing a Report 3. Researching for Points	1. Primary Source: Voices 22.3 2. Researching for Points	1. Primary Source: Voices 22.4 2. ★ Analyzing a Quotation: Alexis de Tocqueville 3. Researching for Points

Chapter Closer	
● **Reteaching Activities**	Outlining, Reading a Map, Summarizing
Chapter Review	Summary, Reviewing the Facts, Basic Skills, Researching and Reporting Skills, Critical Thinking, Perspectives on Past and Present, Investigating History
Chapter Evaluation	Chapter Test 22, Computer Test Bank Chapter 22 Test

cheaper, lighter, and cooler than wool, and could be painted or printed with bright designs. British spinners and weavers could not produce enough cotton cloth to meet the rising demand for it. Enterprising merchants and inventors realized that they could make tremendous profits by finding a way to speed up the work of spinning and weaving. This section describes the inventors and inventions that revolutionized the textile industry.

Teaching Strategies

Skill Building: Making a Chart (Objective 1) Draw a chart with three columns and five rows. Label the columns "Invention/Date," "Inventor," and "What Invention Did." Fill in the chart as a class activity. A completed chart is provided below.

Invention/Date	Inventor	What Invention Did
flying shuttle 1733	John Kay	allowed a weaver to double weaving speed
spinning jenny 1764	James Hargreaves	allowed one spinner to work six or eight threads
water-frame 1768	Richard Arkwright	used waterpower to drive spinning wheels
spinning mule 1779	Samuel Crompton	combined spinning jenny and water-frame, made strong thread
power loom 1785	Edmund Cartwright	speeded up weaving process

Skill Building: Relating Cause and Effect (Objective 2) Call on students to suggest one or more effects of the following technological developments:

1. Spinners and weavers could not keep up with the demand for cloth.
2. The flying shuttle allowed weavers to weave thread faster.
3. Machines became too large and expensive for home use.
4. Eli Whitney invented a machine to remove seeds from raw cotton.

Check for Understanding Call on students to give examples of how factories, inventions, and entrepreneurs contributed to a revolution in the textile industry.

Practice

Guided Practice
Lead a guided discussion of the questions in Section Review 2. (Answers are below.)

Define:
(a) building where machines are set up to produce goods (b) person who organizes, manages, and takes on risk of a business

Identify:
(a) inventor of flying shuttle (b) inventor of spinning jenny (c) inventor of water-frame (d) creator of spinning mule (e) inventor of power loom (f) inventor of cotton gin (g) removed seeds from raw cotton (h) made the steam engine more efficient

Answer:
1. (a) textile (b) to keep up with the great demand
2. (a) flying shuttle, spinning jenny, water-frame, spinning mule, power loom, cotton gin (b) With the invention of the flying shuttle, spinners could not keep up with weavers. The spinning jenny solved that problem, the water-frame added power to drive the spinning wheels, and features of both were combined to form the spinning mule. Cotton gin increased production of raw cotton for factories. Power loom was developed to speed up weaving.
3. (a) ran on waterpower and needed to be located near streams (b) Steam as a source of power could be used anytime and anywhere.
4. Answers should consider that the steam engine provided a source of power where people, raw materials, and markets were already to be found.
5. Look for answers to consider the importance of both inventive talent and financial backing.

Independent Practice
Assign Independent Practice Worksheet 22.2.

Enrichment Activities

1. **Reading a Primary Source** Assign Voices from the Past Resource Book 22.2.

2. **Preparing a Report** Ask students to prepare a report on one of the inventors or inventions discussed in this section.

3. **Researching for Bonus Points** Award bonus points to students who can answer this question: Where did Boulton and Watt manufacture their steam engines? (at the Soho Works in Birmingham)

Industry grew and spread to new lands. 3

Section Objectives

After completing Section 3, students should be able to:

1. describe how Britain's railroad age began.
2. assess the impact of railroads on life in Great Britain.
3. identify factors that slowed the spread of industrialization to America and Europe.

Setting the Stage

Explain that canals and railroads revolutionized transportation and industry during the nineteenth century. For example, before the railroad age began, horse-drawn wagons rarely traveled more than twenty miles in a day. In contrast, the first railroads carried passengers and freight at speeds of more than thirty miles an hour. Tell students that this section describes the impact of canals and railroads on Britain's industrial development. It also explains how industrialization spread to the United States and to the rest of Europe.

Teaching Strategies

Economics and History: The Liverpool-Manchester Railway (Objective 1) Ask students to recall the pioneering work of Richard Trevithick and George Stephenson (page 479). Have students locate the cities of Liverpool and Manchester on the map on page 482. Ask, "Why did merchants want a railway between these two cities?" Explain that by the late 1820's canals carried 1,300 tons of raw cotton and cotton goods from the port of Liverpool to factories in Manchester. The trip required two days. The high cost of transporting goods between Liverpool and Manchester prompted merchants and factory owners to connect their two cities with a railroad line. The line required eight years to plan and construct, and was finally opened on September 15, 1830. A million spectators lined the roadbed to witness the historic event. When the first engine roared by at twenty-four miles an hour, spectators were amazed.

Tell students that the Liverpool-Manchester line was a huge success. Within a short time, a dozen trains carried more than 1,000 passengers between the two cities each day. Freight trains were soon carrying more goods than the canals and road coaches combined. By the late 1840's railways linked most of Britain's major industrial towns. Use Overhead Transparency 96, *The Industrial Revolution in Cotton, Coal, and Pig Iron*, to show the sharp rise in production during the railroad age. Point out that coal and iron were needed for building railways and powering the steam engines.

Writing about History: The Impact of the Railroads (Objective 2) *Prewriting* Ask students what effects railroads had on life in Great Britain, and write students' responses on the chalkboard. Discuss the four major effects described on page 480. *Writing* Ask each student to assume the role of a writer from the *Manchester Guardian* in 1840. The editor has asked for an article entitled "The Age of Railroads—Ten Years of Change." Suggest that students use "quotes" from imaginary interviews with a coal merchant, a textile factory owner, a canal operator, a farmer, a railroad engineer, and a family traveling to a seaside resort.

Geography in History: The Spread of Industrialization (Objective 3) Ask, "What factors slowed the spread of industrialization to Europe and America?" Explain that a combination of restrictive laws, the disruption caused by the Napoleonic wars, and the large supply of cheap British goods slowed the spread of industrialization. Nevertheless, industrialized "islands" soon dotted the European and American landscapes. Distribute Outline Map 9: Physical Europe. Have students use atlases to locate and label the Ruhr Valley, Po Valley, Milan, Frankfort, and Lyons. Ask, "What geographic factors encouraged the development of industry in these areas?" (harbors, rivers for water power, natural resources)

Check for Understanding Ask students to explain how canals and railroads helped promote industrial development.

Practice

Guided Practice

Lead a guided discussion of the questions in Overhead Transparency 96 and in Section Review 3. (Answers are below.)

Identify:

(a) inventor of "macadam" roads (b) made an engine that could pull a cart along a set of rails (c) engine builder and designer of locomotive (d) brought British industrial secrets to the United States (e) built a factory to house Slater's spinning machines (f) built cotton-spinning machines in Belgium

Answer:
1. **(a)** barges; horse-drawn carts **(b)** A network of canals was built; Macadam improved roads by building roadbeds with drainage.
2. **(a)** the railroad **(b)** made an engine that was small and powerful **(c)** designed engines and invented the locomotive
3. **(a)** encouraged industry by giving manufacturers a fast, cheap way to transport raw materials and finished products **(b)** created millions of new jobs **(c)** boosted agriculture by opening markets
4. **(a)** forbade engineers, mechanics, and tool makers to leave the country, or anyone in Britain to sell machines to other countries **(b)** Samuel Slater built a spinning machine from memory. **(c)** through British workers who had left Britain illegally
5. cause: made possible the enlargement of markets necessary for continued expansion; effect: Railroad and canals grew out of industrial needs.

Independent Practice
Assign Independent Practice Worksheet 22.3.
Assign Basic Skills Worksheet 22.

Enrichment Activities

1. **Reading a Primary Source** Assign Voices from the Past Resource Book 22.3.

2. **Researching for Bonus Points** Award bonus points to students who can answer this question: Who was the first person killed by a train? (William Huskisson. He was a Member of Parliament who was accidentally struck by a train during the opening ceremonies of the Liverpool-Manchester Railway.)

Answers to Voice from the Past

1. **(a)** "to toil for their daily bread," earn their own living, and help their families **(b)** children—especially girls—had worked only at home
2. For a while it seemed like fun.
3. Lucy Larcom's work was light, often with free time that allowed her to run home; Coulson's daughters began work at 3 A.M. and ended at 10:30 P.M., with one hour off to eat and drink.

Industry changed ways of life. 4

Section Objectives

After completing Section 4, students should be able to:

1. link industrialization with urbanization.
2. describe the living and working conditions of British factory workers during the early 1800's.
3. support opinions about *laissez-faire* economic policy.

Setting the Stage

Read this excerpt from *The Manchester Guardian*, November 17, 1832. "The manufacturing system as it exists in Great Britain, and the inconceivably rapid increase of immense towns under it, are without previous parallel in the history of the world." Ask what is meant by the phrase "the manufacturing system." Ask, "What other new development was 'without previous parallel?'"

Point out that the Industrial Revolution brought about a major transformation—urbanization. For centuries most Europeans had lived in rural areas, with a small percentage living in towns and cities. The Industrial Revolution reversed this situation. The factory system attracted workers to rapidly growing cities. For example, Manchester's population increased by 41 percent between 1821 and 1831. Ask, "What possible problems might rapid urbanization cause?" This section describes how the Industrial Revolution created both economic progress and urban problems.

Teaching Strategies

Writing about History: Problems of Urbanization (Objective 1) *Prewriting* Have students read, "Problems arose as cities grew" (page 483 and 484). Use students' suggestions to develop concept extensions (clustering) on the chalkboard. Emphasize the sharp contrasts between the technological marvels and wealth of cities and their environmental pollution and human poverty. Tell students that urban life made a vivid impression on the contemporary writers who flocked to see the big cities. *Writing* Divide the class into four groups. Assign each group one of the following roles: business investors from America, farmers from southern England, history professors from

Oxford, and philosophers from France. Ask each group to write a report describing their impressions after visiting Manchester. Have students read their reports to the class and compare and contrast the points of view the reports represent.

Economics and History: A Manchester Family's Weekly Budget (Objective 2) The Factory Commission Report (Vol. XX, pages 39–40) of 1833 contains a wealth of information about living and working conditions in Britain's new industrial cities. For example, the "B" family included five children. They lived in a four-room home in Manchester. The father and his 14-year-old daughter worked in a cotton mill. Reprint and distribute the following "B" family budget. (Costs have been converted into dollar equivalents.)

"B" Family Weekly Budget

Item	Cost
Butter, 1½ lb.	.31
Tea, 1½ oz.	.09
Bread	1.12
Oatmeal	.13
Bacon, 1½ lb.	.18
Potatoes	.33
Milk, one quart a day	.43
Meat on Sunday, 1 lb.	.14
Sugar, 1½ lb.	.18
Pepper, mustard, salt	.06
Soap and candles	.25
Coal	.38
Rent per week	.87
TOTAL	4.47
TOTAL INCOME	6.25
DEDUCT EXPENSES	4.47
Leaves for clothing, sickness of seven persons, schooling, etc., a surplus of	1.78

After students have examined this budget have them answer the following questions: "What item consumes the largest percent of the "B" family budget? Does the "B" family have a well-balanced diet? Does the "B" family income support an adequate standard of living?"

Skill Building: Supporting Opinions (Objective 3) Write the term *laissez-faire* on the chalkboard. Review its origins and meaning with the class. Tell students that Friedrick Engels described *laissez-faire* capitalism as a form of exploitation that "has left no other bond between [people] than naked self interest, ... callous 'cash payment.'" Have students describe the *laissez-faire* policies of the British government in the nineteenth century. Ask, "What were some benefits of *laissez-faire* cap-

italism?" Have students write paragraphs expressing their opinions about the effects of this philosophy. Students should support their opinions with facts from the text.

Check for Understanding Ask students to list three ways in which the Industrial Revolution changed life in Great Britain.

Practice

Guided Practice
Lead a guided discussion of the questions in Section Review 4. (Answers are below.)

Define:
an organization that bargains for better working conditions and higher wages

Identify:
(a) law that regulated child labor in factories (b) law that set limits on the work of children in mining (c) adopted a hands-off attitude toward economic and social developments

Answer:
1. (a) to work in factories (b) poor housing, sanitation, and education; unplanned growth of cities
2. (a) country—family worked as unit, long hours from dawn to dusk, subject to weather; city—depended on factory bell, no seasonal change of pace, children at mercy of overseer (b) performed exhausting, sometimes dangerous work, 12–14 hours daily for little pay
3. (a) middle class (b) looked down on those who made fortunes in the "vulgar" business world
4. (a) great economic and social gaps between rich and poor (b) by not easing plight of poor and by using violence against workers in rebellions
5. (a) to bargain for better working conditions and higher wages (b) denied right to form unions
6. Answers should consider workers' control over their lives in terms of agricultural versus factory work, living standards, family relations, distribution of wealth, and the growing role of education, travel, and leisure.

Independent Practice
Assign Independent Practice Worksheet 22.4.
Assign Geography Skills Worksheet 22.
Assign Critical Thinking Worksheet 22.

Enrichment Activities

1. **Reading a Primary Source** Assign Voices from the Past Resource Book 22.4.
2. **Analyzing a Quotation** After visiting Manchester, Alexis de Tocqueville wrote: "From

this foul drain the greatest stream of human industry flows out to fertilize the whole world. From this filthy sewer pure gold flows. Here humanity attains its most complete development and its most brutish, here civilization works its miracles and civilized man is turned into a savage." Ask advanced students to assess the validity of this statement.

3. **Researching for Bonus Points** Award bonus points to students who can find the answers to these questions: What name was given to the riot that took place at St. Peter's field on August 16, 1819? For what battle was the riot named? (The Peterloo Massacre; the battle of Waterloo)

Concluding the Chapter

1. **Chapter Closer**
   Have students review the industrial developments of the eighteenth century and choose one that they feel was most significant.

2. **Reteaching Activities**
   a. **Outlining** Have students write a sentence outline of Sections 1 and 2, using the headings and subheadings of the sections.
   b. **Reading a Map** Ask students to use the map on page 482 to explain the significance of each item in the map key for industrialization.

3. **Chapter Review Activities**
   Assign Chapter Review 22 activities.

Chapter Evaluation

Chapter Test 22 and Computer Test Bank Chapter 22 Test can be used to evaluate your students' understanding of this chapter.

Answers to Chapter Review 22

Reviewing the Facts

1. **a.** process by which landowners rented land to tenant farmers and fenced in their land **b.** keeping a field fertile by planting different crops on it each year **c.** large building with machines set up to produce goods **d.** person who organizes, manages, and takes on the risk of a business **e.** group of workers speaking for all workers in a trade to bargain for better working conditions and higher wages **f.** scientific approach to farming; improved production and released farm workers for manufacturing jobs **g.** simple machine that allowed one spinner to work six or eight threads at one time **h.** machine that used waterpower rather than human energy to drive spinning wheels **i.** machine combining features of spinning jenny and water-frame; made improved thread **j.** invention that speeded up weaving

2. **(a)** Fewer people went hungry, nutrition improved, and population increased, providing more workers. **(b)** forced many small farmers to move to cities and become part of industrial labor force **(c)** supplied extra workers that new factories and businesses needed; increased demand for goods **(d)** Fine harbors and navigable rivers gave Britain access to raw materials and markets. **(e)** Great Britain was rich in waterpower, coal, and iron ore, all important for industrialization. **(f)** British were interested in science and technology and open to new ideas.

3. From the flying shuttle came a need to produce a better spinning machine, the spinning jenny. Both the spinning jenny and the flying shuttle were hand-operated machines, so a water-frame was invented. Combining the features of the spinning jenny and the water-frame led to the spinning mule.

4. **(a)** increased production of raw cotton needed for British mills **(b)** made it possible for people to have a source of power that could be used anywhere

5. **(a)** Businesses needed improved methods of transporting raw materials and finished products. **(b)** a network of canals which slashed the cost of water transportation; improved British roads with macadam surface; railways which revolutionized transportation **(c)** railways

6. **(a)** As the middle class grew, conditions for workers seemed to decline. **(b)** laissez-faire **(c)** joined together in unions

Basic Skills

1. **(a)** sharp increase in production and consumption **(b)** Technological inventions were a factor in each trend; cotton gin increased consumption of cotton; steam engines needed coal; growth in industry created more demand for railroads, machinery, and buildings, and this in turn increased demand for iron.

2.

TRANSPORTATION REVOLUTION:
London to Edinburgh

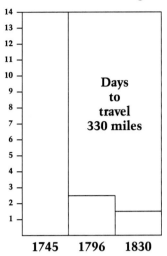

3. **(a)** flying shuttle; spinning jenny; water-frame; spinning mule; power loom; cotton gin **(b)** Flying shuttle enabled weaver to go twice as fast; spinning jenny made up to 80 threads at once; water-frame used water power to drive spinning wheels; spinning mule produced better quality thread; increased weaver's production and factory work; cotton gin increased supply of raw cotton and thus enabled textile mills to work at capacity.

4. **(a)** Railroad and water routes available between London and other three cities. **(b)** All three cities near iron ore fields and accessible by water and rail.

Researching and Reporting Skills
Students' answers will vary.

Critical Thinking
1. Possible answers: **(a)** pride that inventions had spurred growth **(b)** happy over opportunity for enormous profits **(c)** though sometimes difficult conditions arose, it means a comfortable and stable standard of living **(d)** some changes negative; forced into factory; poor working and living conditions; some changes positive; not subject to instability of farm life; possibility of regular wages.
2. **(a)** factory owners, shippers, and merchants **(b)** Landowners forced to share power in Parliament with factory owners, shippers, merchants, and other new members of the middle class.
3. **(a)** laissez-faire: economic role of government should be hands-off **(b)** Entrepreneurs allowed to pursue profit and expansion without concern for resulting working conditions, social conditions and deterioration of environment.

Perspectives on Past and Present
Students should point to technological advances in such things as computers, robotics, communications, CD's, and other changes spurred by electronics.

Investigating History
Students' answers will vary.

Restoration, Romanticism, and Revolution

Chapter Overview

The Congress of Vienna met in 1814 to settle European affairs after the defeat of Napoleon Bonaparte. Led by Metternich—Austria's chief minister—Austria, Great Britain, Prussia, and Russia took steps to encircle France, to restore a balance of power, and to return most rulers to their thrones. After 1815, conservatives once again controlled Europe. However, the political philosophies of liberals and radicals could not be stifled. New movements of nationalism and romanticism also developed. Nationalism was a force for change in Greece, Italy, and Germany. Romanticism, a reaction against the Enlightenment, influenced the arts and politics.

All these forces affected Latin America as well as Europe. Independence movements in the Americas resulted in Spain's loss through war of most of its American colonies, in Brazil's peaceful emergence as an independent country, and in the Monroe Doctrine in which the United States declared the Western Hemisphere closed to future colonization.

Reform and revolution also swept throughout Europe as France overthrew its Bourbon king, Britain broadened voting rights, and Napoleon III came to power in France. The year 1848 stands out as a year of European revolutions that eventually overthrew the agreements made at the Congress of Vienna.

Key Terms

nation-state, caudillos
For additional exercises, see Vocabulary Worksheet 23.

Chapter Focus

Historians have noted that people often cling more strongly to the past during times of rapid social change. Have students speculate on reasons this might be so. Have students read the chapter introduction, and direct their attention to the picture on page 490. Ask why the people who gathered at Vienna were celebrating, and which social classes were represented. Ask students why they think the Congress of Vienna wanted to "turn back the clock." Why were the delegates at the Congress of Vienna frightened by Napoleon Bonaparte? Explain that for the delegates in Vienna, the "good old days" existed when the rights and powers of the aristocracy were not challenged. As they read Chapter 23, have students speculate on the possibilities of returning to the past.

European leaders sought stability. 1

Section Objectives

After completing Section 1, students should be able to:

1. explain the political and social ideals of Metternich.
2. explain the concept of the balance of power as the main goal of the Congress of Vienna.

Setting the Stage

Ask students to imagine the excitement and satisfaction European aristocrats felt as they celebrated in Vienna. Since Napoleon Bonaparte's challenge to their world had been crushed, they expected a reinstatement of the old social order, headed by the aristocratic class. Ask students why political and social change is often met with resistance. Have students recall the changes caused by the Industrial Revolution and by the French Revolution. Tell students that the groups represented at the Congress of Vienna were frightened of revolutionary changes and wanted to reverse the trends that threatened their power. They hoped to restore order in European society.

Teaching Strategies

Discussing History: Metternich (Objective 1)
After students have read Section 1, explain that Vienna was the perfect city to host a meeting that had the main goal of restoring old powers and

ideas. The aristocratic palaces and offices of the monarchy in Vienna suggested stability and order. Suggest that Metternich's aristocratic manner and conservative ideas matched the setting of Vienna. Select a student to read Metternich's statement (page 492). Ask, "Why did Metternich fear democracy?" Explain that Metternich offered Europe peace and stability, and believed that expanding the right to vote to all social classes would lead to chaos. Ask students to speculate on the observations Metternich might make about democracy in the present-day United States.

Relating Past to Present:Balance of Power (Objective 2) Discuss the means by which present-day countries strive to maintain a balance of power. Ask students to explain why a balance is desirable and why it is difficult to maintain. List responses on the chalkboard. Ask "What methods do countries use to maintain a balance of power? (arms treaties and negotiations, trade agreements) Explain that the Congress of Vienna attempted to achieve an equilibrium between European powers so that none could become powerful enough to risk war or to conquer neighboring countries as

Advance Planner

Chapter 23	Restoration, Romanticism, and Revolution 1815–1850			★ Advanced
Focus	Why did the Congress of Vienna want to bring back "the good old days?"			● Basic

	Section 1	Section 2	Section 3	Section 4
Objectives	1. Explain the political and social ideals of Metternich. 2. Explain the concept of the balance of power as the main goal of the Congress of Vienna.	1. Relate the concept of the nationalism to the outcomes of the Congress of Vienna. 2. Evaluate romantic themes in present-day cultures.	1. Name the contributions of Bolívar and San Martín to Latin American independence. 2. Explain how physical and cultural geography affected Latin American political boundaries. 3. Identify the basis of Mexico's nationalist movement.	1. Analyze the causes and effects of the revolutions of 1848. 2. Evaluate the results of the revolutions of 1848 and the failure of French radicals to maintain power.
Setting the Stage	Why political and social change is often met with resistance	The spread of nationalism in Europe	Causes of Latin American independence movements	Charles X's efforts to maintain his power
Teaching Strategies	Discussing History: Metternich Relating Past to Present: Balance of Power Check for Understanding	Writing about History: Nineteenth-Century Nationalism Relating Past to Present: Romanticism Check for Understanding	Writing about History: Bolívar and San Martín Using Geographic Themes: Region Transparency 58 Transferring Ideas: Mexican Nationalism Check for Understanding	Skill Building: Relating Causes and Effects Discussing History: The Revolutions of 1848 Check for Understanding
Guided Practice	Transparency 57 Q&A Section Review 1	Section Review 2	Transparency 58 Q&A Section Review 3	Section Review 4
Independent Practice Worksheets	Independent Practice 23.1 Vocabulary 23 Critical Thinking 23	Independent Practice 23.2 Geography Skills 23	Independent Practice 23.3	Independent Practice 23.4 Basic Skills 23
Enrichment	1. Primary Source: Voices 23.1 2. Researching for Points	1. Primary Source: Voices 23.2 2. Researching for Points	1. Primary Source: Voices 23.3 2. Preparing a Report 3. Researching for Points	1. Primary Source: Voices 23.4 2. Researching for Points

Chapter Closer	
● **Reteaching Activities**	Summarizing, Recalling Information, Explaining
Chapter Review	Summary, Reviewing the Facts, Basic Skills, Researching and Reporting Skills, Critical Thinking, Perspectives on Past and Present, Investigating History
Chapter Evaluation	Chapter Test 23, Computer Test Bank Chapter 23 Test

Napoleon Bonaparte had done. Ask, "How did the Congress' treatment of France demonstrate attempts to achieve a balance of power in Europe?" Explain that after the negotiations in Vienna, Europe remained at peace for thirty years.

Check for Understanding Have students explain how the Congress of Vienna was a response to the French Revolution and how Metternich planned to achieve stability in Europe.

Practice

Guided Practice
Lead a guided discussion of the questions in Overhead Transparency 57 and in Section Review 1. (Answers are below.)

Define:
(a) principle that rulers Napoleon had driven from their thrones should be restored (b) wanted to conserve traditional forms of government (c) wanted more power given to elected but limited parliaments (d) supported democratic government and favored drastic change

Identify:
(a) meeting called by Austria, Great Britain, Prussia, and Russia (b) country that could shape international events (c) minister who dominated Congress of Vienna (d) 39 loosely joined German states, dominated by Austria (e) agreement among rulers of Russia, Prussia, and Austria against liberalism (f) restored Bourbon king of France

Answer:
1. to restore boundaries of Europe as they had existed before Napoleon's conquests
2. Austria, Great Britain, Prussia, Russia, and France
3. strengthen countries surrounding France to prevent French aggression, restore a balance of power, and restore royal families to their thrones
4. (a) forced to give up all territories Napoleon had taken but allowed to keep most of its overseas possessions, its army, and an independent government (b) made stronger (c) loosely joined to form a newly created German Confederation
5. (a) belief in constitutional or even absolute monarchy (b) approval of early reforms of French Revolution and government by an elected, limited parliament (c) support of democratic government and idea of change
6. the only constitutional monarchy
7. Kings and princes were restored.
8. (a) settlement fair enough that no country leaves bearing a grudge and a balance of power

remains intact (b) temporarily (Peace lasted about forty years.) (c) political ideals of liberty, equality, and fraternity introduced by French Revolution

Independent Practice
Assign Independent Practice Worksheet 23.1.
Assign Vocabulary Worksheet 23.
Assign Critical Thinking Worksheet 23.

Enrichment Activities

1. **Reading a Primary Source** Assign Voices from the Past Resource Book 23.1.

2. **Researching for Bonus Points** Award bonus points to students who can answer the following question: Who was the French delegate to the Congress of Vienna? (Talleyrand)

New ideals affected politics and art.   2

Section Objectives

After completing Section 2, students should be able to:

1. relate the concept of nationalism to the outcomes of the Congress of Vienna.
2. evaluate romantic themes in present-day cultures.

Setting the Stage

Recall that Joan of Arc symbolized French nationalism in the fifteenth century (pages 234–235). Joan's victory over the English army at Orleans and her insistence that French kings govern France inspired feelings of nationalism. Tell students that Section 2 describes the spread of nationalism throughout Europe in the nineteenth century. Explain that the nationalist movements in the 1800's continued a centuries-old trend. Nationalist groups fought to establish independent nation-states in Italy, Greece, and Germany. National movements also sparked changes in literature and art that came to be known as the romantic movement.

Teaching Strategies

Writing about History: Nineteenth-Century Nationalism (Objective 1) *Prewriting* Discuss how the growing feelings of nationalism stimulated social unrest throughout Europe. Note that the Congress of Vienna was not interested in nationalist issues. Ask, "How did nationalist ambitions interfere with the Congress' goals of legitimacy and restoration?" Tell students that Europe's aristocrats felt closer ties among themselves than with the middle and lower class members of their own countries. Metternich, for example, considered himself as much a citizen of Europe as of Austria. *Writing* Have students imagine they are members of Young Italy. Ask them to write a letter to Metternich explaining why the Congress of Vienna was wrong in restoring the old political divisions in Italy.

Relating Past to Present: Romanticism (Objective 2) Discuss the themes of nineteenth-century romanticism. Point out that the romantics championed individuality and nonconformity. Byron's person life, for example, became the subject of gossip columns and public speculation. He willingly took the role of a social outcast, which made him a hero in the eyes of rebellious youths. Another romantic poet, Charles Baudelaire, delighted in shocking Parisian society by wearing outrageous costumes and by dyeing his hair green. Ask students how twentieth-century artists, writers, and musicians have expressed romantic themes such as nationalism, individualism, and idealism. Suggest that the romantic movement had a lasting influence.

Check for Understanding Have students explain why nationalist movements found inspiration in romanticism, and why romantic themes supported nationalist movements.

Practice

Guided Practice
Lead a guided discussion of the questions in Section Review 2. (Answers are below.)

Define:
(a) belief that a person's greatest loyalty is to a nation-state (b) group who share traditions, history, and language (c) reaction against Enlightenment

Identify:
(a) battle for Greek independence, 1827 (b) romantic poet who died fighting for Greek freedom (c) founder of Young Italy (d) nationalist group, all under age 40 (e) France's leading romantic novelist, a woman (f) Viennese composer of romantic music (g) British romantic novelist and poet

Answer:
1. (a) traditions, history, and language (b) France and Spain

2. stressed the equality of all French people and gave them opportunity for self-government
3. Greeks revolted against Ottoman rule, and, aided by the great Powers, achieved independence.
4. little mass support; cultural differences between northern and southern Italy; Metternich's suppression of nationalistic groups
5. no all-German army to enforce decision; could make no laws without approval of 39 states
6. Austria consisted of many nationalities.
7. emotion and passion: Goethe; individualism: glorification of heroes; celebration of nature: Turner's landscape paintings; glorification of past: collections of old ballads and folktales
8. (a) geographical conditions, language, literature, and the desires of the people (b) Look for answers to consider the effect of geography on natural boundaries, the role of a common language and literature in uniting a people, and the effect of the French Revolution on the Italian people.

Independent Practice
Assign Independent Practice Worksheet 23.2.
Assign Geography Skills Worksheet 23.

Enrichment Activities

1. **Reading a Primary Source** Assign Voices from the Past Resource Book 23.2.

2. **Researching for Bonus Points** Award bonus points to students who can answer the following question: To whom did Beethoven dedicate his third symphony? (Napoleon Bonaparte)

Answers to Voice from the Past

1. one who has never felt great joy when returning to his native land
2. thinking only of himself and not of his nation
3. (a) to forfeit reknown (b) to be unwept

Latin America won independence. 3

Section Objectives

After completing Section 3 students should be able to:

1. name the contributions of Bolívar and San Martín to Latin American independence.
2. explain how physical and cultural geography affected Latin American political boundaries.
3. identify the basis of Mexico's nationalist movement.

Setting the Stage

Call on students to name the present-day countries in Latin America. Ask students what countries in Latin America are in the news today and for what reasons. Explain that most of these countries gained their independence in the nineteenth century through revolutions. Latin Americans were influenced by the American and French revolutions and viewed their causes as part of the same struggle for liberty and justice. Tell students that Section 3 examines how present-day Latin American countries were established.

Teaching Strategies

Writing about History: Bolívar and San Martín (Objective 1) *Prewriting* Have students compare the personalities and backgrounds of Bolívar and San Martín. Ask, "What was their common goal?" (Latin American independence) "Why had they arranged a meeting?" (To ally forces) Ask students to speculate why San Martín left his army with Bolívar and returned to Argentina. *Writing* Have students summarize the contributions of Bolívar and San Martín to Latin American independence and then offer an explanation of San Martín's departure. Students should review events leading up to the meeting, compare Bolívar's and San Martín's similar concerns about the Spanish army, and speculate on San Martín's reasons for leaving South America.

Using Geographic Themes: Region (Objective 2) Tell students that cultural geography is the study of geographic regions where people share common aspects of culture, such as language or customs. The landforms of Central America and South America encouraged a great diversity of regional cultures. At the same time, the physical and cultural geography of Latin America discourage political unity. Explain that Simon Bolívar wanted to unite the newly independent countries of South America to create a system similar to the United States in North America. However, Latin Americans set up independent, regional governments according to unifying geographic and cul-

tural features. Show Overhead Transparency 58. Point out that Spanish settlements stretched from California to the southern tip of South America, and that then as now the Andes mountain ranges separate coastal and interior regions. Ask, "What geographic features made unification difficult?" (distances, mountains, cultural differences) Have students identify the countries that were established after independence.

Transferring Ideas: Mexican Nationalism (Objective 3) Select a student to read Father Hidalgo's words to the Indian peasants (page 503). Ask, "What did Hidalgo mean by 'lands stolen from your forefathers 300 years ago?'" (land taken by conquistadors) Explain to students that the basis of the Mexico revolution was conflict between wealthy landowners and landless peasants. On the chalkboard, draw a pyramid-shaped diagram illustrating class structure in Mexico during colonial times. Have students label the diagram to show the social status of (a) Indians, mulattoes, and mestizos; (b) creoles; and (c) peninsulars. Ask, "What determined membership in a social class?" (degree of Spanish descent) "Which groups most supported nationalism and why? Why did the creoles refuse to support Hidalgo's revolt?" Direct students to reread Hidalgo's words. Ask, "How did the actions of Spanish conquistadors in the 1500's establish a basis for Mexican nationalism in the 1800's?"

Check for Understanding Ask students to identify the main causes and consequences of Latin America's independence movement.

Practice

Guided Practice
Lead a guided discussion of the questions in Overhead Transparency 58 and in Section Review 3. (Answers are below.)

Define:
(a) lands south of the United States where Spanish, Portuguese, and French are spoken (b) people born in Spain or Portugal (c) people born in Latin America whose ancestors came from Europe (d) people of mixed European and Indian ancestry (e) people of European and African ancestry (f) political strongman who ruled as dictator

Identify:
(a) ex-slave who drove French out of Haiti (b) general who led the struggle for independence in northern South America (c) fighter for independence in southern South America (d) last major

battle of the war for independence against Spain (e) regent of Brazil who agreed to independence (f) priest who led Mexico's war for independence (g) priest who fought beside Hidalgo for Mexican independence (h) creole officer who proclaimed Mexican independence (i) U.S. statement pronouncing Western Hemisphere closed to European colonization

Answer:

1. peninsulars at top; creoles; the common people, including mestizos, mulattoes, blacks, and Indians, at the bottom
2. Black revolutionary leaders defeated French forces with help of slaves.
3. (a) Peninsulars held all high offices; Spain kept tight control over economy, shipping, mining. (b) Napoleon's conquest of Spain
4. (a) through the military accomplishments of Bolívar (b) through the military accomplishments of San Martín
5. peacefully, when Dom Pedro agreed to independence in 1822
6. It began in the countryside, with Indians and mestizos taking a leading role.
7. wealthy creole aristocrats and caudillos
8. to protect Latin American independence and British and American economic interests
9. (a) Answers should note the effects of the Enlightenment and the French Revolution on educated peoples in Latin America and the trend toward nationalism. (b) Answers should consider the general trend toward independence and recognize that, in time, a leader probably would have emerged.
10. Possible answer: all the work can be undone.

Independent Practice
Assign Independent Practice Worksheet 23.3.

Enrichment Activities

1. **Reading a Primary Source** Assign Voices from the Past Resource Book 23.3.

2. **Preparing a Report** Have students report on present-day life in Brazil. They might include information on the Amazon Indians, and on the economic and political problems Brazil faces today. (See *National Geographic*, March 1987.)

3. **Researching for Bonus Points** Award bonus points to students who can answer this question: On what day do Mexican's celebrate their independence? (September 16, the day on which Father Hidalgo's revolt began)

Reform and revolution swept Europe.

4

Section Objectives

After completing Section 4 students should be able to:

1. analyze the causes and effects of the revolutions of 1848.
2. evaluate the results of the revolutions of 1848 and the failure of French radicals to maintain power.

Setting the Stage

Ask students how Americans would react if the President dissolved Congress, shut down newspapers, and limited voting rights. Explain to students that this is what the French king Charles X did in 1829. French citizens were outraged. Explain that Charles was counting on support from the representatives at the Congress of Vienna to suppress challenges to his power. Ask students to find out, as they read Section 4, whether or not Europe's aristocrats came to Charles' aid.

Teaching Strategies

Skill Building: Relating Causes and Effects (Objective 1) Review the political philosophies of conservatism, liberalism, and radicalism (page 493). Ask students to characterize the followers of each philosophy in 1848. Then ask whose interests were ignored at the Congress of Vienna. Explain that the revolutions in nineteenth-century Europe were fought mainly by peasants and workers, who had gained nothing at the Congress of Vienna. Their dissatisfactions were heightened by recurring economic depressions. Ask students how the French reacted to Charles X's policies. (They overthrew him and gave the crown to Louis Philippe) Have students compare events in France with the reform movement in England. Ask, "What liberal goals did the Reform Bill of 1832 demonstrate?" (limited democracy, nonviolent reform)

Discussing History: The Revolutions of 1848 (Objective 2) Tell students that the revolutions of 1848 were violent responses to dissatisfaction with the resolutions of the Congress of Vienna. Ask students which revolts were most inspired by nationalist goals. The aristocrats at Vienna Congress had ignored nationalistic feelings in their haste to restore old monarchies. The revolts attempted to shift power from aristocrats to the middle and lower classes. Ask students which revolts succeeded in expanding rights for citizens. Point out that only in France was democracy the main goal of the revolutionaries. Ask students why the French became disillusioned with the radicals. (They were violent and quarrelsome.) Discuss how the election of Louis Napoleon was a reaction against the French radicals. Select a student to read Napoleon's statement on page 507. Ask, "Why did Napoleon's words appeal to French voters?" (assurances of stability) Have students draw conclusions about the reasons for many of the failures for the revolutions for 1848.

Check for Understanding Have students summarize this section by completing the following sentence. Events in the 1830's and 1840's that undermined the power of conservatism in Europe included....

Practice

Guided Practice
Lead a guided discussion of the questions in Section Review 4. (Answers are below.)

Define:
(a) revolution directed toward overthrowing a system established by a previous revolution (b) sudden overturn of government

Identify:
(a) last Bourbon king of France (b) cousin of Charles X who became citizen king (c) bill which gave almost all middle-class men in Britain right to vote (d) year of European revolutions (e) led temporary government that replaced Louis Philippe's government (f) leader of radical faction that wanted reform (g) took the title Emperor Napoleon III

Answer:
1. (a) actions of Charles X who tried to rule as absolute monarch (b) Riots; king fled to England.
2. gave most middle-class men right to vote, industrial cities represented in Parliament
3. (a) to establish a democratic government (b) to throw off Austrian rule and set up a Hungarian nation-state (c) to unite Germany
4. (a) won many concessions from monarchs (b) Europe returned to its pre-1848 status.
5. (a) by turning a deaf ear to demands that the Chamber of Deputies be made more democratic (b) a split into factions that led to bloody battles

6. by dissolving the French parliament and declaring himself the sole ruler of France
7. (a) that a conservative, absolutist monarch could be elected democratically (b) Answers should note the nature of charismatic leadership, the role of an educated electorate, and the economic benefits of stability.

Independent Practice
Assign Independent Practice Worksheet 23.4.
Assign Basic Skills Worksheet 23.

Enrichment Activities

1. **Reading a Primary Source** Assign Voices from the Past Resource Book 23.4.

2. **Researching for Bonus Points** Award bonus points to students who can answer the following question: What name was given to the reign of Louis Philippe? (the July monarchy)

Concluding the Chapter

1. **Chapter Closer**
   Have students write essays beginning with the following topic sentence: The Congress of Vienna failed to meet its objectives of restoring the old order and maintaining stability. Ask students to trace political development in Europe between 1815 and 1848.

2. **Reteaching Activities**
   a. **Summarizing** Ask students to summarize the resolutions made by the Congress of Vienna.
   b. **Recalling Information** Have students recall the contributions of Bolívar, San Martín, Mazzini, and Byron to nationalist movements.
   c. **Explaining** Ask students to explain how nationalist movements were influenced by romantic ideals.

3. **Chapter Review 23 Activities**
   Assign Chapter Review 23 Activities.

Chapter Evaluation

Chapter Test 23 and Computer Test Bank Chapter 23 Test can be used to evaluate your students' understanding of this chapter.

Answers to Chapter Review 23

Reviewing the Facts

1. **a.** group of people, united under their own government, who also share similar traditions, history, and language **b.** political strongman who ruled as a dictator **c.** loyalty to one's own land and people **d.** intellectual movement that emphasized feeling, individualism, love of nature, and love of the past

2. **a.** settlement at this meeting preserved old political and social order and lasted about 40 years during which there were no wars **b.** chief minister of Austria whose conservative goals were implemented at Congress of Vienna **c.** one of Italy's early nationalists **d.** ex-slave who drove French out of Haiti **e.** brilliant general who led struggle for independence in northern South America **f.** fighter for independence in southern South America **g.** regent of Brazil who peacefully granted independence **h.** priest who was a leader in Mexico's war for independence **(i)** farm worker turned priest who fought beside Hidalgo for Mexican independence **j.** statement announcing that American continents could no longer be colonized by European powers **k.** act that doubled the number of British voters **l.** elected president of France who later declared himself emperor

3. **(a)** restore former monarchies, block France from expanding, and establish a balance of power **(b)** restoration of Bourbon rulers and many Hapsburg princes; creation of Kingdom of Netherlands and German Confederation; keeping France intact and awarding territories to winning power

4. **(a)** Britain had a constitutional monarchy, contrasted with absolute monarchs in eastern Europe. **(b)** Old Bourbon dynasty ruled again but shared some power with Chamber of Deputies.

5. similar traditions, history, language, and own government

6. **(a)** Great Powers sided with Greeks against the Ottoman Turks and destroyed an Ottoman fleet at Battle of Navarino. **(b)** Idea of nationalism won little support from the masses, and deep cultural differences divided northern and southern Italy. Metternich used censorship and arrests to stop the spread of nationalist ideas.

7. glorification of emotion, nature, heroic individuals, and the past

8. **(a)** Haiti **(b)** Slaves and free mulattoes revolted; led by Toussaint L'Ouverture; they drove the French forces from the island.

9. **(a)** creoles **(b)** Peninsulars held almost all the high government offices; Spain controlled colonies' economy; creoles felt no loyalty to King Joseph Bonaparte.

10. **(a)** Bolívar led his soldiers through the Andes to Colombia and defeated the Spanish army there, then freed Venezuela. In Ecuador, with the army of San Martín, he defeated the Spanish army. **(b)** San Martín won victories to free Chile and preserve freedom for Argentina.

11. The regent of Brazil, Dom Pedro, agreed to Brazilian demands for independence.

12. **(a)** In 1810, Father Miguel Hidalgo led an army of Indians toward Mexico City where he was betrayed and executed. The next rebel leader, Morelos, ended up controlling most of Mexico. In 1813, a Mexican congress declared Mexico an independent republic. In 1820, Mexico's creoles, fearing that a new Spanish government would take away their privileges, united in support of independence. Iturbide, a creole officer who had executed Morelos, proclaimed Mexico independent in 1821. **(b)** It began in the countryside with Indians and mestizos playing an important role.

13. **(a)** American continent could not be colonized in the future by any European nation. **(b)** Both wanted to protect their economic interests in Latin America.

14. doubled the number of British male voters

15. Charles X was unseated from his throne and Louis Philippe became a "citizen king" sharing power with the Chamber of Deputies.

16. Violence turned France against radicals and toward a more moderate, liberal government.

Basic Skills

1.

Revolution in Latin America

Countries	European Colonial Power	Social Classes Involved	Leaders	Main Events
Haiti	France	Slaves, Free Mulattoes	Toussaint L'Ouverture	Revolt 1791
Venezuela	Spain	Creoles	Simon Bolívar	Independence declared 1811; Spain defeated Bogotá 1819; Free Venezuela 1821
Argentina	Spain	Creoles	José San Martín	Independence declared 1816; Victories in Chile 1817; Bolívar and San Martín 1821; Battle of Ayacucho safeguards independence 1824

Brazil	Portuguese	Creoles	Dom Pedro	Napoleon invades Portugal 1807; Napoleon defeated; King leaves Dom Pedro regent; Dom Pedro declares independence of Brazil 1822
Mexico	Spain	Indians, Mestizos	Miguel Hidalgo José Maria Morelos	Hidalgo and peasants march 1810; Morelos takes over most of Mexico but creoles oppose. He is executed 1815; Iturbide unites creoles in revolution. Mexican independence declared 1821

2. conservatism—supported the monarchy, rulers have total power to make laws and govern; liberalism—political power in the hands of landowners and educated, against complete democracy; radicalism—supported complete democracy, right of working class to vote, approved use of violence if necessary
3. (a) liberal—Louis Philippe, Bolívar; radical—Lamartine, Morelos, Louis Blanc; conservative—Charles X (b) Louis Philippe—shared power with Chamber of Deputies; Bolívar—represented creoles; Lamartine—wanted political power for French working class; Morelos—represented Mexico's Indians and mestizos in struggle against Spain; Louis Blanc—wanted political and economic reforms for French working class; Charles X—absolute monarch and tried to take power from Chamber of Deputies

Researching and Reporting Skills
Students' answers will vary.

Critical Thinking
1. Possible answers: degree of nationalistic feeling among people, responsiveness of monarch, strength and foresight of leaders
2. (a) opinion (b) yes; from the viewpoint of liberals and radicals it was a political failure. They lost reforms gained during period of French Revolution; the monarchists had strengthened themselves; only landowners and royalty had any rights.
3. (a) to create republics; creole rule (b) Bolívar had only small success; did lead to 16 independent countries and a few wealthy creoles captured power; but by 1830 all countries run by military dictators and people had few political freedoms.

Perspectives on Past and Present
Students' answers will vary.
(a) Nationalism is a significant factor in present-day Africa, Southeast Asia, and Latin America. (b) yes—in North America and much of Europe nationalism takes the form of patriotism and is most likely to surface around economic issues. It is not as much a motivational force as in newly emerging nations or where people are seeking independence from colonial powers, dictators, or dominating foreign nations. Note the Palestinian question in the Middle East, fighting in Nicaragua, political battles in Chile, and struggle in South Africa.

Investigating History
Students' answers will vary.

Economic Expansion and Nationalism

Chapter Overview

By the middle of the nineteenth century, great changes were taking place in Europe and in North America. New inventions were displayed in 1851 at London's Great Exhibition and in 1876 at the Centennial Exposition in Philadelphia. Railroads, steamships, and communications networks were bringing distant parts of the world in closer contact. Global economic ties were developing.

Businesses were growing larger; many became corporations. Workers demanded more rights and protection. Realism in art and literature reflected these changes.

Italy and Germany continued the process of unification. By 1871, Italy was independent and united. Prussia defeated Austria and France and unified the German states into the new German nation, causing the previous balance of power to collapse. Great Britain and Germany emerged as the military and industrial leaders of Europe.

In the United States, the conflict over slavery between the industrial north and the agricultural South finally erupted in civil war. By its hundredth birthday, the United States had a rapidly expanding economy and was becoming a world leader in industrial production.

Key Terms

stock, corporations, monopoly, emigration, immigration, socialism, suffrage
For additional exercises, see Vocabulary Worksheet 24.

Chapter Focus

Tell students that in the 1870's people in Europe and America read about the adventures of Phineas Fogg, the main character in Jules Verne's novel *Around the World in Eighty Days*. Explain that Verne's work was originally a newspaper serial and readers anxiously awaited each new episode to see if Fogg would win his wager to circle the globe in eighty days. Jules Verne was famous for writing stories with curious inventions, such as submarines and spaceships, that foreshadowed actual twentieth-century inventions. In *Around the World in Eighty Days*, however, Phineas Fogg used the new inventions of the nineteenth century, such as the steamship, railroad, and hot-air balloon. These real-life devices were fantastic enough to keep readers interested. Suggest to students that Verne might have gotten some of his story ideas from presentations at London's Great Exhibition of 1851. Tell students that Chapter 24 traces the effects of new inventions on people's lives in the nineteenth century. The chapter also explains how the new technology led to the development of new economic systems and to mass migrations.

Industrialism created a global economy. 1

Section Objectives

After completing Section 1, students should be able to:

1. explain the concept of "global economy."
2. assess the impact of improved communication and transportation in the nineteenth century.
3. analyze the corporation as a new economic institution.
4. identify the causes of immigration and emigration.

Setting the Stage

Economics and History: Global Economy (Objective 1) Ask students to imagine their lives with no foreign products—no oil from the Middle East, no electronic products or automobiles from the Pacific Rim countries, and no music from England. Ask students how events in the Middle East or in Japan can affect economies worldwide. Explain that interdependence among countries for resources and products has created a global economy. Before the technological advances of the nineteenth century, communication between distant countries was limited. Manufacturers waited months for materials and products to be shipped between continents. The invention of steamships and railroads dramatically reduced transportation times. As advances in transportation made longer trade routes more practical, merchants began to expand their operations to eye foreign markets. Ask students to think about the present-day global economy and the importance of transportation and communication technologies as they read Section 1.

Teaching Strategies

Discussing History: Transportation and Communication in the Nineteenth Century (Objective 2) "The world is getting smaller." Ask students what this phase means. Students should refer to present-day advances in transportation and communication. Then explain that before steamships, a trip from New York to England took about four weeks. The steamship cut this time in half. Today, the same trip aboard a supersonic aircraft takes less than five hours. Advances in railroad transportation were also dramatic. Railroads could move people, animals, raw materials and manufactured goods over long distances in any weather. The first transcontinental railroad completed at Promontory Point, Utah, was an achievement of technology and hard work. In one day work crews could build 10.6 miles of track, using 31,000 ties connected with 4,037 iron rails and 120,000 spikes. As a result, a trip from New York to San Francisco was reduced from about three months to seven days.

Tell students that communications were transformed by the telegraph. Before the introduction of the telegraph, the Pony Express was the fastest way for communications to travel. From April 1860 to October 1861 the Pony Express carried mail from St. Joseph, Missouri, to Sacramento, California, in about eight days. Ask students why the telegraph made the Pony Express obsolete. Tell students that before the completion of a trans-Atlantic telegraph cable, news about events in Europe could not reach the united States any faster than ships could carry it.

Discuss with students how advances in transportation and communication changed people's perceptions about distance. Ask, "How did these developments make countries more interdependent?"

Economics and History: Corporations (Objective 3) After students have read Section 1, write *stock,*

corporation, and *monopoly* on the chalkboard. Ask students to imagine that John D. Rockefeller has just discovered his first oil well, but needs to raise money to purchase drilling equipment. Ask students how Rockefeller could raise money without borrowing from banks. (incorporate and sell stock in the oil well) Help students to understand how the stockholders would invest in Rockefeller's company by buying stock, or shares, and would receive a percentage of profits from the sale of the oil. Ask students what it means to incorporate a business. (The business is given an identity that is separate from that of its founder or owners; the company can issue stock; owning stockholders are not personally responsible for the company's debts.) Ask students to summarize the benefits and risks of becoming a stockholder. (Stockholders equally share both profits and losses.) Then ask students to imagine that Rockefeller's corporation must compete with other oil companies. How would competition affect the corporation's profits? (Profits would be reduced.) Explain that corporations such as Rockefeller's tried to reduce competition by forming monopolies. Have students suggest methods of achieving a monopoly. What might be some advantages and disadvantages of a monopoly for workers, for consumers, or for entrepreneurs?

Using Geographic Themes: Movement (Objective 4) Tell students that Europeans immigrated to North America in voyages that were grueling and sometimes fatal. Steamship companies competing for profits overbooked passengers, which resulted in overcrowding and unsanitary, unsafe conditions. Many passengers crowded into airless lower decks fell ill, victims of deadly contagious diseases. Food and fresh water were scarce. To attract customers, one steamship company used a loaf of bread as its advertising logo. However, these hardships did not discourage the flood of emigrants form Europe. Ask students why the 1800's were marked by mass migrations. Recall the effects of the Industrial Revolution and the revolutions of the mid-nineteenth century (overpopulation, poverty, civil strife, political oppression).

Point out that people most often move within a country or from one country to another in order to find better opportunities. Ask, "What opportunity did cities offer for people migrating from rural areas?" (employment) Ask students to speculate on the effects of nineteenth century migrations on the development of the modern world.

Check for Understanding Have students write a paragraph explaining how advances in transportation and communication helped to foster a global economy. Students should mention some of the inventions that stimulated world trade.

Practice

Guided Practice
Lead a guided discussion of the questions in Section Review 1. (Answers are on the next page.)

Advance Planner

Chapter 24 Focus	Economic Expansion and Nationalism 1851–1876 Nineteenth century inventions made the world a smaller place.			★ Advanced ● Basic
	Section 1	**Section 2**	**Section 3**	**Section 4**
Objectives	1. Explain the concept of "global economy." 2. Assess the impact of improved communication and transportation in the nineteenth century. 3. Analyze the corporation as a new economic institution. 4. Identify the causes of immigration and emigration.	1. Discuss the main ideas of socialism. 2. Describe the views of Karl Marx and assess their impact on events in nineteenth-century Europe. 3. Contrast romanticism and realism.	1. Define *realpolitik* and identify its role in nineteenth-century politics. 2. Evaluate the contributions Cavour and Garibaldi made to the unification of Italy. 3. Explain how Bismarck helped to unify Germany.	1. Define the concept of westward expansion. 2. Identify the territorial gains made by the United States between 1783 and 1853 and assess the impact of expansion on economic development. 3. Explain how regional differences between the northern and southern United States affected the Civil War.
Setting the Stage	Economics and History: Global Economy	Workers' struggles to gain greater economic and political power	Discussing History: *Realpolitik*	Using Geographic Themes: Frontier Regions Transparency 61
Teaching Strategies	Discussing History: Transportation and Communication in the Nineteenth Century Economics and History: Corporations Using Geographic Themes: Movement Check for Understanding	Writing about History: Socialism Discussing History: Karl Marx Teaching with Pictures: Realism and Romanticism Check for Understanding	Discussing History: Italian Unification Transparency 59 Writing about History: Unification of Germany Transparency 60 Check for Understanding	Discussing History: American Expansionism Using Geographic Themes: Regions Check for Understanding
Guided Practice	Section Review 1	Section Review 2	Transparency 59 Q&A Transparency 60 Q&A Section Review 3	Transparency 61 Q&A Section Review 4
Independent Practice Worksheets	Independent Practice 24.1 Vocabulary Skills 24	Independent Practice 24.2	Independent Practice 24.3 Geography Skills 24 Basic Skills 24 Critical Thinking 24	Independent Practice 24.4
Enrichment	1. Primary Source: Voices 24.1 2. Creative Writing 3. Researching for Points	1. Primary Source: Voices 24.2 2. ★ Preparing a Report 3. Researching for Points	1. Primary Source: Voices 24.3 2. ★ Relating Past to Present 3. Researching for Points	1. Primary Source: Voices 24.4 2. Creative Writing 3. Researching for Points

Chapter Closer ● Reteaching Activities	Recalling Main Ideas, Outlining, Writing a Paragraph
Chapter Review	Summary, Reviewing the Facts, Basic Skills, Researching and Reporting Skills, Critical Thinking, Perspectives on Past and Present, Investigating History
Chapter Evaluation	Chapter Test 24, Computer Test Bank Chapter 24 Test

Define:
(a) share of ownership in a business (b) business organized by issuing shares of stock to raise capital (c) control of an entire industry by one company (d) movement of people from a region (e) movement of people to an area

Identify:
(a) first world's fair (b) Queen of Great Britain from 1837 to 1901 (c) designer of first practical steamboat (d) canal linking Mediterranean and Red seas (e) inventor of telegraph

Answer:
1. Factory-made goods cost less than handmade items, and lower prices skyrocketed the demand.
2. (a) growth of railroads, invention of a practical steamship, and opening of the Suez Canal (b) helped them flourish by speeding raw materials to factories and finished goods to markets
3. Trains, steamships, and telegraphs speeded communication worldwide.
4. (a) by selling shares of stock (b) by sharing profits and by selling stock at profit
5. (a) brought countries into closer contact (b) Failures had international impact.
6. from Europe to other continents; within Europe, from rural to urban areas
7. (a) Great Exhibition—demonstrated abundance of wares available around the world; Suez Canal—made it possible to obtain goods from Asia without going around Africa; Golden Spike—made possible distribution of goods across the United States in less than a week (b) Countries were economically prosperous and proud of their achievements.

Independent Practice
Assign Independent Practice Worksheet 24.1.
Assign Vocabulary Worksheet 24.

Enrichment Activities

1. **Reading a Primary Source.** Assign Voices from the Past Resource Book 24.1.

2. **Creative Writing** Have students write a first-person account describing the decisions and experiences of a rural family seeking greater economic opportunities in the late nineteenth century.

3. **Researching for Bonus Points.** Award bonus points to students who can answer the following question: What was the country of origin of the largest group of immigrants to the United States in 1854? (Germany)

Working people gained more influence. 2

Section Objectives

After completing Section 2, students should be able to:

1. discuss the main ideas of socialism.
2. describe the views of Karl Marx and assess their impact on events in nineteenth-century Europe.
3. contrast romanticism and realism.

Setting the Stage

Ask students to recall the social problems caused by industrialization (pages 483–487) and the rise of reform movements (page 550). Tell students that in the nineteenth century, members of the working classes felt left out of Europe's economic expansion. Explain that Section 2 describes the workers' struggles to gain greater economic and political power.

Teaching Strategies

Writing about History: Socialism (Objective 1) *Prewriting* Discuss the ideas of Robert Owen and Pierre Proudhon. Ask students why these reformers believed that all injustice stemmed from private property. Why did socialism appeal to many working class people in the nineteenth century? (Workers gained greater economic and social equality.) Invite students to debate the advantages and disadvantages of living in a socialist society. Point out that most present-day capitalist countries have some institutions that reflect socialist ideals, such as national health insurance, social security, and unemployment compensation. *Writing* Ask students to imagine they are members of Robert Owen's planned community in New Harmony, Indiana. Have each student write a letter explaining the benefits of living in New Harmony, and another letter describing conditions that led to the experiment's failure.

Discussing History: Karl Marx (Objective 2) Ask students to clarify the concept of the "means of production." Students might mention capital, land, property or inventories, raw materials, factories or buildings, or capital goods such as machines. Ask students why Marx felt that workers should own the means of production. Recall political developments in Europe between 1815 and 1850 (pages 505–507). Ask, "What did workers in France and England demand?" (political rights, higher wages, better working conditions) Tell students that many revolutionaries were influenced by Marx's view that the Industrial Revolution favored capitalists who grew rich by exploiting workers. Recall, however, that the revolutions of 1848 brought few substantive economic reforms. Explain that as their standard of living rose, workers became more interested in benefiting from economic expansion than in staging revolts. Ask students what other changes in the mid-nineteenth century eased tensions between workers and employers. (unions and suffrage) Ask students how labor unions and suffrage increased workers' influence.

Teaching with Pictures: Realism and Romanticism (Objective 3) Have students compare the paintings on pages 498 and 517 and identify the two movements in art these paintings represent. (romanticism and realism) Ask students how the pictures are different, and what they reveal about changing perceptions of society. (Realism emphasizes day to day struggle; romanticism emphasizes the extraordinary in nature and in human responses.) Select a student to read the quotation by Courbet (page 518). Ask, "Why did Courbet mock Romantic writers?" Then select a student to read the excerpt from Dickens' *Hard Times* (page 518). How does the painting by Daumier illustrate Dickens' description? Invite students to identify realist and romantic themes in present-day art mediums such as music and cinema. Challenge them to determine if our culture emphasizes one viewpoint over the other.

Check for Understanding Ask students to identify trends in the nineteenth century that increased the influence of workers. (the interest in socialist labor reforms, the growth of trade unions, the extensions of suffrage)

Practice

Guided Practice
Lead students in a guided discussion of the questions in Section Review 2. (Answers are below.)

Define:
(a) belief that wealth of a country should be shared equally (b) factory-owning middle class (c) urban working class (d) right to vote (e) artistic approach that focuses on the ordinary and real

Identify:
(a) socialist reformer who founded cooperative village of New Harmony, Indiana (b) co-author of *Das Kapital* and *The Communist Manifesto*

Answer:
1. (a) Wealth of a country should be shared equally among citizens; society as a whole should own most factories and businesses. (b) Owen preached cooperation between classes; Marx believed that the classes were doomed to conflict.
2. Without labor or raw materials, there would be no product and no value.
3. (a) by cheating them out of the wealth created through their efforts (b) Workers would overthrow the bourgeoisie, establish socialist society. (c) Gap between rich and poor failed to widen; everybody's life improved.
4. by uniting workers to obtain higher wages and improved working conditions
5. (a) Middle class men were first given vote in Britain by the Reform Bill; a later bill extended voting rights to nearly all men. In 1871, France granted vote to all men. After Civil War, black men won vote in U.S. (b) women, slaves
6. lives of ordinary people and current social issues
7. (a) agreed (b) agreed (c) probably disagreed (d) disagreed strongly

Independent Practice
Assign Independent Practice Worksheet 24.2.

Enrichment Activities

1. **Reading a Primary Source** Assign Voices from the Past Resource Book 24.2.

2. **Preparing a Report** Have advanced students report on the themes expressed by nineteenth century realists such as Thomas Hardy, Gustave Flaubert, Anton Chekov, Leo Tolstoy, Henrik Ibsen, or George Bernard Shaw.

3. **Researching for Bonus Points** Award bonus points to students who can answer the following question: What was the Fabian Society, founded in Great Britain in 1884? (an organization to promote the gradual spread of socialism)

Answers to Voice from the Past

1. (a) red, unnatural red and black, painted, tall, black, purple, vast, large, small, same (b) rattling, trembling (c) ill-smelling
2. pollution, lack of sanitation, crowded living conditions, monotony
3. (a) the city (b) by using lively, strong adjectives to describe the city and passive, repetitive words to describe the people and their lives

Italy and Germany formed nations. 3

Section Objectives

After completing Section 3, students should be able to:

1. define *realpolitik* and identify its role in nineteenth-century politics.
2. evaluate the contributions Cavour and Garibaldi made to the unification of Italy.
3. explain how Bismarck helped to unify Germany.

Setting the Stage

Discussing History: Realpolitik (Objective 1) Tell students that Section 3 describes a new style of nationalism called *realpolitik*. Ask students what they think the term means. Suggest that the new style of politics echoed the new style in literature and art. Students should be able to identify realism and to infer characteristics of *realpolitik*. Explain that nationalist leaders relied less on romantic ideals and more on practical realities, which led to the successful unification of Italy and of Germany. Tell students that the new style of diplomacy was characterized by ruthlessness, shrewd manipulation, and effectiveness. Ask students to find out, as they read, how *realpolitik* changed Europe's balance of power.

Teaching Strategies

Discussing History: Italian Unification (Objective 2) Show Overhead Transparency 59, *The Unification of Italy, 1850–1870,* and have students note Italy's many political divisions. Explain that each region had its own plans for unification. The two leaders who unified Italy were contrasts in personality and leadership style. Cavour was a purposeful, shrewd politician who practiced the rules of realpolitik. Ask students why Sardinian origins were an advantage for Cavour. (Sardinia was the largest Italian state, and the only one ruled by an Italian dynasty.) Have students explain how Cavour demonstrated realpolitik in his dealings with France and Austria. Ask, "How did Cavour use cunning and diplomacy to drive Austria out of northern Italy?"

Tell students that the unification of southern Italy was accomplished in a different manner. Garibaldi was a romantic nationalist who liked bold, dramatic action. His heroic style endeared him to local populations, who eagerly joined his cause to defeat larger armies in Sicily. Ask, "What did Cavour think of Garibaldi and earlier nationalists such as Mazzini?" (They were too vague, impractical, and emotional.) "Why did Garibaldi's success threaten Cavour?" (Italy might unite under Garibaldi.) Have students explain how Cavour prevented Garibaldi from becoming too powerful and speculate on Garibaldi's reasons for stepping aside. Have students assess the merits of Cavour's and Garibaldi's leadership styles and their importance to Italian unification.

Writing about History: Unification of Germany (Objective 3) *Prewriting* Show students Overhead Transparency 60, *The Unification of Germany, 1865–1871.* Ask, "Which German states formed Prussia in 1865, and which joined Prussia by 1871?" Tell students that unification was carried out under the leadership of Otto von Bismarck, an advocate of realpolitik whose realistic assessment of Austrian strengths and weaknesses guided Prussian foreign policy. Invite students to interpret the quotation on page 521 from Bismarck's address to the Prussian parliament. What "great mistake of 1848" did Bismarck mean? How did Bismarck's words reflect the ideas of realpolitik? Explain that Bismarck's aristocratic background led him to conservative views. His contempt for liberals in the German parliament stemmed from his observation that they endlessly discussed unification but never took action. *Writing* Have students write essays entitled "Iron and Blood" explaining how Bismarck united Prussia. On the chalkboard note the following steps to guide student's writing.

- Explain the rivalry between Austria and Prussia.
- Explain why Bismarck provoked wars with Austria and France.
- Evaluate Bismarck's leadership in terms of effectiveness and fairness.

Check for Understanding Ask students to explain how the unification of Germany and of Italy and conditions in France's Third Republic changed Europe's political boundaries and balance of power.

Practice

Guided Practice
Lead students in a guided discussion of the questions in Overhead Transparencies 59 and 60 and in Section Review 3. (Answers are below.)

Define:
(a) politics of reality (b) member of Prussia's wealthy landlord class (c) system of government in

which Austria and Hungary became two independent and equal states with one ruler (d) emperor

Identify:
(a) early leader of Italian nationalism (b) Italian nationalist; united northern Italy (c) king of Sardinia, first king of Italy (d) emperor of France; made alliance with Cavour (e) Italian nationalist leader of "Red Shirts" (f) Prussian prime minister, united Germany (g) free-trade area; all the major German states except Austria (h) war between Austria and Prussia (i) final step in German unification, in which Prussia crushed France and won Alsace and Lorraine (j) newly formed German empire (k) republican government set up in France in 1875

Answer:
1. was largest and most powerful Italian state with most liberal government
2. (a) Sardinia needed help to drive Austria out of northern Italy. (b) Cavour promised to give France Nice and Savoy. (c) In 1860, Sardinia annexed most of northern Italy.
3. (a) by an Italian parliament which declared Victor Emmanuel II king (b) Venetia, Papal States
4. tensions between industrialized north and agricultural south; lack of strong leadership; lack of well-organized parties within parliament
5. had mainly German population, free-trade area, industry, powerful army, and Bismarck
6. led Prussia to war against Denmark to win Schleswig and Holstein, provoked France into declaring war on Prussia to gain a few southern states outside Germany
7. united French in hatred for Germany
8. great political divisions and frequent changes of government
9. Although five Great Powers had been equal in 1815, by 1871 Britain and Germany had become strongest, economically and politically.
10. (a) In both countries, a strong leader used nationalist sentiment and provoked war when it suited his political goals. (b) Germany was politically and economically stronger than Italy.

Independent Practice
Assign Independent Practice Worksheet 24.3.
Assign Geography Skills Worksheet 24.
Assign Basic Skills Worksheet 24.
Assign Critical Thinking Worksheet 24.

Enrichment

1. Reading a Primary Source Assign Voices from the Past Resource Book 24.3.

2. **Relating Past to Present** Ask advanced students to assess the relevance of Count von Moltke's remarks (page 525) to the realpolitik of nineteenth-century Europe and to the global politics of the present day.

3. **Researching for Bonus Points** Award bonus points to students who can answer this question: What Prussian general effectively used railroads and the telegraph to defeat Austria in the Seven Weeks' War? (Count Helmuth von Moltke)

The United States spread westward. 4

Section Objectives

After completing Section 4, students should be able to:

1. define the concept of "westward expansion."
2. identify the territorial gains made by the United States between 1783 and 1853 and assess the impact of expansion on economic development.
3. explain how regional differences between the northern and southern United States affected the Civil War.

Setting the Stage

Using Geographic Themes: Frontier Regions (Objective 1) Remind students that Section 3 described how the borders of European countries changed as land was shifted between different powers. Explain that in Europe the borderlands separating countries were called frontiers. In America *frontier* referred to borderlands separating settled regions from the "wilderness." Show Overhead Transparency 61, *The Growth of the United States, 1783–1853,* or direct students' attention to the map on page 526. Have students identify the territories added to the United States in the nineteenth century. Explain that because American development started in the east, undeveloped lands were always called "the west." The location of the western frontier continually changed. Until the late 1800's most Americans saw "the west" as a wild, uncivilized, and largely uninhabitable place. Tell students Section 4 explains how and why these perceptions changed.

Teaching Strategies

Discussing History: American Expansionism (Objective 2) Ask students to imagine the excitement of the American ambassador when Napoleon offered to sell the Louisiana territory. Explain that for a year the United States had been trying to purchase the city of New Orleans for its strategic trading location. Suddenly, France was willing to sell New Orleans and an additional 828,000 square miles at a bargain price. Have students use the map on page 526 to identify the regions acquired in the Louisiana purchase. Ask students how this land contributed to the economic development of the United States. Point out that the Louisiana Territory included vast new farmlands, the Mississippi and Missouri river systems, and a strategic port on the Gulf of Mexico.

Next, have students identify the territories acquired from Mexico. Call on students to name the present-day states which include land acquired from Mexico in 1845 and in 1848. Ask students to explain how the United States acquired this land. Ask how the Texas Annexation and the Mexican Cession contributed to the economic development of the United States. Point out, for example, that Texas had valuable ranges for grazing cattle and rich deposits of oil. California had ports on the Pacific Ocean and rich deposits of gold.

Tell students that American expansionism was based on ideas about "Manifest Destiny"—that Americans were destined to bring civilization to undeveloped lands. Students might be interested to know that some American expansionists wanted to annex Mexico and the Caribbean islands, but the American Civil War superceded such plans.

Using Geographic Themes: Regions (Objective 3) Read to students the following passage—William Sherman's advice to a southern friend on why the South should not go to war against the North.

> The North can make a steam engine, locomotive, or railway car; hardly a yard of cloth can you make. You are rushing into war with one of the most powerful, ingeniously mechanical and determined people on earth right at your door. You are bound to fail.

Ask students to identify the main point of Sherman's advice.

On the chalkboard write "North" and "South." Call on students to contrast the economies of the two regions in 1861 at the beginning of the Civil War. Students should consider the main resources, industries, and labor supply of the North and the South. Point out the economic significance of slavery and the fundamental differences between agricultural and industrial regional interests. Point out that besides having economic differences, Southerners and Northerners considered their cultures distinct and in many ways incompatible. The southern aristocracy increasingly felt that their way of life, based on the plantation economy, was being threatened by Northern politicians. Have students draw conclusions about the impact of regional differences on the United States' development as a federal union.

Check for Understanding Ask students to identify the four most significant developments marking the progress of the United States during its first 100 years. (westward expansion, preservation of the union, abolition of slavery, rapid industrialization)

Practice

Guided Practice
Lead students in a guided discussion of the questions in Overhead Transparency 61 and in Section Review 4. (Answers are below.)

Define:
(a) economy with both farms and industry (b) crop for which ready money is offered

Identify:
(a) land west of the Mississippi bought from France in 1803 (b) president during the Civil War (c) 11 southern states that withdrew from the United States (d) war between North and South (e) declaration freeing all slaves in the Confederate states (f) constitutional amendment abolishing slavery

Answer:
1. sold Louisiana Territory to United States
2. (a) broke away from Mexico, was an independent country for 9 years, and became state in 1845 (b) led to quarrel over southern boundary of Texas (c) all land between Rio Grande and Canada plus California
3. North—diversified economy; South—dependent on cash crops, mainly cotton
4. North wanted slavery outlawed in western territories, South wanted laws protecting slavery.
5. South believed states had right to leave; North believed that the Constitution had established a permanent Union.
6. (a) conflict over slavery in western territories, election of Abraham Lincoln in 1860, seces-

sion of Confederate states **(b)** preservation of union, ending of slavery
7. by the Thirteenth Amendment
8. raw materials, growing population, government that put few restraints on business
9. Look for answers to consider the conflicting views of southerners (whose primary commitment was to their state) and northerners (whose primary commitment was to the Union).

Independent Practice
Assign Independent Practice Worksheet 24.4.

Enrichment Activities

1. **Reading a Primary Source** Assign Voices from the Past Resource Book 24.4.

2. **Creative Writing** Have students draw conclusions about the status of American women in the nineteenth century, based on the attractions of the United States Centennial Exposition, described on page 529.

3. **Researching for Bonus Points** Award bonus points to students who can answer the following question: What was the formal name of the United States general nicknamed "Old Fuss and Feathers," who fought in the war against Mexico? Hint: He was also a Union general in the Civil War. (General Winfield Scott)

Concluding the Chapter

1. **Chapter Closer**
Have students summarize the effect of economic expansion and new ideas about nationalism on Europe and on the United States in the nineteenth century. Then ask students to give specific examples of the changes they have summarized.

2. **Reteaching Activities**
   a. Recalling Main Ideas Ask students to explain how Cavour and Bismarck demonstrated the political philosophy of realpolitik.
   b. Outlining Have students outline the main ideas of this chapter by organizing important topics under the following headings: "Inventions," "Events," and "People." Tell students to use the section headings as a guide.
   c. Writing a Paragraph Have students write paragraphs on the impact of the invention of the steamship, the railroad or the telegraph on world history. Students should focus on the question, "How did these inventions make the world a smaller place?"

3. **Chapter Review Activities**
Assign Chapter Review 24 activities.

Chapter Evaluation

Chapter Test 24 and Computer Test Bank Chapter 24 Test can be used to evaluate your students' understanding of this chapter.

Answers to Chapter Review 24

Reviewing the Facts
1. **a.** share of ownership in a business **b.** business organized by issuing shares of stock **c.** movement of people from a place **d.** movement of people to a place **e.** belief that wealth of a country should be shared equally **f.** right to vote
2. **a.** Queen of Great Britain from 1837 to 1901 **b.** socialist reformer who founded cooperative town of New Harmony, Indiana **c.** co-author of *The Communist Manifesto* and *Das Kapital* **d.** what Marx called ideas of socialists who advocated an ideal society **e.** Marx's claim that his ideas were based on scientific study of history **f.** urban working class **g.** Italian nationalist who united northern Italy **h.** Italian nationalist leader of "Red Shirts" **i.** French emperor who made alliance with Cavour **j.** Prussian prime minister who united Germany
3. **(a)** Between 1850 and 1875, coal production in Germany increased from 6 million tons to 35 million tons per year, world output of iron increased fourfold, value of goods bought and sold among countries increased by 260 percent. **(b)** transcontinental railroad, steamships, Suez Canal **(c)** telegraph
4. **(a)** increased capital, limited liability **(b)** could share in the company's profits and profit from selling stocks
5. Possible answer: Shirt manufacturer in Britain could have 1,000 bales of cotton delivered from New Orleans to Manchester factory in 10 days; finished shirt might be on sale in shops in Vienna and St. Petersburg three weeks later
6. **(a)** Workers were slaves to the bourgeoisie. **(b)** Work was the true source of all value. **(c)** Factory-owning middle class took advantage of workers. **(d)** The proletariat were victims of the bourgeoisie.

7. **(a)** Prussia was the most industrial state and had the largest army in the loosely organized confederation. **(b)** Prussia went to war against Denmark to win these two border provinces. **(c)** Prussia defeated Austria to build national pride and crush its rival in the Confederation. **(d)** Defeating France gave Prussia Alsace and Lorraine, the final step in German unification.
8. Italy: lack of national leadership, frequent changes in government, economic problems which led to massive emigration
   France: control of Paris by radicals, political divisions, frequent changes in government
9. In 1815, all the Great Powers were fairly equal in strength. By 1871, Britain and Germany were the strongest, both economically and militarily.
10. **(a)** North had a diversified economy with both farms and industry; South depended on a few cash crops, mainly cotton. **(b)** Southerners depended on slavery to protect their economy, while Northerners considered slavery morally wrong.

Basic Skills
1. **(a)** East and West Germany correspond roughly to what was then Hanover and the South German States; parts of Prussia now Czechoslovakia, Poland, Hungary, and Russia. **(b)** Italy basically the same
2. **(a)** Italy: 1858—war with Austria; 1859–1860—annexation of independent territories; 1866—war with Austria; 1870—takeover of Papal States from Church **(b)** Prussia: 1866—landed in Germany from Austria; 1867—North German Confederation states joined Prussia; 1871—South German states join Prussia; 1871—Alsace and Lorraine conquered from France

Researching and Reporting Skills
Students' answers will vary.

Critical Thinking
1. Industrialization created more goods that could be traded and increased the market for these goods by making them more affordable; advances in transportation made it easier to ship goods to foreign markets.

2. **(a)** socialism—Robert Owen and Pierre Joseph Proudhon; rejects private property; society owns means of production and divides wealth equally among the population; reacting to inequitable distribution of wealth; scientific socialism—Karl Marx and Friedrich Engels; inevitability of class struggle; only work has value; reacting to inequitable distribution of wealth **(b)** socialism—arguments about division of goods and profits; scientific socialism—no large worker revolts; ignored importance of religion, nationalism, ethnic loyalties, and other ideals and concerns not directly related to economics.
3. **(a)** dealt with practicalities and power, not ideals **(b)** Cavour struck a deal with Napoleon III giving France Nice and Savoy for its help in driving Austria out of Italy; Bismarck deliberately deceived or provoked Denmark, Austria, and France into wars in order to acquire land for Prussia.
4. **(a)** Prussia's superior transportation system and ability to manufacture military equipment gave it a decisive advantage. **(b)** Prussia wanted the Alsace and Lorraine regions of France because of their rich coal and iron deposits.
5. Marx was enormously affected by squalor of living conditions and poverty of workers; saw sharp contrast with the wealthy few.
6. **(a)** Foreign trade expanded tremendously both in goods and farm products. **(b)** Industrial development, especially in the North proceeded rapidly.

Perspectives on Past and Present
Students answers will vary. Students could point out that the civil rights of minorities and women's rights have become a major political issue. The right to free speech, a free press, an open and democratic political process, the free practice of religion, individual privacy, and other freedoms are still important issues in countries throughout Eastern Europe, Latin America, Africa, and Asia.

Investigating History
Students' answers will vary.

The Age of Imperialism

Chapter Overview

The nineteenth century was an Age of Imperialism when many European countries competed for overseas colonies, particularly in Africa and Asia. Great Britain was the most successful in establishing a worldwide colonial empire.

In Asia, the British brought some technological advances to India but treated Indians as second-class citizens. Defeat in the Opium War forced China to open its ports to foreign trade. European nations carved China into spheres of influence. Resentment of imperialism led to the Boxer Rebellion and a nationalist movement in China. Japan became a modern, industrialized, imperialist nation.

The United States gained a few colonies in the Caribbean and Pacific after the Spanish-American War and was successful in barring the establishment of new colonies in China and Latin America.

Key Terms

imperialism, protectorate, condominium, sphere of influence.
For additional exercises, see Vocabulary Worksheet 25.

Chapter Focus

Direct students' attention to the painting on page 532. Explain that it shows the huge crowd of Indian rulers, British officials, and curious spectators who gathered outside Delhi to hear the British viceroy read a proclamation declaring Queen Victoria Empress of India. Then ask, "What do these two events reveal about the relationship between Great Britain and India in the 1870's?" Explain that India had lost its independence and was a part of the British empire. Ask, "How could Great Britain control a country that was 6,000 miles from Britain and that had ten times more people and twenty times more territory?" Tell students that the Industrial Revolution gave Great Britain, France, Germany, and the United States enormous economic and military power. This chapter describes how these countries built empires that affected peoples around the world.

Nations competed for overseas empires.

1

Section Objectives

After completing Section 1, students should be able to:

1. explain why the European powers competed for overseas colonies.
2. compare and contrast views on imperialism as a means of advancing civilization.

Setting the Stage

Recall the definition of *colony*. Stress that colonies were thinly populated settlements governed by a "mother country." Direct students' attention to the definition of *imperialism* on page 533. Explain that imperialism involved the attempt by strong countries to dominate the economic, political, and social life of weaker nations. This section describes the reasons European nations chose to build great overseas empires.

Teaching Strategies

Economics and History: The Role of Colonies (Objective 1) Recall that the Industrial Revolution created a demand for colonies that provided raw material and new markets. Supporters of imperialism argued that large self-sufficient empires were economic necessities. Explain that the European powers prized colonies that provided valuable raw materials such as rubber, wool, jute, and coconuts. Jute, for example, was used to make burlap, twine, carpets, and bags. Various parts of the coconut tree could be manufactured into brushes, cables, ropes, and sails. Manufacturers used coconut oil to produce candles, soap and margarine.

The industrialized countries paid for these raw materials by exporting machinery, steel, clothing, arms, railway equipment, and other manufactured goods to their colonies. Point out that the colonies also provided lucrative investment opportunities. By 1914, France and Germany had invested abroad more than 20 percent of their industrial wealth, while Great Britain had invested 25 percent. British investors earned more than $500 million in interest each year. Ask students how colonies helped to reduce over population in European countries.

Skill Building: Comparing and Contrasting Points of View (Objective 2) Explain that many Europeans believed that they had a duty to spread Christianity and the benefits of new technology to less developed regions. However, many people whose homelands were colonized by Europeans did not share this view. Read or distribute the following two viewpoints on the merits of imperialism as a means of advancing civilization:

> We [the British] happen to be the best people in the world, with the highest ideals of decency and justice and liberty and peace, and the more of the world we inhabit, the better it is for humanity.
>
> Cecil Rhodes

> Our whole existence has been controlled by people with an alien attitude to life, people with different customs and beliefs. They have determined the form of government, the types of economic activity, and the schooling which our children have. Even if Europeans had always done their best to do what they believed to be good for us, it would be no less wrong. A man who tries to control the life of another does not destroy the other any the less because he does it, as he thinks, for the other's benefit. It is the principle which is wrong, the principle of one man governing another without his consent.
>
> Julius Nyerere of Tanzania

Ask, "What benefits did Rhodes believe that Britain would bring to its empire?" (ideals of justice, liberty, and peace) "According to Nyerere what important principle did the European imperialists violate?" (the principle that people have a right to self-determination) "How might Cecil Rhodes have responded to Nyerere's statement?" (He might have emphasized that imperialist nations had a responsibility to share their advanced technology, medicine, and agricultural methods with other peoples.)

Check for Understanding Ask students to explain two factors that helped promote imperialism.

Practice

Guided Practice
Lead a guided discussion of the questions in Section Review 1 (Answers follow.)

Define:
policy of conquering and ruling other lands

Identify:
(a) Queen Victoria's son, heir to British throne (b) Englishman who became rich from South African diamond mines (c) ended slave trade in East Africa (d) American reporter who found Livingstone (e) English writer who glorified imperialism

Answer:
1. (a) Germany and U.S. (b) Britain had to find new markets for goods, protect existing markets, and safeguard sources of raw materials.

Advance Planner

Section 1	Section 2
1. Explain why the European powers competed for overseas colonies. 2. Compare and contrast views on imperialism as a means of advancing civilization.	1. Identify the Suez Canal and explain its geographic significance. 2. Identify the Battle of Omdurman and explain its significance. 3. Identify the Kimberly diamond mine and explain its influence on the development of South Africa.
Definitions of colonialism and imperialism	The European division of Africa Transparency 62
Economics and History: The Role of Colonies Skill Building: Comparing and Contrasting Points of View Check for Understanding	Geography in History: The Suez Canal Teaching with Pictures: The Battle of Omdurman Economics and History: The "Big Hole" Check for Understanding
Section Review 1 Independent Practice 25.1 Vocabulary 25 Critical Thinking 25	Transparency 62 Q&A Section Review 2 Independent Practice 25.2
1. Primary Source: Voices 25.1 2. ★ Creative Writing 3. Researching for Points	1. Primary Source: Voices 25.2 2. Preparing a Report 3. Researching for Points

2. (a) Colonies provided new markets. (b) colonies needed for raw materials (c) Race for colonies grew out of a strong sense of national pride.
3. (a) France, Netherlands, Spain, Portugal, Austria-Hungary, Russia, Belgium, Italy, Germany, United States, and Japan (b) by fostering rivalries that could lead to war
4. a sense of duty to pass along what they saw as the progress of their civilization
5. (a) helped spread European values and technology (b) sent reporters to search the globe for stories of mystery, adventure, and excitement
6. (a) the mission to "civilize" non-Europeans

(b) life in the colonies (c) that native populations were in effect prisoners of the Europeans

Independent Practice
Assign Independent Practice Worksheet 25.1.
Assign Vocabulary Worksheet 25.
Assign Critical Thinking Worksheet 25.

Enrichment Activities

1. **Reading a Primary Source** Assign Voices from the Past Resource Book 25.1.

2. **Creative Writing** Ask advanced students to imagine that they are the editors of a large Lon-

| | Chapter 25 | The Age of Imperialism 1876–1914 | | ★ Advanced |
| | **Focus** | The relationship between Great Britain and India in the 1870's as an example of European Empire-Building | | ● Basic |

Section 3	Section 4	Section 5	Section 6	
1. Describe the causes and consequences of the Sepoy Mutiny. 2. Compare a map of British India with maps of India at earlier times. 3. Explain how railroads affected life in India.	1. Explain how European merchants used opium to force open Chinese ports. 2. Locate territories China lost to other nations. 3. Cite reasons for United States endorsement of an Open Door policy in China.	1. Describe the Japanese reaction to the arrival of Commodore Matthew Perry. 2. Identify changes that took place during the Meiji era.	1. Identify causes and consequences of the Spanish-American War. 2. Identify the Panama Canal and explain its significance. 3. Explain why Europeans and Americans competed for control of the Pacific islands.	**Objectives**
Hindi words that were added to the English language during British rule of India	A Chinese emperor's letter to King George III of England rejecting commercial ties	Japan's isolation under the Tokugawa shoguns	Imperialism in Latin America and the basis of United States involvement in Latin American affairs	**Setting the Stage**
Skill Building: Relating Causes and Effects Geography in History: Comparing Maps Transparency 63 Discussing History: Railroads and Indian Life Check for Understanding	Analyzing a Quotation: The Opium Trade Geography in History: Imperialism in East Asia Transparency 64 Outline Map 19 Skill Building: Interpreting a Political Cartoon Check for Understanding	Writing about History: Perry's Arrival in Japan Discussing History: Industrialization of Japan Check for Understanding	Skill Building: Identifying Causes and Effects Teaching with Pictures: The Panama Canal Transparency 91 Discussing History: The Samoan Islands Check for Understanding	**Teaching Strategies**
Transparency 63 Q&A Section Review 3	Transparency 64 Q&A Section Review 4	Section Review 5	Section Review 6	**Guided Practice**
Independent Practice 25.3 Basic Skills 25	Independent Practice 25.4	Independent Practice 25.5	Independent Practice 25.6 Geography Skills 25	**Independent Practice Worksheets**
1. Primary Source: Voices 25.3 2. ★Creative Writing 3. Researching for Points	1. Primary Source: Voices 25.4 2. ★Preparing a Report 3. Researching for Points	1. Primary Source: Voices 25.5 2. Relating Past to Present 3. Researching for Points	1. Primary Source: Voices 25.6 2. Debating a Topic 3. Researching for Points	**Enrichment**

Chapter Closer	
● **Reteaching Activities**	Making a Time Line, Making Comparisons, Listing
Chapter Review	Summary, Reviewing the Facts, Basic Skills, Researching and Reporting Skills, Critical Thinking, Perspectives on Past and Present, Investigating History
Chapter Evaluation	Chapter Test 25, Computer Test Bank Chapter 25 Test

don newspaper. Their assignment is to write an editorial defending or opposing imperialism.

3. **Researching for Bonus Points** Award bonus points to students who can answer this question: In which village on Lake Tanganyika did Stanley find Livingston? (Ujiji)

Imperialists divided Africa.

2

Section Objectives

After completing Section 2, students should be able to:

1. identify the Suez Canal and explain its geographic significance.
2. identify the Battle of Omdurman and explain its significance.
3. identify the Kimberly diamond mine and explain its influence on the development of South Africa.

Setting the Stage

Show Overhead Transparency 62, *Imperialism in Africa, 1913*. Have students compare the map of Africa in 1878 with the inset of Africa in 1913. Ask, "What impact did European imperialism have on Africa between those years?" Explain that in 1875, when the Age of Imperialism began, Europeans controlled less than 10 percent of the continent. By 1913, 90 percent of Africa had been divided into colonies. Tell students that this section describes how the European powers explored, conquered, and divided Africa.

Teaching Strategies

Geography in History: The Suez Canal (Objective 1) Use Overhead Transparency 90, *The World About 1900*, to help students locate the Suez Canal. Then ask, "How did the Suez Canal revolutionize travel between Europe and Asia?" Explain that the canal shortened distances by enabling ships to avoid the long route around Africa. For example, the old voyage from London to Cape Town to Bombay was 10,667 nautical miles. The canal reduced this trip to 6,274 nautical miles—a savings of 41.2 percent.

The Suez Canal promoted trade by shortening distances and cutting travel time. In 1910, 4,533 ships and 234,000 passengers traveled through the canal's calm waters. Ask students to hypothesize why knowledgeable travelers tried to reserve round-trip, north-facing cabins for their journey. Explain that the north-facing cabins sheltered passengers from the hot equatorial sun. Travel agents named these popular but expensive accommodations "POSH"—for "Port Outward, Starboard Home."

Teaching with Pictures: The Battle of Omdurman (Objective 2) After transforming Egypt into a protectorate, the British turned their attention to the Sudan. Use Overhead Transparency 62 to help students locate the Sudan. Explain that the British believed that they had to control the headwaters of the Nile in order to guard Egypt and the Suez Canal. The Sudan was not undefended. A Sudanese army had defeated the British previously in 1884. Tell students that the British were determined to avenge this defeat and to gain control over the Sudan. An Anglo-Egyptian force of 26,000 soldiers commanded by General Horatio Kitchner invaded the Sudan in 1898. They encountered a force of 50,000 Sudanese defenders at Omdurman, a small village near Khartoum.

Direct students' attention to the painting of the Battle of Omdurman on page 538. The British troops are shown wearing scarlet uniforms when in reality they wore khaki uniforms. The British formed a strong defense line behind a stout hedge of thorn bushes. The Sudanese troops boldly attacked, but their swords, spears, and singleshot rifles were no match for the repeating rifles and Maxim automatic machine guns used by the Anglo-Egyptian force.

Explain that the Battle of Omdurman was a decisive British victory. The British suffered fewer than 500 casualties while Sudanese losses included 11,000 dead and an equal number of wounded. The victory established British control over the Nile. It also enabled Kitchner's army to force the French to retreat from Fashoda.

Economics and History: The "Big Hole" (Objective 3) Explain that Cape Colony, Natal, and the two Boer republics were not economic successes. About 45,000 Boer settlers subsisted on farms scattered across the Orange Free State and the Transvaal. Point out that the opening of the Suez Canal in 1869 threatened to end Cape Town's importance as a key port on the route to India.

Soon after the opening of the canal, however, a shepherd found an 85-carat diamond near the Orange River. Known as the "Star of South Africa," this huge white diamond helped to transform

South Africa from a group of impoverished colonies into one of the richest prizes in the British Empire. As members of the Cape Parliament inspected the diamond, Sir Richard Southey proudly announced, "Gentlemen, this is the rock on which the future of South Africa will be built."

Tell students that Southey's prediction proved accurate. Two years later, miners found a rich diamond field on a farm near Kimberly. Thousands of mines soon turned the field into the largest open-pit mine ever dug. The "Big Hole" was more than 700 feet deep and a mile in circumference. During the next forty years, it produced three tons of diamonds including the world famous "Tiffany," "Porter Rhodes," and "Kimberly" diamonds. The Big Hole and other mines helped South Africa become the world's richest supplier of diamonds.

Check for Understanding Have students describe one consequence of the Suez Canal, of the Battle of Omdurman, and of the Kimberly diamond mines.

Practice

Guided Practice
Lead a guided discussion of the questions in Overhead Transparency 62 and in Section Review 2. (Answers are below.)

Define:
(a) country whose foreign policy is controlled by outside government (b) country ruled jointly by two other countries (c) Boer term for foreign settler

Identify:
(a) linked Mediterranean and Red Seas (b) British conqueror of Sudan (c) ruler of Ethiopian empire (d) British-controlled region of Cape of Good Hope (e) Dutch settlers in South Africa (f) emigration of Boers from Cape Colony into African interior

Answer:
1. (a) Henry Stanley claimed most of Congo River valley for Belgium. (b) to lay down rules for competition in Africa (c) European countries agreed to recognize claim based on effective occupation.
2. invaded Algeria in 1830 and gradually took over Tunisia and Morocco
3. (a) Britain took Egypt, making it a protectorate. (b) invaded by Egypt and Britain
4. (a) took France more than six years to conquer (b) independent villages with which Britain made 500 separate treaties (c) region in which Britain was invited to protect a leader or group
5. (a) Liberia and Ethiopia (b) Liberia was closely tied to the United States; Ethiopia had natural protection (mountains), a strong leader, and geographic position as a buffer state.

6. (a) Many traditional rulers continued to hold office. (b) shift to a money economy; made Africans second-class citizens
7. (a) Boers resented British rule; tensions mounted when diamonds and gold were discovered. (b) Boers took up arms in 1899. (c) allowed Boers to keep their language in both schools and courts; helped them rebuild their farms
8. Politics—by denying Africans control of their own governments; taxation—by forcing them to pay taxes, thus requiring them to take low paying jobs in European-owned ventures; ethnic rivalry—by pitting group against group; education—by keeping Africans uneducated

Independent Practice
Assign Independent Practice Worksheet 25.2.

Enrichment Activities

1. **Reading a Primary Source** Assign Voices from the Past Resource Book 25.2.

2. **Preparing a Report** Have students prepare a report on one of these topics: the explorations of David Livingston, the explorations of Henry Stanley, the Belgian Congo, the Suez Canal today, Cecil Rhodes, the Rand gold mines.

3. **Researching for Bonus Points** Award bonus points to students who can answer this question? Who owned the farm where the Kimberly mine was discovered? (Two Boer brothers, Johannes and Diedrich DeBeer.)

The British dominated South Asia. 3

Section Objectives

After completing Section 3, students should be able to:

1. describe the causes and consequences of the Sepoy Mutiny.
2. compare a map of British India with maps of India in earlier times
3. explain how railroads affected life in India.

Setting the Stage

Write the following Hindi words on the board: *pajamas, loot, thug,* and *khaki.* Ask, "Which country contributed these words to the English language?" Explain that the words are derived from the British experience in India. British Prime Minister Disraeli once referred to India as "the brightest jewel in the Royal Crown." Explain that this section describes how the British ruled India during the nineteenth century.

Teaching Strategies

Skill Building: Relating Causes and Effects (Objective 1) Have students read "The Great Rebellion" (page 542). Then ask, "What was the immediate cause of the Sepoy Mutiny?" Explain that the rumors about pig and beef fat on the sepoys' new rifle cartridges was part of a much larger problem. As its power over India increased, the East India Company adopted a policy of trying to reform many aspects of Indian life. These reforms included the abolition of slavery, making *suttee* (the self-immolation of Hindu widows) illegal, legalizing the remarriage of widows, banning female infanticide, requiring English as the official language of education, and insisting that all castes receive equal treatments in the courts. These reforms angered many upper-caste Hindus who resented British interference in their culture. This anger helped fuel the Sepoy Mutiny.

Ask, "What were the consequences of the Sepoy Mutiny?" As noted in the text, the British government assumed direct command of India. Although British leaders continued to promote India's economic development, they refrained from demanding further social reforms.

Geography in History: Comparing Maps (Objective 2) Show students Overhead Transparency 63, *Imperialism in Southeast Asia, 1900*. Then ask students to compare this map with maps of other Indian empires on pages 68, 74, and 285. Ask, "Which empire covered the greatest area?" (British India) "Which areas in British India were not parts of the Maurya, Gupta, or Mughal empires?" (southern India) "Why was this region part of British India and not part of the other empires?" (Help students recall that previous invaders had entered India from the north while the British arrived by sea.)

Discussing History: Railroads and Indian Life (Objective 3) Tell students that the British opened India's first railroad line in 1853. It connected Bombay with the nearby town of Thana. By 1880, the Great Indian Peninsular Railroad connected Bombay with Calcutta. By 1900, India had 30,000 miles of track—more than in all the rest of Asia.

Explain that the railroads helped to promote trade by linking inland regions to the seaports. In addition, the railways helped relieve famines. Food supplies could be moved rapidly to stricken areas. By the end of the century major famines had become less frequent. Finally, railways helped India achieve a degree of cultural unity that the subcontinent had not previously experienced. By bringing Indian intellectuals and political leaders into more regular contact than before, railways helped stimulate Indian nationalism.

Check for Understanding Have students describe how the Sepoy Mutiny and the construction of railroads affected India.

Practice

Guided Practice
Lead a guided discussion of the questions in Overhead Transparency 63 and in Section Review 3. (Answers are below.)

Define:
(a) head of one of India's states (b) Indian soldier

Identify:
(a) Indian empire (b) religious group members who became mainstay of Britain's army (c) part of India under direct British rule (d) nationalist group formed to gain equal opportunities for Indians (e) group formed in 1906 to gain equal opportunities for Indians

Answer:
1. by taking advantage of weakness of Mughals
2. (a) belief that the British-made rifle cartridges were sealed with pork and beef fat (b) princes and maharajahs who had alliances with East India Company and Sikhs (c) In 1858, British government took direct command of Indian affairs.
3. (a) India gained bridges, dams, canals, irrigation, telegraph lines, and railroads. (b) economic exploitation, loss of self-determination.
4. originally, to win equal opportunities for Indians in civil service; later, to gain self-government
5. moved into Burma, helped protect independence of Thailand, and invaded Afghanistan
6. (a) approved because protected raw materials and markets (b) approved because increased wealth, provided labor (c) resented British rule which discriminated against Indians in civil service (d) provided alternative to Muslim rule (e) provided stability among a diverse population

Independent Practice
Assign Independent Practice Worksheet 25.3.
Assign Basic Skills Worksheet 25.

Enrichment Activities

1. **Reading a Primary Source** Assign Voices from the Past Resource Book 25.3.

2. **Creative Writing** Ask advanced students to imagine that they are founding members of the Indian National Congress. Their assignment is to write a list of grievances against British rule.

3. **Researching for Bonus Points** Award bonus points to students who can answer this question: What does the title *Maharaja* mean? ("great ruler")

Imperialism threatened China. 4

Section Objectives

After completing Section 4, students should be able to:

1. explain how European merchants used opium to force open Chinese ports.
2. locate territories China lost to other nations.
3. cite reasons for United States endorsement of an Open Door Policy in China.

Setting the Stage

To illustrate China's traditional lack of interest in the outside world, read aloud the following excerpt from a letter written in 1793 by the Chinese emperor. In it, the emperor politely rejects an invitation by King George III to open trade with Great Britain.

> You, O King, live beyond the confines of many seas, nevertheless, impelled by your humble desire to partake of the benefits of our civilization, you have dispatched a mission respectfully bearing your memorial (message)....
>
> Our dynasty's majestic virtue has penetrated into every country under Heaven, and kings of all nations offer their costly tribute by land and sea. As your ambassador can see for himself, we possess all things. I set no value on objects strange or ingenious, and have no use for your country's manufactures....

Ask students to describe the emperor's view of European culture. Was this view realistic? Recall the new forces that dramatically increased Europe's power in the eighteenth and early nineteenth centuries. Emphasize that the Industrial and Scientific revolutions strengthened Europe while China lagged behind. Tell students that this section describes how the European powers extended their influence over China.

Teaching Strategies

Analyzing a Quotation: The Opium Trade (Objective 1) Read the following passage from a letter a Chinese official wrote to Queen Victoria in 1839.

> Of all that China exports to foreign countries, there is not a single thing which is not beneficial to people.... Take tea and rhubarb, for example, the foreign countries cannot get along for a single day without them.... The goods from China carried away by your country not only supply your own consumption and use, but also can be divided up and sold to other countries, producing a triple profit. Even if you do not sell opium, you still have three-fold profit. How can you bear to go further, selling products injurious to others in order to fulfill your insatiable (greedy) desire?

Have students identify the arguments against the sale of opium in China. Then ask, "Why did the British refuse to stop the opium trade?" Assign "Europeans forced treaties on China" (pages 544–545). Clarify that Europeans use opium to pry open Chinese ports.

Geography in History: Imperialism in East Asia (Objective 2) Show Overhead Transparency 64 *Imperialism in East Asia, 1842–1912*, and have students identify European spheres of influence in China. Then distribute copies of Outline Map 19: China and Japan. Have students use the transparency or the map on page 546 to locate and label territories China lost in the late 1800's. Call on students to name the countries that gained land. Ask students to use the information in Section 4 to explain why China was unable to resist foreign intrusion. Students might write captions based on this discussion to accompany their maps.

Skill Building: Interpreting a Political Cartoon (Objective 3) Have students study the political cartoon on page 547. Ask, "What symbol did the cartoonist use to depict China, and why? How did the cartoonist convey the idea that the imperialist nations regarded the Chinese as unimportant?"

Assign "Foreign influence expanded" (pages 546–547). Ask students to describe how an American official might have responded to the political cartoon. Ask, "How did the United States respond to the partition of China? How did the Open Door Policy prevent China from suffering the same fate as Africa?" (It discouraged European colonization.)

Check for Understanding Have students explain how each of the following events was a reaction against European intervention in China: Opium War, Taiping Rebellion, Boxer Rebellion.

Practice

Guided Practice
Lead a guided discussion of the questions in Overhead Transparency 64 and in Section Review 4. (Answers are below.)

Define:
(a) rights of British citizens to be subject only to British law in China (b) regions in which economic interests of a foreign nation come before those of the home country

Identify:
(a) war Chinese fought against Britain to stop opium trade (b) rebel who took over southern China (c) protected American trade rights in China and protected China from colonization (d) Chinese secret society siege of European section of Peking

Answer:
1. China was practically self-sufficient.
2. (a) provide product Chinese would buy (b) protests, war (c) right to trade at Chinese ports, control over Hong Kong, and damages
3. (a) corruption in government, near bankruptcy, increase in population (b) Modernization was the country's only hope for survival.
4. (a) control of Chinese territory by foreign countries, U.S. fear that it would lose trade (b) American trade rights and China's independence
5. nationalism, republicanism, and land reform
6. Answers should consider China's history of unity and the role of the United States.

Independent Practice
Assign Independent Practice Worksheet 25.4.

Enrichment Activities

1. **Reading a Primary Source** Assign Voices from the Past Resource Book 25.4.

2. **Preparing a Report** Ask advanced students to prepare a report evaluating the effectiveness of

the Open Door Policy.

3. **Researching for Bonus Points** Award bonus points to students who can answer the following question: What was the name of the American Secretary of State who issued the Open Door Policy? (John Hay)

Japan built a modern nation. 5

Section Objectives

After completing Section 5, students should be able to:

1. describe the Japanese reaction to the arrival of Commodore Matthew Perry.
2. identify changes that took place during the Meiji era.

Setting the Stage

Recall that in the 1600's, Japan shunned foreign contact. Between 1616 and 1853, the Tokugawa shoguns stamped out Christianity, expelled foreigners (except for some Dutch), forbade Japanese travel abroad, and dubbed Europeans "hairy barbarians." Explain that in 1853 the United States decided to open up the "Hermit Kingdom." Read the following entry in Commodore Matthew Perry's diary, written as his ship lay anchored in Yedo (Tokyo) harbor:

> We pray God that our present attempt to bring a singular and isolated people into the family of civilized nations may succeed without resort to bloodshed.

Tell the class that this section explains how Japan changed from a feudal, isolated society to an industrialized world power.

Teaching Strategies

Writing about History: Perry's Arrival in Japan (Objective 1) Have students turn to the picture on page 548. *Prewriting* Focus attention on what the Japanese called the "black ship." Ask, "How did the Japanese artist depict Perry's arrival?" Tell students that Perry asked to present the shogun with a letter from the President of the United States. Although the shogun did not appear, he instructed his lesser lords to receive Perry. The Japanese built a pavilion in which the presentation was to take place. More than 5,000 soldiers, dressed in medieval armor and armed with swords and ancient guns, lined the pavilion. Nine samurai warriors hid under the pavilion, ready to attack if Perry or his aides showed any sign of trickery.

Perry marched to the pavilion with a marine escort and a band. The American flag bearer was a black sailor—the first black ever seen by the Japanese. Upon reaching the platform, Perry handed over a letter to a stunningly dressed Japanese official. The letter called for a treaty conference to open relations between the United States and Japan. Perry then announced that he would return in the spring for an answer. *Writing* Using this information and material from the text, ask students to write a news article about Perry's arrival from the point of view of the Japanese. Call on volunteers to share their articles.

Discussing History: Industrialization of Japan (Objective 2) To illustrate the changes that took place during the Meiji era, copy the following data on the chalkboard or on an overhead transparency.

Key Dates in Japanese Industrialization
- 1858, first steamship purchased from the Dutch
- 1859, first foreign loan negotiated with the British
- 1869, first telegraph connected Yokohama and Tokyo
- 1872, first railroad completed, connecting Yokohama and Tokyo
- 1872, first textile factories in operation
- 1900, foreign trade up from zero in 1854 to $200 million a year

Based on this information, have students compare Japan's response to European contact with China's response. Ask students if they think that the Japanese succeeded in the aims of their slogan, "Open the country to drive out the barbarians?"

Check for Understanding Call on students to identify reasons for Japanese imperialism.

Practice

Guided Practice
Lead a guided discussion of the questions in the Section Review 5. (Answers are below.)

Identify:
(a) American commodore who opened Japan to foreign trade (b) emperor after overthrow of the Tokugawa shoguns (c) "enlightened rule" of Mutsuhito (d) Russo-Japanese War battle (e) conflict between Japan and Russia for control of Manchuria

Answer:
1. (a) no contact with industrialized countries (b) fear that foreigners would take over Japan
2. overthrown by a new group of leaders in 1868
3. Feudalism was abolished, Japan adopted a constitution like Germany's; the first railroad line was built; coal production increased.
4. (a) won control of Korean peninsula and Manchuria (b) won Manchuria as well as recognition as a world power
5. Students should note that the leader believed in expediency and was confident the Japanese would make the most of Western technology.

Independent Practice
Assign Independent Practice Worksheet 25.5.

Enrichment Activities

1. **Reading a Primary Source** Assign Voices from the Past Resource Book 25.5.
2. **Relating Past to Present** Have students research Japanese foreign trade today, focusing on aspects of Japanese production that interests the United States.
3. **Researching for Bonus Points** Award bonus points to students who can answer the following question: What Gilbert and Sullivan musical popularized Japanese culture among Americans in 1885? *(The Mikado)*

Imperialism reached the Western Hemisphere. 6

Section Objectives

After completing Section 6, students should be able to:

1. identify causes and consequences of the Spanish-American War.
2. identify the Panama Canal and explain its significance.
3. explain why Europeans and Americans competed for control of the Pacific islands.

Setting the Stage

Begin by writing these four phrases on the chalkboard: "Monroe Doctrine," "Sinking of the *Maine*," "Panama Canal," and "Roosevelt Corollary." Then ask, "With which region of the world are these policies and events associated?" Point out that the chapter has examined imperialism in Africa, India, China, and Japan, and that this section focuses on imperialism in Latin America. Ask students to explain why the United States was concerned with Latin America. Emphasize that American involvement in Latin America was motivated by geographic nearness, economic investment, and a traditional policy of supporting movements for independence from colonial rulers.

Teaching Strategies

Skill Building: Identifying Causes and Effects (Objective 1) Ask students what caused the Spanish-American War. As noted in the text, the war had a number of causes. American newspapers, led by the *New York Journal* and the *New York World*, fanned public outrage by printing stories about alleged Spanish atrocities against the Cuban freedom-fighters. During the height of the controversy, the *Journal* and the *Globe* sold about ten million copies a week. Explain that economic factors were a contributing cause. Americans had invested about $50 million in Cuba, and trade between the two countries exceeded $100 million a year. The sinking of the *Maine* was the immediate cause. An infuriated public helped persuade President McKinley to ask Congress for a declaration of war.

Although the Spanish-American War lasted only five months, it had lasting effects. The war marked the emergence of the United States as a great power with an empire of islands that included the Philippines, Guam, and Puerto Rico. The war also heightened interest in building a canal to connect the Pacific Ocean and the Caribbean Sea. When the war began, the Navy ordered the *U.S.S. Oregon* to steam from San Francisco to the Caribbean. By the time the ship completed its 68-day voyage around Cape Horn, the war was almost over.

Teaching with Pictures: The Panama Canal (Objective 2) Show students Overhead Transparency 91, *The World About 1900* and help students to locate the Panama Canal. Explain that the Canal represented a significant engineering triumph as well as a vital transportation link. More than 40,000 workers labored for ten years to complete the waterway. The painting on page 551 shows a portion of the eight-mile-long Gaillard Cut. This excavation sliced through a narrow 275-foot-high pass over the rugged Continental Divide. Ask students to speculate on the functions of the railroad tracks and trains. Explain that the railroads transported workers, machines, and millions of tons of excavated rock and dirt. More than 150 million cubic yards of soil—nearly twice the amount excavated at Suez—were taken from the Gaillard Cut. The workers sometimes endured temperatures of 120 degrees fahrenheit during their ten-hour shifts. When completed, the Gaillard Cut was 1,800 feet wide and 400 feet deep.

Conclude by emphasizing that the Panama Canal revolutionized travel between the Atlantic and Pacific oceans. Today more than 15,000 ships pass through the canal each year. The 50-mile trip only takes about fifteen hours.

Discussing History: The Samoan Islands (Objective 3) The Samoan Islands form a small archipelago that lies 750 miles west of Tahiti. Explain that on March 15, 1889, a small fleet of German and American warships prepared to fight for control of the islands. A major incident was avoided when a powerful hurricane wrecked both fleets. Ask, "Why were the United States and Germany willing to risk a possible war over a remote group of islands?" Explain that the old wooden sailing ships could travel great distances without stopping for supplies. However, the new steam-driven ironclads needed frequent stops for coal, water, and repairs. As a result, naval planners prized islands such as the Samoans as valuable coaling stations. Tell students that Germany ultimately received control of the Western Samoans while the United States received control of the remaining islands. When Congress annexed the American Samoans in 1900, they became the only United States possession south of the Equator.

Check for Understanding Have students describe the consequences of the Spanish-American War, the significance of the Panama Canal, and the reasons the great powers coveted islands in the South Pacific.

Practice

Guided Practice
Lead a guided discussion of the questions in Section Review 6. (Answers are below.)

Define:
statement declaring right of the U.S. to act as an international police officer in the Americas

Identify:
(a) Western Hemisphere region where Latin-based languages are spoken (b) war between U.S. and Spain over Cuba (c) American president (1901–1909) who wanted to expand American interests abroad (d) site of Panama Canal (e) Queen of Hawaii

Answer:

1. (a) It had resources their factories needed. (b) Foreigners took over ownership of businesses.
2. Unrest in the region threatened its security.
3. (a) Americans did business in Cuba; United States bought sugar from Cuba; Cuba had strategic value; and many Americans identified with Cuba's fight for freedom. (b) United States won many of Spain's Caribbean and Pacific holdings as well as right to build naval bases in Cuba.
4. by encouraging Panama to revolt against Colombia and then leasing the land for the canal from Panama
5. resources and strategic value as naval bases
6. (a) To be truly independent, a country needs to control both its economy and government. (b) One country may need the trade more.

Independent Practice

Assign Independent Practice Worksheet 25.6.
Assign Geography Skills Worksheet 25.

Enrichment Activities

1. **Reading a Primary Source** Assign Voices from the Past Resource Book 25.6.

2. **Debating a Topic** Ask students to debate the following topic: Resolved—President McKinley could have avoided the Spanish-American War.

3. **Researching for Bonus Points** Award bonus points to students who can answer this question: What was the name of the first ship to pass through the Panama Canal? (the *Ancon*)

Answers to Voice from the Past

1. The United States will become entangled in serious conflicts to protect its possessions.
2. (a) need for new markets for industrial products (b) Although we need markets, we do not need to own the countries with which we trade.
3. against, arguing that it represented yet another entanglement and source of conflict

Concluding the Chapter

1. **Chapter Closer**
   Ask students to summarize the events that led historians to characterize the late nineteenth and early twentieth centuries as the "Age of Imperialism."

2. **Reteaching Activities**
   a. Making a Time Line Have students prepare a time line covering the events discussed in this chapter.
   b. Making Comparisons Have students compare and contrast European imperialism in Africa and China.
   c. Listing Have students list the steps Japan took to modernize.

3. **Chapter 25 Activities**
   Assign Chapter Review 25 activities.

Chapter Evaluation

Chapter Test 25 and Computer Test Bank Chapter 25 Test can be used to evaluate your students' understanding of this chapter.

Answers to Chapter Review 25

Reviewing the Facts

1. **a.** policy of conquering and ruling other lands **b.** country outwardly independent but whose real control is in foreign lands **c.** country ruled jointly by two other countries **d.** situation in which people living in a foreign country do not have to obey its laws **e.** region in which the economic interests of a foreign nation come before those of its host country

2. **a.** ended slave trade in East Africa in 1880's **b.** Belgian king who began scramble for African colonies with claim to the Congo River valley **c.** Dutch settler in South Africa **d.** British trading company that became the leading power in India in 1757 **e.** rebellion by Indian soldiers after which British government took direct command in India **f.** religious group that became mainstay of British army in India **g.** nationalist group formed in 1885 to gain equal opportunities for Indians **h.** Muslim group formed in 1906, similar in outlook to the Congress **i.** war waged between Britain and China over opium trade in China **j.** United States policy that protected American trade rights and protected China from colonization **k.** Chinese secret society siege of European section of Peking in China **l.** American commodore who opened Japan to foreign trade **m.** era of industrialization and modernization in Japan **n.** war between United States and Spain over Cuba **o.** statement that Untied States had

right to act as an international police force in the Americas

3. (a) invaded Algeria, built the Suez Canal, and took over Tunisia and Morocco (b) Britain took over Egypt in order to guard the Suez Canal, made Egypt a protectorate, and, with Egypt, invaded Sudan.

4. (a) South Africa had rich resources of gold and diamonds. (b) The British crowded into Boer land in search of gold and diamonds and tried to overthrow the Boer government of the Transvaal. (c) British won but gave rulership of South Africa, as a British colony, to the Boers.

5. (a) Indian resentment of British domination and discrimination (b) by heightening its control and improving the country

6. (b) prosperous agricultural country, practically self-sufficient (b) British smugglers used opium to get China to open trade with Europeans and to weaken Chinese rulers.

7. (a) Japan had little contact with industrialized nations and allowed foreign nations trade rights when it became necessary for protection against conquest. (b) Japan's leaders adopted the best from Western nations, industrialized, modernized the military, and defeated China and Russia, gaining Korea and Manchuria.

8. (a) by lending capital for expansion and then taking over ownership of factories and other business enterprises (b) built the Panama canal and announced the Roosevelt Corollary

Basic Skills

1. (a) France and Britain (b) Britain and France were the world's two dominant colonial powers.

2. (a) to keep foreign nations from recolonizing Latin America (b) negotiator in disputes between Latin American countries and other nations; Roosevelt Corollary said U.S. could use military intervention to keep order; changes due to large economic investments by outsiders, particularly British, and U.S. fear of political influence by those countries on Latin American politics; U.S. wanted to protect its own business interests in Latin America.

Research and Reporting Skills
Students' answers will vary.

Critical Thinking

1. Economic competition from newly emerging industrialized countries, need for raw mater-ials, new markets, and protection of shipping lanes led to race for colonies; politically colonies a sign of national prosperity and international prestige. Examples: imperialists proudly displayed maps of possessions, U.S. and Germany cut into British trade; France, Spain, Portugal, Germany, and Belgium started colonization movements.

2. (a) Africa: many different nations competed for colonies; different types of colonial rule apparent; no major market developed; most improvements benefited only Europeans; India and Southeast Asia: colonial competition primarily between British and French; Britain single power in India, where internal improvements benefited country. In East Asia, China remained independent but was divided into spheres of influence. (b) India and Southeast Asia more valued than Africa because a bigger market and a major supplier of raw materials and resources.

3. The European nations that had the most colonies were likely to have an economic advantage that translated into greater political influence both in Europe and throughout the world. European countries without colonies might align themselves with a particular country for economic reasons and to maintain the balance of power.

4. (a) U.S. one of emerging economic powers that challenged Britain's economic leadership. (b) East Asia and Latin America (c) United States followed example of European nations in pursuing imperialism, though was less imperialist in China and recognized Cuba's independence.

Perspectives on Past and Present
(a) That Africa was considered available to the European powers; African politics and culture were of little importance and Europe was free to divide Africa. (b) no—most African countries are now independent; as Third World nations they have joined with other countries to force the more powerful industrialized nations to deal with their issues; self-determination is accepted by most nations as a worthy goal and the kind of decisions made in Berlin would be strongly criticized in world organizations such as the United Nations.

Investigating History
Students' answers will vary.

The Turn of the Century

Chapter Overview

Just as the Industrial Revolution changed the ways people worked, a wave of new inventions began changing the ways people lived. The Bessemer process ushered in an Age of Steel, Edison perfected the light bulb, and the telephone, radio, automobile, and airplane revolutioned communication and transportation. New ideas in science brought improvements in disease control and public health.

Women demanded the right to vote, more job opportunities, equitable pay, and legal rights. Impressionism, postimpressionism, and expressionism replaced realism in art. Romanticism and nationalism continued to influence music, but some composers experimented with new forms.

At the same time, Europe faced rising tensions. In Germany, Kaiser William II took over the reins of government and forced Bismarck to resign. Great Britain was split over Irish home rule and over the role of the House of Lords. Great Britain and other European nations had wide chasms between social classes.

Political crises arose throughout Europe, especially in the Balkans, as nationalist groups continued to press for independence. In North Africa and along the Rhine, trouble continued to flare.

Key Terms

assembly line, anarchists
For additional exercises, see Vocabulary Worksheet 26.

Chapter Focus

Ask students to pretend that they are professional photographers with a special assignment. Ask, "What scenes, inventions, or technological developments would you photograph to capture the spirit of our time?" Explain that the photographs are to be placed in a time capsule that will be opened in 100 years. After the students have shared their ideas, have them read the opening section (pages 556–557).

Tell students that Lartigue had in a way taken on a special assignment when he enthusiastically photographed the activities of his wealthy family.

Because the Lartigues were members of the rich upper class, they were able to enjoy a period in Europe's history characterized by peace, power, and prosperity. Jacques Lartigue's snapshots captured the images of a new era. Science and technology resulted in remarkable new inventions that dramatically changed human history.

Inventions changed ways of life. 1

Section Objectives

After completing Section 1, students should be able to:

1. identify Thomas Edison and describe how he developed the electric light bulb.
2. identify Henry Ford and explain how he changed the automobile industry.

Setting the Stage

Begin by asking students to explain the distinction between science and technology. Explain that science refers to the systematic methods by which knowledge of nature is sought. Technology refers to the practical application of this knowledge. Point out that before the 1870's, scientific and technological progress had been achieved independently. However, during the 1870's scientific knowledge was increasingly applied to technological problems. This exchange between the laboratory and the factory stimulated an unparalleled increase in the rate of industrial growth. Tell students that this section discusses the inventors and inventions that dramatically changed the way people lived, worked, and traveled.

Teaching Strategies

Discussing History: "The Wizard of Menlo Park" (Objective 1) Ask students if they have experienced a power failure during an electrical storm. Ask, "Can you imagine what life would be like if the lights never came back on?" Point out that few inventions had more impact on the world than Edison's electric light bulb, a convenience that most of us now take for granted.

Explain that Thomas Edison and his researchers worked as much as twenty hours a day for more than a year before their efforts were rewarded. The problem was finding a filament that could burn for a long period of time. They tried dozens of materials including gold, nickel, fishline, and even coconut hair. Finally, in the fall of 1879, Edison found that a charred cotton thread would glow for 13½ hours. Tell students that on New Year's Eve, crowds of excited spectators gathered in Menlo Park, New Jersey, to see the glow of these remarkable new lights shining in Edison's laboratory. By 1900, 24 million bulbs provided what Edison described as "electric light so cheap that only the rich will be able to burn candles."

Economics and History: The Model T (Objective 2) Explain that the first motor-cars were expensive to purchase, and even more expensive to operate and repair. Most cars cost more than $1,000 and half of them were priced above $2,000. The automobile might have remained a toy for the rich had it not been for Henry Ford. In 1903, he founded the Ford Motor Company in Detroit, Michigan. Five years later, after producing eight models including the Model A, Ford reached the revolutionary conclusion that he could produce a dependable and inexpensive car for "the great multitude" of people. Tell students that Ford achieved this goal by becoming the first manufacturer to successfully mass produce automobiles. (For a model of Ford's assembly line see National Geographic's *Historical Atlas of the United States.*)

Ford's new automobile, the Model T, quickly became a success. "Every time I lower the price a dollar, we gain a thousand new buyers," Ford boasted. He was right. In 1914, workers assembled 2,000 cars a day that cost an average price of only $440. That year, Ford also raised his workers' salaries to the unprecedented amount of five dollars a day. He correctly realized that well-paid workers would be able to buy their own Model T's.

Check for Understanding Ask students to explain the contributions made by each these inventors: Henry Bessemer, Thomas Edison, Alexander Graham Bell, Henry Ford, and the Wright brothers.

Practice

Guided Practice
Lead a guided discussion of the questions in Section Review 1. (Answers follow.)

Define:
(a) mixture of purified iron and small amount of carbon (b) machine which generates large amounts of electric power (c) process in which a moving conveyor belt rolls parts past workers

Identify:
(a) developed blast furnace method to make steel (b) inventor of the light bulb, phonograph (c) inventor of the telephone (d) inventor of the radio

Advance Planner

	Section 1
Objectives	1. Identify Thomas Edison and describe how he developed the electric light bulb. 2. Identify Henry Ford and explain how he changed the automobile industry.
Setting the Stage	Defining "science" and "technology"
Teaching Strategies	Discussing History: "The Wizard of Menlo Park" Economics and History: The Model T Check for Understanding
Guided Practice	Section Review 1
Independent Practice Worksheets	Independent Practice 26.1 Basic Skills 26 Vocabulary 26
Enrichment	1. Primary Source: Voices 26.1 2. Analyzing a Quotation 3. Researching for Points

(e) auto manufacturer who pioneered mass production (f) inventors of airplane

Answer:
1. Great Britain, Germany, and the United States
2. (a) Blast furnaces made it easier and cheaper to make. (b) machinery, ships, railroad tracks, buildings, skyscrapers
3. (a) coal and steam (b) electricity, oil, gasoline, and natural gas
4. invented electric light, record player, and developed the industrial laboratory for research and development
5. Telephone and radio communication became essential part of life.
6. use of standardized, interchangeable parts and the assembly line method of production
7. (a) pride in job done with the greatest efficiency in contrast to the pride of personal workmanship (b) advantages: steady job in thriving indus-

Chapter 26 The Turn of the Century 1865–1914			★ Advanced
Focus Jacques Lartigue's snapshots of a new era			● Basic

Section 2	**Section 3**	**Section 4**	**Section 5**
1. Identify Joseph Lister and Louis Pasteur and explain how their medical discoveries saved lives. 2. Define and explain the concept of social Darwinism.	1. Describe economic and legal obstacles women faced in the late 1800's. 2. Explain the goals and strategies of the women's suffrage movement.	1. Describe the new styles of art that developed at the turn of the century. 2. Identify *The Great Train Robbery* and explain the role of movies in mass entertainment.	1. Evaluate the limits to democracy in the industrialized nations. 2. Explain how the issue of Irish home rule divided the British people. 3. Describe the social divisions in *la belle epoque*.
Factors that contribute to increased life expectancy	Attitudes toward women in the late 1800's.	Defining "mass culture"	Were promises of equality kept at the turn of the century?
Relating Past to Present: Antiseptic Surgery Analyzing a Quotation: Social Darwinism Check for Understanding	Skill Building: Comparing Points of View Discussing History: Women's Suffrage Check for Understanding	Teaching with Pictures: New Styles of Art Discussing History: *The Great Train Robbery* Check for Understanding	Analyzing a Quotation: Democracy in Germany Relating Past to Present: Irish Home Rule Discussing History: Social Divisions in *La Belle Epoque.* Check for Understanding
Section Review 2 Independent Practice 26.2 Critical Thinking 26	Section Review 3 Independent Practice 26.3	Section Review 4 Independent Practice 26.4	Section Review 5 Independent Practice 26.5 Geography Skills 26
1. Primary Source: Voices 26.2 2. Preparing a Report 3. Researching for Points	1. Primary Source: Voices 26.3 2. ★Relating Past to Present: The ERA 3. Researching for Points	1. Primary Source: Voices 26.4 2. Researching for Points	1. Primary Source: Voices 26.5 2. Researching for Points 3. Global Perspectives Transparency 91

Chapter Closer ● **Reteaching Activities**	Summarizing, Listing Goals
Chapter Review	Summary, Reviewing the Facts, Basic Skills, Researching and Reporting Skills, Critical Thinking, Perspectives on Past and Present, Investigating History
Chapter Evaluation	Chapter Test 26, Computer Test Bank Chapter 26 Test
Unit VII Review **Geographic Theme:**	Movement: When did a global economy begin?
Unit Perspectives	Understanding History (Explaining, Defining, Relating, Identifying), Critical Thinking, Making Decisions, Continuity and Change
Unit Evaluation	Unit VII Test

try, lack of wasted time and energy, ability to specialize in one task; disadvantages: tedium of repetition, impersonality, and lack of pride in work

Independent Practice

Assign Independent Practice Worksheet 26.1.
Assign Basic Skills Worksheet 26.
Assign Vocabulary Worksheet 26.

Enrichment Activities

1. **Reading a Primary Source** Assign Voices from the Past Resource Book 26.1.

2. **Analyzing a Quotation** The Model T has been described as "the right car at the right time at the right price." Ask students to support their interpretations of this statement.

3. **Researching for Bonus Points** Award bonus points to students who can answer this question: What was the winning speed in the first Indianapolis 500 race, held in 1911? (75 miles per hour)

Science presented new ideas. 2

Section Objectives

After completing Section 2, students should be able to:

1. identify Joseph Lister and Louis Pasteur and explain how their medical discoveries saved lives.
2. define and explain the concept of social Darwinism.

Setting the Stage

Ask students to estimate how long they expect to live. Record students' answers and them compute an average life expectancy for your class. Tell students that in the late 1980's the average American could expect to live 74.8 years. Compare this figure with the average life expectancy of the class. Then tell students that in 1900 the average American could expect to live 47.3 years. Ask students to speculate the reasons people can expect to live so much longer today. Explain that advances in medicine and nutrition account for today's longer life expectancies. Many key medical discoveries were made at the turn of the century. This chapter begins with a description of two doctors—Joseph Lister and Louis Pasteur—whose pioneering work paved the way for future medical discoveries. The chapter then discusses the revolutionary ideas of Charles Darwin, and scientific advances in biology, chemistry, and physics.

Teaching Strategies

Relating Past to Present: Antiseptic Surgery (Objective 1) "What causes diseases to spread?" Explain that in the mid-1800's most doctors believed that a poisonous mist in the air caused disease. Knowing nothing about bacteria, patients reasoned that the dirtier a surgeon's coat, the more operations he must have performed. Many patients asked for the most "experienced" (the dirtiest) doctors to operate on them.

Explain that a Scottish surgeon named Joseph Lister objected to the unsanitary conditions in hospital operating rooms. Influenced by Pasteur's theory that disease was caused by bacteria, Lister began a new program of cleanliness in his hospital ward. After many experiments Lister discovered that carbolic acid could be used to clean bandages and medical instruments. He also insisted that bandages be used only once and that surgeons regularly wash their hands. Explain that since Lister's methods were designed to prevent sepsis, or blood poisoning, they became known as antiseptic surgery. Ask, "What additional procedures do hospitals use today to ensure a germ-free hospital ward?" Explain that modern surgeons use sterile instruments, gauze bandages, and rubber gloves.

Analyzing a Quotation: Social Darwinism (Objective 2) Review the text's discussion of social Darwinism. Then explain that Spencer's ideas quickly spread to America. The following exchange between Yale professor William Graham Sumner and his students can be used to illustrate social Darwinism:

Student: Professor, don't you believe in any government aid to industries?
Sumner: No! It's root, hog, or die.
Student: Yes, but hasn't the hog got a right to root?
Sumner: There are no rights. The world owes nobody a living.
Student: You believe, then, Professor, in only one system, the contract-competitive system?
Sumner: That's the only sound economic system. All others are fallacies.
Student: Well, suppose some professor of political economy came along and took your job away from you. Wouldn't you be sore?

Sumner: Any other professor is welcome to try. If he gets my job, it is my fault. My business is to teach the subject so well that no one can take the job away from me.

Read or distribute this passage to your class. Then ask students to answer these questions:

• Did Sumner believe in government aid to industries? Why or why not? (No. Sumner believed in free economic competition.)
• How would Sumner have felt if another professor tried to take his job? (Sumner believed that the most competent person would be entitled to the job.)

Ask students to explain how Sumner's ideas related to Darwin's theory of natural selection.

Check for Understanding Ask students to name one achievement in each of the following fields: medicine, chemistry, biology, and physics.

Practice

Guided Practice
Lead a guided discussion of the questions in Section Review 2. (Answers are below.)

Define:
(a) substance that kills pain (b) microscopic organisms that cause disease (c) Darwin's premise that fittest individuals are most likely to survive (d) matter containing only one kind of atom (e) tiny particle (f) powerful form of energy

Identify:
(a) suggested relationship between infection and unsanitary conditions (b) discovered heat could destroy harmful bacteria (c) published *Origin of the Species by Means of Natural Selection* (d) idea that every kind of plant and animal was created by God at the beginning of the world and has remained the same ever since (e) idea of change through natural selection (f) idea that those who were fittest for survival enjoyed wealth and success (g) believed that some humans could and should become "supermen" (h) laid groundwork for science of genetics (i) devised the Periodic Table (j) discovered radium and polonium

Answer:
1. inoculation, anesthesia, improved sanitation, control of bacteria
2. (a) Every kind of plant and animal was created by God at the beginning of the world. (b) Change took place through natural selection.
3. contradicted account of creation in the Bible
4. suggested natural selection is at work in the survival of companies that prosper

5. Dalton theorized that all matter is made of atoms and that elements contain only one kind of atom; Mendeleev organized all the known elements and predicted new elements; the Curies discovered two elements for which Mendeleev had left room in his chart.
6. Look for answers to consider the nature of adaptation, the element of luck in entrepreneurship, the fact that wealth can be inherited, and the interdependency of the economic community.

Independent Practice
Assign Independent Practice Worksheet 26.2
Assign Critical Thinking Worksheet 26.

Enrichment Activities

1. **Reading a Primary Source** Assign Voices from the Past Resource Book 26.2.
2. **Preparing a Report** Ask students to prepare a report on one of the scientists discussed in this section.
3. **Researching for Bonus Points** Award bonus points to students who can find the answer to this question: Who discovered that chloroform was a better anaesthetic than ether? (James Young Simpson)

Women sought rights and freedoms. 3

Section Objectives

After completing Section 3, students should be able to:

1. describe economic and legal obstacles women faced in the 1800's.
2. explain the goals and strategies of the women's suffrage movement.

Setting the Stage

Introduce the section by reading the following extract from John Stuart Mill's *Autobiography:*

I saw no more reason why women should be held in legal subjugation [bondage] to other people than why men should be. I was certain that their interests required fully as much protection as those of men, and were quite as little likely to obtain it without an equal voice in making the laws.

Ask students to describe Mill's views on the issue of women's equality. For example, what role did Mill think women should have in making the laws? Why? Then explain that Mill's views were not typical of the late 1800's. That is, few people shared his opinion on the liberty of women. As students read Section 3, tell them to list ways in which, to use Mill's words, women were "held in legal subjugation to other people."

Teaching Strategies

Skill Building: Comparing Points of View (Objective 1) Using the chalkboard or an overhead transparency, write the following quotation from the textbook, spoken by a member of the British Parliament.

"Women are creatures of impulse and emotion. They do not decide questions on the ground of reason as men do."

Have students compare this attitude toward women with that of John Stuart Mill. Ask, "In what ways do the two views differ? On what assumption is each view based?" Then have students divide a sheet of paper into two columns, "Obstacles Faced by Women" and "Gains Made by Women." Tell students to complete this chart as they read, and use the information to determine which view of women was predominant in the late 1800's.

Discussing History: Women's Suffrage (Objective 2) Open discussion of the woman's suffrage movement by reading aloud the following description of Mrs. Emmeline Pankhurst, the fragile-looking widow of a Manchester barrister. Wrote George Dangerfield: "It is known of Mrs. Pankhurst that she never proposed to spend her widowhood behind any scene, if there was the slightest chance of getting in front of it." Ask students what Dangerfield might have meant by this remark. What evidence in the text supports their answers? Then have students review the tactics women used to win the vote. Ask, "Why might women have resorted to such drastic measures as hunger strikes or window smashing?" Conclude the discussion by having students informally debate the following topic: "Resolved: That the most important battle fought by women was waged in the courts."

Check for Understanding Ask students to identify the economic and political advances made by women in the late 1800's and early 1900's.

Practice

Guided Practice
Lead a guided discussion of the questions in the Section Review 3. (Answers are below.)

Define:
right to vote

Identify:
(a) founder of first school of professional nursing (b) organized campaign for women's rights (c) head of the North American Woman Suffrage Association (d) formed Women's Social and Political Union

Answer:
1. lower pay, exclusion from trade unions and skilled jobs
2. (a) domestic work, work in garment or textile factories (b) teaching, nursing, library work, and social work
3. no right to the money they earned; could not sue or make contracts; could not vote
4. by organizing, by demonstrating
5. (a) right to own property, to serve as safety inspectors in factories where women worked, to serve on local boards to oversee schools, poorhouses, and hospitals (b) right to vote
6. (a) Teaching demanded too much of women's intellects, while nursing might expose genteel women to overly harsh realities, and office work would require more "business sense" than women had. (b) Look for answers to cite stereotypes—women's nurturing capability and "capacity for detail."

Independent Practice
Assign Independent Practice Worksheet 26.3.

Enrichment Activities

1. **Reading a Primary Source** Assign Voices from the Past Resource Book 26.3.

2. **Relating Past to Present** Since ratification of the Nineteenth Amendment in 1920, women in the United States have sought to extend their rights by adding an Equal Rights Amendment (ERA) to the Constitution. Ask advanced students to investigate the history of the ERA and its place in the women's movement.

3. **Researching for Bonus Points** Award bonus points to students who can find the answer to the following question: In what year did women in Great Britain win the right to vote? (1928)

Answers to Voice from the Past

1. (a) Each was her political superior. (b) the right to vote

2. the right to trial by a jury of her peers
3. the right to sit on a jury, be admitted to the bar

Art and entertainment took new forms.

4

Section Objectives

After completing Section 4, students should be able to:

1. describe the new styles of art that developed at the turn of the century.
2. identify *The Great Train Robbery* and explain the role of movies in mass entertainment.

Setting the Stage

Ask students to estimate the number of movies they watch in an average month. Then ask students to estimate the number of concerts and professional sporting events they see—in person or on television—each month. Explain that historians refer to these forms of entertainment as examples of mass culture. Point out that in earlier periods, art, music, and most theater had been available mainly to the upper classes. By 1900, however, artists, writers, and musicians reached larger (mass) audiences. Tell students that this section explains how mass culture developed.

Teaching Strategies

Teaching with Pictures: New Styles of Art (Objective 1) Ask students if they have ever seen a tree that contains blue leaves and a pink trunk. Clearly, such a tree does not exist in nature. Then tell students that in 1905 the French artist Henri Matisse unveiled a painting called "Landscape at Collioure" that included multicolored leaves and trees: Ask, "Why did Matisse use these unrealistic colors?" Explain that Matisse used bright colors to express how he felt about a landscape as opposed to what the landscape actually looked like. Have students look at Van Gogh's painting, "The Starry Night," (page 569). Emphasize that Van Gogh, like Matisse, distorted reality to express the ideas or moods suggested by an object or scene. Tell students that the Impressionists tried to paint the light reflecting from objects rather than the objects themselves. Have students find other examples of the art styles described in this section.

Text pages 556–577

Discussing History: The Great Train Robbery (Objective 2) Ask students to describe the scariest scene they have ever seen in a movie. Then explain that in late 1903, audiences in three New York City movie theatres stared intently at the black and white image of a fierce bandit holding a raised gun pointed directly at them. A puff of smoke burst from the gun, causing the spectators to shriek with fearful delight. For the next eight minutes the audience watched in suspense as a band of robbers help up a train, staged a dramatic escape, and were hunted down and finally captured by a hard-riding posse. Within months, this action-packed "western" was drawing large crowds in movie theatres on both sides of the Atlantic.

Explain that the success of *The Great Train Robbery* marks the beginning of the modern film industry. Within a few years other filmmakers added techniques such as fades, close-ups, mobile cameras, and full-length feature films, producing a string of box office hits. By 1916, 25 million Americans watched movies each day, making this the fifth largest industry in the United States. Movies enjoyed almost equal success in Europe. In England, for example, 3,500 new cinemas opened between 1908 and 1914.

Check for Understanding Ask students to give two examples of mass culture and to name three reasons for the rise of mass culture.

Practice

Guided Practice
Lead a guided discussion of the questions in Section Review 4. (Answers are below.)

Define:
culture that appealed to large audience

Identify:
(a) art form attempting to capture the impression of a scene (b) art form concerned with expressing the feelings a scene aroused

Answer:
1. (a) emphasis on light, blending colors to make the work seem to shimmer (b) Manet, Renoir, Monet, Pisarro, Van Gogh, and Gauguin
2. expressionism, cubism
3. Compositions gave people sense of national identity. Wagner's operas took nationalistic themes.
4. (a) increased literacy, improvements in communications, reduction in working hours (b) sports, music halls, recorded sound, movies
5. (a) led to attempts to portray impressions (b) Answers should consider commercial and the aesthetic.

6. **(a)** give rise to thoughts **(b)** defining culture, reflecting society, providing entertainment, exploring the human condition, and celebrating individualism.

Independent Practice

Assign Independent Practice Worksheet 26.4.

Enrichment Activities

1. **Reading a Primary Source** Assign Voices from the Past Resource Book 26.4.
2. **Researching for Bonus Points** Award bonus points to students who can find the answer to this question: Who won the first World Series game and what was the score? (Boston defeated Pittsburgh 5 to 3).

Europe faced rising tensions. 5

Section Objectives

After completing Section 5, students should be able to:

1. evaluate the limits to democracy in the industrialized nations
2. explain how the issue of Irish home rule divided the British people.
3. describe social divisions in *la belle epoque.*

Setting the Stage

Write the following promises of individual liberty on the chalkboard or on an overhead transparency:

Declaration of Independence: "We hold these truths to be self-evident, that all men are created equal...."

The Declaration of Rights of Man and Citizen: "Men are born and remain free and equal in rights."

Call on students to recall the situations that gave rise to each of these promises (the American and French revolutions). Then challenge the class to consider to extent to which the promises of equality were kept during *la belle epoque,* as the early 1900's was called. Have students note, as they read, the limitations and growth of democratic principles and democratic government.

Teaching Strategies

Analyzing a Quotation: Democracy in Germany (Objective 1) Tell students that a short time after Kaiser William II came to the throne in Germany, the 29-year-old monarch declared: "I regard my whole position as given to me direct from heaven." Ask, "What does this quote reveal about William's attitude toward the power of the king? What attitude would you expect him to take toward the prime minister and parliament?" Have students check their answers by rereading "Germany had a hollow democracy" (page 572). Ask, "What were some limits to democracy in the other industrialized nations?"

Relating Past to Present: Irish Home Rule (Objective 2) Assign students tasks in group research on "the Irish question" in Great Britain today. Have one group draw a map showing the division of Ireland into Northern Ireland and the Republic of Ireland. Have other groups use the *Readers' Guide to Periodical Literature* to collect articles on the tensions between Catholics and Protestants in Northern Ireland. Call on students to draw connections between the problems in Ireland today and Britain's failure to grant Ireland home rule in the late 1800's. Using facts to support their views, students might debate the possibility of Ireland's future reunification.

Discussing History: Social Divisions in *La Belle Epoch* (Objective 3) To help students appreciate the inequality of wealth in 1900, write the following facts on the chalkboard or on an overhead transparency:

• In 1900 nearly 41 million people lived in England. Of this number, 175,000 owned 90 percent of the land.
• At the turn of the century, one-third of England's national income went to about 3 percent of the population.

Then read this statement, made by a member of the English working class: "They [the rich] don't have to think of tomorrow. They spend in an hour what would keep me and my little ones for a year."

Ask students to use this information to predict the rise of social tensions in the early twentieth century. Ask, "How did England remain politically stable in light of such economic differences?" Students might suggest that the rise of trade unions and the "People's Budget" were institutionalized ways of managing conflicts. Ask, "Why were anarchists a threat to political stability?"

Check for Understanding Ask students to write two significant facts about each of the following topics: the German Reichstag, "People's Budget," *la belle epoque.*

Practice

Guided Practice
Lead a guided discussion of the questions in the Section Review 5. (Answers are below.)

Define:
(a) more select body of lawmakers (b) body of lawmakers elected directly (c) mob attack against Jews in Russia (d) person who believes governments are evil and should be overthrown

Identify:
(a) lower house of German parliament (b) upper house of German parliament (c) forced Bismarck to resign (d) developed "People's Budget"

Answer:
1. Parties needed tighter organization; leaders had to "communicate" to appeal to voters.
2. Chancellor still had complete control.
3. (a) insurance to help workers in case of accident, old age pensions (b) to prevent revolution, to take support from socialists.
4. (a) whether Great Britain or Ireland should rule Ireland (b) At first both Catholics and Protestants supported home rule, but later the Protestants opposed it.
5. House voted to limit own powers.
6. (a) Austria-Hungary, Russia, Ottoman empire (b) Serbs, Bosnians, Montenegrins, Croats, Slovenes, Albanians, Bulgarians, and Romanians
7. (a) uprisings supported by Russia against Austria-Hungary (b) German gunboat threatened French colony of Morocco. (c) assassinations
8. Bismark's motives were to prevent revolution, so his actions reflected a political philosophy of near-dictatorship; Lloyd George seemed genuinely interested in expanding democracy.
9. (a) It accurately describes wealth of the few. (b) fails to describe widespread poverty

Independent Practice
Assign Independent Practice Worksheet 26.5. Geography Skills Worksheet 26.

Enrichment Activities

1. **Reading a Primary Source** Assign Voices from the Past Resource Book 26.5.

2. **Researching for Bonus Points** Award bonus points to students who can find the answer to the following question: In what year did the Republic of Ireland win its independence from Great Britain? (1949)

3. **Global Perspectives** Have students complete the activities for Overhead Transparency 91, *World about 1900.*

Concluding the Chapter

1. **Chapter Closer**
   Ask students to imagine that they are photographers at the turn of the century. The assignment is to create a photo-essay of the times. Have students describe five scenes or events they would photograph.

2. **Reteaching Activities**
   a. **Summarizing** Ask students to name five turn-of-the-century inventions and explain why each was important.
   b. **Listing Goals** Ask students to list three goals of the nineteenth century woman's rights movement.

3. **Chapter Review 26 Activities**
   Assign Chapter Review 26 Activities.

Chapter Evaluation

Chapter Test 26 and Computer Test Bank Chapter 26 Test can be used to evaluate your students' understanding of this chapter.

Answers to Chapter Review 26

Reviewing the Facts
1. **a.** process in which moving conveyor belt rolls parts past workers **b.** person who believes governments are evil and should be overthrown
2. **a.** provides a cheap way to produce steel **b.** pioneered idea of a laboratory for research and development **c.** invented telephone **d.** invented wireless telegraph **e.** Wright brothers **f.** made surgery routine part of medical care **g.** process of heating liquid to destroy bacteria **h.** style of painting aimed at capturing an impression; replaced realism **i.** style of painting expressing the artists' feelings; replaced realism **j.** conservative chancellor who gave Germany first large-scale social welfare program in the world **k.** Liberal Party and champion of social welfare programs **l.** mob attack on Jews in Russia, symbolic of tensions in eastern Europe
3. **(a)** steel **(b)** electricity

4. **(a)** excited scientific community but caused a controversy still debated today **(b)** natural selection or survival of the fittest; social Darwinism, superiority through power and belief in free economic competition
5. **(a)** periodic chart of elements **(b)** showed that each element contains only one kind of atom **(c)** discovered radioactivity and two new elements **(d)** suggested atoms were made up of smaller particles
6. **(a)** organized campaigns, founded international councils, and organized demonstrations **(b)** widened job opportunities and gained enactment of laws giving married women right to own property and keep own income; right to vote in certain places **(c)** universal suffrage
7. **(a)** home rule for Ireland **(b)** World War I broke out one month before approval of a home rule bill, which Protestants were preparing to fight.
8. When House of Lords vetoed "People's Budget," the king threatened to appoint reform-minded lords. House of Lords voted to limit its powers rather than accept new members.
9. **(a)** nationalistic conflicts and persecutions of ethnic minorities **(b)** German and French hostility over Alsace and Lorraine, also Morocco

Basic Skills
(a) United States, Germany **(b)** Britain, France **(c)** Russia, Austria-Hungary **(d)** Britain losing shares to rising industrial powers of United States and Germany; changes in Russia and Austrian production reflect upheavals in political and social structure.

Critical Thinking
(a) Problems: earned half of what men earned in wages; poor working conditions; confined to work as servants, work in the garment or textile industries, and in a few professions such as teaching and nursing; no legal right to earn money when married. Progress: women formed own unions; gained laws limiting hours and setting health and safety standards in places where women worked; some women allowed into medical schools; jobs opened up in stores and offices (clerical work); laws allowed married women to earn money. **(b)** In terms of actual changes in conditions, relatively little progress was made. However, women had begun to cooperate and organize to improve conditions and to seek the right to vote.

Perspectives on Past and Present
1. **(a)** creation of more democratic governments; to what extent governments should provide public services; social mobility; role of women in public life; living and working conditions for factory workers; rebuilding of cities; and what to do about the national aspirations of various peoples **(b)** All of the above are still controversial issues in many parts of the world. It is unlikely that they will be completely resolved by the end of this century.
2. Possible answers: The impact of the Curie's discoveries can be seen in the development of atomic sources of power and various medical and scientific advances such as the treatment of cancer by radiation.

Investigating History
Students' answers will vary.

Unit VII *Review Activities*

1. Assign Geographic Theme: Movement.
2. Assign Unit Perspectives Questions.

Unit VII *Review Answers*

Geographic Theme: Movement
1. by greatly increasing the need for resources and raw materials and the amount of goods to be sold
2. the increased demand for cotton in the English textile mills
3. Spanish America, Europe, East Indies
4. The flow of resources and raw materials and of manufactured goods to and from all parts of the world is an example of movement. It illustrates the economic interaction between countries distant from each other. It also is an example of economic interdependence.

Unit *Perspectives*

Understanding History
1. **a.** Shuttle allowed faster weaving. **b.** Gin increased cotton production **c.** improved steam engine use in industry **d.** Small powerful engine could pull a cart along rails. **e.** Telegraph speeded up communications. **f.** Telephone made voice communication possible. **g.** Wireless made it possible to send messages across ocean. **h.** Assembly line made mass production possible. **i.** Airplane led to air transportation. **j.** Discovery of radioactivity introduced powerful form of energy.

2. **a.** political philosophies that developed from attitudes toward French Revolution **b.** Laissez-faire policy allowed industrialization to spread without regard for workers' welfare. **c.** Industrialization brought about realism in art. **d.** linked political and artistic movements that grew out of the French Revolution **e.** Entrepreneur sold stock in a corporation to raise capital. When a corporation drove out competition, it became a monopoly. **f.** Social Darwinism justified imperialism.
3. romanticism (**a., c.**); realism (**b., e.**); impressionism (**d., f., g.**)
4. **a.** formed nationalist group **b.** worked to unite Italy **c.** freed Sicily from Spain **d.** freed part of South America from Spain **e.** freed part of South America from Spain **f.** agreed to Brazilian independence **g.** led fight for Mexican independence **h.** drove French from Haiti **i.** united Germany

Critical Thinking
1. **a.** led to start of urban working class, wealthy owners of factories and businesses, and growing middle class; **b.** middle class gained in income; owners of factories and businesses became wealthy; factory workers received low wages and lived in poverty **c.** 1832 Reform Bill gave representation to middle class men and helped to get representation for new cities; later, workers won universal manhood suffrage
2. **a.** both believed in free economic competition; Social Darwinism applied ideas to society as well as to economics; **b.** both were foreign policies of the United States; Monroe Doctrine sought to exclude European nations, but Open Door Policy wanted nations equal in trading with China; **c.** both were possessions of Britain; Canada was given self-government while India was not; **d.** both were varieties of socialism; utopian socialism was evolutionary whereas Marxian socialism was revolutionary.
3. **a.** Imperialism was an expression of nationalism on an international basis; **b.** the idea of social Darwinism that the fittest should survive meant that it was acceptable to subordinate peoples with less political power; **c.** the Enlightenment opened the door to questioning of ideas and the discovery of scientific principles; these concepts were applied in the Industrial Revolution.

4. **a.** political imperialism: Britain's protectorate in Egypt and French takeover of Tunisia and Morocco; economic imperialism: Britain in India, European nations in China
5. **a.** alike in that both sought independence; **b.** different in that the American Revolution was democratic and those in Latin America were not
6. **a.** Japan succeeded in excluding foreigners, whereas China was divided into spheres of interest. **(b)** Africa and Southeast Asia were carved into colonies and run for the benefit of the ruler. Latin American nations were independent, but European nations invested in railroads, mines, and plantations from which they obtained a profit.
7. **a.** Goals included right to vote, end of slavery in the United States, representation in national legislature, legislation reflecting special interests. **b.** Right to vote almost universal for men, but not anywhere for women; slavery ended in the United States; male voters represented in legislatures; some legal protection, such as for the right to strike.

Making Decisions
a. restoration was successful for a time, but conservative Charles IX had to give way to more liberal Louis Philippe; **b.** Bismarck's state socialism was a success; was kept even after the Kaiser dropped Bismarck; **c.** Declaring war on Prussia was a disaster for Napoleon III because Prussia won and exacted hard terms.

Continuity and Change
1. **a.** successful for more than half a century at keeping peace in Europe; **b.** Crimean War and rise of Germany and Italy upset the balance that had existed and led to new rivalries
2. Answers should show the growth of nations in North America, Latin America, Europe, and Australia; staking out of colonial possessions in Africa and in South and Southeast Asia.

Unit Evaluation

Unit VII Test can be used to evaluate your students' understanding of this unit.

Years of Crisis

Unit Overview

Unit VII focuses on the political, social, and economic upheavals that took place throughout the world during the first half of the twentieth century. In 1914, the assassination of Archduke Franz Ferdinand of Austria-Hungary triggered a war between the Triple Entente and the Triple Alliance. The victorious Allies met at Versailles and dictated harsh peace terms to the defeated powers.

As with World War I, the causes of the Russian Revolution had been building for a long time. Between 1900 and 1914, Russia's defeat in the Russo-Japanese War, the events of Bloody Sunday, and the failure of a provisional Duma weakened the power of the czar. In 1917, Lenin's Bolsheviks came to power, signed a truce with Germany, and nationalized all major industries. The civil war that followed left the Russian economy in ruins. Stalin, who succeeded Lenin, launched revolutions in industry and agriculture, imposing harsh totalitarian rule.

Nationalism became an increasingly important force in other parts of the world. In India, Gandhi preached passive resistance and breathed life into the independence movement. In the Middle East, the collapse of the Ottoman empire led to the establishment of Turkey, Iran, and Saudi Arabia. Jews and Arabs fought over Palestine, which had been a British mandate. In Latin America, most countries were politically independent but were ruled by dictators who encouraged economic dependency on foreign investments. Mexico, unlike other parts of Latin America, remained politically stable after the ideas of the 1917 constitution were put into effect.

In 1911, Chinese nationalists established the Republic of China. In time, a civil war broke out between the Communists, led by Mao Tse-tung, and the Nationalists, led by Chiang Kai-shek.

The years following World War I witnessed many changed in technology, culture, and scientific thinking. In the United States, the stock market crash of 1929 set off a worldwide depression, which, in turn, led to Fascist dictatorships in Germany and Italy. The world drifted once again toward war as Japan, Italy, and Germany invaded other nations and Britain and France followed a policy of appeasement.

With Hitler's invasion of the Polish Corridor in 1939, World War II began. The Japanese bombing of Pearl Harbor brought the United States into the war.

Military successes in North Africa, along the Eastern Front, and on the Normandy beaches led to Germany's defeat in June 1945. Japan surrendered in September 1945, following the atomic bombing at Hiroshima and Nagasaki.

Resources

The resources that supplement the study of this unit are:

1. The time line for Unit VIII, found on pages 580–581. The themes for this time line include the patterns and trends leading to the outbreak of World War II, and the social, cultural, and economic changes of the 1920's and 1930's.
2. The Geographic Theme, found on page 686. The theme *Location* teaches the concepts of absolute and relative geographic location. Students work with a map showing the Soviet Union in 1941 and the territories it acquired between 1941 and 1945.
3. The Historical Atlas map on pages 818–819, "The Modern World." The Global Perspectives enrichment activity in Chapter 31 refers to this map, which also appears as Overhead Transparency 91.
4. The Researching and Reporting Skills in chapter reviews, which focus on students' investigations into history as viewed by its contemporaries. Students use oral and visual primary source material in addition to written accounts.

Chapter Titles

Chapter 27

World War I

Ask, '
Then
had ot
tives –
many
War I
stroye
and s
millic
patier
war. H
ence t
lost th
have
for co
neede
anoth

Exp
many
1918,
to pov
Wrote
Prime
by th
people
too m
darke
chair.
punis
injure

Discu
(Obje
faced
class
Britisl
they r
ing iss

• Will
ing V
• Wha
force
• Wha
colo
• Wha
the I
• Shou
for tl

Ask e
five q
decisi
decisi
Versa
Europ
tify cl

Text pε

Chapter Overview

Archduke Franz Ferdinand, heir to the Austro-Hungarian throne, was assassinated in Sarajevo on June 28, 1914. About a month later, Austria declared war on Serbia. A web of alliances among the Great Powers quickly drew virtually all of Europe into the war. Russia backed Serbia and brought France into the conflict as one of the Allies. Germany joined Austria, forming the Central Powers. Britain and Italy joined the Allies, and Turkey and Bulgaria joined the Central Powers.

The belligerents used new technology in warfare, and the war moved to several new fronts. A revolution in Russia led to that nation's withdrawal from the war. The United States and Japan joined the war on the side of the Allies. An armistice ending World War I was signed November 9, 1918.

United States President Woodrow Wilson issued Fourteen Points to try to establish a lasting peace, but France and Britain were eager for vengeance. The leaders of the victorious Allied Powers met at Versailles in January 1919 to establish terms for peace. The United States congress voted against joining the League of Nations. Germany was forced to accept harsh peace terms. The peace treaty created new countries and new territories, but the harsh terms for the losing side nurtured a lasting bitterness.

Key Terms

militarism, ultimatum, mobilize, rationing, propaganda, armistice, self-determination, mandate, reparation
For additional exercises, see Vocabulary Worksheet 27.

Chapter Focus

Begin by asking students what they know about the assassination of John F. Kennedy in 1963. Ask why this event did not lead to war. Students should recall that Kennedy's assassin was an American and that, as far as anyone knew, no foreign power was involved. Have students read the chapter opening (pages 582–583). Ask, "Where was Bosnia? Who was Archduke Franz Ferdinand? Who was Gavrilo Princip? Why did Princip assassi-

nate the Archduke?" Explain that Princip, as a Bosnian Serb, was an Austro-Hungarian subject. Thus, the assassination, like Kennedy's, might have been treated as a purely internal matter. Instead, it precipitated World War I.

Tell students that this chapter explains how the deaths of Ferdinand and Princip set off one of the bloodiest and most catastrophic wars in history.

Conflicts divided Europe. 1

Section Objectives

After completing Section 1, students should be able to:

1. explain the significance of Bismarck's network of alliances.
2. analyze the arms race between the Great Powers.
3. describe the growth of militarism in prewar Europe.

Setting the Stage

Have students imagine that they are advisers to the Austrian Emperor, Franz Josef. His nephew, Archduke Franz Ferdinand, has just been assassinated. They know that the assassin, Princip, belonged to the Black Hand, a terrorist group based in Serbia. They also suspect that the Black Hand is supported by leading members of the Serbian government and army. Ask, "What would you advise the Emperor to do?" After discussing student responses, conclude by explaining that Austria-Hungary decided to punish Serbia.

Teaching Strategies

Discussing History: The Nature of Alliances (Objective 1) Select six students (called A, B, C, D, E, and F) to perform this demonstration. Write the following set of conditions on the chalkboard:

A and F are enemies.
C does not like F.

Enrichment Activities

1. **Reading a Primary Source** Assign Voices from the Past Resource Book 27.4.

2. **Researching a Topic** Ask advanced students to prepare a report explaining the effects of the war on Kaiser William II.

3. **Researching for Bonus Points** Award bonus points to students who can find the answer to this question: Who was the German Foreign Minister who signed the Treaty of Versailles? (Count Ulrich von Brockdorf-Rantzau)

Concluding the Chapter

1. **Chapter Closer**
   Ask students to explain how the deaths of Ferdinand and Princip set off World War I.

2. **Reteaching Activities**
   a. **Supporting a Main Idea** Read aloud the sentence at the top of page 586: "By the summer of 1914, many Europeans believed that war was inevitable." Ask students to name three circumstances that made war seem "inevitable."
   b. **Writing a Paragraph** Ask students to write a paragraph explaining how a war that began between Austria and Serbia became a war that included most of Europe.

3. **Chapter Review Activities**
   Assign Chapter Review 27 activities.

Chapter Evaluation

Chapter Test 27 and Computer Test Bank Chapter 27 Test can be used to evaluate your students' understanding of this chapter.

Answers to Chapter Review 27

Reviewing the Facts

1. **a.** glorification of armed strength **b.** set of demands that, if not met, would end negotiations **c.** to get an army positioned for war **d.** system under which people could buy only small amounts of goods needed for the war effort **e.** one-sided information that aims to convince people of a certain point of view **f.** agreement to stop fighting **g.** allowing people to decide for themselves under what government they wish to live **h.** territory that was administered on behalf of the League of Nations **i.** money to compensate for the costs of war

2. **a.** Archduke of Austria-Hungary whose assassination set off World War I **b.** German Chancellor who attempted to protect German empire by isolating France **c.** German kaiser who forced Bismarck to resign **d.** weakened Turkish empire which Austria-Hungary saw as an opportunity to extend its influence in the Balkans **e.** plan whereby most of the German army would attack France in the west before Russia was mobilized in the east **f.** first major clash on Western Front; stopped German advance and saved Paris **g.** message that Germany would help Mexico regain United States land if Mexico would fight with Germany; brought United States into World War I **h.** United States president whose Fourteen Points outlined a plan for lasting peace **i.** where Allied Powers met to negotiate treaties officially to end war **j.** Article 231 of Treaty of Versailles which placed sole blame for World War I on Germany

3. Europe was divided into two rival factions, and a dispute between any two powers would involve other countries. Slavic nationalism had kept Russia and Austria on the brink of war for years. The assassination of Archduke Ferdinand was the culmination of many years of tension and crises.

4. **(a)** great loss of life but not much gain by either side **(b)** more a war of movement, but stalemate was common

5. **(a)** Revolutionaries drove the czar from power. **(b)** Lacking supplies, the Russian army had felt betrayed by its leaders.

6. German U-boats sank three American ships and Americans were angered over the contents of the Zimmermann telegram.

7. **(a)** restricted the size of the army, banned manufacturing of war material and submarines and airplanes, placement of troops in the Rhineland **(b)** Czechoslovakia now included the border region formerly Germany's; 3 million Germans lived in the border region; anschluss (union) between Germany and Austria was forbidden.

8. **(a)** United States, Britain, France, Italy, and Japan were to be permanent members of the League of Nations Executive Council. There would also be a general assembly at which representatives of 42 Allied and neutral nations would meet. **(b)** Germany, Russia, and the United States **(c)** Germany and Russia were deliberately left out; United States Senate refused to join.

Basic Skills

1.

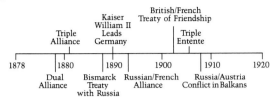

2. (a)

Battles	Objectives	Main Events	Outcomes
Marne (1914)	Germany wanted to knock France out of war before Russia entered	Germany marching on Paris; Allies attack gap in German lines; Germans retreat	Schlieffen Plan fails; Quick victory in west impossible for Germany; Two front war
Verdun (1916)	Germans try to take Paris	300,000 die; British attack Germans at Somme	Stalemate; Germans advance four miles; British advance five miles
Marne (1918)	Deport Allies before impact of American forces can be felt	German shock troops attack France; American troops begin to arrive	German army in disarray and would never recover

(b) Possible answers: Students could say that 1914 Battle of Marne was turning point because it meant Germany would have to fight a two-front war. Students could point to 1918 Battle of Marne as collapse of German military.

Researching and Reporting Skills
Students' answers will vary.

Critical Thinking

1. Possible answer: World War I involved countries from all parts of the world. Outside of European nations the war also involved countries from North America (United States and Canada), Middle East (Ottoman Empire), Asia (Japan), and fighting in Africa (East Africa and Tanzania).

2. The Triple Alliance included Germany, Austria-Hungary, and Italy. The Triple Entente included Great Britain, France, and Russia. The Triple Alliance was formed by Germany as a way of isolating France and neutralizing it as a threat to Germany. Great Britain led in the formation of the Triple Entente. Its purpose was to protect the three countries involved from German aggression.

3. (a) Bismarck's policies went through two very different stages. In the first he used the military and war as tools for unifying and strengthening Germany. It could be said that the Kaiser drew on that legacy when he rejected Bismarck's second-stage policy of peaceful coexistence. (b) Instead of keeping peaceful relations with Great Britain and Russia, the Kaiser let Bismarck's treaty with Russia lapse and directly challenged the dominance of the British navy and Britain's colonial empire. While Bismarck described Germany as a "satisfied power," Kaiser William was far from satisfied with Germany's status in the world community. He sought German dominance, while Bismarck was content with peaceful relations.

4. (a) ending secret treaties, freedom of seas, removing economic barriers to trade, reducing size of national armies and navies, and adjusting colonial claims with fairness toward the colonial peoples (b) For the most part, France's and Britain's goals were similar to Wilson's. The major difference was that France and Britain wanted Germany to pay reparations and demanded that Germany cede some of its lands and agree to sweeping military restrictions.

5. Possible answer: As an era of destruction and despair; as the era of a last generation; as a time like the 1300's with terrible disasters.

6. (a) Possible answer: resolved problems—end secret treaties, freedom of seas, reducing size of military, League of Nations, and self-determination (b) war guilt clause, reparations, and sometimes self-determination. The positive factors tried to open the world to freedom of movement on the seas, an open market where one nation could not shut out others, and self-determination for nationalist groups. They also tried to reduce the threat of war by reducing the size of the military and by establishing the League of Nations. Finally the treaty helped ease tensions in some parts of the world by creating countries that represented the true desires of various minority groups. However, self-determination also had its negative impact. The treaty did not solve all minority problems and often created problems by the way it drew new national lines. Also the demand for reparations and the war guilt clause sowed the seeds of discontent that would eventually lead to the outbreak of World War II.

Perspectives on Past and Present
Students' answers will vary. Students should point to various organizations such as the United Nations, Organization of American States, International Court of Justice, etc.

Investigating History
Students' answers will vary.

Russia in Revolution

Chapter Overview

During the 1800's, Russia lagged behind western Europe. Revolutionary groups began developing after the Decembrists' revolt of 1825, and, by 1900, the country was ripe for revolution. Bloody Sunday, the massacre of petition-bearing workers at the czar's Winter Palace in 1905, provoked a wave of strikes throughout the country, forcing Czar Nicholas II to create a Duma (parliament), which he later dissolved. After the czar led Russia into two disastrous wars, he was forced to abdicate. A provisional government was overthrown by Lenin's Bolshevik party.

Once Lenin took power, he abolished the elected government and established a dictatorship. He agreed to the Treaty of Brest Litovsk and gave up one fourth of Russia's empire in order to withdraw from World War I. Meanwhile, the struggle for control within Russia continued as a civil war. Lenin harshly restored order and instituted new economic policies. After Lenin's death, Stalin took command of both the party and the government.

Stalin forced the country to increase industrial production and replaced privately-owned farms with collective farms. By the time Stalin died, the Soviet Union had made extraordinary progress as a modern power, but that progress had come at the cost of becoming a totalitarian state.

Key Terms

abdicate, autocrat, nihilism, soviet, totalitarianism

For additional exercises, see Vocabulary Worksheet 28.

Chapter Focus

Have students read the introduction (pages 602–603); then ask, "What problem angered the women of St. Petersburg?" As pointed out in the text, a shortage of bread angered the women, causing them to march in the streets. Ask, "Who quickly joined the women and what did they want?" Point out that textile and steel workers, along with the women, demanded bread, an end to war, and the czar's abdication.

Tell students that when city authorities recognized a need for action, they called out the Cossacks—fierce horsemen from southern Russia who were among the czar's most loyal, and most brutal, troops. A shudder went through the crowd as Cossack officers gave their troops the order to charge. Some of the strikers began to pray. The Cossacks, however, were as tired of the war as everyone else. They had no quarrel with these people. As they moved forward, the Cossacks left their swords in their scabbards. Instead of charging, they walked their horses carefully through the crowds. "Some of them smiled," recalled one striker later, "and one of them gave the workers a good wink!"

Explain that the Cossack's wink symbolized the collapse of the czar's authority. Ask, "Why were a wink and a shortage of bread enough to topple a family that had ruled Russia for more than 300 years?" Emphasize that these actions were immediate causes of deep-rooted problems that had been building for almost 100 years. Tell students that this chapter begins with a description of the forces that had been working to weaken the czar's power. It then describes how a moderate democratic government took power and was then overthrown by a communist dictatorship.

Russia struggled to reform. 1

Section Objectives

After completing Section 1, students should be able to:

1. define *autocrat* and give examples of the czar's unlimited power.
2. prepare a graph and chart showing the composition of Russian society and its problems.
3. identify a Fabergé imperial Easter egg.

Setting the Stage

Refer students to the painting and caption on page 604. Ask students to look for two economic problems that are portrayed in this painting. Explain that the painting provides a vivid illustration of

Russia's lack of industrialization and its reliance on the labor of serfs. Tell students that this section describes how the Russian czars tried to reform these two problems.

Teaching Strategies

Discussing History: The Autocracy (Objective 1) Explain that the Russian czars were autocrats with unlimited wealth and power. The czars owned millions of acres and controlled nearly half the peasants. The czars also owned and operated railroads and many industrial plants. They used their wealth to build palaces and to entertain thousands of guests at lavish banquets. The czar's royal throne was encrusted with more than 870 diamonds and hundreds of other precious jewels.

Explain that in addition to wealth, the czars also had absolute power like that wielded in earlier centuries by western European monarchs,

Advance Planner

Chapter 28 Focus	Russia in Revolution 1825–1939 Causes of the Russian Revolution			★ Advanced ● Basic
	Section 1	**Section 2**	**Section 3**	**Section 4**
Objectives	1. Define *autocrat* and give examples of the czar's unlimited power. 2. Prepare a graph and chart showing the composition of Russian society and its problems. 3. Identify a Fabergé imperial Easter egg.	1. Identify the Social Revolutionaries, the Bolsheviks, and the Mensheviks and describe how they wanted to change Russia. 2. Identify and evaluate the mistakes of Nicholas II. 3. Explain why the provisional government failed.	1. Explain how Lenin and the Bolsheviks came to power in 1917. 2. Locate lands Russia lost in World War I. 3. Explain how Stalin defeated Trotsky for control of the Communist party.	1. Contrast the policies of Lenin and Stalin. 2. Explain how Stalin transformed the Soviet economy. 3. Describe how the Soviet Union became a totalitarian state.
Setting the Stage	Russia's lack of industrialization and reliance on serf labor	Reformers vs. revolutionaries in imperial Russia	Observations on Lenin's character	The concept of totalitarianism
Teaching Strategies	Discussing History: The Autocracy Skill Building: Making Charts and Graphs Teaching with Pictures: The Imperial Easter Eggs Check for Understanding	Skill Building: Comparing Revolutionary Groups Writing about History: The Czar's Mistakes Discussing History: Why Did the Provisional Government Fail? Check for Understanding	Writing about History: The Bolsheviks Seize Power Geography in History: Russia's Lost Lands Transparency 67 Outline Map 23 Transferring Ideas: Stalin as a Dictator Check for Understanding	Skill Building: Contrasting Points of View Economics and History: Transforming the Soviet Economy Discussing History: Totalitarianism as a Way of Life Check for Understanding
Guided Practice	Section Review 1	Section Review 2	Section Review 3	Section Review 4
Independent Practice Worksheets	Independent Practice 28.1 Geography Skills 28 Vocabulary 28	Independent Practice 28.2	Independent Practice 28.3 Basic Skills 28	Independent Practice 28.4 Critical Thinking 28
Enrichment	1. Primary Source: Voices 28.1 2. Creative Writing 3. Researching for Points	1. Primary Source: Voices 28.1 2. ★ Creative Writing 3. Researching for Points	1. Primary Source: Voices 28.3 2. Researching for Points	1. Primary Source: Voices 28.4 2. Relating Past to Present 3. Researching for Points
Chapter Closer ● **Reteaching Activities**	Making a Time Line, Identifying			
Chapter Review	Summary, Reviewing the Facts, Basic Skills, Researching and Reporting Skills, Critical Thinking, Perspectives on Past and Present, Investigating History			
Chapter Evaluation	Chapter Test 28, Computer Test Bank Chapter 28 Test			

such as Louis XIV. The czar was the complete master of Russia. There was no parliament or court system to question his decisions. He could appoint and dismiss all government ministers. Finally, the czar commanded the army and was the official head of the Russian Orthodox Church. Nicholas I described the czar's absolute authority when he said, "The czar is a father, his subjects are his children, and children ought never to question their parents." Read this quotation to students. Ask them what kinds of problems could result from this way of thinking.

Skill Building: Making Charts and Graphs (Objective 2) Write the following sentence on the chalkboard: In 1900 about 80 percent of the Russian people were peasants, 15 percent were urban or town dwellers, 3 percent were middle class professionals, and 2 percent were upper class aristocrats. Ask students to make a graph that illustrates the composition of Russian society. What conclusions can they draw from their graphs?

After the students have completed this activity, distribute copies of the following paragraph:

> Russian peasants were discontented because they did not own enough land and frequently did not have enough food. Urban workers were discontented because they earned low wages and had poor working conditions. Middle class Russians were discontented because they wanted a share in the government. These discontents resulted in demonstrations, assassinations, and strikes.

Ask students to read this paragraph and then draw charts illustrating its main ideas. Have students share their charts with the class.

Teaching with Pictures: The Imperial Easter Eggs (Objective 3) Tell students that Easter was the most important holy day in czarist Russia. Russians of all classes celebrated Easter by exchanging eggs. Each year, Nicholas II presented his wife and his mother with a fabulous Easter egg created by Carl Fabergé, a Russian goldsmith. When opened, each egg contained a surprise. For example, the egg shown on page 607 contained a precise replica of the imperial coach, which required 15 months to create. Point out the imperial crown at the center of the roof. It is surrounded by tiny gold eagles. Tell students that Fabergé created fifty-eight eggs for Nicholas II. Some of the other surprises included a model palace, portraits, and miniature animals.

Check for Understanding Ask students to describe Russian society and to list two major economic problems.

Practice

Guided Practice
Lead a guided discussion of the questions in Section Review 1. (Answers are below.)

Define:
(a) king or emperor of Russia (b) resign as ruler (c) ruler with unlimited power (d) peasant community (e) elected council (f) radical belief that everything existing must be destroyed (g) Russian students who went among the peasants to teach reading, provide medical services, and spread the idea of revolution

Identify:
(a) capital of Russia (b) czar who encouraged growth of industry and foreign investment (c) ruling Russian family for more than three centuries (d) northeastern Russia (e) led a revolt when Czar Alexander I died (f) czar of Russia for 30 years (g) freed serfs (h) set out to strengthen "autocracy, orthodoxy, and nationality"

Answer:
1. (a) serfs (b) had no rights; could be bought and sold, beaten or exiled by landholders
2. written constitution giving Russians some rights enjoyed by western Europeans
3. (a) determined to keep reform out of Russia (b) opposed it but needed support of landlords to prevent peasant revolts
4. freed serfs, gave people more rights, expanded educational opportunities
5. (a) Serfs were freed and given farmable land which became the property of the mir. (b) It was almost impossible for a peasant to leave the mir, because other peasants would have to do extra work and pay extra share of taxes.
6. Anyone who questioned the absolute power of the czar, worshiped outside the Russian Orthodox Church, or spoke a language other than Russian was regarded as dangerous.
7. (a) far behind the West (b) growth of industry, cities, and foreign investment; completion of Trans-Siberian Railway
8. (a) preferred rights be guaranteed in a constitution (b) pleased with freedom, frustrated with mir (c) wanted destruction, not reforms, of existing institutions (d) approved expansion of educational opportunities

Independent Practice
Assign Independent Practice Worksheet 28.1.
Assign Geography Skills Worksheet 28.
Assign Vocabulary Worksheet 28.

Enrichment Activities

1. **Reading a Primary Source** Assign Voices from the Past Resource Book 28.1.

2. **Creative Writing** Remind students that the American Declaration of Independence listed grievances against Britain. Ask students to prepare a list of grievances that might have been written by a Russian revolutionary in 1900. Students should follow each complaint with a suggestion for improvement.

3. **Researching for Bonus Points** Award bonus points to students who can answer to this question: What was the name of the revolutionary group that took credit for assassinating Alexander II? (People's Will)

Russia moved toward revolution. 2

Section Objectives

After completing Section 2, students should be able to:

1. identify the Social Revolutionaries, the Bolsheviks, and the Mensheviks and describe how they wanted to change Russia.
2. identify and evaluate the mistakes of Nicholas II.
3. explain why the provisional government failed.

Setting the Stage

Ask, "Would the Russian government benefit the most from gradual reform or from revolutionary change?" Divide the students into pairs. Assign half of each pair the role of "reformer" and the other half the role of "revolutionary." Ask each student to argue the advantages of his or her point of view. Then tell students that this section describes how the reformers and the revolutionaries tried to change Russia.

Teaching Strategies

Skill Building: Comparing Revolutionary Groups (Objective 1) Draw a chart with three columns and three rows on the chalkboard. Label the columns "Social Revolutionaries," "Bolsheviks," and "Mensheviks." Label the rows "Followers,"

"Economic Goals," and "Political Goals." Ask students to review pages 608–609. Then have them fill in the chart as a class activity. When the class chart has been completed, use it as the basis of discussion on the following questions: Which group appealed to the peasants? (The Social Revolutionaries) Which groups appealed to the industrial workers? (The Bolsheviks and the Mensheviks) What were the Bolsheviks' political goals? (to establish a "dictatorship of the proletariat")

Writing about History: The Czar's Mistakes (Objective 2) *Prewriting* Have students read "The czar made serious mistakes" (pages 609–610). Explain that Nicholas II made four serious mistakes. He involved Russia in a disastrous war with Japan, refused to share power with the Duma, entered World War I, and moved his headquarters to the front. *Writing* The text states that "Czar Nicholas made the fateful decision to go to war. It was this decision, more than any other single factor, that cost Nicholas his throne." Ask students to write essays agreeing or disagreeing with this conclusion.

Discussing History: Why Did the Provisional Government Fail? (Objective 3) Explain that the provisional government failed to solve two crucial problems. Tell students that Russian peasants wanted the immediate redistribution of the great landed estates. This "land hunger" of the peasants was a powerful force. Rather than giving in immediately, the provisional government, which included many large landowners, established a commission to collect information on which future legislation would be based. The provisional government also failed to satisfy the popular desire for peace. Explain that the provisional government felt honor-bound by treaties Russia had made with the Allies. In addition, the Allies secretly pledged to give Russia control over the Turkish straits if they remained in the war. Ask students to recall the strategic importance of the Bosporus and the Dardanelles for Russia.

Check for Understanding Ask students to identify the Bolsheviks, Alexander Kerensky, and the provisional government.

Practice

Guided Practice
Lead a guided discussion of the questions in Section Review 2. (Answers are below.)

Define:
elected workers' council

Identify:
(a) German philosopher who argued that the workers of the world would overthrow ruling classes and share equally in society's wealth (b) planned to overthrow the czar and spark a worldwide Marxist revolution (c) Social Democrats who were followers of Lenin (d) Social Democrats who opposed Lenin (e) January 22, 1905, when soldiers killed 500–1,000 workers (f) Russian parliament (g) wife of Nicholas II (h) mysterious peasant who had great influence on the czarina (i) dominant figure in the provisional government

Answer:
1. Social Revolutionaries believed the force to overthrow the czar's government would come from Russia's peasants; Social Democrats believed the urban workers would revolt.
2. (a) He believed a Marxist revolution should begin at once. (b) His policy split the party into Bolsheviks and Mensheviks.
3. (a) shift Russians' attention away from internal problems (b) Korea (c) Russian defeat increased unrest at home and led to the 1905 revolution.
4. (a) Bloody Sunday provoked a wave of strikes that spread across the country. (b) forced czar to promise more freedom and approve creation of a Russian parliament
5. Recurring defeats in battle, the death of many soldiers, and acute shortages led to bread riots and strikes that forced Nicholas to abdicate.
6. (a) chose leaders to act as provisional government (b) more powerful locally than provisional government (c) led provisional government
7. Russian army was no more willing to fight for provisional government than for the czar.
8. Russia was ripe for revolution. On the other hand, if Nicholas had not chosen to enter World War I and had worked closely with the Duma, he might have further split the revolutionaries and avoided being overthrown.

Independent Practice
Assign Independent Practice Worksheet 28.2.

Enrichment Activities

1. **Reading a Primary Source** Assign Voices from the Past Resource Book 28.2.
2. **Creative Writing** Ask advanced students to write a report speculating on what might have happened if Nicholas II had agreed to share power with the Duma.
3. **Researching for Bonus Points** Award bonus points to students who can find the answer to

this question: What was Rasputin's full name? (Grigori Efimovitch Rasputin)

The Bolsheviks led a second revolution. 3

Section Objectives

After completing Section 3, students should be able to:

1. explain how Lenin and the Bolsheviks came to power in 1917.
2. locate lands Russia lost in World War I.
3. explain how Stalin defeated Trotsky for control of the Communist party.

Setting the Stage

Read the following description of Lenin, written by M.J. Olgin in 1924 for the *New York Times*.

> There is nothing remarkable in the appearance of this man—a typical Russian with rather irregular features; a stern but not unkindly expression; something crude in manner and dress, recalling the artisan rather than the intellectual and the thinker. You would ordinarily pass by a man of this kind without noticing him at all. Yet, had you happened to look into his eyes or to hear his public speech, you would not be likely to forget him.

Call on students to identify the character traits mentioned by Olgin. As students read, ask how Olgin's description compares with the material on Lenin in the text.

Teaching Strategies

Writing about History: The Bolsheviks Seize Power (Objective 1) Before beginning the section, write the following statement on the chalkboard: In a revolution, the people rise up spontaneously and take control of government. By a show of hands, determine how many students think this is an accurate statement about revolutions in general. How many think it is not accurate? Record the results next to the statement on the chalkboard. Then assign students to read "The Bolsheviks gained support" and "Lenin took control" (pages 612–614). Based on this reading, have students write paragraphs supporting or qualifying the statement. Call on volunteers to read their paragraphs aloud. Based on events in the Russian Revolution how would students describe the concept of "revolution as a process?"

Geography in History: Russia's Lost Lands (Objective 2) Distribute copies of Outline Map 23: Russia, show Overhead Transparency 67, *Europe after World War I,* or ask students to use the map on page 598 to label areas Russia lost at the end of World War I. Ask, "What territories were recognized as independent nations? What geographic advantage did Russia lose?" Then have students read "Lenin takes control" (pages 613–614). Ask "Why was Lenin unconcerned about the lost lands?"

Transferring Ideas: Stalin as a Dictator (Objective 3) After students have read "Two men struggled to succeed Lenin," reread aloud the following passage from the text: "Trotsky, however, had many enemies within the party. Some feared that he would become a dictator. They likened him to Napoleon in the French Revolution." Then tell students to review the description of Napoleon (pages 458–459). Ask "What traits did Trotsky and Napoleon share? Did Trotsky seem a likely candidate for dictator? Why or why not? How did Stalin manage to mask his own leanings toward dictatorship?"

Check for Understanding Explain the importance of these phrases: (a) "Peace, Land, and Bread" and (b) "dictatorship of the proletariat."

Practice

Guided Practice
Lead a guided discussion of the questions in the Section Review 3. (Answers are below.)

Define:
rule by a small group in the name of the people

Identify:
(a) commander-in-chief of Russian army who tried to seize power and was stopped by the Bolsheviks (b) truce between Russia and Germany (c) opponents of the Bolsheviks (d) army of the Bolsheviks (e) revolt of sailors (f) Lenin's policy calling for a temporary compromise with capitalism (g) name given to Russia by Bolsheviks (h) new name for Bolsheviks (i) founder of Red Army (j) successor to Lenin

Answer:
1. (a) not very popular with the peasants or workers (b) most tightly organized of all the parties

2. The Bolsheviks prevented Kornilov from taking over St. Petersburg and returning the czar. Party membership increased as the people viewed the Bolsheviks as protectors of the revolution.
3. Bolshevik Red Guards took over government offices. St. Petersburg Soviet ordered the arrest of leaders of the provisional government.
4. (a) ordered all farmland divided among the peasants (b) took over all major industries and let workers' councils run factories (c) closed the national assembly (d) signed truce with Germany
5. divided the country and left the economy in ruins
6. (a) used secret police to identify "enemies of the revolution" (b) began a New Economic Policy (NEP)
7. As party secretary, he placed many of his supporters in key positions; when Lenin died, most of the Communist leaders allied themselves with Stalin against Trotsky.
8. All Russians wanted the war to stop, peasants wanted the land to be divided; and all citizens wanted food to be more plentiful.

Independent Practice
Assign Independent Practice Worksheet 28.3.
Assign Basic Skills Worksheet 28.

Enrichment Activities

1. **Reading a Primary Source** Assign Voices from the Past Resource Book 28.3.
2. **Researching for Bonus Points** Award bonus points to students who can find the answer to the following question: What was the fate of Leon Trotsky? (He moved from country to country before settling in Mexico. From here, Trotsky continued to oppose Stalinism until he was killed by an unknown assassin in 1940.)

Answers to Voice from the Past

1. (a) Bolsheviks (b) from his words; is a Marxian student but not a Bolshevik
2. The Germans were backing Lenin and the Bolsheviks, and the revolution was pro-German anarchy and not pro-proletariat.
3. that there are only two classes, the proletariat and the bourgeoisie, and that Lenin was a friend of the proletariat
4. the soldier; portrays the student as rude and arrogant, the soldier as a humble, simple man dedicated to the philosophy of Lenin

Stalin became dictator.

4

Section Objectives

After completing Section 4, students should be able to:

1. contrast the policies of Lenin and Stalin.
2. explain how Stalin transformed the Soviet economy.
3. describe how the Soviet Union became a totalitarian state.

Setting the Stage

Read the definition of *totalitarianism* from the text's Glossary: "A political system in which government has total control over the lives of individual citizens." Ask students to compare this type of government to a democracy. Then list on the chalkboard or on an overhead transparency the following characteristics of totalitarian governments, described by American historian Louis L. Snyder.

• One leader becomes the symbol of government and state.
• All opposition is suppressed.
• Informers and secret police help ensure the power of the dominant party.
• Propaganda, controlled by the government, glorifies the party's leadership.
• Party leaders appeal to nationalism to preserve the party's power.

As students study Section 4, have them list aspects of Stalin's rule that relate to these characteristics.

Teaching Strategies

Skill Building: Contrasting Points of View (Objective 1) To illustrate the change in political thinking after the takeover by Stalin, have students analyze the following passages.

(a) Of course, the socialist idea cannot be attained in one country alone. The workers and peasants who support the Soviet Government are only a fragment of [an] international army...struggling for the common cause of the...international socialist revolution.... [A]nd we can see how the socialist revolution is ripening in every country of the world....

N. Lenin, Report to the
Third Congress of the Soviets

(b) And what do we mean by the possibility of the victory of socialism in one country? We mean the possibility...of the proletariat assuming power and using that power to build a complete socialist society in our country,...but without the victory of the proletarian revolution in other countries....if it is incapable of achieving victory over the capitalist elements in its own economy ...?

J. Stalin, *Problems of
Leninism*

After students have studied the passages, ask them to identify the main difference between Lenin and Stalin on the question of a world-wide Communist revolution. What argument does Stalin use to support his view? Have students find information in the text (pages 616–617) describing Stalin's reasoning on this issue.

Economics and History: Transforming the Soviet Economy (Objective 2) To introduce Stalin's approach to developing the Soviet economy, read aloud two articles from the Soviet constitution of 1936, or "Stalin's Constitution."

ARTICLE 11. The economic life of the U.S.S.R. is defined and directed by the State plan of national economy in the interests of ... strengthening ... the independence of the U.S.S.R.

ARTICLE 12. Toil in the U.S.S.R. is an obligation and a matter of honor to each citizen who is fit for toil, according to the principle: "He who does not work does not eat." In the U.S.S.R. there is being realized the principle of socialism: "From each according to his ability, to each according to his toil."

Ask students to determine the purpose of Stalin's economic plans and his definition of work. Ask, "How might such an economic system affect individual freedoms?"

Have students interpret the following chart to determine to what extent Stalin succeeded in modernizing the Soviet economy.

Industrial Output in the Soviet Union

Industry	1932	1938
Coal	64,000,000 tons	132,000,000 tons
Oil	22,000,000 tons	32,000,000 tons
Pig Iron	6,000,000 tons	14,000,000 tons
Steel	6,000,000 tons	18,000,000 tons
Automobiles	23,000 units	211,000 units
Tractors	50,000 units	176,000 units

Have students assess the human cost of Stalin's economic programs (pages 617–618). Ask, "By what means did Stalin implement his new economy? Why did Soviet peasants resist collectivization and state control of the land? How did Stalin deal with worker dissent?"

Discussing History: Totalitarianism as a Way of Life. (Objective 3) To underscore the extent to which totalitarianism invades the life of a nation, read the following charge printed in a Soviet newspaper in Stalin's time: "Reactionary 'bourgeois tendencies' have been noted in Soviet circuses and persons responsible for it ought to be exposed." Explain that the reporter claimed to have seen what he called "ideologically empty...attractions." That is, he had observed circus performances offering pure entertainment similar to the "decayed circus art of capitalist countries." Ask students what Communist supporters believed circuses should do if not entertain people. Ask "Why was control of all aspects of life, including circuses, critical to the success of Stalin's regime?"

Check for Understanding Have students explain and give examples of totalitarianism.

Practice

Guided Practice
Lead a guided discussion of the questions in Section Review 4. (Answers are below.)

Define:
system of government in which a dictator or small group controls every part of the lives of its citizens

Identify:
Stalin's economic development plan

Answer:
1. Trotsky advocated world revolution; Stalin was only concerned with revolution in Russia.
2. **(a)** set specific production targets for each industry with his Five-Year Plans **(b)** replaced privately-owned farms with collective farms
3. total control of citizens, repression of dissenters
4. repressed all forms of religion, executed members of Communist party, used secret police to find dissenters
5. Look for references to rule by absolute power and lack of personal freedoms in both.

Independent Practice
Assign Independent Practice Worksheet 28.4.
Assign Critical Thinking Worksheet 28.

Enrichment Activities

1. **Reading a Primary Source** Assign Voices from the Past Resource Book 28.4.

2. **Relating Past to Present** Ask students to research and report on changes in the present-day Soviet Union that show a trend away from totalitarian government.

3. **Researching for Bonus Points** Award bonus points to students who can answer the following question: Who was the king of England when Stalin instituted his first Five-Year Plan? (King George V)

Concluding the Chapter

1. **Chapter Closer**
Ask students to identify three long-term causes of the decline of the czars' power and three immediate causes of the Bolshevik Revolution.

2. **Reteaching Activities**
   a. **Making a Time Line** Have students create a time line showing the major events covered in this chapter.
   b. **Identifying** Have students identify the roles of Lenin, Kornilov, the New Economic Policy, the Communist Party, and Stalin in the Bolshevik revolution.

Chapter Evaluation

Chapter Test 28 and Computer Test Bank Chapter 28 Test can be used to evaluate your students' understanding of this chapter.

Answers to Chapter Review 28

Reviewing the Facts
1. **a.** resign as ruler **b.** ruler with unlimited power **c.** belief that everything must be destroyed so new society can be created **d.** elected workers' council **e.** relating to government that controls citizens' lives
2. **a.** rebellion by Russian officers to win a written constitution **b.** believed revolutionary base would be peasants **c.** believed revolutionary base would be urban working class **d.** German philosopher who influenced Social Democrats **e.** Bolshevik leader who gained control of the

government **f.** follower of Lenin **g.** preferred to move slowly towards revolution **h.** last czar to rule Russia **i.** provoked a wave of strikes throughout the country **j.** first Russian parliament **k.** urged czarina to ignore demands for reform **l.** dominant figure in provisional government **m.** lost a power struggle to Stalin **n.** staged by naval officers to demand free elections, free speech, and abolition of secret police **o.** new name of Bolsheviks **p.** ruler after Lenin's death

3. **(a)** swore not to reform **(b)** freed serfs **(c)** rejected reform **(d)** maintained autocracy
4. **(a)** middle class **(b)** The Social Revolutionaries wanted a democratically elected government. The Social Democrats wanted urban workers to revolt. **(c)** Bolsheviks and Mensheviks
5. **(a)** chose provisional government **(b)** allowed provisional government to rule **(c)** dominant figure in provisional government
6. **(a)** Opponents of Bolsheviks formed "White" armies to fight Red Army that won. **(b)** ruined economy
7. **(a)** Trotsky founded the Red Army. Stalin placed friends in important positions and was chosen Lenin's successor. **(b)** Trotsky believed in a world revolution. Stalin was only concerned with revolution inside Russia.

Basic Skills

1. **(a)** Decembrist revolt, freeing the serfs, Russo-Japanese war, revolution of 1905, St. Petersburg bread riots, abdication of Nicholas II **(b)** Decembrist revolt: reaction to lack of political rights of citizens; freeing of serfs: showed that protest could have impact on ruling family; Russo-Japanese war: led to more unrest, showed weakness of czar's government; 1905 revolution: demonstrated that demands of Russian people for more rights would not go away; bread riots: another sign of discontent and government's lack of concern for people; abdication: opened politics to newly formed soviets and various socialist groups who would lead 1917 revolution
2. **(a)** Poland, Finland, Estonia, Latvia, Lithuania **(b)** much unrest among Russian people; Prussia lost her window on the sea and lands closest to western Europe. One result was thus to isolate Russia.

Researching and Reporting Skills
Students' answers will vary.

Critical Thinking
1. Possible answer: The war may have precipi-

tated the final fall of the Russian government, but conditions within the country were the most important factor in the breakdown. The people were disheartened and felt no personal stake in fighting for a government that gave them so little in return for their efforts.

2. **(a)** Lenin: provided strong leadership, consolidated Bolshevik power, organized Red Guard units, captured imagination of public, organized first Communist government, created New Economic Policy, and formed autonomous republics; Trotsky: organizer of 1917 takeover, founded Red Army **(b)** The work of both men was essential. Trotsky led Bolshevik takeover in 1917 when the party's popular support was still low, and he was instrumental in defending the revolution against those who sought its overthrow. However, Lenin was the leader who inspired the people. He organized and conceptualized the new government, forced out opposition, and was adept at adjusting economic and political policy to deal with realities such as NEP and the formation of autonomous republics.
3. **(a)** original goals: rural socialism, distribution of land among peasants, democratically elected government **(b)** Stalin was more concerned with industrial growth; abolished private farms and created collectives, established ruthless dictatorship instead of democracy.
4. **(a)** Lenin adapted from Marx the political and economic ideas of the dictatorship of the proletariat, the start of revolution among urban workers, class conflict, and state ownership of the means of production. **(b)** by leading the workers in revolt, making them the care of the new government, taking over factories for the government, and giving the workers political control.
5. **(a)** to develop USSR's economy **(b)** industrial growth in all parts of country but especially in Siberia; production targets; abolition of private farms **(c)** enormous industrial gains, increased production of energy, increase in farm production
6. powerful secret police, religious repression, execution of party members in disfavor, complete control of workers' lives, censorship

Perspectives on Past and Present
Students' answers will vary.

Investigating History
Students' answers will vary.

Shifts in World Power

Advance Planner

Chapter 29	Shifts in World Power 1900–1939			★ Advanced
Focus	The role of nationalism in independence movements and wars of rebellion			● Basic

	Section 1	**Section 2**	**Section 3**	**Section 4**
Objectives	1. Identify the contributing causes of the Indian independence movement and trace its spread. 2. Describe and evaluate Gandhi's contributions to Indian independence. 3. Contrast the views of Hindu and Muslim nationalists.	1. Locate the Middle East on a map and describe the Middle East as a geographic and cultural region. 2. Compare and contrast the nationalist movements in Turkey, Persia, and Arabia. 3. Explain the sources of Jewish nationalism and of the conflict between Arab nationalists and Zionists. 4. Identify foreign interests in the Middle East.	1. Describe the role of the United States in Latin American Affairs during the early twentieth century. 2. Identify factors affecting the economies of Latin American countries.	1. Compare and contrast the aims and achievements of China's three great nationalist leaders. 2. Explain the outcomes of China's civil war in the 1930's.
Setting the Stage	Indian resentment of British rule	Using Geographic Themes: Region	Political traditions in Latin America	Reasons China rejected western models of government
Teaching Strategies	Skill Building: Identifying Causes Discussing History: Gandhi and Nonviolence Transferring Ideas: Hindu-Muslim Conflict Check for Understanding	Skill Building: Organizing Information in a Chart Discussing History: Zionism Writing about History: Foreign Interests in the Middle East Check for Understanding	Discussing History: The United States in Latin America Economics and History: What Weakens a Nation's Economy? Check for Understanding	Skill Building: Comparing and Contrasting Nationalist Leaders Skill Building: Making Predictions Check for Understanding
Guided Practice	Section Review 1	Section Review 2	Section Review 3	Section Review 4
Independent Practice Worksheets	Independent Practice 29.1 Vocabulary 29	Independent Practice 29.2	Independent Practice 29.3 Basic Skills 29	Independent Practice 29.4 Critical Thinking 29 Geography Skills 29
Enrichment	1. Primary Source: Voices 29.1 2. ★ Relating Past and Present 3. Researching for Points	1. Primary Source: Voices 29.2 2. Preparing a Report 3. Researching for Points	1. Primary Source: Voices 29.3 2. Researching for Points	1. Primary Source: Voices 29.4 2. Researching for Points

Chapter Closer ● **Reteaching Activities**	Summarizing, Comparing
Chapter Review	Summary, Reviewing the Facts, Basic Skills, Researching and Reporting Skills, Critical Thinking, Perspectives on Past and Present, Investigating History
Chapter Evaluation	Chapter Test 29, Computer Test Bank Chapter 29 Test

Chapter Overview

Chapter 29 discusses developments in India, Latin America, the Middle East, and China between 1900 and the outbreak of World War II. During that time, Indian nationalists in the Congress party and followers of Mohandas Gandhi began to challenge British rule. Turkey, Persia, Arabia, and Palestine sought self-rule. The new nations of Iran, Saudi Arabia, and the Republic of Turkey made different choices in entering them modern world. In Palestine, the conflict between Jews and Arabs over a homeland intensified. After ten years of revolution and civil war, Mexico developed a stable republic. Latin American nation-building was slowed by factionalism, economic problems, and foreign intervention. Chinese nationalists overthrew the Ch'ing dynasty. Civil war erupted as the Nationalists and the Communists vied for control of China.

Key Terms

shaykh, nationalized
For additional exercises, see Vocabulary Worksheet 29.

Chapter Focus

Ask students to define nationalism and to explain its role in independence movements and in wars of rebellion they have studied previously. Students might link nationalism with the rise of nations in Europe at the end of the Middle Ages; the American war of independence; the French Revolution; the unifications of Italy, Greece, and Germany; and the Latin American independence movements of the nineteenth century. Tell students that this chapter focuses on the role of nationalism in independence movements and civil conflicts of the early twentieth century in India, the Middle East, Latin America, and China.

Indians organized for independence. 1

Section Objectives

After completing Section 1, students should be able to:

1. identify the contributing causes of the Indian independence movement and trace its spread.

2. describe and evaluate Gandhi's contributions to Indian independence.
3. contrast the views of Hindu and Muslim nationalists.

Setting the Stage

Refer students to the map on page 543, "Imperialism in India and Southeast Asia, 1900." Point out the extent of British colonial rule. Ask students to recall the positive and negative effects of three hundred years of British rule on the Indian people. Ask, "Why did the Indians resent the British? What were some signs of growing Indian nationalism?" Students should recall the founding of the Indian National Congress in 1885 and of the Muslim League in 1906. Tell students that after World War I, Indian public protests increased, and that this section describes India's road to independence under the leadership and inspiration of its hero, Mohandas Gandhi.

Teaching Strategies

Skill Building: Identifying Causes (Objective 1) Write the following sentence fragment on the chalkboard: "… marked the beginning of the end of the British Raj." List on the board students' suggestions for completing the sentence. Students might suggest the rise of Indian nationalism, Gandhi's leadership in the nationalist movement, the Amritsar massacre, the Rowlatt Act, and the Government of India acts. In each case, have students explain how the situation or event contributed to the erosion of British rule in India.

Discussing History: Gandhi and Nonviolence (Objective 2) Ask students why Gandhi was named *Mahatma* and what the poet Rabindranath Tagore meant by "great soul." Have students give examples of Gandhi's application of each of his philosophical principles to the way he conducted his life (page 624).

Point out that Gandhi's strategy for achieving *swaraj* emphasized economic self-reliance and nonviolence. Ask, "How could Indians become economically self-reliant?" (by meeting their own needs while refusing to participate in the British-run economy). "How could Indians gain power through nonviolence?" Point out that Gandhi's fasting and voluntary imprisonment were expressions of passive resistance. Gandhi defined passive resistance as a means of winning rights through personal suffering rather than through force of arms. Refusing to pay taxes, to observe segregation laws, or to attend courts were examples of

civil disobedience. Gandhi referred to civil disobedience as the use of "soul-force" in refusing to
act against one's conscience, regardless of the
consequences. Invite students to express their
opinions of Gandhi's views. Ask, "What made nonviolence a potent moral force? In what aspect of
Indian politics were Gandhi's strategies least effective?" (in uniting Hindus and Muslims)

Transferring Ideas: Hindu-Muslim Conflict (Objective 3) Ask students to recall the historical
precedents for Hindu-Muslim conflict. Students
should be able to trace this conflict to Muslim
invasions of India in the eighth, tenth, and twelfth
centuries, and to the ensuing 400 years of Muslim
domination (pages 287–291). Remind students of
the charts they developed in Chapter 13 contrasting Hindu and Muslim beliefs. Students might
extend the contrast by adding information in this
section to their charts.

Point out that the British used the conflict
between the Hindus and the Muslims to secure
their control over India. In addition, the British
contributed to the conflict by favoring Hindus and
Sikhs for military and government posts and for
social and economic privileges. Conclude by asking students to predict the possible outcomes of
the conflict described in this section between
Hindu and Muslim nationalists.

Check for Understanding Have students identify
the main causes, leaders, strategies, and goals of
the Indian independence movement.

Practice

Guided Practice
Lead a guided discussion of the questions in Section Review 1. (Answers are below.)

Define:
(a) self-rule (b) Gandhi's name for untouchables
(c) Indian name for Ghandi (d) civil disobedience

Identify:
(a) British slaughter of Indians (b) mostly Hindu
national group (c) Muslim nationalist group
(d) leader in Indian independence movement

Answer:
1. (a) original goal was to win equal opportunities
   for Indians in the civil service; by 1935, was
   committed to gaining independence (b) Most
   Indians were uninterested in politics.
2. live simply, be tolerant, serve others, battle
   injustice in nonviolent way
3. (a) Indians put aside nationalism and fought
   with Britain against Germans. (b) made cooperation with Britain impossible

4. use civil disobedience
5. (a) Muslims: one God; all believers equal; Hindus: God manifest in many forms, castes not
   equal (b) wanted the Hindus and Muslims to
   unite (c) separate Muslim nation
6. (a) allowed home rule (b) Congress party was
   committed to full independence; Muslim
   League would settle only for separate Muslim
   nation.
7. Possible answers: personal identification,
   ease of civil disobedience, appeal of belief in
   equality

Independent Practice
Assign Independent Practice Worksheet 29.1.
Assign Vocabulary Worksheet 29.

Enrichment Activities

1. **Reading a Primary Source** Assign Voices from
   the Past Resource Book 29.1.

2. **Relating Past and Present** Ask advanced students to write essays linking the leaders, goals,
   and strategies of the Indian independence
   movement with those of the American civil
   rights movement of the 1950's and 1960's.

3. **Researching for Bonus Points** Award bonus
   points to students who can answer the following questions: What was the Dandi Salt
   March? What was its purpose and its result?
   (Gandhi walked 241 miles from Ahmedabad to
   the sea at Dandi to protest the British salt tax.
   As a result, Indians practiced civil disobedience by distilling salt from sea water rather
   than pay the tax.)

Answers to Voice from the Past

1. to acquire greater self control and inner calm,
   trust one another, consider all as equals
2. stop serving and drinking alcoholic beverages;
   spin cloth at home; wear traditional khadi.
3. division between Muslims and Hindus and
   among castes
4. emphasized moral and spiritual changes

Nationalism spread to the Middle East. 2

Section Objectives

After completing Section 2, students should be
able to:

1. locate the Middle East on a map and describe the Middle East as a geographic and cultural region.
2. compare and contrast the nationalist movements in Turkey, Persia, and Arabia.
3. explain the sources of Jewish nationalism and of the conflict between Arab nationalists and Zionists.
4. identify foreign interests in the Middle East.

Setting the Stage

Using Geographic Themes: Region (Objective 1) Show students a physical map of the Middle East. Explain that the Middle East is a geographic and cultural region that includes the Anatolian peninsula, the lands bordering the eastern Mediterranean and the Tigris-Euphrates, the Arabian peninsula, and the Persian plain. Ask why this region is named the Middle East. Students might note its central location on the Eurasian continent, but point out that Europeans gave the region its name, identifying its location in relation to Europe and to the "Far East."

Review the geographic themes of region and movement, and have students suggest reasons for the integrity of the Middle East as a region. Historically, it was a crossroads for cultural diffusion between Asia and both Africa and Europe. The map on page 177, *The Spread of Islam,* illustrates this point. Note that geographically and culturally, North Africa is part of the Middle East region.

Refer students to the Historical Atlas map, *The World about 1900* (pages 816–817), and ask them to name the territories outside of North Africa that were part of the Middle East at that time. (Arabia, the Ottoman Empire, and Persia) Tell students that this section describes nationalist movements in these territories after 1900.

Teaching Strategies

Discussing History: Zionism (Objective 2) Ask students to explain the reasons for Jewish nationalism. (centuries of exile and persecution) Ask, "How did the Dreyfus case and the Balfour Declaration stimulate the Jewish nationalist movement?" Students should recognize that the Dreyfus case symbolized anti-Jewish prejudice, and that the Balfour Declaration symbolized hopes for a Jewish homeland. Ask, "Why were Arab nationalists opposed to Zionism?" Clarify that Arab opposition was not the result of religious hatred. Muslims regarded Moses as a prophet of Allah and studied the Old Testament as well as the Koran. Arabs and Jews shared a common ancestral language and culture.

Writing about History: Foreign Interests in the Middle East (Objective 3) Have students assess the role of the British in the Palestinian conflict. Ask, "Why was Britain fearful of alienating the Arabs?" Explain that the Arabs controlled a vital strategic resource—oil. The United States, the Soviet Union, and the nations of Europe had economic interests in the Middle East. Ask students to write essays using the information in this section to answer the following question: Why were foreign powers anxious to maintain political stability in the Middle East?

Check for Understanding Ask students to name five significant changes that occurred in the Middle East after World War I.

Practice

Guided Practice
Lead a guided discussion of the questions in Section Review 2. (Answers are below.)

Define:
(a) land governed on behalf of the League of Nations (b) leader of a Bedouin group (c) socialist farm community

Identify:
(a) region that stretches from Turkey to Afghanistan (b) first president of Turkey (c) modernized Persia and changed its name to Iran (d) proclaimed himself king of nation he renamed Saudi Arabia (e) Jewish nationalist movement (f) ambiguous document on issue of Jewish homeland in Palestine

Answer:
1. (a) Scientific Revolution and the Industrial Revolution had made little impact. (b) Ottomans lost control of all their lands outside present-day Turkey; Great Britain and France each received some countries as mandates.
2. (a) Turkish nationalists overthrew the Ottoman emperor. (b) wanted to modernize Turkey; examples: gave women equal rights, set up secular courts and schools
3. (a) aimed to modernize nation and give women more rights (b) Shah kept all power.
4. (a) nomadic herders, lived in family groups with a shaykh at head (b) overthrew local ruling families, united neighboring shaykhs into Saudi Arabia, and held to Islamic and Arab traditions
5. (a) Palestine would be a Jewish homeland. (b) in response to anti-Jewish feeling in Europe
6. demands of Arabs and Jews for own country, Arab-Jewish conflict

7. Countries' drilling rights; foreign countries soon controlled oil industry.
8. **(a)** probably Mustafa Kemal, who tried to adopt democratic, Western ways **(b)** probably Ibn Saud, who retained Muslim traditions

Independent Practice
Assign Independent Practice Worksheet 29.2.

Enrichment Activities

1. **Reading a Primary Source** Assign Voices from the Past Resource Book 29.2.

2. **Preparing a Report** Ask interested students to prepare reports on one of the following related topics: Ataturk's reforms, the role of T.E. Lawrence in the unification of Arabia, the organization and spread of *kibbutzim*, the life and times of Theodor Herzl, and the history of early oil exploration in the Middle East.

3. **Researching for Bonus Points** Assign bonus points to students who can answer the following question: In what year was the first Jewish settlement established in Palestine, and who were its founders? (1882; Russian Jews)

Latin America faced difficult changes. 3

Section Objectives

After reading Section 3, students should be able to:

1. describe the role of the United States in Latin American affairs during the early twentieth century.
2. identify factors affecting the economies of Latin American countries.

Setting the Stage

Refer students to the map on page 502 and review the political problems Latin Americans faced after independence. Ask students to characterize Latin American governments. Suggest that Latin Americans lacked a tradition of democratic values and institutions. They looked to strong dictators, generals, or wealthy landowners to help them achieve unity and progress. Many dictators were reluctant to share power, to plan for succession to power, or to tolerate power in the hands of citizens. In many countries, rebellions and *coups* became a pattern of political change leading to political instability. Tell students that this section focuses on Mexico's struggles to achieve a more democratic government.

Teaching Strategies

Discussing History: The United States in Latin America (Objective 1) Recall the provisions of the Monroe Doctrine (page 504) and of the Roosevelt Corollary (page 553). Ask students to identify United States interests in Latin America. Emphasize that the defense of American property, businesses, and business investments was used to justify military intervention. Point out that American interests centered in Central America and the Caribbean. The United States intervened in Cuba's war of independence from Spain and in the Mexican Revolution. Between 1898 and 1933, the United States took possession of Cuba, Puerto Rico, and the Virgin Islands, ran the economies of Nicaragua, Haiti, and the Dominican Republic, and occupied the Canal Zone in Panama.

Ask students, "Why was the United States anxious to control and protect the Panama Canal?" Students should recall the strategic location of the Panama Canal (page 552) and its great commercial and military value. Conclude by asking how United States policies toward Latin America changed during the 1930's. Students should recall the aims of the Good Neighbor Policy.

Economics and History: What Weakens a Nation's Economy? (Objective 2) Ask students to identify economic indicators that show the strength or weakness of a nation's economy, and list their suggestions on the chalkboard. Then have students find information in the text describing economic conditions in Latin America in the early 1900's.

Help students to understand the basis for the poverty of many Latin American nations: foreign ownership of land and resources, resulting in the drain of profits; reliance on foreign investments, resulting in loss of control over economic policies; dependence on loans from foreign banks, resulting in increased national debt; and the lack of economic diversification, resulting in a dependence on foreign imports to meet basic needs and in a consequent drain of capital.

Explain that countries relying on a single resource were vulnerable not only to changes in the demand for that resource on the world market, but also to competition from other countries that specialized in that resource. Latin American countries could not easily help each other to grow through trade because they were in competition with each other to export the same few products.

Conclude by asking students to infer the characteristics of a strong economy.

Check for Understanding Ask students to name two results of the Mexican Revolution and two results of American intervention in Latin American affairs.

Practice

Guided Practice
Lead a guided discussion of the questions in Section Review 3. (Answers are below.)

Define:
(a) political strongman (b) to bring under government control

Identify:
(a) Mexico's ruler from 1876 to 1911 (b) Mexican leader who instituted many reforms (c) warning to Europe to keep hands off Latin America (d) policy that gave the United States the role of international police officer in the Americas (e) policy in which United States promised to respect rights of Latin America

Answer:
1. (a) political isolation, rule by corrupt caudillos (b) foreign ownership of businesses, dependence on exports
2. (a) economic progress, but no benefits to peasants and factory workers; controlled elections (b) as result of revolution
3. breakup of estates, protective labor code, rules for foreign investments, limits on Catholic Church
4. Obregón put into effect many ideas of 1917 constitution.
5. United States sent in marines or supported dictators to protect American business interests.
6. Good Neighbor Policy led to withdrawing troops.
7. When the price of that resource fell on the world market, the economy of the country collapsed.
8. Students should note that a nation cannot be politically independent unless it is economically independent.

Independent Practice
Assign Independent Practice Worksheet 29.3.
Assign Basic Skills Worksheet 29.

Enrichment Activities

1. **Reading a Primary Source** Assign Voices from the Past Resource Book 29.3.

2. **Researching for Bonus Points** Award bonus points to students who can answer the following question: Who were Pancho Villa and Francisco Madero and what were their roles in the Mexican Revolution? (a bandit cowboy and wayward revolutionary who stole from the rich to give to the poor; President of Mexico from 1911 to 1913 after Diaz' fall, whose weak leadership furthered the civil war)

China overthrew its emperor.

4

Section Objectives

After completing Section 4, students should be able to:

1. compare and contrast the aims and achievements of China's three great nationalist leaders.
2. explain the outcomes of China's civil war in the 1930's.

Setting the Stage

Ask students to recall reasons for the rise of nationalism in China (pages 546–547). Then tell students that the outcomes of World War I gave the Chinese more compelling reasons to reject western models of government. Ask students to find out these reasons as they read. Show students Overhead Transparency 74, *East Asia,* and have them compare the present-day People's Republic of China with colonial China in the early 1900's (page 546). Tell students that this section explains how China's struggle for independent nationhood began.

Teaching Strategies

Skill Building: Comparing and Contrasting Nationalist Leaders (Objective 1) Have students develop charts comparing and contrasting the roles and aims of Sun Yatsen, Chiang Kai-shek, and Mao Tse-Tung. Charts should be organized in terms of the following categories: "Party," "Main Goals," "Main Achievements." (Sun Yat-sen: Kuomintang; independence, nationalism, democracy, socialism; overthrew Ch'ing dynasty, established Republic of China, sided with the Allies in World War I. Chiang Kai-shek: Nationalist; defeat the warlords and unite China, prevent Chinese

Communist party from gaining power, modernize China; unification of China, defeat of Chinese Communists, establishment of the Nationalist Republic of China, improvement of urban economy. Mao Tse-tung: Communist; Communist revolution, economic reforms for workers and rural peasants; established Red Army, fought guerrilla war against Nationalists, survived the Long March.)

Skill Building: Making Predictions (Objective 2) Ask students to describe the effects of China's civil war. Students might note that the Red Army was forced to retreat and that Japan exploited China's disunity by invading Manchuria. Point out that the outcome was inconclusive. Ask, "What events had caused the Nationalists and the Communists to join forces during the course of their struggle?" (warlords' opposition to nationalism, Japan's invasion of Manchuria) Have students give reasons supporting their predictions in answer to the following questions: What effect do you think World War II had on the civil war in China? On what side do you think China fought? Which party, the Nationalists or the Communists, do you think gained more followers during World War II? Which party do you think the United States supported?

Check for Understanding Have students write short essays beginning with the following topic sentence: During the early 1900's, China's nation-building efforts were torn by rival nationalist movements.

Practice

Guided Practice
Lead a guided discussion of the questions in Section Review 4. (Answers are below.)

Identify:
(a) founder and leader of Kuomintang (b) Communist leader (c) established Republic of China (d) wanted to unite China under Nationalists (e) journey Red Army made to escape Chian'g forces

Answer:
1. (a) nationalism, people's rights, livelihood (b) civil war, famine, breakdown of transportation
2. Allies did not give up territories and commercial interests; Japan kept territory seized during war.
3. Lenin sent military advisors and equipment to the Nationalists.
4. (a) He feared they would take over government. (b) killed Communists

5. (a) In cities, it set up new factories and businesses, updated China's laws, and opened new schools and hospitals. (b) Government became less democratic and more corrupt and did nothing to improve life for peasants.
6. Mao felt that peasants, not urban workers, could be the true revolutionaries and that revolution could take place in rural country.
7. (a) guerrilla warfare (b) divided land; had soldiers help farmers (c) Mao fled with Red Army to escape Chiang's army. Mao gained followers.
8. (a) by attacking Manchuria (b) Chiang used resources to fight Mao; Mao fought Japanese.
9. In guerrilla warfare, the army is dependent on people in the area for food, water, information. Without the people, soldiers would die.

Independent Practice
Assign Independent Practice Worksheet 29.4.
Assign Critical Thinking Worksheet 29.
Assign Geography Skills Worksheet 29.

Enrichment Activities

1. **Reading a Primary Source** Assign Voices from the Past Resource Book 29.4.

2. **Researching for Bonus Points** Award bonus points to students who can answer this question: What do the acronyms KMT and CCP stand for? (Kuomintang; Chinese Communist Party)

Concluding the Chapter

1. **Chapter Closer**
   Ask students to compare and contrast the expressions of nationalism in India, the Middle East, Latin America, and China. In what ways were nationalist movements generally similar throughout the world, and in what ways were they different?

2. **Reteaching Activities**
   a. **Summarizing** Have students convert each heading in this section into a question and then answer each question by writing a summarizing sentence.
   b. **Comparing** Write "Nationalists" and "Communists" on the chalkboard. Have students find information in the text that explains the differences between the two parties.

3. **Chapter Review Activities**
   Assign Chapter Review 29 activities.

Chapter Evaluation

Chapter Test 29 and Computer Test Bank Chapter 29 Test can be used to evaluate your students' understanding of this chapter.

Answers to Chapter Review 29

Reviewing the Facts

1. **a.** leader of Bedouin family group **b.** to bring under governmental control
2. **a.** primarily Hindu nationalist group which demanded self-rule **b.** wanted a separate Muslim nation **c.** founder of modern Turkey **d.** leader who modernized Persia and changed its name to Iran **e.** leader who kept Islamic traditions and united Saudi Arabia **f.** belief that Israel is the Jewish homeland **g.** British document that laid foundation for conflict between Arabs and Jews **h.** strongman who ruled as a dictator in Latin America **i.** Mexico's ruler who brought economic progress to Mexico **j.** Mexican leader who instituted many reforms **k.** policy affirming United States respect for rights of Latin American countries **l.** founder and leader of China's Nationalist People's party **m.** Chinese Communist leader **n.** leader of Chinese Nationalist party **o.** retreat of Mao to escape Chiang's forces
3. **(a)** independence **(b)** separate Muslim nation
4. changed from military and political intervention to Good Neighbor policy
5. **(a)** Nationalist party overthrew Ch'ing dynasty. **(b)** civil war, famine, pillaging
6. **(a)** Because many Chinese felt humiliated by treatment at Versailles, they broke with the West and embraced communism. **(b)** distrusted the Communists.

Basic Skills

1. **(a)** drastic decline **(b)** policy kept industry in ruling nation; possession provided new materials and brought back finished goods. **(c)** Gandhi's focus on spinning and wearing homespun was a protest against British policy, since Britain couldn't keep people from spinning and weaving by hand.
2. mastery over themselves, trust for one another, abolishment of untouchable class, outlawing of alcoholic drinks, and use of homespun cloth instead of imported cloth

Researching and Reporting Skills

Students' answers will vary.

Critical Thinking

1. In general, India and the countries of the Middle East were seeking independence from the colonial rule of Britain or France. China and the Latin American countries had already achieved independence from colonial rule but were now faced with internal battles. Authoritarian governments ignored the needs of the people and continued to prevent the establishment of democratically elected governments.
2. **(a)** nonviolence, peaceful refusal to cooperate with British rule, boycotts of British goods, refusal to pay taxes, refusal to obey British laws or attend British courts. **(b)** It was an effective approach because the Indian people did not have the resources to compete with British and military might. Also, because the protest was nonviolent, Britain was at a loss in dealing with it.
3. **(a)** Both Turkey and Iran expanded public education, gave women more rights, and fostered economic growth. Turkey also broke connection between church and state and replaced Islamic law with secular law. Saudi Arabia was slower to modernize and tried to keep traditional ways. **(b)** Islam, lack of education; Saudi Arabia held to Islamic tradition; Ibn Saud ruled country like shaykhdom; laws of Islam were same as laws of state; women had few rights; government frowned on modern technology
4. **(a)** persecution in such places as Eastern Europe and Russia; anti-Jewish sentiment in many Western countries **(b)** Jews and Palestinian Arabs both felt that they had been promised their own country by the British.
5. **(a)** Peasants and factory workers had few rights and lived and worked in terrible conditions; lack of free elections; foreign ownership of businesses; wealth of Catholic church and its alliance with rich and powerful **(b)** Under Obregon, some reforms accomplished: villages took over lands from landlords; public schools were established; and free elections were held.
6. **(a)** Mao believed that revolution could start in a rural setting and be led by peasants. Marx and Lenin were convinced that revolution would be in the cities and led by workers. **(b)** By dividing land among local farmers, having soldiers help with harvest.

Perspectives on Past and Present

Possible answers: **(a)** Fidel Castro, Nasser, Daniel Ortega, Nkrumah **(b)** land reform, control of foreign businesses and political influence, improved education, better living conditions

Investigating History

Students' answers will vary.

The Years between the Wars

Chapter Overview

In the years after World War I, the countries of Europe faced serious economic problems which contributed to political instability. Germany suffered from runaway inflation and massive war debts. However, by the 1920's the European nations had begun to recover. The decade of the 1920's saw great changes in technology, science, and the arts.

The Great Depression of the 1930's brought on new political crises and a loss of faith in democratic government. When the Fascist and Nazi parties gained control of the German government, their leaders, Mussolini and Hitler, began to test their strength against the Western democracies. In response to aggressive action, Britain and France pursued a policy of appeasement, and the United States continued its policy of isolationism.

Key Terms

coalition, isolationism, fascism, appeasement
For additional exercises, see Vocabulary Worksheet 30.

Chapter Focus

Begin by having students read the opening section, which describes the German inflation of 1923. Ask them how they would feel if this sort of extreme inflation happened today. What would they would do if they had to pay for food with wheelbarrows full of money? Who or what would they blame for such a disaster? Then have them imagine that the inflation is taking place only five years after a catastrophic war, in which their country was defeated.

Tell students that 1923 was called the Year of Hunger in Germany. Many Germans despised their new democratic government for having signed the Versailles Treaty. In bitterness and despair, they longed for radical change. Some flocked to the Communist party. Others looked to the Nazis, who were led by Adolf Hitler. The Nazis promised to tear up the Versailles Treaty and to make Germany a great power once again. Point out that in 1923 the Nazis made their first abortive bid for power, the "Beer Hall *Putsch*" in Munich.

Note that the mark regained its former value in 1924, and the crisis ended for a time. However, in 1929 Germany was plunged into the Great Depression, along with the rest of the world. More Germans looked to the Communists or to the Nazis for salvation. Tell students that this chapter explains how Europe achieved an unsteady recovery after World War I, but then collapsed under the impact of the Depression and began to move toward a second world war.

Europe recovered from World War I. 1

Section Objectives

After completing Section 1, students should be able to:

1. analyze Europe's political and economic difficulties faced in recovering from World War I.
2. describe the steps taken to achieve permanent peace in Europe.

Setting the Stage

Remind students that the victory of 1918 was won at a terrible price for the Allies in Europe. The cost was greatest for France. About 1,400,000 men, one-tenth of the adult male population, had perished in the war. Almost every family was in mourning. About 750,000 men had been wounded, many so badly that they were unfit for any kind of work. The streets were filled with casualties. The northeastern part of the country, which contained the richest agricultural land and mining and industrial areas, was heavily damaged. Explain that although France recovered after the war, these losses prevented it from ever fully regaining its former position in world affairs. Tell students that this section shows how Europe emerged from the carnage of World War I.

Teaching Strategies

Economics and History: Inflation (Objective 1)
Ask students to recall the definition of inflation.

Lesson Planner • Chapter 30   **T305**

Then ask, "Why do prices rise faster at some times and more slowly at others?" Explain the difference between an inflated economy and inflated currency. Define monetary inflation as an increase in the amount of money available and a corresponding decrease in its value. Monetary inflation contributes to general inflation by causing a rise in prices. Prices rise even higher if there are shortages in the supply of goods. Point out that inflation often occurs after a political or economic shock. The inflation of the 1970s, for example, was spurred by a rise in oil prices in 1973. Explain that the extreme inflation of 1923 in Germany came as a result of a major shock. In that year Germany failed to keep up its reparation payments to France. In retaliation, the French seized control of the western part of Germany. The German government told the people who lived in this area not to go to work or to cooperate with the French in any way. To support them, the government printed and distributed massive quantities of paper money. With this huge increase in the volume of money, prices began to skyrocket.

Explain that by the end of 1923, four trillion marks equaled the value of a United States dollar. In other words, the mark was essentially worthless. Germans lost all their savings. The only people who benefited were debtors, who could repay their debts in worthless currency. Students might be surprised to learn that the biggest debtors were wealthy businessmen, who had borrowed to invest in their companies.

Discussing History: The "Spirit of Locarno" (Objective 2) Have students read the section "Treaties raised hopes for peace" (pages 644–645). Explain that in 1925 many Europeans fervently hoped that peace would be permanent; almost everyone dreaded the possibility of another world war. The Locarno Pact was an attempt to reduce tensions between Germany, France, and Britain. Tell them that France wanted to make Germany accept the Versailles Treaty as permanent. The French foreign minister, Aristide Briand, knew that as long as the Germans resented Versailles, it would only be a matter of time before they sought revenge. The danger was especially great since Germany's rapidly growing population of 60 million outnumbered France's population of 40 million.

Ask students to recall the terms of the Versailles Treaty: Germany had to pay reparations and declare that it was solely responsible for World War I. French and British leaders hoped that Germany could be reconciled to the Treaty if it was admitted to the League of Nations. Ask, "Was this a reasonable expectation?"

Check for Understanding Ask students to identify the main cause and the main effect of Germany's inflation in the 1920's.

Practice

Guided Practice
Lead a guided discussion of the questions in Section Review 1. (Answers are below.)

Define:
(a) sharp drop in value of currency (b) temporary alliance to form a parliamentary majority

Advance Planner

	Section 1
Objectives	1. Analyze Europe's political and economic difficulties in recovering from World War I. 2. Describe the steps taken to achieve permanent peace in Europe.
Setting the Stage	France's losses in World War I
Teaching Strategies	Economics and History: Inflation Discussing History: The "Spirit of Locarno" Check for Understanding
Guided Practice	Section Review 1
Independent Practice Worksheets	Independent Practice 30.1 Vocabulary 30
Enrichment	1. Primary Source: Voices 20.1 2. Creative Writing 3. Researching for Points

Identify:
(a) postwar democratic government in Germany (b) financial plan to strengthen Germany's economy (c) pledge to renounce war

Answer:
1. European nations were nearly bankrupt; Japan and the United States, economically strong.
2. (a) Democratic government replaced absolute rulers. (b) Citizens had little experience with parliamentary government; many political parties made effective government difficult; coali-

tion governments did not provide leadership.
3. (a) lack of democratic traditions, too many political parties, new government bore the burden of defeat (b) skyrocketing inflation (c) Dawes Plan provided loan and rescheduled reparation payments.
4. (a) They signed a treaty promising not to make war against each other; Germany promised to respect the borders of France and Belgium. (b) Many countries signed the Kellogg-Briand peace pact and joined the League of Nations.
5. a cooperative spirit, which would encourage a lasting peace and economic cooperation

Chapter 30 The Years between the Wars 1919–1939			★ Advanced
Focus Inflation in Germany in 1923			● Basic

Section 2	**Section 3**	**Section 4**	**Section 5**
1. Identify Albert Einstein and explain his theory of relativity. 2. Write a generalization about the 1920's.	1. Identify weaknesses in the American economy that led to the Great Depression. 2. Describe the impact of the Depression on Europe. 3. Compare and contrast the responses to the Great Depression.	1. Compare and contrast the careers of Mussolini and Hitler. 2. Identify *Kristallnacht* and trace its causes and consequences. 3. Describe the impact of the Depression on Japan.	1. Define *appeasement* and explain why Britain and France followed this policy. 2. Locate the Axis powers on a map and identify the nations they invaded. 3. Evaluate the Munich Agreement.
Technological, social, and cultural changes in the United States after World War I	The effects of the stock market crash	The rise of new dictators in Europe	The philosophy of the League of Nations
Discussing History: Einstein's Theory of Relativity Skill Building: Making Generalizations Check for Understanding	Analyzing a Quotation: Overproduction and Unemployment Economics and History: A Global Depression Skill Building: Comparing Responses to the Depression Check for Understanding	Skill Building: Comparing Mussolini and Hitler Discussing History: The *Kristallnacht* Economics and History: The Impact of the Depression on Japan Check for Understanding	Discussing History: Appeasement Geography in History: Invasions of the Axis Powers Outline Map 2 Writing about History: The Munich Agreement Check for Understanding
Section Review 2 Independent Practice 30.2	Section Review 3 Independent Practice 30.3	Section Review 4 Independent Practice 30.4 Basic Skills 30	Section Review 5 Independent Practice 30.5 Geography Skills 30 Critical Thinking 30
1. Primary Source: Voices 30.2 2. ★ Researching a Topic: 3. Researching for Points	1. Primary Source: Voices 30.3 2. ★ Creative Writing 3. Researching for Points	1. Primary Source: Voices 30.4 2. Preparing a Report 3. Researching for Points	1. Primary Source: Voices 30.5 2. Creative Writing 3. Researching for Points

Chapter Closer	
● **Reteaching Activities**	Making a Time Line, Comparing and Contrasting, Identifying Main Ideas
Chapter Review	Summary, Reviewing the Facts, Basic Skills, Researching and Reporting Skills, Critical Thinking, Perspectives on Past and Present, Investigating History
Chapter Evaluation	Chapter Test 30, Computer Test Bank Chapter 30 Test

Independent Practice
Assign Independent Practice Worksheet 30.1.
Assign Vocabulary Worksheet 30.

Enrichment Activities

1. **Reading a Primary Source** Assign Voices from the Past Resource Book 30.1.

2. **Creative Writing** Have students imagine they are reporters assigned to cover the signing of the Kellogg-Briand peace pact in 1928. Have them write an imaginary report describing what took place at the signing and discussing the chances for the pact's success. Encourage students to read background information before writing their reports.

3. **Researching for Bonus Points** Award bonus points to students who can answer this question: Who was the President of the Weimar Republic from 1919 to 1925? (Friedrich Ebert)

Society faced rapid change. 2

Section Objectives

After completing Section 2, students should be able to:

1. identify Albert Einstein and explain his theory of relativity.
2. write a generalization about the 1920's.

Setting the Stage

Direct students' attention to the pictures on pages 645 and 647. Ask, "What kinds of changes do the pictures suggest?" Explain that the picture on page 645 shows the increasing importance of aircraft after World War I. The picture on page 647 shows the increasing prominence of women in politics. Point out that World War I played a major role in stimulating both technological and social changes. Tell students that this section describes important technological, social, and cultural changes that took place in the decade following World War I.

Teaching Strategies

Discussing History: Einstein's Theory of Relativity (Objective 1) Begin by writing the formula $E = mc^2$ on the chalkboard. Ask, "Who wrote this formula and what does it mean?" Explain that this famous formula was written by Albert Einstein, a German physicist. The formula represents a solution to a problem that baffled physicists at the turn of the century.

Explain that scientists had carefully measured the speed of light under different conditions. They found that light travels at exactly the same speed in no matter what direction it travels in relation to Earth. This seemed to make no sense. After all, Earth itself is moving through space.

Einstein put forward the idea that the speed of light is absolute, or unalterable. At the same time, things that seem absolute, such as space and time, are not. They can be different for different observers. He explained that space and time for the spaceship crew are different from space and time for observers on Earth. This difference will arise among any observers who are moving at different speeds or in different directions relative to each other. Because relative motion is the key to Einstein's theories, they are known by the name of *relativity*.

Tell students that Einstein's theories had broad implications. According to the theory of relativity, an object increases both its mass and its energy as it approaches the speed of light. As a result, Einstein suggested, matter can be converted into energy according to the formula $E = mc^2$. (*E* stands for energy, *m* for mass, and c^2 for the speed of light—the constant—multiplied by itself). This meant that even a tiny atom contains an enormous amount of energy. The idea seemed fantastic in the early twentieth century, but became the basis for the development of the atom bomb in the 1940's.

Skill Building: Making Generalizations (Objective 2) Remind the class that the Middle Ages is sometimes called the "Age of Faith," and the late nineteenth century the "Age of Progress." Have students make up names for the decade of the 1920's. Then tell the class that the decade has been called the "Roaring Twenties," the "Golden Twenties," the "Jazz Age," and the "Years of Hope." Have students write essays suggesting how each name is appropriate.

Check for Understanding Have students give six examples of technological, scientific, cultural, and social changes that occurred during the 1920's.

Practice

Guided Practice
Lead a guided discussion of the questions in Section Review 2. (Answers are below.)

Define:
policy of avoiding political ties to other countries

Identify:
(a) German physicist who developed theory of relativity (b) Austrian physician who constructed theory about human mind (c) Czech writer who wrote eerie novels (d) Irish novelist who wrote *Ulysses* (e) writers and artists who tried to draw on the unconscious part of their minds (f) architectural school based on simplicity and functionalism (g) cultural movement of black artists.

Answer:
1. (a) passenger airlines, improved autos and trucks (b) Radio became widespread.
2. (a) Speed of light is constant, but space and time can change when measured in relation to an object moving at high speeds. (b) Matter can be changed into energy according to formula $E = mc^2$.
3. Although the emphasis on sex and the unconscious shocked some, the ideas were very influential.
4. Women won the right to vote and demanded wider career choices.
5. (a) Writers wrote of a world drained of hope and faith; artists tried to draw on the unconscious part of their minds. (b) jazz and movies
6. Though Americans refused to be politically tied to other countries, they still wanted to do business with them.
7. (a) People were willing to consider revolutionary ideas; women won greater rights; U.S. economy prospered. (b) Art expressed pessimism; U.S. turned to isolationism.

Independent Practice
Assign Independent Practice Worksheet 30.2.

Enrichment Activities

1. **Reading a Primary Source** Assign Voices from the Past Resource Book 30.2.

2. **Researching a Topic** Ask advanced students to prepare a report that explains this statement by Sigmund Freud: "The poor ego has a still harder time of it; it has to serve three harsh masters, and has to do its best to reconcile the claims and demands of all three.... The three tyrants are the external world, the superego and the id."

3. **Researching for Bonus Points** Award bonus points to students who can answer this question: Who were the three main characters in James Joyce's novel *Ulysses*? (Stephen Dedalus, Leopold Bloom, and Molly Bloom)

Wall Street's crash opened the Depression. 3

Section Objectives

After completing Section 3, students should be able to:

1. identify weaknesses in the American economy that led to the Great Depression.
2. describe the impact of the Depression on Europe.
3. compare and contrast the responses of the American, British, and French governments to the Great Depression.

Setting the Stage

Have the class read "The stock market fell in 1929." Then ask, "Did the stock market crash destroy America's agricultural farmlands or its industrial facilities?" Explain that America's vast industrial and agricultural resources were physically undamaged and still capable of enormous productivity. The crash appeared to be limited to the million or so speculators who had gambled and lost on the stock market. There seemed to be no reason why the prosperity of the Roaring Twenties could not continue. Yet it didn't. Explain that within a few months after the crash, unemployment rates began to rise at an alarming rate. Meanwhile, industrial production, prices, and wages fell sharply. A prolonged business slump known as the Great Depression had begun. Tell students that this section examines the weaknesses that helped cause the Great Depression and how the Depression spread to western Europe.

Teaching Strategies

Analyzing a Quotation: Overproduction and Unemployment (Objective 1) Explain that the impact of the Great Depression spread to every part of the American economy. The magnitude of the Depression was so great that, as one contemporary economist wrote: "People felt the ground give way beneath their feet." Jobs, homes, and dreams were lost and millions of people asked why. After travelling across the country, Oscar Ameringer told the House Committee on Labor what he had seen:

During the last three months I have visited as I have said some 20 states of this rich and beautiful country. Here are some of the things I heard and saw. A number of Montana citizens told me of thousands of bushels of wheat left in the fields uncut on account of its low price that hardly paid for the harvesting.... While I was in Oregon the *Portland Oregonian* bemoaned the fact that thousands of ewes were killed by the sheep raisers because they did not bring enough in the market to pay the freight on them. And while Oregon sheep-raisers fed mutton to the buzzard, I saw men picking for meat scraps in the garbage cans of the cities of New York and Chicago.... the farmers are being pauperized by the poverty of industrial populations, and the industrial populations are being pauperized by the poverty of the farmers. Neither has the money to buy the product of the other; hence we have overproduction and underconsumption at the same time and in the same country.

Read or distribute the passage and then ask these questions:

- Why was the wheat crop in Montana left uncut? (because the low price of wheat did not pay for the harvesting)
- Why did sheep raisers in Oregon kill their ewes? (because the price of mutton was too low to pay for the cost of shipping the sheep to market)
- What did Ameringer see in New York and Chicago? (people picking for meat scraps in garbage cans)
- What conclusion did Ameringer reach about the causes of the Great Depression? (The United States was suffering from both overproduction and underconsumption.)

Economics and History: A Global Depression (Objective 2) Ask, "Why did the American depression affect Europe?" Remind students that World War I transformed the United States from a debtor nation into the world's leading creditor nation. For example, in 1919 Europeans owed the United States about 10 billion dollars. Explain that after the Wall Street crash, American banks called in their overseas loans. The consequences were immediately felt worldwide. Direct students' attention to the graph and poster on page 651. Ask, "What economic problems does this poster illustrate?" Explain that the poster features the wife and children of an unemployed man. Point out the army of unemployed workers and the smokeless smokestacks in the background. Then direct students' attention to the graph. Ask, "Which coun-

try had the highest rate of unemployment in 1932?" Remind students that the German economy had heavily depended on American loans that were discontinued.

Skill Building: Comparing Responses to the Depression (Objective 3) Draw a chart with three columns and three rows on the chalkboard. Label the columns "United States," "Great Britain," and "France". Label the rows, "Political Leadership," "Programs," and "Results." Ask students to review pages 651–652. Then have them fill in the chart as a class activity. When the class chart has been completed, use it as the basis of a discussion on the following questions: Which country had the most effective leadership? (United States) did any of the programs successfully end the Depressions? (no) How did the public respond to government measures in the United States? (Emphasize that Roosevelt's strong leadership helped preserve America's faith in its democratic political system.)

Check for Understanding Ask students to identify the causes and effects of the Great Depression.

Practice

Guided Practice
Lead a guided discussion of the questions in Section Review 3. (Answers are below.)

Identify:
(a) financial center located in New York (b) financial slump of the 1930's (c) United States president who began New Deal (d) Roosevelt's program of relief, recovery, and reform (e) all-party coalition cabinet in Britain (f) coalition of moderates, Socialists, and Communists in French government.

Answer:
1. (a) everyone wanted to sell stocks and stock prices plummeted; rumors of business failures and suicides were widespread. (b) Unemployment rates rose; industrial production, prices, and wages fell
2. overproduction and underconsumption, bad farm debts, stock speculation
3. Supply raced ahead of demand; owners cut orders from factories; factories cut production.
4. American investors began calling back their loans; trade dropped; unemployment soared.
5. (a) large public works projects to provide jobs; new government agencies to give aid to businesses and farms; insurance for the elderly and the disabled (b) The new Securities and Exchange Commission regulated stock market transactions; the federal government insured bank deposits.

6. (a) passed high protective tariffs, increased taxes, regulated currency, lowered interest rates (b) elected Popular Front coalition, passed reforms
7. (a) wanted to show there would be changes, suggest that all would be new (b) Yes: Government relief program gave people a chance to find work; new stock regulations and bank insurance gave people confidence to invest and save money. No: the economic system remained basically unchanged.

Independent Practice

Assign Independent Practice Worksheet 30.3.

Enrichment Activities

1. **Reading a Primary Source** Assign Voices from the Past Resource Book 30.3.
2. **Creative Writing** In 1933, a presidential adviser told Roosevelt, "Mr. President, if your program succeeds you will be the greatest President in American history." "If it fails," Roosevelt replied, "I shall be the last one." Ask advanced students to write essays speculating on what might have happened had the New Deal failed.
3. **Researching for Bonus Points** Award bonus points to students who can answer this question: On what day did the stock market reach its lowest point? (July 8, 1932)

Fascist leaders formed dictatorships. 4

Section Objectives

After completing Section 4, students should be able to:

1. compare and contrast the careers of Mussolini and Hitler.
2. identify *Kristallnacht* and trace its causes and consequences.
3. describe the impact of the Depression on Japan.

Setting the Stage

Write "Mussolini" and "Hitler" on the chalkboard. Ask students to write two questions asking what they would like to know about these two leaders. List students' questions on the chalkboard.

Explain that Mussolini and Hitler were two dictators who rose to power in the years after World War I. Tell students that this section describes how they seized power and established dictatorships.

Teaching Strategies

Skill Building: Comparing Mussolini and Hitler (Objective 1) Draw a chart with two columns and six rows on the chalkboard. Label the columns "Mussolini" and "Hitler." Label the rows "Attitude toward Versailles Treaty," "Handling of Economic Crisis," "Method of Taking Power," "Style of Leadership," "Goals," and "Enemies." Ask students to review pages 653–657. Then have them fill in the chart as a class activity. When the class chart has been completed, use it as a basis for a discussion of the following questions: What role did the Depression play in the rise to power of Mussolini and Hitler? (Both leaders took advantage of widespread social unrest in their countries.) How did Hitler and Mussolini take power? (Both were legally appointed to office.) What goals did Mussolini and Hitler share? (Both opposed democracy and began to create powerful dictatorships.) In what ways did the social policies of Mussolini and Hitler differ? (Hitler imposed harsh anti-Jewish laws.)

Discussing History: The Kristallnacht (Objective 2) Review the concept of scapegoating—blaming members of a minority for national problems. Ask, "Can you recall an example of scapegoating that we have previously studied?" Remind students that the Roman emperors used the Christians as scapegoats. Explain that Hitler and the Nazis declared that Germans were a superior "Aryan race" and that Jews and others were inferior. The Kristallnacht marked the first systematic action taken by the German government against the Jewish community. Within twenty-four hours, Nazi mobs destroyed 7,500 Jewish-owned shops and businesses, burned 275 synagogues, and arrested more than 30,000 Jews. Have students read the Voice form the Past (page 656), which describes the night of terror as experienced by one family. Tell students that the Kristallnacht signaled the beginning of Hitler's "Final Solution"— the attempt to eliminate all Jews.

Economics and History: The Impact of the Depression on Japan (Objective 3) Explain that moderate democratic leaders ruled Japan during the 1920's. As long as Japan remained economically prosperous, the moderates retained their power. However, Japan had a fragile economy that depended heavily on foreign trade. For example, the nation had to import 79 percent of its oil and all of its rubber.

When the Depression struck, between 1929 and 1931 Japan's export trade fell by almost one-third and industrial unemployment rose to about 25 percent. Japanese militarists believed that the way to solve these economic problems was to create a Pacific empire. Tell students that the militarists seized power in 1930 and promptly launched a program of military expansion.

Check for Understanding Have students describe the role that the Depression played in the rise to power of Mussolini, Hitler, and the Japanese militarists.

Practice

Guided Practice
Lead a guided discussion of the questions in Section Review 4. (Answers are below.)

Define:
(a) form of government based on extreme nationalism and totalitarian dictatorship (b) "the Leader," Italian dictator (c) "leader" in German, Hitler

Identify:
(a) Fascist dictator of Italy (b) German Fascist party (c) Nazi leader (d) guidebook of Nazism (e) Hitler's secret police (f) Hitler's proposed empire

Answer:
1. (a) extreme nationalism; idea that peaceful states were doomed to be conquered by more warlike (b) Both advocated dictatorial one-party rule, denied individual rights, insisted on the supremacy of the state. (c) Communists sought a classless society, but Fascists believed each class had its function. Communists claimed to be a dictatorship of workers, but Fascist parties allied with aristocrats and industrialists. Communists were internationalists, Fascists, nationalist.
2. (a) Italians felt betrayed by Versailles settlement, faced economic crisis and social unrest (b) gathered veterans to combat communism; marched on Rome and took over the government.
3. economic suffering, lack of support for Weimar, belief that Germany would not be prosperous until military power regained
4. Germans were a master race.
5. was named chancellor in coalition government, passed Enabling Act to become dictator
6. (a) provided legal basis for dictatorship (b) deprived Jews of German citizenship, rights
7. Germany would conquer eastern Europe.
8. (a) During the Depression, Japan fell under military rule. (b) to build a Pacific empire

9. (a) Economic problems led Germans and Italians to look toward strong leaders. (b) Hitler: blamed Treaty of Versailles for Germany's troubles, believed in military conquest; Mussolini: favored nationalism and militarism (c) Both were spellbinding speakers. (d) Both had troopers to eliminate opposition.
10. (a) trust the leader, think only of the glory of the nation, believe in the superiority of one's own race (b) seem to promise quick solutions to big problems (c) Students might suggest not believing in easy answers.

Independent Practice
Assign Independent Practice Worksheet 30.4.
Assign Basic Skills Worksheet 30.

Enrichment Activities

1. **Reading a Primary Source** Assign Voices from the Past Resource Book 30.4.
2. **Preparing a Report** Ask students to prepare a report on one of the following topics: the rise of Hitler, the rise of Mussolini, the Reichstag Fire, the Kristallnacht, or Japanese aggression in Manchuria.
3. **Researching for Bonus Points** Award bonus points to students who can find the answer to this question: Who was convicted of setting the Reichstag fire? (Marinus Van Der Lubbe)

Answers to Voice from the Past

1. that the Nazis would take him and his family away
2. that he could not count on a safe and orderly world
3. at least, threats and intimidation; at worst, an unknown and possibly terrible fate
4. the use of intimidation; the lack of accountability on the part of the government; the use of propaganda and prejudice against one group to strengthen the state's power

The world drifted toward war.   5

Section Objectives

After completing Section 5, students should be able to:

1. define *appeasement* and explain why Britain and France followed this policy.
2. locate the Axis powers on a map and identify the nations they invaded.
3. evaluate the Munich agreement.

Setting the Stage

Write the phrase, "all for one and one for all" on the chalkboard. Ask, "How does this phrase reflect the philosophy of the League of Nations?" Explain that the League was founded on the belief that peace could be maintained if the nations of the world acted together to stop aggression. Tell students that this section describes why the League failed to stop Japan, Germany, and Italy from breaking treaties and invading other nations.

Teaching Strategies

Discussing History: Appeasement (Objective 1) Begin by explaining that Britain and France were great world powers in the nineteenth century. However, both declined sharply in strength and importance after World War II. Tell students that France was still determined to uphold the terms of the Versailles settlement. However, France had a small population and a weak industrial base, and therefore was in no position to stand up to Germany alone. The British government of the 1930's wanted above all to avoid a war that would further drain Britain's resources. Moreover, many British people were convinced that the Versailles settlement had been unfair, and that Germany was entitled to a limited amount of geographical and military expansion. Some British leaders argued that a strong Germany would be a barrier against the Communist Soviet Union. British leaders such as Neville Chamberlain therefore favored a policy of appeasement to lessen tensions and avoid war. Ask students if they think the policy of appeasement was realistic or unrealistic. How do they think Mussolini and Hitler interpreted appeasement?

Geography in History: Invasions of the Axis Powers (Objective 2) Distribute copies of Outline Map 2: The World. Have students label Germany, Italy, Japan, Ethiopia, China, Austria, and Czechoslovakia. Tell students to devise a system of arrows and colors as symbols indicating the invasions of each Axis power on neighboring nations. Students should use information in the text narrative to help complete their maps.

Writing about History: The Munich Agreement (Objective 3) *Prewriting* Tell students that Hitler

and Chamberlain signed a joint statement saying: "We regard the Munich Agreement as a sign of the desire of our two peoples never to go to war with one another again." When he returned to England, Chamberlain told cheering crowds: "I believe it is peace in our time." Explain that the British leader Winston Churchill disagreed. Churchill told the House of Commons: "We have been defeated without a war. And do not suppose this is the end. This is only the first taste of a bitter drink which will be forced on us year by year. Unless we arise again. And take our stand for freedom as in olden times." *Writing* Have students imagine that they are members of Parliament. Their assignment is to write statements either supporting Neville Chamberlain's view or agreeing with Winston Churchill's assessment. Have students present their statements to the class.

Check for Understanding Have students explain how Hitler violated the terms of the Treaty of Versailles.

Practice

Guided Practice
Lead a guided discussion of the questions in Section Review 5. (Answers are below.)

Define:
(a) policy of making concessions in hopes of keeping peace (b) government controlled by an outside power

Identify:
(a) international organization that could not maintain a peaceful world (b) region along German-French border (c) British prime minister who advocated appeasement (d) Germany, Italy, and Japan (e) Spain's Fascist dictator (f) mountainous Czech-German border (g) conference at which Britain and France allowed Germany to take the Sudetenland

Answer:
1. At first, the democracies feared the Soviet Union. Later, democracies set aside differences with USSR to fight fascism.
2. United States and Soviet Union were not members; League had no army to enforce position.
3. Neither was strong enough to stand up against Hitler alone; British did not want further to weaken their economy.
4. Japanese forces invaded northern China in 1937.
5. He attacked independent Ethiopia.
6. (a) Franco and the Nationalists were supported by Italians and Germans. The Western demo-

cracies remained neutral. **(b)** Franco became Fascist dictator of Spain.
7. **(a)** When Hitler's troops moved into the Rhineland, the French and British did nothing. **(b)** aligned Hitler with another strong Fascist power **(c)** When the Austrian chancellor resigned, a Nazi puppet took his place. **(d)** gave Hitler more territory without opposition.
8. **(a)** Appeasement—one gives in to another in order to keep peace; compromise—two agree on mutually beneficial terms **(b)** Ethiopia, Austria, Czechoslovakia, and part of China were lost to aggressors. **(c)** Possible answer: Hitler's master plan included conquering other nations, and he would not have agreed to a compromise.

Independent Practice
Assign Independent Practice Worksheet 30.5.
Assign Geography Skills Worksheet 30.
Assign Critical Thinking Worksheet 30.

Enrichment Activities

1. **Reading a Primary Source** Assign Voices from the Past Resource Book 30.5.
2. **Creative Writing** Ask students to choose an event discussed in this section that they would like to have witnessed. Then have them write essays explaining why they chose this event and what they hoped to learn about it.
3. **Researching for Bonus Points** Award bonus points to students who can answer this question: What two leaders attended the Munich Conference other than Hitler and Chamberlain? (French Premier Daladier and Mussolini)

Concluding the Chapter

1. **Chapter Closer**
   Ask students to explain why 1923 in Germany was called the Year of Hunger and how the people responded to the events of that year.
2. **Reteaching Activities**
   a. **Making a Time Line** Ask students to prepare a time line covering the period from 1919 to 1938.
   b. **Comparing and Contrasting** Have students compare and contrast the ways in which the democracies and the dictatorships responded to the Depression.
   c. **Identifying Main Ideas** Ask students to identify and explain four events that helped bring Europe to the brink of war.

3. **Chapter Review Activities**
   Assign Chapter Review 30 activities.

Chapter Evaluation

Chapter Test 30 and Computer Test Bank Chapter 30 Test can be used to evaluate your students' understanding of this chapter.

Answers to Chapter Review 30

Reviewing the Facts

1. **a.** temporary alliance of political parties **b.** avoiding political ties to other countries **c.** totalitarian form of government **d.** making concessions to keep peace
2. **a.** Skyrocketing inflation can lead to weakened economy. **b.** German government that faced severe economic problems after the war **c.** provided loan to stabilize German currency **d.** agreement to renounce war **e.** revolutionary theory of relativity **f.** developed new art form that drew on the unconscious **g.** gave black writers, artists, and composers worldwide recognition **h.** site of stock market crash of 1929 **i.** business slump in the 1930's **j.** Roosevelt's program for recovery from the Great Depression **k.** established the first Fascist government in Europe **l.** right-wing political party in Germany **m.** Nazi dictator of Germany **n.** Hitler's plan for Germany **o.** Hitler's secret police **p.** Hitler's name for his proposed German empire **q.** urged a policy of appeasement **r.** strengthened fascism in Europe **s.** Fascist dictator of Spain **t.** conference at which Britain and France allowed Hitler to take Sudetenland
3. Loss on agreement, Kellogg. Britain Pact.
4. won the right to vote, demanded wider career choices, became more independent
5. The economics of many war-torn European nations depended on American loans which were called back; many countries were trading partners with the United States.
6. **(a)** ended parliamentary democracy, abolished all political parties except Fascists, censored the press, controlled opposition **(b)** forced capitalists and workers to cooperate, set up state corporations to run economy
7. **(a)** conquered Ethiopia **(b)** invaded China **(c)** occupied Rhineland, forced Austria to become German province, took Czechoslovakia

8. (a) defeated elected government (b) showed how devastating the coming war would be

Basic Skills
1. (a) in 1926, 1928, 1930, 1932, 1934, and 1936. (b) In Germany, unemployment declined; in Britain, it remained high.
2. Weimar Republic, burning of Reichstag, Enabling Act, Rhineland, Austria, Munich Conference, Kristallnacht, Czechoslovakia

Researching and Reporting Skills
Students' answers will vary.

Critical Thinking
1. Americans ignored their role as a world leader; wanted to enjoy prosperity by staying out of international politics.
2. (a) More goods were being produced than people wanted or could afford to buy. (b) There was a downward economic spiral; as people bought less, stores bought fewer goods from manufacturers, and inventories rose. Manufacturers then cut back on production and on the number of people employed. Fewer employed people caused further cuts in buying, and this in turn reinforced the downward spiral. (c) Business activity declined, unemployment rose; many people were poor and hungry.
3. (a) loss of territory, including Alsace-Lorraine; France could work Saar mines for 15 years; loss of Polish Corridor, loss of overseas territories, size of army limited, weapons limited, troops forbidden in Rhineland, blame for war, payment of reparations; (b) loss of territory reduced economic strength; loss of Alsace-Lorraine and Saar mines limited industrial growth; loss of colonies took away source of resources and raw materials and the markets for German goods. Limitations on military preparations saved money but hurt national pride; blame for war was a psychological burden. Reparations drained away funds that could have been used for recovery and rebuilding. (c) social effects: lack of opportunity to recover from war; feelings of guilt and hopelessness; economic effects: loss of a major industrial region and large land areas limited ability to recover and become economically strong again; political effects: government's hand limited for rebuilding and leading Germany to a positive future.
4. Germany's coalition president could not have elected a majority of Nazis and their Allies into power in the Reichstag. Once the Nazis became the majority party, it became difficult to stop Hitler within the democratic process because he was legally given dictatorial powers in the Enabling Act.
5. (a) deprived Jews of citizenship; did not allow them to write, publish, act, teach, work in hospitals or banks, or to sell books. Jews had to wear Star of David, endure violence, and were sent to concentration camps. (b) individuals: loss of sense of security; continuing fear; group: sense of being the object of prejudice, with the future uncertain.
6. (a) economic problems from Depression; social instability due in part to economic problems but also to rapid social change; lack of strong and positive political leadership. (b) possible hypothesis: fascism is a response in times of social, economic, and political uncertainty. It offers strong leadership and simple answers that have popular appeal; appears to empower people but actually gives power only to leaders. support for hypothesis: Hitler and Mussolini rose to power in countries that were experiencing severe economic problems and where people had not lived under a long tradition of stable democratic rule. Both the Italians and Germans (particularly the latter) had felt seriously disadvantaged as peoples after World War I. Hitler and Mussolini offered quick solutions, easy explanations, and a sense of pride.

Perspectives on Past and Present
Students answers will vary. However, they should point out that the situation has changed under the United Nations. Several times, the UN has sent troops to the Middle East to prevent the aggression of one group against another. The UN is unable to provide this type of presence when major powers, such as the United States or the Soviet Union, are involved because of their veto in the Security Council. UN peace-keeping action is most successful in limited areas not involving major powers, such as the Greek-Turkish conflict in Cypress or the Iran-Iraq War.

World War II

Chapter Overview

From 1939 to 1941, a string of German victories led to Axis domination of Europe. When Hitler invaded Poland, France and Britain declared war on Germany. Japanese aggression in the Pacific led to the development of an Asian empire that threatened American interests. On December 7, 1941, Japan attacked Pearl Harbor, and the United States entered the war on the side of the allies. Important victories at Midway in the Pacific, Stalingrad in the Soviet Union, and El Alamein turned the tide of the war. On June 6, 1944, Allied forces landed on the beaches of Normandy and began a march to Berlin. Facing British and American forces on the west, and the Soviet army on the east, the German Reich collapsed, and Germany surrendered. War in Asia ended with the dropping of atom bombs on Hiroshima and Nagasaki. The atom bomb, the Holocaust, and the massive loss of civilian life and property made World War II a total war unlike any the world had ever experienced.

Key Terms

genocide
For additional exercises, see vocabulary Worksheet 31.

Chapter Focus

Have students read the introduction to Chapter 31 (pages 664–65). Explain that Martin Gray witnessed the German attack on Warsaw. Then ask, "What were Gray's most vivid memories of this attack?" List students' responses on the chalkboard. Tell students that between 1939 and 1945, people across Europe and Asia experienced the horrors of World War II. This chapter describes how the Axis powers attempted to conquer the world. It also tells the story of how the Allies defeated them.

Germany overran much of Europe. 1

Section Objectives

After completing Section 1, students should be able to:

1. define *blitzkrieg* and explain how Hitler used this new style of attack to defeat Poland, Norway, Belgium, and France.
2. identify Dunkirk and explain how the British rescued the trapped Allied army.
3. identify Winston Churchill and explain how he rallied his people to prepare for the Battle of Britain.

Setting the Stage

Begin by showing Overhead Transparency 68, *Axis Powers in Europe, 1939.* Identify the Axis Powers and review the steps by which Hitler and Mussolini expanded their power. Then locate the Polish Corridor. Explain that the Treaty of Versailles created this strip of land to give Poland access to the Baltic Sea. Ask, "Why would Hitler oppose this arrangement?" Point out that the Polish Corridor divided Germany and stripped it of the important seaport of Danzig. Then direct students' attention to the cartoon on page 667. Ask, "According to the cartoonist what did Hitler want? What impact would that have on Poland? Should Britain and France have offered to protect Poland?"

Tell students that Hitler's new demands convinced Britain and France to reevaluate their policy of appeasement. Meanwhile, Hitler secretly prepared for war. This section describes how Hitler broke the peace by invading Poland, western Europe, and Russia. It also describes how a British leader — named Winston Churchill — rallied his country to meet its greatest challenge.

Teaching Strategies

Discussing History: The *Blitzkrieg* (Objective 1) Begin by explaining that military lessons can be learned from each war. Ask, "What lessons could be drawn from events on the Western Front?" Explain that French generals concluded that their country could best be protected by strong defensive formations. They therefore constructed an elaborate set of fortifications known as the *Maginot Line*. In contrast, German generals concluded

Advance Planner

Chapter 31 Focus	World War II 1939–1945 Martin Gray's account of the German attack on Warsaw			★ Advanced ● Basic
	Section 1	**Section 2**	**Section 3**	**Section 4**
Objectives	1. Define *blitzkrieg* and explain how Hitler used this new style of attack to defeat Poland, Norway, Belgium, and France. 2. Identify Dunkirk and explain how the British rescued the trapped Allied army. 3. Identify Winston Churchill and explain how he rallied his people to prepare for the Battle of Britain.	1. Identify the Lend-Lease Act and explain its importance. 2. Evaluate Japan's decision to attack Pearl Harbor. 3. Explain the consequences of the Japanese attack on Pearl Harbor. 4. Identify the Battle of Midway and explain its significance.	1. Describe how American production rose to meet war needs. 2. Identify the Holocaust and explain how its victims are memorialized.	1. Identify the Battle of Stalingrad and explain its importance. 2. Explain the importance of the D-Day invasion. 3. Evaluate Truman's decision to use the atomic bomb against Japan.
Setting the Stage	Hitler's goals Transparency 68	The threat of Japanese aggression in Asia Transparency 69	The concept of "total war"	The significance of the United States' entry into the war
Teaching Strategies	Discussing History: The *Blitzkrieg* Teaching with Pictures: "The Miracle of Dunkirk" Discussing History: "Their Finest Hour" Check for Understanding	Economics and History: Lend-Lease Discussing History: Japan's Decision to Attack Pearl Harbor Discussing History: Was Pearl Harbor a Japanese Victory? Writing about History: The Battle of Midway Check for Understanding	Economics and History: The Production Miracle Relating Past to Present: The Holocaust Check for Understanding	Discussing History: The Battle of Stalingrad Transparency 70 Discussing History: The Importance of D-Day Writing about History: How to Defeat Japan? Check for Understanding
Guided Practice	Transparency 68 Q&A Section Review 1	Transparency 69 Q&A Section Review 2	Section Review 3	Transparency 70 Q&A Section Review 4
Independent Practice Worksheets	Independent Practice 31.1 Vocabulary 31	Independent Practice 31.2 Critical Thinking 31	Independent Practice 31.3 Basic Skills 31	Independent Practice 31.4 Geography Skills 31
Enrichment	1. Primary Source: Voices 31.1 2. Preparing a Report 3. Researching for Points	1. Primary Source: Voices 31.2 2. Creative Writing 3. Researching for Points	1. Primary Source: Voices 31.3 2. Preparing a Report 3. Researching for Points	1. Primary Source: Voices 31.4 2. ★ Preparing a Report 3. Researching for Points

Chapter Closer	
● **Reteaching Activities**	Making a Time Line, Analyzing
Chapter Review	Summary, Reviewing the Facts, Basic Skills, Researching and Reporting Skills, Critical Thinking, Perspectives on Past and Present, Investigating History
Chapter Evaluation	Chapter Test 31, Computer Test Bank Chapter 31 Test

Unit VIII Review	
Geographic Theme:	Location: How did Soviet territory expand in the course of World War II?
Unit Perspectives	Understanding History (Explaining, Relating, Sequencing), Critical Thinking, Making Decisions, Continuity and Change
Unit Evaluation	Unit VIII Test

that tanks and airplanes gave new advantages to the offensive. Fast-moving tank formations could burst through weak spots or gaps in an enemy line. Meanwhile, fighter bombers and dive bombers could fly over fixed defenses to attack vital command posts and industrial centers. The leaderless enemy forces would then panic and ultimately would be forced to surrender. This highly mobile type of German warfare was called *blitzkrieg* or "lightning war." Have students read pages 666 to 669 and describe how Hitler used the blitzkrieg to defeat Poland, Norway, Belgium, and France.

Teaching with Pictures: "The Miracle of Dunkirk" (Objective 2) Refer students to the map on page 666. Explain that the port of Dunkirk is located just south of the French-Belgian border. Tell students that the German *blitzkrieg* left about 400,000 British, French, and Belgian troops surrounded at Dunkirk. Then direct the students' attention to the picture on page 668. Note that the British organized a rescue fleet of more than 850 vessels that included Royal Navy destroyers, Channel ferries, fireboats, whaleboats, fishing boats, and even private yachts. The fleet sailed through three narrow passageways that had been cleared of mines. German dive bombers repeatedly attacked the fleet. Point out the great columns of smoke in the background, which provided a protective camouflage for the rescue. Dunkirk's sandy beaches also helped in protecting the Allied soldiers. Heavy German bombs buried themselves in the sand before harmlessly exploding. Conclude by emphasizing that the operation rescued 338,000 of the 400,000 trapped soldiers. The "Miracle at Dunkirk" saved the Allied army and rescued commanders such as Brooke, Alexander, and Montgomery.

Discussing History: "Their Finest Hour" (Objective 3) Explain that the fall of France left Hitler in command of western Europe. Tell students that Hitler then offered Churchill peace in exchange for British recognition of the German conquests. Ask, "What do you think should be Churchill's reply to Hitler's offer? What would be the advantages and disadvantages of accepting peace on Hitler's terms?" Discuss student answers. Then tell students that Churchill gave this answer in a radio broadcast to the British people: "We shall defend every village, every town, and every city.... Let us ... brace ourselves to our duties, and so bear ourselves that if the British Empire and its Commonwealth last for a thousand years, men will still say: 'This was their finest hour.'" Ask students to imagine that they are British citizens who have just heard Churchill's speech. Divide the class into small groups and have them discuss their reactions to Churchill's leadership. Then have students read "Germany attacked Great Britain" to find out how the British responded.

Check for Understanding Have students explain the importance of Hitler's Nonaggression Pact with Stalin, the Nazi blitzkrieg tactics, the Battle of Britain, and the German invasion of the Soviet Union.

Practice

Guided Practice
Lead a guided discussion of the questions in Overhead Transparency 68 and in Section Review 1. (Answers are below.)

Define:
(a) making concessions in hopes of keeping peace
(b) lightning war

Identify:
(a) strip of land cut from Germany after World War I to give Poland access to the sea (b) German air force (c) British prime minister during World War II (d) French fortifications built as protection from a German invasion (e) port on English channel from which Allied soldiers were rescued (f) France's Nazi-controlled government (g) underground resistance movement in wartime France (h) leader of French resistance (i) British air force

Answer:
1. (a) that Danzig, plus a German railway and highway route through the Polish corridor, be returned to Germany (b) pledged to defend Poland if Hitler threatened its independence
2. (a) Hitler's Nazis had come to power by attacking communism. (b) He wanted to avoid a two-front war.
3. with a German attack on Poland
4. Estonia, Latvia, Lithuania, and Finland
5. to set up airfields and naval bases from which he could strike at Britain
6. (a) The German army swung west around French defenses and struck through Belgium (b) effectiveness of the German blitzkrieg
7. by a Nazi collaborator who headed the Vichy regime
8. (a) with a seaborne attack called Operation Sea Lion (b) Britain had radar, the ability to crack German codes, and a determined population.
9. (a) to obtain living space and valuable mineral resources (b) conquered the Balkans, destroyed 1,000 Soviet planes on the ground, smashed the lines of the Red Army (c) Hitler's troops were not prepared for the Soviet winter.

10. For: Hitler disliked Communists, wanted the space and valuable mineral resources of USSR. Against: Hitler had signed a ten-year nonaggression pact with the USSR; Hitler could not handle a two-front war.

Independent Practice

Assign Independent Practice Worksheet 31.1.
Assign Vocabulary Worksheet 31.

Enrichment Activities

1. **Reading a Primary Source** Assign Voices from the Past Resource Book 31.1.

2. **Preparing a Report** Ask students to prepare a report on one of the following topics: the Maginot Line, the rescue at Dunkirk, the discovery and use of radon, the Royal Air Force, the "Ultra Secret," the leadership of Winston Churchill, and the German siege of Leningrad.

3. **Researching for Bonus Points** Award bonus points to students who can find the answer to this question: What was the British code name for the rescue at Dunkirk? (Operation Dynamo)

Japan conquered an Asian empire. 2

Section Objectives

After completing Section 2, students should be able to:

1. identify the Lend-Lease Act and explain its importance.
2. evaluate Japan's decision to attack Pearl Harbor.
3. explain the consequences of the Japanese attack on Pearl Harbor.
4. identify the Battle of Midway and explain its significance.

Setting the Stage

Ask students to name the year that World War II began. List responses on the chalkboard. Explain that European history books say that World War II began with the German invasion of Poland in 1939. Then tell students that Chinese history books say that World War II began in 1931. Ask, "What event occurred in 1931 to justify this date?"

Show students Overhead Transparency 69, *World War II in Asia and the Pacific 1941–1945*.

Remind students that the Japanese invaded Manchuria in 1931. Six years later, in 1937, Japanese armies pushed into China. Ask, "What countries were alarmed by Japan's conquests?" Recall that the United States, Britain, and France had vital interests in Asia. Point out that at that time France controlled Indochina, Britain controlled Burma and Malaya, and the Philippines were United States territory. Tell students that this section describes how Japanese expansion led to a confrontation with the United States in the Pacific.

Teaching Strategies

Economics and History: Lend-Lease (Objective 1) Begin by asking students to pretend that a neighbor's house has caught fire. They have a garden hose that could help put out the fire. Would they sell the neighbor the hose, or loan it to help put out the fire? Record students' answers. Then explain that President Roosevelt used this famous analogy to rally public support behind the Lend-Lease Bill. Tell students that at first Britain paid for all United States supplies. However, as the costs of the war rose, British gold reserves fell. By late 1940, the British could not pay for one-twentieth of the supplies they needed. Faced with the possibility of strategic bankruptcy, Churchill appealed to President Roosevelt for help. After a long debate, Congress passed the Lend-Lease Act in March 1941. Relieved Britons celebrated the news by raising American flags over their homes and offices. During the next four years, the United States sent its allies 50 billion dollars in aid to help put out the Axis fires.

Discussing History: Japan's Decision to Attack Pearl Harbor (Objective 2) Divide the class into small groups. Tell each group that they are attending a secret meeting of the Japanese cabinet. Remind cabinet members that Japanese armies occupied French Indochina in July 1941. Great Britain, the Dutch East Indies, and the United States retaliated by cutting off all oil supplies to Japan. If nothing is done, Japan will run out of oil by the Spring of 1942. Explain that the cabinet has three choices: 1. Give in to the American demands by withdrawing Japanese troops from Indochina; 2. Attack the American fleet at Pearl Harbor and then seize the Dutch East Indies; or 3. Attack the Dutch East Indies while avoiding United States territories. Ask each group to make a list of the advantages and disadvantages of these three options and to prepare a statement explaining their final decision.

Discussing History: Was Pearl Harbor a Japanese Victory? (Objective 3) Begin by asking, "Was Pearl Harbor a Japanese victory?" Point out that most would answer yes. The Japanese attack handed the United States the worst naval defeat in its history. Of the 94 ships at Pearl Harbor 19 were sunk or disabled. Suggest that despite their apparent success, the Japanese actually achieved only a limited victory. Japanese bombers failed to destroy Pearl Harbor's repair facilities and huge oil storage tanks. As a result, most of the damaged ships were repaired. In addition, the three aircraft carriers stationed at Pearl Harbor were not in port. Finally, the sneak attack united Americans against Japan and brought the United States into the war.

Writing about History: The Battle of Midway (Objective 4) Tell students that many historians believe that the battle of Midway was an important turning point in World War II. Ask students to write essays explaining why this battle was a turning point and speculating on what might have happened if the Japanese had won it. Have students share and discuss their essays.

Check for Understanding Have students explain the significance of the Lend-Lease Act, the Japanese attack on Pearl Harbor, and the battle of Midway.

Practice

Guided Practice
Lead a guided discussion of the questions in Overhead Transparency 69 and in Section Review 2. (Answers are below.)

Define:
people who did not want the United States to be involved in world politics

Identify:
(a) law authorizing president to send war supplies to any country whose defense was vital to the United States (b) Japanese admiral who planned bombing of Pearl Harbor (c) day Pearl Harbor was attacked (d) American commander of the Pacific troops (e) turning point in the Pacific war

Answer:
1. with Japanese invasion of Manchuria
2. sold them weapons and other goods on a cash-and-carry basis; gave them 50 destroyers in return for leases on bases; passed Lend-Lease Act
3. (a) Roosevelt banned the shipment of American fuel, scrap iron, and steel to Japan, making Japan's war against China more difficult. (b) by striking south against Indochina, Malaya, and the East Indies

4. bombing of Pearl Harbor by Japanese
5. After the attack on Pearl Harbor, the Japanese overran most of the Pacific before the Allies managed to stop them.
6. (a) stopping of the Japanese drive toward Australia (b) Americans stopped the Japanese by destroying their air force.
7. Yes, isolationists were a strong voice in Congress. No, unprovoked attacks on American fleets and conquest of democratic countries would have forced the US into the war.

Independent Practice
Assign Independent Practice Worksheet 31.2.
Assign Critical Thinking Worksheet 31.

Enrichment Activities

1. **Reading a Primary Source** Assign Voices from the Past Resource Book 31.2.

2. **Creative Writing** Ask students to prepare a front page headline and news bulletin on one of the following events: passage of the Lend-Lease Act, the Japanese attack on Pearl Harbor, or United States victory in the Battle of Midway.

3. **Researching for Bonus Points** Award bonus points to students who can answer this question: What were the names of the three United States aircraft carriers that were not at Pearl Harbor on December 7, 1941? (*Saratoga, Lexington,* and *Enterprise*)

World War II was a total war. 3

Section Objectives

After completing Section 3, students should be able to:

1. describe how American production rose to meet war needs.
2. identify the Holocaust and explain how its victims are memorialized.

Setting the Stage

Direct students' attention to the section title, "World War II was a total war." Ask, "What does the phrase 'total war' mean?" Explain that a total war involves the home fronts as well as the war zones. Unlike previous wars, more civilians than soldiers died in World War II. Tell students that civilians on both sides suffered and sacrificed as workers, family members, and victims. This section describes the many ways in which World War II affected civilian life.

Teaching Strategies

Economics and History: The Production Miracle (Objective 1) Ask students to recall the techniques that Henry Ford used to mass produce automobiles. Explain that American industrialists used assembly-line techniques to produce an unprecedented quantity of war materials. For example, Swedish workers required 450 hours to produce a single antiaircraft gun by hand. American engineers used assembly line techniques to cut this time to only ten hours. Tell students that in the five years from September 1940 to September 1945, Americans produced a total of 296,000 warplanes, 102,000 tanks, 372,000 artillery pieces, 87,000 warships, and 2.4 million trucks. Even the Communist leader, Josef Stalin, admitted in 1943 that without United States production, "this war would have been lost."

Relating Past to Present: The Holocaust (Objective 2) Have students read, "Hitler ordered the Holocaust" (pages 677–678). Then read the following passage by Elie Wiesel: "In all their chronicles and testaments, memoirs and prayers, litanies and poems, the victims stressed one single theme over and over again—remember, remember the horror, remember. Bear witness." Ask, "Why did the victims stress this theme?" Tell students that Congress established the United States Holocaust Memorial Council in 1980 to preserve the memory of this terrible tragedy and to provide an early warning against the threat of genocide anywhere in the world. The Council opened a permanent memorial to the Holocaust victims in Washington, D.C. In addition, a Days of Remembrance observance is held annually throughout the United States, and similar observances are held throughout Europe.

Check for Understanding Have students explain the importance of United States war production efforts and define the terms *genocide* and *Holocaust*.

Practice

Guided Practice
Lead a guided discussion of the questions in Section Review 3. (Answers are below.)

Define:
(a) increase in prices resulting from high supply of dollars and low supply of goods (b) ideas deliberately spread for a purpose (c) killing of an entire people

Identify:
(a) law that allowed the United States to draft an army (b) of the Germanic race (c) systematic and deliberate destruction of the Jews by the Nazis

Answer:
1. passed Selective Service Act, increased production of weapons, increased income tax
2. (a) opened employment opportunities to women, blacks, and disabled (b) Consumer goods were scarce and prices became inflated.
3. reminded citizens to support the war effort and that fighting the war was necessary
4. (a) to make them his master race (b) to enslave them
5. with a program of genocide
6. (a) Hitler had control of Germany, the defeated countries, the Gestapo, and the armed forces. (b) He had tacit support from Gestapo and soldiers who carried out orders, from citizens who knew but took no action, and from the powerful nations that did nothing.

Independent Practice
Assign Independent Practice Worksheet 31.3.
Assign Basic Skills Worksheet 31.

Enrichment Activities

1. **Reading a Primary Source** Assign Voices from the Past Resource Book 31.3.

2. **Preparing a Report** Ask students to prepare a report on one of the following topics: Henry Kaiser-master shipbuilder, the impact of World War II on American women, the internment of Japanese-Americans, and German concentration camps.

3. **Researching for Bonus Points** Award bonus points to students who can answer this question: Which executive order authorized the United States Secretary of War to create internment camps for Japanese-Americans? (Executive Order 9066)

Answers to Voice from the Past

1. the Jews
2. because their families were in hiding, confined, or killed in the death camps; that

friends and relatives did not know where the prisoners were.

3. (a) It was unexpected and symbolized their link with loved ones and with the outside world. (b) Rich food after a long period of deprivation could make them sick.

4. They had a strong will to survive and were determined to resist giving in to the Nazi system. Their ability to maintain hope was a triumph of the human spirit.

The Allies launched a drive to victory. 4

Section Objectives

After completing Section 4, students should be able to:

1. identify the Battle of Stalingrad and explain its importance.
2. explain the importance of the D-Day invasion.
3. evaluate Truman's decision to use the atomic bomb against Japan.

Setting the Stage

Explain that Winston Churchill openly rejoiced when he heard the news that the United States had entered World War II. Churchill later explained, "Hitler's fate was sealed. Mussolini's fate was sealed. As for the Japanese, they would be ground to powder. All the rest was merely the proper application of overwhelming force." Read this quotation to the class. Then ask, "Why was Churchill certain that the Axis Powers would be defeated? What did he mean by 'the proper application of overwhelming force?'" Explain that Churchill understood America's enormous industrial and military power. Despite their initial setbacks, he believed that the Allies possessed overwhelming advantages that would ultimately lead to victory. Tell students that this section describes how the Allies used their "overwhelming force" to defeat the Axis Powers.

Teaching Strategies

Discussing History: The Battle of Stalingrad (Objective 1) Show students Overhead Transparency 70, *World War II in Europe and North Africa,*

1939–1945. Help students locate the city of Stalingrad. Explain that Hitler hoped to conquer Stalingrad and then seize the vital Baku oil fields on the Caspian Sea. Artillery bombardments turned Stalingrad into a maze of ruined buildings. Fierce battles were fought for possession of a bakery, an apartment building, or a grain elevator. Tell students that a Soviet army of one million troops surrounded the burning city. The battered German army finally surrendered on January 31, 1943. Twenty-four German generals and 100,000 soldiers became prisoners of war. Only 6,000 of these men are known to have survived. Emphasize that the Battle of Stalingrad marked a turning point in the war with Germany. From that time on, the German army began its long retreat to Berlin.

Discussing History: The Importance of D-Day (Objective 2) Explain that Hitler believed that an Allied invasion of France provided his best hope for victory. Ask, "Why would Hitler actually welcome an Allied attack?" Explain that Hitler believed that the Allied forces would be unable to breach his Atlantic Wall—a 2,400 mile barrier of fortresses, fortifications, and machine gun nests. He predicted that if their invasion failed, the United States and Britain would shift their attention to the Pacific. Hitler would then be free to transfer the fifty-nine German divisions stationed in France to the eastern front for a decisive battle with the Soviet Union. Tell students that Hitler also knew that his scientists were almost ready to unveil deadly new rockets and jet aircraft.

Writing about History: How to defeat Japan? (Objective 3) *Prewriting* Explain that President Truman faced a difficult decision on how best to defeat Japan. As President, he had to choose one of these five options: (a) Use a naval blockade to force the Japanese to starve or surrender; (b) Invade Japan with five million American troops; (c) Ask the Soviet Union to join the fighting against Japan; (d) Demonstrate the power of the atomic bomb by destroying a small unpopulated island; and (e) Drop an atomic bomb on a major Japanese city. *Writing* Ask students to assume the role of President Truman. Their assignment is to make a decision and then write an executive order explaining the reasons for their choice. Have students share and discuss executive orders. Compare students' choices with Truman's decision to use the atomic bomb.

Check for Understanding Have students explain the significance of El Alamein, Stalingrad, and the D-Day invasion.

Practice

Guided Practice
Lead a guided discussion of the questions in Overhead Transparency 70 and in Section Review 4. (Answers are below.)

Define:
Japanese pilot who volunteered for a suicide mission

Identify:
(**a**) German general, "Desert Fox" (**b**) commander of British forces in North Africa (**c**) commander of Allied forces in North Africa; commanded the Allied invasion of France (**d**) Soviet commander at the Battle of Stalingrad (**e**) code name for the day of the Allied invasion of Normandy (**f**) first city to be destroyed by atomic bomb

Answer:
1. (**a**) Whoever controlled North Africa controlled Suez Canal. (**b**) pushed British forces across North Africa to the Suez Canal (**c**) beginning of Allied drive to seize North African coast
2. Soviets trapped the Germans and cut off their supplies.
3. Mussolini was forced to resign, and Italians turned against the Germans.
4. In an all-out effort, Allies invaded Normandy.
5. The German Reich collapsed when German armies had to fight a war on two fronts.
6. (**a**) allowed them to avoid a costly invasion of Japan (**b**) August 6, on Hiroshima; August 9, on Nagasaki
7. Students should note that Okinawa was captured at the cost of 45,000 American lives, and an invasion of Japan would have been even more costly in terms of both American and Japanese lives. One alternative might have been to demonstrate the power of the bomb to Japanese leaders on an uninhabited island.
8. (**a**) does not — Germany allied itself with Russia to avoid a two-front war, used the blitzkrieg, and built its powerful Luftwaffe. (**b**) does — France, expecting another trench-fought war, built the Maginot fortifications. (**c**) does — Except for radar, the British military was ill-equipped for modern warfare. (**d**) does — Soviet Union was surprised by German attack

Independent Practice
Assign Independent Practice Worksheet 31.4.
Assign Geography Skills Worksheet 31.

Enrichment Activities

1. **Reading a Primary Source** Assign Voices from the Past Resource Book 31.4.
2. **Preparing a Report** The United States, the Soviet Union, and Great Britain disagreed over the time and place to open a "second front" against Germany. Ask advanced students to prepare a research report on the causes and consequences of the Allied decision to open a second front in 1944.
3. **Researching for Bonus Points** Award bonus points to students who can answer this question: What was the nickname given to the atom bomb dropped on Nagasaki? ("Fat Boy")

Concluding the Chapter

1. **Chapter Closer**
   Ask students to choose six events described in this chapter that they regard as the most important benchmarks or turning points in the story of World War II. Students should use facts to defend their choices.
2. **Reteaching Activities**
   a. **Making a Time Line** Have each student make a time line of major World War II events between 1939 and 1945.
   b. **Analyzing** Have students develop a list of the major mistakes made by the leaders of Great Britain, Germany, Japan, the Soviet Union, and the United States during World War II. Ask students to evaluate the consequences of each mistake.
3. **Chapter Review Activities**
   Assign Chapter Review 31 activities.

Chapter Evaluation

Chapter Test 31 and Computer Test Bank Chapter 31 Test can be used to evaluate your students' understanding of this chapter.

Answers to Chapter Review 31

Reviewing the Facts
1. **a.** sudden massive attack, lightning war **b.** killing of an entire people
2. **a.** Britain's prime minister during war **b.** land in western Poland taken over by Germany **c.** port

on English Channel **d.** war-time government of France **e.** French resistance organization **f.** led the Free French **g.** won the Battle of Britain **h.** U.S. president who aided the Allies **i.** law allowing U.S. to send war supplies to Britain **j.** day Japan bombed Pearl Harbor **k.** turning point of Pacific war **l.** Hitler's destruction of the Jews **m.** a genius in tank warfare **n.** commander of British in North Africa **o.** commanded Allies on D-day **p.** U.S. president who ordered use of atom bomb

3. **(a)** unprepared for blitzkrieg strike through Belgium **(b)** Vichy government cooperated with Nazis.

4. with Japanese invasion of Manchuria

5. **(a)** persuaded Congress to sell weapons, pass the Lend-Lease; gave Britain destroyers **(b)** Japan's attack on Pearl Harbor

6. **(a)** Europe's factories were destroyed in the war. **(b)** Many Americans began hating all Japanese.

7. **(a)** beginning of the Allied drive to seize North Africa **(b)** Germans were defeated.

8. **(a)** Sicily fell to the Allies, Mussolini was forced to resign, and Italy sided with the Allies. **(b)** the Allies liberated France.

9. **(a)** Faced with Allies to the west and Soviets to the east, the German armies retreated. **(b)** Atom bombs were dropped on Hiroshima and Nagasaki, forcing Japan to surrender.

Basic Skills
1. **(a)** all events following the bombing of Pearl Harbor were Allied victories. **(b)** All events up to and including the bombing of Pearl Harbor were Axis victories. **(c)** Battle of Britain: failure to invade Britain made Hitler turn toward Russia, where German armies suffered major losses; Midway: stopped Japanese expansion; gave U.S. the offensive in naval war.

2. **(a)** It gave Allies naval access to southern Europe from a variety of routes. **(b)** It shows how much more territory Germany would have to protect in a two-front war. It also points out how many enemies it would have to face simultaneously.

Researching and Reporting Skills
Students' answers will vary.

Critical Thinking
1. **(a)** Advantages: had fully prepared military, factories, and people for war; had element of surprise; had time to make pact with Russia to prevent two-front war. Disadvantages: lack of access to raw materials; vulnerable to blocked and air attack; threat of sabotage from subject people such as Czechs; lengthening supply lines. **(b)** Advantages: access to raw materials; possibility of help (destroyers) from U.S.; help from overseas territories. Disadvantages: not prepared; military not in place; factories not geared to produce war equipment; no battle plans or coordination of resources with other friendly countries.

2. **(a)** World War I was typified by trench warfare and corresponding lack of movement. World War II saw the introduction of the German blitzkrieg, with sudden massive attacks that depended on speed and movement. **(b)** fast-moving tanks, planes, motorcycles, other military vehicles

3. **(a)** war with United States seemed inevitable; advantage in striking first; eliminate U.S. as a Pacific power **(b)** destroy U.S. navy **(c)** temporarily harmed U.S. fleet; forced U.S. to declare war; and ultimately faced defeat at hands of rebuilt American navy.

4. **(a)** The decision to bomb Britain should have been reevaluated when it became obvious that Britain could not be bombed into submission; the decisions regarding Russia were both ill conceived. **(b)** Possible answer: not to retreat from Russia was the most instrumental in Germany's defeat. This made it impossible for the German army to recover its losses and still fight the Allies elsewhere. It also prolonged the war and gave the United States time to pull together its resources for the Allied war effort.

5. **(a)** divided humankind into master race and everyone else, deprived Jews of property, and political rights; sent Jews from all over Europe to concentration camps where they either worked at hard labor until they succumbed, or were put to death. **(b)** Genocide is a crime against a people, but no power exists to pass judgment on a people. This is why the UN drew upon international convention making genocide a crime. The U.S. ratified the convention in 1986.

Perspectives on Past and Present
World War II was a struggle to the end between two different political systems, democracy and totalitarianism. Germany—and the Axis powers—set out to conquer the whole world and take it over for their use. Local and regional wars tend to be over more limited and specific issues such as ownership of the Falkland Islands or control of disputed territories or resources.

Investigating History
Students' answers will vary.

Unit VIII *Review Activities*

1. Assign Geographic Theme: Location.
2. Assign Unit Perspectives questions.

Unit VIII *Review Answers*

Geographic Theme: Location
1. **a.** port of eastern Finland, Estonia, Latvia, Lithuania, port of eastern Poland and Czechoslovakia, and Bessarabia; **b.** Soviet territory in Europe was substantially increased between 1941 and 1947.
2. pursued policy of expanding to the west to obtain warm-water ports and territories to serve as buffer against any invasion
3. **a.** The Soviet Union emerged from World War II as a superpower due to success in war, military and industrial power, size of territory and population, and wealth of resources. **b.** new territories added to size, population, resources, industry, and warm-water ports for trade and naval bases.

Unit *Perspectives*

Understanding History
1. **(a)** Alliances divided Europe into two opposing camps. **(b)** Nationalist movements in the Balkan nations threatened Austria-Hungary, while Russia encouraged the Slavic groups in their struggles for independence, thus putting Russia and Austria on a collision course. **(c)** Germany's possessions in China, the Pacific, and in Africa were tempting targets for takeover. **(d)** Nations built up the size of their armies, and militarism won support from the general population.
2. **a.** plan whereby most of the German army would attack France in the west before Russia was mobilized in the east; failed because Russia mobilized more quickly than expected **b.** Austrian province which did not meet Austria's ultimatum and thus triggered World War I **c.** submarine that changed war at sea **d.** France, Great Britain, and Russia formed one side in World War I. **e.** Germany and Austria-Hungary comprised other side in World War I. **f.** battle line formed by Germany and France **g.** battle line formed by Germany and Russia **h.** first

major clash on Western Front; German advance stopped and Paris saved **i.** ended war between Germany and Russia **j.** Wilson's goals for a just and lasting peace
3. **a.** before **b.** before **c.** after **d.** after **e.** before **f.** before **g.** after **h.** after
4. **a.** This lightning war technique stunned Hitler's victims and allowed his army to overcome them. **b.** Hitler announced he wanted the Polish Corridor back; Britain and France declared war on Germany after Hitler invaded Poland. **c.** The German air force bombed Europe's civilian as well as military centers. **d.** The British air force defended Britain and also bombed German cities. **e.** This French fortification was built to prevent an invasion by Germany. **f.** This French government was controlled by the Nazis. **g.** With this law, Roosevelt was able to make America the "arsenal for democracy." **h.** This German defeat signaled the retreat of the Germans from the Eastern Front. **i.** This American victory was the turning point of the Pacific war **j.** This was the day of the Normandy invasion.
5. **a.** before **b.** after **c.** after **d.** before **e.** before **f.** before **g.** after
6. **a.** led independence movement in India **b.** leader of Muslim league **c.** first president of Republic of Turkey who tried to modernize nation **d.** modernized Persia and changed nation's name to Iran **e.** first king of Arab nation (Saudi Arabia) who retained Islamic traditions **f.** leader of Zionist movement in Britain **g.** local leader who inspired Mexican peasants in revolution of 1910 **h.** revolutionary leader who worked to get a more democratic constitution in Mexico **i.** moderate Mexican leader whose presidency marked the beginning of reform **j.** led overthrow of Ch'ing dynasty and became first president of Republic of China **k.** leader of Chinese Nationalists who defeated warlords and then turned against his Chinese Communist allies **l.** leader of Chinese Communist party who led followers on Long March

Critical Thinking
1. **a.** Britain and France weakened but intact; Italy weakened and dissatisfied with peace terms; Austria-Hungary defeated and deprived of most of empire; Germany defeated and in desperate straits; Russia defeated by Germany, forced to accept harsh treaty; devastated by war; tremendous casualties. **b.** Both Italy and Germany in time turned to fascist governments ruled by dictators who promised better

times; Russia underwent total revolution that resulted in a communist dictatorship.

2. Events of the Russian Revolution followed the pattern described. The riots and strikes of 1917 led to the abdication of the czar and the duma's forming of a provisional government led by Kerensky. Kerensky lost popular support when he chose to continue the war. The return of Lenin resulted in a Bolshevik coup that put the radical Bolsheviks in control of the government. They succeeded in keeping control and went on to carry out their objectives for the revolution—the start of a Communist state.

3. (a) similar in that both sought independence; (b) different in that India was one huge country, whereas the Middle East was divided into a number of countries; India had one main leader, while the Middle East had several; some Middle East countries became independent, whereas others and also India did not at that time.

4. a. Mexican revolution: exploitation by landowners and factory owners, masses' lack of representation in government, resistance to foreign ownership of businesses, resentment at wealth of Church; China: foreign control of trade and resources, desire for modernization, nationalist desire to control own affairs. (b) Mexican revolution: short-term effects were making of constitution but dictatorial control; long-term effects were search for reform and more democratic system. China: short-term effects were overthrow of emperor, establishment of nationalist government; long-term effects were dissatisfaction with Nationalists that led to growth of Communist party.

5. a. The Great Depression was the worldwide economic decline that began with the stock market crash in 1929 and that led to business failures, decline of trade, unemployment, and a crisis in the world economy. b. by creating economic, political, and social instability and a search for solutions at any price.

6. (a) World War I grew out of the nationalistic and imperialist rivalries of European nations. World War II grew out of differences in political beliefs — difference between democracy and various totalitarian systems. (b) Conditions after both wars were desperate for the countries where the wars had been fought; there were vast destruction and problems of rebuilding. (c) Civilian populations suffered more in World War II because of bombings and aerial attacks, the length of the war, and the extent of the fighting.

Making Decisions
Answers will vary, but students may well choose b; a was not decisive, and c was already a lost cause. Instead of starting a two-front war, Hitler could have conquered all of Western Europe and then gone after the Soviet Union.

Continuity and Change
1. Answers will vary but should include the threat of totalitarianism, the persecution of the Jews, the use of saturation bombing, and the use of the atomic bomb.
2. Answers will vary but might include such items as the need for new governments in defeated countries, nationalist movements among colonies, and the need for some international system for keeping peace.

Unit Evaluation

Unit VIII Test can be used to evaluate your students' understanding of this unit.

The Modern World

Unit Overview

Unit IX focuses on changes and problems in the world since 1945 and the relationships between the two rival superpowers—the United States and the USSR.

Western Europe moved toward economic cooperation with the formation of the Common Market. Dramatic political and economic changes turned West Germany into an economically prosperous and democratically stable nation. Great Britain attempted to rebuild its economy by becoming a welfare state. France became politically stable and economically successful under de Gaulle. Dictatorships in Spain, Portugal, and Greece ended.

Eastern Europe's recovery, aided by Comecon, was slower than that of Western Europe. Most Eastern Europeans were loyal to their Communist governments, but there was a constant undercurrent of discontent with Soviet control.

In Asia, Japan became an industrial giant, and China a Communist society and modern industrial nation. Independence brought partition to India and Pakistan and a tragic wave of wars and revolutions to Southeast Asia.

By the 1980's, all of Africa except Namibia was independent. The new nations faced economic and political problems. South Africa, though independent, remained under the rule of a white minority. South African blacks sought to end the apartheid system.

Nationalism sparked conflicts in the Middle East. The UN partition of Palestine created the nation of Israel but left the Palestinian Arabs homeless. Nationalism also led to strife in Iran where Iran's political leader, the shah, was overthrown by religious leaders who established an Islamic republic. Lebanon continued to be a patchwork of warring sects.

After 1945, countries in Latin America faced civil strife and political instability. Dictatorships offered stability but at the price of oppression.

Canada overcame a challenge to its unity when voters in Quebec rejected the separatist movement.

Since 1945, Soviet leaders have been confronted with domestic issues of political succession, economic development, the right to dissent, and ethnic variety. In foreign affairs, the USSR has tried to protect its borders and support Communist governments abroad.

The postwar United States has undergone demographic changes, a shift from manufacturing to service industries, a civil rights movement, and political crises. In foreign policy, deep divisions over the Vietnam War and America's involvement in the Middle East and Central America have raised new problems for policymakers.

Resources

The resources that supplement the study of this unit are:

1. The time line for this unit, found on pages 688–689. The themes for the Unit IX time line are the need to preserve the earth and to achieve cooperation and peace among the earth's peoples.
2. The Geographic Theme (page 802): *Region.* Students use statistics to analyze present-day economic changes in the countries of the Pacific Rim.
3. The Historical Atlas map on pages 818–819, "The Modern World." This map, which also appears as Overhead Transparency 92, provides a global perspective of key events following World War II.
4. The Researching and Reporting Skills activities in the chapter reviews. In Unit IX students apply the research and writing skills they have developed to questions about contemporary societies.

Chapter Titles

The Cold War

Chapter Overview

When World War II ended, the United States and the Soviet Union emerged as rival superpowers. At President Franklin Roosevelt's urging, the United Nations, a worldwide peacekeeping organization, was founded. Yet the threats of nuclear arms and "cold wars" loomed.

Soon after the war, Europe was divided into two political camps separated by an "iron curtain." On the west were the generally democratic countries that allied themselves with the United States. To the east were the Soviet-dominated Communist countries. President Harry Truman initiated a policy of containment to prevent further Communist takeovers.

At the end of World War II, Mao Tse-tung's Communists and Chiang Kai-shek's Nationalists fought a civil war in China. By 1949, the Communists had won control, but the United States refused to recognize the People's Republic of China. In 1950, fighting broke out in Korea between the Soviet-dominated north and the south, which was allied with the United States. The United Nations sent forces to stop the North Korean invasion of the south, and Chinese Communists entered the fighting to help North Korea. When the conflict ended in 1953, neither side had gained territory, but the war showed China had become a great power.

Key Terms

buffer zone, satellite
For additional exercises, see Vocabulary Worksheet 32.

Chapter Focus

Have students read the introduction (pages 690–91). Tell them that the Big Three shared a mood of hope and a sense of historic responsibility. At one of their meetings Churchill offered this toast:

> We see that we are on the crest of the hill and there is before us the prospect of open country. Do not let us underestimate the difficulties. Nations, comrades, in arms, have in the past drifted apart within five or ten years of war.... We now have a chance of avoiding the errors of previous generations and of making a sure peace.... I propose the toast to the broad sunlight of victorious peace.

Read or distribute this passage to the students. Then ask, "What 'errors of previous generations' do you think Churchill is referring to?" Remind students that all three Allied leaders had seen the consequences of the punitive peace imposed on Germany by the Treaty of Versailles. Ask, "Do you think that the Allies had a chance of avoiding errors and 'making a sure peace?'"

Explain that the Yalta conference produced a series of compromises. Tell students that this chapter describes how these compromises were implemented and what happened to the wartime alliance between the United States and the Soviet Union.

Two superpowers arose after the war. 1

Section Objectives

After completing Section 1, students should be able to:

1. explain why the United States and the Soviet Union became rivals.
2. identify the United Nations and describe its organization and goals.
3. identify the arms race between the United States and the Soviet Union and discuss if it could have been avoided.

Setting the Stage

Direct students' attention to the picture on page 692. Ask, "What goal united the Soviet and American forces during World War II?" Emphasize that the common goal of defeating Germany united the two powers. Then ask, "After this goal was met, what united the two countries? Were there any problems that they could join together to solve?" Explain that the end of World War II marked the passing of one historic era and the dawn of a new one. Tell students that this section describes why the United States and the USSR changed from wartime allies to unfriendly rivals.

Teaching Strategies

Skill Building: Identifying Causes (Objective 1) Have students read pages 692–693. Then write the following sentence fragment on the chalkboard: "The relationship between the United States and the Soviet Union changed after the war because..." Students might suggest the relative losses the two nations suffered in World War II, the different goals that the two nations had for the future, the Soviet fear of American power, or the American fear of Soviet communism. Encourage students to explain how each of these factors contributed to the growing rivalry between the United States and the Soviet Union.

Relating Past to Present: The United Nations (Objective 2) Have students read the section on the United Nations (pages 693–694). Then review the United Nation's goals and organization. Explain that the United Nations has not yet achieved its goal of ending "the scourge of war." Point out that it

Advance Planner

Unit IX	The Modern World
Theme	The development of rivalry between the United States and the Soviet Union and the end of Europe's colonial empires

Chapter 32	The Cold War 1945–1956	★ Advanced
Focus	The meeting of the Big Three at Yalta as a turning point in history	● Basic

	Section 1	**Section 2**	**Section 3**
Objectives	1. Explain why the United States and the Soviet Union became rivals. 2. Identify the United Nations and describe its organization and goals. 3. Identify the arms race between the United States and the Soviet Union and discuss if it could have been avoided.	1. Identify the Truman Doctrine and describe the conditions that prompted Truman to issue it. 2. Identify and locate on a map the member nations of NATO and the Warsaw Pact in 1955.	1. List reasons the Chinese Nationalists lost power. 2. Locate the Korean peninsula and explain its strategic importance. 3. Locate the armistice line that divides Korea and explain its continuing significance.
Setting the Stage	Changing goals and changing alliances after World War II Unit IX time line	Conditions in Europe at the end of World War II	Nationalist and Communist Leaders in China

Teaching Strategies	Skill Building: Identifying Causes
	Relating Past to Present:
	  The United Nations
	Discussing History:
	  The Arms Race
	Check for Understanding
		Discussing History:
		  The Truman Doctrine
		Geography in History: Political
		  Alliances after World War II
		Transparency 71
		Outline Map 10
		Check for Understanding
			Discussing History: Why Did
			  the Nationalists lose?
			Using Geographic Themes:
			  Location
			Transparency 92
			Relating Past to Present: The
			  Demilitarized Zone
			Transparency 72
			Check for Understanding

Guided Practice	Section Review 1	Transparency 71 Q&A Section Review 2	Transparency 72 Q&A Section Review 3
Independent Practice Worksheets	Independent Practice 32.1 Vocabulary 32	Independent Practice 32.2 Geography Skills 32 Critical Thinking 32	Independent Practice 32.3 Basic Skills 32
Enrichment	1. Primary Source: Voices 32.1 2. ★ Relating Past to Present 3. Researching for Points	1. Primary Source: Voices 32.2 2. ★ Preparing a Report 3. Researching for Points	1. Primary Source: Voices 32.3 2. Researching for Points

Chapter Closer	
● **Reteaching Activities**	Summarizing, Listing
Chapter Review	Summary, Reviewing the Facts, Basic Skills, Researching and Reporting Skills, Critical Thinking, Perspectives on Past and Present, Investigating History
Chapter Evaluation	Chapter Test 32, Computer Test Bank Chapter 32 Test

nevertheless does play a constructive role in global affairs. For example, the General Assembly provides a common forum for the United Nations' 159 member nations to discuss global and regional issues. The United Nations' 10,000 employees administer social, economic, and cultural programs throughout the world. (Many of the United Nations' cultural activities are described in the *UNESCO Courier.*) United Nations peacekeeping forces now play a significant role in patrolling global trouble spots. Tell students that the Nobel Committee recognized this valuable contribution when it awarded the 1988 Nobel Peace Prize to the United Nations soldiers.

Discussing History: The Arms Race (Objective 3) Explain that in 1946 the United States presented a plan to the United Nations to control nuclear weapons. The plan called for the creation of an international agency to control the use of atomic energy for peaceful purposes. The Truman administration pledged to give its nuclear secrets and weapons to this agency. In order to prevent cheating, the agency would have the authority to inspect atomic energy plants in all countries. Have students evaluate the plan's advantages and disadvantages. Ask, "Would this plan have been acceptable to the Soviet Union?"

Tell students that the Soviet Union rejected the proposal. The Soviets insisted that international inspection was unacceptable. They then presented a plan calling for a total ban on the use of nuclear weapons as well as the destruction of all existing bombs. However, the Soviet plan failed to provide for inspections to prevent nations from secretly violating it. Because they disagreed on this important issue, the United States and the Soviet Union accelerated their nuclear programs, thus beginning the nuclear arms race.

Check for Understanding Have students compare and contrast the goals of the United States and the Soviet Union after World War II.

Practice

Guided Practice
Lead a guided discussion of the questions in Section Review 1. (Answers are below.)

Define:
(a) reduce the number of armed forces after a war (b) region between two nations that reduces the threat of open conflict (c) "no" vote (d) weapon getting its power from reactions to atomic nucleus

Identify:
(a) meeting of Big Three focusing on ending the

war (b) conflict between two unfriendly nations that is neither peace nor open warfare (c) succeeded Roosevelt as president (d) worldwide peacekeeping organization (e) main representative body of UN (f) UN group that investigates disputes, keeps peace, and takes emergency action (g) weapons competition between powerful nations

Answer:
1. (a) American factories and cities remained unscathed from bombings. (b) possessed biggest navy, best-equipped army and air force, atom bomb
2. favored international cooperation over political isolationism
3. (a) buffer zone along its western front (b) would give Soviets control of Eastern Europe
4. (a) All major powers joined, and the UN formed a joint peacekeeping force. (b) veto power of Security Council members
5. The Soviet Union and the United States competed to see who could build larger and more powerful nuclear weapons.
6. Both the USSR and the United States emerged from the war economically and militarily strong. The United States had not been occupied during the war, was anxious to disarm, and sought world democracy under its leadership. The USSR had been occupied, wanted world leadership as well as protection from further invasions. Competition for leadership, differing goals, and conflicting ideologies would make the countries rivals.

Independent Practice
Assign Independent Practice Worksheet 32.1.
Assign Vocabulary Worksheet 32.

Enrichment Activities

1. **Reading a Primary Source** Assign Voices from the Past Resource Book 32.1.

2. **Relating Past to Present** America conducted its first postwar atomic tests at the Bikini Atoll. Ask advanced students to prepare a report on these tests and the impact they had on the way of life of the people of Bikini. (See *National Geographic*, "Bikini—A Way of Life Lost," June 1986.)

3. **Researching for Bonus Points** Award bonus points to students who can answer this question: Who was the first Secretary-General of the United Nations? (Trygve Lie of Norway)

Answers to Voice from Our Time

1. No; he is starting to plan for the next war

2. the achievements in science and technology and the high productivity
3. Answers will vary, but will probably support Douglas. This speech was in effect the first round of the cold war.

The war left Europe divided. 2

Section Objectives

After completing Section 2, students should be able to:

1. identify the Truman Doctrine and describe the conditions that prompted Truman to issue it.
2. identify and locate on a map the member nations of NATO and the Warsaw Pact in 1955.

Setting the Stage

Tell students that World War II left Europe in ruins. Britain looked like a defeated country. More than half of its factories lay idle and millions of workers were unemployed. The situation in Germany was even worse. The few remaining factories produced only 29 percent of the nation's prewar output. Shoppers used cigarettes to buy scarce goods. Most Germans had to survive on less than 1550 calories a day—barely enough to survive. Meanwhile, economic conditions in France and Italy also declined. The Communist party gained strength in both countries and threatened to radically change their governments.

Describe these conditions to your students. Then ask, "How would American policymakers of the 1920's have responded to this situation?" Explain that while the United States would have sent humanitarian aid, it would have tried to continue its policy of isolationism. Ask students if this policy could be continued in postwar Europe. Tell students that this section describes how the United States helped to rebuild and defend postwar Europe.

Teaching Strategies

Discussing History: The Truman Doctrine (Objective 1) Tell students that by 1947, Communist governments had seized power in Albania, Bulgaria, Romania, Poland, and Hungary. Explain that these countries became known as satellites because their domestic and foreign policies depended upon the approval of the Soviet government. Point out that Soviet expansion was not limited to Eastern Europe. Stalin placed great pressure on the Turkish government to agree to a treaty that would give Russia control over the strategic Dardanelles strait. The Soviet dictator also sent aid to Communist guerrillas, who appeared to be on the verge of overthrowing the Greek government.

Explain that Britain had been the dominant great power in the eastern Mediterranean. However, the British lacked the economic and military strength to fulfill their traditional commitments to Turkey and Greece. On February 21, 1947, the First Secretary of the British Embassy in Washington delivered two notes to the United States State Department. These notes acknowledged that the British could no longer support the Greek and Turkish governments. The British decisions marked the end of one era and the beginning of another. As an American official later noted: "Great Britain had within the hour handed the job of world leadership with all its burden and all its glory to the United States."

Tell students that the British notes forced the Truman administration to make a decision. Within three weeks President Truman asked Congress for military and economic aid for Greece and Turkey. The President explained his request by saying: "I believe that it must be the policy of the United States to support free peoples who are resisting attempted subjugation by armed minorities or by outside pressures." Read this statement to students and ask, "What problems made countries eligible for American support? What did Truman mean by 'outside pressures?'" Stress that the Truman Doctrine became the cornerstone of America's policy to contain Communist expansion.

Geography in History: Political Alliances After World War II (Objective 2) Show students Overhead Transparency 71, *Postwar Europe*, and discuss the postwar political divisions. Distribute Outline Map 10: Political Europe. Have students refer to the transparency or to the map on page 699 to label the countries of Western Europe and Eastern Europe. Students should identify the NATO countries and the Warsaw Pact countries. Have students draw map keys and add titles to their maps.

Check for Understanding Have students identify the following postwar developments: Truman Doctrine, Marshall Plan, NATO, Warsaw Pact, and the Berlin Airlift.

Practice

Guided Practice

Lead a guided discussion of the questions in Overhead Transparency 71 and in Section Review 2. (Answers are below.)

Define:

(a) country whose politics are controlled by another country (b) Truman's policy to keep communism from spreading

Identify:

(a) trials of Nazi leaders for war crimes (b) Yugoslavian leader who kept his country independent of the USSR (c) alliance of the Western European countries and US (d) alliance of the USSR and seven Eastern European countries (e) moderate but powerful Soviet leader after Stalin's death

Answer:

1. (a) into four occupation zones (b) Three zones controlled by Allies were united under a democratic government, but eastern zone stayed under Soviet control.
2. Soviet troops occupied most of Eastern Europe. Local Communists were strong.
3. Yugoslavia remained independent of USSR.
4. (a) policy of containment (b) United States gave military and economic aid to defeat the Communist rebels in Greece.
5. (a) stabilize currency, increase production, expand exports (b) Europe's economy improved dramatically.
6. (a) military support if attacked (b) formed Warsaw Pact
7. (a) non-Communist island in East Germany (b) The Soviets blockaded West Berlin, but the Allies airlifted supplies to the city.
8. (a) free themselves of Soviet control (b) Rebels were defeated with Soviet tanks.
9. (a) Colonial empires began to crumble. (b) British withdrew peacefully, while the French fought to keep their colonies.
10. Answers might consider magnitude of the crimes, motives of the perpetrators, and methods used to carry out the crimes.

Independent Practice

Assign Independent Practice Worksheet 32.2.
Assign Geography Skills Worksheet 32.
Assign Critical Thinking Worksheet 32.

Enrichment Activities

1. **Reading a Primary Source** Assign Voices from the Past Resource Book 32.2.

2. **Researching for Bonus Points** Award bonus points to students who can answer this question: What is the present location of the headquarters of the NATO alliance? (Brussels, Belgium)

China became a Communist country. 3

Section Objectives

After completing Section 3, students should be able to:

1. list reasons the Chinese Nationalists lost power.
2. locate the Korean peninsula and explain its strategic importance.
3. locate the armistice line that divides Korea and explain its continuing significance.

Setting the Stage

Begin by writing the names "Mao Tse-Tung" and "Chiang Kai-shek" on the chalkboard. Ask students to identify these two leaders. Remind students that Chiang was the leader of the Chinese Nationalists, while Mao was the leader of the Chinese Communists. Tell students that this section begins with a discussion of how China became a Communist country. It then discusses how cold war tensions led to a conflict in Korea.

Teaching Strategies

Discussing History: Why did the Nationalists Lose? (Objective 1) Have students read the sections that discuss how China became a Communist country. Then ask, "Why did the Nationalists lose?" Explain that historians now recognize five key reasons that help explain the collapse of Chiang's government. First, the Nationalist forces had to fight a long and exhausting war against the Japanese and against the Chinese Communists. Second, Chiang failed to carry out needed land reforms, thus losing the support of China's vast peasant population. Third, the Communists carried out land reforms while skillfully hiding their real economic goals. Fourth, the Soviet invasion of Manchuria denied Chiang that province's valuable industrial resources. Finally, Chiang's army misused America's economic and military aid.

The head of the American military mission reported that: "No battle has been lost since my arrival due to lack of ammunition or equipment. Their [the Nationalists'] military debacle, in my opinion, can all be attributed to the world's worst leadership and many other morale-destroying factors that led to a complete loss of the will to fight."

Using Geographic Themes: Location (Objective 2) Show students Overhead Transparency 92, *The Modern World.* Help them locate the Korean peninsula. Ask, "What two countries border the Korean peninsula?" (China and the Soviet Union) Also point out that the peninsula is only about 100 miles from Japan. Then ask students to explain why the Korean peninsula represents a particularly sensitive strategic location. Help students to see that the peninsula forms a partial land bridge linking the Chinese mainland and Japan. Historically, China and Japan have repeatedly used Korea as an invasion route to attack each other. Both countries therefore wanted to make sure that a friendly government controlled the Korean peninsula. Emphasize that these strategic concerns played an important role in the Korean War.

Relating Past to Present: The Demilitarized Zone (Objective 3) Show students Overhead Transparency 72, *The Korean War 1950–1953.* Help students locate the 1953 armistice line. Explain that this line is now a demilitarized zone that separates North Korea and South Korea. The zone remains one of the most heavily guarded boundaries in the world. About 800,000 North Korean troops and 650,000 South Korean troops closely watch each other across the tense boundary. Tell students that the South Korean forces are supported by 43,000 American soldiers.

Check for Understanding Ask students to name three reasons the Communists succeeded in China.

Practice

Guided Practice
Lead a guided discussion of the questions in Overhead Transparency 72 and in Section Review 3. (Answers are below.)

Identify:
(a) Chinese Communist leader (b) Nationalist leader of China (c) island site of Republic of China (d) war that ended in stalement split of Korea (e) commander of UN forces in Korea

Answer:
1. formed political groups in villages, gained support from peasants, recruited large army
2. took aid from United States, fought occasional battles against Japanese
3. recognized only Nationalist China
4. (a) Soviets occupied northern half, American troops southern half. (b) North Korea attacked South Korea.
5. (a) sent troops to stop North Korean invasion (b) ordered its troops to support the South Koreans (c) joined war on North Korea's side
6. stalemate
7. (a) Nationalists had large, well-equipped army and aid from U.S. Communists had strong peasant support, Mao's military strategies. (b) possibly corruption and weakening of Nationalists

Independent Practice
Assign Independent Practice Worksheet 32.3.
Assign Basic Skills Worksheet 32.

Enrichment Activities

1. **Reading a Primary Source** Assign Voices from the Past Resource Book 32.3.

2. **Researching for Bonus Points** Award bonus points to students who can answer this question: What is the name of the square in Peking (Beijing) where Mao announced the formation of the People's Republic of China? (Tiananmen Square)

Concluding the Chapter

1. **Chapter Closer**
   Ask students to assess the extent to which the plans of the Big Three at Yalta were realized in the postwar world.

2. **Reteaching Activities**
   a. **Summarizing** Ask students to tell how the Berlin Airlift, Truman Doctrine, NATO, and Warsaw Pact helped widen the rift between the United States and the USSR.
   b. **Listing** Have students list two reasons the Korean War differed from previous conflicts.

3. **Chapter Review Activities**
Assign Chapter Review 32 activities.

Chapter Evaluation

Chapter Test 32 and Computer Test Bank Chapter

32 Test can be used to evaluate your students' understanding of this chapter.

Answers to Chapter Review 32

Reviewing the Facts
1. (a) area between rival countries (b) country controlled by another
2. (a) planned for end of war (b) warfare without open conflict (c) dropped bomb on Japan, initiated policy of containment (d) trial of Nazis for war crimes (e) kept Yugoslavia free of Soviet control (f) symbolizes division between West and Communists (g) symbolizes division between West and Communists (g) go control spread of Communism (h) rebuilt Europe's economy (i) Western protective alliance (j) Eastern protective alliance (k) democratic half of Germany's former capital (l) gave Soviet satellites more control over their governments (m) led Hungarian revolt (n) leader of Communist China (o) leader of Nationalist China (p) headquarters of Nationalist Chinese government

Basic Skills
1. (a) long Adriatic coastline and water access to Black Sea (b) These countries bordered the USSR and had no access to seas or harbors through which they could get supplies.
2. (a) Role of Government: U.S.—protect democracy, rights of citizens, Constitution; USSR—keep industry and economy nationalized, stop resistance to its programs. Political Parties: U.S.—any formed are allowed; USSR—only Communist party allowed. Economic System: U.S.—free economy, only impacted by government when individuals' rights are affected; USSR—aims to be socially controlled. Role of Individuals: U.S.—all individuals have say in government and are protected by democracy; USSR—individual is part of one body, the collective way of life. International Objectives: U.S.—help build peaceful, democratic world; USSR—increase power of communism and protect itself. (b) Inaccurate; the USSR tends toward totalitarianism especially in economic system.

Researching and Reporting Skills
Students' findings will vary.

Critical Thinking
1. (a) did everything short of war to prevent further Communist takeovers (b) 12 non-communist nations joined together to protect themselves against attack (c) helped Europe recover economically in order to be stronger and more cooperative with one another
2. Eastern Europe became a buffer zone as Communists won powerful posts in Eastern European countries and Soviet satellites were created. The Warsaw Pact strengthened Eastern Europe's unity under the USSR.
3. After World War II, the U.S. worked with other countries to try to gain international peace and democracy. In contrast, after World War I, the U.S. followed a policy of isolationism—avoiding political ties to other countries.
4. (a) aid from U.S., the Marshall Plan, cooperation among countries (b) Countries had stable currency, increased production, and expanded exports. (c) The countries were strong enough to withstand invasion and banded together against communism.
5. (a) UN—51 countries; League—42 countries (b) UN—required consent of all 5 permanent members of Security Council to take action, which rarely happened; League—burden fell on Great Britain and France, who were not strong enough to keep peace except through appeasement (c) UN—U.S. and USSR served on Security Council and so vetoed each other often; league—Germany, Japan and Italy were members, USSR joined in 1934, U.S. never joined.
6. (a) spread of nuclear weapons, disagreements over economics and politics, division of Germany, split between Eastern and Western Europe, rival alliances, failure of UN in peacekeeping, Korean War (b) Students' answers will vary; encourage them to substantiate their opinions.
7. (a) losses suffered by China in war, aid communists gave peasants, corruption among Nationalists (b) Students' answers will vary but might include economic difficulties, lack of support from urban workers, and international distrust.
8. (a) Both situations represented acts of aggression and included requests for UN help. (b) In Hungary, the Soviets were already established in a satellite country; in Korea, the Soviets were not yet established. When pleas for help came to the UN from Hungary, the Soviets vetoed; when pleas came from Korea, the Soviets were absent.

Perspective on Past and Present
Students' opinions will vary.

Investigating History
Students' findings will vary.

Cooperation and Division in Europe

Chapter Overview

After World War II, the nations of Western Europe moved to restore political unity and economic prosperity to the region. The formation of the Common Market in 1957 marked the first step toward reducing internal trade barriers. Another important step will be taken in 1992 when the twelve-member nations embark on a single-market plan. In implementing this program, considerable differences must be overcome among such diverse economies as those of the United Kingdom, France, and the nations of Southern Europe.

Despite Soviet Aid, Eastern Europe experienced slow economic growth after the war. In 1961 the Soviet government reaffirmed its domination by stemming emigration from East Germany to West Germany through construction of the Berlin Wall. It also crushed 1968 efforts at reform in Czechoslovakia in what has become known as "Prague Spring." Similar crack-downs followed in Poland against Solidarity, a workers' union. Under Mikhail Gorbachev, the USSR granted greater freedom to its satellites. However, because of past repressive measures, most Europeans greeted the move with a mixture of happiness and suspicion.

After the death of Joseph Stalin in 1957, Nikita Khrushchev took control of the Communist government. However, even modest reforms, what Khrushchev called "de-Stalinization," cost him the support of party officials. After the loss of prestige abroad, Khrushchev fell from power. For the next twenty years, a series of "hard-liners" held the reins of government. Then, in 1985, Mikhail Gorbachev took over and introduced a policy of *glasnost*—"openness." Both the Soviets and people around the world watched the new policy of toleration with a measure of caution.

Key Terms

import quota, productivity, martial law, dissident, welfare state
For additional exercises, see Vocabulary Worksheet 33.

Chapter Focus

Introduce the chapter by asking students to imagine the United States as a loose confederation of separate, independent nations. Each state may make its own trade laws and enter into treaties with other nations. Passports are required to cross from one "nation" to the other. What problems might arise in such a situation? For example, how would travel and communication be hindered? What would happen to the price of goods shipped from the west coast to the east coast?

Next, write the following sentence from the text on the chalkboard: "Europe has been a nation of boundaries." Call on volunteers to explain what this statement might mean. Then assign students to read the opening paragraphs of Chapter 33 (pages 708–709). Ask "How has the common Market helped strengthen Europe?" Tell students that this chapter explores the ways in which leaders in Western Europe and Eastern Europe have tried to promote regional economic and political cooperation.

Western Europe moved toward cooperation. 1

Section Objectives

After completing Section 1, students should be able to:

1. explain steps Europeans are taking to strengthen economic unity.
2. discuss the meaning of the "Thatcher Revolution."
3. describe the influence of Charles De Gaulle on French government.
4. cite reasons for Southern Europe's rapid economic growth.

Setting the Stage

To introduce students to the Common Market, write the names of the twelve-member nations on the chalkboard or on an overhead transparency: United Kingdom, Ireland, Portugal, Spain, France, Netherlands, Denmark, Belgium, West Germany, Luxembourg, Greece, and Italy. Show Overhead Transparency 73, *Europe Today*, and have students locate the Common Market countries. Then, explain that these nations are bound by treaty to lower all trade barriers by December 31, 1992. The goal is to create a single market, or what supporters of the plan call "a Europe without Frontiers."

Ask students to speculate about some of the practical problems that might arise when this plan goes into effect. To stimulate discussion, tell students that a panel spent five years trying to get all twelve nations to agree on a definition of "white bread." The panel finally gave up, declaring white bread to be anything so named by the country where it was baked. Then point out that Section 1 discusses some of the economic differences that members of the Common Market must resolve to make "1992" a success.

Teaching Strategies

Economics and History: Competing for World Markets (Objective 1) To help students assess the economic clout that the European Community will hold when internal trade barriers come down in 1992, distribute copies of the following statistics.

- In 1987, the European Community exported goods worth just under $400 billion—60 percent more than the United States and nearly 100 percent more than Japan.
- In 1987, the European Community imported goods worth just under $400 billion—roughly equal to United States imports and nearly triple Japanese imports.
- In 1987, the European Community's more than 320 million people made it the largest consumer group in the industrial world.

After students have examined these figures, ask, "Why do many Europeans believe that the 1992 plans for a single market without trade barriers will make Western Europe a world power? Suppose that the European Community decided in 1992 to raise high protective tariffs against foreign competition. What effect might this have on the economies of the United States and Japan?" As a clue, point out the large number of imports consumed by the twelve-member nations. Then challenge students to suggest why foreign critics of a "Euromarket" have nicknamed it "Fortress Europe."

Analyzing a Quotation: The "Thatcher Revolution" (Objective 2) Read aloud the following passage from Marx and Engels to the class: "The modern bourgeois society ... has not done away with class antagonisms. It has but established new classes, new conditions of oppression, new forms of struggle...."

Then read Margaret Thatcher's words from the text: "Capitalism and enterprise is a system which only works by spreading ever more widely to more and more of the population what used to be the privileges of the few."

Use these two quotations to explore Thatcher's attack on socialism. Ask students how Thatcher might answer the charge by Marx and Engels that the rise of a bourgeoisie—a factory-owning middle class—increases class hostilities. Next, assign the text material on Thatcher. Have students evaluate the Prime Minister's success in advancing capitalism.

Skill Building: Interpreting a Political Cartoon (Objective 3) Tell students that Louis XIV once said: "My dominant passion is certainly love of glory." Then have the class turn to the political cartoon on page 715. According to the cartoonist, how would De Gaulle react to this statement? What clues in the cartoon support students' answers.

Next, allow time for students to skim through the material on De Gaulle on pages 714–715. Ask how De Gaulle changed the role of the president in French government. Suggest the following alternative caption for the cartoon, using another quote by Louis XIV: *"L'etat, c'est moi"*—"the state is me." Have students write paragraphs assessing the appropriateness of this caption, based on information in the text.

Discussing History: Southern Europe's Economic Growth (Objective 4) Tell students that a Spanish official recently declared, "We are Europe's California." A Portuguese spokesperson asked, "Could we be Europe's Florida?" To explore the meaning of these statements in terms of economics, ask students to compare the resources of California and Florida with those of Spain and Portugal. The most obvious similarities are climate—the almost year-round presence of the warm sun—and long coastlines with miles of beaches. Then have students find information in the text on other reasons Southern Europeans might compare their nations to California and Florida. What industries do the regions have in common? Point out the importance of tourism and the presence of "high-tech" industries in places such as California's "Silicon Valley" and Italy's Po Valley. If students have had an opportunity to travel in Southern Europe, call on them to make the descriptions of the area's geographic resources more vivid. Ask students to summarize the reasons for Southern Europe's economic growth.

Check for Understanding Ask students to reconsider their predictions about the problems that

Europeans will face when the "single-market" plan goes into effect in 1992. (See Setting the Stage.) What do students think are the biggest obstacles for the Common Market to overcome?

Practice

Guided Practice
Lead a guided discussion of the questions in Overhead Transparency 73 and in Section Review 1. (Answers are below.)

Define:
(a) tax on incoming goods (b) limit one country sets on goods that may be imported (c) country in which government assumes responsibility for people's social and economic well-being (d) worker's hourly output (e) fighters who are not part of a formal army, usually attack by surprise, and withdraw swiftly

Identify:
(a) group formed to encourage trade among Western European countries (b) Eastern European eco-

Advance Planner

Chapter 33	The Cooperation and Division in Europe 1945–Present		★ Advanced
Focus	The effects of political boundaries on commerce and trade		● Basic

	Section 1	Section 2	Section 3
Objectives	1. Explain steps Europeans are taking to strengthen economic unity. 2. Discuss the meaning of the "Thatcher Revolution." 3. Describe the influence of Charles De Gaulle on French government. 4. Cite reasons for Southern Europe's rapid economic growth.	1. Explain how the Berlin Wall became a symbol of Soviet domination in Eastern Europe. 2. Describe how Eastern European's view Gorbachev's new Soviet policies.	1. Identify problems in the Soviet economy and domestic policies. 2. Explain why religion is controversial in the USSR. 3. Discuss how ethnic groups in the USSR pose a challenge to the Soviet government.
Setting the Stage	Problems in implementing the Common Market Transparency 73	Berlin's history of occupation and division	Standards of living in the Soviet Union
Teaching Strategies	Economics and History: Competing for World Markets Analyzing a Quotation: The "Thatcher Revolution" Skill Building: Interpreting a Political Cartoon Discussing History: Southern Europe's Economic Growth Check for Understanding	Teaching with Pictures: The Berlin Wall Relating Past to Present: Soviet Policy in Czechoslovakia Check for Understanding	Writing about History: The Accident at Chernobyl Analyzing Quotations: Religion in the USSR Skill Building: Predicting Trends Transparency 83 Check for Understanding
Guided Practice	Transparency 73 Q&A Section Review 1	Section Review 2	Transparency 83 Q&A Section Review 3
Independent Practice Worksheets	Independent Practice 33.1 Vocabulary 33	Independent Practice 33.2 Basic Skills 33 Critical Thinking 33	Independent Practice 33.3 Geography Skills 33
Enrichment	1. Primary Source: Voices 33.1 2. Relating Past to Present 3. Researching for Points	1. Primary Source: Voices 33.2 2. ★ Skill Building: Making Predictions 3. Researching for Points	1. Primary Source: Voices 33.3 2. Relating Past to Present 3. Researching for Points

Chapter Closer ● **Reteaching Activities**	Summarizing, Making a Time Line
Chapter Review	Summary, Reviewing the Facts, Basic Skills, Researching and Reporting Skills, Critical Thinking, Perspectives on Past and Present, Investigating History
Chapter Evaluation	Chapter Test 33, Computer Test Bank Chapter 33 Test

nomic organization (c) French statesman who proposed economic cooperation (d) leader who rebuilt West Germany's economy (e) Willy Brandt's program to improve relations with USSR and Eastern Europe (f) first woman prime minister of Britain (g) French war hero and strong leader of the Fifth Republic (h) Spanish dictator (i) king of Spain who led his country toward democracy

Answer:
1. wider range of goods, freedom of travel among member countries
2. (a) European Coal and Steel Community (b) by Treaty of Rome
3. (a) rebuilt West German economy, allied West Germany with United States, NATO, and Common Market (b) improved relations with USSR and Eastern Europe (c) expansion of government, peace, environment
4. (a) nationalized transportation, Bank of England, utilities introduced program of social welfare (b) obsolete factories and equipment, low worker productivity, decreased exports, high cost of imports, brain drain (c) reduced government spending and borrowing, lowered interest rates, cut taxes, reorganized some nationalized businesses as private companies
5. conflicts between Protestant majority and Catholic minority, presence of British troops
6. (a) lacked strong executive leadership (b) breakup of colonial empire
7. (a) National Assembly gave him full powers of government for six months. (b) Nationalist stand, independent of United States and NATO
8. increased prosperity with tourism, growth of industry, and foreign investment
9. Political unity can infringe on national self-interests, does not account for different systems of government, and presents problems of leadership.

Independent Practice
Assign Independent Practice Worksheet 33.1.
Assign Vocabulary Worksheet 33.

Enrichment Activities

1. **Reading a Primary Source** Assign Voices from the Past Resource Book 33.1.
2. **Relating Past to Present** Call on volunteers to research life in Spain during the dictatorship of General Francisco Franco. Have students share their findings in oral reports to the class. Then ask the class why present-day Spain might shock someone who has not visited there since 1975, the year of Franco's death.

3. **Researching for Bonus Points** Award bonus points to students who can find the answer to this question: What European city manufactures Ferrari and Maserati sports cars? (Modena, Italy)

Eastern Europe was linked to the USSR. 2

Section Objectives

After completing Section 2, students should be able to:

1. explain how the Berlin Wall became a symbol of Soviet domination in Eastern Europe.
2. describe how Eastern Europeans view Gorbachev's new Soviet policies.

Setting the Stage

To open this section on Eastern Europe, recount the following story: After the division of Berlin into East Berlin and West Berlin, an American returned to visit the city after a sixty-year absence. Asking a taxi driver to explain what had happened during the long interlude, the visitor was told: "The Nazis came, the war came, the Russians came. You didn't miss much."

Have students suggest what this anecdote implies about the experiences of people living in the divided city. For example, why might the driver have felt that the coming of the Nazis and of the Russians was merely "more of the same?" Then tell students that Section 2 examines Eastern Europe in the context of today's world.

Teaching Strategies

Teaching with Pictures: The Berlin Wall (Objective 1) Before discussing material on East Germany, pose the following "What is it?" question to the class:

It is thirteen feet high and twenty-eight miles long. It is steel-reinforced concrete covered with a twisted web of barbed wire. It is guarded by soldiers and police armed with field glasses and machine guns. Guards have orders to shoot anyone who tries to cross it. What is it?

As another clue, tell students that West Berliners call it the "wall of shame." After identifying the

Berlin Wall, point out that before its construction, 2,000 people fled to the West during a single week. Since the Wall was completed in August 1961, only about 5,000 East Germans have successfully crossed to freedom.

To show why a wall was needed, have students study the photo on page 717. Call on volunteers to describe the scene. Why was this photo considered a propaganda "coup" for the West? What did the Soviets hope to accomplish by building the wall?

Relating Past to Present: Soviet Policy in Czechoslovakia (Objective 2) The text points out that most Eastern Europeans have reacted with hope and with caution to Mikhail Gorbachev's new policy of openness. Focus on this idea by telling students the following East European joke:

> "What is the difference between the reform program of Mikhail Gorbachev and that of Alexander Dubcek in Czechoslovakia in 1968? Answer: Nothing—but Gorbachev doesn't know it yet."

Then have students read about Prague Spring in 1968 on page 718. How did Soviets react to reform at that time? How does the information help explain the following comment by a 19-year-old Czechoslovakian construction worker, when asked about Gorbachev's reforms: "We don't look forward to much, and we don't trust anyone." Have students find out about present-day Soviet policies toward satellite countries. Why, do students think, has Gorbachev focused on Czechoslovakia in his plans for dismantling old hard-line policies?

Check for Understanding Ask students to characterize Soviet relations with East Germany, Czechoslovakia, Poland, Yugoslavia, Albania, and Romania.

Practice

Guided Practice
Lead a guided discussion of the questions in Section Review 2. (Answers are below.)

Define:
situation in which military authorities rule a civilian population

Identify:
(a) barrier built between the two halves of Berlin (b) Czechoslovakian leader (c) time of Dubcek's reforms (d) Polish leader installed by Soviets (e) workers' union in Poland (f) leader of Solidarity (g) Yugoslavian leader who broke with USSR (h) Soviet leader who introduced changes in politics and economic policy

Answer:
1. (a) East Germany—shortages of food and goods, buildings left unrepaired; West Germany—rising standard of living, new construction (b) has a higher living standard, expanding economy, and economic contacts with West
2. (a) attempted to create "socialism with a human face" (b) invaded Czechoslovakia
3. (a) rising food prices, nationalist pride (b) Reforms promised were not made. Instead, Polish government declared martial law, arrested Solidarity leaders, and declared union illegal. (c) Because the economy was weakening and it was clear that reforms were needed.
4. (a) Romanians have sought to be neutral; Albania sided for a time with China; Yugoslavia has steered a separate course. (b) Reforms are essential, but they require a loosening of control.
5. (a) USSR did not allow Eastern Europeans to set their own economic priorities. (b) Nationalism has led Eastern Europeans to seek more autonomy from the Soviet Union. To stamp out nationalistic movements, Soviets have invaded Czechoslovakia and declared martial rule in Poland.

Independent Practice
Assign Independent Practice Worksheet 33.2.
Assign Basic Skills Worksheet 33.
Assign Critical Thinking Worksheet 33.

Enrichment Activities

1. **Reading a Primary Source** Assign Voices from the Past Resource Book 33.2.

2. **Skill Building: Making Predictions** Ask advanced students to predict the freedoms Polish workers in the solidarity movement might expect to gain. How much can they pressure the Soviet government before it again takes repressive measures?

3. **Researching for Bonus Points** What is the Polish word for *solidarity*, which workers emblazon on their red and white banners? (*solidarnosc*)

Answers to Voice From Our Time

1. The Communist government controlled the press.
2. to speak the truth
3. cannot suppress thought and the will to resist

Policies changed within the USSR. 3

Section Objectives

After completing Section 3, students should be able to:

1. identify problems in the Soviet economy and domestic policies.
2. explain why religion is controversial in the USSR.
3. discuss how ethnic groups in the USSR pose a challenge to the Soviet government.

Setting the Stage

To open the section, tell students the following anecdote: In 1988 a magazine reporter interviewed Valentina Vladironova Mityushov, a high school physics teacher in the Soviet Union. Valentina takes home approximately $367 a month in pay. Her husband banks his wages, hoping to buy a new car. After more than two years, the couple has managed to save $6,680. However, they still need to save for another year. In the meantime, they live in a two-room apartment with their two sons and do most of their errands on foot or by bus.

Ask students what problems this story suggests about the Soviet economy. Students might note Valentina's small salary and the family's small apartment, which suggests that the standard of living in the Soviet Union is not as high as in the United States. Point out, however, that the Soviet government provides free medical care, education, and other services. Tell students that this section describes the Soviet planned economy and its effects on Soviet citizens.

Teaching Strategies

Writing about History: The Accident at Chernobyl (Objective 1) Ask students to name Soviet economic problems and list suggestions on the chalkboard. Ask, "What domestic issue did the Chernobyl accident force the Soviet Union to acknowledge?" (the issue of environmental quality) Explain that on April 26, 1986, at 1:23 A.M. the worst atomic accident in history occurred at the Chernobyl Nuclear Power Plant. To show the extent of the disaster, write the following statistics on the chalkboard or on an overhead transparency:

- A blast blew off a thousand-ton concrete lid and tore apart one of four working nuclear reactors.
- An increase in radioactivity was recorded as far away as California.
- More than 116,000 people were evacuated from the Soviet republics of the Ukraine and Byelorussia.
- Thirty-one people died in the accident; another 24,000 suffered severe doses of radiation.

Read the following comment from an evacuee: "There is a beautiful nature in that place [the Chernobyl region]—water, forests, berries, and mushrooms to pick.... I was born there and brought up there. After 50 years it is difficult to settle down somewhere else."

Have students use this information and material on page 724 to write a news article on the accident. Call on volunteers to read their articles to the class.

Analyzing Quotations: Religion in the USSR (Objective 2) Read the following passages to the class:

> "[All citizens have] freedom of conscience, that is, the right to profess any religion ... and to perform religious worship."
> —Soviet Constitution

> "The authorities allow the [Eastern Orthodox] church to exist, but it's their [the government's] church. That's why few priests ask to have the laws changed."
> —Soviet religious dissident

Ask, "What does the Soviet Constitution say about religion in the Soviet Union? According to the dissident, why is there less religious freedom than the constitution allows?" Point out that all churches, mosques, and synagogues in the USSR belong to the state. Government propaganda discourages participation in organized religion. Ask students why a totalitarian government might restrict the practice of religion. Recall Karl Marx's views on religion as a barrier to the Communist Revolution.

Skill Building: Predicting Trends (Objective 3) Have students read "The USSR has many nationalities" (page 725). Point out that ethnic Russians are losing their majority status. The United States Census Bureau has projected that other nationalities in the USSR will outnumber Russians by four percent by the year 2000. Challenge students to predict how this change might affect Soviet leaders' policies toward ethnic groups. Ask, "How might a nationalist movements based on a common ethnic identity, language, culture, and history threaten the Soviet Union?" Have students use the map on page 727 to locate the strongly nationalist regions of Kazakh and Soviet Armenia, or use Overhead Transparency 83, *The Soviet Union.*

Check for Understanding Have students identify the views of Nikita Khrushchev, Leonid Brezhnev, and Mikhail Gorbachev on domestic reform.

Practice

Guided Practice
Lead a guided discussion of the questions in Overhead Transparency 83 and in Section Review 3. (Answers are below.)

Define:
(a) policy that attacked Stalin and his policies (b) basic industries that produce metals, farm machinery, trucks, and weapons (c) "self-publishing" (d) person who expresses a differing opinion (e) policy that tries to force other ethnic groups to accept Russian culture

Identify:
(a) Soviet leader who initiated de-Stalinization policy (b) political bureau of the Communist party's central committee (c) Soviet leader who reversed many of Khrushchev's policies (d) present-day Soviet leader (e) site of nuclear power accident in 1986 (f) Russian writer whose books were censored

Answer:
1. (a) no legal, well-defined plan of succession (b) Many party members had suffered under Stalin's dictatorship and wanted leaders to share power.
2. called for reforms many party leaders disliked
3. reversed many of Khrushchev's policies, clamped down on dissent
4. flexible central plans, economic reforms, relaxation of censorship
5. (a) changed its attitude toward economic planning (b) shortage of consumer goods
6. (a) during Khrushchev's and Gorbachev's rule (b) imprisonment, hospitalization, exile
7. (a) frowns on all organized religion (b) tries to force other ethnic groups to accept the Russian culture
8. Advantages may include efficiency and continuity in leadership and policies. Disadvantages are lack of an orderly process for selecting a leader and control by a party not necessarily representative of the people.

Independent Practice
Assign Independent Practice Worksheet 33.3. Assign Geography Skills Worksheet 33.

Enrichment Activities

1. **Reading a Primary Source** Assign Voices from the Past Resource Book 33.3.
2. **Relating Past to Present** Ask interested students to trace the increased freedom of expression in the Soviet Union during the 1980's. Students might focus on art, literature, music, or dress. Have students present their findings in oral reports.
3. **Researching for Bonus Points** Award bonus points to students who can find the answer to this question: Where did Alexander Solzhenitsyn go to live after he left the Soviet Union? (United States)

Concluding the Chapter

1. **Chapter Closer**
   Ask students to identify and discuss the move toward greater cooperation in Western Europe and in Eastern Europe. Have students predict possible long-term consequences of these trends.
2. **Reteaching Activities**
   a. **Summarizing** Have students summarize the achievements and goals of the Common Market.
   b. **Making a Time Line** Have students create a time line that covers the major events described in this chapter.
3. **Chapter Review Activities**
   Assign Chapter Review 33 activities.

Chapter Evaluation

Chapter Test 33 and Computer Test Bank Chapter 33 Test can be used to evaluate your students' understanding of this chapter.

Answers to Chapter Review 33

Reviewing the Facts
1. **a.** limit one country sets on imported goods **b.** country in which government assumes responsibility for people's social and economic well-being **c.** worker's hourly output **d.** military rule over civilian population

2. **a.** Western European economic unit **b.** rebuilt West Germany's economy **c.** Eastern European economic organization **d.** program to improve relations with USSR and Eastern Europe **e.** responsible for improved relations between East and West Germany **f.** West German chancellor during economic slump **g.** took tough measures to improve Britain's economy **h.** site of religious conflict, one of Britain's greatest problems **i.** president of Fifth Republic **j.** socialist president of France **k.** leading Spain toward democracy **l.** barrier between East and West Berlin **m.** Czechoslovakian leader who instituted short-lived reforms **n.** independent trade union in Poland

Basic Skills

1. Students' answers may vary. Suggested responses follow. **(a)** by 1958, West Germany had twice as much production as all of Germany had in 1938; West Germans enjoy a high standard of living; West Germany quickly became a stable democracy; West Germany is internationally respected in technology, economics, and political alliances. **(b)** East German stores and markets had few goods or fresh food; many East German buildings were destroyed; many East Germans left for better conditions in West Germany.
2. **(a)** Holy Roman Empire—East Germany, West Germany, Netherlands, Switzerland, Liechtenstein, Austria, Czechoslovakia, Italy; Byzantine Empire—Yugoslavia, Albania, Greece, Bulgaria, Turkey **(b)** Modern Poland's boundaries are very similar to those of the Kingdom of Poland; modern Hungary is much smaller than the Kingdom of Hungary.

Researching and Reporting Skills
Students' findings will vary.

Critical Thinking

1. **(a)** Economic cooperation has tended to occur more frequently among nations with the same political views, rather than among all nations. **(b)** fundamental differences about political systems, arms race, uncertainty born of constant change; accept other answers

2. **(a)** after World War II—split into two nations, both prosperous and stable; after World War I—lack of stability economically or politically, dissatisfied citizens, desire for military power **(b)** After World War II, Germany was given more aid, trust, and guidance; had better leadership; accept other answers.
3. **(a)** nationalized railroads, coal mines, airlines, Bank of England, electric and gas utilities; extended unemployment and old-age insurance; free medical services **(b)** Bismarck also instituted unemployment and old-age insurance.
4. **(a)** stop flood of people leaving East Germany, isolate East Germany from outside influences; accept other answers **(b)** dissatisfaction of citizens, distrust by other nations; accept other answers **(c)** Students' opinions will vary.
5. **(a)** Eastern Europe is experiencing growing economic problems while Western Europe continues to thrive; this indicates a lack of success with Communist economic policies. **(b)** Dissatisfaction of people is magnified by inflation, unemployment—leading to lowered productivity and political unrest.
6. Both showed citizens' dissatisfaction with Communist regime and their willingness to risk leaders' backlash in order to strive for changes.
7. idea that happier populace might result in higher productivity, idea that more international cooperation might open doors to better economic exchanges, knowledge that USSR should keep up with international technological developments; accept other answers
8. Students' answers will vary.

Perspectives on Past and Present
(a) an empire gained through military conquest **(b)** political balance of power **(c)** Economic unity seems to be more realistic and successful than political unity, especially as the world's economy becomes more interdependent and hope for agreement on style of government becomes more unrealistic.

Investigating History
Students' answers will vary.

Change and Conflict in Asia

Chapter Overview

Enormous changes took place in Asia after World War II. During and after the American occupation, the Japanese economy recovered from the war. By 1970, Japan had become the world's third leading industrial nation. In China, Communist victory in 1949 marked the start of a new era as the nation strove to modernize and develop a Communist society. In 1960, China and the USSR had a serious split, and troops from the two countries began to harass each other. After 1969, China gradually expanded its contacts with the United States and other non-Communist countries.

The former British colony of India was partitioned into two independent nations, India and Pakistan. Obstacles to modernization in predominantly Hindu India included unequal distribution of land and a rapidly growing population. Pakistan, predominantly Muslim, faced problems of lack of leadership and geographical division between West and East Pakistan. After years of rioting, East Pakistan became a separate nation, Bangladesh, in 1974.

In Southeast Asia, former colonies became independent after the war. However, in Indochina, France fought from 1946 to 1954 to keep control. Following defeat by the Vietminh at Dien Bien Phu, the French agreed to a settlement. The United States, viewing the guerrilla victory as a threat to the rest of Asia, became increasingly involved in fighting between Communist North Vietnam and non-Communist South Vietnam. When the Vietnam War finally ended in 1975, the Communists controlled all of Vietnam. Further fighting in Kampuchea and Laos continued.

Key Terms

gross national product
For additional exercises, see Vocabulary Worksheet 34.

Chapter Focus

Have students review "Industrialization in Japan" (page 549). Focus in particular on the passage reprinted below:

Are we to delay the using of steam machinery until we have discovered the principles of steam for ourselves? If we can select examples from them [Westerners] and adopt their contrivances, why should we not be successful in working them out?

Then switch the discussion to Expo 70, described on pages 728–729. Ask students to evaluate the changes that had taken place in Japan since the 1870's. Recall a comment made by Hidetoshi Kato, one of the organizers of the fair. Said Kato, "Expo 70 is a declaration of emancipation. Our people are now convinced that we can do most things without the support of the West." Tell students that this chapter explains how Japan and other nations in Asia tried to achieve economic and political independence in the years after World War II. Use Overhead Transparency 74, *East Asia*, in conjunction with sections 1 and 2 on Japan and China.

Japan became an industrial giant. 1

Section Objectives

After completing Section 1, students should be able to:

1. cite reasons for Japan's economic success.
2. identify problems brought about by Japan's rapid industrial growth.
3. give examples of change and continuity in Japan's society.

Setting the Stage

Ask students to name Japanese products sold in the United States. Students will probably suggest automobiles, computers, radios, televisions, and all appliances. List these items on the chalkboard. Tell students that in the 1950's and early 1960's the label "Made in Japan" meant cheap or inferior goods in the minds of many Americans. However, by the late 1980's, the United States was Japan's biggest market, with Americans buying more then $80 billion a year in good-quality products and services. Explain that Section 1 examines reasons for Japan's tremendous success in producing "high tech" goods that are among the best in the world.

Teaching Strategies

Economics and History: A Productive Labor Force (Objective 1) Ask students what role the United States had in Japan's success. Then have students read "Japan's economy boomed" (pages 730–731). Ask them to identify the four reasons for "Japan's economic miracle." Focus on the importance of human resources—Japan's dedicated labor force. Repeat the following remark, made by a Japanese worker: "They [Japanese managers] believe in peace, brotherhood—and market share." Ask students to interpret this remark which refers to competitiveness among white-collar workers.

Tell students that *sarariman* is the Japanese name for a salaried white-collar worker who looks forward to a lifelong job with a big company. In exchange for loyalty and hard work, a *sarariman* can expect regular promotions and pay increases, job security, medical care, low-interest loans, company housing, and a retirement bonus. The job comes first, the family second.

Challenge students to assess the drawbacks and benefits of a *sarariman's* life from the point of view of a company owner, a *sarariman*, and the *sarariman's* family. Would students prefer a secure position like a sarariman's? Why or why not?

Using Geographic Themes: Human-Environment Interaction (Objective 2) Open this topic by reading aloud the following selection from Alvin Toffler's *Future Shock*.

> Today, with spreading alarm over air pollution, urban crowding, and other such factors, more and more health authorities are coming around to the ecological notion that the individual needs to be seen as part of a total system, and that his health is dependent upon many subtle external factors.

Ask students how this relates to Japan's rapid industrialization in the 1950's and 1960's.

Tell students that the tragic mercury poisoning in the city of Minamata became known as Minamata Disease. Its symptoms include mental retardation, blindness, and severe birth defects. Point out that by the 1980's, almost 1,300 cases of the disease had been confirmed, with 305 deaths. Clarify the concept of *"human ecology"*—the interrelationships between people and their environments. Ask students to identify other positive and negative effects of rapid industrialization on human ecology.

Discussing History: Social Effects of Industrialization (Objective 3) Present the following facts about Japanese society in the 1980's.

- Japanese families earned an average annual income of more than $20,000.
- Unemployment stood at 2.7 percent.
- Two-thirds of all families owned an automobile and at least one tape recorder.
- Roughly 40 percent of all Japanese homes had air conditioning and microwave ovens.
- More than 99 percent of all households owned a refrigerator and at least one color television.
- A single electronics store in Japan might contain no fewer than 100 different models of color televisions, 75 kinds of turntables, and more than 200 types of headphones.

Then have students read "Tokyo became a megacity" (page 731). Ask students to identify aspects of traditional Japanese culture that coexist with modern lifestyles. Ask, "What kind of stresses might old ways and new ways place on young people growing up in Japan? What are some benefits of preserving ancient traditions in a time of rapid change?"

Check for Understanding Ask students to describe three causes and three effects of Japan's "economic miracle."

Practice

Guided Practice
Lead a guided discussion of the questions in Section Review 34.1. (Answers are below.)

Define:
(a) disband a country's armed forces (b) total value of goods and services produced by a country in a year

Identify:
(a) former emperor of Japan (b) general in charge of Japanese occupation (c) Japanese parliament

Answer:
1. showed world that Japan had become industrial powerhouse
2. (a) demilitarize Japan, set up stable democratic government, revive economy (b) demilitarization—arms production halted, armed forces disbanded, war banned in constitution; democracy—constitutional monarchy with power in hands of Diet, universal suffrage; economy—land reforms
3. effective use of imported technology, productive labor force, high rates of savings and investment, government support
4. urban overcrowding, pollution
5. won right to vote and own property, entered work force in large numbers

6. Students might consider such factors as economic power that includes control of large part of world's industrial production and marketplace, role in world affairs, and influences of culture on other parts of the world.

Independent Practice
Assign Independent Practice Worksheet 34.1.
Assign Vocabulary Worksheet 34.

Enrichment Activities

1. **Reading a Primary Source** Assign Voices from the Past Resource Book 34.1.

2. **Researching for Bonus Points** Award bonus points to students who can answer this question: What is the name of the government department responsible for Japan's interna-

Advance Planner

Chapter 34 Focus	Change and Conflict in Asia 1945–Present Expo 70 as a symbol of Japan's rapid industrialization after World War II			★ Advanced ● Basic
	Section 1	**Section 2**	**Section 3**	**Section 4**
Objectives	1. Cite reasons for Japan's economic success. 2. Identify problems brought about by Japan's rapid industrial growth. 3. Give examples of change and continuity in Japanese society.	1. Explain how the Communist party reorganized the government and economy of China. 2. Identify Deng Xiaoping's "four modernizations."	1. Identify the nations of South Asia. 2. Trace trends in conflict among the peoples of India. 3. Explain the significance of the 1988 election of Benazir Bhutto as Prime Minister of Pakistan.	1. Identify Corazón Aquino and explain how she became President of the Philippines. 2. Evaluate President Johnson's decision to escalate the Vietnam War.
Setting the Stage	Japanese products sold in the United States	Problems the Communist faced after taking power.	Jinnah's demand for an Indian Muslim homeland	The break-up of European colonial empires in Southeast Asia after World War II Transparency 76
Teaching Strategies	Economics and History: A Productive Labor Force Using Geographic Themes: Human-Environment Interaction Discussing History: Social Effects of Industrialization Check for Understanding	Economics and History: Economic Mobilization Discussing History: The "Four Modernizations" Check for Understanding	Geography in History: New Nations in South Asia Transparency 75 Outline Map 20 Skill Building: Making a Time Line Writing about History: Election of Benazir Bhutto Check for Understanding	Discussing History: Corazón Aquino Writing about History: Escalation or Withdrawal? Transparency 77 Check for Understanding
Guided Practice	Section Review 1	Section Review 2	Transparency 75 Q&A Section Review 3	Transparency 76 Q&A Transparency 77 Q&A Section Review 4
Independent Practice Worksheets	Independent Practice 34.1 Vocabulary 34	Independent Practice 34.2 Critical Thinking 34	Independent Practice 34.3	Independent Practice 34.4 Geography Skills 34 Basic Skills 34
Enrichment	1. Primary Source: Voices 34.1 2. ★ Preparing a Report 3. Researching for Points	1. Primary Source: Voices 34.2 2. Writing about History 3. Researching for Points	1. Primary Source: Voices 34.3 2. Using Geographic Themes 3. Researching for Points	1. Primary Source: Voices 34.4 2. ★ Preparing a Report 3. Researching for Points

Chapter Closer ● **Reteaching Activities** **Chapter Review** **Chapter Evaluation**	Summarizing, Writing a Paragraph Summary, Reviewing the Facts, Basic Skills, Researching and Reporting Skills, Critical Thinking, Perspectives on Past and Present, Investigating History Chapter Test 34, Computer Test Bank Chapter 34 Test

tional trade? (The Ministry of International Trade and Industry, or MITI)

China changed under a Communist government. 2

Section Objectives

After completing Section 2, students should be able to:

1. explain how the Communist party reorganized the government and economy of China.
2. identify Deng Xiaoping's "four modernizations."

Setting the Stage

Have students recall China's status at the end of World War II. Recall that after the Chinese civil war, Mao Tse-tung and his Red Army triumphed. By 1949 the Communist Revolution was over. The Communists, however, faced a problem. Although the Communist party claimed approximately 4.5 million members, it represented only about 1 percent of the population. Ask students to predict what actions Mao took to bring China under the party's control. What segment of the population probably concerned him—farmers or factory workers? Why?

Record the class's prediction on the chalkboard. Then tell students that Section 2 explains how Mao and the leaders who followed him tried to extend the political revolution to all aspects of Chinese life.

Teaching Strategies

Economics and History: Economic Mobilization (Objective 1) Write the following Communist slogan on the chalkboard: "Let politics rule the farm and factory." Ask students to explain what this statement reveals about Communist plans to reorganize the Chinese economy. Then tell students that the Communists believed that it was impossible to mobilize agriculture and industry without totalitarian methods. This meant promoting the importance of the state over valuing the individual. To illustrate how the party implemented this goal, read the following Communist-approved poem:

The People's Livelihood
The machinery is my husband
The factory is my family
The fruits of my labor are my children
The Party is my father and mother.

Tell students that party officials judged artistic creativity by its "social value." Ask, "Why might Communists think this poem was socially valuable? For example, how would the poem further the goal of economic mobilization?"

After students have discussed the poem, have them read "Communist leaders made reforms" (page 733). Ask, "What specific programs did the Communists undertake to reshape the economy? How did they seek to mobilize China's millions of peasants?"

Discussing History: The "Four Modernizations" (Objective 2) Have students read "A new leader emerged after Mao" (page 736). Have them identify Deng Xiaoping's "four modernizations." Note that in describing his reforms in 1985, Deng, partially deaf in one ear, jokingly commented: "[Karl] Marx sits up in heaven, and he is very powerful. He sees what we are doing, and he doesn't like it. So he has punished me by making me deaf." Ask students to explain why Marx would have disapproved of Deng's changes. In what ways did Deng's reforms depart from strict socialism? Focus on compromises with capitalism. How did Deng's policies initiate what he called a "second revolution" in the Chinese economy?

Check for Understanding Ask students to describe three programs Mao established to propel China into the modern world.

Practice

Guided Practice
Lead a guided discussion of the questions in Overhead Transparency 74 and in Section Review 2. (Answers are below.)

Identify:
(a) head of state and chairman of Chinese Communist party (b) industrial production targets (c) plan to build socialistic society and stronger economy (d) revolution to establish a proletarian culture (e) leader who ended isolationist policy (f) system of spelling Chinese words in roman alphabet (g) leader who encouraged contacts with the West and some private enterprise

Answer:
1. (a) Party sets the policy, and the government carries it out. (b) head of state and chairman of the

Communist party's Central Committee

2. **(a)** Most farmers owned no land. **(b)** Government divided landlords' holdings among peasants.

3. **(a)** Industry experienced rapid growth. **(b)** Poor planning slowed industrial growth.

4. **(a)** to restore purity of the revolution **(b)** Red Guards formed, colleges and schools closed, scientists and doctors were sent to work on farms, Chinese economy headed for collapse

5. made trade agreements with industrial countries; sent students to study abroad, allowed some private enterprise

6. South Korea, Taiwan, Hong Kong, and Singapore have all had major economic growth.

7. **(a)** agrarian reform, nationalization of industries and businesses, Five-Year Plan **(b)** formation of people's communes and urban collective groups, Cultural Revolution **(c)** economic progress as his actions were directed toward improving China's economy rather than enforcing rigid principles of communism.

Independent Practice

Assign Independent Practice Worksheet 34.2.
Assign Critical Thinking Worksheet 34.

Enrichment Activities

1. **Reading a Primary Source** Assign Voices from the Past Resource Book 34.2.

2. **Writing about History** Assign students to research the 1988 Summer Olympics held in South Korea. Have students use this information to write news accounts describing the reactions of South Koreans to the event.

3. **Researching for Bonus Points** Award bonus points to students who can answer this question: What is China's largest industrial city? (Shanghai)

Answers to Voice from Our Time

1. influx of foreigners and imported goods: China's new international interest.

2. improved through better housing and more consumer goods

3. growing economic links, with major rise in trade and U.S. investment in China

4. Because Japan had invaded China in World War II, the U.S. had refused to recognize the communist government in China, and Japan and the U.S. were enemies in World War II. Because of these past conflicts, it is remarkable that the three countries can now work together.

India and Pakistan became Independent. 3

Section Objectives

After completing Section 3, students should be able to:

1. identify the nations of South Asia.
2. trace trends in conflict among the peoples of India.
3. explain the significance of the 1988 election of Benazir Bhutto as Prime Minister of Pakistan.

Setting the Stage

Begin by reading aloud the following quote by Muhammad Ali Jinnah of the Muslim League.

> It is a dream that the Hindus and Muslims can ever evolve a common nationality. Muslims are a nation according to any definition of a nation, and they must have their homelands, their territory, and their state.

Remind students that in Chapter 29 (Section 1) they read about the independence movements led by the mostly Hindu National Congress and by the Muslim League. In 1947 the British finally gave in and agreed to turn over the government of India "into responsible Indian hands" no later than June 1948. Given past hostilities between Hindus and Muslims, ask students to speculate about some of the immediate consequences of independence. Into whose "responsible hands" would India fall? Then tell the class that they will have the chance to check the accuracy of their speculations by reading the material in Section 3.

Teaching Strategies

Geography in History: New Nations in South Asia (Objective 1) Show students Overhead Transparency 75, *South Asia*, and discuss India's border conflicts with China and Pakistan. Distribute copies of Outline Map 20 to the class. Then have students use the map on page 739 to label the following places on the outline map: India, Pakistan, Bangladesh, Nepal, Sri Lanka, Bhutan, Afghanistan, Indus River, Ganges River, Bay of Bengal, Arabian Sea. Point out that prior to 1972, Bangladesh was East Pakistan and present-day Pakistan was West Pakistan. Ask students why the divided country might have been difficult to govern. Have students compare their outline maps with the map on page 543. Ask them to identify nations that have been created since the start of the twentieth century.

Skill Building: Making a Time Line (Objective 2) Assign students to skim Section 3, writing down all important dates mentioned in the text. Next, divide the class into groups, and have each group arrange these dates along a time line for the period from 1945 to the present. Ask students to determine what interval of time is most appropriate for a time line on the period under study. When the groups have completed the project, post the time lines at the front of the classroom. Then repeat Muhammad Ali Jinnah's statement (Setting the Stage). Do students think that the information on the time lines supports or contradicts Jinnah's remarks? What trends in Indian history can students identify on the basis of the time lines?

Writing about History: Election of Benazir Bhutto (Objective 3) Tell students that in 1988 the Pakistani people scored two historic firsts: (a) they conducted a democratic election of a civilian leader, and (b) in that election, they selected the first female ruler in the Muslim world in centuries. The victor in the popular poll was Benazir Bhutto. Next, present the following facts about Bhutto.

- born on June 21, 1953, to one of the most influential and wealthy families in Sind Province
- raised by her father—Prime Minister Zulfikar Ali Bhutto, who was overthrown in 1977 in a military coup and executed two years later
- graduated from Radcliffe College (Massachusetts) in 1969 with a degree in government
- graduated from Oxford University in 1973 with a degree in philosophy, politics, and economics
- returned to Pakistan in 1977 determined to defeat General Mohammad Zia ul-Haq, whom Bhutto claims killed her father
- endured several arrests at the hands of the Zia government
- became an "Eastern bride" in 1988, accepting an arranged marriage
- elected to office after Zia died in a plane crash that same year

Ask students to use these facts in writing biographical descriptions of Bhutto. Students might model their descriptions after entries in *Who's Who*, which is available in the reference section of most libraries. When students have completed the assignment, request volunteers to read their descriptions to the class.

Check for Understanding Ask students to describe three problems India faced after independence and the steps taken to resolve those problems.

Practice

Guided Practice
Lead a guided discussion of the questions in Overhead Transparency 75 and in Section Review 3. (Answers are below.)

Define:
(a) division of British India into two countries (b) policy of not taking sides (c) nonaligned countries, many newly independent and not industrialized

Identify:
(a) first prime minister of India (b) large Muslim province in northern India (c) Nehru's daughter who became prime minister (d) separate Indian religious group (e) present prime minister of India, son of Indira Gandhi (f) nation that was formerly East Pakistan

Answer:
1. (a) emphasize democracy, unity, and economic modernization (b) nonalignment
2. (a) modernized economy (b) unequal distribution of land and constantly growing population
3. (a) Indian leaders thought that partition had mutilated their country; Pakistanis thought their country should include Kashmir. (b) war
4. (a) Their populations were mainly Muslim. (b) differences between ethnic groups; east poorer and more densely populated than west; west controlled army
5. as a result of war between Pakistan and India and resentments toward western Pakistan
6. Students may consider that ethnic and religious loyalties seem to outweigh nationalism or that changes since independence have fostered nationalism.

Independent Practice
Assign Independent Practice Worksheet 34.3.

Enrichment Activities

1. **Reading a Primary Source** Assign Voices from the Past Resource Book 34.3.

2. **Using Geographic Themes: Human-Environment Interaction** Ask interested students to research the effect of monsoons on the poverty-stricken nation of Bangladesh. How has India responded to Bangladesh's pleas for help? Have students report their findings to the class.

3. **Researching for Bonus Points** Award bonus points to students who can answer this question: What rock-and-roll star organized a concert in the 1970's to help starving people in Bangladesh? (former Beatle, George Harrison)

Southeast Asia faced revolution and war.

4

Section Objectives

After completing Section 4, students should be able to:

1. identify Corazón Aquino and explain how she became President of the Philippines.
2. evaluate President Johnson's decision to escalate the Vietnam War.

Setting the Stage

Show students Overhead Transparency 76, *Southeast Asia*. Identify Southeast Asia and help students locate its major countries. Remind the class that foreign powers controlled all of Southeast Asia (except Thailand) during the early 1900's. Point out that the British ruled Burma and Malaya. The United States controlled the Philippines. The Dutch held the East Indies. Finally, France ruled all of Indochina, a region including today's Laos, Kampuchea, and Vietnam.

Have students recall that the European powers lost control over their colonies during World War II. The defeat of Japan in 1945 created a power vacuum in Southeast Asia. The European colonial nations hoped to regain control, but the peoples of Southeast Asia demanded independence. Tell students that this section describes how the former colonies became independent nations.

Teaching Strategies

Discussing History: Corazón Aquino (Objective 1) Ask students if they would risk their lives to support a presidential candidate who had no previous political experience and who listed her occupation as housewife. Explain that in February 1986, millions of Filipinos helped a soft-spoken housewife named Corazón Aquino to overthrow President Ferdinand Marcos. Then have students read the section, "The Philippines sought democracy." Ask, "Why was Marcos unpopular?" Explain that

Marcos and his wife Imelda amassed a personal fortune that exceeded $5 billion, while 70 percent of the people lived below the poverty level. Marcos further enraged Filipinos by apparently ordering the assassination of the popular opposition leader, Benigno Aquino.

After the death of her husband, Corazón Aquino became the leader of the anti-Marcos forces. Despite her lack of experience, she proved to be a determined, shrewd, and courageous leader. On election day, millions of Filipinos ignored Marcos' henchmen to vote for Aquino and democratic government. Unwilling to give up power, Marcos' men ripped up ballots and struck as many as three million names off the voters lists. Tell students that outraged Filipinos then staged a bloodless revolution that forced Marcos to flee the country. Following her triumphant inauguration, Corazón Aquino proudly told her people that, "The world saw and recorded a people who knelt in the path of oncoming tanks and subdued with embraces of friendship the battle-hardened troops sent out to disperse them. All the world wondered as they witnessed … a people lift themselves from humiliation to the greatest pride."

Writing about History: Escalation or Withdrawal? (Objective 2) *Prewriting* Use Overhead Transparency 77, *The War in Vietnam 1957–1973*, to trace the main events of the Vietnam War. Tell students that the deteriorating situation in Vietnam forced President Johnson to make a decision. Despite more than 20,000 American advisers and billions of dollars in aid to South Vietnam, the Viet Cong controlled almost three-quarters of South Vietnam's land and more than half of its people. American observers predicted that South Vietnam would collapse within a short time. The President and his advisers considered these four options: a. The United States could withdraw its forces and negotiate a peace settlement; b. The United States could continue its policy of sending aid and advisers to help South Vietnam; c. The President could escalate or gradually increase the level of American involvement; or d. The President could order an all-out attack on North Vietnam. *Writing* Ask students to assume the role of President Johnson's national security adviser. Their assignment is to write a memo recommending a course of action in Vietnam. Have selected students read their memos to the class. Compare and contrast student decisions.

Check for Understanding Ask students to explain how the United States became involved in the Vietnam War.

Practice

Guided Practice
Lead a guided discussion of the questions in Overhead Transparencies 76 and 77 and in Section Review 4. (Answers are below.)

Identify:
(a) Indonesia's first president (b) corrupt anti-Communist Philippine leader (c) elected president of the Philippines (d) North Vietnamese guerrilla leader (e) unpopular and inept South Vietnamese leader (f) This attack by the North Vietnamese gave President Johnson the authority to send American troops into Vietnam. (g) Cambodian leader (h) leader of Khmer Rouge

Answer:
1. (a) Indonesia (b) Burma, Malaya, Singapore
2. (a) United States promised Philippines complete independence. (b) poverty, rebellion by Huks
3. (a) elected president (b) Charged with fraud, corruption, and misrule, he fled the country.
4. After the French defeat at Dien Bien Phu, the peace settlement divided Vietnam along the seventeenth parallel.
5. (a) sent American advisors (b) increased number of advisors, sent planes and military equipment (c) bombed North Vietnam, escalated war
6. (a) won control after a five-year civil war (b) renamed country Kampuchea, attacked non-Communist enemies
7. (a) highly motivated by nationalism, tactics more successful in jungle terrain (b) corruption, lack of effective leadership, poverty

Independent Practice
Assign Independent Practice Worksheet 34.4.
Assign Geography Skills Worksheet 34.
Assign Basic Skills Worksheet 34.

Enrichment Activities

1. **Reading a Primary Source** Assign Voices from the Past Resource Book 34.4

2. **Preparing a Report** Ask advanced students to prepare reports describing what happened to the following people or groups: Ferdinand Marcos, Norodom Sihanouk, Pol Pot, Nguyen Cao Ky, and the "boat people."

3. **Researching for Bonus Points** Award bonus points to students who can answer this question: What does the hand sign used by the Filipinos stand for, as shown on page 742? (It is an "L" sign that stands for Corazón Aquino's LABAN party. *Laban* means "people power.")

Concluding the Chapter

1. **Chapter Closer**
   Ask students to compare and contrast economic developments in Japan, China, South Asia, and East Asia after World War II.

2. **Reteaching Activities**
   a. **Summarizing** Have students summarize the factors that contributed to Japan's economic revival.
   b. **Writing a Paragraph** Ask students to explain why colonial India became two independent countries in 1947. Have students write paragraphs telling whether partition did or did not settle most problems and giving reasons for their answers.

3. **Chapter Review Activities**
   Assign Chapter Review 34 activities.

Chapter Evaluation

Chapter Test 34 and Computer Test Bank Chapter 34 Test can be used to evaluate your students' understanding of this chapter.

Answers to Chapter Review 34

Reviewing the Facts
1. **a.** disband a country's armed forces and remove its military equipment **b.** total value of goods and services produced by a country in a year
2. **a.** ran Japan 1945–1952 **b.** held political power in Japan under new constitution **c.** instituted the Five-Year Plan, the Great Leap Forward, and the Cultural Revolution **d.** plan that failed to harness energy of peasants and workers **e.** intended to establish proletarian culture but led to violence and near economic collapse **f.** worked to restore order after Cultural Revolution **g.** encouraged contacts with the West and private enterprise **h.** prime minister during first 17 years of independence **i.** helped India become an industrial nation **j.** prime minister after mother assassinated **k.** once part of Muslim Pakistan, world's poorest nation **l.** Indonesia's first president **m.** corrupt Philippine leader forced to flee his country **n.** Benigno—assassinated political foe of Marcos; Corazón—defeated Marcos in election **o.** Communist leader of North Vietnam **p.** Communist guerril-

las who fought South Vietnamese **q.** South Vietnamese dictator killed in military coup **r.** incident that gave President Johnson authority to send American troops into Vietnam **s.** Cambodian Communists who won civil war **t.** local Communists who took control of Laos

Basic Skills

1. Communist leaders made reforms
   A. Changes in government organization
      1. Modeled after Soviet Union
         a. Communist party sets policy
         b. National government carries out policy
      2. Mao Tse-tung authoritarian leader until 1959
   B. Changes in land ownership
      1. Agrarian Reform Law (1950)
         a. Government took land and divided it among peasants
         b. Violent reaction to law resulted in 2 million deaths
      2. Formation of collectives (1953–1957)
   C. Changes in industry
      1. Nationalization of all private industries and businesses
      2. Five-Year Plan (1953–1957)
         a. Set production targets
         b. Very successful
   D. Changes through the Great Leap Forward (1953–1961)
      1. Set up communes, street associations
      2. Failure of plan slowed growth and productivity and caused famine
2. Large numbers of nations formed in the area partly because geographical features (seas, rivers) prevented any unity while also bringing many different influences to the area.
3. These countries bordering seas and having harbors will play large role in trade.

Researching and Reporting Skills
Students' findings and reports will vary.

Critical Thinking

1. **(a)** demilitarization of country; a stable democratic government; revived economy **(b)** demilitarization—American occupation, disbanding of armed forces, halting of arms production, formal renouncing of future war; democracy—all Japanese aged 20 and over could vote, emperor became constitutional monarch, Diet created; economy—land reform, active support of business, stress on job security, effective use of imported technology, high rates of saving and interest
2. **(a)** Japan relied on itself after World War II—achieving high levels of productivity, institut-ing land reforms, and becoming economically strong to achieve a balance of trade. **(b)** Reliance on self and commitment to working toward a new Japan are long-lasting solutions not dependent upon military strength.
3. **(a)** Japan—accepts and contributes to capitalistic world; China—although claims socialism, is starting to allow some capitalist ventures **(b)** Japan—government does not control industries or economy but espouses success and contributes to it through few regulations and low taxes; China—government controls economy **(c)** Japan—economy based on free markets; China—very few free markets allowed
4. **(a)** Students' responses will vary; suggested responses include effective land use, technological knowledge, productivity of workers, government incentives for business. **(b)** Most students will find that China lacks the criteria they list.
5. As international interdependence increases, any emerging nations will have economic significance and be involved in political power struggles. The Third World nations will also impact the world as their cultural heritage gains exposure.
6. Although population growth contributes to a country's work force, it also means more food and housing are needed. In poor countries with limited resources, more people means always trying to stay even rather than modernizing and growing economically.
7. **(a)** imperialism—France did not want to lose colonies **(b)** spread of communism—the U.S. constantly fought for containment **(c)** Neither issue was widely accepted: Many French did not think keeping a colony was worth going to war; many U.S. citizens wanted U.S. to stay out of other countries' affairs.

Perspectives on Past and Present
(a) Suddenly, these countries had a power vacuum and the hope for self-control. **(b)** Korea—U.S. fought possibility of communism by occupying South Korea right after war and joining UN forces as majority of troops; Vietnam—U.S. fought possibility of communism first by offering aid, then by direct involvement. **(c)** similar—Both conflicts became lengthy stalemates representing conflict between communism and the free world. different—Korea remained half Communist, half free; Vietnam fell to communism.

Investigating History
Students' findings will vary.

Nationalism in Africa and the Middle East

Chapter Overview

At the end of World War II, nations in Africa sought to free themselves from colonial bonds. Starting first in the Muslim nations of North Africa, a surge of nationalism spread throughout the African continent. By 1980 all of Africa, except Namibia, had won independence. Colonialism left a legacy of problems, including social instability, ethnic rivalries, and one-crop economies.

In meeting the challenges of independence, African nations adopted a variety of governments including both democracies and dictatorships. Each nation, regardless of its political system, needed to industrialize. Overpopulation and indebtedness slowed progress. In South Africa, where the economy prospered, the issue of apartheid clouded the future. Independence based on white control led to black resistance within South Africa and criticism from other nations.

The fires of nationalism burned in the Middle East as well. In seeking their place among the more developed nations of the world, Arab countries formed the Organization of Petroleum Exporting Countries (OPEC). Oil, a valuable resource in the industrial world, suddenly became a political issue. Oil-rich Arab nations used it to undermine Western support of Israel, setting the stage for conflict in the 1970's. Access to oil, territorial disputes, ethnic and religious strife, and other sources of conflict continued to trouble the Middle East into the 1990's.

Key Terms

apartheid, fundamentalism
For additional exercises, see Vocabulary Worksheet 35.

Chapter Focus

Have students read the description of Ghana's independence ceremony (pages 748–749). Then direct students' attention to the picture on page 748. Identify the Duchess of Kent and explain that she represented Queen Elizabeth II of Britain. Point out that President Nkrumah wore a prisoner's robe as a symbol of his earlier imprisonment

in a British jail. Emphasize that Ghana was the first black African nation to gain independence in the twentieth century.

Divide the class into two groups of reporters—British and Ghanian. Ask each group to write a paragraph that completes this topic sentence: "Ghana's independence ceremony marked..." Compare and contrast the different points of view students present. Explain that this chapter describes how the nations of Africa and of the Middle East won their independence and attempted to solve difficult economic and political problems. It also discusses how nationalism led to conflicts.

The age of imperialism ended in Africa. 1

Section Objectives

After completing Section 1, students should be able to:

1. analyze the factors that hindered nation-building in newly independent African countries.
2. assess some causes and effects of widespread famine in Africa in 1980's.

Setting the Stage

Introduce the section by reading aloud a passage from Kwame Nkrumah's speech before the first session of Ghana's parliament in 1957. To underscore the significance of Nkrumah's remarks, mention that Ghana was the first African nation south of the Sahara to win its independence.

> If we show ourselves disunited, inefficient or corrupt we shall have gravely harmed all those million in Africa who ... looked to Ghana to prove that African people can build a state based on democracy ... and racial equality.

Ask students why Nkrumah might have felt that Ghana was on trial before the world. Have students recall the European view of Africa during the age of imperialism. Given the nature of colonial rule, why was democracy an experiment for most Africans? Then tell students that this section examines some of the problems that confronted new African leaders as they tried to put democratic principles into practice.

Teaching Strategies

Discussing History: Problems of Nation-Building (Objective 1) To open discussion of African independence, tell students that in 1960 Albert Luthuli became the first African to win the Nobel Peace Prize. Luthuli, a Zulu chief, won the prize for his efforts to advance black self-determination in the white-dominated nation of South Africa. Note that Luthuli spoke for all Africans when he delivered his acceptance speech. Read the following extract aloud.

Our continent has been carved up by the great powers; alien governments have been forced upon the African people by military conquest.... Strivings for nationhood and national dignity have been beaten down by force; traditional economies and ancient customs have been disrupted.... But now ... [o]ur people everywhere from north to south ... are reclaiming their land, their right to participate in government, their dignity,... their nationhood...

Ask students what they think Luthuli meant by the disruption of traditional economies. Ask, "What other economic problems did newly independent African nations face?" Have students use information to list all the factors that hampered nation-building in Africa. Then ask the class to

Advance Planner

Chapter 35 Focus	Nationalism in Africa and the Middle East 1945–Present Ghana's independence ceremony as a symbol of 20th century independence movements in Africa		★Advanced ●Basic
	Section 1	**Section 2**	**Section 3**
Objectives	1. Analyze the factors that hindered nation-building in newly independent African countries. 2. Assess some causes and effects of widespread famine in Africa in the 1980's.	1. Compare and contrast African political systems. 2. Identify challenges to African economic development. 3. Discuss the issue of South Africa's policy of *apartheid*.	1. Trace events leading to conflicts and conflict resolutions between Arab nations and Israel. 2. Explain the significance of the rise of Islamic fundamentalism.
Setting the Stage	For most African nations, democracy was an experiment.	Unity, stability, autonomy, and economic development as the problems facing newly independent African nations Transparency 78	Zionism and Arab nationalism Transparency 79
Teaching Strategies	Discussing History: Problems of Nation-Building Skill Building: Making Inferences Check for Understanding	Skill Building: Comparing and Contrasting Political Systems Economics and History: The Sources of Poverty Discussing History: *Apartheid* Check for Understanding	Discussing History: Peace-Keeping Efforts Transparency 80 Discussing History: Islamic Fundamentalism Check for Understanding
Guided Practice	Section Review 1	Transparency 78 Q&A Section Review 2	Transparency 79 Q&A Transparency 80 Q&A Section Review 3
Independent Practice Worksheets	Independent Practice 35.1 Geography Skills 35 Vocabulary 35	Independent Practice 35.2 Basic Skills 35	Independent Practice 35.3 Critical Thinking 35
Enrichment	1. Primary Source: Voices 35.1 2. Preparing a Report 3. Researching for Points	1. Primary Source: Voices 35.2 2. ★Preparing a Report 3. Researching for Points	1. Primary Source: Voices 35.3 2. ★Preparing a Report 3. Researching for Points
Chapter Closer ●**Reteaching Activities**	Summarizing, Identifying Leaders		
Chapter Review	Summary, Reviewing the Facts, Basic Skills, Researching and Reporting Skills, Critical Thinking, Perspectives on Past and Present, Investigating History		
Chapter Evaluation	Chapter Test 35, Computer Test Bank Chapter 35 Test		

distinguish the problems that resulted from Africa's colonial experience and those caused by geographic and environmental conditions.

Skill Building: Making Inferences (Objective 2) Tell students that in the 1980's the worst famine of the twentieth century engulfed much of Africa. To illustrate its causes and effects, distribute copies of the following facts.

• Since independence, Africa's population has increased by 3 percent every year, while food production has increased by only about 1.5 percent.

• In the early 1980's twenty-two African nations suffered famines; by 1990, six nations still needed famine relief.

• In 1983, drought spread across the continent. Some relief came in 1985 when the rains reappeared, but the drought resumed in 1987 and 1988.

• Throughout the 1980's, thousands of people died each day of malnutrition and disease. In 1985 at the height of the famine, about 150 million people faced starvation.

• In 1986, locust swarms defoliated the land in vast areas of Africa, devouring as much as 80,000 tons of crops a day.

• By the late 1980's, efforts to import food increased the total indebtedness of all African nations to more than $100 billion. Countries such as Ethiopia had to depend on foreign aid and worldwide humanitarian famine-relief efforts.

Ask students to infer some of the causes and effects of famine. Then challenge them to suggest long-term solutions. What role do they think the United States should play in helping to implement long-term solutions, and why?

Check for Understanding Have students summarize reasons for the spread of nationalism in Africa after World War II.

Practice

Guided Practice
Lead a guided discussion of the questions in Section Review 1. (Answers are below.)

Define:
(a) the minimum needed to support life (b) a prolonged period of dryness

Identify:
(a) African nation, former British colony known as Gold Coast (b) first president of Ghana (c) first president of the Egyptian republic (d) semiarid region along southern edge of Sahara

Answer:
1. North African Muslims
2. (a) the countries of North Africa (b) followed lead of Muslim countries in the Middle East
3. opposed independence or sought to limit it
4. Africans unprepared for self-government; lack of systems for government; social stability weakened; lack of ethnic unity; lack of income and money for investment; lack of transportation and communication networks; lack of professional classes
5. great distances; lack of harbors and navigable rivers; tropical climate and diseases; droughts, spreading of desert
6. problems resulting from colonialism and the environment were a serious threat to the survival of newly-independent nations.

Independent Practice
Assign Independent Practice Worksheet 35.1.
Assign Geography Skills Worksheet 35.
Assign Vocabulary Worksheet 35.

Enrichment Activities

1. **Reading a Primary Source** Assign Voices from the Past Resource Book 35.1.

2. **Preparing a Report** Have each student select a country in Africa and find out about the events leading to that country's independence. After students have shared their findings, ask them to make generalizations about the differences in Africans' reactions to nationalism.

3. **Researching for Bonus Points** Award bonus points to students who can answer this question: Who is Chinua Achebe? (A Nigerian author of novels about the African experience in changing from colonialism to independence.)

Africans built new nations. 2

Section Objectives

After completing Section 2, students should be able to:

1. compare and contrast African political systems.
2. identify challenges to African economics development.
3. discuss the issue of South Africa's policy of apartheid.

Text pages 748–765

Setting the Stage

Show students Overhead Transparency 78, *The Nations of Africa*, and have them locate the countries mentioned in Section 1. Write on the chalkboard "unity," "political stability," "political autonomy," and "economic development." Tell students that these were the chief problems that newly independent countries faced. Ask, "Why was national unity a problem?" (ethnic rivalries) Have students define *stability* and *autonomy*. Ask, "Why was autonomy a problem?" (foreign interests and spheres of influence, foreign aid) Have students give examples of each problem. Explain that this section describes the different solutions to these problems that African nations have tried.

Teaching Strategies

Skill Building: Comparing and Contrasting Political Solutions (Objective 1) Have students use the information on pages 752–754 to develop headings for a chart comparing and contrasting political systems in selected African countries. Headings might include the following: name of country, former colonial power, leader at independence, dominant ethnic groups, type of government, type of economy, foreign influence. Ask students to define a one-party democracy. Point out that this form of government guarantees civil liberties and elections but limits freedom of choice among leaders representing different political philosophies and goals. Also point out that democratic government developed in countries previously dominated by colonial powers that had democratic traditions, and in countries with stronger economies.

Refer students to pages 632 and 635 on political and economic challenges facing Latin American countries after independence. Ask, "What problems did Latin American and African nations share following their independence?" List responses on the chalkboard. Based on this comparison, have students write generalizations about the challenges of nation-building for former colonies.

Economics and History: Sources of Poverty (Objective 2) Read the following statement by Tom Mboya, a Kenyan diplomat.

The leaders [of Kenya] must establish order to enable the Government to promote economic and social development. The responsibility for virtually all types of development becomes the concern of the Government; for the ... people are poor and they still lack business and commercial skill. On its part, the Govern-

ment finds itself with many projects in hand, but without the capital or technical know-how to sustain development.

Ask, "According to Mboya, what is the main job of government? What factors make it difficult for the government to do its job?" Point out that whatever type of government African nations adopted upon independence, their success depended on how well they met economic needs. Ask students to identify those economic needs. Recall the importance of diversification for establishing a stable economic base. Also emphasize the importance of capitalization for industrializing and reducing foreign debt. Discuss the roles of population growth, literacy, and entrepreneurship in economic development. On the basis of this discussion, ask students to infer and list sources of poverty that potentially affect any nation.

Discussing History: Apartheid (Objective 3) Ask students to define *apartheid*. Clarify that this is a closed system in which the black African majority lacks civil rights, representation in government, and opportunities for economic self-improvement. Refer students to the pictures on page 756. Ask, "What are some effects of racial inequality in South Africa?" Have students suggest possible solutions to the problem of reforming apartheid laws. Ask, "What do white South Africans fear? Why have resistance movements met with little success? Why have foreign pressures had little effect?" Tell students that many white South Africans also oppose apartheid. Also point out that South Africa's economy has suffered inflation, unemployment, and declining productivity as a result of foreign economic sanctions. However, few countries can afford to suspend trade because South Africa's gold and diamonds supply a major portion of the world's wealth.

Check for Understanding Write the following names on the chalkboard, and have students describe the contributions of each to African nation-building: Felix Houphouet-Boigny, Julius Nyerere, Angie Brooks, Nelson Mandela.

Practice

Guided Practice

Lead a guided discussion of the questions in Overhead Transparency 78 and in Section Review 2. (Answers are below.)

Define:

(a) favoring unquestioning of obedience to authority (b) system which separates people of different groups

Identify:
(a) first president of Ivory Coast (b) first president of Tanzania (c) first president of Kenya (d) authoritarian ruler of Zaire (e) ruthless dictator of Uganda (f) white leader in Zimbabwe's independence (g) leader who succeeded Smith in Zimbabwe (h) black South African leader jailed by government (i) President of South Africa (j) black archbishop of South Africa

Answer:
1. (a) Examples: transition peaceful in Côte d'Ivoire and Tanzania; civil war in Zaire led to authoritarian rule; civil war in Nigeria led to military rule; (b) disagreement on form of government; conflict between ethnic groups; lack of money; lack of trained leaders and public officials; (c) solutions varied from one country to another but often led to one-party or one-person rule.
2. new governments not organized for democracy so ended up with one party or authoritarian rulers
3. (a) lacked money or development; (b) by wider range of activities, producing for world markets, producing variety of crops, developing industry
4. Economic development and modern technology were needed to increase productivity and national income and to improve living standards.
5. Rapid population growth made food supplies inadequate, so that food had to be imported. This took money that could otherwise be used for economic development. Also, rapid population growth led to unemployment, urban crowding, and over-grazing of land.
6. Blacks protested the policies of apartheid, homelands, residence laws, registration passes, lack of civil rights, inequality, and discrimination.
7. (a) in being nonaligned and in developing governments to meet their own needs but not necessarily either democratic or communist (b) Many African nations were among the poorest of Third World countries and with the most political and social problems also.

Independent Practice
Assign Independent Practice Worksheet 35.2.
Assign Basic Skills Worksheet 35.

Enrichment Activities

1. **Reading a Primary Source** Assign Voices from the Past Resource Book 35.2.

2. **Preparing a Report** Have advanced students research and report on the efforts of African nations to achieve unity and cooperation for their mutual benefit. Topics should include the Organization of African Unity (OAU) and other Pan-African movements. Have students share their findings and draw conclusions about factors that encourage or discourage international cooperation.

3. **Researching for Bonus Points** Award bonus points to students who can answer this question: What is the name of the black township that serves Johannesburg? (Soweto)

Answers to Voice from Our Time

1. to isolate and silence the individual
2. He could be committing an offense if he spoke to more than one person at a time.
3. It could separate family members and would certainly isolate a family in any community.

Nationalism sparked Mideast conflicts. 3

Section Objectives

After completing Section 3, students should be able to:

1. trace events leading to conflicts and conflict resolutions between Arab nations and Israel.
2. explain the significance of the rise of Islamic fundamentalism.

Setting the Stage

Have students recall the start of the Zionist movement in the late 1800's (page 630). The movement called for Jewish settlement of Palestine and the founding of a Jewish state. Few European Jews had any knowledge of the Middle East. Zionist founder Theodore Herzl noted that most Jews imagined Palestine to be "a land without people waiting for a people without a land." Ask students what was wrong with that idea. Students should recognize that Palestine was not "a land without a people." Palestinian Arabs considered it their homeland as well. Show Overhead Transparency 79, *The Middle East Today* and have students identify the Arab nations that border Israel. Tell students that this section examines the causes and consequences of Arab-Israeli conflict and other conflicts in the Middle East.

Text pages 748–765

Teaching Strategies

Discussing History: Peace-Keeping Efforts (Objective 1) Show students Overhead Transparency 80, *Israel, 1967–1973.* Help students to locate the following contested territories: Sinai Peninsula, Gaza Strip, West Bank, and Golan Heights. Point out the strategic value of these regions to Israel, Egypt, Syria, and Jordan. Tell the class that in 1967 the UN Security Council passed Resolution 242. Write on the chalkboard or on an overhead transparency the following points endorsed by the resolution.

- withdrawal of Israeli armies from territories occupied during the Six-Day War
- political independence for every state in the Middle East
- the right of people to live within secure and recognized boundaries free from external threats
- settlement of the Palestinian refugee problem

Have students use the information on the map and in the text to assess the steps that were taken after 1967 toward fulfilling the UN mandate. Invite students to debate the issue of a Palestinian homeland. Conclude by having students develop a chronology tracing Arab-Israeli conflict and international peace-keeping efforts.

Discussing History: Islamic Fundamentalism (Objective 2) Clarify the concept of fundamentalism as any movement for religious reform that calls for strict adherence to the basic rules and principles of the religion as it was originally practiced. Have students recall the basic rules and principles of Islam (page 176). Ask, "In what ways might strict adherence to Islam conflict with the demands of living in a modern, westernized nation?" Students should recognize practical problems relating to the role and status of women and the conduct of business. Tell students that in present-day Saudi Arabia—a conservative, mainly Sunni Muslim country—businesses and shops are required to close during each of the five daily prayers. Patrolling religious police enforce this rule. Ask what effects such closings would have on businesses in the United States.

Explain that practical differences are only a part of this culture conflict. Muslim conservatives and fundamentalists view many Western ideas and behaviors as immoral. Shi'ite Muslims in Iran reacted most violently to the "corruption" of Western influences, setting off a jihad against Iraq and fundamentalist uprisings throughout the Arab world. Fundamentalists in Saudi Arabia occupied the Kaaba in Mecca until they were overwhelmed by government troops.

Have students use information in the text to assess the impact of Islamic fundamentalism. Ask, "Did Ayatollah Khomeini's regime correct the abuses of the deposed Shah's Western-style government?"

Check for Understanding Call on students to explain how nationalism, terrorism, and Islamic fundamentalism relate to conflicts in the Middle East.

Practice

Guided Practice
Lead a guided discussion of the questions in Overhead Transparencies 79 and 80 and in Section Review 3. (Answers are below.)

Define:
(a) a period of reduced economic activity (b) religion stressing obedience to basic laws (c) conservative Muslim leader (d) a person held as a pledge that terms will be met

Identify:
(a) Organization of Petroleum Exporting Countries (b) Middle East nation, Jewish homeland (c) group of Palestinian Nationalists who seek homeland in region of Palestine (d) branch of Islam

Answer:
1. (a) OPEC was founded to give oil-exporting nations some control over prices. (b) OPEC nations raised price of oil by limiting the supply of it.
2. (a) After the Holocaust, there was an outpouring of support for a Jewish homeland. (b) They felt their land was being given away.
3. Egypt was the first and only Arab country to recognize Israel.
4. (a) modernization in Western European style (b) setting up Islamic republic, ridding Iran of western influence
5. (a) Khomeini called on Iraqi Shi'ites to overthrow their government. Iraq then attacked Iran. (b) Neither side won the war; both suffered heavy losses.
6. No one group held political control; Israel's invasion brought in foreign interests; Muslims wanted more control.
7. (a) Jews wanted a homeland where they could freely practice their religion. The homeland is also significant for Muslims and Christians. (b) In the name of Islamic nationalism, Shi'ite Muslims are fighting Sunni Muslims. (c) Religious convictions make political compromises less acceptable. Religious allegiances are often stronger than political allegiances.

Independent Practice
Assign Independent Practice Worksheet 35.3.
Assign Critical Thinking Worksheet 35.

Enrichment Activities:

1. **Reading a Primary Source** Assign Voices from the Past Resource Book 35.5.

2. **Preparing a Report** Have advanced students prepare reports on conflict and conflict resolution in the Middle East during the 1980's. Suggest that students consult the *Reader's Guide to Periodical Literature* for more recent events. Topics might include the response of the United States to Libyan terrorism, the role of the United States and UN forces in the Persian Gulf War, and the impact of Yasser Arafat's speech to the UN renouncing terrorism.

3. **Researching for Bonus Points** Award bonus points to students who can find the answer to this question: What was Golda Meir's role in Israel's nation-building? (She was Israel's Prime Minister from 1969 to 1974.)

Concluding the Chapter

1. **Chapter Closer**
   Ask students to summarize the main political and economic consequences of independence for African nations.

2. **Reteaching Activities**
   a. **Summarizing** Have students write a paragraph summarizing three problems that confronted the new nations in Africa.
   b. **Identifying Leaders** Have students identify each of the following leaders: Kwame Nkrumah, Gamal Abdel Nasser, Jomo Kenyatta, Desmond Tutu, P.W. Botha, David Ben-Gurion, Anwar Sadat, and Ayatollah Ruhollah Khomeini.

3. **Chapter Review Activities**
   Assign Chapter Review 35 activities

Chapter Evaluation

Chapter Test 35 and Computer Test Bank Chapter 35 Test can be used to evaluate your students' understanding of this chapter.

Answers to Chapter Review 35

Reviewing the Facts
1. **a.** holy war **b.** group whose members share language and culture **c.** policy separating people of different ethnic groups **d.** area set aside for blacks **e.** Southwest Asia from Iran to Arabian Peninsula plus part of North Africa **f.** Shi'ite Muslim leader
2. **a.** one of first African nations to gain independence **b.** first president of Ghana **c.** first president of Egyptian republic **d.** African nation that prospered as one-party democracy **e.** first president of Ivory Coast **f.** authoritarian ruler of Zaire **g.** African nation united as a federal republic **h.** first president of Tanzania **i.** black township in South Africa, scene of a bitter riot in 1976 **j.** group dedicated to returning Palestine to the Arabs **k.** branch of Islam **l.** Mideast nation that has become battleground for many factions
3. **(a)** Colonial powers did not encourage industry and weakened economies dependent on cash crops. **(b)** National borders drawn without regard for ethnic groups encouraged ethnic contact.
4. **(a)** white minority **(b)** apartheid, banning, homelands
5. **(a)** by partition of Palestine according to UN plan **(b)** Many lost their homeland.

Basic Skills
1. **(a)** Nile—Egypt, Sudan, Ethiopia, Kenya; Niger—Guinea, Mali, Niger, Nigeria, Benin; Congo—Angola, Zaire, Congo; Zambezi—Mozambique, Zimbabwe, Zambia, Angola; Limpopo—Mozambique, Zimbabwe,South Africa, Botswana **(b)** The African rivers run mostly east-west across the continent, while the Mississippi River runs mostly north-south through North America.
2. **(a)** colonialism—revolt by African colonies, terrorist tactics by some African nationalists, altered economy of colonies, colonial governments with no relation to African culture, lack of preparation for self-government, borders representing no regard for African groups; environment—drought, famine **(b)** revolt—Morocco, Tunisia, Algeria; terrorism—Kenya; altered economies—Kenya, Ghana; governments with no relation to culture—South Africa; lack of preparation for self-government—Congo; borders—Nigeria; drought—Ghana; famine—

Ethiopia, Somalia, Mozambique, Zambia, Kenya, the Sudan.
3. **(a)** Mediterranean and Red seas: Suez Canal; Persian Gulf and Arabian Sea: Gulf of Oman/ Strait of Hormuz **(b)** Red and Arabian seas (Gulf of Aden)

Researching and Reporting Skills
Students' findings will vary.

Critical Thinking
1. Islamic tradition, ties to Middle East and successes there in gaining nations
2. **(a)** poor soil, drought, famine, tsetse fly **(b)** poor soil—better crop rotation; drought—irrigation; famine—more food crops, better use of farmland, population control; tsetse fly—pest control; accept other answer
3. **(a)** Students' answers will vary, but might include lack of a middle class, political rivalries, ethnic conflict, poor conditions for agriculture, lack of advanced technology, and rapid population growth. **(b)** Students' opinions will vary.
4. **(a)** Israel—Jewish homeland; Palestinians—Arab nation-state, land of Palestine **(b)** Each group has a strong nationalistic vision regarding the same piece of land. **(c)** Students' answers will vary. **(d)** religion, respect for traditions, need for own land; accept other answers
5. **(a)** jihad, restrictions in role of women, Koran laws, etc. in contrast to Western ideas **(b)** Oil-rich nations have taken control, frustrating other nations so that they no longer abide by set production levels.

Perspectives on Past and Present
Imperialism has been replaced with other ideas such as isolationism, detached aid, and protectorate systems. Some factors accounting for this include need to concentrate resources on bettering own country's conditions, dissatisfaction with warlike traits often necessary for imperialism, desire to spread democracy; accept other answers.

Investigating History
Students' findings will vary.

The Americas in the Modern World

Chapter Overview

Since 1945 nations in northern North America have prospered. In the United States the efforts of civil rights activists led to the passage of laws that ended many forms of racial discrimination. In foreign affairs, the Vietnam conflict led to changes in the United States' role as world leader. As European and Asian economies recovered from the effects of World War II, the dominance of the United States began to decline. Canada increased its international role in the 1980's and developed closer economic ties with the United States.

In the past thirty years, Latin American countries have struggled to achieve and maintain prosperity in the face of overpopulation and political instability. Rapid population growth and slow economic growth have contributed to urban poverty and to large foreign debts. Rapid industrialization in Brazil and Mexico has not solved the problems of competing in the world economy.

Progress toward greater democracy has been uneven. Brazil, Chile, and Argentina, for example, have undergone cycles of dictatorship and democracy. Some authoritarian leaders have improved economies at the expense of human and civil rights. In the 1980's Argentina, Mexico, and Chile moved toward more democratic government.

In the Caribbean, Puerto Rico became a commonwealth of the United States. Cuban revolutionaries overthrew a corrupt dictator and established a Communist government. The reactions of the United States and the Soviet Union to the Cuban Revolution led to confrontation in the 1960's. El Salvador, Guatemala, and Nicaragua were torn by civil war. In Nicaragua, the Sandinistas overthrew the dictatorship of the Somoza family and began a program of revolutionary changes with the aid of Cuba and the Soviet Union. The United States, fearing Communist influence in Central America, aided the Contras, rebels fighting against the government. In 1988 a peace plan was proposed by the President of Costa Rica and was supported by other Central American leaders.

Key Terms

multinational corporation, separatism, embargo
For additional exercises, see Vocabulary Worksheet 36.

Chapter Focus

Use a wall map or the map on page 818 to trace the route of the Pan American highway from Alaska south to the tip of Argentina. Call on students to give examples of the geographic and cultural diversity they would see traveling this route. Tell students that political and economic events in the Americas affect the United States. For example, the United States sends hundreds of millions of dollars in aid to Latin American countries and American banks lend billions. Economists predict that Latin America's ability to repay their debts will increasingly affect the United States' economy. Some Latin American countries are able to compete with the United States and other nations in world markets. For example, Brazil, the fifth largest country in the world, produces computers, rockets, satellites, and surgical supplies, and contains the world's largest reserve of iron ore. It is second only to the United States as an exporter of food. Tell students that Chapter 36 examines how the nations of the Americas are changing and are becoming more interdependent.

Two nations prospered in northern North America. 1

Section Objectives

After completing Section 1, students should be able to:

1. describe social changes in the United States and their link to postwar prosperity.
2. evaluate the effects of the 1988 free trade agreement between the United States and Canada.

Setting the Stage

Tell students that in the two decades after World War II the United States and Canada experienced unprecedented prosperity. Rising wages enabled citizens to purchase consumer items, such as refrigerators, washing machines, automobiles, televisions, and radios, which flowed off assembly lines that had been converted to peace time production. Throughout the 1950's and 1960's, however, there was an undercurrent of anxiety and discontent. Black Americans felt left out of the economic boom. Americans continued to fear communism, and went to war to prevent its spread. Explain to students that Section 1 explains how life in Canada and in the United States changed to meet the challenges and opportunities of the postwar period.

Teaching Strategies

Skill Building: Making Generalizations (Objective 1) Ask students to identify social changes in the United States after 1945 and write students' generalizations on the chalkboard. The list should include references to the civil rights movement, the women's movement, and the antiwar movement. Other social changes might refer to efforts to protect the rights of children, senior citizens, Native Americans, immigrants, veterans, disabled citizens, and patients. In each case ask students how changes in perceptions and laws might relate to the conditions of prosperity that followed World War II. Point out that new economic pressures and opportunities after the war were underlying themes in movements for social change.

Tell students that demographic changes included a "baby boom," suburban development, and population movement to southern and western regions. Use Overhead Transparency 84, *The United States Today,* to identify the states in these regions. Point out that new economic pres-

Advance Planner

Chapter 36 Focus	The Americas in the Modern World 1946–Present The Pan American Highway as a symbol of the links between the nations of the Western Hemisphere		★ Advanced ● Basic
	Section 1	**Section 2**	**Section 3**
Objectives	1. Describe social changes in the United States and their link to postwar prosperity. 2. Evaluate the effects of the 1988 free trade agreement between the United States and Canada.	1. Describe the effects of rapid population growth in Latin America. 2. Analyze the reasons Latin American countries lag in achieving prosperity. 3. Identify recent trends toward greater democracy in Argentina, Mexico, and Chile.	1. Identify the forces involved in the Nicaraguan conflict. 2. Trace changes in United States policy toward Latin America.
Setting the Stage	Signs of postwar prosperity in North America	Prewar changes in countries of Latin America Transparency 81	Political geography of the Caribbean Basin
Teaching Strategies	Skill Building: Making Generalizations Transparency 84 Economics and History: The Free Trade Accord Transparency 82 Check for Understanding	Discussing History: Urban Overpopulation Economics and History: Latin American Foreign Debt Skill Building: Comparing and Contrasting Causes Check for Understanding	Discussing History: The Nicaraguan Conflict Writing about History: The United States' Dilemma over Nicaragua Check for Understanding
Guided Practice	Transparency 84 Q&A Transparency 82 Q&A Section Review 1	Transparency 81 Q&A Section Review 2	Section Review 3
Independent Practice Worksheets	Independent Practice 36.1 Vocabulary 36 Geography Skills 36	Independent Practice 36.2 Basic Skills 36	Independent Practice 36.3 Critical Thinking 36
Enrichment	1. Primary Source: Voices 36.1 2. Researching for Points	1. Primary Source: Voices 36.2 2. Researching for Points	1. Primary Source: Voices 36.3 2. ★ Researching a Topic 3. Researching for Points
Chapter Closer ● **Reteaching Activities**	Summarizing, Explaining Main Ideas, Recalling Information		
Chapter Review	Summary, Reviewing the Facts, Basic Skills, Researching and Reporting Skills, Critical Thinking, Perspectives on Past and Present, Investigating History		
Chapter Evaluation	Chapter Test 36, Computer Test Bank Chapter 36 Test		

sures and opportunities changed patterns of family life and created needs for expanded family-support services. Ask students for examples. Conclude by asking students to express opinions on the effects of postwar social changes on Americans' expectations of personal life, family life, and work.

Economics and History: The Free Trade Accord (Objective 2) Show students Overhead Transparency 82, *Canada*, and ask students to determine the approximate length of the border between Canada and the United States (about 3,000 miles). Tell students that this is one of the longest undefended borders in the world. Ask why this border is not defended. Then distribute Outline Map 4: Political North America. Have students refer to the transparency or to the map on page 768 to label the Canadian provinces and main bodies of water. Ask, "Which province threatened to separate from Canada in the 1970's?" Students should be able to identify and locate Quebec and describe the causes and results of the separatist movement.

Tell students that in 1988, goods valued at 131 billion dollars flowed between Canada and the United States, making them the world's largest trading partnership. Explain that by 1999, goods that flow between the United States and Canada will not be subject to trade barriers such as tariffs or quotas. Ask students to evaluate the advantages and disadvantages of free trade for both countries. Recall the goals of Europe's Common Market. Ask, "How might the free trade agreement benefit businesses in both the United States and Canada?"

Point out that some Canadians oppose the free trade agreement on the grounds that Canada's national and cultural identity might be overwhelmed or compromised by American influence. Ask students to discuss this issue from the point of view of Canadians.

Check for Understanding Call on students to identify changes that have taken place in the United States and Canada during the postwar period.

Practice

Guided Practice
Lead students in a guided discussion of the questions in Overhead Transparencies 84 and 82 and in Section Review 1. (Answers are below.)

Define:
(a) a branch of physics that deals with electrons and with electronic devices (b) company with branches in many nations (c) a movement for the creation of an independent state

Identify:
(a) highway that will connect the Americas from Alaska to Argentina (b) civil rights leader (c) Supreme Court justice (d) civil war in Vietnam in which the United States became involved (e) president of the United States

Answer:
1. to encourage communication, tourism, and trade among the nations of the Americas
2. (a) northern North America and Latin America (b) Northern North America is mainly English in heritage; Latin America is mainly Spanish but also Portuguese in its cultural heritage.
3. Lack of wartime destruction, help with postwar rebuilding, growth of foreign trade, leadership in electronics technology
4. civil rights movement, monument for women's rights, issues over the Vietnam War
5. (a) From being a superpower, the United States now held less political and economic power. (b) Canada became more nationalistic and more involved in world affairs.
6. Quebec, being French in heritage, wanted to preserve its culture. To do that, it threatened to separate from Canada.
7. By reducing tariffs between the United States and Canada, the agreement will encourage trade and economic cooperation between the two countries.

Independent Practice
Assign Independent Practice Worksheet 36.1.
Assign Vocabulary Worksheet 36.
Assign Geography Skills Worksheet 36.

Enrichment Activities

1. **Reading a Primary Source** Assign Voices from the Past Resource Book 36.1.

2. **Researching for Bonus Points** Award bonus points to students who can answer the following question: Who designed the Vietnam War Memorial? (Maya Yin Lin)

Latin America searched for stability. 2

Section Objectives

After completing Section 2, students should be able to:

1. describe the effects of rapid population growth in Latin America.

2. analyze the reasons Latin American countries lag in achieving prosperity.

Setting the Stage

Show students Overhead Transparency 81, *The Nations of Latin America*, and have them locate Mexico, the Caribbean Basin countries, and the nations of South America. Ask students to characterize the economies and political systems of Latin America. Ask students to characterize the economies and political systems of Latin American countries before World War II. Explain that Section 2 describes economic and political developments in Latin America in the postwar era.

Teaching Strategies

Discussing History: Urban Overpopulation (Objective 1) Ask students what services a city must provide its inhabitants. (transportation, sanitation, safety, employment) Discuss the difficulty of providing these services in a city where the population increases by nearly 800,000 people every year. Explain that this is the estimated rate of population growth in Mexico City, and that by the year 2,000 an estimated 26 million people will live there. This rapid increase in population has outpaced the ability of the city to provide sufficient jobs and adequate services. For example, in Mexico City 14,000 tons of garbage is produced daily, but the city can dispose of only 8,000 tons per day. This has resulted in large dumps where the city's homeless sift through the refuse for saleable items. Air and water pollution remain unchecked. Doctors estimate that chemical and biological pollutants kill 30,000 children every year. Explain that conditions such as these exist in most major urban areas of Latin America. Discuss the problems of rapid population growth, and challenge students to suggest solutions. Tell them that many countries in Latin America are attempting to relocate populations by creating employment opportunities in rural areas. Ask students to find a specific example of this trend in the text. (Brasília)

Economics and History: Latin American Foreign Debt (Objective 2) Help students to relate the concepts of *principal* and *interest* to the problem of Third World debt. Ask students how much money a country would have to pay a lender in a given year on a $50 million loan at 18 percent interest. ($9 million) Explain that many less-developed countries have difficulty paying the interest on their loans and might never be able to repay the principal. Reasons for difficulty include, for example, devalued currency, inflation, low market prices for the country's main product, costly domestic crises, and political corruption.

Point out that the inability of debtor countries to repay loans threatens the international economy. Large banks use repaid interest as income to loan to other governments and to invest in multinational businesses. Bank failures caused by bad debts can therefore have a global impact. Ask students why governments and banks continue to send foreign aid and to make loans to debtor countries. Explain that cities and countries, like banks and businesses, can go bankrupt. Foreign investments in those countries and in the resources and products of those countries might be lost. Aside from the human suffering that would result, bankrupt countries might face social and political upheaval, which might leave them vulnerable to foreign intervention, which might upset the relationships among world powers. The bankruptcy of a nation can therefore have an even greater global impact than its defaults on international loans. Ask students what steps they think might be taken to help Third World countries to reduce their foreign debts.

Check for Understanding Have students write paragraphs describing the conditions in Latin American countries that have prevented economic prosperity.

Practice

Guided Practice
Lead a guided discussion of questions in Overhead Transparency 81 and in Section Review 2. (Answers are below.)

Define:
failure to pay debts when due

Identify:
(a) new Brazilian capital in interior (b) Argentine dictator from mid-1940's to mid-1950's (c) South Atlantic islands, scene of war between Britain and Argentina in 1982 (d) president of Argentina, chosen in 1983 free election (e) new president of Mexico (f) president of Chile

Answer:
1. has caused very rapid urban growth with vast slums; has slowed economic development
2. (a) They hoped to build industries so that their economies could be more productive and provide more employment; also to provide more social services. (b) Income from new industries was not great enough to pay off the debts.
3. Democracy is limited in that there are property requirements for voting. Also, caudillo rule

and military influence have limited representative government.

4. **(a)** Argentina's defeat in the Falklands War led to the downfall of the despotic leaders and free elections for new officials. **(b)** The 1988 election in Mexico ended one-party rule. **(c)** The 1988 Chilean elections voted that Pinochet should allow open presidential elections in 1989.

5. **(a)** Like most other Third World countries, Latin American nations have rapidly expanding populations, a lack of steady economic growth, and governments that are dominated by one party of the military. **(b)** They differ in that most Latin American nations have been independent for more than one and one half centuries.

Independent Practice
Assign independent Practice Worksheet 36.2.
Assign Basic Skills Worksheet 36.

Enrichment Activities

1. **Reading a Primary Source** Assign Voices from the Past Resource Book 36.2.

2. **Researching for Bonus Points** Award bonus points to students who can answer the following question: "What is the Argentine name for the Falkland Islands?" (Malvinas Islands)

Answers to Voice from Our Time

1. Literature's mission is to disturb, alarm, and also to destroy or purify, which is what fire can do.
2. to stimulate the will to change and improve, to keep people dissatisfied with themselves, agitated, and disturbed
3. He might mean satire and virulent criticism or truths that are too terrible for people to face.
4. religious groups, political groups, military groups
5. Students may consider that literature's function is not only to provide pleasure but also an appeal to conscience.

Caribbean nations took different paths. 3

Section Objectives

After completing Section 3, students should be able to:

1. identify the forces involved in the Nicaraguan conflict.
2. trace changes in United States policy toward Latin America.

Setting the Stage

Tell students that poverty and the policies of dictators also led to revolution, civil war, and foreign intervention, as in Cuba and Nicaragua. Show Overhead Transparency 81, *The Nations of Latin America*, and have students identify the countries of the Caribbean Basin and their capitals. Ask, "How is the political geography of this region different from that of Mexico and South America?" (Countries are smaller and are confined by the sea.) Ask students why political developments in the countries of Central America and the Caribbean are important to the United States. Students should recall the strategic and commercial importance of the region and the traditional role of the Untied States in Latin American affairs.

Teaching Strategies

Discussing History: The Nicaraguan Conflict (Objective 1) Draw a three-column chart on the chalkboard with the following headings: "Somozas," "Sandinistas," and "Contras." Call on students to identify the membership, goals, policies, and alliances of the three groups and add students' responses to the chart. Then ask students to explain why the Sandinistas rebelled against the Somozas and why the Contras rebelled against the Sandinistas. Conclude by asking students to summarize the present-day status of the Nicaraguan conflict.

Writing about History: The United States' Dilemma over Nicaragua (Objective 2) *Prewriting* Tell students that the United States supported the Somoza regimes in Nicaragua, and later aided Nicaraguan Contras against the Sandinistas. Latin Americas and others accused the United States of inconsistency in foreign policy. Have students find clarifying information in the text. *Writing* Ask students to write essays explaining why United States policy was viewed as inconsistent and identifying the concerns that guided American policy choices. Students might conclude their essays with predictions of the concerns that they think will guide United States policy in Latin America in the 1990's.

Check for Understanding Ask students to list the causes of civil conflict in Central American and Caribbean countries after World War II.

Practice

Guided Practice
Lead a guided discussion of questions in Section Review 3. (Answers are below.)

Identify:
(a) policy established by President Theodore Roosevelt that the United States could intervene in Latin America to preserve order (b) caudillo leader and dictator of Cuba (c) revolutionary leader who overthrew Batista and turned Cuba to communism (d) invasion of Cuba by anti-Castro forces in 1961 (e) leader of corrupt ruling family in Nicaragua (f) Nicaraguan group that overthrew Somoza and took over the government (g) group that arose in opposition to Sandinistas (h) governor of Costa Rica; leader in Central American peace movement (i) president of Panama

Answer:
1. Puerto Rico is a commonwealth and has much self-government, although final authority lies with Congress.
2. (a) in land, plantations, mines, oil wells and other businesses (b) by intervening in the internal affairs of countries
3. by leading a political movement against Batista
4. (a) at first, increasing democracy; later, turned to communism and became dictator (b) nationalized oil refineries and sugar plantations; turned to trade with the Soviet Union
5. Castro allowed the Soviets to bring missiles—possibly with nuclear capability—into Cuba. When the United States discovered this, it sought to have the missiles removed, and succeeded.
6. (a) The Sandinistas overthrew Somoza and then turned to redistribution of land, nationalizing of certain industries, and providing more education and social services. (b) The Contras sought greater political freedom, more stable economic policies, and less government control
7. The United States accused Noriega of trafficking in drugs.
8. People to interview include representatives from every economic class, Cuban refugees, Castro, government officials, and people old enough to compare pre-revolutionary and post-revolutionary Cuba. Cuban refugees might be biased, and people living in Cuba might be intimidated.

Independent Practice
Assign Independent Practice Worksheet 36.3.
Assign Critical Thinking Worksheet 36.

Enrichment Activities

1. **Reading a Primary Source** Assign Voices from the Past Resource Book 36.3.
2. **Researching a Topic** Ask advanced students to find out what roles drug trafficking, the Panama Canal, and Oliver North played in United States policies toward Latin America in the 1980's.
3. **Researching for Bonus Points** Award bonus points to students who can answer this question: "On what day of the year do Cubans celebrate their national independence?" (July 26)

Concluding the Chapter

1. **Chapter Closer**
   Ask students to name the regions they would cross if they traveled the length of the Pan American Highway, and to identify some political and economic characteristics of the countries they would see.
2. **Reteaching Activities**
   a. **Explaining Main ideas** Ask students to explain how overpopulation and foreign debts have affected Latin American economies.
   b. **Recalling Information** Ask students to recall the causes and results of the Cuban Revolution and the Nicaraguan conflict.
3. **Chapter Review Activities**
   Assign Chapter Review 36 activities.

Chapter Evaluation

Chapter Test 36 and Computer Test Bank Chapter 36 Test can be used to evaluate your students' understanding of this chapter.

Answers to Chapter Review 36

Reviewing the Facts
1. **a.** Company with branches in many countries **b.** movement aimed at making Quebec independent of Canada
2. **a.** Black civil rights leader in United States **b.** 41st president of the United States **c.** Canadian Prime minister **d.** Argentinean military dictator **e.** islands over which Argentina lost a war to Britain. **f.** democratically elected president of

Argentina. **g.** Mexican president who barely won election in 1988. **h.** military dictator of Chile who lost public referendum in 1988. **i.** Cuban dictator before revolution. **j.** leader of Cuban revolution **k.** corrupt president and dictator of Nicaragua **l.** Nicaraguan rebels who overthrew Somoza government **m.** Nicaraguan rebels who are fighting Sandinista government **n.** Costa Rican president whose five point peace plan proposed a truce between Sandinista government and contra rebels. **o.** United States volunteer organization that works to improve the quality of life in third world countries. **p.** Panamanian leader accused of trafficking in drugs by the United States.

3. **(a)** economic dominance diminished as foreign industrial nations recover from World War II. Exports declined and foreign imports increased. **(b)** Social issues, including the black civil right movement and the women's movement, strove for social equality. American society was divided over differences concerning the Vietnam War.

4. **(a)** population growth, poverty **(b)** economy plummeted; Mexico could not meet debt payments and needed emergency loans

5. Mexican workers illegally entered the U.S.; U.S. banks loaned money.

6. **(a)** by overthrowing the Somoza government **(b)** gave land to the peasants, encouraged health clinics, distributed food **(c)** feared Nicaragua is being used for a Communist take over of Central America

Basic Skills

1. **(a)** Inside tropics: Mexico, Guatemala, Belize, Honduras, El Salvador, Nicaragua, Costa Rica, Cuba, Jamaica, Haiti, Dominican Republic, Panama, Colombia, Venezuela, Guyana, Suriname, French Guiana, Ecuador, Peru, Bolivia, Brazil, Paraguay. Outside tropics: United States, Argentina, Chile, Uruguay **(b)** land in Latin America is tropical savannah, tropical rain forest or a mixture of both; crops are varied and include grains, sugar cane, soy, and coffee; raw materials include large oil and iron ore deposits

2. **(a)** *civil rights movement:* pro arguments— blacks were not participating in economic prosperity, racial discrimination continued to exist; con arguments—white racists resisted black civil rights movement; outcomes—end to racial discrimination, Civil Rights Act, Voting Act; *women's movement:* pro arguments—

discrimination against women kept salaries low and job opportunities limited; con arguments—traditional view of women's roles; outcomes—women gain more access to elected positions, anti-discrimination laws passed, ERA amendment is not adopted; *Vietnam War:* pro arguments—fight against communism; con arguments—war was immoral and unwinnable; outcomes—U.S. withdraws from Vietnam, South Vietnam is taken over **(b)** student answers will vary.

Researching and Reporting Skills

1. Student answers will vary. Suggested topics: Latin American debt payments, struggles between communist and democratic regimes in Latin America, drug trade between Latin America and U.S.

2. Student answers will vary, but should include all Latin American countries and Indian ethnic groups.

Critical Thinking

1. **(a)** escaped WWII devastation, developed foreign trade, technological innovations **(b)** economic prosperity at home, economic dominance abroad led by multinational corporations.

2. **(a)** imports exceed exports as foreign competitors are able to compete with U.S. companies **(b)** U.S. share of foreign markets is diminishing.

3. strong economy, increased nationalism

4. **(a)** encourage trade, made U.S. and Canada more competitive in world markets **(b)** increase trade between U.S. and Canada

5. **(a)** uneven distribution of wealth, caudillo rule, frequent changes in leadership **(b)** democratic elections taking place in Chile and Argentina, one-party domination in Mexico is diminishing

6. employment opportunities must be created to meet the demands of a rapidly expanding population

7. **(a)** communist revolution in Cuba; civil wars in El Salvador, Guatemala, and Nicaragua; corruption in Panama **(b)** broke relations with Cuba, alliance for progress, supported Contras in Nicaragua, shown less tolerance for oppressive regimes, especially in Panama where U.S. has tried to end the rule of Manuel Noriega

Perspective on Past and Present
Answers will vary.

Investigating History
Students' answers will vary.

The World in Change

Chapter Overview

Neil Armstrong's historic mission to the moon marked the first of many dramatic technological and scientific advances. Both the United States and the Soviet Union launched space stations and reusable space shuttles. Personal computers spread from research facilities to offices and homes.

Technology changed patterns of work while also influencing people's appreciation of life. Musicians, writers, and artists now perform for a global audience. Technological advances have also stimulated new surgical techniques and agricultural practices that improve public health and promote better nutrition.

Technology proved to be a double-edged sword. While it improved the quality of everyday life, it also created long-term threats to the global environment. The greenhouse effect and ozone depletion pose serious problems that required international cooperation.

New economic and political trends contributed to an era of extraordinary changes. Led by Japan, the Pacific Rim became one of the most important economic regions in the world. Under the leadership of Mikhail Gorbachev, the Soviet Union launched an unprecedented program of economic and social reform. While nuclear weapons continue to pose a threat to civilization, the United States and the Soviet Union signed a historic treaty reducing their stockpiles of intermediate range missiles. These developments and others indicate that the world is entering a new age of global interdependence.

Key Terms

superconductor
For additional exercises, see Vocabulary Worksheet 37.

Chapter Focus

Begin by having students read the introduction to Chapter 37. Point out that Armstrong's historic trip to the moon is only one of many remarkable advances that have occurred during the past 25 years. Taken together, these changes are producing a new era in human history.

Explain that modern historians are trying to

determine the characteristics of the exciting new age in which we live. Ask students to think about the characteristics of the age in which they now live. Have them write down one or two words they would use to complete this sentence: "We are living in an Age of..." List students answers on the chalkboard. Tell students that modern historians have suggested words such as "Interdependence," "Change," and "Reaction" to describe this era. Explain that this chapter discusses the major technological, economic, cultural, and political trends that are shaping our lives.

Technology led in new directions. 1

Section Objectives

After completing Section 1, students should be able to:

1. identify major achievements of the United States space program and evaluate possible new goals.
2. trace the development of supercomputers and explain the significance of this new technology.
3. explain superconductivity and describe some of its possible applications.

Setting the Stage

Read or distribute the following list of scientific goals:

- send a manned mission to Mars.
- deploy a defense system that could destroy enemy missiles.
- build personal computers that can talk and listen.
- build supercomputers that can mimic the human decision-making process.
- build practical electric cars.

Ask students to select the goal that they would most like to see achieved during their lifetimes and to explain their choices. Explain that new discoveries might enable scientists to achieve all of these goals within the next half century. This section introduces students to the technological and scientific developments that are making the achievement of these goals possible.

Teaching Strategies

Discussing History: The Space Program (Objective 1) Have students identify the major achievements of the United States manned space program. Explain that the Apollo voyages to the moon, the Skylab research station, and the space shuttle mark major achievements. Then divide the class into small groups. Explain that government and NASA officials are debating possible new goals for the United States manned space program. Tell students that their assignment is to prepare a report recommending one of the following three goals:

Space station The construction of a $25 billion orbiting space station. The station would serve as a laboratory for scientific experiments and as a possible staging area for flights to the Moon and to Mars.

Lunar base The construction of a moon base that could serve as an observatory, a laboratory, and a possible launching station for missions to Mars.

Mission to mars The creation of a $300 billion manned flight to Mars. This program could be a joint project with the Soviets.

Relating Past to Present: Supercomputers (Objective 2) Ask students to solve the following mathematical problem as rapidly as they can: $37 \times 43 + 62 + 13 = ?$ (1666). How long did the students take to solve this problem? Explain that before the invention of computers, complex mathematical problems required hours to solve. For example, during World War II, workers at the Army Ballistic Research Laboratory needed forty hours to calculate artillery trajectories. Then, in 1946 scientists at the University of Pennsylvania invented the world's first all-electronic digital computer. Known as ENIAC (Electronic Numerical Integrator and Computer), the new machine could calculate artillery trajectories in just twenty seconds.

Explain that computer scientists have made rapid progress since the invention of ENIAC. By the late 1980's supercomputers could achieve a sustained speed of one billion calculations per second. These powerful machines can simulate weather patterns, crack secret codes, design aerospace vehicles, and create special effects for Hollywood films.

Discussing History: Superconductors (Objective 3) Ask students to describe the coldest temperature they have ever experienced. Explain that minus 460 degrees Fahrenheit represents the total absence of heat and is therefore the coldest possible temperature. Tell students that when metals are cooled to this temperature they suddenly lose their electrical resistance and become superconductors. Although scientists knew about superconductivity, they found that maintaining temperatures near absolute zero was prohibitively expensive.

Then explain that during the late 1980's, scientists discovered new compounds that became superconductors at temperatures as low as $-234°F$. Researchers hope to coat silicon and other wires with a thin film of these new compounds. Scientists believe that by the early 1990's new high-temperature superconductors will speed the passage of electronic signals inside computers. Many predict that superconductors will help save huge amounts of energy.

Check for Understanding Have students explain how the space program, supercomputers, and superconductors are important to both science and society.

Practice

Guided Practice
Lead a guided discussion of the questions in Section Review 1. (Answers are below.)

Define:
(a) a human-made object intended to orbit the earth (b) an electronic device (c) a material with little or no resistance to the transmitting of electricity

Identify:
(a) first astronaut to land on moon (b) space program that landed men on the moon (c) space vehicle that could be launched into orbit and return to earth (d) project for space-based defense against ICBM attack (e) a computer with limited functions

Answer:
1. because they were so great and extensive that they changed basic procedures and processes
2. (a) landing on moon; space probes to explore solar system; putting scientific satellites into orbit (b) explore moon, record and bring back scientific data; learn more about other planets; obtain special astronomical information
3. Space science and technology found many everyday applications, from ceramic kitchenware and special types of clothing to greater understanding of stress and of physical response to changed conditions such as weightlessness.

Advance Planner

Chapter 37	The World in Change 1945–Present			★ Advanced
Focus	The challenge of characterizing the present era in world history			● Basic

	Section 1	**Section 2**	**Section 3**	**Section 4**
Objectives	1. Identify major achievements of the United States space program and evaluate possible new goals. 2. Trace the development of supercomputers and explain the significance of this new technology. 3. Explain superconductivity and describe some of its possible applications.	1. Describe the impact of technology on music. 2. Identify new surgical methods that help doctors repair and replace damaged body parts. 3. Discuss the impact of genetic research on agriculture.	1. Identify the greenhouse effect and explain its consequences. 2. Identify the ozone layer and explain the consequences of ozone depletion.	1. Define and give examples of *perestroika* and *glasnost*. 2. Identify the INF Treaty and discuss its significance. 3. Describe some of the common interests that unite the peoples of our planet.
Setting the Stage	Establishing priorities for scientific goals	Effects of technology on the quality of life	The environmental impact of technological change	The comparative strength of the United States as a world power
Teaching Strategies	Discussing History: The Space Program Relating Past to Present: Supercomputers Discussing History: Superconductors Check for Understanding	Discussing History: Music and Technology Discussing History: Microsurgery Economics and History: Genetic Research and Agriculture Check for Understanding	Using Geographic Themes: Human-Environment Interaction Check for Understanding	Discussing History: *Perestroika* and *Glasnost* Discussing History: The INF Treaty Writing about History: Global Interests Check for Understanding
Guided Practice	Section Review 1	Section Review 2	Section Review 3	Section Review 4
Independent Practice Worksheets	Independent Practice 37.1 Basic Skills 37 Vocabulary 37	Independent Practice 37.2	Independent Practice 37.3	Independent Practice 37.4 Geography Skills 37 Critical Thinking 37
Enrichment	1. Primary Source: Voices 37.1 2. Preparing a Report 3. Researching for Points	1. Primary Source: Voices 37.2 2. Researching for Points	1. Primary Source: Voices 37.3 2. Researching for Points	1. Primary Source: Voices 37.4 2. Researching for Points 3. Global Perspectives Transparency 92

Chapter Closer	
● **Reteaching Activities**	Making a Current Events Bulletin Board, Evaluating Trends
Chapter Review	Summary, Reviewing the Facts, Basic Skills, Researching and Reporting Skills, Critical Thinking, Perspectives on Past and Present, Investigating History
Chapter Evaluation	Chapter Test 37, Computer Test Bank Chapter 37 Test

Unit IX Review	
Geographic Theme:	Region: What changes are happening in the economic region of the Pacific Rim?
Unit Perspectives	Understanding History, (Explaining, Locating, Relating, Matching), Critical Thinking, Making Decisions, Continuity and Change
Unit Evaluation	Unit IX Test

4. (a) provide means for beaming communication signals over long distances (b) provided instant communication to most areas of the world
5. (a) Computers provided a means to store information and retrieve it instantly. (b) Computers provided a data-processing and problem-solving capability.
6. (a) research, industry, capacity for spoken response, design, data storage and retrieval, problem solving, medical diagnosis, and other similar uses.
7. Superconductors are a scientific breakthrough in terms of physics. They have the potential to provide less expensive electricity and, because they are more efficient than present systems, to reduce the pollution caused by fossil fuels.
8. One advance can give insight into related problems, stimulate new thinking and approaches, and provide applications in related areas.

Independent Practice

Assign Independent Practice Worksheet 37.1.
Assign Vocabulary Worksheet 37.
Assign Basic Skills Worksheet 37.

Enrichment Activities

1. **Reading a Primary Source** Assign Voices from the Past Resource 37.1.

2. **Preparing a Report** Have students prepare a report on one of the following topics: uses of superconductivity, new developments in personal computers, new goals for the United States space program, and supercomputers of the future.

3. **Researching for Bonus Points** Award bonus points to students who can find the answer to this question: What is the name of the Soviet space agency? (Glavkosmos)

Technology affected the quality of life. 2

Section Objectives

After completing Section 2, students should be able to:

1. describe the impact of technology on music.
2. identify new surgical methods that help doctors repair and replace damaged body parts.
3. discuss the impact of genetic research on agriculture.

Setting the Stage

Begin by asking students to name an activity that they enjoy doing. Students might mention listening to music, playing a sport, or watching movies. Then ask, "In what ways does technology improve your enjoyment of this activity?" Explain that technology increasingly enhances the potential quality of people's experiences. Tell students that this section describes some effects of technology on the quality of life.

Teaching Strategies

Discussing History: Music and Technology (Objective 1) Tell students that when they hear a string or brass instrument in a radio or television commercial, it is likely that the instrument is not a violin or french horn, but a "digital sample." Instead of a band or orchestra, the music is played by a single musician using a computer and electronic instruments. Musicians are increasingly using computer technology to digitize sounds. In this process, sounds are deciphered into numbers (digitizing) that can then be manipulated by a computer. Using a computer language termed *M.I.D.I.* (Musical Instrument Digital Interface), electronic instruments and computers can "talk" to each other. This technology enables single musicians, with the aid of computers, to reproduce the sounds of an entire orchestra, including "digitally-sampled" Stradivarius violins and soprano voices. Ask students if in their opinion technology is a good or a bad influence in music.

Discussing History: Microsurgery (Objective 2) Ask students if they think it is possible for surgeons to successfully detach a patient's toe and then reattach it to the patient's hand to replace a lost finger or thumb. Explain that in recent years, advances in microsurgery have enabled surgeons to detach and reattach body parts. "In the past," said New York plastic surgeon William Shaw, "you could move tissue around, but you couldn't restore feeling or function. Microsurgery now allows us to reattach tiny veins, arteries, and nerves, and that changes everything." Explain that Shaw and other surgeons believe that they will soon be able to take or "harvest" skin, ligaments, and bone from different body areas, reassemble them into a functioning joint, and attach the joint to the patient's body.

Economics and History: Genetic Research and Agriculture (Objective 3) Begin by pointing out that power-driven machines, artificial fertilizers, and chemical pesticides have dramatically increased the amount of food that farmers can produce and harvest. Then explain that the genetic

engineering of plants could soon lead to a new agricultural revolution. Scientists known as bioengineers have already produced genetically altered
bacteria that can prevent frost damage to plants.
Bioengineers predict that they will soon custom
design plants that can tolerate drought, resist
insects, and withstand salty water. Ask students
to explain the economic benefits of this research.

Check for Understanding Have students explain
how changes in technology are affecting music,
surgery, and agriculture.

Practice

Guided Practice
Lead a guided discussion of the questions in Section Review 2. (Answers are below.)

Define:
(a) basic physical unit of heredity (b) physical
thread-like structure that carry the genes

Identify:
(a) x-rays that give video pictures of internal bodily
activity (b) one of two scientists who researched
the structure of genes

Answer:
1. refers to non-material aspects of living
2. The global orientation of communications technology made music and performers international.
   The technology of recording and broadcasting
   music also improved.
3. by reaching a worldwide audience and expos-
   ing them to the same works
4. Third World writers were able to voice the viewpoints, experiences, traditions, and aspirations
   of their people. They also helped to create a cultural and political identity for newly independent countries.
5. New techniques for surgery made possible
   heart transplants and heart bypass operations.
   Micro-surgery joined severed nerves, and lasers
   treated eye problems, CAT scans and MRI aided
   in diagnosis of internal problems.
6. Worldwide cultural patterns are evidence of
   communications, understanding, and acceptance among people of different cultures.
   There is the potential for enrichment of individual cultures and a reduction in conflict
   between different cultural and ethnic groups.

Independent Practice
Assign independent Practice Worksheet 37.2.

Enrichment Activities

1. **Reading a Primary Source** Assign Voices from
   the Past Resource Book 37.2.

Text pages 782–799

2. **Researching for Bonus Points** Award bonus
   points to students who can answer this question: What is the name of the first artificial
   heart? (the Jarvik-7)

Dangers to the global environment developed. 3

Section Objectives

After completing Section 3, students should be
able to:

1. explain the consequences of the greenhouse
   effect.
2. identify the ozone layer and explain the consequences of ozone depletion.

Setting the Stage

Ask students to discuss the impact of each of the
following events. Have them rate each event in
terms of its effect on the United States, and on the
planet Earth:

• Chinese leaders decide to use coal as their
  nation's primary source of fuel.
• Fast-food restaurants in the United States decide
  to use foam packaging for their take-out orders.
• Brazilian settlers burn Amazon forests to clear
  the land for new farms.

Explain that these three economic activities contribute to global environmental dangers known as
the greenhouse effect and ozone depletion, which
threaten to affect all life on this planet. Tell students that this section examines these and other
dangers to the global environment.

Teaching Strategies

**Using Geographic Themes: Human-Environment
Interaction** (Objective 1) Tell students that many
scientists now predict that the greenhouse effect
will raise global temperatures by three to nine
degrees during the next century. This drastic
change in temperature will have a dramatic
impact on the global environment. As weather patterns change, parched areas in East Africa could
receive more rain, while droughts in the American Midwest could worsen. The warming trend
could also lengthen the growing season in parts of
Canada, the Soviet Union, and Scandinavia.
Explain that rising temperatures will melt polar
icecaps, causing sea levels to rise. Flooding could

threaten low-lying areas and coastal resorts throughout the world. Some experts warn that Manhattan Island would have to build a sea wall to protect itself from rising waters.

Ask students to speculate on ways of reversing the greenhouse effect. Point out that reforms will be difficult. Experts warn that fossil-fuel emissions would have to be cut by 60 percent to stop the current warming of two-tenths of a degree Fahrenheit per decade.

Using Geographic Themes: Human-Environment Interaction (Objective 2) Ask students if they travel in air-conditioned cars, use aerosol sprays, or eat fast-food wrapped in foam packaging. Tell students that each of these products release a chemical known as *chlorofluorocarbon* (CFC) into the atmosphere. Tell students that the chemical emissions eventually reach the ozone layer above the earth's surface. Explain that the ozone layer shields the earth from ultraviolet radiation (UV).

Scientists have proven that CFC's trigger a complex chemical reaction that is destroying the earth's ozone layer. Emphasize that as the ozone layer diminishes, increasing amounts of UV will reach the earth. Scientists believe that increased exposure to this radiation can damage human immune systems, cause higher rates of skin cancer, and harm many crops. Some specialists fear that higher levels of UV will also harm plankton, the tiny organisms that form the base of the marine food chain. Conclude by reviewing the text's discussion of the steps that are being taken to end the use of CFC's.

Check for Understanding Have students list the consequences of the greenhouse effect and of ozone depletion.

Practice

Guided Practice
Lead a guided discussion of the questions in Section Review 3. (Answers are below.)

Define:
(a) a fuel formed in the earth from plant and animal remains (b) a rise of carbon dioxide in the earth's atmosphere that traps heat in the atmosphere, thus causing a warming of the climate (c) a form of oxygen found in the upper atmosphere that shields the earth from ultraviolet radiation (d) rain carrying pollutants such as sulfur that harm the environment

Answer:
1. (a) population growth put a strain on the environment due to the high consumption of resources and the great quantity of waste caused

by people (b) Because modern technology involves use of large quantities of energy, pollutants from energy-producing fossil fuels endanger the environment.
2. burning of fossil fuels and gradual polluting of oceans
3. (a) solar cells, nuclear fusion of safer fission power plants, cleaner ways of burning coal (b) solar cells clean but depend on sunlight; nuclear fusion not yet available; nuclear fission poses danger of accidents; cleaner burning of coal is expensive
4. (a) People began to recognize the environmental cost of high energy use and the over-use of chemicals such as insect sprays. (b) Third World nations began to realize that their environments were vulnerable and needed to be preserved.
5. (a) waste (garbage and trash), carbon dioxide from fossil fuels, acid rain, certain chemicals, oceanic pollution (b) reducing or recycling waste, burning less fossil fuels, regulating sulfur emissions, limiting or banning use of certain chemicals, forbidding ocean dumping

Independent Practice
Assign Independent Practice Worksheet 37.3.

Enrichment Activities

1. **Reading a Primary Source** Assign Voices from the Past Resource Book 37.3.

2. **Researching for Bonus Points** Award bonus points to students who can answer this question: What is UV-B? (A form of ultraviolet light. Each 1 percent drop in ozone allows 2 percent more UV-B to reach the ground.)

A *new era of economic and political change began.* 4

Section Objectives

After completing Section 4, students should be able to:

1. define and give examples of *perestroika* and *glasnost.*
2. identify the INF Treaty and discuss its significance.
3. describe some of the common interests that unite the peoples of this planet.

Setting the Stage

Begin by asking, "Is the United States as strong today as it was at the end of World War II?" List students' answers on the chalkboard. Point out that America's military forces possess thousands of times more firepower today than in 1945. Since the end of World War II, the gross national product has soared from $200 billion to more than $4 trillion.

Then tell students that despite these facts, some historians maintain that America's strength is declining. Ask, "Is it possible for America's economic and military strength to be growing while at the same time the nation's overall international power is declining?" Explain that World War II left the United States with the world's only undamaged industrial base. However, as the rest of the world recovered, America's influence in relation to other countries began to decline. "America is not sinking," stresses one expert. "The rest of the world is rising." Tell students that this section explains how new centers of growth in Europe and Asia began to rival the United States in industrial output, exports, and research development.

Teaching Strategies

Discussing History: Perestroika and Glasnost (Objective 1) Review the definitions of *perestroika* and *glasnost*. Explain that *perestroika* is an attempt to restructure the Soviet economy so that it can be more productive and competitive. To date, Gorbachev's reforms have focused on making factory managers less dependent on central planners. In addition, Gorbachev has encouraged some private initiative. For example, private farm plots occupy only 1.5 percent of Russia's farmland, but now produce 25 percent of all agricultural products.

Explain that *glasnost* refers to a new policy of openness in Soviet society. Remind students that the Communist party has exercised complete control over all aspects of Soviet life. For example, the Party prevented open communications by placing restrictions on who can own telephones and computers. (In 1985, Russia's 278 million citizens owned only 36 million telephones.) Ask, "How might these controls hinder scientific and economic progress?" Explain that *glasnost* is beginning to have an impact on Soviet society. Russian newspapers openly discuss national problems, dissidents have more freedom, and youths are allowed to listen to western music.

Conclude the discussion by pointing out that Gorbachev's new policies have risks for both the Soviet Union and the United States. Ask students to discuss the following questions: Can the Communist party maintain power and still encourage

glasnost? Should the United States ignore or encourage the Gorbachev revolution?

Discussing History: The INF Treaty (Objective 2) Review the text's discussion of the INF Treaty. Explain that intermediate missiles have a range of 300 to 3,400 miles. Point out that the treaty does not affect intercontinental missiles. Stress that the treaty nevertheless marks an important breakthrough in Soviet-American relations. For the first time, both superpowers agreed to allow teams to inspect missile sites in each other's territories. As noted in the text, the treaty also symbolized the hope that superpower cooperation will continue into the coming century.

Writing about History: Global Interests (Objective 3) Divide the class into groups that contain at least seven members. Ask the students to assume the roles of leaders from the following countries: United States, Soviet Union, China, Japan, India, Brazil, and Nigeria. Then direct students' attention to the words of Michael Collins, quoted on page 797. Tell students to pretend that they are attending a conference in a spaceship orbiting the earth. Their assignment is to establish a list of common interests that unite the people on our planet.

Check for Understanding Have students explain the significance of the Pacific Rim, *perestroika*, *glasnost*, and the INF Treaty.

Practice

Guided Practice
Lead a guided discussion of the questions in Section Review 4. (Answers are below.)

Identify:
(a) nations that border the Pacific Ocean (b) Gorbachev's policy restructuring Soviet economy to include incentives, more local control, free markets, and increased productivity (c) policy of openness about political, economic, and social issues (d) nations possessing nuclear weapons (e) Intermediate Nuclear Force Treaty providing for the destruction of certain numbers of missiles capable of carrying nuclear weapons

Answer:
1. rapid economic growth, industrialization, development of modern technology, increased foreign trade
2. modern manufacturing facilities, low wages, efficiency, planned marketing strategies
3. (a) need for more consumer goods, incentives for workers, higher efficiency and productivity, flexible prices, and control of inflation (b) are

intended to meet four needs identified under (a) above and to offer greater freedom as a motivation factor

4. There is great danger (both to the US and the USSR) that nuclear weapons might be used accidentally or irresponsibly.

Independent Practice

Assign Independent Practice Worksheet 37.4.
Assign Geography Skills Worksheet 37.
Assign Critical Thinking Worksheet 37.

Enrichment Activities

1. **Reading a Primary Source** Assign Voices from the Past Resource Book 37.4.

2. **Researching for Bonus Points** Award bonus points to students who can answer this question: At what location did President Reagan and General Secretary Gorbachev sign the INF Treaty? (in the East Room of the White House in Washington, D.C.)

3. **Global Perspectives** Have students perform the activities in Overhead Transparency 92, *The Modern World.* This map also appears on pages 818–819 in the Historical Atlas

Answers to Voice from Our Time

1. greater need to insure human survival and self-preservation

2. Answers will vary; probably that nations should be tolerant of differences and in the face of change.

3. greater openness in words and deeds about differences in political systems, a joint search for answers, more international dialogue and negotiation

4. Answers will vary, but might suggest that the speech can be taken at face value as sincere or that it can be viewed with scepticism.

Concluding the Chapter

1. **Chapter Closer**
   Have students write essays answering the chapter focus question: How would students characterize the age in which they now live?

2. **Reteaching Activities**
   a. **Making a Current Events Bulletin Board** Have students bring in newspaper and magazine aticles and pictures on the following topics: the space program, computers, superconductors, the Pacific Rim, nuclear disarmament talks, and *glasnost.* Have students arrange these materials to create a current events bulletin board.

   b. **Evaluating Trends** Ask students to prepare a list describing the three most important long-term trends discussed in this chapter. Students should explain their choices.

3. **Chapter Review Activities**
   Assign Chapter Review 37 activities.

Chapter Evaluation

Chapter Test 37 and Computer Test Bank Chapter 37 Test can be used to evaluate your students' understanding of this chapter.

Answers to Chapter Review 37

Reviewing the Facts

1. **a.** manmade body put into orbit to receive and send information via radio signals **b.** electronic device that conducts electricity in radios, televisions and computers **c.** materials that carry current with maximum effectiveness **d.** structure in cells that determines characteristics of the organism **e.** long chain of genes **f.** energy source extracted from remains of prehistoric animals **g.** warming of the earth's atmosphere **h.** layer of earth's atmosphere that keeps ultraviolet radiation from reaching planet's surface **i.** restructuring of Soviet economy that provided worker incentives **j.** policy of increased openness

2. **a.** astronaut who landed on the moon in 1969 **b.** space program that sent explorations to the moon **c.** Soviet satellite put into orbit in 1957 **d.** reusable U.S. spacecraft **e.** space-based military defense system using satellites and laser beams **f.** first communications satellite launched in 1962 **g.** information processing device that enables users to organize large amounts of information **h.** computer-enhanced x-rays **i.** controversial manipulation of genetic cell structures **j.** chlorofluorocarbons that destroy earth's ozone layer **k.** Soviet nuclear power plant at which an accident spread a radioactive cloud over Europe in 1985 **l.** nations bordering Pacific Ocean that emerged as economic powers in late 1980's **m.** economic changes that challenged communist traditions in Soviet Union **n.** signaled a change in Soviet attitudes towards their social control and foreign relations **o.** nations who possess nuclear weapons

p. treaty that reduced number of intermediate nuclear forces between U.S. and Soviet Union by 10 percent

Basic Skills

1. **(a)** others 26.8%, USA 18.6%, Germany FRG 9.2%, France 6.2%, U.K. 6.1.%, Japan 6.1%, Italy 4.8%, Canada 4.1%, Netherlands 3.6%, Belg-Lux 3.3%, China PRC 2.1%, USSR 2.1%, Switzerland 2.0%, Hong Kong 1.7%, Spain 1.7%, Korea Rep 1.6%. exporters: all other 27%, Germany 12.2%, USA 10.9%, Japan 10.6%, France 6.3%, Italy 4.9%, Canada 4.5%, U.K. 5.4%, Netherlands 4.0%, Belg-Lux 3.5%, Sweden 1.9%, Switzerland 1.9%, Hong Kong 1.8%, Korea, Rep. 1.8%, USSR 1.7%, China, PRC 1.6% **(b)** USA, USSR, U.K., Switzerland, China PRC, **(c)** Korea, Hong Kong, Netherlands, Italy, Belg-Lux, Germany FRG, France, Canada, Japan **(d)** all countries in answer (b) have negative trade balance, all countries in (c) have positive.
3. **(a)** Negative trade balance has unfavorable effect on economy since it means domestic industry is selling less abroad. **(b)** sample answers: become more competitive in world markets, erect trade barriers such as tariffs and embargoes

Researching and Reporting Skills

1. Presentations will vary.
2. Answers will vary.
3. Answers will vary, though students should note the vast amount of foreign goods sold in American stores.

Critical Thinking

1. **(a)** space travel has provided the military with technology to develop long range nuclear missiles, military satellites and the SDI system **(b)** weather, communications and navigation satellites, space exploration.
2. **(a)** Companies will increasingly do business with foreign companies as global economies become interdependent. **(b)** Multinational companies will expand and become increasingly service oriented.
3. People can experience a variety of art, literature and music from around the world providing a broader perspective and better understanding of different cultures.
4. **(a)** likely to increase population **(b)** environmental pollution, greenhouse effect, depletion of ozone layer
5. **(a)** Countries must cooperate and agree on approaches to environmental problems. **(b)** Answers will vary.

6. **(a)** mutual suspicion, cold war tensions, different political and social philosophies, treaty verification difficult **(b)** Arms reductions must be equitable without giving either side an advantage; treaties must be verifiable.
7. **(a)** providing affordable consumer items, raising worker productivity and workmanship, controlling inflation **(b)** provide worker incentives, give workers more choice and freedom

Perspectives on Past and Present

Sample answer: Stalin's speech took place during the tense period of the Cold War, Gorbachev's is during improving U.S.-USSR relations. Stalin believes conflict is inevitable; Gorbachev believes it must be avoided. Stalin's speech stresses the differences between world nations, Gorbachev's the similarities; Stalin is striving for domination, Gorbachev for cooperation.

Investigating History

1. Answers will vary.
2. Answers will vary.

Unit IX Review Activities

1. Assign Geographic Theme: Region.
2. Assign Unit Perspectives questions.

Unit IX Review Answers

Geographic Theme: Region

1. **a.** Australia, China, and Taiwan **b.** United States, Soviet Union, and Japan
2. **a.** Singapore, South Korea, and Taiwan **b.** China, Canada, and the United States **c.** Singapore, South Korea, and Taiwan **d.** China, United States, and Soviet Union
3. That it is economically very active as a region, with a strongly rising GNP and per capita GNP. The nations of East Asia are doing particularly well.

Unit Perspectives

Understanding History

1. **(a)** policy to contain spread of communism which began with aid to Greece and Turkey **(b)** plan to rebuilt Europe and stop communism after World War II **(c)** defense alliance of Western European nations and United States **(d)** alliance of USSR and its European satellites **(e)**

economic alliance of many Western European countries (f) economic assistance offered by Soviets to Eastern European countries as a substitute for Marshall Plan (g) Brandt's program to improve relations with USSR and Eastern Europe (h) independent Polish trade union that defied Soviet dominance (i) Soviet leaders used this article to justify sending troops to Czechoslovakia.

2. **a.** (e) **d.** (b) **g.** (a) **j.** (g)
   b. (g) **e.** (d) **h.** (c) **k.** (b)
   c. (b) **f.** (f) **i.** (g) **l.** (e)

3. **a.** Indian prime minister who emphasized democracy and economic modernization **b.** made India one of the world's top ten industrial nations **c.** president of Ghana **d.** first president of Egyptian Republic who took over Suez Canal **e.** set up one-man authoritarian rule in Zaire **f.** popular president of Ivory Coast **g.** set up a socialist economy in Tanzania **h.** prime minister of Israel who reached an agreement with Egypt

4. **1.** f **3.** g **5.** c **7.** b
   2. e **4.** a **6.** d

5. **(a)** led fight to free Hungary from Soviets **(b)** initiated set of reforms in Czechoslovakia **(c)** helped force the government to allow rights to Polish workers **(d)** kept Soviets out of Yugoslavia **(e)** began movement to defend French-Canadian rights **(f)** author whose books exposed the brutality of life in Soviet prison camps **(g)** led civil rights movements in United States

Critical Thinking

1. **a.** created division between Eastern and Western Europe; brought Eastern Europe under Soviet domination **b.** North Atlantic Treaty Organization (NATO) included democratic nations of Western and Southern Europe and overseas nations such as United States and Canada. In Eastern Europe, Warsaw Pact linked Soviet Union and seven other countries.

2. land reform, rebuilding of old industries, development of new industries, production of high-quality new-technology goods. The result was an economic boom—Japan's economic miracle.

3. **a.** In 1900 China was politically weak and economically in decay; divided into spheres of interest controlled by European nations. Today, China is a major power with a strong government and expanding economy. **b.** suggests that China will grow in economic and political power

4. **a.** legacy of colonialism and environmental factors make it difficult to build stable governments in Africa; lack of tradition of democratic, representative governments and trend toward strong rulers, often with military support **b.** powerful police and military support and a cohesive white minority government; large majority of nonwhite peoples and the frustration of repressed black majority raise questions about long-term stability

5. Answers will vary, ranging from advising the government to take a hard line to recommending negotiation as a way of achieving lasting peace.

6. End of World War II left U.S. and the Soviet Union as superpowers; as other regions, have recovered from the war, they have gained in political power, approaching that of the U.S. and the Soviet Union.

7. Rapid population growth can lead to population so large that absorbs an undue amount of resource. Rapid growth means an increasing number of people of child-bearing age, even with greater growth in future.

8. Environmental pollution involves the greenhouse effect, ozone layer, oceanic pollution, and possible nuclear radiation involve areas and concerns far greater than those of any single country. Contributing factors are worldwide and must be dealt with globally.

Making Decisions

Truman aided South Korea in order to prevent communist expansion. Attempted expansion was stopped. Johnson's report to congress was of an attack and that defense was necessary. Kennedy's demand was essential to U.S. defense. The outcome was that the missiles were removed. Possible alternatives will vary.

Continuity and Change

Factors include relative balance of power between superpowers; fear of nuclear conflict; conflicts that have occurred being local or regional; desire by all to avoid major war. Existence of UN, extent of WWII destruction, and world opinion may also have contributed.

Unit Evaluation

Unit IX Test can be used to evaluate your students' understanding of this unit.

WORLD
HISTORY

Perspectives on the Past

Authors

Steven L. Jantzen

Author of works on history, government, and classroom-tested teaching strategies; editor of social studies texts; former high-school teacher of government and history

Larry S. Krieger

Social studies supervisor in Edison, New Jersey; coauthor of social studies textbooks and teaching materials; former world history teacher

Kenneth Neill

Author of textbooks on nineteenth- and twentieth-century world history; former history teacher; publisher/editor of *Memphis* magazine, Memphis, Tennessee

Senior Content Consultant
Dr. Lloyd Swenson
Professor of History
University of Houston
Houston, Texas

WORLD HISTORY

Perspectives on the Past

 D.C. Heath and Company

Lexington, Massachusetts   Toronto, Ontario

Teacher Consultants

Lolene Blake
Longmeadow High School
Longmeadow, Massachusetts

Spiro Cora
Wingfield High School
Jackson, Mississippi

John Dare
John Marshall Senior High School
Cleveland, Ohio

Sue Dillard
Shepton High School
Plano, Texas

Michael J. Harkins
Community Unit School, District 300
Dundee, Illinois

James Lange
Bell High School
Los Angeles, California

Eileen Murray
St. Edmunds School
Tonawanda, New York

John Petretich
Boardman High School
Boardman, Ohio

George Rislov
Shepton High School
Plano, Texas

Clint Rouse
Volusia County Schools
Daytona Beach, Florida

Content Consultants

Charmarie Jenkins Blaisdell   Associate Professor of History, Northeastern University, Boston, Massachusetts; specialist in European social and intellectual history; past president of the Sixteenth Century Studies Council

Joan Erdman   Professor of Anthropology, Columbia College, Chicago, Illinois; Research Associate, Committee of Southern Asian Studies, University of Chicago

J. Rufus Fears   Professor of Classics and Chair of the Department of Classical Studies, Boston University, Boston, Massachusetts

Contributions to Chapter 36, *The Americas in the Modern World*, were made by Bert Bower, regional specialist, Stanford University, Palo Alto, California.

Thomas Spear   Professor of African History, Chair of African and Middle Eastern Studies, Williams College, Williamstown, Massachusetts

Leslie Swartz   Specialist in Chinese studies and director of Harvard East Asian Outreach Program, Boston, Massachusetts

Dr. Lloyd Swenson   Professor of History, University of Houston, Houston, Texas

Charles T. Wood   Fellow, Medieval Academy of America; Daniel Webster Professor of History, Dartmouth College, Hanover, New Hampshire; former member of the executive committees of both the New Hampshire School Boards Association and the New Hampshire Joint Educational Council

Published simultaneously in Canada

Printed in the United States of America

International Standard Book Number: 0-669-20189-8

1 2 3 4 5 6 7 8 9 0

Executive Editor	Allen Wheatcroft
Senior Editor	Margaret Kovar
Editor	Cécile Strugnell
Design Manager	Leslie Dews
Designers	Robin Herr, Jane Miron, Cornelia Boynton
Production Coordinator	Joseph Hinckley
Editorial Services	Marianna Frew Palmer Kathleen K. Harvie

Cover illustration: The Roman aqueduct at Segovia, Spain

Contents

Maps

Tables, Graphs, Charts, and Diagrams

Introduction

History is the record of all the hopes, achievements, defeats, victories, discoveries, ideas, and beliefs of human beings since they first appeared on earth. History records the wars, disasters, plagues, and famines that have befallen humankind. Yet history also shows that people are capable of acting with courage, kindness, wisdom, and brilliance.

Every group of people has its own history. To forget that history would be as devastating as loss of memory is to an individual. Knowing who you are means remembering who you were yesterday and all the days before that. The history of a group of people—whether that group is a family, a religious group, or a nation—is part of that group's identity.

As different groups meet, trade, fight, and make alliances, their histories blend into a larger history. Taken together, the histories of all groups make up the history of the largest group of all—humankind.

Stonehenge, a giant arrangement of stones in England, may be more than 3,500 years old. It may have been both a religious center and a huge calendar. On June 21, the longest day of the year, the sun rises directly over a special stone.

Discuss the following views of history. "History is . . . indeed little more than the register of the crimes, follies, and misfortunes of mankind"—Edward Gibbon. "History is more or less bunk"—Henry Ford. "Not to know what happened before one was born is always to be a child"—Cicero.

1

Handbook for Time and Place

Historians work within the dimensions of time and place. Time tells *when* and place tell *where* people have lived and certain events have occurred. Together, time and place provide a frame for the human story that is history.

Historians need ways to represent time.

1

In the entire span of history, events happen on a particular date or during a certain period of time. Dates tell when some person lived, how long a war lasted, how many years passed between events. Dates allow historians to place events in correct sequence.

People use different calendars.

How are specific dates assigned to the passing years? Different groups of people follow different customs. Take, for example, the year that people in the United States and Europe will call 2000. They use that number because the year will come approximately 2,000 years after the birth of Jesus. People call this system of dating "the Christian Era" or "the Common Era."

However, for many Jews, this same year will be called 5761 because, by Jewish tradition, God created the world 5,761 years before. That same year will be numbered 1378 by many Muslims because they began counting from the year Muhammad founded their religion, the year that Europeans and Americans label 622.

In the past, people had even more ways of recording the passage of time. Some numbered their years only by the reigns of kings. Others counted forward or backward from great religious festivals. Historians must often do detective work to determine accurate dates from such sources.

Historians label time in various ways.

The dates given in this text are those of the Christian or Common Era. These dates fall into two groups, B.C. and A.D.

B.C. and A.D. In the early part of the book, many dates are followed by the letters B.C. These letters stand for "before Christ" and mean that the event took place a certain number of years before the birth of Jesus. Thus, the year 500 B.C. was 500 years before the birth of Jesus, or almost 2,500 years ago. As dates get closer to the birth of Jesus, the numbers get smaller. Thus, a person born in 378 B.C. might have lived until 318 B.C.

A few ways of recording time: The carving (left) is a list of Egyptian kings from 1300 B.C. The English sand-glasses below are from 1720; they measure 15-, 30-, 45-, and 60-minute periods. The modern watch shows many time units.

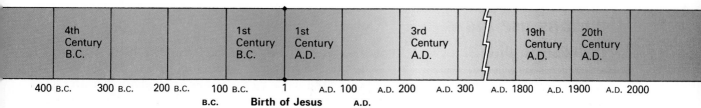

| 4th Century B.C. | | | 1st Century B.C. | 1st Century A.D. | | 3rd Century A.D. | | 19th Century A.D. | 20th Century A.D. | |

400 B.C.   300 B.C.   200 B.C.   100 B.C.   1   A.D. 100   A.D. 200   A.D. 300   A.D. 1800   A.D. 1900   A.D. 2000
                                         B.C.   Birth of Jesus   A.D.

This time line extends from 400 B.C. to A.D. 2000. It shows time in units of a century. The break on the right shows that a period of time has been omitted.

If a year is labeled A.D., it took place after the birth of Jesus. The letters stand for *"anno domini,"* a Latin phrase meaning "in the year of our Lord." These dates are usually written with the letters first: A.D. 939. If a year has no letters with it, you can assume it is A.D.

Other terms for time Besides numbering individual years, historians also group years into useful divisions:

A *decade* is 10 years.
A *century* is 100 years.
A *millenium* is 1,000 years.

We live in the twentieth century, but our years are labeled 19--. Why are these years called the *twentieth* century? Remember that years are numbered from the birth of Jesus. The years A.D. 1 to A.D. 100 were the first century. The years 101 to 200 were the second century, and so on. Thus, when you see *fifteenth century*, you should think of the years from 1401 to 1500.

The same division into centuries is used for the period of time before the birth of Jesus. The years from 100 B.C. to 1 B.C. are the first century B.C. The years from 500 B.C. to 401 B.C. are the fifth century B.C. Thus, an event in 735 B.C. took place in the eighth century B.C.

Broad time periods Sometimes historians talk about periods of time called *ages* or *eras*. An age or era is a broad zone of time. Historians use these terms to describe time periods when people shared certain patterns of life and thought. For example, certain times in history are known as the Bronze Age or the Middle Ages. The Stone Age is the period of time when people made many of their tools from stone.

It is impossible to give one exact date for the end of one era and the start of another. As age follows age, human ways of living change, but there is never a complete break. Every age has deep roots in the past.

Time lines show a certain period of time.

To represent a span of time, historians often use a time line such as the one shown above. A time line is like a graph, with each unit representing an equal amount of time. Together, these units show a period of historic time.

Time lines are based on particular dates that mark the start and end of the line. Between those dates, there usually are other dates to mark important events. Time lines may also serve to trace a historical sequence or the direction of change. By visually representing *when*, time lines are a useful tool for studying history.

Section Review

Define: (a) decade, (b) century, (c) millenium, (d) age, (e) era
Answer:
1. (a) What system do people in the United States use to number the passing years? (b) Why will the year A.D. 2000 be numbered 5761 by many Jews? (c) Why will Muslims number it 1378?
2. Which year in each of the following pairs is more recent? (a) 736 B.C. or 1288 B.C.? (b) A.D. 12 or 416 B.C.? (c) A.D. 1593 or A.D. 1750
3. In what century is each of the following dates? (a) 697 B.C. (b) A.D. 2010 (c) A.D. 1435
4. What are three kinds of information found on a time line?

Critical Thinking
5. Why are the dates for the beginning and end of an age or era only approximate?
6. (a) What label would you choose to describe the present period of history? (b) Would this term apply to all parts of the world or only to certain regions?

Historians use maps to represent place.   2

The events of history happen in a physical setting somewhere in the world. To show these settings, historians use maps, just as geographers do.

Mapmaking has a long history.

From the beginning of time, people have sought to show the world in which they live. If you have ever tried to map a large area, you know how difficult that is.

Early maps When did people first begin to make maps of their surroundings? The earliest known map was made for a Babylonian landowner about 2300 B.C. However, it was the Greeks of ancient times who first studied the world so as to present it in an accurate and systematic way. The word *geography* comes from the ancient Greek words for land (*geo*) and for writing or drawing (*graphien*).

As early as 350 B.C., Greek philosophers conceived of the earth as a sphere. Eratosthenes, a Greek mathematician and geographer, estimated the earth's circumference to be 24,662 miles. (The actual figure is 24,847 miles.) Another Greek geographer, Hipparachus, developed a system of grids, similar to today's lines of latitude and longitude, to locate places on the earth.

The most famous geographer of ancient times, Ptolemy, sought to map all the areas of the world. His map of the then-known world remained the best of its kind until the time of Columbus. Ptolemy also started the practice of putting north at the top of a map, south at the bottom, east at the right, and west at the left.

For more than 1,200 years after Ptolemy, the most complete and accurate maps were made by Arab ship captains and Chinese scholars. Major advances in European mapmaking began after A.D. 1300. As ship captains ventured farther on unknown waters, they charted coastlines and extended the known world. Columbus, for example, drew careful maps of the lands he explored. Gradually, maps became more accurate, detailed, and complete.

Ptolemy's map extends over 180° of longitude, or half the world. It shows more of the northern hemisphere than of the southern. Note that Asia and Africa are joined south of the Indian Ocean. This reproduction of Ptolemy's map was published in Germany in 1486.

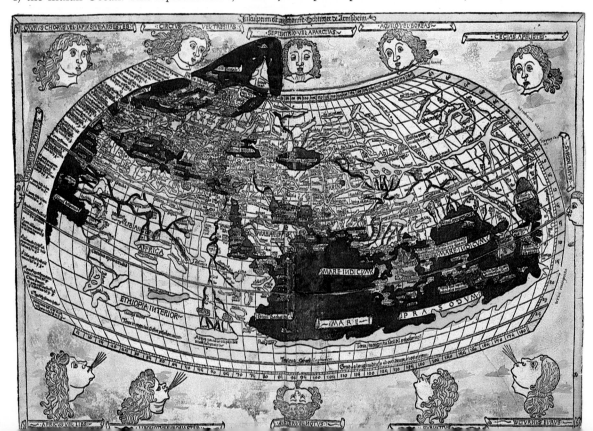

Modern maps In the almost 500 years since Columbus's first voyage, the whole world has been explored and mapped. Today, photos and images of the earth, taken from satellites, confirm the earlier knowledge. In addition, they provide new insights into the world in which we live.

Maps do not show the earth accurately.

The most accurate way to represent the earth is with a globe. Because the earth is a three-dimensional sphere, showing it on a two-dimensional map causes problems.

When a globe is transposed onto a flat surface, some areas are *distorted*, or shown inaccurately. For example, some maps may show the area of continents and oceans out of true proportion. Other maps may distort shapes, such as showing the polar regions as much larger than they actually are. Maps may also distort distance and direction.

Map projections can limit distortions.

Cartographers who design maps have developed a number of different *projections*. Each projection represents the globe in a particular way. As you will see, certain projections tend to meet particular needs. The map chosen for a given task, then, should be the one most suitable for that purpose.

Equal-area projections To show the size of areas accurately, an *equal-area projection* is used. On this projection, the size of one body of land or water is true relative to that of others. One common projection of this type is the *azimuthal equal-area projection*. This projection is always circular. It is centered on a single point on the globe, such as the middle of a continent or one of the poles. An important characteristic of this projection is that a straight line from the center to any other point represents the shortest distance.

Another equal-area map is the Peters projection. Although it shows the true relative size of land areas, you can see that it distorts their shapes.

Projections to show true shape Maps that show the shapes of land areas like those on a globe are said to be *conformal*. On this projection, shapes are true only over small areas. Those of large areas may be greatly distorted.

Landsat Image of Fort Worth and Dallas, Texas

Azimuthal Equal-Area Projection

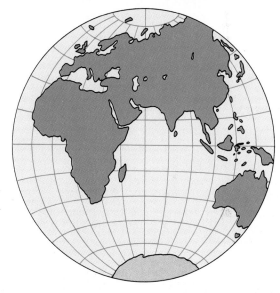

Peters Projection

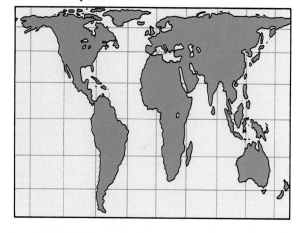

One of the earliest projections of this type is the Mercator projection. It was originated by Gerhardus Mercator, a Dutch cartographer of the sixteenth century. He had the idea of forming a sheet of paper into a cylinder, wrapping it around a globe, and transferring the outlines of land from the globe onto the paper. The shapes of land thus shown are most accurate in low and middle latitudes and least accurate in high latitudes. The island of Greenland, for example, appears on a Mercator projection to be larger than the continent of South America. In reality, it is less than one-eighth the size of South America.

Projections to show true direction The map best known for showing direction accurately is, again, the azimuthal projection. All straight lines drawn through the center of it show true compass direction. These lines, which are straight on the map, form great circles on a globe and show the shortest distance between two points. Great circles are thus the routes used by pilots of airplanes.

Projections to show distances accurately Projections that maintain distances accurately are said to be *equidistant*. However, distances can be kept accurate only over small areas or between two points. No projection can show true distances for the whole globe.

Distance is sometimes combined with other characteristics in a single projection such as the *azimuthal equidistant projection* to show both direction and distance correctly.

Section Review

Define: (a) distort, (b) projection, (c) equal-area projection, (d) conformal projection, (e) azimuthal projection, (f) equidistant projection

Identify: (a) Eratosthenes (b) Hipparachus (c) Columbus (d) Mercator

Answer:
1. Describe the contributions of the ancient Greeks to geography.
2. How did explorers like Columbus add to knowledge of the world?
3. Why is it difficult to show the earth correctly on a map?
4. What kinds of distortions are often found on maps?
5. What advantage does each of the major types of map projection have?

Critical Thinking
6. Why is it important to represent the world as accurately as possible?

Mercator Projection
Mercator maps were valuable to ship captains because a straight line on the map shows a true compass course.

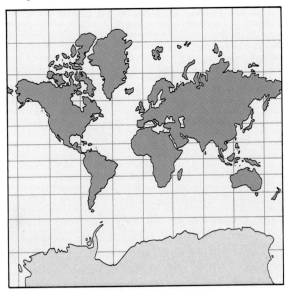

Azimuthal Equidistant Projection
On this projection, a straight line from the center to another point forms a great circle, the shortest route by airplane.

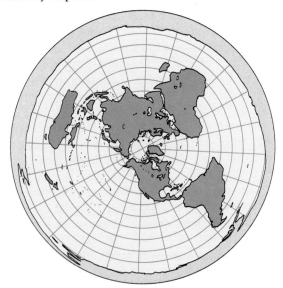

6

Western Europe and North Africa

Historians use ideas from geography.

3

Because *place* is important to historians, they share with geographers many ideas about the world. Among these ideas are five basic themes: *location, place, human-environment interaction, movement,* and *region.* These five themes provide ways for thinking about the world of the past as well as of the present.

Location focuses on where a place is.

The theme of *location* answers the question of where in the world a certain place exists. For example, consider the problem of determining where the place called Gibraltar is located. On the immense sphere that is the planet Earth, how can you tell where this rocky fortress of only 2.3 square miles is found?

Absolute location The location of a place can be described in two different ways. One of these is absolute location, determined by latitude and longitude. A map will show you that Gibraltar is found at the point where the imaginary line of latitude at 36° north of the equator crosses the imaginary line of longitude at 5° west of the prime meridian. An absolute location thus is like an address. Gibraltar's address on Earth is latitude 36° North and longitude 5° West.

Relative location A second method for locating places—the one more often used by historians— is relative location. Where is Gibraltar in relation to other places? On what continent is it found? Near what seas does it lie? Again, a map provides the answers.

Gibraltar is located in southwestern Europe. It lies at the western end of the Mediterranean where that sea meets the Atlantic Ocean. From Morocco in northern Africa, Gibraltar lies across a narrow strait from 8 to 23 miles wide. Describing Gibraltar in these ways shows its location relative to other bodies of land and water.

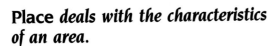

Place *deals with the characteristics of an area.*

Every place on Earth has its own special character. The Sahara is a desert, with a dry climate and little plant and animal life. The Amazon Basin is humid and teems with plants and wildlife. The physical characteristics of a place include its landforms, climate, vegetation, mineral and other resources, and nearness to a river, sea, or other body of water.

In addition to the physical characteristics of a place are its human and cultural characteristics. Is the place lightly or densely populated? What language do the people speak? What are their customs and religious beliefs? How do they earn their living? How are their society and government organized?

Physically, Gibraltar is dominated by the huge Rock of Gibraltar, 1,398 feet tall, from which the whole place takes its name. Culturally, the population of about 33,000 people comes from various countries, but they speak mainly English and Spanish.

Human-environment interaction refers to the relation between people and land.

Wherever people live, the physical character of that place affects their ways of living. People, in turn, change the character of their environment. They cut down forests, plow grasslands, build cities and roads for travel. Interaction between land and people is a central theme of both geography and history.

At Gibraltar, evidence of such interaction is found within the great Rock itself. Its cliffs are honeycombed with natural caves that, thousands of years ago, provided shelter for prehistoric people. The environment thus influenced the way in which people lived. In modern times, British soldiers have blasted within the Rock a network of tunnels for military defense. They have altered their environment to meet a particular need.

Movement concerns the interaction among people.

The theme of *movement* deals with people's efforts to overcome the limits of *place*. History is the story of movement. Armies have marched across plains and over mountain passes. Ships have sailed across seas and oceans on expeditions of trade and war. At times, whole groups of people have migrated from one land to another in search of more favorable environments for living. Ideas, too, spread from culture to culture, thus opening new possibilities for people.

This theme of movement, combined with location, explains the importance of Gibraltar in history. Whoever controls Gibraltar also controls the movement of ships into and out of the Mediterranean Sea. In terms of military and naval power, few places have a more strategic location than Gibraltar.

Moors from North Africa invaded Spain by way of Gibraltar in 711. Spain held the fortress from 1462 to 1704, during the years when that nation was a major power. The capture of Gibraltar by Britain after a naval battle in 1704 marked the growth of British sea power. In time, Gibraltar became a base for protecting British trade with Egypt and India. It remains under British rule today, although Spain would like to take it back.

Regions grow as units with some shared quality.

A region is any area based on some one characteristic. This may be physical—as with landforms and climate—or cultural—as with language, religion, or ways of living. Regions vary greatly in size. They may be larger than some continents, as in the case of Siberia or the South Pacific, or as small as a single community.

One place may be part of several different regions. Gibraltar, for example, is part of Western Europe (a political region). It also is part of the lands bordering the Atlantic Ocean (an oceanic region), lands sharing a Mediterranean climate (a climate region), lands ruled by Britain (a region based on a political unit), and lands speaking the Spanish language (a language region).

Regions change in the course of history. New patterns of interconnections appear and develop. Over time and across the spaces of land and sea, regions of the past have formed the world of today. Changes happening now will shape new regions in the world of tomorrow.

Section Review

Answer:
1. (a) What question does *location* answer? (b) In what ways can the location of a place be described? (c) Give an example of each way.
2. (a) What are the main characteristics used in describing a place? (b) Give examples of each type.
3. (a) What are some ways that the environment affects people? (b) That people affect the environment?
4. Explain the meaning of the sentence "History is the story of movement."
5. (a) Identify two major bases for the development of regions. (b) Give an example of each, explaining how it helps to determine a region.

Critical Thinking
6. Why are the five themes described in this section important to historians?
7. (a) Why are the elements of time and place essential to the study of history? (b) Give examples to support your answer.

9

Unit I

The Beginnings of Civilization

Chapters

3500 B.C.   **2900 B.C.**   **2300 B.C.**

Political and Governmental Life	**3100 B.C.** Upper and Lower Egypt joined	**2500–1500 B.C.** ▶ Cities flourished in the Indus Valley	
Economic and Technological Life	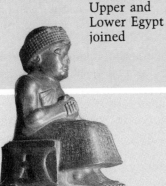	**2800 B.C.** Bronze Age begins	◀ **2000 B.C.** Chinese work bronze and weave silk
Social and Cultural Life	▲ **3500 B.C.** City-states rise in Sumer	**2600 B.C.** Great Pyramid built in Egypt	**2000–1550 B.C.** Babylonians build an empire

10

hange came slowly in early human pre-history and history. During prehistory, people learned to make tools, use language, and raise food. About 3500 B.C., they began to build cities that would become centers of early civilization. There, people first developed systems of rule and law, production and trade, and custom and belief. As cities became empires, ideas also spread and became enriched. These ideas formed a foundation for the achievements of people in later civilizations of both East and West.

1700 B.C.　　　　**1100 B.C.**　　　　**500 B.C.**

1500 B.C.
Shang dynasty begins in China

550 B.C.
Persian empire begins

322 B.C.
Mauryans rule India

1570–1075 B.C.
New Kingdom in Egypt builds wealthy empire

1000 B.C.
Israel becomes a kingdom

1500 B.C.
Hittites learn to use iron

1100–700 B.C.
Phoenicians trade around Mediterranean

130 B.C.
Great Silk Road opens from China to the West

1640 B.C. ▶
Hyksos invade in horse-drawn chariots

Great Wall of China

1700 B.C.
Hammurabi establishes code of laws

550 B.C. ▶
Start of Buddhism in India

1000 B.C.
The Temple is built in Jerusalem

11

Chapter 1

300,000 *B.C.* - 3500 *B.C.*

Prehistoric Cultures

The Paleolithic people of Altamira lived by hunting. Their cave paintings reflect their careful observations of the animals on which they depended for food.

Key Terms

archaeologist
prehistory
society
culture
nomad
technology

Read and Understand

1. Prehistory lacks written records.
2. Paleolithic people hunted and gathered.
3. Neolithic people learned to farm.

In 1868, in a rugged, rock-strewn part of northeastern Spain, a hunting dog became trapped in a pile of boulders. The hunter shoved aside some of the stones to free the dog and found that the rock pile had covered the mouth of a cave.

The cave lay on a farm known as Altamira (AHL-tuh-MIHR-uh). It looked no different from many other caves in that part of Spain. However, in 1879, the owner of the land, Don Marcelino de Sautuola, decided to explore the cave. He was an amateur **archaeologist**. An archaeologist is a person who studies the remains of ancient societies.

Archaeologists look for tools, bones, artwork, jewelry, traces of housing, ashes from ancient campfires—anything that will give them clues to the way people lived in the long-vanished past. Don Marcelino hoped to find traces of early human beings in the cave.

12

Ask students to list some adjectives they associate with prehistoric people. What images do these adjectives call to mind? How were these images formed? Does the cave art pictured above support or contradict these images?

While Don Marcelino searched the floor of the cave, his 12-year-old daughter, Maria, wandered farther into its long, winding passages. As she turned her lantern upward at the cave's low ceiling, Maria suddenly saw something that had been hidden from human eyes for thousands of years. Paintings of bison, horses, deer, wolves, and boars covered the ceiling. The red, black, and violet paints were still vivid. Maria shouted to her father. He too stared in awe. Soon afterward he told other archaeologists of the amazing discovery.

No one had imagined that ancient artists could paint such figures. Most scholars of the 1800's thought that ancient people did not have the ability, the intelligence, or the interest to create such works of art. As a result, Don Marcelino was mocked and criticized by many archaeologists. Some even charged him with fraud, saying he had had the paintings done.

Today's archaeologists, however, believe that the lifelike animals of the Altamira cave were painted by skilled artists who lived between 12,000 and 15,000 years ago. Other caves with similar paintings have been discovered in southern Europe. Carvings of animals and human figures have also been found. Even stone tools such as knife blades and arrowheads were often made in beautiful, leaflike shapes. It seems clear that the people who shaped these tools liked beauty for its own sake, just as people do today.

What can we learn of this very distant part of the human past? How much can anyone today really know about people who lived and died 15,000 years ago? The answer seems to be "not much—but more than you might think." Archaeologists have made a number of discoveries about the distant past, the period of time known as **prehistory**.

Prehistory lacks written records. 1

To reconstruct the human past, historians rely on written records. They examine old letters, diaries, legal documents, business ledgers, ancient clay tablets, scrolls of Chinese silk, bound books, inscriptions on stone monuments—in short, anything with written symbols.

However, writing is a comparatively recent invention. Human beings lived on earth for thousands of years before they learned to record their thoughts in writing. No one knows exactly when the first human beings appeared, but many scientists believe that the most ancient traces of *Homo sapiens* ("thinking man") go back 250,000 or 300,000 years. Of this vast stretch of time, written records cover only the last 5,000 years. Prehistory is the long, long period of time before written records.

In the absence of writings, scholars must look for other kinds of information about prehistoric times. Pieces of stone or bone that were used as tools are clues to early ways of life. A patch of ashes under several layers of soil may show where someone built a fire in ancient times. A place where the ground is slightly softer and darker than the earth around it may show where, long ago, someone put in a post to support a tent.

Sometimes prehistoric stone tools or ancient pieces of bone turn up on the surface of the ground, uncovered when wind or water wears the soil away. Sometimes people find these items by accident when plowing or digging a well. Sometimes archaeologists try to guess where early people might have lived and then dig there.

Much important information about ancient times is undoubtedly buried under our modern work places, housing developments, and shopping centers. Construction crews may uncover traces of ancient buildings when digging for a new subway. Archaeologists must then work quickly to study the clues before they are destroyed.

Dates are difficult to determine.

One of the most important questions archaeologists must answer is, "When did the group of people who made this item live?" Over the years, archaeologists have developed many ways of dating the material they find.

One way of determining dates is by carefully noting just where an object is found. When archaeologists find a prehistoric campsite, they slowly dig downward through layer after layer of soil. Obviously, the items they find in the bottom layer are the oldest of all. The items found closest to the surface are the newest.

Another method of dating is by comparing items from one site to those from another site.

Discussion questions: What policy should a city or country have about archaeology? For example, should a construction project be halted until all useful material is recovered?

13

Suppose someone finds a particular kind of arrowhead at a certain layer in a campsite in France. Later another archaeologist finds a similar arrowhead somewhere else. If the two arrowheads are very much alike, archaeologists may assume that both come from about the same time period.

Such methods can provide *relative* dates—that is, they can tell which of several items is the oldest, which is youngest, and which falls between. However, these methods do not give *absolute* dates. An absolute date is a number, such as 15,400 B.C. or A.D. 1000.

Archaeologists have found several ways of determining absolute dates. One of the best known is called the carbon 14 method. Carbon 14 is a form of radioactive carbon found in all living things. After a living thing dies, the carbon 14 slowly changes to regular carbon. Scientists know the rate at which this change takes place. By measuring how much carbon 14 remains, scientists can tell how long an animal or plant has been dead. Thus, if bits of burned wood or bone turn up at a prehistoric tent site, an archaeologist may be able to tell approximately how long ago the tent builders lived. Several other radioactive elements can be used in similar ways to provide absolute dates.

Archaeologists have also found other ways to pinpoint prehistoric dates. In parts of Europe, scientists have counted the layers of clay deposited year by year at the bottom of lakes. Elsewhere, especially in the southwestern United States, experts can measure dates by counting tree rings. By comparing pieces of wood from prehistoric sites with trees that are still living (some up to 4,000 years old), experts sometimes can tell when the ancient wood was cut.

Archaeologists make deductions about society and culture.

Like people today, prehistoric people lived in social groups. They lived in a network of relationships with other human beings, including family members, neighbors, or nearby groups with whom their paths crossed regularly. Such a network of people who interact with one another is called a **society**.

People who live and work together share many habits, ideas, skills, traditions, and values. All these habitual ways of thinking and acting make up the society's **culture**. Culture is the way of life that a group of people develops and passes on to its children. Every group of human beings—from the most ancient to the most modern, from the smallest to the largest—has a culture. A group's language, tools and skills, beliefs and traditions, ways of organizing itself, and much

An archaeologist in Mexico works painstakingly to remove ancient remains embedded in the rocky soil. Even jeweler's tools are used for this especially delicate work.

Discussion questions: How might early people have passed on their ideas generation after generation? How do people pass on their ideas today? (Look for answers to include the role of formal and informal education.)

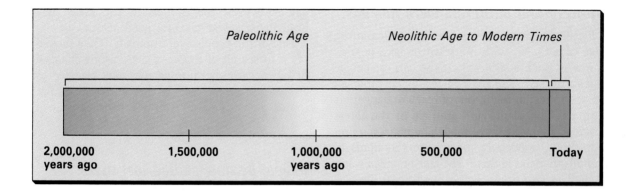

Paleolithic Age		Neolithic Age to Modern Times

| 2,000,000 years ago | 1,500,000 | 1,000,000 years ago | 500,000 | Today |

more are all part of its culture. Culture has been described as "a blueprint for living." From birth to death, most of human life is spent learning, following, and passing on this blueprint.

A single stone tool from prehistoric times tells little about ancient society or culture. However, archaeologists can find clues to social relationships in the way an ancient campsite was arranged. By investigating many, many items, they can begin to find cultural patterns. As you read the following sections, notice the way archaeologists have used clues to make deductions about ancient cultures.

Archaeologists have discovered an amazing amount of information from a wide variety of clues. Because many of the items that survive from prehistoric times are stone tools or bones of animals, archaeologists know a great deal about how ancient people got their food and made their tools. Archaeologists can also make fairly good guesses about prehistoric housing and the number of people who lived together. However, we know very little about prehistoric people's thoughts and feelings, their religious beliefs, or their ideas of right and wrong. Only by careful detective work can modern scholars put together a partial picture of an ancient way of life.

Section Review 1

Define: (a) archaeologist, (b) prehistory, (c) relative date, (d) absolute date, (e) society, (f) culture
Answer:
1. What is the main difference between the study of history and the study of prehistory?

2. How can archaeologists date their findings?
3. (a) What parts of prehistoric culture are best known from their remains? (b) What parts are least known?

Critical Thinking

4. (a) Suggest some reasons why finding the cave paintings of Altamira was more important than finding a large group of stone tools would have been. (b) Why do you think scholars were unwilling to believe Don Marcelino at first?

Paleolithic people hunted and gathered. 2

The earliest part of human prehistory is known as the Paleolithic (PAY-lee-uh-LITH-ik) Age, or the Old Stone Age. (*Paleo* comes from the Greek word for "old," and *lithos* was the Greek word for "stone.") Scholars call this period the Stone Age because people in those years used stone to make many of their basic tools. As the graph on this page shows, the Paleolithic Age was by far the longest part of humankind's past.

The Paleolithic period is sometimes also called the Ice Age. Several times in the past 2 million years, temperatures grew colder all over the world. Each time, huge ice sheets spread out from the polar regions. When these ice sheets were at their greatest extent, they covered much of northern Europe and North America. Then, when the weather warmed, the ice sheets retreated. These climate changes probably forced early people to learn to cope with a variety of conditions.

Question: How did the changes in climate brought on by the Ice Age force early humans to adapt? (Look for answers that include changes in land, vegetation, and animal life.)

Hunters and gatherers were nomads.

Picture a grassy plain in eastern Africa at the edge of a forest, with a stream or lake nearby. It was in such a setting that the earliest people probably lived. The trees in the forest provided a place to rest at night, out of reach of dangerous animals. The plants and animals of the forest provided many kinds of food. The plain too provided food, especially meat from the herds of animals that grazed there. The lake provided water as well as fish, frogs, and other animal life.

By living where different environments met, early humans had a wide choice of food. If they failed to find one kind of food, they could look for another. Variety meant safety from starvation.

Women and children roamed through the tall grasses and clumps of trees to gather roots, berries, nuts, and seeds. Women were the plant specialists of the Old Stone Age. Their work probably provided most of the food people ate every day.

While the women gathered plant foods, small parties of men set out from the camp to track down game. They hunted everything from rabbits to elephants. The hunters' work supplied only a small share of the calories people needed each day. However, the protein in the meat they brought back was vital for good health.

Paleolithic people were **nomads**. They moved often in search of food. As the seasons changed or when game became scarce, they traveled to a new campsite. Probably they followed regular routes, revisiting the same places from year to year. In this way, they would come to know a broad stretch of territory very well.

People became skilled tool users.

Tools and the skills to use those tools make up a group's **technology**. Technology is an important part of a group's culture. Technology is the part of prehistoric culture that archaeologists know most about, because they have found the tools that early people used. In turn, the tools tell much about the skills people must have had.

Tools The earliest tools of the Old Stone Age are crudely made choppers. The toolmaker took a stone and knocked a few chips off one side to make a jagged edge. Such chopping tools probably were used to cut up game after hunters had made a kill. The latest tools of the Old Stone Age are beautifully made knife blades and spearheads that

About 10,000 years ago, someone used the stone at the left to start fires, striking it with flint to make a spark. Other prehistoric tools ranged from crude hand axes (lower right) to antler spears to finely worked arrowheads.

The stone at left is not a tool but rather the core that remained after an ancient toolmaker struck off many sharp flakes. The flakes (such as the one in the center) were used as scrapers. Sometimes people refined the edges of the points by more chipping to make them sharper.

took hours of expert chipping. People's toolmaking skills improved greatly over the long period of time included in the Old Stone Age. The best tools clearly show the makers' pride in their work.

Undoubtedly, people of the Old Stone Age used a wide variety of materials to make tools. Besides stone, they used wood, bone, and hide. However, those materials decay, and so we know less about tools made from them.

The use of fire As hunters and gatherers moved from place to place, they learned to live in many kinds of environments. Ever so slowly, groups spread over the world. Prehistoric campsites in Europe and Asia show circles of ash, burned bones, and heat-cracked rocks. The people who lived in those camps had learned to use fire to help them survive in a cold climate.

Fire greatly changed the way people lived. Of course, it helped to protect them from cold. Just as important, it was a protection against dangerous

Footnote to History

One of the materials that prehistoric people used to make cutting tools was obsidian, a black glass formed naturally by volcanoes. A prehistoric toolmaker could make an obsidian blade that was as sharp as a modern surgeon's knife.

animals. It also provided light, so that people could continue to make tools, prepare food, and talk together after nightfall. Much later, people also learned to use fire to cook their food. Beginning with these ancient campfires, the hearth came to stand for home, for family, and for a warm welcome.

People lived in small groups.

The groups that gathered around these fires probably were fairly small. Groups who lived by hunting and gathering in more recent times usually lived in groups of 25 to 40 individuals. Most were probably blood relatives—parents, children, uncles, aunts, and cousins.

Such groups stayed small for two reasons. First, a given area of land would support only so many people. When a band grew too large to find food within a reasonable distance, people usually divided into two smaller groups and drifted apart. Second, quarrels were less likely to break out while groups stayed small. If individuals found they could not get along together, again the group might divide to prevent violence.

Language One of the most important social developments that took place in the Old Stone Age was the development of language. Although no one knows what Paleolithic languages were like, archaeologists are certain that Paleolithic people could speak. These people hunted large animals that could have been killed only by a group of hunters working together. Some of these hunts involved planning ahead to drive game into dead-end valleys or other areas that were natural traps. Such teamwork probably relied on language. No one knows exactly when people began to develop language, but it was an early and important achievement.

A society of equals Paleolithic hunters and gatherers lived with one another as equals. They had no place for kings, nobles, or chiefs. As nomads, they owned few possessions, and food from the hunt probably was shared with everyone in the group.

Of course, there were differences within the group. The best hunters probably enjoyed extra respect. The oldest members of the group undoubtedly supplied advice, based on their long experience, when food or water was hard to find.

Early hunters and gatherers may have built temporary shelters similar to this dwelling, called a scherm, made by the Kung of the Kalahari Desert.

Some clues to ancient societies come from studies of more recent groups of hunters and gatherers such as the Kung of Africa's Kalahari (KAH-luh-HAHR-ee) Desert and the Aborigines (AB-uh-RIHJ-uh-neez) of Australia. These people are quick to put down anyone who tries to win power over others. Scholars have found that equality and sharing are the rules for survival.

Paleolithic beliefs remain a mystery.

Beliefs and traditions are an important part of every group's culture, yet these are just the parts of Paleolithic culture about which we know the least. Without writing, people in the Old Stone Age could not leave explicit records of their thoughts and feelings. Again, archaeologists must look for other clues.

Hunting magic The cave paintings of Altamira and similar works found at Lascaux (las-KOH) are some of the most important clues to the thoughts of Paleolithic people. However, no one knows for certain how to interpret them. Most scholars assume that the ancient artists created their paintings as a form of magic. Animals as food were vital to the survival of hunters and gatherers. Perhaps people believed that painting a bison or a deer would magically bring the animals close. A few paintings actually show animals that have been speared. Perhaps these were meant to bring luck in the hunt.

The paintings are skillfully done, showing a beautiful sense of movement and line. Few hunters can have had the time or talent to become so skilled at painting. Thus these pictures probably were the work of specialists. The artist-magician may have worked for the whole group and been rewarded with gifts of food.

Treatment of the dead A few tantalizing clues suggest that these very early people may have thought about the question of life after death. In a cave in Iraq, archaeologists found a body that had been buried more than 40,000 years ago. The person had been laid to rest on a bed of pine boughs and bright flowers. Numerous other burials from Paleolithic times show that treasured objects and food were often placed in graves. These may be the first signs of belief in a soul that lives after the body dies.

Cave art rarely includes human figures. When they do appear, they are usually less realistic than the animal figures. Have students speculate on why human figures were not as prevalent or accurate in cave drawings as animal figures.

Hunting and gathering worked well for thousands of years.

People today usually picture life in Paleolithic times as harsh, uncomfortable, and filled with danger. Admittedly, the lives of Paleolithic people often were cut short by accident, injury, or illness. It is true, too, that these people had few possessions because of their nomadic life. Still, in many ways, the hunters and gatherers of the Paleolithic Age lived well. Food was usually plentiful and their varied diet was a healthy one. Moreover, finding food took only a few hours of work each day. There was plenty of time left for storytelling, singing, dancing, and playing.

The hunting and gathering way of life served people well for thousands of years, but it had one great weakness. To be sure of a reliable food supply, hunters and gatherers needed large areas of land. As the number of people in the world slowly increased, less and less land was available for each group. Hunters and gatherers faced the threat of hunger. As a result, the stage was set for the next period of prehistory.

Section Review 2

Define: (a) nomad, (b) technology
Answer:
1. Why was the Paleolithic Age given its name?
2. How did Paleolithic people acquire their food?
3. (a) What conclusions have scholars drawn about the organization of Paleolithic societies? (b) About Paleolithic religious ideas?
4. How did an increasing population eventually cause a problem for hunters and gatherers?

Critical Thinking
5. List three developments of lasting importance that took place during the Paleolithic Age. Explain why you consider each important.

Voice from the Past · *Mysterious Markings*

About 30,000 years ago, a toolmaker in France used a piece of bone to sharpen the edge of stone tools by flaking off chips of rock. Evidently, the toolmaker kept this piece of bone for a long time, using it over and over. When archaeologists found the piece of bone and looked at it very carefully, they saw that it had been used in another way as well. The bone was covered with tiny scratches made over a long period of time, using different points. There was a total of 69 marks, which formed a snakelike pattern back and forth across the piece. Archaeologist Alexander Marschak writes:

It was almost as though someone, 25,000 years before the development of writing and arithmetic, was keeping a record of some process ... The twists and turns [in the line of scratch marks] corresponded to the changing phases of the moon, all the full moons falling at the left, all the half-moons in the middle, and all the crescents at the right. The fit was perfect for an observational lunar notation.

1. What evidence does the archaeologist provide that this item was something like a calendar?
2. What other evidence from the Paleolithic Age might suggest that people then were capable of making a calendar?
3. Why might people have wanted a record of the phases of the moon?

Students may enjoy reading the imaginative and vivid description by Konrad Lorenz (*King Solomon's Ring*) of how the first wild animal was welcomed into a human family.

19

Neolithic people learned to farm.   **3**

Ten thousand years ago, there were fewer people in the whole world than there are today in New York City. Perhaps 10 million people were spread over the entire globe. By the standards of hunters and gatherers, however, the world was already becoming crowded. People began to look for ways to find more food.

This period of time, beginning about 10,000 years ago in Europe and Asia, is called the New Stone Age, or the Neolithic (NEE-uh-LITH-ik) Age. Compared to the Paleolithic Age, the Neolithic Age was a time of rapid change. Many of the discoveries that form the basis for modern life took place in the Neolithic Age. The most important of these discoveries were farming and herding.

Women began to plant seeds.

Wild plants had been an important source of food in the Paleolithic Age. As a result, people already knew a great deal about how plants grew. They knew where different kinds of plants thrived and when each kind ripened. Prehistoric people probably knew how to grow plants from seed long before anyone actually did so.

Because women probably did most of the gathering of plant foods in ancient times, many archaeologists think women were the first farmers. Some sort of farming may have begun while people were still nomads. Women may have sowed the seeds of favorite food plants near a regular campsite. In that way, when the group returned later, they would be able to find the plants easily.

As the world's population increased, wild food became scarcer. These little fields that were planted purposely became more and more important for a group's survival. People began to spend more time caring for their food plants. Children may have been set to work pulling up weeds so that the food plants had a better chance to grow. People also learned not to eat up all the seeds they raised but to save some seeds for planting next year.

Herders domesticated animals.

Just as early gatherers observed plants closely, early hunters were experts on animals. Gradually, some of these animals were tamed for human use. Which animals were tamed first varied from region to region.

In northern Europe, dogs were probably the first animals to be domesticated. Wild dogs may have hung around the edges of human camps in search of meat scraps. Perhaps people found dogs useful for giving warning when dangerous animals or strangers approached.

In Southwest Asia, sheep and goats were the earliest domestic animals. Many times, hunters must have killed a female animal and then found its young. If the hunters had no immediate need for more food, it would have been easy to keep the young animals and let them graze near the camp until they grew larger. Such half-wild, half-tame animals may have been the first herds that humans kept for food. The bones of domestic sheep have been unearthed in Southwest Asia at sites 10,000 years old (8000 B.C.). Pigs were domesticated about 8,500 years ago in that region, and cattle nearly 7,500 years ago. As game became scarcer, these animals became the main sources of meat.

People settled in permanent homes.

As people spent more and more time caring for their food plants, they began to settle near the fields they had planted. Instead of moving whenever the seasons changed or the herds of game migrated, people stayed in one place.

The Neolithic Age was the time when many settled villages sprang up. Farmers needed a place where the soil was fairly fertile. They also needed a steady supply of water. Therefore, most early settlements grew up around a spring or near a stream.

Jarmo A good example of an early farming village is the archaeological site of Jarmo in Southwest Asia. Jarmo is located in what is now Iraq and dates from about 6750 B.C.

How did the people of Jarmo live nearly 9,000 years ago? Evidence shows that the village was made up of about 25 mud houses. Each house had several rectangular rooms divided by mud

Historians consider the beginning of agriculture a major turning point in human history. Have students discuss all the ways in which modern society depends on the ability to grow crops.

The Neolithic way of life spread to many parts of the world. These prehistoric houses are from a village in the islands north of Scotland.

walls. The houses were roofed with brush or reeds plastered with more mud. Jarmo probably was home to about 150 people.

The people of Jarmo did not have as healthy a diet as their ancestors who lived by hunting and gathering. In Jarmo, people grew barley and wheat. (Wild varieties of those grains grow in the nearby hills.) They also had peas and lentils to eat, but it is not clear whether they grew those plants or gathered them from the wild. For meat, the people of Jarmo raised goats and hunted gazelles, wild sheep, and wild pigs. From the number of shells found at Jarmo, it appears that villagers also ate a great many snails.

Çatal Hüyük Not all Neolithic settlements were as tiny as Jarmo. In what is now Turkey, archaeologists found the remains of a larger town, Çatal Hüyük (chuh-**TUL** hoo-**YOOK**). Indeed, with more than 3,000 people, Çatal Hüyük was almost a city.

The residents of Çatal Hüyük had many luxuries that other Neolithic groups lacked. For example, they had mirrors made of obsidian. They also had begun to work with metals, making beads and tubes of copper and lead.

Located high on a plateau, Çatal Hüyük stood in the midst of a region rich in minerals. The people of Çatal Hüyük built up a busy trade based on their mineral wealth. Traders also took finished goods made by Çatal Hüyük's skillful stonecutters. They shaped axes, knives, mirrors, bowls, bracelets and beads.

The town boasted a number of shrines. Some had figures of male and female gods. Others featured figures of stags or leopards. Still others had clay heads of bulls decorated with actual horns from wild cattle. As with the Paleolithic period, however, modern investigators cannot be sure how all these shrines fit together in the religious beliefs of Çatal Hüyük's people.

People developed new skills.

Farming required a different kind of technology from hunting and gathering. To the extent that people still hunted, they continued to need spears, arrows, and bows. However, they also needed tools to scratch and loosen the soil for planting. They needed sickles to harvest their grain and grinding tools to make the grain into flour. When archaeologists find those tools, they know that people were beginning to farm. As a result of these new needs, a number of important technological developments took place in the New Stone Age.

Pottery People who lived as hunters and gatherers found food as they needed it. When people began to live by farming, they harvested their crops once or twice each year. Suddenly, they faced the problem of storing food for use all year long. People needed to protect their harvest from dampness, insects, and also the hungry hordes of rats and mice who quickly moved into the new farming villages.

In many parts of the world, the answer to the food storage problem was pottery. The earliest farmers made containers of stone, wood, or basketry. Pottery jars, however, were easier and faster to make. Moreover, clay was available along many stream banks and riverbeds. The earliest potters shaped their lumps of clay into bowls and jars simply by molding the clay with their hands. Later, people learned to make smoother, rounder shapes by turning the clay on a wheel.

Once people learned to harden the clay by firing it in ovens, clay pots became an important part of everyday life. Broken pottery pieces are so common at ancient living sites that archaeologists often study the pottery to determine the date of the culture.

Ground stone tools Among the many changes that took place in the Neolithic period was a new way of making stone tools. Toolmakers no longer chipped or flaked pieces of stone to make a sharp edge. Instead, they began to grind and polish pieces of stone to sharpen them.

The new kinds of tools had several advantages. First, many of the toughest kinds of rock cannot be chipped or flaked. With grinding, people could use these harder kinds of rocks to make more durable tools. Second, when a ground tool becomes dull, it can be sharpened by regrinding. Thus, the same tool could be used for a much longer period of time. With the new, durable axes, farmers could cut trees and clear even more land for farming.

Farming began in many places.

The changeover from hunting and gathering to farming took place not once but many times. Archaeologists have found evidence that a number of groups learned independently to farm. In Southwest Asia, China, Southeast Asia, Central America, and other places—perhaps some yet undiscovered—people learned how to raise plants from seed. People became food producers rather than food finders.

In each place, early farmers began with foods that grew wild nearby. Thus, farmers in Southwest

This clay model from the Neolithic period shows a potter using a wheel to make jars for storing food. Potters used a variety of natural dyes to decorate their works.

22

Daily Life · *Spinning and Weaving*

At many Neolithic sites, tiny circular objects with holes in the center are a common find. To most modern people, these objects are mysterious, but any Neolithic child would have recognized them. They are spindle whorls, or weights that helped a spindle turn. The presence of these objects shows that people were spinning thread. Archaeologists have also found loom weights, showing that people wove the thread into cloth. Plants such as cotton and flax (for making linen) and wool from sheep were probably the earliest sources of cloth.

Each village household probably made its own clothing, from raw fiber to finished garment. Family members sheared wool from the sheep, spun the wool into thread, wove the thread into cloth, and sewed the cloth into clothing.

Asia raised wheat and barley. In Central America, corn (or maize) became the main crop. In parts of Asia, farmers raised rice. Then, from each of the centers where farming was invented, the idea spread outward.

It is important to remember, however, that the change did not affect the whole world. None of the great changes of history affected everyone, everywhere, once and for all. Even today, a few isolated groups in the world still live by hunting and gathering. The Kung of the Kalahari Desert lived as hunters and gatherers until very recently. Some Inuit (IN-oo-it) of Alaska and northern Canada follow traditional ways and live by hunting. Although the number of hunters and gatherers grew fewer with each passing year, the spread of farming took thousands of years.

Farming led to population growth.

The slow, slow growth of the human population during the Paleolithic Age forced people to look for new ways of providing food. The discovery of farming and herding in the Neolithic Age seemed to solve that problem. But the new food supply had an unexpected result. After the discovery of farming, the world's population began to increase at a much faster pace.

Change piled upon change. The long time span of the Paleolithic Age had been marked by few changes. Beginning in the Neolithic Age, however, people in almost every generation found new ways of living. Many of the changes were tiny, but they added up. All the changes that took people from the nomadic life style of hunters and gatherers to today's giant cities follow step by step from the crucial discoveries made in the Neolithic Age.

Section Review 3

Define: (a) Neolithic Age, (b) obsidian, (c) spindle whorl
Identify: (a) Jarmo, (b) Çatal Hüyük
Answer:
1. How did the knowledge that people had developed as hunters and gatherers help them in becoming farmers and herders?
2. Why did farming lead to the development of villages?
3. How was Çatal Hüyük different from Jarmo?
4. (a) Describe two important advances in technology that took place in the Neolithic Age. (b) How was each related to farming?
5. Why did different types of farming develop in different parts of the world?
6. What was the long-term effect of farming on world population?

Critical Thinking
7. Suggest at least three ways that the change from hunting and gathering might have affected social life within a group. Explain your conclusions.

Chapter Review 1

Summary

1. Prehistory lacks written records. Human beings lived for many thousands of years before they invented writing. Therefore, scholars learn about these prehistoric people through the physical remains of their culture rather than through written records. Archaeologists use scientific methods to determine when an object was made. Archaeologists then make deductions about prehistoric societies based on their investigations of remains and artifacts.

2. Paleolithic people hunted and gathered. The earliest part of prehistory is known as the Paleolithic Age, or Old Stone Age. Paleolithic people traveled from place to place in search of food. They lived in small family groups and made tools of stone, wood, bone, and hide. Eventually, they learned to use fire for cooking and warmth. Scholars believe they also had spoken languages and religions. Hunting and gathering became more difficult as the number of people increased.

3. Neolithic people learned to farm. The Neolithic Age, or New Stone Age, began about 10,000 years ago. During the Neolithic Age, people in many parts of the world gave up a nomadic way of life and settled down in permanent homes to farm. Scholars believe that farming began because early people could no longer find enough food by hunting and gathering. Since farming required a different kind of technology from hunting and gathering, Neolithic people invented pottery and improved their tools by learning to grind stone. The invention of farming marked the beginning of a rapid series of changes that led to modern life.

Reviewing the Facts

1. Define the following terms:
   a. archaeologist
   b. prehistory
   c. society
   d. culture
   e. nomad
   f. technology
2. Explain the importance of each of the following names or places:
   a. Altamira
   b. Jarmo
   c. Çatal Hüyük
   d. Paleolithic Age
   e. Neolithic Age
3. (a) How can archaeologists sometimes determine which of two prehistoric events was the earlier? (b) How can archaeologists sometimes determine actual dates for prehistoric events?
4. How do scholars learn about the cultures of prehistoric people?
5. (a) Why did Paleolithic people move often? (b) Why did they live in small groups? (c) What were some of their religious beliefs?

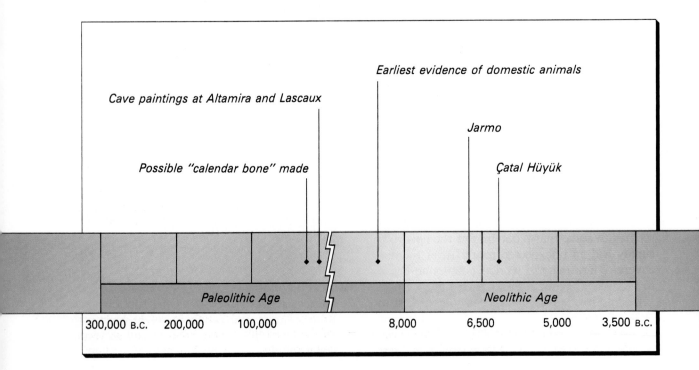

24

6. Why did Neolithic people change to a settled way of life?
7. What differences in technology distinguish Neolithic from Paleolithic groups?

Basic Skills

1. **Reading a time line** (a) On the time line on page 24, what are the starting and ending dates? (b) What change occurs in the scale of measurement starting with 8000 B.C.? (c) Why is a break needed on this time line?
2. **Comparing time periods** (a) Compare the length of the Neolithic Age with that of the Paleolithic Age. (b) How did change in the Neolithic Age differ from that of the Paleolithic Age?
3. **Identifying supporting details** Section headings in this text indicate main ideas, while paragraphs under each heading provide supporting details. For each of the following headings, give two supporting details: (a) "Archaeologists make deductions about society and culture." (b) "Hunting and gathering worked well for thousands of years."
4. **Summarizing** (a) What new skills did people develop as a result of the spread of farming? (b) What needs did these skills meet?

Researching and Reporting Skills

1. **Using a glossary** Use the Glossary in the Reference Section to find the meaning for the italicized words in the following sentences: (a) In Neolithic times, farming was already an *institution.* (b) Though Jarmo's culture was relatively advanced, it was not yet a *civilization.* (c) Neolithic pottery was handcrafted by skillful *artisans.*
2. **Identifying primary sources** Anything that was used or created by people of the past is known as the primary source of evidence. Give two examples of primary sources for each of the following: (a) a prehistoric culture of 10,000 B.C., (b) a Neolithic culture of 3500 B.C.

Critical Thinking

1. **Comparing** Compare the way of life of the cave painters at Altamira with that at prehistoric Jarmo.

What was similar about the two cultures? What was different?
2. **Analyzing a quotation** According to one historian, "About 10,000 B.C. occurred the most important single event in human history. People turned from hunting animals and gathering food to producing it from the earth." (a) Why do you think the historian considers this change so important? (b) Do you agree or disagree with this statement? Why?
3. **Synthesizing** What achievements of Paleolithic and Neolithic societies were particularly significant for the growth of civilization? List them and explain why you think each one was important.
4. **Evaluating** What advantages did life in permanent Neolithic settlements have compared to that of nomadic hunting and gathering?

Perspectives on Past and Present

1. Even today a few groups of people have continued to live by hunting and gathering. Among these groups are the Kung (Bushmen) of southern Africa, the Tasaday of the Philippines, the Inuit of Alaska and Canada, and the Aborigines of Australia. (a) Research the culture of one of these groups. (b) How does this culture compare with that of ancient Paleolithic groups?
2. The hunting and gathering way of life left considerable time for leisure in early Paleolithic societies. How might the use of this leisure compare with your use of leisure time today?
3. If you were to travel back in time to Jarmo or Catal Huyuk, what modern idea, tool, or invention would be most useful to take with you? Give reasons for your answer.

Investigating History

1. The most ancient city archaeologists have excavated so far is Jericho, which was founded about 8000 B.C. Find information on this extraordinary dig. (a) What environmental factors were key to the development of such a city? (b) What findings justify calling Jericho a city?
2. Examples of the cave art of Altamira and Lascaux have been published in many strikingly beautiful books. Look in your library for books on the art of the Paleolithic period. What do the paintings tell about the natural environment of the time?

Civilizations and Empires in Southwest Asia

This panel from a wooden box comes from Ur, an early city in Southwest Asia. The people in the top row are nobles; those in the bottom row are herders.

Key Terms

civilization
artisan
cuneiform
institution
city-state
barter
polytheist
empire
literacy
monotheist
prophet

Read and Understand

1. Civilization arose in the Fertile Crescent.
2. Newcomers contributed to civilization.
3. Conquerors ruled ever larger empires.

About 4,000 years ago, a boy sprinted down a city street, kicking up dust as he ran. The morning sun had just begun to rise above the walls of the city. Even so, the boy knew he was already late for school, which was called the *edubba*.

Historians know of this boy and his school from ancient clay tablets found in Southwest Asia, in what is now the country of Iraq. Part of one tablet tells of a student's typical day:

When I awoke early in the morning, I faced my mother and said to her, "Give me my lunch. I want to go to school." My mother gave me two rolls and I set out. In school, the monitor in charge said to me, "Why are you late?" Afraid and with pounding heart, I entered before my teacher and made a respectful curtsy.

26

The tablet goes on to tell of eight other offenses that the boy committed in school that day, including mistakes in his writing lesson and talking without permission. For each offense, a school official called "the man who holds the whip" lashed the boy across his bare back. In fact, the boy did so poorly in school that his father invited the schoolmaster home for dinner and gave him gifts to keep the boy from failing.

Civilization arose in the Fertile Crescent. 1

The boy and his schoolmates were studying to be scribes—that is, professional writers—in an ancient region known to historians as the Fertile Crescent. On the map on page 28, you can see an arc of land with its eastern end touching the Persian Gulf and its western end lying along the Mediterranean Sea. Inside this arc is some of the best land for farming in Southwest Asia. The region's curved shape and the richness of its land led scholars to call it the Fertile Crescent. (Today this area lies within the nations of Israel, Jordan, Syria, Lebanon, and Iraq.)

In the western part of the ancient Fertile Crescent, the Jordan River watered grapevines, olive trees, and cedar trees. In the eastern part, ducks nested among the marshes created by the Tigris (TY-gris) and Euphrates (yoo-FRAY-teez) rivers. Along the northern curve of the Fertile Crescent, streams flowed down from the mountains. Wherever rivers and streams flowed, people built their villages. In ancient times, the settled life of farmers and villagers was possible only in lands with good supplies of water.

The land where the schoolboy made his home lay at the eastern end of the Fertile Crescent, between the Tigris and Euphrates rivers. This region is known as Mesopotamia (MEHS-uh-puh-TAY-mee-uh), which in Greek means "land between the rivers."

The schoolboy belonged to a group of people known as the Sumerians (soo-MEHR-ee-uhnz). Their homeland, Sumer (SOO-muhr), was in the southern part of Mesopotamia, in the marshes near the Persian Gulf. Sumer was neither a city nor a country in the modern sense of those words.

Rather, it was a collection of separate cities with a common way of life.

Although the cities fought and squabbled constantly, the Sumerian people shared a common culture. Historians believe the Sumerians built the world's first civilization. The next pages will describe what a civilization is and how Sumer was different from any settlements people had ever built before.

Key traits define a civilization.

Every group of people has its own culture—its own way of life including language, tools, customs, and rules. However, not all groups have a way of life that is considered a **civilization.** Civilization is one form of culture—a very complicated form.

The Sumerians stand out in history as the first group of people to become civilized. They developed a new way of life that set them apart from neighboring peoples.

Just what set the Sumerians apart from their neighbors? Historians and other social scientists have struggled with the problem of defining exactly what makes one group of people civilized and another group not. Most scholars agree that the following traits are essential for civilization.

The growth of cities One of the key traits for civilization is cities. (In fact, the word *civilization* comes from the Latin word for *city*.) By 3000 B.C., the Sumerians had built at least a dozen fair-sized cities. For example, Uruk may have had a population of 10,000, and it continued to grow to around 20,000 over the next 200 years. In Lagash, there were about 19,000 people and in Umma, about 16,000. People elsewhere in Asia, Europe, and Africa lived in farming villages, but none of those tiny communities could rightly be called a city.

A city is more than a large group of people living close together. Population size alone does not make a village into a city. One of the most important differences between a city and a village is that a city is a center of trade for a larger area.

Like their modern descendants, ancient city dwellers depended on trade. Farmers, merchants, and traders brought goods to market in the cities. The city dwellers themselves produced a variety of goods for exchange, including pots, tools, and jewelry. Each person specialized in a certain kind

Stress that the ancient Sumerian cities were more or less self-governing. Only in times of war with a common enemy did the cities unite under the leadership of a temporary king, called a *lugal*. Even he, however, did not preempt local administrations.

27

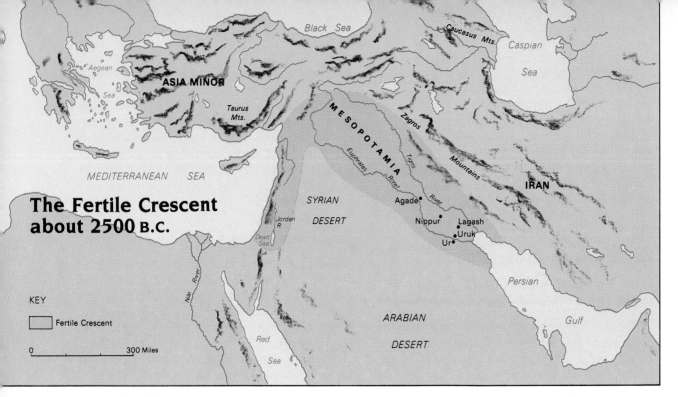

The Fertile Crescent about 2500 B.C.

Black Sea

Caucasus Mts.

Caspian Sea

Aegean Sea

ASIA MINOR

Taurus Mts.

MESOPOTAMIA

Zagros

Tigris River

Mountains

IRAN

MEDITERRANEAN SEA

Euphrates

Agade

SYRIAN DESERT

Nippur   Lagash

Jordan R.

Uruk

Dead Sea

Ur

Nile River

Persian

KEY

Fertile Crescent

ARABIAN DESERT

Gulf

0   300 Miles

Red Sea

Map Study

What major rivers flow through the Fertile Crescent? Into what body of water do those rivers flow? What is the region between those rivers called? What region lies between the Black and Mediterranean seas?

of work and exchanged goods with other people who were also specialists. The importance of trade thus led to another key trait of civilization—specialized workers.

3. **Specialized workers** Think back on the Sumerian schoolboy who was studying to be a scribe. Day after day, scribes in Sumer wrote letters for people, copied down laws, and kept business records for merchants. Scribes were specialists. They traded their services for food, clothing, and roofs over their heads. Some of the other specialists in Sumer were schoolmasters, merchants, priests, and even "the man who holds the whip." Still others were potters, metalworkers, and weavers. Such skilled workers who make goods by hand are called **artisans.** Artisans became an important social group as cities developed.

In earlier human societies, nearly everyone had to spend most of the day getting food, either by hunting and gathering or by raising crops. In Sumer, for the first time in history, farmers were able to raise enough food to have a surplus. They could trade that extra food to a potter for clay pots or to a scribe in payment for writing a letter. Farmers also paid some of their surplus in taxes

to support the city government and the city temple with its priests.

Raising food was no longer a full-time job for everyone in the society. The ability to raise a surplus of food was the key that freed some people to do specialized jobs.

Writing Another essential trait of civilization also made its first appearance at Sumer—writing. Scholars call the Sumerians' way of writing **cuneiform** (kyoo-NEE-uh-fawrm) because of the letters' wedge-like shape. (In Latin, *cuneus* means "wedge.") The scribe's tool, called a stylus, was a sharpened reed with a wedge-shaped point. The scribe pressed the stylus into moist clay to create symbols. Then he laid the clay tablet in the sun to dry and harden.

Sumerians invented writing as a necessity of city life. Priests needed some way to keep track of the grain and other merchandise that moved in and out of the temple storehouses. Merchants needed accounts of debts and payments. The first written symbols, therefore, stood for commonly traded objects—a donkey, an ox, a sack of grain. These signs were called pictographs because they pictured the things they stood for.

Map Study answers: Tigris and Euphrates rivers; Persian Gulf; Mesopotamia; Asia Minor

Eventually, ideas became associated with certain pictures. For example, a house might also stand for the idea of protection or safety. Such signs are known as ideograms.

Still later, signs came to stand for certain sounds. Cuneiform signs did not stand for single sounds, as letters in the alphabet do today. Instead, each cuneiform sign stood for a whole syllable. Thus, a sign might stand for the word *mouth*, which in Sumerian was pronounced *ka*. In that form, the sign was a pictograph. But the same sign also stood for the sound *ka* when that sound was used in other words. By putting groups of signs together, scribes could write full sentences and express many ideas. They could create everything from financial records to poems.

Sumerian writing grew more and more efficient. The earliest tablets used about 2,000 different signs. By 3000 B.C., that number had been reduced to 800. By 2500 B.C., the number had been cut down even further to about 600 written signs. However, this was still such a large number that only a few people learned to read or write.

Advanced technology To their list of civilization's hallmarks, historians usually add another important trait—advanced technology. The Sumerians were skilled in many fields of science and technology. Many of the basic inventions on which humans depend originated in Sumer.

The wheel, the plow, and the sailboat seem like simple devices today. In Sumerian times, however, they were revolutionary. With the plow, farmers could raise more crops, creating the food surplus that Sumer's cities needed to exist. The wheel and the sailboat together vastly improved human ability to move goods over long distances for trade. All these devices were probably in daily use in Sumer by 3000 B.C.

Footnote to History

Sumerian schools taught the use of numbers as well as words. Sumerian mathematicians calculated everything in terms of the number 60. The symbol for 60, written 6 times, equaled 360, almost the number of days in a solar year. The Sumerians also divided circles into 360 parts (or degrees), which helped them measure angles for surveying and architecture. From this use of 60 comes today's circular clock divided into 60 minutes, each having 60 seconds.

Sumerian skill in metalworking shows in this golden helmet, dagger, and sheath from about 2450 B.C. Gold is too soft for use in battle, so these items were ceremonial.

The Sumerians were also skilled in working metal, although they were not the first people to make metal tools. People in Mesopotamia began using copper around 7000 B.C., at least 3,000 years before the Sumerians arrived. However, the Sumerians greatly increased the use of copper. They also used bronze, which is a mixture of copper and tin. Bronze is harder than pure copper and thus more useful for tools and weapons. After 2500 B.C., skilled metalworkers in Sumer's cities turned out bronze spearheads by the thousands. In fact, bronze eventually became so important in making tools of all kinds that the period of history beginning around 2800 B.C. at Sumer is often called the Bronze Age, just as earlier times were called the Stone Age.

Complex institutions As you might imagine, a bustling city required much more organization to run smoothly than did a tiny village or a group of wandering hunters. The long-lasting patterns of organization in a community are known as **institutions**. Complex institutions are another key trait of civilization.

Government is an example of an institution. For hunters and gatherers, family ties and group customs had supplied all the rules that were

Cuneiform needed many symbols because each symbol stood for a complete syllable, not a single sound. Thus the syllables *ba-, da-, ad-, ab-, bad-,* and *dab-* required six symbols, whereas our alphabet requires only three.

necessary. In cities, a new kind of government took shape. The ancient Sumerians were the first people to set up formal governments with officials and laws.

Organized religion is another type of institution. Villagers and hunters and gatherers had worshiped local gods and spirits. With the growth of cities, however, religion was organized in a new way. Most cities had great temples where dozens of priests took charge of religious duties. Priests often kept track of the yearly calendar, managed grain storehouses, and organized important rituals.

Thus, there are five key traits that set Sumer apart from all the human societies that existed before it: (1) the rise of cities; (2) specialized workers; (3) the use of writing; (4) advanced tools; and (5) complex institutions. All the later peoples who lived in this region of the world built upon these key Sumerian traits.

Sumerians faced geographic problems.

Sumer's civilization was shaped in part by the land in which the Sumerians lived. The Sumerians came to Mesopotamia about 4000 B.C. No one knows for sure where they came from. They found that the Tigris and Euphrates rivers flooded their new homeland at least once a year. As the floodwater receded, it left a thick bed of mud. In this rich, new soil, farmers could plant and harvest enormous quantities of wheat and barley.

Good soil was the advantage of living on the flat, swampy land of Sumer. There were three disadvantages.

The water problem The flooding of the rivers was dangerous because nobody could predict when it would happen. Sometimes it came as early as April, sometimes as late as June. Moreover, after the flood receded, the mud quickly dried out. Little or no rain fell, and the land became almost a desert. How could Sumerian farmers get enough water from the rivers during the dry summer months to make their barley grow?

The defense problem Sumer was a small region, only about the size of Massachusetts. It was also as flat as a tabletop. The villages were little clusters of reed huts standing in the middle of an open plain. With no natural barriers for protection, a Sumerian village was almost defenseless. Time

and again, nomadic herders from the nearby mountains and desert swooped down and stole the village's livestock and grain. How could the Sumerian villagers protect themselves?

The resource problem The natural resources of Sumer were extremely limited. Besides the fertile soil, there were huge reeds ten feet tall that grew in dense masses along the river's edge. With bundles of these reeds, people could make primitive boats and one-room huts. But they could not make hammers or axes. Without a good supply of stone, wood, and metal, what were the Sumerians to use for tools or buildings?

The solutions Over a period of 500 years (from about 3500 to 3000 B.C.), the Sumerians worked out ways to handle these problems. To help with the water problem, Sumerians dug irrigation ditches so that they could bring river water into the crop fields. To defend their settlements, they built city walls with mud bricks. To acquire more resources, Sumerians developed a broad trading network with the people of the mountains and the desert. Merchants from Sumer traded grain, cloth, and tools for stone, wood, and metal. By dealing with their problems, the Sumerians cleared the way for the growth of their civilization.

Sumerians created city-states.

Around each Sumerian city lay vast acres of barley and wheat. Each city and the surrounding countryside that it controlled was known as a **city-state.** These city-states included Ur, Kish, Nippur, Lagash, Uruk, and others.

Picture yourself in a field of grain with the mud-brick walls of Ur in the distance. It is early in the morning, but already the summer sun is almost too hot to bear. (By noon, it will be nearly 100°F.) All around, people are working barefoot in the irrigation ditches that run between patches of green plants. With stone hoes, the workers widen the ditches, bringing life-giving water into their fields from the reservoir a mile away. Without this elaborate irrigation network, the crops would die and the city-dwellers of Ur would starve.

Inside the city A broad dirt road leads from the fields up to the city's wall of mud bricks. Inside the city gate, the city dwellers go about their daily lives. A woman walks down a narrow lane with a jug of water balanced on her head.

Her dark hair is braided and coiled around her head. Her dress is a long, white cloth wrapped loosely around her, leaving her arms and one shoulder uncovered. Two men who pass wear skirtlike garments around their waists. Their hair falls down over their bare shoulders in wavy locks. Long, neatly trimmed beards hang low over their chests.

The dusty, unpaved streets are littered with garbage that people throw out their doorways. Most of the houses are small, windowless, one-story boxes packed tightly together along the street. However, a few wealthy families live in two-story houses with an inner courtyard. The courtyard allows some light and fresh air into these houses, but even rich people climb up to the flat roofs on summer nights to escape their stuffy rooms.

Trade The narrow streets finally open out onto a broad avenue where merchants squat under their awnings and trade a necklace for two or three sheep. This is the city's bazaar. People do not use coins to make purchases because money has not yet been invented. However, merchants and their customers know roughly how many pots of grain a farmer must give to buy a jug of wine. (This way of exchanging goods is called **barter**.) More complicated trades require the services of a scribe, who records on a clay tablet how much barley a certain farmer owes a certain merchant for a certain donkey.

The temple Farther down the main avenue stands Ur's tallest and most important building, the temple. Like a city within a city, the temple is surrounded by a heavy wall. Within the temple gate rises a massive, three-tiered structure known as a ziggurat (ZIHG-ur-aht), which means "mountain of god." Leading straight up the outside of the ziggurat is a flight of perhaps 100 mud-brick stairs. Every day, priests with shaved heads climb these stairs, sometimes dragging behind them a plump goat or sheep to sacrifice to Ur's gods.

The ziggurat was central to Sumerian cities.

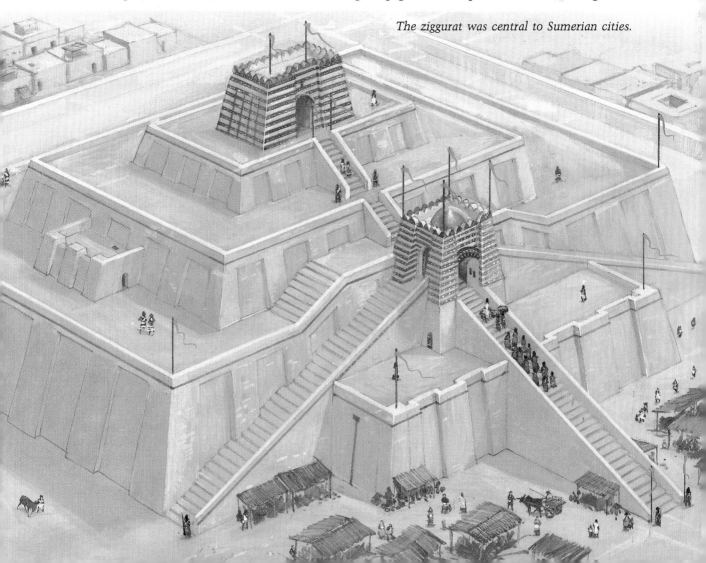

Sumerians believed in many gods.

Like many peoples in the Fertile Crescent, the Sumerians were **polytheists** (PAHL-ee-**THEE**-ists), believers in many gods. Anu (the god of heaven), Enlil (the god of clouds and air), and Ea (the god of water and floods) were the most powerful of their gods. Ranking slightly lower were the gods of the sun, moon, and stars. Then came those gods who inhabited the temple of a particular city-state. Next came the gods who dwelled in every Sumerian home. Lowest of all were demons known as Wicked Udugs, who caused disease, misfortune, and every kind of human trouble. Altogether, the Sumerians believed in roughly 3,000 gods.

Sumerians described their gods as doing many of the same things humans do—falling in love, having children, quarreling, and so on. Yet the Sumerians also believed that their gods were both immortal and all-powerful. The power of the gods was absolute. Humans were nothing but their servants. At any moment, the anger of the gods might strike, sending a fire, a flood, or an enemy army to destroy a city. To placate the gods, the people of Sumer built ziggurats and made rich offerings.

Sumerians worked hard to earn the gods' protection in this life, but they expected little help from the gods after death. The Sumerians believed that the souls of the dead went to the "land of no return," a dismal, gloomy place between the earth's crust and the ancient sea. No joy awaited souls there. According to a Sumerian poem about dead souls, "Dust is their fare and clay their food."

Priests and kings ruled Sumer.

Historians believe that Sumer's earliest governments were controlled by the temple priests. Only the priests knew how to please the city gods and thus keep Ur safe. The ziggurat was far more than a place of worship. It was like a city hall from which priests managed all the major industries of Sumer. They managed the irrigation system and told farmers when to plant and when to harvest. They also demanded a portion of every farmer's crop as taxes. Part of the tax was an offering to the gods, and the rest was used to feed the hundreds of laborers employed at the temple.

In time of war, however, the priests did not lead the city. Instead, the men of the city chose a tough fighter who could command the city's soldiers. At first, a commander's power ended as soon as the war was over. However, as wars between cities became more and more frequent, the commander gradually became a full-time ruler, or king. This ruler usually passed his power on to his sons.

After 3000 B.C., every Sumerian city had both a powerful group of priests and a king. Most cities then had two great buildings, the priests' temple and the royal palace.

Gudea was king of the Sumerian city-state of Lagash about 2100 B.C. He was a pious king who built a great temple to the chief god of Lagash.

Sumerian society had many classes.

With civilization came greater differences between groups in society—between the rich and the poor, noble and peasant, free person and slave. A village farmer who visited Ur would have noticed at once that the priests and nobles were much wealthier than the village leaders back home. Priests and kings made up the highest level in Sumerian society. Wealthy merchants ranked next. The vast majority of ordinary Sumerian people worked with their hands in fields and workshops.

At the lowest level of Sumerian society were the slaves. Some slaves were foreigners who had been captured in war. Others were Sumerians who had been sold into slavery as children to

This small statue of a Sumerian husband and wife from Nippur suggests both affection and equality within marriage.

pay the debts of their impoverished parents. By working obediently day and night, Sumerian slaves could hope to earn their freedom.

Social class affected the lives of both men and women. On the whole, Sumerian women could engage in most of the occupations of city life, from merchant to farmer to artisan. Women could also join the lower ranks of the priesthood. However, none of Sumer's written records mentions a female scribe. Therefore, scholars have concluded that girls were not allowed to attend the schools where upper-class boys learned to read and write. In spite of these limitations, however, women in Sumer possessed more rights than women in many later civilizations.

Warfare brought Sumer's downfall.

For 1,000 years (from 3000 to 2000 B.C.), the city-states of Sumer were almost constantly at war with one another. For a time, the king of Kish was the mightiest ruler in Mesopotamia. But Kish's power gave way to that of the city-state Uruk and then of Lagash, Umma, and Ur.

All these city-states had their brief moments of glory.

Sumerian civilization ended because the constant warfare weakened all the city-states so much that they could no longer ward off attacks from a different enemy. Nomadic raiders from the deserts and the hills looked with envy on the riches of the cities. Around 2000 B.C., these warriors scaled the walls of Ur, swept through the streets, and burst through the gates of the temple. Ur was left in ruins. A grief-stricken scribe speaks for the goddess Ningal in this poem:

Woe is me, my house is a ruined stable,
I am a herdsman whose cows have been scattered,
I, Ningal, like an unworthy shepherd on whose flock the weapon has fallen!
Woe is me, I am an exile from the city that has found no rest;
I am a stranger dwelling in a strange city.

Section Review 1

Define: (a) civilization, (b) scribe, (c) artisan, (d) cuneiform, (e) pictograph, (f) ideogram, (g) institution, (h) irrigation, (i) city-state, (j) barter, (k) ziggurat, (l) polytheist
Identify: (a) Fertile Crescent, (b) Mesopotamia, (c) Sumer
Answer:
1. Explain how life in a Sumerian city differed from life in a small farming village in the same region.
2. (a) What were the advantages and disadvantages of Sumer's natural environment? (b) Explain how Sumerians overcame the disadvantages.
3. Give a brief description of daily life in Sumer, mentioning the activities of at least one member of each social class.
4. Why was this period known as the Bronze Age?

Critical Thinking
5. (a) Writing was a key invention of the Sumerians. Do you think writing is still essential to modern civilization? Explain your answer. (b) Choose another of the Sumerians' inventions and explain how life today would have been different if that invention did not exist.

33

Newcomers contributed to civilization. 2

Around 2000 B.C., many groups of people were on the move through Southwest Asia and neighboring lands. These huge migrations involved thousands of people and lasted hundreds of years. The arrival of new groups brought a wave of warfare and conquest to the Fertile Crescent.

The Sumerians never recovered from the attacks on their cities around 2000 B.C. However, Sumerian civilization did not die. Each new set of rulers adapted the basic ideas of Sumerian civilization to meet their own needs. As kingdoms grew larger and larger, the Sumerian pattern of civilization spread more widely across Southwest Asia. At the same time, the newcomers also made contributions of their own to the development of civilization.

Babylonians wrote a code of laws.

The first conquerors came from the city of Babylon (**BAB**-uh-luhn), a little upstream from Sumer. The Babylonians (**BAB**-uh-**LOHN**-ee-uhnz)

Map Study
Describe the geographic area covered by the Babylonian empire.

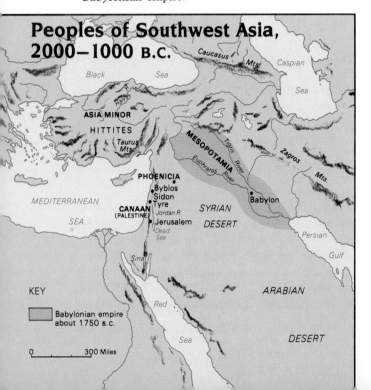

Peoples of Southwest Asia, 2000–1000 B.C.

Caucasus Mts.
Black Sea
Caspian Sea
ASIA MINOR
HITTITES
Taurus Mts.
MESOPOTAMIA
Tigris River
Zagros Mts.
Euphrates River
PHOENICIA
Byblos
Sidon
Tyre
Babylon
MEDITERRANEAN SEA
CANAAN (PALESTINE)
Jordan R
Jerusalem
Dead Sea
SYRIAN DESERT
Persian Gulf
Sinai
Red Sea
ARABIAN DESERT

KEY

Babylonian empire about 1750 B.C.

0   300 Miles

had been nomads, but they quickly adopted the civilized ways of the Sumerians they conquered. They built ziggurats, wrote cuneiform, irrigated fields, and organized society in the same manner as the Sumerians. Most important, by conquering almost all of Mesopotamia, the Babylonians spread civilization over a large area.

The major achievement of the Babylonians was a code of laws. This too was based on earlier Sumerian practices. Several Sumerian kings had set forth the laws of their city-states in writing. The Babylonian law code was more complete than the earlier ones. Moreover, it proclaimed the law not just for one city-state but for an entire **empire**. (An empire is a state that has conquered other lands and now rules them.)

The Babylonian law code was the work of one of history's truly great kings, Hammurabi (ham-uh-**RAH**-bee). The exact years of his reign are unknown. Toward the end of his life (roughly 1750 B.C.), Hammurabi ordered a scribe to chisel a record of his kingly deeds onto an eight-foot slab of black stone.

The stone boasts that Hammurabi gave justice to all the people he ruled. The central and most important part of the stone lists nearly 300 laws. Each one tells how a grievance between wife and husband, master and slave, merchant and customer, or neighbor and neighbor was to be settled. For example, these are five laws in the code:

If a man destroys the eye of another man, they shall destroy his eye.
If he breaks a man's bone, they shall break his bone.
If he destroys the eye of a common man or breaks a bone of a common man, he shall pay one mina of silver.
If a man knocks out a tooth of a man of his own rank, they shall knock out his tooth.
If he knocks out a tooth of a common man, he shall pay one-third mina of silver.

To develop his law code, Hammurabi chose among the many laws of the different city-states he ruled, picking the rulings that seemed best to him. He had to get rid of disagreements and contradictions in the laws. That process is what sets a law *code* apart from a simple list of laws that were enacted one by one.

Map Study answer: land along Tigris and Euphrates rivers including Mesopotamia

In this scene from the top of the stone on which Hammurabi's code was carved, the god of justice (seated) commands the king to write the laws.

Hammurabi's law code was important for the growth of justice in two ways. First, the laws were recorded in writing on the great stone, so that they were public knowledge. (Of course, that knowledge was limited to people who could read.) Second, Hammurabi's idea of justice required balance—an eye for an eye, a tooth for a tooth, a life for a life. Although many of the punishments seem harsh by modern standards, they at least fit the crime. A small crime did not lead to a great punishment.

Around 1550 B.C., 200 years after Hammurabi's rule, the Babylonian empire fell to nomadic warriors. For the next 700 years, the Fertile Crescent broke into small kingdoms as new peoples moved into the region. Small kingdoms and independent city-states sprang up across the region. Despite their small size, some of these groups made important contributions to civilization. Among these peoples were the Phoenicians (fuh-NIH-shuhnz) and the Jews.

Phoenicians invented the alphabet.

About 1100 B.C., the Phoenicians were the most powerful traders and merchants around the Mediterranean Sea. They did not rule a great empire, but they built a number of wealthy cities, something like the independent Sumerian city-states. The first Phoenician cities lay in what is now Lebanon. Later, however, the far-sailing Phoenicians settled widely around the Mediterranean Sea.

Wealth from trade The Phoenicians' wealth began in an unlikely way. Around their island city of Tyre (tire), millions of little snails washed up along the rocky shore. These snails were the resource from which the Phoenicians produced an intensely rich purple dye. To produce just one pound of dye, workers had to squeeze the drops from 60,000 smelly snail glands, a very costly process. All around the Mediterranean, the Phoenicians sold this rare dye at a fabulous price. Indeed, only a king's family could afford to wear "the royal purple" made at Tyre.

All in all, however, Phoenicia was poor in natural resources. Besides the snails, the only valuable item the land produced was fine, tall cedar trees that were in wide demand for building.

Thus, the Phoenicians turned to trade. In addition to purple dye and cedar, they traded goods they got from other lands, including wine, weapons, slaves, cloth, glass, precious metals, and ivory. Tyre competed fiercely with the other Phoenician city-states such as Byblos and Sidon for business that passed through Phoenician ports.

The Phoenicians' desire for trade made them excellent sailors. In narrow, single-sailed vessels equipped with long oars, they traveled all along the Mediterranean coasts of Europe and Africa. They even sailed past the Rock of Gibraltar into the stormy Atlantic Ocean. One Phoenician fleet may have circled the entire continent of Africa around 600 B.C. No other explorers are known to have attempted such a feat until 2,100 years later.

Between 1100 and 700 B.C., the Phoenicians founded trading colonies on almost every Mediterranean island. Perhaps as many as 300 Phoenician cities dotted Africa's Mediterranean coast. By far the greatest was Carthage, built on a fine natural harbor. (In later days, Carthage rivaled Rome in power.)

35

In each province of the Persian empire was a royal governor called a *satrap* (SAY-trap). Darius also appointed an army leader and a tax collector for each province. To make sure his satraps did not rebel against him, Darius sent inspectors known as the "King's Eyes and Ears" to all parts of his kingdom.

The Persian king used two other important tools to hold his empire together. One was an excellent road system and the other was standardized coinage.

The famous Royal Road of the Persian empire ran from Susa, the Persian capital, to Sardis in Asia Minor, a distance of 1,677 miles. An ordinary caravan took three months to travel this distance, but the king's messengers took only about a week. Royal riders dashed along the road. At 111 post stations spaced along the road, new riders on fresh horses took over for tired ones. With this system, royal commands reached all parts of the empire.

Darius's second idea, borrowed from the Lydians of Asia Minor, was to manufacture metal coins. For the first time, coins of a standard value circulated throughout most of the civilized world. People no longer had to weigh and measure bits of gold or silver to pay for their purchases. Like the road system, the wider use of money made trade much easier. Trade, in turn, helped to hold the empire together.

The teachings of Zoroaster By Darius's time, about 2,500 years had passed since the first Sumerian city-states had been built. During those years, people of the Fertile Crescent had suffered often from war, conquest, and famine. Why was there so much evil in the world? A Persian prophet named Zoroaster (ZOH-roh-AS-tuhr) offered an inspirational answer.

Scholars know almost nothing about the life of Zoroaster except that he lived around 600 B.C. His ideas, however, are well-known. Zoroaster taught that two spiritual armies fight for possession of a person's soul. One army is led by

Ahura-Mazda (AH-hoo-ruh-MAHZ-duh), god of truth and light. The other is commanded by Ahriman (AH-ree-muhn), god of evil and darkness. At the end of time, said Zoroaster, all souls would be judged according to the side they had chosen. Followers of Ahura-Mazda would be lifted into a paradise. Followers of Ahriman would suffer forever in a fiery pit.

This belief in a heaven and a hell was radically different from Sumer's gloomy vision of the afterlife. Zoroaster's religion was far more hopeful, because a person's own choice controlled his or her fate. Those who chose the side of goodness were not doomed to a dismal underworld.

The Persian empire lasted about 200 years. Through their tolerance and good government, the Persians brought political order to Southwest Asia. During this long period of comparative peace, the region's great cities prospered. Commerce flourished. Learning and the arts progressed. In other words, all the achievements of civilization were protected and allowed to grow.

Section Review 3

Define: (a) constellation, (b) astronomy, (c) satrap
Identify: (a) Assyria, (b) Assurbanipal, (c) Chaldeans, (d) Babylon, (e) Nebuchadnezzar, (f) Iran, (g) Persians, (h) Cyrus, (i) Darius, (j) Zoroaster
Answer:
1. Explain how the Assyrians succeeded in conquering a great empire.
2. What were the achievements of the Chaldeans in the time of Nebuchadnezzar?
3. What important religious stand did the Jews take during their captivity in Babylon?
4. How was the Persian king Cyrus's way of building an empire different from that of Assyrian kings?
5. How was Zoroaster's philosophy different from earlier religions of Southwest Asia?

Critical Thinking
6. Suppose you lived in a city in Mesopotamia. Would you rather have lived there in the period of the independent Sumerian city-states or in the time of the Persian empire? Explain your answer.

Footnote to History

Satraps lived in luxurious palaces. The Persian name for a satrap's private hunting park was *paradise* (from which comes our own word for a heavenly place).

Chapter Review 2

Summary

1. Civilization arose in the Fertile Crescent. About 5,000 years ago, many groups of people throughout the world were living in small farming villages. In the Fertile Crescent of Southwest Asia, however, the people of Sumer developed a more complex way of life. They built cities in which people worked at a variety of trades. For the first time in history, farmers were able to raise enough food to have a surplus. The ability to raise a surplus freed people to do specialized jobs. Sumerian government and religion were highly organized. Sumerians invented a system of writing, and their technology was advanced for its day. These traits made Sumer the first civilization.

2. Newcomers contributed to civilization. Beginning around 2000 B.C., waves of new peoples swept through the Fertile Crescent. Each new group adopted the ways of life begun in Sumer and added their own ideas. The Babylonians' most famous achievement was a code of law. The Phoenicians invented a system of writing that evolved into our present-day alphabet. The Jews developed a religion based on belief in one God. Between 1500 and 1000 B.C., the Bronze Age gave way to the Iron Age.

3. Conquerors ruled ever larger empires. Between 900 and 350 B.C., the Assyrians, the Chaldeans, and the Persians each took a turn at ruling Southwest Asia. Each group of people imposed its culture and ruling style on the area. Some of the important developments during this time were the increased use of iron, the beginnings of astronomy, the use of money for trade, and the belief in an afterlife.

Reviewing the Facts

1. Define the following terms:

   a. civilization
   b. artisan
   c. cuneiform
   d. institution
   e. city-state
   f. barter
   g. polytheist
   h. empire
   i. literacy
   j. monotheist
   k. prophet

2. Explain the importance of each of the following names, places, or terms:

   a. Fertile Crescent
   b. Mesopotamia
   c. Bronze Age
   d. Iron Age
   e. Sumer
   f. Hammurabi
   g. Phoenicians
   h. Jews
   i. Moses
   j. Solomon
   k. Assyria
   l. Nebuchadnezzar
   m. Persians
   n. Cyrus
   o. Darius
   p. Zoroaster

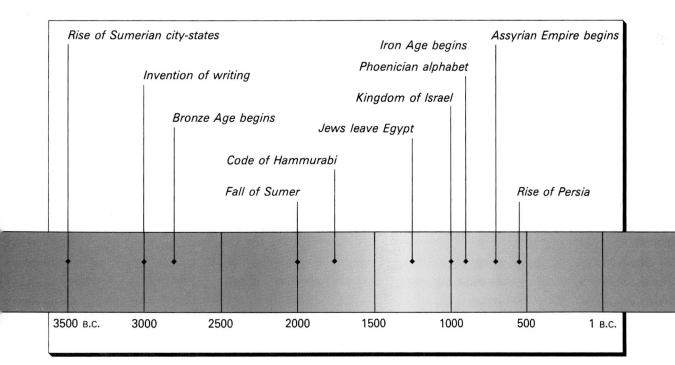

Rise of Sumerian city-states
Invention of writing
Bronze Age begins
Code of Hammurabi
Fall of Sumer
Jews leave Egypt
Kingdom of Israel
Phoenician alphabet
Iron Age begins
Assyrian Empire begins
Rise of Persia

3500 B.C.   3000   2500   2000   1500   1000   500   1 B.C.

45

3. (a) What are the key traits of civilization? (b) Describe how each trait was present in Sumer.

4. What lasting contributions to civilization were made by each of the following groups? (a) the Phoenicians (b) the Jews (c) the Chaldeans

Basic Skills

1. Reading a time line Use the time line on page 45 and information from the chapter to answer these questions: (a) How many years were there between the beginning of the Bronze Age and that of the Iron Age? The invention of writing and of the alphabet? The Jews' exodus from Egypt and their captivity in Babylon? (b) How long did the Assyrian Empire last? The Persian Empire?

2. Reading a map Locate the Fertile Crescent on the map on page 28. Use geographic features such as deserts, mountains, seas, and rivers to define the boundaries of the Fertile Crescent.

3. Outlining Outline the content of the subsection entitled *Persian government* on pages 43 and 44. Your outline should show the main ideas and two or three details supporting each main idea.

4. Using vocabulary Historians often divide their subject into several categories. *Political history* deals with government, laws, and political leaders. *Economic history* sees how society employs labor, money, and tools to make, buy, and sell goods and services. *Social history* studies the way people live, how they relate to each other, how they view the world, and what values they teach their children. *Cultural history* refers to ideas, values, and beliefs and their expression through literature, the arts, and education. For each kind of history, give two examples of information from this chapter.

Researching and Reporting Skills

Of the political and religious leaders described in this chapter, whom do you think is greatest? To learn more about that person, do research in the library.

1. Using the card catalog Identify two books that refer to the person chosen. From each card, copy the book title, author's name, copyright date, and library call number.

2. Acquiring information In each book, read at least ten pages about your subject. Note why each author considers this person important as a leader.

3. Summarizing Write a summary of the historical importance of the leader you chose. Include information from both sources and your own ideas.

Critical Thinking

1. Analyzing cause and effect How did the production of surplus food affect the political, economic, and social life of Sumer?

2. Comparing (a) Compare the origins of Hammurabi's code and the Ten Commandments. (b) How did their ideas for moral conduct differ?

3. Evaluating All conquerors face the problem of gaining obedience from conquered peoples. (a) How did the Assyrians and Persians each solve this problem? (b) Which solution do you consider more effective, and why?

4. Synthesizing (a) In both Sumer and Phoenicia, how did technological advances aid the expansion of trade? (b) Why were new inventions needed for trade to grow?

5. Interpreting What is the significance of the start of monotheism for history?

6. Using visual evidence It has been said that in Mesopotamian art, a seated or reclining figure has a higher social position than does a standing figure. Study the photos relating to Mesopotamia to see whether the statement is true. What conclusion do you draw? On what evidence is it based?

Perspectives on Past and Present

Reread the excerpt from Hammurabi's code of laws on page 34. Do you agree or disagree with the statement, "Although this code was an outstanding example of justice for its day, it would fall short by today's standards"?

Investigating History

1. The Hanging Gardens of Babylon were one of the Seven Wonders of the Ancient World. Use reference books to find out what the others were, and choose one to research further. Write a brief description of that work, or make a drawing or model to show how it may have looked.

2. One monument enduring from the ancient world is the Behistun Rock in Iran. Do research to learn how this landmark aided the translation of early languages.

Ancient Egypt

This golden mask covered the face of Tutankhamon's mummy. Its ears are pierced for earrings. The vulture and the cobra on the head-dress represent two Egyptian gods.

Key Terms

cataract
delta
dynasty
pharaoh
pyramid
maat
hieroglyphics

Read and Understand

1. The Nile River shaped Egyptian life.
2. Egypt's pharaohs ruled as gods.
3. Egypt's way of life endured 3,000 years.

It was late fall in 1922. In northeastern Africa, the sun blazed hot in the Valley of the Kings, which lies in Egypt near a sweeping curve in the Nile River. British archaeologist Howard Carter had spent six years there moving ton upon ton of rock in search of tombs of ancient Egypt's last great rulers. More than 3,000 years had passed since these rulers had been laid to rest. Over the centuries, robbers had opened most of the tombs and taken their treasures. Still, Carter pressed on.

On November 26, 1922, Carter stood before a sealed door. If the wildest of Carter's dreams were true, behind the door lay the mummy and treasure of the ruler Tutankhamon (TOOT-ahngk-**AH**-mun). Carter made a small hole in the door and stuck a candle through. His report told what he saw.

In 1907, Carter had taken part in another expedition, during which seals with Tutankhamon's name were found. Carter became convinced that these seals were from the king's funeral and that the royal tomb was nearby.

At first I could see nothing . . . but presently as my eyes grew accustomed to the light, details of the room within emerged slowly from the mist, strange animals, statues, and gold—everywhere the glint of gold.

The wealth of gold within the tomb included four golden chariots, gilded couches, a golden throne with lions' heads carved in the arms, and much more. All these splendors had been created for Tutankhamon, who ruled Egypt for only a few short years. He became king at the age of 8 in about 1347 B.C. and died 9 years later in 1339 B.C., only 17 years old.

Carter had indeed found the tomb he sought, but where was the royal mummy? The young king's burial chamber lay behind yet another sealed door. When that door was opened, Carter's electric lamp revealed a breathtaking sight—a large, box-shaped shrine of gilded wood that filled the entire room. Nested within the large shrine were three smaller ones, and within the smallest shrine was a great stone coffin.

With a rope and tackle, Carter's crew of workers hoisted the heavy lid off the coffin. From inside, a golden face looked up at them through deep blue eyes of precious stones. Resting lightly on this gleaming mask was a fragile wreath of flowers, placed there by Tutankhamon's young widow. Carter later wrote,

Among all that regal splendour, that royal magnificence . . . there was nothing so beautiful as those few withered flowers . . . They told us what a short period 3,300 years really was.

The Nile River shaped Egyptian life. 1

Tutankhamon's reign was just a brief moment in ancient Egypt's long history. Egypt had already been a united kingdom for 1,700 years when young Tutankhamon came to the throne. The country he ruled was nearly as old as the city-states of Sumer.

Although Egypt existed at the same time as the cities of Sumer and the later empires of Southwest Asia, Egyptian civilization was very different from the ways of life that arose in the Fertile Crescent. Unlike Southwest Asia, Egypt was early united into a single country. That country survived, through good times and bad, for more than 3,000 years. At the center of Egypt's unity was the country's most important geographic feature, the Nile River. Indeed, the story of ancient Egypt begins with the story of the Nile.

The Nile linked diverse lands.

From the highlands of eastern Africa to the Mediterranean Sea, the Nile River meanders over 4,100 miles, making it the longest river in the world. The map on page 49 shows how it winds through Egypt, a thin ribbon of water in a parched desert land.

The cataracts For most of their history, ancient Egyptians knew only the lower part of the Nile—the last 750 miles before it empties into the sea. Their domain ended in the south at Aswan, where jagged granite cliffs pinch inward. The narrowing cliffs and boulders that have fallen from them turn the river into churning rapids called a **cataract** (KAT-uh-rakt). Riverboats cannot pass this spot, known as the First Cataract. (Five other cataracts lie farther upstream to the south.)

Upper Egypt and Lower Egypt Between the First Cataract and the Mediterranean lay two very different regions. Upper Egypt (to the south) was a skinny strip of land from the First Cataract to the point where the river split into many branches. Lower Egypt (to the north, near the sea) began about 100 miles before the river entered the Mediterranean Sea. At that point, branches of the river fanned out over a broad, marshy, triangular area of land. Such a region is called a **delta** (map, page 49).

A transportation link The Nile provided an easy, reliable system of transportation between Upper and Lower Egypt. Going from one end of Egypt to another required no more effort than climbing into a boat. The Nile flowed north, so northbound boats simply drifted with the current all the way from the First Cataract to the marshy flats of Lower Egypt. Southbound boats hoisted a wide sail. The prevailing winds of Egypt blew from north to south, carrying sailboats against the river current.

Upper Egypt ranged from 4 to 20 miles wide along the Nile. Have students compare this distance to some local measurement to appreciate Upper Egypt's extreme narrowness.

Farmers relied on the Nile's floods.

Every year in June, spring rains and melting snow from the mountains caused the Nile River to rise and spill over its banks. This flood was not a menace to the Egyptians. Rather, they depended on it.

The gift of the Nile When the river receded in October, it left behind a rich, wet deposit of fertile black mud. Year after year, Egyptian peasants knew they could count on the flooding Nile to provide this rich layer of soil in time for their next planting.

Before the scorching sun could dry out the soil, the peasants would hitch their cattle to plows and prepare their fields for planting. All summer and fall, they tended the wheat and barley plants. They watered their crops from an intricate network of irrigation ditches. At last came the welcome harvest. This cycle repeated itself year after year—flood, plant, harvest; flood, plant, harvest. As an ancient Greek historian named Herodotus (huh-**RAHD**-uh-tuhs) remarked in the fifth century B.C., Egypt was the "gift of the Nile."

Worshiping the Nile Egyptian farmers were much more fortunate than the villagers of Mesopotamia. Compared to the rampaging, unpredictable Tigris River, the Nile was as regular as clockwork. The Egyptians worshiped it as a god who gave them life and seldom turned against them. They felt secure in their well-being. With nature so much in their favor, Egyptians tended to approach life more confidently and optimistically than their neighbors in the Fertile Crescent.

Even so, life in Egypt had its risks. If the Nile's floodwaters were just a few feet lower than normal, the amount of fresh soil and water for crops was greatly reduced. Thousands of people might starve. If the floodwaters were a few feet higher than usual, the water would spread beyond the fields to the mud-brick villages nearby. The unwanted water might destroy houses, granaries, and the precious seeds that farmers needed for planting.

Thus, the Egyptians were careful to observe all the religious rituals that were supposed to please the gods and keep Egypt safe. In a religious festival on the Nile's banks, they sang: "Hail to thee, O Nile, that issues from the earth and comes to keep Egypt alive."

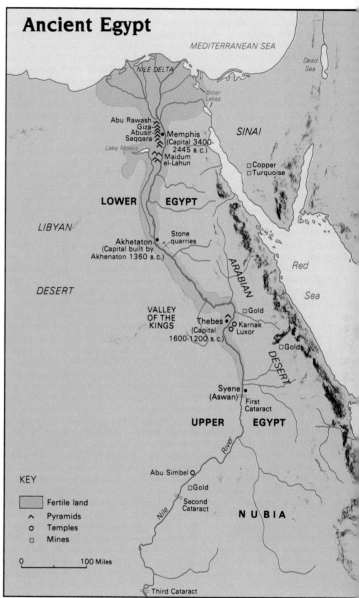

Ancient Egypt

Map Study

In which part of Egypt were most of the pyramids built? What resources did the Sinai contain?

Deserts shielded Egypt from attack.

All of Egypt's villages and cities were built along the Nile on a narrow strip of land made fertile by the river. Beyond that, on either side of the river, the land changed suddenly to desert. To the west stretched the sands of the Libyan Desert, a part of the Sahara. To the east along the Red Sea lay the Arabian Desert, which was

Stone stairs were used to measure the yearly flood and determine its strength or weakness compared to preceding floods.

Map Study answers: Lower Egypt; copper, turquoise

even drier and more barren. The change from fertile land to desert was so abrupt that a person could stand with one foot in each. To the Egyptians, the desert stood for death and the river for life.

The vast and forbidding deserts forced Egyptians to stay close to their lifeline, the Nile. However, the deserts also shut out invaders. For much of its history, Egypt was spared the constant warfare that plagued the Fertile Crescent.

The only possible invasion route into Egypt lay across a narrow corridor called the Isthmus of Suez. In time, invaders would reach Egypt by way of this one geographic link with the outside world. However, for hundreds of years, the deserts kept Egypt secure from any serious attack.

Farm villages joined in nomes.

Egyptians lived in farming villages as far back as 6000 B.C., perhaps even earlier. During those times, they cleared and cultivated the land with stone tools. They domesticated cattle, goats, sheep, and donkeys. They worshiped the wild creatures that swam in the Nile—the hippopotamus and the crocodile. They tried to preserve bodies of the dead by heaping up mounds of sand around them in the desert.

Eventually, the villages united into agricultural districts called *nomes* (nohmz). Each nome had its own rituals, gods, and chieftain. Often people of rival nomes raided one another's territory.

By 3200 B.C., Egyptians were coming into contact with the people of Mesopotamia. Caravans loaded with goods for trade were traveling between the two regions. Even more important, whole groups of people seem to have moved freely from one region to another in search of better land for farming or grazing.

At the same time, important changes were taking place in Egypt. The first kings arose, uniting the territories of many nomes. Egyptians also developed their own system of writing. These ideas may have been borrowed, at least in part, from Mesopotamia. The period of Mesopotamian influence was soon over, however. From then on, Egyptian culture followed its own path, which was very different from Mesopotamia's.

Voice from the Past · *Seven Lean Years in Egypt*

Although the Nile was a dependable, life-giving force in ancient Egypt, the river sometimes withdrew its gifts. In the following account, the ruler Djoser (JOH-suhr) describes one such crisis.

I was in distress on the Great Throne, and those who are in the palace were in heart's affliction from a very great evil, since the Nile had not come in my time for a space of seven years. Grain was scant, fruits were dried up, and everything which they eat was short. Every man robbed his companion ... The infant was wailing; the youth was waiting; the heart of the old man was in sorrow ... The courtiers were in need. The temples were shut up.

[The ruler then tells of a vision that came to him in his sleep.]

I discovered the god standing over me ... I prayed to him in his presence ... His words were:

"I am Khnum, thy maker ... The Nile will pour forth for thee, without a year of cessation or laxness for any land. Plants will grow, bowing down under the fruit."

[Upon waking, the ruler went to the temple of Khnum. He made an offering to the god and prayed for the return of the Nile's floodwaters.]

1. Using the information in the account, describe in your own words what a drought meant for Egypt.
2. (a) How did the ruler handle the disaster? (b) How might a modern government handle a similar natural disaster today?

The Egyptians own name for their country was *Kemet,* meaning "black earth." Black was the color of life, because it represented moisture in the soil.
Answers to Voice from the Past questions appear in the Lesson Planner.

Looking at economics *This wall painting from an Egyptian tomb shows a tax assessor measuring a field of grain to decide how much tax the farmer must pay. Taxes sometimes amounted to 20 percent of the crop.*

Menes united two kingdoms.

By 3200 B.C., the nomes of Egypt were divided into two groups under two kings. One king ruled Lower Egypt and wore a red crown. Another king ruled Upper Egypt and wore a tall white crown shaped like a bowling pin.

This carving shows the large figure of King Menes wearing the White Crown of Upper Egypt as he triumphs over his foes.

Then, about 3100 B.C., a strong-willed king of Upper Egypt named Menes (MEE-neez) united all of Egypt. As a symbol of his united kingdom, Menes created a double crown from the red and white crowns. Menes shrewdly established his capital near the spot where Upper and Lower Egypt met, about 100 miles from the Mediterranean Sea. The capital was called Memphis. Menes was the first of a long series of kings to rule over the united country of Egypt.

Section Review 1

Define: (a) cataract, (b) delta, (c) irrigation, (d) nome
Identify: (a) Howard Carter, (b) Tutankhamon, (c) Nile River, (d) Upper Egypt, (e) Lower Egypt, (f) Menes
Answer:
1. Why was the Nile's yearly flood important to Egyptian farmers?
2. How did the surrounding desert affect life in ancient Egypt?
3. How did Menes alter Egypt's political organization?

Critical Thinking
4. Ancient Egyptians worshiped the forces of nature as gods. Why would they have regarded the Nile River as one of their most important gods?

51

Egypt's pharaohs ruled as gods. 2

The kingdom Menes created held together remarkably well, long after Menes died. Members of Menes's family passed the double crown of Upper and Lower Egypt from father to son to grandson. Such a series of rulers from a single family is called a **dynasty**. When one ruling family died out or lost control, another took its place. Eventually, the history of ancient Egypt would consist of an amazing 31 dynasties, spanning 2,800 years.

Like the Nile flooding and receding, the fortunes of Egyptian kings rose and fell. When strong kings held Egypt together, the region prospered. When the king's control weakened, in-fighting broke out among the nobles of the nomes. Outsiders might spot this sign of weakness and take the opportunity to invade. A century or two of war and misery would follow. Then a strong king would take control of Egypt again. Over and over, strength followed weakness; prosperity followed ruin.

Religion glorified pharaohs in the Old Kingdom.

The history of Egypt's first two dynasties is little known, but records improve with the Third Dynasty. Historians call the period that began with the Third Dynasty the Old Kingdom. This period lasted roughly from 2660 to 2180 B.C. The Old Kingdom set the pattern for Egypt's culture for nearly 3,000 years.

The power of the pharaohs The kings of Egypt are known as **pharaohs** (FAIR-ohz). It is useful to have a special term for Egypt's kings, because they were much more than political leaders to their people. In fact, the role of the king was one of the most striking differences between Egypt and Mesopotamia. In Mesopotamia, kings were considered to be representatives of the gods. But to the ancient Egyptians, pharaohs *were* gods, almost as splendid and powerful as the gods of the heavens.

The god-king stood at the center of Egypt's religion as well as its government and army. Egyptians believed that the pharaoh bore full responsibility for the kingdom's well-being. It was the pharaoh who caused the sun to rise, the Nile to flood, and the crops to grow. It was the pharaoh's duty to foster truth and justice. All the good things of life came from the pharaoh. No wonder Egyptians obeyed the ruler's every word. Who would dare to disobey the commands of a god?

Immortality for the pharaoh Egyptians believed that their pharaoh ruled even after his death. He had an eternal spirit, or *ka* (kah), that continued to take part in the governing of Egypt.

In the Egyptian's mind, the ka remained much like a living pharaoh in its needs and pleasures. To provide for the pharaoh's eternal comfort, artists decorated the walls of his burial chamber with pictures of whatever he might need or like. A picture of many fat geese, for instance, would assure him of endless sumptuous meals. Images of loved ones and devoted servants would keep him company and see that his commands were carried out. The burial chamber was also stocked with such luxuries as fine jewelry, game boards covered with precious stones, and rich clothing. Inscriptions on the tomb walls recounted the pharaoh's achievements.

Even though the ka was a spiritual being, it needed to refresh itself occasionally by entering its human body. Thus, the Egyptians preserved the pharaoh's body by making it a mummy. Scholars still accept Herodotus's description of the process of mummification:

> First, they draw out the brains through the nostrils with an iron hook . . . Then with a sharp stone they make an incision in the side, and take out all the bowels . . . Then, having filled the belly with pure myrrh, cassia, and other perfumes, they sew it up again; and when they have done this they steep it in natron [a mineral salt], leaving it under for 70 days . . . At the end of 70 days, they wash the corpse, and wrap the whole body in bandages of waxen cloth.

The time of the pyramids Since pharaohs expected to reign forever, their tombs were even more important than their palaces. For the pharaohs of the Old Kingdom, home after death was an immense structure called a **pyramid**. The Old Kingdom was the great age of pyramid building in ancient Egypt.

In earliest times, servants were sacrificed to accompany the pharaoh in afterlife. By the Third Dynasty, however, sculpted figures were used instead.

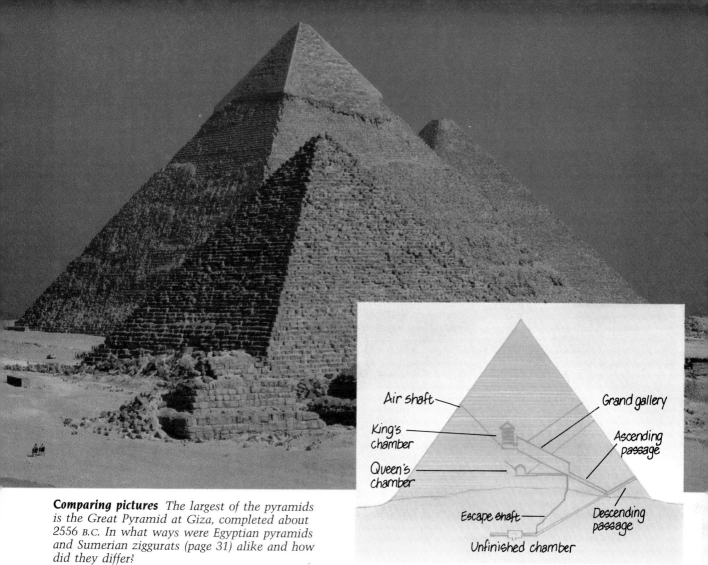

Comparing pictures *The largest of the pyramids is the Great Pyramid at Giza, completed about 2556 B.C. In what ways were Egyptian pyramids and Sumerian ziggurats (page 31) alike and how did they differ?*

Air shaft

King's chamber

Queen's chamber

Escape shaft

Unfinished chamber

Grand gallery

Ascending passage

Descending passage

Today, standing at the foot of the Great Pyramid at Giza, millions of stunned visitors have asked themselves: "How could this mountain of stone have been built by people who had not even begun to use the wheel?" Each perfectly cut stone block weighs at least 2½ tons. Some weigh 15 tons. More than 2 million of these blocks are stacked with precision to a height of 481 feet. The entire structure covers more than 13 acres.

Scholars today no longer believe the famous story told by Herodotus that 100,000 slaves were whipped and driven for 20 years before the last stone of the Great Pyramid was lugged into place. Modern historians think that peasants, not slaves, built the pyramids. Moreover, they did the work willingly for the glory of their god-king. In fact, they needed the work to keep busy and well-fed during the flood season. For cutting and hauling stones, they were probably paid with grain from the king's storehouses. Without work on the royal tombs, temples, and palaces, they would have gone hungry during the flood season.

About 80 pyramids still stand in the Egyptian desert. However, the bodies of the pharaohs no longer rest there. Robbers probably stole the mummies long ago, together with armloads of dazzling treasures.

Footnote to History

Although the ancient Egyptians did not know about the wheel, they did know about the slippery nature of mud. Modern scholars think the Egyptians made huge mud-brick ramps beside the pyramid under construction. One team of workers splashed water over the ramp to make a slick surface. Another team hauled the great blocks of stone up the ramp.

Egyptian pyramids and Sumarian ziggurats were alike in being massive structures built up from the ground. They differed in that pyramids were not solid stone but contained chambers and passages, whereas ziggurats were pyramid-shaped towers culminating in a temple at the top.

The First Illness brought ruin.

Toward the end of the Old Kingdom, the power of the pharaohs declined. More and more power fell into the hands of nobles and officials. Local rulers struggled among themselves for power. Civil war tore Egypt apart.

Some scholars think that these troubles began with a change in climate. Less rain fell in the African highlands, causing the Nile's floodwaters to be too low. Crops died, and the threat of starvation hung over Egypt. Because Egyptians looked to the pharaoh as a god, they expected him to control the forces of nature. When he failed, the people began to doubt his authority.

The Egyptians called this period of weakness and turmoil the First Illness. From 2180 to 2080 B.C., poor harvests, lawlessness, and warfare plagued the region. One Egyptian wrote of this unhappy time:

> . . . The desert is spread over the land. The provinces are destroyed. Barbarians are come into Egypt from without . . . Laughter has disappeared forever. It is wailing that fills the land . . .

Royal power returned in the Middle Kingdom.

Law and order returned to Egypt under the strong kings of the Middle Kingdom (2080–1640 B.C.). Farming revived, trade grew, and the arts flourished. The pharaohs moved the country's capital from Memphis to Thebes and built two massive temples there.

Projects for the public good Some of the prosperity of the Middle Kingdom was brought about by pharaohs who seemed to care about the welfare of the common people. They made trade and transportation easier by having a canal dug all the way from the Nile to the Red Sea. With the wealth that new trade brought in, the pharaohs undertook other public projects. To improve farming, they ordered the building of huge dikes to trap and channel the Nile's floodwaters for irrigation. They also created thousands of new acres of farmland by draining the swamps of Lower Egypt. Harvests were again plentiful; peasants could enjoy a daily diet of bread and beer. One king of this period boasted,

> I was one who cultivated grain and loved the harvest god. The Nile greeted me and every valley. None was hungry in my years, none thirsted then. Men dwelt in peace through that which I wrought, and conversed of me.

Afterlife for commoners During this period, new religious beliefs also showed the increased importance of the common people. During the Old Kingdom, only the pharaoh had expected to live forever. During the Middle Kingdom, Egyptians came to believe that ordinary people had eternal souls as well. People of all classes planned for their burials, so that their place in the afterlife would be assured. This new belief took away some of the pharaoh's grandeur.

The Hyksos ruled during the Second Illness.

The prosperity of the Middle Kingdom did not last. A period known as the Second Illness ravaged the land for about 70 years. Civil war broke out again, leaving Egypt prey to enemies from outside the country. Invaders swept across the Isthmus of Suez into Egypt in horse-drawn chariots. The conquerors were Asian nomads known as the Hyksos (HIHK-sahs), which meant "the rulers of the uplands." They ruled much of Egypt from 1640 to 1570 B.C.

The proud Egyptians despised their less civilized rulers. However, the Egyptians learned several important new skills from the Hyksos. They learned how to make bronze, which was a harder metal than the copper they had used in the past for tools and weapons. They learned to wage war from horse-drawn chariots, shooting arrows from a powerful new kind of bow. And they learned new techniques in the gentler arts of spinning and weaving.

Around 1600 B.C., a series of warlike rulers began to restore Egypt's power. Among those who helped drive out the Hyksos was Queen Ahhotep (ah-HOH-tep), who took over when her husband died in battle. The inscriptions say of her, "She has pacified Upper Egypt and cast out its rebels."

The next pharaoh, Kamose (kah-MOH-suh), won a great victory over the hated Hyksos. Afterward, he described the battle this way:

The benefits and drawbacks of a strong central government are recurring issues in history. Discussion on that topic might begin here and be renewed in later chapters on the fall of Rome, feudal Europe, dynastic change in China, and dictatorships in modern times.

*When day broke I pounced on the foe like
a falcon; at breakfast time I attacked him,
I broke down his walls, I slew his people,
I captured his women. My soldiers were
as lions with the spoils of the enemy; slaves,
flocks, fat and honey. They shared out their
property with merry heart.*

Kamose's successors drove the Hyksos completely
out of Egypt and pursued them across the Sinai
Peninsula into Palestine.

The New Kingdom was an age of empire.

Egypt now entered its third period of power
and glory, the New Kingdom (1570–1075 B.C.).
The kingdom was wealthier and more powerful
than ever before. The buildings were larger and
more lavishly decorated. (This was the period
when Tutankhamon's tomb, with its wealth of
gold, was built.) Showiness was the fashion
throughout Egypt. Yet the art and architecture
of the New Kingdom were not as creative nor
as carefully crafted as in earlier periods.

The Egyptian empire The invasion of the
Hyksos had shaken the Egyptians' confidence in
the deserts as natural barriers for protecting the
country. The pharaohs of the New Kingdom set
out to strengthen Egypt by building an empire.

Equipped with bronze weapons and two-
wheeled chariots, the Egyptians became conquerors themselves. The warlike pharaohs of the
Eighteenth Dynasty (1570–1365 B.C.) set up a
professional army including bowmen, charioteers,
and infantry. The symbols of royal power had
always been the red crown and the white crown.
Now the pharaohs added a new piece of royal
headgear—the blue crown, a war crown shaped
like a battle helmet.

Rule by a queen Among the rulers of the New
Kingdom, perhaps the most surprising was Hatshepsut (hat-SHEP-soot). This remarkable woman
was one of Tutankhamon's ancestors. Although
Egypt had several strong queens who wielded
power through their fathers, sons, or husbands,
custom decreed that the pharaoh be male. Nonetheless, Hatshepsut declared herself pharaoh
around 1478 B.C., while her stepson, Thutmose
(thoot-MOH-suh), was a mere child. On special
occasions, she donned a man's kilt and attached

*This statue of Hatshepsut shows her wearing the
ceremonial beard of a pharoah. Tutankhamon's
golden mask (page 47) has a similar beard.*

the pharaoh's long, braided, ceremonial beard to
her chin.

Hatshepsut ruled boldly for 22 years. Unlike
most New Kingdom rulers, she was better known
for encouraging trade than for waging war. Carved
scenes on her great funeral temple show her
officials on a trade expedition to the east African
coast, buying myrrh, frankincense, ebony, ivory,
and leopard skins.

Hatshepsut's death is still a mystery to historians. No one knows whether she died naturally
or was murdered by her stepson, the impatient-
to-rule Thutmose III.

A warrior pharaoh Thutmose III proved to be
a more warlike ruler than his stepmother. Between the time he took power around 1450 B.C.
and his death in 1425 B.C., he conducted 15 victorious invasions into Palestine and Syria. In addition, his armies pushed south as far as the
Fourth Cataract and returned to Thebes with
thousands of Nubian slaves.

The Jews were made slaves during the New Kingdom. The use of slaves drove down
the value of free labor. For the first time, a wide gap divided rich and poor in Egypt.
Help students understand the economic principle of supply and demand.

55

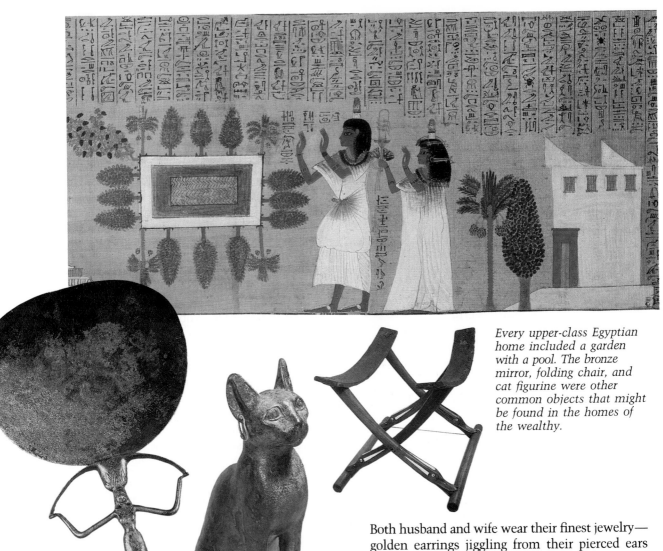

Every upper-class Egyptian home included a garden with a pool. The bronze mirror, folding chair, and cat figurine were other common objects that might be found in the homes of the wealthy.

Both husband and wife wear their finest jewelry—golden earrings jiggling from their pierced ears and broad necklaces glittering with dozens of multicolored gems.

Servants bring in the food—bowls of figs, slabs of bread, platters of roasted duck and lamb. Everyone eats with their fingers and drinks wine from glass goblets. A harpist plays soft music in the background.

Social mobility Most of the wealthy Egyptians who led such pleasant lives had been born as nobles. Some, however, had been born to families of artisans or small shopkeepers. Still others had been born in families of peasant farmers or even slaves.

The way to rise in Egypt was through the pharaoh's service, especially through the army. A soldier who showed courage in battle might win a cash reward, called "the gold of valor." In

visible. You enter through the main gate and cross an open courtyard to the garden where the children are chasing one another around a rectangular pool. Since the children are all under 12 years old, they wear no clothing. Both boys and girls wear golden ornaments around their necks, and the girls wear strings of beads around their waists.

Inside the house, the host and hostess greet you. Their clothes are made of soft, sheer cotton.

58

Egyptian houses were not lavish, even among upper classes, because the Egyptians considered their tombs to be more important than their homes.

time, he might become an officer. After a lifetime of service in the pharaoh's army, he would be rewarded with a small farm, livestock, and some peasants to work his land for him. His sons and grandsons could hold this land as their own, as long as one man in the family continued to serve in the army.

To win the highest posts, either in the army or in the government, people had to be able to read and write. Thus, most high positions went to people who had been born into families wealthy enough to send their children to school. But even humble village scribes taught their own children and perhaps some of their friends' children. In Egypt, unlike Sumer, girls as well as boys were permitted to study to become scribes. Once a person had the skill to read and write, many careers were open in the army, the royal treasury, the priesthood, and the pharaoh's court.

Peasants led a life of toil.

We know less about the peasants of Egypt than about the upper classes. Since the peasants' everyday lives were not considered very important, scribes recorded little about them. Most information about peasant life comes from wall paintings in tombs.

Those paintings show that peasants worked hard and had few comforts. Planting, cultivating, and harvesting in the hot sun were grueling work. Women worked beside men in the fields. Peasants did not even own the land they farmed. The land belonged to the pharaoh and was parceled out by royal officials. These officials hauled away a large share of the harvest as taxes.

Although farming was not possible during the flood season, this time of year rarely brought rest for the peasants. Instead, peasant men—and sometimes women—were called to work on the pharaoh's latest project. A tomb, dike, or canal required many workers.

Nonetheless, it seems that the peasants managed to enjoy life. They were usually left with enough to eat even after taxes. In this respect, they were better off than artisans such as toolmakers and jewelers, who might go hungry during hard times when no one needed their services. Peasants found time for music and games, and they sometimes joined their overseers in a great feast to celebrate the harvest. However, while the rich drank wine, peasants drank barley beer.

Daily Life · *Egyptian Cosmetics*

The dramatic, dark-lined eyes that look out at us from the artwork of ancient Egypt were the height of fashion 3,000 years ago. However, the dark lining was not just a beauty aid. It also softened the glare of the brilliant desert sun. The makeup, called *kohl,* was made from powdered stone—malachite for dark green and galena for black—mixed with water. Men and women applied it to their eyes with small sticks.

Oils were a key ingredient of many other cosmetics the Egyptians used. Some oils came from animal fats, and others were pressed from plant seeds. The Egyptians mixed oil with powdered red ocher (a kind of iron ore) to make lipstick, which they applied with a brush. They steeped flowers and fragrant woods in oil and rubbed the oil into their skin. Sometimes they decked their hairdos with cones of scented oil, which melted slowly in the heat. Like the eye makeup, these fragrant oils had a practical use. They protected skin, lips, and hair from the dry desert air. This glass fish at the right held sweet-smelling oil, and the other container held kohl.

Bring to class a book of Egyptian art. Have students speculate on the practical reasons for the Egyptians' appearance and home furnishings (e.g., style and color of clothing, importance of garden and pool, and so on).

59

Slaves were the lowest class.

Until the time of the New Kingdom, peasants made up the lowest class in Egypt. Then, during the New Kingdom's wars of conquest, thousands of slaves were brought to Egypt from Asia and Nubia, a land to the south of Egypt.

The most fortunate slaves worked in the homes of the rich. They perfomed every kind of service for their wealthy masters—giving them baths, combing their hair, cooking meals, watching their children, feeding their cattle. Through loyal service to a priest or noble, house slaves could hope someday to be granted their freedom.

Other slaves were not so lucky. Whole families of slaves were sent into the mountains of Upper Egypt to work in the gold mines. Often they felt

During the New Kingdom, slavery became common in Egypt. Many slaves were war captives. This slave is carrying a heavy cauldron.

the stinging lash of the overseer's whip. Men, women, and children dropped from exhaustion. According to one account,

> *There is no forgiveness or relaxation at all for the sick, or the maimed, or the old . . . but all with blows are compelled to stick to their labor until, worn out, they die in their servitude.*

Religion taught fairness and hope.

Laws did not forbid Egyptians to mistreat their slaves. However, Egyptian religion taught that it was morally wrong to do so. The Egyptians used the word **maat** (muh-AHT) to speak of the virtues of a good life. Maat was the idea of justice, right, truth, and order. To live according to maat meant always trying to act rightly and justly. Everyone, including the pharaoh, was supposed to uphold this ideal. The idea of maat influenced even the god-king's behavior.

Judgment by Osiris Egyptians believed they would be judged for their deeds when they died. Osiris (oh-SY-rihs), the powerful god of the dead, would weigh each dead person's heart. To win eternal life, the heart could be no heavier than a feather. Each soul was required to come before the great judge, Osiris, and say something like this:

> *Hail to Thee, Great God, Lord of Truth and Justice . . . I have not committed inequity against men. I have not oppressed the poor . . . I have not laid labor upon any free man beyond that which he wrought for himself . . . I have not defaulted, I have not committed that which is an abomination to the gods. I have not caused the slave to be ill-treated of his master . . .*

If the heart tipped the scale, showing that the person was lying, a fierce beast known as the Devourer of Souls would pounce on the impure heart and gobble it up. But if the soul passed this demanding test for purity and truth, it could live forever.

Scenes painted on the walls of tombs showed how Egyptians imagined their future life. Souls journeyed by boat to a pleasant, fertile land, much like Egypt itself. Children in the underworld would still quarrel and pull one another's hair.

Have students compare the Egyptian views of good and bad as expressed in the statement quoted above with the Hebrew and Mesopotamian views of morality.

A priest who has apparently suffered from polio brings an offering to the altar of a goddess. An attendant follows him.

A challenge to tradition Around 1375 B.C., one pharaoh dared to challenge Egypt's religious traditions and also the power of the priests. The name of this bold pharaoh was Akhenaton (AH-kuh-NAH-tuhn).

When the sun rose every morning in the Egyptian sky, Akhenaton worshiped it as a god. This was nothing new. The sun had always been worshiped by Egyptians as one of their many gods. However, Akhenaton made the new and shocking claim that this sun-god, Aton, was the only true god in all the universe. Perhaps the pharaoh truly believed this claim, or perhaps his goal was to lessen the priests' power.

Akhenaton did everything in his power to convert Egyptian religion from polytheism to monotheism. He ordered the religious cults that worshiped the cat-god, the crocodile-god, the baboon-god, and all the other gods to shut down their temples and worship only Aton.

Peasants would still drive oxen over the fields. The rich would continue to enjoy banquets. Nothing would be changed.

The power of the priests What hope was there for those Egyptians who had committed just one mistake—perhaps stealing a jar of grain? How could their souls escape the snapping jaws of the Devourer? They believed their only hope was to employ the services of a priest. Egypt's priests specialized in magical charms and chants to protect both the living and the dead from troubles of all kinds. Many of these prayers were recorded in a text known as the *Book of the Dead*, which was placed in the dead person's coffin.

Because Egyptians believed that their priests could influence the gods with their magic, priests had enormous power and prestige. In fact, in the New Kingdom, the priests probably controlled more land, more slaves, and more wealth than the pharaoh himself.

Akhenaton (right) was the first pharoah to encourage artists to make realistic likenesses of him, rather than idealized, godlike figures. The statue of his wife, Nefertiti (above), is famed for its classic beauty. Many paintings show the couple and their children in everyday family life.

Whatever the motives of Akhenaton, his attempt to impose monotheism from above died with him. In contrast, where monotheism was a truly popular movement with widespread support, as among the Hebrews, it survived all attempts at suppression.

61

Above all, people were commanded to stop worshiping Amon, god of air, wind, and the breath of life. The huge temples around Thebes were all dedicated to Amon. The high priests of Amon were the most powerful rulers in Egypt next to the pharaoh himself. Akhenaton ordered that all the offerings and taxes that had poured into Amon's temples now go to Aton's treasury. Naturally, the priests of Amon were furious.

Workers with chisels and hammers were sent all over Egypt to smash the name of Amon wherever it appeared. The pharaoh changed his own name, originally *Amon*hotep, to Akhen*aton*, meaning "He who serves Aton." Akhenaton then moved the royal capital from Thebes to a new city, which he named Akhet*aton*, "the Place of Aton's Power."

However, many Egyptians refused to abandon their old gods. They defied the pharaoh's laws by secretly worshiping Amon, Osiris, and their other favorites.

When Akhenaton died in 1362 B.C., the priests of Amon regained their power. The new pharaoh, who was only eight or nine years old, took the name Tutankh*amon*, moved the capital back to Thebes, and ordered the names and images of Aton to be destroyed. As a reward, when Tutankhamon died, the priests packed his tomb with the golden treasures that Howard Carter found nearly 3,300 years later.

Egyptians studied many subjects.

The breadth and richness of Egypt's culture impressed early visitors from Greece, Persia, and Mesopotamia. Even then, Egypt gave an impression of great age and secret wisdom that awed travelers from other lands. In many fields, Egypt richly deserved its reputation for knowledge.

Writing Crude pictographs had been the earliest form of writing in Egypt, but scribes quickly developed a better system. For most of ancient Egypt's history, scribes used a form of writing that we call **hieroglyphics** (HY-er-oh-GLIF-ihks). This term comes from the Greek words *hieros* and *glyphe*, meaning "sacred carving."

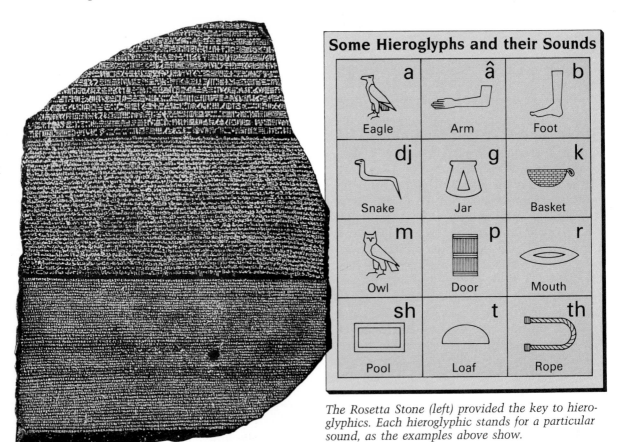

Some Hieroglyphs and their Sounds

a — Eagle	â — Arm	b — Foot
dj — Snake	g — Jar	k — Basket
m — Owl	p — Door	r — Mouth
sh — Pool	t — Loaf	th — Rope

The Rosetta Stone (left) provided the key to hieroglyphics. Each hieroglyphic stands for a particular sound, as the examples above show.

Like other ancients, Egyptians based their measuring system on body parts. A *cubit* was the distance from elbow to fingertips, with the pharoah's arm as the standard. The royal *foot* was also a measure. The Romans adopted this system.

Soon after Egypt's decline, the ability to read hieroglyphics was lost and remained so for 15 centuries. In 1799, near the delta village of Rosetta, some French soldiers found a polished black stone inscribed with a message in three languages. One version was written in hieroglyphics, another was in a simpler form of hieroglyphics, and the third was in Greek. Ancient Greek was a well-known language, yet deciphering the hieroglyphics on the Rosetta Stone still took many years of work. A young Frenchman named Jean François Champollion (shahm-pohl-YAWN) became fascinated by hieroglyphics when he was only a child. By the time he was 16, he had mastered 8 ancient languages. In 1822, at the age of 32, he finally broke the code of the hieroglyphics.

Although hieroglyphics were first written on stone and clay, the Egyptians soon invented a better writing surface. They used the tall stalks of papyrus (puh-PY-ruhs), a reed that grew in the marshy delta. The Egyptians split the reeds into narrow strips, soaked them, and then pressed them into sheets of paperlike material. (The English word *paper* comes from *papyrus*.) Egypt's dry climate preserved papyrus for centuries. Modern scholars can still read writings that are more than 5,000 years old.

Numbers The government of Egypt needed a way of doing arithmetic for the purpose of assessing and collecting taxes. Out of this need, Egyptians invented a system of written numbers for counting, adding, and subtracting. The system was fairly clumsy for numbers greater than 100. To express the figure 999, a scribe had to write 27 symbols. (On the other hand, to express 1 million required only one symbol—a picture of a man striking his hands above his head as if to say, "How in the world could there be such a big number?")

Geometry and surveying One job of the pharaoh's officials was to assign plots of land to peasant families. Because of the Nile's flooding, this job had to be redone every year. The floodwaters wiped out all previous boundaries, and the land had to be measured and marked again. To save time and expense, Egyptians invented an efficient mathematical system for surveying and measuring areas. This method was the origin of geometry.

A calendar To be sure of a good crop, peasants needed to plant at exactly the right time of year. Crops had to be ripe and harvested before the next flood. Therefore, the Egyptians developed a calendar to keep track of the time between floods. Officials had observed that a very bright star, now known as Sirius, began to appear above the eastern horizon just before the floods came. The time between one rising of Sirius and the next was 365 days. They divided this year into 12 months of 30 days each and added 5 days for holidays and feasting. This calendar was so accurate that it fell short of the true solar year by only six hours.

Medicine Egyptian doctors were the most famous in the ancient world. Their medical services were in demand at royal courts in many kingdoms around the Mediterranean Sea. Although Egyptian medical writings contain all sorts of magic charms and chants, Egyptian doctors also had much practical knowledge. They knew how to check a person's heart rate by feeling for a pulse in different parts of the body. They dealt with broken bones, wounds, and fevers. All in all, they approached their study of medicine in a remarkably scientific way.

Section Review 3

Define: (a) maat, (b) hieroglyphics, (c) papyrus
Identify: (a) Osiris, (b) Akhenaton, (c) Aton, (d) Amon, (e) Tutankhamon, (f) Rosetta Stone, (g) Champollion
Answer:
1. (a) What kinds of work might a noble do in ancient Egypt? (b) A peasant?
2. What beliefs influenced the morals of people in ancient Egypt?
3. How was the ability to read hieroglyphics regained in modern times after having been lost for 15 centuries?
4. (a) What practical need led the Egyptians to invent a system of numbers? (b) A branch of mathematics that formed the basis for modern geometry? (c) A calendar?

Critical Thinking
5. As god-kings, Egypt's pharaohs might have ruled through terror, but generally they did not. What attitudes and beliefs in Egypt acted as a check on the pharaohs?

Summary

1. The Nile River shaped Egyptian Life. The Nile River flooded every year, leaving a blanket of rich soil on Egypt's land. The dependability of this pattern made Egypt an excellent farmland. Farming villages flourished as early as 6000 B.C., protected from invasion by the surrounding deserts. Eventually, groups of villages united to form small kingdoms. In 3100 B.C., all of Egypt was united under King Menes.

2. Egypt's pharaohs ruled as gods. Egypt's pharaohs were considered divine and immortal. Over the years, periods of weakness (known as "illnesses") alternated with periods of strength for Egypt. Around 1200 B.C., a wave of invasions began, leading to a decline from which ancient Egypt never recovered.

3. Egypt's way of life endured 3,000 years. Egyptian society was divided into social classes. Upper-class people generally held government jobs and lived in luxury. Peasants did the farming, and slaves served the rich. Egyptians of all classes were polytheists. Egyptian religion emphasized *maat,* or justice. Those who lived according to maat could expect eternal life in the afterworld. Among the Egyptians' cultural achievements were a system of writing and mathematics and a highly accurate calendar. They were also skilled in the field of medicine.

Reviewing the Facts

1. Define the following terms:
   a. cataract
   b. delta
   c. dynasty
   d. pharaoh
   e. pyramid
   f. maat
   g. hieroglyphics
2. Explain the importance of each of the following names, places, or terms:
   a. Upper Egypt
   b. Lower Egypt
   c. Nile River
   d. Isthmus of Suez
   e. Menes
   f. Hyksos
   g. Hatshepsut
   h. Thutmose III
   i. Ramses II
   j. Peoples of the Sea
   k. Osiris
   l. Akhenaton
   m. Tutankhamon
   n. Champollion
3. How did the Nile's yearly cycle affect life in ancient Egypt?
4. (a) Describe the powers of the Egyptian pharaohs. (b) How was the pharaoh different from a Mesopotamian king?
5. (a) Describe the main groups that made up Egyptian society. (b) What skills were necessary for an Egyptian to move up in society?
6. What were some of the basic beliefs of Egyptian religion?
7. List some of the Egyptians' scientific achievements.

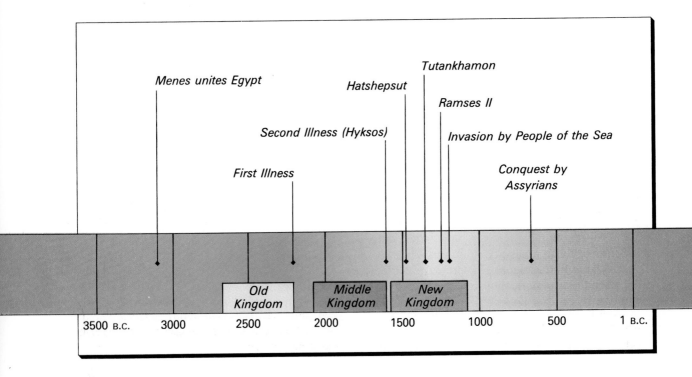

Menes unites Egypt

Hatshepsut

Tutankhamon

Ramses II

Second Illness (Hyksos)

Invasion by People of the Sea

First Illness

Conquest by Assyrians

Old Kingdom

Middle Kingdom

New Kingdom

| 3500 B.C. | 3000 | 2500 | 2000 | 1500 | 1000 | 500 | 1 B.C. |

Basic Skills

1. **Using map symbols** On the map on page 49, locate a pyramid, temple, mine, stone quarry, and cataract.
2. **Identifying directions** (a) In what general direction does the Nile flow? (b) Where is the Valley of the Kings in relation to the Nile Delta? The Second Cataract? The temples of Karnak and Luxor?
3. **Creating a time line** Make a time line for ancient Egypt and Mesopotamia, starting with 2500 B.C. and ending with 500 B.C. Divide the line into five segments. Place these events above the time line, using a pointer to the correct date: Old kingdom pyramids are built; Tutankhamon is buried; Assyrians conquer Egypt. Add these items below the line, using a pointer to the correct date: Sumerian era ends; Hammurabi rules; Babylonians conquer Jerusalem.
4. **Identifying supporting details** Give examples from the political, religious, and economic life of Egypt to support the idea that the Nile River shaped Egyptian life.

Researching and Reporting Skills

1. **Using the encyclopedia** Many historians question whether Akhenaton was sincere in his monotheistic beliefs or whether he had other reasons for wanting his subjects to give up their many gods. Look up articles about Akhenaton in two different encyclopedias. To what extent is the information in the articles similar or different?
2. **Summarizing** Summarize what each article says about Akhenaton's monotheism and the reasons behind it.
3. **Developing a bibliography** Locate three books that discuss the technology that made construction of the pyramids possible. List bibliographical information about these books—including author, title, publisher, date of publication, and the relevant page numbers.

Critical Thinking

1. **Inferring** What influence may the Nile cataracts have had on contacts between Egypt and the lands to the south?
2. **Drawing conclusions** What does the discussion of apparel and cosmetics in this chapter suggest about values in Egyptian society?
3. **Analyzing art** Study the paintings on pages 51 and 58. (a) Describe the way Egyptian artists painted human figures. (b) Compare the style of sculptures shown in this chapter to that of the paintings. What similarities and differences do you find?
4. **Interpreting** (a) Compare the relative location of Egypt and Mesopotamia. (b) How might that location have contributed to the stability of government in Egypt and the change in Mesopotamia?
5. **Comparing** Priests held positions of power in both Sumer and Egypt. (a) Compare the extent of that power in those civilizations. (b) What were the reasons for that power in each case?
6. **Evaluating** Sumer and Egypt both made important contributions to civilization. (a) List the major contributions made by each. (b) Which contribution of each civilization do you consider most important? Give reasons for your answer.

Perspectives on Past and Present

1. Some cultures stress the importance of continuity, using words such as *tradition, time-honored,* and *customary.* Other cultures emphasize the value of change, using words such as *progress, modern,* and *up-to-date* to describe it. (a) Compare the attitudes of ancient Egyptian society toward change with those of society today. Give examples to illustrate your answer. (b) What factors might account for any differences?
2. (a) Describe the position of women in the society of ancient Egypt. (b) Compare this position with that of women in society today.

Investigating History

1. (a) Find out how Champollion succeeded in deciphering the hieroglyphics on the Rosetta Stone. (b) What was the significance of his work?
2. The opening of Tutankhamon's tomb revealed a great variety of treasures. In books on Egyptian art, find out what kinds of treasures were found.
3. Rock paintings in the Sahara indicate that at one time that region had rich grasslands. (a) Find out information about the rock paintings. (b) What can you conclude from them about people's way of life? (c) What climate changes occurred that caused the desert to form?

Ancient India and China

The jagged peaks of the Himalayas dwarf the Buddhist monastery that stands amid them.

Key Terms

subcontinent
monsoon
reincarnation
caste
edict

Read and Understand

1. A new culture arose in northern India.
2. Buddhism spread under Mauryan rulers.
3. Imperial government united China.
4. Ch'in and Han emperors strengthened China.

The two wisest teachers of ancient India and China never heard of each other. The highest, most formidable mountain barrier in the world—the Himalayas (HIH-muh-LAY-uhz)—separated their two civilizations. Yet, by an odd coincidence, these two influential thinkers of ancient Asia were seeking the same goal at nearly the same time. Their common goal was to find wisdom and to know the truth about life. Born within a few years of each other, both wisdom seekers were probably in the prime of life about 525 B.C.

On the southern side of the Himalayas lived Siddhartha Gautama (sih-DAHR-tuh GAW-tuh-muh), later known as the Buddha. The Buddha preached his first sermon to five companions. They were so astonished

Many modern scholars assert that the traditional date of the Buddha's birth is too early and that a correct date would be about 100 years later.

by his wise and gentle words that they exclaimed: "Truly, O Buddha, Our Lord, thou has found the truth!" Thousands of Indians agreed and became his devoted followers.

At the same time, in China, a teacher named Confucius (kuhn-FYOO-shuhs) wandered from village to village offering lessons in wisdom to any family that served him a meal. Young students began writing down his witty replies to their questions. Where, they asked, could you find a perfectly wise person? Confucius said: "I do not expect to find a saint today. But if I find a gentleman, I shall be quite satisfied."

What did it mean to have wisdom? To be wise, said Confucius, was to respect your elders and rulers so that families and kingdoms could live in harmony. The Buddha, on the other hand, said that wisdom lay in giving up all selfish desires so that your soul might escape the pain of life and death. Confucius and the Buddha followed different paths to wisdom in part because each man expressed the ideas of his own civilization. This chapter tells the story of the two remarkable cultures that grew up on either side of the world's highest mountains.

A *new culture arose in northern India.*   1

A great landmass lies between the Himalayan Mountains and the Indian Ocean. Today that region includes the countries of India, Pakistan, and Bangladesh. Historically, however, this land has been divided many different ways. Therefore, when speaking of ancient times, historians generally refer to the entire region as India.

India's outline resembles a diamond-shaped kite. To the north (at the top of the imaginary kite), two mountain chains—the Hindu Kush on the west and the Himalayas on the east—meet at a point. This great wall of mountains separates India from the rest of Asia. As a result, India is sometimes called a **subcontinent** of Asia. Though rugged, the mountains are not impassable. Mountain passes like the 34-mile-long Khyber Pass have been used since prehistoric times by migrants and invaders coming into India.

South of the Himalayas lies an enormous flat and fertile plain formed by two rivers—the Indus River and the Ganges (GAN-jeez) River. These two rivers and the lands they water make up a large arc that stretches 2,000 miles across northern India. This arc is called the Indus-Ganges plain. Because the land is flat, easy to irrigate, and very fertile, this plain has always been the rich heartland of India.

The southern part of the Indian subcontinent (the bottom of the imaginary kite) is a peninsula that thrusts south into the Indian Ocean. The center of the peninsula is a high plateau cut by twisting rivers; this region is called the Deccan (DEK-uhn). Covered by dense forests or scrubby grasses, the Deccan is a harsh land.

A narrow border of lush, tropical land lies along the coasts of southern India. This coastal rim has a wet climate and rich soil. Valuable forests of teak and fragrant sandalwood grow there.

Throughout history, southern India often has been a land apart. Its culture remains very different from that of northern India, even though the two regions are united in one country today.

India's climate is dominated by seasonal winds called **monsoons**. From October to May, winter monsoons from the northeast blow dry air across the country. Then, in the middle of June, the winds shift. Spring monsoons blow from the southwest, carrying moisture from the ocean in great rain clouds. The people of India depend on these monsoons for rain to water their crops of wheat, rice, and cotton. If there is too little rain, plants wither in the fields and people go hungry. If there is too much rain, floods may sweep away whole villages. This climate pattern has shaped life for India's farmers since prehistoric times.

Cities flourished in the Indus valley.

India's first civilization developed on the rich plains of the northern subcontinent. The Indus River flows southwest from the Himalayas through what is now Pakistan. Like the Nile, the Tigris, and the Euphrates rivers, the Indus flooded each year. At each flood, the Indus spread a layer of rich silt across its valley, providing good soil for farming.

Well-planned cities Around 2500 B.C., while Egyptians were building the pyramids, people in

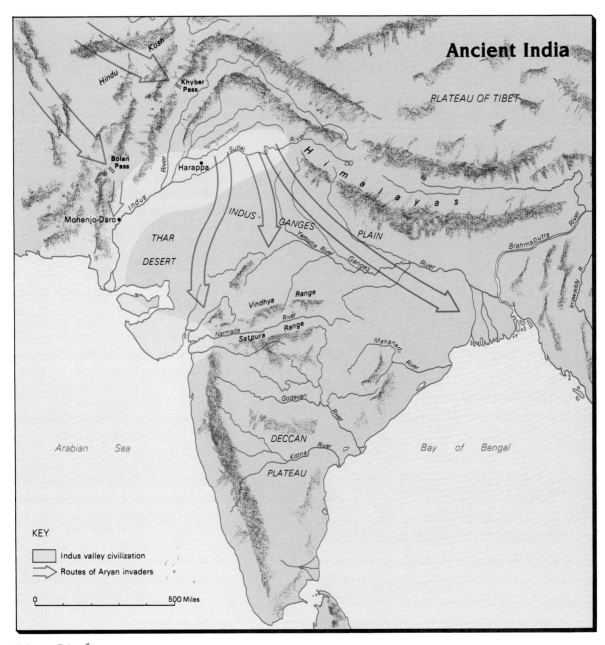

Map Study

From what mountain range does the Ganges River flow? Describe the route by which the Aryan invaders arrived in India.

the Indus valley were laying the bricks for India's first cities. Archaeologists have found the ruins of about 100 settlements along the Indus.

The largest cities were Harappa (huh-**RAP**-uh) and Mohenjo-Daro (moh-**HEHN**-joh-**DAHR**-oh). Each city had a population of roughly 30,000. Although these two cities were 350 miles apart, they were remarkably alike. Each was laid out neatly, with streets running north-south and east-west like a grid. Their mighty walls were built with oven-fired bricks, all of a standard size. To archaeologists, this regular pattern of building suggests that the cities were carefully planned by a strong central government.

68   Because the bricks were oven-fired (rather than sun-baked like those in the Fertile Crescent), the walls of these ancient cities have not crumbled, even though they have been buried in river mud for centuries.

The fine brickwork of Mohenjo-Daro shows in a pool for ritual bathing (left). Cattle such as the one shown on the seal (above) are still common in India today.

Many kinds of specialized buildings lay within the two cities. Each had huge public storehouses for grain, an arrangement that suggests a well-organized government. One large building in Mohenjo-Daro was clearly a bathhouse, with a great brick tub about the size of a swimming pool. Shops lay along main streets.

Housing Dozens of tiny, branching alleys ran off the wide main streets. The doors to people's homes opened out onto these mazelike alleys. Few windows looked out on the street, however. For fresh air, families went to inner courtyards or up stairways to their rooftops. Houses might be two or even three stories high.

The cities of the Indus valley show more concern with cleanliness and sanitation than any other cities of their time. Many houses had brick-floored bathing rooms from which dirty water drained through clay pipes into gutters. Citizens of Mohenjo-Daro disposed of their garbage through narrow slits conveniently cut into the walls of their houses. The garbage fell into containers neatly lined up on the street below.

Everyday life Most people lived by farming. They raised wheat, barley, and perhaps rice for food. They also grew cotton to make cloth. The Indus valley settlers had domesticated cattle, sheep, goats, pigs, and fowl as well as cats and dogs. Some scholars think they may also have tamed elephants.

Next to agriculture, trade was the most important source of prosperity. The Indus valley

city dwellers left hundreds of small clay seals that merchants probably used to mark shipments of goods. Some of these seals have also been found in the ruins of ancient Mesopotamia. Apparently the merchants of Mohenjo-Daro and the merchants of Ur exchanged goods. Perhaps they exchanged ideas as well.

The people of the Indus valley cities worked at a variety of crafts. Archaeologists have found kilns for pottery, vats for dyeing cloth, and many different kinds of metal, including gold, silver, copper, bronze, and lead.

Archaeologists have also turned up relics of everyday pleasures. Little cubes stamped with dots on each side indicate that these early city dwellers enjoyed rolling dice. Children amused themselves with wheeled pull toys made of clay.

A child from Mohenjo-Daro pulled this toy ram.

Have students compare the cities in ancient India with those in Egypt at the same time. Point out that although metalwork, beads, and pottery have been found in India, there are few examples of sculpture besides those associated with the bathhouse.

69

The decline of the Indus valley civilization

Around 1750 B.C., the quality of building in the Indus valley cities became poorer. Mohenjo-Daro grew less and less prosperous. Gradually, the great cities fell into decay.

What happened? Some historians think that the Indus River changed course, as it has been known to do, so that its floods no longer fertilized the fields near the cities. Other scholars suggest that people wore out the valley's land. They overgrazed it, allowing their cattle and goats to eat the ground nearly bare. They overfarmed it, growing the same crops year after year. They overcut its trees, brush, and grass to build their houses and provide fuel for their cooking fires and kilns.

As the Indus valley civilization neared its end, around 1500 B.C., human enemies may have had a hand in the cities' downfall. A half-dozen groups of skeletons were found in the latest ruins of Mohenjo-Daro. Bones of men, women, and children lie together where they fell, seemingly never buried. Two skulls show injuries from a sword or axe. These signs of violence suggest that the city, already weakened by its slow decline, may have been abandoned after a devastating attack. Many historians believe the enemies were newcomers from the north side of the Himalayas.

Aryans moved in from the northwest.

Around 1500 B.C., nomads from central Asia trudged across the Khyber Pass and into the Indus valley. Some of the newcomers called themselves Aryans (AIR-ee-uhnz), which in their language meant "the nobles." Other central Asian groups, whose names and languages are unknown to us, probably drifted into India at the same time.

The newcomers were very different from the people they conquered. For one thing, the Indus valley people lived in cities and were chiefly farmers, artisans, and merchants. The Aryans were nomadic herders who counted their wealth in cattle. The Aryans did not move into the cities they conquered, but left them abandoned. It would be many years before the Aryans became city dwellers. Another major difference was that the Indus valley people were literate. The Aryans had no writing system. Instead, their priests preserved their culture from generation to generation by memorizing long hymns and poems. These poems were in the Aryan language, an early form of Sanskrit. Sanskrit remains a learned and sacred language in India today.

To escape the Aryans, some of the Indus valley people may have fled southward across the Vindhya (VIHN-dee-uh) Mountains to the Deccan. To this day, the people of southern India speak a different group of languages, known as the Dravidian language family.

Not all the Indus valley dwellers fled, however. Many remained as slaves to the newcomers. Although they were conquered, the people of the Indus valley had a lasting influence on Indian culture. Between 1500 and 500 B.C., a new society took shape in northern India. The cultures of the Indus valley dwellers and the Aryans blended into a uniquely Indian civilization. One product of that blending was the religion known today as Hinduism.

Hinduism shaped India's culture.

Hindu practices grew from the mingled beliefs of many groups in India. Figurines from the Indus valley seem to show early examples of some gods that were later important to Hindus. However, the earliest records of Hinduism—the long Sanskrit hymns that the priests memorized—are Aryan.

The Vedic Age When the Aryans migrated to India, they brought a rich collection of myths, or tales of their gods. They had gods of thunder, fire, earth, heaven, the moon, and the sun. Priests made offerings of food and drink to the gods. Everything in nature was believed to be in some way holy.

Footnote to History

Strange as it seems, English is distantly related to Sanskrit. Both are members of a large group of languages called the Indo-European language family. The relationship shows in the roots for some of the most basic words in any language—family terms.

English	Sanskrit
mother	matar
father	pitar
brother	bhratar
sister	svasar
daughter	duhitar
son	sunus

Among the most important Aryan gods was Indra, god of the thunderbolt and a great warrior. In the hymns, Indra is called "destroyer of fortresses" and is said to have torn apart the defenses of a place called Hariyupia, which may have been Harappa.

Aryan priests could sing from memory a great number of long and complicated hymns, each one suited to a different religious ritual. Some of these hymns may date back to 1500 B.C. Priests gathered the hymns into four collections called Vedas (VAY-duhz). The most ancient and important of these collections, the *Rig-Veda*, included 1,028 hymns of praise. It is probably the oldest set of scriptures still in active use. The Vedas were finally written down about A.D. 1400.

Millions of Indians today cherish the Vedas as sacred. Historians cherish them for a different reason. The Vedas are a most important clue to the history of India from 1500 to 500 B.C. This thousand-year period is called the Vedic Age.

The Upanishads Sometime around 400 B.C., the wisest Hindu teachers tried to interpret and explain the hidden meaning of the Vedic hymns. They discussed such questions as these: What is the nature of reality? What is morality? Is there eternal life? What is the soul? The teachers' comments were memorized by their students and later written down as a collection of essays known as the Upanishads (oo-PAN-ih-shadz). Most of our knowledge about Hindu beliefs comes from these writings. Here are the basic ideas expressed in the Upanishads.

1. The one true reality is Brahman, the mighty spirit that creates and destroys. Brahman reveals itself in millions of earthly shapes, from a mountain to a raindrop. Brahman is One, and yet expresses itself as Many.

Brahman is a unifying and all-powerful spirit. In European and American society, people tend to believe that human life is totally different from the life of a turtle or a butterfly. No, declares an ancient Hindu text, everything in nature is tied together by Brahman. The ancient text puts it poetically:

Thou art woman. Thou art man. Thou art the dark-blue bee and the green [parrot] with red eyes. Thou hast the lightning as a child. Thou art the seasons and the seas. Thou dost abide with all pervadingness, wherefrom all things are born.

2. One aspect of Brahman is the Self, or Soul, called Atman. Atman can be compared to particles of salt dissolved in a glass of water. You cannot see the salt, yet it is everywhere in the water—just as Atman is everywhere.

Although this painting was done in the 1700's, it celebrates a battle from the Mahabharata, *a great Hindu poem based on events that took place before 1000 B.C.*

3. Nothing that lives ever dies entirely. When a living thing dies, its inner self is reborn in another form. This passing of the inner self from body to body is known as **reincarnation.** To be reincarnated, say the Upanishads, is much like being given a new coat to wear:

Just as a man, having cast off old garments, puts on other, new ones, even so does the embodied one, having cast off old bodies, take on other, new ones.

4. All wise Hindus must seek to reach a state of perfect understanding called *moksha*. The inner self that attains moksha will never suffer another reincarnation. In moksha, the self disappears to merge with Brahman.

Castes structured Indian society.

During the Vedic Age, Indians began to develop a complicated set of divisions between groups of people. These social divisions were closely linked to the Hindu world view.

According to the *Rig-Veda*, four different groups of people had been created from the body of a Hindu god. First, the Brahmins were created from the god's mouth. They later became the priestly class and were the highest group in Indian society. (Note that a member of this class is a *Brahmin*, while the universal spirit is *Brahman*.) The second group, the Kshatriyas (kuh-SHAHT-ree-uhz), came from the god's arms. They were rulers and warriors. Third, the Vaishyas (VYSH-yuhz) were created from the god's legs. They were landowners, merchants, and artisans. The fourth group, the Shudras (SHOO-druhz), came from the god's feet. They were servants or slaves.

In reality, Hindu society was much more complicated than the myth suggested. There were hundreds of different groups, not just four. Over the years, these divisions in society became more and more defined. Eventually, each group had its own occupation, which was passed down from parent to child. People of each group ate only with each other and usually married only within their own group.

Hindus call these groups within their society *jatis*, a word that means "birth group." When Europeans came to India, they called the groups **castes** (kasts), from a Latin word that meant "pure."

Ritual purity was the basis for the ranking of castes. Hindus considered high castes purer than low castes. Priests were considered the purest group. Farmers were thought to be purer than people who make their living washing clothes. To share food or have any contact with a lower-ranking person was to risk contamination.

The very lowest group in society were those people outside the caste system—the outcastes or untouchables. Even lower than servants, untouchables could not so much as draw water from a caste well, lest their touch contaminate the water. They had to use separate wells or wait for a higher-ranking person to get water for them.

Why was one person born a Brahmin while another was born an untouchable? Hinduism explained it by saying that Brahmins, in former lives, had committed no bad deeds. An untouchable, on the other hand, must have done bad deeds in an earlier incarnation.

Hindus believed in an ethical law of cause and effect called *karma*. It operated as automatically as the law of gravity. By the law of karma, moral behavior in one life guaranteed rebirth in a higher caste. Immoral behavior, on the other hand, automatically dropped a reborn soul to a lower caste. Says a Hindu scripture: "Just as he acts, just as he behaves, so he becomes."

To earn a good rebirth, according to Hindu teachings, a person had to be a good member of his or her caste. Each caste had its particular *dharma*, or duty. Dharma is the set of duties and obligations of each caste. For example, a boy born into the warrior caste had to be willing to fight, kill, and be killed. A woman's dharma was to obey her father while she was a child, her husband after she married, and her sons if she was widowed. The individual's own wishes or talents made no difference. According to an ancient Hindu text, it is better to do one's own duty badly than to do another's duty well.

Section Review 1

Define: (a) subcontinent, (b) monsoon, (c) reincarnation, (d) moksha, (e) caste, (f) untouchable, (g) karma, (h) dharma
Identify: (a) Himalayas, (b) Indus River, (c) Harappa and Mohenjo-Daro, (d) Aryans, (e) Hinduism, (f) Vedas, (g) Upanishads, (h) Brahmins, (i) Kshatriyas, (j) Vaishyas, (k) Shudras
Answer:
1. What evidence has led historians to the following beliefs about India's first cities? (a) The cities were run by a strong central government. (b) People of the cities carried on trade with Sumer. (c) The people were skilled in a number of crafts. (d) The cities' downfall may have been caused by a slow decline, followed by an attack from outsiders.
2. How were the people of the Indus valley different from the Aryans who conquered them?
3. (a) Why are the Vedas of religious importance to many Indians? (b) Why are they important to historians?

4. (a) Explain how the ideas of Brahman, moksha, and reincarnation are all related in Hindu beliefs. (b) Explain how the ideas of reincarnation, karma, and caste are related.

Buddhism spread under Mauryan rulers. 2

Around 530 B.C., near the very end of the Vedic Age, a young man named Siddhartha Gautama challenged the ideas of the Brahmin priests. Even a lowborn person, he said, could gain enough wisdom in one lifetime to escape the cycle of death and rebirth.

The Buddha sought an answer to life's pain.

The date traditionally given for Gautama's birth is 563 B.C. The legends of his life are probably exaggerated. The stories say that Gautama was born into the warrior class and lived in luxury at his family's palaces near the foothills of the Himalayas. Pampered by his wealthy family, he never saw pain, suffering, or death. He married a beautiful woman who bore him a son.

Again according to legend, Gautama's comfortable life was shattered one day when he first saw proof of human suffering. While riding in his chariot, Gautama saw a man who was terribly sick, another who was old and feeble, and a third who had died. He realized that life was an endless cycle of pain and the only way to escape it was by seeking wisdom.

One night, when he was about 29, Gautama took a last look at his sleeping wife and son. Then he left his palace and joined a wandering, homeless band of five other wisdom seekers. For six years, Gautama tried to find wisdom through harsh discipline and suffering. For days at a time, he ate only a single grain of rice each day. His stomach became so empty that, by poking a finger into it, he could touch his backbone. Yet Gautama gained only pain, not wisdom. He decided, therefore, to seek wisdom in other ways.

At last, enlightenment came to him. After meditating deeply for many days in the shade

This Buddha on the island of Sri Lanka was cut from solid rock between A.D. 400 and 500.

of a tree, Gautama suddenly felt that the truth became clear to him. He rose and set out to teach others what he had learned. Thereafter, he was known as Buddha, a title meaning "the Enlightened One."

Buddhism taught nonviolence.

Buddha gave his first sermon to the five wisdom seekers who had been his companions. That sermon was a landmark in the history of world religions. Buddha taught the four main ideas that had come to him in his enlightenment, calling them the Four Noble Truths.

First Noble Truth Everything in life is suffering and sorrow.

Second Noble Truth The cause of all this pain is people's self-centered cravings and desires. People seek pleasure that cannot last and leads only to rebirth and more suffering.

Third Noble Truth The way to end all pain is to end all desires.

Also according to legend, Gautama's father had heard a prophecy that his son would lead a religion if he ever saw misery.

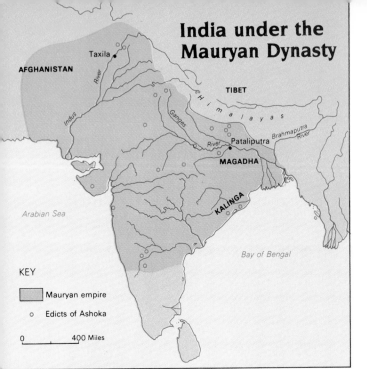

India under the Mauryan Dynasty

TIBET

AFGHANISTAN

Taxila

Indus River

Himalayas

Ganges River

Patliputra

Brahmaputra River

MAGADHA

KALINGA

Arabian Sea

Bay of Bengal

KEY

Mauryan empire

o Edicts of Ashoka

0   400 Miles

Map Study

Describe the extent of Ashoka's empire. What part of India remained outside his control?

Fourth Noble Truth People can overcome their desires and attain enlightenment by following the Eightfold Path.

The Eightfold Path was like a staircase. According to Buddha, those who sought enlightenment had to master one step at a time. The steps of the Eightfold Path were right knowledge, right purpose, right speech, right action, right living, right effort, right mindfulness, and right meditation. By following the Eightfold Path, anyone could attain *nirvana* (nur-VAHN-uh), Buddha's word for release from pain and selfishness.

Buddha taught his followers to treat all living things (humans, animals, and even insects) with loving kindness. A devout Buddhist was not even supposed to swat a mosquito.

Buddhists and Hindus both sought to escape from the woes of this world, but their paths of escape were very different. Unlike traditional Hinduism, Buddhism did not require complex rituals. Moreover, Buddha taught in everyday language, not in the ancient Sanskrit language of the Vedas and the Upanishads, which most Indians in 500 B.C. could no longer understand. Buddha's religion was also unique in its concern for all human beings—women as well as men, lowborn as well as highborn.

Map Study answer: The southernmost tip of India

The Mauryan dynasty built an empire.

Buddha lived near the end of the Vedic Age, around 500 B.C. More than 1,000 years had passed since the fall of the Indus valley cities and the arrival of the Aryans. In all those years, no single ruler had united India's many kingdoms. In Buddha's time, a dozen families had carved the Ganges River valley into little states that were often at war. However, a change was coming. Soon India was to experience a new type of government that brought together large territories under a single king.

In 512 B.C., the armies of the great Persian king Darius I came through the Khyber Pass and conquered northwestern India. For almost 200 years, the Indus valley was ruled by a Persian satrap, or governor. For the first time since the Aryan invasions, Indians felt both the benefits (unity and order) and burdens (heavy taxes) of centralized control.

Then, in 326 B.C., the Greek empire builder Alexander the Great led his armies over the mountain passes into India. The Indus valley passed into Greek hands, but only for five years. When Alexander died, his empire died with him. His ambition to unify all of northern India was finally achieved by another young conqueror—an Indian ruler named Chandragupta Maurya (chuhn-druh-GUP-tuh MOW-ree-uh).

The rise of Chandragupta Around 322 B.C., the young warrior Chandragupta stirred up a revolt against a weak king and thus made himself ruler of the largest kingdom on the Ganges. Over the next 24 years (322–298 B.C.), Chandragupta's army of 9,000 elephants and 700,000 soldiers trampled neighboring kingdoms. He united all of northern India (the Indus valley, the Ganges valley, and the southern Himalayas) under his rule. Chandragupta and his descendants who followed him as kings are known as the Mauryan dynasty.

Chandragupta ruled by force and fear. He planted government spies everywhere to prevent plots against him. He trusted nobody. To avoid being poisoned at a meal, he made servants taste all his food. To avoid being murdered in bed, he slept in a different room every night. People he suspected of plotting revolt were tortured to death. After all, said a political manual of the time, "Government is the science of punishment."

74

Chandragupta loved pomp. For Hindu festivals, he dressed in a dazzling robe embroidered in purple and gold and was carried through the city streets on the shoulders of his attendants. Flapping close to his head was a flock of green and red parrots trained to fan the emperor with their wings.

Chandragupta was succeeded on the throne by his son, about whom little is known. However, Chandragupta's grandson, Ashoka (uh-SHOH-kuh), became the most famous member of the Mauryan dynasty. Ashoka became the complete opposite of his cruel grandfather.

Ashoka's rule Ashoka inherited the throne in 273 B.C. At first, he was as warlike as Chandragupta. His victory against southern tribes ended in the slaying of perhaps 100,000 captives.

The later chronicles say that news of this massacre filled Ashoka with remorse. He decided henceforth to rule according to Buddha's teachings of "peace to all beings." (In fact, Ashoka's acceptance of Buddhism probably took place gradually.) He sent an apology to the southern tribes and promised kind treatment in the future.

Throughout his empire, Ashoka ordered huge stone pillars to be erected. Each pillar was inscribed with a public announcement, or **edict**, of his new policies. Some edicts guaranteed righteous treatment for all Ashoka's subjects. Others urged the people of his empire to live righteously themselves.

Instead of spies, Ashoka employed "officials of righteousness" to look out for the welfare of

Voice from the Past · *The Teachings of Buddha*

Buddha was first and foremost a great religious teacher. The following paired verses explain and illustrate many of his ideas.

All that we are is the result of what we have thought: it is founded on our thoughts, it is made up of our thoughts. If a man speaks or acts with an evil thought, pain follows him, as the wheel follows the foot of the ox that draws the carriage.

All that we are is the result of what we have thought: it is founded on our thoughts, it is made up of our thoughts. If a man speaks or acts with a pure thought, happiness follows him . . .

"He abused me, he beat me, he defeated me, he robbed me"—in those who harbor such thoughts, hatred will never cease.

"He abused me, he beat me, he defeated me, he robbed me"—in those who do not harbor such thoughts, hatred will cease.

For hatred does not cease by hatred at any time; hatred ceases by love—this is an eternal law . . .

As rain breaks through an ill-thatched house, passion will break through an unreflecting mind.

As rain does not break through a well-thatched house, passion will not break through a well-reflecting mind . . .

The thoughtless man, even if he can recite a large portion of the law, but is not a doer of it, has no share in the religious life . . .

The follower of the law, even if he can recite only a small portion of it, . . . possesses true knowledge and serenity of mind; he . . . has indeed shared in the religious life.

1. What basic contrast are the paired verses making?
2. Using the phrase "Thou shalt not," write commandments based on each of the paired verses.
3. What qualities does Buddha think people should seek in life? What phrases show that?

These lions stood atop a pillar set up by Ashoka about 250 B.C. The modern country of India has made this figure its badge.

Indians of every caste. Was anyone imprisoned unjustly? Was a family suffering because of flood or drought? The emperor instructed his officials to furnish necessary aid.

Ashoka sent hundreds of Buddhist missionaries to neighboring lands such as Ceylon (the modern Sri Lanka) and even to kingdoms as far away as Syria. Thanks largely to his encouragement,

Buddhism spread far beyond India and became a major world religion with millions of followers.

Ashoka was the last strong ruler of the Mauryan dynasty. In 180 B.C., only 50 years after Ashoka's death, the Mauryan empire was torn apart by rivalry among local princes. Again, India became a collection of small kingdoms. However, the basic form of Indian civilization—begun in the Indus valley and developed through Hinduism and Buddhism—was already established. This civilization proved strong enough to survive centuries of political disunity.

Section Review 2

Define: (a) nirvana, (b) dynasty, (c) edict
Identify: (a) Siddhartha Gautama, (b) Buddhism, (c) Chandragupta Maurya, (d) Ashoka
Answer:
1. (a) How did Buddhists hope to achieve enlightenment? (b) How was the Buddhist path to enlightenment different from the Hindu path?
2. During what years did the Mauryan dynasty rule India?
3. What were the great contributions of the following rulers? (a) Chandragupta (b) Ashoka

Critical Thinking
4. Both Hinduism and Buddhism accept that human life is filled with suffering. How do the two religions differ in their explanations of human suffering?

Imperial government united China. 3

The walls of China's first cities were built 1,500 years after the walls of Ur, 1,000 years after the great pyramids of Egypt, and 1,000 years after the tidy cities of the Indus valley. Though a late starter, the civilization begun on China's Yellow River 3,500 years ago outlasted all the others and continued into the twentieth century. What gave Chinese civilization its endurance and its unity? Part of the answer lies in China's geography.

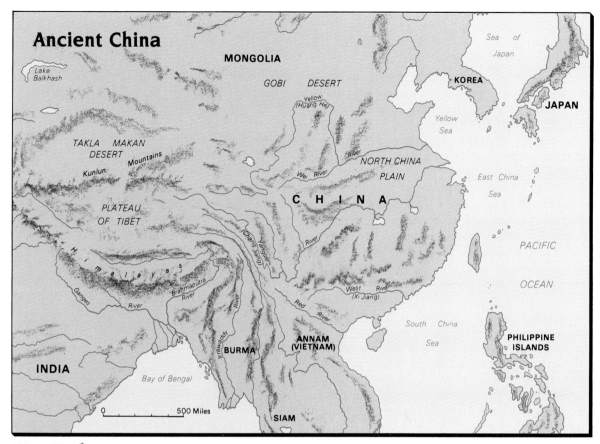

Ancient China

Map Study
What geographic barriers lie to the west and northwest of China? What are the two longest rivers that flow through China?

Geography isolated China.

Chinese civilization grew up in the valleys of two rivers, the Yellow River and the Yangtze River.* On the map on this page, notice that both these long, twisting rivers flow out of the towering highlands of Tibet. The rivers flow east until they reach a broad, flat pocket of land near the Pacific Ocean. This rich plain is cupped on the north, west, and south by hills and mountains. About 90 percent of China's land that is suitable for farming lies within this comparatively small region. This plain was China's heartland.

* This book uses the traditional system for writing Chinese names, sometimes called the Wade-Giles system. This system is used in many standard reference books and in all books on China published before 1979. The new *pinyin* system appears in some current publications, especially newspapers. For place-names, maps in this book show the pinyin form in parentheses after the traditional spelling.

Throughout China's long history, its political boundaries have expanded and contracted depending on the strength or weakness of its ruling families. Yet China remained a center of civilization with all that the word implies—cities, writing, organized government and religion, specialized crafts, and more. In the Chinese view, only barbarians (people who are not civilized) lived outside China's borders. Because the Chinese saw their country as the center of the civilized world, their own name for China was the Middle Kingdom.

Ancient China was isolated from all other civilizations. To its east lay the Pacific Ocean. To the west lay the forbidding Takla Makan Desert and the icy 14,000-foot Plateau of Tibet. To the southwest were the Himalayas. And to the north lived the warlike nomads of Mongolia. For the first 1,000 years of their history, the only foreigners the Chinese met were indeed barbarians.

Students researching the dynasties will want to know their *pinyin* names when they differ from those given in the text. *National Geographic* and the *New York Times* use the *pinyin* names (for example, Chou equals Xhou; Ch'in equals Qin).

77

Strong bonds held Chinese society together.

The culture that grew up in China had strong bonds that made for unity. From earliest times, the group seems to have been more important than the individual. Above all, people's lives were governed by their duties to two important authorities—their family and their king or emperor.

The family In China, the family was central to society. Everyone's role in the family was fixed from birth to death. The elderly had privileges and power; the young had practically none. The oldest man was in charge of all the family's goods and possessions. He also had final approval of the marriages that the women of the family arranged for his children and grandchildren. The oldest woman—usually the grandmother—had authority over all the younger women. Children were expected to obey their parents and grandparents without question. The most important virtue in Chinese society was respect for one's parents.

Women in Chinese society were treated as inferiors. They were expected to obey their fathers, their husbands, and later, their own sons. When a girl was between 13 and 16 years old, her marriage was arranged, and she moved permanently into the house of her husband. A young bride often entered her husband's household with fear and trembling, wondering how her mother-in-law would treat her. Only by bearing sons for her husband's family could a woman hope to improve her status. Eventually, of course, she might be able to rule over her own daughters-in-law.

The importance of family ties is shown by the fact that the Chinese were the first people known to use two names: a personal name and a family name (or surname). Among the Chinese, the first name is the family name. Thus, in a name such as Liu Pang, Liu is the family name and Pang is the personal name.

In China, the family was closely linked to religion. The spirits of family ancestors were thought to have the power to bring good fortune or disaster to living members of the family. The Chinese did not regard these spirits as mighty gods. Rather, the spirits were more like troublesome or helpful neighbors who demanded attention and respect. Every family paid respect to its ancestors and made sacrifices in their honor. Only sons could carry on the traditional religious duties, so sons were valued much more highly than daughters. (Also, only the ancestors in the father's family were so honored; the mother's family did not count.)

View of government In ancient China, a person's chief loyalty throughout life was to the family. Beyond this, people owed obedience and respect to the ruler of the Middle Kingdom, just as they did to their own grandfather. The ruler was like a super-grandfather who had supreme responsibility for the welfare of the Chinese people.

The Chinese believed that royal authority came from heaven. A just ruler had divine approval, known as the Mandate of Heaven. A wicked or foolish king could lose the Mandate of Heaven. The ancestral spirits might show their displeasure by causing a flood, riot, or other calamity. In that case, the Mandate of Heaven might pass to another noble family. This was the Chinese explanation for rebellion and civil war. The fall of one dynasty and the rise of another was never achieved without bloodshed.

Historians describe the rise and fall of dynasties as a cycle. Each dynasty rules vigorously for a while, then weakens and is replaced by a new ruling family. This pattern of strength, decline, and replacement is called the dynastic cycle.

Chinese history is marked by a succession of dynasties until dynastic rule was finally overthrown in the early 1900's. The first historic family to rule the Middle Kingdom (from about 1500 to 1027 B.C.) were the Shang (shahng) kings. The last Shang king was overthrown by the first Chou (jo) king. The Chou dynasty, the longest in Chinese history, lasted for eight centuries (from 1027 to 221 B.C.). It was followed by the shortest and cruelest dynasty, the Ch'in, which in turn was followed by the mighty Han dynasty. These four dynasties—Shang, Chou, Ch'in, and Han—span the first 1,900 years of China's history.

Civilization emerged in Shang times.

Archaeologists have found the remains of China's first civilization along the Yellow River. The river's color is indeed yellowish. From the western mountains, the water picks up a dusty, yellow soil called *loess* (les). The river spreads the loess like a layer of butter over the peasants'

The theory of divine right of kings will be studied in Chapter 18. In Tudor and Stuart England, that theory was interpreted to mean that rebellions were offenses against God as well as king. In China, by contrast, rebellions were seen as part of the dynastic cycle.

fields. Winds from the west bring more rich loess to keep the farmlands of the Middle Kingdom fertile.

The Yellow River is fearfully unpredictable. Its floods can be generous or ruinous. At its worst, when rains are unusually heavy, the river devours whole villages. (The great flood of 1887 killed nearly a million people.) Those who live near the Yellow River know well why it is nick-named "China's Sorrow." Yet the rich farmland constantly draws people back to the river valley.

Early cities China's first cities appeared near the Yellow River about 2000 B.C. Among the oldest and most important was Anyang (ahn-yahng). Anyang was one of the capitals of the Shang dynasty.

Unlike the cities of the Indus valley or the Fertile Crescent, Anyang was built mainly of wood. The city stood in a forest clearing. Nobles lived in large, rectangular wooden houses with thatched roofs. Average families lived in little cone-shaped huts or pit-houses.

Social classes Chinese society was sharply divided between nobles and peasants. Warrior-nobles owned the land. They served in the army and the government of the Shang king. They were skilled fighters with the horse, the chariot, and the bow and arrow. Noble families governed the scattered villages within the Shang lands,

sending tribute to the Shang ruler in exchange for local control.

Meanwhile, peasants tilled the soil for their overlords. In Shang times, the farmers had no plows, only wooden digging sticks and hoes and sickles made of stone. The soil was so rich, though, that it yielded two crops a year of millet, rice, and wheat.

A separate class in Chinese society was made up of people who were skilled in special crafts. At Anyang, these artisans lived outside the city walls. Their houses were smaller than those of the nobles but much more spacious and comfortable than those of the peasants.

Crafts Bronzework was the leading craft in which Shang artisans excelled. Beautiful bronze objects were used in religious rituals and were also symbols of royal power. Some of these objects were small and graceful, such as bronze bells. Others were massive caldrons, weighing almost a ton. The skills of the Shang bronzesmiths, say modern admirers, have never been surpassed.

In earliest Shang times, the Chinese also learned how to draw the fine threads from a silkworm's cocoon and weave them into a light, beautiful fabric. Nobles prided themselves on their finely embroidered silk shoes, which they esteemed as a symbol of civilization. Barbarians, after all, were known to go barefoot.

Shang bronzesmiths made the offering vessel (right) in the form of a tiger protecting a man. The ax (left) was used for beheadings.

79

A *writing system developed.*

The earliest evidence of Chinese writing comes from Shang times. At Anyang and other Shang cities, archaeologists have found hundreds of animal bones and tortoise shells with written symbols scratched on them. These strange objects are known as oracle bones because priests used them to foretell the future. The writing on the oracle bones showed that people 3,500 years ago were part of the same cultural tradition that continues in China today. Some of the characters are very much like those in a modern Chinese newspaper.

In the Chinese method of writing, each character stands for an idea, not a sound. Recall that many of the Egyptian hieroglyphs stood for sounds in their spoken language. Sumerian cuneiform and the Phoenician alphabet also corresponded to spoken language. In contrast, there were practically no links between China's spoken language and its written language. One could read Chinese without being able to speak a word of it. (This seems less strange when you think of our own number system. Both a French person and an American can understand the written equation $2 + 2 = 4$, but an American may not understand the spoken statement, *"Deux et deux font quatre."*)

The Chinese system of writing had one great advantage. People in all parts of China could learn the same system of writing, even if their spoken languages were very different. Thus, the Chinese written language was very important in unifying a large and diverse land.

The disadvantage of the Chinese system was the enormous number of written characters to be memorized. To be barely literate, a person needed to know at least 1,000 characters. To be a true scholar, one needed to know between 5,000 and 10,000 characters. For centuries, this severely limited the number of literate, educated Chinese. As a general rule, a noble's children learned to write, but a peasant's children did not.

Economics in Daily Life · *The Most Treasured Fabric*

According to legend, silk was discovered by the 14-year-old empress Hsi Ling-shi, who lived around 2500 B.C. Hsi Ling-shi was walking one day among the mulberry trees near the palace. A few days earlier, the trees had been covered with caterpillars eating the mulberry leaves. Now the caterpillars hung from the branches in mummylike cocoons.

Curious about the cocoons, Hsi Ling-shi plucked one from a branch and took it home. She dropped it in a pot of water and watched it soften into a loose, tangled web. When she picked up the web, she found she could unravel it like a skein of yarn to form a single long thread of silk.

The legend may or may not be true. The process of making silk became China's best-kept secret for the next 3,000 years. Foreign gold and silver poured into China from the silk trade. To pass on the secret of silk-making to the outside world was treason, punishable by death.

Silk was one of the first items carried in long-distance trade. During the Han dynasty, caravans loaded with silk began to travel the Silk Road, the long route between China and the Mediterranean area. The Chinese monopoly in silk production lasted until about A.D. 550, when Europeans smuggled mulberry seeds and silkworm eggs out of China. Silk still remained important in trade with the East.

The Chou dynasty ruled in troubled times.

In the long parade of dynasties that have ruled China, the Chou followed the Shang. No dramatic changes in civilization marked the change of dynasties. The Chou ruled much as the Shang had. The Chou ruled from around 1027 to 221 B.C. For the first 300 years of this long period, the Chou ruled a large empire including both eastern and western lands. The king's power was wielded locally by mighty lords, but final power still lay in the hands of the king.

Gradually, however, Chou rule weakened. In 771 B.C., the dynasty's weakness brought on a crisis. In this unhappy year, barbarians from the north and west sacked the city of Hao, the Chou capital. They murdered the Chou monarch, but a few members of the royal family escaped eastward to the city of Loyang (loh-yahng). Here in this new capital on the Yellow River, the Chou dynasty pretended to rule the Middle Kingdom for another 500 years.

In fact, the Chou kings at Loyang were almost powerless. Noble families, who supposedly owed allegiance to the king, could not be controlled. Trained as warriors, they sought every opportunity to pick fights with neighboring lords. As their power grew, these warlords claimed to be kings in their own territory. As a result, the later years of the Chou are often called "the time of the warring states."

In this time of bloodshed, traditional values collapsed. At the very heart of Chinese civilization was a love of order, harmony, and respect for authority. Now there was chaos, arrogance, and defiance. How could China be saved? Three solutions were offered by the Middle Kingdom's scholars and philosophers.

Confucius urged social harmony.

China's most influential scholar was K'ung Fu-tzu ("Master Kung"), better known as Confucius. Born in 551 B.C., Confucius was about 12 years younger than the Indian sage Gautama (Buddha). Confucius led a scholarly life, studying history, music, and moral character.

Confucius believed that social order and good government could be restored in China if society were organized around five basic relationships.

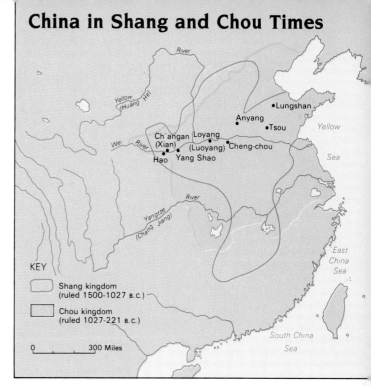

China in Shang and Chou Times

KEY

☐ Shang kingdom (ruled 1500-1027 B.C.)

☐ Chou kingdom (ruled 1027-221 B.C.)

0 ——— 300 Miles

Map Study

Which dynasty—the Shang or the Chou—controlled more land along China's coast? About how far is it from Loyang to Anyang? From Loyang to Tsou?

These were the relationship between ruler and subject, father and son, husband and wife, older brother and younger brother, and friend and friend.

A code of proper conduct regulated each of these relationships. For example, rulers should practice kindness and virtuous living. In return, subjects should be loyal and law-abiding. "If a ruler himself is upright, all will go well without orders. But if he himself is not upright, even though he gives orders, they will not be obeyed."

Three of Confucius's five relationships were based upon the family. Confucius stressed that children should practice what he called *filial piety,* or respect for their parents and elders. "In serving his parents, a filial son renders utmost respect to them at home; he supports them with joy; he gives them tender care in sickness; he grieves at their death; he sacrifices to them with solemnity . . ."

Confucius was not content to be merely a great teacher. He wanted to reform Chinese society by showing a prince or duke how to govern wisely. Impressed by Confucius's wisdom, the duke of Lu appointed him Minister of Crime. According to legend, Confucius so overwhelmed

81

There is no portrait of Confucius that was made during his own time. Like most later portraits, this one suggests his wisdom and kindness.

Taoists sought harmony with nature.

For Confucius, the *social* order (family and government) was most important. For another Chinese thinker named Lao Tzu (low dzu), only the *natural* order was important. If you seek order and harmony, said Lao Tzu, go up into the hills, sit by a stream, and observe a drifting cloud or a soft breeze. Observe that nothing in nature strives for fame, power, or even wisdom. The cloud, the breeze, and the stream move without effort because they follow the Tao (dow), meaning "the Way" or the universal force that guides all things.

Of all the creatures of nature, only humans fail to follow the Tao. They argue about questions of right and wrong, good manners and bad. According to Lao Tzu, such arguments are futile. A simple creature like a turtle is naturally wise because it does not argue, does not strive for personal glory. The turtle simply follows the Tao of its nature. Humans should do likewise, said Lao Tzu. The philosophy of Lao Tzu came to be known as Taoism. Chinese who adopted the Taoist philosophy withdrew from society to live close to nature.

Legalists urged harsh government.

A third group, the Legalists, believed that a highly efficient and powerful government was the key to restoring order. The Legalists taught that a ruler should provide rich rewards for people who carried out their duties well. Likewise, the disobedient should be harshly punished.

In practice, the Legalists stressed punishment more than rewards. For example, anyone caught outside his own village without a travel permit should have his ears or nose chopped off, said the Legalists.

The Legalists believed in controlling ideas as well as actions. They suggested that a ruler should burn all writings that might encourage people to think critically about government. After all, it was for the prince to govern and the people to obey.

Eventually, Legalist ideas gained favor with a prince of a new dynasty that replaced the Chou. A powerful ruler soon put an end to China's long period of disorder, as you will read in the next section.

people by his kindly, courteous ways that almost overnight crime vanished from Lu. When the duke's ways changed, however, Confucius felt compelled to resign.

Confucius spent the remainder of his life teaching. The only record of his ideas are the writings of his students. Only later, 350 years after his death, did millions of Chinese begin to memorize his teachings.

Remind students of the policies of Chandragupta. Discussion question: Would a dynasty following Legalist philosophies last long? Why or why not?

Section Review 3

Define: (a) Middle Kingdom, (b) Mandate of Heaven, (c) dynastic cycle, (d) loess
Identify: (a) Yellow River, (b) Yangtze River, (c) Tibet, (d) Mongolia, (e) Shang, (f) Chou, (g) Confucius, (h) Lao Tzu
Answer:
1. (a) What were the two important bonds that united early Chinese society? (b) What role did religion play in each of those bonds?
2. (a) In the Shang times, what kind of work was done by nobles? (b) By peasants? (c) By artisans?
3. (a) How did writing help to unite China? (b) Why was literacy in China long limited to the wealthy?
4. Why was the traditional way of life in China badly shaken during the late years of the Chou dynasty?
5. What were the basic ideas of the following? (a) Confucius (b) the Taoists (c) the Legalists

Critical Thinking

6. Reread the statement by Confucius on page 81 about the importance of a ruler's character. (a) How does that statement support the Chinese idea of the Mandate of Heaven? (b) In your opinion, how does that statement apply to leadership today?

Ch'in and Han emperors strengthened China. 4

The new dynasty that came to power was the Ch'in. It took its name from the small state of Ch'in, which was the family's home, in western China. In 256 B.C., the Ch'in armies destroyed the Chou forces. In 246 B.C., a new Ch'in king came to the throne. Though he was only a boy of 13 at the time, as he grew older he became as ruthless a ruler as any Legalist could wish.

The Ch'in dynasty built an empire.

This proud ruler was Ch'in Shih Huang-ti (chin shir hwahng-tee), whose name meant "First Emperor." *Huang-ti* was a title that this ruler took for himself in 221 B.C. In earlier times, it had been used only for gods. Because the title means someone even greater than a king, it is translated *emperor.* From this time on, the ruler of China was known as an emperor.

Shih Huang-ti stopped the petty wars that had sapped China's strength. He conquered the barbarians to the south of his kingdom and protected the northern border by building the Great Wall. Most important, he gave China a form of government that lasted more than 2,000 years. His dynasty was even responsible for giving China its name. Nevertheless, Ch'in Shih Huang-ti was hated by one and all. A later Chinese scholar described Shih Huang-ti as having a "high pointed nose, slit eyes, pigeon breast, wolf voice, tiger heart." Furthermore, he was "stingy, cringing, graceless." Nonetheless, Shih Huang-ti was an effective ruler.

Stamping out opposition The First Emperor concentrated all his energies on two tasks: destroying outside rival armies and destroying resistance to his rule from within. His goals were extreme and so were his methods.

His armies struck out in every direction, attacking barbarians north of the Yellow River and south as far as what is now Vietnam. Because of his conquests, the China of the Ch'in dynasty was roughly double the size of China under the Chou dynasty.

At the same time, the Ch'in emperor crushed political opposition within China. To destroy the power of rival warlords, he commanded all the noble families to live at the capital city under his watchful eye. This edict, according to tradition, uprooted 120,000 noble families. To put a stop to wars between states, the First Emperor wiped out the ancient borders of Lu, Ch'u, Ch'in, and other states, and drew new boundaries. China was carved into 36 administrative districts, each of which was controlled by officials from Ch'in.

To prevent criticism of his rule, the emperor ordered the burning of all books that were judged to be either useless or harmful. This included all poetry of the Chou dynasty and all political writings—every book valued by Confucian scholars. Only practical books about medicine and farming were to be spared.

To unite his empire, Shih Huang-ti ordered a gigantic network of highways to be built by peasant work gangs. He also set uniform standards

The Great Wall of China is the only human-made feature on Earth that is visible from the moon. Although Shih Huang-ti built the earliest unified wall, the wall as it exists today dates from the Ming dynasty (1368–1644).

for Chinese law, money, and weights and measures—even the length of cart axles. This last standard ensured that all vehicles fit the ruts of all Chinese main roads.

The Great Wall If scholars most hated Shih Huang-ti for his book burning, peasants most hated him for his Great Wall. This colossal wall, which still stands, was not entirely the idea of the First Emperor. Smaller walls had been built in Chou times to discourage attacks by northern barbarians. Mounted on tough war-horses, the barbarians could not ride through the walls, but of course they could and did ride around them. Shih Huang-ti decided to close the gaps and stretch a new wall so far to the west that an enemy would have to gallop halfway to Tibet to get around it.

Pushing wheelbarrows (a Chinese invention), about a million peasants collected, hauled, and dumped millions of tons of stone, dirt, and rubble. Slabs of cut stone on the outsides of the wall enclosed a heap of pebbles and rubble on the inside. Each section of wall rose to a height of 20 to 25 feet. From the Yellow Sea in the east to the edge of the Gobi Desert in the west, the Great Wall twisted like a dragon's tail for a total distance of roughly 1,400 miles.

The wall builders worked neither for wages nor for love of empire. They worked because it was the law, and to break Ch'in law was death.

Footnote to History

Before his death in 210 B.C., Shih Huang-ti ordered the building of a great tomb for himself. The whole site was as big as a city. Within the burial mound were more than 7,500 life-size clay statues of warriors, charioteers, archers, and spearmen. This royal bodyguard came to light in 1974, in one of the greatest archaeological finds of the century.

Have students compare the Great Wall to the pyramids. What was the attitude of the workers on both projects? Point out that in China, lawbreakers were sentenced to work on the wall.

An army of clay soldiers was buried with Shih Huang-ti in a tomb that covered as much ground as a small city. Archaeologists have roofed over areas as large as two football fields to protect the figures as they are excavated.

Many died anyway from the crushing labor and the freezing winter winds. According to legend, thousands of human bones lie within the wall.

The fall of the Ch'in The Ch'in dynasty was short-lived. Shih Huang-ti's son, though just as cruel as his father, was less able. After three years under the rule of this second Ch'in emperor, the peasants rebelled. One of their leaders, a peasant from the land of Han, marched triumphantly into the capital city. Thus, in 202 B.C., the Ch'in dynasty ended and the Han dynasty began.

Civilization flowered under the Han dynasty.

The Chinese think of the Han years as a time of glory, unity, and peace. The Chinese even call themselves "the people of Han." There were several reasons for the high reputation of the Han. First, though the emperor still had great power, the hated laws of the Ch'in emperors were revoked. Legalist thinkers were expelled from the imperial palace. Second, the Han ruled during a time when barbarians rarely threatened the Chinese. Third, scholars spoke highly of the Han dynasty because these were the years when Confucius's teachings won widespread influence.

The most powerful of the Han emperors was Wu-ti, who ruled from 140 to 87 B.C. Wu-ti was known as the Martial Emperor because of his success in battle. Northern barbarians, the Huns, had earlier broken through the Great Wall and pitched their tents in one corner of the empire. But Wu-ti's armies drove them back beyond the wall. At the same time, the boundaries of the empire were extended westward to central Asia, south to Vietnam, and east into what is now Korea. The armies of the Han struck up to 2,000 miles from their emperor's palace.

Wu-ti and the Confucian scholars During Han rule, there was a renewal of learning. Scholars were again allowed to read the old Chinese classics, the poetry and history so loved by Confucius. Ch'in book burners had destroyed many ancient works, but a few scholars had hidden their classics. Others had memorized them. The most precious books were known as the "Five Classics" because, shortly before his death, Confucius was said to have collected the greatest writings of Chou times and organized them into five books. A sixth book, the *Analects*, contained Confucius's words of wisdom as recorded by his students.

The Han dynasty was contemporaneous with the Roman empire, but the Chinese leaders had many, many more subjects: in A.D. 2, China's population was 59,594,579.

85

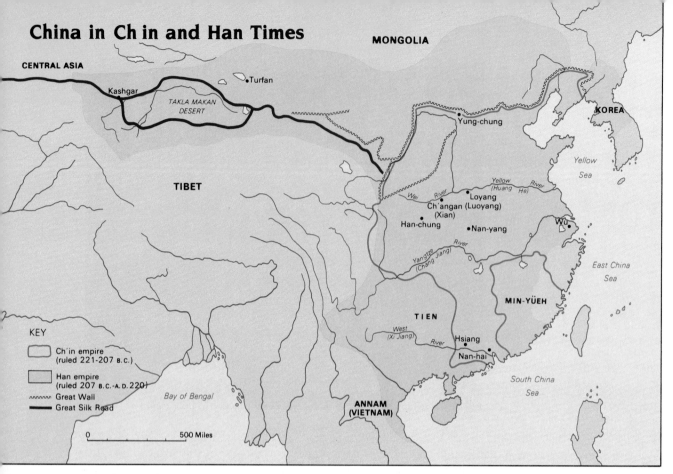

China in Ch in and Han Times

MONGOLIA

CENTRAL ASIA

Turfan

Kashgar

TAKLA MAKAN DESERT

KOREA

Yung-chung

Yellow Sea

TIBET

Yellow (Huang He) River

Wei River

Loyang

Ch'angan (Luoyang) (Xian)

Han-chung

Nan-yang

Wu

Yangtze (Chang Jiang) River

East China Sea

MIN-YÜEH

TIEN

West (Xi Jiang) River

Hsiang

Nan-hai

South China Sea

KEY

Ch'in empire (ruled 221-207 B.C.)

Han empire (ruled 207 B.C.-A.D. 220)

Great Wall

Great Silk Road

Bay of Bengal

0   500 Miles

ANNAM (VIETNAM)

Map Study

During which dynasty did part of Korea become subject to Chinese rule? What areas in the south and west did the Han dynasty add to its empire? What reason might Han emperors have had for wanting to rule the Takla Makan desert?

Wu-ti proclaimed Confucianism the official set of beliefs for his government. In 124 B.C., Wu-ti founded a national university to teach the Five Classics and other great writings of the past. Graduates who passed examinations on the Classics were chosen for high positions in Wu-ti's government. Soon the most powerful officials in China (outside the imperial family) were scholars who had mastered the Classics. In later years, these examinations were a key feature of Chinese government.

The Great Silk Road Wu-ti's conquests to the west of China encouraged the growth of overland trade. According to legend, Wu-ti sent a trusted Chinese official in search of a fresh supply of horses for his armies. Traveling far beyond the Great Wall, the official brought back reports that stunned Wu-ti. Far to the west, he had discovered foreigners (Persians) who were almost as civilized as the Chinese.

It was silk that first linked China with Persia and the rest of the civilized world. Camel caravans carried bundles of silk over a rocky, mountainous route that led past Tibet, across the Takla Makan desert, and into central Asia. This route was known as the Great Silk Road. After a journey of 4,000 miles, Chinese silk reached the great markets of Syria and Asia Minor at the eastern end of the Mediterranean Sea. By that time, the silk had changed hands many times, each time for a higher price.

Collapse of the Han dynasty In the years following Wu-ti's reign, China's prosperity declined. Chinese peasants suffered most in any time of troubles. They lived under a crushing burden of debts and taxes. In times of bad harvests or drought, many peasant families were forced to sell their children into slavery. Famine and plague stalked China's villages. Thousands of peasants fled into the mountains and became bandits.

86

Between the early and later Han rule, the rebel emperor Wang Mang took land away from nobles and ended slavery. His changes led only to more disorder and rebellion.

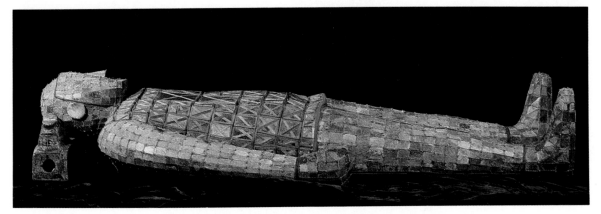

This burial suit is made of 3,000 pieces of jade sewn together with gold thread. It belonged to Liu Sheng, a Han prince who died in 113 B.C. The jade suit was expected to preserve his body for eternal life.

They joined secret societies, each known by a colorful name: the Red Eyebrows, the Green Woodsmen, the Yellow Turbans. Led by these rebels, the peasants revolted.

Twice the Han dynasty was overthrown, partly because of peasant discontent and partly because of rebellious and ambitious warlords. There were therefore two periods of Han rule. The Early Han dynasty lasted from 206 B.C. to A.D 8. The Later Han ruled from A.D. 25 to 220.

A period of peace followed the return of the Han to the throne, but soon the empire was in difficulties again. Cruel and corrupt officials gained power in the government. In the countryside, generals led armies in the emperor's name but, in fact, ruled for themselves. Peasants turned again to banditry. As disorder spread through China, the Han dynasty neared its end.

The spread of Buddhism During the late years of the Han dynasty, between 50 B.C. and A.D. 100, Buddhism became increasingly popular in China. Buddhism came to China with traders on the Great Silk Road or on trade vessels from the Indian Ocean.

In the villages of China, Buddhist monks taught that the Buddha had been a merciful god who came to earth to save human souls. Of course, Buddha himself, dead now for five centuries, had never claimed to be a god. Yet people in both India and China were carving statues of him and bowing before them. In the rocky hills of northern China, huge statues of Buddha were carved into sandstone cliffs and grottos. One such Buddha measured 50 feet from chin to topknot. (The topknot or bun of rolled hair was a Buddhist symbol for wisdom.)

In these bitter times for Chinese of all classes, the need for religious comfort was great. The worship of family ancestors continued, but people were also eager to embrace new beliefs. Millions of Chinese turned to the kindly Buddha. Thus, as the once glorious Han empire collapsed, the religion of Buddhism spread rapidly through the troubled land.

Section Review 4

Define: emperor
Identify: (a) Ch'in, (b) Shih Huang-ti, (c) the Great Wall, (d) Han, (e) Wu-ti, (f) the Five Classics, (g) the Analects, (h) the Great Silk Road
Answer:
1. (a) What were Shih Huang-ti's achievements as a ruler? (b) What methods did he use to reach his goals?
2. (a) How did Wu-ti encourage learning during his reign? (b) How did he expand China's foreign trade?
3. What circumstances encouraged the spread of Buddhism into China?

Critical Thinking
4. Use the idea of the dynastic cycle to describe the rule of the Han dynasty. What characteristics marked each stage of the dynasty's development?

87

Chapter Review 4

Summary

1. A new culture arose in northern India. India's first cities grew up in the Indus valley. Around 1500 B.C., these cities were conquered by Aryans from central Asia. The blending of Indian and Aryan culture produced the religion known today as Hinduism and a caste system of society.

2. Buddhism spread under Mauryan rulers. Around 550 B.C., a new religion known as Buddhism developed in India. Around 300 B.C., the Mauryan dynasty united most of India. The greatest of the Mauryans was Ashoka, who adopted Buddhism and devoted much of his reign to humane causes.

3. Imperial government united China. Chinese civilization began over 3,000 years ago on a plain crossed by the Yellow and Yangtze rivers. A tradition of respect and obedience toward family and government helped the Chinese form a stable society. The teachings of the Chinese scholar Confucius greatly supported these values. Other major schools of thought were the Taoists and the Legalists.

4. Ch'in and Han emperors strengthened China. The harsh Ch'in dynasty strengthened China and paved the way for a period of prosperity under the Han. Near the end of Han rule, during a time of civil strife, Buddhism spread to China.

Reviewing the Facts

1. Define the following terms:
   - a. subcontinent
   - b. reincarnation
   - c. caste
   - d. edict
2. Explain the importance of each of the following names, places, or terms:
   - a. Himalayas
   - b. Indus River
   - c. Mohenjo-Daro
   - d. Aryans
   - e. Vedas
   - f. Buddha
   - g. Chandragupta Maurya
   - h. Ashoka
   - i. Yellow River
   - j. Yangtze River
   - k. Shang
   - l. Chou
   - m. Ch'in
   - n. Han
   - o. Confucius
   - p. Lao Tzu
   - q. Shih Huang-ti
   - r. Wu-ti
3. What signs have archaeologists found indicating that life in India was highly civilized as early as 2500 B.C.?
4. (a) How did Hinduism develop in India? (b) How is Hinduism related to Indian society?
5. (a) How did Buddhism develop in India? (b) What are the main teachings of Buddhism?
6. (a) What important part did Chandragupta Maurya play in India's history? (b) How did Ashoka affect life in India and in countries beyond India?

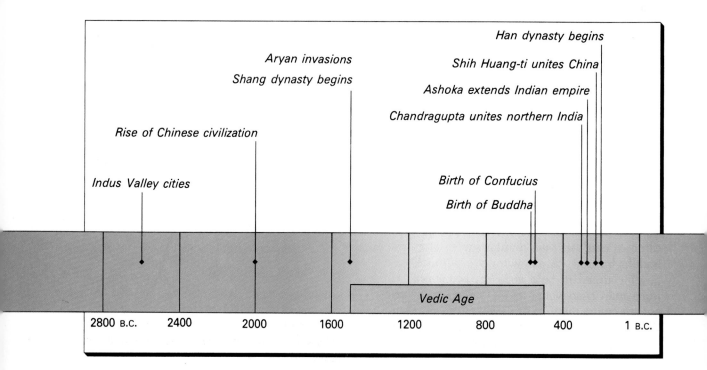

Han dynasty begins

Aryan invasions

Shang dynasty begins

Shih Huang-ti unites China

Ashoka extends Indian empire

Chandragupta unites northern India

Rise of Chinese civilization

Birth of Confucius

Indus Valley cities

Birth of Buddha

Vedic Age

2800 B.C.   2400   2000   1600   1200   800   400   1 B.C.

7. What were the keys to unity in earliest Chinese society?
8. Describe three different philosophies that emerged in China during the troubled years of the Chou dynasty.
9. How did Shih Huang-ti restore order to China?
10. (a) Why are the early years of the Han dynasty considered a golden era in the history of China? (b) What religious change took place in China during the later years of the Han dynasty?

Basic Skills

1. **Comparing maps** (a) Compare the maps of China on pages 77 and 86. What kind of information is included on each map? (b) How may certain features of the first map have influenced the patterns of settlement and conquest shown on the second map?
2. **Charting information** Make a chart comparing ancient India and China. For the vertical rows, use the headings *Geographic Features, Social Patterns, Major Achievements,* and *Philosophies of Life.* Complete the chart by writing several phrases in each space.
3. **Comparing time lines** According to the time lines on pages 45 and 88 and information in the chapter, in what age—Neolithic, bronze, or iron—did cities begin to appear in China?
4. **Reading and interpreting a map** (a) Imagine that you are a citizen of Harappa in 2000 B.C. (a) According to the map on page 68, about how many miles would you travel if you journeyed by river from Harappa to the Arabian Sea? (b) What advantages does the location of your city have for the growth of a civilization? (c) By what routes did the Aryan invaders enter India? (d) As they traveled to the southeast, through what types of land would they be passing?

Researching and Reporting Skills

1. **Using an index** What happened to Buddhism in India and to Confucianism in China after A.D. 100? Find that information by using the Index at the back of this text.
2. **Using the *Readers' Guide*** (a) In the latest *Readers' Guide to Periodical Literature,* find an article about recent archaeological discoveries in China. (b) After

reading the article, write three paragraphs summarizing the information.
3. **Distinguishing between primary and secondary sources** Rearrange the following book titles under the headings *Primary Sources* (written *by* people of the past) and *Secondary Sources* (written *about* people of the past):
   (a) *India: A Short Cultural History*
   (b) *The Analects of Confucius*
   (c) *Introduction to India*
   (d) *Poems of Ancient China: A Collection*
   (e) *Plays of Kalidasa*

Critical Thinking

1. **Comparing** Compare the social classes of ancient China with the caste system in India. (a) What were the underlying principles of each? (b) What were the consequences for the individual?
2. **Identifying viewpoints** Give the viewpoint of each of the following people concerning the topic noted:
   (a) Gautama toward human desires and passions,
   (b) Confucius toward traditional family values,
   (c) Ashoka toward the treatment of his subjects.
3. **Applying a concept** According to an Indian writer of Mauryan times, "Government is the science of punishment." (a) Which rulers and philosophers in both India and China would have agreed with him? (b) Which would have disagreed?
4. **Analyzing** What was the influence of the Vedas on India's civilization and the sayings of Confucius on China's civilization?

Perspectives on Past and Present

1. In what countries are Hinduism, Buddhism, and Confucianism important religions today? On an outline map of Asia, show these areas in color.
2. Religious and philosophical ideas had great influence on political life in ancient China. To what extent do they have an influence on politics today?

Investigating History

1. Writing was not only a form of communication in China but also an important art form. Look up in the library several books on Chinese calligraphy.
2. Why did Shih Huang-ti have an entire army of clay soldiers created for his tomb? An excellent article on this subject appears in the November 1979 issue of *Smithsonian.* Read the article and report on it in class.

Unit I Review

Geographic Theme: Location

Where did ancient cities develop?

The growth of ancient cities reflected the rise of civilization. At first a few cities, then many, showed that a new age had begun.

Geographers describe the location of cities in two ways. *Site* refers to the physical setting of a city. It may be on hills, as with Rome, or on an island, as with Paris and New York. *Situation* refers to a city's location in relation to other features. Is it on a river or harbor? Where a trade route crosses a river? Near mineral deposits or a source of water in the desert? Together, the site and situation of a city tell much about why it has developed and grown.

For ancient cities, the major concerns for *site* were safety and defense. Was the place safe from floods and other natural dangers? Did landforms there provide protection, perhaps through limited access to high places? Was this a favorable place for living?

Situation involved many concerns. Lacking the means for transportation, cities of ancient times were highly dependent upon their immediate environment.

Access to pure water and to food—whether hunted, raised, or harvested—was a basic requirement. If farming was to be the source of food, good soil was essential. Whatever its source, food had to be plentiful enough to support the population. Access to materials for clothing and shelter was another basic need. Although not essential to life, having materials such as obsidian for tools and precious stones for ornaments was an advantage, since these provided a basis for trade. From trade, cities obtained what they lacked. Trade also helped cities to grow.

1. Give a possible reason for the location of each city shown on the map below.
2. Until recently, archaeologists thought that early cities grew on rivers. Yet Çatal Huyuk, one of the earliest cities, rose in the highlands north of Mesopotamia. Give three possible reasons to account for its location there.
3. Using Unit I as a reference, find a reason other than site and situation for the location of one city shown below.

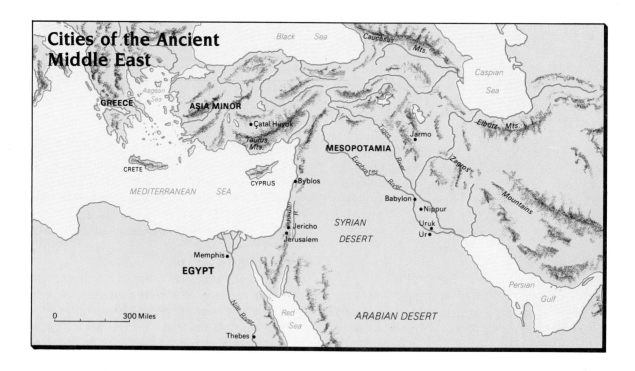

Cities of the Ancient Middle East

Unit Perspectives

Understanding History

1. **Relating** Describe the relationship between or among each of the following sets of terms:
   a. technology
      culture
      civilization
   b. archaeologist
      artifact
      prehistory
   c. cuneiform
      hieroglyphics
   d. pyramid
      pharaoh
   e. Paleolithic
      Neolithic
   f. polytheist
      monotheist
   g. ideogram
      pictograph

2. **Locating** Describe the location and explain the importance of each of the following places:
   a. Jarmo
   b. Çatul Hüyük
   c. Mesopotamia
   d. Nile River
   e. Himalayas
   f. Mohenjo-Daro
   g. Yellow River

3. **Sequencing** Use the text as well as the time lines on pages 45, 64, and 88 to put the events in groups a–d in the correct chronological order.
   a. Rise of Chinese civilization
      Rise of Sumer
      Menes unites Egypt
   b. Old Kingdom in Egypt
      Aryan invasion of India
      Beginnings of Bronze Age
   c. Birth of Buddha
      Rise of Persia
      Conquest of Egypt by Assyrians
   d. Great age of pyramid building in Egypt
      Age of empire building in Egypt
      Second Illness in Egypt

Critical Thinking

1. **Comparing** Describe how the beliefs and philosophies of life of the following people differ: (a) Taoist and Confucian philosophers; (b) an Egyptian pharaoh and a Jewish prophet; (c) Nebuchadnezzar and Buddha.
2. **Using evidence** "Religion played a central role in organizing the ancient civilizations of Egypt, Mesopotamia, and India." For each civilization named, give evidence to support this generalization.
3. **Applying a concept** (a) If no shading were provided on the map on pages 804–805, what indications would there be that Egypt, Mesopotamia, and China were centers of civilization? (b) What conclusions might you draw about Mexico and England?
4. **Making a generalization** What were the principal means by which cultures spread or influenced each other in the earliest civilizations? Make a generalization and support it with examples from India, China, Mesopotamia, and Egypt.

Making Decisions

Evaluate each of the following decisions by describing its impact on the civilization in question: (a) Akhenaton's decision to change Egypt's religion; (b) Cyrus's decision to tolerate the religions of conquered peoples; (c) Shih Houang-ti's decision to destroy Confucian literature; (d) Ashoka's decision to rule according to Buddha's teachings.

Continuity and Change

1. Current activity in archaeology raises the possibility that discoveries made in the next 25 years may alter the world map on pages 804–805. What might some of those changes be? Give reasons for your predictions.
2. Among the institutions that flourished around 1000 B.C. were the following: (a) the Ten Commandments in the Fertile Crescent; (b) the Vedas in India; (c) the Chou dynasty in China; (d) the dynasties of the New Kingdom in Egypt. Of these, which had grown in influence, stayed the same, or diminished in influence by 500 B.C.? Give evidence to support your answers.
3. What are two types of political, economic, and cultural institutions discussed in this unit that you would expect to see developed in the units that follow?

Unit **II**
The Mediterranean World

Chapters

850 B.C.   650 B.C.   450 B.C.

Political and Governmental Life	1100–700 B.C. Phoenicians colonize Mediterranean islands	594 B.C. Solon reforms Athenian government 509 B.C. Rome establishes a republic	336–323 B.C. Alexander of Macedon builds empire
Economic and Technological Life	750–600 B.C. Greek trading colonies develop in Italy	*Greek phalanx* 	264 B.C. Punic Wars begin
Social and Cultural Life	800's B.C. Homer composes *Iliad* and *Odyssey* ▶ 	477–432 B.C. Parthenon built in Athens 461–429 B.C. Pericles leads Athens in Golden Age	380 B.C. Aristotle studies with Plato

The civilizations of Greece and Rome grew to dominate the Mediterranean world for a thousand years. Their achievements gave birth to many of the ideals of today. From Greece came ideas about democracy and individual worth, the use of human reason, and standards of beauty. From Rome came concepts of law and citizenship. During Roman rule, a new religion, Christianity, began and spread. As Rome declined, the Greco-Roman heritage became a part of Western civilization.

250 B.C.

50 B.C.

A.D. 150

218 B.C.
Hannibal invades Italy in Second Punic War

50 B.C.
Caesar becomes consul

27 B.C.
Augustus becomes emperor of Rome

Fasces, symbol of Roman authority

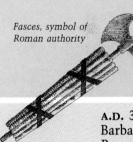

27 B.C.–A.D. 180
Pax Romana prevails; Rome builds roads and aqueducts

A.D. 376–476
Barbarians overrun Roman empire

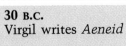

30 B.C.
Virgil writes *Aeneid*

A.D. 312
Roman Emperor Constantine becomes Christian

A.D. 79
Destruction of Pompeii

Pompeiian wall painting

Hellenistic art: Nike of Samothrace

An acropolis was a fortified hilltop at the heart of a Greek city-state. Here the acropolis of Athens is dominated by the ruins of the Parthenon (at right).

Key Terms

epic
arete
polis
aristocracy
hoplite
phalanx
tyrant
colony
democracy
tragedy

Read and Understand

1. Greek culture grew around the Aegean Sea.
2. Greek city-states competed for power.
3. Athens led Greece in its golden age.
4. Alexander's conquests spread Greek culture.

On a June morning in 480 B.C., the male citizens of Athens hiked up a steep hill outside their city. Thousands—perhaps even 10,000—took their seats on rows of stone benches on the hillside. This was the day of decision for Athens. A colossal Persian army, rumored to number more than 2 million soldiers, was marching toward the city. At the same time, a fleet of 1,000 Persian ships was sailing along the coast of Greece.

In size, Athens was no match for the Persian empire. Athens was a Greek city-state of 250,000 people controlling a 117-square-mile plain. The Persian empire, on the other hand, stretched from the Indus River (in what is now Pakistan) to the shores of the Mediterranean and the Black seas. Should the people of Athens fight or run? The citizens on the hill had to decide.

"Pray silence for Themistocles (thee-MIHS-toh-kleez), son of Neocles!" a voice shouted. From the speaker's platform, a stout, bullnecked man addressed the crowd. Themistocles argued that it would be foolish for Athenian soldiers to try to save their city from the Persians. If need be, let the Persians enter the city and burn it. Send the women, old men, and children to safety on a nearby island. Meanwhile, let all men of fighting age row out to meet the Persian fleet with the 200 new Athenian warships. Even though their ships might be outnumbered five to one, said Themistocles, this was the Greeks' only chance.

Naturally, there was strong opposition to this plan. Many Athenians could not bear the thought of allowing the Persians to destroy their city. In the end, though, Themistocles convinced a majority of the citizens to vote his way.

Almost three months later, Persian soldiers walked into a near-empty Athens and burned it to the ground. They destroyed the buildings of Athens, but they could not destroy its spirit. While their city lay in ruins, the Athenians won a complete victory at sea and forced the Persians to withdraw. (You will read the full story of this heroic encounter later in the chapter.) When the stunned Persians finally left Greece, the city of Athens rose from its ashes more glorious than ever before.

This story tells much about the Greek spirit. In Greece, unlike other societies you have studied, civic decisions were made through open debate. That was not the way in Egypt, where a pharaoh spoke with the authority of a god. Neither was it the way in China, where no peasant would dare to contradict the emperor. In Greece, people's freedom to express ideas and leaders' receptiveness to the will of the people did not come about by chance. That was the way the Greeks wanted to live.

In this chapter, you will see how the Greeks overcame a harsh environment to build a remarkable society. The history of ancient Greece is a story of individual thinkers, artists, writers, soldiers, and leaders who contributed to future civilizations. Although in time the Greeks were conquered, their culture spread to distant lands. Their ideas became part of Western civilization, which spread to Europe and the Americas and remains a part of your cultural heritage today.

Greek culture grew up around the Aegean Sea. 1

In ancient times, Greece was not a united country but a collection of lands and islands where Greek-speaking people lived. The mainland of the ancient Greeks was a rugged peninsula that jutted out into the part of the Mediterranean Sea known as the Aegean (ee-JEE-uhn) Sea. The rest of Greek territory consisted of lands on the coast of Asia Minor and hundreds of islands in the Aegean and Ionian (eye-OH-nee-uhn) seas.

Geography shaped Greek civilization.

Physically, Greece is a land of rough mountains, narrow valleys, and no navigable rivers. However, it has a long coastline with many inlets and bays. This combination of physical features had several effects on Greek character and history.

The sea The sea shaped Greek civilization just as rivers shaped the ancient civilizations of the Fertile Crescent, Egypt, India, and China. In fact, some writers have said that the Greeks did not live *on* a land but *around* a sea.

The Aegean Sea and the neighboring Ionian and Black seas were the links that united the Greek people. The "watery ways," as the Greek poet Homer called them, were the best and sometimes the only route between most parts of Greece.

Sea travel was also a link with other societies. The Greek islands formed handy stepping stones across the Aegean Sea. Even in small ships and without compasses, Greek sailors could go from one island to another to reach the older, richer civilizations of Asia and Egypt. Sea travel and trade were vital to the Greeks because their homeland was poor in resources.

The land About three fourths of Greece is covered with mountains, the highest of which is Mount Olympus, the towering, snow-capped "home of the gods." These mountains divide Greece into a number of different regions. In ancient times, rugged terrain made transportation difficult. For example, the city-state of Sparta was only about 60 miles from Olympia, the site of the Olympic games. Yet it took Spartans nearly a week to travel that distance.

Some authors have said that Greece's mild climate encouraged an open, democratic society. Discussion question: Did Egypt's mild climate have the same effect? (Students may be interested to know that the oldest continuous democracy is Iceland!)

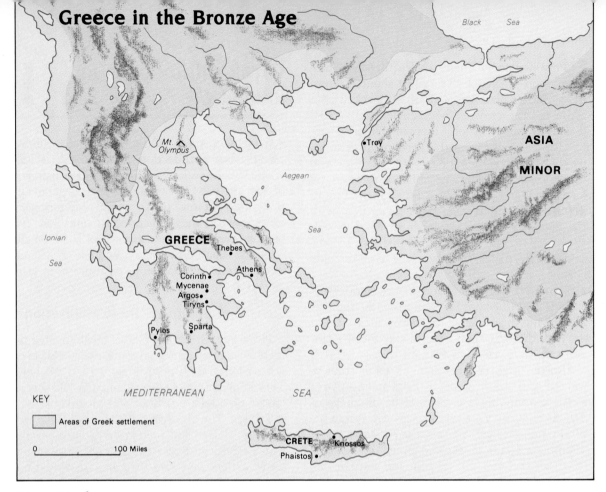

Greece in the Bronze Age

Black Sea

Mt. Olympus

•Troy

ASIA

MINOR

Aegean

Sea

Ionian

Sea

GREECE

Thebes•

Corinth•   •Athens

Mycenae•

Argos•

Tiryns•

•Pylos   •Sparta

KEY

MEDITERRANEAN   SEA

☐ Areas of Greek settlement

0   100 Miles

CRETE •Knossos

Phaistos •

Map Study

Name four seas on which Greek sailors would have sailed in the Bronze Age.
About how far is it from Mycenae to Troy?

The mountains significantly influenced Greek political life. It was very difficult to unite the country under one government. Therefore, the Greeks were content to live in a collection of small independent communities. To most Greeks, home was their own valley and the mountains that enclosed it. It was a small world but one in which self-reliance and individualism could thrive.

Tiny but fairly fertile valleys covered about one fourth of the Greeks' land. These valleys were watered by small streams, not large rivers. Thus, the Greeks had no need for the kind of large-scale irrigation, controlled by powerful priests and kings, that shaped the river valley civilizations.

Greece was never able to feed a large population. It is estimated that no more than 2 million people lived in ancient Greece at one time. Even this small population could not expect the land to support a life of luxury. Fruits and vegetables could grow in only a few places. Meat was rare because the country lacked grasslands to feed large herds of cattle or flocks of sheep. The three principal Greek crops were grains, grapes, and olives. As a result, the Greek diet was light and simple. For instance, a Greek soldier might march through the mountains all morning and fight a battle in the afternoon on a day's meal of a few olives and a small loaf of barley bread.

The climate Climate was the third important environmental influence on Greek civilization. Greece has a Mediterranean climate. Temperatures are moderate, and rain falls only in winter. The Greek way of life, at least for men, was an outdoor life. Men spent almost all their leisure time at the *agora* (**AG**-uh-ruh) or marketplace, at the gymnasium, in political meetings, at the

96

Map Study answers: Ionian Sea, Aegean Sea, Mediterranean Sea, Black Sea; about 250 miles theater, and at civic and religious celebrations. All these public events took place outdoors.

The open gatherings, combined with the small settlements, meant that most people in a city-state knew one another. Citizens met often to discuss public issues and to exchange news. For the Greeks, taking an active part in civic life became both a duty and a virtue.

Rich cultures arose in the Bronze Age.

Across the southern end of the Aegean Sea lies the largest of the Greek islands, Crete. Here an elegant civilization flourished from about 2000 to 1400 B.C. Scholars call it Minoan (muh-NOH-uhn), after Minos, a legendary king of Crete.

Cretan civilization The Minoans were a sea-faring people with great power in the Mediterranean world. They carried on a thriving trade with Greece and other Aegean lands. Safe on their island, they built beautiful palaces without fortified walls.

Life for the Minoans appears to have been very pleasant. Wall paintings in the king's palace-city at Knossos show a lively people with a zest for athletic contests, festivals, and stylish dress. Clad in ruffled gowns, women of the court wore delicate gold jewelry and styled their hair into long, graceful coils. They took part in activities ranging from dancing to strenuous sports. This evidence suggests that Minoan women enjoyed a level of social equality rarely found in the ancient world.

The many flowers, fish, and animals in Minoan paintings reveal that people delighted in the beauty of nature. Another remarkable aspect of Minoan life was its plumbing. At Knossos, pipes carried water for bathing, and even for a flush toilet.

The joys of Crete appear to have ended abruptly some time between 1400 and 1200 B.C. Historians do not know whether the cause was a natural disaster or human conquest. Did a nearby volcanic eruption, with an earthquake and tidal wave, destroy the Minoans' world? Were they overrun by invaders? Evidence shows that the Minoans attempted to rebuild but soon fell to invaders from mainland Greece.

Mainland Greece in the Bronze Age Around 2000 B.C., groups of Greek-speaking people moved into mainland Greece and began to settle there. They were part of the large wave of migrations that swept lands from India to the Fertile Crescent and beyond around that time. The mainland Greeks of the Bronze Age are often known as Mycenaeans (MY-suh-NEE-uhnz), from the name of their leading city, Mycenae (my-SEE-nee).

Mycenae was built to withstand almost any attack. It was located on a steep, rocky ridge and was surrounded by a protective wall up to 20 feet thick. From the citadel of Mycenae, a warrior-king ruled the surrounding villages and farms.

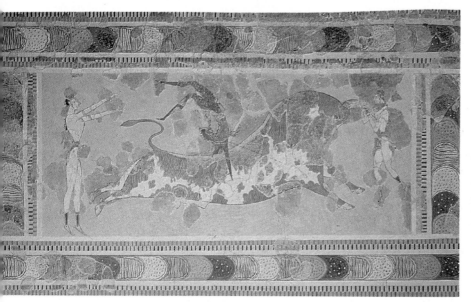

At the Minoan court, young men and women took part in the sport of dancing or leaping over bulls, as shown in this picture. Such rituals may have led to the legend that King Minos of Crete sacrificed young captives to the Minotaur, a monster that was half human and half bull.

Some scholars believe that the volcano that destroyed the island of Thera produced a giant tidal wave that destroyed Minoan shipping and harbors, putting an end to Minoan civilization. Discuss: Can a single event destroy an entire civilization?

Similar palace-forts dotted the southern part of Greece. In each lived a proud, warlike ruler. These kings dominated Greece from about 1600 to 1200 B.C.

Bronze Age society The nobles who lived within the fortresses enjoyed a life of surprising splendor. They feasted in great halls 35 feet wide and 50 feet long. In the center of the hall, a fire blazed on the circular hearth that was ten feet across. During banquets, the firelight glittered from a dazzling variety of gold and silver pitchers, bowls, and cups. When the royal Mycenaeans died, they were buried with their richest treasures. The body of one child was completely covered with a golden suit.

This enormous wealth was won by warrior-kings who led their armies in search of plunder. Trade was also a source of wealth, but Bronze Age trade often was close to piracy.

The warrior kings were only a tiny group at the top of Bronze Age society. The kings had weapons of bronze and jewelry of gold, but ordinary people still used tools of stone and wood. Most people lived as farmers, but there were also weavers, goatherds, shepherds, stonemasons, bakers, metalworkers, nurses, and more.

The Trojan War War was the main business of Greece's Bronze Age kings. Their most famous war was the siege of the great seaport of Troy in Asia Minor. Stories from this war were told hundreds of years later by the Greek poet Homer. According to Homer, a Greek army besieged and destroyed Troy because a Trojan youth had stolen Helen, the beautiful wife of a Greek king.

For many years, historians thought that Homer's stories were imaginary. However, a German archaeologist named Heinrich Schliemann (SHLEE-muhn) thought otherwise. As a boy, Schliemann read Homer's poems over and over. He became determined to find Troy. In 1871, using clues from Homer, Schliemann began to dig for Troy at a site in northwestern Asia Minor. He and his crew unearthed nine layers of city life as well as 8,700 pieces of gold jewelry.

Schliemann's discoveries at Troy, together with the ruins of Mycenae and other cities, showed that Homer's poems had some basis in fact. The Trojan War was probably a great Mycenaean raid against a rival trading city. It took place sometime around 1200 B.C., and it was the last of the Bronze Age Greeks' triumphs.

Dark Ages interrupted civilization.

Not long after the Trojan War, Mycenaean civilization collapsed. Around 1200 B.C., palace after palace was attacked and burned. At Mycenae, a layer of ashes covered the entire palace site, the silent remains of a terrible fire. These were the same years that the Egyptians and Hittites suffered under the attacks of the mysterious "Peoples of the Sea." A tablet from one Mycenaean citadel says, "The watchers are guarding the coast." But guards could not save Mycenaean civilization from destruction.

The Dorian migrations Into this war-torn countryside moved a new group of people, the Dorians (DAWR-ee-uhnz). The Dorians spoke a dialect of Greek and were distant relatives of the Bronze Age Greeks.

The Dorians were far less advanced than the Mycenaean Greeks. Dorian pottery and tools show little skill. The Dorians were not good traders either, and trade came to a standstill with their arrival. Most important to historians, the skill of writing was lost in this time of destruction. There is a 400-year gap in written Greek history from 1150 to 750 B.C. This period is known as Greece's Dark Ages. Without written records, little is known of the Dark Ages, but important events took place during these years.

The poems of Homer Lacking writing, the Greeks of the Dark Ages relied on the spoken word to pass on knowledge to their children. Bards (wandering poets) told stories that glorified the old heroes of Mycenae and Troy. A single tale might last many evenings around a hearth. Such long, heroic poems are called **epics**. The greatest of the bards, according to Greek tradition, was a blind old man named Homer.

We know almost nothing about Homer except his poems. He may have lived as early as 900 B.C. or as late as 750 B.C. His two great epic poems are the *Iliad* (IHL-ee-uhd) and the *Odyssey* (AHD-ih-see).

The *Iliad* is the story of heroes at war. All the action takes place outside the walls of Troy, at the very end of the Trojan War. However, Homer does not explain how the Greek army won the war. He was not interested in groups, only in individuals. Throughout the *Iliad*, the battles that matter are private duels between great heroes, not clashes between armies.

Many countries have some sort of epic tradition—in France "The Song of Roland," in Spain "The Cid," in Sumer "Gilgamesh," in India the "Ramayana" and "Mahabharata." What is the importance of such epics to the people who preserve them?

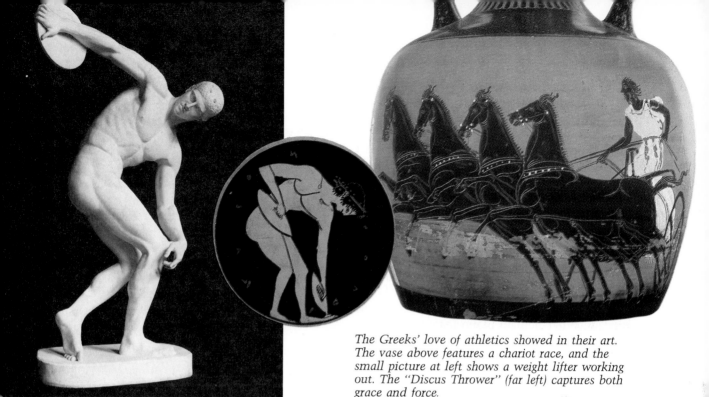

The Greeks' love of athletics showed in their art. The vase above features a chariot race, and the small picture at left shows a weight lifter working out. The "Discus Thrower" (far left) captures both grace and force.

Homer's second epic, the *Odyssey*, concerns the adventures of Odysseus (oh-**DIHS**-ee-uhs), a Greek hero. According to the *Odyssey*, Odysseus spends the ten years after the Trojan War in a series of adventures on his way home. Only through never-failing cunning is he able to survive.

The heroic ideal Listening to Homer's tales, the Greeks of the Dark Ages learned a powerful ideal called **arete** (**AR**-eh-tee). Simply stated, arete meant to strive for excellence, to show courage, and to win fame and honor.

Homer's heroes competed constantly for glory. The two most renowned heroes of the *Iliad* are Hector, Troy's greatest champion, and Achilles (uh-**KIHL**-eez), the Greek champion. In a dramatic

Footnote to History

According to later legends, it was Odysseus's clever scheme that finally brought down the walls of Troy. The Greeks built a gigantic, hollow wooden horse and left it outside Troy's gates. The Trojans convinced themselves the horse must be an offering to the gods and would protect Troy. They dragged the Greek "gift" into the city. Later that night, Greek warriors who had hidden inside the horse's belly leaped out and opened Troy's gates, letting in the Greek army.

scene, Andromache (an-**DRAHM**-uh-kee), Hector's wife, begs him not to fight Achilles:

> "O Hector, your courage will be your destruction; and you have no pity on your little son or on me, who will soon be your widow. For soon all the Greeks will attack you and kill you; and if I lose you, it would be better for me to die . . ."
>
> Then tall Hector of the shining helmet answered, "Wife, I too have thought upon all this. But I would feel deep shame if like a coward I stayed away from battle. All my life I have learned to be brave and to fight always in the front ranks of the Trojans, winning glory for myself . . ."

Hector's answer gives us an insight into the ideal of arete. Confronted with the likelihood of death and tragedy for his family, Hector chooses to live and die by the heroic code. In the following battle, the merciless Achilles slays Hector.

The Olympic games In war, Greek heroes sought glory in battle. In peace, they sought glory in athletic competitions. The most famous games, the Olympics, were held every four years beginning in 776 B.C. Young charioteers, boxers, wrestlers, runners, and javelin throwers came from all parts of Greece to compete on a grassy field at Olympia.

Encourage students to read parts of Homer or the legends on which the poems are based. Discuss the characters of the Homeric heroes: Achilles, Odysseus, Agamemnon, Helen, and Andromache. What parts do the gods play in these stories?

The games lasted five days. The most eagerly awaited event was known as the pentathlon (pehn-**TATH**-luhn). The pentathlon was considered the supreme contest of athletic skill. Contestants took part in five events—a broad jump, a discus hurl, a javelin throw, a stadium sprint (about 200 yards), and a wrestling match. The victor was crowned with the coveted Olympic prize, a wreath of olive leaves. As with the Homeric heroes, the true prize was honor and fame.

Greeks worshiped humanlike gods.

The Olympic games, like many other contests in ancient Greece, were held in part to honor the gods. The Greeks imagined their gods to be very much like humans in most ways. The Greek gods struggled with human passions and weaknesses—love, hate, anger, jealousy. They quarreled constantly with one another. However, unlike humans, the gods were immortal. The 12 most powerful gods and goddesses were believed to gather atop a snow-capped mountain in northern Greece, Mount Olympus. The Greeks also honored local gods and household spirits.

The Greeks developed a rich set of myths or stories about their gods. Through these myths, the Greeks sought to understand the mysteries of nature and the power of human passions.

The Greeks did not develop a powerful priestly class, as the Egyptians and Sumerians did. Instead, priests in Greece were ordinary officials. Serving as a priest was not a lifelong career. Rather, it was only one of many civic duties for a Greek citizen. Thus, religion in ancient Greece was closely linked to government and to civic pride.

Section Review 1

Define: (a) agora, (b) bard, (c) epic, (d) arete, (e) pentathlon, (f) myth
Identify: (a) Aegean Sea, (b) Ionian Sea, (c) Black Sea, (d) Minoan civilization, (e) Mycenaean civilization, (f) Trojan War, (g) Homer, (h) Dorians, (i) Dark Ages, (j) the *Iliad*, (k) the *Odyssey*, (l) the Olympics
Answer:
1. How was ancient Greek society influenced by each of the following geographic factors? (a) the sea (b) the land (c) the climate

2. Describe the society that existed in Greece and on nearby islands in the Bronze Age.
3. How did the Dorian migrations affect Greek civilization?
4. Why were Homer's poems important to Greek society?
5. How was the Greek religion different from the religions of Egypt and the Fertile Crescent?

Critical Thinking
6. (a) What evidence suggests that writing was a skill limited to a small group of specialists in Mycenaean society? (b) Suggest a comparable skill that might be lost today in a society destroyed by war, and explain the consequences of the loss.

Greek city-states competed for power. 2

After 750 B.C., the Greeks began to recover from the Dark Ages. This period was marked by the rise of the city-states, for which the Greek word was **polis** (**PAHL**-uhs). (This is the root of such words as *police*, *politics*, and *politician*.)

A polis included a city and its surrounding countryside. Most city-states controlled between 50 and 500 square miles of territory, although the largest, Sparta, controlled about 4,000 square miles.

The Greeks expected all citizens to share in the discussion of public matters. They held meetings in the agora or on a fortified hilltop called an *acropolis* (uh-**KRAHP**-uh-lihs). The Greeks knew that such general discussion was only possible with a fairly small population. Thus, the ideal polis, to Greek political thinkers, had between 5,000 and 10,000 citizens. (Only free adult men were counted as citizens, however; women, children, slaves, and foreigners living in the city made the whole population of a polis much larger.)

The polis was the central force in Greek life. Citizenship was based on the ideal of human beings as free and rational individuals. Civic decisions were made by open debate, not by a pharaoh or an emperor. In Greece, the freedom to express ideas and the willingness of leaders to listen were not only acceptable but expected.

Power passed from kings to citizens.

Clearly, Greece in the time of the city-states was very different from Greece in the time of the warrior-kings that Homer described. During the Dark Ages, the kings had lost their power. In general, rule passed into the hands of a small group of noble families. Such a government is called an **aristocracy** (AR-uh-STAHK-ruh-see). Yet aristocratic rule soon proved oppressive and un-just. The nobles made laws to suit themselves and forced small farmers into slavery for debts.

A new kind of army Ordinary citizens became dissatisfied with aristocratic rule. The power of those small farmers and artisans was growing because of another change that had taken place in Greece. In the age of Homer, only kings and nobles were warriors. Only the rich could afford great bronze spears, shields, breastplates, and chariots. During the Dark Ages, however, iron became the most important metal for weapons and armor. Not only is iron harder than bronze, but it also is more common and therefore cheaper. Soon, even ordinary citizens could afford iron weapons and armor.

A whole new kind of army developed as a result of the use of iron. Now every citizen was expected to be a soldier for his polis. These soldiers, called **hoplites,** fought on foot. They stood side by side, each man with a spear in one hand and a shield in the other. As the hoplites faced their enemy, the shields formed a solid wall bristling with spears. This fearsome group of soldiers was known as a **phalanx** (FAY-lanks). In its day,

the Greek phalanx was the most powerful fighting machine in the world.

The rise of tyrants It was impossible for rulers to ignore the power of these citizen-soldiers. In many city-states, farmers who had lost their lands and debt-ridden artisans joined in revolt against the nobles. Often the rebels were led by a man from the nobility, perhaps someone who had lost out in a feud among the nobles themselves. With the support of the citizens, such men won power in many city-states.

The ambitious men who came to power through these rebellions were known as **tyrants.** Hated by the nobles, the tyrants usually worked to help the small farmers and artisans. Sometimes tyrants took lands from the defeated aristocrats and divided the property among the poor. To increase their popularity and impress their neighbors, tyrants were great builders. Many Greek cities gained forts, harbors, and temples under a tyrant's rule.

During the time of the tyrants, many Greek city-states also founded **colonies**. Groups of citizens moved abroad to islands and harbors around the Mediterranean. These new settlements were separate city-states, but they retained ties of loyalty to their home city. Colonies became an important source of trade and wealth for many Greek cities.

Some city-states passed from one tyrant to the next, as competing groups took power. Other cities, however, found new ways of governing. Among these city-states were two of the most powerful, Sparta and Athens.

Teamwork was clearly essential in the Greek phalanx. In the Greek polis, every citizen was a soldier.

101

Greece and Its Colonies

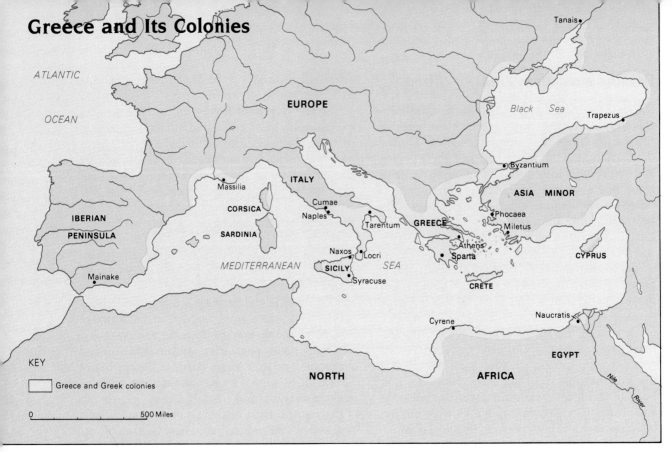

Map Study

Between 750 and 550 B.C., Greek colonies spread around the Mediterranean Sea. What settlement controlled the mouth of the Black Sea?

Sparta built an army state.

Sparta was located in the southern part of Greece, in the large land area known as the Peloponnesus (PEHL-uh-puh-NEE-sus). As the map on page 105 shows, this stretch of land is nearly cut off from the rest of Greece by the Gulf of Corinth.

While other city-states founded colonies abroad, Sparta looked no farther than the fertile fields of neighboring Messenia (muh-SEE-nee-uh). About 725 B.C., the Spartans conquered the Messenians and took over their land.

The Spartans treated the Messenians almost as slaves. Messenians became *helots* (HEL-uhts), peasants forced to stay on the land they worked. Each year, the Spartans demanded half of the Messenians' yearly crop. Around 600 B.C., the Messenians, who outnumbered the Spartans eight to one, revolted. The Spartans put down the revolt, but just barely. From then on, the Spartans lived in fear of a helot uprising. The Spartans concluded that the only way to survive was to make their city-state overwhelmingly strong. Spartan citizens devoted their lives to serving their polis, especially in the army.

To strengthen their city-state, the Spartans adopted a harsh set of laws known as the Code of Lycurgus (ly-KUR-gus). According to legend, Lycurgus gave Sparta its laws, then starved himself to death to save food for his polis. Whether or not the story is true, it shows the Spartan values of self-discipline and endurance.

Footnote to History

Although the Spartans lived on the work of the helots, the Spartan masters certainly did not live in luxury. According to legend, a foreign visitor who shared a meal with the Spartan army remarked after eating the usual dinner of black porridge, "Now I know why the Spartans do not fear death."

Map Study answer: Byzantium

Spartan babies were examined at birth to see if they were healthy. If not, they were left in the hills to die. All fit children stayed with their mothers until their seventh birthdays. Then the boys were sent to army barracks, and their training began. They wore one light tunic, winter or summer, and usually went barefoot. Their beds were hard benches. For food, they had meager servings of coarse black porridge. They were expected to get extra food by stealing from nearby farms, though they would be whipped if caught. Such schooling produced tough soldiers who could fend for themselves in enemy territory.

At the age of 20, a Spartan man was allowed to marry. He continued, though, to live in the barracks for another ten years. After completing full-time military service, men remained on active reserve for another 30 years. Their lives of discipline, loyalty, and training made the Spartan phalanx almost unbeatable.

Spartan girls also led hardy lives. Unlike girls in other city-states, Spartan girls ran, wrestled, and played sports. As adults, they managed the family estates while their husbands served the polis. Spartan women had every right except the vote. As a result of their freedom, they were considered scandalous by other Greeks.

From around 600 until 371 B.C., the Spartans had the most powerful army in Greece. However, they paid a high price for their power. They created little literature, art, or architecture. The Spartans valued duty, strength, and discipline over individuality, beauty, and freedom of thought.

Athens turned to democracy.

In outlook and values, the city-state of Athens stood in sharp contrast to Sparta. An ambassador from Corinth, a city located halfway between the two rivals, once compared the Spartans to the Athenians while he was speaking to the Spartan assembly. With typical Greek frankness, he told the Spartans that even though they had the strongest army in Greece, they were overly cautious and generally lacking in any excitement of the mind. Athenians, he said, were always eager to learn new ideas. They had been educated to think and act as free people.

Like other city-states, Athens went through a power struggle between rich and poor. However, Athenians avoided civil war by making timely reforms. Two of the leading reformers were Solon (SO-luhn) and Cleisthenes (KLYS-thuh-neez). These reforms created a **democracy**, a government in which all citizens took part.

Solon's reforms By 594 B.C., conflict between the rich aristocrats who ruled Athens and the poor farmers who made up most of its population had reached a boiling point. To prevent civil war, the aristocrats asked a middle-aged poet, philosopher, and merchant named Solon to head the government. Solon was well-known for his fairness, and the Athenians gave him full power to reform the laws. Solon's first acts were aimed at improving Athens's economy.

1. He canceled all debts and freed those who had been enslaved for debt.
2. He made farming profitable. The soil of Athens was too poor for grain but good for grapevines and olive trees. Solon refused to allow farmers to sell grain abroad, thus encouraging them to grow more wine grapes and olives. Olive oil and wine became the base of a rich trade for the Athenians.
3. He encouraged industry by requiring every father to teach his son a trade. This gave Athens a better mixture of agriculture and industry. Athenian pottery, for example, was sold all around the Mediterranean Sea.

Solon's political reforms were just as important as his economic ones.

1. He allowed every male citizen to attend the assembly. All important matters were debated there and decided by vote.
2. He began a new legal system in which any citizen could bring charges against anyone who had committed a wrong. Thus, if a citizen saw a crime committed against a slave, the citizen could bring a charge, even though the slave could not. The idea that all citizens were responsible for justice was revolutionary.

After 22 years in power, Solon refused a popular request that he become ruler for life. Instead, he went on an extended tour of Egypt and Asia Minor.

The reforms of Cleisthenes About 60 years later, another Athenian leader, Cleisthenes, introduced further reforms. Beginning in 508 B.C., he convinced the Athenians to enact a series of laws that made Athens a full democracy.

Could the Spartan military system have existed without the helots? Without their labor, what changes would the Spartans have been forced to make? (Consider that full-time soldiers depend on other workers for food, clothing, and weapons.)

Cleisthenes increased the power of the Athenian assembly. He also created the Council of Five Hundred to propose laws and advise the assembly. Members of this council were chosen by lot, so that every citizen had an equal chance of serving.

After all these reforms, Athenians enjoyed nearly a complete democracy. However, it is important to remember that only about one fifth of the people in Athens were citizens. The rest were slaves, foreigners, and women. Women in Athens had no part in government and very little part in its intellectual life.

The Greeks turned back the powerful Persians.

Danger of a helot revolt caused the Spartans to be inhumanly tough. Danger of revolution among poverty-stricken farmers caused Athens to become a democracy. The greatest danger of all—invasion by Persian armies—spurred Athens and Sparta alike to their greatest glory.

The full story of the Persian Wars comes down to modern times in the writings of a Greek scholar named Herodotus (huh-**RAHD**-uh-tuhs). His *History of the Persian Wars* was new and remarkable. Unlike the scribes of Babylon and Egypt, Herodotus did not set out to glorify the deeds of kings.

Instead, he wanted to investigate the past, find out the truth, and report it. He did allow many tall tales to slip into his work, but Herodotus is still justly called the first true historian.

The first invasion The Persian Wars began in Ionia, a thin strip of coastland in what is now Turkey. Greeks had long been settled there, but around 520 B.C., the Persians conquered the area. The Greeks of Ionia submitted to Persian rule for a generation but then revolted. Athens sent ships and soldiers to the Ionians' aid. After the Persian king Darius defeated the rebels, he vowed to destroy Athens in revenge.

In 490 B.C., a Persian fleet carried 25,000 men across the Aegean Sea and landed a little northeast of Athens on a plain called Marathon. There, 10,000 Athenians, neatly bunched into phalanxes, were waiting for them. Shoulder to shoulder, singing as they ran, the Athenians charged. The casualties reportedly numbered 6,400 Persians and only 192 Athenians.

Though the Athenians were victorious, their city was now defenseless. Sailing along the coast, the Persian ships could reach Athens before the Greeks could march overland to defend it. Someone had to race back to Athens to tell people there how badly the Persians had been defeated. Otherwise, the citizens might surrender the city without a fight. A young runner named Pheidippides (fye-**DIP**-uh-deez) stripped off his clothes

Daily Life · Athenian Pottery

"We like beautiful things but don't spend a fortune on them," a leading Athenian remarked about the people of his city. Some of the loveliest objects in Greece, and throughout the Mediterranean for that matter, were easily affordable to almost every family in Athens. These objects were the graceful Athenian vases or pots.

The pottery was made and purchased for practical use as mixing bowls, pitchers, drinking cups, wine jars, and water jars. Different shapes were designed to serve different purposes. Often, Athenians bought new pottery for celebrations, and the scenes on the pottery showed the event they were celebrating—a marriage, an athletic contest, or a voyage.

Athenian potters were dedicated to high quality and beauty in their craft. They proudly signed their finest works. Their products have become a symbol for perfection in art.

Between 490 and 480 B.C., a rich deposit of silver was found in Athens. Themisticles persuaded the citizens to use the windfall for a fleet of warships rather than distribute it as a bonus to all citizens.

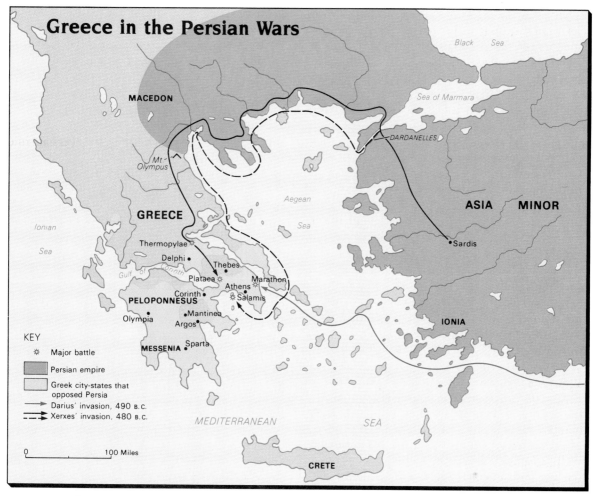

Greece in the Persian Wars

KEY

✴ Major battle

▨ Persian empire

▧ Greek city-states that opposed Persia

→ Darius' invasion, 490 B.C.

⇢ Xerxes' invasion, 480 B.C.

0 ────── 100 Miles

Map Study

Which Persian ruler took a direct sea route to invade Greece? Which ruler brought both a fleet and a land-based army? What two battles did his army fight? What battle did his fleet fight?

and ran 26 miles over the rocky ground from Marathon to Athens. With his last breath, he gasped, "Rejoice, we conquer." Then he collapsed and died. Persian ships arrived much later, saw the situation was hopeless, and sailed away.

The second invasion Ten years later, in 480 B.C., Darius the Great was dead. His son and successor, Xerxes (ZURK-seez), was determined to crush Greece. Xerxes assembled an enormous invasion force of ships and men.

Xerxes' army was like a marching exhibit of all the peoples of the Persian empire. There were Ethiopians in lion skins carrying spears tipped with gazelle horn. Arab soldiers followed him on camels. Scythians from Russia were known by their pointed caps. The Persians sported leather jerkins and fish-scale armor. Xerxes' army was many times larger than any force the Greeks could muster.

The Greeks were badly divided. Some city-states decided to fight the Persians. Others thought it wiser to let Xerxes destroy Athens and return home. Some Greeks actually fought on the Persian side. Thus, Xerxes' army met no resistance as it marched down the eastern coast of Greece. Then, about 85 miles northeast of Athens, Xerxes came to a narrow mountain pass at Thermopylae (ther-MOP-ih-lee). Here he found 7,000 Greeks, including 300 Spartans, blocking his way.

Many Greeks fought on the Persian side, at Marathon, Thermopylae, and later battles. What does this fact show about Greek nationalism or its absence in this period? Where did a person's primary loyalty lie? (polis)

105

Xerxes expected to smash this small army with ease, but he underestimated the Spartans. For three days, the ground at Thermopylae ran red with Persian blood. Finally, a Greek traitor told the Persians about a secret path around the cliffs. Defeat for the Greeks was now inevitable.

The Spartan commander, Leonidas, told the Greeks from other city-states to retreat to safety. He and his Spartans would hold the pass as long as possible and die with honor at Thermopylae. The Persians killed them all. The Spartans' valiant sacrifice made a great impression on all Greeks.

In Athens, the citizens began to plan for the city's defense. It was then that Themistocles convinced Athenians to evacuate their city and pin all their hopes on victory at sea (page 94).

Early one September morning, 310 Greek ships (more than half rowed by Athenians) headed out to sea to face the Persians. Straight ahead was the island of Salamis (SAL-uh-mihs). To the left and right, blocking both ends of the channel, were masses of Persian ships. The Greeks appeared to be trapped.

But Themistocles knew the waters around Salamis better than the foreigners. The channel was too narrow to permit the large Persian fleet to maneuver well. Suddenly, the huge size of the Persian fleet turned into a terrible disadvantage. With lusty shouts, Athenian oarsmen drove straight for the wooden hulls of the enemy. Battering rams protruded from Greek ships below the waterline. These rams punched holes in the Persian ships. The great Persian fleet sank, ship by ship, in the channel.

Xerxes watched it happen. He had set his golden throne upon a rocky height to enjoy seeing the Greeks crushed. Instead, he saw his own navy destroyed. After the battle, Xerxes left Greece hurriedly with about half his army. The remaining half of the Persian army was defeated by the Spartans at a third great battle, which took place on the plain of Plataea (pluh-TEE-uh). Thus ended the second Persian invasion of Greece.

Consequences of the Persian Wars Athens basked in the glory of the Persian defeat. Athens alone had challenged Persian power from the beginning. Athenian heroes had fallen first in Ionia, then at Marathon. Athenian ships had fought at Salamis. The city of Athens, burned to ashes, had suffered the most damage. The Athenians claimed to be the war's greatest heroes.

Their pride in themselves and their city soared to new heights.

After the war, Athens became the leader of an alliance of 140 city-states called the Delian (DEE-lee-uhn) League. The purpose of the league was to ward off further Persian attacks. Soon, though, Athens began to use its powerful navy to control the other members of the league. City-states were forced to join the league and pay yearly dues to Athens. The Delian League thus became just another name for an Athenian empire.

The prestige of victory and the wealth of empire set the stage for a dazzling outburst of creativity in Athens. The city was entering its brief, brilliant golden age.

Section Review 2

Define: (a) polis, (b) acropolis, (c) aristocracy, (d) hoplites, (e) phalanx, (f) tyrant, (g) colony, (h) helot, (i) democracy

Identify: (a) Sparta, (b) Messenia, (c) Lycurgus, (d) Athens, (e) Solon, (f) Cleisthenes, (g) Darius, (h) Herodotus, (i) Marathon, (j) Themistocles, (k) Thermopylae, (l) Xerxes, (m) Gulf of Salamis, (n) Plataea, (o) Delian League

Answer:
1. Why was the polis important to Greeks?
2. How did the Iron Age help ordinary citizens gain power in Greece?
3. How was the rule of tyrants generally different from that of aristocrats?
4. (a) Why was revolt a constant threat in Sparta? (b) How did the Spartans respond to this threat?
5. (a) Why was revolt a threat in early Athens? (b) How did the Athenians respond to this threat?
6. How did the end of the Persian Wars affect the people of Greece, especially the Athenians?

Critical Thinking
7. Choose one of Solon's reforms and explain why it was important to making Athens a democracy.
8. At several major battles in the Persian Wars, there were nearly as many Greeks fighting for the Persians as against them. From your reading, what reasons can you suggest for this division among the Greeks?

(opposite) This city tour features Athens in the time of Pericles. As the center of a polis, Athens was the scene of political, economic, social, and cultural activity. The Parthenon, standing high on the acropolis, dominated the city.

Athens led Greece in its golden age.

3

During Athens's golden age, the arts of drama, sculpture, poetry, philosophy, architecture, and science all reached new heights. For 50 years (from 480 to 430 B.C.), Athens set off sparks of genius in all directions.

Pericles sought glory for Athens.

Among those who evacuated Athens before the Persians arrived in 480 B.C. was a teenager named Pericles (PEHR-uh-kleez). His aristocratic father, a leader of the Athenian assembly, had fought in the Battle of Salamis. When the Persians were finally driven out, much of Athens had been burned. In this bleak, war-scarred city, Pericles prepared to become Athens's leader.

Pericles first attended meetings of the assembly at the age of 20. Soon, his great talent for public speaking won him fame. He did not try to excite his audience but only to reason with them. His arguments made sense to aristocrats, farmers, and artisans alike.

In 461 B.C., the assembly elected Pericles one of Athens's ten generals. He was reelected year after year and became, in effect, the leader of Athens. This one man so dominated the life of Athens for 32 years (461–429 B.C.) that the period often is called the Age of Pericles.

Pericles had three goals: (1) to strengthen Athenian democracy; (2) to build a commercial empire; and (3) to glorify Athens.

To strengthen democracy, Pericles increased the number of public officials who were paid salaries. In earlier times, many public jobs were unpaid, and therefore only the wealthier citizens could afford the time to hold such offices. Under Pericles, members of the Council of Five Hundred, jurors, and all sorts of other public officials were paid for their work. Thus, even the poorest citizens could afford to serve if elected or chosen by lot.

Through the Delian League, Pericles tried to enlarge the wealth and power of Athens. He used money from the league's treasury to make Athens's navy the strongest in the Mediterranean. The navy safeguarded Athenian commerce and settled disputes between league members.

Pericles, shown in his war helmet, was Athens's leading statesman in the city's golden age.

Pericles also used money from the empire to beautify Athens. He persuaded the Athenian assembly (without the league's approval) to vote huge sums of Delian League money to buy gold, ivory, and marble. Still more money went to a small army of artisans who worked for 15 years (447–432 B.C.) on building one of architecture's noblest works, the Parthenon (PAHR-thuh-nahn).

Art flourished in Athens.

The Parthenon was not novel in style. It was built in the traditional style that had been used in Greek temples for 200 years. Neither was it especially large—228 feet by 101 feet. What made it one of the masterpieces of all time was its excellent craftsmanship and design.

Within the temple stood a giant statue of Athena, goddess of wisdom and protector of Athens (which was named for her). Pericles had entrusted much work on the temple, including the statue of Athena, to his friend Phidias (FIHD-ee-us), a sculptor. The great statue of the goddess stood

Eventually, generals were the only officials in Athens who were still elected rather than chosen by lot. Discuss: Why did the Athenians continue to elect their generals? What problems might result if generals were chosen by lot?

107

Comparing Pictures *The Parthenon represented a new style of architecture, known for its proportion and symmetry, that developed in Greece. How does this style differ from that of the ziggurats in Sumer (page 31)?*

about 39 feet tall. A golden helmet crowned her head above her ivory face. A golden robe fell in great folds over her golden sandals. A graceful ivory hand rested on a huge shield. The morning sun rising over Athens briefly lit up the goddess's robe.

Phidias and the other sculptors of the golden age of Athens aimed to create figures that were graceful, strong, and perfectly formed. Their faces showed neither laughter nor anger, only serenity. Greek sculptors also tried to capture the grace of the human body in motion. Their values of order, balance, and proportion became the standards of what is called *classical art*.

Nearly all of the great sculpture and architecture of Periclean Athens was created for the polis. Marble, bronze, and gold went into public temples, not into private homes. The many shrines and temples that the Persians destroyed were rebuilt and made more beautiful than ever.

The importance that Athenians gave to fine public architecture is shown by the temple of Athena Nike (*nike* meant "victory"). This temple was built while Athens was fighting for its life against Sparta. Money was short, and war casualties and plague carried off workers. Yet all through the 30 years of war, the Athenians struggled to complete the temple.

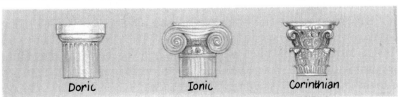

Pillars supported the roofs of the great Greek temples. The three classical styles for the tops (or capitals) of the columns were the Doric, the Ionic, and the Corinthian.

Compare a Greek sculpture with a Roman portrait bust. Which is more realistic? More idealized? Discuss each society's attitudes toward perfection and realism.

The Greeks invented drama.

Like the Parthenon, Athens's theatrical productions were both an expression of civic pride and a tribute to the gods. Writing plays to be performed on stage was a new form of art. Drama as we know it was a Greek invention.

Early in the spring, Athenians rose at dawn and walked to the city's outdoor theater to watch a festival honoring the god of wine, Dionysus. Just as athletes competed in the Olympic games, playwrights competed in this festival. A group of citizens judged the plays and awarded the winner a simple prize: a wreath of ivy.

In the Age of Pericles, two writers dominated these contests. First came Aeschylus (ES-kih-lus), who won the ivy wreath 13 times. Aeschylus shared deeply in Athens's glory; he himself had fought at Marathon and probably at Salamis. He probably wrote more than 80 plays, of which only 7 survive. The second great dramatist, Sophocles (SAHF-uh-kleez), won his first dramatic contest by beating the great Aeschylus in 468 B.C. All together, Sophocles wrote about 100 plays, including the most famous Greek drama of all, *Oedipus* (EHD-uh-puhs).

Greek plays were partly acted and partly chanted. A chorus of singers would comment on the action of the play, helping the plot along. The actors wore masks to identify their roles. The large protruding lips of each mask served as a megaphone to help carry the actor's voice to the back rows.

Both Sophocles and Aeschylus wrote the type of drama known as **tragedy**. To qualify as tragedy, a play had to portray men and women of strong character whose very strength led to their downfall. There was no such thing as a meek hero.

In classic tragedy, strength led the hero to pride, and pride inevitably led to an unforgivable sin. And always, in tragic drama, the gods punished the hero for sinning. The audience who saw these plays left the theater both saddened and uplifted—sad for the fate of mankind and uplifted by the nobility and courage the characters displayed.

Public drama was more than entertainment to the Athenians. It was a form of public education. The plays dealt with great issues that were important to the polis—the power of leaders, the power of the people, questions of justice and morality, questions of war and peace, and the duties owed to the gods, the family, and the city.

The Greek theater at Delphi was set on a hillside with nature as its backdrop. Actors wore masks such as the one at right to show their roles.

For most Greek women, household chores were the main activity. However, Spartan women such as the runner above took part in athletic contests. Sappho, the woman shown on the vase, was considered one of the finest Greek poets.

Drama was so important to public life in Athens that citizens were sometimes paid to attend the plays, just as they were paid for holding public office. As part of their civic duty, wealthy citizens bore the cost for producing the plays.

Athens prospered in the golden age.

The Parthenon and the amphitheater were surrounded by a teeming city. How did it feel to live in such a place?

Athens reeked with the odor of the pigpens most familes kept in their backyards. Foul smells mingled with the raucous noise of the agora. Here merchants in outdoor stalls advertised their goods by shouting. The sound of clanging metal from nearby workshops added to the din. Athens was a city of small shopowners and artisans who specialized in every kind of craft: shoe making, sword making, pottery making, wine making, and so on. The shops were owned by foreigners as well as by Athenian citizens.

Free men and slaves worked side by side in a typical shop and might be given the same meager wages. There were perhaps 100,000 slaves in the city-state of Athens in the 400's, roughly one third the population. Most of them were non-Greeks captured in war. A rich family might own as many as 50 slaves. Even a poor citizen was likely to own one or two. Because poor citizens and slaves dressed much alike, however, it was almost impossible to distinguish them from one another.

The voices in the marketplace were mostly male. A woman's voice rarely was heard outside the home. Cooking meals, nursing babies, and weaving cloth were expected to consume all of a woman's time. If she stepped outside to buy fish at the market, her face was supposed to be veiled. She could not own or inherit land. She had very few legal rights and could not appeal to a jury in her own defense. Unlike her brothers, who started going to school at the age of six, she was educated at home. When she married, she lived in the part of her husband's house reserved for women. She was supposed to retreat there whenever her husband entertained male guests at home.

Most Athenian families lived in tiny, plain dwellings with thin, mud-brick walls. Typical furniture was a few tables and chairs. Often, a family's most valued possessions were the painted pieces of pottery in which they stored their wine and olive oil. The red and black vases made in Athenian workshops were famous throughout the Mediterranean world. In the Age of Pericles, they were Athens's chief export.

Despite its physical discomfort, Athens was in many ways a splendid city. Like the heroes in Sophocles' plays, however, the proud citizens of Athens were soon to suffer a tragic fate.

Sparta defeated Athens in war.

Tension between Athens and Sparta had been building for years. Many people in both cities thought war was inevitable. Instead of trying to avoid war, leaders began to press for a war to begin while they thought their own city had the advantage. Finally, in 431 B.C., the Spartans marched into Athenian territory. They swept over the countryside, burning the Athenians' local food supply.

Athens itself, however, seemed safe. Years before, Pericles had taken the precaution of building the Long Walls, two great ramparts that protected the roadway from Athens to the sea. Thus, Athens was safe from starvation as long as ships could sail into port with food from Athenian colonies as far away as the Black Sea.

Athens was the strongest sea power, but Sparta was the strongest land power. As the leading Athenian general, Pericles did not try to defeat the Spartans on land. Instead, his strategy was to avoid battles with the superior Spartan army and to use Athens's great navy to strike Sparta's territory from the sea.

From the earliest battles, an Athenian named Thucydides (thyoo-SID-ih-deez) wrote about the war in a journal. We still rely on his *History of*

Voice from the Past · *Pericles' Funeral Oration*

In the winter of 431 B.C., Athens honored its war dead with a public funeral. As part of the ceremony, Pericles spoke in praise of the dead and the city for which they had died. His speech is the best expression of the Athenians' pride in their polis.

Our constitution does not copy the laws of neighboring states. Instead, others copy what we do. Our plan of government favors the many instead of the few; that is why it is called a democracy. As for laws, we offer equal justice to everyone. As for social standing, advancement is open to everyone, according to ability. High position does not depend on wealth, nor does poverty bar the way . . .

We take pleasure in the arts, but without extravagance, and in knowledge, but without being soft . . . Our public leaders have their own businesses, as well as politics, to take care of. Our ordinary citizens see to their own livelihoods but are also capable of making political decisions. Unlike other nations, we Athenians do not call a man who takes no part in public life quiet or unambitious; we call such a man useless . . .

In short, our polis is the school of all Greece . . . This is the Athens for which these men nobly fought and died, because they could not bear the thought of losing such a city.

1. How does Pericles define a democracy?
2. According to Pericles, in what aspects of life should a citizen take an interest to lead a full life?
3. (a) How does Pericles describe Athens's position in Greece? (b) What evidence does he offer of its leadership?

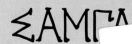

How does the Athens that Pericles describes differ from Sparta? Are Athenians generalists (with wide-ranging interests and abilities) or specialists? (generalists) Are Spartans generalists or specialists? (specialists: warriors)

the Peloponnesian War to understand how this war ruined Athens and weakened all of Greece.

Disaster for Athens Two events were particularly deadly to Athens—a plague and a disastrous military defeat in far-off Sicily. The plague struck in 430 B.C., in the second year of the war. While Spartan soldiers were again laying waste to Athens's farmland, Athenians sought safety behind the city walls. Overcrowding made Athens vulnerable to a frightful plague that killed roughly one third of the population, including Pericles. Thucydides himself fell sick and barely survived.

The second disaster took place in 415 B.C., after the war had gone on for 16 years. The Athenian assembly sent a huge fleet carrying 27,000 soldiers to the island of Sicily, near Italy. Their goal was to destroy the polis of Syracuse, one of Sparta's wealthiest allies. The expedition met overwhelming defeat in 413 B.C. Thucydides reported, "They were destroyed with a total destruction—their fleet, their army—there was nothing that was not destroyed, and few out of many returned home."

Somehow, a terribly weakened Athens managed to fend off Spartan attacks for another nine years. But in 404 B.C., Athens and its allies surrendered. The Spartans then forced the Athenians to join in tearing down the Long Walls, symbol of Athens's strength.

Cultural changes After 27 years of war, Athens had lost its fleet, its empire, its power, and its wealth. It had also lost its self-confidence. This loss of spirit was perhaps the most serious of all for the people of Athens.

Confidence in democratic government began to falter. One leader after another proved weak, corrupt, or traitorous. The assembly began to change its decisions with every shift of the political winds. Leaders and generals were in constant danger of exile if a new speaker persuaded the assembly to turn on them.

Oddly enough, the crisis in public confidence was accompanied by an artistic outburst. As people turned to their private lives, art began to reflect their joys and sorrows. For the first time, the faces of bronze and marble statues began to show emotion.

Drama also underwent a change. It was during the Peloponnesian War that a playwright named Aristophanes (AR-is-TAHF-uh-neez) wrote the first great comedies of the stage. In them, he made fun of the politics, people, and ideas of his time. Athenians laughed at his biting jokes. The fact that Athenians could listen to such criticism of themselves, even in the midst of a great war, showed that the spirit of freedom and public discussion still lived.

Philosophers searched for truth.

In the years after the Peloponnesian War, yet another aspect of Greek culture reached new heights. In this time of questioning and uncertainty, several great thinkers were determined to seek for truth, no matter where the search led them. The name that the Greeks gave to such thinkers was *philosopher*—literally, "one who loves wisdom." The Greek philosophers questioned even the most basic and widely accepted ideas of their time.

Greek thinkers based their philosophy on two original assumptions. First, they assumed that the universe was put together in an orderly way. Land, sky, and sea were all subject to the same laws. These laws were absolute and unchanging. Second, the Greeks assumed that people could understand these laws through reason.

Socrates One of Greece's greatest philosophers fell victim to the frustrations aroused by Athens's defeat in the Peloponnesian War. He was an old Athenian soldier and stonecutter named Socrates (SAHK-ruh-teez). Socrates was not a handsome man, and his clothes and grooming left much to be desired. His agile mind, however, made up for his homely appearance.

Stopping a young man on the street, Socrates would ask if he knew where certain merchandise could be bought. After the youth answered easily, Socrates would ask if he knew where goodness and virtue could be found. No, the youth would reply, he did not know where one could find those. More questions would follow. Soon, Socrates and the young man would be deeply examining some idea like truth or goodness or beauty. (This way of teaching by asking questions is still called the Socratic method.)

Socrates questioned all the accepted values of Athens—democracy, patriotism, religion. He taught that people must examine their ideas by the demanding standards of truth and reason. Those who understood Socrates admired him deeply. The majority of citizens, however, could

This painting, "The Death of Socrates," was painted by the French artist Jacques Louis David in 1787, more than 2,000 years after Socrates died. What impression does the painting give of Socrates?

not understand this strange old man. The bitterness of a long war made them suspicious.

In 399 B.C., when Socrates was 70 years old, he was brought to trial. The father of one of his pupils accused him of "corrupting the youth of Athens" and failing to revere "the gods that the state recognizes." The 501 jurors at his trial listened to Socrates speak in his own defense. He said that his teachings were good for Athens because they forced people to think about their values and actions. In fact, he suggested that the city should give him a pension.

By a majority of 60 votes, the jury voted Socrates guilty as charged. The penalty was death. Friends visited Socrates in prison and pleaded with him to flee into exile. He calmly explained the flaws in their reasoning and drank the slow-acting poison made from hemlock. Athens thus lost one of its greatest citizens.

Plato Among those who had visited Socrates in prison was a brilliant, wealthy idealist named Plato (**PLAY**-toh). He was 28 years old when Socrates died, and the death convinced him that the average citizens of a democracy (who condemned Socrates) were unable to govern wisely.

Plato left Athens in bitterness after Socrates' death. He returned later, however, and established his own school. Plato's school, called the Academy, continued for 900 years.

Unlike Socrates, Plato was a writer as well as a teacher. In his early works, he wrote down the conversations of Socrates as he remembered them. Sometime between 385 and 380 B.C., Plato wrote his most famous work, *The Republic.* In it, he set forth his vision of a perfectly governed society. It was certainly no democracy.

In an ideal community, he wrote, all citizens would fall naturally into three groups. The most common type would be best suited for working as farmers and artisans. A more gifted type had minds and bodies fine enough to be trusted as warriors. Only the third and rarest type should belong to the ruling class. From this highest category, the person with the greatest insight and intellect ought to be chosen philosopher-king. This person might be either a woman or a man.

Answer to caption question: It suggests that Socrates met death calmly and with self control.

113

What mattered most was that the state be ruled by its greatest philosopher.

Plato's writings dominated philosophic thought in Europe for nearly 1,500 years. His only rivals in importance were his own teacher, Socrates, and his own pupil, Aristotle (AR-ihs-tot'l).

Aristotle One of the brightest students at Plato's Academy was a physician's son named Aristotle. Few minds in history were as hungry for knowledge as his. He wanted to know about morals, music, mathematics, biology, botany, geology, medicine, politics, art, drama, language, geography, education, and law. He studied with Plato for 20 years.

Aristotle insisted that every truth followed logically from other truths. You could not miss a step, jumping from truth A to truth C. In the middle, you needed truth B to link the other truths. Aristotle developed a set of logical statements known as a syllogism (SIHL-uh-jihz-uhm). A syllogism consists of three logically related statements. Here is an example:

1. All people are mortal.
2. Socrates was a person.
3. Therefore, Socrates was mortal.

This rigid system for organizing and testing ideas was important for developing rational, scientific thought.

Section Review 3

Define: (a) classical art, (b) tragedy, (c) philosopher, (d) syllogism
Identify: (a) Pericles, (b) the Parthenon, (c) Athena, (d) Phidias, (e) Aeschylus, (f) Sophocles, (g) Peloponnesian War, (h) Thucydides, (i) Aristophanes, (j) Socrates, (k) Plato, (l) the Academy, (m) *The Republic*, (n) Aristotle
Answer:
1. How did Pericles strengthen Athens's position as a leader in Greece?
2. (a) How were the Parthenon and other works of art and architecture examples of Athenian values? (b) How was drama important to the polis?
3. How were the lives of Greek girls and women different from the lives of the boys and men?
4. (a) What were the key events of the Peloponnesian War? (b) What were its results?

5. (a) What topics did Socrates consider important for discussion? (b) How did his views lead to his execution?
6. (a) Why did Plato reject democracy? (b) What type of society did he advocate?
7. How did Aristotle aid the development of scientific thinking?

Critical Thinking

8. (a) Are historians justified in calling this period of Greek history a golden age? Give reasons for your answer. (b) Write a short definition of a golden age that would apply to other civilizations. (Save your definition for reference in later chapters.)
9. How were the assumptions of the Greek philosophers about the universe different from the ideas of earlier civilizations such as the Egyptians and the Sumerians?

Alexander's conquests spread Greek culture. 4

In the years after Athens's defeat by Sparta in 404 B.C., the Greek city-states continued to fight one another. First one polis and then another rose to power, but none was able to bring peace or unity to Greece.

By 350 B.C., the greatest threat to Greek freedom came from a little-known kingdom north of classical Greece called Macedon (MAS-uh-dahn). The Macedonians were a tough, Greek-speaking people who lived in mountain villages, not city-states. Other Greeks looked down on them as uncivilized. They had no great philosophers, sculptors, or writers. However, they did have shrewd and fearless kings.

Philip built Macedon's power.

In 359 B.C., the shrewdest of all the Macedonians, Philip II, became Macedon's new king. Though only 23 years old, Philip knew what he wanted. First, he aimed to unite Greece under his leadership. After that, he planned to invade the Persian empire.

From 356 to 338 B.C., Philip used a combination of war, diplomacy, bribery, and trickery to defeat the Greek city-states one by one. In their continuing squabbles, Philip played them off against one another with great skill. Finally, in 338 B.C., Philip defeated Athens and its ally Thebes at Chaeronea (KAIR-uh-NEE-uh). These two were the last powerful city-states to stand against him. (Sparta was still independent, but it was now so small and weak that it could do nothing against Philip.) The victory at Chaeronea gave Philip control of all Greece.

Although Philip treated Thebes harshly, he was lenient with Athens. One reason for his mild treatment of the Athenians was his respect for Athens as the leader of Greek culture. In fact, around 343 B.C., he had invited Aristotle to tutor the heir to the Macedonian throne, 13-year-old Alexander.

After Chaeronea, Philip began to ready his army for an invasion of Asia. But in 336 B.C., at a great wedding feast for his daughter, Philip was murdered by a Macedonian nobleman. The assassin had a personal grudge against Philip but may also have been in the pay of the Persian king.

Alexander conquered a vast empire.

Philip's son, Alexander, was 20 years old in 336 B.C., when he became king of Macedon. Having studied with Aristotle for seven years, Alexander was steeped in the best traditions of Greek thought. He kept a copy of the *Iliad* under his pillow. He was also a seasoned army commander. He had put down a rebellion in Thrace when he was 16 and commanded a section of Philip's army at Chaeronea when he was 18.

Alexander's conquests Alexander soon showed he meant to keep all that his father had won. When Thebes rebelled, he destroyed the city and sold the survivors into slavery. The other Greek cities, intimidated, quickly fell into line. Then Alexander was free to carry out Philip's plan to invade Asia.

In 334 B.C., Alexander crossed the Dardanelles and set off on a march of conquest that went on for 8 years and covered a route of 20,000 miles. First, he conquered Asia Minor and the eastern coast of the Mediterranean. Then he

This mosaic shows Alexander leading a charge against the Persian army. The mosaic is a Roman copy of a painting done soon after Alexander died.

Gordius, king of ancient Phrygia, tied a knot that could only be undone by the person who would rule Asia. Alexander cut rather than untied the rope. Ask what the story of the Gordian knot reveals about Alexander's character and methods?

115

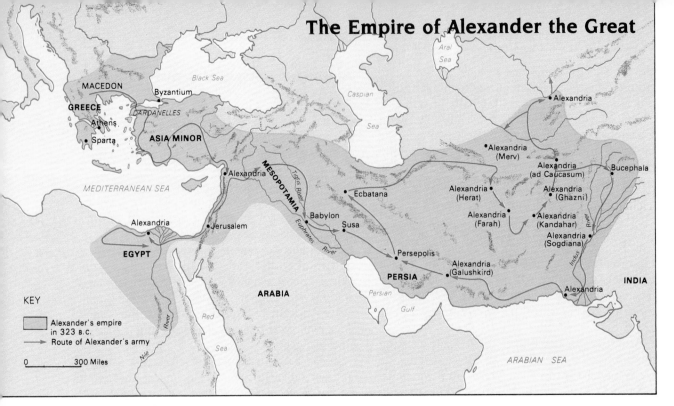

The Empire of Alexander the Great

MACEDON
Byzantium
GREECE
DARDANELLES
Athens
Sparta
ASIA MINOR
MEDITERRANEAN SEA
Alexandria
MESOPOTAMIA
Tigris River
Euphrates River
Alexandria
EGYPT
Jerusalem
ARABIA
Nile River
Red Sea
Ecbatana
Babylon
Susa
Persepolis
PERSIA
Persian Gulf
Black Sea
Caspian Sea
Aral Sea
Alexandria
Alexandria (Merv)
Alexandria (Herat)
Alexandria (Farah)
Alexandria (Galushkird)
Alexandria (ad Caucasum)
Alexandria (Ghazni)
Alexandria (Kandahar)
Alexandria (Sogdiana)
Alexandria
Bucephala
Indus River
INDIA
ARABIAN SEA

KEY
Alexander's empire in 323 B.C.
Route of Alexander's army
0   300 Miles

Map Study

What narrow body of water did Alexander cross to reach Asia Minor? Where did he go after capturing Jerusalem? Where did Alexander build a city to honor Bucephalus, his favorite war horse?

marched into Egypt in 332 B.C. The Egyptians welcomed him as a liberator from Persian rule.

From Egypt, Alexander moved north and east into the heart of the Persian empire around Babylon. Here he smashed the Persian forces. The Persian king, Darius III, fled. Alexander marched into Babylon in triumph. Shortly afterward Darius was murdered by one of his satraps. By 330 B.C., Alexander had become the Great King of Persia.

Alexander continued east, into lands even beyond the reaches of the Persian empire. He conquered the Indus River valley and wanted to go farther. His weary army, however, had faced parching deserts, monsoon rains, and the terrifying war elephants of the Indian armies. The soldiers threatened mutiny, and Alexander turned back.

The army fought its way back, crossing some of the harshest deserts in the world. Shortly after Alexander returned to Babylon, he caught a fever that grew steadily worse. When it was clear he was dying, his loyal Macedonian soldiers filed through the palace past his bedside to bid him farewell. Two days later, on June 18, 323 B.C., Alexander died. He was not yet 33.

The breakup of Alexander's empire Immediately after his death, Alexander's empire broke apart. His three strongest generals each grabbed a piece of it. Ptolemy (TAH-luh-mee) took control of Egypt. Seleucus (suh-LOO-kuhs) took Asia Minor and the Fertile Crescent. Antigonus (an-TIHG-uh-nus) took Macedon.

In Greece itself, individual city-states like Athens and Sparta never recovered their glory. Instead, the city-states grouped themselves into leagues. These leagues and the kingdoms founded by the generals fought with one another almost constantly until a new power farther west—the Romans—came on the scene to rule them all.

Greek culture spread in the Hellenistic Age.

The widespread lands conquered by Alexander were not politically united. However, they developed a common culture known as Hellenism, strongly influenced by Greek civilization. The word *Hellenism* derives from the Greeks' name for their own country, Hellas.

Map Study answers: Dardanelles; Eygpt; near the Indus River

116

A *blending of cultures* Everywhere Alexander had gone, he had established governments run by Greek administrators. Long after Alexander's death, this Greek ruling class continued to spread Greek influence under later kings and queens. The conquered peoples exchanged coins bearing the profile of Alexander the Great. Their public buildings were fashioned in the Greek style. For two centuries after Alexander's conquests, the Hellenizing process affected all lands touching the Mediterranean Sea.

The heart of Hellenism lay in the great cities that Alexander had conquered or founded. Alexander founded more than 70 cities, many of which he named Alexandria in honor of himself. The greatest Alexandria was on Egypt's Nile delta. In its harbor stood a gigantic lighthouse, an estimated 370 feet tall, which greeted ships from all over the Mediterranean. One of the Seven Wonders of the Ancient World, the lighthouse symbolized Alexandria's role as the new center of Mediterranean trade. A huge library containing more than 500,000 papyrus scrolls symbolized Alexandria's fame as the center of learning.

Hellenism was a rich blend of many cultures. In Alexandria, it was part Greek, part Jewish, and part Egyptian. Farther east, it was a blend of Persian and Greek. Although Greek independence was snuffed out by Philip and Alexander, much of Greek creativity was still alive. Hellenistic art, architecture, philosophy, sculpture, and literature showed the influence of many traditions, but its roots were clearly Greek.

Triumphs in science Perhaps the Hellenistic Age's greatest triumphs were in the sciences. Alexander himself had led the way. Even as his armies crossed Asia, he had writers keep records of the plants, animals, weather, and geographic features they found. (Remember, he had been Aristotle's pupil.) Later, the establishment of libraries, the exchange of manuscripts and ideas between cities, and the weakening of ancient Greek religion led to a flowering of science. Two of its geniuses were Euclid (YOO-klihd) and Archimedes (AHR-kih-MEE-deez).

Euclid opened a school of geometry in Alexandria. In his most lasting work, the *Elements*, he logically organized the findings of Greek geometry. The book was used as a geometry textbook in Islamic and European universities well into the 1900's.

Archimedes studied in Euclid's school at Alexandria. He worked with levers, inclined planes, wedges, screws, wheels, and pulleys to find out what laws governed their motions. He discovered that people can use levers to lift objects much larger than themselves. In fact, he once boasted, "Give me a place to stand, and I can move the Earth."

Building on the knowledge of Archimedes, Hellenistic scientists could have started an industrial revolution. They built a force pump, pneumatic machines, and even a steam engine. But they never seem to have considered producing large numbers of these machines. In an age when slaves were plentiful, labor-saving devices had little appeal.

By 150 B.C., Hellenism was losing its strength. A new city, Rome, was at the same time growing and gaining strength. Like Athens, Rome lay on the Mediterranean Sea, but far to the west. Through Rome, the lands of western Europe would soon be introduced to Greek-style drama, architecture, sculpture, literature, religion, and philosophy. These ideas became the heart of Western civilization. How that happened is part of the story told in the next two chapters.

Section Review 4

Define: Hellenism
Identify: (a) Macedon, (b) Philip II, (c) Battle of Chaeronea, (d) Alexander the Great, (e) Ptolemy, (f) Seleucus, (g) Antigonus
Answer:
1. (a) How did Philip II win control of Greece? (b) What was the attitude of both Philip and Alexander toward Greek culture?
2. (a) Describe Alexander's route during his great march of conquest. (b) What happened to Alexander's empire after his death?
3. What changes did Alexander bring to the societies he conquered?
4. (a) What was the importance of Euclid's book, the *Elements*? (b) How did Archimedes build on Euclid's contribution?

Critical Thinking
5. "Alexander's achievements, though brilliant, did not last long." (a) Give evidence to support this statement. (b) Give evidence to refute the statement.

A king asked Archimedes how he could be sure his crown was pure gold. A short time later, while taking a bath, Archimedes realized that gold would displace an amount of water equal to its weight. "Eureka," he shouted, and absent-mindedly ran home naked to test his idea.

Chapter Review 5

Summary

1. Greek culture grew up around the Aegean Sea. Bronze Age cultures on Crete and mainland Greece laid the foundation for later Greek culture. Greek life was also shaped by the mountainous land, the mild climate, and the sea. Adventures of the heroes and gods of the early Greeks have come down to us in the form of epic poems.

2. Greek city-states competed for power. Two of the most powerful city states were Athens and Sparta. Spartans valued military strength above all, whereas Athenians encouraged individualism and creativity. Athens gradually developed a democratic government. After playing an important role in defeating the invading Persian army, Athens became the powerful leader of an alliance of Greek city-states called the Delian League.

3. Athens led Greece in its golden age. Pericles, leader of Greece for 32 years, helped the city grow in military and economic strength. He glorified the city by supporting the work of architects, sculptors, and dramatists. Although Athens's confidence was much shaken by a war with Sparta, the struggle sparked great achievement in the area of philosophy.

4. Alexander's conquests spread Greek culture. Two kings of Macedon, Philip and Alexander, conquered Greece as well as a vast empire beyond. A combination of Greek culture with other cultures, called Hellenism, spread throughout this empire. The Hellenistic Age was marked by important advances in science as well as the arts.

Reviewing the Facts

1. Define the following terms:

   a. epic
   b. arete
   c. polis
   d. aristocracy
   e. hoplite
   f. phalanx
   g. tyrant
   h. colony
   i. democracy
   j. tragedy

2. Explain the importance of each of the following names, dates, places, or terms:

   a. Crete
   b. Mycenae
   c. Trojan War
   d. Homer
   e. Athens
   f. Sparta
   g. Solon
   h. Cleisthenes
   i. Herodotus
   j. 490 B.C.
   k. Peloponnesian War
   l. Pericles
   m. 431–404 B.C.
   n. Aeschylus
   o. Sophocles
   p. Socrates
   q. Plato
   r. Aristotle
   s. Philip II
   t. Alexander the Great
   u. 323 B.C.

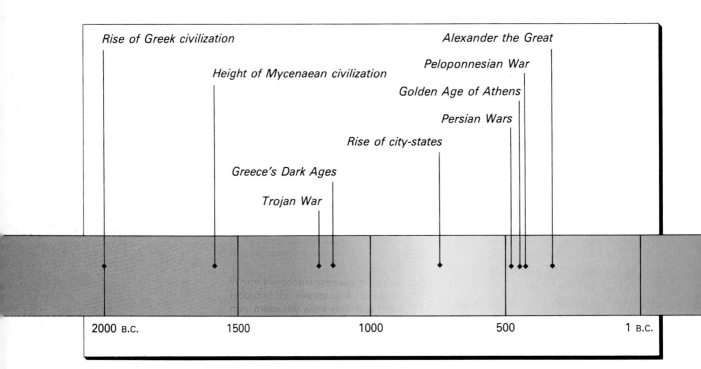

Rise of Greek civilization

Height of Mycenaean civilization

Greece's Dark Ages

Trojan War

Rise of city-states

Alexander the Great

Peloponnesian War

Golden Age of Athens

Persian Wars

2000 B.C.   1500   1000   500   1 B.C.

3. What major changes took place in Greek political organization between 1200 and 500 B.C.?
4. What Greek ideals were expressed both in Homer's poems and in the Olympic games?
5. How did Athens move from aristocratic rule to democracy?
6. Why is the period between 480 and 430 B.C. known as a golden age for Athens?
7. How did the disunity of the Greek city-states lead to their conquest by Philip?
8. How did Greek culture become influential across a broad area outside Greece?

Basic Skills

1. **Interpreting a map** Explain how the map on page 96 illustrates the main idea of that subsection.
2. **Comparing maps** Compare the maps on pages 96 and 102 in terms of title, historical period, region included, and scale.
3. **Sequencing** Arrange the following items in correct chronological order: Dark Ages in Greece, siege of Troy, age of Pericles, reforms of Solon, Persian Wars, death of Socrates, Hellenistic Age, Alexander's empire.
4. **Outlining** Outline the subsection of the text, "Philosophers search for truth," on pages 112–114. Use one heading and three subheadings. Under each subheading, give two items that summarize the major points.

Researching and Reporting Skills

1. **Use the card catalog** In the card catalog in your library, find one book that is a primary source and another that is a secondary source. Use the call numbers to locate the books. Quote a passage from each book to show which type of source it is.
2. **Researching the arts** Greece, together with its overseas settlements and colonies, contains varied examples of Greek architecture. Find information about one of these works. Prepare a report about it, either oral or written, or prepare sketches or diagrams to show the class. List the sources of your information, using proper citations.

Critical Thinking

1. **Giving an opinion** Although Athens and Sparta both had times of greatness, their values and form of government were very different. Which city-state do you think was greater? Give reasons to support your answer.
2. **Evaluating** (a) Compare the ideas of Athenian democracy with those of your country today. (b) In what ways are these ideas alike, and how do they differ? (c) Which do you think is more democratic? Why?
3. **Comparing** Compare the ancient Chinese and Athenian ideas about the role of the individual in society. (a) How are these philosophies alike, and how do they differ? (b) How did the differences affect the development of government in these societies?

Perspectives on Past and Present

1. Pericles said: "Unlike other nations, we Athenians do not call a man who takes no part in public life quiet or unambitious; we call such a man useless." How would Pericles evaluate the behavior of citizens who fail to vote in elections today?
2. If an Olympic athlete of today were to participate in some event of the Greek Olympics, what similarities and differences might that person find?

Investigating History

1. Use the library to find information about the excavations of Heinrich Schliemann at Troy in Asia Minor and Mycenae in Greece and of Sir Arthur Evans at Knossos on Crete. What did those digs show about Aegean civilization?
2. In the library, find books that describe the art of Minoan Crete, Athens at the time of Pericles, and Athens after the Peloponnesian War. (a) How were human and animal figures represented in each period? (b) To what extent might differences in the art of the three eras reflect what was taking place in the society at that time?
3. Find sources on Athenian drama that describe the setting, costumes, and masks that were used. (a) What was the role of song and dance in the theater of Greece? (b) Explain how the role of the audience in the Athenian theater differed from that of an audience today.

The Roman Republic

Warfare was almost a way of life for many Romans.

Key Terms

republic
gravitas
patrician
plebian
consul
veto
senate
dictator
mercenary
proletariat
tribune
triumvirate

Read and Understand

1. The Romans built a great city.
2. The Roman republic spread its power.
3. Republican government collapsed in Rome.

According to an ancient Roman myth, the war god Mars fathered twin sons, Romulus and Remus. Their mother was a Latin princess, Rhea Silvia. A jealous Latin king feared that the twins might some day claim his throne, so he ordered them placed in a basket and set afloat on Italy's Tiber River. The king assumed they would drown. Miraculously, a she-wolf found the half-starved infants and fed them with her own milk. Soon after, a shepherd discovered the babies and brought them up as his sons.

As young men, Romulus and Remus decided to build a city near the spot where they had been abandoned as babies. In the rolling land near the Tiber, each brother chose a hilltop and claimed leadership of the new city. Soon they were quarreling bitterly over their rival claims. In the heat of anger, Romulus struck his brother and killed him. The hilltop Romulus had chosen, the Palatine (PAL-uh-TYN), became the center of the new city. The city itself was called Rome, taking its name from the triumphant and murderous brother.

After a long reign, the myth continues, Romulus disappeared one day during a thunderstorm. A dark cloud enveloped him and lifted him up to heaven. Romulus, now a god, later came back to earth to speak to an old comrade. "Go tell the Romans," he said, "it is heaven's will that my Rome shall be capital of the world. Let them learn to be soldiers. Let them know and teach their children that no power on earth can stand against Roman arms."

Although this story is a myth, it has historic value (as many myths do). It tells how Romans in the days of Rome's greatness viewed themselves and their world. By 27 B.C., Rome had indeed become capital of the world—at least, of the world known to the people of Italy. Rome's ships controlled the entire Mediterranean Sea. Its armies exacted taxes and tribute from people on three continents—Africa, Asia, and Europe.

In the years of Rome's growth, Romans overcame the enemies who surrounded them. At the same time, they developed an effective government and an outstanding system of law. At last, however, disputes among groups of Romans gave way to civil war. The Roman government in which many men had a voice gave way to rule by a single man. This chapter will trace the development of Rome from a small village to "capital of the world."

The Romans built a great city. 1

The map on this page shows the long Italian peninsula. Shaped like a high-heeled boot, it seems ready to kick the nearby island of Sicily. To the east of Italy lies Greece. To the west stretch the southern coasts of modern-day France and Spain. To the south, only 80 miles from Sicily, lies the coast of Africa.

Geography was important to Rome's success. The Italian peninsula is near the midpoint of the

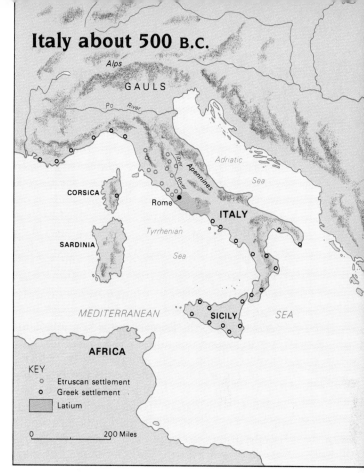

Italy about 500 B.C.

KEY
- o Etruscan settlement
- o Greek settlement
- ▨ Latium

0   200 Miles

Map Study

What mountains lie north of Italy? Where were most of the Greek settlements in Italy?

Mediterranean, dividing the sea into an eastern and a western half. Rome itself is located midway between the Alps and Italy's southern tip. Thus, the city is a central point within a central peninsula. Rome occupies an ideal position from which to send out ships and armies in all directions. Moreover, the city was built about 15 miles inland from the sea, at the first convenient place for crossing the Tiber River. Thus, many key trade routes between northern and southern Italy met at Rome.

Italy's land is mountainous but not as rugged as the land of Greece. The snow-capped peaks of the Alps sharply separate Italy from the rest of Europe. There are, however, passes through the Alps by which invaders and migrating groups could reach the peninsula. A lower mountain range, the Apennines (AP-uh-nynz), runs down the length of Italy. Especially on the western side of the Apennines, the country in ancient times was rolling, wooded, and fertile.

121

Greeks, Latins, and Etruscans battled for Italy.

The earliest settlers of the Italian peninsula arrived in prehistoric times. Around 1000 B.C., Italy's prehistoric period drew to a close. Over the next 500 years, the region's culture was shaped by three dominant groups: the Latins, the Greeks, and the Etruscans.

The Latins The Latins wandered across the Alps into Italy around 1000 B.C. They settled on either side of the Tiber River, a region that they called Latium (**LAY**-shee-uhm). Rome began as a settlement of Latin shepherds, no more than a cluster of round wooden huts perched atop the 300-foot Palatine Hill.

According to the Roman myth, Romulus built his wall around this hill in 753 B.C. At that time, however, Rome barely deserved to be called a city. Its farmers and shepherds lived very simply and wore coarse, homespun clothing. Only a few trade goods from the outside world reached their village. The growth of Rome into a city would soon be influenced greatly by the other two groups that settled in Italy, the Greeks and the Etruscans (ih-**TRUHS**-kuhnz).

The Greeks Between 750 and 600 B.C., settlers from Greece established about 50 colonies on the coast of southern Italy and Sicily. The numerous Greek colonies prompted the Latins to call this area *Magna Graecia*, or Greater Greece. These prosperous and commercially active cities brought all of Italy, including Rome, into closer contact with Greek civilization.

The Etruscans A third group of settlers, the Etruscans, entered northern Italy between 1200

and 800 B.C. Historians have never been sure where the Etruscans originated, but evidence suggests they may have come from Asia Minor.

The Etruscans were much more civilized than their Latin neighbors. The Etruscans had a writing system, which the Latins did not. (Etruscan letters were adapted from the Greek alphabet, which the Greeks in turn had adapted from the Phoenicians.) However, linguists have not yet deciphered the Etruscan language, and so their writings remain unread.

The Etruscans had a great cultural influence on the Latins. Eventually, the Latin settlers of Rome adopted the Etruscan alphabet. Roman buildings show the influence of Etruscan architecture. Etruscans also helped to develop Rome's trade. Several of Rome's kings were of Etruscan background, having migrated to Rome from Etruscan cities.

Romans borrowed religious ideas.

Both the Greeks and the Etruscans had a great influence on the development of Roman religious ideas. Like the Greeks, the Romans were polytheists, believing in many gods and spirits. Unlike Greek gods, however, many early Roman gods had no names or personalities. Instead, they were spirits linked with daily cares such as guarding

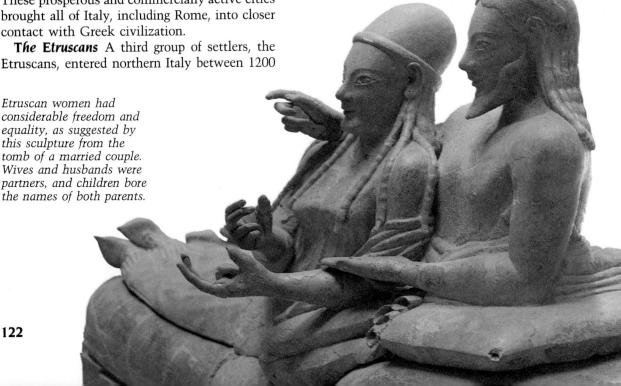

Etruscan women had considerable freedom and equality, as suggested by this sculpture from the tomb of a married couple. Wives and husbands were partners, and children bore the names of both parents.

children's food, protecting the household, and keeping grain supplies safe.

From the Etruscans, Romans learned the practice of "taking the auspices," which literally meant "watching birds in flight." It was auspicious (a good sign) if, before a battle, a vulture or eagle soared overhead. There were also other ways of trying to interpret the will of the gods, including looking at the liver of a slaughtered animal.

Knowledge of Greek gods filtered into Rome through traders. The Romans gave their own names to these gods but kept the legends and personalities of the Greek divinities. The almighty Greek god Zeus became the almighty Roman god Jupiter. The Greek goddess Hera became the Roman goddess Juno.

Romans overthrew their kings and established a republic.

In its early years, Rome was ruled by kings. During the years of royal rule between about 600 and 509 B.C., Rome changed from a collection of hilltop villages to a city. Kings ordered the construction of many of Rome's first temples and public buildings. By royal order, the swampy valley below the Palatine Hill was drained, making a public meeting place. In later years, this valley, known as the Forum (FAWR-uhm), became the heart of Roman political life, as the agora was the heart of the Greek polis.

According to legend, the son of the last king of Rome attacked a Roman woman, Lucretia. The outraged Romans rose in revolt and overthrew the prince's father. Then, the Romans declared they would never again be ruled by a king. Henceforth, any Roman who plotted to make himself king could be killed without trial.

In 509 B.C., Rome set up a **republic,** a government in which citizens who have the right to vote choose their leaders. The word *republic* comes from a Latin phrase, *res publica,* which simply means "public affairs." For the Romans, a republic was not a democracy, because the right to vote and other political rights were not shared by all citizens. Rather, in the Roman republic, various groups struggled for power, sometimes resorting to violence. To understand how the Roman republic worked, we must look first at Rome's social organization.

Romans valued family ties.

Throughout Rome's history, the character of its citizens was influenced by a group of values called "the ways of the fathers." The Romans emphasized discipline, strength, and loyalty. A person with these qualities was said to have the important virtue of **gravitas** (weightiness or seriousness). The Romans honored strength more than beauty, power more than grace, usefulness more than elegance, and steadiness more than quickness of mind. The sober, weighty quality of gravitas left its mark on all aspects of Roman society, from its government to its art.

At the heart of Roman society was the family. By law and custom, power to rule the early Roman household belonged exclusively to one person— the eldest man, known as the *pater familias* (PAY-tur fuh-MIHL-yuhs), or "father of the family." The pater familias had complete power over his family. He controlled all family property. He could sell a family member into slavery or even kill any member of his household without penalty. Usually, of course, the pater familias acted as the protector of his family. It was he who spoke for the family in public assemblies or in the law courts. The pater familias in each household also acted as its chief priest.

Although the pater familias was the legal head of the family, Roman women were in charge of the daily running of the household. A woman in Rome had much greater freedom than in Athens. She was a citizen, with the right to own property and testify in court. She ate meals with her husband, even though he reclined on a couch while she sat upright on a chair. She often advised her husband on business and politics. She did not, however, have the key right, the right to vote. Officially, the Roman woman was expected to remain in the background.

Society was divided into classes.

Not all families were equal in Roman society. Although all male Roman citizens could take part in politics, the city was dominated by a small group of families. Romans of this upper class claimed that their ancestors had been *patres,* or "fathers," who founded Rome. These specially privileged families were known as the **patrician** (puh-TRIH-shuhn) class. They claimed that their

Clans, clusters of families who share a common ancestor, were a key part of Romans' identity. All males in Rome were given three names: a personal name, a clan name, and a family name. Anyone with the middle name Julius (as in Gaius Julius Caesar) was known to belong to one of the oldest, most powerful clans in Rome.

123

ancestry gave them the authority to make laws for Rome and its people.

The common farmers, artisans, and merchants were known as **plebeians** (plih-BEE-uhnz). The plebeians were free citizens with a number of rights, including the right to vote. However, they had far less power than the patricians, who held nearly all important political offices.

Birth alone (not merit or wealth) determined every Roman's social and political status. The line between the patrician and plebeian classes was extremely rigid. In the early years of the republic, for example, marriage between the two classes was forbidden by law.

Rome built a mighty army.

The constant threat of war forced both patrician and plebeian men in Rome to lead double lives as farmers and soldiers. All male citizens were required to serve in the army, and no one could hold public office until he had first served ten years as a soldier.

Learning to fight Roman-style meant being part of a massive military unit called a legion. The Roman legion was made up of 4,000 to 6,000 heavily armed foot soldiers (infantry). A group of soldiers on horseback (cavalry) cooperated with each legion. Every legion was divided into 60 smaller groups, each of which was known as a century.

In battle, the Roman legion proved superior to the Greek phalanx because the legion was more flexible. The wall-like phalanx could move effectively in only two directions—forward and backward. But each century in a legion could move independently. Under a skillful general, a Roman legion could surround and outflank its foes. The legions were the fighting force that spread Rome's power around the Mediterranean.

Daily Life · *The Roman Toga*

Practicality has never been a requirement of fashion. The Roman toga (TOH-guh) was an uncomfortable garment. It was hot in summer, cold in winter, and clumsy for just about any activity but standing still. The toga was, however, practical in one way: It was easy to make, since it involved no sewing. Not even a buttonhole was needed. An adult's toga was basically a large wool blanket, measuring about 18 by 7 feet. It was draped around the body in a variety of ways, without the use of buttons or pins.

In the early days of the Roman republic, both women and men wore togas. Women eventually wore more dresslike garments, called *stolas,* with separate shawls. For men, however, the toga remained in fashion with very little change.

Soon after the republic was formed, the toga became a symbol of Roman citizenship. Different styles of togas indicated a male citizen's place in society. For example, a young boy would wear a white toga with a narrow purple band along the border. When his family decided he was ready for adult responsibilities, he would don a pure white toga. On that day, usually when he was about 16, his family would take him to the Forum, where he would register as a full citizen. For the rest of his life, he would wear a toga at the theater, in court, for religious ceremonies, and on any formal occasion. At his funeral, his body would be wrapped in a toga to mark him, even in death, as a Roman citizen.

The toga had to be sent out for laundering in a large vat in which the agitating action was provided by men's feet.

Section Review 1

Define: (a) republic, (b) gravitas, (c) pater familias, (d) toga, (e) patrician, (f) plebeian, (g) legion, (h) century
Identify: (a) Italy, (b) Rome, (c) Romulus, (d) Palatine Hill, (e) Alps, (f) Tiber River, (g) Apennines, (h) Latins, (i) Etruscans, (j) Forum
Answer:
1. How did geography help Rome?
2. Why was each of the following groups important to Rome's development? (a) Latins (b) Greeks (c) Etruscans
3. What were the values of early Roman society?
4. (a) How was the Roman household organized? (b) What was the role of women in the household? (c) What freedoms did women have in the family and in society?
5. How was the army closely linked to Roman society as a whole?

Critical Thinking

6. Choose one of the earlier civilizations you have studied, such as Egypt or Greece. How did the values of Roman society differ from those of the other society?

The Roman republic spread its power.

2

For 500 years, the Romans governed their city and surrounding farmland as a republic. The history of these five centuries may be divided into two periods of almost equal length.

In the first two-and-a-half centuries (509–265 B.C.), Roman troops battled for mastery of the Italian peninsula. At the same time, in Rome itself, plebeians forced patricians to surrender some of their power.

Footnote to History

Part of a Roman soldier's pay was a special allowance to buy salt. The Latin word for salt was *sal*, and the special allowance was called the *salarius*, from which we get the English word *salary*.

The second half of the republic's history (265–44 B.C.) was marked by civil war, the rising power of army leaders, and the eventual triumph of Julius Caesar. Yet even while Romans fought among themselves, they extended Roman rule around the Mediterranean Sea.

Plebeians slowly won more power.

For centuries, Roman coins bore the letters *SPQR*, which stood for *Senatus Populusque Romanus*—the senate and the Roman people. Together, these two groups were the heart of Roman government. This simple phrase masked years of bitter struggle between patricians (who controlled the Roman senate) and plebeians (who made up the majority of the population).

Conflict between patrician and plebeian After the Romans drove out their kings in 509 B.C., patricians controlled Rome's government. Plebeians were barred by law from holding most important positions in government. Only patricians could command the armies, serve as high priests, or hold the highest political offices. As the years passed, however, plebeians won a greater share of political power.

According to tradition, in 494 B.C., thousands of disgruntled plebeians walked out of the city and camped on a neighboring hillside. They refused to fight in the Roman army unless the patricians agreed to reforms. Between 494 and 287 B.C., the plebeians used this tactic several times. Each time, they won new rights.

Plebeians gradually won the right to hold many political offices that had once been open only to patricians. Laws that had hurt the plebeians were slowly abolished. Enslavement for debt was ended. Plebeians and patricians could marry. Because both sides were willing to compromise, the result was a government in which power was shared.

Twelve Tables Among the first victories of the plebeians was the creation of a written law code. Roman law rested heavily on custom. When laws were unwritten, patrician officials often interpreted the law to suit themselves. Consequently, plebeians demanded that the laws of Rome be published.

In 451 B.C., a special group of ten officials took on the task of writing down Rome's laws. The laws were carved on 12 great tablets, or tables,

The dissatisfaction of plebians came from an economic depression. Many demanded changes in laws that allowed enslavement for debt. Debate: Economic conditions, not idealist concerns, are the prime motivation for political change.

At Roman family meals, the husband reclined on a couch while the wife sat in a chair. The food came from busy shops like the one at the left, which had fruit, chickens, and rabbits.

and hung in the Forum. They became the foundation for later Roman law. Although the laws were sometimes harsh, the Twelve Tables established the idea that all free citizens had a right to the protection of the law. Thus, the Twelve Tables helped to settle the conflict between patricians and plebeians.

Rome achieved a balanced government.

By about 275 B.C., Roman writers boasted that Rome had achieved a balanced government. They meant that their government was partly a monarchy (government by a king), partly an aristocracy (government by nobles), and partly a democracy (government by the people). The Romans believed that this mixture gave them the best features of all kinds of governments.

The office of consul In place of a king, Rome had two officials called **consuls**. The consuls took over many of the powers that the kings had once held. They commanded Rome's army and directed its government. They had the power of life and death over citizens in wartime and great powers in peacetime as well.

The consuls' power was limited, however, by two rules. First, a consul's term was only one year long, and the same person could not be elected consul again for ten years. Second, one consul could always overrule, or **veto**, the other's decisions. (In Latin, *veto* means "I forbid.")

The powerful senate The **senate** was the aristocratic branch of Rome's government. Tradition said that Romulus had named 100 patricians to advise him, thus creating the first senate. Later, the number of senators increased, and plebeians could also be members. Membership was for life. Therefore, the senate provided continuity and stability in the government. It exercised enormous influence over both foreign and domestic policy.

The power of the people The democratic side of Roman government was the assembly. All citizen-soldiers were members of this branch of government. In the early days of the republic, the assembly had little power in comparison to the consuls and the senate. Over the years, however, the powers of the assembly increased. Eventually, its decisions gained the force of law.

The office of dictator In times of crisis, the republic could turn to another type of political leadership, the **dictator**. A man who was named dictator had absolute power to make laws and command the army, but his power lasted for only six months. Dictators were chosen by the consuls and then elected by the senate.

Discussion question: What are the pros and cons of limiting a consul's term to one year in every ten? (Pro: Power cannot remain with one person too long. Con: A consul had little chance to use experience acquired on the job.)

The Roman ideal of a dictator is shown by the story of Cincinnatus (SIN-sih-NAY-tus). In 458 B.C., when Rome's armies were in peril, the senate named Cincinnatus dictator. Cincinnatus was plowing his four-acre farm when messengers brought him the news. He left his plow, defeated Rome's enemies, and stepped down as dictator within 15 days. Then he returned to his farm to finish his plowing.

Rome won control of Italy.

Political struggles between patricians and plebeians were remarkably bloodless during these years. Outside the city walls, however, the blood of both classes was spilled over Italian hills and fields as Rome's legions subdued Italy. City by city, the Romans defeated other Latin groups and the Etruscans. Roman power grew slowly but steadily. And then, Rome suffered a smashing defeat.

The sack of Rome by the Gauls In 390 B.C., Rome's walls were successfully stormed by marauding Gauls (gawlz), a people from the Po River valley, north of the Apennines. The Gauls sacked Rome, leaving it in ruins. Then, the Romans were forced to pay a humiliating bribe to persuade the Gauls to leave.

The Romans recovered rapidly, though. They built a stronger, larger wall around their city. The reconstructed Rome spanned 1,000 acres, making it the largest city in Italy. Foreign troops would not sack the city again for 800 years.

War with the Greeks Eventually, Romans controlled all of the Italian boot except its heel and toe. For centuries, those southern regions of Italy had been colonized by the Greeks.

The Greek cities watched the rise of Roman power with alarm. In 282 B.C., Greek colonists sought aid from Pyrrhus (PIHR-uhs), a king in western Greece. A brilliant general, Pyrrhus brought 20,000 soldiers to fight the Romans. Twice Pyrrhus's army slammed into the Roman legions and drove them from the field. In each battle, however, the Greek army suffered terrible losses. Pyrrhus learned a bitter lesson of warfare (and of life): You can win every battle and still lose the war. In 275 B.C., the Romans drove Pyrrhus's tired and decimated troops back to Greece. Ever since, a victory gained at too high a price has been known as a "Pyrrhic victory."

Rome governed Italy skillfully.

After 275 B.C., the Romans were masters of all Italy except the Po Valley in the north, which was still held by the Gauls. Different parts of the conquered territory were subject to different laws and treatment from Rome.

Latin neighbors on the Tiber were treated as full citizens of Rome. They could marry other Romans, vote in assemblies, and appeal for justice in a Roman court.

In territories farther from Rome, conquered peoples were given the status of half-citizens. They enjoyed all the rights of a Roman citizen except the privilege to vote.

All other conquered groups fell into a third category, allies of Rome. Allies were required to contribute troops to the Roman army. They were forbidden to make treaties of friendship with any state but Rome. An allied city was free, however, to govern its own people without any Roman interference.

Unlike the Athenians, the Romans were willing to extend their citizenship to people outside Rome itself. The new citizens became partners in Rome's growth. This policy helped Rome to succeed in building a long-lasting empire, where Athens had failed.

With most of Italy unified behind it, Rome was now ready to enter the second stage of its astonishing rise to power. In the 250 years after 275 B.C., Roman power spread far beyond Italy.

Rome fought with Carthage.

After the decline of Athens, trade in the Mediterranean region was dominated by two wealthy cities, both on the northern coast of Africa. One was Alexandria in Egypt, still ruled by the Ptolemies. The other was Carthage, the former Phoenician colony. Like Rome, Carthage had the advantage of a location near the midpoint of the Mediterranean coast.

In 264 B.C., Rome and Carthage went to war for control of Sicily and the western Mediterranean. Thus began the first of three periods of struggle known as the Punic (PYOO-nik) Wars. *Punic* comes from the Latin word for Phoenicia.

Let us compare the two cities and their capacity for making war. With a population of 250,000, Carthage was about three times the size of Rome.

Remind students that Carthage was one of the major colonies of the Phoenicians.
Carthage had continued to prosper and controlled all of North Africa and parts
of Spain and Italy.

127

Carthage had a huge navy of 500 ships. Overseas trade had made Carthage an immensely wealthy city. Each year, it collected the equivalent of almost 1 million pounds of gold in tariffs and tribute. With this great wealth, Carthage employed the people of neighboring Numidia as **mercenaries**, soldiers who fight in any country's army for pay.

Rome's resources in ships and wealth seemed meager by comparison. In fact, at the beginning of the First Punic War, Rome had no navy whatsoever. Rome's power had always rested entirely on its armies. However, this great disadvantage was offset by three advantages. First, Rome could draw on a reserve of more than 500,000 troops made available through its conquests in Italy. Second, Rome's citizen troops were generally more loyal and reliable than the mercenaries employed by Carthage. Third, warfare was a Roman specialty. Over the centuries, Romans had directed much of their energy toward winning wars. All of Carthage's energies, on the other hand, had been aimed at winning wealth through trade.

Luck also seemed to favor the Romans. Toward the beginning of the first war, a Carthaginian warship washed up on the Italian shore. Needing a fleet in a hurry, the Romans hastily built 140 ships by copying the Carthaginian design. Unlike the Carthaginian model, however, each Roman warship was equipped with a long gangplank. When not in use, this gangplank was lashed upright to the mast. Attached to the bottom of the gangplank was an iron hook, shaped like a bird's beak and called a raven. When a Roman ship drew alongside a Carthaginian vessel, the gangplank crashed down between the two. Its beak stuck deep in the Carthaginian deck, binding the ships together. Roman soldiers then rushed over the gangplank.

By this means, the Romans won their first two naval battles against the African master of the Mediterranean. Carthage later avenged itself with several shattering victories of its own on land and sea.

The First Punic War dragged on for 23 punishing years before Carthage's last fleet was defeated and sunk in 241 B.C. The defeat marked the end of Carthage as a sea power. Rome took over the rich, grain-growing island of Sicily as the chief prize of victory.

Hannibal sought revenge on Rome.

From 241 to 218 B.C., Carthage and Rome each had other interests. Rome was bent on driving the Gauls out of northern Italy. Carthage set out to win much of southern Spain, which it then turned into a rich colony.

In 218 B.C., however, the uneasy peace between the two cities was broken. The mastermind behind this Second Punic War was a Carthaginian leader named Hannibal, one of the great military geniuses of all time. He was only a boy of nine when his father, a general, made him swear that he would always hate Rome and seek to destroy it. Hannibal grew to manhood on the southern coast of Spain. Here he observed his father's masterful tactics for fighting Spanish tribes and gained experience with troops of his own.

Hannibal's invasion of Italy When Hannibal was 29 years old, in 218 B.C., he assembled an army of 50,000 infantry, 9,000 calvary, and 60 elephants to try to capture Rome itself. He led his army on a long trek from Spain across France and up into the dizzying heights of the Alps. Desertions, battles with Gallic tribes, and blizzards in the mountains killed more than half his men and most of his elephants.

Rome assembled an army to fight this invader, but Hannibal destroyed it. A second Roman army, larger than the first, was also routed. In 216 B.C., a third army of 86,000 Romans found Hannibal's reinforced army of 50,000 men camped at Cannae on the eastern coast of Italy. By brilliant maneuvering, Hannibal drew the attacking army into a deadly trap. In this battle—Hannibal's greatest victory—between 40,000 and 70,000 Romans died.

For the next 13 years, Hannibal marched his armies at will up and down the Italian peninsula. The Romans did not dare to challenge him again in open battle. His soldiers lived off the land, seizing crops and cattle, pillaging farmhouses. However, they could not capture Rome itself. Its walls were too high and their own forces too small even to make the attempt. For years, Hannibal waited for Carthage to send him reinforcements. For years, he waited for Rome's allies to revolt and join his own armies. For years, Hannibal was disappointed.

The Battle of Zama Finally Rome found a general whose boldness and brilliance were nearly

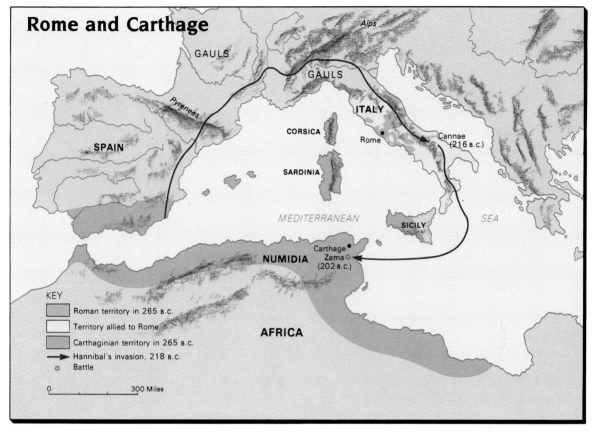

Rome and Carthage

GAULS

Alps

GAULS

Pyrenees

SPAIN

CORSICA

ITALY

Rome

Cannae
(216 B.C.)

SARDINIA

MEDITERRANEAN

SEA

SICILY

NUMIDIA

Carthage
Zama ✿
(202 B.C.)

AFRICA

KEY

Roman territory in 265 B.C.

Territory allied to Rome

Carthaginian territory in 265 B.C.

Hannibal's invasion, 218 B.C.

✿ Battle

0 ———————— 300 Miles

Map Study

How far was Carthage from Rome? Where did Hannibal begin his march to invade Rome? What two mountain ranges did he cross on his way?

equal to Hannibal's. His name was Scipio (SIP-ee-oh). Scipio attacked Carthage itself, forcing Hannibal to rush home to the rescue. The great Carthaginian, unbeaten on European soil, was soundly thrashed by Scipio at the Battle of Zama in 202 B.C. (Hannibal survived and governed Carthage for seven years. He later killed himself to avoid capture by Rome.)

Thus ended the Second Punic War. Zama is one of the few battles that may truly have changed the course of history. Quite possibly, if Hannibal had been the victor, Carthage and not Rome would have become the greatest empire in the world. Because Rome was victorious, it was Rome that passed on its laws, its government, and its culture to Western civilization.

Scipio, in honor of his victory, was named *Africanus* (conqueror of Africa). In the terms of peace, Rome allowed Carthage to keep its lands in northern Africa but nothing more.

Rome made conquests to the east.

Rome now dominated the western half of the Mediterranean Sea. During the next 70 years, Romans also conquered the eastern half.

After the death of Alexander the Great in 323 B.C., his empire had been divided among his generals. Their descendants still ruled the lands around the eastern Mediterranean. The Antigonid dynasty ruled Macedon, the Ptolemaic dynasty ruled Egypt, and the Seleucid dynasty ruled most of what had been the Persian empire. These three—and a few other small kingdoms—were almost constantly at war with one another.

Greece lay nearest Rome, and it was the first to feel Rome's heavy hand. At first, Roman armies marching into Macedon looked like protectors of Greek freedom. The Greeks rejoiced when, in 197 B.C., the Romans freed them from the rule of Philip V of Macedon. Once settled in Greece,

Rome wanted to punish Philip for his alliance with Hannibal.

however, the Romans interfered in Greek politics, crushing all opposition to rulers favored by Rome.

As time passed, the exercise of Roman power in the east became increasingly ruthless. A few Greek city-states tried to free themselves from Rome's tightening grip, but the effort failed. Rome singled out Corinth for punishment as an example to the others. In 146 B.C., its people were massacred or enslaved, its walls wrecked, and its homes and temples burned. The once lovely city was reduced to an ash heap.

Rome finally destroyed Carthage.

In the same year, 146 B.C., Carthage was destroyed. By the time of the Third Punic War (149–146 B.C.), Carthage was no longer a threat to Rome. Yet it was still a prosperous city, and some Romans were filled with hate each time they thought of it. The Roman most responsible for this needless war was a senator named Cato (KAY-toh). Over and over, Cato ended his speeches with the same vindictive message: *"Carthago delenda est"* ("Carthage must be destroyed").

In 149 B.C., Rome forced war on Carthage, seizing on the excuse that Carthage had warred with neighboring Numidia without Rome's permission. The Carthaginians barricaded themselves in their beloved city. For three years, they withstood a Roman siege. Finally, under the leadership of Scipio Aemilianus (uh-MIHL-ee-AY-nuhs)—the grandson of Scipio Africanus—the Roman army broke into Carthage and set it afire. Carthage flamed and smoked for six days, while fighting raged from street to street. Watching the city burn, the Roman general wept. "This is a glorious moment," he said to a friend, "but I am seized with foreboding that someday the same fate will befall my own country." He was right, but Rome's downfall did not come for another 556 years.

Legend says that after Carthage was destroyed, the Romans plowed salt into the soil, so that not even crops would spring up again for Rome's hated rival. The legend, however, is untrue.

After the Third Punic War, Rome continued to expand eastward. In 133 B.C., the western tip of Asia Minor dropped peacefully into Roman hands as the gift of a dying king. This king of Pergamum had welcomed Roman aid against the Seleucids. Dying without an heir, he left his kingdom to Rome. Thus, Rome's Mediterranean empire stretched from Asia Minor to Spain.

Map Study

What territory had Rome gained by 133 B.C. in the region of Asia Minor? Name a city shown on this map that was not under Roman control.

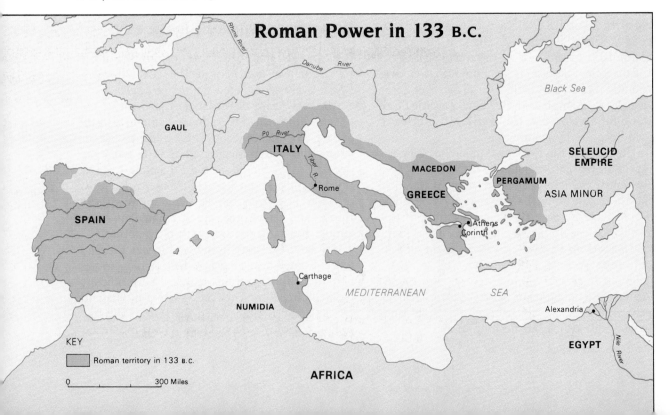

Roman Power in 133 B.C.

Section Review 2

Define: (a) consul, (b) veto, (c) senate, (d) assembly, (e) dictator, (f) mercenary
Identify: (a) SPQR, (b) Twelve Tables, (c) Cincinnatus, (d) Gauls, (e) Pyrrhus, (f) Carthage, (g) Punic Wars, (h) Hannibal, (i) Battle of Zama, (j) Scipio Africanus, (k) Scipio Aemilianus
Answer:

1. (a) Why were many plebeians dissatisfied with Rome's government in the early years of the republic? (b) How did they win reforms? (c) What changes did they bring about in Roman government?
2. Why did Romans consider that they had a balanced government?
3. Once Rome had conquered most of Italy, how did the Roman government win the support of the conquered people?
4. (a) At the start of the Punic Wars, why might Carthage have appeared the stronger power? (b) Why was Rome, in fact, the victor?
5. Why was the Battle of Zama a major turning point in history?
6. (a) Why did the Greeks at first welcome Roman armies? (b) Why did the Greek attitude change?

Critical Thinking

7. (a) How was the Roman republic different from a democracy? (b) What features of the republic were democratic?
8. (a) Give two examples of Rome's increasing ruthlessness as its empire grew. (b) How did Rome's treatment of conquered people outside Italy differ from that of the groups Rome conquered within Italy?

Republican government collapsed in Rome. 3

Carthage was not the only loser of the Punic Wars. Rome was also hurt in many ways. Thousands of men and boys who left their farms to fight in a Roman legion never came back. Those who did return found conditions in Italy drastically changed.

The gap between rich and poor grew.

Hannibal's armies had destroyed farms, homes, and villages. Returning soldiers could rarely afford to rebuild. Many small farmers sold their ruined acres to wealthy citizens. These new landowners treated farming strictly as a business. On their huge estates, known as *latifundia*, they found that raising cattle was more profitable than growing grain. (After the First Punic War, cheap wheat from Sicily had flooded Italian markets.) Labor for the latifundia was cheap because Rome's many wars brought thousands of chained captives to work as slaves.

Battle-scarred farmers could not return to their old way of life. Their land was gone, owned now by wealthy strangers, worked by slaves. Where could uprooted veterans go? Thousands of them sought new homes in or around Rome. They sought city jobs but seldom found them. Wealthy Romans preferred owning slaves to hiring free workers. This new class of urban, landless poor was called the **proletariat** (PROH-leh-TAIR-ee-uht). The people of this class were the poorest of Romans. Without work or hope, they became a dangerous and discontented mob within the city. From this time on, riots were a constant danger in Rome.

While poor farmers lost their land, the rich were corrupted by wealth. Winning a war always meant an opportunity for collecting loot. A victorious general might take a share of the spoils for himself and send the rest to the Roman treasury. After one year's victories, for example, Scipio Africanus displayed in the Roman Forum 123,000 pounds of silver that his army had brought back from Spain and Carthage.

Captured booty was proudly paraded through Roman streets during special holidays called "triumphs." The typical triumph consisted of a victorious general, dressed in purple-trimmed toga and golden crown, riding through a triumphal arch to the cheers of the crowd. He was followed by wagons of loot and bands of veterans.

The spoils of war brought dramatic changes in patrician life. Modest homes turned into ornately furnished mansions. There might be urns from Babylon, silk from China, gold from Carthage, and marble from Athens. While their dress remained rather simple, the rich learned to love exotic foods and lavish entertainment.

Hellenic art and literature were adopted in Rome. How would the new emphasis on luxuries change the valued Roman characteristics exemplified by Cincinnatus?

Slavery became widespread.

The luxury of the rich depended on the labor of slaves. In Rome's slave market, a tablet around the neck of a foreign captive identified his or her special skills and place of origin. Every year, thousands of unhappy captives were inspected and sold. As a result of the First Punic War alone, 75,000 formerly free men and women became Roman slaves. By the year 100 B.C., slaves formed perhaps one third of Rome's total population.

Low-priced slaves, unskilled and uneducated, were assigned to heavy labor in Roman mines, on cattle farms, in vineyards, and in shipyards. The more expensive slaves, usually from Greece and Asia Minor, worked in Roman households as cooks, teachers, musicians, private secretaries, and messengers. In one mansion, a rich Roman kept 11 highly educated Greek slaves just to recite the poems of Homer at his banquets.

Romans lived with the ever-present danger of a massive slave uprising. As the Roman slogan went, "Every slave we own is an enemy we harbor." Three times between 138 and 70 B.C., thousands of slaves rebelled against their masters. The third uprising was by far the most threatening. It was led by the slave Spartacus, who had been trained as a gladiator (a person who fought other warriors or wild beasts as a form of public entertainment). Spartacus raised an army of 70,000 slaves and ravaged the Italian countryside from 73 to 71 B.C. They fought desperately for their freedom, beating the Roman army nine times before their revolt was crushed. About 6,000 of Spartacus's followers were crucified.

The Gracchi attempted reforms.

The worst threat to the Roman republic, however, came from the Roman citizens themselves. The richest families of the city, plebeian as well as patrician, competed for political power. It was a more violent kind of politics than the old struggle between patricians and plebeians. After the Punic Wars, political arguments and rivalries often were settled by bloodshed.

Two brothers, Tiberius and Gaius Gracchus (GRAK-us), attempted to reform Rome's government. The elder brother, Tiberius, was elected to the political office of **tribune** in 133 B.C. Tribunes were officials who spoke on behalf of the plebeians. They were elected by the assembly. Tiberius spoke eloquently about the plight of the landless, dispossessed farmers. "The wolves and the bears have dens to rest and sleep," said Tiberius. "But the men who fight their country's battles have nothing . . . You fight and die only for the wealth and luxury of others. You are called the masters of the world, but you do not have a single clod of earth to call your own." What could be done for these unfortunate citizens? Give them land, said Tiberius. Limit the size of large estates, and distribute lands to the poor people of Rome.

To a poor man, Tiberius's program seemed only fair. To a rich landowner, it seemed like robbery. Tiberius further alarmed the rich by seeking to be reelected as tribune, something never before attempted. On election day, some senators and their followers clubbed Tiberius to death and flung his body into the Tiber.

Gladiators fought to the death in Roman arenas. Political leaders used such games to entertain the proletariat and prevent rebellions.

The Romans had been exposed to the Etruscan practice of slave fights as part of funerals. Originally, gladiator spectacles were scheduled at the funerals of famous Romans.

Ten years later (123 B.C.), the murdered man's younger brother, Gaius Gracchus, was elected tribune. Gaius made the office of tribune the most powerful position in Rome. By his eloquence and political skill, he pushed through a series of laws designed to weaken the senate. He planned programs to deal with unemployment.

The senate's opposition to the younger Gracchus's reforms again led to open violence. Gaius was declared an enemy of the state. The senate offered a large reward for his head. Gaius and his supporters took refuge on one of Rome's hills, where they were attacked by a band of senators with their slaves and foreign mercenaries. Gaius died in the battle. Later, the senate executed 3,000 of his followers.

Army leaders took political power.

After the death of the Gracchi, two army leaders muscled their way to power. First came Marius, whose victories against German tribes made him immensely popular with the people. Then came Sulla, the strong-armed champion of the senate.

Marius and his army saved Rome from a frightening invasion of Germanic tribes in 105 B.C. As a result, he was elected consul five times in a row, breaking the tradition that a consul could not be reelected for ten years. Marius blamed the weakness of Rome's defenses on its dwindling number of citizen-soldiers. Only landowners could serve in the army, and too many farmers had been forced off the land. To make

Voice from the Past · *The Perils of Success*

The Roman historian Sallust lived between 86 and 35 B.C., when Rome was already the greatest power in the Mediterranean region. Sallust had strong views on the course of Roman history, especially on changes he believed had taken place in the character of the Romans.

[In Rome's early years,] good morals were cultivated at home and in the field; there was the greatest harmony and little or no greed; justice and integrity prevailed . . . [Citizens] were lavish in their offerings to the gods, thrifty at home, loyal to their friends. By boldness in warfare and justice in peace, they watched over themselves and their country . . .

But when our country had grown great . . . then Fortune began to grow cruel and to bring confusion into all our affairs. Those who had found it easy to bear hardship and dangers . . . found leisure and wealth, desirable under other circumstances, a burden and a curse. Hence, the lust for money first, then for power, grew upon [Romans]; these were, I may say, the root of all evils. For greed destroyed honor, integrity, and all other noble qualities; taught in their place insolence, cruelty, to neglect the gods, to set a price on everything. Ambition drove many men to become false; to have one thought locked in the breast, another ready on the tongue; to value friendships and enmities not on their merits but by the standard of self-interest, and to show a good front rather than a good heart. At first these vices grew slowly . . . Finally, when the disease had spread like a deadly plague, the state was changed and a government that had been second to none in equity and excellence became cruel and intolerable.

1. According to Sallust, how did Romans show their good moral character in early times?
2. What two evils did Sallust believe were the root of Rome's later problems?
3. To sum up Sallust's ideas, make two lists of words. In the first list, include words that he might have used to describe the early Romans. In the second list, include words he might have used to describe Romans of his own day.
4. Do you agree with Sallust that hard times sometimes bring out better qualities in people than times of prosperity? Explain your answer.

EXEO·OMNIB

up for this loss of manpower, Marius allowed the city's poor to enlist in the army. The new recruits received weapons and armor from the state, unlike the self-equipped citizen-soldiers.

These new soldiers signed up for a period of 16 years—much of their adult lives. In other words, they became professional soldiers. As such, they were willing to fight for any army leader who rewarded them with land and gold. After Marius, Roman armies did not fight for the republic. They fought instead for the military leader who used his political power to give them weapons, food, and loot. More often than not, these leaders used their armies to advance their own political ambitions. It was now possible for rival politicians, each supported by his own army, to win power by force of arms.

In 88 B.C., Marius commanded one army while his rival, Sulla, commanded another. Over the next six years, both leaders used their armies to march against Rome. Each held power for a while and slaughtered the supporters of his opponent. Each forced his own laws on Rome. Sulla, who returned to power in 82 B.C., abolished the six-month limit to a dictator's term and had himself named dictator until he chose to step down. Both Sulla and Marius died peacefully in bed, somehow escaping the violent deaths they had dealt to others. But their pattern of using the army to gain political power outlived them both.

Julius Caesar rose to power.

Among those whom Sulla intended, but failed, to kill was a 20-year-old patrician named Gaius Julius Caesar (SEE-zuhr). Caesar escaped an early death because he understood the uses of money. He bribed Sulla's soldiers to spare his life.

Caesar had little money of his own, but like other ambitious Romans of his day, he knew that the quickest way to wealth was to govern one of Rome's provinces—Spain, Sicily, Gaul, Asia Minor, Macedon, or Africa. A provincial governor could amass a small fortune from just one year's collection of taxes, bribes, and war booty. The position of governor was seldom given to the best administrator. It went instead to the politician who won the good will of the senate and the Roman people.

For more than 20 years, Caesar played hard at the game of Roman politics. In the Forum, he charmed crowds with his brilliant speeches. In his country villa, he threw lavish parties for influential politicians.

To support his extravagant lifestyle, Caesar borrowed huge sums from a man whose well-deserved nickname was Crassus the Rich. Crassus invested in Caesar's political career as a gambler might invest in a racehorse. The gamble paid off handsomely when Caesar was appointed governor of a province in Spain. Caesar collected enough booty there in one year to enrich himself, his soldiers, and Crassus.

The First Triumvirate In 60 B.C., Caesar and Crassus joined forces with Pompey, a popular general. The three men agreed to support one another's political interests. To cement their alliance, Pompey married Caesar's daughter, Julia. With the help of his two allies, Caesar was elected consul in 59 B.C.

Julius Caesar

Victorious Romans usually massacred the relatives of the defeated person. Caesar was one of the few relatives of Marius to escape death at Sulla's hands.

For the next ten years, the three men ruled Rome. The senate and assembly were bribed and bullied into following their decisions. They were known as the **triumvirate** (try-UHM-vuhr-iht), a Latin word meaning "rule of three."

The conquest of Gaul Abiding by ancient tradition, Caesar served only one year as consul. Then he assigned himself the governorship of Gaul. (See the map on page 130.) For eight years, he led his legions in a series of grueling but successful wars in western Europe. He pushed north into the dense woodlands and fertile valleys of central Gaul. He even crossed the English Channel and battled the barbaric tribes who lived in Britannia (present-day England). Back on the continent, he crossed the Rhine River to meet the onslaught of Germanic tribes. According to the historian Plutarch, Caesar's army killed a third of the people in the land it conquered.

Caesar was a tough and dauntless fighter. He drove himself and his troops relentlessly. Carrying 60-pound packs, Caesar's soldiers might march 50 miles in a day. At the day's end, each soldier pulled a shovel from his pack and dug his share of a trench to protect a camp more than one mile square. Inside, two legions (about 9,000 men) could eat and sleep safely before the next day's ordeal. Dinner in Caesar's army was meager: a few handfuls of grain and a cup of sour wine. Caesar himself ate no better. Because he shared fully in the hardships of the march, he won his men's enduring loyalty and devotion.

Never forgetting politics, Caesar sent back regular dispatches to Rome, telling of his victories. Collected into six books, these writings became one of the classics of Latin literature, Caesar's *Commentaries on the Gallic Wars.*

Caesar made himself ruler of Rome.

News from Gaul caused two reactions in Rome. The poorer citizens, who generally adored Caesar, loved him all the more for his conquests. But senators, alarmed at his immense popularity, feared for their own power. By 50 B.C., the triumvirate of Caesar, Crassus, and Pompey had come apart. Crassus was dead, killed in battle while commanding Roman troops in Asia. Pompey had become Caesar's rival rather than his ally. With Pompey's approval, the senate ordered Caesar to disband his legions and return to Rome.

Crossing the Rubicon Caesar's next move led inevitably to civil war. On the night of January 10, 49 B.C., he rode south across the Rubicon River in Italy, the southern limit of his military command. His troops followed loyally behind. Thus, Caesar defied the senate's order and directly challenged Pompey. To this day, "crossing the Rubicon" means making a decision from which there is no return.

Caesar's army marched swiftly through northern Italy and occupied Rome. Pompey barely managed to escape, fleeing eastward to rally his own armies. A year later (48 B.C.), Caesar's troops defeated Pompey's at Pharsalus in Greece. Pompey sailed to Alexandria in Egypt, hoping to win support there for his next campaign against Caesar. Instead, the young pharaoh ordered Pompey to be greeted warmly—and then murdered. When Caesar arrived in Alexandria, he was presented with Pompey's head as a gift. Caesar grieved at the sight, remembering that Pompey had once been both his ally and his son-in-law.

Becoming absolute ruler When Caesar returned to Rome in 46 B.C., he commanded the support of both his armies and the masses. In 44 B.C., the senate appointed him dictator for ten years.

As absolute ruler, Caesar made several sweeping changes. He granted Roman citizenship to many people in provinces outside Italy. Then he expanded the senate to 900 men, adding many of his loyal followers from other parts of Italy and from Gaul. This change made the senate more representative of Rome's empire, but it angered the powerful patricians because it gave Caesar control of the senate.

Some of Caesar's other actions would have pleased the Gracchi. He ordered landowners who used slave laborers to substitute free men for at

Footnote to History

According to legend, while Caesar was in Egypt, a large oriental rug was brought into his quarters. Rolled up inside it was Egypt's 21-year-old queen, the elegant and intelligent Cleopatra. She had herself smuggled into Caesar's presence because she was at war with her brother, the pharaoh. Although Caesar had a wife in Rome, he married Cleopatra under Persian law. With Roman help, Cleopatra defeated her brother and ruled Egypt.

Have students evaluate Caesar's actions as absolute ruler. Were they designed to improve conditions in Rome or to consolidate his power? Are motives important?

135

least one third of their work force. He set up a public works program to create more jobs. He also founded 20 colonies in Spain, France, Switzerland, Africa, and elsewhere to provide land for Rome's landless poor. These programs cut by more than half the number of Romans who lived on government grain handouts.

The calendar Caesar's most lasting reform was to set up a new calendar. He replaced the old Roman calendar, linked to the phases of the moon, with a new solar calendar worked out by the scholars of Alexandria. The new calendar was called the Julian calendar. It counted 365 days in a year and 1 extra day every fourth year. Because the Romans thought February unlucky, they made it the shortest month. The seventh month, July, was named after Julius Caesar, because it included his birthday. The Julian calendar was used in most of Europe until 1582, when slight changes were made for even greater accuracy.

Caesar's death On March 15, 44 B.C., Caesar walked to the Theater of Pompey, where the senate was meeting. Waiting for him were a number of senators with knives hidden beneath their togas.

The chief conspirators, Brutus and Cassius, had been generously pardoned by Caesar for their earlier support of Pompey. Brutus, especially, had been Caesar's friend since then. Even so, both men were still troubled by Caesar's ambitions and his disregard for the old constitution of the republic. They feared that he would make himself king. (According to the ancient laws, you may recall, anyone who plotted to become king could be killed without trial.)

As Caesar approached, the conspirators pressed up against him, pretending to discuss urgent business. Suddenly they struck. Stabbed countless times, Caesar groaned his last words to his old friend Brutus, *"Et tu, Brute!"* ("And you, also, Brutus!") Thus died one of history's most remarkable men.

Civil war followed Caesar's death.

Caesar's assassins thought they had saved the Roman republic. By that time, however, the republic was almost as dead as Caesar himself. Two civil wars (Marius against Sulla and Caesar against Pompey) had crippled the former power of the patricians. Soon after Caesar's death, a third civil war broke out. The final victor of this conflict proved to be an even more astute politician than Julius Caesar. His name was Octavian (ahk-TAY-vee-uhn).

The Second Triumvirate Octavian was Caesar's grandnephew and adopted son. When Caesar was murdered in 44 B.C., Octavian was a frail, sickly youth of 18. Octavian's chief rival, Mark Antony, had been Caesar's trusted comrade. Compared to the young Octavian, Antony was a robust, mature leader and an experienced general.

There was little trust between the two men. For a time, however, they agreed to cooperate in destroying Caesar's enemies. Teaming up with Lepidus, a powerful politician, Antony and Octavian led armies into Rome and forced the assembly to grant them power to rule the state. For ten years (43–33 B.C.), Caesar's three avengers acted together as the Second Triumvirate.

Their vengeance was indeed cruel. A list was drawn up of more than 100 senators and 2,000 businessmen to be killed. One of those murdered was Cicero (SIHS-uh-roh), the senate's greatest orator. Although Cicero had not plotted to kill Caesar, he often had spoken in defense of the republic and against absolute rule. As for Caesar's chief murderers, Brutus and Cassius, they both committed suicide by falling on their own swords after their armies were routed by Antony in 42 B.C. at the Battle of Philippi in Greece.

War between Octavian and Antony The Second Triumvirate ended like the first, in jealousy and violence. Octavian defeated Lepidus and forced him to retire, but Antony's position still seemed secure.

Antony had married Octavian's sister as a political gesture. But while commanding Roman troops in Asia Minor, Antony met the bewitching Cleopatra. (She came to greet him on a barge rowed with silver oars and adorned with purple sails.) Egypt's queen wooed and won Antony as she had won Caesar. Antony sent back word to Rome that he was divorcing Octavian's sister and marrying Cleopatra. In the senate, Octavian accused Antony of plotting to rule Rome from the foreign city of Alexandria. Rome braced itself for a third civil war, this one between Antony and Octavian.

The two forces clashed in a naval battle off the west coast of Greece. In the Battle of Actium (31 B.C.), the fleet commanded by Antony and

Popular opinion of Cleopatra held that she was a dangerous woman who tempted Antony away from his loyalty to Rome. Most of Antony's troops deserted him in the Battle of Actium when Cleopatra demanded to enter the battle herself.

This cameo shows Octavian (Augustus) after he was well established as Rome's sole ruler.

Cleopatra was defeated by Octavian's navy. The couple later committed suicide. To make his triumph even sweeter, Octavian made Egypt another province of Rome.

Octavian became sole ruler.

Like Caesar before him, Octavian was now the sole ruler of Rome. The powers in his hands were as great as a king's or emperor's. However, Octavian remembered what happened to his grand-uncle, Caesar. As a politician, Octavian was more cautious than Caesar, and therefore he lived longer. Instead of seeking a crown, Octavian took only the title of "first citizen."

In 27 B.C., the senate begged Octavian to accept the title of Augustus (aw-GUS-tus). The word means "exalted one" and was normally reserved for the gods. Octavian offered token resistance and then graciously accepted the honor. Afterward, he was known by his honorary title, Augustus, rather than Octavian.

The Roman state under Augustus was no longer ruled by the senate and the assembly as a republic. It was ruled by one man as an empire. However, the senate and the assembly continued to meet and transact business in the old ways. Augustus continued to address the senate as if, at any time, it could strip him of his power and titles.

The senators were not fools. They understood that Augustus held the real power while they held almost none, yet they played along. After all, only by flattering and supporting Augustus could they hope to win appointment to a rich government post in the provinces. Besides, what could they hope to achieve by plotting to overthrow him? Nothing but another civil war, perhaps ending in their own deaths. Thus, Roman politicians found it convenient to let the ancient republic die while pretending that it still lived.

Octavian was to rule Rome for 41 years. His reign marked the beginning of the longest period of peace and prosperity that Rome ever knew.

Section Review 3

Define: (a) latifundia, (b) proletariat, (c) gladiator, (d) tribune, (e) triumvirate
Identify: (a) Spartacus, (b) the Gracchi, (c) Marius, (d) Sulla, (e) Julius Caesar, (f) First Triumvirate, (g) Cleopatra, (h) Brutus, (i) Octavian, (j) Second Triumvirate, (k) Mark Antony, (l) Cicero
Answer:
1. How did victory in the Punic Wars change Roman society?
2. How did slavery undermine Roman society?
3. What reforms did the Gracchi try to make?
4. How were military leaders able to gain political power in Rome?
5. (a) What tactics did Julius Caesar use in his rise to power? (b) What groups supported Caesar? (c) What groups opposed him?
6. (a) Why did Octavian and Mark Antony join forces? (b) How did Rome come under the rule of one man?

Critical Thinking
7. (a) What event do you think was the turning point in Rome's change from a republic to one-man rule? (b) Give two reasons to support your answer.

137

Summary

1. The Romans founded their city. Rome grew up at a location with many geographic advantages. Its early culture was influenced by Latins, Greeks, and Etruscans. At first, Rome was ruled by kings, but in 509 B.C. it became a republic. Roman society was divided into two classes, patricians and plebeians. Over the years, plebeians gradually won more and more rights. By about 275 B.C., Rome claimed to have achieved a balanced form of government.

2. The Roman republic spread its power. Between 509 and 265 B.C., plebeians won increasing political power, leading to a government that blended elements of monarchy, aristocracy, and democracy. Also by 265 B.C., Rome had won control of Italy. At that point, Rome began to expand around the Mediterranean, starting with the defeat of Carthage and extending eastward to Greece and Asia Minor.

3. Republican government collapsed in Rome. The Punic Wars and the spread of slavery brought great changes to Rome. Many Romans became landless and jobless. Political struggles became increasingly violent, and army leaders won control of the government. In 44 B.C., Julius Caesar became sole ruler of the Roman empire. After Caesar's assassination, Octavian held power, becoming king in all but name.

Reviewing the Facts

1. Define the following terms:

a. republic	g. senate
b. gravitas	h. dictator
c. patrician	i. mercenary
d. plebeian	j. proletariat
e. consul	k. tribune
f. veto	l. triumvirate

2. Explain the importance of each of the following names, dates, places, or terms:

a. Rome	k. Battle of Zama
b. Italy	l. 146 B.C.
c. Latins	m. the Gracchi
d. Etruscans	n. Julius Caesar
e. 509 B.C.	o. 49 B.C.
f. pater familias	p. 44 B.C.
g. Carthage	q. Cleopatra
h. Twelve Tables	r. Brutus
i. Punic Wars	s. Octavian (Augustus)
j. Hannibal	t. Mark Antony

3. Explain how each of the following factors influenced life in early Rome.
   a. the geography of Italy
   b. Latin, Greek, and Etruscan settlers
   c. the existence of social classes
   d. the constant threat of war

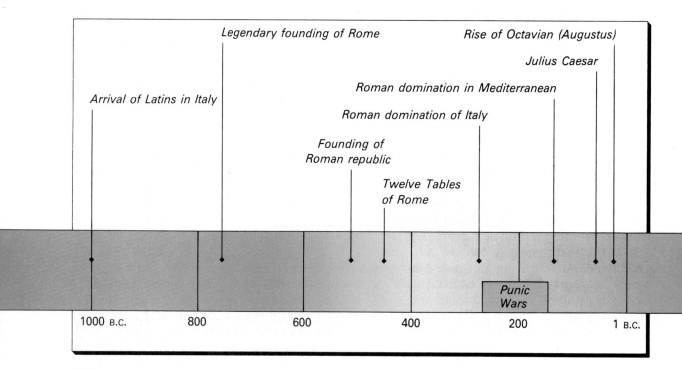

Legendary founding of Rome

Rise of Octavian (Augustus)

Julius Caesar

Roman domination in Mediterranean

Arrival of Latins in Italy

Roman domination of Italy

Founding of Roman republic

Twelve Tables of Rome

Punic Wars

1000 B.C.   800   600   400   200   1 B.C.

4. (a) What was the conflict between patricians and plebeians in the earliest days of the Roman republic? (b) How was the conflict reduced?
5. Describe the structure of Rome's government during the republic. In your discussion, include both the powers and the limitations of each part of the government.
6. How did Rome use its idea of citizenship to unify the lands it won in Italy?
7. (a) How was Rome strengthened by the Punic Wars? (b) How was the Roman republic weakened by the Punic Wars?
8. How was the rise of rulers such as Marius, Sulla, and Julius Caesar different from that of early leaders of the republic?

Basic Skills

1. **Comparing map scales** (a) On the map on page 96, what is the distance from Mount Olympus to Sparta? (b) On the map on page 129, what is the distance from Rome to Carthage? (c) Compare the scale of miles on the two maps. What illusion does the difference in scale create?
2. **Making a time line** Draw a time line for the period from 400 B.C. to 1 B.C., dividing it into eight 50-year segments. On the time line, place the following events in the correct location: first Punic War, destruction of Corinth, sack of Rome by the Gauls, destruction of Carthage, conquest of Gaul, Rome's final victory over Phyrrus.
3. **Identifying supporting details** Give three facts that support the general statement, "The geographic location of Rome offered many advantages for growth."
4. **Making a chart** Make a chart comparing Rome and Carthage at the start of the Punic Wars. For the vertical rows, use the headings *Population, Army, Navy,* and *Resources.* Complete the chart by filling in the information.
5. **Predicting outcomes** (a) On the basis of the information in the previous chart, what would you expect to be the outcome of the Punic Wars? (b) What factors changed the course of events?
6. **Using historical terms** Contemporaries are people who live at the same time, such as Cicero and Julius Caesar. Name a contemporary of each of the following people: (a) Hannibal, (b) Gaius Gracchus, (c) Marius, (d) Sallust.

Researching and Reporting Skills

1. **Using a historical atlas** A historical atlas is an atlas containing maps of places or regions at different times in the past. In a historical atlas, find a map of some period of Roman history and photocopy it. Explain to the class what the map shows.
2. **Reporting on history** Write a news story about the assassination of Julius Caesar. Start with the dateline "Rome, March 15, 44 B.C." In the lead paragraph, tell *who, what, when, where, why,* and *how* in relation to the event. In later paragraphs, give more details about the identity and motives of the assassins and the expected consequences for Rome. Finish by creating a headline for the story.

Critical Thinking

1. **Comparing** (a) Compare the Roman ideal of *gravitas* with the Athenian ideal of *arete.* (b) What do the differences in these ideals tell about the civilization they represent?
2. **Analyzing outcomes** Imagine that you are Julius Caesar deciding whether to cross the Rubicon. (a) What may you achieve if you cross it? (b) What might you lose by crossing it? (c) If you were Caesar, which decision would you make? Why?
3. **Analyzing** (a) Marius changed the Roman army from a body of citizen-soldiers to one of professional soldiers. What advantages did this change have for Rome? (b) What disadvantages?
4. **Analyzing** Rome was the victor in the Punic Wars, but at great cost. (a) What did Rome gain? (b) What were the social and economic costs for Rome?

Perspectives on Past and Present

Reread the quotation from Sallust on page 133. From your knowledge of this period of the Roman empire, evaluate how accurate his assessment is. To what extent might the quotation be applied to society today?

Investigating History

Read the murder scene in Shakespeare's play *Julius Caesar.* Then act out a trial in class to judge whether Brutus and Cassius should be pardoned for acting in defense of the Roman republic or be punished as murderers. Select a prosecuter, a defender, witnesses, and a jury to hold the trial.

Chapter 7

29 *B.C.* - *A.D.* 476

The Roman Empire

The Colosseum in Rome was a center for gladiatorial combats. Its shape is used today for many football stadiums.

Key Terms

civil service
satire
villa
bishop
pope
inflation

Read and Understand

1. Augustus's rule began the Pax Romana.
2. Romans extended Greek culture.
3. Christianity spread through the empire.
4. Rome's empire declined and fell.

In A.D. 80, tens of thousands of spectators poured into Rome's new sports arena, the Colosseum (KAHL-uh-SEE-uhm). To celebrate its opening, spectacles were held every day for 100 days. The Colosseum was the largest building of its kind in the ancient world. A tribute to Roman engineering, it was built so tightly that its arena could be filled with water for mock naval battles.

From the outside, the Colosseum looked truly colossal. Its 160-foot-high walls had 4 tiers of windows, columns, and arches. The Colosseum's 80 entrances were set in the bottom row of arches. As many as 50,000 spectators with numbered tickets entered through 76 of these entrances. Two entrances were reserved for Emperor Titus and his party. The last two were reserved for the gladiators themselves.

The ruins of the Colosseum do not reflect the color and splendor the Romans would have seen. Awnings of brilliant scarlet, blue, and yellow stretched across the top. The sunlight passing through these awnings gave color to all the proceedings.

Once inside, spectators climbed sloping ramps to their seats. The bottom tier featured boxes for the emperor, state priests, and senators. Above them, in rows of marble seats, sat distinguished citizens, members of the middle class, favored slaves, and foreigners, in that order. In the fourth tier, on wooden benches sat women and the poor. No matter where people sat, however, there was a clear view of the arena below. Overhead was a tremendous colored awning that could be rolled out on cables to shield the audience against sun and rain.

The show started early in the morning and lasted all day. Sometimes it opened with a contest between comics, but it soon became bloody. Mornings were devoted to animal shows. Tigers, lions, bears, elephants, and giraffes from distant parts of the empire were released into the arena to fight to the death. In the afternoon, professional gladiators fought animals or one another. Most gladiators were slaves, prisoners of war, or condemned criminals. But others, including a few women, were free Romans who chose to gamble their lives for a short span of glory and public adoration.

The Romans had adopted gladiator contests from the Etruscans. For the Etruscans, such contests had had religious importance. For the Roman government, however, the bloody entertainments in the Colosseum served a political purpose. They were one way to entertain the thousands of unemployed—and potentially dangerous—people who flocked to the city of Rome.

In many ways, the Colosseum is symbolic of the entire Roman empire. From the outside, both were awesome in their size and strength. Within, both combined bravery, honor, and glory with cruelty, sensationalism, and violence.

Rome was at the peak of its power from the time of Augustus's rule to A.D. 180. Then it began a long and uneven decline to the collapse of the western empire in A.D. 476. In the first part of this 500-year period, Rome advanced in architecture, law, philosophy, and literature. At the same time, faith in a new religion, Christianity, spread widely through the empire. Gradually, however, the Roman empire lost the strength to fight off its enemies. In the end, a barbarian king ruled in Rome, and Rome's culture was transferred to a new capital city in the east, Constantinople.

Augustus's rule began the Pax Romana. 1

Pax (paks) is the Latin word for "peace." For 207 years (27 B.C.–A.D. 180), peace was the chief gift that Rome gave the people it ruled. Though legions still fought on the borders of the empire, the immense territory within those borders was largely free of war. This period of peace and prosperity is known as the *Pax Romana*.

The borders of the empire during the Pax Romana measured 10,000 miles and enclosed an area of more than 3 million square miles, about the size of the United States today. The empire extended north to Scotland in the British Isles, south to the Sahara in Africa, east to Mesopotamia in Asia, and west to the Atlantic Ocean. The population of the empire during this period was between 70 and 90 million people. The city of Rome itself was home to about 1 million people.

Augustus set up sound government.

Augustus was perhaps Rome's ablest emperor. He built the foundation for the Pax Romana through a number of far-sighted actions. He encouraged trade, glorified Rome by a splendid building program, and created a system of government that survived for centuries.

Just as important, Augustus set the tone for the empire by extolling the old values of simplicity, sober conduct, and patriotism. Augustus dressed in homemade white togas and lived in a small house on the Palatine Hill.

Trade and transportation In Augustus's time, a silver coin called a denarius (dih-NAIR-ee-uhs) circulated throughout the empire. (It looked very much like an American quarter.) Having a common coinage made trade between different parts of the empire much easier.

Footnote to History

As the adopted son of Julius Caesar, Augustus used *Caesar* as one of his titles. Over the years, the word came to mean "an emperor or ruler." So powerful did the word become that nearly 2,000 years later the ruler of Germany was called kaiser, and the ruler of Russia czar.

Students should note that Greeks also enjoyed contests—the Olympics, for example—but their contests did not involve weapons or a fight to the death.

Augustus also realized that it hurt trade to tax goods as they moved across each province's border. Therefore, he eliminated all such taxes, making Roman lands one large economic empire.

To improve transportation and to bind his empire together more tightly, Augustus began a program of highway construction. Continuing his work, later emperors turned Roman highways into one of the most lasting monuments of their civilization. Roman roads were as impressive in their own way as the pyramids of Egypt. By A.D. 100, there were 50,000 miles of major roads and more than 200,000 miles of secondary roads connecting the cities of the empire.

A *public building program* Marvels such as Rome's roads and bridges were possible through the use of an amazing new building material: concrete. The Romans had learned to mix lime mortar, pour it into a wooden mold, and wait for it to become as hard as stone. Concrete formed the backbone of Rome's bold architecture. The Romans used concrete and decorated its surface with more costly materials, such as marble.

Augustus, however, never bragged about his use of cement. He liked to boast that he had turned Rome from a city of brick into a city of marble. He commissioned Greek artists and architects to build temples similar to the Parthenon throughout the city. During Augustus's reign, Rome began to look like a world capital.

The *civil service* Under Augustus, Rome became the center of an efficient imperial government. Augustus left the senators their titles and money-making positions in the provinces, but he gave much of the real work of running the empire to plebeians and even slaves.

Augustus set up a **civil service**, with salaried, experienced workers to take care of Rome's grain supply, road repairs, the postal system, and all the other work of running an empire. People of all ranks served in this civil service. Hardworking, loyal freedmen (former slaves) won many of the highest and most influential positions. Because these men had a rare opportunity to improve their lot, they served Augustus well.

Peace continued after Augustus died.

Because Augustus had been a sickly youth, his enemies had hoped he would not rule long. But Augustus was more durable than he had looked. He died at the age of 76 in A.D. 14.

When Augustus died, the senate promptly hailed his adopted son and chosen successor, Tiberius (tye-**BIHR**-ee-uhs), as the new ruler. Tiberius and the three emperors after him are known as the Julian emperors because they were descended from the family of Julius Caesar. None of them, however, matched Augustus or Julius Caesar in boldness or skill.

Looking at economics *Aqueducts like this one at Segovia, Spain, carried water to many Roman cities. An adequate supply of water was essential to urban growth and economic development.*

In the years of the Pax Romana, some of Rome's emperors were conscientious, intelligent, and able. Some were corrupt, cruel, or incompetent. One or two were probably insane. (Caligula, for example, appointed his horse consul and talked to statues in the Forum.) Yet the senate and the Roman people put up with each of them and even worshiped them. The system of government set up by Augustus proved to be more stable and effective than its individual leaders.

The problem of succession Rome's emperors never satisfactorily solved the problem of succession. When an emperor died, who was to take his place? Was it to be a person chosen by the senate or a person chosen by the dying emperor himself? Should the favorite candidate of one of the provincial armies be appointed? Or should the Praetorian (pree-TOH-ree-uhn) Guard—the army of 9,000 men stationed in Rome—impose its choice on the empire by force?

At one time or another, each of these methods was tried. Since there was no fixed rule of succession, every time an emperor died there was a potential crisis. When the emperor Nero committed suicide, for example, provincial armies and the Praetorian Guard took turns proclaiming a new emperor, then promptly murdering him, and installing another. In 18 months (A.D. 68–69), Rome had 4 emperors.

The Good Emperors The succession problem was temporarily solved by the men known to history as the Five Good Emperors, or the Adoptive Emperors. When Domitian (doh-MEE-shuhn) was assassinated in A.D. 96, the senate chose Nerva emperor. Nerva made only one vital contribution to the Pax Romana. He adopted as his heir a respected army leader, Trajan (TRAY-juhn). When Nerva died in 98, Trajan was peacefully accepted by armies and senate alike as emperor. Trajan then adopted a distant relative, Hadrian (HAY-dree-uhn), as his successor. Hadrian adopted Antoninus Pius, and Antoninus, in turn, adopted Marcus Aurelius (aw-REE-lee-us), who ruled until the year A.D. 180.

Voice from the Past · A Roman Citizen

"*Civis Romanus sum*" (I am a Roman citizen). Aside from being a proud boast, this statement guaranteed a person the protection of Roman law and also some important privileges in traveling and doing business within the empire. Around A.D. 150, a Greek writer named Aelius Aristides described the idea of Roman citizenship.

Most wonderful of all is your noble idea of citizenship. There is nothing on earth like it. For you have divided all the people of the empire . . . into two groups. The more cultured, better born, and more influential everywhere you have declared Roman citizens. . . . All others are mere subjects. No barrier of sea or land cuts one off from citizenship . . . Everything lies open to everybody, and no one who is worthy to be trusted with public office is considered a foreigner . . .

You have not made Rome a target of envy by letting no one else share in it . . . You have made the word "Roman" apply not to a city but to a universal people . . . As a result, there are many people in each city who are . . . fellow citizens of yours . . . You have no need to keep troops in those cities; the greatest and most influential men everywhere keep watch over their own native places for you. You have a double hold on those cities—from here [Rome] and through the Roman citizens in each.

1. (a) Is everyone within the empire a Roman citizen? (b) What groups in each city are citizens?
2. What military advantage for Rome results from Rome's policy, according to the writer?
3. What benefits might come to a city from being ruled by local people who had become Roman citizens instead of by officials from Rome itself?
4. Do you think this was a wise and fair policy for Rome to follow? Explain.

ΠVIVSQ·ME

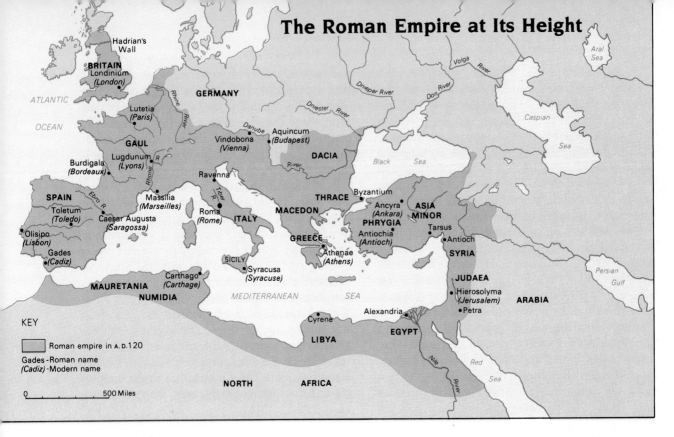

The Roman Empire at Its Height

KEY

☐ Roman empire in A.D. 120

Gades - Roman name
(Cadiz) - Modern name

0 ___ 500 Miles

Map Study

Rome's empire reached its greatest size under Emperor Trajan in A.D. 117. His successor, Hadrian, strengthened its borders. He ordered the building of the wall shown below to keep out barbarians. Where was it located?

Thus, for 85 years, 5 emperors succeeded one another without bloodshed. Although historians call the whole group the Good Emperors, three were perhaps better than good. Trajan, Hadrian, and Marcus Aurelius came close to greatness.

Even during Marcus Aurelius's lifetime, the Pax Romana was severely tested and strained. A dreadful disease—possibly the plague—swept across the eastern provinces into Rome itself, where it killed 2,000 people in a single day. German tribes overwhelmed Roman legions along the Danube River, the empire's northern frontier. After Marcus Aurelius's death in A.D. 180, the Pax Romana collapsed, marking the end of Rome's golden age.

Section Review 1

Define: (a) civil service, (b) succession
Identify: (a) Colosseum, (b) Pax Romana, (c) Augustus, (d) the Julian emperors, (e) the Good Emperors

144

Map Study answer: Britain

Answer:

1. Describe three ways in which Augustus contributed to Rome's success as the center of a great empire.
2. (a) Why was the death of an emperor often followed by violence of some kind? (b) How did the five Good Emperors temporarily solve this problem?
3. Name two events that weakened the empire during the last years of the Pax Romana.

Critical Thinking

4. How might the growth of a civil service make the individual character of a ruler less important to the empire?

Romans extended Greek culture. 2

Under the Roman empire, hundreds of territories were knitted into a single political state. Cities grew in lands where cities had never been known before. Those cities looked very much alike because they had the same model: Rome. Governing lands as different as Britannia and Judaea, Gaul and northern Africa, was in itself a great achievement. The government in one province was set up much like that in another. Goods moved untaxed over Roman roads. Those goods were paid for with Roman coinage. Latin, the language of Rome, could be understood throughout the empire. People who could read shared in a growing body of Latin literature.

The Romans were proud of their ability to rule, but they acknowledged Greek leadership in the fields of art, architecture, literature, and philosophy. Educated Romans learned the Greek language. Emperors and wealthy citizens copied Greek architecture and hired Greek sculptors. The Pax Romana spread Greek as well as Roman achievements. The blend of these two cultures sometimes is called "Greco-Roman" culture.

New schools of philosophy arose.

The tradition of Greek philosophy had continued since the days of Socrates, Plato, and Aristotle. Meanwhile, over the years, traditional Roman religion had lost its meaning for many Romans. In the later years of the Roman republic and the early years of the empire, the Romans turned increasingly to two philosophies.

Epicureanism Epicurus (ep-ih-KYU-rus) lived in Athens between 342 and 270 B.C. He taught that the way to gain happiness was to free the body from pain and free the mind from fear. To avoid pain, Epicurus said that people should avoid all excesses, including those of pleasure. Next, people should accept that death was the end of all existence. Epicurus said there was no life after death and, therefore, nothing to fear.

By the time Epicurus's philosophy reached imperial Rome, the part about avoiding excess had been forgotten. Instead, wealthy Romans used the philosophy to justify pursuing pleasures.

Stoicism A Greek philosopher named Zeno (ZEE-noh) developed a philosophy that had even more influence on Romans than Epicureanism. Zeno gathered his followers on the porch (or *stoa*) near the marketplace in Athens. Hence, his philosophy became known as Stoicism (STOH-ih-SIHZ-uhm). This philosophy was popular in Rome because it encouraged virtue, duty, and endurance.

Zeno (336–263 B.C.) taught that the universe was controlled by a superhuman power, sometimes called the Universal Law, Divine Reason, or simply Supreme Power. The Stoics taught the virtues of duty, reason, and courage. Pain and pleasure were considered unimportant. Stoic ideas supported traditional Roman values. Wealthy families hired Stoic scholars as tutors for their sons. Many of these young men rose to political power as adults, giving the Stoics great influence in politics.

One of the most noted Stoics was the emperor Marcus Aurelius. During the seven hard and lonely years he spent with his armies on the Danube frontier, Marcus Aurelius wrote in the evenings to console himself. His words show his sadness but also his steadfastness.

Ants, loaded and labouring, mice, scared and scampering; puppets jerking on their strings—that is life. In the midst of it all, you must take your stand, good-temperedly and without disdain, yet always aware that a man's worth is no greater than the worth of his ambitions.

Marcus Aurelius's daily jottings were collected into a book called the *Meditations*. This work

Stoics said that all people everywhere share the divine spark and belong to a "world-state." This philosophy was used to bolster Roman imperialism: If there is going to be a world-state, who better to rule than the Romans?

145

Emperors of the Pax Romana

Name	Dates of Rule (A.D.)	Summary of Reign
Julian dynasty—related to family of Julius Caesar		
Tiberius	14–37	A good administrator; improved provincial government and the empire's tax system; later years marked by wholesale treason trials and executions
Caligula	37–41	Mentally disturbed; assassinated after short, brutal reign
Claudius	41–54	Considered slow-witted as a child but became an able, intelligent emperor; added Britannia to empire; set up government departments for accounts, correspondence, and justice
Nero	54–68	Became emperor at 16; devoted to the arts; a good administrator but increasingly vicious in his use of power; responsible for many murders, including that of his own mother; rebuilt Rome after the great fire of A.D. 64; began persecution of Christians; committed suicide
Army emperors		
Galba, Otho, Vitellus	68–69	Succession crisis; three emperors chosen by various factions in the armies
Flavian dynasty		
Vespasian	69–79	Ended civil war of A.D. 69; restored empire's finances; reformed army
Titus	79–81	Opened Colosseum; reign marked by the eruption of Vesuvius that destroyed Pompeii and Herculaneum
Domitian	81–96	Ruled dictatorially but efficiently; later feared treason everywhere and executed many; was assassinated
The Five Good Emperors, or the Adoptive Emperors		
Nerva	96–98	Senator, appointed emperor by senate; began custom of adopting heir
Trajan	98–117	Spanish-born (first emperor from provinces); conquered Dacia (Romania); empire reached its greatest extent during his rule
Hadrian	117–138	Consolidated earlier conquests rather than adding new lands; reorganized bureaucracy and set up postal service; traveled throughout empire
Antoninus Pius	138–161	Uneventful reign marked by public works and expanded programs for education and child welfare; army declined
Marcus Aurelius	161–180	Faced widespread barbarian invasions on Syrian and Danube frontiers; wrote philosophic work, *Meditations;* Pax Romana ended with his death

established his place in literature as one of Rome's great Stoic philosophers.

Stoics believed that human laws, like the Supreme Power itself, should be reasonable and just. Several social reforms during Rome's golden age show Stoic influence. For example, according to a law passed under Hadrian, the pater familias no longer had the power of life and death within the family. New laws also prohibited masters from killing or injuring their slaves.

Latin literature took many forms.

In literature, as in religion, the Romans first looked to the Greeks for inspiration. By the middle years of the republic, however, the Romans had begun to develop an important body of learning of their own. By Augustus's time, there was a group of writers who were able to record the emperor's deeds in glowing and lasting words. As far as Augustus was concerned, however, the skill of the writer was not as important as his patriotism. With patriotic writers, the emperor was generous.

Livy's history One of the most patriotic works sponsored by Augustus was Livy's history of Rome. It covered the years from Rome's founding to the rule of Augustus in 142 Roman-style books.

Livy had a bias typical of many historians. He liked the past better than the present. He thought the heroes of old—Romulus, Scipio, Cato—were more patriotic than Romans of his own time. The old heroes, he said, had been men of honor, courage, discipline, and moral strength. They did their duty toward family, gods, and state. Because of those virtues, Livy explained, they could conquer every foe.

Virgil's epic poem Patriotic virtue was also the theme of the most famous work of Latin literature, the *Aeneid* (uh-NEE-ihd). The poet Virgil devoted ten years of labor to this masterpiece. Often he was unable to write more than a few lines a day. Even then, he was so worried about the poem's flaws that he wanted it destroyed. Luckily, it was saved by Augustus himself.

The *Aeneid* is an epic consciously modeled after the Greek masterpieces of Homer. It traces Roman origins far back before Romulus and Remus to Aeneas, one of the Trojan warriors in Homer's *Iliad*. Reading the *Aeneid*, Augustus perhaps nodded approvingly at these verses:

Remember, Roman, these are your talents:
To rule people by law, and to establish the
ways of peace,
To spare the conquered, and to crush the
haughty.

The silver age of literature Roman literature kept growing and changing during the empire. Historians refer to the 124 years between the deaths of Augustus and Hadrian as the "silver age" of literature. Rome's best writers were still poets and historians, but their work took on a new tone. Criticism replaced patriotism. Praise was replaced by **satire**, writing that mocked society for its foolishness and wickedness. Imagine what Augustus might have thought about these lines from the poet Juvenal:

What should I do in Rome? I am no good
at lying.
If a book's bad, I can't praise it, or go
around ordering copies.
I don't know the stars [astrology]; I can't
hire out as an assassin.

Juvenal lived from about A.D. 60 to 140, during the height of Rome's glory, yet he still found much to satirize.

While Juvenal wrote about the morals of private citizens, the historian Tacitus (TAS-ih-tus) directed his scorn at Roman government. In his major work, the *Annals*, he portrays every emperor from Tiberius to Nero as cruel and corrupted by power. What were the blessings of the Roman peace? "They make a desert and call it peace," accused Tacitus.

Although many of the writers of the silver age made fun of Rome (or worse), they were not banned or sent into exile. By this time, Rome was so secure as capital of the world that it could tolerate criticism. There were moral and spiritual grounds for the writers' charges, but outwardly Rome was thriving.

 ## Majestic buildings adorned cities.

Of the estimated 10,000 cities in the Roman empire, Rome was the most spectacular. The passion for beautifying the capital did not die with Augustus or Nero. Each emperor sought to make his mark on the city. According to one scholar, Rome became "the most spectacular

147

Comparing pictures *The Roman Forum became the showplace of the empire, filled with statues and buildings designed to impress the people Rome ruled. How did the Roman Forum differ from the Athenian acropolis (page 94)?*

tourist attraction in the ancient world." Visitors came from the provinces to see its 10,000 statues, 700 public pools and basins, 500 fountains, 37 monumental gates, and 36 marble arches.

After seeing Rome, visitors from Gaul and Spain went home and imitated its splendor. They too surrounded themselves with Roman buildings and gardens. Soon, new cities in western Europe looked like miniature Romes. Roman governors gladly supported the construction of Roman-style buildings. They saw it as a way of building allegiance to Rome itself. Unlike the Greeks who used architecture to glorify their gods, the Romans used it to glorify their rule.

The crowning achievement of Roman architecture was the dome. Once the Romans had learned to use concrete, they were able to mold on the ground rounded tops for their buildings. Then, when the walls and columns of a building were in place, the dome could be hoisted into place on top.

This is just how one of the most impressive buildings in Rome, the Pantheon (PAN-thee-ahn), was built. The Pantheon was dedicated to all the gods. Its domed roof rested on a drumlike structure called a rotunda. Light streamed into the Pantheon through a small opening or "eye" in the top of the dome.

The Forum was Rome's center of government, including the *Curia* (Senate House) and *Tabularium* (Hall of Records). Although the Forum, like the Athenian acropolis, contained temples, it had less religious significance than the acropolis.

Roman law united the empire.

Rome's most lasting contribution to later civilizations was its law. Early Roman law, such as the Twelve Tables, was concerned mostly with the rights of Roman citizens themselves. As the empire grew, however, the Romans came to believe that law should apply to all people.

Slowly, Roman judges began to recognize certain standards of justice. These standards were based largely on the teachings of Stoic philosophers. Here are some of the most important principles of Roman law:

- No person could be judged guilty of a crime until after the facts of the case were examined.
- All persons accused of crimes had a right to face their accusers and defend themselves before a judge.
- If there was doubt about a person's guilt, he or she should be judged innocent.
- Any law that seemed unreasonable or grossly unfair could be set aside.

Long after Rome fell to barbarian rule, the principles of Roman law endured. Those principles became the basis for law in many European countries and, later, for places that fell under European influence. The Roman empire spread far, but its legal ideas have spread farther.

Contrasts marked Roman society.

Most Roman citizens probably were far more concerned with the pains and pleasures of daily living than with literature, philosophy, or law. To many Romans, spending a day at the Colosseum was the chief benefit of Roman civilization. By A.D. 250, there were 150 holidays celebrating emperors' birthdays, gods' feast days, and other special occasions. On many of these days, the government provided games, races, or gladiator shows at public expense.

These public pleasures were enjoyed by rich and poor alike. In most other ways, however, the rich and the poor had little in common.

Life at the top At home, wealthy Romans lived extravagantly. They spent large sums of money on fancy houses, statues for their gardens, high-priced slaves, and especially banquets. A food's taste was less important than its rarity and cost. These were some of the dishes placed on the tables of wealthy Romans: as appetizers, tree fungi in fish-fat sauce, jellyfish and eggs; as main course, dormouse with pine kernels, boiled ostrich; and for dessert, fricassee of roses with pastry, parrot-tongue pie.

Guests normally arrived for a banquet in the late afternoon and did not stop eating until midnight. They had knives and spoons but no forks, and they picked up most foods with their hands. After each course, a slave stationed behind each guest provided a bowl of scented water for washing sticky fingers.

The eruption of Mt. Vesuvius in A.D. 79 buried the city of Pompeii in ash, killing hundreds. Everyday items —including frescoes, jewelry, and even a loaf of bread—were preserved intact for archaeologists.

149

Life at the bottom Most families in Rome never tasted parrot-tongue pie. They were lucky to eat porridge at daybreak, cold sausage at noon, and porridge again for supper. During Rome's golden age, a large share of the city's population was unemployed most of the time. The imperial government supported these people with daily rations of grain, doled out free or far below market cost.

Only a short distance from Rome's elegant temples were the dingy, run-down, rat-infested homes of the poor. Poor families lived in crowded wooden tenements up to seven stories high. Tens of thousands of such buildings filled Rome's slums. The tenements were so poorly built that roofs and ceilings sometimes collapsed, killing those inside. Worst of all, a poor family faced the ever-present danger of fire touched off by a stray ember from someone's little charcoal stove.

Despite these conditions, the poor of Rome were better off than people without work had ever been in other ancient cities. The Roman poor had food and housing. After the collapse of the empire, no government took such care of its poorest citizens for nearly 1,500 years.

Villas in the countryside Most wealthy city dwellers also had country estates, called **villas**. In Italy, these country homes offered an escape from the noise and dirt of Rome itself. Italian villas had libraries, art galleries, swimming pools, and athletic courts. Fountains sparkled in formal gardens, and Greek statues posed on lawns and terraces.

In provinces such as Gaul, North Africa, and Britannia, villas were more than vacation homes. They were the great estates that grew much of the empire's food supply. Peasant farmers lived on the villas and tilled the soil or tended the owner's livestock. The noble owners managed the villa, served as local officials, and amused themselves by hunting.

In later times, villas became increasingly self-sufficient. The people on a villa raised all their own food and made most of the other goods they needed. Many villas were fortified as protection against bandits (or tax collectors).

Section Review 2

Define: (a) Epicureanism, (b) Stoicism, (c) satire, (d) villa
Identify: (a) Epicurus, (b) Zeno, (c) *Meditations*, (d) Livy, (e) Virgil, (f) *Aeneid*, (g) Juvenal, (h) Tacitus, (i) the Pantheon

Economics in Daily Life · *Tax Reform in Rome*

One of the major reforms made by Augustus was in the Roman tax system. Economic changes during the later years of the republic had led to inequality and irregular collection. To remedy that, Augustus established a census for the empire. The census provided a record of population, land use, flocks and herds, and businesses as a basis for assessing taxes.

Residents of Italy received favored treatment. They paid taxes on inheritances and on the value of freed slaves but not on land or personal property. Residents of the provinces paid taxes on land, personal property, and trade. Taxes from the provinces provided most of the income for running the government.

Most people of Italy and the provinces considered the new tax system fair and just. Efficient and honest collection built public confidence. The taxes gave the government a steady income and helped to strengthen Roman rule, thus adding to the stability of the Augustan age.

Citizens who had struck it rich were expected to give the gift of a bathhouse and money for its upkeep to their fellow citizens. What do the rich do voluntarily today?

Answer:

1. How were the basic ideas of Stoicism well-suited to Roman traditions? (b) How did Stoicism influence Roman law to become more humane?
2. How did Roman literature change from the time of Augustus to the silver age?
3. (a) Describe some of the differences between the lives of the rich and the poor during the Roman empire. (b) What evidence shows that the Roman government took relatively good care of the poor?

Critical Thinking

4. (a) Restate in your own words the ideas of Roman law given on page 149. (b) Explain why each of these four principles is important to justice today.

Christianity spread through the empire. 3

As the Roman empire spread, Romans came into contact with many religions. In the far-flung parts of the empire, most peoples continued to follow their own religious traditions, even though they were under Roman rule. In Rome itself, cults from many lands took root. The Egyptian goddess Isis was especially popular with Roman women. The Persian warrior god Mithra had a wide following in Rome's army.

By the time of Augustus, Rome's traditional gods—Jupiter, Juno, Mars, and others—had no strong emotional or intellectual appeal to most Romans. Nonetheless, these gods were still important as symbols of loyalty to the Roman state. Roman rulers tolerated many religions, but they also expected Roman subjects to respect traditional Roman gods. This Roman attitude was no problem for the empire's many polytheists, but it was a very great problem indeed for the Jews as monotheists.

Jews came under Roman rule.

Most Jews probably saw the Romans as one of a string of pagan conquerors. After their return to Palestine from Babylon (page 43), the Jews had been ruled by Alexander the Great, by the Ptolemies of Egypt, and by the Seleucids of Persia. In general, the Jews tolerated and were tolerated by these rulers. However, in 168 B.C., the Seleucid king decided to build an altar to the Greek god Zeus in the Jewish temple in Jerusalem. The Jews would not stand for that. Led by Judas Maccabee (MAK-uh-bee), they recaptured and purified the temple in 165 B.C. In 142 B.C., the Jews won their independence.

The entire area of Syria and Palestine fell under Roman influence around 65 B.C. However, the Romans at first allowed the Jewish kingdom to remain independent, at least in name. Jewish kings ruled as representatives of Rome. Some Jews became friendly with the Romans and even went along with their plans to "romanize" Jerusalem. The ruler Herod, for example, was a romanized Jew. His loyalties were divided between Rome and his own people. He was also tolerant of polytheistic faiths. These divided loyalties angered many Jews. Rome finally took over the Jewish kingdom and made it the Roman province of Judaea in A.D. 6.

Jesus taught a new religion.

It was about the time of Rome's takeover that Jesus was born, although the exact year is not known. Jesus was both a Jew and a Roman subject. He is not mentioned in any contemporary Roman historic records. Thus, the story of Jesus' life comes from Christian sources, the Gospels of the New Testament. (*Gospel* is the Greek word for "good news.")

Jesus' life According to the Gospels, Jesus was born in the town of Bethlehem, about five miles south of Jerusalem. He grew up in the village of Nazareth. When he was about 30, Jesus began his ministry. For the next three years, he lived as a wandering prophet and teacher. He recruited 12 followers, or disciples, who accepted his teachings and traveled with him. Jesus touched people with his gentleness and challenged them with his message.

Jesus chose the time of Passover, a Jewish holiday, to visit the temple in Jerusalem. Shortly thereafter, Jesus was arrested and taken to the Roman governor, Pontius Pilate. He was accused of the religious crime of blasphemy. He was also accused of plotting to be king, because his teachings had described the coming of the kingdom

According to Jewish tradition, when the temple was rededicated, a miracle of lights occurred. Although there was only enough sacramental oil for one day's worth of ceremony, the oil lasted eight days. Chanukah is a celebration of this miracle.

of God. For these teachings, he was sentenced to death. On a desolate hill called Calvary outside Jerusalem, Jesus was crucified.

Two days later, the Gospels say that Jesus' follower Mary Magdalene visited his tomb and found his body gone. Over the next 40 days, according to the Gospels, Jesus appeared to his disciples several times. "And it came to pass," concludes the Gospel of Luke, "while he blessed them, he was parted from them, and carried up into heaven."

The teachings of Jesus Among the major beliefs of the Christian faith is the idea of the kingdom of God. Jesus taught that God was preparing a new era in which all who repented of their sins and believed in Jesus as savior would live as God's children. Because Jesus taught that God's kingdom was open to all, regardless of wealth or class, he won many followers among the poor.

Jesus taught that God is love and that his followers should love God above all. After that, God's children should love one another. They should treat others as they wish to be treated themselves. This last teaching has come to be known as the "golden rule."

Apostles spread Jesus' teachings.

Jesus' followers believed he was the messiah (muh-SY-uh), or savior, whom God had promised the Jewish people. (The name Christ comes from the Greek word for messiah, *Christos.)*

The disciples who spread Jesus' teachings are known as the apostles. They were leaders of the earliest Christian church. At first, they preached in Jewish synagogues throughout the Hellenistic lands of Palestine, Syria, Asia Minor, and Egypt. In Jerusalem, they established a small but important church led by the apostle Peter.

The apostle who most profoundly influenced the new Christian religion never knew Jesus in person. This man was known by two names—his Jewish name, Saul, and his Christian name, Paul. At first, Saul thought Christianity should be stamped out. One day while traveling to Damascus in Syria, however, he had a powerful religious experience. He told of seeing a blinding burst of light and hearing the voice of Jesus. From that moment, Saul the Jew became Paul the Christian. The apostle Paul dedicated the rest of his life to spreading the teachings of Jesus.

The peace and cultural unity of the Pax Romana provided an ideal opportunity for the spread of the new religion. As a Roman citizen, Paul traveled freely within the empire. For 13 years (A.D. 45–58), he went from city to city around the eastern Mediterranean winning converts.

Paul had an enormous influence on Christianity. His letters, written to churches with which he worked, form a large part of the New Testament. (These letters are known as the Epistles of Saint Paul.) Paul also declared that Christianity was open equally to anyone, Jew or non-Jew. Without this openness, Christianity might have remained a small Jewish sect rather than becoming a world religion. Finally, through Paul's work, Christian churches were established in every major city in the eastern empire, from Jerusalem to Rome.

Christianity grew slowly but steadily. Christian teachings had strong appeal to the poor and powerless. Women, who were barred from some popular Roman cults, had great influence among Christian groups.

Rome struggled with Judaism and Christianity.

As monotheistic religions, both Christianity and Judaism posed a problem for the Roman empire. Good Roman citizens were expected to worship the emperor as a god. Neither Jews nor Christians were willing to do so.

War against the Jews The Romans went far in trying to keep peace with the Jews. The Roman government promised Jews freedom of worship and excused them from worshiping the emperor.

Despite Roman tolerance of Judaism, however, many Jews remained fiercely opposed to Roman rule. In A.D. 66, a band of Jewish revolutionaries called the Zealots (ZEL-uhts) tried to throw off the Roman yoke. When Roman troops finally put down the rebellion four years later, they burned the Jewish temple. All that remained was a western portion of the wall, which is today the holiest of Jewish shrines. Hundreds of fleeing Jews were captured and crucified. The last stronghold, a fortress near the Dead Sea called Masada (muh-SAH-duh), held out until A.D. 73. Half a million Jews died in that war.

The tiny nation made one more attempt to break free of the Romans. In A.D. 130, the emperor

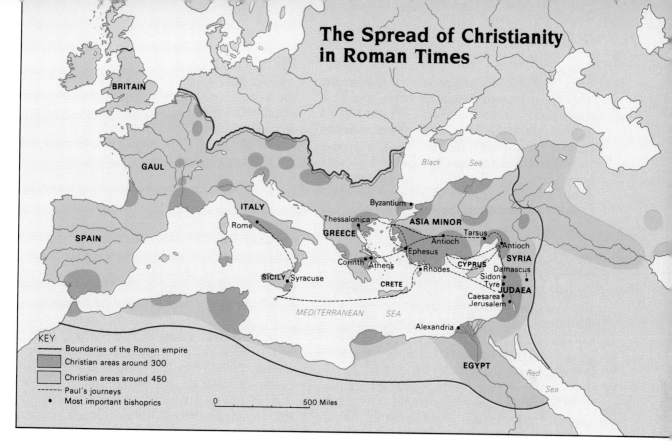

The Spread of Christianity in Roman Times

KEY
- Boundaries of the Roman empire
- Christian areas around 300
- Christian areas around 450
- Paul's journeys
- • Most important bishoprics

0   500 Miles

Map Study

In A.D. 300, was Christianity stronger in the eastern part of the Roman empire or the western part? Name two cities in Greece that Paul visited.

Hadrian ordered that Jerusalem be rebuilt as a Roman colony and that a shrine to Jupiter be built in place of the Jewish temple. The Jews rose in rebellion. In three years of fighting, another half a million Jews died. This war ended the Jewish political state for almost 2,000 years, yet the Jewish religion survived.

Persecution of the Christians As a new religion, Christianity did not win the same respect from Roman rulers as did Judaism. When Christians refused to accept the emperor as a god, Rome struck at them as rebels. In A.D. 64, the year of the great fire in Rome, Nero ordered the first persecution of Christians. According to Christian tradition, the apostles Peter and Paul were killed in Rome on the same day during Nero's rule.

Except for Nero, however, the emperors of the first century did not actively persecute Christians. Later, however, as the Pax Romana began to crumble, the Romans became harsher toward those who would not worship the emperor. Toward the end of the second century, Christians were cruelly persecuted. With Marcus Aurelius's approval, many Christians were brought before Roman magistrates for trial. Those who gave up their religion and accepted the Roman gods were set free without punishment. Those who held to their faith were tortured and executed in the arena. They were regarded by other Christians as martyrs (people who sacrifice their lives for the sake of a cause or belief).

Religious persecutions showed only the growing weakness of the empire, not its strength. Christianity became a formidable religious force at the very time that Roman power was declining. By A.D. 200, around 10 percent of the people in the Roman empire were Christians.

The Petrine doctrine According to many Christians, Jesus had singled out the disciple Peter as the "rock" on which the Christian church would be built. After preaching in Jerusalem, Peter had traveled to Rome where he had acted as Rome's first **bishop**. A bishop was a church official who set moral standards and supervised the finances of several local churches. Peter died in Rome, a fact that became important to later Christians.

Map Study answers: eastern; Thessalonica, Corinth, Athens

153

Eventually, every major city in the empire would have its own bishop. However, later bishops in Rome claimed to outrank all other bishops because Peter had been the leading apostle. Roman bishops argued that Peter was the first **pope**—the father of the Christian Church. This argument, known as the Petrine (PEE-TRYN) doctrine, was accepted by Christians in the western part of the empire but rejected in the eastern part.

Section Review 3

Define: (a) disciple, (b) messiah, (c) apostle, (d) martyr, (e) bishop, (f) pope
Identify: (a) Jerusalem, (b) Herod, (c) Jesus, (d) Gospels, (e) Pontius Pilate, (f) Paul (Saul), (g) Zealots, (h) Masada, (i) Petrine doctrine
Answer:
1. (a) What attitude did the Roman government take toward most religions? (b) Why did Judaism and Christianity not fit into the empire in the same way other religions did?
2. What religious ideas did Jesus teach?
3. What was Paul's importance for the development of Christianity?
4. (a) How did the existence of the Roman empire help the spread of Christianity? (b) How did the Roman government attack Christianity?

Critical Thinking
5. Rome often persecuted Christians after disasters, such as the great fire in Nero's reign, or in troubled times such as Marcus Aurelius's reign. Why might a government turn against a group in such times?

Rome's empire declined and fell.

4

Historians generally agree that the Roman empire began its decline with the rule of Marcus Aurelius's son, Commodus. Instead of adopting an able successor, Marcus Aurelius made the fateful mistake of choosing his own son to succeed him as emperor. Facing a time of troubles, Rome needed a strong, dedicated leader. Instead, it got the vain, irresponsible Commodus.

In A.D. 180, when Marcus Aurelius died, Commodus was a tall, strapping youth of 19. He loved the thrill of sports and hated the duties of government. To show off his athletic talent, Commodus performed regularly as a gladiator. Friends of his father thought Commodus's showmanship disgraced both himself and the empire. They conspired to assassinate him, but he had them executed. After that, Commodus became a cruel ruler as well as a stupid one. Finally, in A.D. 192, he was strangled in his bath.

The decline of the empire, however, continued for almost 300 years. The end of the Roman empire is usually dated as A.D. 476. In that year, a barbarian king took over the rule of Rome.

The process of decline took place in three stages. First, there was a long time of turmoil known by historians as the "crisis of the third century." During these years, the empire was beset by economic, military, and political problems. Second, there was a time of revival, during which the empire was divided into two parts, an eastern half and a western half. As you will see, this change strengthened the Greek-speaking east but weakened the Latin-speaking west. Third, the western half of the empire was overwhelmed by savage invaders. The eastern empire survived these invasions and existed for 1,000 years after the destruction of the western empire.

Crises weakened the empire.

During the third century (A.D. 200–300), a host of problems confronted the Roman empire. Although it survived, these problems left the empire gravely weakened.

Economic decay During the Pax Romana, trade flowed smoothly over sea routes patrolled by Roman navies and land routes patrolled by Roman armies. Rome's treasuries were enriched by huge amounts of gold and silver that the Roman conquerors collected as plunder. Perhaps most basic and most important of all, the empire's farms grew enough grain to feed the population of the cities. During the crisis of the third century, all three sources of prosperity dried up.

Trade was disrupted on both land and sea. Barbarian raids across the Danube River discouraged merchants from driving their oxcarts over Roman roads. At the same time, bands of pirates began terrorizing Mediterranean sea lanes.

When Commodus was murdered, the senate cursed him: "He who killed all men, let him be dragged by the hook! . . . He who set aside wills, let him be dragged by the hook! . . ." Ask how this curse, with its mention of wills, reflects Roman attitudes toward property.

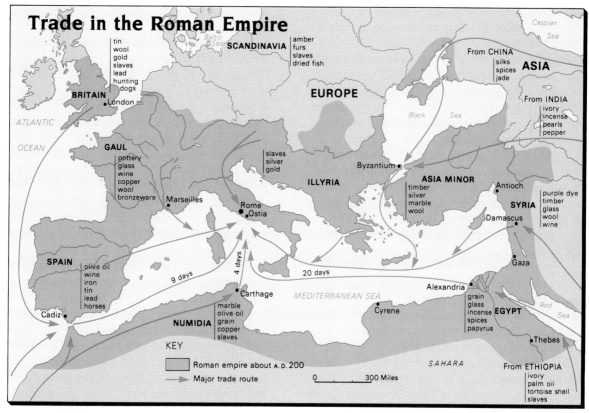

Trade in the Roman Empire

SCANDINAVIA — amber, furs, slaves, dried fish

From CHINA — silks, spices, jade — **ASIA**

From INDIA — ivory, incense, pearls, pepper

tin, wool, gold, slaves, lead, hunting dogs

BRITAIN — London

EUROPE

ATLANTIC OCEAN

Baltic Sea

Black Sea

GAUL — pottery, glass, wine, copper, wool, bronzeware

Marseilles

ILLYRIA — slaves, silver, gold

Byzantium

ASIA MINOR — timber, silver, marble, wool

Antioch

SYRIA — purple dye, timber, glass, wool, wine

Damascus

Rome, Ostia

SPAIN — olive oil, wine, iron, tin, lead, horses

Gaza

9 days

4 days

20 days

Alexandria

Cadiz

Carthage

MEDITERRANEAN SEA

Cyrene

EGYPT — grain, glass, incense, spices, papyrus

Red Sea

NUMIDIA — marble, olive oil, grain, copper, slaves

Thebes

KEY

SAHARA

From ETHIOPIA — ivory, palm oil, tortoise shell, slaves

Roman empire about A.D. 200
Major trade route

0 _____ 300 Miles

Map Study

Trade was crucial to Rome's economy. What goods reached Rome from China? From Scandinavia? How long did a voyage from Alexandria to Rome take?

Rome's gold and silver were drained away to buy luxuries from other lands. Rich Roman families yearned for costly goods from China, India, and Arabia, including spices, perfumes, rubies, pearls, and silk. Rome's small industries produced only wine, cheese, and glass. China, India, and Arabia had little interest in buying such plain goods. Thus, Romans were forced to pay out a fortune in gold and silver every year for the imported luxuries they craved.

Desperate to pay its mounting expenses, the Roman government started minting coins that contained less and less silver. Eventually, Roman coins lost 98 percent of their silver content. As a result, prices shot sky-high. For example, in the second century, a peck of wheat sold for half a denarius. By the end of the third century, the price had risen to 100 denarii. Such an increase in prices is called **inflation.**

Agriculture faced an equally serious crisis. Harvests in Italy and western Europe became increasingly meager. Scholars think that the overworked soil had probably lost much of its earlier fertility.

Military decay The empire's economic troubles were worsened by its growing military troubles. Throughout the third century, tribes of northern barbarians called Goths repeatedly overran the legions guarding the Danube frontier. At the same time, Syria and Asia Minor were threatened by Persia. The Persians' proudest victory (and Rome's most humiliating defeat) occurred in A.D. 260 when the Roman emperor Valerian was captured in battle. For the rest of his life, Valerian was forced to crouch down and allow the Persian king to step on him while mounting a horse.

Roman soldiers now fought strictly for money, not for patriotism. To attract recruits into the army, the government promised ever higher cash awards. These costs put an increasing strain on the treasury. Partly to keep costs down, emperors began to recruit troops from the ranks of the barbarians, who would accept lower pay. However, the loyalty of barbarian troops to the empire could hardly be trusted.

Political decay Loyalty was in fact a key problem, perhaps the most serious of all. At one time, Romans cared so deeply about their republic that they willingly sacrificed their lives for it. In the later centuries of the empire, citizens were not actively disloyal, but they were indifferent.

To hold political office had once been considered an honor (as well as an invitation to profit). But times had changed. By the 200's, local officials usually lost money because they were required to pay for costly circuses and baths out of their own pockets. As the empire's prosperity faded, less and less money came in as taxes. However, the government in Rome continued to require each tax district to send in a certain amount. If the local tax collector could not gather up that much, he had to pay the difference himself. Naturally, few people were willing to serve the government under those conditions.

The only groups actively interested in politics were the armies. In a 50-year period (A.D. 218–268), provincial armies and the Praetorian Guard proclaimed 50 generals emperors of Rome. Of these, 27 briefly won the approval of the Roman senate. Seventeen of these men were murdered. Two others were forced to commit suicide.

The empire might very well have collapsed during the crisis of the third century. Remarkably, it survived for another 200 years. The empire was saved by two men who rank among Rome's greatest emperors, Diocletian (DY-oh-**KLEE**-shuhn) and Constantine (**KAHN**-stuhn-tyn).

Diocletian reformed the empire.

In A.D. 284, Diocletian, a strong-willed army leader and son of a slave, became the new emperor. With amazing boldness, he tried to restore order in the empire and increase its strength. These were Diocletian's reforms:

1. To beat back the Goths and Persians, Diocletian doubled the size of the Roman armies to 500,000. This secured the boundaries of the empire once again.

2. To build economic stability, Diocletian ordered that all sons had to follow the trade of their fathers. Thus, any movement from farm to city workshop was made illegal.

3. To beat inflation, he used price and wage controls. Costs were fixed for everything from a haircut to a bottle of wine.

4. To restore faith in the ancient gods of Rome, Diocletian ordered a general persecution of the Christians.

5. To increase the prestige of the emperor, Diocletian assumed the manner and costume of a Persian ruler. He wore purple robes embroidered with gold, a crown encrusted with pearls, and scarlet boots. Anyone who approached his throne was required to kneel down and kiss the hem of his robe. He took a new title, *dominus et deus* ("lord and god"), abandoning Augustus's modest title of *princeps* ("first citizen").

6. To improve administration, Diocletian divided the empire into the Greek-speaking east (Greece, Asia Minor, Syria, and Egypt) and the Latin-speaking west (Italy, Gaul, Britannia, and Spain). Because the empire had grown too large and too complex for one ruler, each half was to have its own emperor. The eastern half of the empire included most of the great cities and trade centers of the empire. As a result, the east was far wealthier than the more rural west. Diocletian took the eastern half for himself and named another ruler for the west. Each emperor was supposed to name an assistant ruler who would later succeed him. In this way, Diocletian hoped to solve the succession problem as well.

These reforms were not totally successful. Wages for the new troops added to the already crushing load of taxes. Price controls failed. Christianity continued its rapid growth. Yet during his 21-year reign (A.D. 284–305), Diocletian did stop the decline of the empire. The borders were safe again, and the emperor was once more considered an exalted person. Diocletian retired in 305. He spent his last years peacefully tending his garden. But even while he lived, his plans for the succession failed.

Constantine accepted Christianity.

Civil war broke out immediately after Diocletian retired. By A.D. 311, four rivals were competing for power. Among them was a dashing young commander named Constantine. One of the most critical moments in history occurred

Topic for debate: Diocletian's persecution of Christianity may actually have strengthened the religion and helped it gain converts.

Constantine built this triumphal arch to celebrate his victory over Maxentius.

in A.D. 312 when Constantine marched to the Tiber River to fight his chief rival, Maxentius (mak-SEN-shee-uhs). On the day before the battle, Constantine prayed for divine help. What happened next was reported by a Christian bishop, Eusebius (yoo-SEE-bee-uhs):

And while [Constantine] was thus praying, a most marvelous sign appeared to him from heaven. He said that about noon he saw with his own eyes a cross of light in the heavens, above the sun, and bearing the inscription, "In this sign, conquer."

The next morning, Constantine ordered artisans to put a Christian symbol on his soldiers' shields. Then came the clash between the armies of Constantine and Maxentius. Near the Milvian Bridge, two miles outside Rome, Constantine scored an overwhelming victory. He marched into Rome and became emperor of the western half of the empire. He attributed his victory to the power of the Christian God.

The next year, A.D. 313, Constantine announced an end to the persecution of Christians. From Milan, he granted "both to the Christians and to all men freedom to follow the religion that they choose." By this famous Edict of Milan, Constantine changed Christianity from an outlawed sect into a religion approved by the emperor.

Like his conversion, Constantine's decision to choose Byzantium as his capital came about through a vision.

Constantine founded a new capital.

Eventually, Constantine won control of the eastern as well as the western empire. In A.D. 330, he took the momentous step of moving the empire's capital from Rome to the Greek city of Byzantium (bih-ZANT-ee-uhm) in what is now Turkey.

The new capital had four advantages over Rome. First, it stood at a crossroad for trade. Located on a narrow water passageway called the Bosporus (BAHS-puhr-uhs), Byzantium controlled all shipping between the Black Sea and the Mediterranean Sea. The city also dominated the east-west overland trade between Asia Minor and Greece. Second, the city was easy to defend against attack, as it was nearly surrounded by water. Third, the old Rome was a pagan city dedicated to pagan gods. Byzantium was strongly Christian. Finally, Byzantium had the advantage of being in the more prosperous half of the empire, the east.

Thus, the center of empire shifted from west to east. Soon the new capital was protected by massive walls and gleamed with stately buildings. The city even had a new name—Constantinople (KAHN-STANT-uhn-OH-puhl), city of Constantine.

Because of the policies of Diocletian and Constantine, there were now two empires, not one. Because of Constantine's victory at the Milvian Bridge, both empires were Christian.

Barbarians overran the empire.

The third phase of Rome's decline was a century of destruction beginning in A.D. 376 and ending in 476. Many different groups took part in Rome's destruction: Ostrogoths, Visigoths, Franks, Angles, Saxons, Burgundians, Lombards, Vandals. All these groups were semibarbaric peoples who spoke Germanic languages.

Germanic men wore their hair down to their shoulders. They loved to gamble, drink, and fight. They assigned most of the drudgery of farmwork to their sisters, wives, and mothers. The historian Tacitus said they had "blue eyes and reddish hair; great bodies, especially powerful for attack, but not equally patient of hard work." Though the different Germanic groups shared similar ways of life, they hated one another and were frequently at war. Rome often took advantage of this hatred.

Historians debate the reasons for Rome's decline. Some believe the internal crises in the West could, under better conditions, have been energizing and productive, as they were in the East. These historians say Rome fell because of the many invasions.

157

When Rome was still strong, the Germanic tribes generally respected the borders guarded by Roman legions. These borders stretched across Europe from the Black Sea to the North Sea. The longest section of the Roman border followed the Danube River. For many years, the Danube marked the dividing line between the barbaric north and the civilized south.

Though fearless fighters, the Germanic tribes were terrified of the Huns, a nomadic people from central Asia. The following exaggerated description by a Germanic historian, Jordanes, shows how the Huns were feared:

They made their foes flee in horror because their swarthy aspect was fearful, and they had . . . a shapeless lump instead of a head, with pinholes rather than eyes. They are cruel to their children on the very day of their birth. For they cut the cheeks of the males with a sword, so that before they receive the nourishment of milk, they must learn to endure wounds.

When the Huns began to move west, they first attacked the Ostrogoths, the most easterly Germanic tribe. The terrified Ostrogoths fled westward and pressed against their old enemies, the Visigoths. Squeezed off their land, the Visigoths looked for a new home south of the Danube border. Thus began the massive movement of Germanic peoples that eventually destroyed the western half of the Roman empire. In A.D. 378, Visigoths routed a Roman army. This disaster shattered Rome's military reputation.

The Huns kept raiding westward, destroying as they went. Germanic people near the Rhine River—Burgundians, Franks, and Vandals—began to feel the pressure and to move westward also. The Rhine River froze during an especially cold winter in A.D. 406. Bundled in furs, Vandal warriors and their families swarmed across the river ice. They met practically no resistance and so they kept moving westward through the Roman province of Gaul. There were no more than 15,000 Vandal warriors. The population of Gaul was probably 20 million. Yet the Vandals raided the cities of Gaul as if they were defenseless. The empire of the west was now so disorganized that it could not muster even a medium-sized army to stop the barbarians.

Map Study

This map shows the routes of some barbarian groups that invaded the Roman empire. Which group eventually reached North Africa?

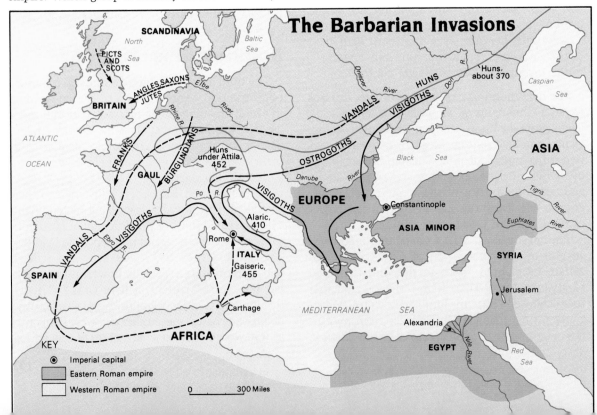

Some say that in the traditions that were passed along through the centuries, Rome actually conquered the barbarians.

Barbarians sacked Rome.

During the first half of the fifth century, Rome was sacked twice by Germanic armies: first by the Visigoths in A.D. 410, next by the Vandals in A.D. 455.

In 410, Alaric (AL-uh-rik), king of the Visigoths, marched across the Alps toward Rome. Rome still was widely regarded as the center of civilization. The news that Alaric and his army stood outside its walls was shocking. A traitor opened Rome's gates, and thousands of Germans stormed in. They plundered the city for three days.

Rome remained rich enough to act as bait for other looters. In 455, the king of the Vandals from North Africa sailed to Rome in pursuit of more treasure. This ruthless leader, known as Gaiseric (GY-zuh-rik) the Lame, sacked Rome more thoroughly than Alaric had. Thousands of Romans were taken captive and shipped back to North Africa as slaves.

Attila the Hun Meanwhile, the Huns, who indirectly began this mayhem, were still on the rampage. In fact, the Huns seemed more dangerous than ever under their new leader, Attila (AT-uhl-uh). The Germanic writer Jordanes described this terrifying chieftain as a short man with a flat nose and thin, graying beard. "He was haughty in his walk, rolling his eyes hither and thither, so that the power of his proud spirit appeared in the movement of his body."

With his 100,000 soldiers, Attila threatened to conquer the entire empire. In the east, his armies sacked 70 cities. (The Huns failed, however, to scale the high walls of Constantinople.)

In A.D. 452, Attila advanced against Rome. But then the barbarian king was stopped in his tracks by a Christian bishop. The first truly powerful pope of Rome, Leo I, journeyed to Attila's camp near the Po River. No record survives of Leo's words to Attila. Perhaps Leo frightened the Hun by telling of the plague that was then ravishing Italy. Perhaps Attila was simply awed by Leo. Whatever the reason, Attila withdrew his forces.

The last emperor of the west By A.D. 455, the Roman emperor in the west was practically powerless. Germanic tribes now fought one another for possession of the western provinces. Spain belonged to the Visigoths, North Africa to the Vandals. Gaul was overrun by competing tribes: Franks, Burgundians, and Visigoths. Britannia was being invaded by Angles and Saxons. Italy was falling victim to raids by the Ostrogoths.

The last Roman emperor was a 14-year-old boy whose name, Romulus Augustulus, recalled 1,000 years of past glory. In A.D. 476, he lost his throne to a barbarian general named Odoacer (oh-doh-AY-sur). Odoacer sent Romulus Augustulus into exile. After 476, no emperor even pretended to rule Rome and its western provinces. Roman power in the western half of the empire had disappeared.

The eastern half, which came to be called the Byzantine empire, not only survived but flourished for another 1,000 years. Its emperors ruled from Constantinople.

Even though Rome's political power ended in the west, its cultural influence was felt for centuries afterward. Latin remained the language of learning in the west. The Christian Church, governed from Rome by a succession of popes, became the chief civilizing force of western Europe. Civilization, though shaken to its roots by the barbarian terror, did not perish.

Section Review 4

Define: inflation
Identify: (a) Commodus, (b) Diocletian, (c) Constantine, (d) eastern empire, (e) western empire, (f) Battle of Milvian Bridge, (g) Edict of Milan, (h) Constantinople, (i) Germanic peoples, (j) Huns, (k) Alaric, (l) Gaiseric, (m) Attila, (n) Leo I, (o) Romulus Augustulus, (p) Odoacer
Answer:
1. What economic problems did the empire face in the third century?
2. By the third century, how had Rome's army changed since the days of the republic?
3. (a) What important religious change did Constantine bring about in the empire? (b) What political change did he bring about?
4. (a) Why did Germanic tribes invade the empire in the 400's? (b) Why was the empire unable to drive the invaders out?

Critical Thinking
5. (a) List three reasons why Diocletian should be considered a successful emperor. (b) List three reasons why he might be considered a failure.

159

Chapter Review 7

Summary

1. Augustus's rule began the Pax Romana. Augustus's wise policies began a period of peace that lasted from 27 B.C. to A.D. 180. Despite some unwise or cruel rulers, Roman government worked well under its civil service. The greatest problem was the lack of a clear way of choosing an emperor.

2. Romans extended Greek culture. Romans continued Greek traditions in philosophy, art, and literature. Epicureanism and Stoicism became influential philosophies. Literature moved from patriotic themes, such as Virgil's *Aeneid,* to criticism of Rome. Roman law established basic principles of justice. Although great contrasts in wealth marked Roman society, the poor at least had some care.

3. Christianity spread through the empire. While Judaea was under Roman rule, Jesus began a new religion known as Christianity. Despite early persecution of its followers, Christianity won acceptance.

4. Rome's empire declined and fell. Rome faced many problems in the 200's but partly recovered under Diocletian, who set up reforms and divided the empire into eastern and western halves. Constantine legalized Christianity and moved the capital to Constantinople. During the 400's, barbarians swept into the empire, sacked Rome, and deposed Rome's last emperor.

Reviewing the Facts

1. Define the following terms:
  - a. civil service
  - b. satire
  - c. villa
  - d. bishop
  - e. pope
  - f. inflation

2. Explain the importance of each of the following names, dates, places, or terms:
  - a. Pax Romana
  - b. Augustus
  - c. Marcus Aurelius
  - d. A.D. 180
  - e. Epicurus
  - f. Zeno
  - g. Livy
  - h. Virgil
  - i. Jesus
  - j. Paul
  - k. Peter
  - l. Zealots
  - m. Diocletian
  - n. Constantine
  - o. Constantinople
  - p. Edict of Milan
  - q. A.D. 476

3. List four major achievements of Roman civilization during the Pax Romana.

4. (a) What were the main teachings of Christianity? (b) How did the position of Christianity within the Roman empire change between the first and fourth centuries A.D.?

5. How did each of the following factors contribute to the decline of the Roman empire? (a) economic problems (b) the issue of loyalty (c) Germanic invasions

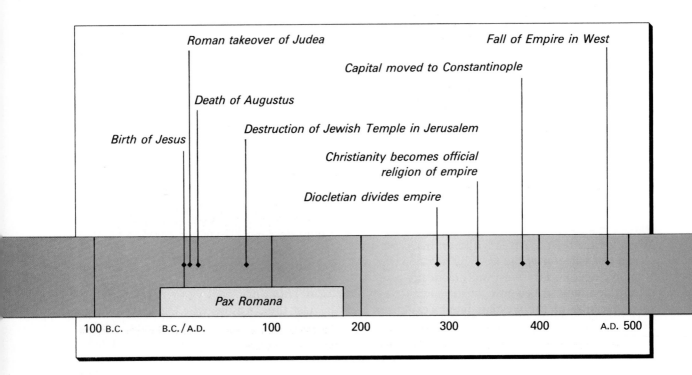

Roman takeover of Judea

Fall of Empire in West

Capital moved to Constantinople

Death of Augustus

Destruction of Jewish Temple in Jerusalem

Birth of Jesus

Christianity becomes official religion of empire

Diocletian divides empire

Pax Romana

100 B.C.   B.C./A.D.   100   200   300   400   A.D. 500

Basic Skills

1. **Comparing time lines** (a) How many years do the time lines on pages 138 and 160 each cover? (b) For what years do the two overlap? (c) How do the scales of the two time lines differ? (d) Which lasted longer, the Pax Romana or the Punic Wars?

2. **Classifying information** Using the map on page 155, make a chart to classify the goods that reached the market in Rome. Make three columns with the headings *Europe, Africa,* and *Asia.* For the vertical rows, use the headings *Minerals, Foods, Building Materials, Clothing/Jewelry, Manufactured Goods,* and *Other.* List items from the map in the appropriate spaces.

3. **Summarizing** Summarize the subsection entitled "Augustus set up sound government" on pages 141–142. Be sure to include all the main ideas and the most important supporting details for each.

Researching and Reporting Skills

1. **Organizing a group project** The chart "Emperors of the Pax Romana" provides the basis for a group research activity. Divide your class into three groups, one to report on the Julian emperors, one to report on the Army and Flavian emperors, and one to report on the Adoptive emperors. Each group should prepare the following: (a) a poster-sized bar graph showing the relative length of each emperor's rule; (b) photocopies of pictures of the emperors; and (c) a summary of each emperor's successes and failures. Groups will then present their materials and findings to the class.

2. **Recognizing primary and secondary sources** Identify each of the following as either a primary or secondary source: St. Paul's Epistle to the Ephesians, Livy's description of the early heroes of Rome, Constantine's triumphal arch (page 157), and Marcus Aurelius's *Meditations.* Give reasons for your answers.

Critical Thinking

1. **Comparing** (a) How did the Roman concept of citizenship differ from that in Athens and Sparta? (b) How does it differ from the concept of citizenship today?

2. **Analyzing** One of the characteristics of early Christianity was its appeal to the poor. What other world religion studied earlier also appealed to poor people? How would the teachings of each religion have this effect.

3. **Evaluating** On page 141, the text states that the Colosseum is symbolic of the entire Roman empire. "Both were awesome in their size and strength. Within, both combined bravery, honor, and glory with cruelty, sensationalism, and violence." (a) Do you think the Colosseum is an appropriate symbol of the Roman empire? (b) To what extent do you agree with the comparison? Why?

4. **Giving an opinion** Page 149 of the text states, "Rome's most lasting contribution to later civilizations was its law." (a) To what extent do you agree with this statement? Why? (b) What other achievements of Roman civilization are enduring?

5. **Applying a concept** At the end of the Roman empire, inflation added to the general economic crisis. (a) Define the term *inflation.* (b) What were its causes? (c) How might it affect society and trade?

Perspectives on Past and Present

1. Elements of Roman architecture have influenced many later styles. Find pictures of the government buildings and monuments in Washington, D.C., and analyze what elements of their style are Roman.

2. The transition of power from one leader to another is a time of crisis for many governments. How was this issue a problem for Rome? How is the problem handled in the United States today? How is it handled in the USSR? Use newspapers or news magazines to find accounts of ways in which new leaders come to power in these and other countries.

Investigating History

1. In A.D. 79, a volcanic eruption destroyed the two Roman towns of Pompeii and Herculaneum. When archaeologists uncovered the towns, they found many details of Roman life perfectly preserved. Find information about these towns and the buildings, activities, and ways of life that existed there.

2. One apparently original feature of Rome's building program was the public bath. (a) Find out how the idea of the Roman bath originated. (b) Why did the baths become a feature of Roman life for both rich and poor?

161

The Byzantine Empire and the Rise of Islam

After the Muslims captured Jerusalem, they built the Dome of the Rock on the spot where they believed the prophet Muhammad had ascended into heaven.

Key Terms

excommunicate
heretic
patriarch
jihad
caliph
sultan

Read and Understand

1. Constantinopole ruled an eastern empire.
2. A new faith spread from Arabia.
3. The Byzantine and Islamic empires influenced Slavs and Turks.

Inside the gates of Jerusalem, a tall, muscular Arab climbed down from the hump of a white camel. From the camel's back, he took down a dusty prayer rug and carried it up the steps of a magnificent, high-domed church, the Church of the Holy Sepulchre. The Arab's name was Omar. The year was 637.

For about 300 years, Jerusalem had been a Christian city, part of the Byzantine empire. Christians considered the ground enclosed by the Church of the Holy Sepulchre to be the most sacred place on earth. According to tradition, the spot where Jesus had been crucified and the tomb in which he had been buried lay beneath the dome of this church.

Map Study answers: The Bosporus; overland from Europe, by river from Scandinavia, by sea from Europe and North Africa, overland from China and Persia, by sea from Palestine, Persia, India, and Southeast Asia

Omar, however, was not a Christian. He was a Muslim, one of the first converts to a new religion called Islam (ihs-LAHM). He had been a personal friend of Islam's founder, an Arab prophet named Muhammad (moo-HAM-uhd).

Omar did not enter the church. Instead, he reverently turned his gaze southeast toward Mecca, the Arab city from which he had come. He knelt on his prayer rug, touching his head to the ground as he prayed toward Mecca. *"Allahu akhbar!"* he cried aloud, meaning "God is most great."

On this day in 637, Omar entered Jerusalem as a conqueror. Some 60,000 Muslim warriors had invaded Palestine to win converts for God —or *Allah*, in the Arabic language. They had defeated the defending Christian armies from Constantinople.

Rising from his prayer rug, Omar asked a Christian priest to show him to the flat stretch of rock where the temple built by the Jewish king Solomon had stood. To Muslims, this plain gray rock was holier than anything else in Jerusalem. Muslims believed that their prophet Muhammad had ascended from this rock into paradise on a golden ladder of light. Omar eagerly followed his guide to the sacred rock, but he found it buried under a mound of garbage and dung. The pious Omar flew into a rage. "Oh, ye men of Greece," he shouted at the Greek-speaking Christians, "ye are the people who shall be slain on this dung-heap."

In the centuries that followed, thousands of Christians and Muslims spilled their blood in wars of religion and conquest. Religious belief can be an immensely powerful force in human affairs. It can inspire great acts of goodness and stunning works of art. It can also drive people to terrible acts against those who hold other beliefs. Both Christians and Muslims claimed theirs was the only true religion. Neither group would allow the other to live in peace.

In this chapter, you will follow the fortunes of two empires, one Christian and the other Muslim. You will see how the Byzantine Christians used their riches to create an artistic masterpiece, the dazzling church of Hagia Sophia in Constantinople. In Jerusalem, the Muslim Arabs erected another architectural masterpiece, the Dome of the Rock, over the very rock on which Christians had dumped garbage. You will see

how Christianity spread from Constantinople into Russia and how Islam spread from Arabia as far west as Spain and as far east as India.

Constantinople ruled an eastern empire. 1

Constantinople was founded by Rome's first Christian emperor, Constantine, in 330. He built the city on the site of a Greek seaport known as Byzantium. It was situated at a point where many major trade routes between Asia and Europe came together, as the map on this page shows.

Between the Black Sea and the Aegean Sea lies a much smaller body of water, the Sea of Marmara. Two narrow straits, like natural gateways, control the shipping routes from sea to sea. The gateway between the Aegean Sea and the Sea of Marmara is the Dardanelles. The gateway between the Sea of Marmara and the Black Sea is called the Bosporus. Whoever controls those gates also controls the shipping from much of Asia to the Mediterranean region.

Map Study

What narrow waterway did Constantinople control? Name five routes by which goods reached the city.

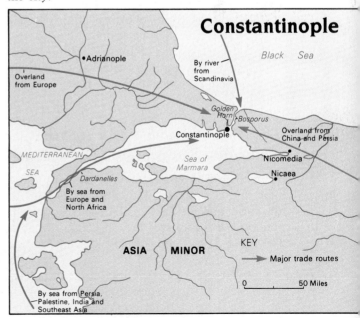

Have students speculate on why three major world religions had their beginnings in Jerusalem.

167

This medieval drawing shows Constantinople's busy harbor, its strong fortifications, its race course, and its great church, Hagia Sophia.

Constantine built his great capital on a peninsula at the southern end of the Bosporus. The city was blessed with a spacious harbor known as the Golden Horn (*horn* because it was shaped like an ox's horn, *golden* because of the wealthy cargoes that floated on its waters).

Constantine liked to call his eastern capital New Rome. Two centuries later, emperors in Constantinople still ruled the eastern part of the old Roman empire. The lands under their control included Greece, Asia Minor, Palestine, Syria, and Egypt. This empire is called the Byzantine empire after the original Greek town on Constantinople's site.

The emperor headed both church and state.

The Byzantine emperors never forgot their Roman heritage. They saw themselves as heirs to the power of Augustus Caesar. To keep up ancient tradition, a senate still met in Constantinople. In truth, however, the power of the emperor was absolute.

Emperors claimed authority from two sources. First, they held the political powers of a Roman ruler. Second, they claimed to rule in Jesus' name

as new apostles. This tradition went back to Constantine, and it gave the Byzantine emperor power similar to that of a pope. Thus, the Byzantine emperor combined political and religious authority in one person.

The Byzantine emperors still considered themselves rightful rulers of all the lands Rome had once held. Even in the 530's and 540's, a hundred years after the plunderings of Visigoths, Vandals, and Huns, one Byzantine emperor tried to reconquer all the western lands that Rome had lost to the barbarians. The name of this ambitious and controversial Byzantine ruler was Justinian (juhs-TIHN-ee-uhn).

Justinian reconquered Roman lands.

Justinian became emperor in 527 and ruled until 565. According to the official court historian, Procopius (proh-KOH-pee-uhs), Justinian was a ruddy-cheeked man of medium height and weight. He never lost his temper and never drank too much wine. He was a conscientious ruler, working from dawn to midnight.

Procopius flattered the emperor in the official histories, but in a *Secret History*, published after Justinian's death, Procopius gave vent to other feelings. Justinian, he wrote, was "deceitful, devious, false, hypocritical, two-faced, cruel, skilled in dissembling his thought, never moved to tears by either joy or pain . . . a liar always."

Whatever the truth may be about Justinian's character, he proved to be an able ruler. He launched three ambitious projects. First, he tried to reconquer Roman lands to the west. Second, he ordered a team of Greek and Latin scholars to compile and simplify the laws. Third, he undertook a massive building program in Constantinople. His works on the city and the laws were of lasting value to civilization. His wars, however, proved to be a waste of men and money.

The campaign to reconquer the Roman empire began successfully. In 533, Justinian sent his best general, Belisarius (BEL-uh-SAIR-ee-uhs), to win back the Vandal kingdom of North Africa. Belisarius broke down the Vandal defenses and rode triumphantly into Carthage. In only a few days, the entire northern coast of Africa beyond Egypt fell under Byzantine rule.

Belisarius's next assignment was to fight the Ostrogoths in Italy. With a tiny army of only

The system by which Byzantine emperors ruled is sometimes called "Caesaropapist." Discuss the meaning of this word. What does such a system imply?

The Byzantine Empire under Justinian

KEY

The Byzantine empire in 528

Areas reconquered by Justinian

0   500 Miles

Map Study

*Name three major areas that Justinian reconquered. For each area, tell what
group or groups his armies had to fight.*

8,000 men, the Byzantine general outmaneuvered
his barbarian foes. Entering Rome in 536, he
received a hero's welcome as the city's liberator.
For the first time in 60 years, wrote Procopius,
"Rome was again brought under the Romans."

The rejoicing, however, quickly turned to sorrow. The Ostrogoths returned and drove out the
Byzantines. The Byzantines struck back. In 18
years of siege and countersiege (535–553), Rome
changed hands six times.

When the Byzantines finally won control of
the city in 553, the triumph was an empty one.
Rome lay in ruins. Fallen statues littered its
streets. No water flowed in its magnificent baths.
Once home to a million people, Rome's population had dropped to a mere 40,000, nearly half
of whom roamed the streets as beggars or looters.
The Byzantines, who had come to save Rome,
ended by destroying it.

To North Africa and Italy, Justinian added part
of Spain as his final conquest. His dream to reunite
Roman lands seemed to have succeeded brilliantly. After his death, however, all the conquered
territory quickly passed back into barbarian hands.
Lombards overran Italy. Muslim Arabs swept
through North Africa and Spain. Ironically, the
destruction of Rome was the one lasting result
of Justinian's costly wars.

Justinian ordered a code of laws.

In the long run, Justinian's legal reforms were
far more important than his conquests. Between
528 and 534, he assigned a group of legal scholars
to an incredible task. They were to codify all
Roman laws and legal opinions since the time
of Hadrian 400 years earlier! If a law made in
Athens in the year 220 contradicted a law made
in Alexandria in 350, which law should be followed in Constantinople in 530? This was the
kind of perplexing question for which Justinian
sought an answer.

The result of his commission's labors was the
Corpus Juris Civilis (Body of Civil Law), known

Despite his short-term victories, Justinian did, in the opinion of historian Joseph
Strayer, reconquer the West "not through his armies but through his law."

169

to later ages as the Code of Justinian. It consisted of four works.

1. *The Codex Justinian* presented nearly 5,000 laws from the Roman empire that Justinian's scholars thought were still useful for Byzantium. The laws were arranged by topic.
2. *The Digest* quoted and summarized the opinions of Rome's greatest legal writers. This massive work had 50 volumes.
3. *The Institutes* was a textbook telling law students how to use the new code.
4. *The Novellae* contained laws made after 534.

Justinian died in 565, but his code lived after him. It was the basis for Byzantine law for the next 900 years. Many centuries later, France and other countries in western Europe turned to Justinian's code as a guide on legal questions concerning justice, property, marriage, and divorce. It was through Justinian's code that western Europe came to know once again the benefits of Roman law.

Constantinople grew in splendor.

While the code was being compiled, Justinian undertook a city building program larger than that of any Roman emperor, including Augustus. When he finished, Constantinople was the wonder of its age. It was known throughout the Eurasian world simply as "The City."

Some 300,000 people made their permanent homes in Constantinople. There were two requirements for citizenship: membership in the Christian church and the ability to speak Greek. The streets, however, were crowded with people from all over the world.

Constantinople was as well protected as any city could be in those dangerous times. Sea walls guarded it from hostile navies. To the west, a moat and three walls blocked the only land route to the city. The outermost wall was just high enough to shield Byzantine archers. The second wall was 27 feet high, and the third was 70 feet high. It is not surprising that Constantinople withstood many foes for more than 1,000 years.

The marketplace The city's main street was the *Mesê* (MEE-zuh), or Middle Way. The tables of merchants lined the Mesê on either side. Some tables were shaded by colorful awnings. Others were set back within colonnaded walkways.

Goods from all over the world found their way here, mostly by ship. Constantinople was noted for its luxury items. There were spices from India; ivory and gold from Africa; honey, timber, and furs from Russia. Cork came from Spain, wine from France, tin and iron from England, and grain and wool from north of the Alps. Bundles of Chinese silk reached the Mesê by camel caravan,

Mosaics were a common Byzantine artform. The one at the left shows Emperor Justinian; above is his wife, Empress Theodora.

a journey of 230 days if all went well. Encouraged by Justinian, two missionaries to China smuggled out a few silkworms and the seeds of mulberry trees. The secret of silk making, guarded by the Chinese for centuries, now belonged to the Byzantines.

The imperial palace The palace was the center of government. Some 20,000 people worked there in the service of the emperor.

In the gardens, peacocks strutted around bubbling fountains. The most impressive fountain was made of gold in the shape of a pineapple. Wine gushed from it into a silver basin filled with pistachio nuts on which a visitor could snack.

In the throne room, a long gold path led from the entrance to the golden throne. Above the throne was a gilded tree with mechanical birds twittering on its branches. Two golden lions stood on either side of the throne, rigged to let forth mock roars. The throne itself was wide enough to seat two persons, a symbol of the emperor's partnership with Jesus. Anyone who approached the throne was expected to lie prone three times, nose down and hands forward. Guests might kiss the emperor's toes or fingertips. The emperor stared ahead, too lordly to speak.

Hagia Sophia Across from the imperial palace stood one of the architectural wonders of the world—the great cathedral called Hagia Sophia (HAY-ee-uh soh-FEE-uh). It was the greatest monument of Byzantine Christianity, a symbol of the Christian city.

Voice from the Past · A *Question of Courage*

In 532, early in Justinian's reign, a great riot broke out in Constantinople. It began as a fight between the Blues and the Greens, rival teams in the city's popular chariot races. It quickly became a full-scale revolt. The crowd burned much of the city and proclaimed a new emperor. Justinian hid in the palace. With him was his beautiful wife, Theodora, a former actress who had spent her girlhood in the circus. Procopius tells of the debate that went on within the palace while the mob raged through the city:

Now the emperor and his court were deliberating whether it would be better to remain or to flee in the ships. And many opinions were expressed on both sides. And the Empress Theodora also spoke as follows: "As to the belief that a woman should not be daring among men or assert herself boldly, I consider the present crisis does not allow us to debate that. My opinion is that now is a poor time for flight, even though it bring safety. For any man who has seen the light of day will also die, but one who has been an emperor cannot endure to be a fugitive. If now you wish to go, Emperor, nothing prevents you. There is the sea, there are the steps to the boats. But take care that after you are safe, you do not find that you would gladly exchange that safety for death. For my part, I like the old saying that the empire is a fine burial cloth." When the queen had spoken thus, all were filled with boldness and began to consider how they might defend themselves from their enemies.

[Made brave by Theodora's speech, Justinian remained in the city, gave orders for his troops to crush the mob, and restored order.]

1. What two courses of action were the emperor and his court considering?
2. (a) What does Theodora say about whether or not a woman should speak out? (b) What does this statement suggest was the usual opinion about women at the time?
3. (a) What course of action does Theodora support? (b) What does she say about the risk of death? (c) What does she warn the emperor might happen if he flees?
4. How do you interpret the proverb, "The empire is a fine burial cloth"?

The palace had a purple bedchamber where all children of the imperial family were born. In their first days of life, everything they saw—walls, carpets, ceilings—was colored purple. "Born to the purple" is still a phrase meaning royal birth.

The great dome of Hagia Sophia was a marvel of engineering. The building has been a Christian church, a Muslim mosque, and a museum.

Hagia Sophia's giant dome rose 180 feet from the floor, an amazing engineering feat. Four acres of gold mosaic tiles covered the dome and the surrounding vaults and arches. The floors, walls, and columns gleamed with every imaginable shade of polished marble—red, white, purple, blue, green, and black. Sunlight poured in the dome's 40 windows by day. At night, light blazed from huge silver candelabra hanging on long chains.

One of the greatest wonders of Hagia Sophia was a magnificent table for preparing the Christian ceremony of Communion. For the making of this table, Justinian ordered pearls and sapphires ground into a rich powder and mixed with molten gold and silver. This extravagant mixture was then poured into a mold for the table.

The university Like several other cities in the Roman empire, Constantinople had a university. Its teachers emphasized the arts of writing and speaking well. The professors included ten Latin grammarians, ten Greek grammarians, three orators, two law professors, and several philosophers. (In later years, Latin fell out of use in Constantinople, and only Greek was spoken at the university.) The university served as a training ground for civil servants and imperial administrators.

Scholars in Constantinople copied the greatest works of the ancient writers—Homer, Plato, Archimedes, Euclid, Livy, Virgil, and others. Had the Byzantines not preserved these works, many would have been lost forever.

Education for both men and women was widespread among the upper classes in the Byzantine empire. Only a few women attended the university, but both boys and girls studied at home with tutors. The learned women of Constantinople included writers, philosophers, and at least one doctor.

The Hippodrome Like Rome's Colosseum, the Hippodrome in Constantinople was the site of extravagant and often bloody scenes for public view. The most important sports events were the chariot races, for which the Hippodrome's 60,000 seats were usually filled.

The Church split into two branches.

Just as the Greeks of Athens spent hours debating politics, the Greeks of Constantinople discussed religion. A shoemaker or a rug seller might argue over the nature of God and Jesus. In the marketplace, icons were sold beside fruit and vegetables. (Icons are small art objects that depict Jesus, Mary, or a Christian saint.)

At one point, conflict over icons had weakened and almost destroyed the Byzantine empire. In the 700's, several emperors tried to end the use of icons in churches. The emperors charged that many people prayed to the icons as if they were idols. Riots and bloody fights broke out between

Many monks earned their livings by making icons for sale. Some of the loudest and strongest protest to the iconoclasts came from the monasteries.

people who wanted to keep the icons in churches and the icon smashers, or *iconoclasts.*

The pope in Rome took the side of those who supported the icons. He **excommunicated** the Byzantine emperor. (That is, the pope declared that the emperor was outside the church, cut off from all Christians.)

Eventually, the Byzantine church again accepted icons, and the iconoclasts were labeled **heretics**. (A heretic is a person whose ideas are incorrect, in the opinion of the Church.)

The most lasting result of the controversy was an increase in bad feeling between Christians in Rome and Constantinople. Over the centuries, differences had developed between Byzantine Christians and the Christians of western Europe. For example, priests in the eastern empire conducted services in the local languages of their members—Greek, Coptic, Ethiopian, or Russian. Priests in western Europe conducted services only in Latin. Byzantine priests were allowed to marry, but Roman priests could not do so by church law.

Most important, the pope in Rome claimed to be supreme head of the Christian church, independent of any king or emperor. The bishop of Constantinople was known as the **patriarch** (PAY-tree-ARK). He accepted the authority of the Byzantine emperor. The pope in Rome claimed to be the leader of all Christians everywhere. The patriarchs, however, refused to accept the pope as their superior.

The break between Rome and Constantinople became final in 1054. That year, the pope and the patriarch excommunicated each other. The western branch of the Christian Church became known as the Roman Catholic Church. (*Catholic* comes from a Latin word meaning "universal.") The eastern branch became known as the Eastern Orthodox Church. (*Orthodox* comes from two Greek words meaning "correct belief.") Thus, the political break between the eastern and western parts of the old Roman empire became a religious break as well.

Byzantium faced many enemies.

Although Constantinople remained a rich and powerful city for hundreds of years, the Byzantine empire suffered many setbacks and dangers. The history of the empire after 565 was marked by a bewildering series of street riots, religious quarrels, palace intrigues, and foreign dangers. Many times, the empire appeared to be on the verge of collapse. Each time, it fought off its enemies and sprang back to renewed life only to be threatened by another crisis.

The first long crisis began with Justinian's death in 565. Plague swept through the empire, weakening its armies. Meanwhile, the Lombards moved into Italy and won much of the land Justinian had reconquered there. The Avars, a Hun-like people, invaded the Balkan peninsula (Greece and Macedon). To the east, the Persians threatened to pounce on their ancient foes, the Greeks. Then armies of Arabs, inspired by the prophet Muhammad, burst forth from the Arabian desert and threatened the Byzantine empire's very survival.

Section Review 1

Define: (a) law code, (b) icons, (c) iconoclast, (d) excommunicate, (e) heretic, (f) patriarch
Identify: (a) Constantine, (b) Constantinople, (c) Bosporus, (d) Justinian, (e) Procopius, (f) Belisarius, (g) Theodora, (h) Hagia Sophia, (i) Balkan peninsula, (j) Eastern Orthodox Church, (k) Roman Catholic Church
Answer:
1. (a) Why was Constantinople's harbor called the Golden Horn? (b) How did activities on the Mesê support this name?
2. What two sources did Byzantine emperors claim for their power to rule?
3. (a) What were Justinian's military goals? (b) Did he succeed? Explain.
4. (a) What was the value of Justinian's Code when it was written? (b) What was its lasting value?
5. (a) What disagreements arose between the Christian Church of Rome and that of Constantinople? (b) What was the result of those disagreements?

Critical Thinking
6. What factors made Constantinople a great city? (Consider geographic, historic, and cultural influences.)
7. If you were writing a history of the Byzantine empire, how would you rate Justinian as an emperor?

173

A new faith spread from Arabia. 2

In the mid-600's, Arab victories swept away enormous chunks of the Byzantine empire, including Palestine, Syria, Egypt, North Africa, and Spain. By 650, only Greece and Asia Minor remained to the Byzantines.

The Arabs threatened to take even Constantinople itself. Every year from 673 to 678, their warships lay outside the great sea wall around Constantinople. What saved the Byzantines was a terrifying weapon that no one else possessed — "Greek fire." Greek fire was a mixture of chemicals (probably naphtha, sulphur, and saltpeter) that the Byzantines squirted through copper tubes at enemy ships. The mixture burst into flames on contact with the Arab ships, turning them into deathtraps. It even burned on the surface of the water.

Who were these Arabs who appeared so suddenly and threatened Constantinople so fiercely? Their story begins in the late 500's. The century in which Justinian lived was also the century in which the prophet Muhammad was born in Arabia.

Arab culture arose in the desert.

The Arabian peninsula stretches 1,400 miles north to south along the Red Sea, the sea that separates Arabia from Africa. The peninsula measures 1,250 miles from east to west at its southern edge. To the traveler, its deserts seem to stretch on forever under a blue sky and merciless sun.

The nomads who lived on this desert were called Bedouin (BEHD-oo-ihn). They slept in tents made from camels' hide and drank camel milk. Mounted on camels, Bedouin traveled between widely scattered oases and trading centers. During much of the year, Bedouin routinely raided one another's camps and caravans. However, certain times were considered holy, for making pilgrimages to a sacred shrine in Mecca.

Mecca was the largest of several towns near the western coast of Arabia. A few generations earlier, these town dwellers had themselves been Bedouin, but by the late 500's, they had left the Bedouin life behind. The leading Meccans were wealthy merchants. Travelers to Mecca brought both goods and ideas from the surrounding Roman, Byzantine, and Persian empires.

Before Muhammad, the Bedouins and the townspeople worshiped hundreds of gods and spirits. Spirits called *jinn* were thought to reside in rocks and other natural objects. Mecca was the home of the most sacred of these rocks. The Black Stone of Mecca was (and still is) embedded within the wall of a shrine called the Kaaba (KAH-uh-buh), which in Arabic means "cube." Besides the Black Stone, the Kaaba contained idols representing 360 gods, including one deity called Allah.

This shrine made Mecca an important religious center. Pilgrims flocked to it during the holy months. In this city, around the year 570, Muhammad was born.

Muhammad taught monotheism.

Muhammad was born into a minor branch of a powerful Meccan family. Orphaned at the age of six, the boy was raised by his grandfather and uncle. He received little schooling and probably never learned to read or write. (Even in well-to-do Arabian families, literacy was unusual.) Muhammad became a trader and business manager for Khadya (KAHD-yuh), a wealthy businesswoman 15 years older than he. When Muhammad was 25, he and Khadya married. It was both a good marriage and a good business partnership.

Muhammad had traveled to Syria as Khadya's business agent. There he may have talked with Byzantine Christians and learned about their religion. Communities of Jews were settled in the Arab towns. Both groups were monotheists. A few Arab holy men, known as *hanifs*, had already turned to the worship of one god.

Muhammad took great interest in religion and often spent time alone in prayer and meditation. At the age of 40, Muhammad's life was changed overnight by a vision that came to him while he meditated in a cave outside Mecca. His description was recorded by a follower:

While I was asleep, with a coverlet of silk brocade whereon was some writing, the angel Gabriel appeared to me and said, "Read!" I said, "I do not read." He pressed me with the coverlets so tightly that I thought it was death. Then he let me go,

Muhammad is said to have spent one month each year meditating in the desert. The Black Stone is said to have fallen from heaven. There is some speculation that it was, in fact, a meteorite.

and said, "Read!" . . . So I read aloud, and he departed from me at last . . . I went forth until, when I was midway on the mountain, I heard a voice from heaven saying, "O Muhammad! Thou art the messenger of God, and I am Gabriel."

Muhammad had other visions in which the angel Gabriel again appeared with messages from Allah (the Arabic word for *God*). Who was Allah? Muhammad believed the messages came from the same God worshiped by Christians and Jews. After much soul searching, Muhammad finally became convinced that he was indeed the last and greatest of the prophets. Khadya and several close friends and relatives were his first followers.

By 613, Muhammad began to preach publicly in Mecca. At first, he had little success. Many Meccans thought his revolutionary ideas were bad for business. They feared that Mecca would lose its position as a pilgrimage center if people accepted Muhammad's beliefs. Some of his followers were stoned in the streets.

The Hegira marked a turning point.

Facing such hostility, Muhammad decided to leave Mecca. In 622, he fled to the town of Medina (muh-DEE-nuh), taking a little band of followers with him. This escape became known as the *Hegira* (hih-JYE-ruh), Arabic for "flight."

The Hegira marked a turning point for Muhammad. In Medina, he attracted many devoted followers. He also won great political influence. Muhammad's new religion became known as *Islam*, which means "surrender to God." Believers became known as *Muslims*, "the surrendering ones." On the Muslim calendar, the year of the Hegira became the year 1, the first year of the Islamic era.

From Medina, Muhammad led raids against Meccan caravans. Later, his armies completely defeated the Meccans. Such victories increased the prestige of Islam. Within ten years, almost all Bedouin had accepted Islam as their faith. In 630, the prophet and 10,000 followers entered Mecca in triumph. Muhammad went to the Kaaba and exultantly declared, "Truth has come and falsehood has vanished." Then, he destroyed the idols in the Kaaba, allowing only the Black Stone to remain. Muhammad died only two years later at the age of 62.

Pilgrims surround the Kaaba in Mecca. The towers in the background are minarets from which muezzins call Muslims to prayer.

The Koran is Islam's holy book.

While Muhammad lived, his followers had listened to his prayers and teachings. The Arabs had a long tradition of oral poetry, and they memorized and recited his words over and over. Muslims who were literate wrote them on scraps of parchment and even on palm leaves. Soon after the prophet's death, a new leader named Abu-Bakr ordered all the words of Muhammad to be gathered into a book. This book is the Koran (koh-RAHN), the holy book of Islam.

The Koran is about the same length as the Christians' New Testament. Its 114 *suras* (chapters) are arranged according to length, not subject. The longest sura comes first, and the shortest comes last.

The Koran was written in Arabic, and only the Arabic version was considered by Muslims to be the true word of God. Only Arabic could be used in worship. Because of this rule, the Arabic language spread widely in the Middle East and North Africa. Wherever Islamic conquerors carried the Koran, Arabic became the language of scholars and poets.

Discussion question: Why might it be difficult for a self-proclaimed prophet to win converts in his own city? (Familiarity might make faith and belief impossible.)

175

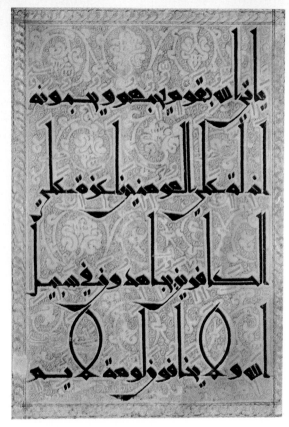

Because their religious art could show no figures of people or animals, Muslims decorated copies of the Koran with fine calligraphy.

The rules of Islam regulated life.

To be a Muslim was both simple and demanding. Muhammad's teachings set forth strict guidelines for right living. Every believer was expected to carry out five duties. These duties were known as the Five Pillars of Islam.

1. *Faith* To become a Muslim, a person had to make a statement of faith: "I testify there is no god but God, and Muhammad is His Prophet."
2. *Prayer* Every day, sleeping Muslims awoke at dawn to the sound of a *muezzin* (myoo-**EZ**-uhn), or crier, calling them to prayer. Their first morning chore was to purify themselves for prayer. They washed their hands and arms up to the elbow, their feet up to the ankles. They used water if it was available, but the Bedouin of the desert washed themselves with sand. Muslims were required to pray five times daily. Each time, they removed their shoes, turned to face the holy city of Mecca, lay flat on the ground, and recited a formal prayer either silently or in a low voice.
3. *Alms* Muhammad strictly commanded the faithful to give a portion of their wealth as alms to help the needy.
4. *Fasting* For one full month—the holy month of Ramadan (RAM-uh-**DAHN**)—Muslims were to eat nothing and drink nothing between sunrise and sunset. Only after sunset could families joyfully sit down together for a meal.
5. *Pilgrimage* Once in a lifetime, any Muslim who could afford the journey was expected to make a pilgrimage to Mecca. For many, this involved a grueling journey across mountains, deserts, and seas.

Along with the Five Pillars, the Koran also established other customs, morals, and laws for Islamic society. Believers were not to eat ham or pork. Believers were forbidden to drink wine or other intoxicating beverages. A man was allowed to marry as many as four wives, but only if he could support them all equally well. Marriage with unbelievers was forbidden. Many such rules regulated daily life for Muslims.

Friday afternoon was set aside for communal worship and prayer. Muslims gathered in the local mosque and prayed in unison, facing Mecca. One person led the prayers in the mosque, but he was not a priest in the Christian sense. Unlike many other religions, Islam had no formal priesthood. Women were sometimes prayer leaders for other women, but few women attended services in a mosque. In Islamic society, women and men led very separate lives.

Muhammad taught that there would be a Day of Judgment, at which time those who followed Islam's law would be rewarded. They would be welcomed into paradise, described by the Koran as a fabulous garden. There believers would bask forever, dressed in silk and drinking from rivers of milk and honey. Unbelievers and Muslims who shirked their religious duties faced eternal punishment. On the Day of Judgment, said the Koran, they would be cast into hell to wear shoes of fire, eat filth, and drink boiling water forever.

Islam expanded east and west.

In 732, exactly 100 years after Muhammad's death, Muslim armies from Spain crossed the Pyrenees into southwestern France. There, at the Battle of Tours, they were defeated by a Christian army commanded by the Frankish leader, Charles

The Arabs were masters of desert warfare, bewildering the enemy with their swift maneuvers, wheeling their camels and horses this way and that. Some historians have compared Arab mastery of the desert to British mastery of the sea.

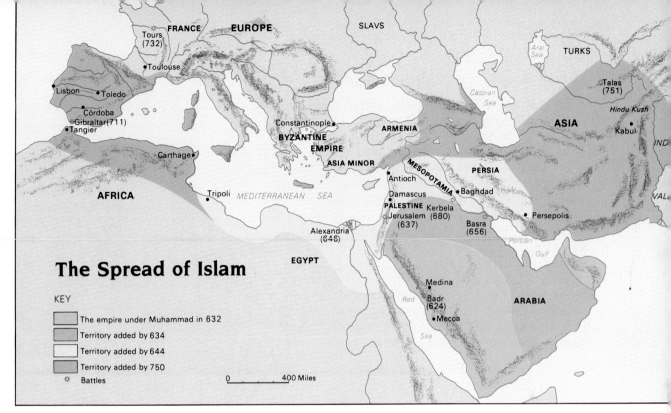

The Spread of Islam

KEY

- The empire under Muhammad in 632
- Territory added by 634
- Territory added by 644
- Territory added by 750
- ☀ Battles

0 — 400 Miles

Map Study

By what year had the Muslims won control of each of the following cities?
(a) Mecca (b) Alexandria (c) Tripoli (d) Kabul (e) Toledo (f) Antioch
What was the northernmost battle that Muslim armies fought in Europe?

Martel. As the crow flies, the Muslims were then 2,500 miles from Mecca. Their advance into Europe was stopped at Tours. But consider how far they had already come.

By 732, Muslim Arabs controlled the Iberian peninsula (Spain and Portugal), the land of the Carthaginians (North Africa), the land of the ancient pharaohs (Egypt), the holy land of the Jews and Christians (Palestine), the land of the ancient Babylonians (Mesopotamia), the land of the once great Persian empire, the land of northwestern India, and of course their own vast land, Arabia. They had conquered more territory than the Romans and all in one century.

Reasons for conquest How did they do it, and why? Several factors help explain the blinding speed with which Muslim armies cut down their foes and spread their faith from India to Spain.

First, the Arabs were passionate in their new faith. The Koran taught that wars fought for God were just. A warrior killed in a **jihad** (jih-HAHD), or holy war, was promised immediate entry into paradise. With this belief, Muslims rushed fearlessly into battle.

Second, the arid Arabian peninsula was badly overpopulated in the 600's. Arab armies were filled with warriors eager to move into more bountiful lands. As new converts accepted Islam, they swelled its armies still more.

Third, resistance was weak. The Byzantine and Persian empires had been fighting each other for centuries. Now they were both exhausted.

Results of conquest The Arabs proved tolerant rulers. They offered their subjects three choices: convert to Islam, pay a reasonable tax, or die. The first two choices were by far the most popular.

As Islam spread, Muslim society changed. Muhammad had taught that all Muslims were equal in the eyes of God. However, as Arab armies conquered new lands, people who were not Arabs began to accept Islam. Gradually, Islamic society came to have two classes: an upper class of Arab Muslims and a second class of non-Arab Muslims.

Christians, Jews, and Zoroastrians ranked below both Muslim groups. These groups paid a tax to avoid converting to Islam. (Indeed, their taxes supported the empire.) All three groups formed important communities within the cities of the

Map Study answers: (a) 632; (b) 646; (c) 644; (d) 750; (e) 750; (f) 644; Tours

177

Daily Life · *Prayer Rugs*

The one piece of art that every Muslim owned was a small, wonderfully patterned carpet called a prayer rug. On this rug the worshiper knelt five times a day to pray. For Persians and Turks, carpet making was both an industry and an art form. A skilled weaver could tie knots at the rate of 900 per hour. Even so, the finest rugs were so densely knotted that an hour's work produced less than three square inches of rug. Ordinary rugs came in many elaborate designs, but prayer rugs followed a particular pattern. Each had a pointed arch in the middle, representing the prayer niche in a mosque. Woven into the border of each rug was a design of flowers, leaves, and vines. Muslims never created pictures of Muhammad or any other human or animal form in their religious art. Such pictures were thought to be an offense to God, who alone can create a living creature. Therefore, weavers used only abstract patterns.

Islamic empire. At least in the early years of the empire, Muslims treated both Jews and Christians with respect because they were also monotheists.

The building of an empire changed Islamic society. No longer was everyone under Muslim rule an Arab or even a believer in Islam. As time went by, the lands under Islamic rule became less a community of believers and more like other empires of history.

Caliphs ruled the Islamic empire.

In Muhammad's last years, he had been a political ruler as well as a religious leader. The leaders who followed him were called **caliphs** (KAY-lihfs), meaning "successors to the prophet." They too had both political and religious power.

The orthodox caliphate (632–661) The first four caliphs were men who had known Muhammad personally, either as friends or relatives. Under their leadership, Islam's wars of conquest were launched. The time in which they ruled is known as the orthodox caliphate.

The first caliph was Abu-Bakr, who ordered the writing of the Koran. The second was Omar, Islam's greatest conqueror. In 636, Syria fell before his fierce Bedouin warriors. We have seen how he entered Jerusalem in 637. By the time of his death in 644, Omar had also won control of Egypt and most of Persia.

Violence plagued the caliphs. Omar was stabbed to death by a Christian slave in 644. The next caliph, Uthman, was murdered by rebel Muslims in 656. Ali, the last of the orthodox caliphs, was also assassinated in 661. These murders sowed the seeds for later civil war and splits within Islam.

The Umayyad caliphate (661–750) With the death of Ali, the office of caliph passed to a new family, the Umayyads (oo-MYE-yads). In their rise to power, however, the Umayyads killed a rival, Husayn, who was Muhammad's grandson. The sin of having killed the prophet's grandson was later to haunt the Umayyad rulers.

The Umayyads continued the wars of conquest. It was under their rule that Arab fleets attacked Constantinople, but their hopes were thwarted by Greek fire. The Umayyad caliphs had much greater success elsewhere. Their armies conquered North Africa and converted the Berber tribes there to Islam. The fierce Berbers then helped the Arabs invade Spain in 711. By 718, Muslim armies had conquered Spain. From Spain, the forces of Islam swept into France but were turned back at Tours in 732. To the east, meanwhile, other Arab armies pushed the borders of the empire out to the Indus River valley. From Asia across Africa into Europe, the Islamic empire stretched over 5,000 miles—about 2,000 miles farther than the distance across the continental United States.

According to tradition, the Arab general who led the invasion of Spain ordered his captains to burn the boats in which the army had come. Then he told his troops that their only hope for life lay in victory. Why might they have been prepared to die? (honor in dying for *jihad*)

The Umayyads were able rulers and administered their vast empire carefully. However, many Muslims never forgave the death of Husayn. Other Muslims called the luxury of the Umayyad royal court sinful. A rebellion broke out against the Umayyads. In 750, the last Umayyad caliph was killed, and so were 80 other members of the family.

The only survivor of the Umayyad family escaped to Spain. There he established his own separate Islamic kingdom.

The Abbasid caliphate (750–1055) The leader of the revolt against the Umayyads was descended from Abbas, an uncle of Muhammad. The new rulers called themselves the Abbasid (uh-BAS-ihd) dynasty, emphasizing the link to the prophet.

The greatest support for the Abbasids came from Persia. Most Persians had accepted Islam. As converts, however, they were still second-class citizens under the Umayyads. With Persia's own proud history of empire, Persians resented the Arab ruling class. The Abbasids promised a return to the early Islamic idea of equality among believers. Yet going back to the past was impossible. Islam and its followers had changed irrevocably in the years since Muhammad's death.

Religious differences split Islam.

By the time of the Abbasids, Islam was no longer a united religion. The killing of Husayn, which helped cause the fall of the Umayyads, also had religious consequences. Muslims who believed that Husayn had been the rightful caliph became known as Shi'ites (SHEE-ytes). The movement began as a political split, but it became a religious one as well. The Shi'ites were especially strong in what is now Iraq.

Shi'ites denied the authority of the Umayyad caliphs and helped the Abbasids win power. The Abbasids, however, refused to tolerate the Shi'ites and sometimes persecuted them. Over the years, hostility increased between the Shi'ites and the Sunni (or orthodox) Muslims.

Baghdad rivaled Constantinople.

Because Persia was the base of Abbasid strength, the Abbasids moved their capital eastward, closer to the heart of the old Persian empire. On the western bank of the Tigris River, they built the city of Baghdad (BAG-dad), as opulent and glittering as Constantinople. Baghdad became the center of Muslim civilization during its golden age.

The Round City Picture three round walls, one inside the other, encircling a perfectly round city. This was Baghdad. At the very center of the inner circle was the famous Green Dome of the caliph's palace. Four broad avenues thrust into the heart of circular Baghdad, carving the city into four equal quarters. Everything in the round city pointed toward and revolved around the caliph's palace.

Under the Green Dome was a grand throne room. There the caliph awaited his visitors behind an ornate curtain, which was drawn with a flourish. Standing behind the caliph's throne was a grim-faced soldier with a sword always drawn and sharpened. Thus, a visitor who displeased the caliph could be beheaded on the spot.

Wealth from trade Between the middle wall and the palace wall lay Baghdad's main business district. Along the four major avenues, merchants tempted passersby with Arabian perfumes, Syrian glassware, Chinese silks, and Indian silver and rubies. There were also swords from Russia, leather goods from Spain, and slaves from Africa and Scandinavia.

By the year 1000, perhaps 100,000 people lived in Baghdad. Their wealth, like the wealth of Constantinople's citizens, was the result of their city's location. The chief caravan routes from India and China passed through Baghdad. Ships from Arabia and India came to the city too. They sailed from the Persian Gulf up the Tigris River to Baghdad's wharves.

To encourage the flow of trade, Muslim money changers set up banks in cities throughout their far-flung empire. Banks offered letters of credit to merchants. Such a letter of credit was called a *sakk*. A merchant with a sakk from a bank in Baghdad could exchange it for cash at a bank in Mecca or in any other major city within the empire. In Europe, the word *sakk* was pronounced "check." Thus the practice of using checks dates back to the Islamic empire.

Arts and sciences flourished.

Under the Abbasids, the Islamic empire enjoyed a brief but brilliant golden age in arts and sciences. The Islamic empire reached the height of its

Founded in 762, Baghdad became the greatest Muslim city and possibly the largest in
the world. Established as a capital, Baghdad also became a center of learning and
trade. Located on the Tigris River, it was for a time the western end of the Great Silk
Road linking the Middle East and China.

179

Muslim astronomers studied the stars at the royal observatory (left). Below is an Arabic astrolabe.

power and prosperity in the reign of Harun ar-Rashid (hah-**ROON** uh-rah-**SHEED**), who ruled from 786 to 809.

Like Hellenistic civilization, Islamic culture was enriched by many groups. The empire included a rich blend of cultures. Christians, Jews, and Zoroastrians played a large part in the empire's intellectual achievements. Yet the Islamic faith and the Arabic language were the bonds that held the empire together. Arabic became the language of scholarship for all who lived within the empire, much as Latin had been for the Romans and as Greek was for the Byzantines.

Islamic science Science thrived in the Islamic empire as it had in Hellenistic times. Scholars were inspired by ancient Greek sources—the ideas of Aristotle and Plato, the geometry of Euclid, and the medical knowledge of Galen. Manuscripts from many lands were brought back to Baghdad's House of Wisdom, a huge library where scholars translated Greek texts into Arabic. After mastering the Greek sources, Muslim scientists went on to make their own discoveries and inventions.

These were some of their most notable works:

First chemical laboratories The first chemists to work in laboratories were Islamic alchemists (**AL**-kuh-mihsts), who tried to turn ordinary metals into gold. It was an impossible task, but as they worked, alchemists found ways to separate one chemical compound from another.

Treatment of disease The greatest names in Islamic medicine were Rhazes (rah-**ZEES**), and Avicenna (**AV**-ih-**SEN**-uh). Rhazes (850–923) wrote more than 100 treatises on medicine. The most famous of these told doctors how to diagnose smallpox and treat it before the patient's condition became hopeless. Avicenna (980–1037) wrote a five-volume encyclopedia that guided doctors of Europe and Southwest Asia for six centuries.

Footnote to History

The alchemists' name for any distilled substance was *alkuhl,* from which comes our word *alcohol.*

Many of the names we use for Arabs are Europeanized corruptions. The Arab form for Rhazes, for example, is ar-Razi; for Avicenna, Ibn Sina.

Islamic doctors also excelled in the preparation of medicines.

Use of the astrolabe First used by ancient Greeks, the astrolabe was rediscovered and improved by Islamic astronomers. A sea captain or caravan leader adjusted the pointer on its brass disk to chart the position of a star, which is the most reliable way to find one's position on Earth.

Mathematics One of Islam's many mathematical wizards was named Al-Khwarizmi (al-KWAH-rihz-MEE). He wrote a textbook in the 800's explaining "the art of bringing together unknowns to match a known quantity." He called this technique *al-jabr*. We call it algebra.

Without the concept of zero, higher mathematics is almost impossible. Neither the Greeks nor Romans had a zero in their number system. The Hindus of India first used a number system based on sets of ten and a symbol for zero. The Muslims adopted the system, and from them it spread to western Europe. We therefore speak today of using Arabic numerals.

Islamic literature The science and mathematics of Islam can be appreciated by people of any culture. However, only people who understand Arabic can fully appreciate its literature. The Arabs considered poetry their greatest art. The thousands of poems created during Islam's golden age were meant to be sung and recited aloud in Arabic. Most often, poets sang of war or of romantic love. The goal of the Arab poets was to compress as much meaning and eloquence as possible into very few words.

Among the Islamic writers was the Persian poet and astronomer, Omar Khayyám (kye-AHM). He lived and wrote around 1100, as Islam's golden age was beginning to fade. Omar Khayyám is best known for a collection of four-line poems called the *Rubáiyát* (ROO-be-aht). This famous stanza shows how the poet celebrated the fleeting pleasures of life:

A Book of Verses underneath the Bough,
A Jug of Wine, a Loaf of Bread—and Thou
Beside me singing in the Wilderness—
Oh, Wilderness were Paradise enow!

Islamic writers produced a great variety of literature. For example, the work known in English as *The Arabian Nights* is a collection of folktales that includes the tale of Aladdin's magic lamp and the stories of Sinbad the Sailor. Islamic scholars also filled volumes on history, geography, law, philosophy, and religion. To devout Muslims, of course, the Koran remains the supreme achievement of Islamic literature.

Islamic architecture Throughout their empire, the Muslims built beautiful mosques. The greatest of these buildings stood in Jerusalem. In 691, a caliph ordered a mosque built over the rock from which Muhammad was believed to have ascended into paradise—the rock that Byzantines had once used for a garbage dump. This mosque became known as the Dome of the Rock because its golden dome was its most striking and beautiful feature. The dome stands 70 feet above the sacred rock. Circling around the dome are bands of black inscribed with a swirling golden script. It is the Arabic script with verses from the Koran.

Below the dome, framed by a circle of marble columns, is the sacred rock itself. Muslim worshipers cannot walk on it—not until the Day of Judgment, when they expect saved souls to be brought to this spot and lifted to paradise. Worshipers spread their prayer rugs at the very edge of the walled-off rock and lie down to pray facing, as always, toward Mecca.

Section Review 2

Define: (a) pilgrimage, (b) jihad, (c) caliph, (d) alchemist, (e) astrolabe

Identify: (a) Arabia, (b) Bedouin, (c) Mecca, (d) Kaaba, (e) Muhammad, (f) Allah, (g) Khadya, (h) Medina, (i) Muslims, (j) Islam, (k) Koran, (l) Hegira, (m) Ramadan

Answer:
1. Briefly describe how Muhammad became a religious teacher.
2. Why is the Hegira important to Islam?
3. What are the Five Pillars of Islam?
4. (a) What lands did the Islamic empire control by 732? (b) Give three reasons for the rapid spread of the empire.
5. Name the three groups of leaders who ruled the Islamic empire between 632 and 1055, and briefly describe each period.
6. How did Islam split into Shi'ites and Sunnis?

Critical Thinking
7. How did the Byzantine and Islamic empires both combine political and religious power?

181

The empires influenced Slavs and Turks. 3

Around the year 800, both the Islamic and the Byzantine empires were strong and stable. The Byzantines had lost much land to the Muslims, but Constantinople still ruled Asia Minor, Greece, and Sicily. At the same time, the giant empire of the Abbasids stretched from Gibraltar to the Indus River valley.

Within both the Byzantine and Islamic empires, the seeds of future trouble had already been sown. Internal divisions weakened the two empires. Enemy attacks eventually destroyed them.

In the meanwhile, the two empires profoundly influenced two groups of invaders—the Slavs and the Turks. The aging Byzantine empire had a powerful cultural impact on the Slavs. Eventually, several Slavic peoples, especially the Russians, adopted the Byzantine form of Christianity. The Turks, on the other hand, became Muslims even while they fought the armies of the Islamic empire.

Byzantine culture influenced the Slavic peoples.

In the 700's, while the Arabs threatened Byzantium from the south, the Slavs struck from the north. The Slavic people were groups of nomads who had migrated into eastern Europe from the plains of Asia. Each group had its own culture, but all spoke related languages. In the 700's and 800's, these groups were perpetually at war with the Byzantines, fighting for possession of the Balkan peninsula and land around the Black Sea.

Conversion of the Slavs While the Slavic rulers coveted Constantinople's wealth and territory, they also admired its civilization. Unlike the Arabs, the Slavs were persuaded to become Christian. Between 850 and 900, Byzantine missionaries began to win Slavic converts. Among the wisest and most statesmanlike of these missionaries was a monk named Cyril (SIHR-uhl). He and other missionaries invented an alphabet for the Slavic languages, so that Slavs could read the Bible in their own tongue. In honor of Cyril, this system of writing is known as the Cyrillic

(suh-RIHL-ik) alphabet. It is still used in some Slavic countries.

The Russian kingdom To the north of the Black Sea, a group of Slavs known as Russians lived in the forests south of the Baltic Sea. The story of Russia's origins comes from the *Primary Chronicle*, an account written around 1050 by an anonymous group of Russian monks who included in their story as much legend as fact.

According to this chronicle, the first Russians were a band of hardy hunters from Scandinavia. They migrated south into forestlands occupied by bands of Slavs. The Slavs called these Scandinavians *Rus* (roos). In 862, says the *Primary Chronicle*, the Slavs invited the Rus to become their protectors and rulers. Thus, 862 is the traditional date for the founding of Russia.

The first Russian prince had a decidedly Scandinavian name: Rurik. His capital city, Novgorod (NAHV-guh-rahd), lay far to the north near the border of present-day Finland. Soon, however, Russian princes moved south to Kiev (KEE-yef), a city better placed for shipping furs, amber, slaves, and honey downriver to Constantinople.

From the *Primary Chronicle* comes a charming—and perhaps true—story of how Kievan Russia was converted to Christianity. Princess Olga, who ruled Kiev from 945 to 955, was the first Russian ruler to become a Christian. However, she did not make Christianity the official religion of her kingdom. In 989, the ruler of Kiev was Vladimir (VLAHD-uh-meer), Olga's grandson. He sent envoys to investigate both Roman and Byzantine Christianity. They found the churches of barbaric Germany drab. Soon afterwards, in Constantinople, the envoys visited Hagia Sophia, the magnificent cathedral built by Justinian (page 172). Stunned by the beauty of its golden mosaics, they reported:

> Then we went on to Greece [Byzantium], and the Greeks led us to the buildings where they worship their God, and we knew not whether we were in heaven or on earth. For on earth there is no such splendor or such beauty, and we are at a loss how to describe it. We only know that God dwells there among men.

Vladimir therefore chose to be a Christian in the Byzantine manner, not in the Roman manner. In 989, he commanded his subjects to go to the

Vladimir wanted a new religion to replace worship of Scandinavian gods. He rejected Judaism because the Jews could not explain to his satisfaction why they had lost Jerusalem. He rejected Islam because it forbade the drinking of wine. "Drinking is the joy of the Russes," said Vladimir.

Dnieper River for baptism. Thus, Russians looked to Constantinople, not Rome, for religious leadership. This choice would have profound consequences for Russia in years to come, as it cut off the kingdom from western Europe.

The Russian kingdom prospered from its ties to Byzantium. By the year 1000, Kiev had a population of 8,000, making it the equal of Paris, the largest city of western Europe at that time. Kiev's gold-domed churches imitated those of Constantinople. Its mosaics too were much like those found in "The City." The pattern of Russian culture—Slavic in language, Byzantine in style—was established for centuries to come.

The Turks struck from the east.

Between the years 1000 and 1100, both the Byzantine empire and the Islamic empire faced new dangers. Chief among them were the ferocious attacks of a nomadic people from central Asia, the Turks.

The breakup of the Islamic empire The Islamic empire had already lost much of its territory. Spain broke away from the Islamic empire in 756, when the Abbasids came to power. After moving their capital east to Baghdad, the Abbasids lost other parts of their empire in the west—Morocco in 788 and Tunisia in 800. After the death of Harun ar-Rashid in 809, parts of Persia also broke away. Then, in 868, the Abbasids lost control of Egypt.

In 945, a local Persian ruler took over Baghdad and ended the caliph's political power. Although the caliph was still the religious leader of Islam, a **sultan** now held all political power. The power of the Abbasids was broken.

Seljuk Turks In this time of weakness and division, a formidable enemy swept out of Asia. On the flat grasslands between the Black and Caspian seas, nomadic Turks grazed their horses and practiced the art of war. Just as Roman emperors had used barbarians in their armies, caliphs in the 800's used the Turks. Finally, just as Rome fell to the barbarians, Baghdad fell to the Turks.

Large numbers of Turks moved into the Islamic empire around 970. This first group of migrating Turks is known as the Seljuk (SEL-jook) Turks, after the family that led them. By 1000, they had converted to Islam, joining the Sunni branch. Conversion did not stop them, however, from

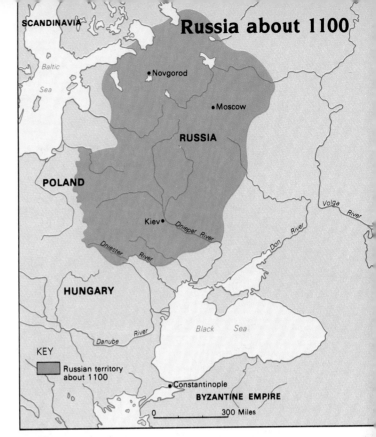

Russia about 1100

Map Study

By what water route would travelers and traders from Kiev have reached Constantinople?

warring with other Muslims. In 1055, they captured Baghdad. Throughout the empire, Turks now replaced Arabs as the ruling class.

Twenty years later, the Seljuk sultans spearheaded a mighty drive against the Byzantine empire. In 1071, at the Battle of Manzikert, the Turks overwhelmed the Byzantines. Within ten years, the Seljuk Turks occupied all of Asia Minor, the eastern heartland of Byzantium. It was a staggering blow to the Byzantines, for even the mighty armies of the Arabs had never come so close to Constantinople by land.

Constantinople fell to the Turks.

After the Battle of Manzikert, the Byzantine empire grew weaker and weaker. Cities in Europe began to take over much of the trade that Constantinople had once controlled.

By 1400, the Byzantine empire was little more than the city of Constantinople itself. All the rest of the empire had fallen to a new branch of Turks, the Ottomans. The Ottoman sultan sent

The Turks stripped Hagia Sophia of its Christian symbols and turned it into a Muslim mosque, which it remains to this day.

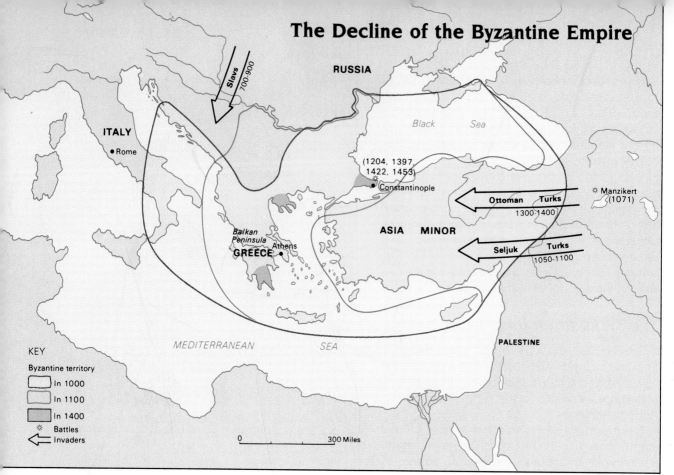

The Decline of the Byzantine Empire

RUSSIA

Slavs 700-900

ITALY

• Rome

Black Sea

(1204, 1397, 1422, 1453)
☼ Constantinople

Ottoman Turks
1300-1400

☼ Manzikert
(1071)

Balkan Peninsula
Athens •
GREECE •

ASIA MINOR

Seljuk Turks
1050-1100

MEDITERRANEAN   SEA

PALESTINE

KEY

Byzantine territory

☐ In 1000
☐ In 1100
☐ In 1400
☼ Battles
⬅ Invaders

0   300 Miles

Map Study

Where was the westernmost boundary of the empire in the year 1000? What territory did the empire control by 1400?

a message to the Byzantine emperor: "Close the gates of the city and rule within it, for I own everything outside the walls." Turkish armies besieged the city in 1397, in 1422, and finally in 1453. By the last siege, the Byzantine soldiers inside the city were outnumbered ten to one by the Turks around their walls.

The last Byzantine emperor, Constantine XI, sent a final plea for peace to the Turkish sultan, 23-year-old Muhammad II. The emperor concluded his letter:

If [God] should inspire you with a desire for peace, I shall be only too happy. However, I release you from all your oaths and treaties with me, and, closing the gates of my capital, I will defend my people to the last drop of my blood.

In May 1453, the Turks captured the city. Constantine XI died fighting. More than 1100 years after its founding, the empire of Constantinople came to an end.

184

Section Review 3

Define: sultan,
Identify: (a) Slavs, (b) Cyril, (c) Rus, (d) Kiev, (e) Vladimir, (f) Turks
Answer:
1. How did the invention of the Cyrillic alphabet help convert the Slavs to Christianity?
2. How did the Russian kingdom begin?
3. What were the long-lasting results of Vladimir's choice of Orthodox Christianity?
4. (a) What conquests did the Seljuk Turks make? (b) The Ottoman Turks?

Critical Thinking
5. The Seljuk Turks and the Ottoman Turks came from central Asia, where they had lived as nomads. (a) What advantages might nomads have in fighting against the Byzantine and Islamic empires? (b) What advantages might the empires have had? (c) Why were the nomads successful?

Map Study answers: Italy; parts of Greece, area around Constantinople

Chapter Review 8

Summary

1. Constantinople ruled an eastern empire. Byzantine emperors claimed both political and religious authority. The most outstanding ruler was Justinian, who tried to restore the glories of the Roman past. He is most noted for his code of laws. After his death, the empire was threatened by revolts, religious quarrels, and invasions. The Roman and Byzantine branches of the Christian Church grew apart and eventually split.

2. A new faith spread from Arabia. Late in the 500's, Muhammad proclaimed the faith of Islam. Gradually, he gained many followers. After his death, Muslim warriors created an empire that spread from Spain in the west to the Indus River valley in the east. Throughout the empire, Muslims followed the same religious duties, which included prayer, fasting, almsgiving, and pilgrimage.

3. The empires influenced Slavs and Turks. By the year 800, both the Byzantine and Islamic empires faced internal and external dangers. The Byzantine empire came under frequent attack from the Slavs, who converted to Christianity, and the Muslims. The Islamic empire was weakened by religious conflict. Baghdad fell to the Seljuk Turks in 1055. Constantinople fell to the Ottoman Turks in 1453.

Reviewing the Facts

1. Define the following terms:
   - a. excommunicate
   - b. heretic
   - c. patriarch
   - d. jihad
   - e. caliph
   - f. sultan

2. Explain the importance of each of the following names, dates, places, or terms:
   - a. Constantinople
   - b. Justinian
   - c. Code of Justinian
   - d. Bedouin
   - e. Mecca
   - f. Muhammad
   - g. 622
   - h. Koran
   - i. Baghdad
   - j. Slavs
   - k. Kiev
   - l. Vladimir
   - m. 1054
   - n. Seljuk Turks
   - o. Ottoman Turks
   - p. 1453

3. Name at least three issues that led to the break between the Roman and Byzantine churches in the year 1054.

4. Explain the importance of each of the following to the development of Islam. (a) Hegira (b) Koran (c) Five Pillars of Islam (d) Shi'ites

5. (a) How did the Umayyad and Abbasid caliphates differ? (b) What were the achievements of each caliphate?

6. (a) How did Byzantine culture influence Slavs? (b) How did the Islamic empire influence Turks?

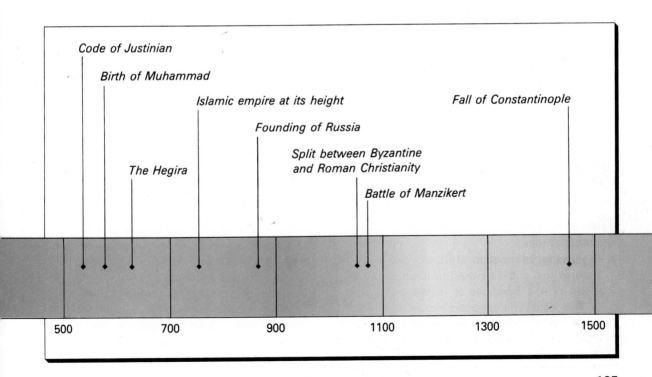

Code of Justinian

Birth of Muhammad

Islamic empire at its height

Founding of Russia

Fall of Constantinople

Split between Byzantine and Roman Christianity

The Hegira

Battle of Manzikert

| 500 | 700 | 900 | 1100 | 1300 | 1500 |

Basic Skills

1. **Explaining a main idea** How does the story about Omar's entering Jerusalem and finding the sacred rock littered with garbage illustrate a main idea of this chapter?
2. **Summarizing** Using the "Voice from the Past" on page 171, write a paragraph summarizing the Empress Theodora's arguments against fleeing Constantinople.
3. **Taking notes** The city tour of Constantinople on pages 170–172 tells much about life in Byzantium. Taking notes will help to clarify that information. Divide a sheet of paper into four equal parts. Label them *People, Defenses, Trade, Public Buildings,* and *Education.* Under each heading, note information about that topic.
4. **Interpreting maps** What parts of the Byzantine empire under Justinian (shown on page 169) had become part of the Islamic empire in 750 (shown on page 177)?
5. **Sequencing** Using the map on page 184, list in chronological order seven events shown on the map. Include both battles and invasions. The completed list summarizes the conquest of the Byzantine empire by Muslim rulers.
6. **Reading a time line** Use the time line on page 185 to calculate how many years it took for the Islamic empire to expand to its fullest extent.

Researching and Reporting Skills

1. **Acquiring information** Islam drew some of its ideas from existing Jewish and Christian beliefs. (a) Do research to find out what aspects of the earlier religions Islam included. (b) What new ideas did Islam add?
2. **Preparing an interview** Imagine that you had the opportunity to interview either Justinian or Harun ar-Rashid. Prepare a list of five questions you would ask Justinian about his Code of Laws or a list of five questions you would ask Harun ar-Rashid about his hopes for the growth of learning in the Islamic empire.
3. **Organizing information** This chapter contains pictures that could be used to illustrate an oral report on the Byzantine or Islamic civilizations. (a) How could you use these pictures to make an oral report on one of these civilizations? (b) Find illustrations pertaining to either civilization and explain how you would use them in a report.

Critical Thinking

1. **Comparing and contrasting** Compare and contrast the teachings of the Jews' Ten Commandments with the rules established for Islamic life by the Muslims' Koran.
2. **Analyzing** (a) Which would you rather have been, a subject of Rome living in Gaul at the time of Augustus or a Greek subject living in the Islamic empire at the time of the Abbasids? (b) What would be the advantages and disadvantages of each?
3. **Synthesizing** In this chapter, you have read about the golden age in arts and sciences under the Abbasid rulers. You have also read about two other golden ages, those of Athens under Pericles and of Rome under Augustus. What are the main characteristics of a golden age?
4. **Evaluating** The Byzantine and Islamic empires were rivals. Which of the two had the greater impact on the world of that time? Evaluate them in terms of their political, economic, religious, and cultural influence.

Perspectives on Past and Present

1. In both the Byzantine and Islamic empires, scholars worked to preserve writings from the past. Why is the perservation of these writings important to people today?
2. Using a world map as a reference, draw in and label the present countries of the Middle East on an outline map of the region. Compare your map to the one of the Islamic empire on page 177. Which countries in the Middle East today were part of the Islamic empire in 750?

Investigating History

1. Sports and politics made an explosive combination in Justinian's Constantinople. Read about the violent rivalry between the Greens and the Blues at the Hippodrome stadium. (A chapter in Edward Gibbon's *The Decline and Fall of the Roman Empire* provides a vivid account.)
2. Using a current traveler's guide from the library, plan a visit to one of the cities mentioned in this chapter. Write a brief description of the places in the city that you want to see. If possible, include a map of the city and your plan for touring it.

The Early Middle Ages

These chessmen show the warlike tone of life in Europe during the Early Middle Ages.

Key Terms

monastery
knight
count
feudalism
lord
vassal
investiture
fief
aid
manor
serf

Read and Understand

1. New ways of life developed in Europe.
2. Charlemagne revived the idea of empire.
3. Vikings terrorized Europe.
4. Feudalism became the basis for government.

A huge cauldron of boiling water steamed and bubbled over an outdoor hearth. Two Christian priests stood near it, preparing themselves for a terrible test. The priests had disagreed over a religious issue. They proposed to settle their quarrel by using the ordeal of boiling water. Each priest was expected to plunge his arm into the cauldron and pick up a small ring at the bottom. Afterward, their arms would be inspected, and the one whose burns healed cleanly would be declared the winner.

As a large group of spectators watched in excitement, the first priest boldly thrust his arm into the water and retrieved the ring. His hand and arm were unharmed. When the second priest tried to do the same,

In the late 1400's, the queen suddenly became the most powerful piece on the chess board, just as strong female leaders were rising in Italy.

Personal ties replaced citizenship.

In the years of upheaval between 400 and 600, Germanic kingdoms replaced Roman provinces. The borders of those kingdoms changed constantly with the fortunes of war. The map on page 189 can give only an approximate idea of which group controlled which lands.

More important than shifting boundaries was that the whole idea of government changed. Family ties and personal loyalty, not public government or public law, bound Germanic society together. The Germanic people did not think of themselves as citizens of a state but as members of a family and followers of a particular leader.

Every Frankish, Saxon, or Visigothic chief had a band of warriors who had pledged their loyalty to him. In peacetime, these followers lived in their lord's hall. He gave them food, weapons, and treasure. In battle, warriors fought to the death at their lord's side. It was the greatest disgrace to outlive one's lord.

Although Germanic warriors would willingly die for a leader they knew, they felt no obligation to obey a king who was a stranger to them. And they certainly would not obey some official sent to collect taxes or administer justice in the name of an emperor they had never seen. This stress on personal ties made orderly government for large territories impossible.

Christianity won new followers.

While Roman roads and Roman law crumbled, there was one institution from Roman times that did not break down: the Roman Catholic Church. Throughout the Early Middle Ages, the Church acted as the strongest civilizing force in western Europe.

The work of missionaries Beginning in the 300's and 400's, many Christian missionaries traveled among the Germanic and Celtic groups that bordered the Roman empire. These missionaries risked their lives to spread their beliefs.

Among the most famous and successful was Patrick of Ireland. Patrick was born of Christian parents in Roman Britannia around 400, shortly before the Anglo-Saxon invasions. When he was 16, his village was raided by pagan Celts from Ireland, and he was captured and taken to be a slave. After six years, Patrick escaped from Ireland to northern Gaul, where he eventually became a bishop. His greatest goal was to convert the Irish to Christianity. In 432, he returned to Ireland as a missionary. Although he was often imprisoned and threatened with death, he established Christian churches throughout the island.

The Franks under Clovis Politics often played an important part in spreading Christianity. In the late 400's, a ruthless Frankish king named Clovis (KLOH-vihs) ruled much of northern Gaul. The Franks were pagans, but Clovis's wife was a Christian who urged her husband to convert.

In 496, Clovis led his warriors into battle against another Germanic army. When the battle began going badly for Clovis, he appealed to the Christian God. "For I have called on my gods," he cried, "but I find they are far from my aid . . . Now I call on Thee. I long to believe in Thee. Only, please deliver me from my enemies." The tide of battle shifted, and the Franks triumphed. Clovis and 3,000 of his warriors asked a bishop to baptize them.

Clovis's conversion was especially welcome to the Roman Church because Catholic bishops wanted his help against other Germanic peoples. The Ostrogoths, Visigoths, and Burgundians were all Christians (and most of them were more civilized than the Franks). However, they were not Catholic Christians. Instead, many Germanic groups had chosen a branch of Christianity known as Arianism (AIR-ee-uh-NIHZ-uhm). The Roman Catholic Church considered Arians heretics. Thus, Clovis's conversion marked the beginning of a special partnership between the Frankish kingdom and the Catholic Church.

By 600, the Roman Catholic Church had succeeded in winning over many of the Germanic peoples who had moved into Rome's former lands. In many places, however, the changeover to Christianity was only on the surface. Some kings even kept two altars, one Christian and one to their earlier pagan gods. Missionaries continued to go out among pagan groups into lands that Rome had never controlled.

Benedict set rules for monasteries.

In the days of the Roman empire, bishops were the most powerful leaders of the Church. Each leading city of the empire had its own bishop. As the population in western Europe shifted away

An Anglo Saxon poet on the loss of a lord: "So have I wandered often in wretchedness/ Fettered my feelings far from my kin/ Homeless and hapless since days of old/ When the dark earth covered my dear lord's face."

from the cities, however, the Church had to adapt to increasingly rural conditions. One effect was the growth of **monasteries**.

Monasteries were communities in which groups of Christian men or women gave up all their private possessions and lived very simply. They devoted their lives to worship and prayer. Women who followed this way of life were called nuns; they lived in nunneries or convents. Men were called monks and lived in monasteries. Like priests, monks and nuns were expected to live according to the threefold rule of poverty, chastity, and obedience.

The Benedictine Rule A monk named Benedict set a pattern for monastic living. Born about 480 in Italy, Benedict went to school in a ravaged Rome. At the age of 15, he left school and hiked up into the Sabine Hills, seeking solitude. He lived as a hermit in a cave for several years. Hearing of his holiness, a group of monks came to him and persuaded him to be their abbot (monastic leader).

Around 540, Benedict wrote a book describing a strict yet practical set of rules for monastic life. These were some of Benedict's rules:

- Once a monk enters a monastery, he is to remain there for life. Monks should not wander from one monastic house to another.
- Daily life in the monastery should follow a strict schedule. Eight times a day are set aside for prayer and worship.
- Monks should spend seven hours a day at manual labor in kitchen, field, or workshop.
- Two hours a day are reserved for reading the Bible and other Christian books.
- Monks should eat one or two meals daily, depending on the season. They may have a little wine, but no red meat.

Benedict's sister Scholastica (skuh-LAS-tik-uh) became head of a convent in which the same rules were adapted for women. Soon almost all Italian, English, and Frankish monks and nuns were living according to the Benedictine Rule.

Benedict's rules were strict but made some allowance for human frailty. Above all, they provided monks and nuns with a workable system for disciplining their lives.

The achievements of the monasteries In the Early Middle Ages, monastic communities were like islands of stability in a sea of chaos. They

Benedict blesses a monk. Behind them is Monte Cassino, the monastery Benedict founded.

were the best-governed communities anywhere in Europe because they followed an orderly, written body of rules.

Monasteries were also the most educated communities. They operated schools, maintained libraries, and copied books. In the 600's and 700's, the monasteries of Ireland and England were the leading scholarly centers of the day. Above all, the monks of these lands excelled in making beautiful copies of religious writings, decorated with ornate letters and brilliant pictures. Through the work of the monks, at least part of Rome's intellectual heritage was preserved.

Gregory I expanded papal power.

Scattered throughout western Europe, monasteries and convents showed the spreading influence of the Catholic Church. At the head of the Church stood the pope in Rome, at first a bishop like other bishops but gradually becoming the strongest single figure in the Church.

One man who greatly increased the power of the popes was Gregory I. As pope, he wore only a rough monk's robe and humbly called himself "the servant of the servants of God." Yet while Gregory was meek on his own behalf, he was mighty on behalf of the papacy.

Monasteries were also the wealthiest communities. Though individual monks and nuns could own nothing, the community as a whole received generous gifts of land and money from Christians.

191

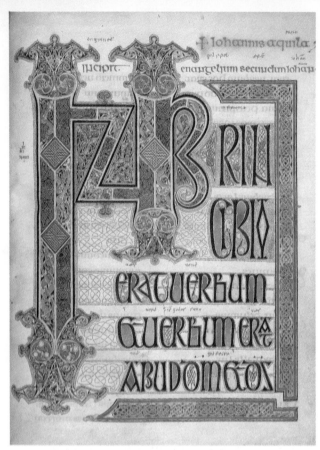

Skilled monks at Lindisfarne, England, made this beautiful gospel about the year 700.

Born in 540, Gregory grew up during the awful days when Justinian's Byzantine armies were driving the Ostrogoths from Rome and, in the process, wrecking the city. In 568, a new group of invaders struck at northern Italy. These were the Lombards, a fierce Germanic people. Conditions in Rome had never been worse. Starving Romans foraged for clumps of grass to eat.

Gregory became pope in 590 and soon made the papacy an office of political as well as spiritual power. The Byzantine emperor was too weak to protect Rome, so Gregory dealt directly with the menacing Lombards. In 599, he persuaded them to sign a peace treaty. At the same time, Gregory's palace became the center of Roman government. He used Church revenues to raise armies, repair roads, and relieve the poor. The pope was now acting as the mayor of Rome.

Gregory worked tirelessly to bring new groups into the Church. He sent missionaries to England under the leadership of a monk named Augustine in 596. This mission spread Christianity among the Anglo-Saxon kingdoms there. Gregory also

wrote two influential books. One was the *Dialogues*, a collection of simply told religious stories, full of miraculous happenings. Most new Christians in this age could not grasp abstract religious ideas, but they understood Gregory's adventurous accounts of saintly lives. The second book, *Pastoral Care*, advised bishops on carrying out their spiritual duties, especially among new converts.

All that Gregory did as pope—writing books, sending out missionaries, governing Rome—expressed a new view of the world. He ignored the political divisions between kingdoms. In his view, the entire region from Italy to England, from Spain to western Germany was his responsibility as pope. Gregory had a vision of Christendom (KRIS-uhn-duhm), a spiritual kingdom fanning out from Rome to the most distant churches. This idea of a churchly kingdom, ruled by a pope, became a central part of the Middle Ages.

Section Review 1

Define: (a) ordeal, (b) medieval, (c) literacy, (d) monastery, (e) monk, (f) abbot, (g) nun
Identify: (a) Patrick, (b) Clovis, (c) Arianism, (d) Benedict, (e) Scholastica, (f) Gregory I, (g) Lombards, (h) Christendom
Answer:
1. What were the three roots of medieval culture in western Europe?
2. Give two examples of ways civilization in western Europe declined after the fall of Rome.
3. (a) How did Christianity spread during the Early Middle Ages? (b) Why was Clovis's conversion to Christianity important?
4. (a) Describe the way of life followed in a monastery. (b) What part did Benedict play in the development of monasteries? (c) How were monasteries important to the preservation of civilization in this period?
5. What were the achievements of Gregory I?

Critical Thinking
6. (a) How did the Germanic ideas of government differ from the Roman ideas? (b) Which set of ideas is closer to those of our own time? Explain your answer.
7. Would it be correct to say that the idea of Christendom was a replacement for the Roman empire? Why or why not?

According to an old story, Gregory I saw some handsome blond men being sold as Roman slaves. "They are Angles," someone told him. "Not Angles, but angels," he replied. When he learned these people were pagans, he sent missionaries to convert them.

Charlemagne revived the idea of empire. 2

After the breakup of the Roman empire, petty kingdoms sprang up all over Europe. For example, England was divided into seven tiny kingdoms, some no larger than the state of Connecticut. By far the largest and strongest of Europe's kingdoms was that of the Franks in what had been the Roman province of Gaul. The foundations for this kingdom were laid by the Franks' first Christian king, Clovis. (As you have probably guessed, the modern name *France* comes from the people of the Franks. *Louis*, the name of 16 later French kings, is a softer-sounding form of Clovis.)

Clovis's descendants lost power.

In 481, when the 15-year-old Clovis became king, the Franks controlled only a small area of flat, marshy land (the present-day Netherlands) on either side of the Rhine River. By the time Clovis died in 511, he ruled most of what is now France.

The Merovingian kings Clovis and his successors are known as the Merovingian (MAIR-oh-VIHN-jee-uhn) dynasty, after a legendary ancestor, Merovech. They were also called "the long-haired kings" because long hair was a symbol of power and authority among the Franks. The Merovingians ruled for about 275 years, but those were not peaceful years.

When a Merovingian king died, his sons treated the kingdom as private property to be divided among themselves. Such divisions weakened the kingdom and often led to civil war as each son tried to seize the whole kingdom. Yet the Merovingians succeeded in keeping the idea of kingship alive.

Mayors of the palace By the year 700, the power of Merovingian kings had dwindled to almost nothing. The most powerful person in the kingdom was not the king but an official known as the *major domo* or mayor of the palace. Officially, a mayor of the palace was in charge of the royal household and estates. Unofficially, he was the power behind the throne. He commanded armies and made policy. In effect, he governed the kingdom in the king's name.

In 714, the position of mayor of the palace was held by Charles, known as *Martel* (the Hammer). Charles Martel was king in all but name. He extended the power of the Franks to the north, south, and east. He even defeated a Muslim raiding party from Spain at the Battle of Tours in 732. (This battle marked the height of Muslim conquests in Europe.) Finally, at his death, Charles Martel passed his power on to his son, Pepin the Short.

Daily Life · Stirrups and Warfare

In Merovingian times, most Frankish warriors were foot soldiers, but during the 700's, warfare changed. The stirrup came into use in Europe. (It may have been invented in India.) As a result, the technology of war changed.

More and more warriors fought on horseback. Without stirrups to brace him, a charging warrior was likely to topple off his own horse. Mounted warriors with stirrups could use heavier armor and weapons. These armored horsemen were known as **knights**. Galloping full tilt at the enemy, a Frankish knight could knock a foot soldier off his feet or an enemy rider off his horse. The horse became essential to a noble warrior. Without a horse, a man was considered a peasant. Gradually, the most important part of an army came to be its mounted knights.

To support the warriors needed to defeat the Muslims, Charles Martel confiscated some church lands, setting up a land-based economy that would prevail for centuries.

The pope named Pepin king.

Pepin was not content to be the power behind the throne. He wanted to be king in his own right. Pepin wrote a shrewd letter to the pope. Pepin asked, Who should be the rightful ruler of the Franks? Should it be the man who had the title of king but no power? Or should it be the man with the power but no title? The pope answered, "It is better that he who possesses power be called king than he who has none." Thus did Pepin the Short obtain the Church's blessing for seizing the throne.

The pope and the new Frankish king needed each other. Only the Church could give legitimacy to the rule of Pepin and his heirs. At the same time, only a strong king like Pepin could protect the pope from the Lombards, who again threatened Rome. In desperation, Pope Stephen II crossed the Alps in 754 to plead for help. Pepin agreed to fight the Lombards on the pope's behalf. Then occurred an event of immense historic importance. In a dimly lighted chapel, the pope anointed Pepin's head with holy oil and declared him "king by the grace of God."

Pepin was the first king ever to be anointed by a pope. Afterward, it became common for kings in western Europe to be crowned "by the grace of God" in a church ceremony. No longer were kings simply political rulers. They now had some spiritual authority as well.

Pepin soon led an army into Italy and defeated the Lombards in one city after another. In 756, he collected the keys to all the cities he had conquered and gave them to the pope. Thus, the popes became political rulers of scattered Italian lands known as the Papal States.

The Frankish kings and the Roman popes had entered into an informal alliance. It was an unstable alliance, however. Much of the later history of the Middle Ages, as we shall see, was the story of popes struggling to control kings, and vice versa.

Charlemagne extended Frankish power.

Pepin the Short died in 768 and left a greatly strengthened Frankish kingdom to his son, Charles. Charles was in his mid-twenties when he became king and in his early seventies at his death. He was king of the Franks for 46 years (768–814), longer than Augustus Caesar had been emperor of the Romans.

In fact, Charles's reign was a glorious time in the Frankish kingdom, just as Augustus's reign had been for Rome. In Latin, Charles was called *Carolus Magnus,* or Charles the Great. In French, his name became Charlemagne (SHAHR-luh-MAYN). His descendants were known as the Carolingian (KAIR-uh-LIN-jee-uhn) dynasty.

Charlemagne's personality Though his father was Pepin the Short, Charlemagne was gigantic, six feet four inches tall. Charlemagne followed the Frankish custom of wearing a mustache but no beard. His secretary and biographer, a monk named Einhard, wrote this description of him:

The upper part of his head was round, his eyes were large and lively, nose a little long, hair fair, and face laughing and merry. Thus his appearance was always stately and dignified, whether he was standing or sitting; although his neck was thick and somewhat short, and his belly rather prominent; but the symmetry of the rest of his body concealed these defects.

Charlemagne was a great sportsman. He especially liked to hunt deer on horseback or to plunge into a river and swim great distances. A king in the Middle Ages needed all Charlemagne's great physical strength and energy.

Charlemagne the conqueror In war, the king himself commanded the armies and fought in the front line. Every spring, Charlemagne called together all the great landowners of the kingdom, both nobles and bishops. They met at Charlemagne's capital, Aachen (AH-kuhn), or at another royal residence. Each noble brought his own followers, equipped for battle. This, for example, was one of Charlemagne's orders to his nobles:

Each horseman is expected to have a shield, lance, sword, dagger, bow, quiver with arrows, and in your carts shall be . . . axes, planes, augers, boards, spades, iron shovels, and other utensils that are necessary in any army. In the wagons shall be supplies for three months, together with arms and clothing for six months.

Summer after summer, Charlemagne led these armies against the enemies that surrounded his

Aachen is the German form of the French name *Aix-la-Chapelle.* Both names are used for Charlemagne's capital, and they show the growing divergence of language within the Frankish kingdom.

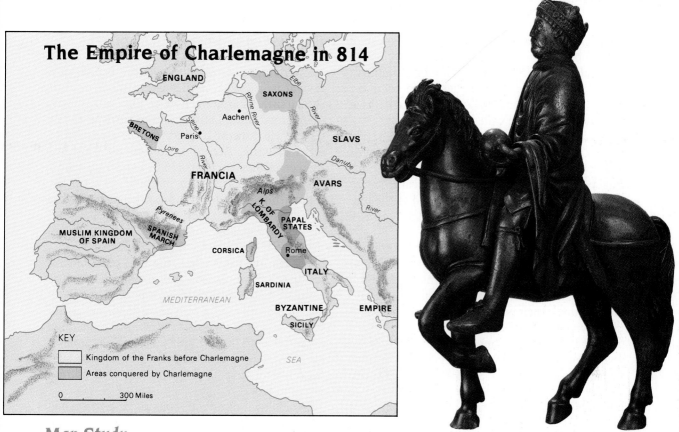

The Empire of Charlemagne in 814

ENGLAND
SAXONS
Aachen
BRETONS
Paris
SLAVS
FRANCIA
AVARS
Alps
K OF LOMBARDY
PAPAL STATES
Rome
MUSLIM KINGDOM OF SPAIN
SPANISH MARCH
CORSICA
ITALY
SARDINIA
MEDITERRANEAN
BYZANTINE
EMPIRE
SICILY
SEA

KEY
☐ Kingdom of the Franks before Charlemagne
▨ Areas conquered by Charlemagne

0   300 Miles

Map Study

Charlemagne, shown at the right, carries an orb as a symbol of imperial power. What enemies threatened his northeastern border?

kingdom. He conquered new lands to both the south and the east.

When a frightened pope again asked for protection against the Lombards, Charlemagne responded. He defeated the Lombards, captured their king, and took over northern Italy in 773.

Five years later, in 778, Charlemagne crossed the Pyrenees Mountains and marched into Muslim Spain. He hoped to win control of northern Spain, but the expedition failed. As the Franks retreated through the mountains, ambushers caught the Frankish rear guard by surprise and slaughtered it. Among the Franks to die was the leader of the guard, Count Roland. This massacre became a Frankish legend, retold in a great epic poem called the Song of Roland.

It was the Franks' eastern frontier, however, where Charlemagne fought his greatest wars. In what is now Yugoslavia and Hungary, an Asian people called the Avars ruled the Slavs. After seven years of brutal warfare, Charlemagne destroyed the Avar kingdom. The Saxons of Ger-

many were even more troublesome. Charlemagne fought them for nearly 30 years before they submitted to his rule and his Christian religion.

Charles did more than encourage missionaries to work among the Saxons and other pagans. He sometimes resorted to baptism by the sword, offering his defeated enemies the choice of becoming Christian or dying on the spot. Not for nothing did Christian chroniclers call him "iron Charles" and "the strong right arm of God."

By the year 800, the Frankish kingdom included two thirds of Italy, all of present-day France, a small part of Spain, and all of German Saxony. It had grown larger than the Byzantine empire. Only a ruler of Charlemagne's energy and ability could hope to govern such an empire.

Charlemagne strengthened his rule.

Like kings both before and after him, Charlemagne needed the help of powerful nobles to govern his kingdom. However, also like other

Map Study answer: Saxons

195

kings, he needed a way to limit the power of those nobles.

Royal officials All of Francia, as the Frankish kingdom was called, was divided into counties. Each county was ruled in the king's name by a powerful landholder called a **count**.

The counts administered justice and raised armies. In theory, the king could dismiss a count at any time. In practice, however, the same count might rule an area for as long as 30 years. Unless the counts were constantly reminded of the loyalty they owed the king, they might quickly become independent rulers.

Wisely, Charlemagne did not trust his counts. He sent out royal agents called *missi dominici* (MIHS-ee doh-MIHN-uh-kee), or "emissaries of the master" to see that counts governed justly and did not abuse their power. Charlemagne also regularly visited every part of his kingdom to judge cases, settle disputes, reward faithful followers, and keep the less loyal in line. By constant watchfulness, he managed to keep his powerful counts under control. (His sons and grandsons, however, were less successful at controlling their nobles.)

The royal estates Much of Charlemagne's power rested on his position as a great landowner. The Carolingian family owned huge estates scattered throughout Francia. Charlemagne and his sons kept a close eye on the management of their lands. This letter, for example, is part of a set of instructions to the overseer of a royal estate.

The greatest care must be taken that whatever is prepared by hand—bacon, smoked meat, sausage, partially salted meat, wine, vinegar, mulberry wine, cooked wine, mustard, cheese, butter, malt, beer, mead, honey, wax, flour, all should be prepared with the greatest cleanliness.

In each of our estates, the chambers shall be provided with counterpanes, cushions, pillows, bedclothes, coverings for tables and benches.

Most of a king's wealth came not from taxes but from goods like those listed in that letter— goods produced on the royal estates. These estates supported the royal court and also paid for the daily working of government. A king who allowed his estates to decline would quickly lose his political power too.

Charlemagne revived learning.

Charlemagne's court became the center for a revival in learning. Earlier Germanic kings had shown little interest in learning. Yet Charlemagne understood some Latin and even perhaps a little Greek. He learned to read, and he struggled to learn to write. According to Einhard, he "used to keep tablets and blanks in bed under his pillow that he might accustom his hand to form the letters; however, as he did not begin his efforts [until] late in life, they met with ill success." He was never able to write more than a word or two.

For his court at Aachen, the king recruited the leading European scholars of his day. There was a music teacher from Italy, a poet from Spain, and many others. By far the most influential of these imported scholars was an Englishman named Alcuin (AL-kwihn) of York. Charlemagne also invited Jews to settle in his kingdom because they were literate and could help with administrative work.

For his own numerous sons and daughters and for other children at the court, Charlemagne began a palace school. There students learned to read, write, and do a little arithmetic. Charlemagne himself visited the classes. On at least one occasion, the king's famous temper was aroused, and he pummeled a lazy student for mistakes in grammar.

By Charlemagne's order, monasteries and cathedrals were expected to open schools to train future monks and priests. (Since only boys could enter the priesthood, only boys attended these schools.)

Monasteries increased their libraries. Monks labored to make handwritten copies of rare Latin books. Each copy took many months of toil. As they worked, the monks developed a new style of lettering. Roman books had all been written in capital letters, and there was no spacing between words. To save time, monks began substituting small letters for the Roman capitals. To make the books easier to read, the monks added spaces between the words. Gradually, writers in monasteries perfected a beautiful and readable style of lettering known as Carolingian miniscule (MIHN-ih-skyool). Most of these small letters look almost exactly like the letters printed in a modern book.

Charlemagne feared that "as the skill in writing was less, so also the wisdom for understanding the Holy Scriptures might be much less than it rightly ought to be," and so he ordered the monasteries to open schools for reading and writing.

The pope made Charlemagne emperor.

By the year 800, Charlemagne was the most powerful king in western Europe. Then he traveled to Rome to help Pope Leo III, who had been attacked by a Roman mob. On Christmas Day in St. Peter's Cathedral, the pope placed a jeweled crown on Charlemagne's head and declared him emperor. The crowd of people in the church (probably coached in advance) shouted, "Hail to Charles the Augustus, crowned by God to be the great and peace-giving emperor of the Romans, life and victory."

What did the title of emperor mean? According to one argument, the title gave Charlemagne new prestige. He could deal as an equal with the Byzantine emperor. The counterargument says Charlemagne gained nothing but trouble from the crowning. The new title added nothing to his power. Moreover, news of the crowning angered the Byzantines and made another enemy on Charlemagne's troubled eastern frontier. After all, in the Byzantine view, the true Roman emperor ruled from Constantinople.

Another theory says that the crowning was the work of the pope and did not please Charlemagne at all. Why would the pope want to make Charlemagne emperor? Perhaps Pope Leo wanted an emperor who would stay in Rome and help govern the unruly city. Perhaps it was a shrewd political move, establishing the pope's power to name an emperor.

Probably Charlemagne's coronation meant different things to different people. Charlemagne and Pope Leo III each had his own motives, which we may never know. However, we do know the long-term consequences of the crowning.

First, the coronation marked another stage in the growing split between the Church of Constantinople and the Church of Rome. After 800, there were two Christian empires, Greek Orthodox in the east and Roman Catholic in the west. Each viewed the other with growing suspicion.

Second, there arose in western Europe a new idea of empire. Later popes repeatedly gave the title "Roman emperor" to one European king or another. In theory, the person entrusted with this title became the protector of all Christendom. The title meant little when held by a weak ruler, but in strong hands it could be a powerful tool.

The Division of the Carolingian Empire, 843

Map Study

The Treaty of Verdun divided Charlemagne's empire among his three grandsons. Which important city lay in Lothair's territory?

Charlemagne's heirs ruled weakly.

When Charlemagne died at his palace in 814, his only surviving son, Louis the Pious, succeeded him as king and emperor. A devoutly religious man, Louis would have made a better monk than a king. As a ruler, he was ineffective. He died in 840.

Louis left three sons: Lothair (loh-THAIR), Charles the Bald, and Louis the German. Like the Merovingian princes, Louis's sons fought one another for the empire. The civil war ended in 843 when the brothers signed a pact called the Treaty of Verdun (vur-DUHN). This document divided Charlemagne's empire into three kingdoms, one for each brother.

Footnote to History

Part of Lothair's central kingdom became known as *Lothair's realm* or *Lotharingia*, a name that was eventually shortened to Lorraine. In the following centuries, as late as World War II, millions of French and German soldiers died in battles over Lorraine.

To publicize the treaty, Louis the German and Charles took oaths of peace before each other's armies. The two kings had to use two different languages—Old French for Charles's army and Old German for Louis's.

Charles the Bald's kingdom would eventually become France. Louis the German's kingdom would become Germany. Lothair, the eldest son, kept the title of emperor and took the land between his brothers' kingdoms, including the imperial capitals of Rome and Aachen. His land became a battleground for the future kings of France and Germany.

After the Treaty of Verdun, Carolingian kings became almost as powerless as the long-haired Merovingians had been. Once again, central authority broke down.

At the same time, all of Europe from Ireland to Italy was repeatedly assaulted and plundered by terrible new invasions. From the south, Muslim pirates seized Sicily and raided Italy, even sacking Rome in 846. From the east struck the Magyars, barbarians from central Asia. Like the earlier Huns and Avars, the Magyar warriors terrorized Germany and Italy. And from the north came the most dreaded attackers of all, the Vikings (VY-kingz). Even before Charlemagne's death, the earliest Viking raids struck Europe.

Section Review 2

Define: (a) knight, (b) count, (c) missi dominici, (d) Carolingian miniscule
Identify: (a) Franks, (b) Merovingians, (c) mayor of the palace, (d) Charles Martel, (e) Pepin the Short, (f) Papal States, (g) Charlemagne, (h) Carolingians, (i) Treaty of Verdun
Answer:
1. (a) What practice weakened the power of the Merovingian kings? (b) Into whose hands did their power pass?
2. (a) Explain how the Frankish king and the pope depended on each other. (b) How did kings gain some spiritual authority? (c) How did the pope become a political ruler?
3. (a) Describe how Charlemagne ruled his widespread lands. (b) Why were his own estates important to his government?
4. How did Charlemagne promote learning?
5. (a) What new title did Charlemagne receive from the pope in the year 800? (b) What were the consequences of this event?
6. How did the Treaty of Verdun affect the Frankish kingdom?

7. What groups invaded Europe in the 800's?
Critical Thinking
8. What do you think was Charlemagne's greatest achievement? Give reasons for your answer.

Vikings terrorized Europe. 3

To the monks on Lindisfarne Island near the northeast coast of England, it seemed to be just another peaceful morning when they awoke to perform their daily rituals. But on this morning in 793, a large sailing vessel lay near the shore, barely visible in the mist. Its square sail was striped red and white. Its prow swept upward in a graceful curve like a swan's neck, but at the top was a dragon's head.

As dawn broke, burly warriors jumped from the ship to the island shore, clutching swords and heavy wooden shields. The monks had no weapons. Some were killed at the altar even as they prayed. Others were dragged to the sea and drowned. The monastery was thoroughly ransacked. Golden crucifixes, silver chalices, ivory boxes, and silk and linen tapestries were all piled in the boat. Laughing and shouting, the attackers heaved on their oars. Soon their striped sail disappeared over the horizon.

News of this outrage soon reached the court of Charlemagne. "Never before," wrote Alcuin, "has such a terror appeared in Britain as this that we have just suffered from a pagan race." In 793, the terror was just beginning. From about 800 until the year 1000, the Vikings raided from Ireland to Russia. In many churches, a new prayer became part of the daily worship: "Save us, O God, from the fury of the Northmen."

Footnote to History

In the heat of battle, some Viking warriors lunged against the enemy howling, snarling, and biting their wooden shields in rage. In this state of hyperexcitement, they felt neither fear nor pain. Such warriors, feared even by other Vikings, were known as *berserkrs,* from which comes the modern word for someone in a violent frenzy, *berserk.*

An Irish chronicler on the Vikings: "If 100 heads of hardened iron could grow on one neck, and if each head possessed 100 . . . tongues of tempered metal, and if each tongue cried out incessantly . . . they would never be able to enumerate the griefs which the people of Ireland . . . have suffered at the hands of these . . . pagans."

By 930, fully 20,000 Norse were raising crops and grazing sheep on the remote island of Iceland.

Vikings were skilled seafarers.

The raiders were known by several names: Northmen, Norsemen, and Vikings. Their home lay far to the north in a wintry, rocky, forested region called Scandinavia (SKAN-duh-NAY-vee-uh). Today, this region consists of Norway, Sweden, and Denmark.

The people of Scandinavia were Germanic with customs and language similar to those of the Franks, Saxons, and Goths who had earlier invaded Europe. The Scandinavians, however, had had almost no contact with Rome. They were still pagans, worshiping warlike gods. Viking leaders took pride in nicknames like Eric Bloodaxe and Thorfinn Skullsplitter.

The Vikings carried out their raids with terrifying swiftness. They would beach their ships, strike, then quickly shove out to sea again. By the time local troops arrived, the Vikings were long gone.

The Viking warships were the technological marvel of their age. Long, lean, and light, the largest of these ships could hold 300 warriors, who took turns rowing its 72 oars. Most ships were smaller, with crews of 30 to 50 fighters. The prow of each ship swept grandly upward, often ending with the carved head of a sea monster or dragon. Although a ship might weigh 20 tons when fully loaded, it could sail in 3 feet of water. Thus, the Vikings could strike villages and monasteries far inland by rowing up shallow rivers and creeks.

Scandinavians settled far and wide.

Despite their fearsome reputation, it is wrong to think of the Vikings merely as ferocious brutes. They were also wily traders and careful farmers. As explorers, they were unsurpassed. They traveled far beyond western Europe, down rivers into the heart of Russia, to Constantinople, and across the icy waters of the northern Atlantic Ocean.

By the year 900, hundreds of Scandinavian families had made the perilous voyage to the distant island of Iceland. There they built a prosperous settlement.

A Norse queen, Asa, was buried in this Viking ship. Among the Vikings, such burials were a common way to honor a leader. The ship shows the high prow and shallow draft of Viking vessels. At sea, Vikings lashed monster heads like the one below to their ship's prow to frighten away evil spirits. In battle, Viking warriors wore helmets such as the one at the left.

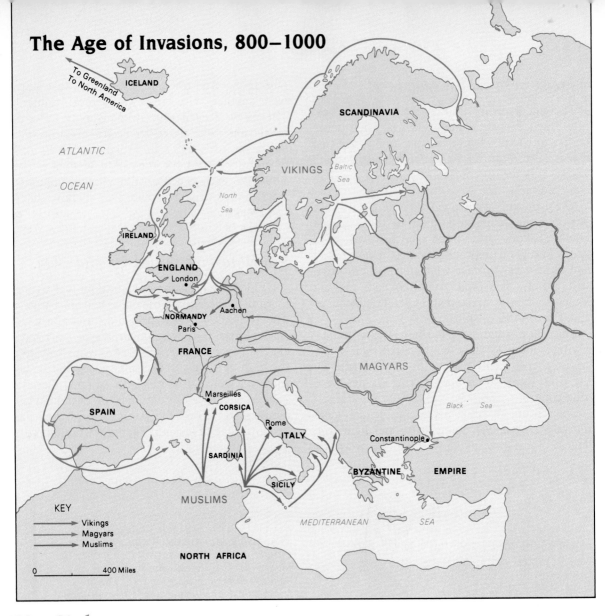

The Age of Invasions, 800–1000

To Greenland
To North America
ICELAND

ATLANTIC

OCEAN

SCANDINAVIA

VIKINGS

Baltic Sea

North Sea

IRELAND

ENGLAND
London

NORMANDY
Aachen
Paris

FRANCE

MAGYARS

Black Sea

SPAIN

Marseilles
CORSICA

Rome
ITALY

Constantinople

SARDINIA

BYZANTINE   EMPIRE

SICILY

MUSLIMS

MEDITERRANEAN   SEA

KEY
→ Vikings
→ Magyars
→ Muslims

NORTH AFRICA

0   400 Miles

Map Study

Of the three great groups of invaders that struck Europe, the Vikings ranged most widely. Name the seas and oceans that they reached. Which group of invaders came overland?

In 982, a red-bearded outlaw named Eric the Red sailed west from Iceland into uncharted Atlantic waters. He came upon an island that was largely buried under a massive sheet of ice. He misnamed the place Greenland. For a while, Norse settlers managed to eke out a living even in that harsh environment. Eventually, however, the settlement was abandoned.

About the year 1000, Eric the Red's son, Leif (leef) Ericson, sailed from Greenland to another unexplored land. This probably was the Canadian island now known as Newfoundland. The Vikings

called it Vinland. There is no question that Leif Ericson reached the Americas before Columbus.

Meanwhile, the Vikings were also settling widely in western Europe. They established their own kingdoms in parts of Ireland and nearly conquered all of England. Only the courage and leadership of the English hero-king, Alfred the Great, finally halted their advance in 886. In northern France, Viking leaders won a rich territory that became known as Normandy.

In all these regions, Viking warriors were the forerunners of Scandinavian settlers. The raiders

200

Map Study answers: Baltic Sea, North Sea, Atlantic Ocean, Black Sea, Mediterranean Sea; Magyars were followed by whole families of farmers, traders, and artisans whose influence spread widely in much of Europe.

The Viking age ended about 1000.

Around the year 1000, the Viking terror, which had raged for two centuries, slowly receded and died. Why? Three facts help to explain it.

First, Europeans finally worked out a way to respond quickly to raids and small-scale invasions. (The way this system worked will be explained in the next section.)

Second, like so many barbarians before them (including Goths, Franks, and Saxons), the Vikings gradually adopted Christianity. For example, King Guthrum of the Danes agreed to become a Christian as part of his peace treaty with England's King Alfred. As Christians, the Vikings were less inclined to raid monasteries.

Third, after 1000, Europe's climate went through a warming trend that lasted several centuries. That trend explains why Viking settlements on Iceland and Greenland prospered. As farming became easier in Scandinavia, fewer Scandinavians turned to the seafaring life of Viking warriors.

The Vikings were the last great raiders to descend on western Europe. While the eastern lands of the old Roman empire were devastated by the Seljuk Turks, the Ottoman Turks, and other warriors from central Asia, western Europe was at last free of invasions.

Section Review 3

Identify: (a) Vikings, (b) Scandinavia, (c) Iceland, (d) Eric the Red, (e) Greenland, (f) Leif Ericson, (g) Newfoundland
Answer:
1. (a) Where did the Vikings come from? (b) How were they different from the earlier Germanic groups who had invaded Europe?
2. What new lands to the west did the Vikings reach?
3. What factors helped to end the Viking terror?

Critical Thinking
4. Why was it very difficult for kings to defend their territory against Viking raids?

Feudalism became the basis for government. 4

In the late summer of 911, two men who had long been enemies stood face to face near the Seine (sayn) River in what is now France. One man was Rollo, the leader of a Viking army that had been plundering the rich river valley for years. The second man was the almost powerless king of France, known to history as Charles the Simple. Though he bore the title *king*, Charles controlled little of the land that is France today.

The two men had come to make peace. In a formal ceremony, Charles granted Rollo a huge piece of French territory. This part of France became the Northmen's land, or *Normandy*. In return, Rollo placed his hands between the king's hands and swore never to make war against the king again.

As part of the ceremony, Rollo was expected to kneel and kiss the king's foot, but this was more than the proud Viking could stand. "No, by God!" he bellowed. Instead, Rollo ordered one of his henchmen to perform the rite. Charles's foot was hoisted into the air so the tall Viking need not bend his knees. The Viking promptly showed his low opinion of royal dignity by tipping the king onto his back in the dirt. Yet Charles grimly swallowed his pride to win Rollo's oath of loyalty.

Other rulers and warriors in many parts of Europe were making similar agreements. The worst years of the invasions (about 850 to 950) were also the years when a new pattern of life emerged in western Europe. No king or pope dictated this pattern. No brilliant thinker proposed the new system. Instead of one solution, there were hundreds, each depending on local circumstances. Villagers in England responded in one way; villagers in northern Italy responded in another.

Yet overall, the pattern was similar. Everywhere, there was an increasing emphasis on local protection, local government, and local self-sufficiency. This new political system is known as **feudalism** (FYOO-duhl-ihz-uhm). Feudalism was a political and military system based on the holding of land. The control of land was the key to feudalism.

Lords and vassals exchanged vows.

At the heart of the feudal system was an agreement between a **lord** and a **vassal**. When Charles the Simple gave Normandy to Rollo the Viking, Charles became Rollo's lord. When Rollo placed his hands in Charles's and swore loyalty, Rollo became Charles's vassal (a person who receives land from a lord).

The bond between lord and vassal The personal bonds of loyalty that tied a vassal to a lord were the key to the feudal system. The oath sworn between them was the equivalent of today's written contract.

Kneeling, bareheaded, and without his sword, the vassal placed his hands in the hands of his lord. In this humble position, he swore to be the lord's man all the days of his life and to defend the lord against "all men who may live or die." The lord then raised him up and kissed him.

Next came **investiture** (ihn-VEST-ih-choor). In a symbolic gesture, the lord presented the vassal with a stick, a small rod, or a clod of earth. The lord thus transferred into the vassal's hands control of a piece of land. Such a piece of land was known as a **fief** (feef).

Redividing a fief By accepting a fief from Charles the Simple, Rollo became a royal vassal—the vassal of a king. But that grant was not the end of the feudal process. Like other royal fiefs, Normandy was huge. To protect such a fief, the vassal needed a private army.

Since the royal vassal had little money but plenty of land, he could afford to divide his fief into, let us say, 70 smaller estates. Keeping the best land for himself, he would give the other 69 estates as fiefs to 69 warriors who agreed to be his vassals. Thus, the royal vassal himself became the lord of other vassals.

These smaller vassals in turn divided their lands and granted fiefs to warriors of their own. Each local lord used grants of land to attract a personal band of warriors. At the bottom of the scale were the knights, men whose parcels of land were too small to be easily subdivided.

The advantages of this system for defense were clear. Every local lord had a force of knights ready to defend the land against all comers—Vikings, Magyars, Muslims, outlaws, or a neighboring lord. Moreover, lords usually fortified their lands, building strongholds at key places.

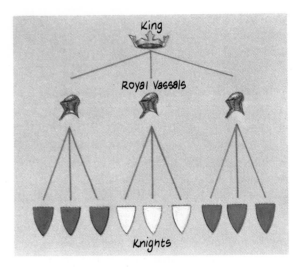

This diagram shows how the feudal system worked in theory. In real life, however, the system became a tangle of conflicting loyalties.

The feudal pyramid In theory, feudal society was a pyramid. At the bottom were many knights, each with a small fief. Above them were their lords, who held larger fiefs. And over all was the king.

In practice, however, the feudal system never worked so clearly. For one thing, an ambitious knight could collect fiefs from several lords by pledging to serve them all. In doing so, he ran a risk. Suppose, as often happened, two of his lords warred with each other. Then the knight would have to choose for whom to fight. His very life might depend on picking the winner. The feudal pyramid often became a complex tangle of conflicting loyalties that both lords and vassals tried to use to their own advantage.

Vassals served in war and peace.

Vassals were required to fight in the lord's army when called. From each of his knights, a lord could demand about 40 days of combat on horseback every year. Weapons, armor, and warhorses were expensive. A vassal needed a certain amount of land so he could afford such gear. Moreover, the skill to use the weapons took training and practice. Gone were the days of citizen-soldiers such as the Greek hoplites or the early Roman legions. Knights in the Middle Ages were specialists in war. Supported by wealth from their fiefs, knights devoted their lives to war.

Discussion question: Why would the gestures of kneeling and placing one's hands in the hands of the lord have been important in an age when few people could read and write? (allowed witnesses to understand the verbal agreement)

Women and church leaders as vassals Feudalism was both a military system and a land-holding system. Noblewomen and church leaders often held great estates. Thus, these groups were part of feudalism even though they usually were not warriors.

A noblewoman might inherit a fief from her parents or her husband, or she might control land in the name of her young son. In such cases, a woman fulfilled the feudal duties that went with the land. She sent her vassal knights to war when the lord called. She might also command and defend her castle if her husband was away.

Church leaders too were part of the feudal system. They owed military service just as other vassals did. In the Early Middle Ages, being a churchman was no bar to being a warrior. Fighting bishops such as Turpin of Reims and Odo of Bayeux were famed for their might in battle. In later times, bishops were more likely to send their vassal knights than to go to war themselves.

Peacetime duties Vassals also owed their lords duties in time of peace. When Rollo was given Normandy, he received not only the land with whatever its farms produced but also the right to rule that land. He was expected to hold courts of justice, to charge tolls on the bridges, to collect taxes, and much more. Justice was the lord's largest peacetime reponsibility.

From vassals who were bishops or abbots, a lord was likely to demand governmental and legal services. Being literate, a bishop or abbot could act as the lord's secretary. He could give learned council, keep written records, and write letters for the lord.

In case of financial emergency, lords could ask their vassals for a grant of money. Such a grant was called an **aid**. Traditionally, a lord could call

Voice from the Past · *Feudalism and Marriage*

Lords controlled the marriages of their vassals, both men and women. In the Middle Ages, marriages were an important part of politics. Marriages cemented alliances between families. When a woman married, her husband usually took over her property. Marriage to a wealthy woman might make a vassal even more powerful than his lord. The documents below come from the royal accounting office in England between 1140 and 1282.

• *Ralph son of William owes 100 marks as a fine, to be allowed to marry Margery who was wife of Nicholas Corbet who [held land of the king], and that the same Margery may be allowed to marry him.*
• *Walter de Cancy renders account of £15 to be allowed to marry a wife as he shall choose.*
• *Emma de Normanville and Roheisa and Margaret and Juliana, her sisters, render account of 10 marks for license to marry where they wish.*
• *Roheisa de Doura renders account of £450 to have half of all the lands which belonged to Richard de Lucy, her grandfather . . . and for license to marry where she wishes so long as she does not marry herself to any of the king's enemies.*
• *Alice, countess of Warwick, renders account of £1,000 and 10 palfreys [women's saddle horses] to be allowed to remain a widow as long as she pleases, and not to be forced to marry by the king . . . and to have the custody of her sons.*

1. Which sections show that the lord (in this case, the king) controlled the marriages of both men and women?
2. What right do most of the vassals seem to want?
3. (a) What fact suggests that Margery may have been a wealthy woman?
(b) What was the probable source of her wealth?
4. What two rights is Roheisa de Doura buying from the king?

quo Rexdeda

Local violence among nobles was a problem. The Church would issue proclamations called *Peace of God* or *Truce of God* outlawing theft, injury, and other crimes and detailing the punishment, including excommunication, for committing them.

203

for aids at three times: (1) when the lord's oldest son was knighted; (2) when the lord's oldest daughter was married; and (3) if the lord was captured in a war and held for ransom. The lord could also travel to a vassal's fief and expect to be housed, wined, and dined for several days.

Historians often describe feudalism as a system in which public power became private. The Roman and Greek idea of public affairs had disappeared. Justice, military power, and political power had all become private possessions. They could be traded among lords or passed down to one's heirs. The duties a person owed were not to a polis or to an empire but to a personal lord.

Manors were the economic side of feudalism.

The great majority of people in the Middle Ages were neither lords nor vassals. Medieval writers said that there were three groups of people: those who fought (the nobles), those who prayed (the men and women of the Church), and those who worked (the peasants). Nobles and church leaders were part of the feudal system. The peasants—horseless, weaponless, and powerless—were outside the political system of feudalism. However, their daily toil lay at the heart of the economic system in the Middle Ages.

The basic economic unit was the **manor**. A manor was a small estate from which a lord's family gained its livelihood. Sometimes a manor was the whole of a fief, sometimes only one part of a fief. If a lord held more than one manor, as was often the case, stewards managed each manor when the lord was absent.

A manor usually covered only a few square miles of land, perhaps with a stream meandering through it. (Fish from streams and ponds were an important source of food.) About one third of the land was cleared for growing grain. Another patch of land was pasture for the peasants' oxen and the lord's horses. The rest was forest.

Self-sufficiency From these meager resources, the laborers on the manor—the peasants—had to produce everything they and the lord needed. Nothing was purchased from outside except salt, iron, and a few unusual objects such as millstones. Everything else—food, fuel, cloth, leather goods, lumber—was produced on the manor. The manor was thus a world unto itself.

Serfs on the land Most peasants were **serfs**. Serfs were not free, but they were not quite slaves either. Unlike slaves, serfs could not be bought, sold, or traded to another lord. Yet serfs could not lawfully leave the manor on which they were born. They were bound to the land. From a different viewpoint, serfs had the right to live on the same manor from birth to death. Although it is hard to understand today, a serf in the Middle Ages may have felt that the right to stay was more important than the freedom to leave.

Free peasants A few peasants enjoyed greater freedom than serfs. They could leave the manor if they wished. These free peasants were not required to do as much work for the lord as the serfs were. Still, one bad harvest or flood could force free peasants to become serfs in exchange for bread and protection. For example, a poor Frankish peasant named William became a serf at the monastery at St. Martin. A monastic document of the eleventh century reads:

> Be it known to all who come after us that a certain man in our service, William, brother of Reginald, born of free parents . . . gave himself up as a serf to St. Martin of Marmoutiers, and he gave not only himself but all his descendants, so that they should forever serve the abbot and monks . . . And in order that this gift might be made more certain and apparent, he put the bell rope round his neck and placed four pennies from his own hand on the altar of St. Martin in recognition of serfdom.

Peasants owed duties on the manor.

All peasants, whether free or serf, were tenants on the lord's manor. They paid dearly for the right to live and grow crops on the lord's land. A typical serf owed the lord the following duties:

- Two or three days' labor every week plowing, planting, and harvesting the lord's own land. (Every sack of grain harvested from this land went to the lord's family.)
- A certain portion of the grain grown on the serf's own land.
- One pig out of every ten pigs raised on the manor, plus the service of slaughtering it.
- As a "gift" at Christmas and Easter, delivery to the lord of so many eggs and chickens.

Discussion question: What is the relation between feudalism and manorialism? (One is a political and military system and the other an economic system. Nonetheless, they were inextricably linked for centuries in many regions.)

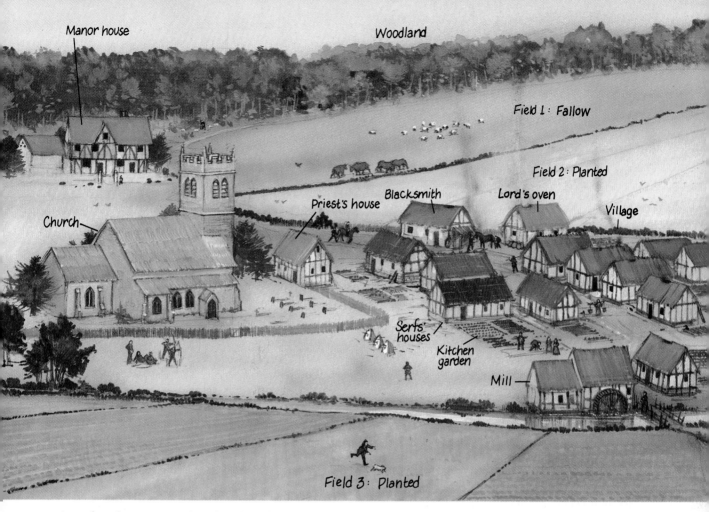

A medieval manor was largely self-sufficient. Its residents raised or made nearly everything they needed for daily life.

- A tax on all grain ground in the lord's mill and all bread baked in the lord's oven. (Any attempt to dodge these charges by baking bread elsewhere was punished as a crime.
- A tax when the serf married. (No marriage could take place without the lord's consent.)

After all these payments to the lord, each peasant's family still owed to the village priest a tithe (church tax), representing one tenth of their income. Together, lord and priest typically collected from each serf six sacks of grain for every ten sacks produced.

Life on a manor was harsh.

Peasant men and women rarely traveled far from their own manor. They could see their entire world at a glance by standing in the center of a plowed field and looking around.

On some manors, the tallest structure on the landscape was a wooden tower set high on a hill and surrounded on four sides by a ditch and a wall. This was the manor's castle, a place of safety for lord and peasant alike whenever Vikings raided or a neighboring lord attacked. (Gigantic stone castles with moats and drawbridges did not exist until later in the Middle Ages.) Not far away was a plain two-story house of rough-hewn timber where the lord's family lived in times of peace.

Across the fields in another direction, one could see the thatch roofs of the peasants' one-room huts in the manor's village. Close by, facing the village well, stood a plain church.

By the stream, the waterwheel of the lord's mill turned slowly and ground the manor's grain into flour. The millwright who built and repaired mills was one of several skilled workers in the

Despite its egalitarian origins, the Church viewed peasants as those whose birth relegated them to a life of back-breaking testing for the future reward of life in heaven.

Looking at economics *This drawing from the mid-1300's shows peasants stacking grain. Farming was the chief medieval economic activity.*

village. Another was the blacksmith, who forged the few metal items used on the manor.

For peasant men and women, probably the most familiar sight was the swishing tails of the oxen that they walked behind as they plowed a field. Since few peasants could afford a whole team of oxen, villagers shared their animals. The same team plowed everyone's fields. Land was shared too. Fields were laid out in long, thin strips because the plow was hard to turn. A peasant family might use strips of land scattered in fields all around the village.

Peasants raised wheat, barley, oats, and rye. Coarse, black bread made from these grains was the main course of many meals. In garden patches, families grew cabbages, onions, beans, and other vegetables. Hens scratched in the dooryards of the houses, more valuable for their eggs than for meat. Half-wild pigs nosed the ground for fallen acorns near the edge of the village woodlands. One slaughtered pig per year might be a peasant family's only source of meat. Honey was used for sweetener. Fruit trees grew apples, pears, cherries, and peaches. Yet after a bad harvest, peasant families lived on the edge of starvation.

In addition to hunger, there was the misery of being chilled to the bone when the winter winds blew. The cold seeped into a peasant's hut through cracks in the log walls. There were no floorboards, only the bare dirt ground. In one corner of the room, in a wooden frame, was a pile of straw crawling with vermin. This was the bed in which the whole family slept, parents and children together. Farm animals (geese, sheep, pigs) were commonly admitted into the hut to increase the general body heat. Though smelly, warming a hut with pig heat was safer than

burning a fire in the center of the room and risking that a spark would fly toward the family's straw bed.

Nobles had more to eat and warmer clothing than peasants did. Yet even nobles had little comfort and no protection from sickness or injury.

The years from 500 to 1000 were harsh for Europeans. Change came slowly. When one bad harvest could spell death, people were reluctant to try new ways. Yet, even by 800, changes were taking place that would improve life on the manor. By 1000, Europe was poised for a revival in farming, trade, government, and learning.

Section Review 4

Define: (a) feudalism, (b) lord, (c) vassal, (d) investiture, (e) fief, (f) aid, (g) manor, (h) serf

Answer:
1. (a) What oath did a vassal swear to his or her lord? (b) What did the lord give in return? (c) How did a vassal become the lord of others?
2. (a) What services could a lord demand of vassals in time of war? (b) In peacetime?
3. (a) How did women become lords or vassals? (b) What part did church leaders have in the feudal system?
4. (a) What duties did a serf owe on a manor? (b) How might a free peasant become a serf?

Critical Thinking
5. (a) How was a local community self-sufficient both militarily and economically in the Early Middle Ages? (b) Why was self-sufficiency important in this age?

Chapter Review 9

Summary

1. New ways of life developed in Europe. By the end of the 400's, the Roman empire had been broken into many Germanic kingdoms. Trade collapsed, towns declined, and the level of learning sank. Germanic leaders and customs replaced Roman government and law. Monasteries stood out as centers of orderly life, where learning was kept alive.

2. Charlemagne revived the idea of empire. The Franks had the largest of the Germanic kingdoms. The greatest of the Frankish rulers was Charlemagne, who conquered pagan lands, set up an effective administration, and encouraged learning. After his death, Europe suffered a new wave of invasions.

3. The Vikings terrorized Europe. From 800 to 1000, raiders from Scandinavia threatened much of Europe. They also explored and settled widely. After 1000, the Viking menace declined.

4. Feudalism became the basis for government. Feudalism developed as a form of local protection and government. Vassals pledged loyalty to a lord; in return, the lord gave each vassal a grant of land. Lords and vassals spent most of their lives training for battle and fighting wars. Peasants worked on manors to supply the goods needed to support themselves and the lords.

Reviewing the Facts

1. Define the following terms:
   - a. monastery
   - b. knight
   - c. count
   - d. feudalism
   - e. lord
   - f. vassal
   - g. investiture
   - h. fief
   - i. aid
   - j. manor
   - k. serf

2. Explain the importance of each of the following names, dates, places, or terms:
   - a. Patrick
   - b. Clovis
   - c. Benedictine Rule
   - d. Gregory I
   - e. Christendom
   - f. Merovingians
   - g. Pepin the Short
   - h. Charlemagne
   - i. missi dominici
   - j. Aachen
   - k. A.D. 800
   - l. Carolingians
   - m. Treaty of Verdun
   - n. Vikings
   - o. Leif Ericson

3. (a) How was learning promoted by Charlemagne? (b) By monasteries?

4. What different methods were used to spread Christianity during the Early Middle Ages?

5. How was Germanic society organized?

6. Explain how the feudal system linked lords and vassals. Include information on investiture, fiefs, and aids.

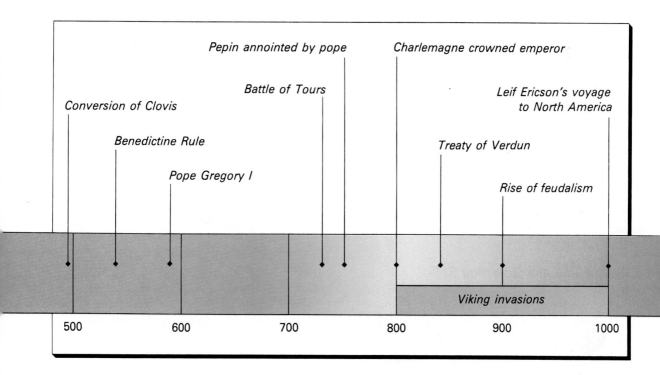

Pepin annointed by pope

Charlemagne crowned emperor

Battle of Tours

Leif Ericson's voyage to North America

Conversion of Clovis

Benedictine Rule

Treaty of Verdun

Pope Gregory I

Rise of feudalism

Viking invasions

500   600   700   800   900   1000

207

7. (a) After 800, what were the titles of the two men who could claim leadership of all Christian Europe? (b) How did leaders depend on each other?
8. (a) What part did the manor play in medieval life? (b) Describe the ways land was used on a manor.
9. (a) What obligations did serfs have? (b) What did they get in return?

Basic Skills

1. **Reading a time line** (a) Using the time line on page 207, tell what event happened at the same time as the start of the Viking invasions. (b) What event happened as the invasions ended?
2. **Classifying** Using the map on page 189, make a chart to classify the peoples who settled in different areas of western Europe. Make four columns with the headings *Spain, France, Germany,* and *Britain.* Under each heading, list the names of the peoples who had settled there by 500. (See page 712 for a map of Europe today. Include both West and East Germany.)
3. **Interpreting a diagram** On the diagram on page 202, assume that the royal vassals are named (from left to right) John, Richard, and William. If one of the white knights owed allegiance to both Richard and William, how would you diagram that relationship? (Draw six shields and two helmets.)
4. **Using historical terms** Political power is *centralized* if it is exercised by a single strong government and *decentralized* if it is divided among many local governments. Illustrate the term *centralized* by describing the rule of Charlemagne and *decentralized* by describing the rule of his successors.
5. **Identifying supporting details** Find details supporting the statement on page 190 of the text, "Throughout the Early Middle Ages, the Church acted as the strongest civilizing influence in western Europe."

Researching and Reporting Skills

1. **Selecting a topic for research** Of the following research topics, which ones would you eliminate as either too broad or too narrow: *The Conversion of Clovis, Feudalism in Western Europe, The Life of Charlemagne, Life in a Benedictine Monastery,* and *Lindisfarne Island during the Roman Empire?* Give reasons for your choices.
2. **Organizing a group project** Feudalism was a complex system organizing many aspects of life. Divide the class into five groups to research and report on the following areas as they are affected by feudalism: distribution of land, military organization, administration of justice, economic activity, and personal relationships.
3. **Role-playing** As a class project, research and role-play the ceremony of investiture between a lord and his vassal. Discuss the significance of this ceremony to the structure of feudal obligations.

Critical Thinking

1. **Analyzing cause and effect** One key to the collapse of Roman civilization was the disappearance of the cities. (a) What were the causes of this disappearance? (b) What were the effects on civilization?
2. **Analyzing** The text stresses the fact that in the Early Middle Ages, ties of personal loyalty replaced citizenship. (a) What would be some of the consequences of this shift for the peace and prosperity of the times? (b) Was this change positive or negative? Why?
3. **Predicting outcomes** In 800, Charlemagne was crowned emperor by the pope. (a) What was the significance of this event? (b) How might it influence future relationships between Church and state?

Perspectives on Past and Present

(a) What generalizations could you make about the relationship between politics and religion in the Middle Ages? (b) Give facts to support your statement. (c) Contrast this generalization about the Early Middle Ages with the principles governing the relationship between church and state in the United States today.

Investigating History

Look up information on Viking ships and sea travel. In what ways did their ships represent technological progress? What other factors enabled the Vikings to become explorers who succeeded in crossing the Atlantic?

The High Middle Ages

Building a cathedral went on for several generations.

Key Terms

burghers
bourgeoisie
guild
apprentice
journeyman
cardinal
interdict
canon law
friar
jury
common law
chivalry
crusader

Read and Understand

1. Farming improved and trade revived.
2. Religious leaders wielded great power.
3. Royal governments grew stronger.
4. Learning revived and spread.
5. Crusaders marched against Islam.

What was this coming slowly down the dirt road through the wheat fields? Who were these people pulling two-wheeled wagons weighted down with stone blocks? A French abbot watching them knew from their rich robes that these haulers of stone were not peasants but nobles. In 1144, the abbot wrote an account of what he saw outside the town of Chartres (shahrt), southwest of Paris:

Who has ever seen! Who has ever heard tell, in times past, that powerful princes of the world, that men brought up in honor and

In 1134, for the fourth time in its history, Chartres Cathedral had been destroyed by fire. Now, in 1144, a new and grander cathedral was rising slowly over the flat countryside.

wealth, that nobles, men and women, have bent their proud and haughty necks to the harness of carts and that, like beasts of burden, they have dragged to the abode of Christ these wagons? . . .

From the stone quarry where the laborers picked up their load, it was a seven-mile trek to the massive structure they were helping to build, the Cathedral of Our Lady of Chartres. The pious workers who dragged the first stones to Chartres never saw the cathedral finished. Few Europeans in the 1100's lived beyond the age of 50. Normally, it took 40 to 60 years to build a cathedral.

In 1180, after two generations of back-breaking labor, the townspeople of Chartres celebrated the dedication of their new cathedral with feasting and bell ringing. Just 14 years later, in 1194, the roof of the great cathedral burst into flame. The work of two generations came tumbling down. Amazingly, the undaunted citizens of Chartres set to work and in just 25 years raised an even more magnificent cathedral, which still stands.

Chartres Cathedral is the symbol of an era. In western Europe, the period from 1000 to 1300 often is known as the Age of Faith. It was an age when hundreds of towering cathedrals were built throughout Europe. Church leaders exerted enormous political and economic influence in Europe. Yet it was not faith alone that built the great cathedrals. The Age of Faith was also a time of increasing material prosperity. In all spheres of life, the High Middle Ages were a time of vigorous growth for European civilization.

Farming improved and trade revived. 1

In the years between 1000 and 1300, dramatic changes were occurring at every level of European society. At the top, new royal families were coming to power. Church leaders were reforming and strengthening the Church. Nobles were creating a glittering society with mock battles and poetry contests. Perhaps the most important changes had begun much earlier at the lowest level of society, with the peasants who worked on the land.

New ways of farming increased food.

A civilization cannot exist without food. Europe's great revival would have been impossible without better ways of farming.

One of the first great improvements in farming had begun in Charlemagne's time. A new, heavier plow slowly came into use. This heavy plow cut deep into the dirt and turned it over. Very gradually, this plow replaced the earlier, lightweight plow that only scratched the top of the ground. With the new plow, farmers could plant crops in the rich, deep soil of Europe's river valleys. This soil produced better harvests, helping peasants get a step ahead in the race with hunger.

Using horsepower For hundreds of years, peasants depended on oxen to pull their plows. Oxen lived on the poorest straw and stubble, so they were easy to keep. However, oxen moved very slowly. Horses needed better food, but a team of horses could plow twice as much land in a day as a team of oxen.

The horse collar and the heavy plow were the newest technology for farming in the Middle Ages.

Horses' hooves were more delicate than oxen's and needed extra protection for the hard work of plowing. The horseshoe appeared in Europe about this time, probably from the plains of central Asia.

The problem was that farmers in the Early Middle Ages did not have the right kind of harness to use on horses. Their harness went around the horse's neck. When the horse pulled against its harness, the poor animal was nearly strangled. Sometime before 900, farmers in Europe began using a harness with a collar that fitted across the horse's chest, taking pressure off its neck and windpipe. Over the next two centuries, the new harness was adopted widely in western Europe. As a result, horses gradually replaced oxen for plowing and pulling wagons.

With horses, a farmer could plow more land in a day. As a result, many farmers cleared new fields from the forests. All over England, France, and Germany, axes rang as the great forests that had covered the land began to fall. Along the marshy coastlands of present-day Belgium, peasants built huge seawalls to drain yet more new land. These new fields supplied enough grain to feed a growing population.

The three-field system At the same time, villagers began to organize their land differently. As you have read, peasants in a village shared the land. Each family had a few strips of land scattered around the village fields.

In the Early Middle Ages, peasants usually divided the village's land into two great fields. One field they planted with crops. The other they left to lie fallow for a year. Fallow land was not planted. It was plowed once or twice to keep down weeds, but otherwise it was let alone. Thus, if a village had 600 acres, each year farmers used 300 for raising food. The following year, farmers would plant the land that had been fallow and leave the other field to rest. This way of dividing a village's land was the two-field system.

Around 800, some villages began to organize their land into three great fields instead of two. With the same 600 acres, they used 200 acres for a winter crop of wheat or rye. In spring, they planted another 200 acres with oats, barley, peas, or beans. The remaining 200 acres lay fallow.

Under this new three-field system, farmers could grow crops on two thirds of their land each year, not just on half of it. The result was an immediate increase in food for the village. Moreover, this change gave peasants a healthier diet because peas, beans, and lentils were good sources of vegetable protein.

Like other farming changes, this one spread slowly. Three or four centuries went by before it was in wide use.

Towns grew larger and richer.

Greater amounts of food meant greater numbers of people. Scholars estimate that between 1000 and 1150, the population of western Europe rose by 40 percent, from around 30 million to about 42 million.

As Europe's population increased, people left the countryside to settle in towns. Compared to great cities like Constantinople or Baghdad, European towns were still primitive and tiny. Europe's largest city, Paris, probably had no more than 30,000 people by the year 1200. A typical town in medieval Europe had only about 1,500 to 2,500 people.

Nevertheless, these small communities became a powerful force for change. Townspeople did not fit into the traditional groups of nobles (those who fight), priests (those who pray), and peasants (those who work the land). In effect, townspeople formed a new social class. A walled town was known as a burgh, and the people who made their homes in such towns gradually became known as **burghers**. In France, burgh dwellers became known collectively as the **bourgeoisie** (BOOR-zhwah-ZEE).

Many of Europe's Jews lived in the growing towns. Because Jews were forbidden to hold land,

In the diagram below, how many acres a year could peasants use to raise crops with the two-field system? With the three-field system?

Planted 300 Acres	Fallow 300 Acres

Two-field System · 600 Acres

Wheat or rye 200 Acres	Barley, peas, oats beans 200 Acres	Fallow 200 Acres

Three-field System · 600 Acres

Medieval shops were often family businesses in which both husbands and wives worked. Here boots, jewelry, and tableware are for sale.

they had never been part of the feudal system. Jews were also barred from many businesses, and so they often did work that Christians could not or would not do. Being literate, Jews sometimes worked as business managers for large landholders. The Church forbade Christians to lend money at interest, yet many people still needed to borrow money. As a result, some Jews became money lenders. From there, it was a short step to all types of banking. When trade began to revive in the later Middle Ages, Jews often were active in long-distance trade. Jewish communities in different cities had the links necessary to arrange credit and transfers of money.

By the High Middle Ages, trade was the very lifeblood of the new towns. Trade and towns grew together. Neither could thrive without the other.

Fairs were centers of trade.

Chartres is a good example of a medieval town. As with any cathedral town, many residents had ties to the Church. Some were priests, monks, or nuns. Others worked for the Church, administering its lands and money. People from the countryside came to town to celebrate religious festivals. Travelers came to the city as pilgrims to honor the holy relics at the cathedral. (A relic was something that people believed had once belonged to Jesus or one of the Christian saints.)

Artisans appeared in the town to meet the needs of all those groups of people. Shoemakers, wheelwrights, candle makers, and others did a lively business in Chartres. At first, these people did not have permanent shops. Instead, they brought their goods to gatherings known as fairs.

The local fair Peasants from nearby manors would travel to Chartres on weekly fair days, hauling wagonloads of grain and baskets of hens. Business might take place in the very shadow of the cathedral. Cloth was the most common item offered for sale, but there were also food-stuffs—fish, meat, bacon, salt, honey, oil, butter, cheese, fruit, and wine. Customers could find leather, fur, iron, steel, dyes, knives, sickles, and ropes. Such local fairs met all the needs of daily life for a small community.

No longer was everything produced on a self-sufficient manor. This was a revolutionary change in the economic life of Europe.

The great fairs Four times a year—during religious festivals, when the most pilgrims would be in town—Chartres held great fairs. People

The two regional markets—northern and Mediterranean—were linked by land routes that crisscrossed Europe. Many of them converged in Champagne, southeast of Paris. Fairs in Champagne continued from early spring to late fall without a break.

came to these fairs from far and wide. Besides buying the wares of local artisans, they could also visit the stalls set up by merchants from as far away as England or Italy.

At great fairs, townsfolk and peasants could taste Russian honey, sample Spanish wine, purchase Flemish cloth, sniff Byzantine perfumes sold by a Venetian, and inspect the handiwork of a local wheelwright. For amusement, people thronged around a pair of jugglers, a strumming minstrel, an acrobat or an animal trainer with a dancing bear.

Guilds controlled crafts and trade.

In a medieval town, even if there were a dozen shoemakers, they all made their shoes the same way and sold them for the same price. Competition was forbidden by the rules of the shoemakers' **guild**. A guild was an association of people who worked at the same occupation.

Merchant guilds The first guilds were formed by merchants. In their hometowns, they erected guild halls where they met to make rules and arrange the details of their business. Members of the merchant guild controlled all the trade in their town. For example, nobody could sell Flemish wool in Chartres except a member of the local merchants' guild.

Craft guilds As towns grew, skilled artisans started another kind of guild, the craft guild. Shoemakers, wheelwrights, glassmakers, wine makers, tailors, grocers, druggists, and others began to meet in their own guild halls. In most crafts, both husbands and wives worked at the family trade. In some guilds, especially cloth making, women were in the majority.

Guild functions Guilds enforced standards of quality. Bakers, for example, were required to sell loaves of bread of a standard size and weight. If a baker cheated a customer with an undersized loaf, his guild might punish him by hanging the loaf around his neck and parading him through the town.

Guilds also fixed the price of everything their members sold. The Church demanded that it be a just price, based on the cost of labor and materials plus a reasonable profit. To make a large profit was thought sinful.

Paying dues to one's guild was a form of insurance. When a member died, the guild paid funeral expenses and also gave some money to support the member's family.

Training new workers The doors of the guild hall were open only to proved masters of the trade. How did someone master a trade? Usually, parents paid a fee to a master to take their child as an **apprentice**. An apprentice lived in the master's home and worked in the shop, which might well be in the same building.

The apprentice worked for the master for 3 to 12 years without pay except for room and board. At the end of this training period, an apprentice went to work for wages as a **journeyman** in the craft. As the final step, a journeyman made an item—whether it was a shoe, a barrel, or a sword—that qualified as a "master piece." Journeymen whose product met guild standards were welcomed into the guild as masters.

Town dwellers won new liberties.

Even a proud master artisan might have begun life as a serf on a manor. Many serfs ran away to town. By the 1100's, according to custom, a serf could become free by living within a town for a year and a day. As the saying went, "Town air makes you free."

At first, feudal lords treated the upstart burghers with contempt. Lords ruthlessly taxed the towns on their lands. Nobles charged fees for everything—the right to hold a fair, the right to use a bridge, or the right to hold a law court.

As time went by, however, burghers worked together to free themselves from the lord or bishop on whose land the town stood. Sometimes they fought for their independence against armies of knights. The greatest weapon the burghers had,

Footnote to History

Many people can trace their last names, or surnames, back to a medieval occupation. Sometimes the name even indicates whether the original worker was a man or a woman. For example, a man who made bread might be surnamed Baker; a woman who did the same job, Baxter. A man who wove cloth was Weaver or Weber; a woman, Webster. Spinning thread was a common job for unmarried women, as the modern use of the word *spinster* implies.

Ask how status and wealth were achieved on the manor and in town. (manor: land ownership and birth; town: money, labor, and bargaining) In a noble's eyes, a merchant could never climb higher than the poorest knight.

213

Voice from the Past · A Town Charter

The growth of towns in the later Middle Ages opened the way for the transition from a rural and feudal society to a more urban and mobile one. Because many townspeople were merchants and artisans, they were outside the rigid class structure of feudalism. Thus they sought new forms of community that involved new traditions of membership. In the towns, members of the merchant guilds often led in creating new approaches to government. With wealth from trade, they were able to bargain with kings for political rights that were granted in the form of charters. The passage that follows is from the charter granted by King Henry II of England to the merchants of the town of Lincoln about 1150. Although granted to the merchants, the charter applied to all the citizens of the town.

Henry, by the grace of God, etc., . . . Know that I have granted to my citizens of Lincoln all their liberties and customs and laws which they had in the time of Edward and William and Henry, kings of England . . . And I have granted them their gild-merchant, comprising men of the city and other merchants of the shire . . . I also confirm to them that if anyone has lived in Lincoln for a year and a day without dispute of any claimant, and has paid the customs, and if the citizens can show by the laws and customs of the city that the claimant has remained in England during that period and has made no claim, then let the defendant remain in peace in my city of Lincoln as my citizen, without [having to defend his] right.

1. What was the importance of a charter?
2. What does the term *citizen* mean as used in the charter?
3. How does this idea of citizenship differ from feudal relationships?
4. What is the significance of the passage about "a year and a day"?

however, was cash. In exchange for a bag of coins, many lords grudgingly granted towns written charters. Such charters listed the towns' special privileges and tax exemptions. In effect, a town charter bearing the lord's seal was a declaration of independence from the feudal system.

Section Review 1

Define: (a) fallow, (b) two-field system, (c) three-field system, (d) burgher, (e) bourgeoisie, (f) fair, (g) guild, (h) apprentice, (i) journeyman
Identify: (a) Chartres, (b) Age of Faith
Answer:
1. (a) Describe three improvements in farming that took place in the Middle Ages. (b) Explain how each helped to increase the food supply.
2. (a) Why did townspeople make up a new social class? (b) What important tasks did Jews perform in the Middle Ages?
3. (a) Why was it no longer necessary for manors to be self-sufficient? (b) How did people get the daily goods they needed? (c) How did they obtain luxury products such as silk?
4. (a) What was the difference between a merchant guild and a craft guild? (b) What regulations did guilds make?
5. How did townspeople become independent of the feudal system?

Critical Thinking
6. Write a series of cause-and-effect statements for the changes described in this chapter. Try to include as many specific changes as possible. Here is an example: "The heavy plow led to farming rich valley soils. Farming rich valley soils led to increased food production."

Religious leaders wielded great power. 2

During the Early Middle Ages, the Church had acted as the preserver of civilization in many ways. Yet the Church had also suffered in the years between 500 and 1000. Vikings had plundered many monasteries. As a result, the level of learning sank. Many priests could barely read their prayers. Church leaders were sometimes corrupt. Italian nobles controlled the election of popes and sometimes chose men whose morals were questionable. Many bishops and abbots cared more about their position as feudal lords than about their duties as spiritual leaders.

During the years between 1000 and 1300, the state of the Church improved dramatically. Religion spread more widely and deeply in society than before. Thousands of men and women became monks and nuns. At the head of the Church, strong popes challenged the power of emperors and kings.

Monks adopted stricter rules.

One of the first signs of reform in the Church was the founding in 910 of a new French monastery at Cluny (KLOO-nee). Cluny was founded by a nobleman, the Duke of Aquitaine. Unlike many lords, the duke did not try to make Cluny a source of personal wealth and power. Instead, he arranged that the monastery be subject only to the pope, not to any nearby lord or bishop.

The abbots of Cluny held strictly to the Benedictine rule. Soon Cluny's reputation for purity inspired the founding of similar monasteries throughout western Europe. By the year 1000, there were 300 houses under Cluny's leadership. Cluny acted as a headquarters for Church reform.

For many men and women, the Benedictine rule no longer seemed strict enough for a holy life. After the year 1000, new groups of monks and nuns chose to live by even stricter rules. For example, the members of the Cistercian (sihs-TUHR-shuhn) order, founded in 1098, vowed to build their monasteries only in the wilderness. The Cistercians often took the lead in the great movement to clear new farmlands. Their life of hardship won many followers.

Reformers ended abuses.

Reformers hoped to purify the Church by freeing it from control by lords and kings. The first step was to free the papacy from the control of Italian nobles. In 1059, a Church decree declared that all future popes would be chosen at a meeting of leading bishops known as **cardinals**. No longer could the Roman mob, the local nobles, or even the emperor choose a pope.

Reformers were also eager to abolish three conditions that were widespread in the Church of the early Middle Ages. First, they wanted to put an end to the *marriage of priests.* Many village priests married and had families, even though such marriages were against Church rulings.

Second, reformers wanted to stop the buying and selling of Church offices, called *simony* (SYE-muh-nee). Many bishops expected to make a profit from their high position. Every Church office brought with it land and a good income. One greedy bishop wrote: "I have gold and I received the [office of bishop] . . . I ordain a priest and I receive gold. I make a deacon and I receive a heap of silver . . ." Like marriage for priests, simony was against Church law but still was widely practiced.

Lay investiture was the third practice Church reformers wanted to end. Just as vassals received their fiefs in a feudal ceremony, bishops and abbots went through a ceremony to receive their Church offices. In both cases, the ceremony was known as investiture. Who should perform this ceremony for Church officials, a layman (feudal lord or king) or a Church leader? If the ceremony was performed by a layman, it was called lay investiture.

Whoever controlled the ceremony held the real power in naming a bishop. Naturally, kings favored lay investiture. Bishops were powerful nobles, and kings wanted to control them. Naturally too, Church reformers frowned on lay investiture. They said that a bishop should not be the political pawn of any king.

Gregory VII clashed with Henry IV.

In 1073, the foremost leader of the reformers became pope. He took the name of Gregory VII. The new pope quickly carried out the aims of the reform movement. He first ordered all married

The Duke of Aquitaine wanted to have masses said for his soul, but he was unhappy with all the available monasteries. That is why he left land for the founding of a new monastery at Cluny.

priests to abandon their wives and children. Then, in 1075, he banned lay investiture.

The young German ruler, Henry IV, flew into a rage. Henry held the title of emperor, passed down since the time of Charlemagne. Henry called a meeting of German bishops, who had all been invested by himself. With their approval, the emperor sent a vicious letter calling Gregory "not pope, but false monk" and ordering him to step down from the papacy.

Gregory replied in the same temper, sending this letter to the German bishops:

> I take from King Henry . . . the government of the whole kingdom of the Germans and the Italians, and I free all Christian people from any oath they have made or shall make to him, and I forbid any to serve the king.

Furthermore, the pope excommunicated Henry.

In this showdown, who would prove the stronger, pope or emperor? Everything hinged on the loyalties of the German bishops and princes. Would they side with their earthly lord or their spiritual lord? They decided to support Pope Gregory. Deserted by his bishops and threatened by rebellious German princes, Henry's position seemed hopeless. The only way to save his throne was to win the pope's forgiveness.

In the middle of winter, 1077, Henry journeyed over the snowy Alps to the Italian town of Canossa (kuh-NAHS-uh). He approached the castle where Pope Gregory was a guest. In Gregory's own words, "He [Henry] presented himself at the gate of the castle, barefoot and clad only in a wretched woolen garment, beseeching us with tears to grant him . . . forgiveness." As pope, Gregory had no choice but to forgive any sinner who came humbly to him. Still, he kept Henry waiting in the snow for three days before ending his excommunication.

This meeting in Canossa was one of the most dramatic confrontations of the Middle Ages, but it solved nothing. It was a master political stroke for Henry, who was free to go home and punish the nobles who had rebelled against him. Yet it was an even greater victory for the pope. He had humiliated the proudest ruler in Europe. The question of investiture was still undecided.

Gregory died in 1085, Henry in 1106. Their successors continued to fight over investiture until 1122. In that year, representatives of the Church and the emperor met in the German city of Worms (vohrms). They reached a compromise known as the *Concordat of Worms*. By its terms, the Church alone would grant a bishop his ring and staff, symbols of Church office. However, the emperor kept the power to grant that bishop the lands that went with his office. Thus, the emperor still had much control over the bishops. (The kings of France and England had reached the same sort of compromise earlier.)

Popes ruled a spiritual empire.

In many ways, the popes who followed Gregory VII exercised greater power than any king or prince. As with Henry IV, a king who quarreled with the pope faced excommunication, which freed all his vassals from their duties to him.

If an excommunicated king or duke continued to disobey, the pope had another weapon—the **interdict**. No Church ceremonies could be performed in the offending ruler's lands. There could be no marriages, no baptisms, no religious services of any sort. In the Age of Faith, fear of the interdict put great pressure on a king to bow to a pope's demands.

Church law and government In the 1100's and 1200's, the Church resembled a kingdom. It was governed by a single ruler (the pope) from a central capital (Rome). A group of advisers, called the papal *Curia*, served as the pope's staff. The Curia supplied him with information, offered advice, and carried out decisions. The pope also had his own diplomats, known as *legates*, who traveled through Europe dealing with bishops and kings.

Outside Rome, the power of the Church was in the hands of bishops. Bishops operated courts of law that rivaled the feudal courts of lords and kings. Bishops' courts ruled on such matters as marriage, divorce, and wills. Thus, all Christians were partly governed by **canon law**, the law of the Church.

The Church was like a kingdom in yet another sense. It collected taxes. Every Christian family was required to give to the Church one tenth of its yearly income as a tithe.

Social services According to canon law, bishops were to use at least one fourth of all tithes to care for the sick and the poor. Orphans, lepers, and beggars received care from Church funds.

216

Christians of the Middle Ages felt a great burden of sin. Only the sacraments, they believed, could save them from the devil's clutches. For this reason, excommunication and the interdict were greatly feared punishments that meant eternal torture.

Most hospitals in medieval Europe were operated by the Church. Around the year 1200, there were 400 hospitals in England and 12 in Paris alone. No needy person could be turned away.

War against heresy Like other rulers in the Middle Ages, popes thought of themselves as warriors. Time and again, as you will read, they urged Christians to go to war against Muslims. The Church also went to war against enemies closer to home—heretics.

With the widespread interest in religion of the 1100's and 1200's, people seriously pondered religious questions. Not surprisingly, some reached answers that differed from the Church's teachings. Many heresies sprang up in Europe during the 1200's. The Church struck back with all its might. In some cases, whole villages of suspected heretics were slaughtered.

The Inquisition (IN-kwuh-ZISH-uhn) was the leading arm of the Church in the war against heresy. The Inquisition was an organization of experts whose job was to find and judge heretics. Beginning around 1225, popes sent many such experts throughout Europe. These men left no stone unturned in their search for heresy, even accepting rumors and gossip. A person who was suspected of heresy might be questioned for weeks and even tortured. It was almost impossible for a suspect to prove his or her innocence.

Friars preached to the poor.

The Church had another weapon in its fight against heresy. In the early 1200's, wandering **friars** traveled from place to place. By preaching, friars tried to carry the Church's ideas more widely and win heretics back to the Church. Like monks, friars took vows of chastity, poverty, and obedience. Unlike monks, however, friars did not live apart from the world in monasteries. Instead, friars preached to the poor, especially in Europe's rapidly growing towns. Friars owned nothing and lived by begging.

The earliest order of friars were the Dominicans. They took their name from Dominic, a Spanish priest who walked barefoot through southern France preaching against heresy. Because Dominic emphasized the importance of study, many Dominicans were formidable scholars.

A second order of friars was founded by an Italian known as Francis of Assisi (uh-SEE-see). The son of a rich merchant, Francis gave up his wealth and turned to preaching when he was about 20 years old. Francis treated all creatures as if they were his spiritual brothers and sisters. Most famous is the episode in which, according to popular legend, he stopped along the road to preach to a flock of birds. Francis placed much less importance on scholarship than did Dominic.

Caring for the sick and needy was the responsibility of the Church in the Middle Ages. These nuns are treating patients in a French hospital of the 1400's.

for your refuge, and the tall trees wherein to build your nests; and for as much as ye
can neither spin nor sew, God clotheth you and your children . . . Therefore beware,
little sisters of mine, of the sin of ingratitude, but ever strive to praise God."

217

Women joined both the Franciscans and the Dominicans, although the Church did not allow them to travel from place to place as preachers. Like the men, these women lived in poverty and worked selflessly to help the poor and sick.

Soon white-robed Dominicans and brown-robed Franciscans were a common sight on the roads of Europe. In this age of reform, friars won wide respect for their poverty and their devout way of life.

Churches rose in a new style.

Although the friars chose to live in poverty, evidence of the Church's wealth could be seen everywhere in the Middle Ages. Between 1000 and 1100, towns in Europe began to build massive stone churches. The huge doors were framed by round arches like the arches on buildings in ancient Rome. The heavy roof pressed down on the thick walls and on two rows of thick pillars within the church. Walls were painted in brilliant colors. This style of architecture was called *Romanesque* (ROH-muh-NEHSK).

Romanesque churches were certainly impressive, but at least one man was not satisfied with them. That man was Suger (soo-ZHAY), abbot of the monastery of Saint Denis (sahn duh-NEE) near Paris. To Suger's eye, Romanesque churches had two great faults. First, they looked heavy and earthbound. Second, their tiny windows set in thick walls let in little light.

In 1137, Suger began to direct the rebuilding of the church at Saint Denis. He wanted the new building to thrust upward as if reaching toward heaven. He wanted light to stream in from all sides, reminding worshipers that God was the light of the world.

Suger's goals—more height and more light—seemed to defy the laws of medieval architecture. To lift a heavy roof higher and higher meant that you had to make the walls supporting it thicker and thicker. But thicker walls meant smaller and fewer windows, hence less light.

For several decades, master builders in France had been experimenting with new techniques. Under Suger's guidance, these ideas came together at Saint Denis. The result was a new style of architecture known as the *Gothic* style. Three new building techniques were the key to Gothic architecture:

1. *Pointed, ribbed vaults* In the new Gothic churches, narrow bands of stone called ribs ran from the roof to the columns below and helped support the roof's weight. The sections of walls between the pillars carried no weight at all. These walls became frames for huge stained-glass windows.
2. *Flying buttresses* Stone roofs pushed not only downward but outward. To support this outward pressure, Gothic builders made braces of beautifully carved stone. These braces slanted up against the outside walls of the cathedral. They were called flying buttresses.
3. *Pointed arches* To emphasize the height of a Gothic church, all the arches rose to points. The highest arch was the vaulted ceiling itself, where all lines came together as if pointing toward heaven.

Soon Gothic cathedrals were rising in many towns of northern France. In 1163, the people of Paris set out to build the tallest church in Christendom. The vaulted ceiling of the Cathedral of Notre Dame (NOH-truh DAHM) eventually rose to 114 feet. Then Chartres, Reims, Amiens, and Beauvais built even higher cathedrals.

The Gothic style spread to other parts of Europe. In all, nearly 500 Gothic churches were built between 1170 and 1270. All were beautiful, but none had windows quite as beautiful as those of Chartres. The stained-glass windows at Chartres illustrated stories from the Bible. As illiterate peasants walked past the 176 windows, they could "read" those stories. The thousands of stone carvings that framed every door in the cathedral showed more Bible stories. Scholars called Chartres "a Bible for the poor."

Section Review 2

Define: (a) cardinal, (b) simony, (c) lay investiture, (d) interdict, (e) legate, (f) canon law, (g) heretic, (h) friar
Identify: (a) Cluny, (b) Cistercian order, (c) Henry IV, (d) Gregory VII, (e) Canossa, (f) Concordat of Worms, (g) Curia, (h) Inquisition, (i) Dominic, (j) Francis of Assisi, (k) Suger, (l) Romanesque, (m) Gothic
Answer:
1. What were the major changes that Church reformers tried to achieve?

(opposite) The cathedrals at Chartres and Bourges represent the Gothic style of architecture. The focus on height and light gave a sense of soaring space. Although the vault came from Roman architecture, both Roman and Byzantine architecture were better known for the dome and Byzantine, for its interior decoration.

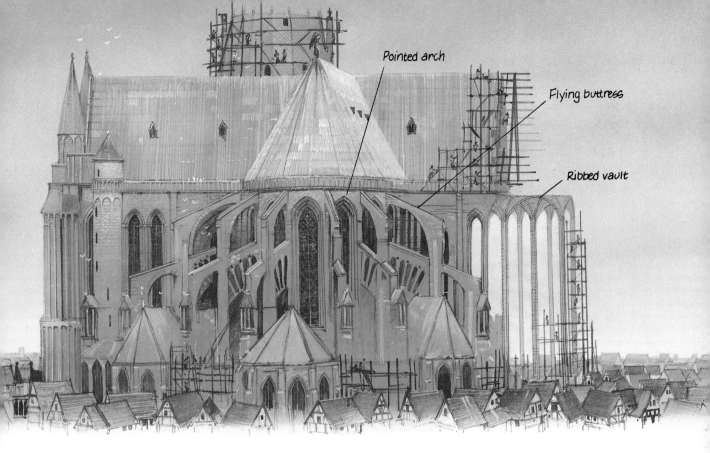

Pointed arch

Flying buttress

Ribbed vault

Comparing pictures *One of the glories of the Chartres cathedral is its rose window (below left). The Bourges cathedral (below right) clearly achieves the goals of Gothic architecture, height and light. What features set these cathedrals apart from Roman and Byzantine architecture (pages 148 and 172)?*

2. (a) Why did Henry IV favor lay investiture? (b) Describe the main events in the conflict between Henry IV and Gregory VII.
3. How was the Church similar to a kingdom?
4. (a) In its fight against heresy, how did the Church use the Inquisition? (b) The work of the friars?
5. How was Gothic architecture different from Romanesque architecture?

Critical Thinking
6. Why was the Concordat of Worms a compromise settlement?
7. Suppose you visited a medium-sized town in France around 1250. What evidence might you see in daily life that this was the Age of Faith? List as many examples as you can.

Royal governments grew stronger. 3

In part, Europe owed its prosperity to the coming of more peaceful times. By 1000, the great invasions of Vikings, Magyars, and Muslims had come to an end. Law, order, and peace were slowly gaining ground. By the 1050's, kings, dukes, and counts were winning greater control over their lands, ending petty wars between vassals, driving out nests of bandits, and in general, keeping the peace.

Kings had little more power than other great lords. In the words of the time, the king was "first among equals." Yet, like other lords, kings began to strengthen their control over their own lands. In doing so, they laid the groundwork for the growth of royal power.

Norman conquerors ruled England.

Surprisingly, the king who laid the foundations for royal power in England was not English at all. He was William, Duke of Normandy. Although William was a descendant of Rollo the Viking, by 1050 the Normans were French in language and culture.

The Norman Conquest How did a French duke become king of England? The story began when England's aged King Edward the Confessor died without an heir in January 1066. As Edward's second cousin, William claimed the English crown. William was ambitious, tough, and brave. Yet so was his rival, the English nobleman Harold Godwinson. Harold had been named king by a council of English lords. In the end, perhaps what helped William most was plain luck.

By the summer of 1066, William had gathered an army to invade England. The story of William's invasion is vividly recorded on the famous Bayeux (by-YOO) Tapestry, woven soon after the event. On this piece of linen 231 feet long, the drama unfolds scene by scene. The Norman knights and their horses crowded onto ships. They disembarked on English shores. Then came the battle that changed the course of English history—the Battle of Hastings.

On October 14, 1066, King Harold's English foot soldiers grouped themselves on the top of a small hill. The Norman knights on horseback charged. At the front of the Norman army went Taillefer, the Norman bard, spinning his sword in the air and singing the Song of Roland.

The battle raged from morning till dusk. Several times, the English seemed on the edge of victory. Then, luck stepped in for William. Late in the day, Harold fell dead with an arrow in his eye. The Normans broke through the English lines, and the Battle of Hastings ended in a decisive Norman victory.

William the Conqueror (1066–1087) After his victory, William (now called "the Conqueror") declared all England his personal property. The English lords who had supported Harold lost their lands. William then granted fiefs to about 200 Norman lords who swore oaths of loyalty to him. He also granted lands to the Church, appointing Norman bishops who were his loyal

Footnote to History

As a result of the Norman conquest, French became the language of the upper class in England and remained so for nearly 300 years. About one fourth of the words in modern English are of French origin. In many cases, modern English has two words for the same thing, one French and one English. For example, *flower* comes from a French word, but *blossom* has an English root word.

England had been conquered many times—by the Romans, the barbaric Angles and Saxons, and the Danish Vikings. The invasion by warriors from the French duchy of Normandy was the last conquest of England by a foreign foe.

This scene from the Bayeux Tapestry shows Harold's English footsoldiers forming a shield wall against the mounted Norman knights at Hastings.

vassals. England suddenly had a new ruling class of French-speaking nobles.

William kept about one fifth of England for himself, a powerful base for any king. Thus, William made England the most centralized feudal kingdom in Europe.

Henry II (1154–1189) Thanks to William's harsh but efficient rule, later kings of England had a strong base on which to build. William's great-grandson, Henry II, became king in 1154 and further increased royal power.

Henry's greatest achievement lay in strengthening the royal courts of justice. He sent royal judges to visit every part of England at least once a year. These judges collected taxes, settled lawsuits, and punished crimes. Henry also introduced the use of the **jury** in English courts. A jury in medieval England was a group of local people—usually 12 neighbors—who answered questions about the facts of a case for a royal judge.

Suppose Knight X and Knight Y both claimed a certain piece of land. In earlier times, such a case might have been settled in trial by combat at a lord's court. In Henry's royal court, the judge would call together 12 nearby landholders who were the knights' social equals, or peers. The 12 were sworn to tell the judge what they believed to be true in the case. (The word *jury* comes from the French *juree*, meaning "oath.") Then the judge would decide which knight was in the right. Jury trials became a popular way of settling disputes. Only the king's courts were allowed to conduct them.

As the king's courts gained in importance, the lords' feudal courts declined. Thus, the king of England won power from the nobles.

Over the centuries, case by case, the rulings of England's royal judges formed a unified body of law. Because this law was common to the whole kingdom, it was known as **common law**. Today, the principles of English common law are the basis for law in many English-speaking countries, including the United States.

The Capetian dynasty ruled France.

The kings of France, too, looked for ways of increasing their power. In theory, all French lords were vassals of the French king. In fact, however, after the breakup of Charlemagne's empire, French counts and dukes ruled their lands as if they were independent. By the year 1000, France was divided into about 30 feudal territories.

In 987, the last member of the Carolingian family—Louis the Sluggard—died. To succeed him, France's most powerful nobles chose Hugh Capet (**KAP**-uht), an undistinguished duke from the middle of France. The Capet family ruled only a small territory, but at its heart stood Paris, on a well-protected island in the Seine River. Hugh Capet ruled from 987 to 996. He began the Capetian (kuh-**PEE**-shuhn) dynasty of French kings.

When the French lords chose Hugh Capet, they assumed he would be a weak king. (They had no national loyalties to the region we call France. Such feelings did not exist until centuries later.)

Henry II was brilliant in the role of king, but he failed as father, husband, and French duke. His French wife, Eleanor of Aquitaine, plotted revenge against him for his ill treatment of her, and all four of his sons led armies of rebellion against him.

221

What they wanted was someone they could control. Hugh Capet did not disappoint them; neither did his son and grandson. The first three Capetian kings were little more than petty feudal lords.

Though weak rulers, the Capetians survived. The first six Capetians ruled for nearly 200 years (987–1180), an average of 32 years per reign. For many generations, Capetian queens bore healthy sons. Thus, bloody civil wars over the succession were avoided.

Time and geography were on the side of the Capetian kings. Their territory, though small, sat astride important trade routes in northern France. For 200 years, Capetian kings tightened their grip on this strategic area. The power of the French king gradually spread outward from Paris. Eventually, the growth of royal power would unite France.

German kings failed to unite their lands.

After the death of Charlemagne, Germany was the strongest of the kingdoms that arose from the ruins of his empire. Yet in building royal power, the rulers of Germany faced a different set of problems than did the kings of England and France. When the last Carolingian died in 911, the German nobles claimed the right to elect the next king.

Otto the Great (936–973) In 919, the Duke of Saxony, known as Henry the Fowler, was elected king. He ruled until 939, winning several important victories over the Slavs and the Magyars. (One of Henry's distant descendants was the emperor Henry IV, who begged the pope's forgiveness at Canossa.)

Map Study

Which ruler appears to have been more powerful, the king of France or the king of England? What are the two largest empires shown?

The Kingdoms of Europe in 1160

KEY
Lands held directly by the Capetian family
☼ Battle

Map Study answers: the king of England; Holy Roman and Byzantine empires

The strongest ruler of medieval Germany was Henry's son Otto I, known as Otto the Great. Otto, who became king in 936, consciously copied the policies of his boyhood hero, Charlemagne. He even chose to be crowned king at Charlemagne's old capital, Aachen.

Otto ended the threat of Magyar raids by crushing the Magyars at the Battle of Lechfield in 955. He also set about building up his own power within Germany.

Like other medieval kings, Otto's greatest problem was the power of the nobles within his kingdom. To limit that power, Otto turned for support to the bishops and abbots of the Church. These churchmen were themselves feudal lords with armies of knights at their command.

Otto was able to dominate the Church in Germany by granting fiefs only to loyal bishops and abbots. He made his brother archbishop of Cologne and his son archbishop of Mainz. With armies drawn from Church lands, Otto overpowered the great princes of Germany.

Despite this success, Otto still yearned to be crowned emperor as Charlemagne had been in 800. In 951 and again in 962, he invaded Italy. Italian towns such as Genoa, Pisa, and Venice had grown wealthy from trade with Asia, and they were a powerful bait for the German emperor. During his second invasion, Otto entered Rome to defend the pope from an Italian duke. This time, the pope rewarded Otto with the imperial crown he coveted.

The German-Italian empire created by Otto was known first as the Roman Empire of the German Nation and later as the Holy Roman Empire. It remained the strongest state in Europe until about 1100. In the long run, though, Otto's attempt to revive Charlemagne's empire caused trouble for later German kings. Italian nobles resented German rule. Popes too came to fear the political power of the German kings in Italy. As you have read, Henry IV of Germany nearly lost his crown in a long power struggle with the pope over lay investiture (page 216).

During that struggle, German princes regained much of the power they had lost under Otto. Thus, a later German ruler would have to begin again to build up royal authority. That ruler was Frederick Barbarossa.

Frederick Barbarossa (1152–1190) Seven German princes had the right to elect the German king. By 1152, even these princes realized that Germany needed a strong king to keep the peace. They chose Frederick I. A handsome, golden-haired man and a great warrior, Frederick was the ideal medieval king. His red beard earned him the nickname *Barbarossa* (Italian for "red beard").

Frederick was the first ruler to call his lands the Holy Roman Empire. Yet what he really ruled was not so much an empire as a patchwork of feudal territories. By his own forceful personality and his skill as a soldier, Frederick was able to control the German princes. But whenever he was out of the country, disorder returned.

Frederick did not concentrate on building royal power in Germany. Instead, like Otto the Great, he turned his attention south to the rich cities of Italy. Frederick invaded Italy repeatedly, spreading destruction wherever he went. His brutal tactics led Italian merchants to set aside their differences and unite against him. Also fearful of Frederick, the pope joined with the merchants. Together, Frederick's enemies formed an alliance called the Lombard League.

In 1176, the foot soldiers of the Lombard League faced Frederick's army of mounted knights at the Battle of Legnano (lay-NYAHN-oh). The German knights suffered a smashing defeat. For the first time, foot soldiers defeated feudal knights. The Battle of Legnano showed that towns could wield military as well as economic power. It was an omen for the future.

In 1179, Frederick made peace with the pope and returned to Germany. By that time, however, he had lost his chance to limit the power of the German princes. Their power continued to grow in spite of Frederick's efforts. After he drowned in 1190, his empire was torn to pieces.

Therefore, unlike England and France, Germany did not become a united country during the Middle Ages. There were several reasons why German kings failed to unite their country. First, the system of electing the king weakened Germany. It made the nobles more powerful than the king. Second, German rulers had fewer royal lands to use as a base of power than did the kings of France and England. Third, German kings continued to try to revive Charlemagne's empire by involving themselves in Italian politics. This policy led to wars not only with Italian cities but also with the pope.

Frederick Barbarossa remained a popular figure of folklore. Legend grew up after his death that, like Arthur of England, he was not dead but was sleeping somewhere in a German cave, ready to awake when Germany needed him again.

223

Section Review 3

Define: (a) jury, (b) common law
Identify: (a) William the Conqueror,
(b) Harold Godwinson, (c) Battle of Hastings,
(d) Henry II, (e) Hugh Capet, (f) Otto the
Great, (g) Holy Roman Empire, (h) Frederick
Barbarossa, (i) Battle of Legnano
Answer:
1. How did William the Conqueror lay the basis
   for strong central government in England?
2. How did Henry II's royal courts strengthen
   the king's power over the lords?
3. Describe the proceedings at a jury trial in
   medieval England.
4. Give two factors that strengthened the Capetian dynasty.
5. How did German rulers succeed to the throne?
6. (a) How did Otto the Great make the crown
   stronger than the German nobles? (b) What
   problems did Otto's policies create for his
   successors?

Critical Thinking
7. Look at a map of modern Europe. Suppose
   that the descendants of William the Conqueror
   and of Otto I had succeeded in holding the
   lands these two men ruled. How might the
   map of Europe be different today?

Learning revived and spread. 4

As kings grew more powerful, they needed
officials trained in law and record keeping for
their growing governments. At first, most royal
officials came from the Church, because few
others could read or write. By the late 1100's,
however, literacy was spreading to people outside
the Church. Just as Europe's material prosperity
was growing, so was European interest in learning.

Scholars gathered at universities.

At the center of the new growth of learning
stood an institution that was new to Europe—
the university. Athens, Alexandria, Baghdad, and
Constantinople had all had their universities,
but never before had such a center of learning
existed in western Europe. The first universities
in Europe were not ivy-covered buildings on green
campuses. The word *university* originally meant
a group of scholars. People, not buildings, made
up the medieval university.

Universities had arisen at Paris, France, and
Bologna, Italy, by the end of the 1100's. (The
exact dates are uncertain.) Others followed at
Oxford, England, and Salerno, Italy.

Most students came from middle-class families,
not from the nobility. They were the sons of
burghers or well-to-do artisans. (Girls could not
attend.) For most students, the goal was a job
in government or the Church.

Since the university had no buildings, classes
met in rented rooms or in the choir section of
a church. Lucky students sat on a bench. Most
squatted on the straw-covered floor as they tried
to memorize the master's lecture. Because writing
materials were scarce, all exams were oral.

As much as they might love books, few students
could afford to own even one. Because all books
were handwritten, a single book cost the equivalent of $600 or $700. Many students rented
their textbooks, but even this was too costly for
some. Often the only textbook for a course belonged to the teacher who read it aloud, line by
line, and offered his own comments.

To earn a bachelor's degree, students spent 3
to 5 years in school before taking a final exam.
A master's degree required an additional 3 to 4
years (in Paris, as long as 15 years). With such
a degree, however, a scholar could teach anywhere
in Europe. There was no language barrier since
scholars everywhere spoke Latin.

Scholars rediscovered Greek writings.

The revival of learning made Europeans more
interested in the works of ancient scholars. At
the same time, the growth of trade brought Europeans into contact with Muslims and Byzantines. In those empires, the writings of the old
Greek philosophers had survived.

Christian scholars from Europe began visiting
Muslim libraries in Toledo, Spain. There, Jewish
scholars translated Arabic copies of Aristotle and
other Greek writers into Latin. From Constantinople, Europeans brought home Latin translations of Justinian's code of laws. All at once,

Henry I of England who ruled from 1100 to 1135 was known as Beaclerc or "Good
Scholar" because he could write his name. His great grandson, Richard I, who
ruled from 1189 to 1197, was a skilled poet. Thus the progress of learning was apparent
even in the royal family.

Europeans acquired a huge new body of knowledge on science, philosophy, law, and religion.

Christian scholars were excited by the Greek writings but also deeply troubled by them. After all, the ancient Greeks had been pagans. Their knowledge was not based on the Bible but on their own powers of reasoning. Could a Christian scholar use Aristotle's logical approach to truth and still keep faith with the Bible? This was the debate that shook scholars in the 1100's.

Aquinas linked faith and reason.

In the mid-1200's, the scholar Thomas Aquinas (uh-KWYE-nuhs) found no conflict between faith and reason. He believed that the most basic religious truths could be proved by logical argument.

Born in 1225 in Italy, Thomas Aquinas joined the Dominicans when he was about 18 years old. He then went to the University of Paris. After his studies, he stayed to teach there.

Between 1267 and 1273, Aquinas created a scholarly work of colossal scope called the *Summa Theologiae*. In its 21 volumes, he attempted to answer 631 philosophical questions about God and the universe. For each question, he used logic and reason to show the truth of the Church's answer and to refute any other answers. The *Summa Theologiae* was like a cathedral of scholarship. Its stones were reasoned arguments, but it rose from the same foundation as Chartres Cathedral—a foundation of faith.

Poems praised knightly heroes.

Learning was also reviving outside the Church. Most feudal lords cared little about the debate over reason and faith, but they enjoyed the heroic poems known as *chansons de geste* (songs of deeds). Sung to the accompaniment of a lute, each song celebrated a warrior-hero. Unlike learned writings, these poems were not in Latin but in the languages people spoke every day.

One of the earliest and most famous of the heroic poems was the Song of Roland. It praised the courage of the band of French soldiers led by Roland who perished in battle during Charlemagne's reign (page 195). Although the actual battle had been against bandits, the poem transformed it into a battle between a few French

Daily Life · *Medieval Writing Materials*

"Finished, thank God." Medieval students, who sometimes acquired books by renting and then copying them letter by letter, often added these words of relief to their last page. The process of copying a book was indeed a long and painstaking one. It began with the purchase of the paperlike material called parchment or vellum, made from the skin of lambs, calves, or kids. However, a student could not simply sit down with his sheets of vellum and begin to write. The vellum was usually rough when he bought it. The student had to scrape it with a knife or razor, sprinkle it with chalk, and rub it smooth and white with a rough stone. Then, with a ruler and a pointed tool, he drew grooves in the vellum to mark off lines and margins.

The student made his own ink from black soot, charcoal, or bark. His inkwell was a cow's horn set into a round hole in his writing board, and he wrote with the point of a goose feather. He would dip his pen into the ink, write a line, and then, if the weather was damp, dry the ink with the heat from a basin of coals. If he made a mistake, he would scrape it off with a knife and rub the area smooth again with a boar's tooth.

mover, and God is the First Mover. All things are caused by something else, and God is the First Cause. The work of Aquinas is still the foundation of Catholic theology today.

225

Guests at this wedding banquet in the 1400's ate almost everything with their fingers. For cutting, they used the daggers that they carried all the time. For entertainment, minstrels played from a gallery above the banquet hall.

knights and an overwhelming army of Muslims from Spain. Many an evening, lords and knights heard the familiar tale. They applauded the valor of Roland's friend, Turpin, a warrior-bishop. Surrounded by enemies, Turpin fights on:

Turpin of Reims feels himself overcome,
His body pierced by four spears.
Yet he gets quickly to his feet,
Looks for Roland, runs to him,
And says one thing: "I am not beaten yet.
While life remains, no good knight gives up."

The Song of Roland celebrated courage in battle, but later tales had wider scope. Stories about King Arthur and his knights dealt with battle but also with issues of pride, loyalty, and justice. The story of Tristan and Isolde, like many poems of the period, dealt with ill-fated love.

Poems show how the ideals of noble society were changing. In the early days, little was asked of a knight other than courage in battle and loyalty to his lord. By the High Middle Ages, however, knights were expected to live up to a complex set of ideals. These ideals became known as the code of **chivalry** (SHIH-vuhl-ree).

Knights lived by a code of chivalry.

The word *chivalry* comes from the French word *cheval* (horse) and *chevalier* (horse-riding lord). The code demanded that a knight fight bravely in the defense of three masters: his earthly feudal lord, his heavenly Lord, and his chosen lady. Furthermore, a knight should aid the poor and defend the weak. Few knights actually met these standards. Even so, the ideals of chivalry helped raise European civilization to a new level.

A knight's education The education of a young nobleman began at age seven when his parents sent him off to the castle of another lord, possibly a relative. Here he acted as a page, waiting on his hosts and learning manners. In his free hours, he played with fellow pages at fencing, hunting, and chess. Before 1250, pages seldom were taught to read, since this skill was thought unmanly. (Girls learned music and weaving because these were judged to be feminine arts.)

At around the age of 14, the page was raised to the rank of squire. He now waited on a knight of the household, helping him with his armor and weapons. The squire also practiced his own skills with sword and lance on horseback. The

226

Castles were cold, uncomfortable places to live. Flies and mosquitoes swarmed into the open slits in walls that served as windows. Only a few rooms had fireplaces and beds. Most people in castles slept on mats in corners, halls, and courtyards.

squire accompanied the knight on the hunt and in battle.

Becoming a knight A squire became a full-fledged knight when he was about 21 years old. First, to wash away impurities of soul and body, he had an elaborate bath. He spent a day fasting and a night praying in church. Then he knelt before the lord of the manor, who dubbed him a knight by slapping him on the shoulder with the flat of a sword. The new knight was hoisted onto his horse and galloped joyously around the church.

Mock battles for glory After being dubbed a knight, most young men traveled with companions for a year or two. They gained experience fighting in local wars or taking part in mock battles called tournaments.

In a tournament, two armies of knights charged each other, accompanied by the blare of trumpets and the cheers of lords and ladies. As in real war, prisoners captured in the tournament were held for ransom by their captor.

The idea of romantic love arose.

Before 1100, knights seemed interested only in winning the admiration of fellow men. In the Song of Roland and other heroic poems, women played a minor role. Then, in the 1100's, a whole new set of ideals evolved. Under the code of chivalry, a knight's duty to his lady became fully as important as his duty to his lord. Indeed, in many poems, the hero's difficulty resulted from a conflict between the two duties.

Poets called troubadours (TROO-buh-DOHRZ) sang the praises of noble ladies and the knights who loved them. Sometimes troubadours sang their own verses in the castles of their lady. Other times they sent roving minstrels to carry their song to court.

Southern France was the homeland of the first troubadours. The most celebrated woman of the age was Eleanor of Aquitaine (1122–1204). Troubadours flocked to her court in the French duchy of Aquitaine. Later, as queen of England, Eleanor was the mother of Richard the Lionheart. Richard himself composed romantic songs and poems. Eleanor's daughter, Marie of Champagne, made love into a subject of study like logic or law. She presided at a famed Court of Love to which troubled lovers brought their grievances.

The role of women changed.

The idea of romantic love placed women on a pedestal where they could be worshiped. Yet women in the High Middle Ages probably had less real power than in earlier years. It is true that Eleanor of Aquitaine ruled England at times for her husband, Henry II, and later for her sons Richard and John. Few other women, however, had such opportunities.

As society became more peaceful and organized, women's roles were increasingly limited to the home and the convent. More and more often, lords passed down their fiefs only to their sons. Women held less property. As royal judges and officials gained power, queens shared less in ruling the land.

Girls from noble families were usually married around the age of 16, often to men in their 30's, 40's, or 50's. (Young men could not marry until they had property of their own, usually after their fathers died.) The girls themselves had little to say in the choice of a husband.

After marriage, a woman had her greatest power and independence while her husband was away at war. After 1100, as you will read in the next section, many knights left home for years to fight in the Crusades. In their absence, women often held power, but usually unofficially.

These women are breaking flax to get fibers to spin into thread and then weave into cloth.

Discuss: How is castle-siege warfare different from the type of wars Europe suffered during the barbarian invasions of the late Roman empire? The Viking raids? Modern war? Focus attention on civilian involvement.

Section Review 4

Define: (a) university, (b) chivalry, (c) page, (d) squire, (e) tournament, (f) troubadour
Identify: (a) Thomas Aquinas, (b) *Summa Theologiae*, (c) *Song of Roland*, (d) Eleanor of Aquitaine
Answer:
1. Why was learning difficult for students in a medieval university?
2. (a) How did scholars in western Europe become familiar with the writings of the ancient Greeks? (b) What problem did Christian scholars see in these writings? (c) What was the importance of the *Summa Theologiae?*
3. Describe the process by which a young nobleman learned to become a knight.
4. How did the role of women change during the Middle Ages?

Critical Thinking
5. Explain why the ideas of chivalry and romantic love were signs of a less warlike age.

Crusaders marched against Islam. 5

Near Clermont in southern France, a crowd of nobles and churchmen gazed upward at Pope Urban II as he addressed them from a wooden platform. His voice boomed forth:

From the confines of Jerusalem and from Constantinople, a grievous report has gone forth that an accursed race has violently invaded the lands of these Christians, and has depopulated them by pillage and fire.

The year was 1095. The "accursed race" was the Seljuk Turks who had recently stormed Baghdad, taken Jerusalem, and conquered all of Asia Minor from the Byzantine Greeks. The Byzantine emperor, Alexius Comnenus, appealed for assistance against the Turks. In response, the pope called on the knights of Christendom to rescue Jerusalem and the Holy Land (that is, the lands where Jesus had lived) from the Muslim Turks. Urban II's speech—one of the most influential in history—concluded:

Jerusalem is a land fruitful above all others, a paradise of delights. That royal city, situated at the center of the earth, implores you to come to her aid. Undertake this journey eagerly for the remission of your sins, and be assured of the reward of imperishable glory in the Kingdom of Heaven.

A feeling of intense excitement swept through the crowd. "God wills it!" someone shouted. Soon everyone was roaring, "God wills it! God wills it!" Thus began the First Crusade. Over the next two centuries, there were eight official Crusades and countless unofficial ones.

The Crusades had many causes.

In 1096, between 50,000 and 60,000 knights became **crusaders.** A crusader is someone who fights on behalf of a religious cause. The crusaders painted red crosses on their armor and marched eastward on a journey from which few would return. The ambitions of three groups fueled the Crusades.

The pope's goals Urban II, like Gregory VII before him, claimed to be the leader of all Christendom. What better way to show the pope's power than to send an army of knights from all Europe's kingdoms on a holy war?

Urban II also hoped to reunite Byzantine and Roman Christians. The Byzantine empire, though Christian, denied that the pope was the supreme head of the Church. Urban II still hoped to heal this breach. Perhaps a successful Crusade would persuade the Byzantines to unite with Roman Catholics under Urban's banner.

The knights' goals Most knights probably had mixed motives for joining the crusaders' army. Especially in the First Crusade, many were fired by religious zeal. If they died on the Crusade, the pope promised forgiveness for their sins. For other knights, the Crusades were a chance to win glory in battle. Earthly rewards were also tempting. Rich plunder awaited any army strong enough to conquer the cities of the Holy Land.

The merchants' goals Merchants played little part in the early Crusades, but after 1200 their influence grew. Some merchants supported the Crusades with gifts or loans of cash. Others used their ships to transport armies over the sea, often for a hefty fee. The merchants of Pisa, Genoa,

Historian Edward Gibbon called the Crusades "the world's debate." Have the class discuss the meaning of this and also the extent to which the debate continues today.

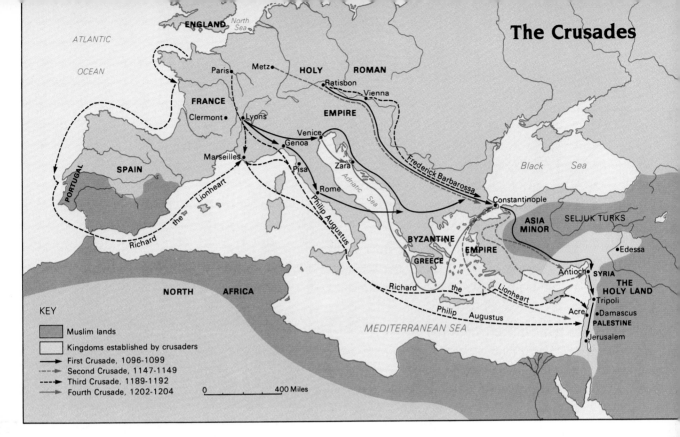

ENGLAND
North Sea
ATLANTIC
OCEAN
Paris
Metz
HOLY ROMAN
Ratisbon
Vienna
FRANCE
Clermont
Lyons
EMPIRE
Venice
Genoa
Marseilles
Zara
Black Sea
Pisa
Frederick Barbarossa
SPAIN
PORTUGAL
Rome
Adriatic Sea
Constantinople
Richard the Lionheart
Philip Augustus
BYZANTINE
ASIA MINOR
SELJUK TURKS
GREECE
EMPIRE
Edessa
Antioch
SYRIA
NORTH AFRICA
Richard the Lionheart
THE HOLY LAND
Philip Augustus
Tripoli
Damascus
Acre
PALESTINE
MEDITERRANEAN SEA
Jerusalem

KEY
Muslim lands
Kingdoms established by crusaders
First Crusade, 1096-1099
Second Crusade, 1147-1149
Third Crusade, 1189-1192
Fourth Crusade, 1202-1204
0   400 Miles

Map Study

Of the three great kings who set out on the Third Crusade, which one took an overland route? Which crusade never reached the Holy Land?

and Venice were eager to win control of key trade routes. For centuries, Muslim traders had ruled the cities of Antioch, Damascus, and Jerusalem. If Christians held those trade centers, more wealth would flow to European merchants.

The First Crusade won Jerusalem.

By early 1097, three huge armies of knights had gathered outside the walls of Constantinople. Most of the crusaders came from France, but there were Germans, Englishmen, Scots, Italians, and Spaniards. They were led by French counts and bishops, not by kings.

The crusaders were well prepared for battle. However, they were woefully unprepared for the trek over the desert to Jerusalem. For two years, they suffered from heat, thirst, hunger, and fever. Yet they somehow mustered enough strength to capture several cities along their route. (Many of their victories were made possible by the fact that the Muslims were fighting among themselves, Arab against Turk.)

Finally, a bedraggled troop of about 12,000 knights (less than one fourth the original army) approached Jerusalem. They besieged the city for a month, sometimes praying and marching barefoot around its walls. Finally, on July 15, 1099, they captured the city.

A dreadful slaughter followed, as Muslim men and women were chased through the streets and murdered. The Jews of the city were rounded up, herded into a temple, and burned to death. One eyewitness reported:

Piles of heads, hands, and feet were to be seen in the streets of the city . . . But these were small matters compared to what happened at the Temple of Solomon [where] men rode in blood up to their knees and bridle reins.

All in all, the crusaders had won a narrow strip of land stretching about 400 miles from Edessa in the north to Jerusalem in the south. Four feudal states were carved out of this territory, each ruled by a French duke or count.

Crusaders defended their conquests in the Holy Land by building great castles like Krak des Chevaliers in Syria (above). At left, a wife welcomes her husband home; he wears a cross, the symbol of a crusader.

Later Crusades accomplished little.

The crusaders' states were extremely vulnerable to Muslim counterattack. In 1144, Edessa was reconquered by the Turks. The Second Crusade was organized to recapture the city, but its armies straggled home in defeat.

In 1187, Europeans were shocked by the news that Jerusalem itself had fallen to a Muslim conqueror named Saladin (SAL-uh-dihn). This event touched off appeals by the Church for yet a third Crusade.

The Third Crusade was known as the Kings' Crusade because three of Europe's most powerful monarchs took the cross: the French king Philip Augustus, the German emperor Frederick I (Barbarossa), and the English king Richard I (the Lionheart). Of these three, only Richard won fame. Crossing a river, the 67-year-old Barbarossa fell from his horse and drowned. Philip Augustus caught a fever and went home.

King Richard fought valiantly to regain the Holy Land. In the process, he discovered that his foe, Saladin, could be as chivalrous as himself. Hearing that Richard was ill, Saladin sent his own personal physician and a refreshing gift of snow and peaches. The two leaders came to respect each other and in 1192 agreed to a three-year truce. Jerusalem remained under Muslim control, but Saladin promised that unarmed Christian pilgrims could freely visit the city's holy places.

Crusaders sacked Constantinople.

In 1202, a powerful pope named Innocent III appealed for still another Crusade to rescue Jerusalem from the Muslims. But the knights who took part in this Fourth Crusade never came close to Jerusalem. Instead, they became entangled in Byzantine and Italian politics.

The merchants of Venice were the main culprits in this disaster. They promised to furnish the crusaders with ships and money for their journey to the Holy Land. In exchange, the crusaders were to attack one of Venice's trading rivals—the island of Zara in the Adriatic Sea. The pope protested this diversion but was ignored. The crusaders took Zara. The pope struck back by excommunicating them.

The pope withdrew his excommunication of the crusaders shortly afterward and allowed them to continue.

Next, the crusaders moved against Constantinople and the unfriendly Byzantine emperor. The city, split between rival leaders, could not defend itself well. When the crusaders entered the city, they went on a savage spree of looting. They stole the relics from Hagia Sophia and loaded the jewel-studded communion table onto a Venetian ship. (The ship sank and its priceless cargo was never recovered.) The looters set fires that burned much of the city, including libraries with priceless ancient manuscripts. The sack of Constantinople in 1204 ended the Fourth Crusade.

European crusaders controlled Constantinople for 57 years, until the Greeks drove them out in 1261 and restored the Byzantine empire. The breach between the Eastern Orthodox Church and the Roman Catholic Church widened into an ugly and permanent split.

The crusading spirit dwindled.

In the 1200's, Crusades became almost as common as medieval fairs and tournaments. In several later Crusades, armies marched not to the Holy Land but to North Africa. The Fifth Crusade (1218–1221), the Seventh Crusade (1248–1254), and the Eighth Crusade (1270) were all aimed at Islamic cities in Egypt and North Africa. The French king who led the last two Crusades, Louis IX, won wide respect in Europe and was later declared a saint. None of these attempts accomplished much, however.

Of all the later Crusades, the Sixth Crusade (1228–1229) came nearest to success. The Holy Roman emperor, Frederick II, led an army to the Holy Land. There Frederick met with Saladin's nephew and peacefully negotiated a treaty by

which Jerusalem was returned to Christian rule. The pope, however, was not pleased. He called the treaty a pact with the devil and excommunicated Frederick.

The Christians' last stronghold in the Holy Land, the city of Acre, fell to the Muslims in 1291. By that time, many Europeans had become cynical about Crusades. Several popes had tried to use them against their religious or political enemies in Europe. For example, Innocent III declared a crusade against the emperor Frederick II.

In the Crusades, all the forces of Europe's revival had come together with explosive energy. The Crusades grew from the forces of religion, feudalism, and chivalry. Yet by 1300, fewer and fewer people were answering the crusading call. People expected their kings to rule wisely at home rather than to set off on knightly adventures. Merchants did not want their flourishing trade interrupted by war. People's loyalty to the idea of Christendom lessened as new loyalties to their own lands of England, France, or Spain grew. The end of the Crusades signaled that the Middle Ages were drawing to a close.

Footnote to History

In 1212, a German boy named Nicholas convinced many children that they could succeed where armies of knights had failed. Some 20,000 German children set out for Jerusalem believing that the Holy Land would fall to them without a fight. As they crossed the Alps into Italy, many died of hunger. Finally, a bishop persuaded some to go home. Others remained in Italy, where some fell into the hands of dishonest shipowners who sold the young crusaders into slavery in North Africa.

Section Review 5

Define: crusader
Identify: (a) Urban II, (b) Jerusalem, (c) Holy Land, (d) Byzantine empire, (e) Saladin, (f) Richard the Lionheart, (g) Constantinople, (h) Frederick II, (i) Innocent III
Answer:
1. What were the Crusades?
2. What reasons did each of the following have for supporting the Crusades? (a) the pope (b) knights (c) merchants
3. Based on the original goals of the crusaders, which crusade was the most successful?
4. (a) Why was the Third Crusade called the Kings' Crusade? (b) What new view might it have given the crusaders of the Muslims?
5. What happened on the Fourth Crusade?
6. What caused interest in crusading to die down after 1200?

Critical Thinking
7. What factors may have contributed to the crusaders' violence when they reached Jerusalem on the First Crusade?

231

Chapter Review 10

Summary

1. Farming improved and trade revived. Better farming methods made it possible for farmers to grow more food, which brought a population increase in the High Middle Ages. People began to move into towns. Trade expanded, and guilds formed for both merchants and artisans.

2. Religious leaders wielded great power. The great Gothic cathedrals that soared heavenward in many cities were symbols of the Church's power. Yet this power did not go unchallenged. For decades, kings and popes engaged in power struggles.

3. Royal governments grew stronger. England and France developed the basis for strong central governments. Despite the efforts of some strong German rulers, however, Germany did not become united.

4. Learning revived and spread. Europe's first universities developed in the High Middle Ages. Interest in learning grew in part as a result of the rediscovery of ancient Greek writings. Medieval society became more refined as chivalry and romantic love brought changes in knighthood and the view of women.

5. Crusaders marched against Islam. In 1095, the pope called for Christians to go to war to regain the Holy Land. Although the First Crusade captured Jerusalem, later ventures accomplished little.

Reviewing the Facts

1. Define the following terms:
   a. burghers
   b. bourgeoisie
   c. fair
   d. guild
   e. apprentice
   f. journeyman
   g. cardinal
   h. interdict
   i. canon law
   j. friar
   k. jury
   l. common law
   m. chivalry
   n. crusader

2. Explain the importance of each of the following names, dates, places, or terms:
   a. three-field system
   b. Cluny
   c. Canossa
   d. Concordat of Worms
   e. Inquisition
   f. Gothic
   g. William the Conqueror
   h. 1066
   i. Henry II
   j. Hugh Capet
   k. Otto the Great
   l. Frederick Barbarossa
   m. Holy Roman Empire
   n. Thomas Aquinas
   o. Constantinople
   p. Jerusalem
   q. Saladin

3. How did changes in farming lead to an overall change in medieval life?

4. What purposes did guilds serve?

5. Why did the appointment of bishops become the issue in a struggle between kings and popes?

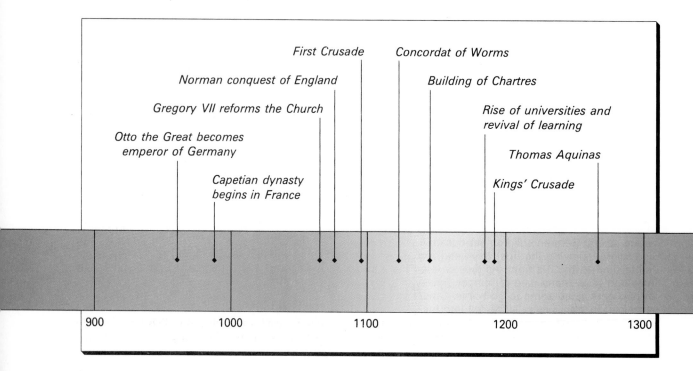

First Crusade

Norman conquest of England

Concordat of Worms

Gregory VII reforms the Church

Building of Chartres

Otto the Great becomes emperor of Germany

Rise of universities and revival of learning

Capetian dynasty begins in France

Thomas Aquinas

Kings' Crusade

900   1000   1100   1200   1300

6. How did the development of Germany differ from that of England and France?
7. (a) Explain how medieval builders solved the problem of supporting the weight of a church roof without using thick walls. (b) What changes did this improvement allow?
8. What debt did universities owe to each of the following? (a) Jewish and Muslim scholars (b) Byzantine scholars (c) monks
9. (a) Why did the Crusades win wide support in Europe? (b) What did they achieve?

Basic Skills

1. **Acquiring information**   Study the photos on pages 209, 210, and 212 to find information on medieval trades and occupations. (a) Identify as many of these as possible. (b) Describe the various tools and technologies shown.
2. **Summarizing**   Summarize the changes in European civilization during the High Middle Ages by writing a paragraph on political changes, another on economic changes, and a third on social changes.
3. **Reading a map**   Using the map on page 229, identify for each of the four Crusades the points of origin, the routes taken, and the destinations.

Researching and Reporting Skills

1. **Translating information**   Write a 50-word advertisement or make a poster for a medieval fair to be held in Chartres on October 25, 1250.
2. **Identifying sources**   If you were researching the Crusades, which of the following sources would you consult: (a) a history of Europe in the tenth century, (b) a history of Venice in the Middle Ages, (c) a biography of Peter Abelard, (d) an article on women in the twelfth century, (e) a history of the Church in English society from 1400 to 1600, (f) a history of medieval armament? Give reasons for your choices.

Critical Thinking

1. **Inferring**   (a) What do you think caused the growth of chivalry in the Middle Ages? (b) What were some of the consequences?
2. **Synthesizing**   Give a brief assessment of the role of women during the Middle Ages. Provide two examples of situations in which they could exercise power or rights and two examples of situations illustrating their lack of power or rights.
3. **Evaluating**   The heading on page 222 states that German kings failed to unite their lands. Yet the map on the same page shows the Holy Roman Empire covering the Germanic kingdom as one unified block. How can you explain these apparent differences?
4. **Analyzing outcomes**   The growth of cities and trade aided the development of guilds. (a) How might the growth of guilds affect the relationship between the king and the nobles? (b) How might it affect personal rights?
5. **Interpreting**   According to your text, the medieval Church resembled a kingdom in many ways. (a) Identify three activities of the Church that resembled those of a government. (b) What powers did the pope have that could intervene between a king and his subjects?

Perspectives on Past and Present

1. If you were a student at a medieval university, how would your experience differ from that of a student today?
2. Two excellent movies, *The Lion in Winter* and *Becket*, depict the struggle for political power by Henry II of England. Watch the videotape of one film. What problems does Henry face? How does he deal with them?

Investigating History

1. Investigate the medieval past of London, Paris, Brussels, Antwerp, Cologne, or some other European city of your choice. For that city, locate a traveler's guidebook that identifies cathedrals, castles, guild halls, or other sites dating back to medieval times. Prepare an oral report or written description of your findings.
2. Two powerful leagues of cities were formed during the Middle Ages—the Hanseatic League and the Lombard League. Find information about one of these leagues. What were its objectives? What cities were members? Where did its members trade, and what products did they trade?
3. Look up the *Song of Roland* or the tales of King Arthur and his Knights of the Round Table. Write a short essay describing how that literary work expresses the ideal of chivalry.

Chapter 11

The Origin of European Nations

There are no pictures of Joan of Arc that were drawn during her lifetime. This picture is one of the earliest. It appeared in a book called Lives of Famous Women, written in 1505, about 75 years after her death.

Read and Understand

1. England and France developed as nations.
2. The Church faced a crisis in the 1300's.
3. The 1300's brought plague and war.
4. New monarchs ruled in western Europe.
5. A new empire arose in Russia.

Key Terms

nation-state
nationalism
czar
boyar

In April 1429, French peasants peered from their houses and fields as a small army of perhaps 4,000 soldiers moved across the war-torn countryside of northern France. Armies were no novelty to these peasants. France and England had been at war since 1337, and English armies had tramped all over France. This particular army, however, was something new. It was French. Its leader was not a hard-bitten captain but a black-haired, fair-faced peasant girl of 17 who called herself Joan the Maid. She is known to history as Joan of Arc.

Before accepting the aid of Joan of Arc, Charles VII, taken aback by the young girl who heard voices from heaven, had her questioned and found trustworthy by a committee of clergy.

Joan had come to save the French city of Orleans, which the English had been besieging for the past six months. Without help, the city's defenders could not hold out much longer. When Joan reached the threatened city, she sent a message to the English:

You, men of England, who have no right in the kingdom of France, the King of Heaven sends the order through me, Joan the Maid, to return to your own country.

The arrival of this heroic young woman had an electrifying effect on the townspeople of Orleans. They hailed her as champion of all France against the English enemies.

Early in the morning of May 7, 1429, Joan buckled on her white armor. She took up her white linen banner decorated with angels and the lilies of France. The English had built forts blocking the roads into Orleans. Marching against these forts, following Joan's banner into battle, the French army attacked.

You will read later in the chapter whether Joan of Arc and her soldiers won or lost their fight for France. From a historical point of view, the outcome of the battle was less important than its cause. Joan and the men who followed her in 1429 were fighting for a cause that was new to Europe and the world. They were *not* fighting for one feudal lord against another. Unlike the crusaders of an earlier century, they were *not* fighting for Christianity against Muslim enemies. Instead, they were French people fighting in defense of their homeland, France, against a foreign enemy, England.

Joan of Arc had a feeling of loyalty to a nation—a feeling that we call nationalism. It was a new and powerful force in history. How that feeling of national loyalty arose in France and in England during the 1300's and 1400's is a major theme of this chapter.

In part, the growth of national feeling began with the power struggles of medieval kings from about 1200 to about 1500. These rulers fought against the Church, against powerful lords within their own realms, and against rival kings of other countries.

Slowly, these struggles shattered the power of two great medieval institutions—the Church and feudalism. In their place, we see the beginnings of a powerful new institution—the nation.

By 1500, for the first time, we can speak of nations in the modern sense of the word, not just of feudal kingdoms.

Such a fundamental change took a long time to develop. To see how France and England became separate nations—not just separate kingdoms—we must go back in time 300 years before Joan of Arc put on her white armor. The story begins with the feudal wars of England's King Henry II.

England and France developed as nations. 1

In the late 1100's, France and England were a mixture of interconnected feudal lands. In the early 1200's, however, the two countries began to follow separate paths.

England's king lost his French land.

Henry II, king of England from 1154 to 1189, was also feudal lord of more than half of France. From his great-grandfather, William the Conqueror, Henry had inherited Normandy and other lands in northern France. Henry added to his holdings by marrying Eleanor of Aquitaine, the richest heiress in Europe. She brought him fiefs in southern France. For his French lands, Henry was the vassal of France's Capetian king, Louis VII. However, Henry was a better soldier than Louis and often defeated him.

When Henry and Louis died, the story took a different turn. Henry was succeeded first by his son Richard I, the hero of the Third Crusade. A fearless fighter and skilled general, Richard the Lionheart was able to defend his French lands. When Richard died in 1199 after only ten years as king, he was followed by his younger brother, John, who ruled from 1199 to 1216. John was a complete failure as a military leader; indeed, he won the nickname John Softsword. He soon proved to be no match for the wily king who now wore the French crown, Philip II, known as Philip Augustus.

As a child, Philip had watched his father lose battle after battle to Henry II. When Philip became

After one humiliating scene, the boy Philip warned Henry: "I can't hinder you, my lord, but I tell you now that when I am grown up, I will take back all of which you have deprived him." Discuss the motives of other powerful leaders.

235

king in 1180, at the age of 15, he set out to weaken the power of the English kings in France. His greatest triumphs came during John's reign. In 1204, Philip Augustus took Normandy from John. Within two years, he had also won the rest of John's lands in northern France. Only Aquitaine and Gascony in southern France remained loyal to John. By the end of his reign, Philip had tripled the lands under his own direct control. For the first time, a French king was more powerful than any of his vassals. Philip's victories set the stage for England and France to develop as two separate countries.

The barons rebelled against King John.

John's losses in France were just the beginning of his troubles. He soon faced another crisis in England. Some of John's problems stemmed from his own character. According to one historian, John was "selfish, cruel, shameless, cynical, lustful, dishonorable, and utterly false." These character flaws made John's subjects dislike him all the more after his defeats.

In some ways, John's defeats in France proved valuable to England. First, England was gaining an identity as a distinct nation. After John lost Normandy, many lords had to choose whether to hold lands in France or in England. Philip Augustus gave them a year to decide. For those who chose to keep their English lands, England became more important than before. No longer were their interests divided between lands in France and lands in England. Though their ancestors had been Norman, they grew more and more English in customs and loyalty.

John's losses were England's gain for another reason. His unsuccessful wars led directly to the most celebrated document in English history, the Magna Carta.

How did John's wars in France lead to a landmark in English liberty? Wars are always costly. In trying to win back his French lands, John raised taxes to an all-time high. He tried every possible way of squeezing money out of his barons. (The term *barons* includes all the nobles of England who were direct vassals of the king, regardless of their rank. Some were great lords, some were bishops, and a few were simple knights.)

In 1214, John tried again to recover his lands in France. Once again, Philip Augustus defeated him. Soon after John returned to England, his barons revolted. They demanded that John promise to change his ways of governing.

John's situation was hopeless. To keep his crown, he was forced to agree to the barons' terms. Seething with anger, he rode to the appointed meeting place, a broad meadow called Runnymede on the Thames (tehms) River. The barons presented their demands. The date was June 15, 1215, a date that marks a milestone in English history. Four days later, the negotiations between the barons and the king were finished, and John affixed his seal to the document later known as the *Magna Carta* (Great Charter).

The Magna Carta limited royal power.

The English barons were thinking mostly of themselves when they drew up the 63 clauses of the Magna Carta. They wanted to protect themselves from unjust taxes and to safeguard their own feudal rights and privileges. In later years, however, English people of all classes argued that certain clauses in the Magna Carta applied to every citizen.

In the Magna Carta, John made a variety of promises. For example, he agreed to respect the rights and privileges of the city of London. He promised merchants the right to travel freely in and out of England. The most important promises, however, guaranteed what are now considered basic legal rights, both in England and in the United States.

Guarantee of basic rights Clause 12 of the Magna Carta declared that taxes "shall be levied in our kingdom only by the common consent of our kingdom." This clause meant that the king could not arbitrarily demand taxes. He had to have the agreement of his advisers, usually at a meeting of barons called the king's Great Council. In other words, said later generations of English men and women (and eventually, people in the United States), there shall be *no taxation without representation*.

Another important guarantee was stated in Clause 39: "No free man shall be arrested or imprisoned . . . except by the legal judgment of his peers or by the law of the land." In other words, people later claimed, a person had the right to a jury trial and to the protection of the law. (This right to have the law work in known, orderly ways came to be known as *due process of law.*)

The idea of limited monarchy The underlying idea of the Magna Carta was not stated in so many words. It is the idea of limited monarchy. The barons at Runnymede forced their king to recognize limits on his powers. They said that he must follow the established laws and customs of the land. As Winston Churchill, England's great leader of the twentieth century, wrote: "Throughout [Magna Carta] it is implied that here is a law which is above the King and which even he must not break. This [idea] of a supreme law . . . is the great work of Magna Carta; and this alone justifies the respect in which men have held it."

Parliament became part of English government.

John died in 1216, the year after he signed the Magna Carta. He left a young son, only nine years old, who became Henry III. Henry's long and unhappy reign (1216–1272) was marked by more losses in France and further conflicts with the barons.

For a time, it appeared that the strong foundations of England's royal government laid by William the Conqueror and Henry II would be washed away. Near the end of the 1200's, however, one of England's ablest kings restored royal power. Edward I, the son of Henry III and grandson of John, became king in 1272.

During Edward's long reign (1272–1307), he improved administration and strengthened the royal courts. His laws clarified the division of power between the king and the nobles, usually to the king's advantage.

Edward was able to limit the power of the troublesome barons. One reason for the barons' power had been the king's dependence on them for money. Now times were changing. Edward I was perhaps the first king to realize it. With the growth of towns and trade, it was easier to raise taxes from the middle-class burghers (or *burgesses* as the English called them) than from the upper-class barons.

In the past, people of the towns had been left out of the king's Great Council, the gathering that approved the royal plans for taxes. Only the great barons and bishops were ordinarily summoned to hear the king's requests for more money. Edward I was the first king to see the advantages of including townspeople in the meeting.

The Model Parliament In 1295, Edward I was planning another war to prevent his last remaining French lands from being conquered by the French king. To raise taxes for that war, Edward needed the support of all influential groups—not just the barons but the townspeople as well. Therefore, the king summoned two burgesses from every borough and two knights from every county to a parliament. According to Edward's royal writ,

The Magna Carta

Edward I sits above the Model Parliament, with churchmen at the left, barons at the right, and burgesses seated on wool sacks in the center.

The strength of Parliament Under Edward I, Parliament was in part a royal tool that weakened the great lords. The knights and burgesses generally sided with the king even when the nobles opposed him. As time went by, however, Parliament became strong enough that, like the Magna Carta, it provided a check on royal power.

England was not the only country to develop something like a parliament. France, as you will read, had a similar group called the Estates General. Spain had an assembly called the Cortes. There were also assemblies in parts of Germany and Italy in the Late Middle Ages. However, England's Parliament proved stronger and longer-lasting than any of the others.

The English Parliament was truly a national assembly. Although its members came from different parts of England, they generally put their loyalty to England ahead of local ties. Their laws applied to the whole country.

Even so, England in 1300 was not yet a true nation. Its kings and barons were bound by the old feudal obligations of lord-to-vassal and vassal-to-lord. As we shall see, it would require 200 years of strife before the feudal order in England finally broke down.

French kings expanded their power.

While England was limiting the power of its kings by the Magna Carta and Parliament, French kings were increasing their power. Early in the 1200's, John's old enemy Philip Augustus did for France what Henry II had already done for England. He gave France a strong central government.

Royal officials called bailiffs (**BAY**-lifs) were sent out from Paris to every district in Philip's kingdom. These bailiffs presided over the king's courts and collected the king's taxes.

Louis IX France's central government was made even stronger during the reign of Philip's grandson, Louis IX. Louis ruled from 1226 to 1270. He came to the throne as a boy of 12, and in his early years, France was actually ruled by his mother, Blanche of Castile. Blanche carried on the work of Philip Augustus, putting down revolts by the nobles and defeating the English.

When Louis IX began to rule on his own, he showed that his mother had taught him well. Better known as Saint Louis, this immensely pious and popular king had a passion for justice.

the so-called commoners of the kingdom were being summoned because "what affects all should be approved by all." (That is, since taxes affected everyone, all groups should be consulted.)

Thus, in November 1295, knights, burgesses, bishops, and lords met together at Westminster in London to consult with the king. Historians refer to this famous gathering as the *Model Parliament* because its new composition (commoners as well as lords) served as a model for later kings.

Over the next century, from 1300 to 1400, the king called the knights and burgesses whenever a new tax was needed. In Parliament, these two groups gradually formed an assembly of their own called the House of Commons. Nobles and bishops met separately as the House of Lords.

Footnote to History

Because the king's councils involved a lot of talk and discussion, they took their name from the French word *parler* (talk); the meetings became known as *parliaments.*

By 1300, England had three unique institutions: its court system, which relied on juries and the Common Law; its tax system, with townspeople and nobles in Parliament; and its monarchy, forced by Magna Carta to respect subjects' rights.

So great was his reputation for honor and fairness that even the king of England, a traditional enemy, once appealed to him to settle a dispute.

Louis created a supreme court for France called the Parlement of Paris. This Parlement could overturn the decisions of local courts. The royal courts of France (like those of England) had a double impact: They strengthened the monarchy while weakening feudal ties.

Philip IV and the Estates General In 1302, the king of France was involved in a quarrel with the pope. The French king was Philip IV, a handsome man whose nickname was Philip the Fair. As in England, the French king usually called a meeting of his lords and bishops when he needed support for his policies. To win wider support against the pope, Philip IV decided to include members of the middle class in the meeting.

In France, church leaders were known as the First Estate and great lords as the Second Estate.

The middle-class representatives that Philip invited to the council became known as the Third Estate. The whole meeting was called the Estates General.

The Estates showed the growing power of the townspeople and the middle class as a whole. Like Parliament in its early years, the Estates helped to increase royal power against the nobility. Unlike Parliament, however, the Estates never became an independent force that limited the king's power.

Nation-states began to arise.

By 1300, France and England were slowly taking new shapes, both geographically and politically. Geographically, each country was beginning to reach the borders that it would have, more or less, for the next 600 years. Politically, the kings of each country were becoming more powerful

Voice from the Past · St. Louis, the Ideal Medieval King

Louis IX was a pious and popular king. In this reading, a French noble, Jean de Joinville, describes him.

This holy man loved God with all his heart, and imitated his works. For example, just as God died because He loved his people, so the king risked his life many times for the love of his people . . . He said once to his eldest son: ". . . I beg you that you make yourself loved by the people of your realm, for truly, I would rather that a Scot came from Scotland and governed the people of the kingdom justly and well than that you should govern them badly . . ." The holy king loved the truth so much that he kept his promises even to the Saracens.

A friar told the king . . . that he had never read that a kingdom was destroyed or changed rulers except through lack of justice . . . The king did not forget this lesson but governed his lands justly and well, according to the will of God . . . Often in summer he went to sit down under an oak-tree in the wood of Vincennes . . . and made us sit around him. And all those who had suits to bring him came up. And he would ask them: "Does anyone here have a suit?" And those who had requests would get up . . . And then he would call Lord Pierre de Fontaines and Lord Geoffroi de Villette and say to one of them: "Settle this affair for me." And if he saw anything to correct in what they said on his behalf, he would do so.

1. What did Louis consider a king's greatest duty to be?
2. Describe the way that Louis dispensed justice.
3. What effect would a ruler like Louis IX have on the monarchy in France?

than the feudal lords beneath them. In both countries, the middle classes—especially the townspeople—were winning a larger share of political power.

Between 1300 and 1500, France and England slowly became a new type of country—a **nation-state**. A nation-state is a group of people who occupy a definite territory and are united under one government. The people of a nation-state are culturally united as well. For example, they generally all speak the same language. Most important, they have a feeling of belonging together and a sense of loyalty to their country.

Section Review 1

Define: (a) baron, (b) limited monarchy, (c) burgess, (d) commoner, (e) bailiff, (f) nation-state
Identify: (a) Henry II, (b) John, (c) Philip Augustus, (d) Magna Carta, (e) Edward I, (f) Model Parliament, (g) Geoffrey Chaucer, (h) Louis IX, (i) Philip IV, (j) Estates General
Answer:
1. Explain why the histories of France and England were tightly interwoven during the Late Middle Ages.
2. (a) Why was John of England called John Softsword? (b) What happened when he tried to increase taxes?
3. (a) List two basic rights that the Magna Carta guaranteed. (b) How did the Magna Carta affect the king's power?
4. (a) How did Edward I change the makeup of England's Parliament? (b) How did the House of Lords and the House of Commons differ?
5. How did each of the following French king's increase royal power? (a) Philip Augustus (b) Louis IX (c) Philip IV

Critical Thinking
6. Why is the Magna Carta called a "landmark of English liberty"?
7. What evidence shows that the power of the middle classes was growing both in France and in England?
8. How did the work of Geoffrey Chaucer show that France and England were becoming two separate countries in the 1300's?

The Church faced a crisis in the 1300's. 2

Feudalism and the Church were the two great forces that shaped society in the Middle Ages. As the Middle Ages drew to a close, feudal loyalties were being replaced by national loyalties. The Church too faced a crisis. At the beginning of the 1300's, the papacy seemed as strong as ever. Soon, however, both pope and Church were in desperate trouble.

Boniface VIII overreached himself.

The pope in 1300 was an able but stubborn Italian named Boniface VIII. Boniface well remembered the triumphs of past popes over kings and emperors. He did not realize, however, that these earlier power struggles had weakened the spiritual prestige of the pope. Boniface VIII tried to force the rulers of Europe to obey him as they had obeyed earlier popes.

Already, in 1296, Boniface had issued an official order stating that kings were not to tax the clergy. (Official statements by the pope were called *bulls*.) The bull of 1296 was aimed at the French king Philip IV, who was taxing Church property in France to pay for a war against England. Philip shrugged off the order and continued to tax the Church. Boniface was forced to back down.

A more cautious pope might have taken this setback as a warning. Boniface, however, still believed that the pope was stronger than any king. In 1302, he issued another bull known as *Unam Sanctam*. This bull declared that there were two powers on earth, the temporal (earthly) and the spiritual (heavenly). The spiritual power, he said, was always supreme over temporal power. In short, kings must always obey popes.

Philip merely sneered at this bull. Before Boniface could excommunicate him, the king sent a small army to Italy to kidnap the pope and bring him to France for trial. The pope was taken by surprise when, in September 1303, soldiers burst into his palace at Anagni (ah-NAHN-yee) outside Rome and took him captive. The townspeople of Anagni rescued the pope, but the shock was too much for the elderly Boniface. He died a month later.

240

When his captors arrived at Anagni, Boniface stood firm and told them to murder him if they wanted. So confused were they at the suggestion that they stalled for time, giving the townspeople sufficient time to rescue the pope and drive the captors away.

Never again would a pope be able to force monarchs to obey him. For more than 100 years (1303–1417), the papacy suffered a serious decline.

The popes moved to Avignon.

Philip the Fair went on boldly to capture the papacy itself. In 1305, he persuaded the College of Cardinals to choose a French archbishop as the new pope, Clement V. In 1309, Clement announced that political violence in Rome threatened his life. Therefore, he was moving to the city of Avignon (AV-een-YOHN), right on the borders of France.

Avignon remained the home of the popes for the next 67 years. Yet could a pope rightly rule from any city except Rome? Throughout Europe, Christians were tormented by this question.

Many people concluded that the Avignon popes were mere hirelings of the French kings. The English, the Germans, and the Italians were especially unhappy. They complained that the Church was held captive in Avignon just as, centuries before, the Jews had been held captive in Babylon. Thus, this period in Church history came to be called the "Babylonian captivity."

Visitors to Avignon were shocked by papal extravagance. The pope served dinner on gold and silver plates to guests dressed in costly furs and brocades. He slept on pillows lined with ermine skins. A Spanish churchman wrote, "Whenever I entered the chambers of the churchmen of the papal court, I found brokers and clergy weighing and reckoning the money that lay in heaps before them."

A great schism divided the Church.

The move to Avignon had badly weakened the Church. When reformers finally tried to move the papacy back to Rome, however, the result was even worse.

In 1378, Pope Gregory XI died while visiting Rome. The College of Cardinals then met in Rome to choose a successor. As they deliberated, they could hear a mob outside screaming, "A Roman, a Roman, we want a Roman for a pope, or at least an Italian!" Finally, the cardinals announced to the crowd that an Italian had been chosen: Pope Urban VI. (By his very choice of name, Urban made it clear that he planned to keep the papacy in "the city"—that is, Rome.)

Many cardinals regretted their choice almost immediately. They had not counted on Urban VI's reforming zeal and overbearing personality. After a few months, 13 French cardinals decided to elect another pope. They chose Robert of Geneva, who spoke French. He took the name Clement VII.

Now there were two popes. Each declared the other to be a false pope. Each excommunicated his rival. The French pope moved back to Avignon while the Italian pope remained in Rome. Thus began the split in the Church known as the Great Schism (SIHZ-uhm).

Which was the rightful pope? For political reasons, the French supported the pope in Avignon. On the same basis, the English, the Germans, and the Italians favored the Roman pope. In many parts of Europe, two bishops (one loyal to Clement, the other to Urban) claimed to represent the

Economics in Daily Life ◆ Religion and Trade

The beliefs of the medieval Church directly affected economic activity. Two of those beliefs concerned just price and the prohibition of usury. The concept of just price was stated by Thomas Aquinas: ". . . to sell dearer or to buy cheaper than a thing is worth is in itself unjust and unlawful . . ." Opposition to usury—that is, to interest (payment for the use of money)—was based on the idea that money was lifeless and so could not produce wealth. The Church's focus on real value and the need for charity reflected the insecurity of medieval life.

The cardinals who chose Urban VI actually feared for their lives if they did not elect a Roman.

241

"true" Church. Churchmen at all levels excommunicated one another. People wondered if they had been baptized or married by a true priest.

After Urban and Clement died, rival groups of cardinals in Rome and Avignon continued to elect two popes. The Great Schism lasted from 1378 to 1417.

Two scholars challenged the Church.

Often, when an old source of authority collapses, new ideas arise. In the late 1300's and early 1400's, the most famous thinkers to respond to the crisis of the Church were two professors. One was an Englishman named John Wycliffe (WIHK-lihf), the other a Bohemian named John Huss.

"Christ was meek," wrote John Wycliffe in one of his many pamphlets. But "the pope sits on his throne and makes lords to kiss his feet." From 1360 to 1382, Wycliffe taught religion at the University of Oxford. His radical ideas were discussed widely throughout England. These were Wycliffe's major ideas:

1. The true head of the Church was Jesus Christ, not the pope.
2. Like Jesus and his disciples, the clergy should own no land or wealth. Poverty was better for the Church than riches.
3. The Bible alone—not the pope—was the final authority for Christian life.

How could an English Christian be guided by the Bible when, as late as 1360, it could be read only in Latin or French? Wycliffe answered by translating the New Testament into English.

Because the popes since 1306 had been French and England was often at war with France, Wycliffe became a kind of English national hero by attacking the pope. When an English archbishop tried to charge him with heresy in 1377, there were riots in the London streets. The archbishop was forced to free Wycliffe. Instead of being burned at the stake, he died peacefully in 1384.

John Huss of Bohemia (now part of Czechoslovakia) was not so lucky. Influenced by Wycliffe's writings, Huss taught that the authority of the Bible was higher than that of the pope. Huss became a spokesman for Czech national feeling as well as for religious reform. He preached his sermons in Czech rather than in Latin. In 1411, Huss was excommunicated.

In 1414, Sigismund, the newly elected emperor of Germany, arranged a Church council to end the Great Schism. He urged Huss to attend and even gave him safe conduct. When Huss arrived at the meeting, however, he was seized and tried as a heretic. In spite of the safe conduct, he was burned at the stake in 1415.

A Church council ended the schism.

The gathering that condemned John Huss was known as the Council of Constance (named for the German city where it met). The council's major task was to end the Great Schism by choosing a new pope.

In 1414, when the Council of Constance began its meetings, there were a total of *three* popes. There was the Avignon pope, the Roman pope, and a third pope elected by an earlier council. With the help of the Holy Roman Emperor, the council forced all three popes to resign. In 1417, the council chose a new pope, Martin V. He made good his claim to being the only pope, thus ending the Great Schism.

Where, Christians wondered, was true religious authority—with the pope, with a Church council, or in the Bible? In a later chapter, we shall see how this confusion led to a violent upheaval in the 1500's known as the Reformation.

Section Review 2

Define: (a) papal bull, (b) schism, (c) excommunicate, (d) heretic
Identify: (a) Boniface VIII, (b) Philip IV, (c) Clement V, (d) Avignon, (e) Urban VI, (f) Great Schism, (g) John Wycliffe, (h) John Huss, (i) Council of Constance
Answer:
1. (a) What power did Boniface claim in *Unam Sanctam?* (b) What actions did Philip IV take in response?
2. Why was the period from 1309 to 1376 called the Babylonian captivity?
3. (a) How did the Great Schism begin? (b) What effects did it have? (c) How did it end?
4. What were Wycliffe's three major teachings?
5. (a) How did Huss inspire national feelings among the Czechs? (b) What happened to Huss?

Of the three popes, the pope at Avignon clung the tightest to his title. He retired to Spain where, according to historian Edward Gibbon, he passed his time "excommunicating his enemies three times a day."

6. During the earlier part of the Middle Ages, most European Christians had unquestioning faith in the authority of the Church. How did events in the 1300's change this outlook?

The 1300's brought plague and war. 3

A modern historian has called the 1300's "a violent, tormented, bewildered, suffering, and disintegrating age." During the 1300's, Europeans suffered from a series of disasters including crop failures, a terrifying new disease, and a war that dragged on for years.

Artists of the 1300's depicted death as the Grim Reaper, a skeleton on horseback whose scythe cut people down. It was an apt view. Consider what happened to the city of Barcelona in Spain. Famine struck in 1333; then came the plague in 1347, plague again in 1351, and two more years of famine in 1358 and 1359, followed shortly by another two years of plague in 1362 and 1363.

What brought on these catastrophes? Europe's population had been increasing steadily for more than 300 years. Using new methods such as the horse collar and the three-field system, Europeans had begun farming much new land. By 1300, however, almost all the great forests had been cleared and the swamps had been drained. The soil in many places was losing its fertility. Of course, medieval peasants knew nothing about chemical fertilizers. Year by year, the old fields produced smaller crops.

Moreover, a change was taking place in Europe's climate, though Europeans did not know it. From 1000 to 1300, Europe had enjoyed a time when temperatures were warmer than average. Around 1300, that period ended and temperatures dropped. During this "little ice age," as geologists call it, glaciers slowly advanced over Greenland and parts of Scandinavia. Fall frosts came early to the fields of Europe. The shorter growing season meant smaller harvests and a reduced food supply. Hunger paved the way for even grimmer events.

The great plague of 1348, called the Black Death, killed about a third of the people in Europe. In some cities, nine tenths of the population died. Here the people of Tournai (Belgium) bury their dead.

The Black Death struck in 1347.

In 1347, four Genoese ships arrived in Sicily from the Black Sea. Besides trade goods from Asia, the ships brought a dread cargo—a disease that became known as the Black Death. Soon the illness was sweeping through Italy. From Italy, the outbreak followed trade routes to France, Germany, England, and other parts of Europe.

The victims of this terrible plague had a raging fever. Black swellings grew at their necks and joints. The name *Black Death* came from these swellings. Many victims died within 24 hours. No one had any idea what caused this terrifying outbreak, and medieval doctors were helpless against it. (Modern scholars know that fleas from infected rats spread one form of the plague. Thus, the terrible sanitary conditions in Europe's cities were an important cause of the high death rate.)

Death carts loaded with plague victims soon became a common sight in Europe. Whenever plague broke out, people fled in terror. Yet many were already infected and carried the disease with them to new places.

The death rate was appalling. A churchman visiting Avignon in 1348 wrote:

To put the matter shortly, one half, or more than a half, of the people of Avignon are already dead. Within the walls of the city there are now more than 7,000 houses shut up; in these no one is living, and all who inhabited them have left; the suburbs hardly contain any people at all.

This massive disaster tore medieval society apart. Whole villages disappeared as people either died or fled in fear. Even families were split. Fear of the plague was so great that some parents abandoned their sick children. The Church too failed. Priests were too few (and often too fearful) to give last rites to the dying.

Historians estimate that the plague killed 25 million people—about one third of Europe's population—in the 5 years between 1347 and 1352. The Black Death claimed more lives than any war until the twentieth century. Even more terrible, the plague came back again and again. New outbreaks occurred in 1361, 1369, 1374, 1390, and on into the 1600's. Though never again as severe as the first outbreak, plague became a constant danger.

Peasants rose in revolt.

The decline in population had far-reaching effects. Workers were scarce everywhere. Serfs could demand wages for their work. Thus, landlords could no longer collect their traditional rents and services. As a result, in many places serfdom began to disappear. The manor's economy, based on a fixed labor supply of workers who could not leave, was doomed.

The ruling class fought these changes. Nobles fiercely resisted peasant demands for higher wages. In 1381, peasants in England revolted, burning manors and killing local lords. Similar uprisings took place in France, Italy, and Belgium. In each case, nobles ruthlessly put down the revolts.

Although the peasants did not win the lower taxes or other reforms they wanted, the revolts were important nevertheless. The ideal society of the Middle Ages was gone. No longer was there peace among those who worked, those who prayed, and those who fought.

France and England fought the Hundred Years' War.

War added to the miseries of people in England and France. In 1337 (ten years before the first outbreak of the Black Death), war broke out once more over an English king's claims to land in France. The war lasted, off and on, for 116 years, not ending until 1453. It was called, somewhat inaccurately, the Hundred Years' War. Except for one futile French raid on English shores, the war was fought entirely on French soil.

The Hundred Years' War can be divided into four stages:
1. *1337–1360* Ably led by King Edward III, English forces invaded France. They captured the French king and gained control over much of France.
2. *1361–1396* The French reconquered almost everything the English had won.
3. *1397–1420* The English invaded France again. They conquered the northern half of the country. England's Henry V forced the French king to sign a humiliating treaty.
4. *1421–1453* The French rallied. In 1429, inspired by Joan of Arc, they began a drive that forced the English out of all France, except the western port city of Calais.

Discuss the Grim Reaper as a creation of the medieval imagination. In what ways does the figure represent the interests and concerns of the medieval person?

New weapons changed warfare.

The Hundred Years' War dealt a deathblow to feudal warfare. During the war, new weapons caused a revolution both in warfare and in society.

The longbow The weapon that gave England its early victories in the war was known as the longbow. Before battle, skilled English bowmen ranged themselves, side by side, along a wide arc. Into the ground they drove long, iron-tipped stakes that pointed outward to impale an enemy's charging horse. As the French attacked, the English bowmen drew their six-foot longbows. Then, as one French chronicler wrote, the sky became so thick with arrows that "it seemed as if it snowed." The arrows were dangerous at a range of 300 yards. They were absolutely fatal within 100 yards.

The result was disaster for the French. Slain and wounded horses tumbled over each other. Thrown on their backs, the French nobles in their heavy armor could not rise. They were as helpless as upside-down turtles. Foot soldiers killed them with long knives. Thus, the finest French cavalry was wiped out. The victors were English foot soldiers, mere commoners.

Such disasters befell the French knights at the Battle of Crécy (1346), the Battle of Poitiers (1356), and the Battle of Agincourt (1415). The age of feudalism, based on the power of warriors on horseback, could not survive long.

The cannon The second weapon that battered down the feudal system was the cannon. The sound of exploding gunpowder was first heard in Europe sometime after 1250. The English fired small cannons at the Battle of Crécy, but these did little more than scare the horses.

After 1400, however, European cannons grew huge and powerful. They could shoot stone balls 20 inches in diameter. In the last years of the Hundred Years' War, both sides used cannons to batter down the walls of each other's castles. Thus, the castle—like the knight's suit of shining armor—became an outdated relic.

National feeling grew in Europe.

Faith in feudalism and in the Church were both shaken by the upheavals of the 1300's. Among the peoples of Europe, they were replaced by a new feeling called **nationalism**.

During the Hundred Years' War, armies began to use cannons against the walls of enemy castles.

Nationalism is a feeling of loyalty to one's own land and people. It is a feeling that cuts across all class lines. During the Hundred Years' War, for example, English barons and peasants alike rejoiced at news of their king's great victories in France. After the Battle of Crécy, a jubilant throng greeted King Edward III when he returned to London. One proud Englishman wrote: "A new sun seemed to have arisen over the people in the perfect peace, in the plenty of all things, and in the glory of such victories."

No longer did people think of the king as simply a feudal lord. Instead, he was seen as a national leader fighting for the glory of the nation-state.

During the third stage of the war, English nationalistic feeling soared when people heard what had happened near the castle of Agincourt in France. In 1415, against 50,000 French troops, England's King Henry V urged his 8,000 soldiers into battle. "Hurrah! Hurrah! Saint George and Merrie England!" shouted the English as they strung their bows. The Battle of Agincourt ended in a stunning English victory.

Five years later, in 1420, Henry V forced the French king, Charles VI, to sign away his kingdom. (Henry was greatly aided by the fact that Charles suffered from periods of insanity.) By the Treaty of Troyes, Charles gave his daughter Katherine to Henry in marriage. Charles also agreed that Henry would inherit the French crown

Discussion questions: What impact did nationalism have on the Holy Roman Empire?
On Christendom?

245

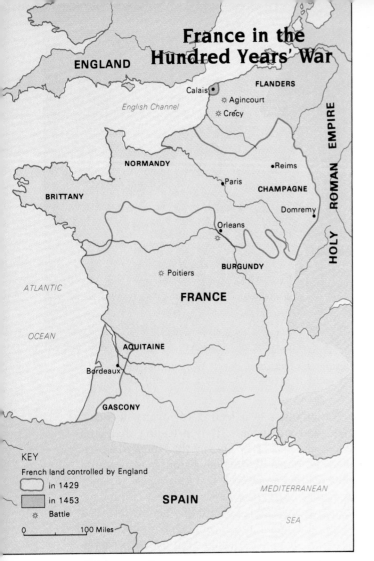

France in the Hundred Years' War

Map Study
What regions of France did the English control in 1429? What land did they hold in 1453?

KEY
French land controlled by England
☐ in 1429
▨ in 1453
✳ Battle

0   100 Miles

when Charles himself died. Thus, it seemed that France and England would become one kingdom.

However, Henry V died in 1422, just before Charles's death. Henry's son, Henry VI, was only nine months old. An English duke ruled northern France in the name of the baby king. Then, in 1429, a French girl felt moved by God to rescue France from its English conquerors. Her name, as you read on page 234, was Joan of Arc.

Joan of Arc turned the tide of war.

Perhaps no one in history accomplished so much in such a short time against such overwhelming odds as did Joan of Arc. In only six months, Joan changed a pathetic prince into a

king, led the French army to victory, and awakened the national spirit of a defeated people.

Yet Joan herself was not surprised by these events. She believed in miracles. She believed that several times, while she was tending her father's sheep, heavenly voices had spoken to her. Her mission, as dictated by those voices, was to drive the English army out of France and give the French crown to France's true king, Charles VI's son.

In February 1429, Joan made a hazardous journey to the court of the prince, Charles the Dauphin (DAW-fuhn). (*Dauphin* was the title given to the eldest son of a French king.) The Treaty of Troyes had robbed Charles of his kingdom. Though the Dauphin still pretended to be king, he lacked both spirit and confidence. He was dumbfounded when a crudely dressed peasant girl entered his court and said to him:

> *God send you long life, gentle Dauphin . . .*
> *I have been sent by God to take you to*
> *Reims to be anointed. Give me soldiers*
> *and I will raise the siege of Orleans, for it*
> *is God's will that the English shall leave*
> *France and return to their own country.*

As you read (page 234), on May 7, 1429, Joan led the French army into battle against the English forts that blocked the roads to Orleans. It was a hard-fought battle for both sides. The air was filled with arrows and the stinking smoke of cannon. Joan stayed always at the thick of the fighting. About noon, the French fought their way close to the main fort and threw up ladders to scale its walls. As Joan climbed swiftly up the first ladder, an English arrow tore into her shoulder. She pulled it out and urged her troops to fight on. The French threw up more ladders, but the English flung them down, throwing French fighters to their deaths. By sunset, the weary French had still not taken the fort. Despairing, their commanders sounded the retreat. The English looked out in victory from the safety of their walls.

Suddenly, Joan and a few soldiers charged back toward the fort. The entire French army stormed after her. This time, there was no stopping the French. They swarmed up their ladders and into the English fort. A mass of English soldiers tried to retreat across the nearby river, but the French set the bridge afire. When the bridge broke, the

Joan herself thought it was strange to hear voices. She tried to deny them for a while, but when she saw her king's power weakening, she finally gave in.

terrified English, weighed down by heavy armor, drowned in the river beneath.

Over the crackle of the flames and the cries of the dying, the bells of Orleans rang out in joy. The siege of Orleans was broken. Joan of Arc had guided the French onto the path of victory.

After that victory, Joan persuaded Charles to go with her to be crowned king. The route led through enemy territory, and Charles quaked with fear. Yet Joan brought him safely to Reims. At the cathedral on Sunday, July 17, 1429, he was crowned King Charles VII.

Joan had one year of triumph, 1429. Her last two years were years of betrayal and anguish. The English hated her and believed her to be a witch. In 1430, she was captured in battle and turned over to Church authorities to stand trial. Although Charles VII owed his crown to her, he did nothing to rescue her. Condemned as a witch and a heretic, Joan was tied to a stake and burned to death on May 30, 1431. One Englishman, wiser than the rest, cried out, "We are lost. We have burned a saint."

Joan's execution did the English no good. French nationalism did not die. Charles VII overcame his cowardice to become a strong king. By 1453, his troops had won back every part of France except Calais.

Joan of Arc is still revered by the French as their greatest patriot. In 1920, nearly 500 years after her death, the Church retracted its judgment of heresy and declared Joan a saint.

Section Review 3

Define: (a) nationalism, (b) dauphin
Identify: (a) Black Death, (b) Hundred Years' War, (c) Henry V, (d) Battle of Agincourt, (e) Joan of Arc, (f) Orleans, (g) Charles VII
Answer:
1. (a) What was the Black Death? (b) How did trade encourage its spread? (c) What effects did it have on Europe?
2. What was the Hundred Years' War about?
3. (a) What did Joan of Arc believe to be her mission in life? (b) What did she accomplish? (c) How did her life end?
4. (a) What new weapons came into use during the Hundred Years' War? (b) How did each change warfare?

Critical Thinking
5. Why did the Black Death weaken the manorial economy?
6. How did the Hundred Year' War weaken the feudal system?
7. Give evidence that each of the following people was a *national* hero, not just a feudal leader. (a) Henry V (b) Joan of Arc

New monarchs ruled in western Europe. 4

Throughout this chapter, we have seen how the medieval world came apart in the 1300's. Out of that turmoil and pain, however, three strong nation-states of western Europe arose.

France was no longer a patchwork of lands, some attached to the French king, others to the English king. England, stripped of its holdings in France, was now a compact country surrounded by the sea. And, to the south of France, Spain had developed by 1500 as a third nation-state.

New monarchs replaced feudal kings.

Medieval kings had ruled according to feudal custom. To fight wars and govern their kingdoms, they had relied mainly on the support of their vassals. The strong rulers who arose between 1450 and 1500 did not base their power on feudalism (although they certainly used their rights as feudal lords when it suited them). Historians often call these rulers the "new monarchs." The new monarchs had three important new sources of power: control of taxes, a professional army, and professional officials.

Broad taxing power Feudal kings had received most of their income from their own estates and from the feudal aids of their vassals. (Remember that an aid was a grant of money for a specific purpose, such as ransoming the lord from captivity or fighting a war.) The new monarchs demanded every penny of those aids too, but they also received money from other groups. Every class in society—nobility, clergy, townspeople, and peasants—paid some kind of tax to the king.

Professional army Medieval rulers marched to war followed by an army of vassals, who owed

Have students briefly review the histories of France, England, and Spain.

247

military service in exchange for their land. The new monarchs hired soldiers from any class in society. No longer was fighting the specialized work of the nobility, although nobles still commanded most armies. Soldiering became a trade open to all, and professional soldiers were paid from the royal treasury.

Professional officials The new monarchs surrounded themselves with a new class of advisers and officials. Some were nobles, but many were middle-class townspeople. Educated officials from the middle class gave the king loyal service. They were the ruler's natural allies against the haughty and quarrelsome nobles.

Crafty kings strengthened France.

Charles VII, who had won the French throne with Joan of Arc's help, set the French monarchy on the road to recovery. By 1453, he had driven the English out of France, except for the single city of Calais. He set up a royal council, using middle-class men as his officials. He chose his advisers so wisely that he won the nickname "Charles the Well-Served." He also set up the first permanent royal army.

Charles found new sources of money for the royal treasury. Most of his money came from two taxes. One was called the *taille* (TAH-yuh), a tax on land. The other was called the *gabelle* (guh-BEL), a tax on salt. For more than 300 years, these two taxes on basic necessities of life were the main source of money for French kings.

Charles's son became king in 1461. Louis XI was known as "the Spider King." To achieve his ends, Louis resorted to trickery, intimidation, bribery, and espionage. He had spies in almost every noble's court in Europe. A cardinal who once betrayed him was locked up in a small cage for 11 painful years, unable either to stand up or lie down. Nobles who resisted Louis's rule usually were bribed or bullied into submission.

Like his father, Louis wanted to weaken the power of the great lords within France—above all the Duke of Burgundy. Burgundy had long been a thorn in France's side. This mighty dukedom included southeastern France, Flanders, Luxembourg, and other territories. During the Hundred Years' War, the Burgundians often had sided with the English. Louis XI regarded Duke Charles the Bold of Burgundy as his chief enemy.

Perhaps nothing pleased the Spider King more than the news in 1477 that the duke had been killed in battle. By 1482, Louis had added Burgundy to the French state. It was a sizable and critical addition.

Money flowed into Louis's treasury through the taille and the gabelle. Therefore, Louis needed to call together the Estates General only once in his 22-year reign. He did not need its approval for his policies. Thus, Louis passed on to his heirs a monarchy of almost unlimited power. Unlike the kings and queens of England, French rulers after 1500 collected taxes without the consent of their subjects.

The Wars of the Roses split England.

While France was building its strength after the Hundred Years' War, England went through another time of turmoil. The Hundred Years' War was scarcely over when England was split by a civil war beginning in 1455.

Two branches of the royal family claimed the English crown. One branch, headed by the dukes of York, took a white rose as their emblem. The other branch, descended from the dukes of Lancaster, had a red rose as their symbol. Thus, the civil war came to be called the Wars of the Roses. These battles were really a bloody family quarrel.

The wars disrupted the reign of three kings: Henry VI, Edward IV, and Richard III. Finally, Richard III was killed at the Battle of Bosworth Field in 1485. This battle marked the end of the Wars of the Roses and a turning point for England. Richard III often is called England's last medieval king. The man who defeated him set England on a new path.

Henry Tudor made peace in England.

The victor at Bosworth Field was another Henry. By marriage and inheritance, he was connected to both the Lancastrians and the Yorkists. His own family name, however, was Tudor (TOO-duhr). Crowned Henry VII, he began the most renowned dynasty in English history: the Tudor dynasty. (His granddaughter, Elizabeth I, would later become England's greatest queen.)

Henry VII (1485–1509) ruled as a new monarch. His chief ministers were not great lords but members of the middle class. In every part of

The horse of Richard III was slain in battle. Shakespeare had him exclaim, "A horse! A horse! My kingdom for a horse!" Interested students may wish to read *Richard III* and report to the class.

Henry Tudor became Henry VII of England, a shrewd and power-hungry new monarch.

his kingdom, he used local landowners as officials called justices of the peace. In doing so, he continued a long tradition of local government that served England well. (As these justices were unpaid, they were no burden on the royal treasury.)

Henry VII made himself as king the richest man in England. Much of his money came from feudal dues, which he collected with truly modern efficiency. Still more money came from "tonnage and poundage," taxes on imported goods. The more trade grew, the more money flowed into Henry's hands. So Henry was eager to encourage trade, and business prospered during his reign. He made treaties with other rulers to open new markets for English merchants.

To safeguard the money he was piling up, Henry VII carefully avoided expensive wars. Thus, he did not need to keep—or pay—a standing army.

Many of England's great nobles had died or fled abroad during the Wars of the Roses. Henry completed the job of destroying their power. He limited their military might by having Parliament outlaw the private armies of paid fighters many lords had kept.

Henry also used the Court of Star Chamber to destroy over-mighty subjects. This court got its name from the starry ceiling in the room where its judges met. The Court of Star Chamber violated most ideas of fairness and justice. It met in secret. People accused of crimes had no right to know what evidence was being used against them. People were tortured so that they would confess. Yet most people in England accepted the Court of Star Chamber because Henry used it to keep peace after years of strife.

It is probably fair to say that Henry was respected but not loved. Unheroic and miserly, he was far from the Middle Ages' idea of a great king. Yet when he died in 1509, England was prosperous and peaceful. The benefits of the new monarchy were plain.

Isabella and Ferdinand strengthened Spain.

As far back as 1063, well before the First Crusade, the pope had urged Christian knights to drive the Muslims (or Moors) out of Spain. This drive became a centuries-long effort known as the *Reconquista* (ray-kahn-KEES-tuh) or reconquest. By the late 1400's, Muslims held only the tiny kingdom of Granada.

Four other kingdoms on the Iberian peninsula were ruled by Christians. The kingdom of Portugal faced the uncharted waters of the Atlantic Ocean. The small kingdom of Navarre sat astride the Pyrenees, bordering France. The large kingdoms of Castile (ka-STEEL) and Aragon (AR-uh-gahn) spanned the neck and midsection of the peninsula. (See the map on page 250.)

A capable and aggressive princess named Isabella was heir to the throne of Castile. Likewise, a determined and crafty prince named Ferdinand was heir to Aragon. Their marriage, in 1469, brought their two kingdoms into close alliance.

The conquest of Granada Beginning in 1482, Ferdinand and Isabella set out to conquer the last Muslim kingdom, Granada. It took ten years, but in 1492, Granada fell to a Christian army. In the final battle, Isabella personally led her army, wearing the red cross of a crusader.

This crusading spirit linked religion closely with Spanish nationalism. To be a "true Spaniard"

Ferdinand and Isabella expelled about 280,000 Jews from Spain, depleting the country of many of its skilled workers in trade, farming, and industry.

249

The Growth of Spain

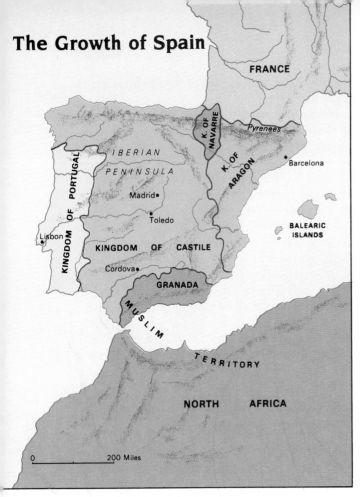

FRANCE

K. OF NAVARRE

Pyrenees

IBERIAN

PENINSULA

K. OF ARAGON

Barcelona

KINGDOM OF PORTUGAL

Madrid

Toledo

BALEARIC ISLANDS

Lisbon

KINGDOM OF CASTILE

Cordova

GRANADA

MUSLIM

TERRITORY

NORTH AFRICA

0   200 Miles

Map Study

What Spanish kingdom nearly surrounded the Muslim territory on the Iberian Peninsula?

came also to mean being a "true Christian." The result was disastrous for Spaniards who were not Christian.

The Inquisition Spain had a long history of religious diversity and tolerance. Since the height of the Islamic empire in the 700's, Muslims, Jews, and Christians had all lived there. The three groups had often lived together in peace. Jews held high positions as bankers, merchants, scholars, physicians, and government officials. Under Ferdinand and Isabella, however, Spain's religious tolerance ended.

As a devout Roman Catholic, Isabella decreed that in a Christian state, there could be only "one king, one law, one faith." She and Ferdinand won permission from the pope to revive the Inquisition, the arm of the Church that had tracked down heretics in the Middle Ages (page 217).

All over Spain, boards of priests met to hear cases of suspected heresy. The primary suspects were Jews and Muslims who had converted to Christianity. Assuming the suspects were guilty, the priests would demand that they confess. If the suspects refused, they often were tortured. Once they confessed, they were burned at the stake. A report by Isabella's secretary shows that 2,000 men and women were executed in this way between 1478 and 1490.

The expulsion of the Jews In the same year as the conquest of Granada (1492), Isabella and Ferdinand began a new campaign against the 200,000 Spanish Jews who openly practiced their religion. They were forced to become Christians or leave the country. The great majority, about 150,000, chose exile.

Jewish families, now homeless, set out from Spain to other lands. The departure of their ships was witnessed by another captain who recorded the event in his diary. That captain was Christopher Columbus, who sailed from the Spanish port of Palos in August 1492.

Columbus was just setting out on a voyage that he hoped would lead to Asia. In fact, his historic voyage took him to the Americas. Some exiled Jews sailed with him. Among them were the expedition's doctor and interpreter. Later, a few Jews became early settlers in the Americas. Most of the exiles, however, went to the Muslim countries of Southwest Asia, including lands that are now Iran, Syria, Israel, and Jordan.

Expelling the Jews and Muslims made Spain a religiously united nation, but it hurt the country economically. Many of Spain's leaders in business and trade had been Muslims or Jews.

After Isabella's death in 1504, Ferdinand seized the part of Navarre south of the Pyrenees. By his death in 1516, Spain had reached its modern borders.

Section Review 4

Define: (a) new monarch, (b) feudal aids, (c) taille, (d) gabelle, (e) tonnage and poundage
Identify: (a) Charles VII, (b) Louis XI, (c) Wars of the Roses, (d) Henry VII, (e) Reconquista, (f) Ferdinand, (g) Isabella
Answer:
1. In general, how did the new monarchs strengthen their powers?
2. List three accomplishments of Charles VII.

250

Map Study answer: Castile

3. (a) How did Louis XI win the nickname "the Spider King"? (b) Why did Louis XI and his successors have more power than English rulers of the same period?
4. (a) What part did the middle classes play in Henry VII's government? (b) What methods did Henry use to keep the peace within his kingdom?
5. (a) How did a political marriage begin Spain's development as a nation? (b) How did the position of Spanish Muslims and Jews change in the late 1400's?

Critical Thinking

6. Compare the policies of medieval rulers with the policies of the new monarchs with regard to (a) sources of money, (b) the army, and (c) choosing officials. In each case, explain why the new policies increased royal power.

A new empire arose in Russia. 5

At the eastern end of the European continent, in the land known as Russia, another country was taking shape in the 1400's. To understand how Russia developed, you must know something of its geography. The Ural (YOOR-uhl) Mountains divide Europe and Asia. Russians first settled on the European side of the mountains, and the European part of Russia remained its heartland. Later, Russians pushed eastward into the vast wilderness of northern Asia known as Siberia (sye-BIHR-ee-uh).

European Russia is mostly flat. The northern part, near the Baltic Sea, is covered with an immense forest of pine, spruce, and other cone-bearing trees. The southern part is a sweeping, grassy steppe with rich black soil.

The rivers of European Russia seem to twist and turn in every direction. Eventually, they empty into one of four bodies of water—the Caspian Sea, the Black Sea, the Baltic Sea, or the Arctic Ocean. In the warm months, barges floated easily over these broad and abundant rivers. In the freezing Russian winters, horse-drawn sleds glided safely over the thick river ice. Thus, in every season, Russians depended on their rivers for transportation and trade.

The Mongols conquered Russia.

During the 700's and the 800's, groups of people who spoke Slavic languages migrated from Asia into eastern Europe. They fought a series of bitter battles with the Byzantine empire. Yet these Slavs also accepted Eastern Orthodox Christianity along with other Byzantine influences (page 182). In the Early Middle Ages, the group of Slavs who became known as Russians built a rich trading kingdom centering on the city of Kiev.

In the middle 1200's, a fierce group of horsemen from central Asia slashed their way into Russia. These nomads were the Mongols. (You will read more of them in Chapter 12.) In 1240, they completely destroyed Kiev. Its churches were burned, its rich treasures were plundered, and even its tombs were broken open and the bones scattered. By 1241, the Mongols ruled all of Russia. From that time on, Russian history followed a new course.

In some ways, the Mongols actually began the work of uniting Russia. Kievan Russia had been a collection of small, independent kingdoms. The Mongols forced all the kingdoms of Russia to pay them tribute. In each kingdom, a Russian prince ruled under the Mongols and collected tribute for them. As long as a prince was obedient, the Mongols allowed him to rule as he wished. Russian historians call the period of Mongol rule from 1240 to 1480 "the Mongol yoke."

Moscow's princes united Russia.

Moscow, located in the northern forests, suffered less from Mongol raids than did the cities of the steppe such as Kiev. Moscow was first settled in the 1100's. By 1250, it was a primitive hamlet enclosed by a crude log wall. It took the princes of Moscow 240 years (1240–1480) to build a strong and independent state (map, page 252).

Note the location of Moscow near the headwaters of three great rivers: the Volga (VAHL-guh), the Dnieper (NEE-puhr), and the Don. If the ruler of Moscow could gain control of these rivers, he could control nearly all of European Russia.

Moscow began its rise to power under the Mongols. Its prince from 1328 to 1341 was Ivan I. As tax collector for the Mongols, he became known as Ivan Moneybags. He served the Mongols so well that they gave him the title of "Great

The Mongols lived in camps called *ordu*, from which comes the English word *horde*. One branch of the Mongols ruled the Khanate of the Golden Horde in Russia.

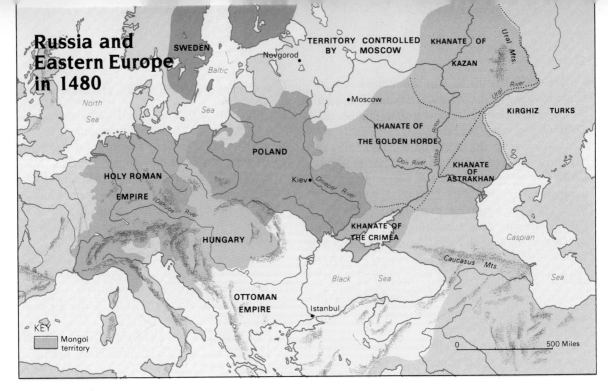

Map Study

Mongol rulers were known as khans. What areas shown on the map were ruled by Mongols? What power bordered Moscow's lands on the southwest?

Prince." In 1328, the head of the Russian Orthodox Church made Moscow his residence. The Church became a major ally of Moscow's princes.

Ivan and his successors gradually enlarged their kingdom by purchase, war, trickery, and clever marriages. Generation after generation, they plotted to win control of the small states that encircled Moscow. By the 1400's, Moscow had become the strongest of the Russian states under the Mongols.

The prince of Moscow became czar.

The Russian state became a true empire during the 43-year reign of Ivan III (1462–1505). Born in 1440, Ivan was a boy of 13 when Constantinople fell to the Turks in 1453. In 1472, Ivan married the niece of the last Byzantine emperor. At that time, he began calling himself **czar**, the Russian word for *caesar* or *emperor*.

In 1480, Moscow finally freed itself from the Mongol yoke. Ivan III refused to pay the Mongol's their tribute. Rising to the challenge, the Mongol ruler led his army to the banks of the Ugra River. The Russian army stood on the opposite bank. The two armies glowered at each other, neither daring to cross the river. Finally, without shooting

a single arrow, the Russians and the Mongols turned around and marched back home. After this bloodless face-off, Moscow was free of Mongol control.

Ivan wanted to make Moscow a fitting capital for an emperor. The center of the city was a walled citadel or fortress known as the *Kremlin*. Ivan tore down the old triangular wall around the Kremlin and erected a massive new wall 60 feet high and 15 feet thick. Inside, he built a palace for himself, another palace for the head of the Russian Church, and three great churches.

Moscow became the capital of a new and aggressive empire. By the time of his death in 1505, Ivan had tripled the territory under Moscow's control. Ivan III was both the first czar and the first leader of a united Russian nation. Russians call him Ivan the Great.

Ivan IV ruled through terror.

The next important figure in Russian history also had a well-earned nickname: Ivan the Terrible. He came to the throne as Ivan IV in 1533, when he was only three years old. His youth was marked by struggles for power among Russia's nobles. These nobles, themselves often minor

252

Ivan's marriage in 1472 to the niece of Constantinople's last emperor and the strict Orthodoxy of the Russian church helped him build his claim to [continued below]

princes, were known as **boyars**. Like the feudal lords of western Europe, they held large estates. Just as the feudal lords struggled against the growing power of the kings in England and France, the boyars opposed the growing power of Russia's czars.

Ivan's mother, who acted as regent, died in 1538 when he was eight, probably poisoned by her boyar enemies. For the next eight years, the boyars kept Ivan a virtual prisoner, poorly fed and badly clothed. As a result, Ivan mistrusted and hated the boyars for the rest of his life.

In 1547, when he was 16, Ivan took power into his own hands, having himself crowned czar. He married the beautiful Anastasia, related to an old boyar family, the Romanovs. (You will hear more of this family later.)

The years from 1547 to 1560 are often called Ivan's "good period." He won great victories against the Mongols and destroyed the Mongol khanate on the Volga River. He also gave Russia a code of laws in 1550 and ruled justly. Hoping to increase Russia's trade with Europe, he began a long war to win access to the Baltic Sea.

Ivan IV is probably better remembered for his later "bad period," which began after his beloved Anastasia died in 1560. Little is known about these years because the records were lost in a great fire that swept Moscow. Some historians believe Ivan was insane part of the time. Others say his acts of cruelty were little different from those of other European rulers—for example, the use of the Inquisition by Ferdinand and Isabella in Spain.

Whatever the explanation, Ivan turned brutally against the boyars. He accused them of poisoning his wife. He organized his own police force whose chief duty was to hunt down "traitors" and murder them. The members of this police force were called *oprichniki* (oh-PREECH-nihk-ee), or "separate class." They dressed in black and rode black horses with dogs' heads on their saddles as symbols of terror. Thousands of boyars and ordinary people as well died in this reign of terror.

Ivan's uncontrollable rage at last led him to an act that was both the greatest personal tragedy and the greatest political disaster of his reign. In 1581, during a violent quarrel, he killed his older son and heir. Thus, when Ivan himself died in 1584, only his unintelligent younger son remained to succeed him as czar.

Ivan IV built St. Basil's Cathedral in Moscow to celebrate his victories over the Mongols.

Russia at the time of Ivan's death was an isolated and primitive empire. The story of how this empire became a major European power is left to a later chapter.

Section Review 5

Define: (a) czar, (b) boyars, (c) oprichniki
Identify: (a) Ural Mountains, (b) Slavs, (c) Kiev, (d) Ivan I, (e) Kremlin, (f) Ivan IV
Answer:
1. Describe the geography of Russia.
2. (a) When did the Mongols conquer Russia? (b) How did they rule it?
3. (a) What geographic advantages helped Moscow's rise to power? (b) What other factors helped the city?
4. What achievements explain why Ivan III is known as Ivan the Great?
5. (a) What were the accomplishments of Ivan IV? (b) How did he come to be known as Ivan the Terrible?

Critical Thinking
6. (a) How was the czars' situation like that of the new monarchs? (b) How was it different?

being the heir to Constantinople. Moscow as the seat of power became a "third Rome," and "Holy Russia" carried on the traditions of Byzantium.

Chapter Review 11

Summary

1. England and France developed as nations. In England, the signing of the Magna Carta limited royal power. The middle class grew stronger when townspeople were included in Parliament. In France, Philip II won much English-held land and strengthened royal power. Later rulers set up royal courts and included the middle class in the Estates General.

2. The Church faced a crisis in the 1300's. The Babylonian captivity and the Great Schism weakened the authority of the Church. John Wycliffe, John Huss, and their supporters called for changes in the Church.

3. The 1300's brought plague and war. The Black Death killed millions and weakened the manorial economy. The Hundred Years' War further diminished feudal power, as the longbow and cannons doomed armored knights and castles. During the war, national loyalties increased in England and France.

4. New monarchs ruled in western Europe. Rulers in France, England, and Spain found new sources of tax money, hired professional soldiers, and chose middle-class officials. The Tudor dynasty came to power in England. French kings strengthened royal control. In Spain, the Reconquista linked Spanish nationalism with the crusading spirit, ending religious toleration for Jews and Muslims.

5. A new empire arose in Russia. The Mongol invasion destroyed Russia's old Kievan civilization. Beginning in the 1300's, Moscow became the new center of Russian power. Moscow's rulers eventually drove out the Mongols and added to their own territory.

Reviewing the Facts

1. Define the following terms:
   a. nation-state
   b. nationalism
   c. czar
   d. boyar
2. Explain the importance of each of the following names, dates, places, or terms:
   a. 1215
   b. Model Parliament
   c. Estates General
   d. Babylonian captivity
   e. Great Schism
   f. Council of Constance
   g. Black Death
   h. Hundred Years' War
   i. Joan of Arc
   j. Wars of the Roses
   k. Henry VII
   l. Charles VII
   m. Ferdinand of Aragon
   n. Isabella of Castile
   o. Reconquista
   p. 1492
   q. Moscow
   r. Ivan III
3. (a) How did the Magna Carta come to be signed?
   (b) Why is it important?
4. (a) What was new about the Model Parliament?
   (b) When did it first meet?

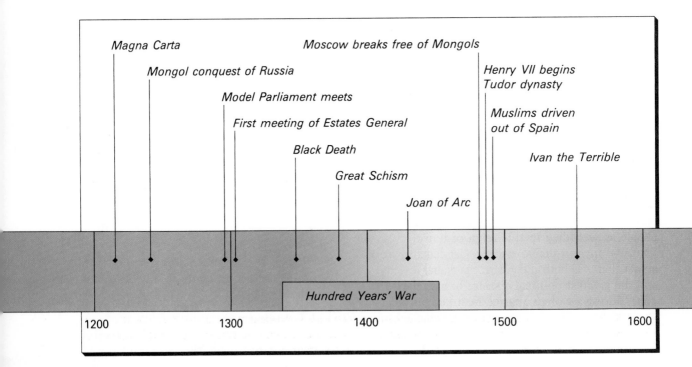

Magna Carta

Mongol conquest of Russia

Model Parliament meets

First meeting of Estates General

Black Death

Great Schism

Joan of Arc

Moscow breaks free of Mongols

Henry VII begins Tudor dynasty

Muslims driven out of Spain

Ivan the Terrible

Hundred Years' War

1200   1300   1400   1500   1600

5. Briefly describe how each of the following kings helped France become a strong nation-state. (a) Philip Augustus (b) Louis IX (c) Charles VII (d) Louis XI
6. (a) How was the Church's authority weakened by the Babylonian captivity? (b) How was the Church's authority weakened once again by the Great Schism?
7. Identify three factors that led to a population decline in the 1300's and explain the part each played in the decline.
8. How did the Hundred Years' War contribute to the rise of nationalism?
9. Briefly describe the new policies that were followed by the monarchs who came to power between 1450 and 1500.
10. How did Russia begin to become a unified empire?

Basic Skills

1. **Making a time line** (a) Using 20-year segments, make a time line of the Hundred Years' War. (b) Use shading or color to indicate the four stages described on page 244. (c) Include the following events: Battle of Crecy, Battle of Poitiers, Battle of Agincourt, Joan's victory at Orleans, and Joan's death at the stake.
2. **Making a chart** Between 1100 and the early 1300's, the kings of England and France faced many changes. (a) Make a chart to compare the changes in these countries. For the vertical headings, use *Taxes, Parliament/Estates General,* and *Royal Courts.* Fill in the appropriate information for each country. (b) What conclusions do you draw on the basis of the chart?
3. **Comparing maps** Between 1160 and the late 1400's, the boundaries of many European nations changed. Compare the maps on pages 246, 250, and 252 with that on page 222. What major change has occurred in each of the three countries?
4. **Summarizing** Summarize the section "New monarchs replaced feudal kings" on pages 247–248. For each paragraph, write a sentence describing the feudal customs and the new conditions that replaced them.

Researching and Reporting Skills

1. **Preparing an interview** If you could have interviewed Joan of Arc at the time of her trial, what three questions would you have asked?

2. **Surveying** Combine the questions about Joan asked by everyone in the class and analyze them. (a) What question was asked most frequently? (b) Into what different categories can the questions be divided?
3. **Interpreting primary sources** The primary sources in this chapter include both pictures and quotations. (a) Identify three visual sources and three quoted passages from the chapter that represent the times. (b) What does each source contribute to historical understanding?

Critical Thinking

1. **Distinguishing fact from opinion** Page 236 contains the statement, "John's losses were England's gain . . ." (a) Is this statement fact or opinion? Why? (b) Is there evidence to support the statement? If so, what?
2. **Analyzing cause and effect** (a) What factors caused the middle class to grow in power in England and France during the late Middle Ages? (b) What were the effects of this change in each country?
3. **Inferring** The Moors and Jews of Spain included many merchants and scholars. What effect might the policies of religious intolerance have had on Spain's economic and social development?

Perspectives on Past and Present

1. According to Winston Churchill, the great contribution of the Magna Carta was that it established the idea of a supreme law that even the king may not break. What are several examples of the use of this concept in the United States?
2. Religious dissenters like John Wycliffe and John Huss challenged a Church that considered itself the final authority in religious matters. To what extent have attitudes about religious dissent changed since that time? Give examples to support your answer.

Investigating History

Increased trade, which encouraged contacts among different peoples, helped spread the Black Death. Organize a debate on the following issue: A highly contagious disease such as the Black Death would or would not spread even more rapidly today than in the Middle Ages.

Unit III Review

Geographic Theme: Interaction

How did people use resources to develop trade?

The Pax Romana enabled a remarkably productive economy to develop, linked by the bonds of trade. That economy illustrates what geographers call *interaction*—the relation of people and their environment. From the resources around them, people of the empire produced goods to sell. Trade carried those goods to market and brought back what the local environment could not provide.

The collapse of the empire destroyed this network of production and trade. Roads fell into disrepair, routes became unprotected, and cities declined. As a result, economic units became local and self-sufficient. Long-distance trade and even regional exchange ceased.

Almost 500 years passed before an awakening of economic life began. Among the early signs of revival was the rise of towns in Italy and northwestern Europe. Venice, Genoa, and other cities grew through Mediterranean trade. In northern France and Flanders, towns such as Bruges and Antwerp became centers of cloth manufacture. Access to the sea gave both regions an advantage in sea-borne commerce.

For a time, the Mediterranean and northern European centers were separate. Eventually Venetian ships reached Flanders to start a new trade connection. Meanwhile, merchants rediscovered the Alpine routes leading to France and Germany. A third trading region, the Hanseatic League, grew to extend from Flanders across the Baltic Sea into Russia.

Once again, Europeans began to sell their natural resources and products. Using the means available in their environment, they made contact with the wider world. Whether from resources, manufacture, or trade, goods once again made the journey to distant markets. A new economic era had begun.

1. List four trading cities of Italy, four of northwestern Europe, and four of the Baltic area.
2. List the major products of the Italian cities, Flanders and northern France, Spain, England, and the Baltic region.
3. Compare the economic development of the Italian and Flemish cities with that of Spain, England, and the Baltic region.
4. What changes do you think would happen in the new era?

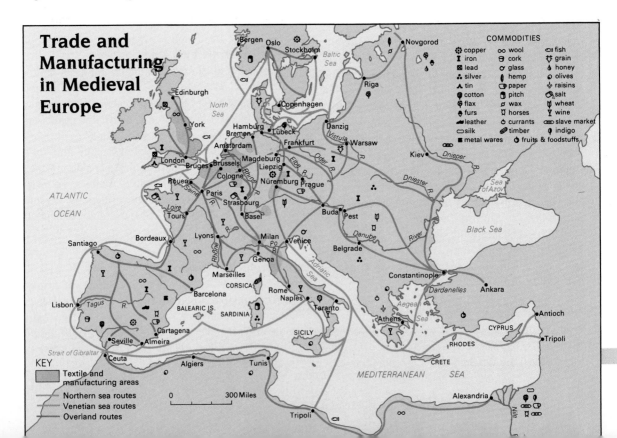

Trade and Manufacturing in Medieval Europe

COMMODITIES

copper · iron · lead · silver · tin · cotton · flax · furs · leather · silk · metal wares · wool · cork · glass · hemp · paper · pitch · wax · horses · currants · timber · fruits & foodstuffs · fish · grain · honey · olives · raisins · salt · wheat · wine · slave market · indigo

KEY

Textile and manufacturing areas
Northern sea routes
Venetian sea routes
Overland routes

0   300 Miles

Unit Perspectives

Understanding History

1. **Relating** Identify the religion (Islam, Eastern Orthodoxy, or Roman Catholicism) with which each of the following people, places, or things is associated. Describe the significance of each.

   a. friar
   b. Constantinople
   c. Koran
   d. patriarch
   e. canon law
   f. cardinal
   g. Gregory I
   h. Baghdad
   i. Concordat of Worms
   j. caliph
   k. Hagia Sophia
   l. Great Schism

2. **Sequencing** Draw a time line that extends from 500 to 1500. Divide the time line into 200-year increments. Place the following events on the time line.

   a. Fall of Constantinople
   b. Beginning of Viking invasions
   c. Birth of Muhammad
   d. Battle of Tours
   e. Treaty of Verdun
   f. Revival of learning
   g. Charlemagne crowned emperor
   h. Norman conquest of England
   i. Magna Carta
   j. War of the Roses

3. Explain the significance to world history of each of the events on your time line.

Critical Thinking

1. **Comparing** For each of the following pairs of topics, give one similarity and one difference: (a) Christian crusade and Islamic jihad; (b) the influence of Theodora on Justinian and that of Joan of Arc on Charles VII; (c) Hagia Sophia and Chartres cathedral; (d) English government under Henry II and under Henry VII.
2. **Applying concepts** (a) What schism occurred in the Islamic religion? (b) How did Joan of Arc violate the code of chivalry? (c) How did the nation-states of England and France differ from Charlemagne's empire?
3. **Evaluating** (a) List four events that in your view had a generally destructive or negative effect on Europe in the Middle Ages. (b) List another four events that had a generally constructive or positive effect. (c) Which event do you consider most constructive? Most destructive? Explain your choices.
4. **Synthesizing** (a) What factors favored the rise of a middle class in France and England? (b) What factors discouraged the growth of a middle class in Spain and the Holy Roman Empire?

Making Decisions

1. Evaluate and comment briefly on each of the following decisions in terms of its effect on the relative power of Church and state in western Europe: (a) Henry IV's decision to plead for forgiveness at Canossa; (b) Clovis's decision to be baptized; (c) Pope Urban II's decision to organize a crusade to conquer Jerusalem; (d) Ferdinand and Isabella's decision to revive the Inquisition.
2. Decisions often have far-reaching consequences. What were the consequences of each of the following decisions: (a) King John's signing the Magna Carta; (b) King Edward's calling the Model Parliament; (c) Louis IX's creating the Parlement of Paris?

Continuity and Change

1. (a) Name five major new institutions that emerged in the Middle Ages. (b) Which of these do you think is most influential today?
2. How did the Middle Ages provide a cultural link between the ancient world and modern times?

Unit IV

An Age of Empires

Chapters

	100	400	700
Political and Governmental Life		**320–467** Gupta rulers bring golden age to India	**600's–700's** Ghana gains power in West Africa	**800's** Rajputs build new kingdoms in India

Yoruba pendant

Economic and Technological Life	**300's** Axum in Ethiopia trades from interior to Red Sea	**500's–1600's** Gold and salt trade thrives in West Africa	**794** In Heian, Japan, a golden age begins

Detail from The Tale of Genji

Mohica earspool

Social and Cultural Life		**400's** India uses decimal systems and concept of zero	
	250–900 Maya civilization flourishes in Central America	**500's** Buddhism reaches Japan	**850–1250** Khmer empire peaks during Angkor period

Before 1500, cultures in different regions of the world tended to grow in isolation. Of all the cultures, those of the Americas were most separate. During Europe's Middle Ages, dynasties rose and fell in China. Both China and India enjoyed a golden age of learning. In Africa, trade led to mighty empires and thriving city-states. In the Americas, the empires of the Aztecs and the Incas were at their height. Just before 1500, this pattern of isolation ended, and a new age began with European voyages of discovery.

1000   **1300**   **1600**

◄ **1200's**
Shogunate
established
in Japan

1400's
Incas build empire
in Andes

1600's
Japan bans foreigners

1644
Manchus set up Ch'ing
dynasty in China

Inca weaving from Peru

1100's–1500's
East African coastal cities
centers of trade

1275–1292
Marco Polo visits China

1433
Great Fleet sails from
China to Africa

*Pueblo pottery:
glazed polychrome jar*

1100's
Yorubas in Africa
are skilled
craftspeople

1300's
China develops public
elementary schools

1325
Aztecs build capital,
Tenochtitlán

1653
Shah Jahan builds
Taj Mahal in India

259

Golden Ages in China and Japan

Emperor Yang-ti rides through the imperial gardens with some attendants, while others care for his water lilies.

Key Terms

gentry
steppe
khan
clan
samurai
shogun
daimyo

Read and Understand

1. Two great dynasties ruled China.
2. The Mongols conquered a vast empire.
3. China chose stability over change.
4. Japan developed a unique civilization.
5. Japan turned to isolation.

Day after day, the golden leaves of autumn fluttered lazily to the ground outside the palace of the Chinese emperor Yang-ti. Yet the trees in Yang-ti's garden remained as green as in the summertime. How could this be?

Watchful peasants were seated in the branches of every tree. Each peasant held a basket filled with artificial leaves made of green silk. Whenever a natural leaf fell, a peasant instantly replaced it with a silken leaf.

At the same time, on Yang-ti's huge artificial lake, other peasants paddled boats among the thousands of floating lotus flowers. Blossoms that had withered overnight were plucked off and replaced by delicate petals of white and pink silk. Thus did the ambitious Yang-ti, who ruled China from 605 to 618, try to bring even the seasons under his control.

What was happening elsewhere in the world? In the year 618, the prophet Muhammad was just beginning to preach about Allah. The golden age of Islamic civilization lay 200 years in the future. The golden age of Rome lay 500 years in the past. Nowhere else in the world was there a monarch who could equal the power and wealth of Yang-ti. China in the 600's enjoyed a golden age of political unity and artistic splendor.

This chapter covers 1,300 years in the history of two Asian peoples, the Chinese and the Japanese. From 300 to 1650, both China and Japan passed through ages of extraordinary cultural vitality and richness.

Two great dynasties ruled China.   1

As you read in Chapter 4, the Han dynasty collapsed in A.D. 220. For 350 years, no emperor was strong enough to hold China together. More than 30 local dynasties rose and fell. A Chinese poet wrote, "The land was divided like a melon, or shared like beans."

Under the Shang, the Chou, and the Han, the center of China's civilization had been in the north, in the plains along the Yellow River. After 220, however, barbarians from beyond the Great Wall conquered much of northern China. Chinese nobles moved to the safer south, along the Yangtze River. During this long time of troubles, the south slowly became the new center of Chinese civilization.

The Sui dynasty reunited China.

In the late 500's, a new dynasty united China once again. In 581, Sui Wen-ti took over the north and then conquered the south. He brought China once again under the rule of a strong central government.

The new ruling family called themselves the Sui (sway) dynasty. (Recall the Chinese custom of giving the family name first and then the personal name.) There were only two Sui emperors, Wen-ti and his son, Yang-ti. Their dynasty

was short (589–618), but it laid the foundation for the golden age that followed.

The Grand Canal The second Sui ruler, Yang-ti, completed the work of reuniting China. His greatest single accomplishment was the building of the Grand Canal. The canal cut across the center of China, tying together its two great rivers, the Yellow River in the north and the Yangtze River in the south.

The canal helped to unite northern and southern China both politically and economically. From his capital in the north, the emperor demanded obedience and tribute from the people of southern China. Barges carried tons of food from the rich rice fields of the south to the less fertile north.

The digging of this 1,000-mile waterway was a prodigious feat. Tens of thousands of peasant men and women toiled on the project for five years between 605 and 610. Perhaps as many as half the workers died on the job. (Yet more died on Yang-ti's project of rebuilding the Great Wall to keep out raiding Turks.)

The overthrow of the Sui The endless work of building canals, walls, and palaces turned people against the Sui dynasty. Yang-ti ranks as one of the most hated emperors in China's history. Overworked and overtaxed, the peasants rebelled. Rebel armies arose all over China. In 618, his own servants strangled Yang-ti.

T'ai-tsung founded the T'ang dynasty.

A young rebel general soon won the throne. He took the name T'ai-tsung (tye-dzoong), which meant "Grand Ancestor." The dynasty he founded was the T'ang. The T'ang dynasty ruled a united China from 618 to 907, nearly 300 years. T'ai-tsung's brilliant reign (627–649) ushered in a golden age when China was the richest, most powerful country in the world.

T'ai-tsung led armies northwest against the Turks of central Asia and northeast against the Koreans. His soldiers, clad in armor of rhinoceros hide, reconquered the northern and western lands that China had lost since the decline of the Han dynasty. Korea fought off T'ai-tsung's invasion, but it fell to his son in 660. For the next 90 years, Korea was forced to pay tribute to China.

T'ai-tsung remembered the Sui dynasty's mistake of overtaxing peasants. He lowered taxes.

Have students compare the Sui dynasty to the Ch'in (Chapter 4). (Both were short-lived and harsh. Both overstrained the kingdom's resources and fell, but both paved the way for succeeding periods of strength and prosperity—the Han and the T'ang.)

261

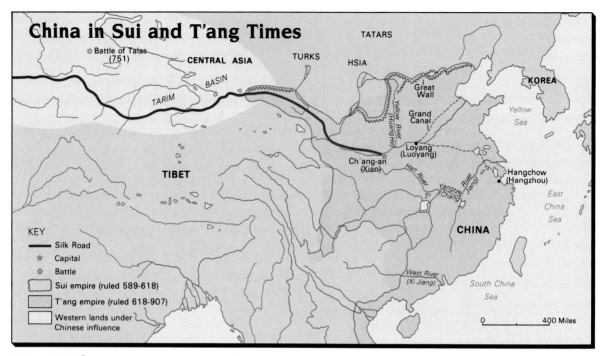

China in Sui and T'ang Times

KEY
— Silk Road
☆ Capital
✿ Battle
▢ Sui empire (ruled 589-618)
▢ T'ang empire (ruled 618-907)
▢ Western lands under Chinese influence

Map Study

Which dynasty controlled a larger area, the Sui or the T'ang? What region was under Chinese influence but was not part of China during this period? Name two regions shown here that were independent of China.

He also took lands from wealthy landlords and gave those lands to peasants.

Wu Chao strengthened T'ang rule.

Another able T'ang ruler was Empress Wu Chao (woo jaow). She became the only woman ever to rule China in her own name.

In 635, when she was 13, the beautiful Wu Chao left her family for T'ai-tsung's court. When T'ai-tsung died in 650, his son succeeded him. The new emperor made Wu Chao his chief wife and empress. After his death in 683, she ruled in her sons' names. Finally, in 690, Wu Chao took the throne herself.

China benefited from the empress's strong leadership. Her armies won victories in Korea. She lowered taxes. She also encouraged the spread of Buddhism in China.

Scholar-officials governed China.

The T'ang dynasty's most important reform was a system for choosing government officials. As early as the first century B.C., the Han emperor

Wu-ti had begun granting government jobs to scholars who passed an examination on the Five Classics of Confucius. Now, 700 years later, the system was revived and expanded.

Candidates for high office had to pass three grueling exams. Any man, from peasant to noble, could take the first exam. (Women could not compete except during Wu Chao's reign.) In theory, even a peasant could rise in government by doing well on the exams. In practice, however, the system favored wealthy men, because only they could afford an education.

The fortunate few who made it through the first test were known as Budding Scholars. They journeyed to their provincial capitals to take a second exam. If successful again, they traveled to the T'ang capital of Ch'ang-an. Here, locked in windowless cells, they spent days of mental torture taking the final exam.

The successful scholar became a member of China's elite class of scholar-officials. He might serve as a teacher or an administrator. In return, he was freed from paying taxes or serving in the army. He could adopt the fashion of growing his fingernails long. (A two-inch fingernail showed clearly that its owner did no manual labor.) Finally, the scholar-official could use his special privileges to gain land and amass a fortune.

China continued to use the examination system for over 1,000 years. The system had its weaknesses. It did not weed out selfish or corrupt officials. Also, training in writing poetry and quoting Confucius was not always helpful in collecting taxes or supervising canal repairs.

With all its faults, however, the system gave China a remarkably intelligent governing class. No longer did a few ruling families control the country. Now talent was more important than high birth in winning power. As a result, many moderately wealthy families shared in China's government. Scholar-officials and their families formed a new class in Chinese society. This class is often described as the **gentry**, a large, well-to-do group of people who rank below nobles but above the common people.

Some scholars struggle with their exams, while others wait outside to learn if they passed.

Ch'ang-an (known today as Xian) reflected the highly structured and regulated life of T'ang China. Located at the eastern end of the Great Silk Road and on the Wei River, Ch'ang-an was a center of trade and of wealth that supported a sophisticated civilization.

Ch'ang-an was the T'ang capital.

The capital of T'ang China was Ch'ang-an, a city of about 2 million people. Ch'ang-an's layout showed the Chinese passion for order. Its walls, 18 feet high, formed a rectangle 6 miles long and 5 miles wide. The walls were carefully aligned with the cardinal points of the compass. In each wall were three evenly spaced gates. The streets within the city formed neat, rectangular blocks. The main avenue was almost 500 feet wide, about 5 times wider than New York's Fifth Avenue.

The imperial palace lay within a complex of palaces and beautifully landscaped parks. The stone-paved road that led to the main palace curved in the shape of a dragon's tail.

Booming drums regulated daily life in Ch'ang-an. At daybreak, the police who patrolled the streets beat on their drums to announce the opening of the city gates. At sunset, the markets closed and people scurried home to the beat of drums as the police locked the city gates. Anyone caught on the streets after the evening drums had sounded could be severely punished.

Within the city, more than 200 different trades and professions had their own sections. So did the various groups of foreigners—Jewish traders and shopkeepers, traders from India, musicians and dancers from Burma, Buddhist pilgrims from many lands, and caravan leaders from the deserts.

Shops in Ch'ang-an sold rugs from Persia, glassware from Syria, lapdogs from Samarkand (in central Asia), pine nuts from Korea, peacock feathers from Burma, and ivory and gems from Vietnam. Chinese women took up foreign fashions. Their silk gowns (tight bodice, plunging neckline, winglike shoulderpads) were modeled after Persian styles. Their hair was done up in the elaborate fashion begun by the princesses of Samarkand.

Once, China had been cut off from the rest of the world by oceans, mountains, and deserts. The T'ang emperors did not isolate themselves behind such barriers. Imperial armies guarded the Great Silk Road, which linked China to the west. Merchandise and travelers moved safely across it in both directions. Sea trade connected China to India and Southeast Asia. In fact, China was more open to foreign trade and influence during the T'ang years than at any other time in history.

Drums such as this one regulated the lives of Chinese city dwellers. The booming of the drums announced daybreak and curfew.

Poets captured moments of beauty.

In earlier times, Chinese nobles had enjoyed rural pastimes such as horseback riding and hunting, much as the feudal lords of Europe did. In T'ang times, however, the gentry preferred living in the sophisticated atmosphere of cities. There the scholar-officials enjoyed the pleasures of literature and art.

During the golden years of T'ang China, every educated person was expected to write poems. For the gentry, it was almost a daily habit. "At this age," wrote a Chinese chronicler, "whoever was a gentleman was a poet." (Of course, educated people were still a tiny minority.)

Three qualities marked the Chinese poetry of this period. First, images from nature filled nearly all the poems. Mention of a butterfly's wing or a mountain stream subtly suggested the poet's mood. Second, each poem focused sharply on a single moment. Third, poems were brief, seldom longer than a dozen lines.

Li Po (lee boh) and Tu Fu were the most celebrated poets of the 700's. They were friends, but their poems were quite different. Li Po often wrote about the pleasures of life, whereas Tu Fu praised orderliness and the Confucian virtues.

Tu Fu's masterly touch shows in this poem titled "Welcome Rain One Spring Night":

> *A good rain knows its season*
> *And comes when spring is here;*
> *On the heels of the wind it slips secretly*
> *into the night;*
> *Silent and soft it moistens everything.*

The T'ang dynasty lost power.

By the early 700's, the T'ang dynasty was weakening. Crushing taxes brought hardship to the people but still failed to meet the rising costs of government. In times of famine, peasants fled their villages and ranged the countryside in bandit gangs.

Moreover, the T'ang could not control the vast empire they had built. In 751, Arabs soundly defeated the Chinese on China's western frontier at the Battle of Talas. Central Asia passed out of Chinese control and into Muslim hands.

To the Chinese, these troubles showed that the T'ang dynasty was losing the Mandate of Heaven. In 755, an army general led a revolt against the emperor. Although a new T'ang emperor regained the throne in 766, the T'ang dynasty never recovered its power and prestige. The government lost control over the more distant parts of China. At the same time, the Chinese began to turn away from foreign contacts, so trade declined. Finally in 905, Ch'ang-an was sacked and burned by rebels. In 907, the last T'ang emperor, a child, was murdered.

The Sung ruled a smaller empire.

After the end of the T'ang dynasty in 907, rival warlords divided China into unstable kingdoms. A poet summed up the chaos of these times: "States rose and fell as candles gutter out in the wind."

In 960, an able army leader proclaimed himself Emperor Sung T'ai-tsu (soong tye-dzoo). The Sung dynasty, like the T'ang, lasted about three centuries (960–1279).

Military decline The Sung dynasty was never as strong as either the Han or the T'ang. The Battle of Talas had marked the beginning of 500 years of military decline for China. Sung armies never regained the western lands lost at Talas in

Topics for review: dynastic cycle, mandate of Heaven (see Chapter 4).

751. More serious, they never regained the northern lands lost to the nomadic Hsia (shee-ah) and Tatars (TAHT-uhrz) during the T'ang decline.

Sung emperors tried to buy peace with their northern enemies. Beginning in 1004, they paid to the Tatar khan (chieftain) 6,250 pounds of silver and 200,000 bolts of silk each year. To appease the Hsia, they sent a yearly "gift" of 4,375 pounds of silver, 150,000 bolts of silk, and 30,000 pounds of tea. This policy worked for over 100 years.

Move to the south In the end, however, bribes failed to stop the barbarians. In 1126, the Tatars galloped as far as the Yellow River and captured the Sung capital of K'ai-feng (kye-fung).

The emperor was taken prisoner, but his family fled south across the Yangtze River to Hangchow (hahng-joh) in southern China. Thus the traditional center of Chinese civilization, the Yellow River valley, was lost to the Tatars. After 1126, the Sung emperors ruled only southern China.

Merchants thrived in Hangchow.

Despite its military troubles, the Sung dynasty was truly a golden age in southern China. Merchants prospered by selling rice, tea, fish, and other wares in the markets of Hangchow.

Unlike the orderly Ch'ang-an, Hangchow was a marvel of noise and confusion. There were no nightly curfews. Wine flowed all night in the city's restaurants. The canals that twisted through every section of Hangchow were choked with barges piled high with cargo. Mules laden with sacks clattered across the "rainbow bridges" that arched over the canals.

Paper money In the busy markets, two kinds of money passed from hand to hand. First, there were copper coins with square holes cut through the center. The standard unit for trading was "a thousand cash," a thousand coins fastened together on a long string. However, these strings of coins were clumsy and burdensome.

Therefore, between the years 1000 and 1100, the Sung government began to print paper money—the first such money in the world. The merchants of Hangchow could leave their strings of metal cash with bankers in exchange for paper bank notes. Each note carried the warning, "Counterfeiters will be beheaded."

Trade in silk and porcelain Merchants from Hangchow sent trade goods south to the Malay

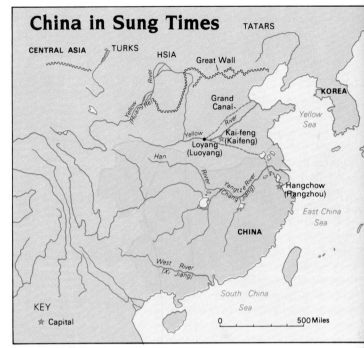

Map Study

Compare this map with the one on page 262. What lands has China's emperor lost?

Peninsula and west to India, the Persian Gulf, and even the coast of Africa. Two luxury items were especially easy to trade for a profit in any Asian or African port. One, of course, was Chinese silk. The other was porcelain.

For hundreds of years, the Chinese were the only people who knew the secret formula for combining certain clays and minerals to produce the fine, bone-hard substance called porcelain. Even today, people call such fine cups and dishes "china." The porcelain of Sung times was famous for its delicacy and its subtle colors with such delightful names as plum-colored blue and crushed-strawberry red.

Artists painted beauties of nature.

Like the T'ang period, Sung times were an age of artistic brilliance. The T'ang dynasty was the golden age of the poet. The Sung dynasty was the golden age of painting.

Every well-to-do family had a cherished collection of silk scrolls tucked away in a cabinet. When a scholar wished to escape the hustle and bustle of court life, he could find peace and

Graceful lines and subtle colors were characteristic of Chinese landscape painting during the Sung dynasty. In pottery, colors were soft but rich, as in this bowl for narcissus bulbs.

comfort by unrolling a scroll to view the beauties of nature. When he had sat long enough with trees, waterfalls, and mountain mists, he rolled up the scroll and returned it to the cabinet.

Sung artists did not use brightly colored paints. Black ink was their favorite paint. Said one Sung artist, "Black is ten colors." Grace of line was at the heart of Sung art.

China led the world in technology.

During the years of the T'ang and the Sung dynasties, no other area of the world was China's equal in skilled workers, science, and technology. Three Chinese inventions—printing, gunpowder, and the compass—were destined to have a revolutionary impact on the rest of the world. All three originated during the T'ang dynasty and were fully developed during the Sung.

Printing The Chinese began to print books around the year 600. Printers first cut a block of wood the size of two book pages. Over the block they pasted a sheet of thin paper on which the text was written. Using the writing on the paper as a guide, they carved around the characters so that they stood out in relief. By brushing ink onto the carved block and pressing it onto blank sheets of paper, a printer could produce a copy

of the original page. In one day, an expert printer could make 2,000 copies.

Sometime in the Sung dynasty, probably in the 1040's, an inventor named Pi Sheng (bee shung) took the next logical step—movable type. He arranged the individual characters on an iron plate coated with sticky resin and tar to hold them in place. Thus, the same characters could be used over and over, instead of carving a new set for each page. (Europeans did not discover how to print books until 1450.)

Magnetic compass The Chinese also learned that a magnetized needle floating in a bowl of water always points north-south. They first used

Footnote to History

Beginning in Sung times, the Chinese considered it beautiful for women to have very tiny feet. Upper-class parents would wrap their daughter's feet in tight bandages when she was about five years old. As the child grew, the wrappings forced her foot to curl painfully until the toes and heel came together. Women whose feet had been bound could hobble only a few steps. For a man, having such a wife was a sign of wealth because she could do little household work.

Discussion question: What attitude toward women is suggested by the value placed on long fingernails and bound feet?

this device to make sure their houses faced south, as custom required. By 1119, traders from south China had discovered how useful the compass could be for finding directions at sea. Eventually, Arab traders carried the compass to the Mediterranean Sea.

Gunpowder As early as the 600's, fireworks lit up the evening sky over Ch'ang-an during festivals. The Chinese called their thrilling firecrackers "fire trees," "flame flowers," and "peach blossoms."

Sometime after the year 1000, the Chinese experimented with explosive weapons. They made a kind of hand-grenade and shot off small rockets. However, gunpowder remained a minor invention until Europeans learned of it, probably by way of the Arabs and Mongols.

Eventually, the Sung dynasty collapsed. It had already abandoned the northern half of China to the Tatars. In the 1200's, it lost the southern half as well to the Mongols, a warlike people akin to the Tatars. The destructive fury of the Mongols affected much of Asia and Europe.

Section Review 1

Define: (a) gentry, (b) porcelain
Identify: (a) Sui dynasty, (b) Grand Canal, (c) T'ai-tsung, (d) T'ang dynasty, (e) Wu Chao, (f) Ch'ang-an, (g) Great Silk Road, (h) Battle of Talas, (i) Sung T'ai-tsu, (j) Sung dynasty, (k) Hangchow
Answer:
1. (a) What made the Sui dynasty important? (b) Why was it short-lived?
2. (a) How did Chinese officials earn their jobs? (b) What were the good points of this system? (c) The weaknesses?
3. (a) What part did the Tatars and the Hsia play in Chinese history? (b) What was the policy of the Sung toward them?
4. Describe the role of trade in China under the T'ang and Sung dynasties.
5. What political and military changes took place between T'ang and Sung times?
6. Describe three important inventions that the Chinese developed during the T'ang and Sung periods.

Critical Thinking
7. Explain why you agree or disagree with the following statement: "T'ang poetry and Sung painting share some basic values that were important in China."

The Mongols conquered a vast empire. 2

Who were the Mongols? To their enemies, they were "the devil's horsemen"—the ugliest, filthiest barbarians that ever lived. Of course, the Mongols saw themselves differently. In their own view, they were a noble people whose warlike, nomadic way of life was superior to the soft ways of city people. They felt nothing but contempt for the rich civilizations of India, China, and Persia.

Between 1200 and 1350, the Mongols conquered lands from the Pacific Ocean to the Adriatic Sea. Sweeping out of central Asia, they conquered much of the Islamic empire and destroyed Baghdad. They sent their armies westward to Russia, eastward to China, and south to the Himalayas. They ruled the largest unified land empire in history.

The Mongols came from the steppe.

The homeland of the Mongols was a vast grassland north of China's Great Wall. The hardy grasses there supported huge herds of horses, cattle, yaks, and sheep. Except for grass, the land was bare. One could travel for weeks without seeing a single tree. Savage winds swept the plain.

Mongolia lies at the eastern end of an enormous belt of **steppe**, or dry grassland, that stretches all across Asia and into eastern Europe. In this huge region lived a bewildering number of nomadic bands. You have already read some of their names—Huns, Avars, Turks, Tatars.

Whether called Hun, Tatar, or Mongol, the people of the eastern steppe followed basically the same way of life for centuries. They practically lived on horseback, following their huge herds of cattle, sheep, and horses over the steppe. They camped at night in great circular tents made of felt. Mare's milk was the one staple of their diet.

An Arab historian of the 1300's suggested the idea of cycles of warfare between the desert and the town. How were the early Arab armies examples of this conflict, first described in Chapter 2? The Turks? The Mongols?

The Mongols were fearsome warriors. Mounted on tough war ponies, their armies could cover great distances while living off the land. A Mongol warrior's most important weapon was his bow made of wood, horn, and sinew. Pulling the bow took over 100 pounds of force, and the Mongol archer pulled it while riding at a full gallop. He could hit an enemy over 200 yards away.

Genghis Khan united the Mongols.

For centuries, the Mongols had lived in loosely organized groups. Each group had its own leader, known as a **khan**. Around 1200, however, they suddenly united under the leadership of one of history's greatest conquerors. His name was Temujin (TEM-yoo-jin), but he is better known by his title, Genghis (JENG-gihs) Khan.

Temujin was born sometime around 1160. The first 20 years of his life were a struggle for survival. When he was 13, his father was murdered and Temujin nearly met the same fate at the hands of a rival Mongol family. However, he survived to become a minor chieftain.

Temujin spent the next 20 years fighting for power on the Mongolian steppe. He defeated his rivals one by one, showing no mercy. (After one victory, he slaughtered every person in the defeated group who was taller than a cart axle. Only the youngest children survived. They were brought up as his followers.)

In 1206, Temujin became the accepted ruler of all the steppe people. He took the title Genghis Khan, meaning "ruler of all between the oceans."

Between 1206 and his death in 1227, Genghis Khan conquered most of Asia.

Several traits lay behind Genghis Khan's stunning success as a conqueror. First, he was a brilliant organizer. He grouped his warriors in armies of 10,000, which in turn were organized into brigades of 1,000. Brigades were broken down into companies of 100, and companies were divided into 10-man platoons. Each group had its own commander. This organization meant that the army could carry out orders swiftly.

Second, Genghis Khan was shrewd as well as warlike. He never plunged recklessly into battle against an unknown enemy. He employed spies brilliantly to find out enemy weaknesses.

Finally, Genghis Khan used cruelty as a weapon. He believed in terrifying his enemies into surrender. If a city refused to open its gates to him, he might kill the entire population when he finally captured the place. The terror that the Mongols spread led many towns to surrender without a fight.

The Mongol empire divided.

Genghis Khan died in 1227, but the Mongol conquest continued. The sons and grandsons of Genghis Khan were responsible for the massacre of untold millions and the destruction of some of Asia's greatest cities. In about a 50-year period (1229–1279), they overthrew the Abbasid dynasty in Persia, burned Baghdad, conquered Kievan Russia, terrorized eastern Europe, and defeated China's Sung dynasty.

Mongol horsemen sharpened their riding skills in swift games of polo. Their small ponies were nimble enough for such games, but they were also hardy enough for long treks across the harsh lands of central Asia.

Another brilliant stroke was Genghis Khan's system for expanding his army with Turkish recruits. As Mongol hordes swept westward over the central steppe, defeated Turks were forced to fight for the Great Khan.

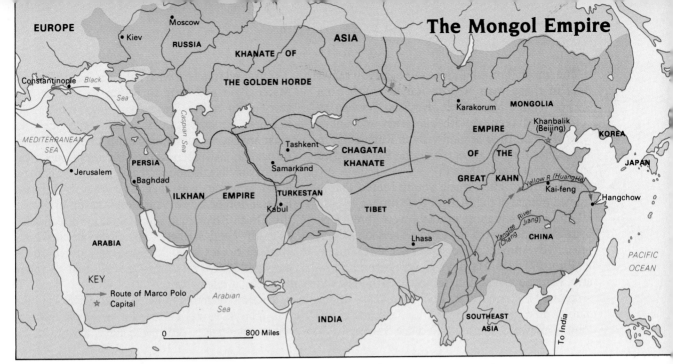

The Mongol Empire

Map Study

Name two cities that Marco Polo visited on his way to China. Which khanate controlled Russia? Persia? Korea?

By 1259, there were four khans, each ruling a different part of the empire. One khan ruled the central steppes of Turkestan. A second held the lands of the fallen Islamic empire in Persia. A third ruled Russia. These three khans owed loyalty to the fourth khan, known as the Great Khan, who ruled China. As time went by, however, each khan became more and more independent.

Kublai Khan ruled China.

The conqueror of Sung China was Genghis Khan's grandson, Kublai (KOO-blye) Khan. He ruled China from 1260 to 1294, taking the Chinese name Yüan for his dynasty. Unlike his barbarian ancestors, Kublai Khan spent almost his entire life within China. Far from the Mongolian steppe, he did not share his ancestors' hatred for civilization. On the contrary, he rather enjoyed living in the luxurious manner of a Chinese emperor. He ruled from a square capital in northern China that he called Khanbalik (City of the Great Khan). Today it is called Peking.

Failure to conquer Japan Kublai Khan tried to extend his rule to Japan. In 1281, the Great Khan sent two fleets carrying a total of 150,000 warriors against Japan. It was the largest seaborne invasion force in history until World War II. The Japanese

warriors fought the invaders to a standstill for 53 days. Suddenly, the sky darkened and a typhoon swept furiously across the Sea of Japan. Mongol ships were upended, swamped, and dashed to bits against the shore. Many Mongols drowned and others were quickly slain by the Japanese. For centuries afterward, the Japanese spoke reverently of the *kamikaze*, or "divine wind" that had saved Japan.

Marco Polo at the Mongol court Though warlike and cruel, the Mongols made the caravan routes across central Asia safe again for trade and travel. Ever since the decline of the T'ang dynasty, robbers and warring tribes had nearly shut down those routes. The Mongol empire put an end to such dangers. For about a century (1250–1350), Mongol armies kept peace across central Asia, just as Roman armies had once done around the Mediterranean Sea.

Footnote to History

In his quiver, a Mongol archer carried long-range arrows, short-range arrows, arrows to pierce armor, arrows to shoot fire into enemy camps, arrows with explosive tips, and even whistling arrows to use as signals.

Map Study answers: Jerusalem, Baghdad; Khanate of the Golden Horde; Ilkhan empire; Empire of the Great Khan

269

The most famous European to travel across Asia in these years was an Italian youth from Venice named Marco Polo. He was 17 when he set out from Venice with his father and uncle, who were on their second visit to Khanbalik. In 1275, after three years of travel, the Polos reached the court of Kublai Khan.

The shrewd khan made young Marco Polo a trusted official of the Mongol government. Nearly all the khan's highest officials were foreigners, because he distrusted the Chinese and kept them out of government. Polo served the Great Khan well for 17 years. He traveled across the Yellow and Yangtze rivers and returned with detailed reports of the empire. In 1292, two years before Kublai died, the Polos left China and made the long homeward journey to Venice by sea.

Captured in a war with the rival city of Genoa, Marco Polo had time in prison to tell the full story of his travels and adventures. To his awed listeners, he spoke of China's fabulous cities, its great armies, its fantastic wealth, and the strange things he had seen there. He mentioned the burning of "black stones" (coal) in Chinese homes. (Coal as a fuel was then unknown in Europe.) He told too of a new year's celebration in which the Great Khan received 100,000 white horses as a gift. He described a postal service in which 200,000 horses sped messages on paved roads between 10,000 relay stations. He told all these marvelous tales and more.

A fellow prisoner gathered Marco Polo's stories into a book. It was an instant success in Europe, but most readers did not believe a word of it.

Voice from the Past · *The City of the Great Khan*

After Marco Polo was released from prison in Genoa, he spent the rest of his life quietly in Venice. He died in 1324 at the age of 70. According to legend, he was asked on his deathbed to take back the so-called tall tales in his book. He answered that he had told less than half the wonders he had seen on his travels. Here is his description of Khanbalik.

The new royal city is a perfect square, each of its sides being 6 miles long. The city wall has 12 gates, 3 on each side of the square. The whole city was laid out by line. The streets are so straight that if you stand at one gate, you can see the gate on the other side of the city.

The throngs of inhabitants and the number of houses in Khanbalik are greater than the mind can grasp. The suburbs have even more people than the city itself. Within each suburb, there are many hotels at which merchants can stay.

Everything that is most rare and valuable in the world finds its way to this city. This is particularly true for rich goods from India, such as precious gems, pearls, and spices. From other parts of Cathay [China] itself, at least 1,000 carriages and packhorses loaded with raw silk enter the city each day.

In the center of the city is a great bell, which is rung every night. After the third stroke, no one dares to be found on the streets, except for some emergency. In such necessary cases, the person is required to carry a light. Groups of 30 or 40 guards patrol the streets all night, looking for people who are out of their houses after the great bell has rung.

1. What features show that the city was carefully planned?
2. What evidence shows that Khanbalik was larger than cities in Europe?
3. What statements show that trade was important in Khanbalik's economy?
4. Compare this description to that of Ch'ang-an (page 263). How are the two cities alike?

per que excita

Map Study answer: The Great Wall and the Grand Canal were longer; more cities had grown up.

They thought Polo's account was a marvelous collection of tall tales. It was clear to Marco Polo, however, that the civilization he had visited was the greatest in the world.

Section Review 2

Define: (a) nomad, (b) steppe, (c) khan, (d) kamikaze

Identify: (a) Mongols, (b) Genghis Khan, (c) Kublai Khan, (d) Yüan, (e) Marco Polo

Answer:

1. (a) Describe the Mongols' way of life. (b) How did this way of life make them strong warriors?
2. List three factors that helped Genghis Khan conquer an empire.
3. (a) What conquests were made by Genghis Khan? (b) What did his descendants add to the empire? (c) Identify the four areas the khans ruled after 1259.
4. How did the spread of Mongol rule affect trade between Europe and Asia?
5. Name at least three things in China that impressed Marco Polo.

Critical Thinking

6. (a) What evidence is there that the Chinese way of life influenced the Mongol conquerors? (b) What evidence is there that the Mongol rulers partly resisted Chinese influence?

China chose stability over change. 3

After Kublai Khan's death in 1295, Mongol rule weakened. Between 1295 and 1333, seven Mongols schemed and murdered their way to the Dragon Throne. China was beset by famines and revolts. The Yuan dynasty of the Mongols was near its end.

The Ming dynasty brought peace.

The leader who freed China from the Mongols was a commoner named Chu Yuan-chang (joo yoo-ahn-jang). Born into a peasant family in 1328, he was orphaned at the age of 16 and lived as a

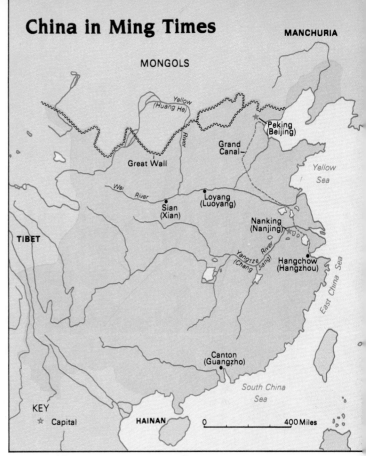

China in Ming Times

Map Study

What evidence shows that the Ming dynasty was more powerful than the Sung (map, page 265)?

beggar. He entered a Buddhist monastery where he learned to read and write. In 1352, Chu joined one of the secret groups resisting the Mongols. He proved to be a brilliant military leader. In 1368, Chu proclaimed himself the emperor of the new Ming (meaning "brilliant") dynasty. For himself, he took the name Ming T'ai-tsu, meaning "Grand Progenitor." By 1382, Ming T'ai-tsu had succeeded in bringing all of China under his rule.

China was divided into two major geographic zones. The southern, rice-growing zone followed the Yangtze River and centered on the seaports along the East China Sea. The northern zone was traditionally considered the true heartland of China. It had been the home of Confucius and of the Han and T'ang emperors. The first Ming emperor, Ming T'ai-tsu, was a southerner. He built his capital at Nanking (which meant "southern capital") on the Yangtze River and ruled there until his death in 1398.

Ming T'ai-tsu's son, Yung-lo, ruled from 1403 to 1424. He decided that he wished to rule from

Map Study answer: The Great Wall and the Grand Canal were longer; more cities had grown up.

Ming emperors such as Ch'eng-tsu (below) lived in the Forbidden City. The drawing above shows one of the city's hundreds of courtyards. Because the emperor stood for peace and harmony in China, the plan of the city emphasized balance, order, and symmetry.

the north, and he chose Kublai Khan's city of Khanbalik. Yung-lo gave Khanbalik a new name—Peking ("northern capital").

Peking was laid out in the traditional manner of a Chinese walled city. Gates facing north, south, east, and west pierced a high wall that enclosed the outer city. Broad avenues led from the outer gates to a smaller rectangular wall that surrounded the inner Imperial City. This city within a city was the center of routine government business.

Inside the Imperial City was yet another walled city with pagoda-like towers at its four corners. This was the Forbidden City—forbidden to everyone except the emperor and his court. Most residents of Peking lived and died without ever seeing what lay inside. The 250 acres of the Forbidden City held reception halls, private palaces, libraries, theaters, gardens, and athletic fields. More than 6,000 cooks prepared lavish meals for the 10,000 to 15,000 people who ate at the Court of Imperial Entertainments.

Ming scholars looked to the past.

From earliest times, the Chinese honored the ways of their ancestors. When a new dynasty came to power, its goal was not to bring new ways but to rule according to the good traditions of the past. Thus, China generally progressed by small adjustments, not by great changes.

The Ming emperors brought China's scholar-officials back to power. The Mongol emperors had deliberately excluded the scholar-officials (the gentry) from government. Ming T'ai-tsu restored the examination system (page 262).

Ming T'ai-tsu prized education so much that he opened public elementary schools in many cities. The use of printing made books easier to obtain in China than anywhere else in the world. Few rural children learned to read or write, but China's cities probably had a higher literacy rate than any other civilization in the 1300's.

To preserve the wisdom of the past, the second Ming emperor, Yung-lo, commissioned an encyclopedia of worthy Chinese writings from past ages. More than 2,000 scholars worked on the project for 4 years. When completed in 1408, the *Yung-lo Encyclopedia* filled 11,095 hand-written volumes. (The project was so huge that it was never printed.)

Such works of scholarship were impressive, but they also showed an overwhelming concern with the past. During the Ming dynasty, scholars held rigidly to Confucian ways of thinking. They did not strive for original ideas. Compared to their earlier achievements in science and technology, the Chinese of Ming times made few advances. Gradually, China lost its position of world leadership in those fields.

China limited foreign contacts.

During the first century of the Ming dynasty, from about 1350 to 1450, China was the greatest naval power in the world. In 1433, China's Grand Fleet crossed the Indian Ocean and sailed south along Africa's eastern coast. This immense fleet had over 100 ships manned by 27,500 sailors. Its commander, the 62-year-old Cheng Ho (jehng huh), had made seven such voyages since 1405. The ships of the Grand Fleet carried silks, porcelain, and art objects to exchange for ivory, rhinoceros horns, pearls, and jewels.

Cheng Ho's seventh voyage was the largest naval expedition launched by the Ming dynasty. It was also the last. Later Ming emperors decided such voyages were a waste of money. The Grand Fleet decayed. Even Cheng Ho's records were burned.

China's abandonment of its Grand Fleet marked an important turning point in world history. At the very time that China lost interest in exploration, the European kingdoms of Portugal and Spain began sending ships south around Africa. Eventually, European ships sailed east to Asia and west to the Americas. The story of these voyages is told in Chapter 15.

This turnabout suggests the different paths that western Europe and Asia took beginning in the 1400's. While China was turning inward, western Europe was ready to turn outward. Europeans wanted such Asian products as spices and silks. Christians from Europe also wanted to teach their religion to the people of Asia.

Europeans reached China in the 1500's.

The first Europeans to reach China by sea were the Portuguese. In 1513, a small fleet of Portuguese ships sailed into the South China Sea and anchored near Canton. Eager to make a quick fortune, the Portuguese grew impatient when the Chinese showed little interest in trade. The Portuguese sank Chinese vessels with their cannon. Horrified Ming officials closed their harbors to the "ocean devils" from Europe.

The Portuguese persisted in their efforts to trade for Chinese silk. At last, in 1557, the Chinese allowed them to operate a trading base at Macao (ma-COW). The base lay on an island near Canton and could be closely watched. For the next 200 years, the Chinese forced Europeans to conduct all their trade with China from Macao.

At first, Christian missionaries were more welcome in China than were Portuguese merchants. In 1583, a scholarly young Italian priest named Mateo Ricci (muh-TAY-oh REE-chee) went to China. Ricci learned Chinese and dressed like a scholar-official. Ming officials conceded that Ricci was less barbaric than other "ocean devils." In 1601, Ricci was at last permitted to travel north to Peking. He entered the Forbidden City and presented gifts of tribute to the emperor.

In a poem celebrating Cheng-Ho's voyages, the poet tells of "barbarous" people in Java: "Strange the people are./With unkempt heads and naked feet,/a barbarous tongue they speak;/dresses and hats they use not,/nor right nor virtue seek."

273

The scholars at court were not impressed with the missionary's gifts, but they were fascinated by two mechanical clocks that Ricci showed them. They were also impressed by his knowledge of astronomy. Because of his knowledge and his respect for Chinese ways, Ricci was accepted as a fellow scholar.

Within the Forbidden City, Ricci wrote in classical Chinese a Christian tract titled *The True Doctrine of God*. It was widely printed in China and helped other Roman Catholic missionaries convert thousands of Chinese. Ricci died in Peking in 1610.

The Ming dynasty collapsed.

By 1600, the Ming had ruled for more than 200 years and the dynasty was weakening. Ming officials were corrupt. The government was out of money, despite crushing taxes. High taxes and bad harvests pushed millions of peasants toward starvation. Many were reduced to a homeless life of begging and banditry. As in the past, they joined secret societies and plotted revolt.

Dangers also threatened from outside China. To the north and east of China lay Manchuria (man-CHOOR-ee-uh). The people of that region were called the Manchus (MAN-chooz). Though the Chinese considered them barbarians, the Manchus had already adopted many Chinese ways. Indeed, they had set up a kingdom modeled after China. By the late 1500's, the Manchus were a threat on China's northern border.

Peasant revolt and Manchu invasion combined to bring down the Ming dynasty. As an army of peasant rebels approached Peking, the last Ming emperor despaired. "I have incurred the wrath of the gods on high," he wrote. "My ministers have deceived me. I am ashamed to meet my ancestors." Setting aside his brush, the emperor hanged himself from a locust tree. Thus, in 1644, the Ming dynasty ended.

A foreign dynasty took power.

Soon after the death of the last Ming emperor, Manchu armies entered China and took over Peking. The Manchu ruler was declared China's new emperor. As the Mongols had done, the Manchus took a Chinese name for their dynasty— the Ch'ing dynasty.

The Manchu conquerors tried to keep themselves separate from the Chinese people. Manchus could hold government positions without taking the civil service examinations. Marriage between Chinese and Manchus was barred. The Manchu rulers forced all Chinese men to braid their hair into a long pigtail as a sign of low status.

In most respects, however, life under the Ch'ing was much the same as life under the Ming. The Ch'ing dynasty ruled for more than two centuries (1644–1912). In Chapter 29, you will see how revolutionary changes began to transform Chinese society under the later Ch'ing rulers.

Section Review 3

Define: literacy
Identify: (a) Ming T'ai-tsu, (b) Ming dynasty, (c) Nanking, (d) Peking, (e) Forbidden City, (f) Cheng Ho, (g) Macao, (h) Mateo Ricci, (i) Manchuria, (j) Ch'ing dynasty
Answer:
1. (a) How did Peking become the capital of China? (b) What was the difference between the Imperial City and the Forbidden City?
2. What factors encouraged learning in Ming China?
3. (a) What evidence indicates that the Chinese lost interest in contacts with other peoples after 1433? (b) Why did they make an exception for Mateo Ricci?
4. What factors, both within China and outside its borders, contributed to the downfall of the Ming dynasty?

Critical Thinking
5. Suggest some reasons why many Chinese rulers thought it important to build a grand capital city for their dynasty.

Japan developed a unique civilization. 4

Japan lies east of China, in the direction of the sunrise. In fact, the name *Japan* comes from the Chinese words *jih pen*, which mean "origin of the sun." The islands of Japan are separated from China by 500 miles of ocean. The nearest part of the Asian mainland is Korea, across 100 miles of water. In their early history, the Japanese were close enough to feel the civilizing influence of China. Yet they were far enough away to be reasonably safe from invasion.

About 3,000 volcanic islands make up the Japanese island group, but many are very tiny. Most of Japan's people have always lived on the four largest islands: Hokkaido (hah-KYE-doh), Honshu (HAHN-shoo), Shikoku (shih-KOH-KOO), and Kyushu (kee-YOO-shoo).

Japan's total land area is about equal to California's. The climate is temperate and the land is wooded. The islands are so mountainous, however, that only one fifth of the land is suitable for farming.

Clans dominated early Japan.

The first historic mention of Japan comes from Chinese writings of about A.D. 300. Archaeological evidence shows that people had lived in the Japanese islands for many centuries before that. However, because the early Japanese had no writing system, they left no historic records of their own.

Japan in the year 300 was not a united country. Instead, each **clan** controlled its own territory. A clan was a group of people who believed they were descended from the same ancestor.

The Yamato emperors The leading clan was the Yamato. The Yamato chiefs came to be called the emperors of Japan. Yet these emperors had no real power over the country as a whole. When rival clans fought for power, the winner gained control of the emperor and then ruled in the emperor's name.

The Shinto religion The Yamato rulers claimed the sun goddess as their ancestor. Other clans worshiped their own nature gods and goddesses. In different parts of Japan, people honored thousands of local gods and spirits. Their varied customs and beliefs eventually combined to form Japan's earliest religion. It was called Shinto (SHIHN-toh), meaning "the way of the gods."

The central idea of Shinto was the worship of nature. The sun goddess was the chief deity, but hundreds of lesser gods and spirits were thought to dwell in nature. Any unusual tree, rock, waterfall, or mountain was considered the home of a *kami*, or nature god.

The Japanese adapted Chinese ideas.

Around the year 500, the Japanese began to have more contact with mainland Asia. They were soon influenced by Chinese ideas and customs, about which they first learned from Korean travelers.

Buddhism in Japan For centuries, Korea had been in close touch with China. During the 500's, many Koreans migrated to Japan, bringing Chinese influences with them. One such group of Korean travelers brought with them a bronze statue of the Buddha. Within 50 years, the new religion had spread widely in Japan. For many centuries, the greatest Japanese scholars and sages lived as Buddhist monks.

The Japanese did not give up their Shinto faith. Shinto and Buddhism comfortably coexisted. Some Buddhist rituals became Shinto rituals, and some Shinto gods were worshiped in Buddhist temples.

Cultural borrowing The most influential convert to Buddhism was Prince Shotoku (shoh-toh-koo). In 607, Prince Shotoku sent a group of scholars to study Chinese civilization firsthand

Map Study

At the narrowest part of the sea, how far is Japan from Korea? From China? What sea lies east of Korea? West of Korea?

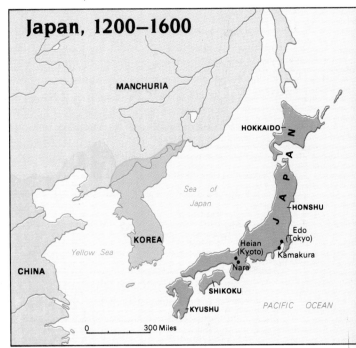

Japan, 1200–1600

For a noble family in Japan, amusements included music, games, and writing poetry or love letters. The screen in the background, with its view of a landscape, shows the Chinese influence on Japanese art.

at Ch'ang-an. These scholars braved the dangers of shipwreck and storm without even a compass to guide them on the 500-mile voyage. Over the next 200 years, while the T'ang dynasty was at its height, the Japanese sent many such groups to learn more of Chinese ways.

The Japanese adopted the Chinese system of writing. Japanese artists painted landscapes in the Chinese manner. The gracefully curved, winglike roofs of Japan's Buddhist pagodas imitated Chinese roofs. The Japanese even followed Chinese styles in the simple arts of everyday living such as cooking, gardening, drinking tea, and hairdressing.

Imperial government For a time, Japan also modeled its government on China's. Prince Shotoku drew up a written plan of government based on the teachings of Confucius. Shotoku and his successors tried to build a strong central government like that of the T'ang rulers. Shotoku also tried to introduce China's examination system in Japan. However, the attempt failed. In Japan, noble birth remained the key to winning a powerful job. Unlike China, Japan continued to be a country where a few great families held power.

In imitation of Ch'ang-an, Japanese builders laid out a magnificent square city on the island of Honshu. This city, called Nara, was the first capital in Japanese history.

The Japanese adapted and changed Chinese ways to suit their own needs. While they learned much, they also retained their own traditions. Then, in the 800's, Japan's ruling family abruptly broke contact with the T'ang court. Japanese leaders felt they had nothing more to learn from China. Japan's own culture was about to come into full flower.

🏯 Court society developed at Heian.

Nara was the Japanese capital from 710 to 784, less than a century. In 794, Emperor Kammu built a new capital city called Heian (**HAY**-ahn). Its modern name is Kyoto (kee-**OHT**-oh). Japan's 400-year golden age from 794 to 1185 is known as the Heian age.

"Dwellers among the clouds" Historians estimate that there were about 5 million Japanese in the year 800. Most were farmers and fishers living in tiny villages. Heian itself had a population of about 100,000 of which only 3,000 belonged to the noble class. These families lived so far above the common people that they were called "dwellers among the clouds."

Men and women of noble birth in Heian lived outdoors as much as possible. They gossiped and sipped tea around the fishponds of their beautiful gardens. A Japanese woman seated in her garden was as colorful as the surrounding cherry blossoms. She wore up to 12 silk gowns, one over the other. As the breezes blew, the various colors showed in shifting patterns. If one color of her dress was off by a mere shade, people at court might snicker about it.

Men and women alike used cosmetics heavily. They blackened their teeth because white teeth were considered ugly. They covered their faces

The capital of Japan from 794 to 1868, Kyoto became a center of learning and the arts. A city of tradition, it is known for its Buddhist temples and Shinto shrines.

with white powder. Women plucked out their eyebrows and painted artificial brows high on their foreheads. Sometimes they gilded their lips. Men used perfumes as a mark of identification.

To be accepted in Heian society, one had to write poetry. To start a romance, a man or woman composed a short poem showing the writer's fine taste and artistry. The poem had to be written on a sheet of colored paper with a shade and texture that perfectly suited the feeling of the poem. The other person replied in the same way. If each person liked the other's poem, the man and woman went on with their flirtation. The slightest blunder with the brush might end the romance.

Leading women authors The best accounts of this elegant society come from the diaries, essays, and novels written by women of the court. The women writers of the Heian court were far more noteworthy than the male writers of the time.

Why? Two reasons have been suggested. First, Japanese women in the Heian Age were held in high esteem, unlike women in China or the Greco-Roman world. Men deferred to their artistic taste and their intellect. Second, Japanese men were bound by custom to use only Chinese characters when they wrote. Women wrote in a simpler script called *kana* that was better suited to the Japanese language. Thus, ideas flowed much more smoothly from a woman's brush.

The leading writer of this period was Lady Murasaki Shikibu (moo-rah-sah-kee shee-kee-boo). Around the year 1000, she wrote *The Tale of Genji*, which has been called the world's first true novel. It tells a long, involved story about the countless loves of its hero, Prince Genji, "the Shining Prince." A modern edition of it fills over 4,000 pages. Japanese scholars have so valued Lady Murasaki's masterpiece that their commentaries on it fill 10,000 volumes.

Feudal lords divided the land.

During the Heian Age, Japan's central government was strong. However, this strength was soon to be challenged by great landowners and clan chiefs who acted more and more as independent local rulers.

Between 1000 and 1200, Japan developed a feudal system much like the one in Europe during the Middle Ages. Each lord surrounded himself with a bodyguard of loyal warriors. Wars between rival lords became commonplace. Lesser lords pledged to fight for greater lords in exchange for protection. Peasants began to pay taxes to the lords, not to the central government.

The warriors who fought for the lords were called **samurai** (SAM-yuh-RYE), meaning "one who serves." The samurai lived according to a harsh code called *bushido*, which meant "the way of the warrior." A samurai's honor was constantly on the line. He had to prove his absolute courage in battle and absolute loyalty to his lord. Dying an honorable death was judged more important than living a long life.

A samurai's armor was one of the most elaborate costumes ever worn. It consisted of leather shinguards, billowing pantaloons, a kimono, broad thigh guards tied over the pantaloons, metal-cased shoulder guards, a chest protector, an iron collar, a cotton skullcap, an iron facemask, and a visored helmet. The samurai trained himself to get into this outfit in a minute. This armor weighed much less than the chain mail worn by European knights, and it provided good protection in battle.

Shoguns ruled puppet emperors.

By the 1100's, two clans, the Taira (tah-ee-rah) and the Minamoto (mee-nah-moh-toh), had gathered the largest armies of samurai. Up and down the island of Honshu, the armies of the two clans fought murderous battles. Heian was burned several times. After almost 30 years of fighting, the war ended in 1185 with a Minamoto victory.

In 1192, the emperor gave a Minamoto leader named Yoritomo the title of **shogun** (SHOH-guhn). The title meant "supreme general of the emperor's army." In effect, the shogun had the powers of a military dictator. Officials, judges, taxes, armies, roads—all were under his authority.

The emperor still lived in Kyoto, rebuilt on the ruins of Heian. Although the emperor enjoyed great prestige, the real center of power was at the shogun's military headquarters at Kamakura. The 1200's are known in Japanese history as the Kamakura shogunate. The system of central government led by the shoguns lasted in Japan until 1868, nearly 700 years.

Under the early shoguns, the local lords still held great power. Instead of trying to wipe out

Have students compare and contrast the samurai and the medieval knight.

In addition to this impressive suit of armor, a samurai wore two razor-sharp swords as symbols of his profession and high rank.

Section Review 4

Define: (a) clan, (b) kami, (c) kana, (d) samurai, (e) bushido, (f) shogun
Identify: (a) Yamato, (b) Shinto, (c) Shotoku, (d) Nara, (e) Heian, (f) Kyoto (g) Murasaki Shikibu, (h) Minamoto, (i) Kamakura
Answer:
1. (a) Where is Japan located? (b) Give a brief geographic description of Japan.
2. (a) Name at least five things the Japanese borrowed from China. (b) What did Shotoku do to make Japan more like China?
3. (a) What was the Heian Age? (b) Briefly describe Heian society.
4. (a) How was Japan's feudal system organized? (b) What were the most important characteristics of the samurai?
5. (a) What powers did the shoguns have? (b) How did the shogunate affect feudalism in Japan?

Critical Thinking
6. Compare Japan's system of government to that of China. (a) Why might a casual observer think the two were similar? (b) What were the fundamental differences?

Japan turned to isolation. 5

A Japanese Buddhist once wrote, "The proud do not last long, but vanish like a spring night's dream. And the mighty ones too will perish, in the end, like dust before the wind." Japan's history from 1300 to 1600 was filled with the rise and fall of proud and mighty lords.

Feudal lords controlled Japan.

After the decline of the Kamakura shoguns, the most powerful of the feudal lords became nearly independent rulers in their own areas. They were known as **daimyo** (DYE-mee-OH), which means "great name." Each daimyo commanded his own army of sword-wielding soldiers. Peasants as well as samurai took up arms. Dangerous bands of lordless samurai roamed the land.

feudalism, the Kamakura shoguns chose to build upon it. They worked with the local lords. A lord who loyally served the shogun was given almost a free hand to rule his own province.

The Kamakura shoguns were strong enough to turn back the two naval invasions sent by the great Mongol ruler Kublai Khan in 1274 and 1281 (page 269). However, the Japanese victory over the Mongols drained the shogun's treasury. Loyal samurai were bitter when the government failed to pay them. The Kamakura shoguns lost prestige and power. Samurai attached themselves more closely to their local lords, who soon fought one another as fiercely as they had fought the Mongols. Civil war shook the land.

The years from 1467 to 1568 were known as the Age of the Country at War. Rival armies repeatedly attacked and burned Kyoto, the imperial capital. The powerless emperors lived in poverty amid the ruins of their city. (One emperor was so poor that, when he died, his burial was delayed for six weeks until money could be scraped up for a funeral.) Disorder spread through the country. At the same time, Japanese pirates terrorized both their own seacoast and the coastal cities of southern China.

Europeans reached Japan.

The first European ships arrived in Japan in 1543, during this time of fighting and disorder. As in China, these first Europeans were Portuguese. Unlike China, Japan had no strong central government to bar or limit contact with Europeans. Thus, some daimyo welcomed the first Portuguese merchants and missionaries. If one daimyo turned against the Europeans, they could always find another daimyo to help them.

The Japanese looked with amusement at the Portuguese sailors, who dressed in button-down jackets and baggy trousers, or pantaloons. The Japanese called the strange-looking newcomers *nampan*, meaning "southern barbarians." As other ships arrived on their coast, the Japanese received the visiting nampan (mainly Portuguese and some Dutch) with courtesy. Japanese merchants eagerly traded silks for guns. For a brief time (around 1600), rich daimyo thought it stylish to wear pantaloons, smoke tobacco, and play cards in the European manner.

From swords to guns The novelty that most intrigued the Japanese were the Europeans' guns. One Japanese writer described his experiment with a musket:

> Set up a small white target on a bank, grip the object [musket] in your hand, compose your body, and closing one eye, apply fire to the hole. The pellet hits the target squarely. The explosion is like lightning and the report like thunder. Bystanders must cover their ears.

Japanese craftsmen quickly learned how to make guns in their own workshops. Power-hungry daimyo began to equip their troops with muskets and bullets.

Catholic missionaries As in China, Catholic missionaries came to China close on the heels of European merchants. The leader of the first Christian mission to Japan later became one of the Church's most beloved saints, Francis Xavier (ZAY-vee-uhr). During Xavier's two years in Japan (1549–1551), he baptized hundreds of converts.

For almost 90 years, Catholic missionaries traveled freely in Japan. With amazement, they noted the Japanese habit of taking daily baths. (In Europe at this time, people rarely washed.) With some shame, the missionaries tried to change their own European table manners because these offended the Japanese. "They are much amazed," wrote one priest, "at our eating with the hands and wiping them on napkins, which then remain covered with food stains, and this causes them disgust."

Strong leaders restored order.

Soon after the Europeans arrived, a series of determined rulers strengthened Japan's central government. In the 1560's, a ruthless daimyo named Oda Nobunaga (oh-dah noh-boo-nah-gah) used firearms to defeat armies ten times larger than his own. He entered Kyoto in triumph in 1573. Nobunaga won and held the area around Kyoto, although he did not control all Japan.

After Nobunaga was assassinated by one of his own generals in 1582, two other ruthless but able men completed the process of uniting Japan. First Nobugnaga's best general, Toyotomi Hideyoshi (toh-yoh-toh-mee hee-deh-yoh-shee), killed the assassin. Then Hideyoshi went on to win control over the shogunate at Kyoto. Many Japanese historians regard him as the greatest of their country's founding fathers. Although he never took the title of shogun, Hideyoshi was in fact the absolute ruler of Japan.

In 1588, Hideyoshi ordered a "sword hunt," in which he commanded all peasants to surrender their swords. Other decrees set up strict barriers between social classes. Hideyoshi himself had risen from common foot soldier to ruler of the country, but he did not intend for others to follow that path. Never again could a peasant or merchant hope to wear the armor of a samurai.

Hideyoshi's armies crushed any daimyo who defied him. He even had ambitions to conquer Ming China. However, his armies were defeated

Nobunaga's killer also burned down his palace. A European wrote. "Of this man, who made everyone tremble not only at the sound of his voice but even at the mention of his name, there did not remain even a small hair that was not reduced to ashes."

279

in Korea in 1597. The great Hideyoshi died a year later of natural causes.

The last of Japan's three unifiers was Tokugawa Ieyasu (toh-koo-gah-wah ee-yeh-yah-soo), one of Hideyoshi's strongest supporters. In 1600, Ieyasu defeated his rivals at the Battle of Sekigahara. He assumed the title of shogun in 1603. He then moved Japan's administrative center east to the place where his own support was strongest— the small town of Edo, later named Tokyo.

To keep the daimyo from rebelling, Ieyasu required that they spend at least half their time at his capital. Even when they returned to their own lands, they were forced to leave their families in Edo.

Ieyasu founded the Tokugawa shogunate. On his deathbed in 1616, Ieyasu advised his son and successor, "Take care of the people. Strive to be virtuous. Never neglect to protect the country." For the most part, his advice was well followed. Tokugawa shoguns gave Japan stability until 1868.

Japan's door slammed shut.

By 1600, as many as 300,000 Japanese (out of a population of 20 million) had become Christian. The growing influence of the missionaries worried Japan's leaders. Hideyoshi threatened Christians with banishment. Ieyasu, the Tokugawa shogun, was alarmed by reports that the Spanish had conquered an island in the Philippines. Might these aggressive Europeans soon turn their guns against Japan? Might the missionaries plot with Japanese Christians to overthrow him?

In 1614, Ieyasu banned Christianity in Japan. Over the next 20 years, Tokugawa officials rounded up Christians and subjected them to torture and execution. In 1638, about 36,000 Japanese Christians made a final, desperate stand behind the walls of an old fortress. Their futile defense ended tragically. Only 105 of the Christians came out alive.

The Tokugawa shoguns also banned all European merchants except the Dutch. Just as the Chinese had limited the Europeans to Macao, the Japanese now confined Dutch merchants to the port of Nagasaki. For the next 200 years, Japan remained closed to Europeans. (It did not, however, break off contact with China.)

The Tokugawa policy of isolation from Europe had far-reaching effects on Japan. Gradually, Japan fell behind Europe in science, technology, and military power. On the other hand, isolation gave Japan a long period of peace and stability. During the years of the Tokugawa shogunate, Japanese culture was rich and creative. Buddhist monks developed a unique religious outlook, and artists perfected an exquisite style of painting.

Zen Buddhism stressed meditation.

Buddhism in Japan followed a path of quiet contemplation. *Zen* was the Japanese word for meditation. Though there were other forms of Buddhism in Japan, Zen Buddhism had the greatest influence on Japanese culture.

Zen Buddhists seek spiritual enlightenment through meditation. Strict discipline of mind and body was the Zen path to wisdom. Young monks would sit rigidly for hours, staring straight ahead with unblinking eyes. If they fidgeted or showed signs of losing concentration, a Zen master might

Daily Life · *The Tea Ceremony*

The Zen spirit appeared in the popular tea ceremony. A small group of close friends gathered in a plain, low-ceilinged room to share tea. The tea was not intended to quench their thirst but to lift their minds. A tea master served them, using the host's tiny tea utensils. The master first poured hot water into a ceramic cup containing green powdered tea. A guest would meditate before and after sipping, then another friend would do likewise. When the cup was finally empty (after at least an hour of sipping), the friends would admire it as a fragile symbol of eternity.

Japan always had difficulty deciding how to deal with other peoples. Recall that for about 200 years (607–838), the Japanese were eager to learn all they could about Chinese civlization. But then abruptly, they turned their backs on Chin and removed their ambassadors from the Ch'ang-an court.

Tranquil Zen gardens are still maintained in Japan today. Sand patterns, carefully chosen rocks, and subtle blends of leaf color and texture are the main features of such a garden.

shout at them and beat them with a stick. Some Zen masters helped their disciples to free themselves from ordinary ways of thinking by asking unanswerable riddles. The master might say, for example, "When both hands are clapped, they make a sound. What is the sound of one hand clapping?"

Art suggested nature.

Japanese paintings, like tea, were made for meditation and spiritual enlightenment. Japanese artists followed the style of painting that arose in China under the Sung dynasty (page 265). Japan's greatest master of the Sung style was a Zen monk named Sesshu (sehs-shoo), who worked during the late 1400's. Sesshu's most famous surviving work is a silk scroll 55 feet long. It shows the four seasons in shades of black, white, and gray. To appreciate this great work, one must roll it open slowly and meditate on the differences between appearances and reality with each passing image of tree and rock.

Nature played a key role both in Japanese art and in Zen meditation. During the 1400's, a small garden of jagged rocks and clipped shrubs became a common feature of the Zen temple. These gardens had symbolic meaning. Instead of seeing merely a gray rock surrounded by raked white pebbles, a Zen meditator might see a lofty mountain peak towering above a vast sea. The garden was always starkly simple. As one gardener-artist of medieval Japan warned, "Take caution not to . . . overcrowd the scenery to make it more interesting. Such an effect often results in a loss of dignity and a feeling of vulgarity."

The artistic traditions that developed during Japan's period of isolation had lasting importance for the country. For 200 years, Japan was able to continue on its own path, with little influence from the outside world.

Section Review 5

Define: (a) daimyo, (b) nampan
Identify: (a) Francis Xavier, (b) Oda Nobunaga, (c) Toyotomi Hideyoshi, (d) Tokugawa Ieyasu, (e) Zen, (f) Sesshu
Answer:
1. Describe the political situation in Japan during the 1400's and 1500's.
2. (a) When did the first Europeans reach Japan? (b) How were they received?
3. What part did each of the following play in unifying Japan? (a) Oda Nobunaga (b) Toyotomi Hideyoshi (c) Tokugawa Ieyasu
4. (a) What was Tokugawa Ieyasu's policy toward the daimyo? (b) Toward Europeans?
5. (a) What policy did later Tokugawa shoguns adopt toward other countries? (b) How did this policy affect Japan?

Critical Thinking
6. (a) How did Japanese policy toward Christianity change between the 1550's and the early 1600's? (b) Give several reasons to explain this change.

Sesshu was a contemporary of Leonardo da Vinci.

Chapter Review 12

Summary

1. Two great dynasties ruled China. After the Sui reunited China in the late 500's, the country experienced a golden age. The T'ang, noted for poetry, expanded the examination system. Printing, the compass, and gunpowder were invented. The Sung dynasty, noted for its art, moved the capital to southern China.

2. The Mongols conquered a vast empire. After Genghis Khan united the nomadic Mongols, they conquered most of Asia. China's ruler, Kublai Khan, encouraged trade and hired non-Chinese officials. Among them was Marco Polo, whose tales increased European interest in Asia.

3. China chose stability over change. The Ming dynasty at first encouraged trade but later limited foreign contacts. Under the Ming, traditional values were stressed. The Manchus, who succeeded the Ming, followed similar policies.

4. Japan developed a unique civilization. From the 500's to the 800's, Japan borrowed heavily from Chinese culture. Japan enjoyed a golden age, especially for literature, during the Heian period. Gradually, powerful landowners built up samurai armies in a feudal system. A shogun replaced the emperor as effective ruler.

5. Japan turned to isolation. Following the Kamakura shoguns, strong local lords called daimyo challenged the authority of the shogun. After a period of disorder, Japan was reunited. Under the Tokugawa shoguns, Japan cut off European contacts and banned Christianity. During this time, Japan fell behind Europe.

Reviewing the Facts

1. Define the following terms:
   a. gentry
   b. steppe
   c. khan
   d. clan
   e. samurai
   f. shogun
   g. daimyo

2. Explain the importance of each of the following names, places, or terms:
   a. Sui
   b. T'ang
   c. Ch'ang-an
   d. Buddhism
   e. Sung
   f. Great Silk Road
   g. Mongolia
   h. Genghis Khan
   i. Kublai Khan
   j. Marco Polo
   k. Khanbalik
   l. Ming
   m. Peking
   n. Ch'ing
   o. Shinto
   p. Heian
   q. *The Tale of Genji*
   r. Francis Xavier
   s. Tokugawa Ieyasu

Koreans bring Buddhism to Japan

Sui dynasty reunites China

Heian Age begins in Japan

Kublai Khan rules China

Genghis Khan conquers Asia

Manchus conquer China

Europeans reach East Asia

Daimyo control Japan

Kamakura shoguns repel Mongol invasion

T'ang dynasty

Sung dynasty

Ming dynasty

500   700   900   1100   1300   1500   1700

3. (a) How did a person become a member of the gentry in China? (b) What benefits did that position bring?
4. What major T'ang inventions became important outside China?
5. (a) What methods did the Mongols use to build an empire? (b) What areas did they conquer?
6. (a) What was the Japanese attitude toward Europeans in the early 1500's? (b) After 1600?

Basic Skills

1. **Comparing maps** Compare the size of the Mongol Empire, shown on page 269, with that of Alexander the Great, shown on page 116. Use the scale of miles to estimate their length from east to west, their width in the center, and their area (length times width). How much larger was the Mongol empire?
2. **Making a time line** Make a time line to show Mongol expansion in Russia to the west and in China and Japan to the east. Indicate the dates of major expansion, consolidation of empire, and checks to Mongol expansion or control.
3. **Making a chart** Make a chart to show the various achievements of the T'ang, Sung, and Ming dynasties, using a column for each. For the vertical rows, use the following headings: *Political, Economic, Cultural,* and *Social.* Fill in the appropriate information.

Researching and Reporting Skills

1. **Using reference books** Locate in your library the reference work called *Books in Print.* Information is listed in separate volumes for book titles, authors, and subject. Using the "Subject" volume, look up books on the early history of Japan. Give the titles and authors of at least five books in which you might find information about Japanese shoguns and samurai.
2. **Writing an essay** Use the chart on the T'ang, Sung, and Ming dynasties to evaluate them. (a) Which civilization do you think was superior? (b) Write a brief essay expressing your opinion and providing supporting evidence.
3. **Formulating research questions** Buddhism had great influence in both Chinese and Japanese civ-

ilization. What questions would provide a framework for learning more about Buddhist influence on those societies?

Critical Thinking

1. **Comparing** (a) Compare the feudal system of medieval Europe with that in Japan between 1300 and 1600. (b) How did the two systems develop, and how did they end?
2. **Identifying viewpoints** (a) How did the Chinese look upon the Mongols? (b) How did the Mongols look upon the Chinese? (c) How would you characterize the Mongols?
3. **Drawing conclusions** This chapter describes the rise and fall of four Chinese dynasties. (a) What recurring patterns occur in the decline of these dynasties? (b) What advice might you give a Chinese emperor, based on these patterns?
4. **Synthesizing** (a) Identify and list some of the common characteristics found in Chinese and Japanese art through the ages. (b) Discuss what influences may have had this effect.

Perspectives on Past and Present

1. What factors led China to turn away from foreign contact? What reasons did Japan have for its policy of isolation? What countries today place strict limits on trade and foreign contact? What advantages and disadvantages do you see in such a policy?
2. In China, long fingernails and bound feet became fashionable. Why were these styles regarded as signs of wealth and status? What are some modern examples of status symbols?

Investigating History

1. One of the vital connections between East and West was the Great Silk Road. Look for information on this trade route in historical atlases, college texts, *National Geographic Magazine,* or other sources available to you. Describe the cities and landscapes a traveler would encounter along this road. How did the road change over time? What other uses did it have besides trade?
2. Read Marco Polo's description of China in the time of Kublai Khan. Write a brief report explaining why his fellow Venetians would have trouble believing what he described.

Civilizations of India and Southeast Asia

Although the Taj Mahal was built by a conquering dynasty in the 1600's, it has become a symbol of India. The four outer towers are minarets, from which leaders call Muslims to prayer.

Key Term

purdah

Read and Understand

1. India flourished under the Guptas.
2. Mughals ruled India in splendor.
3. Kingdoms arose in Southeast Asia.

Shah Jahan, the ruler of northern India, was one of the wealthiest kings in the world. He was also a heartbroken man. In 1631, after 19 years of marriage, his beloved wife, Mumtaz Mahal (moom-**TAHZ** mah-**HAHL**), had died. She had given her husband 13 children but died giving birth to the fourteenth. The grieving monarch commanded that a tomb be built "as beautiful as she was beautiful."

Those events were the beginning of the romantic story of the Taj Mahal. Fine white marble and jewels were gathered from many parts of Asia and brought to a spot near Agra. For 22 years, 20,000 workers labored on Shah Jahan's last gift to his queen.

The ivory-white beauty of India's greatest monument is difficult to describe. Artists have praised it for its perfect proportions. Visitors

British poet Edward Lear wrote, after visiting the Taj Mahal in 1874: "Come to the Taj Mahal; descriptions of this wonderfully lovely place are simply silly, as no words can describe it at all. . . . Let the inhabitants of the world be divided into two classes—them as has seen the Taj Mahal; and them as hasn't."

have marveled at the way the towering dome and four minarets seem to change colors as the sun moves across the sky. Inside are thousands of carved marble flowers inlaid with tiny sapphires, bloodstones, rubies, and lapis lazuli.

Shah Jahan dreamed of building an identical tomb of black marble for himself nearby. The two tombs were to be linked by a bridge of polished silver, a symbol of the royal couple's love. However, the black tomb was never built. One of Shah Jahan's sons revolted and imprisoned his aged father not far from the Taj Mahal. When the old emperor died in 1666, a mirror was found in his prison room. It was angled so that the dying man could gaze at the reflection of the Taj Mahal. When he died, Shah Jahan was buried in the Taj Mahal next to the bejeweled casket of Mumtaz Mahal.

During their lives, Shah Jahan and Mumtaz Mahal prayed to Allah, the Muslim name for God. In the 1600's, Islam was fairly new to India. The religion of ancient India had been Hinduism (pages 70–72), not Islam. At the point where Chapter 4 ended, with the fall of the Maurya dynasty in 180 B.C., the prophet Muhammad (founder of Islam) had not been born.

In this chapter, we must go a long way back in time to a dynasty of Hindu rulers called the Guptas. These powerful kings lived more than 1,000 years before the building of the Taj Mahal. We will see how Hinduism developed during this early period. Then we will see how Islamic Turks swept in from central Asia, slaughtering Hindus and destroying their temples. These conquerors brought the Muslim religion to India.

In the 1,400 years described in this chapter, there was much violence. However, there was also much splendor and beauty. The marble domes and minarets of the Taj Mahal stand as a monument to the achievements of these years.

India flourished under the Guptas. 1

In India, 500 years of disunity followed the end of the Mauryan dynasty (page 76) in 180 B.C. In northern India, waves of invaders continued to arrive from Persia, Afghanistan, and the plains

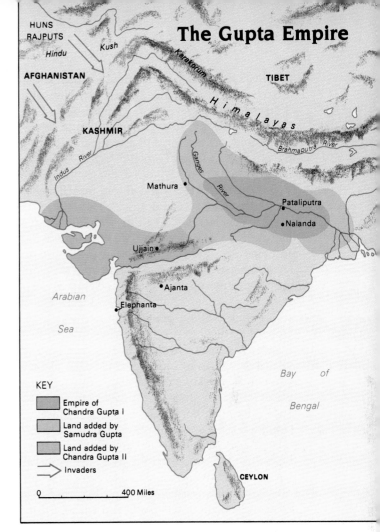

The Gupta Empire

Map Study

What river valley formed the heartland of the early Gupta empire? Under what ruler did the empire reach its greatest size?

of central Asia. These newcomers set up many warring states and kingdoms. Southern India was not affected by those invasions. Politically, the south remained a land apart.

The Gupta dynasty ruled the north.

In A.D. 320, a Hindu prince named Chandra Gupta (CHUHN-druh GOOP-tuh) was crowned king of the upper Ganges valley. (He was no relation to the long-dead Chandragupta Maurya.) The new king was the first in a line of remarkable rulers who brought a golden age to India.

The Gupta dynasty ruled a mighty empire for nearly 150 years (320–467). After the founder of the line, Chandra Gupta I, came Samudra Gupta, called the Poet King. Samudra Gupta

285

extended his kingdom to the mouth of the Ganges River, winning another nickname—"exterminator of all other kings."

The third Gupta ruler, Chandra Gupta II, was both a man of learning and a conqueror. During his reign, the Gupta empire stretched across northern India from sea to sea. For the first time in 500 years, northern India was united under one government.

Indian scholars in Gupta times left few written histories. To a Hindu, the passage of worldly time from past to present was unimportant. Therefore, few Indian scholars bothered to record current events. Instead, Indians celebrated their past in oral accounts called *itihas* (meaning "so it was told"). These oral records were very accurate, but they do not emphasize dates. Thus, modern historians have problems pinpointing when key events in Indian history took place.

Much of what we know about India comes from Chinese monks who traveled to India to study Buddhism in the land where it had begun. Around A.D. 405, the Chinese monk Fa-Hsien traveled widely in India and greatly marveled at the peace and prosperity he saw. He reported that the government supported free hospitals for the sick. He was especially impressed that as a stranger, he could travel freely and without fear.

Science and learning advanced.

Learning thrived during the Gupta period. Young Hindus of the priestly (Brahmin) castes attended school from the age of 9 to 30. The university at Nalanda on the Ganges River was famous throughout Asia and attracted students of philosophy from faraway kingdoms. Gupta scholars made many advances in science. The following list details only a few.

Inoculation Indian doctors were the first to give injections. Cowpox injections helped to stop epidemics of the deadly disease smallpox. In India's free hospitals, inoculation was widely used 1,000 years before Europeans first tried it.

Surgery Indian surgeons were remarkably advanced. They sterilized their cutting tools. They knew how to set broken bones. They repaired injured ears and noses by techniques of plastic surgery.

Number system Hindu mathematicians were the first to use a system of numbers based on

ten. (Muslims of Baghdad adopted the system and passed it along to Europe, so Europeans called these numbers Arabic numerals.) Hindu philosophers understood the concept of zero and wrote it as a number. They also had a symbol for infinity.

Kalidasa wrote great drama.

The greatest literature of India's golden age was drama. Imagine an Indian actor wearing a sparkling, richly embroidered costume and the jeweled crown of a king. Standing beside him is an actress in the plain cotton gown of a poor hermit's daughter. The actress is playing the title role in one of the most famous plays in world literature, *Shakuntala.* The plot involves an unfortunate accident by which the king, though married to Shakuntala, loses all memory of her.

Shakuntala was written by the poet and dramatist Kalidasa (KAH-lih-DAH-suh), whose genius has been compared to Shakespeare's. Unlike Shakespeare, however, Kalidasa wrote no tragedies. There might be moments of sorrow during the play, but all his plays ended happily.

Emotion is the key to Indian drama. Audiences at the Gupta court recognized eight pure emotions known as *rasas.* One scene might make them feel the emotion of laughter, another sadness, a third pride. The other five rasas were love, anger, fear, loathing, and wonder. Then the final scene of a drama swept the audience up in an overpowering emotion that combined all the others.

Huns destroyed the Gupta empire.

The last Gupta rulers faced the same frightening challenge as the last Roman emperors. During the 400's, the Huns rampaged across Asia and Europe. While Attila was terrifying Rome, other Hun chieftains crossed the rocky passes of the Hindu Kush into India. Under constant attack from the Huns, the Gupta empire shrank. The Gupta dynasty disappeared from history during the 600's.

For the people of northern India, the next six centuries (650–1250) were ones of turmoil. First, several proud, warlike tribes from central Asia crossed the Hindu Kush mountains and settled in northwestern India. The local Hindus called this new ruling group Rajputs, a name that meant "sons of kings."

The Gupta empire never extended into the rough, southern region called the Deccan. This region was, in a sense, like a separate country with its own distinct history. It too passed through an age of great creativity, which was recorded in stone monuments.

Inside each cave, colonies of Buddhist monks slept on stone pillows in a series of small chambers that opened out into the central chapel area. Twenty-nine such temples were created, the last just as India's golden age was coming to an end.

The Rajputs built new kingdoms.

In the 800's and 900's, northern India once again became a land of small kingdoms, ruled by Rajput warrior-kings. Soon after coming to India in the 500's, the Rajputs converted to Hinduism. They claimed membership in Hinduism's second highest caste, the Kshatriyas (or warriors).

Like European knights and Japanese samurai, Rajput men lived by a code of honor and bravery. Women were respected and had some property rights as well. However, both poetry and drama stressed that a woman's highest virtue was devotion to her husband. If her husband died, a faithful wife could show her love by a Hindu rite known as *suttee*. As her husband's body burned on a funeral pyre, she would remain at his side and die honorably in the flames.

An age of great temples By the 800's, three gods had risen to new importance in Hinduism: Brahman the Creator, Shiva the Destroyer, and Vishnu the Preserver. Poems, tales, and songs honored these gods and told of their deeds.

The 800's and 900's were a great age of temple building. Hindus could worship at a temple dedicated to the energetic Shiva, or they might become devotees of Vishnu, a loving god. (The creator-god, Brahman, though greatly honored, was seldom worshiped directly.) Among the great temples were those on the island of Elephanta, off India's west coast. Here, towering sculptures of Hindu gods fill caves that were cut into solid rock.

Decline of Buddhism During the Rajput centuries, Buddhism almost ceased to exist as a separate faith. Indians still worshiped figures of the Buddha, but they now worshiped him in Hindu temples. Hindu priests taught that the gentle Buddha had come to earth as an incarnation of the loving god, Vishnu. Thus, Indian Buddhism slipped quietly back into Hinduism.

Hindus and Muslims met in war.

In the 700's, Hinduism was one of the oldest religions in the world. Islam was the newest. The fierce conflict between Hindu and Muslim that began in this century has been called "probably the bloodiest story in history."

Arab Muslims conquered a major portion of the Indus River valley in 712, just as other Arab armies were conquering Spain. This first Muslim invasion, however, was mild compared to what followed.

In 997, a Turkish chieftain named Mahmud (muh-**MOOD**) became sultan of a little state in eastern Afghanistan called Ghazni. Mahmud of Ghazni was no barbarian. He loved Persian poetry and the Koran. He also loved gold and silver, and he made a solemn vow to plunder India

The Buddhist temples at Ajanta were hollowed out of granite cliffs between 100 B.C. and A.D. 500. Within the caves, the walls are covered with magnificent paintings.

287

every year. For 17 successive years, Mahmud's troops sacked India's cities and destroyed Hindu temples. They massacred and enslaved thousands. The Rajputs resisted bravely, but their slow-moving war elephants were no match for the lightninglike attacks of the Turkish cavalry. Mahmud of Ghazni died in 1030, leaving behind a legacy of hatred between Hindu and Muslim.

Muslim sultans ruled from Delhi.

About 160 years later, in 1191, another Turkish sultan named Muhammad Ghuri (GOO-ree) rode into India bent on conquest. A desperate stand by the Rajputs defeated him. The next year he returned and took a terrible revenge. His armies conquered city after city. At Nalanda, he destroyed the famous university. Much of northern India was conquered by Turkish armies and ruled by Turkish generals from the city of Delhi.

Thus began what is called the Delhi sultanate. For over 300 years (1200–1526), northern India was ruled by Turkish sultans from their courts in Delhi. These Turkish rulers were Muslims, and they treated the Hindus as a conquered people. Hindu kingdoms survived as independent states only in the Deccan, to the south.

The conquest of the Muslim Turks, though cruel, may have saved India from the Mongols. Although the Mongols raided and threatened India, the Turkish rulers were strong enough to turn them back.

Section Review 1

Define: (a) itihas, (b) caste, (c) inoculation, (d) rasa, (e) suttee, (f) sultan
Identify: (a) Shah Jahan, (b) Mumtaz Mahal, (c) Taj Mahal, (d) Chandra Gupta, (e) Gupta

Voice from the Past · *The Harshest of Sultans*

The most powerful of the Delhi sultans was the harsh Ala-ud-din (ah-LAH-ood-DEEN), who took the throne by murdering his uncle in 1296. A Muslim historian wrote the following account of Ala-ud-din's cruel measures.

The people were pressed and [taxed] and money was exacted from them on every kind of pretext . . . The people became so absorbed in trying to keep themselves alive that rebellion was never mentioned. Next [Ala-ud-din] set up a system of espionage so minute that nothing done, good or bad, was hidden from him . . . Nobles dared not speak aloud even in thousand-columned palaces, but had to communicate by signs. In their own houses, night and day, dread of spies made them tremble . . .

The Hindu was to be [made so poor] as to be unable to keep a horse, wear fine clothes, or enjoy any of life's luxuries. No Hindu could hold up his head . . . "I am an unlettered man," [Ala-ud-din] said, "but I have seen a great deal. Be assured that the Hindus will never become submissive and obedient till they are reduced to poverty. I have therefore given orders that just enough shall be left to them of [grain], milk, and curds, from year to year . . . Although I have not studied the science or the Book, I am a Muslim of the Muslims. To prevent rebellion, in which many perish, I issue such ordinances as I consider to be for the good of the State and the benefit of the people."

1. (a) What measures did the sultan use to prevent the nobles from plotting against him? (b) To prevent the common people from rebelling against him?
2. (a) What was the religion of the sultan? (b) What did he mean by "the Book"?
3. What was his policy toward Hindus?
4. What justification did the sultan give for his policies?

dynasty, (f) Arabic numerals, (g) Kalidasa, (h) Huns (i) Rajputs, (j) Turks

Answer:
1. (a) How did Gupta rule affect northern India? (b) What were some of the key achievements in the arts and sciences under the Guptas?
2. What brought the Gupta empire to an end?
3. (a) In the Rajput kingdoms, what virtues were expected of a man? (b) Of a woman?
4. What changes in religion took place in Rajput times?
5. (a) What was the Delhi sultanate? (b) How did it come into being? (c) What was its effect on the Hindu population?

Critical Thinking
6. Briefly summarize the status of each of the following religions in northern India about the year 1200. (a) Hinduism (b) Buddhism (c) Islam

Mughals ruled India in splendor.

2

The greatest menace to the Delhi sultans came from their own homeland, the steppes of central Asia. Late in the 1300's, a fearsome conqueror rode out over the dusty steppe of Turkestan. He was Timur the Lame, or Tamerlane.

Tamerlane destroyed Delhi.

Tamerlane boasted descent from Genghis Khan, even though he was more Turk than Mongol. He led his forces westward into Persia, northward into Russia, and westward again into Mesopotamia and Asia Minor. From his capital in Samarkand, Tamerlane terrorized all of western Asia. To mark his victories, he erected heaps of human skulls where villages had been.

In 1398, Tamerlane led his armies south through the mountain passes into India. Within a few months, he had taken Delhi itself. Although he was a Muslim, he massacred Muslims and Hindus alike. About 100,000 people were sold into slavery. A witness wrote, "The city was utterly destroyed . . . for two whole months, not a bird moved in the city."

Unlike Genghis Khan, Tamerlane failed to build an empire that outlasted his own life. After his death in 1405, nothing remained of his conquests. Delhi was rebuilt, but the Turkish sultans who ruled there for the next century were weaker than their predecessors. To the west, Rajput princes strengthened their Hindu states. No single ruler was able to dominate India. Wars among the rival states and kingdoms were frequent.

Babur founded the Mughal dynasty.

In 1526, another Turkish-Mongol conqueror from central Asia ended the feeble Delhi sultanate for good. His name was Babur (BAH-buhr), which meant "the tiger." He traced his descent from Genghis Khan on his father's side and from Tamerlane on his mother's side. Babur was a hulking, broad-shouldered, big-bellied man. As his son testified, "He never hit a man whom he did not knock down." He was also a wily politician, a skilled general, and an educated man who wrote an autobiography.

Babur conquered India with cannon and firepower. His troops carried a supply of gunpowder, muskets, and several hefty cannon across the mountain passes from Afghanistan into northern India. Soon Babur captured Delhi and Agra in north-central India. The Delhi sultanate was thus overthrown after 320 years (1206–1526).

The new empire established by Babur came to be known as the Mughal (MOO-gahl) empire. (*Mughal* was another form of the name *Mongol*.) Mughal rule became a byword for wealth and splendor.

Akbar enlarged the Mughal empire.

By far the greatest and most talented of India's Mughal monarchs was Babur's grandson. Though his Muslim name was Muhammad, he was known as Akbar, which means "most great." Akbar was 13 when his father (Babur's son) had a fatal fall down a flight of palace stairs. Akbar ruled the Mughal empire with wisdom and fairness from 1556 to 1605.

Early in his reign, Akbar added new lands to the Mughal empire. Dressed in golden armor and mounted on an elephant, he fought countless battles against tough Rajput challengers. By the end of his reign, the Mughal empire covered

The dates of Akbar's reign coincide almost exactly with those of England's Elizabeth I (1558–1603).

almost all of northern India and much of the Deccan.

Like the Delhi sultans, the Mughal rulers were Muslims. However, Hindus in Mughal lands outnumbered Muslims by at least four to one. To unify his empire, Akbar decided that he needed Hindu support. Therefore, after defeating the Rajput princes, he did not seek revenge. Instead, he spared the Rajputs' lives and invited them to help rule. He married a Rajput princess and entrusted Hindus with high government offices. Akbar also removed the special taxes that Hindus had paid their Muslim rulers. His tax system stressed fairness. For example, in years of famine, taxes were dropped.

Akbar's wise policy toward Hindus was based on his personal religious tolerance. In his adult years, he ceased to believe that Islam was the only true faith. What Hindus taught might also be true, he thought. He was interested, too, in the teachings of Christian missionaries.

After learning about all these faiths, Akbar concluded that a new religion could embrace them all. He called his new religion *Din Ilahi* (Divine Faith) and made himself its leader. He made few converts, however, and his religion died with him in 1605.

Splendor disguised a weakening empire.

Under Akbar's successors, the strong empire he had built began to weaken. Later rulers were neither as tolerant nor as skilled in administration as Akbar had been.

A strong queen Akbar's son was named Jahangir (juh-HAHN-geer), meaning "world-grasper." He was sadly misnamed, however. Addicted to both wine and opium, he played little part in governing. His reign (1605–1627) might have been an even greater disaster for India if he had not married an able woman.

In 1611, Jahangir married a Persian princess whom he called Nur Jahan ("the light of the world"). Nur Jahan was probably the most powerful woman in India's history before modern times. For many years, she was the true ruler of the empire.

Religious intolerance You have already read about the next Mughal monarch—Shah Jahan, the builder of the Taj Mahal. In his 30-year rule (1628–1658), Shah Jahan was as cruel toward his enemies as he had been loving toward his wife. He was followed by his even more ruthless son, Aurangzeb (OH-rung-zeb), who imprisoned his aging father as you have read.

Shah Jahan and especially Aurangzeb turned away from Akbar's policy of treating Hindus and Muslims as equals. Aurangzeb tried to make his empire an Islamic state. In 1669, he ordered the destruction of Hindu temples. He also returned to the policy of taxing non-Muslims more heavily than Muslims. No longer did Hindus serve the empire in high positions. By his intolerance, Aurangzeb weakened his government.

Extremes of wealth and poverty During Shah Jahan's reign, the Mughal empire was at its peak. Its glittering treasures amazed European visitors. For example, at the Red Fort at Agra (one of three royal residences built of red sandstone) the Mughal treasury contained these items:

> *750 pounds of pearls, 275 pounds of emeralds, 5,000 gems from Cathay (China) . . . 200 daggers, 1,000 gold studded saddles with jewels, 2 golden thrones, 3 silver thrones, 100 silver chairs, 5 golden chairs, 200 most precious mirrors . . .*

The list goes on and on. And it was said that the treasury at Lahore, the Mughals' third capital, was three times the size of Agra's.

India's poor, however, had few comforts. A European traveler left a description of a poor family's house that was not far from the great treasury of Agra:

> *Their houses are built of mud with thatched roofs. Furniture there is little or none except some earthenware pots to hold water and for cooking and two beds . . . Their bed*

Footnote to History

Akbar was an intelligent and cultured man who was eager for all kinds of knowledge, but he never learned to read or write. He mastered many fields of knowledge, from science to poetry, through conversation with scholars at his court. Some recent historians suspect he had the learning disability known today as dyslexia, which makes it difficult for a person to perceive letters and words.

Akbar slept only three hours a night. Many of his waking hours were spent thinking of new projects. Among his many inventions were a huge cannon, a cleverly designed war tent, and a kind of crude machine gun that fired fourteen muskets at once.

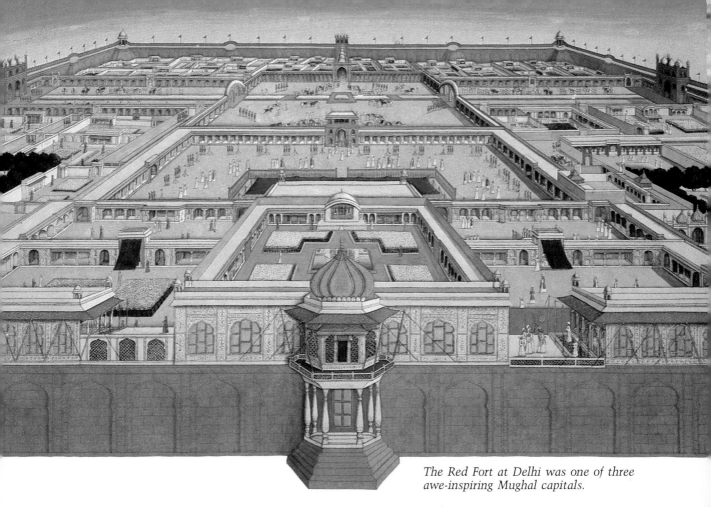

The Red Fort at Delhi was one of three awe-inspiring Mughal capitals.

cloths are scanty, merely a sheet or perhaps two . . . This is sufficient in the hot weather, but the bitter cold nights are miserable indeed . . .

In 1630 (during Shah Jahan's reign), a Dutch merchant visited northern India during one of the region's frequent famines. He wrote, "As the famine increased, men abandoned towns and villages and wandered helplessly . . . wherever you went, you saw nothing but corpses."

Hinduism and Islam were rivals.

All India's earlier conquerors had eventually blended into the Hindu system, but the Muslims did not. Their strong monotheism kept them from being absorbed by the Hindu majority.

Yet Hinduism and Islam did affect each other. For example, Hindus began to dress in the same styles as Muslims. Hindu women in northern India began to veil their faces as Muslim women did. Northern Hindus also adopted the idea of **purdah**. Purdah was a Muslim practice of keeping women in seclusion. Women were not allowed to go out in public or meet socially with any man outside the family.

Some Hindus converted to Islam. Islam's idea of the equality of all believers had a strong appeal to lower-caste Hindus and to untouchables.

A few thinkers tried to blend the ideas of Hinduism and Islam. One such thinker was Nanak, who lived from 1469 to 1539. Nanak became the *guru* (religious teacher) of a new religion. His teachings combined the strict monotheism of Islam with the Hindu idea of a mystical union with God. Followers of Nanak became known as Sikhs (seeks), meaning "disciples."

The Mughal rulers persecuted the Sikhs and killed two of their gurus. As a result, the Sikhs became a community of soldiers, ready to defend themselves or to attack. Many Sikh men took the last name Singh, meaning "lion," while women took the name Kaur, meaning "lioness." When Mughal rule weakened, the Sikhs set up an independent military state in northern India.

Interested students may wish to report on the relation of Sikhs to other sects in India today.

Europeans reached India's coast.

While Shah Jahan concentrated on building lavish tombs and palaces, Europeans were increasing their influence in Asia. In 1498, a Portuguese captain and adventurer, Vasco da Gama, arrived in India after sailing all the way around Africa. He reached India in 1498. For the first time, powerful newcomers had arrived in India by sea rather than through the mountain passes of the Himalayas to the north.

Da Gama's voyage marked a great turning point in India's history. After 1500, control of the seas around India became the key to controlling India itself. The Mughal rulers, however, took little interest in building warships. In the end, the weakness of their navy proved fatal to both the Mughal empire and the smaller Hindu kingdoms to the south.

The spices Da Gama took back from his voyage sold in Europe for 27 times their cost in India. Obviously, there were fortunes to be made in the Indian Ocean. Portuguese merchants were quick to go after them.

The Portuguese did not try to conquer India or the spice-producing islands south of China (the East Indies). Instead, they set up strong bases at strategic points all along the major Asian sea lanes.

A Portuguese sea captain named Alfonso de Albuquerque (al-buh-KEHR-kay) seized the western Indian port of Goa in 1510. In 1511, his fleet sailed to the East Indies and occupied the strategic port of Malacca (muh-LAK-uh) on the Malay peninsula. (See map on page 293.) In 1515, he captured his last great prize, the Muslim city of Hormuz (hor-MOOZ). It lay at the entrance to the Persian Gulf. From these three bases and the East African city of Zanzibar, the Portuguese dominated the Indian Ocean trade for the remainder of the 1500's. For the time being, however, the Europeans were not a serious threat to the Mughal emperors.

Section Review 2

Define: (a) purdah, (b) guru
Identify: (a) Tamerlane, (b) Babur, (c) Mughal dynasty, (d) Akbar, (e) Aurangzeb, (f) Sikhs, (g) Da Gama
Answer:
1. (a) How was the Delhi sultanate affected by Tamerlane? (b) By Babur?
2. List two major achievements of Akbar.
3. Compare the home of a poor family with the royal residences of the Mughals.
4. What are some customs that Hindus adopted from Muslims?
5. (a) What important change was marked by Da Gama's arrival in India? (b) How did the Portuguese come to control trade in the Indian Ocean?

Economics in Daily Life · *Cloth from India*

Indian farmers raised cotton to make cloth as early as 3000 B.C. By 300 B.C., Indian clothmakers were printing unique designs on their fabrics. Although European merchants at first were dazzled by India's jewels, they soon found that they could make even greater fortunes in the cloth trade. From Indian looms came cloth of many different weights and patterns. In Europe, each type of cloth came to be known by the name of the Indian city or region where it was woven. For example, the fabric madras takes its name from the Indian city Madras, calico from the city Calicut, cashmere from the region Kashmir. *Chintz* comes from a Hindi word whose root means "bright" or "many-colored." Even the word *dungaree* comes from the name of a section of Bombay where sturdy blue denim was woven.

The Brooklyn Museum

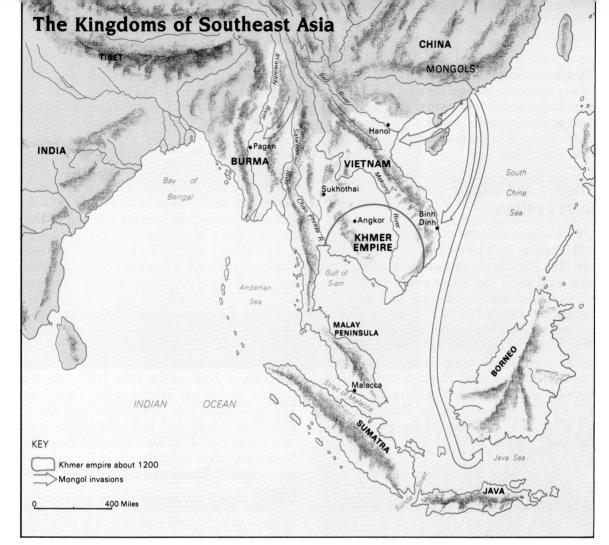

The Kingdoms of Southeast Asia

Map Study

What geographic reason helps to explain why Vietnam was more heavily influenced by China than other countries in Southeast Asia?

Critical Thinking

6. (a) What were the critical differences between the beliefs of Hindus and Muslims? (b) What effect did the policies of Akbar, Aurangzeb, and Shah Jahan have on relations between Hindus and Muslims?

Kingdoms arose in Southeast Asia. 3

East of India, across the Bay of Bengal, lies Southeast Asia. It includes the modern countries of Burma, Laos, Kampuchea, Vietnam, Malaysia, Indonesia, Thailand, Singapore, and Brunei.

Many groups settled Southeast Asia.

For thousands of years, many groups of people passed through Southeast Asia on routes linking Asia and the Pacific islands. As a result, the region has a great variety of languages and cultures. Burma alone includes more than 100 different language groups.

Southeast Asia has never been united either politically or culturally. Seas and straits separate the islands. On the mainland peninsula, five great rivers flow from the north and cut valleys to the sea. Between the valleys rise hills and mountains, making travel and communication difficult.

Southeast Asia lies on the most direct sea route between India and China. Throughout Southeast Asia's history, the key to political power has

Africa and the Americas

More than a thousand years old, these stone temples at Tikal in Guatemala were built during the height of Maya civilization.

Key Terms

oasis
savanna
lineage

Read and Understand

1. Early civilizations arose in Africa.
2. African empires thrived on trade.
3. Indians developed many ways of life.
4. Empires flourished in the Americas.

High over the rain forest of northern Guatemala, airplane pilots in the 1950's saw the tops of five stone pyramids piercing the canopy of green leaves. The pilots realized that the pyramids had to be tall. The vine-woven treetops were at least 100 feet high. Archaeologists later learned that the towering pyramids were the remains of the ancient city of Tikal (tih-**KAHL**).

Beginning about 200 B.C., Central America's Mayas (**MY**-uhz) built layer upon layer of city on the site of Tikal. At its height around A.D. 750, the city had about 40,000 people. The people who lived around Tikal were good farmers. They also traded from the Gulf of Mexico to the Pacific. By the year 900, however, only a few squatters remained in the decaying city. Archaeologists are still trying to learn more about this once-magnificent city.

Leave the rain forest now and travel in time and space to the steely gray Nubian desert in Africa. Here, too, stand rows of crumbling pyramids, the remains of a lost civilization.

The city here was Meroë (MEHR-uh-WEE). Meroë was the capital of a kingdom called Kush. Its four-century golden age ended about A.D. 150, while Tikal was still new. The people of Meroë, who were known as Kushites, traded with Egypt. They also traded indirectly with Greece, Rome, and India. Some of Meroë's buildings had columns much like those in ancient Rome. The Kushite lion god had four arms and three faces. Some archaeologists think it resembles the Hindu god Shiva. The Kushites also worshiped some of the same gods as the Egyptians.

After Meroë fell, it was forgotten by people in other lands. A Scottish traveler who reported its ruins in the 1700's had trouble convincing Europeans of its existence.

Until 1500, the people of the Americas had almost no contact with Africa, Asia, or Europe. During much of that time, large parts of Africa were also isolated. Our knowledge of early civilizations in Africa and the Americas is limited. In some cases, linguists have not been able to decipher the writings from these cultures. In others, particularly in Africa, knowledge was passed on orally and is just now being written down and analyzed.

Though our knowledge is incomplete, we do know that rich civilizations developed on all three continents—Africa, North America, and South America. This chapter traces the rise and fall of some of those civilizations, spanning thousands of years.

Early civilizations arose in Africa.
1

The lands of North Africa have long been part of the Mediterranean world—the world of the Phoenicians, Greeks, Romans, and later the Arabs. South of Africa's Mediterranean coast, however, the land becomes drier and more barren. Eventually, the landscape becomes an empty waste of sand and gravel. This is the Sahara, the largest desert in the world.

Historically, the Sahara has been a great dividing zone in Africa. The lands south of it followed different patterns of development from the Mediterranean cultures. All the African societies described in this chapter had their centers south of the Sahara, although many traded with lands to the north.

Africa has four major regions.

Africa is the second largest continent. (Only Asia is larger.) Africa covers 11.7 million square miles, giving it about 20 percent of Earth's land surface. Geographers divide Africa into four general regions.

The northern and southern coasts Narrow strips of fertile land border both the northern coast and the southern tip of Africa. In these two areas, rainfall is moderate and temperatures are warm. Summers tend to be hot and dry. Though these areas make up only a small part of the vast continent, they support dense populations.

The deserts Altogether, deserts make up about one third of Africa's land. The largest desert, the Sahara, is roughly the size of the United States. The Sahara is one of the hottest, driest, and most forbidding territories on Earth. *Sahara* come from the Arabic word *sahra*, meaning "desert." It suggests the gasping sound made by parched travelers.

The Sahara was not always a desert. Before 5000 B.C., rain fell regularly there. Herds of elephants and giraffes roamed through fields of tall grass. Over the centuries, many groups of people made their homes on the Saharan plain. Some hunted wild animals and fished in the streams. Later, others grazed herds of domesticated sheep and cattle along rivers. Farmers raised grain. These cultures vanished, however, as the climate grew drier and drier. By 2000 B.C., the Sahara had become the desert it is today.

Because the Sahara is so vast, it has been likened to a waterless ocean. People have used camels, the "ships of the desert," to cross it since about A.D. 400. Travelers follow time-honored routes between **oases**. An oasis is a place where underground water comes to the surface in a spring or well. Marked by tall date palm trees, oases dot the desert like islands in the sea.

The savannas Another third of the continent consists of grassy plains with a few scattered trees. Such plains are called **savannas** (suh-VAN-uhz).

Unlike Europeans, Arabs and North Africans had many contacts with Africa south of the Sahara. They were accustomed to desert travel and crossed the Sahara by camel caravan. Their ships sailed along the East African coast, trading silks and spices for ivory and gold.

299

Regions of Africa

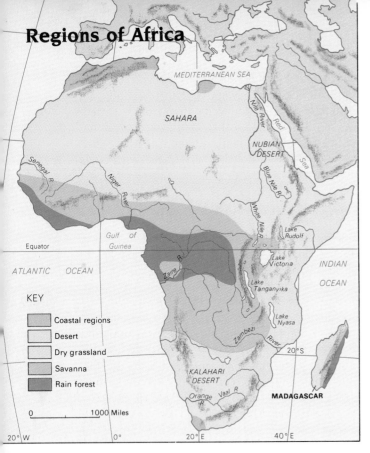

KEY
- Coastal regions
- Desert
- Dry grassland
- Savanna
- Rain forest

Map Study answers: Zaire River; Gulf of Guinea

Map Study

What river flows through the rain forest? Into what body of water does the Niger River empty?

Savannas cover much of central Africa, both north and south of the equator.

In the savanna, rainy seasons alternate with dry seasons. When the land is drenched with rain, tall grasses and umbrella-shaped acacia trees come to life. Farming is difficult on the savanna because heavy rains can strip minerals from the soil. Then, when the dry season comes, the ground turns almost as hard and dusty as the desert.

Nevertheless, the savannas have always supported the largest share of Africa's population. In most years, early farmers had enough rainfall to raise their crops of millet (a type of grain) and African rice. On lands close to the desert that were too dry to farm, nomads lived by herding.

The rain forest About one fifth of Africa is rain forest. The forest zone stretches inland from the Atlantic Ocean, straddling the equator. Twisting through the forest are the branches of Africa's second longest river, the Zaire (zah-EER).

Rain falls almost daily in the rain forest. Mahogany and teak trees tower 200 feet above the forest floor. Their leaves form a canopy that blocks sunlight from reaching the forest floor. At ground level in a rain forest, the earth is nearly bare.

In early times, fishing villages grew up along the rivers in the rain forest. Later, farmers raised such root crops as yams. Grains would not grow in the damp climate. Farmers did not keep cattle or other livestock because of a tiny but deadly creature known as the tsetse (SET-see) fly. This blood-sucking insect carries sleeping sickness. The disease may weaken or kill people, and it is absolutely fatal to most livestock.

Societies developed many ways of life.

By the earliest historic times, a wide variety of societies existed in Africa south of the Sahara. Groups differed in their ways of governing themselves, in their family organizations, and in their ways of making a living.

Family ties As in other parts of the world, family organization was central to African society. In many African societies, families were organized in groups called **lineages** (LIHN-ee-ihj-uhz). The members of a lineage believed they were descended from a common ancestor. Besides its living members, a lineage also included past generations (spirits of ancestors) and future generations (children not yet born).

In some African societies, lineage groups took the place of kings or other rulers. For example, a people called the Tiv in what is today Nigeria had no formal government. If a dispute arose among them, it was settled by respected elders from the lineages.

People in a lineage felt strong loyalties to one another. The lineage helped members in times of trouble, negotiated marriages for them, and supported members politically. Members of a lineage also had religious duties.

Religions African religions blended monotheism (belief in one supreme God) and polytheism (belief in many gods). Most African groups honored a large number of gods and spirits. Above these lesser gods was the principal creator of the universe. However, this High God or Supreme Spirit was thought to be too powerful and distant to listen to human appeals.

In daily life, the spirits of departed ancestors were especially important. As part of the lineage, they were the guardians of traditions, values, and laws. Most families believed that the spirits could

300

The Zaire River is 2,700 miles from the tip of its longest tributary to its Atlantic outlet. (The Nile is longer. The Amazon in South America carries more water than either.)

either make trouble or bring good fortune, depending on how well their living relatives honored them. Thus, the lineage was a religious group as well as a social and political unit.

At least one member of a village was trained in the magic art of communicating with both good and evil spirits. This important person, known as the *diviner*, called on the spirits for aid whenever there was an illness or village crisis. The diviner also tried to cure sickness or anger within the village by religious rituals.

After North Africa became part of the Islamic empire, traders brought the Muslim religion to many parts of Africa south of the Sahara. Even in places where Islam became strong, however, African religious traditions often survived too.

The arts flourished in many forms.

The arts linked religion, politics, and everyday life. Some types of art honored the king or the spirits of ancestors. Other forms of art included music for daily life or everyday objects made with fine craftsmanship.

Sculpture Artists in the rain-forest kingdoms used the beautifully grained woods that grew there to create works of art. The long tradition of metalworking in Africa likewise led to striking sculpture in gold and bronze. Most wooden sculptures from ancient times have crumbled to dust, victims of dampness or hungry insects. Ants could not devour bronze or gold, however, so some of these marvelous works have survived.

Some of the most famous African sculptures were created by the Yoruba (YOR-uh-buh), a group of people in the rain forest of what is now Nigeria. Two successive groups of Yoruba people made fine bronze sculptures between 1100 and 1600 (Europe's late Middle Ages). One group governed a forest kingdom called Ife (EE-fay). The bronze heads of Ife were wonderfully natural and lifelike. As Ife declined, a second Yoruba group formed the state of Benin (buh-NEEN). Metalworkers in Benin made a series of bronze plaques that hung in the palace of their *oba* (king). The plaques showed people commonly seen at the royal court: acrobats, warriors, royal sentries, drummers, and others.

Music and dance Many kinds of African music had very complex rhythms. For example, several drummers might play together, each following a different rhythm. Such music is called *polyrhythmic* (having many rhythms).

Music often accompanied dance. In many societies, dancers wore masks to honor spirits or family ancestors. Thus, the art of the carved masks, the music of the drums, and the dancing of the villagers shared a common religious purpose. They bound a community together and enabled it to pass its heritage on through the centuries.

Oral history Most African languages had no writing systems. Instead, each group handed down its history and laws by word of mouth.

In many West African societies, specially trained people known as *griots* (GREE-ohz) were the record keepers. Griots memorized the great deeds of past kings, family histories, and important events in their village. Young griots studied with older ones so that knowledge of the past was handed down accurately. Even after Arab traders brought Arabic writing to sub-Saharan Africa, griots remained the historians of their people.

A sculptor at the royal court of Benin in what is now Nigeria created this bronze figure. The man is wearing a leopard skin and blowing a horn. It was made about 1600.

The syncopated rhythms of modern ragtime are believed to have their roots in African music.

301

Section Review 1

Define: (a) oasis, (b) savanna, (c) lineage,
(d) monotheism, (e) polytheism, (f) diviner,
(g) griot
Identify: (a) Sahara, (b) Zaire River
Answer:
1. What are the four general geographic regions of Africa?
2. (a) How did people make a living on the savannas? (b) In the rain forest?
3. What functions did the lineage perform in African society?
4. How did African religions embrace polytheism and monotheism?
5. How did many West African societies keep records?

Critical Thinking
6. How did the lineage system ensure that society's values would be upheld?

African empires thrived on trade.

2

Many powerful states arose in Africa before 1500. The states of eastern Africa date as far back as ancient Egypt. Among them was the kingdom of Kush, with its capital at Meroë. Other African states arose in the savanna and the forests of western Africa.

Kush was an ironworking center.

The first group of people to build cities in sub-Saharan Africa were the Kushites. They lived south of Egypt along the Nile River. The great ruins of Meroë are the remains of their work.

Egypt dominated Kush from about 2000 to 1000 B.C. Egyptian armies raided and even occupied Kush for a brief period. More important, the people of Kush learned about Egyptian civilization through trade. The Kushites adopted the Egyptian idea of a god-king. They wrote with Egyptian hieroglyphics and built pyramids.

In 751 B.C., a Kushite king named Piankhi (**PYANG**-kih) led an army down the Nile and conquered Egypt. Piankhi and his descendants became

Egypt's Twenty-fifth Dynasty. After a century of power, Assyrians drove the Kushite rulers out of Egypt around 650 B.C. The Assyrians never conquered Kush itself, however.

The Kushites had long known the use of iron. After facing the iron weapons of the Assyrians, the Kushites began to make more use of the metal. The mining and smelting of iron soon became the base of Kush's economy. Around 590 B.C., the Kushites moved their capital south to Meroë to be near supplies of iron ore. There Kush enjoyed a golden age from 250 B.C. to A.D. 150.

The ironworkers of Meroë were so busy that their slag heaps encircled the city. Traders took donkeyloads of iron ingots, tools, and spearheads from Kushite foundries to the Red Sea. There the Kushites exchanged iron goods for luxuries from India and Arabia, including jewelry, glass bottles, fine cotton cloth, and lamps of bronze and silver.

The kingdom of Kush began to decline around A.D. 150. Finally, around A.D. 325, an Ethiopian king from the city of Axum destroyed the city.

Christian kings ruled in Ethiopia.

Meroë's conquerors lived about 400 miles to the southeast in what is now Ethiopia. In ancient times, Axum was the capital of this rugged country of high plateaus.

Axum's King Ezana celebrated his triumph over the Kushites with this inscription carved on a tall stone pillar:

Meanwhile I burnt their towns, [both] those built of brick and those built of reeds, and my soldiers carried off their food, as well as copper, iron, and brass; they destroyed the statues in their temples as well as their storehouses for food, and their cotton trees, casting them in the river Sida [the Nile].

By A.D. 300, Axum had grown rich and powerful by controlling trade between the African interior and the Red Sea. Persian and Arab merchants sailed to the Ethiopian port of Adulis. Here they exchanged their wares for gold, ivory, and spices.

Byzantine Greeks also traded with Axum. They were astonished at the splendor of the Ethiopian royal court. One Byzantine visitor to Axum described the king riding through the streets of his

The Kushites also developed a writing system of their own. Unfortunately, it has not been deciphered. Thus, historians know less about Kush's golden age than about its earlier periods, when people used Egyptian writing.

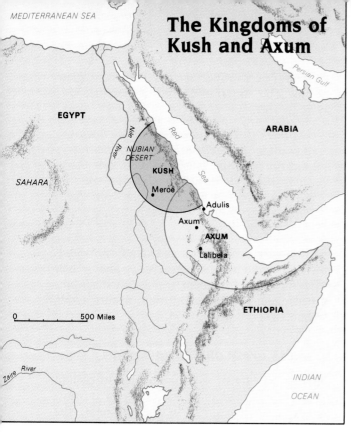

The Kingdoms of Kush and Axum

MEDITERRANEAN SEA

EGYPT

ARABIA

SAHARA

NUBIAN DESERT

KUSH

Meroë

Adulis

Axum

AXUM

Lalibela

ETHIOPIA

0 — 500 Miles

INDIAN OCEAN

Map Study

Ethiopia's famous rock churches (right) are near the town of Lalibela, named for the king who built them. On what sea did Axum's major port lie?

capital in a four-wheeled, gold-plated chariot pulled by four elephants. The linen garment around the king's waist glittered with beautiful gold embroidery.

King Ezana became a Christian in A.D. 324, shortly before he destroyed Meroë. Ethiopia's rulers remained Christian through the centuries. When Islamic armies swept through Egypt in the 600's, Ethiopia remained independent.

During Europe's Early Middle Ages (500–1000), Ethiopia's kings lost contact with Christian lands to the north. Then, in 1520, a Portuguese explorer named Francisco Alvares journeyed into the Ethiopian highlands. He was amazed to find Christians worshiping in handsomely decorated churches. Built around 1200, many of the churches had been hollowed out of solid rock at the command of a devout king named Lalibela (LAH-lee-BAY-luh). Instead of towering skyward, each church was carved into bedrock below ground. Worshipers reached the church door by climbing down a flight of stairs about 30 to 40 feet deep.

Coastal cities traded with Asia.

Trade was vital to the growth of cities on the East African coast of present-day Kenya and Tanzania. Today, beachcombers in Tanzania find multicolored chips of pottery in the sand. These are fragments of Chinese porcelain that was traded centuries ago in East Africa.

From 1100 to 1500, there were more than 35 African city-states strung out over a coastal strip 1,000 miles long. These cities bore lovely sounding names: Malindi (muh-LIHN-dee), Mombasa (mahm-BAHS-uh), and Zanzibar (ZAN-zuh-bahr).

The ancestors of the people who lived in these cities had migrated to the East African coast during the 700's. Most came from inland Africa and spoke languages from the Bantu language family. Other settlers on the coast were Arab Muslims who fled their homeland to escape political enemies.

The two peoples, Bantu and Arab, intermarried, and their cultures fused. Their language was mostly Bantu but later gained many Arabic words.

Map Study answer: Red Sea

In 1417, a fleet of Chinese ships came to Malindi, bringing a message of thanks from the Chinese emperor. The emperor, said the fleet's captain, was pleased with the gift shipped to him earlier by Malindi's sultan. It was a giraffe.

Islam became the major religion of the cities on Africa's eastern coast. This new culture came to be known as *Swahili* (swah-HEE-lee), from an Arabic term meaning "people of the coast."

Most of the Swahili people lived by farming, fishing, and trading. They built small houses with walls of smoothed, sun-dried mud. Such houses clustered in villages all along the coast.

At the best harbors, large towns grew up. The tiny homes of the common people formed a ring around the stone buildings of the central town. The beauty of these central towns, where the oldest and richest trading families lived, impressed all who visited them. A Portuguese traveler in the early 1500's described Mombasa as having high, handsome houses of white-washed stone. He noted that the women wore silks and gold.

At Swahili ports, trading vessels regularly arrived from Arabia, India, and China. The most common ships in a Swahili harbor were triangular-sailed Arab vessels called *dhows* (dowz). For centuries, the Arabs acted as the chief middlemen in the Indian Ocean. They brought Asian luxuries to Africa and African luxuries to Asia. In the marketplaces of Kilwa, Mombasa, and Zanzibar, Arab merchants exchanged porcelain bowls and vases from China, jewels and cotton cloth from India, and African ivory, gold, tortoise shells, and rhinoceros horns.

The African gold and ivory in Swahili markets came from the interior. Gold mines, for example, were located 300 miles inland near a great African city called Zimbabwe (zihm-BAHB-way). This city, whose stone ruins still rise grandly over the southern savanna, was once the capital of an inland kingdom.

The kings of Zimbabwe and the sultans of the coastal cities enjoyed power and wealth for many centuries. Then their lives were violently upset by the coming of the Portuguese.

The Portuguese reached East Africa.

Portuguese explorers first arrived in the early 1500's, sailing north along Africa's east coast on their way to India. The Portuguese were eager for Asian wealth. They were also old enemies of the Muslims, who controlled trade in eastern Africa. The Portuguese came with cannons, a weapon previously unknown to the peoples of East Africa.

One by one, the Swahili cities fell to Portuguese attacks. The sultan of Mombasa described this scene in 1505:

He [the Portuguese] raged in our town with such might and terror that no one, neither man nor woman, neither the old nor the young, nor even the children however small was spared to live . . . The stench from the corpses is so overpowering that I dare not enter the town.

Although the Portuguese conquered the Swahili towns, they did not succeed in ruling them. Their heavy taxes and frequent wars with the Arabs ruined trade. The coastal cities went into a long decline.

Empires arose on the savannas.

While city-states were flourishing in eastern Africa, other kingdoms were developing in western Africa. They arose in the savannas, the sweeping grasslands between the Sahara and the tropical rain forests. Three empires—Ghana, Mali, and Songhai—rose to power there between A.D. 300 and 1600.

The wealth of the savanna empires was based on two precious substances: gold and salt. The gold came from a forest region south of the savanna between the Niger (NYE-juhr) and Senegal (SEHN-ih-GAHL) rivers. Miners dug gold from shafts up to 100 feet deep or sifted it from river sands. Until about 1350, at least two thirds of the world's supply of gold came from West Africa.

Despite this wealth in gold, however, the savanna and the forest were poor in salt, and salt is essential to the human diet. The Sahara, on the other hand, was rich in salt. Deep in the desert lay a salt-mining village called Taghaza. Salt was so common there that miners used slabs of it to build huts. Arab and Berber traders carried Taghaza's salt across the Sahara by camel caravan.

After a frightful six-month journey, these traders reached the market towns of the savanna. Meanwhile, other traders brought gold north from the forest region. The two sets of merchants met in Jenné (je-NAY), Timbuktu (TIM-buhk-TOO), and other trade centers. There they exchanged goods under the watchful eye of the tax collector. Kings taxed this trade heavily. In return, royal guards kept peace in the markets. Royal officials made

The king of Zimbabwe was regarded as partly divine. If he sneezed, others in his presence were required to sneeze also as a gesture of respect. If he fell ill, however, tradition required that he commit suicide for the good of his people.

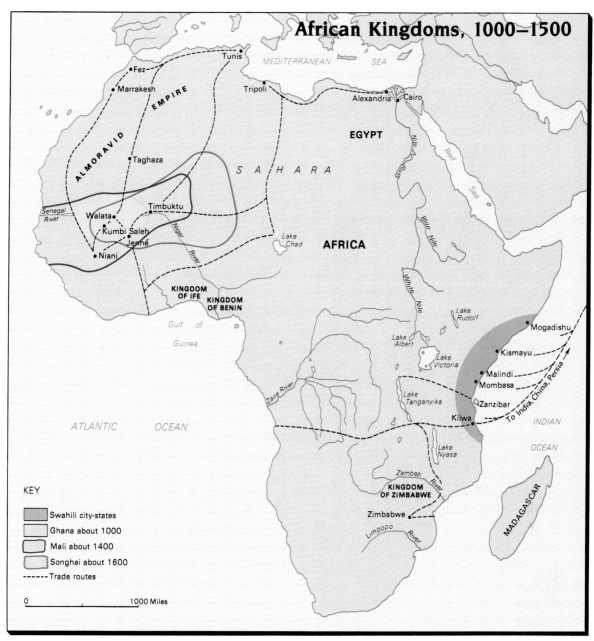

African Kingdoms, 1000–1500

KEY

- Swahili city-states
- Ghana about 1000
- Mali about 1400
- Songhai about 1600
- - - - - Trade routes

0   1000 Miles

Map Study

Which savanna empire reached Africa's west coast? What towns would a caravan go through on the shortest route from Tunis to Niani?

sure that all traders weighed goods fairly and did business according to law.

Some traders took part in a fascinating exchange called the silent trade. At a spot near the Niger River, Arab traders would pile their slabs of salt in neat rows. Pounding on drums, they would invite the gold merchants to trade. Then the Arabs would mount their camels and ride off a few miles. The gold merchants would arrive, look over the piles of salt, leave some of their gold, and withdraw into hiding. Next the Arabs would return and decide whether enough gold had been offered for their salt. If so, they would take the gold and leave the salt. If not, they would beat their drums, suggesting a second round of trading. Thus, the traders swapped salt for gold without either group meeting the other.

No one knows for certain why the traders chose to work in this way. Most likely they hoped to keep the sources of their precious goods secret. At the same time, the silent trade helped prevent the fighting that may break out when two groups of strangers try to bargain.

Ghana taxed the gold-salt trade.

The trade routes lay across the savanna farmed by the Soninke (soh-NIHN-keh) people. The Soninke king demanded a heavy tax in both gold and salt from the Arab traders. The Soninke title for their king was *Ghana*. The Arabs applied this name to the entire territory from which the Ghana collected taxes. By the year 700, the empire of Ghana was well established.

Ghana's ruler demanded taxes and gifts from the chiefs of surrounding lands. As long as those chiefs made their payments, the king of Ghana left them in peace to rule their own people. When Ghana had a strong king, it controlled a wide territory. If the king was weak, Ghana's kingdom shrank. For much of its history, Ghana dominated a region about the size of Texas. Its capital city, Kumbi Saleh, was home to about 30,000 people.

In 1076, an Arab geographer named al-Bakri wrote a description of Ghana's royal court:

The king adorns himself like a woman, wearing necklaces and bracelets, and when he sits before the people he puts on a high cap decorated with gold and wrapped in turbans of fine cotton . . . Behind the king stand ten pages holding shields and swords decorated with gold, and on his right are the sons of the vassal kings of his country wearing splendid garments and their hair plaited with gold.

Gold nuggets and slabs of salt (collected as taxes) were stashed away in the royal palace.

Footnote to History

One gold nugget belonging to the ruler of Ghana weighed 30 pounds, and he tethered his horse to it.

Only the king had the right to own gold nuggets, although gold dust freely circulated in the marketplace. By this means, the king limited the supply of gold and kept its price from falling.

The Ghana acted as chief priest, judge, and military commander. His people believed he spoke to the gods on their behalf. When his subjects approached him, they showed their respect by falling on their knees and throwing dust over their heads. In war, the Ghana could gather an army of 200,000 warriors.

In 1076, Ghana's northern borders were overrun by zealous Muslim Berbers from the Almoravid (al-MOHR-uh-vihd) kingdom to the north. Although Ghana's armies eventually drove the Berbers out, the gold-salt trade was badly disrupted by the war. Ghana never regained its power.

Mali won control of trade.

As old supplies of gold near the coast ran out, miners found new deposits farther east. As a result, the most important trade routes shifted eastward too. By 1200, a different group of people—the Mandingo—controlled the gold trade.

To this day, Mandingo legends celebrate the rise to power of Sundiata (suhn-dee-AH-tuh), the founder of the empire of Mali. The Mandingo griots say that Sundiata's 11 brothers were all put to death by a ruthless king named Sumanguru. Sundiata alone was spared because, as a child, he was sickly and seemed likely to die anyway. As he grew to manhood, he gained strength. He became the leader of a village and raised an army. In 1235, he destroyed Sumanguru's capital. After that battle, in the words of a Mandingo griot, "the world knew no other master but Sundiata."

Sundiata's empire was known as Mali (again not to be confused with the modern country of the same name). Its capital was the city of Niani. Like Ghana, Mali collected taxes from many local chiefs who were otherwise independent.

The influence of Islam in the savanna region was growing. Muslim traders and officials held high positions in Mali as they had in Ghana. Yet most people worshiped traditional African gods. Many people who converted to Islam still kept some of their old ways.

Influenced by Arab traders, some of Mali's kings became Muslims. The most famous of these was

Discussion questions: How are the king and court of Ghana like the pharaoh and court of ancient Egypt? How are they different?

Looking at economics *The first European map of western Africa, drawn in 1375, showed Mansa Musa (lower right) holding a giant nugget of gold. Most European coins of this time were made of gold obtained from Africa. An African goldsmith of the Baule people made the pendant mask (upper left).*

Mansa Musa (MAHN-suh MOO-suh), Sundiata's grandnephew. Mansa Musa ruled Mali from 1307 to 1332. He set out from Timbuktu on a remarkable pilgrimage to Mecca in 1324. According to one report, his caravan consisted of 60,000 people. In front of Mansa Musa went a troop of 500 slaves, each carrying a 6-pound staff of gold. Piled on the backs of 80 camels were 12 tons of gold.

Songhai conquered Mali.

By the late 1300's, Mali's empire was weakening. Once more, the trade routes were shifting eastward as old mines ran out of gold and new mines were discovered. Between 1350 and 1450, the Songhai (SONG-hye) people replaced the Mandingo as controllers of trade. The Songhai farming, fishing, and trading villages lay along the banks of the middle Niger.

The Songhai had two extraordinary kings. One was a ruthless conqueror named Sunni Ali. The other was an excellent administrator whose name was Askia Muhammad.

"Always conqueror, never conquered"—thus did an Arab writer describe Sunni Ali, founder of the Songhai empire. First he attacked and sacked the Malian cities of Timbuktu and Jenne. Then he extended his control over the surrounding savanna and into the rain forest.

After Sunni Ali's death, one of his generals seized power. The new king, Askia Muhammad, divided his huge empire into provinces ruled by governors. He set up an efficient tax system and chose able officials. Under his rule, the Songhai empire was prosperous and well governed.

Timbuktu was among the cities that flourished at this time. A famous university there attracted Muslim scholars from afar. One wrote:

Here are a great store of doctors, judges, priests, and other learned men that are bountifully maintained at the king's cost and charges. And hither are brought diverse manuscripts of written books out of Barbary

In Europe at the time of Mansa Musa's pilgrimage, Dante was writing *The Divine Comedy* and Giotto was painting frescoes.

Voice from the Past · *Ibn Battuta's Travel in Africa*

One of the greatest travelers in history was an Arab named Ibn Battuta (IHB-uhn bat-TOO-tah). Born in 1304 in Morocco, Ibn Battuta spent his entire adult life traveling through Muslim lands. He visited Mecca and Baghdad, Mombasa, and Kilwa. He traveled to India, Southeast Asia, and China. In 1352, this world traveler made the rugged trip across the Sahara to the savanna kingdoms. Here he found a number of things that surprised him.

My stay in Walata lasted about 50 days . . . It is an excessively hot place and has only a few small date palms . . . The women are treated with more respect than the men, an amazing state of affairs. A man's heirs are his sister's sons, not his own sons. I have never seen such a custom anywhere else in the world except among the Indians of Malabar. But the Indians are heathens, while the people of Walata are Muslims, most careful about making their prayers, studying books of law, and memorizing the Koran. Yet their women show no shyness before men and do not veil themselves, though they go to prayers faithfully . . .

[Ibn Battuta then went on from Walata to Mali and described the people there.]

They are seldom unjust and have a greater hatred of injustice than any other people . . . There is complete security in their country. Neither the traveler nor the man who stays at home has anything to fear from robbers or men of violence.

1. What did Ibn Battuta find most surprising about the customs in Walata?
2. (a) List the customs in Walata and Mali that Ibn Battuta seemed to admire. (b) What did he think of their practice of Islam?
3. From Ibn Battuta's reactions, what can you deduce about the way women lived in other Muslim countries he had visited?

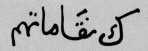

(northern Africa), which are sold for more money than any other merchandise.

Despite its wealth and learning, however, the Songhai empire lacked gunpowder and cannon. In 1591, a Moroccan sultan named El Mansur led an army of about 4,000 men over the Sahara. Most of the invaders collapsed and died as they hauled their heavy guns across the desert. The 1,000 survivors used their cannon to destroy 27,000 Songhai warriors armed only with swords and spears. Thus ended the great savanna empire of Songhai.

Section Review 2

Identify: (a) Kush, (b) Ethiopia, (c) Swahili, (d) Ghana, (e) Mali, (f) Songhai, (g) Soninke, (h) Mandingo, (i) Sundiata, (j) Mansa Musa, (k) Sunni Ali

Answer:
1. How did Kush's relations with Egypt change over the years?
2. (a) How did Axum become a powerful city? (b) What set Ethiopia apart from other African kingdoms?
3. Describe Swahili trade.
4. What effect did the Portuguese have on East Africa?
5. How did Ghana, Mali, and Songhai profit from trade?
6. What factor brought about the downfall of Songhai?

Critical Thinking

7. The use of new technology plays a large part in history. Show how the Kushites, the Portuguese, and the Moroccans used new technology to their advantage.
8. Describe some of the effects of trade on African society.

Indians developed many ways of life.

3

Medieval Europeans were dimly aware of Africa south of the Sahara. However, they were totally unaware that two giant continents lay west of the Atlantic Ocean.

The Americas have many environments.

Together, the American continents stretch more than 9,000 miles from north to south. North America includes all the land north of the Isthmus of Panama. Thus, Mexico and Central America are part of North America. So are the islands in the Caribbean Sea. South America includes all the land south of the isthmus.

North America has almost every kind of land and climate. There is tundra in the far north—a frozen, treeless land where only moss and stunted bushes grow. In contrast, rain forest covers much of the Isthmus of Panama. Between these two extremes lie thousands of square miles of mountains, plains, and plateaus.

South America is much smaller and lies farther east than North America. Both continents have mountains in the west. However, the Andes of South America are higher and narrower than the Rocky Mountains and the Sierra Nevada of western North America. The Andes are the world's longest mountain chain.

Both continents have great river systems. In North America, the Mississippi and its tributaries drain the central plains. Through South America flows the Amazon River, which carries more water than any other river in the world—more than the Mississippi, Yangtze, and Nile rivers combined.

The first Americans came from Asia.

Most scientists believe that the first human beings to settle in the Americas came during the last Ice Age, between 20,000 and 40,000 years ago. During that period, great ice sheets covered much of northern Europe, Asia, and North America. So much water was locked in the ice sheets that the level of the oceans dropped. The

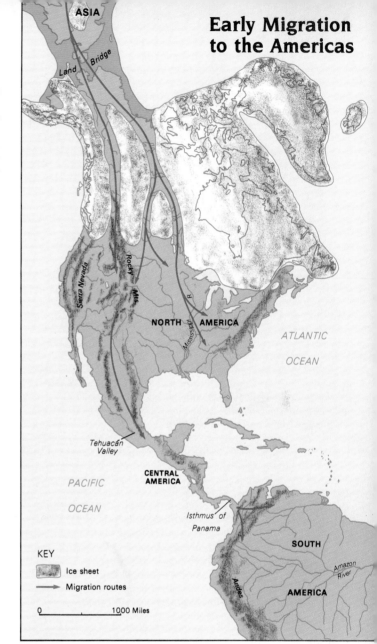

Early Migration to the Americas

KEY
Ice sheet
→ Migration routes
0 _____ 1000 Miles

Map Study

What narrow bridge of land links North and South America?

low sea levels uncovered land that formed a bridge between Asia and North America.

Bands of Paleolithic hunters and gatherers wandered across this land bridge from Asia. Without knowing it, they became the first Americans. Today, they are usually called Indians. (The name *Indian* came into use, as you will read later, after Christopher Columbus reached the Americas in 1492 and mistakenly thought he was near some islands in Asia, the Indies.)

This pottery figurine from ancient Mexico shows a woman grinding corn on a stone slab called a metate. Her child reaches under her arm to take one of the tortillas she has made.

The two continents offered plenty of living space. Groups of Indians fanned out over mountains, woodlands, plains, deserts, and rain forests. They adapted to the demands of each environment. About 7000 B.C., a band of Indians reached the most distant tip of South America. By that time, the land bridge to Asia had sunk under Arctic waters.

Farmers learned to raise corn.

The first people to reach the Americas lived by hunting game and gathering wild foods. Their descendants, however, discovered a new way of life. Like the people of ancient Egypt and Southwest Asia, the Indians learned to farm.

America's earliest farmers lived in the Tehuacán (TAY-wuh-KAHN) Valley, about 150 miles southeast of modern Mexico City. Around 5000 B.C., Indians there raised avocados, squash, beans, and chili peppers. Gradually, they added another crop—corn, or maize.

Corn became the most important crop in the Americas. Over the centuries, corn growing spread to most parts of the two continents. The people of Mexico and Central America revered corn as "the food of the gods."

Corn gave Indian farmers a stable food supply. They began to build permanent villages. Even farmers, however, continued to use wild foods for part of their diet. Many groups chose not to farm. They continued to hunt and gather.

Many cultures developed in North America.

Many Indian groups lived in the present-day lands of the United States and Canada. Each group had its own language, customs, and way of life. Along the northern Pacific coast, some groups fished for salmon, hunted for seals, and carved tall totem poles from giant evergreen trees. Along the Atlantic coast, Indian peoples farmed, hunted deer and rabbits, and made canoes of birchbark. The languages of the Indians were as varied as their ways of life. There were about 30 languages, with perhaps 2,000 dialects, spoken by Indian peoples.

The Hopewell of the eastern woodlands In the well-watered woodlands of what is now the eastern United States, Indians lived by a combination of farming, hunting, fishing, and gathering wild foods. One group, known to archaeologists as the Hopewell culture, lived in southern Ohio. They flourished from about 100 B.C. to A.D. 300. Family groups of 30 to 40 people lived together in large, rectangular houses made of bent saplings covered with bark, skins, or grass mats. They raised corn, squash, and tobacco.

The Hopewell people traded widely to get the beautiful, glossy green and black stones they used for beads and spear points. They also valued items from the seacoast—seashells, turtle shells, and shark teeth. They worked copper to make jewelry and shaped clay into fine pottery.

The spectacular achievements of the Hopewell can still be seen today—great cone-shaped burial mounds that rise 30 or 40 feet high. These Indians also made other great earthworks in geometric shapes. The scope of their public projects show that Hopewell society was organized with strong leaders. The quality of Hopewell crafts suggests that they had many specialized workers.

The Hohokam of the Southwest In the dry southwestern part of what is now the United States, Indians followed a very different way of life from that of the woodlands. One group of Indians who lived in the Southwest was named

People as well as goods were buried in the Hopewell mounds. Archaeologists have found pearls, carved shells, mica jewelry, and clay figurines in them. Ask what view of the afterlife is suggested by the burial of goods.

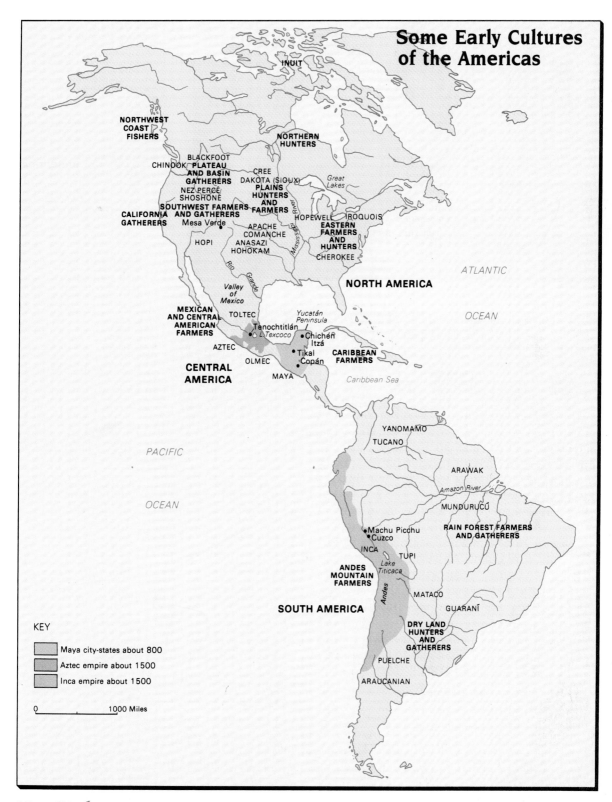

Some Early Cultures of the Americas

INUIT

NORTHWEST COAST FISHERS

NORTHERN HUNTERS

BLACKFOOT
CHINOOK PLATEAU AND BASIN GATHERERS
CREE
DAKOTA (SIOUX)
NEZ PERCE SHOSHONE
PLAINS HUNTERS AND FARMERS
SOUTHWEST FARMERS AND GATHERERS
CALIFORNIA GATHERERS   Mesa Verde
HOPEWELL   IROQUOIS
EASTERN FARMERS AND HUNTERS
APACHE COMANCHE
HOPI   ANASAZI HOHOKAM
CHEROKEE

Great Lakes

Mississippi River

NORTH AMERICA

ATLANTIC

OCEAN

Rio Grande

Valley of Mexico

MEXICAN AND CENTRAL AMERICAN FARMERS
TOLTEC
Yucatán Peninsula
Tenochtitlán
L. Texcoco
•Chichén Itzá
AZTEC
•Tikal
OLMEC   •Copán
MAYA
CARIBBEAN FARMERS

CENTRAL AMERICA

Caribbean Sea

PACIFIC

OCEAN

YANOMAMO
TUCANO

ARAWAK

Amazon River

MUNDURUCÚ

•Machu Picchu
•Cuzco
INCA
TUPI
RAIN FOREST FARMERS AND GATHERERS

Lake Titicaca

ANDES MOUNTAIN FARMERS

Andes

MATACO
GUARANÍ

SOUTH AMERICA

DRY LAND HUNTERS AND GATHERERS

PUELCHE

ARAUCANIAN

KEY

Maya city-states about 800

Aztec empire about 1500

Inca empire about 1500

0 ——————— 1000 Miles

Map Study

Which of the three major Indian empires described in this chapter was the largest? In what areas of the Americas did Indians get most of their food by a combination of hunting and farming?

311

The Hopewell trading network reached as far west as the Rockies, as far east as the Atlantic, as far south as the Gulf of Mexico, and as far north as present-day Canada.

This giant earth mound in the shape of a serpent lies in the Ohio River valley. It was built more than 2,000 years ago by a group of woodland Indians that scholars call the Adena. The Hopewell lived later in the same geographic area.

the Hohokam (ho-**HO**-kahm). The name *Hohokam* means "those who have vanished" in the language of the Pima Indians, modern descendants of the Hohokam.

The Hohokam culture arose about 100 B.C. between the Gila (**HEE**-luh) and the Salt rivers in what is now Arizona. The Hohokam triumphed over their harsh desert environment. They built dams on the rivers and dug irrigation canals up to 25 miles long. With these irrigation canals, they were able to bring water to their fields of corn and cotton.

The Hohokam people seem to have lived in peace, for their villages show little provision for defense. A Hohokam house began with a pit dug in the dry, firm ground. Above the pit, the builders raised a structure of branches and brush. Besides such houses, a Hohokam village also had a ball court. Players used rubber balls imported from Central America.

The Hohokam developed many skills. They made fine red-and-tan pottery and wove cloth from the cotton that they grew. They used turquoise and shells to make jewelry.

The Hopewell and Hohokam societies were only two of the hundreds of Indian groups in the northern part of North America. The map on page 311 shows where some of the other groups lived by 1500. Yet such a map can only suggest what territory each group occupied, because many groups traveled widely. Related groups might live far apart.

312

Section Review 3

Define: (a) tundra, (b) isthmus
Identify: (a) Tehuacán Valley, (b) Indians, (c) Hopewell, (d) Hohokam
Answer:
1. How do most scientists believe that the first humans reached the Americas?
2. When and where did farming begin in the Americas?
3. (a) What kind of houses did the Hopewell build? (b) What can be inferred about Hopewell society from their burial mounds?
4. How did the Hohokam grow food?

Critical Thinking
5. What characteristics did the Hopewell and Hohokam societies share, in spite of the great differences in their environments?

Empires flourished in the Americas.   4

By A.D. 1500, only about 1 million Indians lived in what is now Canada and the United States. The lands farther south were much more heavily settled. Population figures vary widely, but recent scholars estimate that between 50 and 60 million Indians lived in Mexico, Central America, and South America by 1500.

The Olmecs lived in Mexico.

The first major American civilization seems to have arisen in the swampy lowlands of Mexico's Gulf Coast around 1200 B.C. The creators of this civilization were the Olmecs.

By slashing and burning the trees of the dense rain forest, the Olmecs cleared enough land for farming. Yet the forest was never far away. Late at night, the Olmecs doubtless heard the howls of the wild jaguar, a spotted cat that still lives in the area. The Olmecs carved stone figures that were half jaguar and half human, suggesting that they worshiped the jaguar's spirit. Among their many achievements, the Olmecs produced fine pottery, invented a system of writing, and developed a calendar. Ceremonial ballgames, which were important to nearly all later Indian societies in the region, began with the Olmecs.

The Olmec civilization flourished for about 800 years. It perished around 400 B.C. Our knowledge of the Olmecs is limited. However, later civilizations of Mexico and Central America clearly show the influence of the Olmecs.

The Mayas built great cities.

Around 500 B.C., the Mayas began to create their civilization in the southern Gulf Coast region and present-day Guatemala. In the insect-infested rain forest, the Mayas built a brilliant civilization. Historians call the years from 500 B.C. to A.D. 250 the Formative Period of Maya civilization. The Mayas reached their height during their Classic Period, from A.D. 250 to 900.

Slashing trees with stone tools, the Mayas cleared the rain forest to grow corn. Although they had no wheeled vehicles and no beasts of burden such as horses or oxen, they moved great pieces of stone to build their temples. They had no iron tools, yet they shaped their stone blocks so skillfully that their pyramids still stand.

The pyramids were the center of Maya religious ceremonies. Around them, cities grew up where priests, government officials, some merchants, and artisans lived. Peasant farmers probably lived outside the cities in thatched huts. The farmers came to town for religious events and to visit the market.

Like the ancient Greeks and Phoenicians, the Mayas built city-states. The ruins of at least 80 have been found. Each city-state had a hereditary ruler, nobles, and priests. Four or five of the most powerful city-states dominated their smaller neighbors.

Tikal Tikal was the largest Maya city. In its heyday, five pyramid-temples towered over its plazas and avenues. The tallest, the Temple of the Giant Jaguar, was as high as a 20-story building. A flight of stairs led up one side of each pyramid to a small temple at the top. Intricately carved panels over the temple entrances were painted bright red, blue, and orange. The priests who climbed to these temples offered sacrifices of corn, cocoa beans, and an occasional monkey to the gods.

The calendar Maya priests also measured the nightly movements of the moon and stars. Keeping track of time was crucial to the Maya priests. The calendar allowed them to predict what their

Daily Life · Ball Games of the Mayas

In Tikal's sports plaza, priests and others attended ball games. The games were something like a combination of modern basketball, soccer, jai alai, and volleyball. The ball court was a narrow alley flanked by two high walls. Players used a solid ball made from the sap of Yucatan rubber trees. Using only their hips, knees, and forearms, players on two teams passed the ball up and down the court, trying to put the ball through one of the stone rings on each wall. Because the ball weighed about five pounds, players protected themselves with helmets, gloves, knee pads, and broad belts.

313

heavenly gods (sun, moon, planets) would be doing from day to day. It also foretold dramatic events, such as eclipses of the sun.

The Maya calendar was both accurate and complex. The Mayas kept track of time on three different calendars. They measured the solar year to 365 days, very close to our own. They also counted a sacred year of 260 days. Third, they kept track of what was called the Long Count, in which a full cycle lasted about 400 years. After 13 such cycles, the Mayas believed, the world would be destroyed and created again.

Clearly, the Mayas were skilled mathematicians. As early as 300 B.C., they discovered the concept of zero, an idea unknown to Greeks and Romans. For numbers, the Mayas used a system of dots and bars. Five dots were equal to one bar. A shell symbol represented zero.

New cultures replaced the old.

Most Maya cities declined after the year 700. By 900, Maya civilization had collapsed. No one knows exactly why. Some scholars believe that peasants revolted against the ruling class. At the same time, invaders from the north disrupted the fragile economy of all of Mexico and Central America. Crop failure and famine may also have played a part in the Maya decline.

North of the fertile Valley of Mexico lay a dry and barren plain of scrubby grasses and cactus, a semi-desert. For centuries, this area was the homeland of warlike peoples, including the Chichimecs, the Toltecs, and the Aztecs. These groups were like the Huns and Mongols of Asia. They raided the richer, more settled civilizations whenever they could.

Between 900 and 1300, successive waves of northern warriors swept into the Valley of Mexico. One of these groups, the Toltecs, established an empire. The Toltecs learned to build pyramids and ball courts in the style of their more civilized

Footnote to History

The wealthiest Mayas showed off their high status by nibbling cocoa beans. These tasty, chocolate-flavored beans served as a common medium of exchange in Tikal's marketplace. Thus, to eat them was like eating money.

predecessors. They dominated the Valley of Mexico for 200 years. Around 1160, their capital of Tula was destroyed by new invaders.

The Aztecs built an empire.

Among the invaders was a fierce and desperately poor band of barbarians. These invaders were known by two names: Mexicas and Aztecs.

According to their own legends, the Aztecs came from a northern land called Aztlan. Migrating to the Valley of Mexico, they wandered until their god of war showed them where to build a city. "Look for an eagle perched on a cactus and holding a snake," said the god.

The Aztec priests stood on the shore of a great salt lake, Lake Texcoco (tehs-KOH-koh), and looked out over the water. They saw the eagle with a snake wriggling in its beak. The cactus on which the bird perched grew on one of Lake Texcoco's islands. (The eagle, snake, and cactus appear today on Mexico's flag.)

Tenochtitlán The Aztecs settled on the island, probably about 1325. Their island city was called Tenochtitlán (tay-NOCH-tee-TLAHN), which meant "Place of the Prickly-Pear Cactus." As the Aztecs gained power and wealth, Tenochtitlán became one of the most magnificent cities in the world.

Scholars guess that about 300,000 Aztecs may have lived in Tenochtitlán in 1500. (That figure would make the Aztec city five times larger than London at the same time.) People traveled to and from the lake city over three long causeways. Within the city, the quickest way to get from one's home to the Great Temple was to paddle a boat up one of the major canals that crisscrossed the island. The royal palace boasted wonderful gardens, fountains, baths, and a well-stocked zoo.

Human sacrifice The legendary god that led the Aztecs to their city was also the god of the sun. Aztec priests believed it was their sacred duty to feed human hearts to him. The Aztecs thought that the sun's life-giving light could flicker out at any time. They believed the sun could burn brightly only as long as they fed its god human blood. The Aztecs fought their wars in the Valley of Mexico in part to get victims for sacrifice.

After some 200 years of nearly constant war, the Aztecs triumphed over almost all their neighbors. By the year 1500, the Aztec king was

This Aztec drawing shows Tenochtitlán beneath the legendary eagle on the cactus.

taking tribute in gold, silver, fine cloth, feathers, cocoa beans, and furs from an immense area. Perhaps as many as 11 million Indians were subjects of the Aztec ruler. Yet within a few years, the mighty Aztec empire would come to an end, as you will read in Chapter 17.

The Incas built an empire in Peru.

Some 2,800 miles south of the Aztec capital was an even larger empire. The Incas built their capital of Cuzco high in the Andes in what is now Peru. Separated by immense geographic barriers, the Aztecs and the Incas probably never knew of each other. Yet the rise of the two empires was similar.

Civilization in the high valleys of Peru was already at least 1,000 years old when the Incas started their climb to power around the year 1200. The Incas had learned from earlier peoples how to build fortress walls using gigantic blocks of stone. Inca stonemasons had no mortar, but they cut the stones so carefully that many of their walls still stand, despite earthquakes.

Like earlier Peruvians, the Incas grew corn at elevations up to 11,000 feet. On even higher lands, they planted potatoes on terraced fields.

Unlike the Aztecs, the Incas treated fairly the peoples they conquered.

Like the Aztecs, the Incas worshiped the sun as their main god. Inca princes proudly called themselves "Sons of the Sun."

The Incas were excellent adminstrators, even though they never developed a system of writing. They kept records by tying knots in a bundle of strings, a device called a *quipu* (**KEY**-poo). The position of the knots indicated payment to the government of so many baskets of corn, so many bags of gold, and so on.

A 10,000-mile network of stone highways held the Inca empire together. Swift runners used these highways to carry the commands of the Inca ruler to all his officials. After memorizing a message from the emperor, a courier from Cuzco would run to a relay station. Here a second courier would jog alongside the first. After learning the message, the second runner carried it to the next relay point. Inca messages traveled this way at the brisk rate of 140 miles a day.

For the Incas as for the Aztecs, the 1400's were a time of conquest. By 1493, their empire stretched about 2,500 miles from present-day Ecuador to the middle of Chile. The Inca ruler had the power of life and death over his 6 million subjects. Soon, as you will read in Chapter 17, the 200-year-old empire would fall. Its defeat by Europeans came as a total surprise.

Section Review 4

Define: (a) city-state, (b) quipu
Identify: (a) Olmecs, (b) Mayas, (c) Aztecs, (d) Tenochtitlán, (e) Incas
Answer:
1. Where did the first major American civilizations begin?
2. (a) How was the Maya society organized? (b) What shows that the Mayas were skilled mathematicians?
3. How did the Aztec empire begin?
4. How did the Inca rulers control their empire?
5. Describe the architectural achievements of the Mayas, Aztecs, and Incas.

Critical Thinking

6. Why do you think so little is known about the Mayas when a great deal is known about some people who lived during the same centuries in other parts of the world?

315

Summary

1. Early civilizations arose in Africa. Sub-Saharan Africa has four geographic regions: the northern and southern coasts; the deserts; the savannas; and the rain forest. A variety of societies developed in those regions. In many groups, lineages were central to both family organization and religion. Art and music expressed the values of these societies.

2. African empires thrived on trade. The Kushites built the first cities south of the Sahara. Meroë was conquered by Ethiopia, a Christian kingdom. In cities along the eastern coast of Africa, the Swahili culture arose. In the 1500's, the Portuguese destroyed the Swahili cities. In western Africa, the empires of Ghana, Mali, and Songhai developed on the savanna.

3. Indians developed many ways of life. Most scientists believe that the first Americans came from Asia by crossing a land-bridge about 20,000 to 40,000 years ago. Groups of Indians spread out over North and South America, creating many different ways of life. Corn became the basic crop of many farming groups, while other groups continued to hunt and gather food.

4. Empires flourished in the Americas. The largest Indian civilizations developed in Mexico and in Central and South America. The Mayas are known for their huge stone pyramids and accurate calendar. The Aztecs built an empire in the Valley of Mexico. The Incas ruled an empire in Peru, uniting it by skilled administration and good roads.

Reviewing the Facts

1. Define the following terms:
   a. oasis
   b. savanna
   c. lineage

2. Explain the importance of each of the following names, places, or terms:
   a. Sahara
   b. Yoruba
   c. griots
   d. Kushites
   e. Ethiopia
   f. Ghana
   g. Mali
   h. Songhai
   i. Mansa Musa
   j. Tehuacán Valley
   k. Hopewell
   l. Hohokam
   m. Olmecs
   n. Mayas
   o. Aztecs
   p. Tenochtitlán
   q. Incas

3. Describe the climate and vegetation of Africa's major geographic regions.

4. (a) Who were included in a lineage? (b) How did the lineage system help to organize society?

5. Compare the ways of life of the Hopewell and the Hohokam.

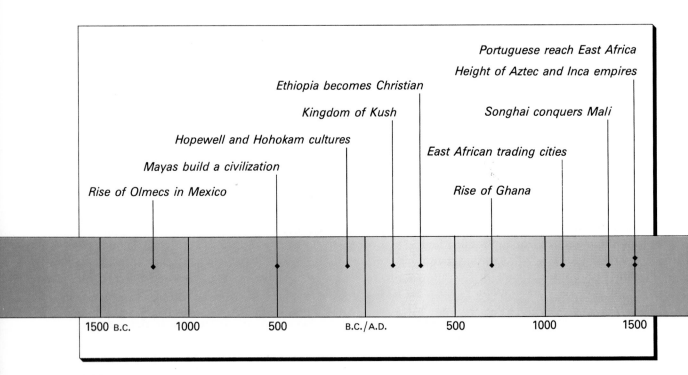

Portuguese reach East Africa

Height of Aztec and Inca empires

Ethiopia becomes Christian

Kingdom of Kush

Songhai conquers Mali

Hopewell and Hohokam cultures

East African trading cities

Mayas build a civilization

Rise of Ghana

Rise of Olmecs in Mexico

1500 B.C.   1000   500   B.C./A.D.   500   1000   1500

Basic Skills

1. **Interpreting time lines**   Refer to the time line on page 316. For each event on the line, tell whether it occurred at the precise time shown or over a period of many years.
2. **Comparing time lines**   Using the time lines on pages 282 and 296, find out what was happening in Asia during each of the following periods: (a) when Ghana was at its height in Western Africa; (b) when Aztec civilization was at its height in Central America.
3. **Stating main ideas**   Give one main idea (other than the section headings) on each of the following topics: (a) the kingdom of Kush, (b) the kingdom of Axum, (c) the coastal cities of East Africa, (d) the empire of Ghana, (e) the empire of Mali, (f) the empire of Songhai.
4. **Making a comparison chart**   Make a chart comparing the Aztec and the Inca. For the vertical column, use the headings Location, Political Organization, Religion, and Major Achievements.

Researching and Reporting Skills

1. **Identifying primary sources**   Identify from the text one primary source mentioned for each of the following: (a) Kush, (b) Axum, (c) coastal cities, (d) Ghana, (e) Mali, (f) Songhai, (g) the Hopewell, (h) the Hohokam, (i) the Maya.
2. **Evaluating sources**   Discuss the value of the various types of sources in number 1 above, based on the following criteria: (a) objectivity, (b) type of information provided, (c) amount of interpretation needed.
3. **Finding and listing references**   To prepare a report on one of the groups of people mentioned in this chapter, you might use a college textbook on world history to locate references. Find such a textbook in your library and look up in the index the name of the group you have chosen. Using the page references and end-of-chapter bibliographies, list three references that give information on your subject. For each reference, prepare a citation that includes author's name, title of reference, name and location of publisher, and date of publication.
4. **Choosing a title**   Based on the sources you have identified, select one aspect of your subject's history

as the topic for a possible report. Choose a title that conveys what your report will cover.

Critical Thinking

1. **Analyzing**   What geographic and environmental factors contributed most to the rise of the various African kingdoms? Give examples to support your answer.
2. **Synthesizing**   Trade was of major importance in the economy of the various African kingdoms. (a) What were the main resources and products exported from Africa? (b) What were the main kinds of imports and where did they come from?
3. **Inferring**   What factors besides iron working aided the prosperity of Kush?
4. **Analyzing**   Choose two of the societies described in this chapter and explain how each adapted to its geographic environment.
5. **Comparing**   How did Maya pyramids differ in design and function from those of Egypt?
6. **Evaluating**   The Maya, Aztec, and Inca developed distinctive civilizations. (a) List four major achievements of each civilization. (b) Which do you consider most advanced in terms of European civilization?

Perspectives on Past and Present

This chapter has highlighted certain characteristics of African civilization—such as the importance of family ties, religion honoring the spirits of ancestors, and music and dance that bound communities in a traditional heritage. Read about a contemporary African nation to find whether these characteristics still apply.

Investigating History

1. Alex Haley's book *Roots* gives an account of a present-day griot. Read that description and report to the class on the role of the griot in helping Haley to identify his ancestors.
2. The earliest known civilization in Peru was that of the Moche. Preceding the Inca by some 1,200 years, they rivaled their Maya contemporaries in art and technology. Read in the October 1988 *National Geographic* or news magazines of that date about the extraordinary discovery of a Moche ruler's tomb and what it tells of this early civilization.

Unit IV Review

Geographic Theme: Place

What are the characteristics of three cities of the past?

Geographers are concerned with the special character of a place. Their interest includes both the nature of the land and the customs of the people. Historians share this interest when they study cities of the past.

In this unit, you have read accounts written by two of history's great travelers. Marco Polo described the "new royal city" of Khanbalik. The other traveler, the Arab Ibn Battuta, described the African city of Walata, then in the kingdom of Mali.

Another great city of the past is Tenochtitlán in Mexico. It is known today through the writings of a Spanish soldier, Bernal Diaz, who accompanied Cortés. Diaz had a chance to tour the city before it was destroyed. In his old age, Diaz recorded his recollections of the Aztec capital.

"We saw the fresh water which came from Chapultepec [by aqueduct] to supply the city, and the bridges that were constructed at intervals on the causeways so that the water could flow in and out from one part of the lake to another ... We saw *cues* [temples] and shrines that looked like gleaming white towers and castles: a marvellous sight ...

Having examined and considered all that we had seen, we turned back to the great market and the swarm of people buying and selling. The mere murmur of their voices talking was loud enough to be heard more than three miles away. Some of our soldiers who had been in many parts of the world, in Constantinople, in Rome, and all over Italy, said that they had never seen a market so well laid out, so large, so orderly, and so full of people."

1. (a) What is Diaz's impression of Tenochtitlán?
   (b) What does his description tell about Aztec civilization?
2. What can you tell about the site and situation of Tenochtitlán?
3. Compare the accounts of Diaz with those of Polo and Battuta. Which description conveys the most vivid impression? In which city would you have preferred to live?
4. What does each description show about the culture and society of that city?

Tenochtitlán in about 1500

Unit Perspectives

Understanding History

1. **Relating** With what civilization is each of the following people associated? What role did that person play in the civilization?
   - a. Kublai Khan
   - b. Tokugawa Ieyasu
   - c. Sesshu
   - d. Chandra Gupta I
   - e. Akbar
   - f. King Ezana
   - g. Mansa Musa

2. **Matching** Match the term in the first column with the correct definition in the second.
   - a. dynasty
   - b. clan
   - c. caste
   - d. gentry
   - e. samurai

   1. people descended from the same ancestors
   2. series of rulers from the same family
   3. a large, wealthy group of people who rank below nobles
   4. a Japanese warrior
   5. a Hindi birth group

3. **Locating** Describe the location of each of the following cities. Why was each city important?
   - a. Peking
   - b. Heian
   - c. Ch'ang-an
   - d. Axum
   - e. Timbuktu
   - f. Mombasa
   - g. Tikal
   - h. Tenochtitlán

Critical Thinking

1. **Comparing** For each of the following pairs of topics, give one similarity and one difference: (a) Marco Polo and Ibn Battuta; (b) Shah Jahan of India and Mansa Musa of Mali; (c) Islam in northern Africa and northern India; (d) Nalanda in India and Timbuktu in Africa; (e) the messenger service of the Inca and the postal service in China under the Great Khan.

2. **Analyzing** From the chapters in this unit, give three examples of the importance of interaction between people and their environment in shaping a people's culture.

3. **Identifying viewpoints** Explain what each of the following people might have thought about the subject given: (a) a Delhi sultan on Hinduism; (b) a Portuguese explorer on Ethiopia; (c) a scholar of the Ming court on tradition; (d) a Maya priest on mathematics.

4. **Identifying causes and effects** Give one cause and one effect of each of the following: (a) the decision to discontinue the voyages of China's Grand Fleet; (b) the migration of Paleolithic tribes from Asia to America; (c) the wars between Hindus and Muslims in India.

5. **Forming a hypothesis** What factors might explain the religious tolerance between Muslims and Africans, in contrast to the persecution of Hindus by Muslims in India? Explain the reasons for your hypothesis.

6. **Comparing** (a) How were the men of Rajput India similar to European knights and Japanese samurai? (b) What happened to Buddhism and Hinduism in India during the Rajput centuries?

7. **Analyzing** (a) How has the location of Southeast Asia impacted life there? (b) What present-day countries make up Southeast Asia?

8. **Comparing** Compare the economic life of the city-states of East Africa with that of the savanna kingdoms in western Africa between 1100 and 1500.

Making Decisions

The Sui ruler Yang-ti faced many important decisions during his reign. (a) Should he build the Grand Canal? (b) Should he pay tribute to the Mongols? (c) Should he make Marco Polo a court official? (d) Should he move his capital to the south of China? What factors did Yang-ti have to consider in making each of these decisions?

Continuity and Change

1. In the Historical Atlas, pages 810–813, compare the world about 1250 (pages 810–811) with that of about 1500 (pages 812–813). (a) Outside of Europe, what groups gained power between the two dates? (b) What groups lost power? (c) In which Asian empire did territories change the least?

2. Comparing the Unit III time line (pages 164–165) with that of Unit IV (pages 258–259), what might you conclude about the changes in centers of civilization?

Unit V

The Spread of New Ideas

Chapters

	1300	**1360**	**1420**
Political and Governmental Life	**1300's** Rise of independent cities in Northern Italy		**1434** Medici control Florence **1430's** Prince Henry the Navigator sponsors exploration
Economic and Technological Life	**1300's** Florence is financial center of Europe		**1400's** New technology opens way to exploration
Social and Cultural Life	**1300's** Renaissance begins in northern Italy **1321** Dante writes *The Divine Comedy*		**1455** Gutenberg prints Bible with movable type

Bronze doors of
Baptistry in Florence

Detail from Giotto's
The Crucifixion

Printing shop

The end of the Middle Ages saw Europe entering a new age of creativity and prosperity. Artists and writers were inspired by new knowledge of Greek and Roman art and learning. The old isolation of cultures ended as explorers crossed unfamiliar oceans in search of trade. The new era led to the questioning of long-held beliefs in religion and science and the affirming of the importance of each person's mind and soul. It thus opened the way to the growth of modern thought.

1480   **1540**   **1600**

1485–1603
Tudor dynasty rules England

1519
Cortés conquers Mexico

Conquistador's helmet

1566–1581
The Netherlands gains independence

1538
England defeats the Spanish Armada

1618–1648
Religious wars divide Germany

1500's–1600's
Scientific Revolution brings new ideas

1490's
Explorations of Columbus and Da Gama

Copernicus' sun-centered theory

1600's
Dutch merchants develop capitalism

1600's
Amsterdam becomes a center of art

1508–1512
Michelangelo paints in Sistine Chapel

1521
Luther begins religious revolt

1605
Cervantes publishes *Don Quixote*

Chapter 15
1300 - 1600

The Renaissance and Exploration

Renaissance Florence lay on the Arno River. It was a city of about 100,000 people. Notice the various styles of architecture in the palaces and churches. (The artist has shown himself, or another painter, drawing the city from a hilltop.)

Read and Understand

1. The Renaissance began in northern Italy.
2. Florence led the way in arts.
3. Three artistic giants led the Renaissance.
4. Explorers opened new sea routes.

Key Terms

vernacular
humanist
caravel

An intriguing idea darted into the mind of Leonardo da Vinci (LAY-uh-NAHR-doh duh VEEN-chee). Eagerly he flipped open his notebook and wrote this message to himself: "Dissect the bat, study it carefully, and on this model construct the machine."

The machine that Leonardo imagined had huge, batlike wings measuring 80 feet from tip to tip. Below the wings, he imagined a person standing on a wooden framework and pedaling furiously. By ropes and pulleys, the pedals would make the wings flap. With this device, thought Leonardo, a person could fly.

We know about Leonardo's ideas for flying machines from the many sketches he drew in his books. Unfortunately, the notebooks show only what he planned to do. They do not tell whether he ever tried to build his great bat machine.

The flying machine was only one idea among hundreds that excited Leonardo. Looking through his notebooks (5,700 pages of which have survived), we can track Leonardo's lifelong quest for knowledge. He wanted to know the physical universe inside and out—how it worked and how its hidden laws could be mastered by the human mind.

On one page are drawings of the muscles and tendons of a man's arm as it swings forward. On another page, Leonardo made a rough sketch of a falling man clinging to a tent-shaped cloth. A note next to it explains its purpose:

> If a man has a tent made of linen of which the [openings] have all been stopped up . . . he will be able to throw himself down from any height without injury.

Here, in other words, is the first design for a parachute.

Leonardo knew he was a genius. In 1482, he wrote a letter offering his services to the duke of Milan in northern Italy. Leonardo assured the duke that there was no better weapons designer, military engineer, painter, or architect than he was. He concluded, "I commend myself to Your Excellency with all possible humility."

Another Italian of this time, Christopher Columbus, had fewer ideas than Leonardo. However, he believed in his one great idea as firmly as Leonardo believed in parachutes and flying machines. Columbus thought he could reach Asia by sailing west across the Atlantic Ocean. He was looking for a patron to pay for his voyage at the very time that Leonardo was trying to interest the duke of Milan in new ideas for bridges and armored vehicles.

Columbus (born in 1451) and Leonardo (born in 1452) were only two of many individuals whose genius and daring made the years from 1300 to 1600 a golden age. They lived during the time we call the Renaissance (REN-uh-SAHNTS). The word means "rebirth."

What was being reborn? The educated men and women of Italy hoped to bring back to life the classical culture of Greece and Rome. Yet bringing back a past golden age is never possible. In striving to revive the past, the people of the Renaissance in fact created something new.

The Renaissance was a time of great intellectual and artistic creativity. Above all, people of the Renaissance had a new view of themselves and their world.

The Renaissance began in northern Italy. 1

Like other great changes in history, the Renaissance did not replace the Middle Ages overnight. Nor did the change take place at the same time everywhere in Europe. The Renaissance began in Italy around 1300. Later, its new styles of art, writing, and thought spread northward to the Netherlands, France, Germany, and England.

It is important to remember that early writers and artists of the Renaissance were creating their masterpieces in Italy while France and England were still locked in the Hundred Years' War. The bustling cities of northern Italy seem to be in a different world from the feudal villages of northern Europe, but both existed at the same time.

Italy offered new opportunities.

The Renaissance began in the city-states of northern Italy, especially Florence. The region of Italy that lies north of Rome and south of the Alps was different from the rest of Europe in two ways.

Urban centers First, northern Italy was a highly urban region. By 1350, three cities there had

This sketch from one of the Leonardo da Vinci's notebooks shows an idea for a flying machine.

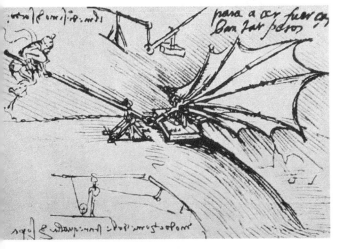

Renaissance Italy

Map Study answers: Adriatic; the Papal States; Savoy, Milan, Modena

Map Study

What sea did Venice control? Who ruled Rome and the surrounding territory? What states bordered Genoa?

populations of about 100,000, a huge figure by medieval standards. Two of those cities—Genoa in the west and Venice in the east—were major seaports whose merchants dominated the rich Mediterranean trade. The third city, Florence, was located inland on the Arno River. Its thriving economy was based on the making of fine woolens, leathers, and silks.

Aside from those three large cities, northern Italy had a number of other good-sized towns, as the map on this page shows. Thus, northern Italy was urban while the rest of Europe was still mostly rural. (The Black Death of 1348 struck Italy's cities hard, but they recovered quickly.)

The power of merchants Second, northern Italy was a merchant's region. In these cities, wealthy merchants dominated politics and society as well as business. You have read how the Lombard League defeated the Holy Roman Emperor, Frederick Barbarossa, in 1176 at the Battle of Legnano (page 223). After that defeat, the Holy Roman emperors had little control over Italy's cities.

The popes had left Rome for Avignon and were later weakened by the Great Schism. They could not dominate Italy's cities either.

Milan, Genoa, Florence, Venice, and the other independent city-states ran their own affairs. Each collected taxes and supported an army. Within these cities, merchants were the wealthiest and most powerful class.

Unlike feudal nobles, merchants did not inherit their social rank. Success in business depended mostly on the merchant's own wits. As a result, successful merchants took pride in their achievements. They believed they were great because of their merit as individuals. The theme of individual achievement is an important one in the Renaissance, as you will see.

Just as these merchants competed with one another in business, they also competed as patrons, or sponsors, of the arts. A Florentine merchant was as proud of spotting a promising young painter as of making a profitable deal in silks. Throughout northern Italy, wealthy families spent their money lavishly for the glory of helping artists create works of genius.

Such was the setting for the Renaissance. Like the blossoming of a flower, the Renaissance first showed itself as a lovely bud in the 1300's. Three of the earliest geniuses in this golden age were a painter, a poet, and a letter writer.

Giotto painted lifelike figures.

Giotto di Bondone (JOHT-oh dee bohn-DOH-nay) was 38 years old when, in 1304, he carried his paints and brushes into a small, empty building in Padua, Italy. The building, called the Arena Chapel, was owned by a wealthy merchant who had commissioned Giotto to decorate it with scenes from the Bible. Giotto dabbed his brush in pigment and applied his first masterly stroke to the wet plaster. (The technique of painting on wet plaster was known as *fresco* painting.)

Most painters of the time would have covered the walls with flat, stiff-looking figures like those painted throughout the Middle Ages. Giotto had a different style. He painted human figures that looked real and lifelike, with bodies and faces that seemed fully rounded. When Giotto painted on a flat wall, he created an illusion of depth. The people in his paintings all seemed to be interacting with one another. Their faces showed

324

One scene in the Arena Chapel, for example, shows a group of grief-stricken women whose children had been killed by Roman soldiers. Though Giotto painted for another 30 years, the frescoes in the Arena Chapel were his greatest achievement.

realistic emotions. Giotto's acclaimed frescoes began a revolution in art.

Dante wrote *The Divine Comedy*.

Dante Alighieri (DAHN-tay AH-lee-GYAY-ree) was to the world of poetry what Giotto was to the world of painting. Dante was born in Florence in 1265, only a year before Giotto's birth. At the age of 9, Dante met an 8-year-old girl, Beatrice Portinari. Although he did not see her again for 10 years, she became his spiritual ideal. "From that time forward," he wrote later, "love quite governed my soul." He continued his spiritual love for her from afar, although he rarely saw or spoke to her. She died in 1290, at just 24 years old. Yet Dante worshiped her memory until his own death in 1321. For Dante, Beatrice was his muse—that is, the guiding genius of his writing. In his poems, he spoke of her as a kind of goddess.

Dante's most famous work was *The Divine Comedy*. (In this sense, *comedy* refers to a literary work with a joyous ending.) This long poem has three parts. In the first part, Dante imagines that the ancient Roman poet Virgil is guiding him on a tour of "the inferno" (hell). In the second part, Dante and Virgil visit a zone called purgatory, which lies between hell and heaven. Finally, in the third part, Dante is guided through paradise by the famous medieval monk, St. Bernard. Eventually, he meets Beatrice there.

Dante filled his poem with real people. He called dead friends and enemies by name and told of their earthly adventures. *The Divine Comedy* is full of comments on the political events of Dante's time. He showed a keen interest in human personalities.

Dante's masterpiece showed both the religious ideas of the Middle Ages and the worldly concerns of the Renaissance. *The Divine Comedy* was a kind of philosophic bridge between Europe's past and its future.

At a time when other serious poets wrote in Latin, Dante wrote *The Divine Comedy* in the **vernacular**, or everyday language of his homeland. By his work, Dante gave the Italian language new prestige, and he is sometimes called the creator of modern Italian. His example encouraged other poets to write in their own vernacular languages, as England's Geoffrey Chaucer did later in the 1300's.

Petrarch wrote poems and letters.

Another Italian poet, Francesco Petrarch (PEE-trahrk), was born in 1304, the year that Giotto began work on the Arena Chapel. Petrarch wrote both in Italian and in Latin. In Italian, he wrote beautiful sonnets in honor of a mysterious woman named Laura, who was his muse and spiritual ideal as Beatrice had been Dante's. (Little is known of Laura except that she died of the plague in 1348.) In classical Latin, he wrote letters to his many influential friends.

In Petrarch's letters, he imitated the graceful style of his favorite classical author, Cicero, the ancient Roman senator. Petrarch's writing showed a new idea of beauty. Instead of the complexity of medieval poetry, Petrarch strove for the classical virtues of simplicity and purity. If Dante's works were a bridge between the Middle Ages and the Renaissance, Petrarch had crossed that bridge and stood fully within the new age.

New values shaped the Renaissance.

No age or time breaks completely with the past. Yet the men and women of the Renaissance came to have a new outlook on life. Here are some of the characteristics that set the Renaissance apart from the Middle Ages.

Celebration of the individual Artists in the Middle Ages did their work skillfully. In general, however, they did not win fame as individuals. The glassmakers, stonecutters, and wood-carvers of the great cathedrals worked for the glory of God, not for personal glory. Even the author of the *Song of Roland* is unknown.

By the 1300's, however, artists and writers in northern Italy were eager to be known and remembered as individuals. From this time on, we know the names of people who created works of art. Fame was the final reward for superior talent.

Two new art forms show this interest in individual fame: portrait painting and autobiography. Wealthy patrons wanted their faces recorded for all time. Artists often painted self-portraits too. Autobiographies were the written equivalents of self-portraits. People believed that their own lives were interesting and important not just to themselves but to others. They wished to share their lives with the world.

How is the celebration of the individual shown in Giotto's epitaph: "I am he through
whose merit the lost art of painting was revived . . . But what need is there for
words? I am Giotto, and my name alone tells more than a lengthy ode."

325

Admiration for the classical culture of Greece shows in this Renaissance painting, "The School of Athens." Under the central arch, Plato talks with his pupil Aristotle. They are surrounded by important figures from both ancient and Renaissance times. (This work is by Raphael, who is discussed on page 334.)

Love of classical learning Renaissance scholars despised the art and literature of the Middle Ages. Since the fall of Rome in 476, they said, the people of Europe had lived in darkness and ignorance. Even the beautiful Gothic cathedrals were dismissed as the work of barbarians. Admiring only Greek and Roman art, a Renaissance artist once cried, "Cursed be the man who invented this wretched Gothic architecture!" Petrarch summed up the Renaissance attitude by calling the medieval years "the Dark Ages."

Petrarch and other Renaissance scholars loved the writings of ancient Greece and Rome. Scholars who studied classical texts were called **humanists**, from the Latin word *humanitas*. According to Cicero, humanitas meant the learning that every educated, civilized person should have. Petrarch himself is considered the first humanist. He and his followers were the cultural leaders of the Renaissance. Under their influence, all painting, sculpture, and architecture carried on the traditions of ancient Greece and Rome.

Enjoyment of worldly pleasures In Renaissance Italy, almost everyone with money openly enjoyed material luxuries, fine music, tasty foods, and beautiful surroundings. For example, clothing itself became almost a work of art. Women's gowns were sometimes so encrusted with pearls or golden beads that the fabric underneath was nearly hidden. Men wore colorful stockings, fancy jackets called doublets, and plumed hats. Both men and women perfumed their clothing and hair.

This enjoyment of worldly goods showed a new attitude. In the Middle Ages, devoutly religious people had proved their piety by wearing poor, rough clothing and living on the plainest foods. Renaissance humanists suggested that a person might love and enjoy life without offending God. Most historians agree that Renaissance art and literature show a growing interest in earthly and human subjects.

Ideals differed for men and women.

For Renaissance thinkers, the ideal individual strove to master almost every art. Those who excelled in many fields were admiringly known as "universal men." Later ages called such people "Renaissance men."

A book called *The Courtier* became widely popular because it told young people how to become an accomplished person whom everyone would admire. Its author was Baldassare Castiglione (KAHS-tee-LYOH-nay).

The ideal man A young man, said Castiglione, should be well educated in the Greek and Latin classics. He should be charming, polite, and witty. He should be able to dance, write poetry, sing, and play music. In addition, he should be physically graceful and strong, a skilled rider, wrestler, and swordsman.

Renaissance men tried to live up to this ideal. In his autobiography, Leon Battista Alberti (1404–1472) boasted of his many skills. Here, in the

Young men and women of the upper classes in the Renaissance studied history, rhetoric, literature, and moral philosophy. These subjects were called the liberal arts because their purpose was to liberate the students' minds.

third person, is Alberti's description of his accomplishments and interests:

> He played ball, hurled the javelin, ran, leaped, wrestled, and above all delighted in climbing steep mountains . . . As a youth, he excelled in warlike games. With his feet together, he could leap over the shoulders of men standing by . . . He delighted in the organ and was considered an expert among the leading musicians.

In addition, Alberti designed and built several churches and made a scientific study of perspective. Alberti summed up the spirit of his times when he wrote, "Man can do anything if he will."

The ideal woman Upper-class women of the Renaissance were as well educated as the men. According to *The Courtier*, women too were expected to know the classics, to write well, to paint, to make music, to dance, and to be charming. Yet they were not expected to seek fame as men did. Like Beatrice and Laura, they were expected to inspire poetry and art but rarely to create it.

The most honored woman of the Renaissance in northern Italy was probably Isabella d'Este. Born into the ruling family of the city-state of Ferrara, she married the ruler of another city-state, Mantua. Her art collection was famous throughout Europe. She brought many of the greatest Renaissance artists, including Leonardo da Vinci, to the court of Mantua. She was also skilled in politics. She defended Mantua when her husband was taken captive in war and won his release.

Isabella d'Este and a few other women such as Caterina Sforza (who ruled Milan from about 1488 to 1500) exercised real political power. For the most part, however, women were expected to create a charming court and home but not to take part in public life. Although upper-class women of the Renaissance were far better educated than the women of the Middle Ages, most Renaissance women had less political, economic, and social influence than medieval women.

Renaissance individualism shows in these realistic portraits. The Duke of Urbino, who fought his way to a dukedom by his military skill, suffered a broken nose in battle. His wife, Battista Sforza, came from the ruling family of Milan. Behind them lies their duchy.

A young artist named Sandro Botticelli (1444–1510) tried to express Plato's ideals with his brush. Botticelli's most famous painting, "The Birth of Venus," pictured ideal beauty in the shape of a woman rising from a shell.

Section Review 1

Define: (a) Renaissance, (b) fresco,
(c) vernacular, (d) humanist
Identify: (a) Leonardo da Vinci, (b) Giotto di
Bondone, (c) Dante Alighieri, (d) *The Divine
Comedy*, (e) Francesco Petrarch, (f) *The
Courtier*, (g) Isabella d'Este
Answer:
1. What conditions in northern Italy encouraged the beginning of the Renaissance?
2. How did Giotto revolutionize painting?
3. (a) What are the topics of the three major parts of *The Divine Comedy?* (b) How did Dante change the writing of poetry?
4. How did Petrarch draw on the classics in his writings?
5. What new art forms showed the Renaissance interest in the individual?
6. List three characteristics of the Renaissance.
7. (a) What was the Renaissance ideal for a young man? (b) For a young woman?

Critical Thinking
8. The wealth of northern Italy was important in fostering the many artists of the Renaissance. How were money and art related?
9. Which of the characteristics of the Renaissance do you consider most revolutionary? Explain your answer.

Florence led the way in arts. 2

The Renaissance burst into full flower in the 1400's. This century was called the *Quattrocento* (kwah-troh-**CHEN**-toh) in Italian. During the Quattrocento, dozens of the most talented painters and sculptors in history competed for fame in the thriving cities of northern Italy. In the forefront of artistic developments was Florence, the City of Flowers.

Cloth and banking enriched Florence.

The golden age of Florence was based on the golden florins (the city's coin) of its merchants and bankers. Florentines made their wealth chiefly through two industries—textiles and banking.

In 1338, one Florentine writer boasted that 200 workshops in Florence produced more than 70,000 pieces of cloth. Merchants in the various cloth guilds employed 30,000 Florentines, one third the city's population. As a result of the general prosperity, Florentines were well fed, consuming 110,000 sheep, goats, and pigs and 70,000 casks of wine in a year.

The riches gathered by the cloth guilds gave Florence a second major industry, banking. By 1300, wool merchants routinely deposited their gold coins in Florentine banking houses.

Florentine bankers grew rich loaning their depositers' money to borrowers. By the 1300's, Florence was the financial center of Europe. From London to Rome, merchants figured their losses or gains in terms of one coin: the florin. Kings, princes, nobles, and merchants throughout Europe depended on loans from Florence's banks. At times during the Hundred Years' War, both French and English armies were paid with loans from Florentine bankers.

Among Florence's leading merchants, the pursuit of wealth and the scramble for political power went hand in hand. Florentines boasted that they had a republican form of government like that of ancient Rome. In theory, any citizen who belonged to one of the city's 21 guilds could hold office. However, membership in the guilds was tightly restricted. As a result, only about 3,500 men were eligible to vote—about 3 percent of the total population. Among these citizens, the competition for office never ceased.

Although ruled by a wealthy elite, Florence had a democratic social atmosphere. Visitors in Florence were amazed to hear a lowly journeyman address a leading citizen by his first name.

The Medici ruled Florence.

As the golden age of the Quattrocento began, Florence came under the political rule of one powerful family, the Medici (**MEHD**-uh-chee). The Medici had made a fortune in trade and banking.

Cosimo (**KOH**-see-moh) de Medici was the wealthiest man of his time. In 1434, he won control of the government of Florence. He did not seek political office for himself, realizing that he could rule more effectively behind the

By the mid-1400's, the city-states of Venice, Milan, and Florence dominated northern Italy. There, interest in culture was stimulated by the recovery of classical works, brought by refugees from Constantinople after that city fell to the Turks in 1453.

scenes. He made sure, however, that all eight members of the city council were loyal to him. The lower classes of the city loved him because he championed popular causes. For 30 years, Cosimo de Medici was virtually dictator of the city of Florence.

Like Pericles of ancient Athens, Cosimo took pleasure in beautifying the city he ruled. From his personal fortune, he spent 400,000 florins on artistic and scholarly projects. He paid off the staggering debts of a bankrupt friend and took in exchange the friend's collection of 800 books by classical authors. To house this rare collection, he built the first free public library in western Europe.

Cosimo de Medici died in 1464, but his family remained in control of Florence. After a brief rule by Cosimo's sickly son, power passed in 1469 to Cosimo's 21-year-old grandson, Lorenzo. He soon became known as Lorenzo the Magnificent. Lorenzo ruled with absolute power, yet he kept up the appearances of a republican government. He held the goodwill of the common people with balls, festivals, carnivals, and celebrations of all sorts. Like his grandfather, Lorenzo continued the tradition of beautifying his city.

Artists beautified Florence.

Florence entered its golden age through a set of gleaming metal doors. In 1401, the wool manufacturers' guild wanted an artist to create new doors for the Baptistry of the local cathedral, an old eight-sided building. The guild held a contest, inviting Florence's most promising artists to submit designs for the doors. With great fanfare, the judges announced the winner. The guild had bestowed the honor upon a 23-year-old goldsmith named Lorenzo Ghiberti (gee-BEHR-tee).

Ghiberti spent the next 50 years creating two pairs of bronze doors for the Baptistry. At a time when 200 florins was a princely sum, the wool merchants and the city council spent 22,000 florins on the first pair alone. The new doors were so magnificent that the artist Michelangelo later likened them to the gates of paradise.

The finished doors were divided into panels, each showing a scene from the Bible. Each scene looked like a deep stage with the background trees and buildings far behind the people in the foreground. Yet the sculptured metal is only four inches deep at most. Ghiberti died in 1455, just three years after completing the doors.

Meanwhile, an architect named Brunelleschi (BROO-nuh-LAYS-kee) was working on the Cathedral of Florence, directly across the street from the Baptistry. Brunelleschi had been one of the losers in the contest to make the Baptistry doors. By 1420, however, his genius was recognized. Brunelleschi proposed to cap the cathedral with a gigantic dome. Such a dome had not been built in Europe since Roman times. Between 1420 and 1436, admiring Florentines watched his dome rise slowly. When it was completed, the cross at its top stood 370 feet above street level. It was twice as high as the famous dome of Constantinople's Hagia Sophia.

Donatello revolutionized sculpture.

Florence was also home to a host of younger artists. The most talented was a 17-year-old sculptor named Donatello (DAHN-uh-TEHL-oh). He came to work in Ghiberti's workshop just after 1400.

Donatello (1386–1466) left Ghiberti's workshop and journeyed to Rome to study its ancient ruins. When he returned to Florence, he was eager to make free-standing statues like those of the ancient Greeks and Romans. He rejected the style of medieval stonecutters, who usually carved only the front of their human figures. The back side merged into a cathedral's walls. Above everything else, Donatello wanted his figures to seem real and alive.

Like the ancient Greeks, Donatello wanted to show the strength and grace of the human form. In his statue "David," Donatello was the first European sculptor since ancient times to make a large, free-standing human figure in the nude. He was also famous for his heroic statues of men on horseback.

Footnote to History

Every year, in his country villa, Lorenzo invited the finest scholars of Italy to a banquet in honor of Plato's birthday. While sipping wine and listening to music, they tried to equal the intellectual discussions of the ancient Athenians.

In 1425, Donatello was putting the finishing touches on a statue of a biblical prophet. The prophet's expression seemed so thoroughly human that Donatello looked his creation in the eyes and shouted at it, "Speak! Speak or the plague take you!"

A diagram shows how perspective works in this fresco by Masaccio. Lines come together at a vanishing point near the center. The horizontal line running through the vanishing point shows the eye level of the viewer.

Masaccio developed perspective.

To Ghiberti, Brunelleschi, and Donatello, we must add the name of a fourth genius of Florence's golden age: Masaccio (mah-ZAHT-choh). Last of the four to be born (1401), Masaccio was also the first to die (1428). Yet in his 27 years, he changed painting as profoundly as Donatello changed sculpture.

One hundred years earlier, Giotto had started a revolution in the arts by giving a sense of depth and roundness to his paintings. Masaccio carried the revolution further by using a technique called perspective that Brunelleschi had developed.

Commissioned in 1425 to decorate a chapel in Florence, Masaccio used his new technique in a fresco called "The Healing of the Cripple and the Resurrection of Tabitha" (above). The picture shows two events in the life of the apostle Peter. Buildings stand at each side of the picture. Their upper stories slant downward, and the ground level slants up. People in the foreground look much larger than those in the distance. The slanting lines of the buildings and the relative sizes of human figures give the scene an illusion of depth.

Masaccio realized that objects look smaller the farther they are from the viewer. He also realized that parallel lines, like the edges of a road, seem to come together in the distance. These are the principles of perspective. As a result of his new ideas, Masaccio has been called the "father of modern painting."

Machiavelli wrote about politics.

The golden age of Florence lasted nearly a century. Lorenzo the Magnificent died in 1492. Then, just two years later, a shocking event shattered the self-confidence of the Florentines. In 1494, King Charles VIII of France led an army across the Alps into northern Italy. His main goal was to claim Naples in the south, but his invasion route led past Florence, which he attacked.

Piero de Medici (son of Lorenzo) surrendered without a fight. Outraged by their ruler's weakness, a mob of Florentines stormed the Medici palace and drove Piero into exile.

330

People began to think of artists as geniuses, not just artisans, and their status rose sharply. While the Holy Roman Emperor Charles V was visiting the workshop of the great painter Titian in Venice, the artist dropped one of his paintbrushes. The emperor, who ruled half of Europe, bent down and picked up the brush for Titian.

For the next two generations, Florence and other Italian cities suffered from war and political upheavals. Spain's King Ferdinand of Aragon contested the French king's claim to Naples. In the early 1500's, French and Spanish armies attacked all along the Italian peninsula. All the great Italian cities—Florence, Milan, Venice, Rome—were forced to ally themselves with one foreign power or the other. Diplomacy and war became the keys to survival.

One result of the turmoil was a provocative book called *The Prince*. Its author, Niccolò Machiavelli (MAH-kyah-VEHL-ee), was bitter about the invasion of Italy by foreigners. Born in Florence in 1469, Machiavelli spent his youth under the rule of Lorenzo the Magnificent. As an adult, he saw the golden age begin to crumble. He served his city as a diplomat to many courts, where he observed dukes and kings. He tried to understand why one ruler succeeded while another failed.

In 1513, Machiavelli wrote a book of advice to rulers. *The Prince* is a book about power. How can a ruler gain power and keep it despite his enemies? asked Machiavelli. In answering this question, he began with the idea that most people are selfish, fickle, and corrupt. To succeed in such a wicked world, Machiavelli said, a prince must be strong as a lion and shrewd as a fox:

> *. . . for the lion cannot protect himself from traps, and the fox cannot defend himself from wolves. One must therefore be a fox to recognize traps, and a lion to fight wolves.*

Machiavelli said that a prince might have to trick his enemies and even his own people for the good of the state. His ideal ruler was the crafty Spanish king, Ferdinand of Aragon. When the king of France complained that Ferdinand had deceived him twice, Ferdinand boasted, "He lies, the drunkard. I have deceived him more than ten times!"

In *The Prince*, Machiavelli was not concerned with what was morally right but with what was politically effective. He believed that, in politics, the end justifies the means. According to *The Prince*, even immoral acts were justified if they served the interests of the state. Thus, although Machiavelli was himself an upright, honest, and religious man, his name has come to stand for trickery and double dealing.

Voice from the Past · *The Dangers of Flattery*

In *The Prince*, Machiavelli advised rulers that they must always *seem* to be honest, merciful, and true to their word, even if they were not always so. However, he warned princes that they must beware of people who tried to flatter them.

I must not leave out . . . a mistake that is hard for princes to avoid . . . And this is with regard to flatterers, of which courts are full . . . There is no other way of guarding oneself against flattery except by letting men understand that they will not offend you by speaking the truth. But when everyone can tell you the truth, you lose people's respect. A prudent prince must therefore take a third course, by choosing for his council wise men and by giving them alone full liberty to speak the truth to him. And they may speak the truth only of those things that he asks, so he must ask them about everything . . . A prince, therefore, should always take advice, but only when he wishes, not when others wish . . . He ought to be a great asker and a patient hearer of the truth . . . Indeed, if he finds out that anyone has hesitated to tell him the truth, he should be angry.

1. (a) Why might a prince's court be full of flatterers? (b) Why would flatterers be dangerous to a prince?
2. How does Machiavelli say a prince can avoid being fooled by flatterers?
3. Why must a prince be "a great asker"?
4. Why might it be difficult for a prince to follow Machiavelli's advice?

Eloque re ergo

Discussion questions: How might the emphasis on humanism (as opposed to the intense Christianity of the Middle Ages) in part explain the political theories of Machiavelli?

331

Define: Quattrocento
Identify: (a) Cosimo de Medici, (b) Lorenzo de Medici, (c) Ghiberti, (d) Brunelleschi, (e) Donatello, (f) Masaccio, (g) Machiavelli

Answer

1. What were the main businesses of Renaissance Florence?
2. (a) Describe the government of Florence. (b) How did Cosimo de Medici control the city for 30 years?
3. (a) What were Donatello's goals in sculpture? (b) How did he accomplish these goals?
4. What contributions did Masaccio make to painting?
5. (a) What was Machiavelli's view of human nature? (b) Describe the advice he gave to rulers.
6. What political events threatened the Italian city-states in the 1500's?

Critical Thinking

7. In many ways, the achievements of the Renaissance were linked to civic pride. Explain how this statement applies to Florence during the Quattrocento.

Three artistic giants led the Renaissance.

3

In 1513, while Machiavelli was writing *The Prince*, Leonardo da Vinci took regular walks in the pope's garden in Rome. Leonardo was an old man now with a flowing white beard. Though born in Florence, he had spent his most productive years as a painter in Milan. Now, in his last years, Leonardo sought the favor of the pope. After the death of Lorenzo de Medici, the popes became the foremost patrons of art.

In Rome, during the early 1500's, Renaissance art reached new grandeur. This period is known as the High Renaissance. Three artists lifted Renaissance art to unsurpassed brilliance. The three were Leonardo, Raphael Santi (RAF-ay-el SAHN-tee), and Michelangelo Buonarroti (MYE-kel-AN-juh-loh BWOH-nahr-ROH-tee).

Popes supported the arts.

In the Middle Ages, Rome had fallen into a sad state of disrepair. Goats grazed among the ruins of ancient palaces. The Forum, where great orators had once spoken, became a pig market. When the Babylonian captivity and the Great Schism (page 241) were over, however, Rome began to recover. In the mid-1400's, Renaissance popes were determined to beautify the city.

In their tastes and ambitions, these Renaissance popes were much like the Medici and other Italian princes of their time. They loved fine foods and fine wines as well as fine arts. Pope Nicholas V, for example, spent vast sums collecting classical texts for the Vatican library.

One Renaissance pope in particular stands out. Julius II, who was pope from 1503 to 1513, loved art and power in equal measure. He longed for Rome again to become, in Livy's phrase, "the capital of the world." To glorify his city, Julius enlisted Italy's greatest artists including a brilliant Florentine named Michelangelo.

Michelangelo excelled in many arts.

Born in 1475, Michelangelo was apprenticed at the age of 13 to a painter. Soon, however, Michelangelo turned from painting to sculpture. He quickly surpassed his famous predecessor,

"Let us enjoy the papacy," said Pope Leo X (son of Lorenzo de Medici) to his brother, "since God has given it to us."

Michelangelo's many-sided genius shows in his "Pieta" (far left), "David," (left) and the Sistine Chapel (above). Recently, 400 years of grime was cleaned from the chapel ceiling to reveal the original beauty of Michelangelo's colors.

Donatello. In 1498, he was commissioned by a Roman cardinal to create "a Virgin Mary clothed, with the dead Christ in her arms, of the size of a proper man, for the price of 450 golden ducats of the papal mint." The result was a marble sculpture known as the "Pieta" (pee-ay-TAH).

In 1504, another masterpiece by Michelangelo was hoisted onto a pedestal in a public square in Florence. His white marble statue of David, the Biblical warrior and king, stood 16 feet tall. It showed a strong young athlete whose muscles rippled with power. Even more awesome than the body was the face, which seemed to radiate strength and vigor. Better than any other single work of art, Michelangelo's mighty statue of David summed up the Renaissance belief in human dignity and greatness.

In 1505, Pope Julius II invited the 30-year-old Michelangelo to Rome. Despite quarrels between the two high-tempered men, Michelangelo did some of his best work for Julius. When the pope wanted him to paint the ceiling of the Sistine (sihs-TEEN) Chapel, Michelangelo grumbled that he was a sculptor, not a painter. Finally, however, he agreed to undertake the task.

Every day for four years (1508–1512), Michelangelo climbed the scaffolding in the Sistine Chapel about 65 feet above the floor. Lying flat on his back, he covered the ceiling with more than 300 massive human figures. It was messy, tiring work. Michelangelo, who also wrote poetry, vividly described his daily agony:

My stomach is thrust towards my chin,
My beard curls up, towards the sky,
My head leans right over onto my back,
My chest is like that of an old shrew,
The brush endlessly dripping onto my face
Has coated it with a multi-colored paving.

Yet even as paint trickled into his eyes, Michelangelo never lost sight of his grand design. Toward the center of the ceiling, he painted the scene that was to command the viewer's attention. This scene showed God reaching out to infuse spirit into Adam, the first man.

Within his own lifetime, Michelangelo was recognized as a universal genius. He worked as sculptor, painter, and architect. (His poetry did not come to light until after his death.) In his last years, he designed a huge dome for the new St. Peter's Cathedral. A younger artist called him "the divine Michelangelo" and wrote, "The world has many kings, but only one Michelangelo." Michelangelo died in 1564. He was 89.

A contemporary describing Michelangelo: "He generally went to bed with his clothes on, even to the tall boots . . . He kept these boots on for such a length of time, that when he drew them off the skin came away together with the leather."

Raphael perfected painting.

In 1508, the same year Michelangelo began painting the chapel ceiling, a young artist named Raphael started painting the walls of Julius II's private library. It was a short walk from library to chapel. Raphael, always eager to learn from older artists, often dropped in on Michelangelo.

The pope's library held both Christian and classical works. Raphael's assignment was to celebrate this knowledge and show its underlying unity.

Gradually, Raphael transformed the library into a kind of Renaissance hall of fame. On one wall, in a painting called "The School of Athens," were the white-bearded Plato and the black-bearded Aristotle in deep discussion. Around them were groups of listeners, including the greatest figures of both classical and Renaissance times. Among them, the pope certainly would have recognized the face of young Raphael and the brooding figure of Michelangelo. Another wall, dedicated to poetry and music, showed Homer and Dante.

Besides artistic genius, Raphael was blessed with a pleasant personality. His easy temper made him the favorite painter of Julius II's successor, Pope Leo X (a son of Lorenzo de Medici). For his patrons, Raphael painted dozens of lovely madonnas and flattering portraits. His death in 1520, when he was only 37, plunged the papal court into sadness.

Leonardo was both scientist and artist.

When Leonardo da Vinci came to Rome in 1513, he was 61. The aging artist, curious as ever, still filled his notebooks with inventions and new observations. As a painter, however, his best years lay behind him. In Milan, while he was experimenting with bicycles, hydraulics, masonry, and countless other things, he produced one of the most famous paintings in history.

Leonardo's fascination with the human personality shows in the "Mona Lisa," completed in 1506. It was a portrait of a Florentine woman, probably Lisa Gheradini del Giocando. Though only 24, she had been married 3 times. The picture fascinates viewers because the woman's face seems to change expression. Is she smiling in

Leonardo da Vinci's "Mona Lisa"

welcome or smirking in disdain? Are her eyes friendly or cold? One scholar has called this painting "the first distinctly psychological portrait of the Renaissance."

Section Review 3

Identify: (a) Raphael, (b) Michelangelo, (c) Pope Julius II
Answer
1. (a) What was the condition of Rome in the early 1400's? (b) Who took on the task of beautifying the city?
2. Name three major works of Michelangelo and briefly describe each one.
3. What was Raphael's task in the work he did for the library of Julius II?
4. Why is the "Mona Lisa" a significant painting?

Critical Thinking
5. Why is it common for powerful rulers to begin massive projects in building and the arts?
6. Which of the three artists discussed in this section do you consider the greatest? Explain your answer.

The reason for Mona Lisa's smile may be mathematical: the smile is a segment of the same arc as the top of her forehead.

Explorers opened new sea routes.

4

You have seen how Renaissance artists looked at human life in a new way. Running parallel with this human discovery was the geographic discovery of lands beyond Europe.

During Leonardo's lifetime (1452–1519), Europeans greatly expanded their knowledge of the world. Portuguese sea captains charted the entire coast of Africa. Europeans crossed the Atlantic Ocean and reached two vast continents—the Americas—of which they had known nothing. In 1519, the year of Leonardo's death, five ships sailed from Spain. One of those ships eventually made its way completely around the world.

Was it just coincidence that great explorers lived during the same period as the great artists of the High Renaissance? No, like the artists, the explorers were confident, ambitious, and eager for individual glory. In short, they shared many values of the Renaissance.

New ideas made exploration possible.

In the late 1200's, a Venetian named Marco Polo had written a book about his adventurous travels to the court of Kublai Khan in China (page 269). Two centuries later, an Italian sea captain named Christopher Columbus read Marco Polo's book. Columbus resolved to reach Cipangu (Polo's name for Japan) by sailing west across the Atlantic.

Why did 200 years go by before someone took up the challenge of finding a new route to Asia? By the late 1400's, Europe had changed in a number of ways since Marco Polo's time.

Economic need As merchants from the Italian seaport of Venice, Marco Polo's family had no need to discover a new trade route to Asia. The old route was good enough for them. During the Middle Ages, Venice and Genoa controlled the only practical route by which Asian goods reached Europe. For centuries, Arab and Turkish caravans had carried Chinese silks and Indian spices overland to the bazaars of Antioch and Alexandria. There Italian merchants bought the goods and carried them west to Europe. Every time the Asian goods changed hands, their price went up.

By the 1400's, the "new monarchs" of France, England, Spain, and Portugal wanted a share of this profitable trade. They wanted routes that they themselves could control. (Many of these rulers were also heavily in debt to Italian bankers.) Thus, the rulers of many European countries began to seek new routes to Asia.

Technological skills In the 1200's, it would have been nearly impossible for a European sea captain to cross 3,000 miles of open water and find the way home again. Medieval ships and navigational tools were adequate for the sheltered waters of the Mediterranean Sea, but they were hopelessly inadequate for the Atlantic Ocean.

In the 1400's, however, shipbuilders designed a new vessel called a **caravel**. The caravel had triangular sails for tacking into the wind. It had square sails for running before the wind. Its carefully designed hull could ride out an ocean storm.

Two other inventions were critical for crossing the Atlantic Ocean—the compass and the astrolabe. Muslim mathematicians and instrument makers had perfected both (page 181). Italian sailors knew of the magnetic compass as early as 1200, but it became more useful as Europeans made more charts of coastlines and currents. The astrolabe was a brass circle with carefully adjusted concentric rings marked off in degrees. Using these rings to sight the stars, a sea captain could tell how far north or south of the equator he was. Without the astrolabe, Columbus would almost certainly have been lost at sea.

Geographic knowledge In 1410, a humanist translated a manuscript dating from about A.D. 150. Written by the Greek geographer Ptolemy (TAHL-uh-mee), the work described Africa, Asia, and Europe. Scholars of the 1400's believed that these three were Earth's only continents. Ptolemy also said that Earth is a sphere. By the 1400's, most educated Europeans accepted that idea too.

Based on Ptolemy's writings, Renaissance mapmakers figured that about 3,000 miles of Atlantic Ocean lay between Europe and China. They were wrong. The actual distance was closer to 11,000 miles, including the Atlantic Ocean, the American continents, and the Pacific Ocean.

Columbus believed the writings of Ptolemy and the estimates of the mapmakers. He thought a skillful navigator such as himself could sail straight across the western ocean and return in a few months with a rich cargo of spices.

Voyages of Discovery

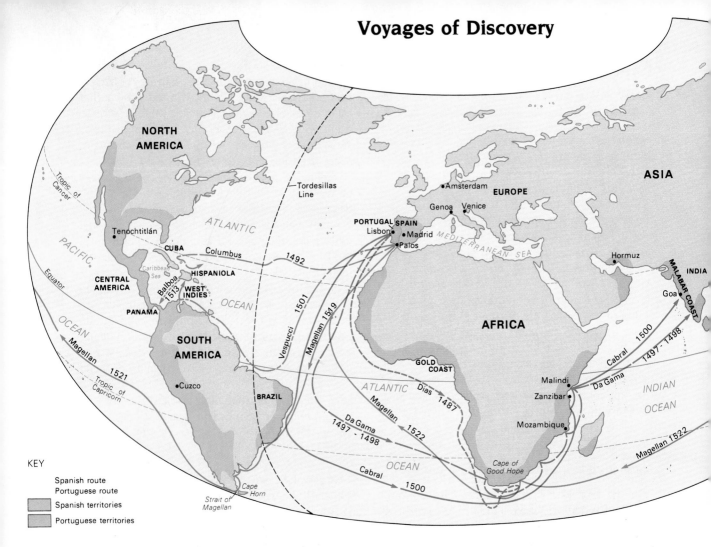

NORTH AMERICA

Tropic of Cancer

ATLANTIC

PACIFIC

Tenochtitlán

CUBA — Columbus 1492

CENTRAL AMERICA — Balboa 1513 — HISPANIOLA — WEST INDIES

Caribbean Sea

Equator

OCEAN — Magellan

PANAMA

SOUTH AMERICA

Tordesillas Line

Vespucci 1501 — Magellan 1519

Tropic of Capricorn — Magellan 1521

•Cuzco

BRAZIL

Cape Horn — Strait of Magellan

Amsterdam — EUROPE
Genoa Venice
PORTUGAL SPAIN
Lisbon — •Madrid
•Palos
MEDITERRANEAN SEA

ASIA

Hormuz

MALABAR COAST — INDIA
Goa

AFRICA

GOLD COAST — Dias 1487

Cabral 1500 — Da Gama 1497-1498

Malindi
Zanzibar•
Mozambique•

INDIAN OCEAN

Magellan 1522

Magellan 1522

ATLANTIC — Da Gama 1497-1498
Cabral 1500

OCEAN

Cape of Good Hope

KEY

Spanish route
Portuguese route
Spanish territories
Portuguese territories

Remember the cocky statement by Alberti, "Man can do anything if he will." Columbus had the Renaissance spirit of self-confidence and its passion for fame. He and Europe's other explorers needed all their confidence to face the dangers of the sea.

The Portuguese explored Africa.

The Portuguese took the lead in exploration. For several centuries, they had been sailing and fishing farther and farther south along Africa's west coast.

Henry the Navigator The man who began the great age of exploration never sailed into unknown waters himself. Like the patrons who supported Renaissance artists, Portugal's Prince Henry the Navigator organized and paid for voyages.

Henry, third son of a Portuguese king, devoted his life to sending ships south along the west

coast of Africa. At first, his goal was to find gold. Legend said that a "river of gold" lay south of the Sahara, the vast desert that divides northern Africa from southern Africa. In the 1440's, Henry's ships passed one cape after another. Soon he began to think of Asian spices. He began to hope that a Portuguese caravel might sail around Africa to Asia. He never saw it happen, however. Prince Henry died in 1460.

Bartholomeu Dias and Vasco da Gama In 1488, a Portuguese captain named Bartholomeu Dias (DEE-ahsh) finally reached the southernmost tip of Africa. His ships were so battered by storms that Dias named the spot the Cape of Torment. King John II of Portugal, however, was so pleased at the thought of his ships rounding Africa and sailing to Asia that he renamed it the Cape of Good Hope.

Then, in 1497, four Portuguese ships sailed around the Cape of Good Hope. Commanded by

In 1476, a red-headed Italian sailor was shipwrecked off the Portuguese coast. By this stroke of fortune, Christopher Columbus changed his home from Italy to Portugal.

Map Study

What explorers rounded the Cape of Good Hope going east? Going west? Many of the ships on those voyages were caravels such as those shown above. What sea did Columbus (top) reach?

a tough and able captain, Vasco da Gama, the ships traveled north along Africa's east coast as far as Zanzibar. From there, Da Gama steered boldly eastward with the monsoon winds across the open Indian Ocean. Finally, the ships arrived at the Malabar Coast of India on May 20, 1498.

As the Portuguese sailors wearily stepped ashore, they were met by Arab merchants. "May the devil take you!" the Arabs exclaimed menacingly. "What brought you here?" The Arabs had long controlled India's spice trade. They rightly saw the Europeans as a threat.

Although the Indian merchants thought the Europeans' trade goods were of poor quality, the Portuguese were able to load their ships with pepper and cinnamon. They then set sail on the long voyage home. Only 54 of the original 170 sailors returned to Portugal two years later in 1499. The spices they brought back sold for 60 times the cost of the entire expedition.

Columbus reached the Americas.

While Dias and Da Gama were charting the route around Africa, Christopher Columbus made

three voyages across the Atlantic Ocean. He claimed that the land he reached there was part of Asia. But had he truly found a shorter way to Asia than Da Gama's?

Columbus's first Atlantic crossing was in 1492, and it was by far his happiest voyage. King Ferdinand and Queen Isabella of Spain gave him three ships. On the morning of August 3, Columbus set sail from Palos, Spain. He had a crew of 90 men and boys on the *Santa Maria* (his flagship) and two smaller ships, the *Niña* and the *Pinta*. Strong winds briskly drove the little fleet westward. Weeks passed with no sight of land. The crew was growing impatient. On October 9, Columbus promised his fearful crew that he would turn back unless they sighted land in the next three days.

On October 12, two hours after midnight, a lookout on the *Pinta* saw in the distance what seemed to be a white cliff shining in the moonlight. They had reached land at last. Columbus believed he had reached the East Indies, near Japan and China. Therefore, he called the people he met "Indians." In fact, he was nowhere near Asia. He had reached the Bahamas.

Map Study answers: DaGama, Cabral; Magellan; Caribbean

337

When Columbus returned to Spain in 1493, Isabella and Ferdinand gave him a hero's welcome and the title Admiral of the Ocean Sea. They promised him a larger fleet for his next trip.

The thrill of discovery soon wore off. Columbus crossed the Atlantic three more times (in 1493, 1498, and 1502). He explored all the major islands of the Caribbean—Cuba, Hispaniola, Jamaica, and Puerto Rico. On his fourth voyage, he explored the coast of Central America. Nowhere did he find the fabulous civilization described by Marco Polo.

The hurricanes and hardships of his fourth voyage nearly killed Columbus. He returned to Spain white-haired and arthritic. He died in 1506, insisting to the bitter end that the lands he had explored were Asia.

Other explorers reached the Americas.

Columbus's mistake was soon corrected. A Florentine merchant named Amerigo Vespucci (AHM-uh-REE-goh veh-SPYOO-chee) crossed the ocean in 1499 and 1501. In his letters, he described the coastline of the land we know as Brazil. This was not Asia, he wrote, but a newly discovered continent.

One of Vespucci's letters fell into the hands of a German publisher, Martin Waldseemüller (VAHLT-zay-MOO-luhr). In 1507, Waldseemüller published a new map of the world, showing a great blob of land west of the Atlantic. He labeled this land *America* to honor Amerigo Vespucci.

If this was indeed a new continent, how big was it? How far was it from Asia? Was there a way either through it or around it? For a Renaissance explorer, these were urgent questions.

In 1513, a Spaniard named Vasco Nuñez de Balboa slashed through the rain forests of Panama. He climbed over a hill and beheld a vast ocean. Dressed in full armor, Balboa plunged into the water up to his knees and claimed the entire ocean for Spain. Balboa had reached what is now called the Pacific Ocean.

Portugal claimed Brazil.

When Columbus first reached the Americas, it was not clear what lands he had found. The king of Portugal suspected that the Spanish might be taking over some lands that Portuguese sailors had reached first. Soon rivalry between Spain and Portugal reached a dangerous level.

In 1493, to keep peace, Pope Alexander VI ruled that Spain and Portugal might divide the

Economics in Daily Life · The Spices of Life

"Take ginger, clove, and a little pepper, and crush together." So began a French recipe from 1393 for making a "black pudding." Indeed, without these spices, the pudding would have been little more than tasteless mush. Europeans craved spices partly because their food would have been so monotonous otherwise. In summer, most people depended on foods that were raised locally. In winter, they had only what could be dried or pickled for storage.

The poor flavored their foods with herbs from their own dooryard gardens: garlic, thyme, marjoram, bay leaf, and savory. The rich bought spices from distant lands: cinnamon, nutmeg, ginger, turmeric, cardamom, clove, mace, saffron, and—above all—pepper.

The start of Portugal's trade with the Indies in 1498 increased the supply of spices. In 1503, Portuguese ships brought back 1,300 tons of pepper. Although the price of pepper fell, the trade was so profitable that the Dutch took it away from Portugal in the 1600's.

so-called "Indies" between themselves. He ordered a line drawn from north to south through the Atlantic Ocean. This line was known as the Line of Demarcation. All newly discovered lands east of that line would be Portugal's. All such lands west of that line would be Spain's.

In 1494, the Portuguese persuaded the Spanish to move the line a few degrees farther west. Their agreement of 1494 was called the Treaty of Tordesillas (tor-duh-SEE-yahs). Explorers later found that the line cut across South America near the mouth of the Amazon River. Since the mouth of the Amazon lay east of the line, Portugal claimed that river and the lands around it. Here lay Portugal's only share of the Americas.

In 1500, a second event strengthened Portugal's claims. A Portuguese sea captain named Pedro Alvares Cabral explored the forest along the mouth of the Amazon River. Cabral's men cut down a tree and found its wood was as red as a glowing coal from a charcoal brazier. They called it "brazil" wood from the Portuguese word for a brazier—hence the name of the country that Portugal later colonized.

Magellan's crew rounded the globe.

In 1519, a Portuguese nobleman named Ferdinand Magellan (muh-JEHL-uhn) decided he could reach Asia by sailing around the southern tip of the new continent. The king of Spain agreed to pay for the voyage. He gave Magellan five old ships that were barely seaworthy.

With 230 men aboard, Magellan's ships sailed in September 1519. For three years, nothing was heard from them, and they were given up for lost. Then, in September 1522, a lone ship with tattered sails limped into a harbor in Spain. The 18 men who staggered ashore were the only survivors of Magellan's crew. All the others had died of hunger, cold, disease, or shipwreck.

As planned, Magellan had crossed the Atlantic and led his fleet south along the South American coast. One ship had capsized in a storm. The crew of another had mutinied. Three ships remained. In August 1520, Magellan reached a strait near the southern tip of South America. Vicious winds and jagged rocks made passage difficult. Somehow, after 38 days of struggling, the three ships reached the other side safely. This strait is now called the Strait of Magellan.

Magellan explored the western coast of South America. Then he headed out into the Pacific Ocean in search of Asia. Little did he realize that the Pacific was almost three times wider than the Atlantic. (It is 9,300 miles from Panama to the Philippine islands.) After three months, the sailors were so short of food that they ate rats, leather, and sawdust. Many died of hunger or of diseases brought on by malnutrition.

Finally, they reached the Philippines. Here was Asia at last. Unfortunately, Magellan joined in a war between local groups. He was killed by a poisoned arrow. One of the Spanish ships was destroyed there too.

The remaining crew members set out for home in the last two ships. One was captured by the Portuguese while sailing toward India. That left only one ship and a sickly crew to sail home around Africa.

In 1522, as the survivors recounted their three-year adventure, it became clear what they had achieved. They had sailed around the world. They had proved that the Americas were separate continents that lay thousands of miles from Asia. Perhaps most important, they had learned that the world was much larger than any European had thought.

To the Europeans, this world seemed ready to be conquered by ambitious men. Renaissance sea captains had demonstrated in their own way that "man can do anything if he will." Spaniards made themselves rulers of the lands once held by the Aztecs and the Incas. First Spain and later Portugal, France, and England built great colonial empires in the Americas.

Worldwide contact brought hazards and benefits.

In the early 1500's, for the first time in history, all the continents around the Atlantic came in regular contact with one another. Sea lanes now connected Europe, Africa, North America, and South America. This development brought change on both sides of the Atlantic. In Europe, the changes were generally welcomed. For the peoples of the Americas and later the people of Africa, life was brutally disrupted.

Epidemics Before the Spanish came, the deadly germs of smallpox, measles, and influenza were unknown in the Americas. The Indians did not

Epidemics of smallpox, measles, and influenza were followed by new epidemics. As African slaves arrived, the Indians fell victim to the worst African diseases: yellow fever and malaria.

339

have the immunities that Europeans had developed through long contact with those diseases. Columbus's voyages ended the Americas' isolation. Suddenly, Indians were exposed to germs carried by European explorers and colonizers.

Deadly epidemics swept over the Caribbean islands. Smallpox wiped out whole villages in a matter of months. Hispaniola had an estimated population of 250,000 Indians in 1492. Twenty years later, the population had fallen to 60,000. Just 50 years after that, Spaniards on Hispaniola counted only 500 Indians. Smallpox spread to Mexico where it helped destroy the Aztec empire. In the first century of Spanish rule (1500–1600), Indians in Central and South America sickened and died by the millions. By 1650, the population of central Mexico had declined by 85 percent.

The impact of corn and potatoes European ships also carried a great number of beneficial goods across the Atlantic. Before Columbus's voyages, people in the Americas had never seen horses, cows, chickens, pigs, sheep, goats, donkeys, or oxen. In the 1500's, these farm animals came to the Americas with European settlers.

Spanish colonists also brought a wide variety of new plants to the Americas, including wheat, barley, rye, oats, rice, oranges, apples, bananas, apricots, peaches, pears, coffee, sugarcane, and olive trees.

Crossing the Atlantic in the other direction were plants that Europeans, Asians, and Africans had never before used. Among those plants were corn (or maize), manioc (or tapioca), potatoes, tomatoes, kidney beans, lima beans, squash, avocados, pineapples, melon, tobacco, quinine, and cacao (for chocolate).

In time, the potato—a staple of the Inca diet—was transported in European ships to almost every part of the Eastern Hemisphere. Both in Asia and in Africa, it became a tremendously important food. In Europe, crops of potatoes and corn yielded more calories per acre than the traditional crops of wheat, barley, or rye.

This revolution in the world's food supply eventually enriched the diets of people the world over. History books often dwell too much on the rise and fall of empires. The planting of the first white potato in Ireland and the first sweet potato in China probably changed more lives than the deeds of a hundred kings.

The slave trade began in the 1500's.

The settlement of the Americas affected Africa in an unexpected way. Ever since the time of Prince Henry the Navigator, trade between Europeans and Africans had been increasing. In western Africa, the powerful kings who ruled the forest kingdoms controlled trade with the Europeans for a time. The African rulers refused to allow Europeans to travel inland. Instead, the Portuguese traders paid rent to the Africans for small posts near the coast.

Looking at economics *The West African slave trade was highly profitable. Control of that trade, known as the asiento, passed from Spain to Britain in 1713. To maximize their profits, slave traders loaded their ships with as many captives as possible. The diagram below shows how a ship was filled. Under such inhuman conditions, many people died during the voyage.*

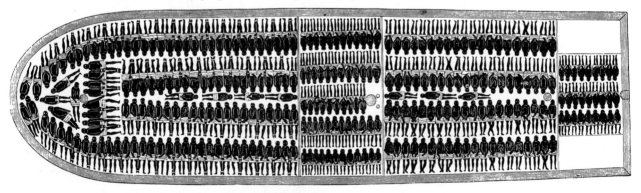

Nonetheless, European influence had far-reaching effects. Some African rulers traded for guns, which they used to expand their power over their neighbors. In this way, kingdoms arose that depended on a steady supply of guns and gunpowder from Europe. In exchange, more and more European traders wanted slaves. The effects of the slave trade were devastating to some African societies.

In 1441, while exploring the West African coast for Prince Henry the Navigator, a sea captain returned to Portugal with 12 slaves. The unfortunate Africans were readily sold to Portuguese nobles for use on their estates. This was the beginning of the Atlantic slave trade.

The growth of the slave trade was linked closely to the growth of European colonies in the Americas. Europeans began gold mines, silver mines, and plantations to raise sugar and other crops. Who was to work on these enterprises? European immigrants were too proud and too few to do the heavy work themselves. After the great epidemics, there were not enough Indian workers either. The solution seemed to be captives from Africa.

Ships with chained men and women aboard were soon a regular sight in the harbors of Cuba, Hispaniola, and the Bahamas during the 1500's. By 1540, about 10,000 Africans each year became slaves in the Americas. The slave trade peaked in the 1700's. In that century, between 6 and 7 million Africans were shipped to the Americas as slaves. European trade in African slaves continued for 400 years before it finally came to an end in Brazil in 1870.

The human cost of the slave trade was terrible. Besides the approximately 10 million Africans who reached the slave markets, millions of others died in the hands of their captors.

Usually, a person captured for the slave trade was first made prisoner by other Africans. Some powerful African groups made a business of raiding inland villages and marching their captives to the coast for trade. The march was brutal, and many died along the way. At trading stations along the coast, the survivors were sold to European sea captains for rum, guns, and gunpowder. Many more captives died in the crowded, stinking holds of the slave ships. Modern historians estimate that for every two Africans sold in the Americas, at least one died on the way.

Europe's power touched many lands.

The Age of Exploration marks the beginning of a period when Europe dominated much of the world. That period lasted more than 400 years, from the 1500's to the 1900's.

The people of Europe had gained political mastery over two huge continents, North and South America. Europeans were also the undisputed masters of the ocean routes across the Atlantic. Africa, the Americas, and Europe were now bound together by new economic and political ties. Until the mid-1900's, Europe controlled those ties for its own advantage.

Section Review 4

Define: caravel
Identify: (a) Columbus, (b) Henry the Navigator, (c) Dias, (d) Da Gama, (e) Vespucci, (f) Balboa, (g) Line of Demarcation, (h) Magellan
Answer
1. What is the link between Marco Polo and Columbus?
2. (a) Describe the route of trade goods from Asia to Europe in the late Middle Ages. (b) Why did the monarchs of France, Spain, Portugal, and England want to find new routes to Asia?
3. What technological improvements made long sea voyages possible in the 1400's?
4. (a) What was the goal of Prince Henry the Navigator? (b) Who achieved that goal?
5. (a) What was Columbus's goal in 1492? (b) Why did later voyages disappoint him?
6. What two events enabled Portugal to claim Brazil?
7. What was the significance of Ferdinand Magellan's voyage?
8. (a) What were the major results of exploration and colonization for Europe? (b) What changes took place in the Americas as a result of European exploration and settlement?
9. (a) How did the African slave trade begin? (b) Why did the slave trade increase with the growth of European colonies in the Americas?

Critical Thinking
10. How did Columbus exemplify the spirit of the Renaissance?

341

Chapter Review 15

Summary

1. The Renaissance began in northern Italy. Northern Italy was a highly urban region. Merchants dominated the cities and competed as patrons of the arts. Painting and poetry changed greatly owing to the work of early Renaissance artists. Some of the characteristics of the Renaissance were a celebration of the individual, a love of classical learning, and an enjoyment of worldly pleasures.

2. Florence led the way in arts. During the 1400's, or Quattrocento, Florence was a wealthy city with a thriving textile industry and a strong banking business. Florence was under the control of the Medici family for most of the 1400's, although the city continued to call itself a republic. Such artists as Ghiberti, Brunelleschi, Donatello, and Masaccio beautified the city with their work. After the death of Lorenzo de Medici, while Florence was in a period of turmoil, Machiavelli wrote a book of advice to rulers called *The Prince.*

3. Three artistic giants ruled the Renaissance. Leonardo da Vinci, Raphael Santi, and Michelangelo Buonarroti were the leading artists of the High Renaissance. Pope Julius II commissioned Michelangelo and Raphael to glorify the Vatican.

4. Explorers opened new sea routes. During the late 1400's, rulers of many European nations were eager to find new trade routes to Asia. Advances in shipbuilding and navigation made possible long ocean voyages. The Portuguese explored the African coast and reached India by sailing around Africa. In 1492, Columbus reached the Americas while trying to sail to Asia across the Atlantic Ocean. Other explorers quickly followed him. The pope divided the newly discovered lands between Spain and Portugal. In 1519, Magellan began a voyage around the world that was completed by some of his crew in 1522. Huge numbers of Indians died from diseases brought by the Europeans. New food crops were introduced to both the Americas and Europe. The African slave trade began in the 1500's.

Reviewing the Facts

1. Define the following terms:
   a. vernacular
   b. humanist
   c. caravel
   d. Renaissance
2. Explain the importance of each of the following names, dates, places, or terms:
   a. Leonardo da Vinci
   b. Giotto
   c. Dante
   d. Petrarch
   e. *The Courtier*
   f. Isabella d'Este
   g. Quattrocento
   h. Florence
   i. Cosimo de Medici
   j. Lorenzo de Medici

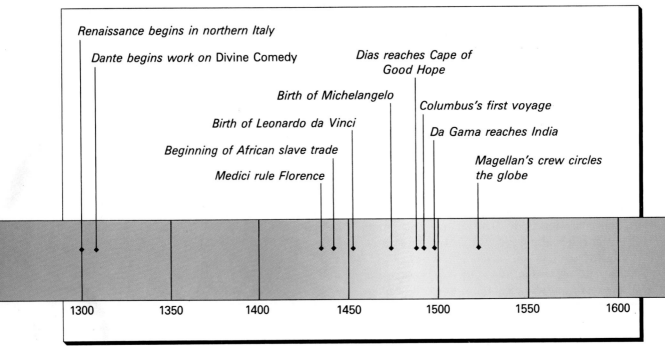

Renaissance begins in northern Italy

Dante begins work on Divine Comedy

Dias reaches Cape of Good Hope

Birth of Michelangelo

Columbus's first voyage

Birth of Leonardo da Vinci

Da Gama reaches India

Beginning of African slave trade

Medici rule Florence

Magellan's crew circles the globe

1300 1350 1400 1450 1500 1550 1600

k. Donatello
l. Masaccio
m. *The Prince*
n. Sistine Chapel
o. Raphael
p. Henry the Navigator

q. 1488
r. 1492
s. Amerigo Vespucci
t. Line of Demarcation
u. Magellan
v. Cabral

3. (a) What was the Renaissance? (b) Where did it begin?
4. How did the Renaissance emphasis on the individual affect each of the following groups? (a) Italian merchants (b) artists and writers (c) explorers
5. (a) Why were many European monarchs eager to find new trade routes to Asia in the 1400's? (b) Describe the two different routes explorers eventually found.
6. What changes did European exploration and settlement bring to each of the following continents? (a) Europe (b) the Americas (c) Africa

Basic Skills

1. **Classifying information**   The map on pages 336–337 shows the major voyages of discovery of the late 1400's and early 1500's. List the explorers for each nation, together with the places they explored.
2. **Outlining**   (a) Make an outline of the subsection "New values shaped the Renaissance" on pages 325–326. (b) For each new value, give an example of a Renaissance person who illustrates that value and why.

Researching and Reporting Skills

1. **Making an oral report**   Locate in the library a copy of the notebooks of Leonardo da Vinci. Study one invention that interests you and report on it to the class. Include the purpose and design of the invention, with visuals to illustrate it.
2. **Writing headlines**   Write three different headlines announcing to the world Columbus's discovery of America. Take into account the knowledge and values of the time.

Critical Thinking

1. **Synthesizing**   The ideals of humanism during the Renaissance were in strong contrast to the values

of the Middle Ages. (a) Explain how the two differed. (b) How were these differences reflected in the art, architecture, and life-styles of each period?
2. **Recognizing a thesis**   (a) Identify the author's thesis on page 335 concerning the explorers' relationship to the Renaissance. (b) What ideas and arguments support this thesis?
3. **Inferring**   (a) From the information about Julius II on page 332, what can you infer about his leadership in the Church? (b) From the information on page 325, would you infer that Petrarch was more modern in outlook than Dante? Why or why not?
4. **Analyzing economics**   During the Renaissance, Florence was both the financial and artistic center of Europe. (a) What hypothesis might you develop about the relationship between economic prosperity and artistic activity? (b) Is your hypothesis supported by evidence from other golden ages? Give examples to support your answer.
5. **Comparing**   (a) How does the position of women in society during the Italian Renaissance compare to that during the age of chivalry? (b) In which era do you think women were better off? Give reasons for your answer.

Perspectives on Past and Present

Americans are said to be an individualistic people. They are expected to be self-reliant and, as one advertisement puts it, to "be all that you can be." How is the Renaissance ideal of individualism similar to or different from that of today?

Investigating History

Find information on the expeditions to America by the Vikings and Columbus. Compare the navigating and sailing technology used, including features of the ships, nautical instruments, and geographic knowledge that made their venture successful. Two fine sources are the volumes by Samuel E. Morison, *European Discovery of America: The Northern Voyages* and *The European Discovery of America: The Southern Voyages*. Present either a written or oral report with illustrations and captions.

The Reformation and the Scientific Revolution

This painting is a symbolic picture of Luther and his supporters. Using a giant quill, they are writing their demands for religious reform on the door of All Saints Church in the German town of Wittenberg.

Key Terms

predestination
theocracy

Read and Understand

1. Martin Luther began a religious revolt.
2. Protestantism spread in northern Europe.
3. The Catholic Church made reforms.
4. Scientists challenged old assumptions.

Sweat glistened on the brow of a black-robed friar, Martin Luther. Torches lit the great hall in which he stood. Jammed together, craning their necks to see Luther, were the princes and bishops of Germany. They were members of the Imperial Diet (or assembly) of the Holy Roman Empire. At the head of the diet was the newly elected Emperor Charles V. The 21-year-old emperor stared grimly from his throne at the 37-year-old friar.

It was early evening on April 18, 1521. The setting was the town of Worms (vawrms) in Germany. Though they did not know it, the dignitaries who packed the hall were witnesses to a great turning point in European history.

About 20 books were stacked on a table near Luther. Europeans from London to Rome knew of the radical ideas these books contained. In them, Luther accused bishops, archbishops, and the pope of straying

The people of Worms sided with Luther. When Charles V passed judgment against Luther, signs were posted throughout the streets of Worms saying, "Woe to the land whose king is a child."

dangerously far from the teachings of Jesus. Throughout Germany, Luther's books sold out as fast as they were printed. The German people regarded Luther as a national hero. The Church considered him a dangerous heretic.

At the Diet of Worms, Luther and his ideas were on trial. A Church official named Eck pointed at the stack of books. Were these Luther's work? he asked. "Yes," said Luther. Would Luther take back the heretical ideas in these books? Luther's reply rang through the hall:

> Unless I am convinced by Scripture and plain reason . . . my conscience is captive to the Word of God. I cannot and I will not recant [take back] anything, for to go against conscience is neither right nor safe. Here I stand. I cannot do otherwise. God help me. Amen.

Luther's defiant words led to a revolutionary change in the Christian religion. Many Europeans stopped accepting the pope as the head of a united Church. In this chapter, you will read about the split between the Catholic Church and a new group of Christians called Protestants.

Religious leaders such as Martin Luther were not the only ones to challenge the Catholic Church's authority in the 1500's and 1600's. Scientific thinkers too began to question traditional ideas. This challenge led to a new way of thinking called the scientific revolution.

Comparing these two revolutions, we could say that Protestantism changed the way many Christians thought of God, heaven, and the soul. The scientific revolution changed the way Europeans thought about Earth and the universe.

Martin Luther began a religious revolt. 1

Martin Luther's dramatic stand at Worms grew out of a long history of protest within the Church. Leaders such as Wycliffe (page 242) and Hus (page 242) were part of that history. By 1500, many forces had weakened the power of the Catholic Church. The most important of these forces were the new ideas of the Renaissance and the new technology of the printing press. The greatest

changes took place between 1517 and 1555. Thus, the new religious movement began during the last years of the High Renaissance in Italy.

The Catholic Church faced problems.

The Renaissance popes who ruled Rome from 1447 to 1534 patronized the arts, collected ancient manuscripts, and vigorously defended the Papal States from French and Italian armies. These worldly concerns left the popes little time for spiritual duties. It was a serious failing. One Renaissance pope, Pius II (1458–1464), wrote:

> People say that we live for pleasure, gather wealth, bear ourselves arrogantly, ride on fat mules and handsome palfreys [horses] . . . And there is some truth in their words: many among the cardinals and other officials of our court do lead this kind of life. If the truth be confessed, the luxury and pomp of our court is too great.

There were abuses among the lower clergy as well. Many priests and monks were so poorly educated that they could scarcely read. Some village priests had semi-official wives. How could such a pope as Alexander VI (1492–1503) condemn them? He publicly acknowledged his own five children, born before he became pope.

Many people were devoutly religious.

People had come to expect higher standards of conduct from priests and church leaders. During the 1400's and early 1500's, groups of Christians throughout Europe set increasingly strict standards for their own lives. In the Netherlands, for example, a group called the Brethren of the Common Life attracted many men and women. They lived very simply while helping the poor, the hungry, and the sick. Such groups spread to Germany, France, and Italy.

Likewise, Europeans in the 1500's expected a higher level of learning from priests. In the Middle Ages, when few people were literate, a priest who could read even a little was respected. During the Renaissance, however, learning spread more widely in society. By 1500, well-educated people sneered at the priest who was a poor reader.

Two groups of people led the demand for reform and for higher standards of religion. One group

Discussion question: How might a religious revolution and a scientific revolution go hand in hand?

345

included popular religious leaders who roused the people with fiery sermons. The other group consisted of Renaissance writers who became known as Christian humanists.

Savonarola An Italian friar named Girolamo Savonarola (jih-ROHL-uh-moh SAV-uh-nuh-ROH-luh) came to Florence to preach in 1490. In eloquent sermons, he called for reform of the Church. Florentines flocked to hear him. In 1494, he helped overthrow Florence's ruler, Piero de Medici. From 1494 until 1498, Savonarola virtually controlled Florence.

In 1497, Savonarola demanded that the people of Florence gather their personal "vanities" and burn them in a giant bonfire. People threw wigs, velvet gowns, and even rare manuscripts and paintings into the flames. Only a year later, however, Florentines turned against Savonarola. Before a jeering mob, a hangman executed him.

The case of Savonarola showed how easily a leader could turn people's religious passions in revolutionary directions. Yet more moderate voices also called for change. Popular books by humanist authors called attention to corruption in the Church and the need for reform.

Erasmus and More Around 1475, Renaissance ideas began to spread beyond Italy to northern Europe. This development is often called the Renaissance of the North. Scholars in northern Europe valued the Greek and Roman classics just as much as Italian humanists did. However, northern scholars showed more interest in religion. Thus, the leaders of the northern Renaissance are often called Christian humanists.

The best known of the Christian humanists were Thomas More of England and Desiderius Erasmus (DEZ-uh-DAIR-ee-uhs ih-RAZ-muhs) of Holland. The two were close friends.

Born in Rotterdam, Erasmus (1466–1536) was honored by princes, kings, and cardinals for his brilliant writings. In 1509, while he was a guest in More's house, Erasmus wrote his most famous work, *In Praise of Folly*. This short book poked fun at greedy merchants, heartsick lovers, quarrelsome scholars, and pompous priests. Erasmus's most stinging barbs were aimed at the clergy.

Voice from the Past · *Gold and Silver in Utopia*

In *Utopia*, Sir Thomas More described a society in which everyone had enough food, clothing, and possessions for a comfortable life. No one had more than necessary or sought wealth for its own sake.

Silver and gold get no more respect from anyone than their intrinsic value deserves—which is obviously far less than that of iron . . . [The author then describes the Utopians' way of making sure that people do not prize precious metals or jewels too much.] According to this system, plates and drinking vessels, though beautifully designed, are made of quite cheap stuff like glass or earthenware. But silver and gold are the normal materials . . . for the humblest items of household equipment, such as chamber-pots. They also use chains of solid gold to immobilize slaves. And anyone who commits a really shameful crime is forced to go about with gold rings on his ears and fingers, a gold necklace round his neck, and a crown of gold on his head . . .

It's much the same with jewels . . . If they happen to come across one, they pick it up and polish it for some toddler to wear. At first, children are terribly proud of such jewelry—until they are old enough to notice that it's only worn in the nursery. Then . . . they give it up.

1. What reasons do you think a Utopian could give for thinking that iron was more valuable than gold or silver?
2. How did the Utopians use psychological methods to keep people from valuing gold and jewels?
3. *Utopia* is a satire, a form of literature that makes fun of foolishness or wickedness. What forms of foolishness or wickedness in European society is More mocking in this passage?

glass

This drawing of a printing shop in the 1500's shows the steps in the printing process. At the left, handwritten copy is taped to the wall. Workers take letters from type cases to make up a page. Another person (center, rear) inks a page of type that has been set. At the right, a man pulls the handle of the press that prints the sheets. A young apprentice (front) carries away the freshly printed pages to dry.

For example, he wrote, "One of their chief beliefs is that to be illiterate is to be of a high state of sanctity [holiness], and so they make sure they are not able to read."

How might a truly good society be organized? In 1516, Thomas More tried to answer this question in a book called *Utopia*. It told about a peace-loving people who lived in the imaginary land of Utopia, a Greek word meaning "nowhere." Utopia was a nearly perfect society based on reason and mercy. Greed, corruption, war, and crime had been weeded out.

Thousands of Europeans read the works of More and Erasmus. The reason that these authors could command such a wide audience was a remarkable technological breakthrough—the printing press.

The printing press spread new ideas.

The impact of the printing press on European society was revolutionary. It might be compared to the combined impact of television and the computer in recent times.

The first Europeans to use movable type were some printers in Mainz (mynts), Germany, between 1440 and 1450. The most famous of them was Johann Gutenberg (GOOT-uhn-burg), who printed a Bible around 1455. This Bible was the first full-size book printed with movable type.

Printing spread quickly to other cities in Europe. Print shops opened in Rome (1467), Venice (1469), and Paris (1470). By 1500, presses in about 250 cities had printed between 9 and 10 million books. For the first time, books were cheap enough that many Europeans could buy them.

How did printing prepare the way for a religious revolution? First, many writers criticized the corruption of the Renaissance popes. Erasmus, for example, wrote a savage satire about Pope Julius II.

Second, printed books on religion encouraged popular piety. Many printed books were illustrated with woodcuts and engravings. In Germany, an artist named Albrecht Dürer (DYOOR-uhr) drew Jesus and other biblical figures as if they lived in a German town. His beautiful pictures deeply stirred people's religious feelings.

Third, the printing press made the Bible available to all Christians who could read. When books were scarce, most Christians had depended completely on priests to interpret the Bible. After the Bible was printed, people could read it for themselves. Some, like Luther, interpreted what they read differently from the Church.

Footnote to History

Europeans had already learned from the Arabs how to make paper from old, shredded rags. Rag paper was much cheaper than parchment (made from sheepskin) or vellum (made from calfskin). Before the use of paper, a bookmaker had needed about 25 sheepskins to make a 200-page book.

Durer studied in Italy, but his subjects and his style remained distinctly German. His woodcut, *The Knight, Death, and the Devil*, reminded German Christians that the Devil—evil personified—was constantly beckoning to them.

Fourth, with the printing press, new ideas spread more quickly than ever before. Remember the stack of books for which Luther stood trial at the Diet of Worms. The ideas in them were similar to earlier writings of John Wycliffe and John Huss. Luther's books caused a revolution partly because so many people read them in a short time. With the printing press to spread a writer's ideas, the pen could indeed be mightier than the sword.

Luther challenged the Church.

All his life (1483–1546), Martin Luther wished only to be an obedient, God-fearing Christian. He did not set out to lead a religious revolution. What led this strongly religious man to defy the pope and Church traditions?

Luther's background The son of a copper miner, Luther was born in a tiny town in the German region of Saxony. As a child, he felt guilty and fearful much of the time. His father's bursts of anger terrified him. The stern teachings of local priests deeply impressed Luther.

When Luther was 21, he narrowly escaped death. During a storm, a great bolt of lightning struck near him, knocking him down. Afraid for his life, Luther cried, "Saint Anne, help me! I will become a monk." Luther's father, who wanted his son to be a lawyer, was furious.

As a monk, Luther tried desperately to win peace of mind. He confessed his sins at great length. He fasted regularly. He slept without a blanket until he nearly froze. Nevertheless, he still felt sinful, lost, and rejected by God.

Sometime between 1512 and 1515, Luther was alone in his study puzzling over a phrase in the Bible: "The just shall live by faith." In a flash, Luther thought he understood. Praying and fasting were not the keys to salvation. Instead, a strong faith in God was all that mattered. He wrote later, "Thereupon I felt myself to be reborn and to have gone through open doors into paradise."

The 95 theses Martin Luther might have lived quietly after finding peace. In 1517, however, something occurred that made him take a public stand. Like many other citizens of Wittenberg, he was offended by the deeds of a friar named Johann Tetzel. Tetzel was raising money in nearby towns to rebuild St. Peter's Cathedral in Rome by selling letters of indulgence.

This portrait of Martin Luther, drawn by one of his friends, shows him thoughtful and serious.

Indulgences were pardons from the Church for certain sins. Strictly speaking, an indulgence could free a sinner only from the penance a priest had set, such as saying a certain number of prayers. The sinner would still have to pay the penalty set by God. Unfortunately, Tetzel was overeager to collect money. He gave people the impression that they could buy their way into heaven.

Luther was deeply troubled by Tetzel's tactics. On October 31, 1517, he took up his pen and wrote 95 theses (formal statements) attacking the "pardon-merchants." He posted his theses on the door of the castle church in Wittenberg and invited fellow scholars to debate him. Excited by the challenge, someone copied Luther's words and took them to a printer. Within six months, Luther's name was known all over Germany. The religious crisis later known as the Reformation had begun.

The pope tried to silence Luther.

Soon Luther went far beyond criticizing indulgences. He wanted a full reform of the Church. Luther's teachings rested on three main ideas:

1. *Salvation by faith alone* In Luther's view, people could not win salvation by their own efforts—what the Catholic Church called "good works." Faith in God was the only way to salvation.
2. *The Bible as the only authority for Christian life* All Church teachings, said Luther, should be clearly based on the words of the Bible. The pope, he said, was a false authority. (The Catholic Church accepted both the Bible and Church traditions as authorities.)
3. *The priesthood of all believers* According to Luther, each person had a relationship with God and all people with faith were equal. Therefore, people did not need priests to interpret the Bible.

On June 15, 1520, Pope Leo X issued a bull (an official statement) threatening Luther with excommunication unless he recanted. Luther did not take back a word. Instead, his students at Wittenberg gathered around a bonfire and cheered as he threw the bull into the flames. Leo answered by excommunicating Luther.

Charles V opposed Luther.

The pope seemed powerless to touch Luther. However, the young Holy Roman Emperor, Charles V, had greater authority in Germany. We have seen how Charles summoned Luther to Worms in 1521 to stand trial. Charles promised Luther safety from arrest while at Worms. Would Luther back down at last? As you have read, he did not.

Luther made his famous speech on Thursday, April 18. The next day, Charles replied: "A single friar who goes counter to all Christianity for a thousand years must be wrong . . . I will proceed against him as a notorious heretic." On May 26, Charles issued an imperial order, the Edict of Worms. It declared Luther an outlaw and heretic. According to this edict, no one in the empire was to give Luther food or shelter. All his books were to be burned. Legally, there was no place in Germany for Luther to hide.

However, Luther lived comfortably in Germany for almost 25 years after his trial at Worms. Charles V, the most powerful ruler in Europe, could neither capture Luther nor stamp out his ideas. What accounts for this extraordinary failure?

First, Charles's huge empire was simply too much for him to govern effectively. Charles belonged to a family called the Hapsburgs, who had risen to power in Austria. After the 1400's, most Holy Roman emperors were chosen from the Hapsburg family. By a series of careful marriages, the Hapsburgs won more and more lands. In 1521, their holdings included not only Austria and lands in Germany but also the Netherlands, parts of Italy, Spain, and Spain's empire in the Americas.

Charles had another problem. The German people, although divided politically, had a strong national spirit, and they resented sending German money to Rome. Luther's attacks on the pope's "greed" were popular with many Germans. An Italian churchman visiting Germany in 1521 wrote, "Nine tenths of the people are shouting 'Luther!' And the other tenth shouts 'Down with Rome!' "

Luther's ideas spread in Germany.

For almost a year after the Diet of Worms, Luther shut himself away in a castle owned by Prince Frederick the Wise of Saxony. While there, Luther translated the New Testament into German. Now even Germans who did not know Latin could read the Bible.

Luther returned to Wittenberg in 1522. There he discovered that many of his ideas were already being put into practice. Town priests had given up their colorful robes. They dressed in ordinary clothes and called themselves ministers. They led services in German instead of in Latin. Some ministers had married, because Luther taught that the clergy should be free to wed.

Luther and his followers had taken the long step from wanting reform within the Catholic Church to becoming a separate religious group. They became known as Lutherans.

The revolt against the papacy became much broader. In 1524, German peasants, excited by reformers' talk of Christian freedom, demanded an end to their economic and political bondage. Serfdom, they cried, must be abolished. Bands

Throughout Germany, nuns and monks were leaving their cloisters, exchanging their monastic robes for everyday clothes, and marrying. A former nun named Katherine von Bora (aged 26) became the wife of Martin Luther (aged 42) in 1525.

349

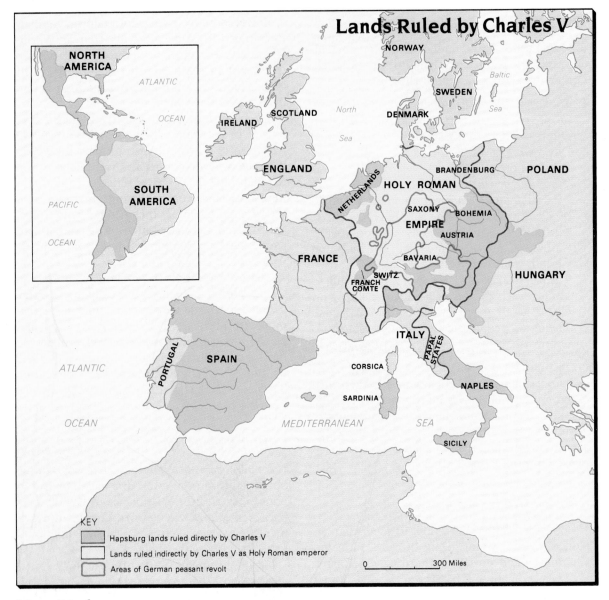

Lands Ruled by Charles V

KEY
- Hapsburg lands ruled directly by Charles V
- Lands ruled indirectly by Charles V as Holy Roman emperor
- Areas of German peasant revolt

0   300 Miles

Map Study

On what three continents did Charles V control lands? Name three European areas of which Charles was the ruler.

of angry peasants went about the countryside raiding monasteries, pillaging, and burning.

Luther was horrified by the peasants' revolt. He insisted that he wanted only peaceful reform, not violence and lawlessness. To the German princes, he wrote a savage letter urging them to show the peasants no mercy.

With brutal thoroughness, the princes' armies crushed the peasant revolt of 1524–1525. Perhaps 100,000 people were massacred. The lower classes

felt betrayed by Luther, and many turned away from his religious leadership.

After 1525, the success of Lutheranism depended increasingly on the support of German princes. Some princes liked Luther's ideas for selfish reasons. They saw his teachings as a good excuse to seize Church property. Other princes, however, genuinely shared Luther's beliefs.

In 1529, princes loyal to the pope agreed to join forces against Luther's ideas. Princes who

Luther wrote: "If the peasant is in open rebellion, then he is outside the law of God, for rebellion is not simply murder, but it is like a great fire which attacks and lays waste a whole land . . . nothing can be more poisonous, or devilish than a rebel."

supported Luther signed a protest against that agreement. From that time on, these protesting princes came to be known as Protestants.

Eventually, the term *Protestant* was used for many Christians who turned away from the papacy and the Catholic Church. Their movement was commonly known as the Protestant Reformation.

Section Review 1

Define: (a) heretic, (b) excommunicate, (c) indulgence, (d) minister
Identify: (a) Martin Luther, (b) Diet of Worms, (c) Savonarola, (d) Erasmus, (e) Thomas More, (f) *Utopia*, (g) Gutenberg (h) Charles V, (i) Hapsburg family
Answer:
1. What criticisms were made of many popes and lower clergy during the 1400's and 1500's?
2. Identify four ways in which the printing press prepared the way for the Reformation.
3. (a) What events led Luther to take a stand against the Church? (b) Summarize his three main ideas.
4. (a) What was the Edict of Worms? (b) Why was it unsuccessful?
5. (a) To whom was the term *Protestant* first applied? (b) What broader meaning did the term acquire?

Critical Thinking
6. Politics and religion were closely intertwined in the 1500's. How did each of the following political factors affect the spread of Luther's ideas? (a) the size of the Holy Roman Empire (b) German nationalism (c) the ambition of the German princes
7. Would you define Luther as a revolutionary? Why or why not?

Protestantism spread in northern Europe.

2

Martin Luther continued to write pamphlets and deliver sermons until his death in 1546. As time passed, however, the Protestant Reformation depended less and less on his leadership. Other reformers were also clamoring for change. Among them were John Calvin of France and John Knox of Scotland. Soon the Catholic Church was being challenged in many parts of Europe, especially in England.

Henry VIII *broke with the pope.*

When Henry VIII became king of England in 1509, he was 18 years old. He was the son of the "new monarch" Henry VII (page 248). Young Henry was handsome, strong, and intelligent. He loved tennis, classical literature, music, and food.

In religion, Henry VIII was a devout Catholic. He detested Luther. In 1521, Henry wrote a pamphlet calling Luther "a great limb of the Devil" and many other such names. Impressed by Henry's loyalty, the pope gave him a special title, "Defender of the Faith."

Yet political needs soon proved more important to Henry than religious loyalty. Henry was only the second king of the Tudor family, and he was anxious about the future of his line. Henry and his wife, Catherine of Aragon, had only one child—a daughter named Mary, born in 1516. Their five other babies, including three boys, had died in infancy. Henry feared that another civil war like the Wars of the Roses (page 248) would occur unless he had a male child to inherit his crown.

By 1527, Henry was convinced that Catherine would have no more children. He wanted a new queen to give him a son. He had already picked her out: a dark-eyed 20-year-old named Anne Boleyn (boo-LIHN).

How could Henry legally end his marriage to Catherine? Church law did not allow divorce, but the pope might set aside Henry's marriage by saying that it had never been legal in the first place. Such matters were often arranged.

In 1527, the king asked the pope to end the marriage. Unfortunately, 1527 was a very bad year to ask the pope for a favor. Pope Clement VII had taken the losing side in a war against Holy Roman Emperor Charles V. Charles's armies swept into Rome in 1527 and held the pope prisoner in the Vatican. Henry's unwanted wife, Catherine of Aragon, was the emperor's aunt. Charles would not allow his prisoner, the pope, to end his aunt's marriage. The pope turned down Henry's request.

Catherine of Aragon was the daughter of Spain's Isabella and Ferdinand. Their other daughter, Juana "The Mad," was the mother of Charles V.

351

Henry VIII, the second Tudor king of England, broke with the Roman Catholic Church in 1534.

The king sought Parliament's help.

Henry soon looked for more radical answers to his marriage problem. In 1529, he called Parliament and asked it to pass a group of laws that stripped away the pope's power in England. This Parliament is known as the Reformation Parliament. It met whenever the king summoned it for seven years (1529–1536).

Parliament soon legalized Henry's divorce from Catherine. In January 1533, Henry married Anne. Parliament passed a law stating that the king was not responsible "to any foreign princes or potentates of the world." (In other words, the pope was not to interfere with the king's divorce and remarriage.)

After being crowned queen in May, Anne gave birth to Henry's child in September. Imagine the king's frustration when he learned that the child was a girl. (Little did he realize that this daughter, Elizabeth, would be the greatest Tudor monarch of all.)

In 1534, Henry's break with the pope was made complete when Parliament voted to approve the Act of Supremacy. This act declared, "The king's majesty justly and rightly is and ought to be . . . the only supreme head in earth of the Church of England."

The English king, not the Roman pope, was now the official head of England's Church. Henceforth the king's agents collected all Church moneys. All priests and bishops were subject to the king's appointment and approval. Thus began the church that is called the Church of England.

The acts of the Reformation Parliament strengthened both the king and Parliament itself. The king won control of the Church of England. At the same time, Parliament gained power. Never before had a ruler asked Parliament to act on such fundamental questions.

Henry VIII *enforced his changes.*

Only a few people in England proved more loyal to the pope than to the king. The most famous of them was Thomas More. He refused to take an oath supporting the Act of Supremacy. For this refusal, Henry VIII ordered More beheaded. At his execution, More forgave his executioner and asked spectators to pray for the king. He said, "I die the king's good servant, but God's first." His death shocked people all over Europe.

The closing of the monasteries Soon after making himself supreme head of the Church of England, Henry made another sweeping change in religion. He closed all English monasteries and seized their wealth and lands. The monasteries had owned almost one third of the land in England, so this act vastly increased royal power and enriched Henry's treasury.

To raise money, Henry sold much of the land he had seized to nobles and to members of England's rising middle class. Suddenly there were many English landowners who stood to lose property if England returned to the Catholic Church. This group formed a solid base of support for the Protestant Reformation in England.

In most other ways, Henry remained more Catholic than Protestant. He insisted that English

The Protestant archbishop of Canterbury, Thomas Cranmer, created a *Book of Common Prayer* to be read aloud in church by all English Christians. Soon English priests were being called "ministers" in the Protestant manner, and their approach to the bread-and-wine sacrament was more like Luther's than the pope's.

priests make no changes in Catholic rituals and doctrines.

Henry's later marriages Meanwhile, Anne Boleyn had fallen rapidly out of favor with the king. Henry ordered her imprisoned in the Tower of London and later beheaded in 1536.

Within a month of Anne's death, Henry VIII married a third time. His new wife, Jane Seymour, lived just long enough to fulfill his dearest wish. On October 12, 1537, she bore a son, Edward. Then she died 12 days later.

Henry VIII married three more times. To win an alliance with Germany's Lutheran princes, he arranged to marry Anne of Cleves, a German princess he had never met. After only a few months, he had that marriage set aside. The king's fifth wife, Catherine Howard, was young and beautiful but foolish. She was executed on charges of adultery after less than a year as queen. In 1543, he married Catherine Parr. A mature woman, she loyally cared for Henry, who was now so fat and ill that he could hardly move, until his death in 1547.

Henry's children After Henry's death, all three of his children eventually inherited the throne. Edward VI was the first to rule. As he was a staunch Protestant, the Protestants gained power during his reign. Edward's half-sister Mary ruled England next. She was a Catholic who returned the English Church to the rule of the pope. England's next ruler was Anne Boleyn's red-headed daughter, Elizabeth. Elizabeth I returned her kingdom to Protestantism.

Women influenced the Reformation.

Mary and Elizabeth Tudor could force their religious ideas on their subjects because they were queens. However, many other women also played prominent roles in the Reformation.

Some women of the nobility protected Protestant leaders who lived and taught within their lands. In France, one of the most influential Protestants was Marguerite of Navarre, the sister of King Francis I. Besides protecting several Protestant preachers, she passed her Protestant ideals on to her descendants. Her grandson, Henry of Navarre, later became Henry IV of France.

Educated women wrote treatises on religious issues that were widely read. Margaret More, daughter of Sir Thomas More, was a recognized

Marguerite of Navarre, sister of France's king, protected French Protestants.

scholar. Likewise, Catherine Parr, the last wife of Henry VIII, wrote a book that discussed such questions as justification by faith.

Protestant ideas also spread widely among middle-class women. Protestantism appealed to the middle classes—both men and women—partly because preachers spoke in the vernacular, not in Latin. In addition, nationalist feelings against Rome were as strong among women as among men in Germany, England, and the Netherlands.

Women, like men, often suffered for their religious views. In the bitter struggles over religion, many women died for their beliefs.

Women's influence on the Protestant movement was greatest in the early years, between 1519 and 1580. As the Protestant religion became more firmly established, its organization became more formal. There were fewer opportunities for women to act as leaders. Women once again found themselves in the background.

Catherine Parr proved herself a kind stepmother to Henry's three children by his other marriages. She saw to their educations and helped reconcile Henry to his two daughters.

Calvin formalized Protestant ideas.

The Church of England remained close to the Catholic Church in many of its doctrines and ceremonies. Meanwhile, other forms of Protestantism were developing elsewhere in Europe.

When Luther stood trial at Worms, John Calvin was a boy of 12 in Noyon (nwah-**YOH**), France. No one could have guessed that this shy, studious child would in some ways have even greater influence than Luther. Luther had sparked the religious revolution. A generation later, Calvin gave order to the new faith.

Calvin studied law and philosophy at the University of Paris. Early in the 1530's, he came under the influence of French followers of Luther. When King Francis I ordered these Protestants arrested, Calvin fled. Eventually, he made his way to Switzerland.

In 1536, Calvin published a book called the *Institutes of the Christian Religion*. This work set forth a systematic Protestant philosophy. The first edition of the *Institutes* was completely sold out in a year.

Calvin taught that men and women are by nature sinful. By God's grace, however, a very few people will be saved from sin. Calvin called these few the "elect." Because God is all-knowing, Calvin said, He has known since the beginning of time who will be saved. Calvin's doctrine is called **predestination**.

Calvin said that the duty of the elect is to rule society so as to glorify God. Therefore, he taught, the church should dominate the state. Calvin hoped for a **theocracy**, a government controlled by church leaders. This idea was a major difference between Calvinism and Lutheranism, for Luther preached obedience to earthly rulers. Calvin's ideas gave more support for revolt against an "ungodly" ruler, an idea that later influenced events in Scotland and several other countries.

Calvin did more than write about his ideas. He actually set up the kind of theocracy he had described in his book. In 1541, Protestants in the French-speaking city of Geneva, Switzerland, asked Calvin to lead their community. When Calvin arrived there in the 1540's, Geneva was a self-governing city of about 20,000 people.

To many Protestants, Geneva under Calvin's rule became a "city of saints." Calvin and his followers regulated the lives of everybody who lived in the city. Everyone in Geneva attended classes in religion. No one wore brightly colored clothing or played cards. No one could argue in defense of the pope. No one could visit a public inn after nine o'clock at night. For breaking such rules, a person might be imprisoned, excommunicated, or banished from the city. Moreover, in Protestant Geneva as in Catholic Rome, anyone who preached a different set of doctrines might be burned at the stake.

Knox led the Scottish Reformation.

Protestants from everywhere in Europe came to Geneva to see how a sober, purified city was organized. Among the admiring visitors was a preacher from Scotland named John Knox. When he returned to Scotland in 1559, Knox put Calvin's ideas on church organization to work in Scottish towns. Each community church was governed by a small group of laymen called elders or presbyters (**PREHZ**-buh-tuhrs). From this organization, followers of Knox became known as Presbyterians.

In 1567, Protestant nobles led by Knox overthrew the Catholic queen of Scotland, Mary Stuart, in a nearly bloodless revolt. They put her one-year-old son, James VI, on the throne. Real power, however, was in the hands of the Protestant nobles. They created a national church and made Calvinism Scotland's official religion.

Protestant churches spread widely.

Elsewhere in Europe, the Calvinist form of church organization was widely adopted by Swiss, French, and Dutch reformers. Except for Scotland, no other kingdom officially converted to Calvinist belief. However, as the map on page 355 shows, communities of Calvinist Protestants were to be found from England to Italy.

In Sweden, Norway, and Denmark, Lutheranism became the official religion. Denmark had ruled both Sweden and Norway until 1523. In that year, Sweden revolted against the Danish king. The leader of the Swedish independence movement, Gustavus Vasa, became Sweden's new king. He soon ended papal power in Sweden and seized Church lands. Norway remained under Danish control and became Lutheran when Denmark made Lutheranism the official religion of the country in 1536.

The doctrines of the Anabaptists, founded in 1525 by Conrad Grebel, horrified Lutherans and Catholics alike. Anabaptists interpreted the Bible literally, saying that "Thou shalt not kill" commanded them to avoid weapons at all times, even in defense of their country.

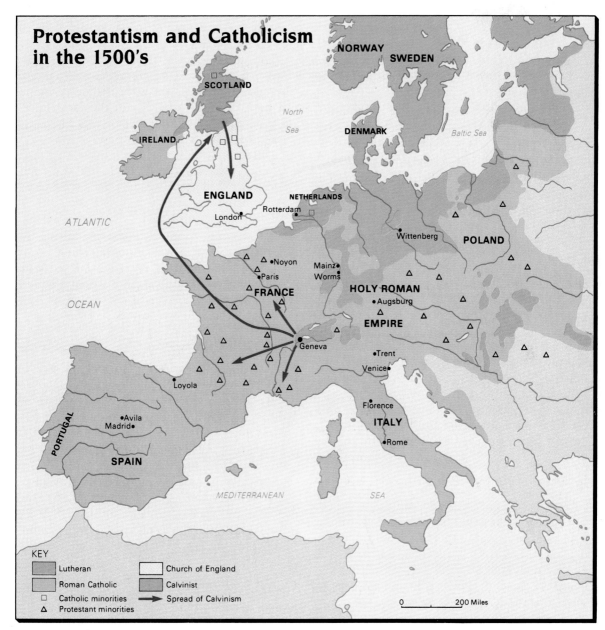

Protestantism and Catholicism in the 1500's

KEY

▨ Lutheran	☐ Church of England
▨ Roman Catholic	▨ Calvinist
☐ Catholic minorities	→ Spread of Calvinism
△ Protestant minorities	

0 _____ 200 Miles

Map Study

Where was Protestantism stronger, in northern Europe or in southern Europe?
Where was the center of the Calvinist movement?

Section Review 2

Define: (a) elect, (b) predestination,
(c) theocracy, (d) presbyters
Identify: (a) Henry VIII, (b) Catherine of Aragon, (c) Anne Boleyn, (d) Reformation Parliament, (e) Edward VI, (f) Mary Tudor,
(g) Elizabeth I, (h) John Calvin, (i) John Knox

Map Study answers: northern Europe; Geneva

Answer:
1. Why did Henry VIII of England want to end his first marriage?
2. What part did Parliament play in the English Reformation?
3. (a) What changes did Henry make in the English Church? (b) What changes did each of his children make when they succeeded him?

4. (a) Briefly describe Calvin's idea of the elect and their place in society. (b) How were Calvin's political ideas different from Luther's?
5. How did Calvinism become the official religion of Scotland?
6. Where in Europe did Lutheranism become the official religion?

Critical Thinking

7. (a) What did Thomas More mean by his statement, "I die the king's good servant, but God's first"? (b) How does this statement show the dilemma that many people faced in the 1500's?

The Catholic Church made reforms.   3

While Protestants won many followers, millions of Catholics held fast to their traditional beliefs. Catholics in the 1500's had their own religious reformers. One great champion of Catholic reform was Ignatius (ig-NAY-shus) of Loyola, later canonized as Saint Ignatius.

Ignatius began the Jesuits.

Born in 1491, Ignatius grew up in his father's castle in Loyola in eastern Spain. The great turning point in his life came in 1521 when he was in the Spanish army fighting the French. A cannonball shattered his right leg, leaving him an invalid for months. During his recovery, Ignatius thought about his past sinfulness and the events of the life of Jesus. His daily devotions seemed to cleanse his soul. In 1522, he began writing a book. Titled *Spiritual Exercises*, his book laid out a day-by-day plan of meditation, prayer, and study.

Over the next 18 years, Ignatius gathered a band of followers. Eventually, he won the support of Pope Paul III. In 1540, the pope made Ignatius's company a new monastic order called the Society of Jesus. Those who later joined the order were commonly called Jesuits (JEHZ-uh-wuhts).

What made the Jesuits unique was their emphasis on absolute discipline and obedience. They were like a spiritual army. These disciplined Catholics were willing to go anywhere in the world in the service of the pope.

The Jesuits concentrated on three activities. First, they founded superb schools throughout Europe. Jesuit teachers were rigorously trained in both classical studies and theology. Priests who attended the Jesuit schools were far better educated than many other priests.

The second mission of the Jesuits was to convert non-Christians to Catholicism. Jesuit missionaries risked their lives preaching Christianity in the Americas, Africa, and Asia.

The Jesuits' third goal was to prevent Protestantism from spreading. The zeal of the Jesuits overcame the drift toward Protestantism in Poland and southern Germany (Bavaria). These regions today are overwhelmingly Roman Catholic because of the work of the Jesuits.

Reforming popes led the Church.

Two popes of the 1500's, Paul III and Paul IV, took the lead in reforming the Catholic Church. They had two goals. One was to strengthen and purify the Catholic Church for its own sake. Their other goal was to combat Protestantism.

Pope Paul III (1534–1549) took three important steps in reforming the Catholic Church. First, he directed a council of cardinals to make a thorough investigation of simony, indulgence selling, and other abuses within the Church. Second, he approved the Jesuit order. Third and most important, he decided to call a great council of Church leaders.

In 1545, Catholic bishops and cardinals met in the town of Trent in northern Italy. After much heated discussion, they agreed on the following doctrines:

1. The pope's interpretation of the Bible was final. Any Christian who substituted his or her own interpretation was a heretic.
2. Christians were not saved by faith alone, as Luther argued. They were saved by faith *and* by good works.
3. The Bible and Church tradition shared equal authority for guiding a Christian's life.
4. Indulgences, pilgrimages, and venerations of holy relics were all valid expressions of Christian piety. (But the false selling of indulgences was banned.)

356

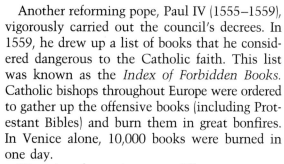

The picture above shows the interior of a Protestant church with the minister at the pulpit. At the right is a ceremony in a Roman Catholic church. Bishops are gathered in front of the pope. What differences do the pictures show between the two styles of worship?

Another reforming pope, Paul IV (1555–1559), vigorously carried out the council's decrees. In 1559, he drew up a list of books that he considered dangerous to the Catholic faith. This list was known as the *Index of Forbidden Books.* Catholic bishops throughout Europe were ordered to gather up the offensive books (including Protestant Bibles) and burn them in great bonfires. In Venice alone, 10,000 books were burned in one day.

Historians have given two different names to this wave of reform in the Catholic Church. Protestant historians have generally called it the Counter-Reformation. They argued that its goal was to stamp out Protestantism. Catholic historians usually called this period the Catholic Reformation. They stressed the sincere desire of popes, cardinals, nuns, and monks to end Church corruption.

Religion divided Europe.

While the popes tried religious measures to strengthen the Church and crush Protestantism, Holy Roman Emperor Charles V turned to military measures. In 1544, Charles finally felt safe enough from his French and Turkish enemies

to take up arms against the Protestant princes of Germany.

These Protestant rulers had joined together in a defensive group called the Schmalkaldic (shmahl-**KAHLD**-ik) League. In 1547, Charles's troops met the Schmalkaldic princes in battle and badly trounced them. However, the Catholic princes of Germany refused to join Charles in his war against Protestantism.

Weary of fighting, Charles ordered all German princes, both Protestant and Catholic, to assemble for an Imperial Diet in the city of Augsburg. At that meeting, the princes agreed that the religion of each German state was to be decided by its ruler. This famous religious settlement, signed in 1555, was known as the Peace of Augsburg.

By the terms of the Peace of Augsburg, German princes could choose either Lutheranism or Catholicism. Calvinism and other forms of Protestantism were outlawed.

From the point of view of Charles V, the Peace of Augsburg was not a happy settlement. After all, it led to religious division, not unity. All his life, Charles V had been deeply attached to the great institutions of the Middle Ages—feudalism, chivalry, and the Catholic Church. As Holy Roman emperor, he had hoped to preserve these

Luther was still under ban during the Diet of Augsburg so a friend, Melanchthon, went on his behalf. Some historians believe that the outcome of the Diet might have taken longer to achieve if Luther, less able to compromise than Melanchthon, had been present.

357

institutions. However, the forces of historical change were too powerful for him to stop.

Charles was sick of troubles. He was eager to give up his crown, which had brought him little but grief. To his son, Philip II, he gave Spain, parts of Italy, the Netherlands, and Spain's holdings in the Americas. He turned over the Holy Roman Empire to his brother, Ferdinand. Then Charles V, once ruler of the largest empire in the world, retired to a monastery in Spain. He died there in 1558.

Section Review 3

Identify: (a) Ignatius Loyola, (b) Society of Jesus, (c) Council of Trent, (d) Index of Forbidden Books, (e) Peace of Augsburg
Answer:
1. (a) Who were the Jesuits? (b) What were their goals and achievements?
2. How did each of these popes strengthen the Catholic Church? (a) Paul III (b) Paul IV
3. What conclusions did the Council of Trent reach?
4. How did the Peace of Augsburg affect the states of Germany?

Critical Thinking
5. (a) What are the two names for this period of reform in the Catholic Church? (b) How do these two names show different attitudes on the part of historians? (c) Why might such differences arise?

Scientists challenged old assumptions. 4

The other revolution that began in the early 1500's developed more slowly and quietly than the Reformation. In fact, this revolution in scientific thinking was so gradual that it went nearly unnoticed for about 100 years. Eventually, however, the new scientific ways of thinking profoundly changed the whole world.

Before 1500, scholars generally decided what was true or false by quoting an ancient Greek or Roman author. For example, medieval scholars assumed that whatever Aristotle said about the natural universe was true unless the Bible said otherwise. Few European scholars tested Aristotle's ideas by looking at nature for themselves.

In the late 1500's, however, a few scholars published works that challenged the ideas of the ancient thinkers. A profound change in European thought was beginning. Historians call it the Scientific Revolution.

Copernicus and Kepler studied the solar system.

Among the first of the ancient theories to be challenged in the Scientific Revolution were the ideas of the astronomer Ptolemy (TAHL-uh-mee). About A.D. 150, during Roman times, Ptolemy wrote that Earth was the center of the universe. Ptolemy said that the sun, the moon, the stars, and five planets—Mercury, Venus, Mars, Jupiter, and Saturn—all circled around Earth. Scholars accepted Ptolemy's ideas for 1,400 years.

In 1543, a Polish scholar known by the Latin name of Nicolaus Copernicus (koh-PUHR-nih-kuhs) published a book challenging Ptolemy's theory. Copernicus's book was called *On the Revolutions of the Heavenly Bodies.* It argued that Earth and the other planets moved around the sun. Furthermore, said Copernicus, Earth was constantly spinning or rotating, which explained why the sun appeared to rise and set each day.

At first, Copernicus's book caused little excitement. Only a few scholars knew about it, and most of them did not agree with him. Copernicus himself wrote no more. Born in 1473, he had not published his book until he was on his deathbed. Furthermore, his arguments were based strictly on logic and geometry, not on direct observation.

Early in the 1600's, a German named Johannes Kepler (1571–1630) made careful observations of Mars and other planets. His data showed that Copernicus's ideas were right. Kepler concluded that Earth did in fact move around the sun, and so did the other planets.

Kepler worked out a series of mathematical equations that described how each of the planets moved around the sun. His three principal equations are known as Kepler's laws of planetary motion.

Luther on Copernicus: "The fool will overturn the whole art of astronomy. But as Holy Writ declares, Joshua commanded the sun to stand still and not the earth."
Discuss: Does a literal interpretation of the Bible conflict with scientific exploration?

Galileo used a telescope.

In 1610, an Italian scientist named Galileo Galilei (GAL-uh-**LEE**-oh GAL-uh-**LAY**-ee) published a little book called *Starry Messenger*. This book began a controversy that went on for years.

European scholars had long believed that the universe was made of two totally different substances. Earth, they thought, was made of impure material that changed and decayed with time. They thought that the moon and the stars, on the other hand, were made of a pure, eternal substance that was smooth and perfect.

Galileo's observations of the heavens Galileo argued in his book that the moon was not smooth at all. It had mountains and plains on it just as Earth did. Moreover, Galileo said that the sun was not a perfect ball of heavenly light. Instead, it had many dark spots on it.

How did Galileo know? He had seen the sunspots and moon mountains while gazing through a telescope. The telescope was not entirely Galileo's invention. A Dutch lensmaker was the first to make an instrument to enlarge far-off objects. However, Galileo was the first astronomer to study the night sky through a telescope. Nobody else had ever seen the moon and planets as Galileo saw them through his telescope. Enlarged, they looked more Earthlike than heavenly. Galileo's observations, like those of Kepler, strongly supported the Copernican theory of a sun-centered solar system.

Galileo's experiments in physics Besides his important work in astronomy, Galileo started a whole new field of scientific investigation. This was the modern science of dynamics, which studies matter in motion.

As a youth of 18, Galileo watched the movements of a cathedral's chandelier as it swung back and forth on its chain. Aristotle had said that a pendulum swings more slowly as it approaches its resting point. Galileo tested this idea and found it wrong. Feeling his pulse to keep time, he found that each swing of the pendulum took exactly the same amount of time, from the first long sweep to the last tiny quiver.

Galileo performed other experiments in this careful way. For days, he rolled balls down a slope and measured the speed at which they moved. His data led him to conclude that a falling object accelerates at a fixed and predictable rate.

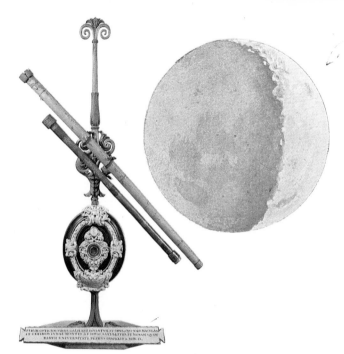

Galileo used this telescope to observe the moon. His drawings showed that the moon's surface is rough, not smooth as others thought.

Scientists used precise tools.

During the Scientific Revolution, scholars developed ways to make precise, reliable observations. Galileo's telescope was only one of the important instruments that aided science during the early 1600's. Other scientists and artisans developed more such tools.

Microscope The first microscope was invented by a Dutch maker of eyeglasses, Zacharias Janssen (**YAHN**-sen) in 1590. In the 1650's, Anton van Leeuwenhoek (**LAY**-vuhn-**HOOK**) used a microscope to observe bacteria swimming in his own saliva. He also described red blood cells.

Thermometer Galileo made the first thermometer in 1603, using alcohol for measuring temperatures. A German physicist named Gabriel Fahrenheit (**FAHR**-uhn-hyte) made the first thermometer using mercury. Fahrenheit's thermometer showed water freezing at 32° and boiling at 212°. A Swedish astronomer named Anders Celsius (**SEL**-see-uhs) created another scale for the mercury thermometer. Celsius's scale showed freezing at 0° and boiling at 100°.

Barometer One of Galileo's students developed the first mercury barometer, a tool for measuring atmospheric pressure and predicting weather. Evangelista Torricelli (TOR-uh-**CHEL**-ee) made this advance in 1655.

Later in the 17th century, an English scientist named Isaac Newton would further Galileo's work. Newton would show that all the universe is subject to the same laws of motion and would speak of a physical law called gravity (see Chapter 20).

Daily Life · *Pendulums and Clocks*

Since Greek times, people had marked the passing hours with water clocks—clocks in which water dripped at a steady rate from one container into another. In winter, however, these water clocks froze. In the 1200's and 1300's, European inventors worked on clocks that were driven by weights. In the 1400's, they turned to spring-driven clocks. Yet none of these timepieces was very accurate.

When Galileo saw that a pendulum always took the same amount of time, the way was open to a new method of measuring time. In 1656, a Dutch astronomer, Christian Huygens (HYE-guhnz), built a clock using a pendulum. It was more accurate than earlier ways of measuring time. Pendulum clocks were not surpassed in accuracy until the use of electricity.

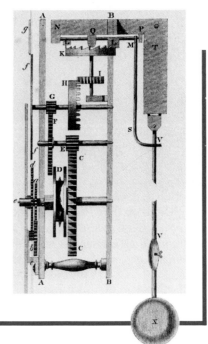

New ideas caused conflict.

Rarely are new ideas accepted right away. In fact, they are more likely to be treated at first with deep suspicion. Many early scientists found themselves in conflict with the Catholic Church. By far the best known of these conflicts was the case of Galileo. As you have read, Galileo's observations convinced him that Copernicus was right. Yet, after a Church ruling banned Copernicus's ideas in 1616, Galileo was not free to say so.

Galileo thought he had a solution. In 1632, he wrote a book presenting the ideas of *both* Copernicus and Ptolemy. He himself, he said, was neutral. Yet Church officials saw clearly that Galileo gave all the strongest arguments to the Copernican theory. In fact, he seemed to be mocking the Church-approved ideas of Ptolemy.

Jesuit leaders charged that Galileo's ideas threatened to do the Church more harm "than Luther and Calvin put together." The pope decided to suppress the opinions of this famous scientist. Therefore, in 1633, the aged Galileo was called to Rome to stand trial.

Under the threat of torture, Galileo knelt before the cardinals and read aloud a signed confession. In it, he called the ideas of Copernicus "a false opinion." He said, "I abjure, curse, and detest the aforesaid errors and heresies."

Galileo was never again a free man. He was allowed to return to his home near Florence, but he was kept under house arrest until he died in 1642. Nevertheless, the revolution that Galileo helped to start could not be stopped.

Section Review 4

Define: Scientific Revolution
Identify: (a) Ptolemy, (b) Copernicus, (c) Kepler, (d) Galileo, (e) Leeuwenhoek, (f) Fahrenheit, (g) Celsius, (h) Torricelli
Answer:
1. (a) According to Ptolemy, what was Earth's position in the universe? (b) How did Copernicus's view differ? (c) Which theory did Kepler's observations support?
2. What revolutionary conclusion about the sun and moon did Galileo reach by gazing at the heavens through a telescope?
3. List four new instruments that came into use during the Scientific Revolution. After each, write its purpose.
4. (a) How did Galileo arouse the Church's anger? (b) What was the result?

Critical Thinking

6. (a) How did Galileo, Kepler, and other scientists of this period try to determine scientific truth? (b) How was this method different from that used by medieval thinkers? (c) Give an example of how each method might be used in everyday life today.

Discussion question: What effect would the Church's trial of Galileo have on other scientific thinkers of the time?

Chapter Review 16

Summary

1. Martin Luther began a religious revolt. The early 1500's brought two kinds of revolution—one in religion, the other in science. The Protestant Reformation, which split Europe into Catholic and Protestant states, began with Martin Luther's criticism of the selling of indulgences. Luther was later excommunicated and outlawed for teaching ideas that conflicted with Church doctrine. He gained the support of many Germans, however, and the new technology of the printing press spread his ideas throughout Europe.

2. Protestantism spread in northern Europe. Several countries turned to Protestantism. Henry VIII of England broke with the Catholic Church when the pope would not set aside his first marriage. John Calvin set forth a systematic Protestant theology based on the doctrine of predestination. One of his followers, John Knox, led a revolt that made Calvinism the official religion of Scotland.

3. The Catholic Church made changes. At the same time, the Catholic Church experienced reforms. Ignatius of Loyola formed the Society of Jesus to serve the pope. Pope Paul III called the Council of Trent, which reaffirmed Church doctrine. Paul IV enforced the new decrees and drew up a list of books believed dangerous to the Catholic faith.

4. Scientists challenged old assumptions. In the Scientific Revolution, scientists broke with the ancient teachings of Ptolemy. Knowledge of the universe increased. Copernicus proclaimed that Earth moved around the sun. The observations of Kepler and Galileo supported his theory.

Reviewing the Facts

1. Define the following terms:
   - a. theocracy
   - b. predestination
2. Explain the importance of each of the following names, places, or terms:
   - a. Savonarola
   - b. Erasmus
   - c. More
   - d. *Utopia*
   - e. Gutenberg
   - f. Dürer
   - g. Luther
   - h. Charles V
   - i. Diet of Worms
   - j. Henry VIII
   - k. Catherine of Aragon
   - l. Reformation Parliament
   - m. Mary Tudor
   - n. Calvin
   - o. elect
   - p. Geneva
   - q. Knox
   - r. Ignatius Loyola
   - s. *Index of Forbidden Books*
   - t. Peace of Augsburg
   - u. Copernicus
   - v. Kepler
   - w. Galileo

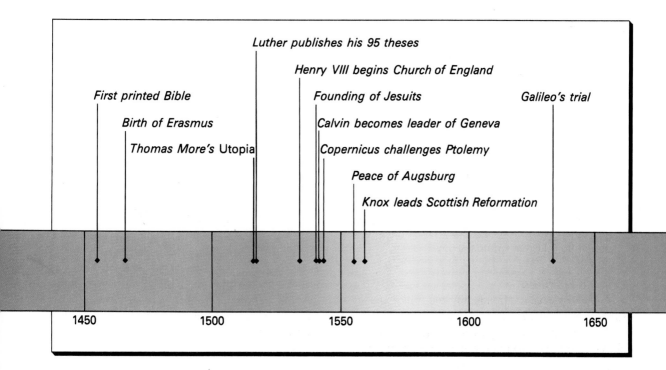

First printed Bible
Birth of Erasmus
Thomas More's *Utopia*
Luther publishes his 95 theses
Henry VIII begins Church of England
Founding of Jesuits
Calvin becomes leader of Geneva
Copernicus challenges Ptolemy
Peace of Augsburg
Knox leads Scottish Reformation
Galileo's trial

1450   1500   1550   1600   1650

3. (a) What was the peasant revolt of 1524? (b) What were its results?
4. (a) How did Henry VIII strengthen Protestantism in England through the Act of Supremacy? (b) By his policy toward monasteries? (c) How did the religious outlooks of his children vary?
5. (a) What was Calvin's view on salvation? (b) How did Calvinism become established in Scotland in the 1500's?

Basic Skills

1. **Interpreting maps** Use the maps on pages 350 and 355 to answer the following questions: (a) What religious groups did Charles V have to contend with in the Holy Roman Empire? (b) What countries were the main centers of Calvinism, Lutheranism, and Catholicism in the 1500's?
2. **Sequencing** List the following events, together with their dates, in chronological order: Savanarola holds power in Florence, *In Praise of Folly,* Luther's 95 theses, *Utopia,* Edict of Worms, Act of Supremacy, Peace of Augsburg, Index of Forbidden Books.
3. **Making a comparison chart** Make a chart comparing Luther and Calvin. For the vertical column, use the following headings: Role in Reformation, Ideas about Religion, Political Ideas, and Writings.

Researching and Reporting Skills

1. **Having a roundtable discussion** Historians differ in their interpretation of the relation between the Renaissance and the Reformation. Some historians think the Reformation was a reaction against the Renaissance. Others think it was the result of the humanistic thinking of the Renaissance. Have a roundtable discussion to decide which thesis is more valid, based on the evidence.
2. **Writing a pamphlet** Imagine that Ignatius Loyola asked you to write a pamphlet to recruit people into the Society of Jesus. How would you present this organization and its goals so as to persuade people to join this spiritual army?

Critical Thinking

1. **Analyzing causes** (a) Identify the major causes of the Reformation. (b) Which were immediate causes and which were remote causes?
2. **Identifying arguments** (a) List the practices and beliefs of the Catholic Church that Luther opposed. (b) What argument did Luther use against each of them?
3. **Identifying issues** Identify and explain briefly the religious issues addressed (a) by the Council of Trent and (b) by the Peace of Augsburg.
4. **Analyzing economics** The Reformation was a religious movement, but its success in different countries was influenced by economic factors. (a) Identify three economic changes related to the Reformation. (b) How did those changes affect the establishment of Protestantism?
5. **Applying a concept** In the late 1500's, scientific thought underwent a revolution. (a) What old ideas and beliefs were challenged? (b) What new ideas and beliefs emerged to replace the old? (c) What impact did this change have on society?
6. **Relating** The Reformation and the Scientific Revolution occurred at the same time in Europe. (a) To what extent were they related and how? (b) Which had the greater impact on the lives of most Europeans in the seventeenth century? Give reasons for your answers.

Perspectives on Past and Present

1. The text suggests that the impact of printing in the 1500's was comparable to the modern-day invention of television and the computer combined. Evaluate this comparison, giving your own opinion about it.
2. The text on page 359 describes advances in technology that helped to make the Scientific Revolution possible. What is the state of each of these inventions today? That is, how has modern technology improved upon the original inventions?

Investigating History

For refusing to obey one of the Reformation laws of Henry VIII, Thomas More was executed. Read the award-winning play *A Man for All Seasons,* by Robert Bolt, or watch a videotape of the movie, which dramatizes More's defiance of his former friend, the king.

The Spanish Empire and Shifts in European Power

BOLCAN DE MEXICO
Nº 3

In full royal splendor, the Aztec ruler Montezuma greeted the Spanish explorer Cortés and his translator, Doña Marina. According to tradition, the Aztec ruler's feet could not touch the ground, and his subjects could not look directly at his face.

Key Terms

conquistador
viceroy
inflation
capitalism

Read and Understand

1. Spain built an overseas empire.
2. Spain was a Catholic bulwark.
3. The Netherlands won independence.
4. France's crown changed hands.
5. Religious wars split Germany.

For several months, messengers had been bringing frightening reports to Montezuma, emperor of the Aztecs, in his capital city of Tenochtitlán in the Valley of Mexico. The reports told of white-skinned, bearded men arriving at the coast in winged towers. Were these strangers merely men from distant lands? Or was their leader, as Montezuma feared, the ancient ruler-god of the Aztecs, Quetzalcoatl (ket-suhl-**KWAH**-tuhl), returning to claim the Aztec kingdom?

In fact, the strangers were a small force of Spaniards under the leadership of Hernán Cortés (air-**NAHN** kor-**TEHZ**). Cortés had sailed in March 1519 from the Spanish settlement on Cuba with about 600

In Nahua, the language of the Aztecs' forebears, Quetzalcoatl meant a combination of a bird and a snake (*quetzal*, a bird; *coatl*, a snake), or a feathered serpent.

Spaniards, 11 ships, 16 horses, and a few brass cannon. His goal was to explore and colonize the North American mainland. Without knowing it, Cortés's little group of Spaniards was approaching the vast Aztec empire with its 11 million people (pages 314–315).

Montezuma soon sent his own ambassadors to see these newcomers. Whether they were gods or men, he hoped rich gifts would persuade them to go away. Aztec ambassadors presented Cortés with ornaments of gold and turquoise. The most impressive presents, in the eyes of the gold-hungry Spaniards, were two discs as big as the wheels of a cart. One, made of gold, represented the sun. The other, of silver, represented the moon.

Far from persuading Cortés to leave, the sight of so much gold and silver only stiffened his determination to win more. So that none of his men could sail home with the treasure, he ordered all his ships sunk.

For the Spaniards, it was now conquer or die. If they failed, they might be carried up the steps of an Aztec temple and sacrificed to the sun god. Torn between hope and terror, Cortés's small force set off on the 250-mile march to Tenochtitlán. Never in history had so small an army planned to topple so great an empire.

As you will see in this chapter, Cortés's actions in the spring of 1519 had far-reaching results. His handful of Spaniards destroyed the Aztec empire, and this conquest laid the foundation for an empire that made Spain the richest power in Europe.

Spain quickly put its great wealth at the service of Catholicism in the religious wars that shook Europe throughout the 1500's and 1600's. There was little peace between Catholics and Protestants in those years. Armies from Catholic Spain fought for 80 years against Protestants in the Netherlands. France was torn apart by assassinations, massacres, and civil wars—often fueled by religious hatred. In Germany, Protestants and Catholics fought one of the most destructive wars in European history, the Thirty Years' War (1618–1648).

The period of time covered in this chapter was a time of violence. However, it was also a time of great creativity. Dutch and Spanish artists produced some of the greatest treasures of European art. Literature too flourished, especially in Spain and France.

Spain built an overseas empire. 1

In the 1490's, Christopher Columbus (page 337) founded the earliest Spanish settlements in the Americas on the islands of Hispaniola and Cuba. Within a generation, Spain's lands in the Americas grew to a great empire. Sailing out from the islands, daring Spanish fortune hunters called **conquistadors** (kohn-KEES-tuh-dohrs) searched the Americas for gold and precious gems. Hernán Cortés was one of the earliest, and most successful, of these conquistadors.

Cortés conquered the Aztecs.

After Cortés's fateful decision to sink his ships, he was committed to war against the Aztecs. The Spaniards were overwhelmingly outnumbered, but they did have several advantages. They were equipped with weapons the Aztecs had never seen. There were horses, steel swords and armor, crossbows, and light artillery.

Cortés also had another advantage. Traveling with him was a young Indian woman who had been given to him as a slave when his group first landed. Her name was Malinche, and she spoke the Aztec language and several others. She learned Spanish rapidly. The Spaniards gave her a Christian name, Marina.

Doña (Lady) Marina soon became Cortés's invaluable aide. She explained that the Aztecs were hated and feared by most of the Indians they ruled. She helped him win allies among these Indians. Later, she played on Montezuma's fears to keep him from taking a strong stand against the Spaniards.

On November 8, 1519, Cortés reached Tenochtitlán. Montezuma invited the Spaniards into the city as his honored guests. Much impressed with the place, Cortés would later call Tenochtitlán "the most beautiful city in the world."

Why did Montezuma let the Spaniards enter his capital? He still feared that Cortés might be Quetzalcoatl, a light-skinned god who had once ruled the lands around Lake Texcoco. One day he had vanished mysteriously, but he vowed to return and claim his kingdom. As fate would have it, Cortés arrived in exactly the same year

Research project: Compare the religion, language, territory, and art of the Aztecs and the Incas. How does their art reveal their view of the universe?

Quetzalcoatl was expected to return. As the legend had foretold, Cortés came in "white-winged ships" from across the eastern sea. Thus, Montezuma feared Cortés as a god. His fear led to the fall of the Aztec empire.

After several days of sight-seeing in Tenochtitlán, the Spaniards boldly took Montezuma prisoner and kept him in their quarters. Despite his apparent success, however, Cortés was still in an explosive situation. While he was out of the city, one of his lieutenants interfered with an Aztec religious ceremony. An uprising broke out against the Spaniards.

When Cortés returned, he and Marina forced Montezuma to go out on the roof of the Spanish barracks to calm the crowd. The Aztecs flung stones at their former ruler, now the puppet of Cortés. Soon after, word came that Montezuma was dead. The Spaniards said he had been killed by a stone from the mob. Not surprisingly, the Aztecs believed the Spanish had killed him. The Spaniards were now surrounded by thousands of Aztecs demanding their blood.

On the night of June 30, 1520, the Spaniards tried to sneak out of the city, but a guard spotted them. The Aztecs swarmed out to attack the hated foreigners. Many Spaniards, slowed by the loot they carried, were either clubbed to death or carried away for sacrifice. Among those who escaped were Cortés and Doña Marina.

The Aztecs might have pursued Cortés and destroyed his small force, but another disaster befell the Aztecs just then. The morning after Cortés's flight, smallpox broke out in the city. This terrible disease, brought by the Spaniards, killed many Aztec leaders (page 340). Partly for that reason, the Aztecs failed to follow the fleeing Spaniards and wipe them out.

A year later, in 1521, Cortés returned. This time he had with him a huge army of Aztec-hating Indians. Trapped in their island city, the Aztecs refused to surrender. Cortés's army had to fight its way into the city, block by block. After an 85-day siege, Tenochtitlán lay in ruins. When it was rebuilt, it was as a Spanish capital for an empire called New Spain.

Voice from the Past · *An Aztec Poem*

An anonymous Indian poet voiced the grief that the Aztecs felt for the ruin of their once beautiful capital, Tenochtitlán.

Broken spears lie in the roads;
we have torn our hair in our grief.
The houses are roofless now, and their walls
are red with blood.

Worms are swarming in the streets and plazas,
and the walls are splattered with gore.
The water has turned red, as if it were dyed,
and when we drink it,
it has the taste of brine.

We have pounded our hands in despair
against the adobe walls,
for our inheritance, our city, is lost and dead.
The shields of our warriors were its defense,
but they could not save it.

We have chewed dry twigs and salt grasses . . .
we have eaten lizards, rats, and worms . . .
Gold, jade, rich clothes, quetzal feathers—
everything that once was precious
was now considered worthless.

1. The poet tells a whole story in the first stanza. What information can you deduce from reading just four lines?
2. During the siege, the city's defenders had no way of bringing food into the city. What were the consequences?
3. (a) Which parts of this poem might apply to the fall of Troy, Carthage, or another great city? (b) What details are specific to Tenochtitlán?

High in the Andes lie the ruins of the great Inca city Machu Picchu. Though the Spaniards searched for it, no outsider found it until 1911.

Pizarro conquered the Incas.

Cortés was only one of many Spanish adventurers who hoped to win a large fortune in the Americas. Another was Francisco Pizarro (puh-ZAHR-oh). A gray-bearded man of 62, Pizarro landed on the coast of Peru in 1532 with about 200 soldiers. The Spaniards panted up the western slopes of the Andes and followed the Inca road to the city of Cajamarca (kah-huh-MAHR-kuh). They found the city deserted.

The Inca ruler, Atahualpa (AHT-uh-WAHL-puh), and his army were camped close by. Atahualpa had won the throne after a bitter war with his brother. The war between the two brothers severely weakened the Inca empire. Even so, Atahualpa had 30,000 men to fight Pizarro's small troop. Pizarro, on the other hand, had horses and superior weapons.

Through a messenger, Pizarro invited Atahualpa to Cajamarca for a friendly visit. The Inca ruler agreed. Meanwhile, the Spaniards hid themselves and their horses in the narrow alleys of the city. They waited in silence as Atahualpa was carried into the city on a gold litter. He was accompanied by a guard of between 5,000 and 6,000 men. The guards were not armed.

A Spanish priest greeted Atahualpa. Suddenly a shot rang out. From all directions, the Spaniards charged their startled visitors. Not one Spaniard died, but the slaughter of Inca guards was dreadful. Most important, Atahualpa was taken prisoner. Since only the emperor could lead the Inca army, no one could rescue him. The emperor's absolute power was his empire's fatal flaw.

Atahualpa offered a huge ransom for his release. He promised to fill a large room with gold and another with silver. Pizarro agreed to free the Inca when the ransom was paid. Soon the rooms were filled as promised. Pizarro melted down the finely crafted objects into gold and silver bricks. Then, breaking his promise, he ordered Atahualpa strangled to death.

A few months later in 1533, Pizarro's horses clattered down the streets of Cuzco (KOOZ-koh), the Inca capital. The Spaniards were now rulers of Peru, and Pizarro was rich beyond measure. However, the Spaniards began to fight among themselves. In 1541, a group of Pizarro's old comrades broke into his home and killed him.

Pizarro laid out the city of Lima and planned its cathedral, where his bones now rest. How do these actions demonstrate one role of the conquistador in settling the Americas?

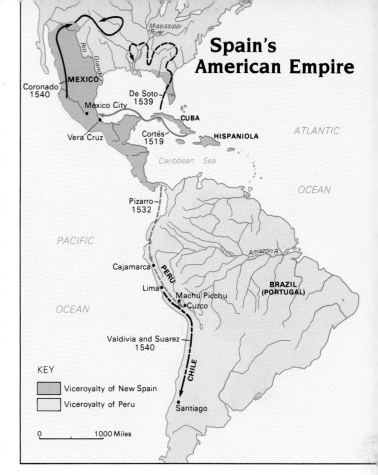

Spaniards explored widely.

Map Study answers: New Spain; Coronado; 1532

Emboldened by the riches of Cortés and Pizarro, other soldier-adventurers set out in search of more treasures. Hernando de Soto sailed north from Cuba in 1539. He landed on the Florida coast and marched inland as far as the Mississippi River. He claimed the river and the land along it for Spain. Having fought with Pizarro, he dreamed of conquering another glittering empire. Instead, he died of sickness in 1547, and his soldiers dropped his body into the Mississippi.

Another Spaniard, Francisco Coronado, crossed the Rio Grande in 1540. He explored as far north as the plains of Kansas. One of his captains discovered the spectacular beauty of the Grand Canyon. Yet like De Soto, Coronado found no gold. He returned to Mexico bitterly disappointed.

Meanwhile, far to the south, a man and a woman extended Spain's conquests in the Andes Mountains. In 1540, Pedro de Valdivia (vahl-**DEE**-vyah) and Ines Suarez (**IH**-nehz **SWAH**-rayth) led a small army south from Spain's strongholds in Peru. They marched along the coastal desert of what is now Chile. In 1541, they founded the city of Santiago, Chile's modern capital. Between 1540 and 1547, they rode and fought together, conquering much of Chile for Spain.

By 1550, Spanish territory reached all the way from present-day Kansas to Chile. Spain's American lands were larger than the empires of Alexander the Great or Julius Caesar. This was also the first empire in history that was separated from its capital by an immense ocean. Its ruler was Spain's Charles I, who also held the title of Holy Roman Emperor as Charles V.

Colonists enslaved the Indians.

The king of Spain claimed absolute power over his American lands. He entrusted the power to make laws for these lands to a group of officials called the Council of the Indies. The council met in Spain and sent its laws to two capitals in the Americas. One capital was Mexico City, which the Spanish had built over the ruins of Tenochtitlán. The other capital was Lima, Peru. Pizarro founded Lima in 1535 and made it the capital of Peru because communication with Spain was easier from the coastal Lima than from the inland Cuzco.

Map Study

What viceroyalty included the former land of the Aztecs? Which Spanish explorer traveled farthest north? When did Pizarro go to Peru?

In both Mexico City and Lima was a royal agent called a **viceroy**. The viceroy in Mexico City ruled Spain's North American territory, called New Spain. The viceroy in Lima ruled Spain's South American lands, called Peru. Viceroys were noblemen born in Spain. No Spaniard born in the Americas could hope to reach such high office.

The viceroy's authority did not matter much to the average Aztec, Inca, or Maya. For the conquered Indians, the only rulers who mattered were the ruthless conquistadors who seized their villages. The Council of the Indies granted to certain settlers a privilege called an *encomienda* (**EHN**-koh-mee-**EHN**-duh). The holder of an encomienda became master of a particular area. He could force Indians in his lands to work long hours in his cornfields, sugar plantations, or silver mines. In effect, the Spaniards treated the Indians as slaves. Abuse in Spanish silver mines killed thousands of Indians.

Some Spaniards, especially missionaries, were deeply concerned about the Indians. One, Bartolome de las Casas, convinced the Spanish monarch to enact laws protecting them. The laws met with opposition from the *encomienderos* and were soon repealed.

367

Section Review 1

Define: (a) conquistador, (b) viceroy,
(c) encomienda
Identify: (a) Montezuma, (b) Tenochtitlán,
(c) Cortés, (d) Doña Marina, (e) New Spain,
(f) Pizarro, (g) Atahualpa, (h) De Soto,
(i) Coronado, (j) Valdivia, (k) Suarez
Answer:
1. (a) What was the legend of Quetzalcoatl?
   (b) How did it help Cortés?
2. How did Cortés finally conquer Tenochtitlán?
3. Why was the conquest of the Incas relatively easy after the capture of Atahualpa?
4. (a) How was Spain's American empire governed? (b) What qualified a person to become a viceroy?
5. (a) What types of economic enterprises did Spanish settlers establish in the Americas? (b) What workers did they use there?

Critical Thinking
6. List five factors that contributed to Cortés's success and explain how each one helped him. Be sure to consider political and social factors as well as military ones.

Spain was a Catholic bulwark.

2

The riches of Spain's new empire were fabulous. By 1600, the amount of gold taken from American mines and shipped to Spain was estimated at 750,000 pounds. American silver mines yielded even greater treasure. Between 1550 and 1650, roughly 16,000 *tons* of silver bullion (metal bars) were unloaded from Spanish galleons and carted over Spanish roads. Between a fifth and a fourth of every shipload of treasure went to the king of Spain as his royal share. With the vast wealth of its American territories, Spain began to play a commanding role in Europe.

Philip II *ruled an empire.*

In 1556, Charles V divided his empire, giving Spain to his shy and serious son, Philip II, who ruled from 1556 to 1598. Under Philip's rule, Spain became the staunchest supporter of Catholicism and the most dangerous enemy of Protestantism.

Europe was entering a time of violent conflict over religion. In 1559, Spain and France signed a treaty ending the long series of wars they had fought over lands in Italy. Thereafter, for nearly 100 years, most of the wars in Europe were fought over religion.

Philip's inheritance from Charles V included more than Spain and its American colonies. He also ruled the duchy of Milan in northern Italy, the kingdom of Naples in southern Italy, the territory called Franche-Comté on France's eastern border, and all 17 provinces that made up the Netherlands.

Toward the middle of Philip's reign, another great prize fell into his hands. In 1580, the king of Portugal died without an heir. Philip quickly seized the small but important Portuguese kingdom. Counting Portuguese strongholds in Africa, India, and the East Indies, he now had an empire that circled the globe.

Spain's wealth and its power grew together. Minted into coins, Spain's gold and silver supported an army of about 50,000 soldiers. Through the late 1500's, Spain had by far the largest and best-equipped army in Europe. Looking at Spain's awesome military machine, people said, "When Spain moves, the whole world trembles."

The nerve center of the Spanish empire was Philip's palace, the Escorial (es-**KOHR**-ee-uhl). All the roads and ship lanes in Spain's far-flung empire led ultimately to its massive, gray stone walls about 26 miles northwest of Madrid, the capital. The Escorial's outer gates were so huge that the keys to open them weighed half a ton. Within the gigantic walls, there were 86 staircases to climb, 1,200 doors to open, and 84 miles of corridors to explore.

In a small, candle-lit room within the Escorial, Philip II worked far into the night. The most powerful ruler in Europe, he was also the hardest working. He demanded reports, reports, and more reports from his chief advisers. Then, in his tiny office, he would agonize over decisions. Much of the time, he could not bring himself to choose one policy over another. At such times, the government of Spain ground nearly to a halt. Yet Philip would not allow anyone to help him. Deeply suspicious, he trusted no one for long.

Some students may wish to report on recent efforts to salvage riches from sunken Spanish galleons.

As a palace, the Escorial served a worldly, political purpose rather than a religious one, as the Gothic cathedrals did. The Escorial was divided into many sections, often grouped around courtyards. The dome, towers, classical columns, and decoration show the influence of Renaissance architecture, in contrast to that of the Gothic cathedrals.

Comparing pictures *The Spanish architects who planned the Escorial (above) were influenced by the buildings of Renaissance Italy. Yet they created a much plainer, sterner palace, well suited to the character of Spain's Philip II (right). How does the architecture of the Escorial differ from that of a Gothic cathedral (page 219)?*

As his own court historian wrote, "His smile and his dagger were very close."

The Escorial was more than a palace. It was also a monastery. From his bedroom, Philip II could slide open a hidden window that allowed him to watch the monks' church services. There, in private, he took part in their prayers.

The two functions of the Escorial—palace and monastery—show clearly the character of Philip II. Throughout his reign, he doggedly sought to strengthen both his monarchy and the Catholic Church.

Spain battled for Catholicism.

Philip II was eager to see Catholicism triumph over its religious rivals, the Muslim Ottoman Turks and the Protestants. Against the Ottomans, Philip achieved a stunning victory. However, Philip's struggles against Protestantism caused him only frustration.

War against the Ottoman Turks   In 1571, the pope called on all Catholic princes to take up arms against the mounting power of the Ottoman empire. Philip responded like a true crusader. Huge Spanish galleons joined Venetian ships in the Mediterranean Sea and rowed toward the coast of Greece.

On October 7, 1571, near the Greek seaport of Lepanto (lih-**PAN**-toh), 200 Spanish-Venetian ships met the Ottoman fleet of 300 ships in a ferocious battle. Philip II's half-brother, Don John of Austria, commanded the Christian forces. His ships slammed into the Turkish galleys. Then the Spaniards and Venetians swarmed aboard and slaughtered the foe with sword and musket. The Battle of Lepanto crushed the Ottoman navy. It was a major victory for Christendom.

War against Protestant forces   As the champion of Catholicism, Philip wanted first and foremost to crush Protestantism in his own lands. He also worked constantly to weaken or overthrow Protestant rulers throughout Europe.

No other place on the map of Europe gave Philip as much trouble as a tiny corner of his own empire, the Netherlands. Later in this chapter, you will read how the Dutch rose in revolt against Philip (page 372). In his efforts to crush

Discussion question: To what extent might Philip's character have prevented his victory over Protestant forces? (Students may want to review the previous page for help.)

369

the revolt, Philip spent a fortune in Spanish gold to no avail.

After the Dutch, Philip's greatest Protestant enemy was Elizabeth I of England. Philip had once been married to Elizabeth's Catholic sister, Mary (page 353). After Mary's death in 1558, he hoped to keep England as an ally and a Catholic country. For a while, he even hoped to marry Elizabeth. Gradually, however, Elizabeth showed that she intended to keep England Protestant and that she did not intend to repeat her sister's mistake of marrying an unpopular foreign king. Later, Elizabeth openly assisted the Dutch rebels with money and troops. She also encouraged English sea captains to raid Spanish treasure ships for gold.

In 1588, Philip struck at England. He assembled a fleet of 130 ships with 31,000 men. This fleet was known as the Armada (ahr-MAHD-uh). Philip had high hopes for his mighty Armada, but the skilled English sea captains destroyed it. For England, the victory was the high point of the Elizabethan age (Chapter 18).

Spain had a golden age in art and literature.

Despite these military setbacks, Spain remained a mighty nation. Philip's reign marked the beginning of a golden age for Spanish culture.

El Greco and Velázquez The works of two great artists showed both the pride and the piety of Spain during its golden age. The first of these artists was El Greco (GREH-koh). The second was Diego Velázquez (vay-LAHTH-kayth).

El Greco (1541–1614) was not a Spaniard by birth but a Greek from the island of Crete. His real name was Kyriakos Theotokopoulos, but the Spanish gave him the name El Greco, which means "the Greek." His major works were all painted in Spain.

El Greco painted Catholic saints and martyrs as huge, long-limbed figures. The backgrounds of his paintings were usually a mass of swirling gray clouds. The use of deep, vibrant colors heightened the drama and religious intensity of El Greco's paintings.

El Greco's saintly figures showed the strength of the Catholic faith in Spain. The paintings of Velázquez (1599–1660) showed the pride of Spain's royal family. Velázquez was best known for his

The dramatic sky in this painting of Saint Bernardino is typical of El Greco's work.

portraits of Spanish kings and princes mounted on rearing stallions.

Cervantes In 1605, an unsuccessful Spanish playwright named Miguel de Cervantes (suhr-VAN-teez) published a book that many critics call the first modern European novel. The book was named for its main character, Don Quixote (kee-HOH-tee) of La Mancha. In his own life, Cervantes had had his ups and downs. He had been wounded in the Battle of Lepanto and jailed for debt. He worked for a time as a tax collector. These varied experiences seem to have made Cervantes tolerant of humankind.

Valazquez was the court painter to Philip IV and also the master of the king's collections. In this latter role, he managed to acquire for the king some of the greatest masterpieces of European art.

Don Quixote de la Mancha was a gentle satire of chivalry. Don Quixote was a Spaniard of noble birth and noble mind who went a little crazy after reading too many books about heroic knights. Hoping to "right every manner of wrong," he rode forth in a suit of rusty armor, mounted on a feeble nag. At his side, through all his adventures, was a stout and comical little squire named Sancho Panza.

Because of his romantic ideals, Don Quixote never saw things as they were. He saw a common tavern by the road as a grand castle. To him, a windmill became a hostile giant to be challenged and fought. Of course, Don Quixote's wild notions caused no end of trouble. Strangers laughed at his chivalric speeches, knocked him off his horse, and left him in the mud.

Sancho Panza, more sensible than his master, objected to everything the foolish knight proposed, but Don Quixote never listened. This bit of dialogue was typical:

"What the devil kind of vengeance are we going to take," asked Sancho, *"seeing there are more than twenty of them and not more than two of us, or maybe only one and a half?"*

"I," replied Don Quixote, *"am worth a hundred."*

So saying, the knight charged to the attack, only to receive another beating.

Don Quixote's misadventures made it clear that the age of knights in shining armor had passed. By 1600, chivalry seemed outdated and somewhat foolish to Cervantes's readers, even though its ideals still had some sentimental appeal, especially to kings and queens.

Spain's economy weakened.

With a prayer on his lips, Philip II died in his palace bed in 1598 after a reign of 42 years. His successors were weaker kings, notable mostly because Velázquez painted their portraits.

In the next 50 years, Spain's golden age gradually lost its glitter. By 1650, the Spanish economy was in a dreadful state. The king was hopelessly in debt to foreign creditors. In every Spanish town, prices soared wildly.

Strangely, Spain's great wealth in the 1500's was the direct cause of its poverty later. Boatloads of gold and silver from the Americas flooded Spain—and later the rest of Europe—with precious metals. As a result, the value of gold and silver dropped, and prices doubled and redoubled. Such an upward spiral of prices is called **inflation**.

Spain was most seriously affected by these skyrocketing prices. Spaniards found that they could neither eat gold nor hammer it into shoes.

Unlike many other parts of Europe, Spain never had a large middle class. The most powerful group in Spanish society was still the great feudal landholders. No class of burghers or bourgeoisie won political influence in Spain as such groups did in England and France.

Spain's methods of manufacturing were also old-fashioned. The guilds that had grown up in the Middle Ages still dominated business. These guilds did not produce enough manufactured goods for Spain's use. Instead, Spaniards imported much of what they needed from the Netherlands, France, and England. Thus, Spanish gold and silver tended to flow right out of Madrid into the pockets of Spain's worst enemies—the hard-working, hard-bargaining Dutch burghers of Amsterdam.

Section Review 2

Define: inflation

Identify: (a) Philip II, (b) Escorial, (c) Battle of Lepanto, (d) the Armada, (e) El Greco, (f) Velázquez, (g) Cervantes, (h) Don Quixote

Answer:

1. (a) What lands did Philip II inherit? (b) What lands did he add to his empire?
2. What made Spain's government inefficient?
3. What were Philip's two goals?
4. (a) What action did Philip take toward the Ottoman empire? (b) What Protestant lands caused difficulties for Spain?
5. How did Spain's wealth from the Americas weaken its economy?

Critical Thinking

6. Cervantes, El Greco, and Velázquez present very different outlooks on life. What might Philip II have thought of the works of each man, if he had known of them? (Only El Greco's works were actually produced during Philip's lifetime.)

371

The Netherlands won independence. 3

Of Spain's many enemies in the late 1500's, the most stubborn (and successful) were the people who lived in the low marshlands between northern Germany and northern France. Today, this region is divided into two nations, Belgium to the south and the Netherlands to the north. In the 1500's, the whole region was known as the Netherlands, or the Low Countries. The northerners, known as the Dutch, took the lead in the battle with Spain.

It is not surprising that the Dutch rebelled against Spanish rule in the late 1500's. In culture, customs, and religion, the Dutch were strongly at odds with Spain and its ruler, Philip II. Broadly speaking, Spain still held to the great institutions of the Middle Ages: the Catholic Church, the feudal system of landholding, and the guild system for producing goods. The Netherlands, on the other hand, had many Protestant congregations. The feudal system had little influence on the busy towns of the Netherlands. Moreover, as Spain's economy faltered, the Dutch were taking the lead in new ways of doing business.

The Dutch revolted against Spain.

The Netherlands had long been part of the Holy Roman Empire. When Charles V divided his lands, he gave the Netherlands to Philip II along with Spain. Thus, the only link between the two lands was that they shared a ruler.

Spain, as you have read, was a thoroughly Catholic country. In the Netherlands, about one third of the people were Calvinists. Although they were a minority, the Calvinists were a strong, tightly knit group that included many powerful nobles and wealthy merchants.

In 1559, Philip II sent his sister Margaret to govern the Netherlands with the twin goals of stamping out Protestantism and raising taxes. These policies soon antagonized many Dutch.

In 1566, mobs of angry Calvinists rampaged through Catholic churches in many parts of the Netherlands. Calling themselves the Sea Beggars, they smashed windows, burned books, destroyed altars, and ruined all the rich ornaments.

In response, Philip II sent 20,000 soldiers under the Spanish Duke of Alva to destroy Protestantism in the Netherlands. The duke's troops broke into Dutch homes and carried off suspected heretics. On a single day in 1568, Alva executed 1,500 people. Between 1568 and 1578, the Netherlands flamed as war raged between Catholics and Protestants, Dutch and Spaniards.

The greatest leader of the revolt against Spain was Prince William of Orange. (He was also known as William the Silent for his remarkable ability to keep his plans secret.) Born a Lutheran but raised a Catholic, William's motives for fighting the Spaniards were political, not religious. He hated to see his country ruled by foreigners and wanted to free the Netherlands from Spain.

At first, William and the Dutch lost battle after battle, town after town to the Spaniards. Then, at the town of Alkmaar, the Dutch took a desperate step. Their lands were called the Low Countries because much of the land was actually below sea level. Only great dikes kept the seawater from flooding over the fields. To drive out the Spanish, the Dutch opened the floodgates, covering the land around Alkmaar with water. Thereafter, the Dutch took this terrible step several times, destroying their countryside to save their towns from Spain.

By 1579, the Dutch were in control of the northern part of the Netherlands. Seven provinces, led by the province of Holland, united and declared themselves independent of Spain in 1581. This country became the United Provinces of the Netherlands.

Meanwhile, the southern part of the Netherlands (which is modern-day Belgium) remained under Spanish control. The majority of people in this region were Catholics, and their language was closer to French than to German.

William the Silent hoped to establish a country where both Protestantism and Catholicism were tolerated. Few people, however, were ready to accept this idea. William himself was murdered in 1584 by a fanatic. Today, Dutch Catholics and Protestants alike honor him as the "father of his country."

Gradually, the idea of religious toleration did take root in the Netherlands. Somehow the Dutch managed to overcome the religious hatreds stirred up by their war for independence. In the 1600's, the United Provinces was the one country in

The city of Antwerp was completely destroyed by unpaid Spanish soldiers after their leader, the Duke of Alva, resigned.

Europe that accepted people of almost all faiths. Jews, unable to practice their religion in most parts of Europe, found a haven in Amsterdam and other Dutch cities. Scholars from many parts of Europe also came to live in the United Provinces or sent their books there to be published. For the times, this kind of religious toleration was rare.

The Dutch established a republic.

Another distinctive feature of the United Provinces of the Netherlands was its government. Unlike most states of Europe, the United Provinces was not a kingdom but a republic. Each province had an elected governor called a *stadtholder*. The power of this official depended on the active support of the province's leading merchants and landholders.

Each of the seven provinces sent delegations to a legislative body called the States General. These lawmakers had few powers because each province jealously guarded its independence. Nevertheless, members of the States General were so proud of themselves that they insisted on being called "Their High Mightinesses."

The Dutch built a trading empire.

While Spain lived on the gold and silver from its colonies, a new economic system was thriving in the Netherlands. The Dutch took the lead in the development of a new way of organizing business, a system that later came to be called **capitalism**.

Capitalism and the commercial revolution What were the features of this new economic system? Capitalists were people who invested large sums of money (or *capital*) in business ventures. Their goal was to make enough money to pay all the costs of the venture plus some additional money (or *profit*).

A capitalist who made a profit on a trading expedition did not spend all the money on luxury items. Instead, the successful capitalist reinvested the profit in another, probably larger, venture. Of course, there was always the risk of failure. Capitalists risked losing not only the chance for profit but all the capital they had accumulated as well. During the 1660's, however, the hope of profit kept the Dutch economy booming.

This painting by Vermeer shows the three-story houses that were common in Dutch towns. The top floor often served as the owner's warehouse.

The merchants of Amsterdam traded in many goods. They bought surplus grain in Poland and crammed it into their warehouses. Then, they waited for news of poor harvests in southern Europe so they could ship the grain south while prices were highest. Tons of smoked and pickled herring also found a ready market. Western Europe was short of timber, a fact that Dutch merchants were quick to exploit. They shipped great quantities of Scandinavian lumber to Spain, France, Italy, and England, all in ships owned by Dutch capitalists.

The Dutch had the largest fleet of ships in the entire world—10,000 ships in 1600. Even merchants of other countries often sent their cargoes in Dutch ships and, of course, paid dearly for it.

Banking As the trade routes of the Atlantic became more important than those of the Mediterranean, the Dutch replaced the Italians as the bankers of Europe. Soon after its founding in 1609, the Amsterdam Exchange Bank won a reputation as the safest, soundest bank in Europe.

Dividends paid by the Dutch East Indies Company were sometimes as high as 63 percent above a backer's initial investment. Compare this rate to current dividend rates to help students appreciate the lure of venture capitalism.

373

Princes and merchants from many countries deposited money there. They also borrowed from the Dutch banks, and the interest on such loans enriched Amsterdam's bankers.

The Dutch East Indies Company Among the most prized luxury items in Europe were the spices imported from Asia. Ambitious Dutch merchants knew that the spice trade could bring enormous wealth to their country. They also knew that entering the spice trade was dangerous as long as Portugal controlled the routes around Africa and across the Indian Ocean.

In 1602, 17 of Amsterdam's wealthiest merchants pooled their money to form the Dutch East Indies Company. The firm had enough capital to outfit a heavily armed fleet far superior to Portugal's. Within 20 years, the Dutch had displaced the Portuguese in the East Indies, Ceylon, and the Cape of Good Hope. Shiploads of pepper, cloves, and nutmeg sold in Amsterdam brought huge profits to the company. The merchant owners used these profits as capital to invest in new trading ventures and in banks that financed other undertakings. Any Dutch citizen, however, could buy shares in the company, and those shares could be bought and sold.

Dutch merchants took the lead in their capitalist approach to trade, but merchants in other nations soon followed. English and French merchants in particular also invested in bold enterprises and expanded their markets. This system of trade, profit, and investment became so important to Europe that historians have called it the Commercial Revolution. It marked the beginning of the economic system later known as capitalism.

Amsterdam became a great city.

Holland was the wealthiest Dutch province, and Amsterdam was Holland's largest, most flourishing city. In fact, by 1650, Amsterdam had become the financial and commercial center of Europe, far surpassing the Italian cities of Venice and Florence.

Amsterdam's growth through the early 1600's was spectacular. In 1610, there were 50,000 people living in Amsterdam. Only 10 years later, the population had doubled to 100,000. By 1660, the figure had swollen to 200,000. This phenomenal growth was due partly to Amsterdam's location on a sheltered bay, the Zuider (ZYE-duhr) Zee. However, human skill did far more than geography to account for Amsterdam's wealth.

Hoping to boost their city's commerce, a group of Dutch engineers designed a remarkable network of canals. The plan was approved in 1610 and completed in 1663. Three 80-foot-wide semicircular canals ran from the Zuider Zee into the heart of the fan-shaped city. A web of 600 smaller canals fed into the larger ones so that every dwelling in the city could be reached by water.

The Dutch merchants even designed their houses so that they could move merchandise efficiently. The top floor of each three-story house usually served as the owner's warehouse. It was equipped with a hoisting beam that jutted out over the water. When a barge tied up below, the merchant could lower a hook from the hoisting beam and thus quickly gather in a shipment of wheat, beer, or herring.

Imagine that it is a winter morning in the 1630's. Let us take an early stroll along a narrow

Daily Life · *Tulips and Trade*

Amsterdam in the 1600's was a hotbed of financial speculation. People bought and sold goods of all sorts in hopes of making a profit. In the mid-1630's, a new money-making craze swept the city—tulip bulbs. Everyone in Amsterdam, it seemed, had gone mad over exotic strains of tulips imported from Turkey. It was common for a single tulip bulb to be bought and sold ten times in one day, always for a profit. A wealthy Dutchman once traded his mansion for three tulip bulbs and considered it a bargain!

Rembrandt van Rijn's dramatic painting, "The Night Watch," shows the civic leaders of Amsterdam keeping guard over their city.

lane beside one of Amsterdam's canals. In the soft light of dawn, the milk pails of a milkman clank loudly. Moments later, the neighborhood baker drags a cart along the lane and calls out to the homeowners opening their shutters, "Hot white bread! Rye bread rolls! Barley biscuits!"

In the frosty air, as Dutch neighbors greet one another across the canal, their bodies seem oddly round and bulky. To keep warm, they bundle up in layer upon layer of woolen clothing. Men wear seven or eight waistcoats and pairs of trousers. Women pile on layer after layer of petticoats.

In one of the narrow houses, a family is taking the first meal of the day. The family members begin with a solemn Calvinist prayer before settling down to a standard Dutch breakfast: bread, cheese, butter, and beer. When finished, all stand to pray again. In the course of the long day, they look forward to three more meals. For the main feast at midday, a prosperous family will set out plates of herring, almonds, fruits, and a rice pudding dessert. The poor usually make do with four meals of cheese, bread, broth, and many tankards of beer.

Dutch artists developed a new style.

During the 1600's, Amsterdam became what Florence had been during the 1400's. It boasted not only the best banks but also the best artists in Europe.

The greatest Dutch artist of the period was Rembrandt van Rijn (REHM-brant vahn ryne), who lived from 1606 to 1669. Rembrandt's paintings realistically captured moments of drama. In 1632, a wealthy physician commissioned Rembrandt to paint a group portrait. The artist showed the distinguished doctor standing over the corpse of an executed criminal, lecturing a group of fellow surgeons. Rembrandt's most famous group painting, "The Night Watch," showed his mastery of light and shadow.

Dozens of other artists worked in Amsterdam. The older master Franz Hals (1580–1666) painted brighter and less somber works than Rembrandt. His merry spirit showed itself in the vigorous faces of the people he painted.

The Dutch often chose domestic, indoor settings for their portraits. They apparently enjoyed

Wealthy merchants and bankers wanted portraits, landscapes, and scenes from day-to-day life in their homes both to offer tranquility and to reflect their prosperity.

Both this painting and the one on page 373 are by Dutch artist Jan Vermeer. How are the two pictures similar in style and content?

seeing themselves doing chores in their homes and workshops. For example, the young artist Jan Vermeer (1632–1675) became famous for his paintings of middle-aged women doing such tasks as pouring milk and sewing. In his paintings, light from an open window seemed to flood the room.

Dutch art showed more interest in groups than in heroic individuals such as Michelangelo's "David" or Velázquez's Spanish monarchs. Frequently, Dutch artists painted group portraits of people—families, civic leaders, military units. As many as 40 people may appear in one painting. Taken as a whole, Dutch art revealed the prosperity, the civic spirit, and the values of a new age in Europe.

Section Review 3

Define: (a) republic, (b) capitalism, (c) capital, (d) profit, (e) Commercial Revolution
Identify: (a) the Netherlands, (b) Sea Beggars,

(c) William of Orange (the Silent), (d) stadtholder, (e) Dutch East Indies Company, (f) Amsterdam, (g) Rembrandt
Answer:
1. (a) List three ways in which the Netherlands differed from Spain. (b) How did the Netherlands become a part of Spain?
2. (a) What policies did Philip's sister Margaret and the Duke of Alva follow in the Netherlands? (b) What were the results?
3. (a) What was William the Silent's political goal? (b) His religious goal? (c) What did he achieve?
4. How were the Dutch able to stop the Spaniards at Alkmaar?
5. (a) What part of the Netherlands declared itself independent of Spain in 1581? (b) What happened to the rest of the Netherlands?
6. (a) Describe the government of the Netherlands. (b) Briefly describe the way businesses in the Netherlands were organized.
7. (a) Why was the Dutch East Indies Company formed? (b) What help did the Dutch government give the company?

Critical Thinking
8. How was the United Provinces of the Netherlands unusual for its time in both politics and religion?

France's crown changed hands. 4

In 1559, France's future looked bleak. Its long series of wars with Spain for control of Italy had come to an end, with Spain the clear winner. France was exhausted by the wars. Moreover, the French king, Henry II, was severely injured in a jousting tournament and died from his wounds in 1559. Henry II had been a member of the Valois (va-LWAH) dynasty, the family that had ruled France since 1328.

Not content with defeating France, Philip II worked for the rest of the 1500's to weaken the French monarchy. His efforts helped bring about the downfall of the Valois. Yet, by destroying the Valois, Philip II unwittingly helped bring to power a strong new king, Henry IV.

Catherine de Medici ruled France.

Henry II left four young sons, all of whom were incompetent. All had short lives, so that three of Henry's boys briefly wore the French crown. Their strong-willed mother, Catherine de Medici, really ruled France in their name.

Catherine came to power at a time when France was deeply divided over religion. Calvinist ministers had made thousands of converts in France. French followers of Calvinism were known as Huguenots (HYOO-guh-nahts). By 1559, about one sixth of France's population was Calvinist.

Most of the major towns and cities in France were divided between Catholics and Huguenots. Intense hatred between the two groups frequently led to violence. Groups attacked each other's churches. Thousands of people were tortured, burned, or beaten to death for their beliefs.

Two ambitious French families further inflamed these religious hatreds. On one side was the House of Bourbon (BOOR-buhn), a family of French nobles who had become Protestants. On the other side was the House of Guise (geez), a noble family who staunchly championed Catholicism. The Bourbon and the Guise families hated each other, and each hoped to overthrow the Valois monarchy and start a dynasty of its own. Between 1562 and 1589, there were nine civil wars between Bourbons and Guises, Huguenots and Catholics.

The worst outbreak of fury began in Paris on August 24, 1572—the date known on the Catholic calendar as St. Bartholomew's Day. With the first light of dawn, Catholic mobs in Paris hunted for Protestant neighbors, dragged them from bed, and murdered them. The massacres spread to other cities and went on for over a month. About 12,000 Huguenots were killed.

The queen mother herself, Catherine de Medici, was largely to blame for the massacre. Catherine was Catholic, but her motives were not religious. Politics concerned her far more than religion. In 1572, she feared she was losing her influence over her weak son, King Charles IX. The Admiral de Coligny (koh-lee-NYEE), a Protestant noble, had become the king's closest adviser. To keep her position as the power behind the throne, she arranged for Coligny to be killed.

At first, the weak king objected to his mother's scheme. Finally, however, he yielded to her browbeating. He shouted in a fit of temper, "I consent. But then you must kill all the Huguenots in France so that none shall be left to reproach me. Kill them all! Kill them all." With Catherine's complete approval, the St. Bartholomew's Day massacre of the Huguenots began. On the same day, a hired killer assassinated Coligny.

The Valois dynasty ended.

After the St. Bartholomew's Day massacre, French politics became even more violent and confused. In 1574, Charles IX died of tuberculosis. His younger brother, Henry III, was destined to be the last Valois king of France. Though Henry reigned for 15 years, he did not rule. Nobody ruled France in these years of civil war.

Just as some German nobles supported Lutheranism to weaken the emperor, some French nobles became Protestants to weaken their Catholic king. Among the upper classes, religion and politics were closely linked.

For a while, it appeared that the Guise family might triumph and place their Catholic duke on the throne. Catholics both inside and outside France rallied around the Guise banner. Spain's Philip II supported the Catholic cause by sending Spanish armies into France. His French ally, the Duke of Guise, marched triumphantly into Paris.

Many French people—Catholics as well as Protestants—were outraged. Had France fought Spain for years only to have Spain handpick France's king? Nationalism began to outweigh religion for some French Catholic leaders. These leaders, known as the *politiques* (poh-lih-TEEKS), wanted peace for France. They wanted a king strong enough to stop the wars that were tearing France apart. The politiques worked for religious toleration and a strong monarchy.

In 1589, Catherine de Medici died. Shortly afterward, King Henry III ordered nine of his soldiers to murder the Catholic Duke of Guise. In revenge, a Dominican friar stabbed the king to death.

Henry IV brought peace.

The heir to the French throne was Prince Henry of Navarre. He was descended from the popular medieval king, Saint Louis (Louis IX). Henry was robust, athletic, and handsome. He soon showed

Catherine de Medici was a patroness of the arts. She initiated the building of a new wing on the Louvre, the construction of the Tuileries, and the building of the chateau at Monceau.

himself to be decisive, fearless in battle, and a clever politician as well. He was the leader of the House of Bourbon and therefore a Huguenot. With the support of both the Protestants and the Catholic politiques, he became the first Bourbon king of France, Henry IV. Yet it took him nine more years of fighting to secure his crown.

Many Catholics, including the people of Paris, still opposed Henry. For the sake of his war-weary country, Henry chose to give up his religion. In 1593, he became a Catholic. Shortly afterward, the Catholics of Paris warmly welcomed him as their king. Explaining his religious turnabout, Henry IV is sometimes quoted as saying: "Paris is well worth a Mass."

In 1598, Henry took another giant step toward healing France's wounds. He declared that the Huguenots could henceforth worship in peace. In every district, Huguenots could set up at least one house of worship. Paris was the only large French city where Protestant worship was strictly banned. This declaration of religious toleration was known as the Edict of Nantes.

Henry devoted the rest of his reign to rebuilding France and restoring its prosperity. "I hope to make France so prosperous," he said, "that every peasant will have chicken in the pot on Sunday." Although chicken dinners remained beyond the reach of most peasants, no other French king had cared so much for the welfare of the common people. Aided by an able finance minister, the Duke of Sully, Henry restored the French monarchy to a strong position. Spanish armies no longer invaded French soil. After a generation of war, most French people welcomed Henry's peace.

Some people, however, hated the compromising spirit of their Bourbon king. In 1610, one such fanatic leaped into the royal carriage and stabbed Henry to death.

Cardinal Richelieu controlled France.

Henry's nine-year-old son, Louis XIII, became the second Bourbon monarch. Louis reigned from 1610 to 1643. Even after he became an adult, Louis XIII lacked the ability and strength of his father. However, he at least had the good sense to turn over the business of government to someone more gifted than himself.

In 1624, Louis appointed a Catholic cardinal named Richelieu (RISH-uh-loo) to be his chief

Richelieu was the power behind the French throne from 1624 to 1642. A shadowy figure, he was sometimes called "the gray eminence."

minister. Richelieu became virtual ruler of France. No statesman in Europe could match the iron will and cunning mind of this lean-faced, hawk-nosed cardinal.

The wily Richelieu devoted himself to two goals: increasing the power of the Bourbon monarchy and making France the strongest state in Europe. He saw three dangers to the French state: (1) the independence of the Huguenot cities, (2) the power of the French nobility, and (3) the

Footnote to History

Richelieu, plagued by ill health, often shunned the hectic social life of the royal court. He retreated to the peace and quiet of his own household and the companionship of his 14 cats.

By persuading the king to banish his own mother from the court, Richelieu demonstrated his control of the country. The king, however, always insisted that Richelieu seek his approval on state matters. Richelieu did, and he was never denied.

encircling armies of the Hapsburgs. He fought relentlessly against all three.

First, Cardinal Richelieu feared a provision in the Edict of Nantes that gave Huguenots the right to fortify their cities. A walled city could defy the king. Indeed, several Huguenot cities had already rebelled, including the stronghold of La Rochelle. In 1627, royal troops besieged La Rochelle and starved it into submission. The loss of La Rochelle and other walled cities was a major setback for French Protestantism. Huguenots continued to worship freely while Richelieu lived, but later even this privilege was revoked.

The French nobles were the next group to lose their privileges under Richelieu. Many were ordered to take down their fortified castles. Richelieu's spies reported those who resisted or plotted against the king. In addition, Richelieu strengthened the powers of government agents to collect taxes and administer justice. These officials, called *intendants,* came from the ranks of the French middle class. They were staunchly loyal to the crown. Thus, the French ruler no longer needed the military and political services of the nobility. For the next 100 years, Bourbon kings would rule France as absolute monarchs, and no nobles would be strong enough to resist.

Richelieu triumphed over the Spanish and Austrian Hapsburgs as well. His successes formed part of the story of the Thirty Years' War (pages 380–381).

French thinkers questioned authority.

As France regained its political power, a new French intellectual movement began as well. The leading French thinkers of the 1500's witnessed France's religious wars with horror. What they saw turned some of them into skeptics (doubters) about the doctrines of all religions. To doubt old ideas, they thought, was the first step toward finding truth. The work of three French writers— François Rabelais (RAB-uh-**LAY**), Michel de Montaigne (mahn-**TAYN**), and René Descartes (day-**KART**)—marked another sharp break from the ideas of the Middle Ages.

Rabelais (1483–1553) François Rabelais was a monk who loved to laugh at human folly. He fled the monastery to pursue a career in medicine. Between 1532 and 1535, he published two satires on European society, *Gargantua* and *Pantagruel.* The comic heroes of these books were keen-witted giants with immense appetites for food and fun. Rabelais ridiculed everything that restricted the human spirit. People, he wrote, should live by one rule: "Do as you wish."

Montaigne (1533–1592) A later writer and thinker, Michel de Montaigne lived during the worst years of the French religious wars. Early in his life, the death of a dear friend caused him overwhelming grief. He shut himself away in his private library and thought deeply about life's meaning.

Montaigne set forth his thoughts in a new form of literature, the essay. An essay is a short written work on a single topic. It usually expresses the personal views of the writer. In his essays, Montaigne told about himself, his lost friend, the meaning of friendship, the books that he loved, the doctors that he shunned, and many other topics.

In the first edition of his *Essays* (published in 1580), Montaigne warned readers that his subject goes no deeper than himself:

> *This is an honest book, reader . . . I want to be seen here in my simple, natural, ordinary fashion, without pose or artifice; for it is myself that I portray. My defects will here be read to the life . . .*

In fact, Montaigne's essays showed him to have more virtues than defects. An admirer once called him "the wisest Frenchman that ever lived."

Descartes (1596–1650) The third important French writer and thinker of this age was René Descartes. Descartes was both a mathematician and a philosopher. In his mathematical writings, he developed the basic ideas of analytic geometry. He also studied optics, astronomy, and natural philosophy in its connections with what is now called psychology.

Descartes is considered the founder of modern philosophy. His most famous work was his *Discourse on Method*, which he wrote as a guide for "seeking truth in the sciences." Descartes believed nothing should be accepted on faith. Everything should be doubted until proved by reason. How could he prove his own existence? Descartes knew himself to be thinking, doubting. The one thing each person knows for certain, wrote Descartes, is, "I think, therefore I am."

Gargantua and Pantagruel appealed to the masses and sold many more copies during Rabelais's lifetime than he ever imagined. His books, however, were placed on the Index of Forbidden Books and for many years could not be published in France.

Define: (a) politiques, (b) intendants, (c) essay
Identify: (a) Valois, (b) Catherine de Medici, (c) Huguenots, (d) Henry IV, (e) Edict of Nantes, (f) Richelieu, (g) Rabelais, (h) Montaigne, (i) Descartes

Answer:

1. (a) What political problems did France face in 1559? (b) How did religion divide the French people?
2. (a) What two noble families wanted to overthrow the Valois? (b) What was the religion of each?
3. (a) How did Catherine de Medici use religious hatreds to maintain her political power? (b) What role did she play in the St. Bartholomew's Day massacre?
4. What were the goals of the politiques?
5. (a) Why did Henry IV change his religion? (b) What did he do to establish religious toleration in France?
6. (a) What were Richelieu's two goals? (b) Why did he fear the Huguenot cities? (c) How did he weaken the French nobles?

Critical Thinking

7. Henry IV defined his own religion this way: "Those who follow their consciences are of my religion, and I am of the religion of those who are brave and good." Why was this a wise political statement for him to make as France's king?
8. Explain why Richelieu is generally considered a politique, even though he was a cardinal in the Catholic Church.

Religious wars split Germany.

5

For a time, the German princes and electors had settled their religious differences by the Peace of Augsburg in 1555 (page 357). They had agreed that the churches in Germany could be either Lutheran or Catholic, but not Calvinist. Furthermore, the prince of every state was to decide the religion of that state.

The Catholic and Lutheran princes of Germany watched each other warily. As tension mounted, the Lutherans joined together in the Protestant Union in 1608. The next year, Catholic princes formed the Catholic League. It would take only a spark to start a war.

Germans fought the Thirty Years' War (1618–1648).

The spark came in 1618. A Protestant mob rioted in the streets of Prague in the Czech kingdom of Bohemia. These Czechs were angry that their king, Ferdinand II, was both a foreigner—a German-speaking Austrian—and an ardent Catholic. Ferdinand was also a leader of the Hapsburg family. (He was a nephew of Charles V, a cousin of Philip II.) In 1619, he became Holy Roman Emperor.

As an Austrian, Ferdinand II aroused the Czechs' national hatred. As a Catholic, he menaced the religious freedom of the Lutheran princes of Germany. As a Hapsburg, he posed a threat to the Bourbon kings of France. Ferdinand's many enemies soon united against him.

In 1618, Ferdinand sent an army into Bohemia to put down the Protestant revolt. Several German Protestant princes took this chance to challenge their Catholic emperor.

Thus began the struggle known as the Thirty Years' War. This war was as confusing as it was vicious. To simplify it, we can divide the Thirty Years' War into two major phases: the phase of Hapsburg triumphs and the phase of Hapsburg defeats.

Between 1618 and 1630, Hapsburg armies from Austria and Spain crushed the troops hired by the Protestant princes. The Czech uprising also failed, and its leaders were executed. In 1625, the king of Denmark entered the war on the Protestant side. On the Catholic side, Ferdinand II hired a ruthless soldier of fortune, Albrecht von Wallenstein. Wallenstein raised an army of 125,000 men. He paid them by allowing them to plunder German villages. Wallenstein's huge armies destroyed everything in their path. By 1629, the Protestant cause in Germany looked weak indeed.

Then the tide of war suddenly shifted as the Protestants found a new leader. In 1630, a tall Swedish king named Gustavus Adolphus landed

Gustavus Adolphus was not only a great general but also a capable adminstrator who did much to develop the natural mineral resources of his country. He was succeeded by his daughter, Christina, 1626–1689.

on the north coast of Germany. With him was a tough, tightly disciplined army of 13,000 men. For two years (1630–1632), Protestant princes rallied around his banner. Gustavus Adolphus outmaneuvered the Hapsburg armies and drove them out of northern Germany. Then Gustavus Adolphus was killed in battle in November 1632. Wallenstein died soon after, murdered by his own officers.

The remaining years of the German war were dominated by Cardinal Richelieu, the power behind the French throne. Richelieu cared nothing that the Hapsburgs were Catholic as he was. He loved France and feared the Hapsburgs, so he brought France into the war on the Protestant side. In 1635, he sent French troops into Germany to join Swedish and German Protestants.

The war dragged on for 13 more years. It left Germany ravaged. The German population sank from 20 million to 13.5 million. Only a small share of these died in battle. Many died of hunger, as armies burned and destroyed the crops. Others died of such diseases as plague, dysentery, and typhus that spread from army camps to the people nearby. Still others simply fled. Whole villages disappeared. Many peasants were forced back into serfdom after marauding armies destroyed their homes. Both trade and agriculture were in a shambles. Germany's economy was ruined.

The Treaty of Westphalia ended the war.

Gradually, the French and their Protestant allies wore down the Austrian Hapsburgs and their Spanish allies. In 1648, Ferdinand II's son (the new Holy Roman Emperor) agreed to a peace treaty that heavily favored his Swedish, French, and Protestant enemies.

The Thirty Years' War ended with the Treaty of Westphalia. These were its major terms:

1. France took Alsace, a fertile strip of land along the west bank of the Rhine River.
2. Sweden took a piece of northern Germany on the North Sea and another piece on the Baltic Sea.
3. The princes of Germany won almost total independence from the Holy Roman Empire. Each German state could sign treaties and go to war without the approval of the emperor.
4. Calvinism gained equal privileges with Lutheranism and Catholicism. A Calvinist prince in Germany could now dictate the religion of his state.
5. The Dutch Republic (or United Provinces) won recognition as an independent state.

The long-term consequences of the treaty were more important than its terms. In effect, Germany lost what little unity it once had. Its 300 states became virtually independent. The Holy Roman Empire, which had earlier held the German princes together, survived only in name.

As the big losers of the Thirty Years' War, the Hapsburg states of Austria and Spain declined in power. As the major winner of the war, France emerged as Europe's strongest state.

Another European nation, England, was fortunate to stay out of the ruinous Thirty Years' War. However, England was going through serious religious and political troubles of its own. England's troubles as well as its growing strength will be described in the next chapter.

Section Review 5

Identify: (a) Ferdinand II, (b) Bohemia, (c) Thirty Years' War, (d) Wallenstein, (e) Gustavus Adolphus, (f) Treaty of Westphalia
Answer:
1. (a) Why did the Protestants of Bohemia riot in 1618? (b) What happened when Ferdinand II tried to put down the revolt?
2. What was the turning point in the Thirty Years' War?
3. Why did France, a Catholic kingdom, join the Protestant side?
4. (a) What were the economic and social effects of the Thirty Years' War on Germany? (b) What was the political effect on German unity?
5. What did each of the following gain from the war? (a) France (b) Sweden (c) Dutch Republic (d) German Calvinists
6. (a) Which powers were the major losers in the war? (b) Which was the major winner?

Critical Thinking
7. Give evidence to support the following statement: The Thirty Years' War was more a political conflict than a religious one.

381

Chapter Review 17

Summary

1. Spain built an overseas empire. Early in the 1500's, Spain began building a vast empire in the Americas. Cortés conquered the Aztecs of Mexico, and Pizarro defeated the Incas of Peru. Explorations by others extended Spain's empire from what is now Kansas to Chile. Spain prospered, and its art and literature flourished.

2. Spain was a Catholic bulwark. At the center of Spain's empire was its emperor, Philip II, who ruled his lands absolutely. Determined to support Catholicism, Philip played a large part in the defeat of the Ottomans at Lepanto. His attempt to invade England with the Armada failed. He also failed to put down a revolt against Spanish rule in the Netherlands. Spain's prosperity, based only on gold and silver from its empire, soon collapsed.

3. The Netherlands won independence. Successful in their revolt against Spain, the Netherlands had a thriving trade and a capitalist economy. The Dutch established a republic in which many religious viewpoints were accepted. The artists of the Netherlands reflected its prosperity and civic spirit.

4. France's crown changed hands. After 1559, France was mired in a series of wars between Catholics and Huguenots as well as a power struggle between the reigning Valois kings and the competing houses of Bourbon and Guise. The civil war ended when Henry IV won the throne, changed his religion to Catholicism, and passed laws granting toleration to both Catholics and Huguenots. The skillful governing of Richelieu, minister to Louis XIII, made the French monarch an absolute ruler. During this era, French thinkers developed new literary forms and laid the basis for modern philosophy.

5. Religious wars split Germany. Germany became more disunited when conflicts between Catholics and Protestants led to the Thirty Years' War. The war caused great suffering in Germany, led to the decline of Hapsburg Spain and Austria, and left France the strongest state in Europe.

Reviewing the Facts

1. Define the following terms:
   a. conquistador
   b. viceroy
   c. inflation
   d. capitalism
2. Explain the importance of each of the following names, dates, places, or terms:
   a. Cortés
   b. Pizarro
   c. encomienda
   d. Philip II
   e. Lepanto
   f. Armada
   g. Cervantes
   h. El Greco

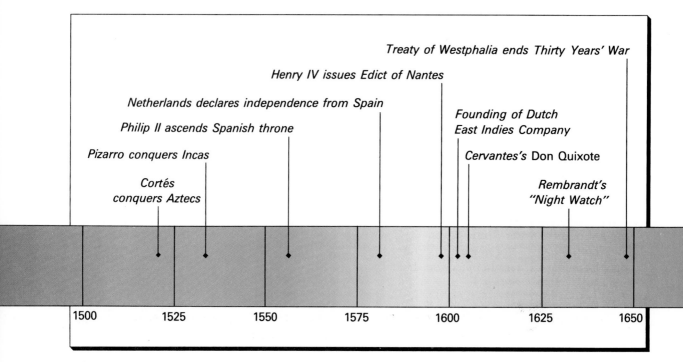

Cortés conquers Aztecs

Pizarro conquers Incas

Philip II ascends Spanish throne

Netherlands declares independence from Spain

Henry IV issues Edict of Nantes

Treaty of Westphalia ends Thirty Years' War

Founding of Dutch East Indies Company

Cervantes's Don Quixote

Rembrandt's "Night Watch"

1500   1525   1550   1575   1600   1625   1650

i. William the Silent q. intendant
j. Rembrandt r. Rabelais
k. Huguenot s. Montaigne
l. Catherine de Medici t. Descartes
m. politique u. 1618–1648
n. Henry IV v. Hapsburg
o. Edict of Nantes w. Treaty of
p. Richelieu Westphalia

3. (a) What was the outcome of Spain's attack on the Ottoman empire? (b) Of the Spanish Armada? (c) Of Spain's war in the Netherlands?
4. What was the Commercial Revolution?
5. (a) How did the Thirty Years' War begin? (b) What were the results of the war?

Basic Skills

1. **Interpreting statistics** Shipments of gold and silver from America to Spain peaked between 1591 and 1600 to a total of 2,707,626,528 grams of silver and 19,451,420 grams of gold. (a) If the value of silver is currently $.23 per gram and the value of gold is $15.00 per gram, what was the value of those shipments of silver and gold by today's standards? (b) Based on information in the chapter, how was most of this wealth used?
2. **Applying a concept** Review the concept of inflation on page 371. (a) As imports of silver and gold increased, what happened to prices in Spain? (b) How was the economy affected?
3. **Using maps** (a) Using the maps on pages 336–337 and 384, identify the parts of the Portuguese empire taken over by the Dutch. (b) What purposes did these territories serve for the Netherlands?

Researching and Reporting Skills

1. **Writing an editorial** Imagine that you are the editor of either an English or a Spanish newspaper at the time of the Spanish Armada. Write an appropriate editorial about the outcome of the battle.
2. **Writing a speech** After seeing examples of their wealth, Cortés was determined to conquer the Aztec, even to sinking his ships so there would be no turning back. Write a speech that Cortés might have made to his men before they attacked the Aztec, inspiring them to fight. What arguments might he have used to urge them to conquer?

Critical Thinking

1. **Comparing** Compare the leadership of Philip II of Spain and Henry IV of France. (a) What were the objectives of each? (b) How well did each succeed? (c) What legacy did each leave to his kingdom?
2. **Analyzing a quotation** A sixteenth-century diplomat summed up the motivation of the conquistadors with the words, "Religion supplies the pretext and gold the motive." (a) Explain the meaning of this quotation. (b) To what extent do you think it accurately describes Spanish conquests in the Americas?
3. **Forming a hypothesis** Spain and Portugal were the two countries that first explored the Americas and staked out empires there. Why were these two countries the leaders? (a) Form a hypothesis to answer this question. (b) Explain your reasoning.
4. **Analyzing economics** (a) What role did interest and profit have in the Commercial Revolution? (b) How did these ideas differ from those of the medieval Church?
5. **Evaluating** (a) List the causes and outcomes of the Thirty Years' War. (b) To what extent did the merit of the causes justify the outcomes? (c) What old problems did the Treaty of Westphalia solve and what new ones did it create?

Perspectives on Past and Present

1. People's values today differ greatly from those at the time of the Spanish conquest. (a) At that time, how was the conquistadors' treatment of the Indians judged? (b) How would it be judged today?
2. During the 1500's, political thinking in France developed in two different directions—one of centralizing authority and the other of questioning authority. What was the outcome for France? Can you think of countries today where this has happened?

Investigating History

Read about the work of one of the artists of the period—such as Velasquez, El Greco, Hals, Vermeer, or Rembrandt. Choose one painting you particularly like. How does it relate to the society of its day and why does it appeal to you?

Unit V Review

Geographic Theme: Movement

How did European civilization spread around the globe?

The age that began with the voyages of Diaz, Columbus, Da Gama, and Magellan saw the spread of European influence around the world. Before 1450, European nations had no direct contact with the Americas, sub-Saharan Africa, and the Far East. Within less than a century, European influence would circle the globe.

The discovery of a sea route to the East and another to the newly discovered continents to the West caused a revolution in trade. Often political control became necessary to gain a monopoly of trade. Nations therefore staked out claims to strategic places and areas for trade.

European ships loaded with goods also carried an unseen export—the culture of their homelands. The governing of colonies was done in the language of the ruler. Colonial laws reflected those of the parent country. Religion too followed the flag. The efforts of French, Spanish, and Portuguese priests spread Catholicism worldwide.

Ideas know no boundaries. Their spread through trade, migration, and conquest is known as *cultural diffusion*. Thus, the expansion of European economic and political power after 1500 brought with it the diffusion of European culture. A Spanish cathedral rose where Tenochtitlán had stood, and Portuguese forts overlooked the trading cities of East Africa.

Often the spread of European thought and traditions overshadowed what was native to a place. Subject peoples everywhere faced the problem of adapting to foreign ways without losing their own culture and traditions.

1. List the overseas lands owned or held by the major European nations in 1650.
2. Using the maps on pages 732, 739, 741, 753, and 772, give the names of those places today.
3. From the information on the map, make a generalization about the influence of European civilization in the seventeenth century. Give examples to illustrate your answer.
4. What ways might subject peoples use to preserve their own culture and traditions?

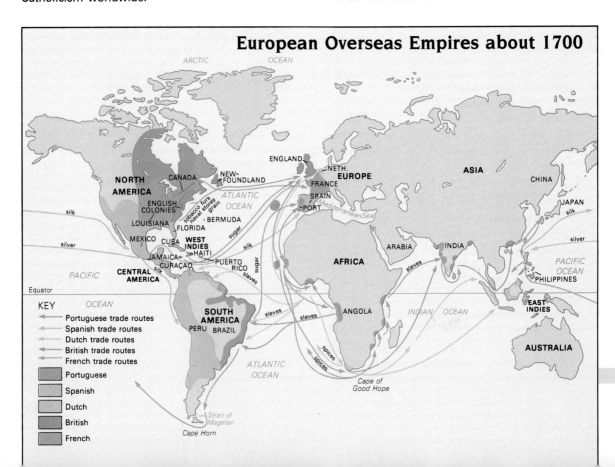

European Overseas Empires about 1700

KEY
- Portuguese trade routes
- Spanish trade routes
- Dutch trade routes
- British trade routes
- French trade routes

- Portuguese
- Spanish
- Dutch
- British
- French

Unit Perspectives

Understanding History

1. Classifying Put each set of terms below in one of the following categories: the Renaissance, the Reformation, the Age of Exploration. Then define each term.
   a. viceroy; conquistador
   b. theocracy; predestination
   c. vernacular; humanist
   d. capitalism; commercial revolution

2. Identifying Tell whether each of the following people was a religious leader, an explorer, or a Renaissance artist. Then describe a major contribution of each person.

   a. Leonardo
   b. Luther
   c. Loyola
   d. Calvin
   e. Cortés
   f. Magellan
   g. Raphael
   h. Knox
   i. Michelangelo
   j. Pizarro
   k. Cervantes
   l. Vespucci

3. Relating Explain how each of the following impacted religion during the 1500's and 1600's.
   a. Act of Supremacy
   b. Council of Trent
   c. Peace of Augsburg
   d. Edict of Nantes
   e. Treaty of Westphalia

Critical Thinking

1. Comparing For each of the following pairs of topics, give one similarity and one difference: (a) Peace of Augsburg and Edict of Nantes; (b) Machiavelli's *Prince* and Richelieu's political actions; (c) Calvinists and Jesuits; (d) Michelangelo and Rembrandt; (f) the contribution to scientific thought of Galileo and Descartes.

2. Synthesizing What were the major characteristics of the Renaissance? (b) Give an example to illustrate each one.

3. Analyzing (a) In what ways was the geographic discovery of new lands related to the Renaissance?

(b) What economic motives encouraged exploration?

4. Inferring How does the golden age of painting in Italy, Spain, and the Netherlands in the fifteenth and sixteenth centuries reflect the values of each society?

5. Inferring (a) What action concerning the Reformation did England, France, and the Holy Roman Empire take? (b) In each case, what was the effect on the monarchy?

6. Comparing Compare the attitudes of merchants in the sixteenth and seventeenth centuries with those of the medieval Church concerning capital, investment, and profit.

7. Evaluating How valid do you consider each of the following statements and why? (a) The Scientific Revolution began with Copernicus. (b) The Renaissance ended with the death of Michelangelo. (c) By 1650, France had become more powerful than Spain.

Making Decisions

Identify one significant decision made by each person listed below. What other options did that person choose not to take? Considering the outcome, do you think the decision was a wise one? (a) Martin Luther, (b) Charles V, (c) Cardinal Richelieu, (d) Galileo

Continuity and Change

1. Unit IV emphasized the isolation of the great civilizations existing on different continents. (a) Looking at the time line for this unit on pages 320–321, how much did that isolation change? (b) What new elements brought about such changes? (c) What far-reaching results might those changes have for future world history?

2. (a) What factors contributed to the growth of national power among most countries of western Europe between 1300 and 1650? (b) How do you think that power will influence events in the next century?

Unit VI

The Transition to Modern Times

Chapters

	1560	1600	1640
Political and Governmental Life	Queen Elizabeth I	**1603–1713** Stuart dynasty rules England	 Louis XIV
Economic and Technological Life	**1570** Drake raids Spanish ships and sails around the world	**1607** England founds Virginia colony **1600** English East India Company founded	**1650's** Inflation ruins Spanish economy
Social and Cultural Life	**1576** First permanent theater is built in London	**1600's** Painting flourishes in Amsterdam	 **1660's** France cultural center of Europe *Rubens'* Autoritratto con Isabella Brandt

etween the Renaissance and the late 1700's, people's ideas about government underwent great change. When the age opened, monarchs in most countries—with the exception of England—ruled with absolute control. In time, some people questioned that power and instead emphasized the values of human reason and liberty. People in America and France rebelled against their rulers. Americans set up a republic, with a Constitution that upheld both law and liberty. Events in France left the outcome there unclear.

1680　　　　　　**1720**　　　　　　**1760**

1689
Glorious Revolution
leads to Bill of Rights

1682
▼ Peter the Great modernizes Russia

1687
Newton discovers
law of gravity

1700's
Parliamentary rule
emerges in England

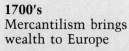

1700's
Mercantilism brings
wealth to Europe

1700's ▲
Age of Enlightenment
brings new ideas

◀**1776**
United States declares
its independence

1795–1814
Napoleon rules France

1768–1779
James Cook explores the Pacific

1776
Adam Smith writes
The Wealth of Nations

1789
Parisian women
march on Versailles
◀

England: Tudor Queen and Stuart Kings

Queen Elizabeth sits in triumph, her hand on the globe. The ships shown in the background symbolize the English victory over the Armada.

Key Terms

joint-stock company
divine right

Read and Understand

1. Elizabeth I faced many challenges.
2. The Elizabethan era was a golden age.
3. England had a civil war.
4. Parliament won political power.

As she rode through the ranks of the cheering soldiers, Elizabeth Tudor planned her speech to stir their fighting spirit. As queen of England, she was their leader, and she bore the fearful responsibility for the crisis that threatened all England.

On this day in August 1588, the Spanish fleet that Philip II called his Invincible Armada was somewhere off the English coast. Everyone knew that the Armada was coming to invade England, but nobody knew when or where it would strike.

An English army of 10,000 men was camped along the Thames River 20 miles east of London to defend their country from the invaders.

Now the queen herself was in the camp, and the soldiers were wildly excited to see their high-spirited, beloved sovereign seated proudly on her white horse. For this special occasion, Elizabeth wore her brightest red wig adorned with two white plumes that were easy for all to see above the soldiers' long pikes.

From her horse, the queen called to her troops, "My loving people!" They stopped their shouts and listened to her words.

My loving people . . . Let tyrants fear! I have always so behaved myself that, under God, I have placed my chiefest strength and safeguard in the loyal hearts and good will of my subjects. Therefore, I am come amongst you . . . being resolved, in the midst and heat of battle, to live or die amongst you all—to lay down for my God, and for my kingdom, and for my people, my honor and my blood even in the dust! I know I have the body of a weak and feeble woman, but I have the heart and [courage] of a king, and a king of England too, and think foul scorn that . . . any prince of Europe should dare to invade the borders of my realm.

As you will read in this chapter, Elizabeth's navy had already destroyed the Spanish Armada, even as she spoke. This stirring victory raised English pride in their nation and their queen to new heights.

Elizabeth I was the last and greatest of the Tudor dynasty. She ruled England for 46 years, from 1558 to 1603. During her reign, daring English captains roamed the seas in search of treasure. English writers, scholars, and poets produced great works of art.

Yet, for all of its glory, the Elizabethan Age was not without troubles. In fact, political and religious conflicts raged frequently. By the end of Elizabeth's reign, England was on the brink of a great crisis. The central question was, Who would rule England—Parliament or the monarch? To answer that question, much English blood was spilled.

This chapter traces English history from Elizabeth's golden age through the troubled reigns of the Stuart kings. Finally, a revolution led to the beginning of a new era with a new philosophy of government.

Elizabeth I faced many challenges.   1

The 25-year-old Elizabeth came to the throne in 1558 at the death of her half-sister, Mary Tudor. Elizabeth was the third of Henry VIII's children to rule England. Like her father, Elizabeth had a fierce temper and a robust nature. Athletic as a girl, she showed amazing energy and strength into her old age.

One courtier who observed Elizabeth closely concluded that she was "more than a man, and (in truth) sometimes less than a woman." At times, she was quite crude. She would spit on the floor and swear in an astonishing manner. When her temper boiled over, she sometimes cuffed an offending courtier with a sharp blow to the head.

The other side of Elizabeth's character was graceful, witty, and refined. Her wardrobe included 2,000 velvet and jewel-encrusted gowns. She composed poetry and strummed a lute. She boasted of being as well-read in the classics as any prince in Europe. She had a scholar's command of Greek and Latin and spoke fluently in French, Italian, and Spanish. Her mind was remarkably quick, and nothing escaped her keen, penetrating eyes. One observer wrote of her:

All her faculties were in motion, and every motion seemed a well-guided action; her eyes were set upon one, her ears listened to another, her judgment ran upon a third, to a fourth she addressed her speech.

Elizabeth understood all too well the widespread prejudice against a woman ruler. All during her reign, Parliament urged her to marry a suitable man, either foreigner or Englishman. Yet she always resisted these pressures for the good of England and the preservation of her own power. Though she had many suitors, she remained unmarried until her death. She was nicknamed the "Virgin Queen."

This gifted queen needed all her intelligence and energy to guide England safely through the troubles of the late 1500's. These troubles came from four directions at once: religious conflicts, a rival queen, Spanish ambitions, and financial difficulties.

During Mary Tudor's reign, Elizabeth became the target of complex plots. She was imprisoned in the Tower of London, accused of involvement in a rebellion. These early experiences taught Elizabeth to guard her thoughts and measure every word.

Religious issues divided England.

Elizabeth inherited the religious problem from her father, King Henry VIII. Henry had broken with the papacy in 1534 (page 351). In that year, he had persuaded Parliament to enact a law that made him, not the pope, head of the Church of England.

Since then, royal policy on religion had changed directions several times. Protestantism gained strength under Elizabeth's young half-brother, Edward VI (1547–1553). Then, her half-sister, Mary Tudor (1553–1558), made every effort to return the country to Catholicism. At first, no one knew which religion Elizabeth would choose. After all, she had been Protestant when Edward ruled and Catholic during Mary's reign.

When Elizabeth came to power, she knew she could not hope to satisfy either the extreme Catholics or the extreme Protestants. She decided, therefore, to establish a state church that moderate Catholics and moderate Protestants might both accept, however grudgingly.

In 1559, the first Parliament of Elizabeth's reign granted her request for two religious laws. The first, the Act of Uniformity, set up a national church much like the one under Henry VIII. This was to be the only legal church in England. People were required to attend its services or pay a fine. The second law, a new Act of Supremacy, declared Elizabeth the Supreme Governor of England's institutions, its church as well as its state.

As a concession to Protestants, priests in the Church of England were allowed to marry and to deliver sermons in English, not Latin. As a concession to Catholics, the Church of England kept all the trappings of a formal priesthood such as rich robes and golden crucifixes. To avoid controversy over doctrine, the wording of the queen's Book of Common Prayer was intentionally vague.

What mattered most to Elizabeth was not the religious beliefs of her subjects but their loyalty and obedience. She wanted no religious wars in England. It was not her intention, she said, "to pry windows into men's souls." Even so, during her long reign, Elizabeth ordered several dozen people burned at the stake for openly defying the official religion.

Catholics were unhappy with the Protestant aspects of the new Church of England. Still, it was more than ten years before the pope took action against Elizabeth by excommunicating her. That he waited so long was partly a tribute to the moderation of Elizabeth's policies.

Mary Stuart plotted against Elizabeth.

Outside England, devout Catholics looked for a champion to overthrow the Protestant queen. They found such a champion in Mary Stuart, Queen of Scots, Elizabeth's Catholic cousin.

In the 1560's, England and Scotland were separate kingdoms ruled by female cousins, Elizabeth Tudor in England and Mary Stuart in Scotland. As the great-granddaughter of England's Henry VII, Mary Stuart had a good claim to the English throne. She hoped some day to be England's queen as well as Scotland's.

French, Spanish, and Irish Catholics, and even the pope himself actively supported Mary in her quest to unseat Elizabeth. In fact, Mary received more support from these outsiders than she did from her own Scottish subjects. The Scots were fast converting to the Presbyterian creed preached by John Knox (page 354).

In 1567, an army of Scottish Presbyterians rose in revolt against Mary. To escape, Mary was forced to flee south to England. She thus placed herself at Elizabeth's mercy. For 20 years, Mary lived as part guest and part prisoner at an English estate set aside for her use.

Even as a prisoner, Mary could not rid herself of the itch for power. She foolishly became the center of some Catholic plots to overthrow Elizabeth. Finally, English spies intercepted a message from Mary agreeing to a scheme for murdering Elizabeth. The letter sealed her fate.

Elizabeth ordered Mary beheaded in 1587. Mary went to her death in a robe of black satin and a bodice of crimson velvet. English Protestants lit bonfires of celebration when they heard that the ax had fallen. Elizabeth, however, wept at the thought of having shed the blood of a cousin and fellow queen.

Philip of Spain threatened England.

When Mary Queen of Scots died, Philip II of Spain also grieved but for a different reason. He had been one of Mary's strongest supporters in

Time after time, Elizabeth looked for a way to avoid having Mary put to death. Even after reluctantly signing the death warrant, she postponed its delivery. Finally royal aides did what she could not and delivered the warrant for Mary's death.

her bid for the throne. With Mary's death, relations between England and Spain reached their lowest point.

The marriage question When Elizabeth first came to the throne in 1558, Philip II had seemed to be her ally. In those days, Philip had been more concerned with the power of Catholic France than with the threat of Protestant England. Moreover, he had been Elizabeth's brother-in-law, the husband of Mary Tudor. After Mary's death, Philip let it be known that he hoped to marry Elizabeth.

Elizabeth deliberately kept Philip (and dozens of other suitors) waiting. In fact, Elizabeth never had any intention of marrying Philip. She charmed, dazzled, and raised hopes in first one king or prince and then another. She used the hopes of a marriage to win diplomatic advantages with many European countries. Eventually, it became clear to all that the strong-willed sovereign would not marry anyone.

Drake and the sea dogs After Elizabeth turned down Philip as a husband, relations between England and Spain grew cool. By the 1570's, the two countries were enemies.

While still pretending friendship for Philip, Elizabeth secretly encouraged English adventurers to attack Spanish treasure fleets. These fleets sailed regularly from the Americas to Spain with rich cargoes of gold and silver. The bold English captains who raided them were known as "sea dogs." To the Spanish, they were simply pirates.

The greatest of the sea dogs was Francis Drake. On his most daring expedition (1577–1580), Drake raided Spanish ships in the Caribbean and along the eastern coast of South America. Then he did what no English captain had done before. He sailed through the Strait of Magellan around the tip of South America and captured Spanish treasure along the coast of Chile and Peru as well. From there, Drake sailed as far north as San Francisco Bay, crossed the Pacific Ocean, and returned triumphantly home with stolen prizes valued at 600,000 pounds. (This sum was more than twice the *yearly* revenue of the English crown.)

Drake thus became the first person since Magellan's crew to sail around the world. Instead of apologizing to Spain for his piracies, Queen Elizabeth knighted him aboard his ship, the *Golden Hind.*

The Armada In the 1580's, Elizabeth further angered Philip by aiding Dutch Protestants in their revolt against Catholic Spain (page 369). Elizabeth's decision to execute Mary Queen of Scots was the final straw, provoking Philip to wage war against England.

In 1588, Philip struck. He assembled a fleet of 130 ships with more than 31,000 men. This Invincible Armada, as Philip called it, sailed for

Economics in Daily Life · A *Share* in Trade

Queen Elizabeth recognized the growing importance of trade. She granted charters to a number of trading companies. These companies were organized as joint stock companies, a new form of business. Unlike Dutch companies, which were based on the merchants who did the actual trading, the English companies were based on the capital that was invested. By investing money in the company, anyone could obtain a share of ownership and receive a share of the profits. Drake's around-the-world voyage was a joint stock venture in which the queen herself owned shares. Most investors, however, came from the urban middle class.

The greatest of the joint stock companies was the East India Company, chartered in 1600. Although its main purpose was trade, it provided the foundation for the growth of British power in India.

A Spanish ship from the Armada (left) turns its guns on an English ship. In the distance, five English fireships drift toward the Spanish fleet.

England. In late July, it boldly entered the English Channel.

Warily keeping their distance, the English captains—including Sir Francis Drake—set fire to a few of their own ships. Winds and currents carried the burning ships into the closed ranks of the Armada. To avoid these blazing hazards, the Spanish broke up their tight formation.

Now the smaller, faster English ships with their better guns began pounding the giant Spanish ships. As guns boomed and masts broke, a furious storm came up and scattered the damaged Armada. The Spanish commander decided to give up the invasion and run for home. However, more storms wrecked many of his ships. Barely half the Invincible Armada made it back to Spain.

Elizabeth had financial problems.

Another problem for Elizabeth was money. The yearly income of the English ruler was about 200,000 pounds. This was a meager sum indeed compared to the tons of gold collected by her rival, Philip II. The House of Commons always balked at a ruler's request for new taxes. How then was the queen to find enough money for the costly business of defending her country?

Elizabeth was, first of all, extremely tight-fisted. Soldiers in her army had cause to grumble about their poor wages and lack of supplies. The queen was always generous with her compliments but stingy with her cash.

Much of Spain's wealth came, as the English knew well, from its American colonies. England had played little part in the early voyages of exploration. In the late 1500's, however, the English began to think about building an American empire of their own.

Who had the funds to support such a venture? Certainly the queen did not, nor did a single merchant or even a partnership of merchants. Instead, English business leaders set up a special organization to attract capital from many people. It was known as the **joint-stock company**.

Investors in a joint-stock company bought shares of ownership. If the company went bankrupt, its owners lost the money they had invested. If the company prospered, the investors' shares

The more secular world of the English is reflected in the names of their ships against the Armada: *Lion, Tiger, Dreadnought,* and *Revenge.* The Spanish, in contrast, were depending on the grace of God: *San Mateo, San Cristobal,* and so on.

of ownership entitled them to collect a proportional share of the profits. (Drake's voyage around the world in 1577 was a joint-stock enterprise that returned a 4,600 percent profit to its stockholders.) The joint-stock company was a sign that the Commercial Revolution (page 373) that began in the Netherlands had spread to England.

In 1589, a London merchant named Sir Thomas Smyth began to organize a company to settle the part of North America known as Virginia (named in honor of the Virgin Queen). The continuing threat of war with Spain, however, delayed such plans. Not until after Elizabeth's death did the English found permanent colonies in North America.

The most successful of England's joint-stock companies received its charter from the queen in 1600. Known as the English East India Company, its ambitious goal was to carve out a share of the rich East Indies spice trade.

Among the company's 101 owners were a London ironmonger, a vintner, and a leather seller, each of whom invested 200 pounds in the venture. They and their fellow owners waited through three suspenseful years before the company's four ships returned from the East Indies. As hoped, the ships carried tons of pepper, cloves, and other spices. In its first 21 years of business, the East India Company increased its capital 50 times over. Its owners became rich beyond their wildest imaginings.

While such ventures did not enrich the queen directly, they strengthened England economically. Moreover, the deeds of the sea dogs and the merchants weakened Spain at minimum cost to Elizabeth. Nonetheless, the queen's constant need for money would carry over into the next reign and lead to bitter conflict between the monarch and Parliament.

Parliament began to assert itself.

Toward the end of Elizabeth's reign, conflicts between Elizabeth and Parliament arose more and more often. Her religious compromise, which had kept peace for so many years, was no longer satisfactory. The people who objected most strongly were Puritans—men and women who wished to purify the Church of England of practices that they thought were too close to Catholicism. Puritans hated to see gold crucifixes

at the altar and bishops dressed in richly ornamented robes.

The Puritans were a minority in the English population, but they were active in politics. When Parliament met, they formed a strong group in the lower house, the House of Commons. Puritan members of Parliament were outspoken in their demands for changes in the Church of England. Their bold speeches and petitions sent the queen into a towering rage. The rituals and organization of the church, she said, were her business. She wanted no suggestions about it from Commons.

Puritans were not the only outspoken members of Parliament. Others in Commons also wanted to be heard. Elizabeth, however, would have none of it. Instead, she left her successor, James I, a legacy of doubt and resentment. The question of who would rule England was yet to be resolved.

Section Review 1

Define: joint-stock company
Identify: (a) Elizabeth I, (b) Act of Uniformity, (c) Act of Supremacy, (d) Mary Stuart, (e) Philip II, (f) Francis Drake, (g) Armada, (h) Virginia, (i) English East India Company, (j) Puritan
Answer:
1. (a) Describe the religious problem that Elizabeth inherited from her father. (b) How did Elizabeth deal with the problem at the beginning of her reign?
2. (a) What threat did Mary Stuart pose to Elizabeth? (b) How did Elizabeth deal with that threat?
3. How did each of the following contribute to worsening relations between England and Spain? (a) English sea dogs (b) Dutch Protestants (c) Mary Stuart
4. What solution helped Elizabeth ease England's financial problems?
5. (a) Why did some members of Parliament begin demanding changes in policy? (b) How did Elizabeth respond?

Critical Thinking
6. Despite the advice of her councilors, Elizabeth chose never to marry. From a political point of view, do you think her decision strengthened or weakened her position as queen? Why?

393

Church spires formed the skyline of Elizabethan London. The grandest was St. Paul's, the large building at the top left. The Globe Theater and the Bear

The Elizabethan era was a golden age.

2

For England, the defeat of the Armada produced a burst of pride and self-confidence. The late 1500's became a golden age economically, politically, and culturally. The center of this age was England's greatest city, London.

London was a bustling city.

In 1588, the year of the Spanish Armada, London was the most populous city in Europe. There were probably 200,000 Londoners who celebrated Sir Francis Drake's exploits. More than most cities at the time, London was densely populated and hummed with activity. Its medieval walls enclosed a space of only one square mile. Within that square mile, houses were so close together that neighbors could reach out their second-story windows and shake hands across the narrow streets.

Velvet-clad merchants dominated the commercial life of the city. However, they daily rubbed elbows with swarming masses of ragged poor.

Standing in the doorways of their little shops, sellers of odds and ends would yell at a well-dressed man or woman: "What do you lack?"

That was a standard cry heard by everyone throughout the city.

Another constant sound was the roar of the Thames River as it rushed through the great stone arches of London Bridge. This famous bridge spanned the river for 350 yards at one of its roughest parts. "The bridge at London," wrote one Englishman, "is worthily to be numbered among the miracles of the world."

The crowds passing over the bridge heard the water below but could not see it. Blocking their view were rows of shops and houses built right on top of the bridge. Like every other part of London, the bridge was a place of commerce.

The character of the city during its golden years was at once elegant and raw. We can best see this by observing a few of the many ways Londoners earned a living.

Boaters Because the streets of London were clogged with carts and crowds, the fastest way through the city was the Thames. Boaters waited along each bank of the Thames to offer rides, much as taxi drivers do today. Passengers in a hurry might order the boater to take a chance and shoot the rapids under London Bridge. More prudent souls heeded the old proverb: "London Bridge was made for wise men to walk over and fools to go under."

Water carriers In the days before pipes and plumbing, water carriers were a common sight

394

The Elizabethan age was a time of change for London. The growth of overseas trade brought new wealth to the city. During this time the first public theaters appeared, built in the suburbs to keep their noise outside the city.

Garden, octagonal buildings, stood on the south side of the Thames. Above the gate to London Bridge, traitors' heads were displayed on pikes.

on city streets. Of course, only the well-to-do could afford to hire water carriers or "cogs" to bring fresh water to their homes. The poor went out to the city wells and the river to carry home their own water.

Because even the homes of the wealthy lacked plumbing, buckets were stashed in dark, closetlike rooms to collect human waste. Though there was a law against it, the buckets were usually emptied out the front door. A more sanitary contrivance, the flush toilet, was invented in 1596, but only the queen and a few others had such a luxury.

Cappers Those who followed the hat-making trade were popularly known as cappers. To keep cappers in business, the government of London passed a law in 1571 requiring that everyone over seven years of age wear a hat on Sundays and other holidays. The law was designed to prevent masses of idle cappers from rioting.

Barbers The barbers of London did a nice business catering to English gentlemen. The style of a Londoner's hair and beard received as much attention as his brightly colored doublets, stockings, hats, gloves, and knee-breeches. A writer of the period has left us this picture of the beard-trimmer's art:

And therefore if a man have a lean and straight face, a Marquess Otto's cut will make it broad and large; if it be platterlike,

a long, slender beard will make it seem the narrower; if he be weaselbeaked, then much hair left on the cheeks will make the owner look big like a bowdled hen and so grim as a goose.

Rogues and vagabonds Lacking an honest trade, many young Londoners fell into a life of crime. Lurking everywhere on London's streets were the coneycatcher, the nip, the foist, the wild rogue, the ruffler, and the angler. These were just some of the nicknames for the city's horde of petty criminals. Each name indicated a special branch of thievery.

The angler, for example, literally fished for stolen goods. Attaching a hook to the end of a long pole, the thief would stick the pole through a victim's window and then pull out whatever it caught. One angler was said to have stripped the bedclothes right from under the nose of a snoring man.

Jailers and executioners The many criminals of London gave employment to jailers and executioners. Petty thieves, for example, were normally punished by painful mutilation. A judge might tell the jailer either to cut off the thief's right ear or to brand it with a red-hot iron. Executioners also had much to do, because there were 200 crimes in Elizabethan England that were punishable by death. Some 800 English citizens were hanged every year.

There may have been as many as 10,000 vagabonds in England during this period. What to do with this poor fraternity was a problem that plagued the cities. During Elizabeth's reign, the first law recognizing that the poor were a public responsibility was passed.

Shakespeare wrote drama and poetry.

Nowhere in England could one see a greater variety of people—both high and low—than in London. Watching this pageant of human life was a man who became a master at revealing human nature in all its forms: the good and the evil, the wise and the foolish, the gentle and the terrible. No one better symbolizes England's golden age of literature than the poet and dramatist William Shakespeare. Many people regard him as the greatest writer of all time.

William Shakespeare was born in 1564 in Stratford-upon-Avon, a small town about 75 miles northwest of London. He spent an unremarkable childhood in this little town, attending grammar school with other boys and taking part in some of the town's lively fairs and pageants. At the age of 18, Will married Anne Hathaway. Records show that by 1592 he and Anne and their three children were living in London. It was in London that Shakespeare displayed his great genius both as a poet and a playwright.

It is difficult to define Shakespeare's genius. To some, it lies in his remarkable understanding of human nature. William Shakespeare revealed the souls of men and women brilliantly in scenes of dramatic conflict. However, Shakespeare was more than a skilled observer of human nature. He was also a poet who understood the sound and weight of every word. These lines from the tragedy *Macbeth* show Macbeth's despair:

> *Tomorrow and tomorrow and tomorrow*
> *Creeps in this petty pace from day to day*
> *To the last syllable of recorded time*
> *And all our yesterdays have lighted fools*
> *the way to dusty death.*

The theater was popular in London.

English people enjoyed plays and drama long before William Shakespeare. As early as the Middle Ages, companies of actors traveled from town to town, performing in the courtyards of inns. The inn's guests watched from upper windows, either hooting or applauding the performance.

There were no fixed stages or theaters until 1576. In that year, an enterprising actor named James Burbage built the first permanent playhouse just outside the walls of London. He called it simply "The Theater." Londoners quickly got

William Shakespeare (1564–1616) wrote 38 plays, including Hamlet, Othello, *and* Romeo and Juliet.

into the habit of packing the house every afternoon. (Evening shows were impossible because audiences could not see actors by moonlight.)

The number of theaters in England grew rapidly. In 1599, Richard and Cuthbert Burbage (sons of James) built the Globe Theater about half a mile from London Bridge. The Globe soon became home to a company of actors, one of whom was Shakespeare.

Shakespeare's most famous plays were first performed at the Globe. As in other theaters of the day, the audience sat around a central yard that was open to the sky. A wooden platform or stage jutted out into this yard, and a curtain

Footnote to History

Shakespeare invented new words and used old words in new ways. Among the more than 1,700 words that he was first to use are *bump, courtship, critic, dwindle, gnarled, hurry, lonely, majestic,* and *road.* It is hard to imagine English without them!

In addition to his greatness, Shakespeare had good circumstances for fame: by 1592, virtually all the other famous playwrights of the time—Marlowe, Greene, Kyd, Lodge, and Peele—had either died or given up writing for the stage.

This drawing shows the stage areas and seating galleries of the Globe Theater. No picture exists of the original Globe, which burned in 1613.

was placed at the back of it (not in front as in modern theaters). Actors performed scenes in three places: on the main stage, in a space behind the drawn curtain, and on a balcony above the stage. Thus, as one scene ended on the balcony, the next could begin immediately on the main stage. There was no painted scenery, but actors used a great variety of props, including swords, cannon, cages, live animals, and artificial heads.

The Globe seated about 2,300 people. For a penny, one could sit or stand on the ground itself as a so-called groundling. For two or three pennies, one was admitted to the sheltered galleries three stories high that encircled the yard. Those who came to the theater to show off their fine clothes and good looks could be seated on the stage itself. Of course, such seats cost more.

Shakespeare's plays were written during the reigns of two English monarchs, Elizabeth I and her successor, James I. Shakespeare died in 1616. His friend and fellow playwright, Ben Jonson, said of him: "He was not of an age, but for all time."

Section Review 2

Identify: (a) London, (b) William Shakespeare, (c) James Burbage, (d) Globe Theater
Answer:
1. How do do each of the following livelihoods reflect the character of London during the mid-1500's? (a) boater (b) water carrier (c) capper (d) barber (e) rogue (f) jailer

In 1613, a cannon was set off in the Globe during a play. A spark from it landed in the thatched roof of the gallery, setting the straw on fire. In less than an hour, the theater had burned to the ground. Although it was rebuilt within a year, the Globe was pulled down in 1644 when the Puritans closed all theaters.

2. Why do many scholars consider William Shakespeare the greatest English writer of all time?
3. Describe the stage and seating arrangements of an Elizabethan theater.

Critical Thinking

4. What did Ben Jonson mean when he wrote, "He [Shakespeare] was not of an age, but for all time"?

England had a civil war.

3

On a cold day in March 1603, the reign of Queen Elizabeth I quietly came to an end. Elizabeth was dead at the age of 69. Never having married, she left no child to inherit her throne. The Tudor dynasty died with her.

Elizabeth's nearest relative was her Scottish cousin, James Stuart. James was the only son of Mary Stuart, whom Elizabeth had executed for treason 16 years earlier. James Stuart was already King James VI of Scotland when Elizabeth died. In 1603, he became King James I of England as well. Although England and Scotland remained separate countries for another 100 years, they now shared the same king.

James I clashed with Parliament.

With the throne, James inherited all the unsettled problems of Elizabeth's reign. Key among these was the question of how much say Parliament would have in governing England.

As king, James believed he had absolute authority to govern England as he saw fit. Royal authority, James declared, came directly from God, and kings were answerable only to God, not to the people or Parliament. This theory that royal power came from God is called the **divine right** of kings.

Elizabeth too had believed in her divine right to rule, but Elizabeth had had more tact than James. Often, she flattered Parliament in an attempt to get her way. James had no such tact. In addition, Parliament was growing impatient. It was an explosive combination.

Quarrels with Parliament James's worst struggles with Parliament revolved around money. Despite Elizabeth's frugal habits, she had left behind a sizable debt. James needed money, and Parliament had no desire to give it to him. James's manner with Parliament did not help. He felt it was beneath his dignity to bargain over money.

Puritan members of Parliament were especially offended by their new Stuart king. They complained that the Church of England was too Catholic. They urged James to make major changes in church rituals. The king angrily refused. Like Elizabeth, he insisted that the Church was strictly the ruler's business, not Parliament's.

The King James Bible Indeed, James was very interested in religion, and scholarship was his great strength. It bothered him that although there were many translations of the Bible, none was fully satisfying. Therefore, he gave to several committees of Bible scholars the task of creating a single authoritative text. The new version of the Bible was first printed in 1611. As befits a book produced in the age of Shakespeare, the King James Bible is noted for the elegance and power of its language. The King James Bible is still read by millions of English-speaking Protestants throughout the world.

The English founded American colonies.

Another achievement of James's troubled reign was the founding of the first permanent English colonies in North America. In 1604, James concluded a peace treaty with Spain. As a result, English joint-stock companies could go ahead with their plans for colonies without fearing that the Spanish would attack their settlements.

James granted a charter to the Virginia Company in 1606. The first English settlers arrived in Virginia in 1607 and named their community Jamestown in honor of their king. The colony was a disaster for these newcomers. Four out of every five died of hunger, disease, or Indian attacks.

Jamestown was also a financial disaster for its English backers. Far from winning profits, the company's organizers had to put more and more money into the venture to keep the colony going. In 1624, the London investors finally gave up. They turned over Virginia to the king's rule.

On her deathbed, Elizabeth confirmed James's succession to the throne: "Who should that be," she said, "but our cousin of Scotland?"

Looking at economics In 1629, Charles II granted a charter to the Massachusetts Bay Company to settle and trade in America. In time, it became the basis for a colonial constitution. A portion of the charter is shown above.

Nonetheless, the colonists in North America did not give up. Despite untold sufferings, they had gained a foothold in their new land. Other English settlers soon followed. Settlements began at Plymouth and Boston in Massachusetts.

By the end of Stuart times, England controlled much of the Atlantic coast of what is now the United States. English explorers had also claimed much of Canada. A rival power, France, was also building its power in North America. These developments set the stage for later conflicts between France and England.

The policies of Charles I led to war.

In 1625, James I died. His son, Charles I, became the second Stuart king to rule England. He inherited his father's problems with Parliament and made them even worse.

Charles was a firm believer in the divine right of kings. He had courage and intelligence. Like his father, however, he had too much pride and not enough common sense. Also like his father, he was always in need of money. As a result, the king and Parliament clashed constantly.

In 1626, a costly war with Spain forced Charles to go to Parliament for money. When Parliament refused to grant him the needed funds, Charles responded by dismissing it. The following year, the country became involved with a war with France as well as Spain. To pay for the war, Charles demanded forced loans from knights and nobles. He promptly imprisoned those who refused to pay. He also quartered troops in private homes at the homeowners' expense.

By 1628, financial needs forced the king to call Parliament again. Parliament, however, had had enough. It refused to grant Charles any money unless he signed a document that was known as the Petition of Right. In this document, the king made the following concessions:

1. He would not imprison subjects without due cause.
2. He would not force loans or levy taxes without the consent of Parliament.
3. He would not house soldiers in private homes without the owner's consent.
4. He would not impose martial law in peacetime.

The next year, weary of dealing with Parliament, Charles dissolved it. For the next 11 years, from 1629 to 1640, he refused to call Parliament at all. During these years, the king resorted to all kinds of fees and fines on the English people to raise money. His unpopularity grew greater every year.

England reached the brink of war.

Although Charles's taxation policies enraged the English people, it was his religious policies that eventually cost him his head. During his reign, thousands of Puritans fled England to escape persecution. Worse still, Charles chose William Laud to be archbishop and lead the Church of England. In truth, Laud was a staunch Protestant. However, his love of ceremonies and rich robes was so great that many Puritans thought he might be a secret Catholic.

In 1639, Laud foolishly decided to force Charles's Presbyterian subjects in Scotland to follow the Church of England's style of worship. To defend their religion, the Scots gathered a huge army and threatened to invade England.

Charles needed money to meet this danger —money he could get only from Parliament.

One historian said: James I had "a genius for getting into difficulties, but was not without a certain shrewdness in stopping just short of catastrophe. If he steered the ship straight for the rocks, he left his son to wreck it."

Between gritted teeth, he called a new Parliament. It turned out to be a mistake for the king.

Throughout the autumn of 1641, Parliament passed laws to limit the king's power. Charles was furious. In January 1642, he decided to take drastic action. Accompanied by 400 swordsmen, he strode into the House of Commons and demanded the arrest of five of its leaders. Alerted ahead of time, the men had escaped and were hiding in London. "I see that the birds are flown," said the embarrassed king as he stomped from the House.

News of the king's action angered Londoners. A mob raged outside Charles's palace. The city was now too dangerous for the king. He abandoned it and raised an army in lands in the north where people were still loyal to him.

Cavaliers and Roundheads fought a civil war.

The king's flight to the north in 1642 marked the beginning of the English civil war. Two groups of English people squared off to fight.

Those who remained loyal to King Charles were known as Royalists or *Cavaliers*. (The term was an insult because it was linked to the Spanish *cavaliero*, suggesting that a person was a Spanish sympathizer.) In general, the Cavaliers included English nobles and church officials.

On the other side were the Puritan townspeople and merchants who supported Parliament. Puritans cropped their hair short over their ears, instead of wearing it long and curled as the fashionable Cavaliers did. For this reason, Cavaliers mockingly called the Puritans *Roundheads*.

A Roundhead soldier summed up the issues this way:

The question in dispute between the King's party and us was whether the King should govern as a god by his will, and the nation be governed by force like beasts; or whether the people should be governed by laws made by themselves and live under a Government derived from their own consent.

At first, the Cavaliers held the advantage, controlling about three fourths of the country. They also had most of England's experienced military leaders. However, Parliament had great financial resources on which to draw. All the Puritans

needed was a general who could win, and by 1644, they had found a military genius—Oliver Cromwell.

Cromwell was a country gentleman who had served in the House of Commons. Now he organized an army of zealous Protestants and inspired each soldier with the thought that God favored the Roundheads. "Truly," said Cromwell to his troops, "I think he that prays best will fight best." His military machine was called the New Model Army.

At first, most English people went on with their lives, untouched by the civil war. As the war dragged on, however, more and more villages were destroyed, more crops were ruined, and more hatreds were aroused. By the end of the war, 100,000 people had died in battle. The hatreds and the sufferings of the war had made people on both sides much more radical in their ideas than they had been at the beginning.

In 1646, Cromwell's New Model Army defeated the king's forces. Charles himself was a prisoner in Scotland. It seemed that Parliament had won, but the fighting was not over.

In 1647, Parliament tried to dissolve the New Model Army, but the army refused to obey. The army and its leaders were much more strongly Puritan and much more radical politically than members of Parliament. The army did not intend to give up control of the country.

In desperation, some members of Parliament joined forces with the king. Cromwell defeated them and captured Charles in August 1648. Then, Cromwell and his army marched into London and surrounded Parliament. Army leaders ordered the expulsion of 143 members of the House of Commons.

In 1649, Cromwell and the Puritans brought Charles to trial for treason. The king listened as the sentence of death was read aloud. Parliament's makeshift court declared, "Charles Stuart, as tyrant, traitor, murderer, and public enemy to the good people of this nation, shall be put to death by the severing of his head from his body."

The execution was set for Sunday, January 30, 1649. It was a cold day. As Charles was dressing, he asked his attendant to bring him an extra shirt to wear. He did not wish to tremble from the cold, he said, and have people think he was afraid. He went calmly to the place of execution,

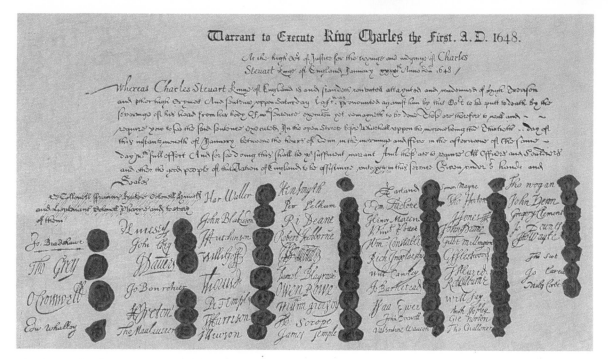

Charles I's death warrant, signed by 59 Puritans, accused him of treason.

laid his head on the block, and himself gave the signal to the headsman.

The execution of Charles was revolutionary. Kings had often been overthrown, killed in battle, assassinated, or put to death in secret. Never before, however, had a monarch faced a public trial and an official execution.

Cromwell ruled as military dictator.

With the king gone, Oliver Cromwell now held the reins of power. Of Parliament's original members, only a few remained. They had lost the respect of the nation and the army. In 1653, Cromwell announced to them, "You are no Parliament, I say you are no Parliament, and I will put an end to your sitting." His soldiers then drove the members out of the building.

To set up a new government, in 1653 Cromwell drafted a constitution, the first written constitution of a major European nation. This constitution set up a republic in which Cromwell ruled England as Lord Protector. In fact, his protectorate was little more than a military dictatorship, thinly disguised by talk of English liberty.

Now that the Puritans were in power, they set about reforming English society. Puritan laws shut down theaters and forbade sporting events. Under Cromwell, merrymaking and amusement became illegal. Many English people bitterly resented the Puritan dictatorship.

The conquest of Ireland Harsh as Cromwell's policies were in England, they were far harsher in Ireland. The island of Ireland had fallen under English rule during the reign of Henry VIII, but the Irish rebelled frequently against their English overlords. Elizabeth, James, and Charles each faced the problem of putting down Irish revolts.

After Charles was beheaded, the Irish rose again. In August 1649, Cromwell himself landed on Irish shores with a Protestant army. The English laid siege to the town of Drogheda. When it fell, Cromwell's army put all of its 9,000 inhabitants to the sword. They took special satisfaction in killing the town's Catholic priests and friars.

The Irish suffered more than a single massacre. Their lands and homes were taken from them and given to English soldiers as spoils of conquest. Several counties were set aside as strictly English property, and all Irish families who lived there were driven out. The general misery and homelessness took a frightful toll. One scholar estimates that 616,000 Irish, nearly half the island's population, perished from famine and plague between 1641 and 1652.

The death of Cromwell Oliver Cromwell ruled until his death in 1658. Next, his son Richard briefly held the title of Lord Protector. However,

Cromwell's view on religious toleration is expressed in the following words: "Notions will hurt none but them that have them." Ask students to compare this view with the actions the army took under Cromwell's direction.

401

Richard did not command the same respect as his father. His enemies laughed at him behind his back, calling him "Tumbledown Dick." The army deserted him. The English people, even many Puritans, yearned for the days when their government was headed by a king.

Section Review 3

Define: divine right
Identify: (a) James I, (b) King James Bible, (c) Jamestown, (d) Charles I, (e) Petition of Right, (f) William Laud, (g) Cavalier, (h) Roundhead, (i) Oliver Cromwell, (j) New Model Army
Answer:
1. (a) Why did James I clash with Parliament? (b) Name two things that he achieved during his reign despite such clashes.
2. (a) Why did Charles I clash with Parliament? (b) Why did he agree to sign the Petition of Right?
3. (a) What action of Archbishop Laud led to a confrontation between the king and Parliament? (b) What event marked the beginning of civil war?
4. (a) What two groups opposed each other during the war? (b) Over what issue did they fight?
5. (a) Who took control of England after the king's death? (b) Describe life for the English and Irish under his rule.

Critical Thinking
6. How do you think the death of Charles I affected other European monarchs who believed as he did in the divine right of kings? What advice would you give those monarchs?

Parliament won political power.

4

In 1659, an army general named George Monck decided the time had come for the English people to restore the monarchy. He marched into London and recalled Parliament. To no one's surprise, Parliament promptly voted to bring back a Stuart to rule England.

Charles II restored the monarchy.

Parliament invited Prince Charles Stuart, the elder son of Charles I, to return from exile. On a fine day in May 1660, Prince Charles sailed up the Thames. The crowds in London welcomed him with joyous shouts. Church bells rang throughout the realm. On this jubilant note, the reign of King Charles II began. Because he restored the monarchy, the period of his rule (1660–1685) is known as the Restoration.

Charles restored more than the monarchy. He also restored the theater, sporting events, dancing, and merrymaking in general. Life at Charles's court was elegant, colorful, and scandalous. It was not long before people were calling their new king "the merry monarch."

Drama and poetry Theater and the arts flourished during the Restoration. Not surprisingly, comedy dominated the stage. High society flocked to see amusing plays that poked fun at the manners and morals of the times. For the first time, women appeared on the English stage to play female roles. (In Shakespeare's time, beardless boys had played women's parts.)

The greatest writer of the period, however, was not a dramatist but a poet. John Milton, aged and blind, was a devout Puritan. He had worn out his eyesight writing propaganda for Cromwell. He took no joy in the Restoration, but his greatest poem, *Paradise Lost*, was published under Charles II. It was a work of Christian philosophy, an attempt to explain why life's suffering and pain are justified in God.

A moderate ruler Although Charles restored the monarchy, he did not try to restore the idea of the divine right of kings. Unlike his father and grandfather, Charles II had the good sense not to push himself or others too hard.

In religion, as in other things, Charles tried to steer a middle path. He wanted to give both Puritans and Roman Catholics some measure of religious freedom. In this, however, he met with firm opposition from Parliament. The Church of England remained the only legal religion.

The passage of habeas corpus Although England did not have religious freedom, the English people did win another important guarantee of freedom during Charles's reign. In 1679, Parliament passed a law known as habeas corpus. (*Habeas corpus* is a Latin term that means "you

Paradise Lost dramatizes the story of Adam and Eve and Satan's treachery. Milton worked feverishly on his masterpiece, sometimes waking his three daughters in the middle of the night to dictate to them another set of inspired verses.

have the body.") This law gave every prisoner the right to obtain a writ or document ordering that the prisoner be brought before a judge. The judge could then decide whether the prisoner should be brought to trial or set free.

The Habeas Corpus Act meant it was no longer possible for the king or queen to put someone in jail simply for opposing the ruler. It also made it impossible for the monarch to hold someone in jail indefinitely without a trial. Today habeas corpus remains one of the most important guarantees of personal freedom in both the United States and England.

Problems over religion and money Although Charles had learned many lessons from his Stuart predecessors, in the end the very issues that ruined his father and grandfather returned to haunt him. Those issues were, of course, religion and money.

Charles had had Catholic leanings for many years. In addition, he was unable to live on the money that Parliament provided him. In secret, he turned to the Catholic and wealthy king of France, Louis XIV. Charles and Louis entered into a secret agreement. Louis promised to give Charles a lump sum of money every year. In return, Charles agreed to become a Catholic at some time in the future.

Although the people of England did not know of the agreement, they did know that their king was sympathetic to Catholicism. They also knew

Voice from the Past · *The London Fire*

On the night of Sunday, September 2, 1666, a disastrous fire broke out in London. It began in a baker's shop and raged for 3 days, destroying more than 13,000 houses and leaving 100,000 Londoners homeless. The following account comes from the diary of Samuel Pepys (peeps), a royal official.

Jane [woke] us . . . about three in the morning to tell of a great fire they saw in the City . . . [Pepys soon goes down to see for himself.] Everybody endeavoring to remove their goods, and flinging into the river . . . poor people staying in their houses as long as till the very fire touched them, and then running into boats . . . Having stayed, and in an hour's time seen the fire rage every way, and nobody, to my sight, trying to quench it, but to remove their goods, and leave all to the fire . . . So I was called for and did tell the King . . . that unless his Majesty did command houses to be pulled down nothing could stop the fire . . . [Carrying the King's command, Pepys finds London's Lord Mayor.] At last met my Lord Mayor in Canning-Street, like a man spent, with a handkercher about his neck. To the King's command he cried, like a fainting woman, "Lord! What can I do? I am spent. People will not obey me. I have been pulling down houses, but the fire overtakes us faster than we can do it" . . .

As it grew darker, [the fire] appeared more and more, and in corners and upon steeples, and between churches and houses, as far as we could see up the hill of the City, in a most horrid malicious bloody flame . . . it made me weep to see it. The churches, houses, and all on fire and flaming at once; and a horrid noise the flames made, and the crackling of houses at their ruin.

1. How did Londoners try to save their possessions?
2. (a) What step did Pepys recommend for stopping the fire? (b) How would this step have halted the fire?
3. What two reasons did the Lord Mayor give for his inability to stop the fire?
4. What service that almost every town has today was evidently lacking in London in the 1600's?

Pepys

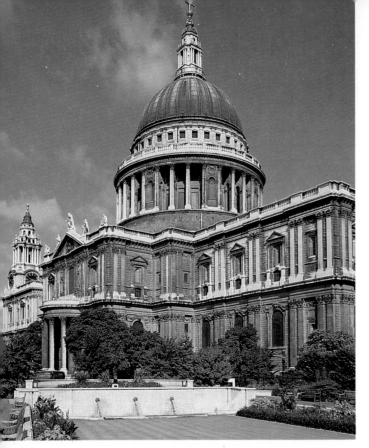

After the great fire of London, St. Paul's Cathedral and many other churches were rebuilt by the noted architect, Sir Christopher Wren.

James II lost his throne.

In 1685, Charles II died, and James II became king of England. Like his father, Charles I, James asserted his divine right to rule without Parliament's consent.

At first, the Tories in Parliament supported James. Soon, however, he antagonized even his firmest friends by appointing several Catholics to high office. This action openly violated the laws passed earlier by the Restoration Parliament. Tories as well as Whigs protested. James responded by dissolving his first Parliament and never calling another.

Three other events excited the fears of English Protestants. First, in 1687, James announced that government posts would be open to Catholics as well as Protestants. Second, James stationed 13,000 soldiers just outside London. Many Londoners feared that he was preparing to force England to accept Catholicism as the state religion. Third and most disturbing, James announced in 1688 that his second wife had given birth to a son. English Protestants were terrified at the prospect of a line of Catholic kings.

The infant prince was not James's only possible heir, however. James's first wife had been a Protestant. She had raised their eldest daughter, Mary, as a Protestant. Now an adult, Mary was the wife of William of Orange, a powerful Protestant prince of the Netherlands.

Whigs and Tories seized on a bold plan. They invited William and Mary to overthrow James II for the sake of Protestanism. William and Mary accepted the challenge.

William landed on English shores in November 1688 and led his army north to London. Nobody tried to stop him. The general of the English army, John Churchill, deserted James and joined William. Without any troops to fight for him, James sailed for France where he remained in exile until his death. Compared to Cromwell's civil war, this revolution was peaceful. The English still celebrate it as the Bloodless Revolution or the Glorious Revolution.

that he had no legitimate child to inherit the kingdom. Therefore, when Charles died, the throne of England would pass to his brother, James, who was openly Catholic.

Political parties developed.

The debate in Parliament over James's succession was fierce. Those who opposed James formed a group dedicated to keeping him off the throne. Those who defended both the king and his Catholic brother formed another group.

Each group invented a scornful label for the other. James's opponents were labeled "Whigs" (a Scottish word for assassins). His supporters were mockingly called "Tories" (the nickname for Irish bandits). These two groups were the ancestors of England's first political parties.

Long after the deaths of Charles and James, members of Parliament continued to identify with either Whigs or Tories. The two-party political system in both the United States and England today has its roots in this conflict.

The English won a Bill of Rights.

In 1689, Parliament asked William and Mary to rule England as joint sovereigns. At their coronation, they solemnly vowed "to govern the

For all its majesty, in Elizabeth's day St. Paul's was a bustling center of social commerce. No urgings from the Church could keep people from using the cathedral as a place to sell their wares and as a shortcut for themselves and their horses and mules.

people of this kingdom of England . . . according to the statutes in Parliament agreed on and the laws and customs of the same." This oath shows the significance of the Glorious Revolution. William and Mary recognized Parliament as the leading partner in ruling England.

To make clear the limits of royal power, in 1689 Parliament drafted a Bill of Rights. This document listed many things that a ruler could *not* do. These were the major prohibitions:

- No suspending of Parliament's laws
- No levying of taxes without a specific grant from Parliament
- No interfering with a member's freedom of speech in Parliament
- No penalty for a citizen who petitions the king about grievances
- No standing army to be kept in time of peace
- No posting of excessive bail in royal courts

William and Mary officially consented to these limits on their power.

Political ideas grew from conflict.

Did the English people have a right to rebel against Charles I in 1642 and against James II in 1688? Could a ruler lawfully be overthrown by his subjects?

The revolutionary events of the 1600's challenged two English philosophers to think about these questions. No, said Thomas Hobbes, there was no such thing as a right to rebel. Yes, said John Locke, people oppressed by their government had every right to rebel against it.

Thomas Hobbes wrote his most famous work, *Leviathan* (lih-**VYE**-uh-thuhn), in 1651, two years after the beheading of Charles I. The horrors of civil war convinced him that all humans were naturally wicked. Left to themselves, he thought, people would give free rein to their evil ways. Governments were created, said Hobbes, to protect people from their own selfishness. The best government was one that had the awesome power of a leviathan (sea monster). Since the chief purpose of government was to stop society from falling into disorder, Hobbes reasoned, an absolute monarchy was best.

John Locke held a different, more positive, view of human nature. He believed that people had the gift of reason. As reasonable beings, they had the natural ability to govern their own affairs and to look after the welfare of society.

Governments were formed, said Locke, to protect three basic human rights: the right to life, the right to liberty, and the right to property. These rights were absolute, belonging to all people everywhere as their birthright. What was government? It was a contract in which the rulers promised to safeguard people's natural rights. If any government abused these rights instead of protecting them, said Locke, then the people were justified in rebelling.

Locke's ideas were published in 1690, only two years after the Glorious Revolution. His two *Treatises on Government* served to justify the overthrow of James II.

Locke's theories had immense importance for future revolutionaries. Less than 100 years later, on the other side of the Atlantic Ocean, a young lawyer named Thomas Jefferson would use Locke's ideas to justify the rebellion of 13 American colonies against their English king, as you will read in a later chapter.

Section Review 4

Identify: (a) Charles II, (b) Restoration, (c) John Milton, (d) habeas corpus, (e) Tory, (f) Whig, (g) James II, (h) William and Mary, (i) Glorious Revolution, (j) Bill of Rights, (k) Thomas Hobbes, (l) John Locke

Answer:
1. Besides the monarchy, what else was restored in the Restoration?
2. (a) In what way was Charles II a moderate leader? (b) How did religion and money cause problems for him toward the end of his reign?
3. How did the succession of James II lead to the development of political parties?
4. (a) Why did Parliament invite William and Mary to rule England in 1588? (b) Name three ways the Bill of Rights limited royal power.

Critical Thinking
5. Explain why habeas corpus was an important landmark for personal freedom.
6. Hobbe's *Leviathan* was written two years after Charles I was beheaded. Locke's *Treatises on Government* was written two years after the Glorious Revolution. How was each work influenced by events of the time?

Summary

1. Elizabeth I faced many challenges. The last of the Tudor rulers, Elizabeth I was a gifted queen who guided England through the troubles of the 1500's. These included religious conflicts between Catholics and Protestants; a plot against her life by her Scottish cousin, Mary Stuart; the threat of Philip II's Invincible Armada; and severe financial difficulties. Toward the end of her reign, Parliament began demanding rights that Elizabeth was not prepared to grant.

2. Elizabethan England was a golden age. Under Elizabeth I, England had a golden age. The center of this golden age was London, the most populous city in Europe. Elizabethan London bustled with trade and was filled with people from every class, from the well-to-do to criminals. This human pageant was brilliantly captured by William Shakespeare, whom many regard as the greatest writer of all time.

3. England had a civil war. Elizabeth's cousin, James Stuart, King of Scotland, succeeded her at her death in 1603. His reign is remembered for the King James Bible, the establishment of the first English colony in the Americas, and bitter quarrels with Parliament over money and religion. His son, Charles I, had even more difficulty with Parliament. Eventually, those difficulties led to a civil war in which Puritan members of Parliament fought the king's supporters. Oliver Cromwell led the Puritans to victory. After the beheading of the king, Cromwell established a severe military dictatorship.

4. Parliament won political power. In 1660, Charles II, son of Charles I, was recalled from exile to restore the monarchy. Although Charles II followed moderate policies and saw the passage of habeas corpus, his death sparked hostilities over the Catholic religion of his successor, James II. Eventually, James's harsh policies and staunch Catholicism led to a Glorious Revolution, in which Parliament forced James II off the throne and invited James's Protestant daughter, Mary, and her Dutch husband, William, to rule England. In 1588, William and Mary signed the Bill of Rights, which limited royal power and recognized Parliament as the real ruler of England.

Reviewing the Facts

1. Define the following terms:
   a. joint-stock company   b. divine right
2. Explain the importance of each of the following names or terms:
   a. Elizabeth I   d. Philip II
   b. Puritan   e. Francis Drake
   c. Mary Stuart   f. Invincible Armada

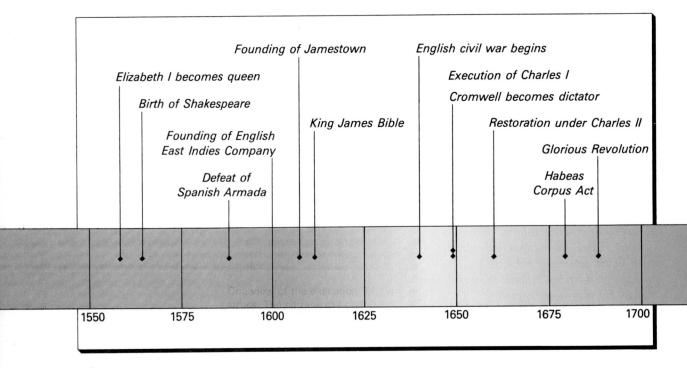

Elizabeth I becomes queen

Birth of Shakespeare

Founding of English East Indies Company

Defeat of Spanish Armada

Founding of Jamestown

King James Bible

English civil war begins

Execution of Charles I

Cromwell becomes dictator

Restoration under Charles II

Glorious Revolution

Habeas Corpus Act

1550   1575   1600   1625   1650   1675   1700

g. William Shakespeare   l. Roundhead
h. James I   m. Oliver Cromwell
i. Charles I   n. Charles II
j. Petition of Right   o. Whig
k. Cavalier   p. Tory

3. (a) How was the vitality of Elizabeth's reign reflected in the city of London? (b) How do the writings of William Shakespeare symbolize the golden age of English literature?
4. What social changes took place in England during the protectorate of Oliver Cromwell and after the Restoration?
5. (a) Why did Hobbes oppose the civil war? (b) Why did Locke support the Glorious Revolution?

Basic Skills

1. **Sequencing** Certain parallels exist in the sequence of events of the two English revolutions. (a) List the main events from 1625 to the execution of Charles I. (b) List the main events from 1685 to the conclusion of the Glorious Revolution. (c) What similarities and differences do you observe in these two critical periods?
2. **Solving problems** The text on page 389 states that Queen Elizabeth faced four kinds of problems—"religious conflicts, a rival queen, Spanish ambitions, and financial difficulties." Explain how Queen Elizabeth dealt with each problem.

Researching and Reporting Skills

For a group research project on the English civil war, divide your class into two groups: Roundheads and Cavaliers.

1. **Finding primary and second sources** In your library's card catalog, find books relating to the period of the English civil war. Try to find both primary and secondary sources and to get several perspectives on the subject.
2. **Compiling a bibliography** From this research, prepare a group bibliography. References should be classified as primary or secondary sources and identified according to viewpoint on the conflict.
3. **Listing supporting arguments** From the complete bibliography, each group should select the materials pertaining to its side in the conflict. Each group should then divide the reading, take notes, and list arguments supporting its cause.

4. **Debating viewpoints** When the lists of arguments are complete, each group should prepare its full case. One or two members from each group may then be chosen to debate whether the civil war was essential to limiting royal power in England.

Critical Thinking

1. **Analyzing viewpoints** How might each of the following people have regarded the queen: (a) Mary Queen of Scots, (b) an English sea captain, (c) a Puritan member of parliament? Explain your answers.
2. **Identifying fact and opinion** From Elizabeth's speech to her troops on page 389, list the phrases that are fact and those that are opinion.
3. **Interpreting economics** What was the significance of the chartering of joint stock companies in England?
4. **Synthesizing** (a) What precedents existed before the Tudors for limits on royal power? (b) To what extent did the Tudors respect those precedents? (c) Give examples from the reigns of Henry VIII and Elizabeth to illustrate your answer.
5. **Applying concepts** James I, Charles I, and James II believed in and acted according to the concept of the divine right of kings. (a) For each of these reigns, give an example of an act based on this principle. (b) Explain how the Habeas Corpus Act and the Bill of Rights limited this concept.
6. **Synthesizing** In what ways did the Elizabethan Era represent an English renaissance?

Perspectives on Past and Present

The Glorious Revolution in England ended with the adoption of the Bill of Rights. (a) Which of those rights are also included in the Bill of Rights of the United States Constitution? (b) What reasons might account for any differences?

Investigating History

From a historical perspective, is Oliver Cromwell a tyrant, a liberator, or both? (a) Read a selection about Cromwell and analyze what its author thinks of him. (b) To what extent do you agree or disagree with the author? (c) What is your own evaluation of Cromwell's leadership?

Chapter 19

Europe in the Age of the Absolute Monarchs

Louis XIV's grand palace at Versailles was a monument of beauty and splendor. It also stood at a safe distance from the dangerous mobs of Paris.

Key Terms

absolute monarch
mercantilism
balance of trade
tariff
balance of power

Read and Understand

1. The Sun King ruled France.
2. Peter the Great changed Russia.
3. Austria and Prussia rose to power.

"Sire, it is time."

In the privacy of his bedroom, the French king awoke, as he always awoke, to the whispered announcement of his chief valet. It was 7:30 A.M. at the royal palace of Versailles (vair-SYE), 11 miles southwest of Paris. From this moment until midnight, King Louis XIV understood that his every move would be watched and commented on a thousand times by the courtiers who lived at Versailles.

Louis had trained them all to depend on his little favors. A kingly nod to one courtier, a glance at another, a kind word to a third were treasured by the French nobles. Now, outside the curtains of his canopy bed, the 100 nobles on whom he had conferred his greatest favors were waiting. Every morning, these 100 privileged ones were permitted to enter the royal bedchamber and help the great king dress for the day.

Louis was the son of a loveless marriage. He claimed that his parents were so neglectful that once he almost drowned. The best friends of his youth were servants in the palace. They were the only common people he ever knew.

First, the four highest-ranking nobles would approach the bed. Only one of these four was judged worthy enough to draw the curtain of the king's bed. For the next two hours, different groups of honored courtiers would file into the room to aid the king as he dressed. One noble would receive the king's discarded nightcap from the royal hand. Another would present Louis with his royal slippers. A third and a fourth would hold the two sleeves of Louis's nightdress as he stepped out of it.

Meanwhile, outside the king's bedchamber, thousands of lesser nobles would station themselves in palace halls. They hoped the king might see them as he passed and perhaps favor them with a nod or a look.

At exactly 10:00 A.M., Louis would be carried in a sedan chair into his chapel to attend the Catholic mass. Hundreds of nobles stood ready to greet him there and bow toward him just as he bowed toward the holy altar. It was as if the king, not God, was the true object of their worship.

For French nobles, success or failure in life depended on winning Louis's favorable attentions. A single blunder at court might doom their hopes of advancement. Thus, they were careful to follow the intricate rules of etiquette laid down by their demanding king. For example, whenever they met a procession of servants carrying the king's dinner, they were required to doff their hats and bow low. Knocking on someone's door was considered rude. The proper way to announce one's presence was to scratch lightly at the door with the little finger of the left hand.

Louis XIV, who ruled France from 1643 to 1715, was the most powerful monarch in French history. He was an **absolute monarch**, a ruler with unlimited power. Unlike England's ruler, Louis did not share his power with a parliament. In Louis's view, he and the nation were one and the same. He reportedly boasted, "*L'état, c'est moi,*" meaning "I am the state."

Although Louis XIV was the most powerful monarch of his time, he was by no means the only absolute ruler. Of all the major nations of Europe, only England (as you have seen) and the Dutch Netherlands resisted absolute rule. Elsewhere in Europe—France, Russia, Prussia, and Austria—powerful rulers dominated their lands. This chapter looks at Europe during the brief age (1648–1763) of absolute monarchs.

The Sun King ruled France. 1

Just as the sun is the center of the solar system, Louis was the center of France's government. Just as the sun dazzles people's eyes, so Louis dazzled France (and indeed all of Europe). "The Sun King" was the flattering description Louis liked best.

Louis XIV was the third king of the Bourbon dynasty. His father, Louis XIII, had been a weak ruler who left government in the hands of the powerful Cardinal Richelieu (page 378). Richelieu died in 1642, followed six months later by Louis XIII in 1643.

The heir to the throne, little Louis XIV, was only five years old. Although technically he became king in 1643, real power rested in the hands of his mother, Anne, and her prime minister, the ruthless Cardinal Jules Mazarin (MA-za-RAN).

Violence marred Louis's childhood.

Like Richelieu, Mazarin worked steadily to increase France's power. Mazarin's greatest triumph came in 1648 when he represented France at the peace conference after the Thirty Years' War. The terms of the Treaty of Westphalia (page 381) made France the strongest nation in Europe.

Although France was at the peak of its power, its king was still a frightened, lonely ten-year-old boy. In fact, the young Louis XIV had much to fear. Many people in France hated Mazarin and his harsh policies. In 1648, this hatred broke out in a revolt led by nobles who feared that Mazarin was stripping away their powers and privileges. A series of terrifying riots began in Paris and spread to the countryside. These violent outbreaks were called the *Fronde*. (*Fronde* meant "slingshot" and was a scornful term suggesting that the rebels were naughty children.) The riots and revolts continued for five years.

During the years of rioting, Louis's life was often in danger. In 1651, a group of rebels broke into the royal palace in Paris and roughly demanded to see the 13-year-old king. The terrified queen mother led them to the chamber where they found Louis sleeping—or rather, pretending to sleep. Satisfied that the king had not escaped

Louis had an all-absorbing concern to see that every noble idolized him. He was constantly checking to see who put in a regular appearance at court. Failure to appear meant certain disgrace.

409

Paris, the rebels stomped out. Ever after, the king hated Paris. His later move to Versailles was partly caused by bitter memories of Paris.

In the end, the Fronde rebellion failed because its leaders distrusted one another even more than they distrusted Mazarin. Peasants and townspeople grew weary of disorder and fighting. For many years afterward, the people of France accepted the oppressive laws of an absolute king, because they were convinced that the alternative, rebellion, was even worse.

Louis ruled in grand style.

In 1661, Cardinal Mazarin died. Louis XIV, now 23, was glad to be rid of him. The king wished to rule France himself, to be king in fact as well as name. For the next 54 years, from 1661 to 1715, Louis dominated France.

Louis was indeed an impressive figure. Although he stood only 5 feet 5 inches tall, many people who saw him commented on his imposing height. His erect and dignified posture made him appear tall. (It also helped that he wore high-heeled shoes.)

Louis had very strong likes and dislikes. He hated cities but loved to travel through France's countryside. Because he hated delays, the people who traveled with him were at his mercy. Louis allowed no stopping except for his own comfort.

As king, Louis lived in a grand style. Eating was one of his chief pleasures. Nearly 500 cooks, waiters, and other servants worked day and night to satisfy his tastes. An observer claimed that the king once consumed four plates of soup, a whole pheasant, a partridge in garlic-flavored sauce, two thick slices of ham, a salad, a plate of pastries, fruit, and hard-boiled eggs in a single sitting!

The form of service was as important to Louis as the food itself. For example, three cupbearers busied themselves for eight minutes in the ritual of refilling the royal wineglass.

Colbert improved France's economy.

To Louis, all the pomp and ceremony of his court glorified France as well as himself. He wanted to make France the leader of Europe. As king, he devoted himself to helping France attain economic, political, and cultural brilliance.

Early in Louis's reign, France made impressive economic gains, thanks largely to the efforts of his dour, humorless minister of finance, Jean Baptiste Colbert (kohl-BAIR). Like other economists of his time, Colbert believed in the theory of **mercantilism** (MUHR-kuhn-TEE-lihz-uhm). According to this theory, a country's economic strength rested on certain conditions. These included acquiring gold and silver, expanding manufacturing, exporting more than was imported, encouraging commerce, owning colonies, and building up shipping and a navy.

In 1665, when Colbert became Louis's minister of finance, the economy of France was weak. For the next 20 years, Colbert worked tirelessly to strengthen it. To expand manufacturing—for example, glassmaking, weaving, and silk production—he gave subsidies and tax benefits to French companies. Colbert also sought to develop mining and agriculture. To obtain skilled workers, he encouraged those from other countries to settle in France.

Having more manufactured products enabled France to start exporting more than it imported. This gave it a favorable **balance of trade** that brought more gold and silver into France than went to other countries. To protect France's industries, Colbert placed a high **tariff**, or import tax, on goods coming into the country.

Colbert also recognized the importance of colonies. They provided a source of raw materials for French industry and a market for manufactured goods. The government encouraged people to migrate to Canada, where the fur trade added to French commerce and brought more wealth to France.

Colbert knew that transportation was vital to trade. To improve travel within France, he encouraged the building of roads and canals. By adding more than 100 warships to the French navy, he increased protection for French shipping. Colbert's mercantilist measures were successful—so successful that by 1683 France had become the industrial leader of Europe. To Colbert, the purpose of this expanded economic activity was to serve the state.

Many of France's skilled workers and business leaders were Huguenots (French Protestants). They took a leading role in commerce, banking, and industry—the economic activities that Colbert had encouraged. Both France and the Huguenots prospered from Colbert's policies.

Sadly, a single mistake by Louis undid much of Colbert's work soon after the minister's death in 1683. Louis, a devout Catholic, revoked the Edict of Nantes (page 378). For almost 100 years, the Edict of Nantes had protected the religious freedom of the Huguenots. Suddenly, Huguenots could no longer attend their own churches or schools. Instead, they could be imprisoned as enemies of the state.

Louis paid a high price for his religious intolerance. To escape persecution, 200,000 Huguenots fled France. Thus, the country lost many of its skilled workers and business leaders. The mercantilists of rival countries gloated over Louis's economic blunder.

The French court set styles.

Louis was more successful in his cultural goals. During Louis's reign and long after his death, the French practically dictated the artistic tastes and fashions of Europe, extending eastward even into Russia. Every ruler in Europe, from great kings to petty dukes, tried to imitate Louis's life style, especially his grand palace at Versailles.

In 1661, as one of his first decisions after Mazarin's death, Louis ordered his royal country house at Versailles to be enlarged on a colossal scale. For years, thousands of marble blocks littered the grounds as Louis and his architects rode about directing workers to place a statue here or there.

Louis officially moved his court from Paris to Versailles in 1682. However, the palace was far from complete. Nobles living at Versailles seldom had any rest from the incessant banging of the stonemasons' hammers. In 1685, for example, the palace grounds swarmed with 46,000 workers busily building the Sun King's dream palace.

Footnote to History

When Louis built his Hall of Mirrors, the only mirror-makers in Europe lived in Venice. The Venetian rulers jealously guarded this profitable business. Colbert sent spies to Venice to lure mirror-makers to France with the secrets of their trade. The result was a valuable new French industry.

The gold fleurs-de-lis that adorn Louis XIV's cape in this portrait were the emblem of the Bourbon dynasty. The high heels on his shoes made him appear taller.

The most dazzling of all the rooms was the Hall of Mirrors. Along one wall of this room, 17 towering windows gave a splendid view of the palace gardens. Light from these windows flooded the room and reflected the gardens in 17 huge, gold-framed mirrors on the opposite wall. In the Hall of Mirrors, Louis entertained foreign princes. Here his daughters' wedding guests danced by the light of thousands of candles that sparkled and reflected in the windows and mirrors.

Although a courtier's life at Versailles was glamorous, it was far from comfortable. Nobles from all over France flocked to Versailles to seek favors from the king. About 1,000 nobles and their 4,000 servants crowded into the palace's 226 rooms. Even the best rooms were cramped and uncomfortable. Smells from the outdoor latrines seeped through the windows—in the few

Just to decorate the gardens of Versailles, the following materials were needed: 1,400 fountains, 100 marble statues of Greek gods, 2 million flowerpots, and 4 million tulips—half crimson, half yellow.

Parquet floors, marble walls, and gilded wood gleamed in the Hall of Mirrors where Louis XIV held his most lavish receptions.

rooms that had windows. Many lower-ranking nobles settled for windowless, closetlike cubicles. In the summer, they roasted in these stifling quarters; in the winter, they froze.

Yet thousands of French nobles gladly endured discomfort to share the glamour of Louis's court with its spectacular entertainments. One famous party in July 1689 lasted all day and night. After feasting and dancing to the music of the royal orchestra, awed onlookers watched as fireworks rocketed into the night sky. Some of the rockets twisted and turned to write the royal monogram, double L's, in fiery letters against the darkness.

France led Europe in the arts.

For his entertainment, Louis XIV demanded good music. At times, he could be heard humming the operas composed by the chief musician at his court, Jean Baptiste Lully (loo-**LEE**). Italian composers had written the first European operas around 1600. Now, thanks to Louis, operas became popular throughout Europe. They combined music, dance, and drama with the opportunity for spectacular costumes and special stage effects.

Comedies and tragedies Another of the king's favorite entertainers was comic actor and playwright Jean Baptiste Poquelin, better known by his stage name, Molière (moh-**LYAIR**). Molière lived from 1622 to 1673. This witty dramatist wrote some of the funniest and most popular plays in French literature: *Tartuffe, The Miser, the Misanthrope, The School for Wives.* Each play is a biting satire on French society.

While comedy was Molière's specialty, tragedy was the specialty of his two friends and fellow dramatists, Pierre Corneille (cor-**NAY**) and Jean Baptiste Racine (rah-**SEEN**). These authors modeled their tragedies on the works of the ancient Greek playwrights Aeschylus and Sophocles (page 109), whom they greatly admired.

Like the classical Greek dramatists, the French playwrights always observed the "three unities" of classic drama. First, all action was related to a single plot; there were no subplots. Second, all the action took place in a single setting. Third, all the action took place in a single day. (These strict rules made French tragic dramas very different from the English tragedies of Shakespeare, whose work was not admired at the French court.)

Corneille and Racine often drew the plots of their plays from Greek mythology. One of Racine's masterpieces, for example, was *Andromaque,* based on the story of Andromache, the wife of the great Trojan hero Hector.

Royal patronage Louis XIV was the principal patron of these artists. Not since Augustus of Rome had there been a monarch who aided the arts as much as Louis. He treated Racine, for example, as one of his favorite courtiers and gave him a generous pension for life. He brought hundreds of pieces of Renaissance sculpture from Italy to exhibit in his Versailles gardens. The "Mona Lisa" by Leonardo da Vinci was one of the smaller paintings that hung in his bedroom.

All of Versailles was a monument to the king's classical tastes in art. The buildings and grounds of the palace gave an impression of perfect balance, elegance, and classical grandeur. The chief purpose of art was no longer to glorify God, as it had been in the Age of Faith. Now the purpose of art was to glorify the king.

Louis fought costly wars.

By any measure, France was the most powerful country in Europe. In 1660, France had about 20 million people—4 times as many as Spain or England and 10 times as many as the Dutch republic. The French army, numbering 100,000 in peacetime and as many as 400,000 in wartime, was far ahead of other nations' armies in size, training, and weaponry.

By comparison, all of France's rivals were in decline or disorder. England was still recovering from its civil war. Spain continued its long decline. The Thirty Years' War had left most of Germany devastated.

Despite France's strength, however, Louis XIV failed in many of his military goals. Between 1667 and 1713, Louis fought a series of wars to expand France's boundaries to the Rhine River and to the Alps. Rather than bringing glory to France, these wars brought the country to the brink of bankruptcy.

Alone, no other country was a match for France. However, by joining together, weaker countries could equal or even exceed French power. This defensive strategy is known as a **balance of power**. In such a balance, no one country or group of countries can dominate others. Many smaller countries banded together to stop France's aggression.

Three times in 30 years (1667–1697), Louis sent French armies into the Netherlands to try to extend his borders to the Rhine River. Each time, he was stopped. At various times, England, Sweden, the Netherlands, Spain, Austria, and several German states joined forces against Louis. By the time the third war ended in stalemate in 1697, Louis had almost emptied the French treasury. His only important gain had been the German province of Alsace.

In 1700, the balance of power was once again threatened when the childless king of Spain, Charles II, died. On his deathbed, Charles bequeathed the Spanish throne and the huge Spanish empire to Louis's 17-year-old grandson, Philip. The two greatest powers in Europe, enemies for so long, were now linked by bonds of blood.

Smaller countries felt threatened by this sudden increase in the power of the Bourbon dynasty. In 1701, England, Austria, the Dutch republic, Denmark, Portugal, several German states, and the Italian duchy of Savoy all joined together against France and Spain. They fought a long and painful struggle known as the War of the Spanish Succession.

The War of the Spanish Succession was a disaster for Louis. Several times he sued for peace. Each time, negotiations broke down because Louis insisted that his grandson must keep the Spanish throne. The costly war dragged on for 13 years.

At last, in 1713, a peace treaty was signed in the Dutch city of Utrecht. In the Treaty of Utrecht, France and Spain managed to win only two points. First, Louis's grandson, Philip V, was allowed to remain king of Spain as long as the thrones of France and Spain were not united. Second, France kept the disputed territory of Alsace. On all other matters, France and Spain were the losers.

Great Britain,* on the other hand, was one of the victors in the war. From Spain, Britain took an important fortress at the southern tip of Spain known as the Rock of Gibraltar. This fortress gave Britain control of the strategic gateway to the Mediterranean Sea. (The British still hold Gibraltar today.) From France, Great Britain won several colonies in North America, including Nova Scotia, Newfoundland, and the Hudson Bay territory.

The Austrian Hapsburgs, also victors in the war, gained the Spanish Netherlands (what is

*In 1707, the kingdoms of England and Scotland were united by law. After that date, the kingdom was called Great Britain.

Louis persecuted the Huguenots, a Protestant group, causing almost 400,000 of them to leave the country. Among the Huguenots were many of France's best craftspeople.

413

now Belgium). They also took over Spain's Italian lands, including Sardinia, Naples, and Milan.

Two smaller states on the winning side gained power and prestige. The German state of Prussia and the Italian duchy of Savoy were both recognized as kingdoms. These ambitious kingdoms later proved important in the development of Germany and Italy as nations.

The Treaty of Utrecht set up a new balance of power in Europe. On one side stood France and Spain, weakened but still imposing, both ruled by Bourbon kings. On the other side were the combined forces of Britain, Austria, and the Netherlands. The balance, however, was delicate. Any shift in power could tip Europe into a war.

Louis XIV's reign came to a sad end.

The War of the Spanish Succession left France near ruin, and Louis's last years were more sad than glorious. He still went through the same daily rituals at Versailles. In his old age, however, he was sorry for the great suffering his wars and high taxes had caused the people of France. Louis had suffered personal losses too. His only legitimate son died in 1711, and his favorite grandson died a year later.

In 1715, the saddened Sun King, now 77, developed gangrene in one leg. Gracious to the end, he said farewell to his wife, his courtiers, and his weeping servants. Then he called to his bed his five-year-old great-grandson, the future Louis XV. "My child," said the dying king, "do not imitate me in the taste that I have had for building or for war. Try, on the contrary, to be at peace with your neighbors ... Try to comfort your people, which unhappily I have not done."

Section Review 1

Define: (a) absolute monarch, (b) mercantilism, (c) balance of trade, (d) tariff, (e) balance of power
Identify: (a) Louis XIV, (b) Jules Mazarin, (c) Jean Baptiste Colbert, (d) Versailles, (e) Molière, (f) Corneille, (g) Racine
Answer:
1. (a) What was the Fronde? (b) How did it affect Louis XIV? (c) How did it make the people of France feel about absolute rule?

2. Why was "the Sun King" a fitting title for Louis XIV?
3. (a) What did Colbert do to improve France's economy? (b) How were his achievements undermined by Louis XIV?
4. (a) How did Louis XIV promote culture in France? (b) What purpose did art serve during his reign?
5. (a) What was the War of the Spanish Succession? (b) How did the Treaty of Utrecht affect each of the countries involved in the war?

Critical Thinking
6. Under Louis XIV, France succeeded in dominating Europe culturally but failed to dominate it militarily. Suggest some reasons for both its success and its failure.

Peter the Great changed Russia. 2

Like the king of France, the czar of Russia was an absolute ruler. In 1682, the year that Louis moved his court to Versailles, Peter Romanov became Czar Peter I. The log houses and onion-domed churches of Moscow, capital of Russia, were very different from the elegant corridors of Versailles. Yet in many ways, Peter I was like the Sun King.

Like Louis, Peter I came to the throne as a child. Also like Louis, Peter had a boyhood filled with violence, as older people used him in a struggle for power. Later, when Peter held power in his own hands, he avenged himself on his enemies, torturing them without mercy.

In some ways, Peter Romanov grew up to be a bullying brute. However, he was also a brilliant and able czar. His impact on Russian culture was probably even greater than the impact of Louis XIV on French culture. Peter I, called Peter the Great, made Russia a major European power for the first time.

Russia was isolated from Europe.

Peter I was neither the first czar to rule Russia nor the first to earn the title of "great." Both distinctions had gone in the 1400's to Ivan III (page 252). In 1480, Ivan had freed Moscow from

414

the Mongol overlords who ruled Russia. Ivan took the title of czar (emperor) and began to widen Moscow's rule.

The rise of the Romanovs Peter's family, the Romanovs, came to power in a time of troubles during the early 1600's. After the death of Ivan IV (Ivan the Terrible; page 253) in 1584, Russia was torn by power struggles among the nobles, or boyars.

In 1613, representatives from 50 Russian cities met to choose the next czar. Their choice was Michael Romanov, grandnephew of Ivan the Terrible. Thus began the Romanov dynasty, which was destined to rule the Russian empire for 300 years (1613–1917).

A land of boyars and serfs When the Romanov family came to power, Russian society was still dominated by the great, landowning families of the nobility, the boyars. Their vast estates were worked by serfs.

Serfdom in Russia lasted much longer than it did in western Europe. In France, England, and other parts of western Europe, serfdom developed in the late days of the Roman empire and began to weaken in the late 1300's and 1400's. In Russia, however, serfdom developed much later and continued to thrive into the late 1700's.

Serfdom in Russia was not much different from slavery. When a landowner sold a piece of land, the serfs were sold with it. Landowners could give serfs away as presents or to pay debts. It was against the law for serfs to run away from their owners.

An isolated land When Peter I came to the throne in 1682, most Russian boyars knew little of western Europe. In the Middle Ages, Russia had looked to Constantinople, not to Rome, for leadership. During most of the Renaissance, Russia was under the rule of the Mongols and remained cut off from western Europe. Thus, the ideas of the Renaissance, the Age of Exploration, and the Scientific Revolution had scarcely touched Russia.

Geographic barriers also kept Russia closed in on itself. Its only seaport was Archangel on the White Sea, which was choked with ice much of the year.

Religious differences widened the gap between western Europeans and Russians. The Russians had adopted the Byzantine, or Eastern Orthodox, branch of Christianity. Western Europeans were

Peter the Great planned to make Russia a westernized nation and a naval power.

mostly Roman Catholics or Protestants, and the Russians shunned them as heretics. The few travelers from western Europe who reached Moscow were mostly Germans, and they stayed in the so-called German quarter of the city.

Peter dreamed of modernizing Russia.

In the 1670's and 1680's, people in the German quarter often saw the young Peter Romanov striding on long legs through their part of town. He was fascinated by the modern tools and machines in the foreigners' shops. Above all, he had a passion for ships and the sea.

Peter's love of ships was more than a boyhood fancy. The young czar believed that Russia's future depended on having a warm-water port. Only then could Russia compete with the more modern nations of western Europe.

After his troubled childhood, Peter I finally took full power in his own name in 1696, when

Russia grew eastward from 1500 to 1650. In the 1500's, Cossacks crossed the Urals following fur animals into the Siberian forests. They were eventually organized into a cavalry. By the 1640's, the boldest pioneers had reached the Pacific Coast.

he was 24 years old. He had the mind of a genius, the body of a giant, and the ferocious temper of a bear. One could not help but look up to Peter, who stood about 6 feet 8 inches tall.

Peter I came to the throne determined to modernize Russia. In 1698, at the age of 25, he went with 200 servants and 55 nobles on an overland journey to western Europe to learn about European customs. Never before had a czar traveled among western heretics.

On his journey, Peter insisted on keeping his identity a secret. He went to the Netherlands in the plain clothes of an ordinary worker. Pretending to be just another shipyard worker, he rose at dawn every morning and carried his own sack of carpenter's tools to the worksite. Nobody was fooled. A Russian giant in a Dutch seaport was a conspicuous sight. Yet if a fellow worker addressed him as "Your Majesty" or "Sire," he would not answer. No, he was just plain "Carpenter Peter," and for four months in Amsterdam, the czar insisted that everyone honor his disguise.

Traveling to England to see more ships, Peter presented himself to the king, toured London, and brushed off the gaping crowds that dogged his footsteps. An English gentleman who loaned Peter his house returned to find that the czar and his friends had played wild games with his property. Among other acts of destruction, they had thrown things at his paintings and flattened the hedges in his garden with a wheelbarrow.

Peter made many changes in Russia.

Peter admired everything that he saw in Europe—its ships, its industries, its cities, its elegant music, its fashions in clothing, even the way men shaved their faces. What would it take to make Moscow more like the countries of western Europe? Gentle persuasion would not do it. What was needed, in Peter's view, was to hammer Russia into a modern mold. "For you know yourself," said Peter to an official, "that, though a thing be good and necessary, our people will not do it unless forced to." Few rulers in history have attempted reforms as sweeping as Peter's.

The status of women Until 1700, Russian women followed the Byzantine custom of secluding themselves at home and veiling their faces in public. Peter set a new fashion by inviting noblewomen to social gatherings. Moreover, he demanded that they come without veils. The czar also decreed that parents could no longer marry off their daughters and sons unless the young people agreed to the match.

The Russian calendar Though Russian Orthodox priests opposed the change, Peter forced his people to give up their old calendar. No longer would Russians celebrate the new year on September 1. Henceforth, said Peter, Russians would follow the European custom of starting their year on January 1. In addition, Russians would date each year from the birth of Jesus, not from the

Daily Life · The Barber King

Surprisingly enough, the first thing Peter reformed when he returned to the Kremlin was not the army or industries but beards. To Peter, the Russian custom of wearing beards symbolized everything that was backward about his country. When his nobles fell on their knees to welcome him home, the czar raised them up, whipped out a long European razor, and commanded them to hold still while he shaved off their beards. The boyars were horrified. Russian men of the time treasured their beards as symbols of manhood and Christianity. Yet Peter decreed that all Russian nobles must shave off their beards. To make sure his decree was obeyed, he posted barbers at Moscow's gates. Noblemen who wished to keep their beards had to pay a beard tax every year and hang a metal tag from their necks to prove that they had indeed paid it.

The fine arts of western Europe did not interest Peter as much as the practical arts of shipbuilding and iron mining. Even so, he imported companies of German actors and put together an orchestra of foreign musicians.

creation of the world as their old calendar had done. Thus, the czar's decree changed the Russian year 7208 into the European year of A.D. 1700.

Agriculture From Europe, Peter brought back specimens of potatoes and encouraged landowners to grow the new crop. Potatoes became a staple food in Russia because they grew well in its cold climate.

Factories and mines To strengthen Russia's economy, Peter adopted the mercantilist ideas fashionable in Europe. He encouraged exports and discouraged imports. As a good mercantilist, Peter favored factories and subsidized their growth. Peter's factories were really more like centralized workshops, with perhaps a few machines run by hand. Still, when he came to the throne, Russia had only 13 such factories, and by the time of his death, there were about 200.

Peter also aided Russia's iron industry. With rich deposits of iron ore and large forests that supplied charcoal for smelting the ore, Russia soon was selling iron to other countries.

Newspapers Even literate Russians knew little of events outside their own country. To combat this ignorance, Peter started Russia's first newspaper and edited its first issue himself.

Peter I was an absolute ruler.

Like Louis XIV, Peter I of Russia was an absolute monarch. Many of the changes he made in his country were for the sake of increasing his own power.

For example, Patriarch Hadrian, the head of the Russian Orthodox Church, died in 1700. For more than 20 years, Peter neglected to appoint another patriarch. Then, in 1721, he abolished the office of patriarch altogether. In its place, he set up a group of high priests called the Holy Synod. At its head was Peter himself. The Russian church was now the czar's church, much as the English church had been made into the king's church by Henry VIII (page 351).

Peter also reduced the power of the great landowners, the boyars. He rarely gave high posts in government to the most powerful boyar families. Instead, Peter recruited able men from lower-ranking families, promoted them to positions of authority, and rewarded them with grants of land. Because these men owed everything to the czar, they were loyal to him.

When Peter first came to power, the Russian army was made up of cavalry (soldiers on horseback) who fought with sabers. They served only on a part-time basis. The armies of western Europe, on the other hand, were made up of highly trained infantry (foot soldiers) who marched forward while firing a constant barrage of bullets. These expert marksmen were full-time, professional soldiers.

To modernize his army, Peter hired European officers who drilled his soldiers in European tactics with European weapons. Russian soldiers no longer served on a part-time basis. Instead, as in western Europe, being a soldier became a lifetime job. By the time of Peter's death, the Russian army numbered 200,000 men. To pay for this huge army, Peter laid heavy taxes on nearly everyone in Russia.

Peter expanded Russia's empire.

Peter used his huge army to crush peasant revolts within Russia. He also turned it against neighboring countries to satisfy his greatest ambition—winning a warm-water seaport for Russia. He wanted, as he put it, a "window on the sea."

Peter believed that Russia needed a good navigable strip of coastline both on the Baltic Sea to the northwest and on the Black Sea to the south. The Swedes held the Baltic coast. The Ottoman Turks and their Tatar vassals held the Black Sea.

To win a warm-water port, Peter's first goal was to take Azov on the Black Sea from the Turks. His earliest campaign in 1695 failed badly. Undaunted, he saw that he needed warships. He helped build one with his own hands and besieged Azov again in 1696. This time the city fell to the Russians, though the Turks regained it several years later.

Peter then turned north to fight for a piece of the Baltic coast. His war against the Swedes, known as the Great Northern War, lasted 21 years (1700–1721).

At first, this war too went badly for the Russians. Early in the war, the Swedish King Charles XII scored a brilliant victory against the Russians. Then, in 1708, the Swedes suddenly invaded the Ukraine, a region on Russia's southwestern border. At first, Peter did not oppose the invaders. Instead, he left the Swedes to be starved and demoralized

Under Peter, all Russians were required by law to give service to the state. Such service included working in industries as well as serving in the army.

Although St. Petersburg lay farther north than Moscow, the new city's location on the coast gave it a somewhat milder climate than the old capital.

by Russia's most potent weapon, the winter cold. In the spring of 1709, Peter's army set upon the weakened, frostbitten Swedes and annihilated them at the Battle of Poltava.

The remaining 12 years of the Great Northern War went well for Peter. Sweden's Charles XII died in battle in 1719, and Peter successfully invaded both Finland and Sweden. The treaty of peace, signed in 1721, finally gave Russia a broad belt of land on the Baltic Sea.

Peter built a new capital.

Actually, Peter had secured his "window on the sea" many years before Sweden officially surrendered it. In 1703, he began building a new city on Swedish lands occupied by Russian troops.

The site for this city was a low-lying swamp at the mouth of the Neva River. The climate was damp and unhealthful, and the drinking water caused dozens of diseases. On the whole, the location was fine for wolves and wild ducks but terrible for people. To Peter, however, the location seemed ideal because ships could sail down the Neva into the Baltic and on to western Europe. Here at last, as Peter said, "a great window for Russia to look out at Europe" could be built. He called it St. Petersburg after his patron saint.

To build a city on this desolate swamp was no easy matter. Every summer, the czar's officials forced thousands of luckless serfs to leave home and trudge to the work camps on the Neva River. They had only the crudest tools and a few wheelbarrows. Workers lugged soil and stones across the swamp to make the city's foundations. Thousands of people perished from the terrible working conditions and rampant diseases. Estimates of the dead range from 25,000 to 100,000. St. Petersburg well deserved to be called "a city built on bones." Peter himself shared some of the hardships. He lived at the building site in a house that was little more than a log cabin.

In 1712, the czar proclaimed St. Petersburg his new capital. Russian nobles groaned when Peter ordered them to leave the comforts of Moscow and settle in St. Petersburg. Peter, however, was delighted with his new capital. "Truly," he wrote, "we live here in heaven."

So western a city was St. Petersburg that French—not Russian—was often the preferred language.

In the fall of 1724, Peter was with his army along the Gulf of Finland. A ship ran aground, and the soldiers on it were about to drown. The 52-year-old czar plunged into the icy water to help, heedless of his own safety. He caught a cold that grew worse through the winter, and he died early in 1725. Near his death, he said, "I hope God will forgive me my many sins because of the good I have tried to do for my people."

For better or for worse, Peter the Great had tried to transform the culture and government of Russia. To an amazing extent, he had succeeded. By the time of his death, Russia was a power to be reckoned with in Europe.

Section Review 2

Define: (a) boyar, (b) serf
Identify: (a) Peter the Great, (b) Russian Orthodox Church, (c) St. Petersburg
Answer:
1. (a) When did the Romanovs come to power? (b) Describe Russian society under the early Romanovs.
2. (a) Why had Russia been cut off from western Europe? (b) What was Peter's goal for his country?
3. (a) Describe three reforms that Peter made for the sake of modernizing Russia. (b) Describe three reforms he made for the sake of his own power.
4. (a) Why was the Great Northern War fought? (b) What was its outcome?

Critical Thinking
5. (a) What cultural obstacles did Peter I face in his attempt to make Russia more like the countries of western Europe? (b) Why are rulers usually more successful in making political and military changes than social changes?

Austria and Prussia rose to power. 3

Between France in the west and Russia in the east lay the rolling plains of eastern Europe. The major powers of the region were the Holy Roman Empire, the kingdom of Poland, and the Ottoman empire. Unlike France and Russia, which were highly centralized monarchies, the three powers of eastern Europe were not well organized.

Weak empires ruled eastern Europe.

Geographically, eastern Europe is a sweeping plain that extends from the Elbe River in what is now Germany to the Ural Mountains in Russia. The lack of mountains or other natural frontiers left this region open to constant warfare, migration, and shifting boundaries. Rulers in eastern Europe had trouble establishing firm borders.

Socially, eastern Europe followed a different path of development from western Europe. During the late Middle Ages, serfs in western Europe slowly won freedom, and the middle-class townspeople gained power. In eastern Europe, the landowning aristocracy gained more and more control over their serfs. By 1700, Polish landowners could demand as much as five days' work a week from their serfs, leaving the serfs only two days to grow their own food. There was a great gap between the aristocracy and the serfs, with few middle-class merchants or free artisans between the two extremes.

Politically, eastern Europe fell under the rule of the Holy Roman emperor, the Ottoman emperor, and the king of Poland. Each of these rulers had more power in theory than in fact.

Poland On the map on page 420, the kingdom of Poland appears to be a large, united country. However, the king of Poland was elected by the Polish nobility, who allowed him practically no power. Poland's king had little income, no law courts, no officials, and no standing army. Usually, the nobles chose a foreigner as their king because they were too jealous of one another's power to choose someone from their own ranks.

The Ottoman empire The sultan of the Ottoman empire still exercised some power. He collected taxes and had a large standing army. The greatest of the sultans, Sulieman the Magnificent, had conquered Hungary and threatened Vienna. Since his death in 1566, however, the mighty empire had been steadily declining. The government in Istanbul (once Constantinople) was corrupt, and the large army was poorly equipped.

The Holy Roman Empire The Holy Roman Empire in the early 1700's was little more than

Poland's lawmaking body, called a *diet*, was virtually powerless. Rarely could it enact a law code since each member had the right to break up or "explode" the diet at any minute for any reason. From 1652 to 1764, 55 diets met and 48 were exploded.

419

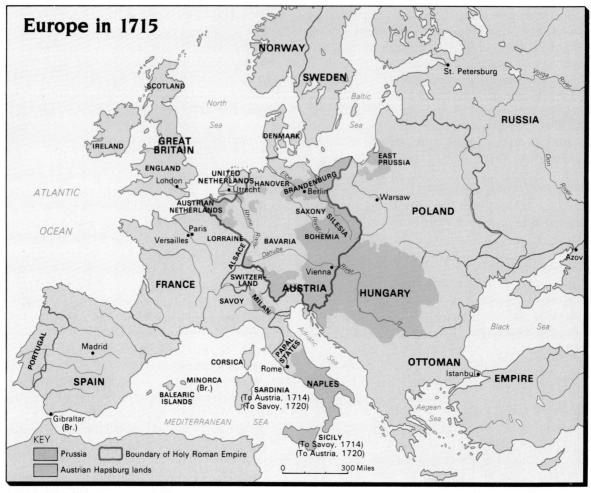

Map Study

What mainland regions of Italy did the Hapsburgs hold? What regions made up their largest single piece of territory? Why was Gibraltar a key point?

a name. In fact, after the Thirty Years' War, it consisted of about 300 states, each of which jealously guarded its rights and liberties.

In short, eastern Europe was a region of old, weakening empires and kingdoms. Historians call this situation a power vacuum. Such weakness tempts ambitious leaders to move into the area to fill the power vacuum. That was not long in happening.

In the late 1600's, two German-speaking families were eager to take advantage of eastern Europe's power vacuum. One was the Hohenzollern (HOH-ehn-TSAHL-uhrn) family of north Germany; the other was the Hapsburg family of Austria. Their ambitions threatened to upset Europe's delicate balance of power.

Austria regained power in the 1700's.

Even after the terrible losses in the Thirty Years' War, Austria still remained the most powerful and important state within the empire. Its ruling family, the Hapsburgs, was one of the oldest and most distinguished dynasties in Europe. As far back as the 1400's, most of the Holy Roman emperors were Hapsburgs.

The Hapsburg ruler in 1713 was Charles VI. Austria had just won much territory in the War of the Spanish Succession (page 413). Despite this victory, however, Charles's empire was not an easy one to rule. It had three main parts. First, there was the dukedom of Austria on the middle stretches of the Danube River. Second, to the

420

west, there was the kingdom of Bohemia. Third, to the east, lay the kingdom of Hungary. In addition, there were other German states and scattered lands in Italy.

Nothing about this patchwork empire was either natural or logical. Within its border existed a diverse assortment of peoples—Czechs, Hungarians, Croatians, Italians, and Germans. What held the empire together, generation after generation, was the fact that the Austrian, Hungarian, and Bohemian crowns were all worn by the same ruler, a Hapsburg.

How could the Hapsburgs make sure that they never lost claim to the lands that formed their empire? Charles VI spent his entire reign (1711–1740) working out an answer to this problem. By endless arm twisting, he persuaded the other rulers of Europe to sign an agreement known as the Pragmatic Sanction. By its terms, all the countries recognized Charles's only child as the heir to all his Hapsburg territories. That heir was a young woman named Maria Theresa.

In theory, the Pragmatic Sanction guaranteed Maria Theresa a peaceful reign. Instead, she faced years of war. Her main enemy was Prussia, a new state to the north of Austria. Like Austria, Prussia rose to power in the late 1600's. Soon Prussia's ruling family, the Hohenzollerns, challenged Maria Theresa and the Hapsburgs.

The Hohenzollerns ruled Prussia.

Like the Hapsburgs of Austria, the Hohenzollerns built up their state from a number of scattered holdings. At first, the small duchy of East Prussia in northern Poland was of little importance to the Hohenzollerns. Their most valued possession was a small state in the Holy Roman Empire called Brandenburg.

Brandenburg was never very powerful, but in the middle 1600's it enjoyed one distinction. Its ruling prince held the cherished title of elector. He was one of the seven electors who chose the Holy Roman emperor.

Maria Theresa (1717–1780) became ruler of the Hapsburg lands in 1740, when she was 23 years old. Although she lost Silesia and later Naples, she strengthened Austria by reforming administration and finance. Her father, her husband, and her son were all Holy Roman emperors. She was denied the title because she was a woman, but she was generally called empress anyway.

In 1640, a 20-year-old Hohenzollern named Frederick William inherited the title Elector of Brandenburg. Frederick William, later called the Great Elector, had the unhappy experience of seeing Brandenburg overrun by rival armies during the Thirty Years' War. His capital, Berlin, was so badly devastated that its population fell from 14,000 to 6,000.

Frederick William, a tall and muscular man with piercing blue eyes, concluded that there was only one way to safety. Brandenburg, he decided, must have a strong standing army. At first, with his almost empty treasury, he could equip and feed only about 8,000 men. Yet even this small force gave him some leverage in dealing with other states.

With a keen eye for his own advantage, the Great Elector made alliances with the French, the Swedes, the Dutch, and the Poles. He offered the services of his army to any power that paid him well and granted him a little slice of territory. In some wars, he got money from Louis XIV, and in other wars, from Louis's enemies. So well did Frederick William play the diplomatic game that his armies rarely went into battle. Thus, he saved a great deal of money, which he used to build a larger army. The larger army, of course, allowed him to strike even better bargains.

The Prussian army grew in strength.

The three Hohenzollerns who followed the Great Elector were all named Frederick or Frederick William. They all followed his formula for success: Build a bigger and better army.

Frederick I The Great Elector's son was the first Hohenzollern to call himself a king. By the Treaty of Utrecht in 1713, his duchy of East Prussia (which lay outside the Holy Roman Empire) was recognized as a kingdom. Thereafter, all the Hohenzollern territories, including Brandenburg, were grouped under the name Prussia. To live like a true king, Frederick I built ornate country palaces in imitation of Versailles.

Frederick William I Frederick I's son and successor, Frederick William I, was a harsh and mentally unbalanced character who loved only his army. In his 27-year reign (1713–1740), he refused to spend money on anything but his soldiers. He dressed in an army uniform and prowled the streets of Berlin, barking out commands to soldiers and civilians alike. The Sergeant-King, as he was called, had a vicious temper. When displeased, he would fly into a rage and clobber the offending person with his walking stick.

Frederick William's obsession with his army had a lasting effect on Prussia. He more than doubled the size of the army, from 40,000 to 85,000 soldiers. He promoted his officers only from Prussia's landowning nobility, called the *junkers* (YUNK-uhrs). These army officers were far superior in social status and power to any civilian. Thus, more than any other country in Europe, Prussia became a military society. In fact, as a foreigner said, "Prussia is not a state that possesses an army, but an army that possesses a state."

Frederick II (the Great) The Sergeant-King worried that his son, another Frederick, might turn out badly because he enjoyed too many nonmilitary interests—music, philosophy, and literature. The scholarly young prince hated his father and tried to run away to France, but he and a companion were caught. As punishment, the furious father ordered Frederick, age 18, to witness the beheading of his friend. Despite such bitter quarrels, however, Frederick II followed many of his father's policies when he came to the throne in 1740.

Frederick II invaded Hapsburg lands.

In 1740, the same year that Frederick II became king of Prussia, Austria's Maria Theresa succeeded her father as the Hapsburg monarch. The newly crowned Prussian king scorned the Pragmatic Sanction, which his father had signed. Frederick wanted Austria's iron-rich land of Silesia. He assumed that, being a woman, Maria Theresa would lack the forcefulness to defend her lands.

The Prussian army invaded and occupied Silesia in December 1740. Thus began the War of the Austrian Succession. Following Prussia's lead, other countries leaped to take advantage of Maria Theresa's supposed weakness. France, Spain, and the German state of Bavaria all sent armies across Austria's western border.

Austria's young queen reacted quickly. She had recently given birth to her first son, but nonetheless she made a dashing journey across Austria to her Hungarian lands. There, Maria Theresa appeared in person before an assembly

As a boy, Frederick II of Prussia hated the army. After he became king, however, he valued the power his army gave him. Prussian troops were the best armed and best drilled in Europe.

of Hungarian nobles, who were not especially friendly to their Hapsburg rulers. Holding the infant prince, she delivered a stirring speech that instantly won over the assembly. The Hungarians pledged to give her an army of 100,000 men.

Maria Theresa also got help from Great Britain. Britain entered the war to fight its archrival France, which was allied with Prussia. With Great Britain, Russia, and the Dutch Netherlands on her side, Maria Theresa managed to stop Prussia and its allies from swallowing Austria and her other lands. She was not able, however, to turn the Prussian fighting machine out of Silesia. In 1748, at the Treaty of Aix-la-Chapelle, Austria lost Silesia.

Maria Theresa resolved to regain Silesia. Her determination to strike back at Frederick led to both a "diplomatic revolution" and a second Austrian-Prussian war.

Alliances shifted in Europe.

For more than 200 years, the Bourbon kings of France had been the chief enemies of the Austrian Hapsburgs. But was France still a threat to Austria? No, decided Maria Theresa's foreign minister, Count Kaunitz (KOW-nits). Austria's chief foe was now Prussia. Recognizing this, Kaunitz worked tirelessly to make France an ally. Aware of Austria's shrewd maneuvering, Britain decided its wisest move was to make an alliance with Prussia. After all, Britain had Europe's strongest navy and Prussia the strongest army. Together, they should be unbeatable.

By 1756, a so-called diplomatic revolution had taken place. Austria, France, and Russia were now allied against Britain and Prussia. With powerful enemies on three sides, Prussia's Frederick II decided to strike first.

Once again, Prussia and Austria were at war. This time, almost every country in Europe took part. In Europe, the war was known as the Seven Years' War (1756–1763). In North America, where France and Great Britain battled for colonies, it was known as the French and Indian War. Even Asia was involved, for there too France and Britain were rivals for colonies. Many historians refer to this war as the first true world war.

In 1763, the war on three continents ended with the signing of the Peace of Paris. Maria

At this time, the French held parts of Canada and several islands in the Caribbean Sea. The British held several other Caribbean islands, Nova Scotia, Newfoundland, the Hudson Bay territory, and 13 colonies on the North American coast.

423

Voice from the Past · A Call to Arms

The year was 1741. Maria Theresa had lost Silesia. Prague, the capital of Bohemia, had also fallen. The future looked grim, as this letter from the queen to her chancellor, Prince Kinsky, reveals.

So Prague is lost, and perhaps even worse will follow unless we can secure three months' supplies. It is out of the question for Austria to supply them, and it is even doubtful if Hungary will be able to do so.

Here then, Kinsky, we find ourselves at the sticking point where only courage can save the country [Bohemia] and the Queen, for without the country I should indeed be a poor princess. My own resolve is taken: to stake everything, win or lose, on saving Bohemia; and it is with this in view that you should work and lay your plans. It may involve destruction and desolation that 20 years will be insufficient to restore, but I must hold the country and the soil, and for this all my armies, all the Hungarians shall die before I surrender an inch . . . You will say that I am cruel; that is true. But I know that all the cruelties I commit today to hold the country I shall one day be in a position to make good a hundred-fold. And this I shall do. But for the present I close my heart to pity . . .

1. Maria Theresa refers to Austria, Bohemia, and Hungary in this letter. How are the three countries connected?
2. (a) What is Maria Theresa's resolve? (b) What alternative, if any, does she have?
3. (a) How do the sentiments expressed by Maria Theresa compare with those of Elizabeth I at the time of the Armada? (page 389) (b) What traits do these women share?

Maria Theresia

Theresa gained nothing from the war. Silesia remained in Prussian hands. France lost Canada and most of its lands in India to Britain.

Of the five major powers that fought the Seven Years' War, only one emerged with major prizes. This was Britain, the only country of the five whose king was *not* an absolute monarch. In the next chapter, we will see how new ideas began to replace absolutism in Europe.

Section Review 3

Define: junker
Identify: (a) Holy Roman Empire, (b) Hapsburg, (c) Hohenzollern, (d) Pragmatic Sanction, (e) Great Elector, (f) Frederick I, (g) Frederick William I, (h) Frederick the Great, (i) Maria Theresa
Answer:
1. (a) Describe the geography of eastern Europe. (b) How did the region's geography make it difficult for strong states to develop there?

2. (a) Identify the three main parts of the Austrian Hapsburg empire in 1713. (b) How did Charles VI try to keep the title to these lands for his daughter?
3. How did Frederick William build up the power of Brandenburg after the Thirty Years' War?
4. (a) What distinguished Frederick I from earlier Hohenzollern rulers? (b) What happened to the Hohenzollern territories during his reign?
5. (a) Why was the War of the Austrian Succession fought? (b) Describe the diplomatic revolution that took place after the war.
6. (a) Why was the Seven Years' War fought? (b) What country was the chief loser in the war? (c) Who emerged as the winner?

Critical Thinking
7. One observer of Prussia in the 1700's commented, "Prussia is not a state that possesses an army, but an army that possesses a state." Explain what this statement means.
8. Maria Theresa ruled a very large empire. Did the size of her empire add to or diminish its strength? Explain your answer.

Summary

1. The Sun King ruled France. Louis XIV of France became king in 1643 at the age of five. For the next 17 years, real power rested in the hands of his minister, Cardinal Jules Mazarin. After Mazarin's death, Louis became the most powerful monarch in French history.

During his reign, Louis succeeded in some areas and failed in others. He wisely chose Jean Baptiste Colbert as his minister of finance but foolishly undid much of Colbert's work by forcing thousands of Huguenots out of France. As king, he patronized the arts and made France the cultural center of Europe. He also tried to expand France's power through wars but witnessed the defeat of his armies time and time again. Louis died regretting the costliness of his court and his wars.

2. Peter the Great changed Russia. Peter I of Russia came to the throne in 1682. At the time he came to power, Russia was a backward, isolated nation. Peter set out to win a warm-water port for Russia and modernize his country.

Like Louis XIV of France, Peter was an absolute ruler. During his reign, he made sweeping reforms that both modernized Russia and increased his own power. Peter also extended his country's borders. He won from Sweden a broad belt of coast on the Baltic Sea. There he built St. Petersburg, the new capital of Russia.

3. Austria and Prussia rose to power. Both Austria and Prussia lay on the sweeping plains of eastern Europe. Prussia was the creation of the Hohenzollern rulers of Brandenburg, who had extended their power by offering their armies' services in exchange for land. Austria, the most powerful state in the Holy Roman Empire, was ruled by the Hapsburgs. In 1740, the ruler of Prussia, Frederick the Great, invaded Silesia, a territory of Austria. One war followed another as the Hapsburg queen Maria Theresa tried to block Prussia's advances. The other countries of Europe, trying to protect the delicate balance of power, took part as well. In the end, a war was fought on three continents. Maria Theresa lost Silesia while her ally France surrendered much of its overseas empire to Prussia's ally, Great Britain.

Reviewing the Facts

1. Define the following terms:
   a. absolute monarch
   b. mercantilism
   c. tariff
   d. balance of trade
   e. balance of power

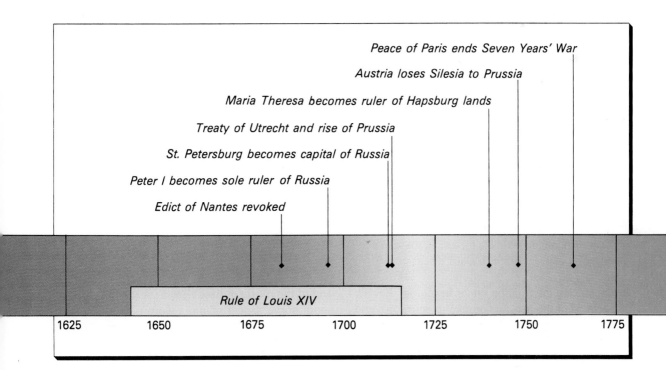

Peace of Paris ends Seven Years' War

Austria loses Silesia to Prussia

Maria Theresa becomes ruler of Hapsburg lands

Treaty of Utrecht and rise of Prussia

St. Petersburg becomes capital of Russia

Peter I becomes sole ruler of Russia

Edict of Nantes revoked

Rule of Louis XIV

1625   1650   1675   1700   1725   1750   1775

2. Explain the importance of each of the following names, places, or terms:
   a. Louis XIV
   b. Cardinal Mazarin
   c. Jean Colbert
   d. Molière
   e. Peter I
   f. Charles XII
   g. Hohenzollern
   h. Hapsburg
   i. Maria Theresa
   j. Prussia
3. (a) Describe Russia when Peter I came to the throne. (b) What two goals did Peter have for Russia? (c) What did he do to accomplish each goal?
4. (a) Explain how Austria became a strong power. (b) Why were its lands difficult to rule?
5. (a) Explain how Prussia became a great power. (b) Why did it become a military state?

Basic Skills

1. **Organizing information**   Make a chart of the wars fought by France, Prussia, Austria, and Britain from 1701 to 1763. For each war, include in the vertical column the headings Dates, Causes, Countries on Each Side, and Outcome.
2. **Interpreting a time line**   Using the time line on page 425, identify the three new powers that were emerging as the reign of Louis XIV ended.

Researching and Reporting Skills

Writing a Historical Essay

In this chapter and the two that follow, you will be writing a historical essay. The purpose of a historical essay is to present a point of view, or thesis, on a historical subject.

Phase 1: Choosing a topic and developing a working thesis   If possible, the topic should be a subject about which you can develop a point of view. Two examples might be "The role of individual X in the development of Y" or "The implications of C for D and E." The most interesting topics are those that highlight recurring patterns. After choosing a topic, you will analyze information in order to develop a viewpoint for a working thesis.

1. **Brainstorming about a topic**   Look over Chapters 18 and 19, noting possible topics. Share your suggestions with others in a class discussion. Then make your final choice of topic.
2. **Organizing information under headings**   Review sections of the text that pertain to your topic and take notes. Organize this information under headings.

3. **Developing a working thesis**   Form an opinion that you believe is supported by your information. Write a sentence that expresses your opinion. This becomes the main idea of your essay.

Critical Thinking

1. **Applying a concept**   In France, Louis XIV was the prime example of the absolute monarch. In England, the Stuarts asserted the divine right of kings but were unable to enforce that principle. (a) Give examples of Louis XIV's absolutism. (b) Explain what made absolutism possible in France and unacceptable in England.
2. **Analyzing an economic concept**   Explain the concept of mercantilism. (a) What was its aim? (b) How did Colbert's policies apply the ideas of mercantilism?
3. **Synthesizing**   In 1685, Louis XIV revoked the Edict of Nantes. Two centuries earlier Ferdinand and Isabella had expelled the Muslims and Jews from Spain. Compare the effect of these decisions on each country.
4. **Analyzing causes**   Geographical factors had considerable impact on the history of Russia. Identify two ways in which they helped to shape events in the time of Peter the Great.
5. **Comparing**   Both Peter the Great and the Hohenzollerns greatly increased the power of their countries. Compare the methods they used to achieve their goal.

Perspectives on Past and Present

In the time of Louis XIV, Europeans imitated the clothing styles and tastes of the court at Versailles. (a) To what extent is Paris still the fashion and cultural capital of the world? (b) What economic advantages does a nation derive from having a reputation for cultural leadership?

Investigating History

The age of the absolute monarchs was the era of baroque architecture—displayed in ornate castles—and of the music of Bach, Haydn, and Handel. Read about some aspect of the culture of the time and report on it or plan an audio presentation of music of the era.

Enlightenment in Europe, Revolution in America

As the most famous writer of his day, Voltaire (leaning forward at left) was an honored guest at courts throughout Europe. Here, dining at the Prussian palace, he conversed with Frederick II.

Key Terms

philosophe
executive
legislative
judicial
separation of powers
enlightened despot
constitutional monarchy
cabinet
prime minister
federal

Read and Understand

1. European thinkers expressed new ideas.
2. Writers advocated liberty and reason.
3. Enlightened despots sought progress.
4. Britain developed new forms of leadership.
5. Americans created a republic.

It was a sad and shocking tale that the young man told, and the old Frenchman who listened to it was deeply moved. The young man was Donat Calas, a youth whose family had been forced to flee in poverty and disgrace from the French city of Toulouse. His hearer was Voltaire (vohl-**TAIR**), whose name was famous throughout Europe for his brilliant letters, pamphlets, plays, and satires.

Donat Calas told how, in 1761, his older brother Marc had been found hanged from the rafters of the family linen shop. Neighbors quickly accused the boy's father, Jean Calas, of killing his son.

The story of murder was all lies, said Donat Calas. He explained that Jean Calas was a Huguenot, hated as a heretic by the Catholic citizens of Toulouse. Because they thought his religion was evil, they

427

believed he would act in evil ways. Young Marc had planned to become a Catholic, said the neighbors, and so his father killed him.

The neighbors told this story in court, and the judges of Toulouse believed them. Jean Calas was tortured and then executed. The judges ordered all his property to be confiscated. The surviving members of the Calas family, including Donat, were driven from their home and fled to Switzerland.

Donat Calas wept as he described the misfortunes of his family. Of course, he repeated, his father was innocent. What had really happened was obvious, Donat concluded. His moody and unhappy brother Marc had taken his own life. Jean Calas was executed only because of prejudice against the Huguenots.

Donat Calas had indeed found a sympathetic listener. Few people hated injustice and prejudice more than Voltaire. Now 68 years old, Voltaire had written thousands of letters and pamphlets denouncing intolerance and bigotry of all kinds.

Voltaire had hundreds of influential friends in Europe. From his country estate near Geneva, Voltaire sent forth a barrage of letters about the execution of Jean Calas. Friends rallied to the cause and wrote letters of their own.

French officials felt the sting of Voltaire's pen. In 1765, three years after the execution of Jean Calas, King Louis XV's council overruled the Toulouse judges and declared Calas innocent of murder. His family could return to Toulouse, reclaim their property, and collect a huge payment for the wrongs done to them.

Voltaire wept for joy at the news. In a long, happy letter to a friend, he exclaimed, "What great victories reason is winning among us!" Note that he did not take credit for the victory himself. No, the true victor in the struggle for justice was a higher power that he called reason.

Voltaire and his scholarly friends honored reason as if it were a kind of divine force. They hoped that, through the power of reason, society would make steady progress toward liberty and justice. In a society ruled by reason, they thought, injustice would disappear.

In this chapter, we will say more about Voltaire and his fellow thinkers. The period of their greatest influence was known as the Age of Enlightenment and spanned the middle years of the eighteenth century (roughly 1720–1790).

In the English colonies of North America, the ideals of the Enlightenment played a large part in sparking a revolution against Great Britain. These ideals of liberty and reason helped to shape the government of the new country created by that revolution—the United States of America.

European thinkers expressed new ideas. 1

The Age of Enlightenment brought together the ideas of the Renaissance and the Scientific Revolution. Remember that Renaissance artists and writers adopted a secular outlook on life instead of the more spiritual outlook of the Middle Ages. They were also among the first Europeans to look critically at society in an effort to improve it. These new attitudes found their way into the Enlightenment.

Now recall the ideas of the Scientific Revolution. Copernicus, Kepler, and Galileo showed that the idea of an Earth-centered universe was wrong. Descartes had created a scientific philosophy for seeking truth. Everything had to be tested by the standard of reason. This idea too was basic to the Enlightenment.

Newton discovered the law of gravity.

In the history of ideas, as in other kinds of history, beginnings are seldom clearly marked. Isaac Newton may be called either the last and greatest figure of the Scientific Revolution or the first figure of the Enlightenment. Newton recognized what he owed to such earlier thinkers as Galileo and Kepler when he said, "If I have seen farther than others, it is because I have stood on the shoulders of giants."

Isaac Newton was born in England in 1642, while conflict was raging between the king and Parliament. Newton studied at Cambridge University and became a professor there. By the time he was 24 years old, he was certain that all physical objects (stones, birds, planets, stars) were affected equally by the same forces. However, he could not yet prove his ideas mathematically, and it was more than 20 years before he published these ideas.

Newton created the first reflecting telescope, using mirrors. In addition, he analyzed light by shining it through prisms and discovering its separation into bands of color. He thus became one of the founders of the science of optics.

In 1609, the astronomer Kepler had worked out laws for a planet's motion around the sun (page 358). Galileo had studied the motion of pendulums and the acceleration of balls rolling down a slope (page 359). Newton's great achievement was to discover that the same force ruled the motions of the planets, the rolling balls, the pendulum, and all matter on Earth and in outer space. He disproved the idea that one set of physical laws governed Earth and another set governed the rest of the universe.

All objects attract one another, said Newton. He called this attraction "gravitation." The attraction varies both with the mass of the objects and with the distance between them. In 1687, Newton at last published his fully developed theories in a book titled *Mathematical Principles of Natural Philosophy*. In a single sentence, he summarized the workings of the universe:

Every particle of the universe attracts every other particle with a force varying inversely as the square of the distance between them and directly proportional to the square of their masses.

European scientists who read Newton's work were overwhelmed by its brilliance. Newton's laws became the starting point for investigating everything in nature.

The philosophes advocated reason.

In the early 1700's, a group of thinkers set forth the idea that people could apply reason to all aspects of life just as Newton had applied reason to science. These thinkers were known as **philosophes** (FEE-luh-sohfs). At the heart of their philosophy were five ideas:

1. *Reason* Enlightened thinkers such as Voltaire regarded reason as a sort of divine force, as we have seen. Reason, they said, was the absence of intolerance, bigotry, or prejudice in one's thinking.
2. *Nature* The philosophes referred to nature frequently. To them, what was natural was also good and reasonable. They believed that there were natural laws of economics and politics just as there were natural laws of motion.
3. *Happiness* A person who lived by nature's laws would find happiness, the philosophes said. They were impatient with the medieval notion that people should accept misery in this world to find joy in the hereafter. The philosophes wanted well-being on Earth, and they believed it was possible.
4. *Progress* The philosophes were the first Europeans to believe in progress for society. Now that people used a scientific approach, they believed, society and humankind could be perfected.
5. *Liberty* The philosophes envied the liberties that the English people had won in their Glorious Revolution and Bill of Rights (page 404). In France, there were many restrictions on speech, religion, trade, and personal travel. Through reason, the philosophes believed, society could be set free.

Voltaire combated prejudice.

Thousands of Europeans in the 1700's shared these five ideas and thought of themselves as enlightened. None, however, was as widely admired (or as widely hated) as a Frenchman who called himself by an invented name, Voltaire.

Voltaire's real name was François Marie Arouet (AH-rweh). Born in Paris in 1694, he nearly died in infancy. He remained frail all his life and complained of almost every ailment: smallpox, fever, gout, a chronic itch, coughing fits, partial deafness and blindness, lost teeth, dropsy, paralysis, and grippe. He often ended his letters to friends by saying that he expected to die soon. Yet he did not put down his pen until death finally took him at the age of 84.

As a young writer, he adopted the name Voltaire, possibly because Arouet sounded too close to the French word for king. Voltaire's sharp tongue made him enemies at the French court, and twice King Louis XV had him jailed in a Parisian prison called the Bastille (ba-STEEL). All his life, therefore, Voltaire held a grudge against the French monarchy.

After one stay in prison, Voltaire was exiled to England for two years. While there, he read the works of John Locke, with their emphasis on reason and the natural rights of all human beings (page 405).

Voltaire came to admire the English government much more than his own. After he returned to Paris, much of his work mocked the laws and

Alexander Pope, an English poet of the early 1700's, summarized Newton's achievement in two famous lines: "Nature and Nature's laws lay hid in night/ God said, Let Newton be; and all was light."

429

customs of France and even dared to raise doubts about the Christian religion. The French king and France's Catholic bishops were outraged. In 1734, fearing another unpleasant stay in the Bastille, Voltaire fled from Paris to a spot near the French border.

In his later years, Voltaire was less a French citizen than a citizen of the world. He moved to Switzerland, seeking freedom to write and publish his works. There, in 1758, Voltaire wrote his most famous work, *Candide,* a short, satiric novel that he dashed off in three days. Voltaire spent his last years living with his niece in the little Swiss village of Ferney.

From his study overlooking a lovely garden, Voltaire used his quill pen as if it were a deadly weapon in a thinkers' war against humanity's worst enemies—prejudice, superstition, and intolerance. Such attitudes were, he said, *l'infame*—infamous or shameful things. He often ended his letters with a fighting slogan, *"Écrasez l'infame!"* (ay-crah-zay lahn-fam). The phrase meant "Crush the infamous thing!" Soon it was the battle cry of every enlightened thinker in Europe.

Salons were intellectual centers.

In the 1700's, Paris was the cultural and intellectual capital of Europe. There, it was the fashion among wealthy hostesses to invite the best poets, the keenest wits, and the most charming conversationalists to their mansions for refined conversation.

Such social gatherings were known as *salons.* One guest might be invited to read a poem or play a piece on the flute or harpsichord. The other guests would comment on the performance, showing off their good taste and broad understanding. The women who organized the salons were, in effect, the drama and music critics of their age.

The most influential of the salon hostesses in Voltaire's time was Marie Thérèse Geoffrin (zhoh-**FRAHN**). In her autobiography, Madame Geoffrin explained how her tastes and education were shaped early in life by her grandmother:

> She taught me to think, and made me reason; she taught me to know men, and made me say what I thought of them, and told

Mme Geoffrin (third from right in front) hosts a salon at which an actor reads from a play. Enlightenment culture was limited to the wealthy class.

The royal court at Versailles had lost some of its prestige after the death of the Sun King, Louis XIV, so his court did not attract the leading thinkers of the time.

me how she herself judged them ... She could not endure the elegancies that dancing masters teach; she only desired me to have the grace that nature gives to a well-formed person.

Every Monday the great artists of Paris assembled in the Geoffrins' drawing room. Every Wednesday, the foremost writers and scientists dined at her elegant table. Her husband, a much older man, sat politely through these dinners and rarely spoke.

Diderot planned an encyclopedia.

Marie Thérèse Geoffrin also sponsored one of the most ambitious intellectual projects of the Enlightenment. The philosophe Denis Diderot (dee-DROH) imagined a set of large books to which all the leading scholars of Europe would contribute articles and essays. This *Encyclopedia,* as he called it, would bring together all the most current and enlightened thinking about technology, science, mathematics, music, art, medicine, government, law, geography, and more. Madame Geoffrin was so fond of the project that she contributed nearly half the total cost. Other hostesses also gave money to the effort. The first volume of the set was published in 1751 and distributed to 1,431 subscribers.

In a dingy attic room in Paris, Diderot labored for 20 years to complete the project. His seventh volume provoked the French king, Louis XV. Therefore, government censors banned further volumes. Fearing arrest, some leading philosophes withdrew from the project and urged Diderot to quit. Diderot pressed on, however, and found ways around the ban on publishing. The last volume under his editorship, number 28, was finally printed in 1772.

The popularity of the *Encyclopedia* soon spread to French-reading buyers all over Europe. It also inspired English and Scottish writers to produce their own *Encyclopedia Britannica* in the 1770's.

Scientific knowledge advanced.

In the 1700's, it was fashionable for wealthy families to display scientific instruments in their homes. They invited their guests to observe the planets through a telescope or an insect's wing under a microscope. Most educated men and women only dabbled at science. A few, however, pursued their observations and experiments seriously and made breakthroughs in every branch of scientific inquiry.

The discovery of oxygen Before the Enlightenment, no one knew that air was made up of a mixture of gases (mostly oxygen, nitrogen, and carbon dioxide). Then, in 1774, an English minister and scientist named Joseph Priestley separated one pure gas from air. He noticed how good he felt after breathing this special air and watched how alert two mice were while breathing it. Wrote Priestley, "Who can tell but that, in time, this pure air may become a fashionable article of luxury? Hitherto only two mice and I have had the privilege of breathing it."

Meanwhile, in France, during the 1770's, Antoine Lavoisier (lah-vwah-ZYAY) was performing similar experiments. In 1779, Lavoisier named the newly discovered gas oxygen.

Electricity Electricity mystified the scientific thinkers of the 1700's. Why, they wondered, did electric sparks sometimes jump between objects and give people a shock? In the British colony of Pennsylvania, a printer named Benjamin Franklin thought there might be a connection between a lightning bolt in a thunderstorm and the puzzling little electric sparks.

To test his theory, Franklin performed one of the most famous—and dangerous—experiments in the history of science. In 1752, he sent up a kite during a thunderstorm. At the end of the kite string was an iron key. A bolt of lightning struck the kite, and in a flash, the key emitted an electric spark. Wrote Franklin:

When the rain has wet the kite twine so that it can conduct the electric fire freely, you will find it stream out plentifully from the key at the approach of your knuckle.

Enthralled by Franklin's experiment, a number of Europeans tried to repeat it, and several were killed instantly by the shock.

Geography Two centuries after the voyages of Columbus and Magellan, vast stretches of the Pacific Ocean were still unknown to Europeans. In 1768, the English navigator and mapmaker James Cook set out on the first of three voyages to explore and chart the South Pacific.

Cook was not in search of gold, as Dias, Da Gama, and Columbus had been. Instead, Cook's

In 1781, William Herschel, builder of powerful telescopes, discovered a distant body beyond Saturn. It was Uranus. He also observed that the Milky Way was not a mass of stellar gas but a collection of stars.

431

Daily Life · *A Defense against Smallpox*

In the 1600's and 1700's, few words conjured up as much dread as smallpox. An infectious disease, it struck 60 of every 100 people. Of those 60, at least 20 died, and another 20 were horribly disfigured by scars.

Then, in the early 1700's, Lady Mary Wortley Montagu made an amazing observation. While traveling in Turkey, she saw that mothers there deliberately infected their young children with smallpox by breaking the skin and applying some liquid taken from the sore of a victim. (Such a process is called inoculation.) Children who were inoculated caught smallpox, but they had a good chance of getting only a mild case that protected them from ever having the disease again. Lady Montagu bravely had her son inoculated. She then returned to Britain and spread news of the procedure. By the middle 1700's, inoculation, although still dangerous, was being used all over Europe.

In 1796, British physician Edward Jenner discovered that an inoculation with the less dangerous disease cowpox (taken from a cow) gave permanent protection from smallpox for humans. Because cowpox was a much milder disease, the risks for this form of inoculation were much lower. Jenner used cowpox to produce the world's first vaccination.

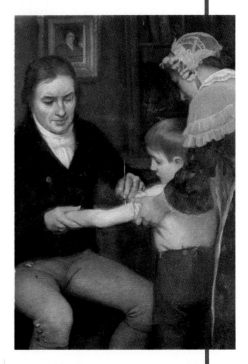

voyages were scientific expeditions. They were sponsored by the Royal Society of London, a group founded in the mid-1600's to encourage the growth of scientific knowledge. Astronomers, artists, and a botanist went with Cook to gather information about distant parts of the world.

Captain Cook became the first European to reach and chart the east coast of Australia and the islands of Tahiti, New Zealand, and Hawaii. He died in 1779 during a fight with the Hawaiian islanders.

New forms dominated music.

Educated men and women of the Enlightenment were as interested in music as in literature and science. This age produced some of Europe's most brilliant musicians.

The baroque period Music of the late 1600's and early 1700's is called *baroque,* which in French means "odd." The term was first used for art that was more ornate than the art of the Renaissance. Baroque music is noted for its drama and complexity.

Two musical techniques, the fugue and counterpoint, reached their height in baroque music. In a fugue, the composer repeats a single melody, or two or three melodies, with slight variations on different musical instruments. We may hear the theme first on a horn, then on a violin, and later on a cello.

Counterpoint is the weaving of two or more melodies together. Probably the plainest example of counterpoint is a simple tune—"Three Blind Mice," for example—sung in rounds. Musicians in the 1700's created very intricate counterpoint.

Baroque music reached its height in the early 1700's. The greatest of the baroque composers were Johann Sebastian Bach (1685–1750) and George Frederick Handel (1685–1759).

The classical period By the time Bach and Handel died in the mid-1700's, the age of baroque music was passing. New composers wrote less ornate works. Unity, clarity, and balance became more important than the intricate patterns of baroque music. New forms, such as the symphony, the concerto, and the sonata, came to dominate music.

Beethoven composed many of his best-known works after he had lost his hearing. His hearing loss and a turbulent relationship with his nephew were sources of profound suffering for Beethoven.

The period from 1750 to 1820 is known as the classical period in European music. Its most noted composers were Joseph Haydn (HYE-d'n), Wolfgang Amadeus Mozart (MOH-tsahrt), and Ludwig van Beethoven (BAY-TOH-vuhn).

Haydn, born in 1732, was not the first European to write full symphonies for strings and woodwinds. However, his compositions were so superior to earlier works that he is honored today as the "father of the symphony."

Mozart was a child prodigy who began composing music at the age of five and performed for Britain's King George III at the age of eight. At 12, he wrote his first opera. Mozart's operas baffled audiences with their originality and brilliance. His great operas—*The Marriage of Figaro, Don Giovanni,* and *The Magic Flute*—are widely performed today. In 1791, at the age of 35, Mozart died in poverty.

Beethoven (1770–1827) is considered by many to have been the greatest European composer of all time. While his earlier works were in the

Wolfgang Amadeus Mozart, 7 years old, and his sister Maria Ann, 12, toured the capitals of Europe giving recitals with their father.

same classical style as Mozart's, the music of Beethoven's later years began new trends, which carried music on into the Age of Romanticism (Chapter 23).

Section Review 1

Define: (a) philosophe, (b) salon

Identify: (a) Age of Enlightenment, (b) Newton, (c) Voltaire, (d) Marie Thérèse Geoffrin, (e) Diderot, (f) *Encyclopedia,* (g) Priestley, (h) Lavoisier, (i) Franklin, (j) Cook, (k) baroque, (l) Bach, (m) Handel, (n) Haydn, (o) Mozart, (p) Beethoven

Answer:

1. Describe the five ideas that were at the heart of the Enlightenment.

2. (a) Describe an evening in a Parisian salon. (b) What role did French women play in these salons?

3. (a) What was the purpose of the *Encyclopedia?* (b) What British work did it inspire?

4. (a) Describe three scientific accomplishments of the Englightenment. (b) Describe the two periods of music that flourished during the Enlightenment.

Critical Thinking

5. "If I have seen farther than others," said Newton, "it is because I have stood on the shoulders of giants." Who were the giants to whom Newton was referring? Could this be said of any scientific accomplishment? Explain.

Writers advocated liberty and reason. 2

Diderot once wrote, "I am a good citizen, and everything that concerns the welfare of society and the life of my fellow men is very interesting to me." The Age of Enlightenment was a time for thinking about the welfare of society, the freedom of the individual, and the happiness of humanity. In the opinion of the philosophes, these three ideals were almost identical. People could only be truly happy, they said, in a good society that allowed economic, religious, and political liberty.

433

The champion of economic liberty was a Scottish professor named Adam Smith. The champions of political liberty were a French aristocrat named Montesquieu (MOHN-tes-KYOO) and a Swiss commoner named Rousseau (roo-SOH). All three claimed to have discovered the "natural laws" by which society works.

Adam Smith supported free trade.

As a professor at the University of Edinburgh, Adam Smith (1723–1790) devoted almost every waking hour to philosophic questions. Often, he was so busy with his own thoughts that he dressed in rumpled, mismatched outfits.

In Diderot's *Encyclopedia*, Smith read the ideas of French economic theorists who called themselves "physiocrats." The physiocrats argued that the old mercantilist ideas about wealth were wrong. Did nations become wealthier by placing heavy tariffs on foreign goods? No, said the physiocrats. All such governmental regulations actually interfered with the production of wealth.

Instead, said the physiocrats, the government should give merchants a free hand to produce and sell their goods openly in the world market. The economy would prosper by itself if the government left it alone. The French phrase for "leave alone" was *laissez faire* (LAY-zay FAIR).

Adam Smith defended the idea of a free economy in his book *The Wealth of Nations*, published in 1776. He argued that a free economy could produce far more wealth than an economy regulated by governmental laws. His arguments rested on three so-called natural laws of economics.

The law of self-interest People act for selfish reasons, said Smith. They work for their own good, not for their neighbor's good. For example, bakers do not bake bread out of concern for hunger. Bakers bake bread to make money. Their motives are selfish. In his second and third laws, Smith explained how both the buyer and the seller gain from the other's selfish motives.

The law of competition In a free market, every baker competes with other bakers. To stay in business, each baker must try to make bread more efficiently and sell it at a lower price than rival bakers can. In other words, competition forces people to make a better product. Thus, competition among selfish individuals leads naturally to economic progress for all.

The law of supply and demand What happens if bakers make more bread than people want to buy? In other words, what happens when the supply of bread exceeds the demand for it? In that case, said Smith, bakers would have to lower their prices to attract more customers. The low price would drive the least efficient bakers out of business. This process would continue until there were just enough bakers to meet their customers' demand for bread.

According to Smith, in a society where these natural laws were free to operate, plenty of goods would be produced at the lowest possible price. On the other hand, if the government interfered in the economy, none of the natural laws could operate. Economic liberty, said Smith, was essential to economic progress.

Montesquieu advocated separation of powers.

A French nobleman, the Baron de Montesquieu (1689–1755), devoted himself to the study of political liberty. For years, he studied the history of ancient Rome. He concluded that Rome's collapse was directly related to its loss of political liberties.

Montesquieu believed that Britain was the best-governed country of his own day. Here was a government, he thought, in which power was balanced among three groups of officials. The British king and his ministers held **executive** power. They carried out the laws of the state. The members of Parliament held **legislative** or law-making power. The judges of the English courts held **judicial** power. They interpreted the laws to see how each applied to a specific case. Montesquieu called this division of power into three branches **separation of powers**.

Although Montesquieu oversimplified the British system, it gave him the idea for his most famous book, *On the Spirit of Laws*. Published in 1748, it contained such maxims on government as these:

- When the legislative and executive powers are united in the same person . . . there can be no liberty.
- Again, there is no liberty if the judiciary power be not separated from the legislative and executive [power].
- Power should be a check to power.

Encourage a class debate on Montesquieu's conclusion about the fall of Rome.

(This last statement meant that each branch of government would limit the power of the other two branches. Thus, no branch could become a threat to liberty.)

Montesquieu's book was admired by political leaders in the British colonies of North America. His ideas about separation of powers became the basis for the United States Constitution.

Rousseau championed freedom.

The third great champion of liberty during the Enlightenment was a strange figure indeed. His name was Jean Jacques Rousseau.

Rousseau (1712–1778) was born in the Swiss city of Geneva, the son of a watchmaker. When he was 13 years old, he was apprenticed to an engraver, a harsh and unkind man. After three unpleasant years, Rousseau fled to Italy. Thereafter, he worked at many jobs, including music teacher, tutor, and secretary.

Eventually, Rousseau made his way to Paris and won recognition as a writer of essays. Diderot and other Enlightenment leaders tried to befriend him. Yet Rousseau felt out of place in the elegant salons of Paris. He much preferred walking in the woods. Sooner or later, Rousseau quarreled

Adam Smith saw the market as an invisible hand that guided the production of goods and services.

with almost everyone. At times in his later years, he was undoubtedly insane. Nonetheless, his ideas about government were brilliant.

Rousseau's best known book on government was *The Social Contract*, published in 1762. The book begins with the declaration, "Man is born free, yet everywhere he is in chains." In other words, liberty was every person's natural birthright, and yet most people were oppressed.

How did this unnatural state of things come about? In brief, this was Rousseau's answer: In the earliest times, people had lived as free and equal individuals in a primitive "state of nature." As people became civilized, however, the strongest among them forced everyone else to obey unjust laws. Thus, freedom and equality were destroyed.

Like Locke, Rousseau argued that the only legitimate government was one that ruled with the consent of its people. However, Rousseau believed in a much broader democracy than Locke had advocated. The people, not monarchs or aristocrats, should be sovereign (dominant), said Rousseau. He believed that liberty and justice would thrive in a state where the "general will" of the people was all-powerful.

Section Review 2

Define: (a) executive, (b) legislative, (c) judicial, (d) separation of powers
Identify: (a) physiocrat, (b) laissez faire, (c) Adam Smith, (d) Montesquieu, (e) Rousseau
Answer:
1. (a) How did the philosophes feel about economic, religious, and political liberty? (b) Who was the greatest champion of economic liberty? (c) Who were the leading champions of political liberty?
2. What were Adam Smith's three natural laws of economics?
3. (a) What did Montesquieu believe led to the fall of Rome? (b) What did he admire about the government of Great Britain?
4. (a) What was Rousseau's view on government? (b) How did it differ from Locke's?

Critical Thinking
5. (a) What did Montesquieu mean when he said, "Power should be a check to power?" (b) How did his viewpoint reflect enlightened ideas?

We know of Rousseau's inner feelings and wild changes of mood from his autobiography. It begins: "I desire to set before my fellows the likeness of a man in all the truth of nature. I believe that I am not made like any of those who are in existence."

435

Enlightened despots sought progress.

3

What did the kings and queens of Europe think about the ideas of the philosophes? The French king, Louis XV (1715–1774), liked to be entertained but not enlightened. He was openly hostile to the philosophes and often ordered their writings censored.

Other monarchs, however, were enchanted by the new ideas about reason and progress. Several rulers conducted scientific experiments, played musical instruments, dabbled at poetry, read books of philosophy, and corresponded with Voltaire. They were what historians call **enlightened despots**. A despot is an absolute ruler, one who controls all the powers of government. Enlightened despots, therefore, were absolute rulers who supposedly used their great power for the good of the people they ruled.

The philosophes were willing to consider a ruler enlightened if he or she (1) favored religious tolerance, (2) made economic and legal reforms, and (3) could justify his or her reign by its usefulness to society rather than by divine right. In the 1700's, Frederick II of Prussia and Catherine II of Russia were the foremost of Europe's enlightened despots.

Frederick II made reforms in Prussia.

Frederick II was the young Prussian king who invaded Austria in 1740 and began the War of the Austrian Succession (page 422). Born in 1712, Frederick ruled Prussia from 1740 to 1786 during the Enlightenment. He is known as Frederick the Great.

Frederick was brilliant. He had a keen ear for music and a passion for witty conversation. He always carried his flute with him, even on military campaigns. He wrote long, flattering letters to his intellectual hero, Voltaire. Voltaire, who loved to be flattered, answered Frederick's letters with flowery phrases of his own.

Frederick invited Voltaire to come to Prussia so that they might talk of philosophy. Voltaire consented, and for three years (1750–1753) he lived in Frederick's palace at Potsdam. At first, the two men seemed like ideal companions. Both were witty. Both cared nothing for appearances and dressed in shabby, rumpled clothes. Each friend paid the other elegant compliments.

Before long, however, the king and the philosophe got on each other's nerves. Voltaire disliked editing Frederick's mediocre poetry. Frederick suspected Voltaire of some shady business dealings. Eventually, Voltaire tried to sneak out of Potsdam, but Prussian soldiers captured him and made him spend the night in jail. Both men were now thoroughly angry. Returning to France, Voltaire described the Prussian king as "a nasty monkey, perfidious friend, wretched poet." Frederick returned the abuse, calling Voltaire a "miser, dirty rogue, coward."

Was Frederick truly an enlightened ruler? His opinions were generally liberal and humane, but his deeds were not always so. He granted religious freedom to Catholics and Protestants, but he discriminated against Polish and Prussian Jews. He reduced but did not abolish the use of torture in his kingdom. He allowed freedom of the press. He admitted that serfdom was wrong. Yet he did nothing to end it because he needed the support of landowners.

Perhaps Frederick's most important contribution was his attitude toward being king. He called himself "the first servant of the state." From the beginning of his reign, he made it clear that his goal was to serve and strengthen his country. This attitude was clearly one that appealed to the philosophes.

Catherine the Great ruled Russia.

Catherine II of Russia was another monarch who wrote letters to Voltaire and claimed to rule by enlightened principles. Voltaire, in turn, flattered Catherine, calling her "the star of the north," "benefactress of Europe," "first person in the universe."

Catherine was born in 1729, the daughter of an unimportant German prince. At 15, she was sent to the distant Russian court at St. Petersburg to be married to the Grand Duke Peter, heir to the Russian throne.

Peter the Great's daughter, Elizabeth, was the ruler of Russia when Catherine arrived. The Grand Duke, whom Catherine was to wed, was her nephew. Peter was mentally unstable. His chief pleasures were playing with toy soldiers and torturing dogs and cats.

Despite his reforms, "Old Fritz" (as Frederick came to be called) was not popular in Prussia by the end of his reign. He openly despised most people and showed real affection only for his pet dogs. His last wish was that he be buried beside his dogs.

Catherine soon saw that Peter's weakness and cruelty gave her an opportunity to seize power. She made important friends among Russia's army officers, and she became known as the most intelligent and well-informed person at court. In 1762, only months after her husband became czar as Peter III, Catherine had him arrested and imprisoned. Soon afterward, Peter conveniently died in prison, probably by murder. In September 1762, Catherine was crowned Catherine II of Russia, beginning a reign that lasted 34 years.

Though Russia was not her native land, Catherine II dedicated herself totally to the country's welfare. In 1767, she called a large convention of nobles, free peasants, and townspeople to frame a constitution for Russia. To guide them, she wrote a brilliant essay suggesting many reforms. She wanted to stop capital punishment, end the use of torture, and abolish serfdom. Unfortunately, the delegates to the convention debated and quarreled for months. Finally, Catherine lost patience and dismissed them. Though they had accomplished nothing, Catherine had tried to listen to the wishes of the common people.

Even without a constitution, Catherine put several of her enlightened ideas into effect. She limited the use of torture (but kept the death penalty). She allowed greater religious freedom to Roman Catholics and Jews. She encouraged education.

Catherine honored the great writers of the Enlightenment. (She herself wrote a large number of plays, fairy tales, and satiric essays.) Learning that Diderot desperately needed money, she wrote to him offering to buy his personal library for any price he named. He suggested a figure. She paid him twice what he asked and allowed him to keep the books during his lifetime.

In spite of her sympathy for enlightened ideas, however, Catherine did little to improve the life of the peasants in her empire. A great turning point in her plans for reform came in 1773. In that year, there was a massive uprising of Russian serfs, soldiers, and escaped prisoners. The leader of the rebellion was a soldier named Pugachev, who claimed to be the dead Peter III. As in the peasant revolts of western Europe in the 1300's, serfs burned manor houses and murdered landowners. When Pugachev promised to end serfdom, the revolt spread like wildfire. His mobs threatened Moscow itself.

As wife of the heir to the throne, Catherine (shown here at 19) had the title Grand Duchess.

With great brutality, Catherine's army crushed the rebellion. Her soldiers destroyed whole villages. The roads of Russia were lined with gallows for hanging rebels. Pugachev was brought in an iron cage to Moscow and was executed.

After the revolt, Catherine saw that she could not keep her throne without the nobles' support. She dropped her plans for ending serfdom and gave the Russian nobles absolute control over their serfs. Thus, under the "enlightened despot" Catherine, Russian serfs lost their last traces of freedom. By the end of her reign, nearly 95 percent of Russia's people toiled as serfs for all-powerful landlords.

Catherine expanded Russia's lands.

Like Frederick II, Catherine ignored the philosophes' arguments against war. She waged war relentlessly against Russia's southern neighbor, the Ottoman Turks.

In 1773, Diderot traveled to St. Petersburg to visit his benefactress. He became excited as he talked and gestured wildly—thumping on her knees and pounding her shoulders—to make a point. Catherine finally put a table between them.

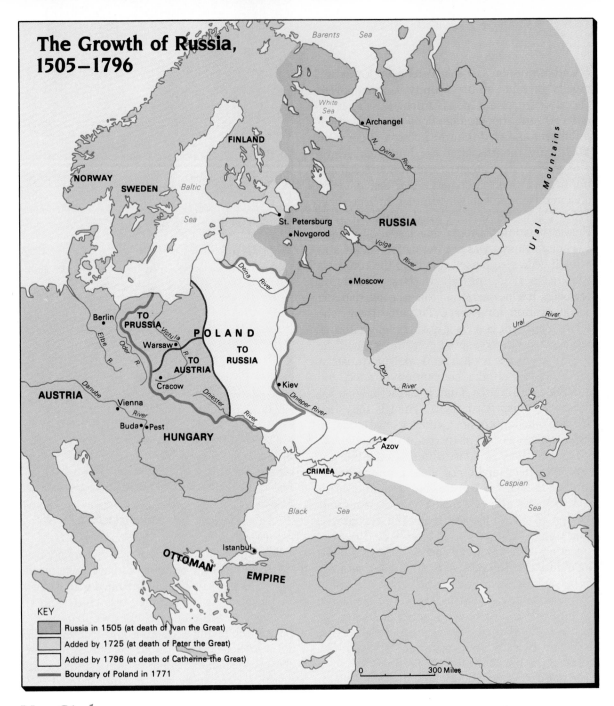

The Growth of Russia, 1505–1796

NORWAY
SWEDEN
FINLAND
NORWAY
Baltic
Sea
Barents Sea
White Sea
• Archangel
N. Dvina River
Ural Mountains
• St. Petersburg
• Novgorod
RUSSIA
Volga River
Berlin •
TO PRUSSIA
Dvina River
• Moscow
Elbe R.
Oder R.
Vistula R.
Warsaw •
POLAND
TO RUSSIA
Ural River
TO AUSTRIA
• Cracow
Dniester River
Don River
Ural River
AUSTRIA
Danube River
• Vienna
Buda • • Pest
HUNGARY
Dnieper River
• Kiev
• Azov
CRIMEA
Caspian Sea
Black Sea
Istanbul •
OTTOMAN
EMPIRE

KEY
Russia in 1505 (at death of Ivan the Great)
Added by 1725 (at death of Peter the Great)
Added by 1796 (at death of Catherine the Great)
Boundary of Poland in 1771

0   300 Miles

Map Study

What port did Russia have on the White Sea? On the Baltic? Along what seas did Catherine II win land? What three countries divided Polish lands?

Just as Peter the Great had fought for years to win a port on the Baltic Sea, Catherine was determined to win access to the Black Sea. In 1783, her armies won the Crimean Peninsula on the Black Sea. This victory brought Russia a giant step closer to Catherine's goal of reaching the Mediterranean Sea.

Catherine's conquests of Turkish territory threatened the delicate balance of power that existed in eastern Europe. Prussia's Frederick the Great and Austria's Maria Theresa both feared that Russian armies might grab the strategic straits leading to the Mediterranean Sea, the Bosporus, and the Dardanelles.

438

Map Study answers: Archangel; St. Petersburg; Black Sea, the Baltic Sea, and the Caspian Sea; Austria, Prussia, and Russia

The partition of Poland It was a dangerous situation until Frederick suggested a scheme that satisfied all three countries—Austria, Prussia, and Russia. Frederick proposed that the three powerful countries should take chunks of territory from the weak kingdom of Poland, rather than fight a costly war over Turkish lands.

Catherine and Maria Theresa agreed to Frederick's plan. In 1772, Austria, Russia, and Prussia each took a generous slice of Poland and sent troops to occupy it. Poland's wishes in the matter were ignored. This flagrant land grab was known as the First Partition of Poland.

There were two later partitions, both suggested by Catherine. In 1793, Russia and Prussia took more of Poland's land. Two years later, in 1795, the three greedy neighbors took the rest. On a map of Europe, Poland no longer existed. It did not appear again as an independent country until after World War I.

Catherine's achievement Catherine was the only monarch who lived long enough to participate in all three partitions of Poland. By war and diplomacy, she had vastly enlarged the Russian empire, adding 200,000 square miles of Turkish and Polish lands.

At the end of her remarkable reign (1762–1796), Catherine the Great wrote the epitaph for her own tomb: "Enthroned in Russia, she desired nothing but the best for her country and tried to procure for her subjects happiness, liberty, and wealth. She forgave easily and hated no one." She exaggerated only a little.

Section Review 3

Define: enlightened despot
Identify: (a) Frederick II, (b) Catherine II
Answer:
1. According to the beliefs of the philosophes, what did a ruler have to do in order to earn the title *enlightened?*
2. (a) In the 1700's, what despots were the foremost of Europe's enlightened rulers? (b) In what respect did each try to be an enlightened ruler? (c) In what respect did each fail?
3. (a) How did Catherine the Great expand Russian lands? (b) Why did this concern Prussia and Austria? (c) What solution did Frederick II propose?

Critical Thinking
4. What did Frederick II mean when he called himself the "first servant of the state?" Was he? Explain.
5. Was the partition of Poland in accord with the principles of the Enlightenment? Why or why not?

Britain developed new forms of leadership. 4

The philosophes looked on England's government as the most progressive in Europe. England's ruler was no despot, not even an enlightened one. The Glorious Revolution of 1688 had given England a **constitutional monarchy**. The power of the ruler was limited by law.

Even while the English monarch's power was being limited at home, the power of the English nation was spreading overseas. During the 1600's and 1700's, England won colonies in many parts of the world, including North America and India. Indeed, after 1707 (when the kingdoms of England and Scotland were officially joined), the country even had an impressive new name—Great Britain. To rule this far-flung empire, Britain's monarch and Parliament developed new ways of working together.

Britain was a limited democracy.

After 1688, no British monarch could rule without the consent of Parliament. At the same time, Parliament could not rule without the consent of the monarch. Thus, there was danger of a stalemate if the crown and Parliament disagreed.

During the 1700's, that problem was gradually solved by the development of an executive committee called the **cabinet**. This committee acted in the ruler's name but in reality represented the majority party of the House of Commons. Only temporary and makeshift at first, the cabinet eventually became one of Britain's most durable institutions.

The development of the cabinet Under William and Mary, the cabinet was nothing more than a group of the monarchs' most influential ministers. Like earlier rulers, William III, who was

The French Revolution and Napoleon

Rebellious Parisians and soldiers dragged cannons toward the Bastille on July 14, 1789. The fall of the Bastille marked the beginning of the French Revolution.

Key Terms

estate
bourgeoisie
coalition
coup
plebiscite
guerrilla

Read and Understand

1. The French monarchy faced a crisis.
2. Revolution brought reform and terror.
3. Napoleon conquered much of Europe.
4. Napoleon's empire collapsed.

Beneath the towering gray walls of an old fortress, a shouting mob of Parisians brandished their stolen muskets. They had been rioting for several hours on this gray and misty day, July 14, 1789. The muskets in their hands and the ammunition in their pockets had been taken that morning from a military hospital on the other side of Paris. Now they were clamoring at the gates of the fortress called the Bastille.

Built in the Middle Ages, the Bastille served in the 1700's as a jail for political prisoners. It was guarded by 114 soldiers loyal to the French king. Their aristocratic commander, the Marquis de Launay (mahr-**KEE** duh loh-**NAY**), firmly refused to turn over the fortress and its 20,000 pounds of gunpowder to the mob. After several tense hours

The Bastille was located in a middle class neighborhood and its imposing presence was a daily reminder of the taking of political prisoners.

of waiting, he gave the order to fire. Cannons thundered from the battlements.

Some of the rioters were killed, and hundreds of others quickly took cover. They loaded their stolen weapons. It was a battle now between the soldiers' heavy cannons and the civilians' light muskets, and the civilians were taking a beating.

However, other soldiers in Paris sympathized with the mob. A few blocks from the Bastille, an ex-officer in the French Guard pleaded with his comrades:

> Brave guards, can't you hear the cannons? ... That villain De Launay is murdering our brothers, our parents, our wives and children who are gathered unarmed around the Bastille. Will you allow them to be massacred? ... Will you not march on the Bastille?

Tears streamed down the man's face as he spoke. Moved to fury by his speech, 60 soldiers followed him to the Bastille, dragging 4 cannons with them. Facing these heavy guns, the Marquis de Launay had no choice but to surrender.

It was a moment of triumph for the working people of Paris, a moment of stark terror for the marquis and his men. The mob dragged the captive soldiers through the narrow lanes of the city. "Stones were thrown at me," said one soldier, "and women gnashed their teeth and brandished their fists at me." That soldier survived the fury of the mob, but De Launay and others were hacked to death.

Meanwhile, in his palace at Versailles, France's King Louis XVI was peacefully asleep. Awakened by a duke, he heard the horrifying news of the fall of the Bastille. "Why, this is a revolt!" exclaimed the king. "No sire," the duke replied. "It is a revolution."

It was indeed a revolution that confronted Louis in the summer of 1789. Historians generally divide this revolution into four stages. First, there was a relatively moderate stage (1789–1792) in which the leaders wrote a constitution and a bill of human rights. Second came a radical and bloody stage (1793–1794) called the Reign of Terror. Third, there was a period of reaction against the violence of the revolution (1794–1799). In the fourth and final stage (1799–1815), an ambitious young general named Napoleon Bonaparte made himself France's dictator and later its emperor.

In this story of violent change and upheaval, the storming of the Bastille was only one episode. Yet it was a crucial one, as we shall see.

The French monarchy faced a crisis. 1

Why did millions of French people suddenly revolt against institutions that their ancestors had accepted for hundreds of years? Ways of life that once served people well can become rigid over time. New conditions change the way people see their world. What seems reasonable in one age may later seem hateful and unnecessary.

By the 1770's, the old institutions of monarchy and feudalism no longer worked for France. As a group, these institutions were known as the Old Regime.

The Old Regime had three estates.

Since the Middle ages, the people of France had been divided into three large social classes, or **estates.** The Roman Catholic clergy formed the First Estate. The nobles made up the Second Estate. The commoners were the Third Estate. In the 1300's, these three groups had begun meeting as the Estates General (page 239), a French institution much like the early English Parliament.

The Old Regime worked well for the members of the First Estate and the Second Estate. They enjoyed wealth and special privileges under law. The Third Estate, however, had many reasons for dissatisfaction.

The First Estate The Catholic Church held about 10 percent of all the land in France. The highest officials of the French Church—the archbishops, bishops, and abbots—were enormously wealthy. Parish priests, on the other hand, were nearly as poor as the peasants to whom they preached.

French clergy paid no direct taxes to the royal government. Instead, they gave the government a "free gift" of about 2 percent of their income.

The Second Estate Although nobles made up less than 2 percent of France's population, they owned about 20 percent of the land. They also

449

held all the highest offices in the church, the army, the government, and the courts of law. For centuries, the people of this estate had enjoyed the privilege of paying no taxes. Their refusal to pay taxes was one cause for revolution.

The Third Estate About 98 percent of France's people belonged to the Third Estate. There were actually three groups in the Third Estate: (1) a city-dwelling middle class called the **bourgeoisie** (boor-zhwah-ZEE), (2) urban lower classes, and (3) peasant farmers. Although these three groups belonged to the same political classification, they were very different economically.

The bourgeoisie had been growing slowly in numbers and power since the Middle Ages. By profession, its members were lawyers, doctors, manufacturers, bankers, merchants, and shop-keepers. Many were well educated and believed strongly in the Enlightenment ideals of liberty and equality. Some of the bourgeoisie were as rich as nobles. Like nobles, wealthy middle-class men dressed in powdered wigs, fine waistcoats, and tight-fitting knee breeches called *culottes* with silk stockings below the knee. Yet the law treated them as peasants. Members of the bourgeoisie yearned for social status and political power equal to their wealth.

The workers of France's cities—butchers, brewers, weavers, tanners, peddlers, cooks, ser-vants, and others—formed a second group within the Third Estate. They were poorer than the bourgeoisie, and their poverty showed in their clothing. Unlike the nobles and the bourgeoisie, poor men wore shirts and loose-fitting trousers that came down to their ankles. As a class, these urban workers were called *sans-culottes* (those who are without knee breeches).

The poor people of France's cities often went hungry. Most of Paris's poor people ate three pounds of bread a day and very little else. If the cost of bread rose, hungry mobs attacked carts of grain and bread to steal what they needed. In 1788, grain harvests were small. The price of bread doubled. Thus, the sans-culottes were in a dangerous mood in the spring of 1789.

The largest group within the Third Estate were the peasants. They made up more than four fifths of France's 26 million people. As a rule, French peasants in the 1700's lived better than peasants elsewhere in Europe. Even so, they lost about half their income in taxes. They paid feudal dues to the nobles, tithes to the church, and royal taxes to the king's agent.

Besides taxes in money, peasants owed the *corvée*. The corvée was a form of tax that was paid with work rather than money. Every year, the law required the peasants to work without pay on government roads for a certain number of days.

Thus, the bourgeoisie, the sans-culottes of the cities, and the peasants of the countryside all had reasons to hate the Old Regime. The French Revolution was partly the outcome of these re-sentments from the lower classes. It was also the result of weak leadership at the top.

Louis XVI was a weak ruler.

Louis XVI, who became king in 1774, was good-hearted and generous. However, he was not a strong leader. He was indecisive and allowed matters to drift.

Louis and his wife, Marie Antoinette, were a devoted couple. They married when he was 15 years old and she was 14. Marie Antoinette was pretty, light-hearted, and charming. However, she was unpopular from the day she set foot in France because she came from the royal family of Austria, France's longtime enemy. The queen made herself even more unpopular by her habit of buying ex-pensive gowns and jewels while the poor went hungry and the government treasury was empty.

Louis's government was deeply in debt. Part of the debt arose because Louis had borrowed heavily to help the American revolutionaries in their war against Great Britain. Britain was France's chief rival, and Louis had seized the chance to strike at the British.

Louis's ministers hoped to avoid bankruptcy by taxing the nobles. The nobles, however, refused to pay taxes unless the king called a meeting of the Estates General, which had not met since 1614. Reluctantly, Louis called a meeting of the estates at Versailles on May 1, 1789. As it proved, his order was nothing less than an invitation to revolution.

The National Assembly took power.

The First and Second estates (clergy and nobles) had dominated the Estates General in the Middle Ages. They still expected to do so in 1789. Under

A French writer of the period described the poor wage earners of Paris: "The people are like a man wading in a pond with water up to his mouth: the slightest dip in the ground, the slightest ripple, makes him lose his footing—he sinks and chokes."

On June 20, 1789, the king locked the Third Estate out of its meeting hall. Furious, members met at an indoor tennis court nearby, where they vowed to stand fast until a constitution was established.

the estates' medieval rules, each estate was to meet in its own hall and vote either for or against a given proposal. In the final decision, each estate was to have one vote. Thus, the First and Second estates could always outvote the Third Estate two to one.

In 1789, the Third Estate demanded that all three estates meet together. The votes of all members would count equally. The 610 members of the Third Estate would thus outnumber the 591 members of the combined First and Second estates.

Siding with the nobles, the king ordered the estates to follow the old rules. The representatives of the Third Estate, however, became more and more determined to wield power. The leading spokesman for their viewpoint was a clergyman sympathetic to their cause, the Abbé Sieyès (ah-**BAY** syay-**YAS**). In a bold pamphlet, he had written, "What is the Third Estate? Everything. What has it been up to now in the political order? Nothing. What does it demand? To become something herein."

On June 16, the Abbé Sieyès rose to address an excited gathering of bourgeois deputies. He suggested that the Third Estate change its name to the National Assembly. He called on the new assembly to pass laws and reforms in the name of the French people.

After a long night of excited debate, the deputies of the Third Estate agreed to Sieyès's idea by an overwhelming majority. The vote of June 17, 1789, created the National Assembly. In effect, the deputies proclaimed an end to absolute monarchy and the beginning of representative government. This vote was the first deliberate act of revolution.

Parisians stormed the Bastille.

In this crisis, Louis XVI acted indecisively. He tried to make peace with the Third Estate by yielding to their demands. He ordered the nobles and clergy to meet as one law-making body with the Third Estate (now the National Assembly). At the same time, the king sent orders for his mercenary army of Swiss guards to march toward Paris. He called on these Swiss troops because he could no longer trust the loyalty of French soldiers. The bourgeois deputies feared, with good

The tennis court had been built for the amusement of the king's courtiers. When the members of the Third Estate found it empty, they entered noisily and ripped off one of its doors to make a table for their assembly leader.

Comparing pictures *A Parisian woman (left) and Marie Antoinette symbolize two different classes. What role and rights did each have in French society?*

reason, that the troops were coming to break up the National Assembly.

In Paris, mobs were already rioting over the high price of bread. The riots reached their peak in the storming of the Bastille. What the mob wanted was the Bastille's supply of gunpowder to defend Paris and the National Assembly against the king's foreign troops.

The fall of the Bastille was important for several reasons. Militarily, it forced Louis to give up his plan of bringing his foreign troops into the city. Politically, it reduced the king's power and saved the National Assembly.

Perhaps most important, the fall of the Bastille became a great symbolic act of revolution in the minds of French people. Ever since 1789, they have celebrated July 14 as a national holiday similar to the United States' Fourth of July.

The Great Fear swept France.

Before long, rebellion was spreading from Paris into the countryside. From one village to the next, wild rumors circulated about a plot against the common people. People said that nobles were hiring brigands to terrorize the peasants.

A wave of panic, called the Great Fear, swept France. Peasants banded together and hid in forests and caves. When they met no enemy brigands, they became brigands themselves. Waving pitchforks and torches, they broke into nobles' manor houses. Once inside, they tore up the old legal papers that bound them to pay feudal dues. Then they burned the manor houses as well.

In October 1789, thousands of Parisian women rioted over the rising price of bread. Their anger quickly turned against the king and queen. Why was the royal couple living in luxury at Versailles while the people starved? The women demanded that Louis and Marie Antoinette come to Paris.

Seizing knives and axes, the women marched on Versailles. They broke into the palace, ransacked the queen's apartments, and killed three guards. Finally, the king appeared on a balcony and told the angry mob below, "My friends, I will go to Paris with my wife and children." Never again would Louis and his family see the beautiful palace at Versailles.

As queen, Marie Antoinette had a ceremonial role, with great influence in society and the culture and fashion of the court but with no direct political rights. The Parisian woman—a member of the lower class—had neither rights nor influence. Parisian women in the Revolution, however, showed their concern for political matters and economic conditions.

Section Review 1

Define: (a) estates, (b) bourgeoisie, (c) sans-culottes, (d) corvée

Identify: (a) July 14, 1789, (b) Bastille, (c) Louis XVI, (d) Old Regime, (e) Estates General, (f) Marie Antoinette, (g) National Assembly, (h) Great Fear

Answer:

1. (a) What were the three estates in France? (b) What part did each play in French society and government?

2. (a) Briefly describe each of the groups that made up the Third Estate. (b) Why was each dissatisfied with the Old Regime?

3. How did the characters of King Louis XVI and Queen Marie Antoinette add to the crisis that France faced?

4. Why did the king need to call a meeting of the Estates General?

5. (a) What was the voting system in the Estates General before 1789? (b) How did the Third Estate wish to change this system? (c) How did Louis react? (d) What was the result?

6. (a) Why was the fall of the Bastille important militarily? (b) Politically? (c) Symbolically?

7. What happened during the Great Fear?

Critical Thinking

8. At first, Louis XVI called the fall of the Bastille "a revolt," but he was told it was "a revolution." What is the difference?

Revolution brought reform and terror.

2

The night of August 4, 1789, was one of the most astonishing nights in the history of France. In a matter of hours, the National Assembly swept away the ancient privileges of the nobility and the clergy.

One by one, the nobles in the assembly gave impassioned speeches declaring their love of liberty and equality. The nobles who made these grand speeches were moved by fear as well as idealism. The Great Fear was at its height, and peasant bands were terrorizing the countryside.

The Assembly adopted many reforms.

The emotional speeches went on through the night. By morning, the National Assembly had voted to end feudalism, serfdom, church tithes, and the special privileges of nobles and clergy. The Old Regime was dead. "Liberty, Equality, Fraternity" became the slogan of the revolution.

The Rights of Man Three weeks later, on August 27, 1789, the National Assembly adopted a set of revolutionary ideas called *A Declaration of the Rights of Man and of the Citizen.* The first article of the document declared, "Men are born and remain free and equal in rights." The second article stated:

> The aim of all political association is the preservation of the natural . . . rights of man. These rights are liberty, property, security, and resistance to oppression.

Other articles of the famous document guaranteed citizens equal justice, freedom of speech, and freedom of religion.

A limited monarchy For two years, the National Assembly argued over a new constitution for France. By 1791, they had made huge changes in France's government and society.

The National Assembly created a limited, constitutional monarchy somewhat like the British government. An elected assembly held the law-making power. Although the monarchy lost its absolute powers, the king and his ministers still held the executive power to enforce laws.

Departments The National Assembly abolished France's traditional provinces, which had existed since the Middle Ages. Instead, the assembly divided France into 83 districts called departments. A council of officials elected by the local citizens administered each department.

A state-controlled church The Catholic Church lost both its lands and its political independence. The government took over church lands. The assembly also ruled that church officials and priests were to be elected by property owners and paid as state officials. This law alarmed millions of devout French peasants, who rallied to the support of their parish priests.

These changes in the Catholic Church drove a wedge between the peasants and the bourgeoisie. From this time on, the peasants often opposed further revolutionary changes.

453

The king reluctantly approved the constitution and the Declaration of the Rights of Man. Then, in June 1791, Louis and his family tried to escape from France to the Austrian Netherlands. Just as they neared the French border, however, a postmaster recognized the king from his portrait on some paper money. The royal family returned to Paris under guard. As a result of this attempted escape, Louis XVI discredited both himself and the plan for constitutional monarchy. His action increased the influence of his radical enemies and sealed his own doom.

In September 1791, having completed its new constitution, the National Assembly stepped down from power. It was followed by a newly elected group called the Legislative Assembly.

France was split by factions.

Despite the new government, the old problems remained. Angry cries for more liberty, more equality, and more bread soon caused the leaders of the revolution to turn against one another.

The Legislative Assembly split into three general groups. Each group tended to sit together in its own part of the meeting hall. On the benches to the right sat the conservatives, those who opposed more changes in government. In general, they trusted the king and upheld the idea of limited monarchy. On the left side of the hall sat the radicals, those who clamored for more sweeping changes. They hated the king and wanted to set up a republic in which the common people had full power. In the center sat the moderates. They wanted some further reforms but not as many as the radicals demanded.

To this day, radical politicians are commonly described as being "on the left," and conservative politicians are said to be "on the right." Moderates are called "centrists." These terms began with the French Revolution.

Outside the government, there were far more extreme groups, both on the right and on the left. People on the extreme right hoped to undo the revolution and restore the Old Regime. Among this group were the emigrés (EHM-uh-grayz) —nobles who had fled during the peasant uprisings. They lived abroad and plotted against the revolution. On the extreme left were the sans-culottes of Paris. Their radical leaders set

Voice from the Past · *The Rights of Woman*

In 1791, a woman revolutionary named Olympe de Gouges (goozh) demanded the same rights for French women that French men were demanding for themselves. Here is part of her "Declaration of the Rights of Woman."

Woman is born free and lives equal to man in her rights. Social distinctions can be based only on the common utility . . .

The law must be the expression of the general will; all female and male citizens must contribute either personally or through their representatives to its formation; it must be the same for all: male and female citizens, being equal in the eyes of the law, must be equally admitted to all honors, positions, and public employment according to their capacity and without other distinctions besides those of their virtues and talents . . .

No one is to be [persecuted] for basic opinions; woman has the right to mount the scaffold; she must equally have the right to mount the rostrum [a public speaking platform].

1. What legal rights does De Gouges ask for women?
2. What political positions does she say should be open to women?
3. (a) What is implied by "the right to mount the scaffold"? (b) By "the right to mount the rostrum"?

les femmes

Olympe de Gouges was a playwright who turned her talents to political writing when the conflicts began. The work excerpted here was dedicated to Marie Antoinette.

up a new city government with representatives from each of Paris's 48 sections. This powerful city council, known as the Paris Commune, became a dominant force in the revolution.

France went to war with Austria.

France faced not only a revolution at home but also a disastrous foreign war. The ruler of Austria, Marie Antoinette's brother, threatened to attack France.

French radicals were delighted at the idea of war with Austria. They hoped that the war would give them a chance to spread their revolution to all the peoples of Europe. On April 20, 1792, the Legislative Assembly declared war on Austria. Soon Prussia joined Austria against France.

The war began badly for the poorly equipped French armies. By the summer of 1792, enemy armies were advancing toward Paris.

On July 25, the Prussian commander threatened to destroy Paris if the revolutionaries harmed any member of the royal family. This rash statement provoked the fury of the mob. On August 10, about 70,000 men and women surged into the palace in Paris where the royal couple was staying. The king's Swiss guard of 900 men fought desperately to defend Louis. The mob brutally massacred them and swarmed through the palace. Louis and Marie Antoinette were imprisoned in a stone tower.

Under the threat of the Parisian radicals, the Legislative Assembly gave up the idea of a limited monarchy. The lawmakers set aside the Constitution of 1791 and declared the king deposed. The assembly then ended its own existence by calling for the election of a new legislature.

The new governing body, elected in September, was called the National Convention. Just as the new government took office, France had a stroke of luck. A French army managed to defeat the Austrians and Prussians. For the moment, France was out of danger from abroad.

The radicals executed Louis XVI.

During the desperate summer of 1792, the leaders of the frenzied mobs on the streets had more real power than any governmental assembly. Although the mobs were poor, their leaders came from the bourgeoisie.

Both men and women of the middle class joined political clubs. The most radical of these clubs in 1792 was the Jacobin (JAK-uh-buhn) Club, where violent speechmaking was the order of the day. Its members wanted to remove the king and establish a republic.

One of the frequent speakers before the Jacobin Club was Georges Danton (dahn-TOHN), a leader of the Paris Commune. Fearless and devoted to the rights of Paris's poor, Danton used his talent for speechmaking to win political leadership.

Another prominent radical leader was Jean Paul Marat (muh-RAH). The very opposite of the strong, bull-like Danton, Marat was a thin, high-strung, sickly man who had hoped to win fame for his scientific research. After the revolution broke out, he edited a radical newspaper called *The Friend of the People*. His fiery editorials called for "five or six hundred heads cut off" to rid France of the enemies of the revolution.

By August 1792, Danton and Marat were two of the most powerful of the radical leaders. Together with the Paris mob, these men set the revolution on a new and more violent path.

The National Convention met in Paris on September 21. It quickly abolished the monarchy. Next, the assembly declared France a republic. Every adult male citizen had the right to vote and hold office. Women could not vote, however, despite the important part they had already played in the revolution.

Louis XVI was king no longer. Under the new republic, he was just a common citizen and prisoner. What was to be done with this dangerous citizen? The delegates to the National Convention tried him for treason and found him guilty.

The radicals demanded that Louis be condemned to death. They won by a single vote. On the morning of January 21, 1793, the ex-king walked with calm dignity up the steps of the scaffold to be beheaded by a machine called the guillotine (GIHL-uh-TEEN). Thousands died by the guillotine during the French Revolution.

France created a citizen-army.

The new republic's first problem was the hostile armies of Austria and Prussia. In the fall of 1792, Britain, Spain, and Portugal joined Prussia and Austria in an alliance known as the First Coalition. (A **coalition** is a temporary alliance between

Groups of national guardsmen from the provinces marched to defend Paris against the Prussians. Among them were men from the seaport of Marseilles who marched into Paris singing "La Marseillaise," which later became the French national anthem.

The guillotine was invented by a doctor as a more humane form of execution than the ax.

groups who are usually on different sides.) In the face of so many enemies, France suffered a string of defeats.

The Jacobin leaders took extreme steps to meet the new danger. In February 1793, the convention drafted into the army 300,000 men between the ages of 18 and 40. By 1794, this number had grown to 800,000. Women too asked for the right to form regiments to defend France. The government never granted their request. However, a number of women fought beside men in France's armies during the revolution.

Most armies in Europe were made up of mercenaries, but the new French army was a people's army of loyal patriots. Led by dedicated officers, the French scored victory after victory.

Robespierre began the Terror.

Foreign armies were not the only enemies of the French Republic. The Jacobins had thousands of enemies within France itself—peasants who were horrified by the beheading of the king, priests who would not accept control by the government, and rival leaders who were stirring up rebellion in the provinces.

As dozens of leaders struggled for power, one man slowly gathered control into his own hands. His name was Maximilien Robespierre (ROHBZ-pihr).

Robespierre was one of the few members of the Jacobin Club who did not dress like a revolutionary. He wore a powdered wig in the old style, knee breeches, and stockings. Nicknamed "the Incorruptible," Robespierre never enriched himself at the public expense, unlike many of the men around him. In his fanaticism, however, Robespierre was merciless. His period in power is fittingly known as the Reign of Terror.

Robespierre and his supporters set out to build a Republic of Virtue. They tried to wipe out every trace of France's past monarchy and nobility. Many families named Leroy (king), for instance, changed their names to something less political. (Even if they did not support the monarchy, it was safer to take a new name.) Decks of cards no longer had kings, queens, and jacks. Instead, they had cards called liberties, equalities, and fraternities.

Firm believers in reason, the radicals wanted to make the calendar scientific. They divided the year into 12 months of 30 days and gave each month a new, "reasonable" name. October, for instance, was renamed Brumaire, or Fog Month. The new calendar had no Sundays because the radicals considered religion old-fashioned and dangerous. The Paris Commune closed all churches in the city. Towns all over France soon did the same.

In the summer of 1793, Robespierre formed the Committee of Public Safety. As head of the committee, Robespierre decided who should be judged an enemy of the republic. Those he accused were often tried in the morning and guillotined that very afternoon. From July 1793 to July 1794, he governed France nearly as a dictator.

The widowed queen, Marie Antoinette, was the most famous victim of the Terror. Calm and dignified, she rode in the death cart past jeering crowds. On the scaffold, she accidently stepped on her executioner's foot. "Monsieur," she apologized, "I beg your pardon. I did not do it on purpose." These were her last words.

However, the so-called enemies of the republic who most troubled Robespierre were not monarchists like Marie Antoinette. They were fellow revolutionaries who challenged his leadership. In October 1793, many of the leaders who had first helped set up the republic were executed. Their only crime was that they were less radical than Robespierre.

In the mid-1790's, many saw the Old Regime as the "good old days" and yearned for its return. Royalists pinned their hopes on Louis XVI's brother. The middle class wanted order restored but did not want to give up the power they had gained.

By the beginning of 1794, even Danton found himself in danger. (Marat had already been stabbed to death by a young woman from another political faction.) Danton's former friends in the National Assembly, afraid to defend him, joined in condemning him to death. On the scaffold, he told the executioner, "Don't forget to show my head to the people. It's well worth seeing."

Besides leading political figures, thousands of obscure people were sent to death on the flimsiest of charges. An 18-year-old youth was guillotined for sawing down a tree that had been planted as a symbol of liberty. A tavern keeper died because he had sold sour wine "to the defenders of the country."

During the Terror, at least 3,000 people were executed in Paris. Some historians believe as many as 40,000 were killed all together. Fully 80 percent were peasants, sans-culottes, or bourgeoisie—common people for whom the revolution had supposedly been fought.

Robespierre fell from power.

By July 1794, members of the National Convention knew that none of them was safe from Robespierre. To save themselves, they turned on him. A group of conspirators demanded his arrest, shouting "Down with the tyrant!" Robespierre tried to speak in his own defense, but delegates to both left and right shouted him down. Within two days, the revolution's last powerful leader went to the guillotine.

With Robespierre's execution, the radical phase of the French Revolution ended. Robespierre died on July 28, 1794. On the new revolutionary calendar, July was called *Thermidor* from the French word for "heat." Hence, the revolt against Robespierre is called the *Thermidorian reaction.*

Moderates ruled in the Directory.

Public opinion in France now shifted dramatically to the right. People of all classes were sick of the Terror. They were also sick of the skyrocketing prices for bread, salt, and other necessities of life.

In 1795, moderate leaders of the National Convention drafted a new constitution. This new plan of government put power firmly in the hands of the upper bourgeoisie. This constitution, the third since 1789, called for a two-house legislature and an executive body of five men known as the Directory.

The five directors were moderates, not revolutionary idealists. Some of them freely enriched themselves at the public's expense. Despite their corruption, however, they gave their troubled country a period of order.

The Directory also found the right general to command France's armies. With a string of astounding victories, this general crushed France's foes. The name of this supremely talented young man was Napoleon Bonaparte.

Section Review 2

Define: (a) emigrés, (b) guillotine, (c) coalition

Identify: (a) *Declaration of the Rights of Man and of the Citizen,* (b) Legislative Assembly, (c) Paris Commune, (d) Jacobin Club, (e) Danton, (f) Marat, (g) Robespierre, (h) Committee of Public Safety, (i) Reign of Terror, (j) Directory

Answer:
1. What rights were proclaimed in *A Declaration of the Rights of Man?*
2. (a) What reforms did the National Assembly make in France's government? (b) In the Catholic Church?
3. What was the result of the royal family's attempt to escape France?
4. (a) What were the basic political divisions within the Legislative Assembly? (b) How did seating arrangements there affect the labels given to political groups?
5. (a) How did the limited monarchy come to an end? (b) What was the fate of Louis XVI?
6. After 1793, how did the French army differ from the armies of its enemies?
7. (a) Briefly describe the Reign of Terror. (b) How did it end?
8. What political outlook did the Directory represent?

Critical Thinking
9. There is a saying, "Revolutions devour their own children." (a) What evidence from the French Revolution supports that proverb? (b) Why might revolutions in general have such an effect?

Napoleon conquered much of Europe. 3

Napoleon was a small man (five feet six inches tall) who cast a long shadow over the history of modern times. As a military genius, he ranks with Alexander the Great of Macedonia, Hannibal of Carthage, and Julius Caesar of Rome. In only four years (1795–1799), Napoleon rose from obscurity to mastery of France.

Napoleon rose through the army.

Napoleon Bonaparte was born in 1769 on the island of Corsica in the Mediterranean Sea. In that same year, French troops invaded Corsica and crushed a movement for Corsican independence. "I was born," wrote Bonaparte later, "when my country was dying."

When Bonaparte was ten years old, his parents sent him to a military school outside Paris where his French schoolmates snubbed him as a foreigner. Cut off from other students, Bonaparte devoted himself to mastering military tactics. In 1785, when he was 16, he finished school and became a lieutenant in the artillery. When the revolution broke out, he joined the army of the new government.

In October 1795, fate handed the young officer a chance for glory. An army of royalists threatened the palace where the National Convention was meeting, and a government official told Bonaparte to defend the palace. Bonaparte and his gunners greeted the thousands of royalists with a deadly cannonade. Within minutes, the attackers fled in panic and confusion. Napoleon Bonaparte was the hero of the hour. He was hailed throughout Paris as the savior of the French Republic.

In 1796, the Directory appointed Bonaparte to command a French army against Austria and the Kingdom of Sardinia. Crossing the Alps, the young general swept into Italy and won a series of remarkable victories. The French marched into Milan and made it the capital of a new Italian republic dominated by France.

Though Bonaparte posed as the liberator of northern Italy, he was in fact its conqueror. After a year of triumphant campaigning (1796–1797), Bonaparte was the most famous general in Europe.

Napoleon seized power in France.

Watching the early disorders of the French Revolution, a British statesman made this astute prediction:

In the weakness of authority . . . some popular general shall draw the eyes of all men upon himself. Armies will obey him on his personal account . . . The person who really commands the army is your master.

In 1799, the prediction came true.

By 1799, the Directory had lost the confidence of the French people. They were accused of corruption. In several elections, voters rejected the Directory's candidates. Only the directors' control of the army kept them in power.

Bonaparte decided that the time had come to seize political power. On November 9, 1799, he ordered 500 of his troops to occupy one chamber of the national legislature and drive out its elected members. The second chamber of the legislature, terrified by this show of force, voted to end the Directory. The chamber turned over power to three officials known as consuls. Bonaparte was one of the three.

Soon Bonaparte assumed dictatorial powers as the First Consul of the French Republic. Such a seizure of power is known as a **coup** from the French phrase *coup d'état* (koo day-TAH) or "stroke of state."

A Second Coalition attacked France.

At the time of Bonaparte's coup, France was still at war. Bonaparte's Italian campaign of 1796–1797 had forced Austria and Prussia to make peace, thus ending the First Coalition. The British navy, however, continued its damaging attacks against French shipping. In 1799, British diplomats arranged a Second Coalition of anti-French powers. The Second Coalition consisted chiefly of Britain, Austria, and Russia.

Once again, Napoleon rode out from Paris at the head of his troops. Once again, he led a huge French army over treacherous Alpine passes into northern Italy. Once again, he was victorious. The Austrians were forced to accept his peace terms. The Russians also made peace.

The British fought on, but in 1802, they agreed to Bonaparte's conciliatory peace terms. The

Like Alexander, Hannibal, and Julius Caesar, Napoleon overwhelmed his enemies by striking swiftly at their weakest point, whether on the battlefield or in government.

British and the French signed a peace treaty at Amiens (ahm-YAN) in March 1802. For the first time in ten years, Europe was at peace. Sadly, however, this peace did not last long.

Napoleon became emperor.

At first, Bonaparte pretended to be the constitutionally chosen leader of a free republic. In 1800, he and his two fellow consuls asked the French people to approve a new constitution, the fourth in eight years. They held a **plebiscite** (PLEHB-uh-syte), an election in which all citizens vote yes or no on an issue.

In the plebiscite of 1800, the French showed how desperate they were for strong leadership. They voted overwhelmingly for Bonaparte's constitution, which gave all real power to Bonaparte himself as the First Consul.

Bonaparte saw that he could take as much power as he wanted. In 1802, yet another plebiscite made him consul for life. French voters approved the change by a staggering majority (3,568,885 voting yes and only 8,374 voting no).

Two years later, in 1804, Bonaparte decided to make himself emperor. Again, the French voters agreed to his decision. Dressed in a splendid robe of purple velvet, Napoleon walked down the long aisle of Notre Dame Cathedral in Paris on December 2, 1804. The pope waited for him with a glittering crown. As thousands watched, the new emperor took the crown from the pope's hands and placed it on his own head.

Napoleon restored order.

At his coronation, Napoleon Bonaparte became Emperor Napoleon I. The French Republic was dead. In its place stood an absolute monarchy known as the French empire. Yet Napoleon did not try to return France to the days of Louis XIV. He kept many of the changes that had come with the revolution.

Economic order Napoleon managed to slow inflation by balancing the government's budget and setting up a national bank. The sans-culottes of Paris were finally able to buy bread.

Social order Noble emigrés returned to France by the thousands. Napoleon welcomed them as long as they behaved themselves politically. The bourgeoisie were also well pleased with Napoleon

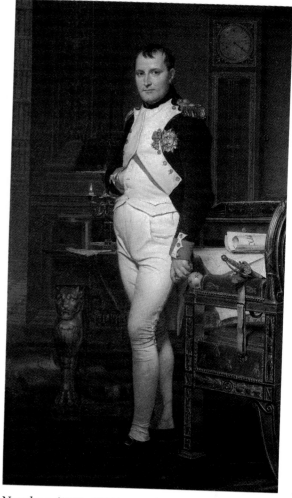

Napoleon (1769–1821) rose through the army to become emperor of France. His loyal troops affectionately nicknamed him "the little corporal."

because he promoted officials according to merit, not according to noble family.

Religious order Both the clergy and the peasants wanted to restore the Catholic Church's position in France. In 1801, Napoleon signed a *concordat* (agreement) with Pope Pius VII. It spelled out a new relationship between church and state.

Napoleon agreed to recognize Catholicism as the faith of "the great majority of Frenchmen." The French government would appoint Catholic bishops, but those bishops could appoint parish priests without government interference. Everyone in France was free to worship as he or she wished.

For his part, the pope stopped trying to win back the lands that the revolutionary government

After crowning himself, Napoleon also crowned his beloved Josephine, whom he had married in 1795 and to whom he wrote passionate love letters whenever his military duties separated them.

Summary

1. The French monarchy faced a crisis. Under the Old Regime, French society was divided into three estates. The First and Second estates had both political power and special privileges. The Third Estate—the majority of the people—had a wide variety of grievances against the Old Regime. When Louis XVI called a meeting of the Estates General in 1789, the Third Estate proclaimed a constitutional monarchy. The Paris mob stormed the Bastille.

2. Revolution brought reform and terror. By 1791, the National Assembly had proclaimed the equality of all men, reformed the government, and weakened the Church. In 1793, radicals won power, declared a republic, and executed Louis XVI. Their citizen-army defeated a coalition of enemies. Led by Robespierre, the radicals condemned thousands to death as enemies of the republic during the Reign of Terror. In 1795, the radicals were overthrown by the more moderate Directory.

3. Napoleon conquered much of Europe. General Napoleon Bonaparte overthrew the Directory in 1799. In 1804, he made himself emperor. He brought stability to France and set up a single legal system under the Napoleonic Code. Napoleon expanded his control over most of Europe.

4. Napoleon's empire collapsed. Napoleon's Continental System weakened European economies. A guerrilla war in Spain drained money and men from France's army. Napoleon's invasion of Russia ended in a disastrous retreat. In 1814, Napoleon was defeated by an alliance of powers. Although he returned briefly in 1815, he met his final defeat at Waterloo.

Reviewing the Facts

1. Define the following terms:
   - a. bourgeoisie
   - b. coalition
   - c. coup
   - d. plebiscite
   - e. guerrilla

2. Explain the importance of each of the following names, dates, places, or terms:
   - a. July 14, 1789
   - b. Louis XVI
   - c. Old Regime
   - d. estates
   - e. sans-culottes
   - f. Marie Antoinette
   - g. Great Fear
   - h. emigrés
   - i. Jacobin Club
   - j. guillotine
   - k. Robespierre
   - l. Reign of Terror
   - m. Bonaparte
   - n. Continental System
   - o. Waterloo

3. What were the four stages of the French Revolution, from 1789 to 1815?

4. Describe French society under the Old Regime.

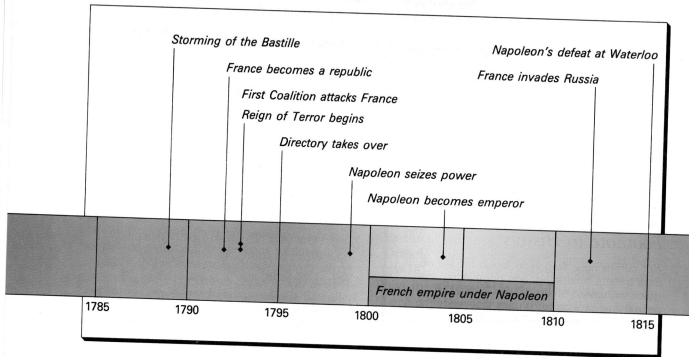

Storming of the Bastille

France becomes a republic

First Coalition attacks France

Reign of Terror begins

Directory takes over

Napoleon seizes power

Napoleon becomes emperor

Napoleon's defeat at Waterloo

France invades Russia

French empire under Napoleon

1785 1790 1795 1800 1805 1810 1815

5. (a) Why was Louis XVI forced to call a meeting of the Estates General in 1789? (b) What was the result?
6. What form of government did the National Assembly set up?
7. (a) Explain how the revolution steadily grew more violent. (b) What form of government did the Jacobin National Convention establish? (c) Briefly describe the Reign of Terror.
8. Trace the steps by which Napoleon rose to power.

Basic Skills

1. **Summarizing** Write a paragraph summarizing the information on page 450 on the makeup of the Third Estate.
2. **Interpreting a map** Answer the following questions, using the map on page 461 and your text for reference: (a) What countries were a basic part of Napoleon's empire? (b) What countries were under his control and how much support could he count on from them? (c) Which were the allied countries and to what extent could he depend on them?
3. **Interpreting a time line** Explain the significance of each of the items on the time line on page 466.

Researching and Reporting Skills

Writing a Historical Essay

Phase 3: Writing the Essay The essay should include a title, introductory paragraph, supporting paragraphs, and concluding paragraph. The tone should be persuasive.

1. **Selecting paragraph topics** Based on your notes, make an outline indicating the main idea of each paragraph and the details that will support your thesis.
2. **Writing an introductory paragraph** Write an introductory paragraph, stating your topic and your thesis.
3. **Writing expository paragraphs** Write supporting paragraphs as needed to present the points that support your thesis.
4. **Writing a concluding paragraph** Write a paragraph that will persuade the reader that the points presented support your thesis. Choose a title that will interest the reader in your topic. List your

bibliographical references, using standard citation form.

Critical Thinking

1. **Interpreting** The Abbé Siéyès suggested that the meeting of the Third Estate be renamed the National Assembly. What was the significance of this change?
2. **Identifying viewpoints** For each of the following people, write a sentence describing that person's point of view on the revolution: (a) Louis XVI, (b) Robespierre, (c) a highly placed member of the clergy, (d) the wife of a sans-culotte.
3. **Analyzing economics** Identify three economic factors that contributed to the revolution in France and describe their impact.
4. **Synthesizing** The revolution in France promoted a new sense of nationalism. (a) What examples of this can you find? (b) How did these events increase nationalistic feelings?
5. **Evaluating conflicting opinions** The last paragraph of the chapter comes to several conclusions about Napoleon's achievements. The quotation from Napoleon expresses a different opinion. (a) Write a paragraph discussing each opinion. (b) Write a third paragraph expressing your own conclusions.

Perspectives on Past and Present

Napoleon's invasion of Russia was neither the first nor the last that ended in defeat. (a) What invasions in the early eighteenth and mid-twentieth centuries met the same fate? (b) What similarities in purpose and outcome can you find among those invasions?

Investigating History

1. Dickens's novel *A Tale of Two Cities* is set in the context of the French Revolution. (a) Read a portion of the book to see how it presents events. (b) Write a brief report on its accuracy and particular point of view.
2. Select one of the important battles of the Napoleonic wars (Austerlitz, Trafalgar, Waterloo, or others). Study the battle thoroughly in a historical atlas and other sources. Describe the military strategy and tactics of the battle, using a diagram on the chalkboard to illustrate your talk.

Unit VI Review

Geographic Theme: Place

How did planning change the growth of cities?

Every city has its own unique character. Located in a particular kind of natural environment, it also has patterns of human use specific to that location. The physical and cultural characteristics that give a locale its identity are known to geographers as *place*.

The map of a city reveals much about its character. The maps of Paris and Versailles are a contrast in setting. To historians, they also show the difference between one historic era and another.

Paris began as a Gallic settlement on an island in the Seine River. Its location where roads join to cross the river made it a center of trade. When its feudal lord Hugh Capet was chosen king of France in 987, Paris became the royal capital. The construction and restoration of public buildings in the 1500's improved the central city, but most of it remained crowded and run-down. Even though Paris in 1789 was Europe's second largest city, its narrow and twisted streets reflected its medieval past rather than its future as a modern capital.

Eleven miles from Paris, the city of Versailles came into being after Louis XIV built his royal residence there. The site was not a favorable one. One courtier described it as "the saddest, the most unattractive of places, without views, any woods or streams, nothing but shifting sand and swamps." That was before Louis brought architects, designers, and landscape gardeners to transform the area into a new capital away from Paris. Swamps became gardens, and a landscape that improved upon nature provided a view. In the midst of this scene stood the great palace, with a planned town nearby. The gardens and orderly avenues of Versailles anticipated the modern city and the new age of urban planning.

1. (a) Compare the sites of Paris and Versailles. (b) How do the physical layouts of Paris and Versailles differ?
2. Paris is centered around the Cathedral of Notre Dame, whereas Versailles is centered around the palace. What do those facts show about the character of the cities?
3. In what ways does the town of Versailles represent the transition to a new age?

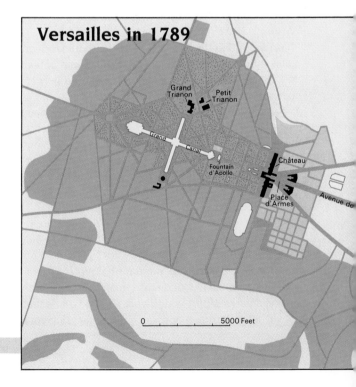

Paris in 1789

Champs Elysées
Palais des Tuileries
Louvre
Champs de Mars
Hôtel des Invalides
Hôtel de Ville
Faubourg
Palais de Justice
Notre Dame
Bastille
École Militaire
St. Antoine
0   3000 Feet

Versailles in 1789

Grand Trianon
Petit Trianon
Grand Canal
Château
Fountain d'Apollo
Place d'Armes
Avenue de
0   5000 Feet

Unit Perspectives

Understanding History

1. Relating Identify each person listed below. Include dates. Then describe the relationship between the people in each group.
   a. Elizabeth I; Philip II
   b. Oliver Cromwell; Charles I
   c. James II; William of Orange
   d. Louis XIV; Cardinal Mazarin
   e. Peter I; Charles XII
   f. Maria Theresa; Frederick II
   g. Catherine II; Voltaire
   h. George III; Thomas Jefferson
   i. Robespierre; Louis XVI

2. Matching Match the book, document, play, or opera in the left column with the correct author in the right column.
   1. Pragmatic   a. Newton
      Sanction   b. Mozart
   2. *Macbeth*   c. Rousseau
   3. *Mathematical*   d. Adam Smith
      Principles   e. Montesquieu
   4. *Candide*   f. Voltaire
   5. *The Miser*   g. Shakespeare
   6. *The Wealth*   h. Charles VI
      of Nations   i. Molière
   7. *On the Spirit*   j. John Milton
      of Laws
   8. *The Social Contract*
   9. *The Marriage of Figaro*
   10. *Paradise Lost*

3. Defining Describe the difference between each set of terms:
   a. balance of power; balance of trade
   b. divine right of kings; constitutional monarchy
   c. Roundheads; Cavaliers
   d. radicals; conservatives

4. Explaining Describe the theories of government held by each of the following men:
   a. Thomas Hobbes
   b. John Locke
   c. Montesquieu
   d. Rousseau

Critical Thinking

1. Applying a concept (a) What is meant by the term *balance of power?* (b) Of the European wars between 1650 and 1815, which one do you think posed the most serious threat to the balance of power? (c) How effective was the balance of power in giving peace and stability to Europe? Give reasons for your answers.

2. Interpreting a quotation Identify the source for each of the following quotations and explain what it means: (a) L'état, c'est moi; (b) Écrasez l'infame; (c) a window on the sea; (d) laissez-faire.

3. Analyzing Your text states on page 428, "The Age of Enlightenment brought together the ideas of the Renaissance and the Scientific Revolution." (a) What ideas from the Renaissance were reflected in the ideas of the philosophes? (b) What ideas from the Scientific Revolution were developed further in the 1700's and what new scientific discoveries were made?

4. Comparing Two monarchs, England's Charles I and France's Louis XVI, were executed by revolutionaries. What common mistakes did they make in dealing with the forces of change in their countries?

Making Decisions

Select one of the following decisions to analyze in terms of its wisdom and outcome: Philip II's decision to attack England; Louis XIV's decision to seek control of Spain; Napoleon's decision to invade Russia.

Continuity and Change

1. (a) Between 1500 and 1800, what major ideas about government and the role of the ruler prevailed in Europe? (b) What new ideas emerged in the late 1600's and 1700's that might influence later thinking?

2. Compare the Historical Atlas maps on pages 812–813 and 814–815. Identify three major changes that occurred between 1500 and 1800.

Unit VII

The Age of European Dominance

Chapters

1700   **1740**   **1780**

Political and Governmental Life

◀ **1740–1780**
Maria Theresa, ruler of the Hapsburg empire, queen of Hungary and Bohemia, and archduchess of Austria

◀ **1811–1824**
Bolívar leads Latin American struggle for freedom

Economic and Technological Life

1700's
Britain modernizes agriculture

1700's
Inventions mechanize the textile industry

1763
Britain wins India from France

1815
Congress of Vienna ▼

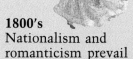

Social and Cultural Life

Spinning jenny

1750's–1900's
Industrialism brings rise of middle class

1800's
Nationalism and romanticism prevail

470

In the late 1700's, a massive economic change known as the Industrial Revolution began in Europe. It involved the use of steam power and machines to produce goods cheaply and in great quantity. This change transformed the ways people lived and worked. At the same time, a political movement known as nationalism changed the political scene. New nations emerged, and some older nations gained in power. Together, the Industrial Revolution and growing nationalism increased Europe's prosperity at home and its influence throughout the world.

1820   **1860**   **1900**

1857
Sepoys rebel against British rule in India

1875–1900
Imperial powers divide Africa into colonies

1900–1914
Nationalist uprisings in Balkans

1871
Germany united as a nation

The luxury liner Mauretania

1840's
Famine in Ireland causes emigration

1873
Japan begins to industrialize

Chinese emperor's robe

1848
Marx views history as class struggle

1869
Suez Canal opens

1914
United States opens Panama Canal

1865
Slavery ends in the United States

Charles Dickens's Oliver Twist

Renoir's Lady with a Parasol

471

Chapter 22

1700 - 1850

The Industrial Revolution

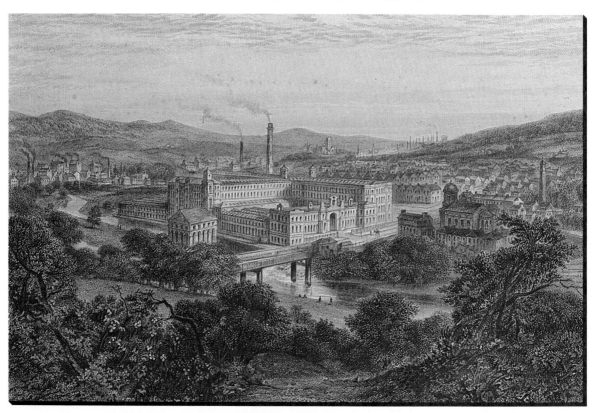

In many parts of Great Britain, industrial towns sprang up almost overnight around 1800. Smoke rising from the factories came to symbolize both plentiful jobs and unhealthy working conditions—some of the pluses and minuses of industrialism.

Key Terms

enclosure
crop rotation
factory
entrepreneur
union

Read and Understand

1. Many factors aided industrial growth.
2. Britain led in the rise of industry.
3. Industry grew and spread to new lands.
4. Industry changed ways of life.

One day in 1828, a British businessman named Joseph Pease stood clutching his hat and eyeing a windswept marshland near the mouth of the River Tees in northeastern England. The only other sign of human life was a scattering of farmhouses where fewer than 40 people lived. This was the small village of Middlesbrough, England.

Pease was one of a group of businessmen who planned to create a coal port and industrial city on the spot. That evening, he wrote in his diary that he could picture "a coming day when the bare fields ... will be covered with a busy multitude, and numerous vessels crowding to these banks denote the busy seaport." That day was not long in coming.

By 1840, only 12 years later, Middlesbrough had been transformed from a sleepy farming village into a bustling seaport that exported 1.5 million tons of coal a year. Its population had mushroomed from

The Industrial Revolution, like the introduction of farming and the beginning of cities, is considered by most historians to be one of the few genuine turning points in world history.

40 to 4,000. Thirty years later, in 1870, the population had grown to 40,000.

Such transformations took place in many parts of England during the period known as the Industrial Revolution. This was a different kind of revolution from the political revolutions that changed the governments of the United States and France. The Industrial Revolution was a series of dramatic changes not in the way a country was governed but in the way work was done.

Before the Industrial Revolution, most work was done by hand. People planted crops, wove cloth, and made shoes all by hand. Then, beginning in the middle 1700's, people began to use machines to do more and more jobs. No longer was muscle power (whether of people, oxen, or horses) the main way to get work done. Waterpower, once used only to run tiny grain mills, came into use for all kinds of machinery. By 1800, steam power was replacing waterpower. In hundreds of factories, steam engines chugged away, turning wheels, pumping water, and driving the great forge hammers in iron mills.

In the 80 years between 1760 and 1840 in Great Britain, one invention led to another with a swiftness for which there is no parallel in history. The average British person born in 1760 saw more changes in his or her lifetime than ten generations of ancestors had seen in theirs.

Though the Industrial Revolution began in Britain, its effects soon spread outward. Eventually, it touched the lives of people worldwide.

Like all great changes, the Industrial Revolution had both good and bad results. Some of its changes led to healthier, more comfortable, and more productive lives for people. Sometimes, however, industrialization caused immense suffering. In this chapter, we will see what a mixed blessing the Industrial Revolution was in the land of its birth, Great Britain.

Many factors aided industrial growth. 1

The Industrial Revolution began in the middle 1700's in the lowland parts of eastern England and southern Scotland. Why industry arose in England at that particular time involves many factors—from England's geographic advantages to the resourcefulness of the British people. Let us look at some of these factors.

Changes in farming led the way.

The Industrial Revolution might not have taken place without the dramatic improvements in farming that began in the early 1700's. This agricultural revolution started sooner than the Industrial Revolution. Then, once industrialization began, the two revolutions went hand in hand.

The enclosure movement By 1700, small farms were disappearing in Great Britain. Wealthy landowners were buying up much of the land that village farmers had once worked. Then the landowners rented fields to families of tenant farmers who worked the land. This process was called **enclosure**, because the new owner sometimes put up a fence or hedge around his land.

The villagers who shared common fields generally kept on with traditional ways of farming. It was difficult to persuade everyone in the village to try a new method. A landowner with a large estate, however, was free to experiment.

In the 1700's, many of these wealthy landowners began to look for ways to increase the size of their harvests. Influenced by the ideas of the Scientific Revolution and the Enlightenment, they applied a scientific approach to their farms. They kept careful records of the methods they used on their land. With such records, they could compare one year's harvest with the next. They also exchanged ideas with one another about land use and crops.

Jethro Tull was one of the first of these scientific farmers. He saw that the usual way of sowing seed by scattering it across the ground was wasteful. Many of the seeds failed to take root. He solved this problem with an invention called the seed drill in 1721. The seed drill allowed farmers to sow seeds in well-spaced rows at specific depths. A larger share of the seed germinated, boosting crop yields.

Crop rotation The most revolutionary discovery of these scientific farmers was a new system of **crop rotation**. For centuries, the chief way to keep a field fertile had been to let it lie fallow every two or three years. This practice arose in the Middle Ages with the two-field and three-field systems on medieval manors (page 211). As

Discuss: What is the role of farms in an industrial society? (to feed growing population, to provide surplus of laborers who move to cities for jobs, and become profit centers themselves, available for sale so new money can be invested in industry)

473

These surveyors are measuring a field so that the landlord can enclose it. The drawing decorates a map of Bedfordshire in southeastern England.

a result, at least a third of the country in any one year was producing nothing but weeds.

After much experimenting, the gentleman farmer Viscount Charles Townshend found that it was not necessary to let the land lie fallow. The secret, he told people, was to rotate crops. One year, a farmer might plant a field with wheat or barley, which tended to wear out the soil. The next year, the farmer could plant turnips or clover, which restored the soil. Not surprisingly, the viscount was nicknamed Turnip Townshend in honor of his favorite crop.

Improved livestock Thanks to the efforts of other farmers, raising livestock also became more productive. For example, in the 1700's, Robert Bakewell began trying to raise larger sheep to provide more meat and wool. By allowing only the best animals to breed, he increased the weight of his sheep and also greatly improved the taste of the mutton.

As more and more farmers followed his lead, farm animals increased dramatically in size and quality. In 1700, the average weight of a steer sold for slaughter was 370 pounds. By 1786, that weight had more than doubled to 840 pounds. The average weight for sheep rose from 28 to 100 pounds over the same period.

Effects on population Scientific farming had a twofold effect. Better livestock and rising crop production meant more food. Fewer people went hungry, and nutrition improved.

On the other hand, the enclosure movement forced many small farmers off the land. Many lost fields that their families had worked for centuries. Some simply left Great Britain and moved to the British colonies in North America. Others crowded into British cities looking for work. They became the labor force for industry.

A *rise in population helped industry.*

Mystery still surrounds another change that played a part in the Industrial Revolution. During the 1700's, the population of Europe began to increase more rapidly than at any earlier time.

Since the great plagues of the Middle Ages (page 244), Europe's population had grown. That growth, however, was very slow.

In the 100 years from 1750 to 1850, the numbers increased at a phenomenal rate. It had taken 400 years from 1350 for the European population to double. Then it nearly doubled again in just a century.

Historians have long debated the causes of this population explosion. Some point to new farming methods that increased food supplies and improved health. Others point to medical advances such Edward Jenner's discovery of a smallpox vaccine in 1796. Still others suggest that larger food supplies and better living conditions meant that people lived longer and married younger. These young couples soon had children, shortening the time span between generations.

Was the population explosion a direct cause of the Industrial Revolution? Probably not. After all, the population also rose rapidly in nearby Ireland, where little industrial development took place. Nevertheless, rapid population growth certainly helped quicken industrial progress. With more people, there was an increasing demand for food and other goods. At the same time, population growth supplied the extra workers that the new factories and businesses needed.

Great Britain had many advantages.

In 1700, Great Britain was neither the largest country in Europe nor the smallest. It was, however, rich in all the factors needed for industry.

Abundant natural resources The Industrial Revolution depended on three important natural resources. Two of these were waterpower and

(opposite) **Reading a graph** Exports increased the most to the Atlantic economy (North America, West Indies, Spanish America, and West Africa).

Great Britain also led the way because the feudal system, tying peasant workers to the land, had long since been done away with. In France and Prussia, the feudal system clung longer and made the change to an industrial society slower.

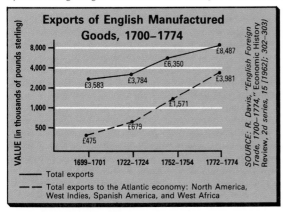

Exports of English Manufactured Goods, 1700–1774

VALUE (in thousands of pounds sterling)

£8,487
£6,350
£3,583   £3,784
£3,981
£1,571
£679
£475

1699–1701   1722–1724   1752–1754   1772–1774

—— Total exports
- - - Total exports to the Atlantic economy: North America, West Indies, Spanish America, and West Africa

SOURCE: R. Davis, "English Foreign Trade, 1700–1774," Economic History Review, 2d series, 15 (1962): 302–303)

Reading a Graph *How much did total exports increase between 1699–1701 and 1772–1774? To what regions did exports increase the most?*

coal, which supplied the energy for the new machines. The third was iron ore, used for machines, tools, and buildings. Great Britain was rich in all three.

A *favorable geography* Geography also gave Great Britain an advantage over other countries. An island nation with many fine harbors, its fleet of more than 6,000 merchant ships sailed to almost every part of the globe. This overseas trade gave Britain access to raw materials and markets. Both were essential to industrial growth. Trade also gave Britain a wealthy class of ship-owners and merchants who had money to spare for new projects at home.

A *favorable climate for new ideas* In the 1700's, British people in many walks of life were interested in science and technology. The Royal Society, founded in London in 1660, had become a world-famous "club" for the exchange of scientific ideas and practical inventions. Smaller clubs sprang up in other parts of the country. In Birmingham, for example, there was a scientific group known as the Lunar Society. Its members (who cheerfully called themselves Lunatics) met about once a month at the full moon.

New ideas were not only encouraged but also rewarded. Business people were willing to invest in the manufacture of new inventions. In fact, the business person and the inventor were often the same person.

A *good banking system* By the 1700's, Great Britain had the most highly developed banking system in Europe. Making loans was by far the most important service of British banks. By lending money at reasonable interest rates, banks encouraged business people to invest in better machinery, build new factories, and expand their operations.

Political stability Although Britain took part in many wars during the 1700's, none was fought on British soil. For ordinary people, it was a century of peace. This freedom from war and bloodshed gave Britain a tremendous advantage over its European neighbors. British business people did not have to worry about a hostile army destroying their property.

At the same time, the British government favored economic growth. Merchants and business people had considerable influence in Parliament. The government supported laws that encouraged new investment both at home and abroad.

Section Review 1

Define: (a) enclosure, (b) crop rotation
Identify: (a) Tull, (b) seed drill, (c) Townshend, (d) Bakewell, (e) Royal Society
Answer:
1. (a) What was the Industrial Revolution? (b) When did it take place? (c) How did it differ from other revolutions?
2. (a) How did the enclosure movement help scientific farming? (b) What effect did scientific farming have on the labor force? (c) How did a rise in population help the Industrial Revolution?
3. Describe the five factors that contributed to industrialization in Great Britain.

Critical Thinking
4. In what way was Middlesbrough a symbol of the Industrial Revolution in England?
5. Was the revolution in agriculture necessary to the Industrial Revolution? Explain.

Britain led in the rise of industry. 2

In the middle 1700's, the situation in Britain was ripe for the development of industry. The country had a good food supply, a large work force, and plenty of people with money to invest.

All the forces that had been slowly building suddenly came together in a giant burst of inventiveness. The changes appeared first in the textile industry.

Inventions revolutionized the textile industry.

Britain had long been one of the leading sheep-raising areas in the world. Raw wool and wool cloth had been Britain's major trade goods as far back as the Middle Ages. All this cloth was produced by hand. Spinners and weavers (mainly women) worked in their own homes, using spinning wheels and hand looms.

British clothmakers produced other fabrics as well as wool. Linen, a cloth woven from the fiber of the flax plant, was popular for lighter-weight clothing. Even more popular was cotton, which was also light but more durable and easier to care for than linen.

Working by hand at their wheels and looms, spinners and weavers could not keep up with the demand for cloth, especially cotton. Since they could not make as much cotton cloth as people wanted to buy, its cost remained relatively high. Cloth merchants saw that they could make greater profits if they found a way to speed up the work of spinning and weaving.

One invention led to another.

By 1800, six major inventions had totally transformed the cotton industry. The first invention came in 1733, when a watchmaker named John Kay made a shuttle that moved back and forth on wheels. The flying shuttle, as it was called, was little more than a boat-shaped piece of wood to which yarn was attached. Yet it allowed a weaver to work twice as fast.

Now weavers were working so quickly that spinners could not keep up. A prize was offered to anyone who could produce a better spinning machine. The prize went to a textile worker named James Hargreaves.

In 1764, Hargeaves invented a new spinning wheel. He called it the spinning jenny in honor of his wife. This simple machine allowed one spinner to work six or eight threads at a time. Later models could spin as many as 80 threads at once.

Both the flying shuttle and the spinning jenny were hand-operated machines. Richard Arkwright's water-frame, invented in 1768, brought a new breakthrough. The water-frame used the waterpower from fast-flowing streams to drive spinning wheels.

In 1779, Samuel Crompton combined features of the spinning jenny and the water-frame to produce the spinning mule. (It was so named because, just as a mule is the offspring of a horse and a donkey, this machine was the offspring of two inventions.) The mule made thread that was stronger, finer, and more even than earlier spinning machines.

The water-frame and the spinning mule were too large and expensive for people to use at home. Spinning and weaving slowly stopped being work that families did together in their homes. Instead, wealthy textile merchants set up several of the new machines in large buildings called **factories**. At first, the new factories needed waterpower, so they were built near a stream or waterfall.

With so many new machines for turning out thread, the weavers soon fell behind in their jobs. In 1785, a new invention promised to restore the balance by speeding up weaving. This was Edmund Cartwright's power loom, run by waterpower. Early power looms were inefficient, but steady improvements meant that by 1813 more than 2,000 were in use. By 1833, there were more than 100,000, most of them in large factories where they rattled away under the same roof as spinning machines. By the late 1700's, both spinners and weavers were working so fast that cotton growers could not keep up with them.

Much of England's cotton came from the southern part of the United States. In Virginia, Georgia, North Carolina, and South Carolina, farmers raised cotton on large plantations worked by slaves. One of the most time-consuming jobs on the plantation was removing the seeds from the raw cotton. In 1793, American educator Eli Whitney invented a machine to do this tedious chore. His cotton gin made it possible for slaves to pick and clean ten times as much cotton daily as they had before.

Whitney's invention spurred a dramatic increase in American cotton production: from 9,000 bales in 1791 to 987,000 in 1831. Now there was enough raw cotton to keep the factories of Britain humming.

The money to be made in the cotton industry was so staggering that many small investors rushed in. In 1789, a draper named Robert Owen borrowed 100 pounds to start a mill. Twenty years later, he bought out his partners for 84,000 pounds.

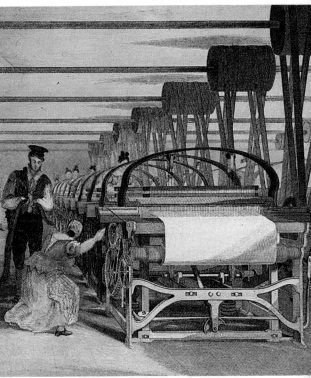

Comparing pictures *During the Industrial Revolution, jobs such as spinning and weaving gradually moved out of home workshops (left) and into factories (right). How did the nature of the work and the working environment change?*

Thanks to continuous technological improvements in spinning and weaving, however, English merchants used all this cotton and still called for more. The output of cotton cloth from British factories rose from 40 million yards in 1785 to more than 2 billion yards in 1850—a staggering 5,000 percent increase.

Watt improved the steam engine.

The early power looms and spinning machines had one large drawback. They ran on waterpower, and so every factory that used them had to be near rushing water. Such places were often far from raw materials, workers, or markets. Therefore, many factory owners were eager for a new source of power. They found it in steam.

As early as 1705, coal miners were using steam-powered pumps to remove water from deep mine shafts. However, this early steam engine, called the Newcomen engine after its inventor, worked very slowly. It also took great quantities of fuel, making it expensive to run.

In 1763, the problem came to the attention of James Watt. Watt was a mathematical instrument maker at the University of Glasgow in Scotland. He helped science professors make the equipment they used in their experiments. Watt pondered the problem for two years. Then, one day in the spring of 1765, as he was strolling along the Glasgow Green, a solution suddenly came to him. Watt saw how to make the steam engine work much faster and more efficiently while burning less fuel.

In the 1770's, Watt went into partnership with a farsighted businessman named Matthew Boulton. Watt and Boulton were both **entrepreneurs** (AHN-truh-pruh-NUHRZ). An entrepreneur is a person who organizes, manages, and takes on the risks of a business.

With Boulton's financial backing, Watt continued to make better and better engines. By 1800, almost 500 steam engines were huffing and puffing in various British factories. James Watt, once a modestly paid craftsman, had become a millionaire.

The work changed from being a highly skilled craft, done within the familiar home environment, to being a less skilled tending of machines within the highly controlled, noisy, and polluted factory environment. In the factory, women could no longer carry on household activities or care for children while producing goods.

Watt's improvements made the steam engine much more practical for use in industry. For the first time in history, people had a source of power that could be used anywhere and anytime.

Section Review 2

Define: (a) factory, (b) entrepreneur
Identify: (a) John Kay, (b) James Hargreaves, (c) Richard Arkwright, (d) Samuel Crompton, (e) Edmund Cartwright, (f) Eli Whitney, (g) cotton gin, (h) James Watt
Answer:
1. (a) What British industry did the first inventions of the Industrial Revolution affect? (b) Why were merchants in this industry looking for ways to speed up production?
2. (a) Name the six inventions that transformed the cotton industry. (b) How did each of these inventions lead to another?
3. (a) What drawback did early power looms and spinning machines have? (b) How did the invention of the steam engine solve this problem?

Critical Thinking
4. The steam engine has been called the greatest invention of the Industrial Revolution. Do you agree or disagree? Explain.
5. Could the Industrial Revolution have taken place without entrepreneurs? Why or why not? What role do entrepreneurs play in business today?

Industry grew and spread to new lands. 3

In 1800, a businessman could walk through his mill and look with pride at the latest model of the Watt steam engine. He could see the power looms and other machines to which it was connected by drive shafts and belts. Yet most of these mechanical wonders had been delivered to the factory by horse-drawn cart. When the businessman finished his inspection, he rode home in a horse-drawn carriage over mud-rutted roads that dated back to the Middle Ages. Great changes, however, were on the way.

Engineers built roads and canals.

Before the Industrial Revolution, the cheapest and most reliable way to travel in England was by water. Besides its good harbors, England also had many navigable rivers. Barges laden with coal, iron, bricks, and other goods floated up and down the rivers of England. Since a barge drawn by horse could carry a far greater load than a cart pulled by the same horse, water transportation was much cheaper than land transportation.

Yet water transportation had a major drawback. There was only one way to take goods across the stretches of land that lay between rivers. Workers had to unload the boats, put the goods into wagons, drive the wagons to the next river, and move the cargo again onto boats.

To solve this problem, the British built a network of canals. (A canal is a human-made waterway.) In the late 1700's and early 1800's, British workers built more than 4,000 miles of inland waterways. The new canals slashed the cost of transportation. Now coal and other raw materials could be carried by water to more places in Britain.

British roads also improved. John McAdam, a Scottish engineer, was largely responsible for the better roads. Working in the early 1800's, he built roadbeds with a layer of large stones for drainage. Over that bed, he put a carefully smoothed layer of crushed rock. Roads with the "macadam" surface were not nearly so muddy or dusty as the old ones. Heavy wagons could travel over them even in rainy weather without sinking to their axles in mud.

The Railway Age began.

The biggest change in transportation came with the use of steam power. Just as the steam engine itself was a key breakthrough in the late 1700's, the steam engine on wheels gave a tremendous boost to English industry after 1820. This invention is better known, of course, as the railroad locomotive. The railroad revolutionized transportation first in England and later in many parts of the world.

The idea of running wagons on iron tracks was not new. For centuries, horses had pulled carts of iron and coal along railway tracks in and around mines. Before 1800, however, no one succeeded in using steam power to run such a cart.

Henry Cort's improved smelting methods (1784) moved the British iron industry away from small forges toward much larger, much more efficient blast furnaces, which boosted British iron production from 68,000 tons in 1790 to 677,000 tons in 1830.

The Industrial Revolution in Cotton, Coal, and Pig Iron

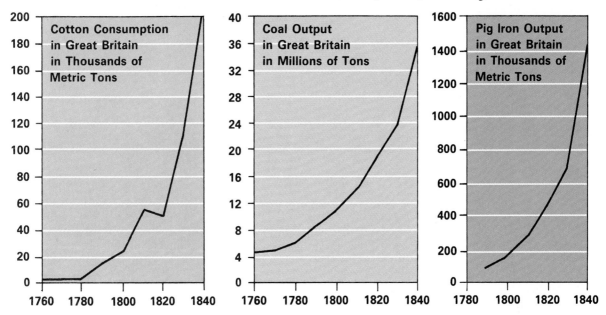

Reading graphs *In what 20-year period did the use of cotton first show an increase? About how much pig iron did Britain produce in 1800? In 1820?*

These vehicles needed smaller, more powerful engines than the ones that Watt was producing for factory use.

In 1804, an English engineer named Richard Trevithick made an engine that was both small and powerful. In fact, it ran at such high pressures that Watt and others expected it to blow up. Trevithick claimed his engine could pull a cart along a set of rails. A mine owner in Wales bet Trevithick the equivalent of several thousand dollars that such a feat was impossible. Trevithick won the bet by running his locomotive over ten miles of track, hauling ten tons of iron as well. "The public until now called me a scheming fellow," wrote Trevithick at the time, "but now their tone is much altered."

Other British engineers soon built improved versions of Trevithick's locomotive. By 1820, several hundred such vehicles were in operation in and around British mines. One of these early railroad engineers was George Stephenson, who gained a solid reputation by building some 20 engines for mine operators in northern England.

In 1821, Stephenson began work on the world's first railroad line. It was to run 27 miles from the Yorkshire coalfields to the port of Stockton on the North Sea. In 1825, the railroad opened,

using four locomotives that Stephenson had designed and built.

News of this success quickly spread throughout Britain. The entrepreneurs of northern England were especially interested. They wanted a railroad line to connect the port of Liverpool on the northwestern coast of England with the inland city of Manchester, the heart of the spinning and weaving industry. The track was laid, and in 1829, trials were held to choose the best locomotive for use on the new line.

Five engines entered the competition, but none could compare with the Rocket, designed by Stephenson and his son. With smoke pouring from its tall smokestack and its two pistons pumping to and fro as they drove the front wheels, the Rocket hauled a 13-ton load at an unheard-of speed—more than 24 miles per hour!

Footnote to History

In 1745, it took two weeks to travel from London to Edinburgh, a distance of 330 miles. By 1796, better roads cut the traveling time to two and a half days. In 1830, a passenger on a coach could make the trip in 36 hours.

Railroads captured the imagination of people everywhere. In a very brief time, short lines were opened in the United States (1826), France (1828), Germany and Belgium (1835), and Russia (1837). Cross-country lines, of course, took a long time to complete.

First-class passengers on the Liverpool-Manchester Railway rode in covered carriages (top). Second- and third-class passengers rode in open cars.

Railroads spread across England.

The Liverpool-Manchester Railway opened officially in 1830. It was an immediate success. Thousands of passengers traveled between the two cities every day on a dozen separate trains. Freight trains soon carried more goods back and forth along this route than canals and road coaches combined.

Confident that there were great profits to be made in railroads, British business people began building new lines all over the country. Hundreds of different railroads opened during the 1830's and 1840's. Soon such lines linked nearly all the major cities and towns of Britain. In 1850, only 25 years after the first line had been built, Great Britain had 16,200 miles of railroad track.

Perhaps the only business people who did not welcome the Railroad Age were the owners of canals and freight wagon lines. The "iron horse" soon drove many of them out of business.

Not everything went smoothly on these early railroads, of course. Breakdowns, accidents, and delays were frequent. At first, most passengers traveled in open cars where they were exposed to rain, wind, and the black clouds of soot that poured from the engine smokestack. Despite such drawbacks, however, railroads offered faster and more reliable transportation than anything known in earlier times.

Railroads had far-reaching effects.

No other industrial development had a greater effect on life in Great Britain than the railroads. In fact, the invention and perfection of the locomotive had at least four major effects.

First, railroads encouraged further industrial growth by giving manufacturers a fast, cheap way to transport both raw materials and finished products. Moreover, entrepreneurs could now build factories in many more locations. They no longer needed to be close to supplies of raw materials. Trains could deliver such supplies wherever there were tracks.

Second, the railroad boom provided millions of new jobs. Thousands of people did the back-breaking work of leveling hills, laying track, digging tunnels, and building bridges. Railroads used so much coal and iron that they boosted the demand for workers in those two industries as well. One mile of railroad track, for example, required 300 tons of iron.

Third, railroads gave a further boost to progress in agriculture. Now farmers could send milk and fruit to market in distant cities. In the same way, trains opened new markets for the fishing industry. Fresh fish could now be sold daily even in cities far from the sea.

Last but not least, railroads had enormous influence on the attitudes that ordinary people had about travel. Until this time, most people had thought of travel as something one did only when it was absolutely necessary. By offering quick and reasonably cheap transportation, railroads completely changed this view. Country people, for example, were now more willing to take jobs in distant cities, because they knew they could make regular visits home. At the same time, railroads began to open up a new world of travel for enjoyment. The spread of the railroads through Britain led directly to the growth of such popular seaside resorts as Brighton (south of London) and Blackpool (on the northwestern coast).

Railroads boosted the coal and iron industries even more. From 1830 to 1850, Britain's iron output tripled, from 677,000 to 2,250,000 tons. Each mile of railroad track required 300 tons of iron. Coal output also tripled, leaping to 49 million tons.

Industrialization spread to other countries.

For many years, the Industrial Revolution was limited mostly to the country of its birth, Great Britain. The reason was simple: Britain wanted to keep the secrets of industrialization to itself. Until 1825, it was against the law for engineers, mechanics, and toolmakers to leave the country. Until 1843, it was against the law for anyone in Britain to sell the new machines to people in other countries. Despite such laws, however, the ideas of the Industrial Revolution did spread beyond Britain.

The spread to the United States In 1789, a young British mill worker named Samuel Slater disguised himself as a farmer and boarded a ship headed for the United States. There he built a spinning machine from memory. The next year, a Rhode Island businessman named Moses Brown began work on a factory to house Slater's machines. In 1793, this factory—the first one in the United States—opened for business in Pawtucket, Rhode Island.

Early factories in the United States made only thread. The thread was then given to weavers who worked in their homes. Later, mills combined the spinning of thread with the weaving of cloth. The number of mills grew slowly at first and then more rapidly. By 1850, they had spread over much of the northeastern United States.

The spread to Europe Industry made little headway on the European continent before 1815. The French Revolution and the Napoleonic wars disrupted business all over Europe. By the time peace returned, Britain had a commanding lead.

Goods from Britain's factories flooded European markets. British woolens and cottons were much cheaper than anything textile workers in Europe could make by hand. As a result, many European spinners and weavers found themselves out of work. The countries along the North Sea coast were especially hard hit.

Belgium was one of the first countries in Europe to respond to the British challenge. Like Britain, Belgium had good supplies of coal and fine waterways for transportation. At first, the know-how to build industrial machines in Belgium

Voice from the Past · A Girl in the Mills

In 1823, a New England businessman named Francis Lowell built a model factory town at Lowell, Massachusetts. His idea was to hire young women from farming villages. He offered safe, attractive living quarters and opportunities for education as well as jobs. At the age of 13, Lucy Larcom became a mill girl. Years later, she described her life at Lowell.

That children should be set to toil for their daily bread is always a pity; but in the case of my little workmates and myself there were imperative reasons, and we were not too young to understand them. And the regret with which those who loved us best consented to such an arrangement only made us more anxious to show that we really were capable of doing something for them and for ourselves. The novelty of trying to "earn our own living" took our childhood fancy; the work given us was light, and for a few weeks it seemed like beginning a new game with a new set of playmates. Replacing the full spools of bobbins with empty ones on spinning frames was the usual employment given to children. It was a process which required quickness but left unoccupied intervals . . . during which we were frequently allowed to run home.

1. (a) Why did Lucy and other mill girls probably go to work? (b) Why was the idea of young women earning their living a novel one for its time?
2. How did the mill girls feel about their work?
3. In time, Lowell followed the grim path of factory towns in Britain. Describe how Lucy's account differs from the one given by Samuel Coulson on page 485.

The Industrial Revolution in Great Britain, 1850

ATLANTIC
OCEAN

SCOTLAND

North
Sea

Glasgow
New
Lanark
Edinburgh
Firth
of Forth
Firth of
Clyde
IRON
SHIPBUILDING

Carlisle

Newcastle
Sunderland
Durham
IRON

LEAD

COTTONS

IRELAND

Irish Sea

Preston Halifax
Liverpool Manchester
Leeds York
WOOLENS
Hull
Sheffield
METAL
GOODS

The
Wash

POTTERY

Wolverhampton
Birmingham

WALES

IRON
COTTONS

Norwich

ATLANTIC
OCEAN

Bristol
Channel
Cardiff
Bristol
Bath

Thames
River

ENGLAND

London

COPPER

Southampton

English Channel

Plymouth

KEY

- Major industrial areas
- Coal fields
- ✕ Iron ore fields
- ----- Major canals
- ——— Major railways

0   50 Miles

FRANCE

Map Study

The industrial area in central England is known as the Midlands. What goods were produced there?

came from British workers who left England illegally. In 1799, a British carpenter named William Cockerill began building cotton-spinning machines in Belgium while it was still under French rule. Later, Cockerill's sons opened factories that turned out steam engines, locomotives, and other machinery.

Soon, industrialized "islands" began to dot the European landscape. Among these areas were the

coal-rich Ruhr Valley in northwestern Germany and the Po Valley in northern Italy. Cities such as Milan, Frankfurt, and Lyons expanded rapidly on the continent during the middle 1800's.

Britain led the world in industry.

Despite such growth, no other European country came close to rivaling Britain as an industrial power before 1850. In 1850, Britain still produced most of the world's iron and coal. British factories and mills accounted for 70 percent of Europe's cotton cloth production.

Yet another measure of British dominance was railroad development. With 9,797 miles of track in operation in 1850, Britain had more railroad lines than France, Russia, Austria, and all the German and Italian states combined. With its highly developed industrial economy and splendid merchant fleet, Britain made foreign trade a major feature of its economy. During the 1840's, the value of British exports increased at an amazing rate. Little wonder that the country earned the title of "workshop of the world."

Section Review 3

Identify: (a) John McAdam, (b) Richard Trevthick, (c) George Stephenson, (d) Samuel Slater, (e) Moses Brown, (f) William Cockerill
Answer:
1. (a) Name two ways goods were transported before the Industrial Revolution. (b) How was each method improved during the Industrial Revolution?
2. (a) What new invention revolutionized transportation? (b) What role did Trevithick play in this new invention? (c) What role did Stephenson play?
3. How did railroads affect each of the following? (a) the growth of industry (b) employment (c) agriculture
4. (a) What did Britain do to prevent the spread of industrialization? (b) How did the ideas of the Industrial Revolution spread to the United States? (c) How did they spread to Europe?

Critical Thinking
5. How was improved transportation both a cause and an effect of the Industrial Revolution?

Discuss: How might the sudden surge of wealth and the growing middle class have weakened royal power?

Industry changed ways of life.

4

As the pace of industrialization quickened, life changed in many ways. By the 1800's, more people could afford to heat their homes with coal from Wales and to dine on Scottish beef. They had more clothing too, much of it from cloth made on power looms in Manchester or Liverpool. Industrialization affected every part of life.

More people lived in cities.

Perhaps the most obvious change brought about by the Industrial Revolution was in where people lived. For centuries, most Europeans had lived in rural areas. A much smaller share had lived in towns and cities. Now that balance began to shift toward the cities.

The growth of the factory system brought people flocking into cities and towns. Between 1800 and 1850, the number of European cities with more than 100,000 inhabitants rose from 22 to 47. Most of Europe's urban areas at least doubled in population during this period. Some, such as Glasgow and Berlin, tripled or even quadrupled in size.

Factories tended to develop in clusters because entrepreneurs built near sources of power. Major new industrial centers sprang up between the coal-rich area of southern Wales and the Clyde River valley in Scotland (map, page 482). The biggest of these centers developed in England, from the Midlands north along the Pennines and on the northwest and northeast coasts.

London, of course, remained the most important city in Great Britain. Among other things, it was Europe's largest city (twice as populous as Paris, its nearest rival) and was growing larger all the time. This population gave London a vast labor pool for industry. Though lacking nearby sources of raw materials, London thus shared in Britain's industrial growth.

However, new cities were challenging London's leadership. Perhaps the most famous of the new industrial cities was Manchester, which along with the port of Liverpool formed the hub of Britain's cotton industry. "What Manchester thinks today, London thinks tomorrow," declared the city's proud entrepreneurs.

Problems arose as cities grew.

The pride of Manchester's business leaders was typical of their go-ahead spirit. Yet Manchester was also typical of the new industrial cities in other ways. These cities grew so quickly that little thought or planning was given to housing, sanitation, or education for the people who poured in from the countryside to seek jobs. Let us look at life in Manchester in the early 1800's.

It is 5 A.M. on a chilly fall day in 1840. Men, women, and even small children are spilling out of the city's courtyards and alleys to make their way on foot to the cotton mills. Some have already had a cup of tea and a plate of oatmeal, but others

Reading a table *Which town was largest in 1685? In 1881? From information in the text and on the map (page 482), what geographic feature helped the latter?*

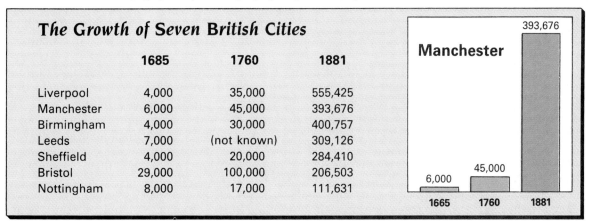

The Growth of Seven British Cities			
	1685	**1760**	**1881**
Liverpool	4,000	35,000	555,425
Manchester	6,000	45,000	393,676
Birmingham	4,000	30,000	400,757
Leeds	7,000	(not known)	309,126
Sheffield	4,000	20,000	284,410
Bristol	29,000	100,000	206,503
Nottingham	8,000	17,000	111,631

Manchester

393,676

45,000

6,000

1665 1760 1881

Manchester grew in the 1800's as a center for producing cotton textiles. Raw cotton came to Liverpool and from there to Manchester by canal. This flow was reversed as the Manchester mills shipped cotton cloth to Liverpool and from there, to markets overseas. Note on page 578 the Geographic Theme based on the cotton trade.

483

will wait until the 8 A.M. break for tea and a piece of bread. The sky is dark, but gas lamps gleam along the alleys, where taverns are already open for business.

Although many of the brick buildings along the streets are new, they are blackened by the smoke and soot that hang over the city all the time. Manchester sprawls alongside the Pennine Hills, which are capped by bare, windswept moors. However, smoke from the clusters of cotton mills that ring the city blot out any glimpse of these open spaces.

Most of the streets are unpaved and have no drains. The larger streets are cleaned from time to time, but the alleys are not. These streets collect heaps of filth and excrement. In courtyards, some of the workers keep pigs that root as best as they can among the garbage. The stench that rises from these areas is almost unbearable.

The smell in other parts of the city is little better. Gasworks, bone works, breweries, and tanneries add their various odors to the smoky air. The city's main river, the Irwell, is filled with so much waste that, in the words of one visitor, it is "considerably less a river than a flood of liquid manure."

In 1760, Manchester had been a market town with a population of around 30,000. It became the center for the expanding British cotton industry for two reasons. First, Manchester was close to the port of Liverpool, where most of the raw cotton from the United States entered Great Britain. Second, the town had abundant sources of power. Streams tumbling down from the nearby Pennines supplied waterpower, and nearby coalfields offered fuel for steam power.

By 1800, there were more than 50 cotton mills in Manchester. By 1830, there were 130. By 1850, Manchester was home to some 300,000 people, 10 times the number that had lived there a century earlier.

This tremendous growth brought great wealth to Manchester—and also enormous social problems. The city was built almost overnight, without plans, without any kind of sanitary codes or building controls. Not until the 1830's did the city have a municipal government to keep order. Before then, Manchester was little more than "a huge overgrown village," as one observer said.

Not all quarters of the city were miserable, of course. Well-to-do merchants and factory owners made their homes in Alderley Edge, a pleasant suburb on the east of the city. For the working people of Manchester, however, Alderley Edge must have seemed light-years away. One person wrote:

> The dwellings of the poor in the back streets and alleys are as woeful as they are degrading. The amount of room occupied by many families is miserably small; great numbers have only one bedroom for the whole family.

Not surprisingly, sickness was rampant. Cholera epidemics regularly swept through the slums of Manchester and other industrial cities. A British government study in 1842 showed that the average lifespan for working-class people in Manchester was 17 years, as compared to 38 years in a nearby rural area.

By the 1840's, changes were in sight. Streets were being paved and drains installed. The city's first three parks were created. Yet many of the grim conditions spawned by rapid industrial expansion would linger for a long time.

Manchester was indeed a city of contrasts. "From this foul drain, the greatest stream of human industry flows out to fertilize the whole world," wrote the French journalist Alexis de Tocqueville after visiting Manchester in 1835.

The Industrial Revolution changed working conditions.

Faced with such living conditions, why did people continue to pour into Britain's cities from the countryside? One reason was that life was harsh in the country too. The cities at least offered plenty of jobs. Moreover, a factory worker could hope for regular wages, rain or shine. In contrast, a spell of bad weather could wipe out a farmer's whole crop.

Families in the the country were used to working from dawn to dusk. Parents expected their children to work long and hard as well. The family worked as a unit, both at farm tasks and at home industries such as spinning and weaving. When such a family moved to town, however, they found that working conditions were different.

In the city, work hours depended on the factory bell or whistle, not on the season or the weather. Factory owners wanted to keep their machines

Despite their long experience in the textile trade, women in textile factories were generally paid lower wages than men.

Child labor was one of the most shocking abuses of the early Industrial Revolution. Perhaps the worst conditions were in the mines, where boys and girls dragged cartloads of coal through dark, cramped passages.

running for as many hours a day as possible. As a result, the average worker spent 14 hours a day at the job, 6 days a week. Instead of changing with the seasons, the work was the same week after week, year after year. Workers could not change their pace; they had to keep up with the machines.

Industry also posed new dangers in work. Factories were seldom well-lit or clean. Machines injured workers in countless different ways—a boiler might explode or a drive belt might catch an arm. The most dangerous conditions of all were found in the coal mines, where frequent accidents, damp conditions, and the constant breathing of coal dust combined to make the average miner's life span ten years shorter than that of other workers.

Children suffered in mills and mines.

In the factories as on the farms, whole families worked. Again, however, there were important differences. In the country, children worked side by side with their parents. In factories, family members often worked separately. In such cases, young children were at the mercy of impersonal overseers. During the early 1800's, children as young as six or seven years worked long hours in factories and mines.

Children were especially useful in the mines, where small size was a great advantage in moving about in narrow shafts and tunnels. Many were employed as "trappers," whose job was to keep the ventilation shafts in the mines clear. "It is a most painful thing to contemplate the dull, dungeon-like life these little creatures are doomed to spend," noted one mine visitor, "a life for the most part passed in solitude, damp, and darkness."

Orphan children faced the worst plight. Factory owners employed large numbers of these children in return for room and board. The child workers were seldom fed properly. Their lodgings might be nothing more than piles of straw beside the machines at which they worked 12 or 14 hours a day.

In 1831, Parliament set up a committee to investigate abuses of child labor. A worker named Samuel Coulson told the committee that in busy times, his small daughters started work at 3 A.M. and ended at 10:30 P.M. What rest periods did they have during those 19 hours? "Breakfast a quarter of an hour, and dinner half an hour, and drinking a quarter of an hour."

As a result of this committee's findings, Parliament passed the Factory Act of 1833. The new law made it illegal to hire children under 9 years old. Children from the ages of 9 to 13 were not to work more than 8 hours a day. Young people from 14 to 18 could not be required to work more than 12 hours. In 1842, the Mines Act placed similar limits on the work of children in mining.

While such acts limited the worst abuses, children continued to do exhausting work, often under unhealthy or dangerous conditions. They worked because the money they earned was essential to

Most mill owners, according to Peter Gaskell in 1833, considered the workers no more than "so many accessories in his machinery, destined to produce a certain quantity of work at the lowest possible outlay of capital."

485

Radicals sometimes came from the working class. The Parisian sans-culottes are a good example. Radicalism also drew support from intellectuals and students. However, support for radicalism was not widespread.

Conservatives controlled Europe.

The Congress of Vienna was a victory for conservatives. Kings and princes were restored in country after country, in keeping with Metternich's goals. However, there were important differences from one country to another.

Britain's constitutional monarchy Britain was the only one of the Great Powers with a true constitutional monarchy. Parliament actually had far more power than the ruler. Yet Britain was far from a democracy. Most members of Parliament were wealthy landowners. They were elected by a tiny fraction of the population. Only men who owned a substantial amount of property were qualified to vote. Nevertheless, Britain's form of government was much more open than anything found in eastern Europe.

Absolute rulers in eastern Europe Generally speaking, governments were more conservative in eastern Europe than they were in western Europe. The rulers of Russia, Prussia, and Austria were absolute monarchs. Late in 1815, the rulers of those three countries drew up an agreement called the Holy Alliance. In this agreement against liberalism, Czar Alexander I, Emperor Francis I, and King Frederick William III promised to help one another if any of them were threatened by reformers or revolutionaries.

Tension in France Among the Great Powers, France's position was unique. The old Bourbon dynasty ruled once more, but an elected Chamber of Deputies shared some power with Louis XVIII. This parliament was even less democratic than Britain's. Only about one of every 300 French men (and no French women at all) had the right to vote.

France after 1815 was deeply divided politically. Conservatives were happy with the Bourbon restoration and determined to make it last. Liberals wanted the king to share more power with the Chamber of Deputies and to grant the middle class the right to vote. Many people in the lower class, especially in Paris, remained committed to the ideals of liberty, equality, and fraternity. They were determined to overthrow the Bourbons and make France a republic once again. It was an explosive mixture of ideas and factions that would contribute directly to revolutions in 1830 and again in 1848.

Section Review 1

Define: (a) legitimacy, (b) conservative, (c) liberal, (d) radical
Identify: (a) Congress of Vienna, (b) Great Power, (c) Metternich, (d) German Confederation, (e) Holy Alliance, (f) Louis XVIII
Answer:
1. What was the purpose for which the Congress of Vienna met?
2. Which countries were the Great Powers of Europe?

Daily Life · City of Waltzes

A princely visitor to Vienna in 1815 remarked, "The congress doesn't march—it dances." Indeed it did, to lilting tunes in three-quarter time, written for the new dance that was sweeping Vienna, the waltz. The aristocratic visitors found the waltz far more exciting than the formal minuet that they had danced for years. Adapted from a country dance, the waltz appealed to dancers of all social classes. The word *waltz* came from the German word for "revolving." Partners whirled across the floor with their arms wrapped around each other in a way that many people thought indecent for public view.

3. What were Metternich's three goals at the Congress of Vienna?
4. (a) What were the results of the congress for France? (b) For the small states around France? (c) For the German states?
5. (a) In general, what were the political ideas of conservatives? (b) Liberals? (c) Radicals?
6. How was the British government different from governments in the rest of Europe?
7. How was the Congress of Vienna a triumph for conservatism?

Critical Thinking
8. (a) What are the factors that make a peace conference successful? (b) By those standards, was the Congress of Vienna a success? (c) What trends or movements did the congress fail to recognize?

New ideals affected politics and art.

2

Liberals, conservatives, and radicals debated the roles of kings, parliaments, and people in government. Meanwhile, two new movements were arising that blurred the lines between these political theories. One of the new movements was nationalism. The other was romanticism.

Nationalism was a force for change.

Nationalism is the belief that a person's greatest loyalty should be to a nation-state. In the years after 1800, this belief fired the hearts of millions of Europeans and reshaped the map of Europe.

To understand nationalism, let us review the meaning of the word *nation*. A group of people who share similar traditions, history, and language make up a nation. Usually, they live in the same geographic area as well. If such a group is united under its own government, it is known as a **nation-state.** For nationalists of all groups, forming such a nation-state became the goal of their lives.

In 1815, there were very few nation-states in Europe. A quick glance at the map shows no countries called Italy, Germany, Greece, Hungary, or Poland. Only France and Spain qualified as nation-states. England, like France, had developed as a nation during the late Middle Ages (page 239). However, England was now part of Great Britain, along with Ireland and Scotland. Many Irish and Scots definitely did not think of themselves as part of an English nation.

Modern nationalism was born during the French Revolution. The leaders of the revolution stressed the equality of all French people. Overjoyed at the chance to govern themselves, the French felt a burst of national pride. "Our life, our goods, and our talents do not belong to us," cried one French army volunteer. "It is to the nation, to France, [that] everything belongs." This national pride was an important factor in Napoleon's remarkable victories.

Ironically, France's military success sowed the seeds of its own downfall, because nationalism grew quickly too among the people France conquered (page 463). Fired by national pride, Spaniards, Italians, and Germans rebelled against their French conquerors.

The downfall of Napoleon did not lead immediately to the creation of new nation-states in Europe. In 1815, many national groups were ruled by larger, more powerful states. Most Poles, for example, lived under Russian rule. Hungarians and many Slavs lived under Austrian rule.

As nationalism spread, such groups became more and more unhappy with their situation. They formed nationalist societies, often meeting in secret. These societies published books and newspapers that stressed each group's unique character and the glories of its past.

Greece won its independence.

The first new nation-state to win its freedom was Greece. For centuries, Greece had been part of the Ottoman empire, which controlled most of southeastern Europe. As nationalism spread across Europe, the Greeks were among the first to be affected. Greek nationalists demanded that Greece take its place among the nation-states of Europe. A major revolt against Ottoman rule broke out in 1821.

The Greek war for independence was a difficult struggle. However, the Greeks had two great advantages that other rebellious groups such as the Poles and the Irish did not. First, the Ottoman army was much weaker than the Russian or the British armies. Second, the cause of Greek

Belgium also gained its independent status early, winning freedom in 1830, the same year as Greece.

Lord Byron, a leading romantic poet, posed for this portrait dressed as a Greek nationalist.

independence was popular with many Europeans whose education had given them tremendous respect for ancient Greek culture. "Fair Greece! Sad relic of departed worth!" lamented Lord Byron, a British poet. "Immortal, though no more; though fallen, great!" Byron went to Greece as a volunteer soldier and died there in 1824.

Eventually, the Great Powers took the side of the Greeks. In 1827, a joint British, French, and Russian fleet destroyed an Ottoman fleet at the Battle of Navarino. In 1830, a treaty granted Greece full independence. This success encouraged other nationalities to seek independence.

Mazzini sparked Italian nationalism.

The situation in Italy was much more complicated than that in Greece. Italy was divided into many different states. Some parts were ruled by Austria. Others were fiercely independent, in the traditions of the Renaissance city-states. Part of Italy was ruled by the pope. Unity was the great ambition of Italian nationalists.

Modern Italian nationalism began with Napoleon. In 1805, he combined the many separate Italian states into a single French-controlled Kingdom of Italy. The Congress of Vienna restored most of the old divisions. Yet the idea of a united Italy survived.

Among Italy's early nationalists was Giuseppe Mazzini (maht-TSEE-nee). "A people destined to achieve great things," argued Mazzini, "must one day or other form a nation-state. Italy therefore will be one. Her geographical conditions, her language, her literature, and the desires of her people all point to this aim."

In 1831, the 26-year-old Mazzini formed a nationalist group called Young Italy, which no one older than 40 was allowed to join. At its peak during the 1830's, Young Italy claimed 60,000 members. Most were of middle-class backgrounds. Unfortunately for Mazzini, the idea of nationalism won little support from the Italian masses. Deep cultural differences divided northern and southern Italy. An urban worker in Milan had little in common with a peasant farmer in Sicily.

Austria proved an even bigger obstacle to Italian unity. The Austrian emperor ruled Lombardy and Venetia in northern Italy. Several of his Hapsburg relatives ruled other Italian states. Metternich saw Italian nationalism as a serious threat to Austria, so he made every effort to suppress such groups as Young Italy. Austrian officials arrested Mazzini many times.

In Italy, as in other European countries, nationalism was closely connected to liberalism. Both ideas appealed to people who were educated and eager to govern their countries. In most cases, both nationalists and liberals came from the middle class. Teachers, lawyers, and business people often led the struggle for more liberal government and the formation of nation-states.

Germany was disunited.

As in Italy, there was tremendous interest in nationalism in the German states during the early 1800's. However, unity seemed far away in 1815. The area where most Germans lived was divided into 39 separate countries. The Congress of Vienna had set up a loose union known as the German Confederation.

Every year, each German state sent representatives to Frankfurt to attend a Federal Diet. The diet was a kind of all-German parliament that discussed the problems of member states. The

Like the Greeks, the Italian people could point to a glorious past. Ancient Rome had, of course, ruled a sweeping empire around the Mediterranean Sea. Latin was the ancestor of most languages in western Europe.

German Federal Diet was almost powerless. It had no all-German army to enforce its decisions. It could make no laws unless all 39 states approved. Such agreement was almost impossible because the two largest states—Austria and Prussia—rarely agreed on anything.

Nevertheless, the German Confederation was an important first step toward a German nation. The Federal Diet became a rallying point for liberals and nationalists who wanted unity.

The largest and most powerful member of the German Confederation in 1815 was the Austrian empire. Its Hapsburg emperors ruled peoples of a dozen different nationalities.

The dominant national group within the empire was German. The Hapsburgs themselves were German. So were most of the empire's political and military leaders. Most Germans in the empire lived in and around the city of Vienna. Elsewhere in the empire, there were millions of Hungarians, Czechs, Serbs, Poles, Italians, Romanians, and other peoples.

Metternich was well aware that nationalism posed an enormous threat to the Austrian empire. Throughout his long tenure as Austrian foreign minister, he used censorship and arrests to stop the spread of nationalist ideas. While such tactics slowed nationalism, they did not wipe it out. The result was a constant buildup of pressure as the various peoples moved closer and closer to rebellion against the Hapsburgs.

Romanticism rejected reason.

Nationalism was strongly linked to a second great intellectual movement that began around 1800. That second movement was romanticism. Romanticism affected literature, art, and music, but it also touched politics. Many romantics were also nationalists. Lord Byron, who died fighting for Greek freedom, was a leading romantic poet.

Romanticism was a reaction against the Enlightenment. It was a reaction against the orderly, rational approach of writers such as Voltaire and musicians such as Mozart.

Romanticism was marked by four distinctive characteristics. One was its heavy emphasis on emotion and passion. The romantics stressed feeling over thinking. As the German novelist Johann Wolfgang von Goethe wrote, "What I know, anyone can know, but my heart is my own, peculiar to itself."

Voice from the Past · *Poetry and Patriotism*

Britain's most popular romantic novelist and poet was Sir Walter Scott (1771–1832). Many of Scott's writings told heroic stories of the Middle Ages. This poem shows the link between romanticism and nationalism.

Breathes there a man with soul so dead,
Who never to himself hath said,
  'This is my own, my native land!'
Whose heart hath ne'er within him burn'd
As home his footsteps he hath turn'd
  From wandering on a foreign strand?
If such there breathe, go, mark him well;
For him no Minstrel raptures swell;
High though his titles, proud his name,
Boundless his wealth as wish can claim;
Despite those titles, power, and pelf,
The wretch, concentred all in self,
Living, shall forfeit fair renown,
And, doubly dying, shall go down
To the vile dust from whence he sprung,
Unwept, unhonor'd, and unsung.

1. According to Scott, what sort of man is dead in his soul?
2. What do you think the phrase "concentred all in self" means?
3. (a) What is the fate of such a person in life? (b) In death?

Some students may be able to recount the story of *Ivanhoe,* one of the more famous Romantic novels.

497

Romantic painters emphasized dramatic aspects of nature and the human soul
(right). Among the leading figures of romanticism were George Sand (top),
Beethoven (bottom), and Mary Shelley (center), author of Frankenstein.

A second characteristic of romanticism was its emphasis on the individual. Romantics celebrated individuals, especially heroic rebels. Romantic writers and artists glorified such legendary heroes as the English King Arthur and also such powerful historic figures as Napoleon. It mattered little whether the hero was a revolutionary or a king. It was heroic action that counted.

A third feature of romanticism was its celebration of nature. France's leading romantic novelist, Amandine Aurore Dupin, lovingly described the French countryside and rustic life. (To win a wider audience for her novels, Dupin took the male pen name George Sand.) British writer Emily Brontë made the windswept moors of northern England the setting for her powerful romantic novel, *Wuthering Heights*.

Last but not least, romanticism glorified the past. Romantics yearned for "the good old days," a past that seemed more noble than anything the modern age had to offer. They looked back longingly to a preindustrial age. The deeds of past kings, knights, and outlaws seemed more worthy of song and story than those of factory owners and railway engineers.

Romanticism touched many arts.

Similar ideas—the emphasis on emotion, individual expression, nature, and the glories of the past—affected all the arts. Painting and music as well as literature followed the romantic path.

Romanticism in music In music, Ludwig van Beethoven was a key figure. In his early years, he wrote music in the classical manner (page

Footnote to History

Beethoven never heard his Ninth Symphony. During his last years, he was completely deaf. When he finished conducting the first performance of the Ninth, the audience burst into thunderous applause. Beethoven, facing the orchestra, heard nothing. Only when a singer turned him around did he realize that he was being given a standing ovation.

498

433). In his later symphonies and concertos, however, Beethoven turned away from the tightly controlled compositions he had written in the 1700's. His ninth and last symphony is an overwhelmingly emotional celebration of freedom, dignity, and spiritual triumph. Later romantic composers such as Robert Schumann and Felix Mendelssohn similarly appealed to the hearts and souls of their listeners.

Romanticism in painting Emotion dominated the work of painters as well. Some painters, such as the English painter Joseph Turner and the German Caspar David Friedrich, used landscape scenes to convey moods. Other artists, including France's Eugene Delacroix, painted dramatic scenes from history to arouse the emotions of the viewer.

Romanticism fueled nationalism.

Many romantics were also whole-hearted nationalists. The celebration of past glories appealed to both romantics and nationalists. So did the strong emotions aroused by nationalism.

Writers collected the ballads and folktales of their national group. Such stories, said romantic nationalists, expressed the time-honored spirit of their people. In Germany, for example, the Grimm brothers gathered a collection of fairy tales, which they published in 1812.

In art, romantics often showed their country as a human figure. The French painter Delacroix, for example, portrayed France as a beautiful woman in such works as "Liberty Leading the People" and "Liberty on the Barricades."

Section Review 2

Define: (a) nationalism, (b) nation-state, (c) romanticism
Identify: (a) Battle of Navarino, (b) Byron, (c) Mazzini, (d) Young Italy, (e) George Sand, (f) Beethoven, (g) Scott
Answer:
1. (a) What are the common characteristics of a nation? (b) Which countries in Europe were nation-states in 1815?
2. Explain how the French Revolution brought about the beginning of modern nationalism.
3. How did Greece become a nation?

4. What were some of the obstacles to Italian unification?
5. Why was the German Federal Diet weak?
6. Why was nationalism a threat to Austria?
7. Name four characteristics of romanticism and give an example of each.

Critical Thinking
8. Reread the quotation by Mazzini on page 496. (a) What four factors does he list as developing Italian nationalism? (b) How would each of those factors help Italy become a nation-state?

Latin America won independence. 3

Just as nationalism became a major force in Europe during the early 1800's, it also became important in the Western Hemisphere. As you know, 13 of Britain's North American colonies became independent in the late 1700's, forming the United States of America (page 443). Between 1800 and 1825, similar wars for independence were fought in the region called Latin America.

The term *Latin America* applies to the lands south of the United States where Spanish, Portuguese, and French are spoken. All these languages developed from Latin. The region includes Mexico, Central America, South America, and the islands of the Caribbean.

Several events outside Latin America helped to spark the drive for independence. The ideals of the Enlightenment spread to the educated people of Latin America. When the French Revolution broke out, many Latin Americans applauded its early reforms, if not its later violence. The American Revolution showed that determined rebels could defeat a European government. Finally, Napoleon's conquests in Europe set off a wave of nationalism that affected Latin Americans as well as Europeans.

Latin American society was divided.

On the surface, the Latin American revolutions of the early 1800's appear similar to the American Revolution. In every case, revolutionaries overthrew a government controlled by a European

499

country. The leaders of the revolution then set up a new national government.

However, there were important differences between conditions in Latin America and in the United States. In Latin America, colonial society was sharply divided into classes based on birth. Struggles among these classes played an important part in the revolutions.

At the top of Latin American society were the *peninsulars*, people who had been born in Spain or Portugal. They held the most important positions in colonial government and in the Roman Catholic Church.

Creoles (**KREE**-ohls) ranked next after the peninsulars. Creoles were people who were born in Latin America but whose ancestors came from Europe. This class included many wealthy landowners and lesser government officials.

The peninsulars and the creoles formed an aristocracy in Latin American society. Together, they made up less than one fifth of the population. Below them ranked the common people who had few political rights and little share in the region's wealth.

The common people included mestizos (meh-**STEE**-zohs), mulattoes (myoo-**LAT**-ohs), blacks, and Indians. Mestizos were people of mixed European and Indian ancestry. Mulattoes were of European and African ancestry. Some mestizos and mulattoes owned small farms or businesses. Most rented small farms from landlords. Most blacks worked as slaves on large plantations, although there were free blacks in many Latin American towns. Lowest ranking of all were the millions of Indians. They were legally free, but they were usually treated no better than slaves.

Slaves revolted in Haiti.

The first Latin American country to free itself from European rule was the French colony on the island of Hispaniola in the Caribbean Sea. Slaves and free mulattoes there rose in revolt against France in 1791.

In 1794, the revolutionaries found a skilled general in an ex-slave, Toussaint L'Ouverture (too-**SAHN** **LOO**-vuhr-TYOOR). Toussaint (1743–1803) drove the French forces from the island. Then, in 1802, he attended a peace meeting where he was treacherously taken prisoner. He was then sent to France, where he died in prison. However, the French could not retake the island. Black revolutionary leaders set up the independent country of Haiti in 1804.

Creoles wanted independence.

Elsewhere in Latin America, creoles took the lead in battles for independence. The creoles had a number of long-standing grievances against Spain. Peninsulars held almost all the high government offices in Spain's Latin American lands. Of the 170 viceroys who held office between 1492 and 1810, for example, only 4 were creoles.

Spain also kept tight control over the economy of its colonies. Merchants in Spanish colonies could trade only with Spain. They could send their goods only on Spanish ships. The valuable mines of Mexico and Peru were under direct Spanish control, which the creoles resented.

The direct cause of the Latin American revolts, however, was Napoleon's conquest of Spain in 1808. Napoleon made his brother Joseph king of Spain (page 463). Many creoles might have remained loyal to a Spanish king, but they felt no loyalty at all to a Frenchman placed on the Spanish throne by force.

Toussaint L'Ouverture

Napoleon's defeat in Haiti led to the Louisiana Purchase. Napoleon had hoped to use Louisiana for growing food for his West Indian colonies. When he lost the largest one, Haiti, he agreed to sell Louisiana to the United States for a mere $15 million.

Fighting broke out in 1810 in several parts of Latin America. The wars for independence were complicated and confusing. Loyalties were divided. The viceroys and their armies remained loyal to Spain, as did some creoles. Indians and mestizos fought on both sides, often forced into armies against their will.

Bolívar and San Martín led the struggle.

The South American wars of independence produced two brilliant generals whose leadership was largely responsible for the success of the rebels. One was Simón Bolívar (see-**MOHN** buh-**LEE**-vahr). The other was the Argentinian José San Martín (hoh-**SAY** san mahr-**TEEN**).

Bolívar in the north Simón Bolívar (1783–1830) was a wealthy Venezuelan creole. He had traveled in Europe and read the works of Voltaire, Rousseau, and Montesquieu, even though they were banned in Latin America. Bolívar was both romantic and practical, a writer and a fighter, handsome and brilliant. He won admiration from friend and foe alike. Above all, he was tireless in the struggle for independence.

Bolívar's native Venezuela declared its independence from Spain in 1811. However, the struggle seesawed back and forth. The revolutionaries suffered many defeats, and Bolívar was twice forced into exile.

The turning point came in 1819. Bolívar built up an army from many sources. He promised to end slavery, winning many black volunteers. Other volunteers came from Europe. In January 1819, Bolívar led his 2,500 soldiers on a daring march through the towering Andes into what is now Colombia. Coming from this unexpected direction, he took the Spanish army completely by surprise in Bogotá and defeated them.

Bolívar went on to free Venezuela in 1821. Next, he marched south into Ecuador. In the coastal city of Guayaquil, he met with the other great hero of the independence movement, San Martín.

San Martín in the south When the wars for independence broke out in Latin America, José San Martín (1778–1850) was in Spain fighting Napoleon. Hearing of the revolt in his homeland, Argentina, he returned at once. Soon he commanded a creole army there. While Bolívar was

Simón Bolívar

freeing the northern part of South America, San Martín freed the south.

Argentina declared its independence in 1816. However, the new country was not safe as long as Spanish forces had strongholds in nearby Chile and Peru. Thus, in 1817, San Martín led an army on a grueling march across the Andes to Chile. There he won several decisive victories and freed the country.

Next, San Martín took his army north by sea to Lima, Peru, in 1821. The Spanish army retreated into the mountains of Peru. To drive them out, San Martín needed a much larger force. Otherwise, the Spaniards would remain a threat to all of independent South America. This was the problem that faced San Martín and Bolívar when they met at Guayaquil.

The Spanish were finally defeated.

Mystery has long surrounded the meeting between these two great generals. They differed in many ways. San Martín was a less dashing and romantic leader than Bolívar. San Martín wanted

Bolívar had little time for the day-to-day business of government. He was always at the front. As soon as independence was secured for one country, he moved on to the next. He was honored everywhere. What South American country is named for him?

501

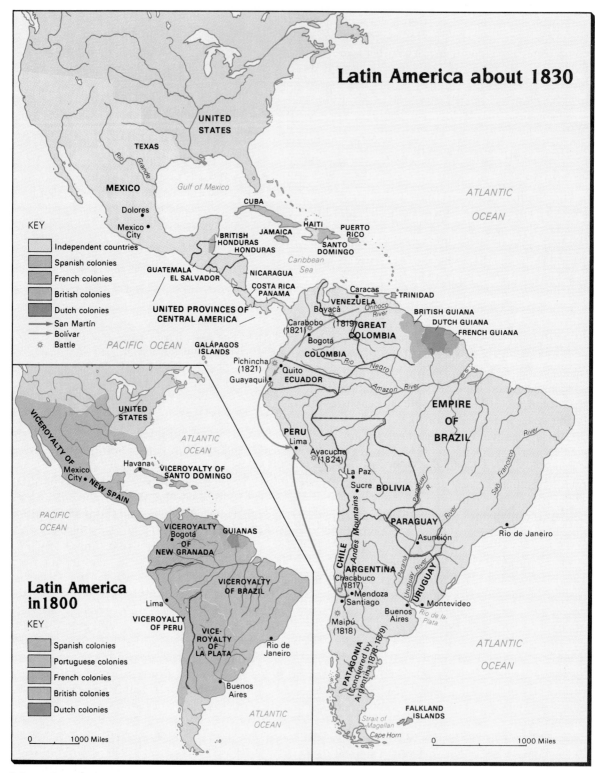

Latin America about 1830

UNITED STATES

TEXAS

MEXICO

Dolores

Mexico City

Gulf of Mexico

CUBA

JAMAICA

HAITI

PUERTO RICO

SANTO DOMINGO

BRITISH HONDURAS

HONDURAS

Caribbean Sea

ATLANTIC OCEAN

GUATEMALA

EL SALVADOR

NICARAGUA

COSTA RICA

PANAMA

UNITED PROVINCES OF CENTRAL AMERICA

Caracas

TRINIDAD

VENEZUELA

Boyacá

Orinoco River

BRITISH GUIANA

DUTCH GUIANA

FRENCH GUIANA

Carabobo (1821)

(1819) GREAT COLOMBIA

Bogotá

COLOMBIA

Rio Negro

Pichincha (1821)

Quito

Guayaquil

ECUADOR

Amazon River

EMPIRE OF BRAZIL

PERU

Lima

Ayacucho (1824)

La Paz

Sucre

BOLIVIA

Paraguay R.

Sab. Francisco River

Andes Mountains

PARAGUAY

Asunción

Rio de Janeiro

CHILE

ARGENTINA

Chacabuco (1817)

Mendoza

Santiago

Paraná River

Uruguay River

URUGUAY

Montevideo

Buenos Aires

Rio de la Plata

Maipú (1818)

PATAGONIA (Conquered by Argentina 1878-1879)

ATLANTIC OCEAN

FALKLAND ISLANDS

Strait of Magellan

Cape Horn

PACIFIC OCEAN

GALÁPAGOS ISLANDS

KEY

	Independent countries
	Spanish colonies
	French colonies
	British colonies
	Dutch colonies

→ San Martín
→ Bolívar
✸ Battle

0 _____ 1000 Miles

Latin America in 1800

UNITED STATES

ATLANTIC OCEAN

VICEROYALTY OF NEW SPAIN

Mexico City

Havana

VICEROYALTY OF SANTO DOMINGO

PACIFIC OCEAN

VICEROYALTY OF NEW GRANADA

Bogotá

GUIANAS

VICEROYALTY OF BRAZIL

Lima

VICEROYALTY OF PERU

VICE-ROYALTY OF LA PLATA

Rio de Janeiro

Buenos Aires

ATLANTIC OCEAN

KEY

	Spanish colonies
	Portuguese colonies
	French colonies
	British colonies
	Dutch colonies

0 _____ 1000 Miles

Map Study

By 1830, in what region were most of the lands that were still colonies? In what country did Bolívar and San Martín meet?

502

the newly independent countries of South America governed as monarchies. In contrast, Bolívar hoped to establish republics that would be dominated by the creoles. Nonetheless, both knew that the first step was to defeat the Spanish.

Although no one knows what the two leaders said to each other, the results were dramatic. San Martín left his army for Bolívar to command and returned to Argentina. Some historians think San Martín left in anger after a quarrel with Bolívar. Others say San Martín deliberately stepped aside in favor of Bolívar, so that the independence movement could unite behind a single leader. Whatever his reasons, San Martín soon sailed for Europe, where he died almost forgotten in 1850. Only later was he recognized as a true Argentinian hero.

Bolívar followed the Spaniards into the heights of the Andes. His forces defeated the Spanish army at the Battle of Ayacucho on December 9, 1824. This was the last major battle of the war for independence. South America was free of Spanish rule.

Brazil freed itself peacefully.

Meanwhile, Brazil won its independence peacefully. In 1807, Napoleon invaded Portugal. As his armies neared Lisbon, the Portuguese royal family fled to Brazil. After Napoleon's defeat, the king of Portugal returned to Europe. However, he left his son, Dom Pedro, as regent of Brazil.

When Brazilians demanded their independence in 1822, Dom Pedro agreed. He defied the Portuguese government's command to sail for Lisbon. On September 7, 1822, he issued the call, "Independence or death!" Brazilians celebrate this day as their national independence day.

In December 1822, Dom Pedro was named emperor. Brazil, South America's largest country, became South America's only monarchy.

Mexicans struggled for freedom.

In most Latin American countries, revolution began in the cities, but in Mexico, it began in the countryside. Only in Mexico did Indians and mestizos take a leading part in the struggle for independence.

The first outbreak of the Mexican revolution came in 1810. A group of creoles plotted a revolt, but the government learned of their plans. One of the leaders was Father Miguel Hidalgo (ee-THAHL-goh), a priest in the small mountain village of Dolores. Hidalgo was a poor but well-educated man, steeped in the ideals of the French Revolution. On September 16, 1810, he called on the Indian peasants of his parish to rebel against their Spanish masters. "My children," he asked them, "will you be free? Will you make the effort to recover from the hated Spaniards the lands stolen from your forefathers 300 years ago?"

Hidalgo's Indians began a 200-mile march toward Mexico City. Armed with sickles, stones, and clubs, this unruly army moved southward, picking up thousands of new recruits and weapons along the way. Creole landlords fled for their lives. Soon Hidalgo had a force of 60,000 men behind him. He declared an end to slavery and called for other reforms.

At Mexico City, however, the main Spanish army and the creoles joined forces against Hidalgo's army. Hidalgo was betrayed by one of his officers, captured, and executed.

The rebels found another strong leader in José María Morelos (moh-RAY-lohs). Morelos was a farm worker turned priest who had fought beside Father Hidalgo. He proved a far better general than Hidalgo had been. By 1813, Morelos's army controlled all of Mexico except for the largest cities. A Mexican congress, called by Morelos, declared Mexico an independent republic in 1813. Morelos wanted to set up a democratic government, tax the wealthy, and distribute lands to the peasants.

Many creoles supported the idea of independence, but they were not willing to accept Morelos's social reforms. A creole officer, Augustín de Iturbide (EE-toor-BEE-thay), captured and executed Morelos in 1815. A few scattered groups of rebels fought on as guerrillas.

Suddenly, events took a new turn. In 1820, a revolution in Spain put a new group in power. Mexico's creoles feared that this Spanish government would take away their privileges. At once, the creoles united in support of independence. The very man who had killed Morelos, Iturbide, made peace with the last guerrilla leader. Then Iturbide proclaimed Mexico independent in 1821. Iturbide later made himself emperor, but he was soon ousted. When he tried to return to power in 1824, he was shot.

"More than anyone," wrote Bolívar, "I desire to see [Spanish] America fashioned into the greatest nation in the world." In this great hope he was disappointed. Venezuela, Colombia, and Ecuador were briefly united as Gran Colombia, but they soon divided.

Caudillos dominated governments.

By 1830, Latin America was home to 16 independent countries, but the citizens of these new countries had few political freedoms. All the countries were dominated by a small group of wealthy creole aristocrats. "Independence," said Bolívar shortly before his death in 1830, "is the sole benefit we have gained, at the sacrifice of all others ... He who serves a revolution plows the sea."

Army leaders had come to power during the long struggle with Spain, and they continued to control Latin America after independence. By 1830, nearly all the countries of Latin America were run by **caudillos** (kow-THEE-yohs). Caudillos were political strongmen, usually army officers, who ruled as dictators. Many caudillos cared only for their own power and wealth. They did little to improve the lives of the common people. Changes of government most often took place at bayonet-point, as one caudillo was forced to give way to another.

Foreign interests dominated Latin America's economies.

In one way, Latin America was luckier than other nonindustrial parts of the world. Despite the political confusion, Latin America was never again carved into colonies as Africa and Asia were in the late 1800's. Having won independence, Latin America succeeded in keeping it.

The Monroe Doctrine Spain did not give up hope of winning back its former colonies. France too saw a chance to take over land in Latin America. Both Britain and the United States, however, were determined not to allow such a development.

In 1823, President James Monroe of the United States announced, "the American continents ... are henceforth not to be considered as subjects for future colonization by any European powers." This statement is known as the Monroe Doctrine. Alone, the United States was not strong enough to enforce the Monroe Doctrine. However, Great Britain also wanted to protect Latin American independence.

British and American economic interests Britain had no political ambitions in Latin America, but it did have large economic interests. During the wars for independence, many Latin American countries began trading with Britain rather than with Spain. British banks and businesses invested heavily in South America, especially in Argentina and Brazil.

Britain's only real economic rival in Latin America was the United States. However, most United States' exports in the early 1800's came from the farm rather than the factory. Thus, there was little direct competition between the United States and Great Britain. Both countries were happy with the economic advantages they gained by Latin American independence.

Section Review 3

Define: (a) Latin America, (b) peninsulars, (c) creoles, (d) mestizos, (e) mulattoes, (f) caudillo
Identify: (a) Toussaint L'Ouverture, (b) Bolívar, (c) San Martín, (d) Battle of Ayacucho, (e) Dom Pedro, (f) Hidalgo, (g) Morelos, (h) Iturbide, (i) Monroe Doctrine
Answer:
1. Describe the divisions in Latin American society under Spanish rule.
2. How did Haiti gain independence?
3. (a) What economic and political grievances did the creoles have? (b) What was the direct cause of revolt in Latin America?
4. (a) How was independence achieved in northern South America? (b) In southern South America?
5. How did Brazil become independent?
6. How did the Mexican revolt differ from revolts in other Spanish colonies?
7. What groups dominated Latin America after independence?
8. Why was the Monroe Doctrine drawn up?

Critical Thinking
9. Historians have often debated the importance of individual leaders in history. (a) Would the Latin American revolts have taken place without Toussaint, Bolívar, San Martín, and Hidalgo? Explain your answer. (b) Which, if any, of the revolts would have succeeded without these leaders?
10. What did Bolívar mean when he said, "He who serves a revolution plows the sea"?

Reform and revolution swept Europe. 4

As we have seen, new ideas had widespread impact in Europe during the early 1800's. Nationalism and romanticism roused people's emotions. Liberalism gained ground with the growth of the middle class in western Europe. Members of this class were eager to have greater political power. They won large gains in Great Britain and France, but they failed, for the time being, in most other parts of Europe.

France overthrew its Bourbon king.

In 1830, a short and almost bloodless revolution ended the rule of France's Charles X. Charles, the last Bourbon king of France, brought on the revolution by his own stupidity. He ignored both middle-class liberals and Parisian radicals and tried to rule as an absolute monarch. He had nothing but contempt for the idea of a limited monarchy such as the one in Britain. "I would rather be a woodcutter," he once said, "than be the king of England."

Charles sparked the revolution by trying to take away what few powers France's Chamber of Deputies held. Riots broke out in Paris as liberals and radicals joined together to rid the country of this impossible king. Charles fled as an exile to Great Britain.

Within a few days, a group of liberal leaders offered the French crown to Charles's cousin, Louis Philippe, who was sympathetic to liberal reforms. Louis Philippe accepted, promising to rule as a "citizen king" who would share power with the Chamber of Deputies. France enjoyed almost two decades of peace and stability before another revolution broke out in 1848.

Britain's middle class won the vote.

Peaceful debate in the British Parliament, not armed revolution, won the most important liberal victory of these years. After a decade of pressure from factory owners and merchants, Parliament passed the Reform Bill of 1832.

The Reform Bill of 1832 set up new districts for electing members of Parliament. Many of the old districts had existed for hundreds of years. Some had been medieval villages but were now empty fields. Yet the owner of that field could elect a member of Parliament. In contrast, new cities such as Manchester and Sheffield had no representatives because those cities had grown up after the districts were formed. The reform bill put an end to such injustices. For the first time, the thriving new industrial cities had representation in Parliament.

The reform bill also gave more men the right to vote. Before 1832, only men who owned a substantial amount of property could vote. After 1832, men who paid a certain amount of rent could also vote. (Around the same time, Catholic men also won the right to vote.)

The Reform Bill of 1832 doubled the number of British voters. Nearly all middle-class men could now take part in elections. Still, this was less than 20 percent of the men in Great Britain.

The working class had little power.

Although Britain had the most liberal government in Europe, working class people still had no political influence. Daniel O'Connell, an Irish nationalist and liberal leader of this time, was asked to explain a political issue to some road-workers. "Whatever happens," O'Connell told them, "you will still be breaking stones." Nevertheless, the working class was beginning to demand some say in politics.

As the Industrial Revolution progressed, working conditions improved a little. Workers' wages were rising, and ordinary people were better fed and better clothed. Life was no longer a grim struggle to survive. Workers began to organize.

By the 1840's, the Industrial Revolution was sweeping across the continent. It particularly affected the Ruhr and Rhine valleys in western Germany and the Po valley in northern Italy. Factories sprang up in cities such as Frankfurt, Cologne, and Milan. Radical political organizers in these cities were determined that the working-class voice would be heard.

1848 was a year of revolutions.

By 1848, working-class radicals and middle-class liberals in Europe were convinced that the Metternich system—the political agreements of

The Industrial Revolution brought large numbers of workers together in the cities, where they could see how unfairly the fruits of their labors were divided. Slowly but surely, they realized that if they united, they would become more powerful.

In 1848, revolts shook many European capitals. Here, troops fire on protestors in Vienna.

the Congress of Vienna—had long outlived its usefulness. Nationalists believed the time had come to sweep away old-fashioned empires and replace them with nation-states.

With such widespread discontent, it was only a matter of time before a violent outburst occurred. The explosion came in 1848. In January of that year, there was a revolution in the Kingdom of the Two Sicilies. Over the next 4 months, almost 50 similar revolts rocked Europe. "What remains standing in Europe?" asked Czar Nicholas I of Russia in April. His empire and Britain were the only major countries not touched by revolt.

The revolts meant different things in different places. In France, the revolutionaries planned to establish a democratic government. In Hungary, they wanted to throw off Austrian rule and set up a Hungarian nation-state. In the German states, rebels hoped for a united Germany.

At first, the revolutions caught Europe's rulers by surprise. Many monarchs granted concessions to the rebels. Even Prussia's King Frederick William IV agreed to the election of a democratic parliament. He also agreed to support an all-German parliament that would meet in Frankfurt. Hungary and several states in northern Italy won temporary freedom from Austria.

The Austrian empire seemed to be falling apart. After 30 years as Europe's most powerful political figure, Metternich resigned. As he left Vienna for exile in Britain, he told a friend, "Everything is finished."

Everything was not finished, however. As spring turned to summer, the revolutionaries seemed to run out of steam. The rebels shared the common aim of overthrowing the conservative order, but they disagreed strongly over what to do next. Meanwhile, the rulers regained their courage. With the strength of their armies behind them, they began a counterrevolution. German princes called their representatives home from Frankfurt, and the all-German parliament vanished almost as suddenly as it had appeared. Elsewhere, Austrian armies crushed the rebels in northern Italy and put down the revolt in Hungary. By 1849, Europe had practically returned to its pre-1848 status.

On the surface, therefore, the revolutions of 1848 brought about little reform. However, the forces of change had not been destroyed, only contained. The demands for independence and an end to the old empires would be heard again and again.

France again overthrew its king.

Radicals were involved in many of the 1848 revolts, but only in France was the demand for democratic government the main point of revolution. Only in France—particularly in Paris—were radicals the moving force behind revolution.

During the late 1840's, King Louis Philippe turned a deaf ear to demands that the Chamber of Deputies be made more democratic. "Get rich by work, and you will have the vote," his chief minister scornfully told the working classes.

Paris rose up against the king in February 1848. Louis Philippe's government collapsed almost overnight. It was replaced by a temporary government led by Alphonse de Lamartine (lahm-ahr-TEEN), one of France's leading romantic poets. "Down with royalty!" shouted the Paris mob.

Preceding the revolutions of 1848 were several years of bad harvests across the continent and a business slump that had led to the loss of thousands of factory jobs.

Lamartine and his colleagues declared France a republic once more.

Things went sour for the new republican government almost from the start. A quarrel split the radicals into factions. One side, led by Lamartine, wanted only political reform. The other, led by Louis Blanc, wanted economic reform as well. Blanc's group demanded that the government set up national workshops to make jobs for the unemployed. Such workshops were indeed set up in Paris, but Lamartine's government soon closed them. This order led to bloody street battles in Paris. More than 10,000 workers were killed before the government subdued the rebels.

A *new Napoleon came to power.*

The violence turned France against the radicals toward a more moderate, liberal government. The new constitution drawn up later in 1848 called for a parliament and a strong president elected by the people.

France held a presidential election in December 1848, and the winner was none other than Louis Napoleon Bonaparte. Nephew of the great emperor, Louis Napoleon lacked his uncle's intelligence and strength of character. However, he had a name that French voters linked with past glories. "How could I help voting for this gentleman," said one old man in 1851, "I whose nose was frozen at Moscow?"

Louis Napoleon won widespread support from the peasants, who resented the dominance of Paris in French politics and wanted peace and order. Nationalists saw in him a man who could unite all of the country's political factions. Thus, a second Bonaparte came to power swearing to "remain faithful to the democratic Republic and to defend the Constitution."

Like his uncle, Louis Napoleon soon broke that oath. In December 1851, he dissolved the French parliament and declared himself sole ruler of France. Remarkably, an election held later that month (in which all French men had the right to vote) approved his deed by an overwhelming 92 percent. Adopting his uncle's constitution, Louis Napoleon then took the title Emperor Napoleon III.

Why did the French people accept this coup? Louis himself gave perhaps the best explanation: "The Empire means peace. It means peace because France wishes it, and when France is satisfied, the world is quiescent [quiet]."

From his exile in London, the 78-year-old Metternich was puzzled by events in France. Louis Napoleon's success seemed to break all the political rules that Metternich knew. How could a conservative, absolutist monarch come to power in a democratic election? It seemed impossible. Said Metternich:

He must choose between grasping the reins of government either as heir of Napoleon the First or as one elected by universal suffrage. He will destroy himself upon this contradiction.

Time proved Metternich wrong. Napoleon III governed France for the next 20 years.

The times had changed. The rules of politics were changing too. Over the next century, other absolute rulers would come to power through the ballot box. As we shall see, democracy proved to be a form of government that could destroy itself.

Section Review 4

Define: (a) counterrevolution, (b) coup
Identify: (a) Charles X, (b) Louis Philippe, (c) Reform Bill of 1832, (d) 1848, (e) Lamartine, (f) Blanc, (g) Louis Napoleon
Answer:
1. (a) What brought on the French revolt of 1830? (b) What were its results?
2. Explain two ways that the Reform Bill of 1832 broadened the right to vote in Great Britain.
3. What goals did the revolutionaries of 1848 have in each of the following places? (a) France (b) Hungary (c) the German states
4. (a) What did the revolutions of 1848 achieve at first? (b) What happened in the counterrevolution?
5. (a) How did Louis Philippe fall from power? (b) What problems did the new French government face?
6. How did Louis Napoleon become emperor?

Critical Thinking
7. (a) What contradiction did Metternich think would lead to Napoleon III's downfall? (b) Could a leader follow such a path to power today? Explain your answer.

Said one of Napoleon III's chief advisers: "I am willing enough to be baptized with the water of universal suffrage, but I don't intend to live with my feet in it."

Chapter Review 23

Summary

1. **European leaders sought stability.** In 1815, representatives from Europe met in Vienna to make a peace settlement. Led by Metternich, they restored former monarchies, blocked France from expanding, and established a balance of power. Many parts of the settlement were opposed by middle-class liberals and by radicals.

2. **New ideals affected politics and art.** After 1815, European politics were heavily influenced by nationalism, particularly in countries that were divided or ruled by foreign powers. Nationalism was closely linked to romanticism, which glorified emotion, nature, heroic individuals, and the past.

3. **Latin America won independence.** The early 1800's saw a series of wars for independence throughout Latin America. In Haiti, slaves revolted against France and set up an independent country. Bolívar and San Martín led independence movements in South America. In Mexico, Indians and mestizos played a large part in the war for independence. Brazil won independence peacefully. Although free, Latin American countries were still dominated by a small wealthy class. Many countries fell under military rule. Independence was aided by the Monroe Doctrine.

4. **Reform and revolution swept Europe.** In Britain, reforms expanded voting rights. Elsewhere in Europe, however, nationalism and the desire for reform led to revolt. France overthrew one king in 1830 but remained a monarchy. In 1848, a wave of revolts swept Europe but were soon put down. Radical demands for reform in France led to the establishment of a republic, but violence soon turned people against the new government.

Reviewing the Facts

1. Define the following terms:
   a. nation-state
   b. caudillo
   c. nationalism
   d. romanticism

2. Explain the importance of each of the following people or events:
   a. Congress of Vienna
   b. Metternich
   c. Mazzini
   d. L'Ouverture
   e. Bolívar
   f. San Martín
   g. Dom Pedro
   h. Hidalgo
   i. Morelos
   j. Monroe Doctrine
   k. Reform Bill of 1832
   l. Louis Napoleon

3. (a) What were Metternich's goals at the Congress of Vienna? (b) How was each met?

4. How were nationalist goals blocked in Italy and the German states?

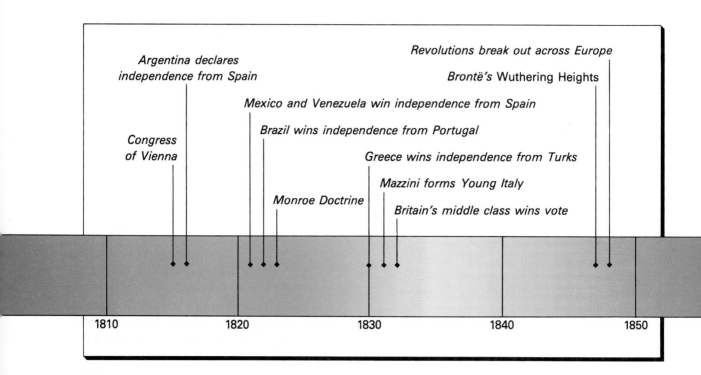

Argentina declares independence from Spain

Revolutions break out across Europe

Brontë's *Wuthering Heights*

Mexico and Venezuela win independence from Spain

Brazil wins independence from Portugal

Greece wins independence from Turks

Congress of Vienna

Mazzini forms *Young Italy*

Monroe Doctrine

Britain's middle class wins vote

1810   1820   1830   1840   1850

5. (a) What was the first Latin American country to become independent? (b) How did it do so?
6. (a) Describe Bolívar's achievements in South America. (b) Describe San Martín's.
7. (a) Briefly describe the war for independence in Mexico. (b) How did it differ from revolts in South America?
8. (a) What stand did the United States take in the Monroe Doctrine? (b) Why did both the United States and Great Britain support this doctrine?
9. What were the effects of the Reform Bill of 1832 in Great Britain?
10. How did the events of 1848 help Louis Napoleon win power?

Basic Skills

1. **Making a chart** Make a chart of the revolutions in Latin America. In the left-hand vertical column, list the main Latin American countries involved (Haiti, Venezuela, Argentina, Brazil, and Mexico). In the horizontal columns, use the headings European Colonial Power, Social Classes Involved, Leader(s), and Main Events.
2. **Paraphrasing** Briefly explain the ideas and goals of conservatism, liberalism, and radicalism in Europe in the early 1800's.
3. **Classifying** (a) Classify the following individuals according to the categories of liberal, radical, conservative: Bolívar, Lamartine, Louis Philippe, Morelos, Charles X, Louis Blanc. (b) Give a reason for each choice.

Researching and Reporting Skills

Writing a Research Paper
Phase 2: Consulting sources and writing a working thesis statement
1. **Taking notes** Using the research questions you wrote in Phase 1, look for information in the sources you have located. Take notes on cards, identifying the subject of each note and the source and page number of the information. If other information unrelated to your questions seems important to your topic, frame a new question and record the information. Your notes should summarize the main ideas in your own words. You should also include quotations, graphs, and references to art or literature that may be useful in your report.
2. **Organizing notes** Use the research questions to help in organizing your notes. Identify three or more categories of information. Group the cards in the appropriate categories. Save cards that do not fit for possible use later.
3. **Drafting a working thesis** Based on your notes, establish what main idea emerges from your information. Write a sentence that states this thesis.
4. **Outlining** Review your categories and decide in what order they should be presented to support your thesis. Then go back over your notes to identify and add subtopics and supporting points. Make an outline of the major topics and subtopics.

Critical Thinking

1. **Inferring** Identify three factors that influenced the success or failure of the national uprisings in Europe in the 1800's.
2. **Identifying fact and opinion** Reread on page 492 the paragraph beginning, "The Congress of Vienna was a political triumph . . ." (a) Does it express fact or opinion? (b) Would it be possible to come to different conclusions? If so, what are they?
3. **Evaluating** (a) What were the goals of Bolívar for South America? (b) To what extent did he accomplish those goals? Support your answer with facts and examples.

Perspectives on Past and Present
Nationalism was a driving force in the political events of the 1800's. (a) How important is it in the world today? In what regions is it most active? (b) Is it more active in some regions than others? Give examples and explain how they illustrate the statement.

Investigating History

1. Using art history books for reference, identify three painters who belonged to the Romantic tradition. Choose a painting by each artist and explain how it characterizes that style.
2. Read about the revolution for independence in one Latin American country. How did the revolution begin? Who were the leaders? What were the main events? What new type of government was established?

509

Economic Expansion and Nationalism

The skill of Britain's ironworkers and engineers showed in the towering iron framework of the Crystal Palace. This building housed the Great Exhibition of 1851, a display of inventions and products from around the world.

Key Terms

stock
corporation
monopoly
emigration
immigration
socialism
suffrage

Read and Understand

1. Industrialism created a global economy.
2. Working people gained more influence.
3. Italy and Germany formed nations.
4. The United States spread westward.

It was May 1, 1851—a date thousands of British people had been eagerly awaiting for months. By noon, more than 500,000 people had gathered in London's Hyde Park to witness the opening of the Great Exhibition. On display were arts, crafts, and inventions from all over the world. This exhibit was, in many ways, the first world's fair.

The 25,000 people lucky enough to have tickets for the opening ceremonies were crammed inside the Crystal Palace. This remarkable building had been designed especially for the exhibition. It looked like a gigantic greenhouse. More than 1 million square feet of glass on a framework of bare iron formed its walls and roof. The main hall was as long as six football fields and high enough to house several fully grown elm trees.

The Crystal Palace was the first major building prefabricated with a framework of bare iron. It pointed toward a new and easier way of constructing large buildings.

Promptly at noon, a flourish of trumpets announced the arrival of Queen Victoria and the royal family. Although the queen's political power was limited, her symbolic importance as head of the British empire was immense. During her long reign (1837–1901), Victoria skillfully used ceremonial occasions such as this exhibition to foster national spirit.

Prince Albert, Victoria's German-born husband, stood proudly by her side. He was an intelligent, energetic man who was fiercely devoted to his adopted country. The Great Exhibition had been his idea, a way of showing the world the awesome power of the British empire. It would also, Albert said, "give us a living picture of the point of development at which the whole of mankind has arrived."

Visitors to the Great Exhibition exclaimed over stuffed elephants from India, fine lace from Spain, diamonds from the Netherlands, cigars from Cuba, perfumes from Turkey, cannons from Germany, birchbark canoes from Canada, and porcelain from China and France.

Exhibit after exhibit showed the strength of British industry. Among the wonders on display were a printing press that could turn out 5,000 newspapers per hour and a locomotive engine that could pull a train at 60 miles per hour. While the Great Exhibition celebrated the height of civilization to which the "whole of mankind" had risen, it left no doubt as to which country was in the lead. More than half the exhibits came from Great Britain and its territories.

Many of the 6 million visitors felt that the Great Exhibition marked the dawn of a new age of progress. Indeed, the years after the Great Exhibition were a period of tremendous economic growth. Perhaps the most striking advances during this time were in travel and communications. Railroads, steamships, and the telegraph made the world seem smaller than ever before. News, goods, and people traveled faster.

People responded to the spread of industrialism in a variety of ways. Some groups demanded a new division of wealth, with equal shares for all. Others believed that the path to a better future lay in building strong nation-states. In Europe, nationalism led to the birth of two new nation-states, Germany and Italy. In North America, the United States added new lands and grew to be an industrial power.

Industrialism created a global economy. 1

The people who visited the Great Exhibition of 1851 lived in a world that their grandparents could not have imagined. It was a world of booming factories, speeding trains, and mile-long bridges. Above all, it was a world of change.

The pace of industrialization continued to quicken. In 1858, a German economist wrote, "Railroads and machine shops, coal mines and iron foundries, spinneries and rolling mills seem to spring up out of the ground, and smokestacks sprout from the earth like mushrooms." Between 1850 and 1875, coal production in Germany grew from 6 million tons to 35 million tons per year. During the same years, the total world output of coal nearly tripled. The world output of iron increased fourfold.

Because factory-made goods cost less than handmade items, mass-produced items found their way into every home. Thus, the demand for manufactured goods skyrocketed along with the supply of such goods.

Finally, the great boom brought a tremendous increase in world trade. Between 1850 and 1870, the value of goods bought and sold among countries increased by a staggering 260 percent. In other words, world trade more than tripled during these 20 years. Trade increased more rapidly during this period than at any other time in history.

Steam revolutionized transportation.

By 1850, the same changes that had swept Great Britain in the early 1800's were happening on a global scale. Leading the way were advances in transportation and communication.

The growth of railroads The late 1800's were a golden age for railroad builders. They laid thousands of miles of new track every year, spanning rivers with iron bridges and carving tunnels through mountains. Between 1850 and 1880, the length of railroad track in the world grew from 23,600 miles to 228,400 miles—almost the distance from Earth to the moon!

Although most railroad building took place in Europe and North America, the "iron horse" soon reached every inhabited continent. By 1875, even

Steam engines were the driving forces of the great boom. In 1850, the steam engines of the world had a total capacity of some 4 million horsepower. By 1870, their combined horsepower had surged to over 18 million.

Looking at economics *The opening of the Suez Canal in 1869 provided a direct route between Europe and the East. In 1875, Britain purchased the Egyptian ruler's stock in the Suez Canal Company. As a shareholder, Britain could protect the shipments of Indian and Egyptian cotton bound for British mills.*

such nonindustrial countries as Brazil and Egypt had more than 1,000 miles of track. Swashbuckling railroad tycoons such as the Englishman Thomas Brassey became giants of industry. At one time, Brassey employed 80,000 workers and was building railroads on 5 continents.

Railroads boosted trade and industry wherever they spread. The iron and coal industries grew to meet the railroads' endless need for tracks, trains, and fuel. Other industries flourished as railroads brought them raw materials and carried their finished products to market.

Steamships Meanwhile, similar changes were taking place with water transportation. In 1807, an American named Robert Fulton designed the first practical steamboat. By the 1840's, more than 500 steamboats were chugging up and down the Mississippi River.

For ocean crossings, the changeover from wind power to steam power was slow. Early steamships needed to stop for fuel too often to make ocean travel practical. In 1850, only 5 percent of all oceangoing ships used steam power. By 1870, however, that figure had grown to 40 percent.

Breakthroughs in transportation Two celebrations in 1869 highlighted the dramatic advances in transportation. One took place in the United States and the other in Egypt.

On May 10, a crowd gathered in a lonely part of Utah to celebrate the opening of the first transcontinental railroad. At Promontory Point, a work crew laying track from the east met the crew laying track from the west. Amid cheers and brass bands, officials hammered a golden spike to mark the meeting place. On the new railroad, travelers could journey from Boston to San Francisco in less than a week.

Six months later, on November 17, a parade of 69 ships sailed out of the harbor of Port Said, Egypt. Led by the yacht of France's Empress Eugenie, the ships sailed southward through the just-completed Suez Canal. This 100-mile canal, planned by French businessman Ferdinand de

Footnote to History

In 1872, French writer Jules Verne published a novel called *Around the World in Eighty Days.* Just 20 years earlier, the journey would have taken about 11 months. Real-life travelers would not have shared all the adventures of Verne's hero, who fought off an Indian attack in the United States and rescued a princess in India. However, travelers *could* have made the trip in the same time. The novel was based on actual railroad and steamship schedules.

A telegraph message carried the news of the railroad link at Promontory Point across the nation: "One, two, three—done!" Parades and fireworks greeted the news in cities and towns across the United States.

Lesseps, linked the Mediterranean and Red seas. No longer did ships from Europe have to go around Africa to reach Asia. The canal shortened the travel time between Europe and India by at least one month.

The telegraph speeded communication.

Trains and steamships carried letters, newspapers, and other kinds of information. However, by the mid-1800's, the field of communications was already far ahead of transportation in terms of speed. The telegraph could send information at the speed of electricity.

Electricity had fascinated the scientists in the Age of Enlightenment (page 431). During the 1840's, several inventors made telegraph systems using wires that carried low-voltage currents. The most successful telegraph was invented by an American artist, Samuel F.B. Morse. His system used a key (which looked something like a stapler) to make and break an electric circuit. Morse developed a code in which short bursts of current (dots) and longer bursts (dashes) stood for letters.

By 1850, all the major cities in the eastern United States were connected by telegraph lines. In 1851, a telegraph cable was laid under the English Channel to connect London and Paris. In 1866, the first successful transatlantic cable was completed, linking Newfoundland and Ireland. By 1875, it was possible to send messages around the world—from London to Calcutta, from New York to Melbourne, from Paris to Tokyo—in less than five minutes.

Business leaders formed corporations.

As world trade and industry expanded so did the size of businesses. Building transcontinental railroads and telegraph systems took a huge supply of money for investment, or capital. Many entrepreneurs needed help in raising the capital to start their businesses. To raise this money, an entrepreneur could sell shares of **stock** in the new company. Everyone who bought stock became a part-owner of the business.

By the mid-1800's, most major companies had thousands of owners. For example, Ferdinand de Lesseps set up a corporation to raise money to build the Suez Canal. He sold nearly 400,000 shares, which were purchased by several governments and more than 20,000 individuals.

If a company did well, stockholders stood to make money in two ways. First, each stockholder shared in the company's profits in proportion to the amount of stock he or she owned. Second, stockholders could often sell their shares of stock at a higher price than they had paid for them, because other people were eager to own a share of a thriving business. On the other hand, if the company did poorly, stockholders might lose the money they had invested. However, they could never lose more than they had originally paid for the stock.

Businesses organized in this new way were called **corporations**. They operated under charters obtained from the government. Countless businesses formed corporations and added the term *incorporated* (in the United States) or *limited liability* (in Great Britain) to their names.

Businesses were soon operating on a larger scale than ever before. These vast enterprises yielded correspondingly great profits. Investment banks, concentrated in London, specialized in channeling that income into new ventures all over the world.

Some corporations became so successful that they drove rivals out of business. For example, the American entrepreneur John D. Rockefeller began his rise to wealth by building an oil refinery in 1863. His business incorporated as the Standard Oil Company of Ohio in 1870. Soon Rockefeller owned not only oil refineries but also oil wells, oil pipelines, and oil sales agencies. He controlled every step of the business from the ground to the customer. By the 1880's, Standard Oil was the only major oil company in the United States. When a single company controls an entire industry, the situation is called a **monopoly.** In the late 1800's, monopolies arose in many industries, both in the United States and in Europe.

Economic ties circled the globe.

The transportation revolution, the growth of trade, and the huge increase in industrial production brought countries around the world into closer contact than ever before. A shirt manufacturer in Britain, for example, could have 1,000 bales of cotton delivered from New Orleans to his factory in Manchester in 10 days. The finished

In the 1890's, Standard Oil controlled 90 percent of the nation's oil refineries. It also enjoyed special favors from the railroads, which made large amounts of money from shipping Rockefeller's oil. Shortly after 1900, Rockefeller became a billionaire.

shirts might be on sale in shops in Vienna and St. Petersburg three weeks after they left the factory.

Industrial countries depended on a steady stream of imports from many parts of the world. To keep their factories running, most industrial countries needed far more raw materials than they themselves could provide. As their cities swelled in size and population, most industrial countries also needed more food than they could grow. By 1875, for example, Britain imported more than 75 percent of the wheat its people consumed.

Much of this food and the resources for industry came from countries that had few factories of their own. In turn, those countries bought their manufactured goods from the industrial countries. The world was rapidly becoming interdependent.

The growth of a world economy brought risks along with benefits. In 1857, for example, the collapse of a major insurance company in the United States led to the failure of dozens of other businesses across the country. Within months, this financial crisis had shaken businesses in Britain, France, Argentina, and Australia. Such "crashes" took place repeatedly in the late 1800's. Crop failures or financial problems in one part of the world now had international impact.

People relocated in search of work.

As we saw in Chapter 22, the Industrial Revolution was accompanied by a population explosion. In 1850, about 266 million people lived in Europe. By the end of the century, the population had risen above 400 million, an increase of more than 50 percent. That figure would have been even larger if many Europeans had not left the continent for other lands.

The 1800's were marked by great shifts in population. Some parts of the world had large-scale **emigration**—that is, many people left those places to settle elsewhere. In other places, there was large-scale **immigration**—that is, many people settled in that area. Between 1850 and 1900, an estimated 25 million people sought to escape poverty or oppression by emigrating to the United States, Canada, South Africa, Australia, New Zealand, and Latin America.

The migration within Europe, as rural people flocked to the cities, was even greater. For every seven children born in the rural areas of western Europe after 1850, one stayed at home, one emigrated to another country, and five moved to cities in their own country. These massive shifts in population played a large part in the development of the modern world.

Reading a table Which nation's manufacturing had the largest relative increase?

Reading a graph During what two periods did trade increase most rapidly?

Relative Shares of World Manufacturing Output, 1750–1900

	1750	1800	1830	1860	1880	1900
United Kingdom (Britain)	1.9	4.3	9.5	19.9	22.9	18.5
France	4.0	4.2	5.2	7.9	7.8	6.8
German States/Germany	2.9	3.5	3.5	4.9	8.5	13.2
Russia	5.0	5.6	5.6	7.0	7.6	8.8
United States	0.1	0.8	2.4	7.2	14.7	23.6
Japan	3.8	3.5	2.8	2.6	2.4	2.4
China	32.8	33.3	29.8	19.7	12.5	6.2
India/Pakistan	24.5	19.7	17.6	8.6	2.8	1.7

SOURCE: P. Kennedy, The Rise and Fall of the Great Powers. *Random House, New York, 1987, p.149.*

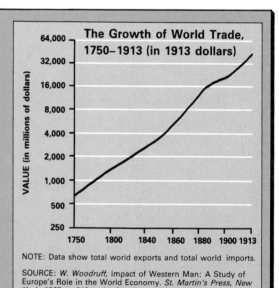

The Growth of World Trade, 1750–1913 (in 1913 dollars)

VALUE (in millions of dollars)

NOTE: Data show total world exports and total world imports.

SOURCE: W. Woodruff, Impact of Western Man: A Study of Europe's Role in the World Economy. *St. Martin's Press, New York, 1967, p. 313 and references cited therein.*

Section Review 1

Define: (a) stock, (b) corporation, (c) monopoly, (d) emigration, (e) immigration
Identify: (a) Great Exhibition, (b) Victoria, (c) Fulton, (d) Suez Canal, (e) Morse
Answer:
1. How did industrialization encourage the demand for goods?
2. (a) What changes occurred in transportation? (b) How did the growth of transportation affect other industries?
3. What changes took place in communications?
4. (a) How did entrepreneurs raise money for investment? (b) In what two ways could stockholders make money?
5. (a) What were the advantages of the increase in world trade? (b) What were the drawbacks of the world economy?
6. Briefly describe the major shifts in Europe's population in the late 1800's.

Critical Thinking

7. The text describes three ceremonial occasions—the Great Exhibition, the opening of the Suez Canal, and the driving of the golden spike at Promontory Point. (a) What was the significance of each for trade? (b) What do these celebrations suggest about the spirit of the age?

Working people gained more influence.

2

By 1850, some of the worst abuses of the Industrial Revolution were slowly being corrected. From a modern point of view, however, workers still had many grievances. A number of people tried to solve these problems in new ways.

At first, many reformers came from the middle and upper classes. For example, a few British aristocrats championed laws limiting child labor (page 485). Such upper-class reformers saw themselves as protecting the common people from the greed of the new entrepreneurs. In the late 1800's, however, working people themselves became more active in politics. Gradually, they made their voices heard.

During the 1800's, demands for reform grew louder. However, reformers often disagreed with one another on how to improve society.

Socialists planned to share wealth.

Industrial society "may truly be said to be a miserly, selfish system," wrote a British reformer named Robert Owen in 1857. "Under this system, to support life you must be tyrant or slave. It is all about individual wealth and power, with which the most successful are maintained with considerable hazard and gross injustice." A French writer, Pierre Joseph Proudhon (proo-**DON**), put it more simply. "Property," he said, "is theft."

The ideas of Owen, Proudhon, and similar thinkers came to be called **socialism**. Socialists believe that the wealth of a country should be shared equally among all its citizens. Under a socialist system, society as a whole owns most factories and businesses. Some socialists believe that there should be no private property at all.

Robert Owen tried to put his socialist ideals into practice. Owen began his working life as a shop clerk. By the time he was 30, he was the owner of a cotton mill with 2,000 employees at New Lanark, Scotland. Owen treated his workers well. He built houses near the factory and rented them to his employees at low rates. He did away with child labor, giving his workers' children free schooling instead.

New Lanark prospered, but Owen's later attempts to set up socialist villages failed. His most ambitious experiment was the cooperative village of New Harmony, Indiana, founded in 1825. It lasted only four years and then broke up from constant quarrels about the sharing of goods and profits.

Marx urged workers to revolt.

Robert Owen preached cooperation among social classes. A later socialist, Karl Marx (1818–1883), said that such cooperation was impossible. "The history of all . . . society is the history of class struggles," wrote Marx in 1848. "Freeman and slave, patrician and plebeian, lord and serf . . . stood in constant opposition to one another."

Marx called Owen and others like him *utopian socialists*. As you may recall, the word *utopia* means "nowhere" and was the title of a book

The gap between rich and poor is demonstrated in the following statistic: in the French manufacturing city of Lille, 9 percent of the population in 1875 controlled 90 percent of the community's wealth.

Karl Marx

describing an ideal society (page 346). Marx described his own ideas as *scientific socialism* because he claimed that they were based on the scientific study of history.

Marx was born in Germany in 1818. While a student, he became a radical activist and a journalist. Marx outlined his ideas in *The Communist Manifesto*, published in 1847. A short book, it sowed the seeds for several later revolutions. By 1848, Marx had been exiled from France, Belgium, and Germany. He finally found a haven in Britain, where he spent the rest of his life writing. His major work was *Das Kapital*, a three-volume study of economics and political power.

Marx's co-author for both the *Communist Manifesto* and *Das Kapital* was a fellow German socialist, Friedrich Engels (page 486). Engels came from a well-to-do family with international economic interests. Indeed, Marx and his family were so poor that they often depended on Engels for support.

Marx believed that economics was the key to understanding both the past and the present. Economic goals—the need for food, shelter, clothing, and other goods—were the forces that determined people's actions, said Marx. Thus, the most basic question in history was this: Who controls the means of producing goods? In a farming society, Marx reasoned, land was the most important source of wealth. Therefore, landowners dominated society and government. In an industrial society, factory owners had the greatest economic power. As a result, they soon won political power as well.

Marx said that work was the true source of all value. For example, the work of a shoemaker changed a piece of leather into a pair of shoes for which a buyer would pay money. Without the shoemaker, the leather had no value. According to Marx, workers were being cheated out of the wealth created through their efforts. Workers in a shoe factory got only part of the money for which each pair of shoes sold. The rest of the money went to the factory owner as profit.

According to Marx, the Industrial Revolution was making the rich richer and the poor poorer. Marx used the word *bourgeoisie* to describe the factory-owning middle class. These people were capitalists, people who invest money in businesses. Marx used the Latin word *proletariat* to describe the urban working class. These workers, said Marx, had nothing to sell but their labor. They had no choice but to work for whatever wages the bourgeoisie offered.

Sooner or later, Marx predicted, workers would join together to overthrow the bourgeoisie and establish a true socialist society. "Workers of the world, unite!" wrote Marx. "You have nothing to lose but your chains."

Despite Marx's predictions, however, workers showed little sign of rebelling. Except for a brief outburst in Paris in 1871 (page 524), there were no large workers' revolts in the late 1800's. Most workers did not want to overthrow the system but to share in its benefits.

Moreover, some of Marx's key ideas proved wrong. The gap between the rich and the poor did not widen as he had expected. The rich certainly got richer, but the lives of the poor also improved. The tremendous growth of trade and production brought benefits to almost everyone. Marx also underestimated the noneconomic forces that influence people. He ignored the importance of religion, nationalism, ethnic loyalties, and other ideals in people's lives.

Another reason workers did not erupt in the way Marx predicted was that emigration gave millions of discontented workers a chance to improve their lives in new lands.

Working men won the vote.

Although workers did not revolt, many did strive for changes in society. Brought together in factories, mines, and mills, workers soon saw that there was strength in numbers.

As you have read, workers began to form trade unions in the early 1800's (page 487). Trade unions did not try to remake society, as the socialists did. Instead, unions tried to raise wages and improve working conditions. By 1875, British trade unions had won the right to strike and picket peacefully and had built up a membership of 1 million people. In many other European countries, however, unions remained illegal.

The basis for workers' growing influence was the right to vote. The right to vote is often called **suffrage**. By the end of the 1800's, several industrial countries had universal manhood suffrage (the right of all adult men to vote). No country, however, allowed women to vote.

In the United States, nearly all adult white men had the right to vote by 1850. However, the great numbers of blacks who were slaves had no voting rights. In some places, free blacks had once had the right to vote, but it was taken away from them. As you will read later in this chapter, black men won the right to vote after the Civil War. It was many years, however, before either black or white women could vote.

In Great Britain, as you have read, the Reform Bill of 1832 (page 505) gave the vote to most men in the middle class. In 1867 and 1875, further reform bills gave the vote to nearly all men.

In France, Napoleon III (page 507) broadened voting rights during the 1850's and 1860's. In 1871, France became the first European country to allow universal manhood suffrage.

Realism replaced romanticism in art.

Just as the working class was becoming more important in politics, it was also becoming more visible in the arts. Artists and writers turned away from romantic, idealized views of the past and of nature. Instead, novels and paintings began to reflect the lives of ordinary people and current social issues. This new artistic approach is called realism. Realists tried to observe and report what they saw in a precise, objective fashion.

Realism in painting In 1855, artists in Paris held a grand exhibit of French paintings. The works on display were mainly romantic landscapes, formal portraits, battle scenes, and figures from ancient myths.

Just outside the exhibit hall, an artist named Gustave Courbet (koor-**BAY**) set up a large wooden shack labeled the Pavilion of Realism. The paintings within were all by Courbet and included a huge, stark funeral scene that had been turned

The realist painters emphasized everyday life, especially among the lower classes. This painting by Daumier shows travelers in a third-class railroad carriage. Compare it with the romantic painting on page 498.

Another of Courbet's paintings, ''The Stone Breakers,'' shows the style of the realists. These laborers are real workers doing a real job.

down by the official exhibit. Realist painters such as Courbet scorned romantic art. Courbet called the romantics "painters of angels" and asked, "What do those look like? I've never had the luck to see one in the flesh."

Another outstanding artist of the realist school was Honoré Daumier (doh-MYAY). He became famous for his scathing pictures of what he saw as the pompous and self-satisfied middle class.

Realism in literature Realist authors turned to the novel as the form best suited to their goals. "The only reason for the existence of a novel," wrote American author Henry James, "is that it does attempt to represent life." Many European countries produced realist authors. France had Gustave Flaubert (floh-BAIR) and Honoré de Balzac (BAHL-zak). In Russia, there were Fyodor Dostoevsky (DAHS-tuh-YEF-skee) and Leo Tolstoy (tahl-STOY). William Thackeray, Charles Dickens, and Thomas Hardy wrote in Britain.

Section Review 2

Define: (a) socialism, (b) bourgeoisie, (c) proletariat, (d) suffrage, (e) realism
Identify: (a) Robert Owen, (b) Karl Marx
Answer:
1. (a) What were the general beliefs of socialists? (b) How did Marx's approach to socialism differ from Owen's?
2. Marx stressed the importance of work as the source of value. Explain what he meant.
3. (a) According to Marx, how did bourgeois business owners take advantage of workers? (b) What did he predict would happen? (c) Give two reasons why the events he predicted failed to occur.
4. How did trade unions increase the power of working people?
5. (a) Briefly describe how the right to vote grew broader in Europe and the United States.

Voice from the Past · *An Industrial City*

Charles Dickens was the most widely read of the English realists, largely because he mixed his realism with plenty of sentiment and melodrama. At the same time, he vividly reminded his readers that they lived in a world where much was grim, ugly, and unjust. Here is how he describes an industrial town in his 1854 novel, *Hard Times*.

It was a town of red brick, or of brick that would have been red if the smoke and ashes had allowed it; but, as matters stood, it was a town of unnatural red and black, like the painted face of a savage. It was a town of machinery and tall chimneys, out of which interminable [endless] serpents of smoke trailed themselves for ever and ever, and never got uncoiled. It had a black canal in it, and a river that ran purple with ill-smelling dye, and vast piles of buildings full of windows where there was a rattling and a trembling all day long, and where the piston of the steam-engine worked monotonously up and down, like the head of an elephant in a state of melancholy madness. It contained several large streets all very like one another, and many small streets still more like one another, inhabited by people equally like one another, who all went in and out at the same hours, with the same sound upon the same pavements, to do the same work, and to whom every day was the same as yesterday and tomorrow, and every year the counterpart of the last and the next.

1. Dickens uses strong sensory words. What adjectives relate to each of the following senses? (a) sight (b) hearing (c) smell
2. What real social problems does Dickens mention in this description?
3. (a) Which seems more alive and powerful, the city or the people in it? (b) How does Dickens create this impression?

518

(b) What groups were still denied the vote?

6. What new themes did art and literature begin to portray in the mid-1800's?

Critical Thinking

7. How might each of the following people have reacted to Proudhon's statement, "Property is theft"? (a) Robert Owen (b) Karl Marx (c) a trade unionist (d) a stockholder in a business

8. How was the change in socialist ideas from Owen to Marx similar to the change in literary styles during this period?

Italy and Germany formed nations. 3

Many early nationalists had been romantics like Byron and Mazzini. In politics as in art, however, realism was replacing romanticism. During the late 1800's, a new group of national leaders practiced what they called *realpolitik*. This German term meant "the politics of reality." People used the word to describe a tough, calculating brand of politics in which idealism played no part.

As nationalism grew in strength, it destroyed the balance of power that Metternich had so carefully set up in 1815. In France, Napoleon III was bent on reviving French glory. In Germany and Italy, people were determined to form united nation-states. Austria wanted to preserve its empire. These conflicting goals touched off five wars among the Great Powers between 1854 and 1871.

Cavour united Italy.

The Congress of Vienna left Italy divided and almost entirely under foreign control. In the north, Austria ruled Venetia and Lombardy and also dominated the small states of Tuscany, Modena, Parma, and Lucca. In the south, Spain ruled the Kingdom of the Two Sicilies (map, page 520).

During the fateful year of 1848, revolts broke out in eight separate states on the Italian peninsula. Giuseppe Mazzini, the early leader of Italian nationalism (page 496), briefly headed a republican government at Rome. However, the 1848 rebellions failed in Italy just as they did elsewhere in Europe. Within months, the former rulers of the Italian states returned and drove Mazzini and other nationalist leaders into exile.

After 1848, Italian nationalists looked to the Kingdom of Sardinia for leadership. Sardinia was the only Italian state ruled by an Italian dynasty. This kingdom included the Piedmont, Nice, and Savoy as well as the island of Sardinia. It was the largest and most powerful of the Italian states and had the most liberal government.

In 1852, Sardinia's King Victor Emmanuel II named Count Camillo di Cavour (kuh-**VOOR**) his prime minister. Cavour (1810–1861) was a wealthy aristocrat and a moderate nationalist. He made uniting Italy his highest priority.

Cavour considered Mazzini and the earlier nationalists vague and impractical. He believed that careful diplomacy and well-chosen alliances were more useful than grand proclamations and romantic rebellions. In turn, nationalists such as Mazzini called Cavour a "pale ghost of Machiavelli." They feared his main goal was not to unite Italy but to broaden the power of Sardinia.

An alliance with Napoleon III The greatest roadblock to Italian unity was Austria. Cavour knew that Sardinia was going to need help from another Great Power to drive Austria out of northern Italy.

Cavour found an ally in France. Napoleon III hoped to make France Europe's greatest power, as it had been under his uncle, Napoleon I. However, Napoleon III lacked his uncle's brilliance, and most of his schemes backfired.

Napoleon III believed that France could dominate Italy if Austria were out of the way. In 1858, the French emperor and Cavour had a secret meeting at which Napoleon agreed to help drive Austria out of Lombardy and Venetia. In return, Cavour promised to give France the border regions of Nice and Savoy.

Cavour soon provoked a war with Austria. A combined French-Sardinian army won two quick victories against the Austrians. Meanwhile, Italian nationalists staged revolts against Austria all across northern Italy. They demanded that Sardinia take over their lands.

A strong, united Italy was not what Napoleon III had expected. For a time, he considered going to war against Sardinia. However, Cavour had been careful to maintain good relations with the other Great Powers so that France was isolated.

Cavour published a newspaper called *Il Risorgimento* (The Resurgence), which eventually gave its name to the whole movement for Italian unity.

The Unification of Italy, 1850–1870

FRANCE

AUSTRIAN EMPIRE

SWITZERLAND

SAVOY

LOMBARDY
Milan
Turin
Po River
PIEDMONT
To France, 1860
NICE
Genoa

PARMA
MODENA

VENETIA
Adige R.
Venice

Drave River
Save River
Danube River

Florence
Pisa
Arno R.
TUSCANY

PAPAL
STATES

OTTOMAN
EMPIRE

Adriatic Sea

CORSICA
(Fr.)

Tiber R.
Rome

MEDITERRANEAN
SEA

SARDINIA

Naples

KINGDOM

Tyrrhenian
Sea

OF

THE

Palermo

TWO SICILIES

SICILY

MEDITERRANEAN
SEA

0   100 Miles

AFRICA

KEY
- Kingdom of Sardinia, 1858
- Added to Sardinia, 1859–1860
- Added to Italy, 1866
- Added to Italy, 1870

Map Study

By skillful maneuvers, Cavour (above) led Italy to national unity. What border territories did he give up in 1860? What territory was the last to be added to Italy?

Napoleon backed down, accepting Nice and Savoy as Cavour had promised. In 1860, Sardinia annexed all of northern Italy except Venetia.

Garibaldi and the Red Shirts While Cavour was uniting the north, he was also secretly helping nationalist rebels in southern Italy. In May 1860, a small army of about 1,100 Italian nationalists sailed from Genoa to Sicily. They were led by a bold and romantic soldier, Giuseppe Garibaldi (GAR-uh-BAHL-dee). In battle, Garibaldi always wore a bright red shirt. Since his followers imitated him, they became known as the "Red Shirts."

Garibaldi was victorious in Sicily and began marching north. Volunteers flocked to his banner. Everywhere he was greeted as a liberator. Garibaldi spoke excitedly of freeing the rest of Italy, especially his beloved birthplace, Nice.

Now it was Cavour's turn to feel that his schemes had backfired. He had given Nice to France as a consolation prize, and he did not want to provoke Napoleon III again. "Garibaldi

has become intoxicated with success," Cavour complained to an adviser. "He is planning the wildest schemes."

Knowing that war against France would lead to disaster, Cavour arranged for King Victor Emmanuel II to meet Garibaldi in Naples. "The Red One" willingly agreed to step aside and let the Sardinian king rule the areas he conquered.

In March 1861, an Italian parliament met at Turin and declared Victor Emmanuel II king of Italy. The new nation thus had a government headed by a constitutional monarch and an elected parliament.

A united Italy faced problems.

Worn out by years of work, Cavour died shortly after Victor Emmanuel II became king. He never saw his country fully united. Venetia did not become part of the new nation until 1866. In 1871, Italy took over the Papal States. Rome became the national capital of a united Italy.

520

(According to a treaty called the Law of Guarantees, the pope kept the section of Rome known as Vatican City.)

The movement of the capital to Rome was a triumphant moment for Italian nationalists. However, unification did not cure all the country's problems. Many centuries had passed since the peninsula had last been united, and fierce rivalries flared between different provinces. The greatest tension arose between the industrialized north and the agricultural south. The people of these two regions had very different ways of living. They scarcely understood each other's versions of the Italian language.

After Cavour's death, Italy lacked strong national leadership. Garibaldi tried to head a government, but he lacked the political skill. Within the Italian parliament, there were no well-organized parties with clear-cut policies. As a result, prime ministers and cabinets changed frequently.

Italy also faced severe economic problems. There were bloody peasant revolts in the south and strikes and riots in the northern cities. One result of Italy's problems was massive emigration, particularly from the south. Between 1860 and 1910, 4 million Italians moved to the United States and another 1 million went to Argentina. "I had hoped to evoke the soul of Italy," wrote the old patriot Mazzini shortly before his death in 1872, "but all I can see is a corpse."

Austria and Prussia were rivals.

Like Italy, Germany finally achieved unity in the mid-1800's. Since 1815, 39 German states had formed a German Confederation. The two largest states, Austria and Prussia, dominated this loose grouping.

Austria, earlier the home of the Holy Roman emperor, was still considered the natural leader of Germany. Vienna, Austria's capital, was an important cultural center for German music, art, and literature. However, Austria faced serious problems. Most of the people in the Austrian empire were non-Germans who yearned to break away. Austria also lagged behind Prussia in industrial development.

Prussia, on the other hand, had everything to gain from nationalism. It had a mainly German population. As early as 1834, Prussia had taken the lead by forming the Zollverein (TSOHL-vur-eyn), a free-trade area that included all the major German states except Austria. Prussia was also the most industrial of the German states. Moreover, Prussia's army was by far the most powerful in central Europe.

Prussia was a conservative state. Although most adult men could vote, the Prussian parliament had little control over policies. The king, William I of the Hohenzollern family, had almost unlimited power. His ministers and army officers all came from Prussia's wealthy landlord class, the junkers. Prussia's middle class, although wealthy, had little political influence.

In 1862, William I chose as his prime minister a junker and a staunch conservative named Otto von Bismarck (1815–1898). A master of realpolitik, Bismarck set out to make Prussia the head of a united Germany. He saw Austria as Prussia's major rival. "Germany," he said, "is clearly too small for us both."

Bismarck had only contempt for the liberals who had led the movement for German unity in 1848. In his first speech as prime minister, he told the Prussian parliament, "The great questions of our day cannot be solved by speeches and majority votes—that was the great mistake of 1848 and 1849—but by blood and iron."

Bismarck united Germany by blood and iron.

In 1864, Bismarck took the first step toward increasing Prussian power. He led Prussia into war against Denmark to win two border provinces, Schleswig and Holstein. The quick victory increased national pride among Prussians and won Prussia new respect from other Germans.

The Seven Weeks' War In 1866, Bismarck purposely provoked Austria into declaring war on Prussia. This conflict was known was the Seven Weeks' War. As the name suggests, the war was quickly over. Thanks to Prussia's efficient railroad network, Prussian generals could move their troops to the battlefield more quickly than Austrian leaders could. Once there, the Prussians used their superior training and equipment to win one smashing victory after another.

Austria was humiliated. It lost some German lands to Prussia. It also lost Venetia to Italy, which had fought alongside Prussia. Worst of all,

Austria, afraid to sit idly by while Prussia grew in size and strength, joined the war on Prussia's side. It was the Prussian army, however, that defeated Denmark.

The Unification of Germany, 1865–1871

DENMARK

North Sea

SCHLESWIG

HOLSTEIN

MECKLENBURG

Hamburg

OLDENBURG

H A N O V E R

BRANDENBURG

• Berlin

WEST PRUSSIA

EAST PRUSSIA

Memel •

Baltic Sea

Niemen River

River

RUSSIAN

Vistula

• Warsaw

EMPIRE

Oder River

Elbe River

SILESIA

NETHERLANDS

WESTPHALIA

Ruhr River

Rhine River

BELGIUM

HESSE

Ems •

Frankfort •

SAXONY

BOHEMIA

• Prague

LUX.

Sedan •

LORRAINE

FRANCE

ALSACE

WÜRTTEMBURG
HOHENZOLLERN

BAVARIA

Danube River

• Munich

AUSTRIAN

Vienna •

EMPIRE

ITALY

Adriatic Sea

KEY

- Prussia, 1865
- Annexed by Prussia, 1866
- Joined Prussia in North German Confederation, 1867
- South German States (joined Prussia to form German empire, 1871)
- Conquered from France, 1871
- — German empire, 1871

0 ____ 100 Miles

Map Study

Prussia's chancellor, Otto von Bismarck (right), created a united German empire under Prussian leadership. When did Prussia take over Hanover? Saxony and Mecklenburg? What were some of the German states that joined with Prussia to form the German empire in 1871? What territories were conquered from France?

522

Austria was forced to withdraw from the German Confederation.

Prussia now took control of northern Germany. For the first time, the eastern and western parts of the Prussian kingdom were joined. In 1867, the remaining states in the north joined the North German Confederation, which Prussia dominated completely.

Reeling from this defeat, the Austrian empire set out to rebuild its strength. The empire's biggest problem was the discontent of the many nationalities it ruled. The Hungarians, who had rebelled in 1848, were the largest of these groups. They wanted more independence.

In 1867, Austria agreed to a *dual monarchy*. Austria and Hungary became two independent and equal states with one ruler. Each state had its own parliament and officials. The two states still had a united army, however, and they acted as one in foreign policy. The new empire was known as Austria-Hungary.

The Franco-Prussian War By 1867, only a few southern German states remained independent of Prussia. Because most people in southern Germany were Catholics, they did not want to be dominated by Prussia, which was largely Protestant. However, Bismarck felt certain he could win their support if they faced a threat from outside Germany. He believed his best chance was to provoke a war with France.

Napoleon III of France, whose clumsy diplomacy had helped Cavour unite Italy, soon gave Bismarck a chance to win southern Germany. In 1868, Spanish revolutionaries overthrew Spain's Queen Isabella II and offered the throne to Leopold of Hohenzollern, a distant cousin of Prussia's William I. Napoleon III protested, as he did not want France surrounded by Hohenzollern rulers. The Prussian prince turned down the Spanish offer, but tensions remained high.

During this crisis, the French ambassador met with the Prussian king. Bismarck deliberately gave German newspapers a misleading account of the two men's conversation. Bismarck made it sound as if the king and the ambassador had insulted each other.

As Bismarck hoped, this news story caused an uproar. Soon public opinion in both countries demanded war. On July 15, 1870, France declared war on Prussia.

The Prussian army struck at once. Before most French soldiers had even left their hometowns, Prussian troops poured into northern France. In September 1870, the Prussian army surrounded the main French force at Sedan. Among the 100,000 French prisoners was Napoleon III himself, a beaten and broken man.

Only the city of Paris held out against the Germans. For four months, Parisians withstood a German siege. Finally, hunger forced them to surrender.

France was crushed. It had to pay Prussia the huge sum of 5 billion francs. As an even greater blow to French pride, France had to give Prussia the two border provinces of Alsace and Lorraine, which contained France's richest coal and iron deposits.

The Franco-Prussian War was the final step in German unification. Now people in southern Germany as well as those in the north were caught up in nationalistic fever. Despite their earlier doubts, they accepted Prussian leadership.

The Second Reich On January 18, 1871, at the conquered French palace of Versailles, King William I of Prussia was crowned *kaiser* (**KYE**-zuhr), or emperor, of the newly formed German empire. To Germans, the empire was known as the Second Reich (ryke). (They considered the Holy Roman Empire the First Reich.) Bismarck became the new nation's first prime minister.

The new German nation had a solid economic foundation. By 1870, Germany was the world's third biggest producer of manufactured goods, after Britain and the United States. After unification, German industry grew even faster. Soon it overtook Britain.

France formed the Third Republic.

In the aftermath of the Franco-Prussian War, France went through a series of crises. After being released by Prussia, Napoleon III spent his last years in exile in Britain. France's National Assembly met to decide on a new government.

Footnote to History

Food was so scarce in besieged Paris that people ate sawdust, leather, and rats. Even the animals in the Paris zoo were slaughtered for food by starving Parisians.

A French man called Bismarck "the craftiest of foxes, who had the art of making truth itself an instrument of falsehood; to whom gratitude and respect were as entirely unknown as all other noble sentiments save one: devotion to his country's ambition."

Meanwhile, in March 1871, a radical government called the Paris Commune took control of Paris. Once again, Paris faced war, this time a war against France's own National Assembly. When the assembly's troops marched into the city, Parisian workers threw up barricades in the streets and fought block by block. Thousands died, and much of the city burned. In May 1871, the National Assembly defeated the last Communards, as supporters of the Commune were called. The following week, more than 20,000 Parisians were executed.

Not until 1875 could the National Assembly agree on a new government. Eventually, the members voted to set up a republic. In the words of a leading French politician, it was "the system of government that divides us least." The Third Republic, as this new system was called, lasted nearly 60 years. However, France remained bitterly divided, with a dozen political parties jockeying for power. Between 1871 and 1914, France averaged a change of government every ten months.

Despite these divisions, the French were united in their hatred of Germany. Nearly all French people agreed that France must regain Alsace and Lorraine. As French political leader Léon Gambetta declared, "We shall demand each day before Europe our rights and our ravished provinces. France is at the mercy of Germany. We are in a state of latent war; neither peace nor freedom nor progress is any longer possible in Europe."

The balance of power broke down.

For 40 years after the Congress of Vienna in 1815, the countries of Europe had remained at peace with one another. The first crack in the peace settlement had come with the Crimean (krye-MEE-uhn) War in 1853. That war pitted Britain and France against Russia. These three countries had competing interests in the Ottoman empire, now weak and crumbling. In a pointless struggle, British and French armies attacked the Crimea, a Russian peninsula in the Black Sea. Although the Crimean War cost the lives of 500,000 men, it was fought far from most European capitals. It did not lead to general warfare in Europe. Its most important result was to reveal the military weakness of the huge but backward Russian empire.

The first battles after 1815 to strike close to home were the wars of Italian and German unification. However, these wars were short, and many countries took no part in them. Europe had not known a major war since the fall of Napoleon.

Meanwhile, the political situation in Europe had changed greatly since 1815. At the Congress of Vienna, there had been five Great Powers—Britain, France, Austria, Prussia, and Russia. The wars of the late 1800's changed one Great Power, as Prussia became Germany, and added a sixth, Italy.

In 1815, all the Great Powers had been fairly equal in strength. By 1871, however, Britain and

Daily Life · *Balloons in War*

When Prussian troops surrounded Paris in 1870, French political leader Léon Gambetta was desperate to escape. If only he could get out of the city, he hoped to raise new armies to defend France. Gambetta took the only way not blocked by the Prussians—he left Paris by balloon. More than 160 other people did the same. During the four months of the siege, balloons also carried ten tons of mail in and out of Paris.

For a brief period, balloons were very important in war. During the United States Civil War, the North used its balloon corps to observe enemy troops and direct cannon fire. After the Franco-Prussian War, many countries added balloon corps to their armies.

Another reason for France's slow economic growth was its relatively slow population growth—the slowest in Europe.

Germany were clearly the strongest, both economically and militarily. Austria, Russia, and Italy lagged far behind. France struggled along somewhere in between. The balance of power had broken down, and the risk of a major war was increasing.

It is no coincidence that Britain and Germany, the two countries with the greatest military power, were also the industrial leaders. The Industrial Revolution had military as well as economic impact. In war, industrial countries had enormous advantages over nonindustrial countries. Victory usually went to the side with the most advanced weapons and the best transportation network.

As war became industrialized, it also became nationalized. France built a citizen-army during the French Revolution. By the end of the 1800's, all industrial countries relied on such armies.

Germany's military leader, Count Helmuth von Moltke, wrote:

The days are gone by when, for dynastic ends, small professional armies went to war to conquer a city or a province. The wars of the present day call whole nations to arms. The entire financial resources of the state are appropriated to the purpose. In the interest of humanity, it is to be hoped that wars will become less frequent, as they have become more terrible.

Section Review 3

Define: (a) realpolitik, (b) junker, (c) dual monarchy, (d) kaiser
Identify: (a) Mazzini, (b) Cavour, (c) Victor Emmanuel II, (d) Napoleon III, (e) Garibaldi, (f) Bismarck, (g) Zollverein, (h) Seven Weeks' War, (i) Franco-Prussian War, (j) Second Reich, (k) Third Republic
Answer:
1. What made Sardinia the leader in the Italian nationalist movement?
2. (a) Why did Cavour make an agreement with Napoleon III? (b) What were the terms? (c) What were the results?
3. (a) How was the kingdom of Italy established? (b) What additional territories were joined to it later?

4. What problems did the united Italy face?
5. Why did Prussia rather than Austria take the lead in uniting Germany?
6. Briefly describe the major steps that Bismarck took to unify Germany.
7. What lasting effect did the Franco-Prussian War have on relations between France and Germany?
8. What political problems did France face under the Third Republic?
9. How had the balance of power in Europe changed since 1815?

Critical Thinking
10. (a) In what ways were the unification of Italy and Germany alike? (b) How was the outcome different for the two countries? Explain.

The United States spread westward. 4

Across the Atlantic Ocean from Europe, another country was also establishing itself as a nation. When the United States of America declared its independence in 1776, all 13 states lay along the Atlantic coast. By the time the nation celebrated its hundredth birthday in 1876, its borders had reached the Pacific coast. To unite this territory, Americans fought bitter wars with the Indians and with Mexico. The bloodiest war of all on the path to nationhood, however, was a war the people of the United States fought among themselves. It is known as the Civil War (1861–1865). Within ten years after the Civil War, it was clear that the United States was on its way to becoming a world power to rival Britain and Germany.

Americans moved westward.

At the end of the Revolutionary War, the Mississippi River marked the western boundary of the United States. Surprisingly, it was Napoleon who gave the United States its first chance to expand west of this river.

The Louisiana Purchase Ever since 1763, when Great Britain drove France out of North America, Spain had held the lands west of the Mississippi. Then in 1800, Spain made a secret treaty with

European settlers were lured to America by descriptions like these: "So at last I was going to America. Really, really going, at last! The arch of heaven soared. The winds rushed in from outer space, roaring in my ears, 'America! America!'"

525

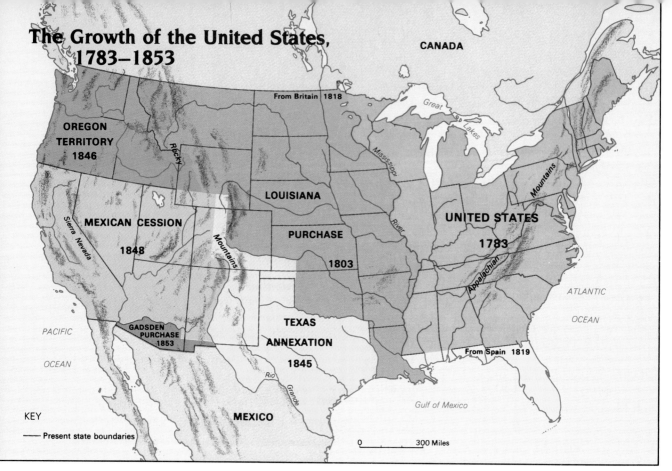

The Growth of the United States, 1783–1853

CANADA

OREGON
TERRITORY
1846

From Britain 1818

Great Lakes

Rocky

Mississippi

Mountains

LOUISIANA

PURCHASE

1803

UNITED STATES

1783

Appalachian

Mountains

MEXICAN CESSION

1848

Sierra Nevada

River

ATLANTIC

OCEAN

PACIFIC

OCEAN

GADSDEN
PURCHASE
1853

TEXAS

ANNEXATION

1845

From Spain 1819

Rio Grande

Gulf of Mexico

KEY

MEXICO

—— Present state boundaries

0   300 Miles

Map Study

What was the first territory to be added to the United States after 1783? What lands were added between 1805 and 1840? Between 1840 and 1860?

Napoleon, giving those lands to France. The region was known as the Louisiana Territory.

Napoleon dreamed of building a French empire in the Americas as well as in Europe. However, as you read in Chapter 23, Toussaint L'Ouverture led a revolt against French rule in Haiti. Toussaint's fighters and yellow fever all but wiped out a French army of 10,000 soldiers. Discouraged, Napoleon gave up the idea of an American empire and decided to sell the Louisiana Territory. The United States, under President Thomas Jefferson, was eager to buy.

In 1803, the United States bought the entire territory—828,000 square miles—at the bargain price of $15 million. The cost came to about three cents per acre.

The war with Mexico For the next 40 years, the Rocky Mountains were the western boundary of the United States. Then, during the 1840's, a new idea took hold. Some Americans began to argue that the Pacific Ocean was the country's natural boundary.

The lands west of the Louisiana Territory belonged to Mexico, which had won its independence from Spain in 1821 (page 503). However, a number of people from the United States had settled in the area, with Mexico's acceptance. Some settlers were unhappy with Mexican rule.

The largest number of American settlers were in Texas. In 1836, Texans revolted against Mexican rule. For nine years, Texas was an independent country. Then, in 1845, it joined the United States.

Mexico was angered by the United States' decision to annex Texas. The two countries soon quarreled over the new state's southern boundary. Both sides sent troops into the disputed area near the Rio Grande. In 1846, there was a skirmish between Mexican and American soldiers. Within a few days, the United States Congress declared war on Mexico.

The war lasted from May 1846 to September 1847. American troops invaded Mexico and advanced on Mexico City. In bitter fighting, they

526

Map Study answers: Louisiana Territory; Florida from Spain and territory below Canada just west of Great Lakes; Oregon Territory, Texas, Mexican Cession, Gadsden Purchase

captured the city, and Mexico was forced to surrender. The United States won not only the western part of Texas but also all the land between the Rio Grande and Canada.

Just as the war began, people in California revolted against Mexico and set up their own republic. In the treaty that ended the war, California too became part of the United States.

Meanwhile, the United States had been negotiating with Great Britain over the Oregon Territory in the northwest. In 1846, the two countries agreed to set the northern boundary of the United States at 49° north latitude.

Conflict grew between North and South.

As people settled these western lands, questions arose over the laws and customs to be followed there. Ever since the nation's early days, the northern and southern parts of the United States had followed different ways of life. Each section wanted to extend its own way of life to the western lands.

The North had a diversified economy with both farms and industry. Northern farmers raised a variety of crops that fed the thriving northern cities. Mills and factories in the North competed with Britain in making cloth, shoes, iron, and machinery. For both its farms and factories, the North depended on free workers. Such workers could move from place to place to meet the needs of industry. They could also be laid off when business slumped.

The South depended on just a few cash crops, mainly cotton. To raise cotton, planters needed a large labor force year round. They relied on slave labor. Southerners traded their cotton for manufactured goods from Europe, especially Great Britain. The South had little industry of its own.

The economic differences between the two sections soon led to political conflicts. The bitterest of these conflicts arose over slavery. Many people in the North considered slavery morally wrong. They wanted laws that would outlaw slavery in the new western territories. Some wanted to abolish slavery altogether. Most white southerners believed slavery was necessary for their economy. They wanted laws to protect slavery in the west so that they could raise cotton on the fertile soil there.

Southerners feared the North's rising industrial power and growing population. Soon, they reasoned, the North would completely dominate the federal government. The election of 1860 seemed to confirm their worst fears. Abraham Lincoln, a northern candidate who opposed the spread of slavery, was elected president.

In the months after the election, 11 southern states made the fateful decision to withdraw from the United States. They established a separate nation called the Confederate States of America. On April 12, 1861, Confederate guns opened fire on Fort Sumter, a fort in South Carolina held by soldiers of the federal government.

The Civil War preserved the Union and ended slavery.

The Civil War lasted from 1861 to 1865. Counting losses on both sides, about 720,000 Americans died in the war. Many were killed in combat, but even more died of diseases such as yellow fever and dysentery that swept through army camps. No other war has taken so many American lives.

Clara Barton (1821–1912) helped the wounded in the American Civil War and the Franco-Prussian War. She founded the American Red Cross.

527

In part, the North and the South fought over their different views of the Union (the country as a whole). The South believed that the states had formed the Union. Therefore, said southerners, states were free to leave the Union if they wished to do so. Northerners believed that the Constitution of the United States had established the Union once and for all.

To European observers, it was clear that the struggle between North and South was a war for the survival of the United States. It was as much a war of nationalism as the conflict between Prussia and Austria over the future of Germany.

From the beginning of the war, President Abraham Lincoln was determined to preserve the Union. In his inaugural speech, Lincoln reminded his hearers that he had taken an oath to "preserve, protect, and defend" the Union.

Although Lincoln was deeply opposed to slavery, he said repeatedly that the purpose of the war was to save the Union and not to end slavery. Yet many northerners believed that the war was a crusade against slavery. Lincoln eventually decided that ending slavery would help to save the Union. In late 1862, he issued the Emancipation Proclamation, declaring that all slaves in the Confederate states were free.

At first, the proclamation freed no slaves, because the Confederate states did not accept it as law. As Union armies advanced into the South, however, they freed slaves in the lands they conquered. The Emancipation Proclamation also made clear to people in Europe that the war was being fought against slavery. The proclamation made many Europeans, especially the British, less sympathetic to the South. They did not send the money and supplies that the South had hoped they would.

The longer the war went on, the more important the North's advantages in population and industry became. Its bigger population allowed it to raise larger armies. Its factories and railroads kept those armies supplied.

Worn down by lack of food and supplies, the major Confederate army surrendered on April 8, 1865. The Civil War was over.

The Union had been preserved at a tremendous cost. In the aftermath of the war, Congress passed

Lincoln visited the Union army near Antietam, soon after the bloodiest battle of the war. He had just decided to issue the Emancipation Proclamation.

Discuss Lincoln's views: "Must a government . . . be too strong for the liberties of its own people, or too weak to maintain its own existence? . . . It is now for [us] to demonstrate to the world that those who can fairly carry an election can also suppress a rebellion . . . and that when ballots have . . . decided, there can be no . . . bullets."

the Thirteenth Amendment to the Constitution. That amendment forever abolished slavery in all parts of the United States.

Industry developed rapidly.

After the war, the American economy expanded at a rate never before seen in the history of the world. There were three main reasons for this rapid growth. First, the United States had a wealth of raw materials. Second, it had a rapidly growing population to provide workers. (During the 1870's, immigrants arrived at the rate of nearly 2,000 a day.) Third, the nation had a democratic political system that put few restraints on its business development.

As early as 1870, the United States had 53,000 miles of railroad track and 5.5 million horsepower in steam engines, more than any other country in the world. American factories led the world in the production of clocks, rifles, sewing machines, and copper wire. American farms led world production of corn, wheat, cotton, and cattle. Never before had so much real and potential wealth been concentrated within one country.

The nation celebrated its first century.

Americans were proud of their country and its achievements. They celebrated its hundredth birthday in 1876 with a magnificent Centennial Exposition in Philadelphia. Like the British exhibition of 1851, this celebration drew visitors from all over the world.

The exposition stood in an enormous 400-acre park on the outskirts of Philadelphia. The main exhibition hall—the United States' answer to the Crystal Palace—covered more than 21 acres. At the time, it was the largest building in the world. Another enormous building, the Machine Hall, held mechanical marvels from all over the world. Among them were several "automatic-writing machines" (the first typewriters) and an amazing new invention that could transmit a human voice by wire. Its inventor, Alexander Graham Bell, called it the telephone.

In the Agriculture Hall, visitors could watch self-rising flour in action and marvel at Gail Borden's new product, canned condensed milk. Other buildings included a Shoe and Leather Hall, a glassworks, a butter and cheese factory, an art gallery, and a Women's Building. In this last building, among exhibits of embroidery, knitted work, and other domestic arts, there were also machines invented by women. These included a machine for washing blankets, a steam iron, and an early dishwashing machine.

Between May and November 1876, more than 9 million people attended the Centennial Exposition—more than had visited any previous world's fair. Most were Americans, of course, but those who came from abroad undoubtedly went away impressed. The United States had made remarkable progress during the 100 years since its founding. Over the next 50 years, it would take its place as a major power in the world.

Section Review 4

Define: (a) diversified economy, (b) cash crop
Identify: (a) Louisiana Purchase, (b) Abraham Lincoln, (c) Confederate States of America, (d) Civil War, (e) Emancipation Proclamation, (f) Thirteenth Amendment
Answer:
1. What part did Napoleon play in the expansion of the United States?
2. (a) How did Texas become part of the United States? (b) How did the annexation of Texas lead to war between the United States and Mexico? (c) What additional territories did the United States gain as a result?
3. How did the economies of the North and the South differ?
4. How was the issue of slavery related to the new western lands that the United States had gained?
5. How did the North and the South differ in their views of the Union?
6. (a) Briefly describe the political events that led to the outbreak of fighting. (b) What was the outcome of the war?
7. How was slavery ended in the United States?
8. What three factors promoted rapid industrial growth after the Civil War?

Critical Thinking
9. How might the Civil War be viewed as a conflict over nationalism?

529

Chapter Review 24

Summary

1. Industrialism created a global economy. Industry boomed in the mid-1800's. Railroads, the Suez Canal, and the development of steamships speeded transportation. The telegraph made global communication possible. Many businesses became corporations to get new funds for investment. Production and the demand for raw materials soared, causing the growth of worldwide trade. Industrialization also brought about great shifts in population.

2. Working people gained more influence. As industry spread, socialists urged equal distribution of wealth. While Robert Owen tried to set up cooperative villages, Karl Marx called for a revolt against capitalists. Workers made gains through trade unions, and working men won the right to vote in some countries. The working class also became more visible culturally as realism replaced romanticism.

3. Italy and Germany formed nations. Under the leadership of Cavour, Italy formed a united kingdom. Problems plagued the new nation, however. Guided by Bismarck, Prussia became the center of a new German nation after winning wars against Austria and France. The rise of Germany signaled the collapse of the balance of power in Europe.

4. The United States spread westward. During the 1800's, the United States bought the Louisiana Territory, annexed Texas and California, won vast lands from Mexico, and negotiated with Britain for the Oregon Territory. Conflict between the industrial North and the agricultural South led to a Civil War. The North's victory ended slavery. After the war, the economy of the United States grew rapidly.

Reviewing the Facts

1. Define the following terms:
   a. stock
   b. corporation
   c. emigration
   d. immigration
   e. socialism
   f. suffrage
2. Explain the importance of each of the following names or terms:
   a. Victoria
   b. Owen
   c. Marx
   d. utopian socialism
   e. scientific socialism
   f. proletariat
   g. Cavour
   h. Garibaldi
   i. Napoleon III
   j. Bismarck
3. (a) Give examples of the way industry expanded after 1850. (b) What advances took place in transportation? (c) Communication?
4. (a) What was the advantage of incorporation for a business? (b) For stockholders?

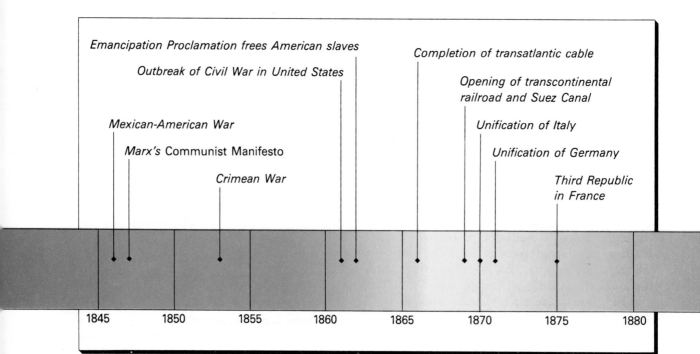

Emancipation Proclamation frees American slaves

Outbreak of Civil War in United States

Completion of transatlantic cable

Opening of transcontinental railroad and Suez Canal

Mexican-American War

Unification of Italy

Marx's Communist Manifesto

Unification of Germany

Crimean War

Third Republic in France

1845 1850 1855 1860 1865 1870 1875 1880

5. Give specific examples to show that a world economy had developed by the late 1800's.
6. Briefly summarize Marx's ideas on the following topics. (a) relations between social classes (b) work and economic value (c) the bourgeoisie (d) the proletariat
7. Briefly describe the part each of the following played in the unification of Germany. (a) German Confederation (b) Schleswig-Holstein (c) Seven Weeks' War (d) Franco-Prussian War
8. Describe the problems that France and Italy faced after 1870.
9. How did the balance of power in Europe change between 1815 and 1875?
10. (a) How did the North and the South differ economically? (b) Why was the issue of slavery especially divisive?

Basic Skills

1. **Comparing maps** (a) Compare the size and location of Prussian territory in 1871 (page 522) with that of East and West Germany in 1945 (page 699). (b) Compare the size and location of Italian territory in 1870 (page 520) with that of Italy today (page 712). What differences do you note in each case?
2. **Translating information** Using the maps on pages 520 and 522, explain how (a) Italy and (b) Prussia acquired their territories by the dates specified by the keys. In each case, note from whom the different territories were acquired.

Researching and Reporting Skills

Writing a Research Paper
Phase 3: Drafting the paper

1. **Revising the thesis statement** Check your thesis statement to be sure that it states the main idea of the paper, covers the main topics of your outline, and is supported by your information.
2. **Choosing a title** Choose a title that suggests the subject of the paper.
3. **Writing an introduction** Your introduction should capture attention, provide brief background information, and contain your thesis statement.
4. **Writing the body of the paper** The body of your paper should support the thesis statement with information drawn from your research. Following your outline, write paragraphs that state a main idea and give supporting details. Paragraphs should be linked by transitions that support the flow of your thinking. Your finished paper should be about five pages long. Make your draft longer by one or two pages so that it can be trimmed down in editing.
5. **Using and citing sources** As you cite information from different sources, paraphrase the information or use quotations. Cite each source in a footnote and in the bibliography.
6. **Using visuals** Insert visuals such as pictures, graphs, diagrams, or charts where they can enhance or clarify your meaning. Make sure that they are integrated in the paper by an introduction or comment and cite your sources.
7. **Writing a conclusion** Your conclusion should restate the thesis, emphasizing how earlier ideas support it.

Critical Thinking

1. **Synthesis** How did industrialization lead to the growth of a global economy?
2. **Summarizing** During the 1800's, improving conditions for workers became an important issue. (a) Summarize the major approaches, including people involved and the problems to be solved. (b) What were the advantages and limitations of each approach?
3. **Applying a concept** Cavour and Bismarck were representatives of realpolitik. (a) What is realpolitik? (b) How did each leader use this approach?
4. **Analyzing economics** (a) What economic factors were involved in Prussia's Seven Day War with Austria? (b) In the Franco-Prussian War?
5. **Analyzing** To what extent might the living and working conditions Marx saw around him account for his theory of revolution?
6. **Evaluating** (a) What were the effects of the Civil War on United States foreign trade? (b) On industrial development?

Perspectives on Past and Present

In the late 1800's, the right of all men to vote was a major issue. What political rights have become important issues in the late 1900's?

Investigating History

The Footnote to History on page 512 mentions Jules Verne's novel *Around the World in Eighty Days.* Either read the book or watch a videotape of the movie. Write a summary of the plot.

The Age of Imperialism

Red-coated British soldiers stand at attention around a royal pavilion during a ceremony in India. Britain's Queen Victoria took the title Empress of India in 1876.

Key Terms

imperialism
protectorate
condominium
sphere of influence

Read and Understand

1. Nations competed for overseas empires.
2. Imperialists divided Africa
3. The British dominated South Asia.
4. Imperialism threatened China.
5. Japan built a modern nation.
6. Imperialism reached the Western Hemisphere.

On a warm November afternoon in 1875, the H.M.S. *Serapis* steamed into Bombay harbor as British battleships formed two long lines to greet the vessel. On the bridge stood His Royal Highness Edward, Prince of Wales. He was Queen Victoria's eldest son and the heir to the British throne. Smiling, he waved to the cheering sailors and bowed to the captain of each ship as his own glided by.

When the *Serapis* finally docked, brass bands played and cannons fired salutes. Lord Northbrook, the queen's representative in India, welcomed the future king. Together they rode through streets crowded with cheering Indians. The *Times* of London reported, "The whole population of Bombay swarmed along the road," giving the Prince "a welcome such as an Indian city has seldom seen."

The crown of the Guicowar of Baroda alone was said to be worth more than $3 million, and he brought a gift of six heavy gold cannon. When the prince asked about his schooling, the boy replied that his favorite "studies" were hunting and cricket.

The following day, his thirty-fourth birthday, Prince Edward officially greeted dozens of Indian princes who came to pay their respects. Seated on a silver throne, dressed in royal robes, and flanked by British officials in scarlet and gold uniforms, the prince received his guests one by one. Each was magnificently dressed for the occasion. One guest, the nine-year-old ruler of Baroda, wore so many jewels that he was compared to "a crystallized rainbow."

The prince spent four days in Bombay, attending state banquets, receiving visitors, and watching a spellbinding performance by magicians and snake charmers. Then he began a grand tour. Over the next three months, he visited Calcutta, Madras, and other major Indian cities. At each stop, he reviewed troops, inspected railway lines and stations, visited prisons, palaces, and sacred ruins, and attended countless balls, banquets, and fireworks displays.

Throughout his stay, the heir to the British throne was treated as if he were the next emperor of India. In many respects, he was. Shortly after his return home, Parliament would add *Empress of India* to his mother's long list of titles.

Only a century earlier, the British East India Company had been building a trading network based on forts in major Indian cities. Now this enormous country was part of the British empire. In the words of Prime Minister Benjamin Disraeli, India was "the brightest jewel in Her Majesty's Crown."

Disraeli had not always viewed British colonies as jewels. In 1852, he referred to India and other colonies as a "millstone round our neck." In this chapter, we will see why Disraeli and other Europeans changed their views of colonies in the late 1800's. The chapter will also explain how the empires Europeans built affected people around the world.

Nations competed for overseas empires. 1

In 1901, when Queen Victoria died and Edward became king, Britain and other industrialized nations controlled virtually the entire world. They ruled some lands directly; they governed others indirectly through treaties or trade agreements. As empires grew in size and number, people needed a word to describe this new policy of conquering and ruling other lands. The word they invented was **imperialism**.

Imperialists proudly displayed world maps with their nation's empire in bright colors. The British empire usually appeared in red. It was the largest empire the world had ever known, covering an area nearly 100 times larger than Britain, with a population of more than 400 million. Britain controlled territory on every continent but Antarctica. About one fourth of the world's land and people lived under British rule.

Britain's lead was challenged.

As late as 1870, many Britons believed that colonies were more trouble than they were worth. They noted that trade with their former colonies in North America had grown tremendously since the United States won its independence. Many Britons were eager to rid themselves of their remaining colonies.

Throughout the 1800's, Britain granted many of its colonies more freedom. By the 1840's, Canadians had a measure of self-rule. Soon after, Australians also won the right to govern themselves. Yet even as the British were granting some colonies more freedom, the British empire was adding more territory elsewhere. By the turn of the century, a majority of Britons had come to believe that colonies were essential to their nation's prosperity and prestige.

Britain's attitude toward empires changed as Britain's role in the world changed. In the mid-1800's, Britain was the most powerful nation in the world. Its factories produced more goods than those of any other country, and the British navy guarded the oceans so that those goods could be shipped safely to ports around the world. The British exported more than just goods. They also exported capital, the money needed to build factories, mines, railroads, and other businesses. Britain became the world's banker. The money its banks loaned came from the profits earned by manufacturers, merchants, and shippers.

By the late 1800's, however, Germany and the United States were challenging Britain's economic leadership. Although British factories continued to increase their output each year, Britain's share

533

of the world's total production fell sharply. In 1870, it produced one third of the world's total. By 1900, British factories were turning out just one fifth.

At the same time, countries that had once welcomed British goods were now taxing those goods to protect their own factories. Increasingly, Britain had to find new markets for its goods or protect existing markets. It also had to safeguard sources of raw materials. The British Isles had only a few of the resources its factories needed. Most were imported.

Faced with economic decline, Britain looked to its colonies for markets and resources. In the late 1800's, the British government tightened its hold over India and other colonies. It also added new colonies in hopes of guarding critical trade routes and business interests.

Imperialism fostered rivalries.

Other countries followed Britain's lead. They too came to see colonies as necessary for their economic well-being. France, which had been a colonial power since the 1600's, greatly expanded its holdings in the late 1800's. By 1900, it had an empire second in size only to Britain's. The Dutch expanded too. Spain and Portugal, both of which had lost most of their original empires, tried to build new empires in Africa. At the same time, Austria-Hungary moved into the Balkans, and Russia expanded into the Caucasus, Central Asia, and eastern Siberia.

Countries that had no colonies set out to acquire them. Belgium, Italy, and Germany all took over lands in Africa. Germany also tried to control parts of East Asia and islands in the south Pacific. At the same time, German bankers made loans to governments in Latin America, and German capitalists were building a Berlin-to-Baghdad railway. Their hope was that where business went, the German flag would soon follow.

Two non-European countries, the United States and Japan, also became involved in overseas expansion during this period. Both were interested in East Asia. The United States was also deeply involved in Latin America.

Increasingly, Europeans viewed an empire as a measure of national stature. "There has never been a great power without great colonies," proclaimed one French writer. Thus the race for

colonies grew out of a strong sense of national pride as well as from economic competition. As the competition for colonies intensified, many countries claimed land that had little economic value. Pride, not profit, was their motive. Each country was determined to plant its flag on as much of the world as possible.

Europe believed in its own superiority.

Thanks to the Industrial Revolution, each European country had not only the weapons needed to win an empire but also the means to control it. Steamers, railroads, telegraph cables, and other inventions allowed nations to keep in close touch with even the most distant colony.

At the same time, the new technology encouraged Europeans to think that they had a right to conquer other countries. They regarded their steamships and factories as proof of their progress. They believed that they had the right and the duty to bring the results of that progress to other peoples.

Many Europeans went abroad with a strong sense of mission. One such European was Cecil Rhodes, a young Englishman who became rich in the diamond mines of South Africa. He boasted:

I contend that we Britons are the first race in the world, and the more of the world we inhabit, the better it is for the human race. I believe it is my duty to God, my Queen, and my country to paint the whole map of Africa red [the color of the British empire on maps], red from the Cape of Good Hope to Cairo.

The push for expansion also came from missionaries who worked among the peoples of Asia, Africa, and the Pacific islands. Many missionaries believed that European rule was the best way to end evil practices such as the slave trade.

Perhaps the most famous of these missionaries was David Livingstone (1813–1873). A minister from Scotland, Livingstone went to Africa in 1841 to preach the Gospel and heal the sick. He grieved to see East Africans carried off to be sold as slaves in Arabian, Turkish, and Persian lands. Over the years, he became convinced that only the British government was strong enough to end the trade. As a result of his efforts and those of his followers, the slave trade was abolished in East Africa in the 1880's. At the same time, much of the region became part of the British empire.

Imperialism had mass appeal.

Stories of adventure in distant places have always appealed to people. In the late 1800's, Europeans and Americans were eager to read about soldiers who guarded the empire against fierce enemies in far-off lands, sailors who roamed the open sea, and merchants who traded for silks and spices in mysterious Asian ports. When David Livingstone wrote a book about his work in Africa, thousands of people in Europe and the United States bought copies.

Newspapers competed for readers by hiring reporters to search the globe for stories of adventure, mystery, or excitement. For example, in the late 1860's, David Livingstone and a group of Africans traveled deep into the heart of the continent in search of evidence against the slave trade. When several years passed with no word from him or his party, many people feared he was dead. An American newspaper hired reporter Henry Stanley to find Livingstone. Stanley arrived in Zanzibar in January 1871. Ten months later, he caught up with Livingstone on the shores of Lake Tanganyika.

Stanley's account of the meeting made headlines around the world. Stanley became a celebrity. Queen Victoria gave him a jeweled snuffbox. Cities across the United States held banquets in his honor.

Novels and poetry also glorified imperialism. The most popular writer of the day was Joseph Rudyard Kipling (1865–1936). Children and adults alike were fascinated by his poems and stories, many of which were set in India. Kipling appealed not only to his readers' spirit of adventure but

also to their feelings of superiority. He saw imperialism as a mission to "civilize non-Europeans" and urged his readers to:

Take up the White Man's Burden—
   Send forth the best ye breed—
Go bind your sons to exile
   To serve your captives' need . . .

In answering the call of imperialism, Europeans altered life on every continent.

T 256 – 257

Section Review 1

Define: imperialism
Identify: (a) Prince Edward, (b) Rhodes, (c) Livingstone, (d) Stanley, (e) Kipling
Answer:
1. (a) What countries challenged Britain's economic leadership? (b) How was the search for colonies a response to Britain's declining share in world trade?
2. What part did each of the following play in imperialism? (a) markets (b) raw materials (c) national pride
3. (a) What countries joined the competition for colonies? (b) How did this competition set up a potentially explosive situation?
4. What attitude did people in industrialized countries have toward other peoples?
5. (a) What part did missionaries play in imperialism? (b) How did newspapers and writers encourage imperialism?

Critical Thinking
6. Reread the lines from Kipling's poem on this page. (a) What did he mean by "the White Man's Burden"? (b) What was the exile of which he spoke? (c) What does the word *captives* indicate?

Footnote to History

When Stanley finally reached Livingstone's camp, he reported that his first impulse was to rush over and throw his arms around Livingstone. Then, perhaps remembering that he had come without an invitation and that the missionary was a reserved Scot, Stanley settled for a simpler greeting. He held out his hand and said, "Dr. Livingstone, I presume?"

Imperialists divided Africa. 2

Nowhere was the competition for colonies more intense than in Africa. When the Age of Imperialism began in 1875, Europeans controlled less than 10 percent of the continent. By 1900, 90 percent of Africa was divided into colonies.

Age of Imp. began 18

Europeans explored Africa.

For centuries, Europeans had considered Africa the "dark continent" because they knew so little about it. Although European ships had traded at ports along the coasts for centuries, the vast interior of the continent was unknown to Europeans until well into the 1800's.

Beginning with the Scotsman Mungo Park's exploration of the Niger River in 1805 and 1806, European explorers slowly penetrated the African interior. The Frenchman René Caillié (kah-**YAY**) was the first European to cross the Sahara (1827–1828), while the German Heinrich Barth traveled widely in western Africa during the 1850's. Best-known of the explorers was David Livingstone, the Scottish missionary who spent 30 years in central Africa.

Explorers such as Barth and Livingstone gave Europeans their first detailed information about Africa and its peoples. In the mid-1800's, Africa south of the Sahara contained more than 700 different ethnic groups, each with its own language and customs. Most were organized into communities based on ties of tradition and kinship. Occasionally, a powerful group formed a state that was strong enough to conquer neighboring groups and form an empire.

These communities and states had been trading with Europeans for hundreds of years. Africans had no reason to expect any change in those relationships. Yet by the late 1800's, traditional relationships were changing rapidly.

Europeans scrambled for colonies.

The scramble for African territory began after 1879. In that year, Henry Stanley, the reporter who found David Livingstone, returned to Africa and claimed most of the Congo River valley in the name of King Leopold II of Belgium. The Belgian Congo, as the colony later became known, was 80 times larger than Belgium.

Leopold's action alarmed France. The French responded in 1882 by taking the north bank of the Congo River. Soon Britain, Germany, Italy, Portugal, and Spain were also staking claims to parts of Africa.

The competition was so fierce that countries feared a war. To prevent fighting, representatives from European countries met in Berlin in 1884

and 1885 to lay down rules for this new competition. No African ruler attended this meeting, yet it sealed Africa's fate. Europeans agreed that any European country could claim land in Africa simply by sending troops to occupy strategic points there. As a result, by 1913 a map of the continent looked like a patchwork quilt of imperial colors.

North Africa   Europeans had already moved into North Africa. There, the once-powerful Ottoman empire had become too weak to prevent local rulers from taking control in Morocco, Algeria, Tunisia, and Egypt. These local rulers were no match for the Europeans bent on conquest.

As early as 1830, France had invaded Algeria. Its aim was to build its prestige and to stop Algerian pirates who attacked French ships. Until 1869, no other European country paid much attention to North Africa. That year, a French company built a canal across the Isthmus of Suez at the northern end of the Red Sea. The canal linked the Mediterranean and Red Seas, providing a much shorter route from Europe to the Indian Ocean.

As the fastest route to India and Australia, the Suez Canal was crucial to Britain. It was so important that the British government bought stock in the company that owned the canal in 1875. Guarding the canal became a critical part of Britain's foreign policy. Therefore, when fighting broke out in Egypt in 1882, Britain took over the area. Egypt became a British **protectorate**—a country whose foreign policy is controlled by an outside government.

Next the British turned their attention to Sudan, which lay along the Nile River south of Egypt. Because water from the Nile was essential to the people of Egypt, the British believed that they had to control the headwaters of the Nile to guard Egypt and the canal. Many Britons also now shared Rhodes's dream of ruling all of Africa from Cairo to Cape Town. Thus, in 1896, Britain and Egypt invaded Sudan. The Sudanese defended their country fiercely, but in 1898, General Horatio Kitchener conquered the country. The following year, Britain and Egypt made Sudan a **condominium**—a country ruled jointly by two other countries.

France also dreamed of a great African empire. It would stretch from Dakar in the west to French Somaliland in the east. To fulfill that dream, the

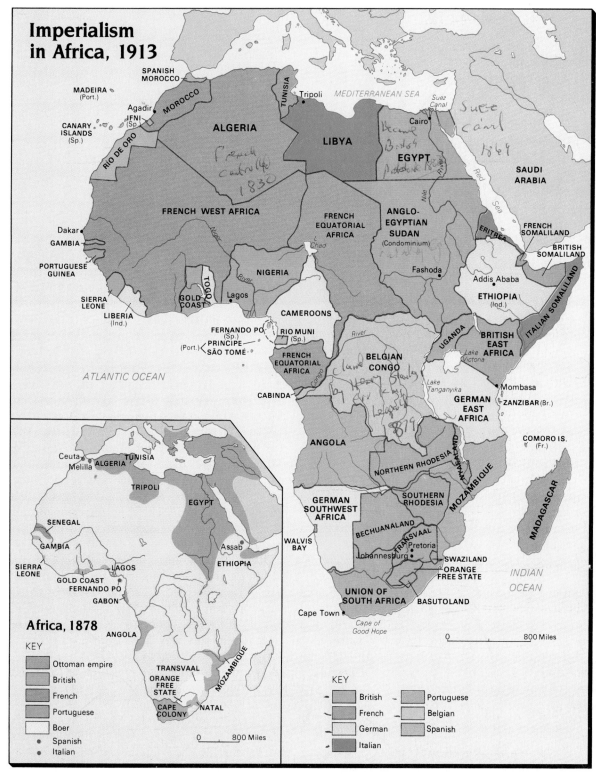

Imperialism in Africa, 1913

SPANISH MOROCCO
MADEIRA (Port.)
Agadir
IFNI (Sp.)
MOROCCO
CANARY ISLANDS (Sp.)
RIO DE ORO
ALGERIA
TUNISIA
Tripoli
LIBYA
MEDITERRANEAN SEA
Suez Canal
Cairo
EGYPT
Red Sea
SAUDI ARABIA
FRENCH WEST AFRICA
Dakar
GAMBIA
PORTUGUESE GUINEA
SIERRA LEONE
LIBERIA (Ind.)
GOLD COAST
TOGO
Lagos
NIGERIA
L. Chad
FRENCH EQUATORIAL AFRICA
ANGLO-EGYPTIAN SUDAN (Condominium)
Fashoda
ERITREA
FRENCH SOMALILAND
BRITISH SOMALILAND
Addis Ababa
ETHIOPIA (Ind.)
ITALIAN SOMALILAND
CAMEROONS
FERNANDO PO (Sp.)
RIO MUNI (Sp.)
PRINCIPE (Port.)
SÃO TOMÉ
FRENCH EQUATORIAL AFRICA
CABINDA
BELGIAN CONGO
UGANDA
Lake Victoria
BRITISH EAST AFRICA
Mombasa
ZANZIBAR (Br.)
Lake Tanganyika
GERMAN EAST AFRICA
COMORO IS. (Fr.)
ATLANTIC OCEAN
ANGOLA
NORTHERN RHODESIA
NYASALAND
MOZAMBIQUE
MADAGASCAR
GERMAN SOUTHWEST AFRICA
SOUTHERN RHODESIA
WALVIS BAY
BECHUANALAND
TRANSVAAL
Pretoria
Johannesburg
SWAZILAND
ORANGE FREE STATE
BASUTOLAND
INDIAN OCEAN
UNION OF SOUTH AFRICA
Cape Town
Cape of Good Hope
0   800 Miles

Africa, 1878

Ceuta
Melilla
ALGERIA
TUNISIA
TRIPOLI
EGYPT
SENEGAL
GAMBIA
SIERRA LEONE
LAGOS
GOLD COAST
FERNANDO PO
GABON
Assab
ETHIOPIA
ANGOLA
TRANSVAAL
ORANGE FREE STATE
MOZAMBIQUE
CAPE COLONY
NATAL
0   800 Miles

KEY
- Ottoman empire
- British
- French
- Portuguese
- Boer
- • Spanish
- • Italian

KEY
- British
- French
- German
- Italian
- Portuguese
- Belgian
- Spanish

Map Study

*Britain long planned a Cairo-to-Cape-Town railroad. In 1913, what British
colonies could it have gone through? What other powers blocked its way?*

At the Battle of Omdurman, fought in the Sudan in 1896, Sudanese casualties were
11,000, with 16,000 more wounded, while the British totaled only 48.

At the Battle of Omdurman in 1898, 26,000 British troops defeated about 50,000 Sudanese. The key to victory was Britain's 20 machine guns.

French gradually took over Tunisia and Morocco. In 1898, they also pushed east into Sudan. There they encountered British troops at Fashoda. For weeks, Britain and France were at the edge of war. Then France suddenly backed down. It now turned its attention south of the Sahara.

Africa south of the Sahara European control south of the Sahara began in the mid-1800's around trading posts such as the French port of Dakar in the west or the British port of Cape Town in the south. From such outposts, European control spread inland.

The push toward colonization often came from European officials and merchants. Many were tempted to use force whenever they came into conflict with an African state. Often, Europeans found it easier to shoot first and ask questions later than to negotiate with the group involved. As a result, home governments sometimes found themselves in the middle of wars about which they knew little or nothing.

European conquest took many forms.

Equipped with superior weapons, European armies usually had no great difficulty defeating African soldiers. Such defeats, however, did not always result in an easy conquest. It might take years to conquer a large empire. Samori Touré,

a Malinke, built an empire that stretched across the northern Ivory Coast into present-day Ghana. To protect that empire, he bought arms from Europeans along the coast. He also set up his own weapons factory. As a result, he was able to hold off the French for more than six years.

Some parts of Africa were not organized into states or empires. Here, each village was independent. Therefore, Europeans had to conquer every community to take over the region. Britain made 500 separate treaties before it won control of eastern Nigeria.

Other African states accepted European rule without going to war. In some cases, an alliance with Europeans seemed to be a smaller threat than conquest by a neighboring people. Such alliances, however, gradually led to a European takeover. In this way, for example, the British won control of Africa's Gold Coast.

Elsewhere, Europeans were sometimes invited into a region to protect a leader or a group against internal enemies. One of the best-known examples is Buganda, the African kingdom on the north shore of Lake Victoria. In the 1880's and 1890's, Buganda was in the midst of civil war as Muslims, Catholics, Protestants, and followers of the traditional Ganda religion competed for power. With British help, however, the two Christian groups removed the king and seized

538

For the location of the present-day nations of Ghana and the Ivory Coast, see the map of Africa on page 749.

power. In 1900, they signed an agreement that gave them a privileged position in the British colony of Uganda.

Africa became a continent of colonies.

By 1900, Europeans controlled most of Africa. Only two countries remained free from European control, Liberia and Ethiopia.

Liberia, founded during the 1820's by former American slaves, was closely allied with the United States. This alliance kept the West African nation safe from conquest.

The kingdom of Ethiopia in East Africa owed its independence to a variety of factors. Geography gave it some protection. It was located at a place where the rival empires of Britain, France, and Italy met. Each was determined to keep the others from expanding further, and Ethiopia could stand as a buffer state. Ethiopia also had the natural protection of mountains. Most important, it had a leader capable of using these advantages to protect his kingdom.

Menelik II, who ruled Ethiopia from 1889 to 1913, took advantage of international rivalries to get the most modern weapons. With these, he turned back an Italian invasion in 1896. Then he went on to conquer neighboring peoples to create an empire.

Colonial rule European rule of the rest of Africa was mostly indirect. Relatively few Europeans settled in their African colonies, except in Algeria and South Africa. In 1900, for example, only 2,000 of Uganda's 3 million people were British. Thus, all colonial governments had to have some African administrators.

Wherever possible, Europeans turned to Africans already in authority. Many traditional rulers continued to hold office. However, this policy did not mean that life continued as usual for the people of Africa.

Europeans wanted African workers for mines and plantations. At first, Europeans simply used their superior weapons to force Africans into work crews. Later, however, most colonial governments used an economic weapon—taxes. Africans had long paid taxes to their rulers in goods and services. Now, however, they were required to pay taxes in money. The need for money forced many Africans to work on plantations or in mines, all owned by Europeans.

Other Africans began to raise crops that Europeans wanted to buy rather than food crops for themselves. This shift marked the beginning of a money economy.

Colonial governments used tax money to provide a range of services that led to better health care, improved farming methods, European-style education, and other changes. In some cases, Africans benefited from these services. Often, however, the new services were only for European settlers or traders.

The African people were now second-class citizens in their own lands. Many African leaders came to believe that only by borrowing from European cultures could they regain control over their own country. "The blacks had slept long; perhaps too long," observed Blaise Diagne, a Senegalese leader. "But beware! Those who have slept long and soundly, when once they wake up, will not easily fall back to sleep again."

Europeans were fearful of such an awakening. To guard against it, some colonial officials encouraged rivalries among ethnic groups. As long as Africans were divided, Europeans could keep control. Many nations also kept education to a minimum in their colonies. Rather than train Africans, Europeans often brought in Indians, Chinese, and other Asians to handle jobs requiring special skills.

In setting up their colonies, Europeans had two main goals. One was to keep order and prevent rebellions. The other was to see to it that their colonies paid for themselves.

Economic disappointments When the scramble for Africa began, many believed that the African people would soon be buying European goods in great quantities. Shortly after his return from Africa in 1872, Henry Stanley, for example, told a group of Manchester business leaders, "There are 40 million people beyond the gateway of the Congo, and the cotton spinners of Manchester are waiting to clothe them." Stanley estimated that if each of these Africans bought just one Sunday dress or suit every year, the merchants of Manchester would enjoy a tremendous boost in sales.

However, those sales never materialized. Most Africans were too poor to buy European goods. Europeans also found that much of Africa was too wet or too dry for commercial farming to succeed. Minerals and good farmland were often

The quality of European-run government in Africa varied. In French-controlled Senegal, the native population elected representatives to Paris. In the Congo, Leopold II had ruthlessly exploited the rubber forests for his personal profit.

539

too far from transportation routes to ship goods profitably to market. Only a few powerful business groups such as traders and shippers prospered from imperialism. Leaders in those businesses urged governments to continue imperialism.

Few European nations grew rich from their colonies. Only in South Africa did Europeans find the wealth of which they dreamed. As a result, South Africa's history differed sharply from that of the rest of the continent.

South Africa supplied great wealth.

The British first took control of the Cape of Good Hope in 1806, during the Napoleonic wars. They called the region Cape Colony. There the British found not only a variety of African peoples but also a well-established community of about 40,000 Dutch settlers. The Dutch called themselves *Boers* (from the Dutch word for farmer). Most Boers were strict Calvinists who believed that God had selected a small group, of which they were a part, for salvation. They used this belief to justify their harsh treatment of African peoples in the region.

The Boers disliked being ruled by Britain. They wanted their own government. Thousands migrated from Cape Colony during the 1830's into the African interior. This Great Trek brought the Boers into conflict with the Zulu people, who had built a great empire in southern Africa. After years of fighting, the Boers finally defeated the Zulu and set up three countries—Natal, Transvaal, and the Orange Free State.

At first, Britain accepted the independence of the three Boer states. At the time, Britain's main interest was the Cape Colony, which was an important stop on the route around Africa to India. In 1845, the British annexed Natal to guard Africa's southern coast but allowed the other two states to remain independent.

Then, in 1867, diamonds were discovered on a farm at Kimberley, on the border of the Orange Free State. Within weeks, Kimberley became a boom town. "Men who set out to work in the morning, not knowing where their dinner was to come from," noted one reporter, "became richer than any member of their family had ever been before it was time for an eleven o'clock snack."

Most of the miners were British. Among them was Cecil Rhodes, who gradually won control of the entire Kimberley diamond field. By 1889, his company controlled 90 percent of the world's diamond output.

As British miners crowded onto Boer land, tension between the Boers and the British mounted. In 1886, gold was discovered in a ridge of mountains called the Rand in the heart of Transvaal. Again British fortune-seekers stampeded into Boer territory. By 1895, the Boers were outnumbered by *uitlanders* (AYT-lahn-duhrz), the Boer term for foreign settlers.

When the Boers tried to keep their way of life by restricting uitlanders, the newcomers were outraged. They had the support of Cecil Rhodes. In 1895, one of his associates tried to overthrow the government of Transvaal. Although the attempt failed, the Boers blamed Britain for the uprising. As tensions mounted, the Boers took up arms against Britain in 1899.

On the surface, it appeared a hopelessly uneven match—100,000 Boers against the largest empire the world had ever known. The Boers, however, successfully used guerilla tactics against the British army. Britain struck back by burning farms and destroying food supplies in the Boer regions. British troops captured and imprisoned Boer women and children. At last, the Boers were forced to make peace in 1902.

To prevent future trouble with the Boers, the British allowed the Dutch-speaking settlers to keep their language in both schools and courts. The British even helped Boers rebuild their farms. (On the other hand, the British did nothing to help Africans whose farms had been destroyed.)

Both the Transvaal and the Orange Free State became self-governing British colonies, much like Australia and Canada. In 1910, they were joined with Cape Colony and Natal. The new country had equal status with Canada and Australia within the British empire.

After the mining boom tapered off, the Boers were once more the majority of the Europeans in the new state. Two Boers, Louis Botha and Jan Christian Smuts, served as South Africa's first prime ministers.

In the end, the British bought peace with the Boers at the expense of the black African population. Blacks made up 75 percent of South Africa's people. Under Boer rule, the millions of black Africans who lived in the country were reduced to a life little better than slavery.

When Europeans first arrived in South Africa, they encountered a native population of more than seven million, made up of dozens of different groups, including Bushmen who lived by hunting and gathering, the pastoral Bantus, and the warlike Zulus.

Define: (a) protectorate, (b) condominium, (c) uitlander
Identify: (a) Suez Canal, (b) Kitchener, (c) Menelik II, (d) Cape Colony, (e) Boers, (f) Great Trek
Answer:
1. (a) How did the scramble for colonies in Africa begin? (b) Why did representatives of European countries meet in Berlin? (c) What was the result of the meeting?
2. Briefly describe France's expansion in North Africa.
3. (a) What were the effects of the building of the Suez Canal on Egypt? (b) What were the effects on Sudan?
4. How did each of the following exhibit a different pattern of colonization? (a) the empire of Samori Touré (b) Nigeria (c) Buganda
5. (a) What two African countries remained free of European control? (b) Why?
6. (a) What did the policy of indirect rule mean for Africa? (b) What were some of the effects of colonial rule on African society?
7. (a) How did the Boers and the British come into conflict? (b) What were the results? (c) What concessions did the British make to the Boers?

Critical Thinking

8. How did colonization make Africans second-class citizens in terms of role in politics, taxation, ethnic rivalry, and education?

The British dominated South Asia.

3

India was the cornerstone of the British empire. The Industrial Revolution had turned Britain into the world's workshop, and India was a major supplier of raw materials for that workshop. Its 300 million people were also a large potential market for British-made goods. It is not surprising, then, that the British valued India above their other colonies and that other nations envied Britain's control of that country.

British rulers in India built English-style homes where they lived surrounded by Indian servants.

Britain expanded control over India.

British economic interest in India began in the 1600's, when the British East India Company set up trading posts at Bombay, Madras, and Calcutta. At first, India's ruling Mughal dynasty kept European traders under control. By 1700, however, the Mughal empire was collapsing. Dozens of small states, each headed by a ruler or *maharajah*, broke away from Mughal control.

The growth of the East India Company The East India Company was quick to take advantage of the growing weakness of the Mughals. By 1757, the company was the leading power in India. It governed directly or indirectly an area that included modern Bangladesh, most of southern India, and nearly all the territory along the Ganges River in the north.

Officially, the British government regulated the company's efforts both in London and in India. In fact, the company ruled India with little interference from the British government. The company even had its own army, which was led by British officers and staffed by *sepoys* (SEE-poyz), or Indian soldiers. One early company official referred to this army as "a delicate and dangerous machine, which with a little mismanagement may easily turn against us."

British India was made up of dozens of different ethnic groups speaking over 200 different languages. There were also a half-dozen major religions represented, of which Hinduism and Islam were dominant.

The Great Rebellion The army did indeed turn against the company in 1857. In that year, word spread among the sepoys that their British-made rifle cartridges were sealed with beef and pork fat. Soldiers had to bite off the seal to use the cartridges. Both Hindu and Muslim soldiers were outraged by the news. (Muslims are forbidden to eat pork, and Hindus are not allowed to eat beef.) Although the British quickly corrected the error, they could not quiet the soldiers' suspicions.

On May 10, 1857, the sepoys at Meerut rebelled. They marched to Delhi, where they were joined by Indian soldiers stationed there. Together, the soldiers captured the city. From Delhi, the rebellion spread to much of northern and central India. Fighting was widespread and fierce.

The British called this outbreak the Sepoy Mutiny, but in fact it was a full-scale rebellion. Muslim rebels even tried to place a descendant of the last Mughal emperor on the throne.

It took the East India Company more than a year of hard fighting to regain control of the country. The British government sent troops to help the company. The British were also helped by serious splits between Hindus and Muslims. Hindus did not want the Mughal empire restored. Indeed, many Hindus preferred British rule to Muslim rule.

At the same time, nearly all the princes and maharajahs who had made alliances with the East India Company remained loyal. Also loyal were the Sikhs, a religious group that had long been hostile to the Mughals (page 291). Indeed, from then on, the bearded and turbaned Sikhs became the mainstay of Britain's army in India and fought loyally for the British.

India after 1857 The mutiny marked a turning point in Indian history. In 1858, the British government took direct command of India. A cabinet minister in London directed policy, and a British governor-general in India carried out the government's orders. (After 1877, this official held the title of viceroy.)

To reward the many princes who had remained loyal to Britain, the British promised to respect all treaties the East India Company had made with them. They also promised that the Indian states that were still free would remain independent. Unofficially, however, Britain won greater and greater control of those states. For example, if rival princes claimed a throne, the British often interfered to make sure the prince they preferred won.

The part of India that was under direct British rule was called the *Raj*. The Raj was divided into 10 provinces and some 250 districts. Sometimes a handful of district officials were the only Britons among the million or more people in their districts.

Convinced that they knew what was best for India, British officials set out to improve the country. They built bridges, dams, canals, and European-style public buildings. Their irrigation projects opened millions of acres of land to farming. The British also created a network of telegraph lines and railroads that linked major Indian cities. By 1900, India had more than 30,000 miles of track—the third largest rail network in the world.

As in Europe, the development of railroads boosted trade, especially in inland areas that now were directly connected with seaports. The tea industry, for example, blossomed almost overnight

Daily Life · A New Look for the Army

In 1850, a British soldier's uniform had a brilliant red coat, a shiny black hat, and white breeches. Such uniforms made a splendid sight on the parade ground—and a splendid target on the battlefield. During the sepoy revolt, British soldiers in India found that they were much safer after their bright uniforms were covered with a layer of yellow-brown dust (in the dry season) or mud (in the wet season). Dirt-colored uniforms made fine camouflage. Eventually, the British adopted this drab color as their official combat uniform. They called it *khaki,* from the Indian word for dust.

542

Discuss the remarks of Jawaharlal Nehru (later to become prime minister of India): "The memory of [the discrimination] hurts and what [continued on next page]

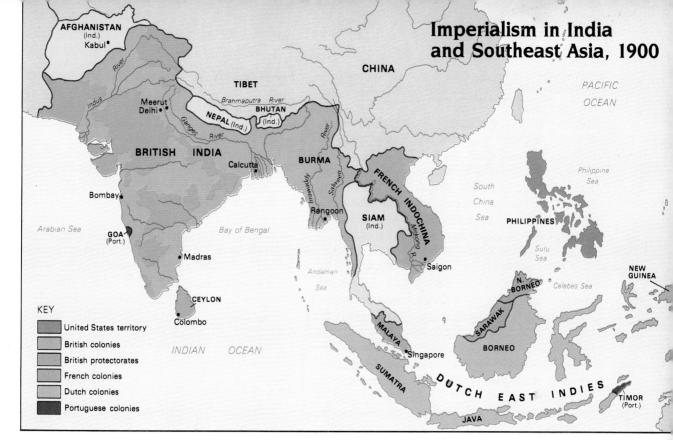

Map Study
What country separated British and French colonies? What was its status?

in the hilly regions of the northeast. Between 1850 and 1871, Indian tea exports soared from 200,000 pounds to more than 6 million pounds annually. Other major export crops such as jute, cotton, and indigo also benefited from railway development.

The beginning of Indian nationalism The British were proud of the changes they brought to India. They boasted of the many improvements they had made. Indians quietly noted, however, that money for the new roads, telegraph cables, and irrigation projects came from Indian taxpayers. Only the railroads were built by private British companies. Yet they too got help from taxpayers. Nor did the British do the work of digging roadbeds and laying track. Rather, they directed the projects and supplied the technical skills. Indians did the hard work. Yet the Indians had no opportunity to manage future projects.

Increasingly, Indians resented a system that made them second-class citizens in their own country. They resented the many signs that read, "For Europeans only." Such signs were everywhere—at doorways, in railroad cars and waiting rooms, and even on park benches. Even Indians with a European education faced discrimination. They were barred from top posts in the Indian Civil Service. Those who managed to get middle-level jobs were paid less than Europeans. A British engineer on the East India Railway, for example, made nearly 20 times as much money as his Indian counterpart.

A spirit of Indian nationalism slowly began to grow. This feeling led to the founding of the Indian National Congress in 1885 and the Muslim League in 1906. At first, such groups were mainly concerned with winning equal opportunities for Indians in the civil service. Gradually, however, their demands broadened. By the early 1900's, they were calling for self-government.

Britain protected the Raj.

Britain had no desire to give the Indians more control over their own country. Instead, as the competition for colonies in other parts of the world grew more fierce, the British tightened their control in South and Southeast Asia. The

hurts still more is the fact that we submitted for so long to this degradation." Why did Indians submit for so long? In what ways did European and even British values influence their demand for independence?

British saw two threats to their control of India—France on the southeast and Russia on the northwest.

In the late 1800's, France took over much of what is now Vietnam, Laos, and Kampuchea. To keep the French from advancing farther west, the British moved into Burma. By 1885, Burma was a province of India. The British also helped protect the independence of Siam, now Thailand. Britain hoped Siam would be a buffer between French colonies in the east and British colonies in the west.

The British were also concerned about India's northern border. There they feared a Russian advance. As early as 1839, the East India Company had invaded Afghanistan in the hope of creating a buffer zone, but the invasion failed. In 1878, the British decided to try again. The Second Afghan War, which lasted three years, finally established India's northern border. It also checked Russian influence in the region.

Section Review 3

Define: (a) maharajah, (b) sepoy
Identify: (a) Mughal, (b) Sikhs, (c) Raj, (d) Indian National Congress, (e) Muslim League
Answer:
1. How did the British East India Company win control of much of India?
2. (a) What caused the sepoys to revolt? (b) What groups supported the British during the revolt? (c) What were the results?
3. (a) From a British point of view, how did British rule benefit India? (b) From an Indian point of view, what were the drawbacks of British rule?
4. What were the goals of the Indian National Congress and the Muslim League?
5. What steps did Britain take to protect its control of India?

Critical Thinking
6. What point of view might each of the following people have taken on British rule of India? (a) a textile manufacturer in Britain (b) a British railroad executive in India (c) an Indian official in the civil service (d) a Sikh soldier (e) a maharajah educated in Britain

Imperialism threatened China. 4

To the east of India lay China. Here too Europeans were eager to win colonies. Indeed, at one time it seemed as if a scramble for China might follow the one for Africa.

Europeans forced treaties on China.

In the 1800's, the Manchus still ruled China as the Ch'ing dynasty (page 274). For many years, China had been a prosperous country, with a highly developed agricultural system. Farming was critical because, by 1800, China had some 300 million people—more than the entire population of Europe. China was not industrial, but workers in small workshops were able to produce most of the goods the Chinese needed.

Because China was practically self-sufficient, its emperors had little interest in trading with Europeans. For decades, Europeans could do business only at the port of Canton. Despite pleas from Britain and other nations, China refused to open other ports to foreigners. The Chinese regarded European goods as inferior to their own and bought few goods from the European merchants at Canton.

European merchants were determined to find a product the Chinese would buy in large quantities. Eventually, the British East India Company discovered such a product—opium. Opium is a habit-forming narcotic made from the poppy plant. The use of opium was strictly controlled in India, Europe, and China. Now, however, British merchants smuggled in so much opium that the weak Chinese government was powerless to control its flow.

In 1836, the Chinese government tried to stop the opium trade by appealing to Queen Victoria for help. A leading official wrote to her:

Suppose there were people from another country who carried opium for sale to England and seduced your people into buying and smoking it; certainly your honorable ruler would deeply hate it and be bitterly aroused.

When such pleas went unanswered, the quarrel over opium grew into a war. The Opium War

Canton was the first port where China granted Europeans trading rights. By 1800, flags of many European countries flew over Canton's busy harbor. In the harbor were both Chinese and European vessels.

of 1839 was fought mostly at sea. Chinese fleets, armed with a type of cannon in use since the 1300's, proved to be no match for well-armed British gunboats. In 1842, the two sides signed a treaty at Nanking.

For China, the Treaty of Nanking marked the beginning of a century of humiliation. The treaty was a clear victory for Britain. The British won the right to trade at four Chinese ports besides Canton. In each of these ports, British citizens would enjoy *extraterritorial* rights. That is, Britons did not have to obey Chinese law. They were subject only to British law and to British courts. Furthermore, China was required to pay damages for the opium it had destroyed. The trade in the deadly drug continued.

The Treaty of Nanking was the first of many unequal treaties China would be forced to make as one European country after another established **spheres of influence**. These were regions in which the economic interests of a foreign nation came before those of China. In these regions, foreigners did much as they pleased.

A revolt weakened southern China.

By 1850, the Ch'ing dynasty was losing control of the country. The government was riddled with corruption. China was on the verge of bankruptcy as a result of the unequal treaties. Most serious of all, the population was increasing quickly while food production grew little. China's population reached about 430 million in 1850, nearly half again as large as 50 years before. The result was widespread hunger even in good years. In a bad year, such as 1852 when the Yellow River flooded, millions starved. As one Chinese official lamented:

Today there are law-breaking soldiers and greedy officials everywhere who encourage the bandits and indulge them. Whenever one thinks of it, one's heart goes cold. Right and wrong are turned upside down.

It was in this upside-down world that a man named Hung Hsiu-ch'uan (hoong sh'yoo-chwan) attracted a following. Hung, a teacher in a small village in southern China, claimed to have a divine mission to save the world. He told the peasants that with their help he would establish on Earth a "Heavenly Kingdom of Great Peace." Hung's revolt was called the Taiping Rebellion from the Chinese words for "great peace." By 1853, his ragtag army had about 1 million people.

Chinese officials were unable to keep the rebels from taking control of all of southern China. In Nanking, Hung established a government for his Heavenly Kingdom, but it did not stay in power long. With British help, the imperial army won back the south from the rebels in a 10-year war that took 20 million lives.

The rebellion convinced many Chinese officials that modernization was the country's only hope

Shang period, Greece and other countries came under the influence of the Orient.... Before long, writing and civilization began to flourish." Discuss cultural bias in telling history.

545

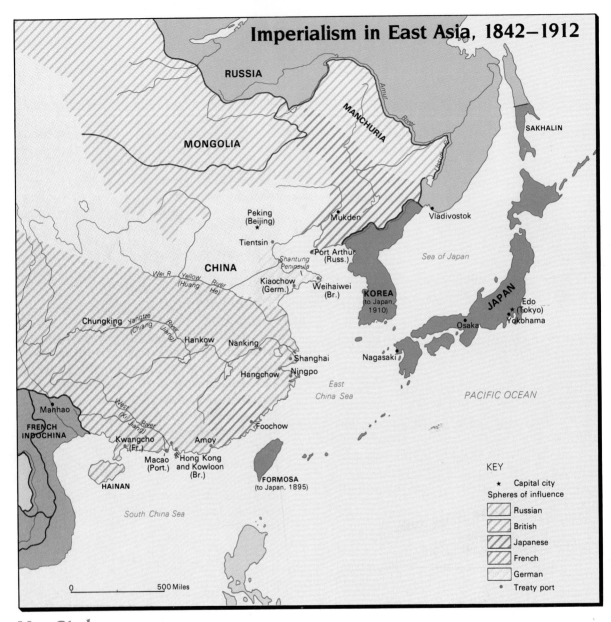

Imperialism in East Asia, 1842–1912

RUSSIA

MANCHURIA

MONGOLIA

SAKHALIN

Peking (Beijing) ★

Mukden

Vladivostok

Tientsin

Port Arthur (Russ.)

Shantung Peninsula

Sea of Japan

CHINA

Wei R. Yellow River (Huang He)

Kiaochow (Germ.)

Weihaiwei (Br.)

KOREA (to Japan, 1910)

JAPAN

Edo (Tokyo) ★
Yokohama

Osaka

Chungking

Yangtze (Chiang) River Jiang

Hankow

Nanking

Shanghai

Hangchow Ningpo

Nagasaki

East China Sea

PACIFIC OCEAN

West (Xi Jiang) River

Manhao

FRENCH INDOCHINA

Kwangcho (Fr.)

Amoy

Foochow

Macao (Port.)

Hong Kong and Kowloon (Br.)

HAINAN

FORMOSA (to Japan, 1895)

South China Sea

KEY

★ Capital city
Spheres of influence

- Russian
- British
- Japanese
- French
- German
- • Treaty port

0 ____ 500 Miles

Map Study

What European power might rival Japan in northern China and Korea?

for survival. During the 1860's and 1870's, these officials tried to upgrade the army and navy, improve transportation and communication, and broaden China's educational system to include technical subjects and foreign languages.

Such efforts, however, met with strong opposition. A number of officials believed that China should borrow little if anything from the West. China's emperors seemed to agree. As a result, China continued to weaken.

Foreign influence expanded.

Outsiders were quick to take advantage of China's weakness. A second opium war with Britain and France from 1857 to 1860 gave foreigners even more trading rights. About the same time, the Russians forced China to give up the Ussuri territory, where the Russians built their major Pacific naval base of Vladivostok. In 1879, Japan annexed the Ryukyu Islands.

546

The most powerful figure in nineteenth-century China was Tzu Hsi, mother of one of several boy emperors. Out of touch with reality, she once used funds for naval construction to build a marble "ship" to adorn her Summer Palace.

By 1885, much of China's empire was gone. The rest fell in the 1890's when Japan took over Formosa and the Liaotung Peninsula. Japan was able to keep only Formosa, as several European countries joined together to force Japan out of the peninsula. Once they did so, however, the Europeans demanded some Chinese territory for themselves. Russia took Port Arthur and the Liaotung Peninsula in 1896, and France took Kwangchow. By 1898, Germany controlled Kiaochow, and Britain held Weihaiwei.

The United States began to fear that China would be carved into colonies and American traders would be shut out. Therefore, in 1899, the United States declared the Open-Door Policy. This policy proposed an "open door" to China for merchants of all nations. A number of nations agreed to the policy. As a result, American trade rights were protected in China, and China was protected from colonization. Yet, though it was not carved into colonies, China remained at the mercy of outsiders.

In this French cartoon, Britain, Germany, Russia, France, and Japan carve up China.

Nationalism grew in China.

Although China kept its freedom, Europeans dominated most of China's largest cities. There, resentment simmered beneath the surface as some Chinese formed secret societies pledged to rid the country of the "foreign devils."

The most famous of these secret groups was the Society of Righteous and Harmonious Fists, better known simply as the Boxers. In 1900, the Boxers rebelled in Peking, shouting the slogan, "Death to the Foreign Devils." The Boxers surrounded the European section of the city and kept it under siege for several months. Eventually, an army made up of troops from eight nations (Britain, France, Germany, Austria, Italy, Russia, Japan, and the United States) arrived. It quickly defeated the Boxers.

Despite the failure of the Boxer uprising, a nationalist movement began to take shape in China. It drew its strength from the many humiliations the Chinese suffered at the hands of imperialists. Its goals were nationalism, republicanism, and land reform.

Section Review 4

Define: (a) extraterritorial rights, (b) sphere of influence
Identify: (a) Opium War, (b) Hung Hsiuch'uan (c) Open-Door Policy, (d) Boxer Rebellion
Answer:
1. Why were China's emperors uninterested in trading with Europe?
2. (a) Why did the British import opium to China? (b) What was the Chinese response? (c) What did the British gain from the treaty ending the Opium War?
3. (a) What conditions led to the Taiping Rebellion? (b) What change in outlook did the revolt cause among China's leaders?
4. (a) What events caused the United States to announce the Open-Door Policy? (b) What did this policy protect?
5. What were the goals of Chinese nationalists?

Critical Thinking
6. Despite its losses in the 1800's, China remained an independent country. Why was China not carved into colonies as Africa was?

Europeans had little influence on most Chinese—those who lived in the countryside. A nineteenth-century proverb: "The people fear the officials; the officials fear the foreign devils; the foreign devils fear the people."

547

Japan built a modern nation.

5

When imperialists threated China, the Chinese fought to keep their traditional way of life. Japan chose a different course. It responded by becoming a powerful rival of European nations.

Americans ended Japanese isolation.

Japan in 1850 was almost as it had been in the 1600's when the Tokugawa family took control of the country and ushered in an era of peace. For 250 years, Tokugawa shoguns ruled over a remarkably stable society. During this period, the Japanese had almost no contact with the industrialized countries of the world. Japan continued to trade with China, but the only Europeans allowed in the country were Dutch traders who kept an outpost at Nagasaki.

1853

Then, in 1853, four United States ships commanded by Commodore Matthew Perry steamed into what is now Tokyo harbor. Perry came to ask the Japanese to open their country to foreign trade. The Japanese who lined the harbor were astounded by the foreigners' black ships made of iron and powered by steam. They were also shocked by the cannons and rifles that could have wiped out hundreds of the fiercest samurai in a matter of seconds.

The Japanese felt that they had no choice but to give in to Perry's demands and sign a treaty with the United States. They were not strong enough to force the foreigners to leave. The treaty the Japanese signed was the first of many with the Western powers. By 1860, Japan, like China, had granted permission to trade and extraterritorial rights to many foreign nations.

The Japanese feared that foreigners would take over Japan unless some changes took place. Therefore, in 1868, a new group of leaders overthrew the last of the Tokugawa shoguns. The new leaders ruled in the name of Emperor Mutsuhito, who was just 15 years old. Mutsuhito chose the name *Meiji* for his reign, meaning "enlightened rule."

Industrialization transformed Japan.

The Meiji era was a revolutionary time in Japan. During the 45 years of Mutsuhito's reign, one change followed another. Feudalism was ended,

Commodore Matthew Perry arrived in Japan in 1853. His huge warships dwarfed the Japanese boats that went out to meet them. With this show of strength, Perry forced Japan to open its ports to American merchants.

Compare and contrast the approaches the following countries took to Western influence: India (adapted its culture to fit the European model), China (resisted), Japan (transformed itself into a powerful rival).

Japan responded to the threat from the West by developing its own industries.

and Japan adopted a constitution much like Germany's. As in Germany, real power was in the hands of a small group of men who were determined to build a powerful nation.

Industrialization in Japan "Open the country to drive out the barbarians" was the slogan of leaders such as Tomomi Iwakura (toh-moh-mee ee-wah-koo-rah). To do so, he vowed to seek knowledge throughout the world. In 1873, Iwakura led the first of many missions to Europe and North America. On these missions, the Japanese studied foreign ways of life and chose the best Western civilization had to offer. Observed one Japanese leader:

> *Are we to delay the using of steam machinery until we have discovered the principles of steam for ourselves? If we can select examples from them [Westerners] and adopt their contrivances, why should we not be successful in working them out?*

Over the next 30 years, the Japanese economy became as modern as any in the world. The country's first railroad line was built in 1872, connecting Tokyo, the nation's capital, with the port of Yokohama some 20 miles away. By 1914, Japan had more than 7,000 miles of railroad track. Coal production grew from half a million tons in 1875 to more than 21 million tons in 1913. Meanwhile, large state-supported companies built thousands of factories. Japan's government took an active part in the development of industry.

Little help came from the outside. Fearful of economic dependence, the Japanese borrowed as little money as possible from European or American bankers. Any money they did borrow was quickly repaid. Japan earned most of the capital it needed to modernize by the sale of such traditional products as silk.

Japanese imperialism Economic development was only one part of Japan's plan to become a world power. Another part of the plan was military reform. Japan's new leaders believed that military strength was essential for a strong and independent nation. In modernizing its army and building a navy, the Japanese chose the best that Europe had to offer. Japanese leaders patterned their army after Germany's and their navy after

Modernization brought many of the same problems to Japan that the Industrial Revolution had brought to other countries. Tokyo had wretched slums, and women and children in Japanese textile factories worked in deplorable conditions like those of early Manchester.

Britain's. By 1890, Japan had several dozen warships and 500,000 soldiers.

Japan was now strong enough to renegotiate the unequal treaties it had signed in the 1850's. In 1899, the Japanese persuaded Western powers to give up their extraterritorial privileges in Japan.

As Japan became stronger, it also became more imperialistic. Like many European nations, Japan saw empire building as a way of meeting its economic needs. As in Europe, national pride also played a large part in Japan's imperialism. The Japanese were determined to show the world that theirs was a powerful nation.

From the start, Japan's leaders saw opportunities to expand at China's expense. In 1894, the two countries went to war. As a result of that war, China was forced to grant Korea independence. Soon, the Japanese began to take over Korea. They also moved into Manchuria, China's northeastern province, which was rich in iron and coal. Japan's growing interest in Manchuria alarmed the Russians, who were also eager to take over the province. In 1904, the conflict exploded in the Russo-Japanese War.

Most Europeans expected Russia to defeat Japan easily. To their surprise, the Japanese won victory after victory. At the Battle of Tsushima (soo-shee-muh), fought in the straits between Japan and Korea, the Japanese navy sank 38 of the 40 ships in the Russian Far Eastern Fleet.

With their victory in the war, the Japanese won control of all Russian business interests in southern Manchuria. Though still technically part of China, Manchuria was now a part of Japan's sphere of influence. More important, Japan won recognition as a great power. It was the only Asian country that was able to deal with the West as an equal.

Section Review 5

Identify: (a) Matthew Perry, (b) Mutsuhito, (c) Meiji, (d) Battle of Tsushima, (e) Russo-Japanese War
Answer:
1. (a) What was the policy of the Tokugawa shoguns toward other nations? (b) What changed this policy?
2. How did the reign of the Tokugawa shoguns come to an end?
3. What changes took place in Japan during the Meiji era?
4. (a) How did Japan become an imperialist nation? (b) What was the importance of the Russo-Japanese War?

Critical Thinking
5. Reread the quotation on page 549. What attitude toward modernization did Japanese leaders take?

Imperialism reached the Western Hemisphere. 6

Europeans and Americans brought many changes to countries such as China and Japan. Contact with the West also changed life in places that once seemed very remote and isolated. In some of these places, Westerners took political control and started colonies. In others, they were interested only in economic power.

Outsiders dominated Latin America.

By 1870, a number of European nations were eyeing Latin America with new interest. It had many of the resources their factories needed. Suddenly there was a demand for tin from Bolivia and copper from Chile. There was also a market for Latin American food products. The revolution in land and sea transportation helped open those markets. For example, the development of refrigerated railroad cars and refrigerated ships enabled countries such as Argentina to ship huge quantities of refrigerated beef and mutton to Europe.

Latin Americans responded to the growing demand for raw materials and crops by increasing their output. In doing so, however, they needed capital to build railroads, docks, processing plants, and other facilities. Latin American governments borrowed money for improvements from banks in Europe and the United States. Latin American landowners and business people also borrowed money to expand their enterprises.

Gradually, however, outsiders took over ownership of plantations, mines, processing plants, and other key businesses in Latin America. By

The United States had long had its eye on Cuba. In 1858, Senator Stephen A. Douglas said, "It is our destiny to have Cuba, and it is folly to debate the question."

1914, Britain had invested more than $5 billion in Latin America. The United States, which had only a very tiny investment in the region in 1870, had more than $1.6 billion invested by 1914. As outsiders became more involved in Latin America's economy, their political influence also increased.

The United States had the greatest stake in Latin America. Leaders in the United States believed that unrest in the region threatened the security not only of American businesses there but also the security of the United States itself. These leaders were especially fearful that Europeans might take over unstable governments in Latin America to protect their investments.

Since the 1820's, the United States had been using the Monroe Doctrine (page 504) to keep foreigners out of the Americas. In the 1890's, the United States began to use that doctrine in new ways. The United States government acted as a negotiator in disputes between Latin American nations and European powers. It was even willing to go to war to protect its interests in the region.

Spain and the United States fought a war.

Cuba was one of the last Spanish colonies in the Americas. The Cubans rose up against Spain in 1895. American newspapers printed daily reports of the conflict, shocking their readers with tales of Spanish brutality and Cuban heroism. While the Spanish efforts to put down the revolt were indeed brutal, many of the news accounts were exaggerated. As a result of these stories, the American public clamored for war against Spain to free Cuba.

The United States had several reasons for watching the revolution closely. A number of Americans did business in Cuba. They had plantations, factories, and warehouses on the island. In fact, the United States bought most of its sugar from Cuba. Cuba had strategic importance as well. It guarded the entrance to the Gulf of Mexico.

Many people in the United States identified with the Cubans. They saw Cuba's fight for freedom as similar to their own war for independence.

United States' interest in Latin America increased after 1900 with the building of the Panama Canal. Here, workers dig the 8-mile-long Gaillard Cut.

The "yellow press" newspapers played a large part in this war. On February 9, about a week before the explosion of the battleship *Maine,* the New York *Journal* printed a letter stolen by a Cuban in which the Spanish insulted President McKinley.

Thus, when the United States battleship *Maine* mysteriously blew up in Havana harbor on February 15, 1898, the United States was quick to blame Spain. On April 24, the two nations went to war.

The war lasted five months. When it was over, the United States had won much of Spain's empire in the Caribbean and the Pacific. Although Cuba was allowed its independence, the United States insisted on the right to intervene in Cuban affairs. The United States also claimed the right to build naval bases on the island.

The United States built a canal.

In the years after the Spanish-American War, the United States increased its involvement in Latin American affairs. The United States government worked closely with investors to protect and expand trade in the region.

No president was more enthusiastic about expanding American interests abroad than Theodore Roosevelt, who led the nation from 1901 to 1909. He was especially eager to build a canal across the narrow Isthmus of Panama, which was then part of Colombia. Such a canal would shorten the sea route from New York to San Francisco by more than 5,000 miles. The United States Navy could move more quickly to defend either of the nation's coasts.

In 1903, the United States offered Colombia $10 million plus a yearly payment for the right to build a canal across Panama. The Colombian senate thought the price was ridiculously low for what would soon be an extremely valuable trade route. They demanded a higher price.

Roosevelt responded by encouraging a revolution in Panama. Panamanians had often tried to break away from Colombia. With help from the United States Navy, rebels in Panama quickly

Voice from the Past · *A View of Imperialism*

Carl Schurz came to the United States from Germany after fighting in the revolutions of 1848. He was elected to the United States Senate in 1869. The following excerpt is from a speech he gave in 1899, when the United States was preparing to take over the Philippines, Pacific islands that had belonged to Spain.

If we take those new regions, we shall be well entangled in that contest for territorial aggrandizement [expansion], which distracts other nations and drives them far beyond their original design. So it will be . . . with us. We shall want new conquests to protect that which we already possess. The greed of speculators, working upon our government, will push us from one point to another, and we shall have new conflicts on our hands, almost without knowing how we got into them . . . We are told that our industries are gasping for breath; that we are suffering from over-production; that our products must have new outlets, and that we need colonies and dependencies the world over to give us more markets. More markets? Certainly. But do we, civilized beings, indulge in the absurd and barbarous notion that we must own the countries with which we wish to trade? Here are our official reports before us telling us that of late years our export trade has grown enormously . . . Trade is developed, not by the best guns, but by the best merchants.

1. What does Schurz predict will happen if the United States begins to follow an imperialist policy?
2. (a) What economic argument in favor of imperialism does he summarize? (b) How does he respond to it?
3. If Schurz had still been a senator, how do you think he would have voted on the annexation of the Philippines? Explain your answer.

Yellow fever and malaria were serious threats to those working on the canal. Posters telling how to fumigate to get rid of the mosquitoes were widely circulated.

won their independence. They then leased the United States a ten-mile-wide zone in which to build a waterway.

For the next ten years, American engineers battled floods, heat, and mosquitos while building the canal. In 1914, the canal was finally opened. Ships from all nations began to use it. Latin America become a crossroads of world trade.

As interest in Latin America grew, Roosevelt issued a *corollary* to the Monroe Doctrine. (A corollary is a natural result of another statement.) In 1823, the Monroe Doctrine had warned Europeans that the Americas were closed to further colonization. Now, Roosevelt's corollary said that as a result of that warning, the United States had the right to act as an international police officer in the Americas.

The Roosevelt Corollary was used to justify American intervention in Latin America on several occasions. The United States sent troops to such countries as Haiti, Nicaragua, the Dominican Republic, and Cuba.

The situation in Latin America showed the link between political and economic independence. To be truly independent, a country needed to control both its own economy and its own government. The presence of foreign interests spurred a new growth of nationalism in Latin America.

Interest in Pacific islands grew.

Even before the Panama Canal opened, interest in the islands that dotted the Pacific was growing. By the late 1800's, Europeans and Americans were competing fiercely for control of the larger islands and island groups.

Rivalry grew for a variety of reasons. Some islands were rich in resources. Others were valued as coaling stations and naval bases. Steamships ran on large amounts of coal. Therefore, every trading nation needed places where its huge freighters could stop and refuel. Naval bases were also needed, where a ship could stop for repairs if necessary. The great engines that powered steamships required trained technicians with special equipment. Few nations were willing to rely on their rivals for coal or repairs. Each country wanted its own islands in the Pacific.

In 1876, Europeans and Americans controlled fewer than half the islands in the Pacific. By

1900, nearly all the islands had lost their independence. Britain was the leader here as elsewhere. It held Australia, New Zealand, Fiji, the southern Solomons, and many other islands in the Pacific. Germany took the northern Solomons and a number of islands once held by Spain. France controlled Tahiti.

The United States was mainly interested in Hawaii. By the 1880's, Americans dominated the islands and were eager for the United States to annex them. When Queen Liliukalani refused to give up her country's freedom, she was overthrown. In 1898, Hawaii became part of the United States. The following year, as a result of the Spanish-American War, the United States also won control of Guam and the Philippines.

No part of the world was too remote for trade and colonization. The industrial nations were willing to compete for even the most distant island. By the early 1900's, explorers from several nations were racing to claim even the frozen wastes of Antarctica.

Section Review 6

Define: Roosevelt corollary
Identify: (a) Latin America, (b) Spanish-American War, (c) Theodore Roosevelt, (e) Panama, (f) Liliukalani
Answer:
1. (a) Why were European countries interested in Latin America? (b) How did European economic influence in Latin America increase?
2. Why was the United States concerned about events in Latin America?
3. (a) Give four reasons for the United States' interest in the Cuban revolt. (b) What was the result of the war between the United States and Spain?
4. How did the United States gain the right to build a canal in Panama?
5. Why were industrialized nations interested in Pacific islands?

Critical Thinking
6. (a) How are political and economic independence linked? (b) If two countries, such as Brazil and Great Britain, are trading, how can one trading partner be more dependent than the other?

Senator Henry Cabot Lodge on the Philippines: "... American law ... American civilization and the American flag will plant themselves on shores [once] bloody and [backward]."

553

Chapter Review 25

Summary

1. Nations competed for overseas empires. The need for new markets, the desire to foster national pride and spread European values, and the lure of adventure all fostered imperialism. By 1900, European powers, the United States, and Japan had colonial empires in Africa, India, China, and the Pacific islands.

2. Imperialists divided Africa. Armed with superior weapons, European nations conquered all of Africa except Liberia and Ethiopia. Under colonial rule, Africans became second-class citizens.

3. The British dominated South Asia. By 1757, the British East India Company was the leading power in India. In 1857, following the Sepoy Mutiny, the British government forced the East India Company to turn over the rule of India to the British crown. Benefits of British rule were reaped mainly by Europeans. Discrimination against Indians caused the rise of nationalism in the late 1800's.

4. Imperialism threatened China. Defeat in the Opium War of 1839 forced China to open its ports to British traders. In the following years, one country after another established spheres of influence in China. By 1850, China was on the verge of bankruptcy. Corruption in the civil service, foreign control, and famine lead to a rebellion against the Ch'ing dynasty.

In 1899, the United States proposed the Open-Door Policy to protect American trading rights in the country. Resentment of imperialism fostered secret societies and nationalism in China.

5. Japan built a modern nation. Japan's isolation ended when American Commodore Matthew Perry sailed into Tokyo Harbor in 1853. The Meiji era of modernization that followed gave Japan a strong economy. Military reforms fostered imperialism.

6. Imperialism reached the Western Hemisphere. Although Latin American countries maintained their independence, foreign investments tied Latin American economies to outside powers. United States control of Latin America increased after a war with Spain in the late 1800's. In 1904, the United States used the Roosevelt Corollary to justify intervention in Latin American affairs. Not long after, the United States began work on the Panama Canal. By the late 1800's, outsiders were also competing for control of Pacific islands.

Reviewing the Facts

1. Define the following terms:
   a. imperialism
   b. protectorate
   c. condominium
   d. extraterritorial rights
   e. sphere of influence

Treaty of Nanking weakens China

Perry opens Japan to foreign trade

British government takes control of India

Meiji era begins in Japan

European powers agree to divide Africa

Spanish-American War and annexation of Hawaii

Open-Door Policy in China

Russo-Japanese War

Japan wins control of Korea

Opening of Panama Canal

| 1840 | 1855 | 1870 | 1885 | 1900 | 1915 |

2. Explain the importance of each of the following names or terms:
   a. Livingstone
   b. Leopold II
   c. Boer
   d. East India Company
   e. Sepoy Mutiny
   f. Sikh
   g. Indian National Congress
   h. Muslim League
   i. Opium War
   j. Open-Door Policy
   k. Boxer Rebellion
   l. Perry
   m. Meiji era
   n. Spanish-American War
   o. Roosevelt Corollary

3. (a) How did France gain control of parts of North Africa and West Africa? (b) How did Britain gain control of Egypt and the Sudan?

4. (a) Why did the history of South Africa differ from that of the rest of the continent? (b) What led to war between the British and the Boers? (c) What was the outcome?

5. (a) What led to the rise of nationalism in India? (b) How did the Raj respond?

6. (a) Describe China in 1800. (b) What were the goals of Chinese nationalists? *Nationalism/Republicanism and reform*

7. (a) How did Japan keep from becoming a colonized nation? (b) How did it become an imperialistic power?

8. (a) How did outsiders gain control of Latin America? (b) Name two ways the United States increased its power there.

Basic Skills

1. **Interpreting maps** (a) Using the maps on pages 537, 543, and 546, tell what two major European powers dominated in Africa, India and Southeast Asia, and East Asia. (b) What would you conclude from these observations?

2. **Sequencing** The Monroe Doctrine was formulated in 1823, and it was reinterpreted twice. (a) Explain its original provisions and intent. (b) Explain the two reinterpretations, including what led to the changes and their impact on the role of the United States.

Researching and Reporting Skills
Writing a Research Paper
Phase 4: Completing the research paper

1. **Revising** Check your paper against the following questions: Does the introduction contain background information and a clear thesis statement? Does the body of the paper support the thesis statement? Are paragraphs introduced by a transition? Is the paper coherent? Does your conclusion provide a strong ending, focused on the thesis statement?

2. **Trimming for length** Reducing the length of the paper to the required five pages by deleting unnecessary words and phrases will help to sharpen the focus.

3. **Writing a bibliography** List your sources alphabetically. Entries for the bibliography do not have the first line indented, but the other lines are; the author's last name is listed first; periods are used in place of commas, and parentheses are deleted; no specific page reference is necessary. If many articles are used, you may want to make separate lists for books and articles. Place the bibliography at the end of your paper.

4. **Editing** Check spelling, grammar, and punctuation. For quotations, check that you have used the exact words, that they are in quotation marks (or inset if longer than five lines), and that the author and source have been identified.

Critical Thinking *↑ 266*

1. **Analyzing** What political and economic factors led to the race for colonies in the late 1800's? Give examples.

2. **Comparing and contrasting** (a) How did colonialism differ in Africa, India and Southeast Asia, and East Asia? (b) What factors may account for the differences?

3. **Inferring** How might the race for colonies affect the balance of power in Europe?

4. **Synthesizing** (a) What was the role of the United States during the age of imperialism? (b) In what parts of the world did it gain power? (c) What impact did it have on the spread of imperialism?

Perspectives on Past and Present

In 1884, representatives from European countries met in Berlin to determine how colonial powers could claim lands in Africa. (a) What attitudes did this approach imply? (b) Would this kind of decision making be possible today? Give reasons for your answer.

Investigating History

Make a study of one country in Africa, including its peoples, culture, precolonial history, and period of colonial rule. What modern nation emerged from that colony?

The Turn of the Century

9. Place Pigalle
P. Sescau
Photographe

Photography was in vogue at the turn of the century, whether it was the work of professional portrait photographers (as shown in the poster above) or enthusiastic amateurs such as young Jacques Lartigue.

Key Terms

assembly line
anarchist

Read and Understand

1. Inventions changed ways of life.
2. Science presented new ideas.
3. Women sought rights and freedoms.
4. Art and entertainment took new forms.
5. Europe faced rising tensions.

"Photography is a magic thing! A magic thing with all sorts of mysterious smells, a bit strange and frightening, but something you learn to love very quickly." So wrote seven-year-old Jacques Lartigue (lahr-**TEEG**) in his diary in 1901. His father, a wealthy Parisian banker, bought Jacques his first camera.

Photography had come a long way since Louis Daguerre (duh-**GARE**) had made the first hazy photographs in the 1830's. By the 1850's, homes all over the world were decorated with solemn, black-and-

Another Frenchman, Nicephore Niepce, had used light-sensitive silver compounds to create the world's first photographs during the 1820's. Daguerre's main contribution had been the discovery of a fixative that would keep the photographs from fading.

white family photographs. Known as daguerreotypes, such pictures cost as little as 25 cents each. By 1900, simple box cameras like the one Jacques owned could produce black-and-white photographs as good as those today.

Armed with his camera, young Jacques set out to capture the world around him. His pictures give a glimpse of life in a well-to-do family of the time.

By 1900, the upper classes in France and other industrialized countries had luxuries that earlier generations had never known. Electric lights or gaslights lit their houses at night. Coal furnaces or gas heaters warmed them in winter. Hot and cold running water, flush toilets, and bathtubs made their lives easier, cleaner, and more comfortable than ever before. The telephone kept them in touch with distant friends and relatives. Their servants—for even middle-class households had help—cooked meals on huge, iron stoves and washed clothes in machines.

Jacques's photos show not only his friends and relatives but also the new machines of the early 1900's. With his father, Jacques went to the military airfield outside Paris and saw France's first flimsy airplanes take to the sky. Most of all, however, Jacques loved automobiles. In 1912, his father bought a 35-horsepower Peugeot—"a big, open monster," Jacques called it. The Lartigue family, wearing goggles and rubber coats in case it rained, roared along the dirt roads at 30 miles per hour.

Sitting next to Yves, the family chauffeur, Jacques waited eagerly for the chance to pass another car.

We see a car ahead of us. Yves accelerates. We are coming closer . . . We see the white cloud behind the wheels of the car, smell the dust . . . Oh, what a fantastic moment . . . There we go, past the other car! I feel cut off from the rest of the world, wonderfully superior to everybody else; I wish we would never stop!

Such an event, Jacques wrote sadly, "doesn't happen too often . . . there are still so few cars on the road."

In this chapter, we will see some of the new inventions and scientific developments that altered Jacques Lartigue's life in the early 1900's. We will also see how the writers and artists of this exciting age viewed their world. Finally, we will see how governments responded to the challenge of this new age.

Jacques Lartigue (left) skillfully photographed scenes from daily life in the early 1900's. At right, the Lartigue's chauffeur changes a flat tire.

557

Inventions changed ways of life. 1

Worldwide industrial production more than tripled between 1870 and 1914. The Industrial Revolution touched lands from Europe to Japan and Australia. Three countries dominated the world economy—Great Britain, Germany, and the United States. Together, these countries produced two thirds of all the world's manufactured goods in 1913. This economic growth was accompanied by rapid advances in technology.

Bessemer began an Age of Steel.

In the mid-1800's, despite all the advances of science and industry, iron was still the basic metal for tools and machines. In the 3,000 years since the Iron Age began (page 38), nothing had replaced iron. In the late 1800's, however, a new age began—the Age of Steel.

Steel is a mixture of purified iron and a small amount of carbon. It is tougher, lighter, and more flexible than iron. For hundreds of years, metalworkers made steel in small quantities for swords and knives. (Steel can hold a sharp edge, and iron cannot.) Purifying steel took weeks of steady heating, making the metal very expensive.

In the 1850's, an Englishman named Henry Bessemer developed a less costly way to make steel. He forced blasts of hot air through the molten iron to burn out impurities. Bessemer began using this new "blast furnace" in 1859 in his factories at Sheffield. Operating around the clock, the huge furnaces lit up the night sky with an eerie glare.

By the turn of the century, steel was widely used for machinery, ships, and railroad track. Steel rails lasted up to 15 times longer than iron ones. Steel girders replaced stone and iron as the supports for buildings. The first building with a steel frame was Chicago's ten-story Home Insurance Building, completed in 1884.

New sources of power came into use.

Before 1890, the tallest buildings stood about 20 stories high. With steel girders, architects could plan much taller buildings, but how would people reach the top floors? In 1889, the invention of the electric elevator made possible a new kind of building for crowded cities—the skyscraper. By 1913, New York City was a city of skyscrapers. Its 60-story Woolworth Building, completed that year, was the world's tallest building. It rose 792 feet above the shadowy streets.

Electricity was one of the new kinds of energy that were coming into use in the late 1800's. Just as iron was giving way to steel for some uses, coal and steam were giving way to electricity, oil, gasoline, and natural gas.

To many people, electricity seemed the most magical of the new kinds of energy. Early in the 1800's, Alessandro Volta and Michael Faraday had discovered ways to make small amounts of electricity. In 1872, the Belgian electrician Zenobe Gramme developed the first industrial dynamo. Dynamos generated electric power by using steam engines to spin electromagnets. With the invention of the dynamo, electricity moved out of the laboratory and into daily life.

Edison set up a research laboratory.

If electricity seemed like magic, without doubt its greatest magician was the American inventor, Thomas Alva Edison (1847–1931). Edison worked on everything from movie projectors to household irons, from phonographs to doorbells. Altogether, he patented more than 1,000 inventions.

As a 12-year-old boy in Michigan, Edison had sold newspapers and candy on commuter trains to and from Detroit. While the commuters were at work, he taught himself mathematics and science in the public library. He also set up a laboratory in one of the boxcars on the train.

By the time he was 20 years old, Edison was working as a telegrapher, but he regarded inventing as his real career. In 1870, he went from poverty to wealth in a single bound when he sold his invention of a stock ticker for $40,000.

The wizard of Menlo Park Edison used his money to start a laboratory in Menlo Park, New Jersey, where he worked full-time as an inventor. Indeed, the idea of a laboratory for industrial research and development was Edison's most important invention.

A steady stream of inventions flowed from Edison's laboratory. People began calling him "the wizard of Menlo Park." Actually, Edison was not

Edison's goal was to turn out "a minor invention every ten days and a big thing every six months or so." Partially deaf since the age of 12, Edison believed his impairment helped him concentrate on his inventions.

Daily Life • *Music for the Home*

"Mary had a little lamb," bellowed Thomas Edison into the mouthpiece of his newest invention. The device recorded the sound vibrations on a sheet of tin foil wrapped around a cylinder. When Edison turned the crank, a scratchy imitation of his own voice came back through the funnel-shaped speaker. It was the first phonograph.

Like Edison's prototype, the earliest record players needed no electricity. To hear a record, you simply wound up the phonograph with a crank. It played until it ran down. The earliest records were wax cylinders, later replaced by disks. On such recordings, people could hear all kinds of music, from music-hall entertainers to world-famous opera singers, in their own homes.

so much an inventor as a perfecter of already existing inventions. "The first thing," he said, "is to find out what everyone else knows and begin where they leave off."

The electric light In 1879, Edison developed the first practical electric light bulb. As early as 1808, an English scientist named Humphrey Davy had made a bulb in which a piece of thin metal would glow. The problem, which baffled inventors for years, was to find something that would glow but would not quickly burn itself out.

After months of trial and error, Edison discovered an answer—thin cotton thread coated with carbon. Making sure that a vacuum existed inside the bulb, Edison turned on the current.

It lit up ... We sat and looked, and the lamp continued to burn. None of us could go to bed, and there was no sleep for any of us for 40 hours. We sat and just watched it, with anxiety growing into elation.

Within three years, Edison perfected light bulbs that would burn for 1,400 hours. He also designed and guided the construction of New York City's first electrical system. On September 4, 1882, as the sun set, New York's first electric streetlight glowed to life.

Telephones and radios carried voices.

Electricity had powered the first great advance in modern communications, the telegraph. In the late 1800's, it powered two more advances, the telephone and the radio.

Bell and the telephone Alexander Graham Bell (1847–1922) was a Scot who emigrated to the United States. He studied speech and sound to teach deaf students to talk. He was also interested in transmitting sound electrically. After several years of experimenting, he succeeded in changing the sound waves of the human voice into electric impulses, sending them through a wire and then changing them back to sound waves at the other end. Bell patented his invention, which he called a telephone, in 1876.

At the Philadelphia Exposition in 1876, Bell displayed his telephone to the astonished crowd. Among those watching was the emperor of Brazil, who used Bell's machine to speak with an aide in another room. "My word!" the emperor exclaimed when his aide answered, "It speaks Portuguese!"

The telephone quickly became an essential part of modern life. By 1900, there were nearly 2 million telephones in the United States, and by 1912, there were 8.7 million. The telephone also spread rapidly in the cities of western Europe, especially in Germany and Britain.

Marconi and the radio The next challenge was to send messages without using wires. Many people contributed to the invention of the radio. Physicists James C. Maxwell and Heinrich Hertz made the theoretical discoveries about electromagnetic waves, or radio waves. Then, in 1895, inventor Guglielmo Marconi used these waves to send telegraph signals directly through the air, without the use of wires. He used transmitters that sent out electromagnetic signals at certain

Discussion question: Did the harnessing of electricity have as great an impact on the way people live as did the ability to control fire?

559

frequencies and receivers that could be "tuned in" to pick up the signals. In 1901, Marconi's wireless telegraph sent Morse code across the Atlantic. Primitive radios were soon standard equipment for ships at sea. Not until later could radios transmit human voices.

A *new engine burned gasoline.*

During the 1870's, many inventors experimented with an engine that would run on gasoline. Like the steam engine, the gasoline engine had a piston that moved inside a cylinder. Instead of steam pressure to move the piston, the gasoline engine used a series of small explosions inside the cylinder. Because the gasoline burned inside the cylinder, the new machine came to be called an *internal combustion engine.* It was much smaller than a steam-powered engine. Steam-powered vehicles were large because they had to carry coal, water, and a furnace in which the coal burned to heat the water. By contrast, the gasoline engine needed no furnace and no water, only a tank to hold the gasoline.

In 1885, German inventor Gottlieb Daimler mounted a gasoline engine on a bicycle to produce the world's first motorcycle. In 1890, he founded the Daimler Motor Company. He manufactured cars that he named for a friend's daughter, Mercedes.

Ford *built cars on an assembly line.*

By 1900, about 13,000 automobiles were sputtering and clattering along the roads of Europe and North America. Some of these vehicles could reach speeds of 10 to 15 miles per hour. Nearly all of them had been assembled by hand. Such cars were expensive to buy and to repair. As a result, they remained luxuries that the average worker never dreamed of buying.

One of the mechanics who built such cars was an American named Henry Ford. Ford decided to make cars that many people could buy. "The way to make automobiles is to make them all alike," he said, "just as one pin is like another pin when it comes from the pin factory, or one match is like another." Ford's solution was the Model T, a homely but reliable car. By 1913, it was selling for just $500, less than half the usual price of a car.

How did Ford lower prices? Part of the answer was mass production. Ford's Tin Lizzies were made from standardized, interchangeable parts. Thus, they were easier to assemble and repair than other cars.

Ford's major innovation was to improve efficiency in his factory. He watched his workers and noticed that they spent much of their time carrying parts and tools to the car they were working on. To put an end to this wasted time and motion, Ford set up an **assembly line**.

The assembly line was a moving conveyor belt that rolled unfinished automobiles past the workers. Workers did their tasks one after the other while the chassis moved slowly past. By 1914, workers on Ford's assembly line could put a car together from start to finish in less than two hours. Soon, Ford's Detroit factory was producing 2,000 cars every hour.

By 1914, there were more than 600,000 cars in operation around the world. Of these, 75 percent were in the United States, where the Automobile Age had gotten off to a roaring start.

The *Wrights built an airplane.*

Meanwhile, in 1903, two brothers from Dayton, Ohio, had put the gasoline engine to a spectacular new use. At Kitty Hawk, North Carolina, on a cold, windy December morning, Wilbur and Orville Wright launched the age of powered flight. This first airplane flight lasted only 12 seconds and covered 120 feet. By 1905, the Wrights' third plane, *Flyer III*, could do all kinds of maneuvers and stay aloft for half an hour.

In 1908, Wilbur Wright went to Paris to demonstrate the airplane. The American pilot was greeted as a conquering hero. Crowds cheered as they watched him fly rings around the Eiffel Tower and stay aloft as long as two hours at a time.

Unlike the automobile, which blossomed almost overnight, the airplane developed slowly. Even in 1914, the total number of airplanes in the world was less than 1,000.

Inventions *became group efforts.*

The Wright brothers were among the last in a long line of independent inventors. Many early inventions of the Industrial Revolution were the

Scientific management, developed by American Frederick W. Taylor, became widespread in industry. This endeavor seeks to use workers, tools, and procedures to achieve maximum efficiency. Production increased greatly under scientific management.

In the Wright Flyer, the pilot lay prone to minimize wind resistance. To take off, the plane rolled along a track made of two-by-four boards.

work of one or two people experimenting in their basements, backyards, or small workshops. After 1900, however, most major technical advances resulted from group effort. Technology had become too complex and too expensive for one person to undertake a project from start to finish.

Therefore, after 1900, it is seldom accurate to name one person as *the* inventor of a complex device such as the computer or the television. As the twentieth century progressed, most new inventions came from research laboratories such as the one that Edison founded at Menlo Park.

Section Review 1

Define: (a) steel, (b) dynamo, (c) assembly line
Identify: (a) Henry Bessemer, (b) Thomas Edison, (c) Alexander Graham Bell, (d) Guglielmo Marconi, (e) Henry Ford, (f) Orville and Wilbur Wright
Answer:
1. What countries dominated world industry in the year 1900?
2. (a) Why did steel become more common in the late 1800's? (b) What were some of its most important uses?
3. (a) What were the major sources of energy in the early Industrial Revolution? (b) In the later Industrial Revolution?
4. Briefly describe the contributions of Thomas Edison.
5. How did communications change in the late 1800's and early 1900's?
6. What changes did Henry Ford bring to the auto industry?

Critical Thinking
7. (a) Using the quotation from Ford on page 560, explain how his attitude on making goods differed from those of a traditional craftsperson. (b) From a worker's point of view, what would be the advantages and disadvantages of an assembly line?

Science presented new ideas. 2

Theoretical scientists such as Volta, Faraday, Maxwell, and Hertz laid the groundwork for Edison and Marconi. In a similar way, other scientists in the late 1800's and early 1900's were pushing the frontiers of knowledge forward.

Medical discoveries saved lives.

At the beginning of the 1800's, doctors had few weapons in the fight against disease. Some of their "cures"—such as bloodletting—did more harm than good. Thanks to advances during the 1800's, more and more diseases could be cured or even prevented. By 1875, Europeans lived an average of 15 years longer than their grandparents had lived.

As you have read, Edward Jenner discovered a way to prevent smallpox (page 432). By 1875, widespread inoculation had nearly wiped out smallpox in western Europe.

Another major discovery came in the 1840's. Several American doctors and dentists began using the gases ether and chloroform to "knock out" their patients during painful operations. With this discovery of anesthesia, surgery became a routine part of medical care rather than a last-resort remedy.

Lister Although anesthesia made surgery less painful, nearly half of all surgical patients still died of infection. No one knew why. A Scottish surgeon, Joseph Lister (1827–1912), suggested that infection might be connected with the filthy conditions that were normal in hospitals. Patients were seldom bathed. Doctors worked in their street clothes and went from one patient to the next without even cleaning their instruments.

In 1865, Lister began a new program of cleanliness in his hospital ward. He insisted that his staff keep the place spotlessly clean. He began using carbolic acid to clean medical instruments. As a result, 85 percent of his patients survived. By 1890, other European and American hospitals were trying to live up to Lister's standard of cleanliness.

Pasteur Although Lister believed that tiny, invisible particles caused infection, he had no proof at first. Then, in 1865, Lister read of the work that French scientist Louis Pasteur (pas-TUHR) was doing. (The two scientists later became good friends.)

Pasteur (1822–1895) was experimenting to find out why milk soured and alcohol fermented. He discovered that the causes were microscopic organisms he called bacteria. He found that heat could destroy many harmful bacteria. The process of heating a liquid to kill the bacteria in it is now called *pasteurization*.

Pasteur also found ways to weaken the microorganisms that caused disease. Among other diseases, he worked with the virus that caused rabies, which was always fatal. In 1885, grief-stricken parents brought him their nine-year-old son who had been bitten by a rabid dog. Pasteur hesitated to use his new methods on a person without more tests, but there was no other hope. He inoculated the boy, and the youngster recovered.

Armed with the new knowledge of bacteria, later scientists found the causes of many diseases. Slowly, they also began to find cures. Moreover, when people saw how closely disease and filth were connected, they began to be more careful with city water supplies and food products. As a result, such diseases as cholera and typhus claimed fewer lives.

Darwin developed the theory of evolution.

No scientific idea of the 1800's caused a greater upheaval than the work of British biologist Charles Darwin (1809–1882). Darwin's research dated from the mid-1800's, but the controversy about his writings reached a peak in the latter part of the century. The cause of the controversy was Darwin's answer to the most challenging and important question that faced biologists: How can we explain the tremendous variety of plants and animals on Earth?

The most widely accepted answer in the 1800's was the idea of *special creation*. According to this view, every kind of plant and animal had been created by God at the beginning of the world and had remained the same since then.

Darwin challenged the idea of special creation. In 1859, he published a book titled *The Origin of Species by Means of Natural Selection*. Interest was so great that the book sold out immediately. In his book, Darwin put forward three major premises:

1. Within every species, more individuals are born than can survive. Therefore, every living thing takes part in a constant struggle for survival.

2. Variations—differences among individuals—make some members of a species better fitted to their environment than others. The fittest individuals are most likely to survive. Darwin called this idea *natural selection*.

In industrial areas of England, supporters of Darwin found evidence for the evolutionary process by observing moths. Originally white, these moths gradually mutated to gray and black as industrial soot changed the color of their habitat.

3. Because the fittest individuals are more likely to live to become adults, they are therefore more likely to have offspring. Thus, they pass on their differences to a new generation.

This process, Darwin reasoned, explains how species change over time and how new species gradually arise from old ones. Thus, over time, many different kinds of living things could have developed from a few early ones. Darwin's idea of change through natural selection came to be called the *theory of evolution.* (Darwin himself did not use the term evolution.)

The Origin of Species caused great excitement among scientists. Naturalist Thomas Henry Huxley wrote, "It is doubtful if any single book, except the *Principia* [of Sir Isaac Newton], ever worked so great and rapid a revolution in science." By 1900, nearly all biologists and botanists accepted the theory of evolution as the best explanation of variety among living things.

At the same time, Darwin's ideas roused a storm of debate outside the scientific community. Many people believed that the idea of evolution directly contradicted the account of creation in the Bible. The bishop of Oxford, for example, accused Darwin of "a tendency to limit God's glory in creation." In 1871, Darwin fueled the conflict when he published *The Descent of Man.* In this new book, he said that humans too had evolved from earlier forms of life.

The evolution controversy continued for decades. Even today, well over 100 years after *The Origin of Species* was first published, Darwin's ideas are not universally accepted.

Social Darwinists favored competition.

Darwin was a biologist, but a number of nineteenth-century thinkers applied his ideas about plants and animals to economics and politics. The leader in this movement was Herbert Spencer, an English sociologist.

Footnote to History

In 1901, a London newspaper polled its readers, asking for lists of the 10 most influential books of the past 100 years. Of the hundreds of different lists that the paper received, every one included *The Origin of Species.*

Free economic competition, Spencer argued, was natural selection in action. The best companies, for example, make profits, while inefficient ones go bankrupt. Spencer applied the same rules to individuals. Those who were fittest for survival enjoyed wealth and success, while the poor remained poor because they were unfit. This idea became known as *social Darwinism.* Social Darwinists believed that governments should not upset the "natural" system of rich and poor.

Others carried Darwin's ideas even further. The German philosopher Friedrich Nietzsche (**NEE**-chuh) believed that some humans could and should evolve to a higher level by the use of willpower and courage. Such people would become *übermenschen* (supermen) above the common herd. "I am opposed," Nietzsche wrote, "to parliamentary government . . . because [it is] the means whereby cattle become masters."

Many nationalists and imperialists seized on both Darwin's and Nietzsche's ideas to support their own views. They argued that their own nation should prove its superiority through power, especially military power. As we will see in later chapters, several dictators used nationalism and scorn for democracy to justify their oppressive governments.

Science advanced in many fields.

Just as Copernicus and Galileo began a scientific revolution around 1600, Darwin was part of a new age of science that began in the late 1800's. Thanks to the work of many men and women, the foundations of modern biology, chemistry, and physics were established by 1914.

Biology Although Darwin said that living things passed on their variations from one generation to the next, he did not know how they did so. In the 1860's, Gregor Mendel discovered that there is a pattern to the way that certain traits are inherited. Although his work was not widely known until 1900, Mendel laid the groundwork for the science of genetics.

Other biologists took up the study of bacteria where Louis Pasteur left off. The German scientist Robert Koch, for example, discovered the organisms that caused tuberculosis and cholera.

Chemistry In chemistry, most of the major elements and compounds found in nature had been identified by the end of the 1800's. In 1803,

Many other scientists in the 1700's and 1800's already accepted the general idea of evolution—it was not a new idea. Darwin's contribution was suggesting a mechanism—natural selection—to account for evolution.

563

Marie Curie was Polish, born in a part of Poland ruled by Russia. She named the mineral polonium *in honor of her country.*

Marie Curie eventually died of the effects of radioactivity, which caused her to have leukemia.

the British chemist John Dalton had theorized that all matter is made of tiny particles called atoms. Dalton showed that elements contain only one kind of atom, which has a specific weight. Compounds, on the other hand, contain more than one kind of atom.

In 1869, Dmitri Mendeleev (MEN-duh-LAY-yef), a Russian chemist, organized a chart on which all the known elements were arranged in order of weight, from lightest to heaviest. He left gaps where he predicted that new elements would be discovered. Later, his predictions proved correct. Mendeleev's chart, called the Periodic Table, is still used by scientists today.

A husband and wife team working in Paris discovered two of the missing elements. Marie and Pierre Curie found that a mineral called pitchblende released a powerful form of energy. In 1898, Marie Curie gave this energy the name *radioactivity*. The Curies discovered two new

elements that they named radium and polonium. Both were highly radioactive. In 1903, the Curies shared the Nobel Prize for Physics for their work on radioactivity. In 1911, Marie won the Nobel Prize for Chemistry for the discovery of radium and polonium. The prizes awarded to the Curies show how closely the fields of chemistry and physics were linked.

Physics Physicists around 1900 were trying to unravel the secrets of the atom. Among the leaders in this field were two British physicists, Ernest Rutherford and J. J. Thomson. Earlier scientists believed that the atom was the smallest particle that existed. Rutherford suggested that atoms were made up of yet smaller particles. Each atom, he said, had a nucleus surrounded by one or more particles called electrons.

Soon other physicists such as Max Planck, Neils Bohr, and Albert Einstein were studying the forces that held atoms together. Their discoveries, as we shall see in Chapter 30, were fully as revolutionary as Darwin's ideas.

Section Review 2

Define: (a) anesthesia, (b) bacteria, (c) natural selection, (d) element, (e) atom, (f) radioactivity

Identify: (a) Joseph Lister, (b) Louis Pasteur, (c) Charles Darwin, (d) special creation, (e) theory of evolution, (f) social Darwinism, (g) Friedrich Nietzsche, (h) Gregor Mendel, (i) Dmitri Mendeleev, (j) Marie and Pierre Curie

Answer:
1. List four developments that improved health care during the 1800's.
2. (a) How did the theory of special creation explain the variety of living things? (b) How did the theory of evolution explain this variety?
3. Why did Darwin's ideas arouse controversy?
4. How did some thinkers apply Darwin's ideas to industrial society?
5. How were the contributions of Dalton, Mendeleev, and the Curies related?

Critical Thinking
6. Darwin did not fully agree with the social Darwinists. How do natural selection and economic competition differ?

Because working women were still expected to do the household chores, it is not suprising that in Britain the campaign for women's rights began in Manchester, not London.

Women sought rights and freedoms. 3

In 1906, Marie Curie became the first woman ever to teach at France's prestigious Sorbonne. She won two Nobel Prizes and was acknowledged as one of the foremost scientists of her time. Yet she could never become a member of the French Academy of Sciences because she was a woman. During the years when she was making her great discoveries, she could not even vote.

The massive changes that the 1800's brought to Europe and North America affected everyone's lives. By the late 1800's, however, it was clear that the Industrial Revolution and the social changes that went with it had had different results for women than for men.

Women faced economic problems.

In some ways, the Industrial Revolution opened economic opportunities to women. Factory work offered higher wages than work done at home. Women spinners in Manchester's cotton factories, for example, received much higher pay than women who spun cotton thread at home.

On the other hand, women factory workers usually earned only half as much as men. Employers claimed that women needed less money than men because women did not have to support families. This argument ignored the many women who worked because their husbands had died or deserted them or were too ill to work.

Trade unions began to win better wages for working men in the mid-1800's. However, these unions seldom accepted women as members. Unions fought to keep women out of skilled jobs that offered better pay. Men feared that if women worked at such jobs, employers would lower the wages for everyone doing the work. During the mid-1800's, women formed several unions of their own in the trades where they dominated. Still, by 1907, only 15 percent of the unions in Great Britain admitted women.

When reformers began demanding better conditions for workers, the laws often applied first to women and children. Lawmakers were more willing to protect women and children than men. Beginning in the 1830's, some laws limited the hours women and children could work. Other laws set health and safety standards in factories.

Sometimes, these laws backfired against women. If the law said that women could not work 16 hours a day, some employers simply fired women and hired men instead. Eventually, however, the reforms spread to all workers and benefited both men and women.

Women entered new fields.

The years around 1900 were a watershed for working women. A gradual shift took place in the kinds of jobs that were open to them. In the late 1800's, working women were clustered in three kinds of jobs. The largest share worked as servants in other people's homes. In industry, most women were either garment workers or textile workers.

Middle-class women with an education had other job possibilities. Some were teachers. There was a demand for teachers in the late 1800's because countries in western Europe were beginning to offer free public schooling. France began public education in the 1860's. The British government began to organize schools in 1870, although they were not free to all children until 1891.

Nursing was another career open to women. British nurse Florence Nightingale (1820–1910) took the lead in winning professional training

Florence Nightingale organized British army hospitals during the Crimean War.

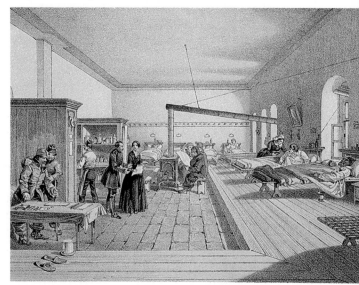

By 1875, more than one third of France's primary schoolteachers were women. Discuss the sexual balance of the teaching profession today and ask students to speculate on possible causes.

565

for women as nurses. In 1854, she went to Turkey and later Russia to help British soldiers in the Crimean War. Making her night rounds in the hospitals, she became known to hundreds of sick and wounded soldiers as "The Lady with the Lamp." When she returned to Britain, she used money that was donated in her honor to found the Nightingale School for Nurses. It was the first school of professional nursing in the world.

Teaching, nursing, library work, and social work were service professions in which many women worked. Opportunities for women in other professions were limited. In 1898, for example, there were only two women lawyers in all France.

In the late 1800's, a number of women's medical schools opened. Faced with this competition, several large medical schools for men began to admit women as well. By 1900, 10 percent of the medical students in the United States were women.

New jobs were also appearing for less educated women. After 1900, many women worked as shop clerks and office workers. (Before 1870, nearly all office clerks were men.)

While jobs in offices, stores, and schools were opening to women, jobs in industry were closing. The traditional women's industries—textiles and garment making—fell on hard times after 1900. Thus, the share of women in manufacturing jobs dropped sharply.

Women had few legal rights.

Working women of the middle 1800's faced yet another problem. They had no legal right to the money they earned. An unmarried woman's wages legally belonged to her father. If she married, everything she owned or earned became her husband's property.

Women could not sue or make contracts. Often, if a woman's husband died, she could not even act as guardian of her children.

In 1900, no country in Europe allowed women to vote. Even in Britain, where Queen Victoria was perhaps the most popular monarch the country had ever had, women could not vote or serve in Parliament. "Women are creatures of impulse and emotion," declared one British member of Parliament in 1906. "They do not decide questions on the ground of reason as men do." Thousands of women (and men) throughout the developed world disagreed.

Women sought the right to vote.

In the United States, women such as Lucretia Mott and Susan B. Anthony organized a campaign for women's rights as early as 1848. By the 1880's, women were working internationally to win more rights. In 1888, women activists founded the International Council for Women. Delegates and

By 1900, women in many countries were organizing to demand the right to vote. They believed that this right was the basis for other steps toward legal equality.

As early as 1848, Elizabeth Cady Stanton led a group of women reformers at a meeting in Seneca Falls, New York. There supporters of women's rights drafted a declaration of independence, asserting that "All men and women are created equal."

observers from 27 countries attended the council's 1899 meeting, coming from lands as far apart as the United States, New Zealand, Argentina, Iceland, Persia, and China.

Even among activist women, however, the question of suffrage (voting rights) for women remained controversial. Not all women were in favor of it; not all men were against it.

In Britain and the United States, there had been decades of peaceful efforts to win the right to vote for women. Around 1900, more militant organizations sprang up. In the United States, Carrie Chapman Catt headed the North American Woman Suffrage Association. In Britain, Emmeline Pankhurst formed the Women's Social and Political Union (WSPU) in 1903.

The WSPU became the most militant organization for women's rights. Besides peaceful demonstrations and parades, its members cut telegraph wires, heckled government speakers, chained themselves to railings at public buildings, and smashed windows. Their goal was to draw attention to the cause of woman's suffrage.

Emmeline Pankhurst and her daughters Christabel and Sylvia were arrested and imprisoned dozens of times. When she was jailed, Emmeline Pankhurst turned to hunger strikes to keep her cause before the public. British officials force-fed her to keep her alive.

The authorities could not stop another woman who was determined to become a martyr to the cause of woman's suffrage. In June 1913, the cream of European society was watching the English Derby at Epsom Downs. Suddenly, a young WSPU member, Emily Davison, threw herself in front of the king's horse and was killed.

Voice from the Past • *A Citizen's Right to Vote*

In 1872, Susan B. Anthony and 50 other women were arrested for trying to vote in the presidential election. After she was found guilty, Anthony made the following statement.

Of all my prosecutors, from the corner grocery politician who entered the complaint, to the United States marshal, commissioner, district-attorney, district-judge, your honor on the bench—not one is my peer, but each and all are my political superiors; and had your honor submitted my case to the jury . . . even then I should have had just cause of protest, for not one of those men was my peer but, native or foreign born, white or black, rich or poor, educated or ignorant, sober or drunk, each and every man of them was my political superior; hence in no sense my peer . . .

Precisely as no disfranchised person [person without the right to vote] is entitled to sit upon a jury, and no woman is entitled to the franchise, so none but a regularly admitted lawyer is allowed to practice in the courts, and no woman can gain admission to the bar—hence, jury, judge, counsel, all must be of the superior class.

[Here, the judge stated that the trial had been handled according to the established forms of law.]

Yes, your honor, but by forms of law all made by men, interpreted by men, administered by men, in favor of men and against women; and hence your honor's ordered verdict of guilty, against a United States citizen for the exercise of the "citizen's right to vote," simply because that citizen was a woman and not a man.

1. (a) According to Susan B. Anthony, why are none of the people who brought her to trial her peers? (b) What right do they have that makes them her political superiors?
2. What traditional right in American and British law does she imply she was denied in her trial?
3. Besides the right to vote, what other opportunities and civic responsibilities were closed to women, according to this speech?

At her funeral, thousands of women in white dresses carried banners supporting woman's suffrage. "Thoughts have gone forth whose power can sleep no more," read one banner. "Victory! Victory!"

In fact, victory was still many years away. Though the woman's suffrage movement commanded wide attention between 1880 and 1914, its successes were few. Women won the right to vote in New Zealand (1893) and Australia (1902). Only in two European territories—Finland (1906, then part of the Russian empire) and Norway (1913)—did women gain voting rights before World War I. Several western states in the United States also granted women the right to vote. Often, women won voting rights for local elections before they won statewide or national rights.

On other issues, women's rights made faster progress. Britain and most states in the United States enacted laws giving married women the right to own property. In Britain, women began to serve as safety inspectors in factories where women worked. Women also served on local boards to oversee schools and hospitals.

Section Review 3

Define: suffrage
Identify: (a) Florence Nightingale, (b) Susan B. Anthony, (c) Carrie Chapman Catt, (d) Emmeline Pankhurst
Answer:
1. What economic problems did women face?
2. (a) What fields of work employed most women in the late 1800's? (b) What new fields opened around 1900?
3. What were some of the restrictions on women's legal and political rights?
4. How did women try to secure their rights?
5. (a) In what areas did they achieve some success by 1914? (b) In what areas were they less successful?

Critical Thinking
6. In the 1850's, teaching, office work, and professional nursing were unusual jobs for women. (a) From the point of view of an employer of that time, explain why each of these jobs is "unsuitable" for women. (b) From the point of view of an employer in 1900, explain why each job is a "natural" one for women.

Art and entertainment took new forms. 4

The late 1800's and early 1900's saw great changes in the world of the arts. The period was also marked by new forms of art and entertainment for a mass audience.

New styles in art replaced realism.

Although France lagged behind Britain and Germany in economic and military power, its capital, Paris, still dominated European culture. Rebuilding carried out under Napoleon III had transformed central Paris from a maze of crumbling medieval streets into a magnificent urban center. Artists from Europe and America flocked to Paris. There they could enjoy unequaled cultural resources while exchanging ideas about a new style of painting, Impressionism.

Impressionism Like other styles of art, Impressionism involves a choice of subjects, an attitude toward these subjects, and techniques for presenting them. Impressionists concentrated on scenes from everyday life—crowded city streets, the arrival of a train at its station, or Sunday picnics on the Seine. Perhaps influenced by photography, they hoped to capture their impressions of a certain instant in the ever-changing world about them.

To convey their impressions of a scene, these painters adopted the new technique of painting thousands of dabs of pure color onto their canvas. As Edouard Manet explained, light could become "the principal personage of a painting." Impressionist works by Manet, Claude Monet, and Auguste Renoir do indeed seem to shimmer and sparkle.

Postimpressionism During the 1890's, a new group of painters, sometimes called the postimpressionists, carried this emphasis on light and color even further. Among these artists were Vincent van Gogh (van GOH) and Paul Gauguin (goh-GAN). Gauguin explained his colorful style this way:

By the combination of lines and colors, under the pretext of some motif taken from nature, I create symphonies and harmonies that represent nothing absolutely real in

While France lagged behind Britain and Germany in economic and military power, Paris still dominated European culture. It became a city of broad, tree-lined boulevards, opera houses, art museums, and galleries.

Like many impressionists, Monet favored outdoor scenes for their natural light. A detail from his "Gladioli" (left), a tranquil garden scene, shows the impressionists' use of light and color. In "Starry Night" (right), the postimpressionist Van Gogh painted the sky as an overwhelming display of fireworks.

the ordinary sense of the word but are intended to give rise to thoughts as music does.

Expressionism Other early twentieth-century painters, such as the Norwegian Edvard Munch and the Russian Vasily Kandinsky, were mainly concerned with expressing the feelings that a scene aroused. They were therefore known as expressionists. Because the feelings they expressed were often grim and anguished, their paintings were unsettling and frightening.

New directions Even with wild colors and distortions, the paintings of Van Gogh and Munch could still be recognized as objects from the real world. Other artists, however, were beginning to change the shapes they painted beyond all recognition. One group of painters, for example, was nicknamed the cubists because their work featured geometric planes and angles. A picture of a person might look at first sight like an intricate stack of boxes.

One of the cubists was a young Spaniard working in Paris, Pablo Picasso. He explained why he rejected realism: "Nature and art, being two

different things, cannot be the same thing, period. Through art, we express our concept of what nature is not."

Music often took nationalistic themes.

Romanticism was still the leading style of music in the late 1800's. These years were a golden age of opera. Composers such as Giuseppe Verdi (**VERD**-ee) and Giacomo Puccini (poo-**CHEE**-nee) wedded their emotional music to melodramatic plots.

Nationalism also played a strong role in music. The German composer Richard Wagner (**VAHG**-nuhr), for example, based many of his operas on old German legends. Nearly every European country had a composer whose work gave people a heightened sense of national identity.

Just as painters were branching out from tradition, some composers began to experiment with different kinds of music. The French composers Claude Debussy (deb-yoo-**SEE**) and Maurice Ravel (ruh-**VEL**) wrote loosely structured musical impressions such as *The Sea* (Debussy) and *The*

Other nationalist composers included the Czech Anton Dvořák, the Finn Jan Sibelius, and the Spaniard Isaac Albéniz. You may wish to play some of their music for the class.

Waltz (Ravel). In fact, music critics compared them to the impressionist painters.

Other composers, such as the Russians Alexander Scriabin (skree-**AHB**-uhn) and Igor Stravinsky (struh-**VIHN**-skee), produced even more complex harmonies and rhythms. The Austrian Arnold Schönberg (**SHUHN**-buhrg) began to base his music on mathematical patterns rather than upon sounds that were pleasing to the ear.

Most of this experimental music did not appeal to a wide public. When Stravinsky's ballet *The Rite of Spring* was first performed in Paris in 1913, the audience rioted against what they thought was an insult to their ears.

The turn of the century also saw the beginnings of modern popular music. In Britain, singers with Cockney accents sang ballads at popular theaters known as music halls. In the United States, ragtime—a musical style based on a rapid melody and strong beat—was becoming very popular thanks to black musicians such as Scott Joplin.

The arts reached new audiences.

In earlier periods, art, music, and most theater had been largely the concern of the upper classes. By 1900, however, artists, writers, and musicians were appealing to a much larger audience. For the first time, we can speak of *mass culture*. There were at least three causes for the rise of mass culture around the turn of the century.

First, the spread of public education broadened literacy in both Europe and North America. The millions of new readers created an enormous market for newspapers, magazines, and books that were written in simple, colorful language.

Second, improvements in communication made it possible to meet this broad demand for information and entertainment. The new, high-speed presses and linotype machines could turn out thousands of pages in a few hours. The phonograph brought music directly into people's homes.

The third cause was a gradual reduction in working hours. By 1900, most industrial countries had limited the working day to ten hours. Most people worked Monday through Friday and half a day on Saturday. Thus, men and women of the lower and middle classes had more leisure time than ever before. They could take part in activities that their grandparents never had time to enjoy.

Sports entertained millions.

The five-and-a-half-day work week created the "weekend," a special time of relaxation and fun. All kinds of new leisure activities became popular. Millions flocked to beaches on summer weekends. Golf and tennis were a hit among the well-to-do, who could afford to join clubs with playing areas. People with less money took up soccer or baseball, which they could play with simple equipment on vacant lots.

For every person who played sports, there were 20 who enjoyed watching. In the United States, football and baseball skyrocketed in popularity. Teams from the rival American and National leagues played baseball's first World Series in 1903. Soccer became popular in Europe.

As a result of the growing interest in sports, the international Olympic Games began in 1896. They revived the Greek tradition of holding an athletic competition among states every four years. Fittingly, the first modern Olympics were held in Athens.

Baseball's popularity grew swiftly in the 1890's.

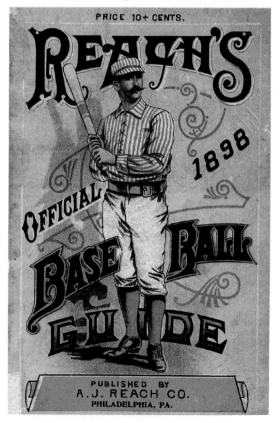

570

People flocked to see movies.

One of the most popular new leisure activities was an evening visit to the movie theater or the music hall. With names such as the Gaiety, the Grand, or the Orpheum, music halls offered a dozen or more different acts. Such variety shows often included singers, dancers, comedians, acrobats, and even trained parakeets.

During the 1880's, dozens of inventors worked on moving-picture cameras and projectors. One successful design came from France. Another came from Thomas Edison's laboratory.

The earliest films caused a sensation only because of their novelty. They were in black and white, lasted less than a minute, and had no plot. One, for example, showed a man sneezing—that was all!

In 1903, an American filmmaker named Edwin S. Porter offered the first feature film. As the lights dimmed, a fierce bandit appeared on the screen and fired his revolver directly at the audience. People shrieked with fear and delight. In the next eight minutes, they watched as a band of outlaws held up a train and fled, only to be hunted down by a white-hatted sheriff and his hard-riding posse. The film was *The Great Train Robbery*, and it packed theaters on both sides of the Atlantic.

Movies quickly became big business. By 1910, 5 million Americans attended some 10,000 theaters across the country each day. The European movie industry enjoyed similar growth.

The people who saw *The Great Train Robbery* were watching the beginnings of both a new industry and a new art form. Movies made possible a new kind of visual storytelling. Moving images, together with recorded sound, came to dominate mass culture in the twentieth century.

Section Review 4

Define: mass culture
Identify: (a) impressionism, (b) expressionism
Answer:
1. (a) What were the major characteristics of impressionist and postimpressionist painting? (b) Name the leading painters of these schools?
2. What trends in painting followed the impressionist period?
3. How did some music of the late 1800's reflect political trends of the time?
4. (a) What were the causes of the development of mass culture around 1900? (b) Give some examples of the new forms of art and entertainment for wide audiences.

Critical Thinking
5. (a) How did the development of photography change the function of painting? (b) What is the importance of each today?
6. Reread the statement by Gauguin on pages 568–569. (a) What purpose do painting and music share? (b) In your opinion, what is the importance of the arts in society?

Europe faced rising tensions.   5

More than ever before, the views of ordinary people were making an impact on society. By 1914, most industrialized countries allowed all adult men to vote. This development brought about two major changes in European politics.

First, political parties became more tightly organized than before. In earlier times, political parties had been loose-knit clubs. Now they were (or tried to be) well-oiled machines for winning elections. Major parties had branches in every election district. Those branches reported to a central committee. The central committee set party policies and made sure that party members in parliament supported those policies.

Second, the spread of democracy brought forward a new kind of political leader. Besides commanding the respect and support of fellow party leaders, a successful politician now had to appeal to large numbers of voters. As a result, politicians found they had to be part actors and part salespersons, able to win widespread support.

By itself, the right to vote did not guarantee democratic government. Much depended on the political system of each country. Even in the United States, for example, only the House of Representatives was elected directly by the voters. Senators were not directly elected. Until 1913, they were chosen by the state legislatures. France had a similar system with a Chamber of Deputies

571

and a Senate. In Britain, members of the House of Lords were not elected at all.

Such *upper houses* could reject bills passed by the *lower houses* and also frame bills of their own. In some other countries, the powers of elected legislatures were restricted both by an upper house and by a monarch who still made many major governmental decisions.

Germany had a hollow democracy.

Germany was a good example of the limits on democracy. The Reichstag (RYKES-tahg) was the lower house of the German parliament. It was elected by universal manhood suffrage. Members of the upper house, the Bundesrat (BOON-duhs-raht), were appointed by each of Germany's 25 states. Often, they were chosen by local princes and dukes.

Furthermore, the German kaiser (emperor) named his own chancellor (prime minister). Neither the Reichstag nor the Bundesrat had any control over the chancellor. Thus, if the Reichstag voted against raising the army budget, the chancellor might simply raise the budget anyway. "The Reichstag does not make history," said one German political leader, "but is merely playing a comedy."

Otto von Bismarck continued to govern Germany as chancellor until 1890. As we have seen, Bismarck was a staunch conservative who distrusted both democracy and socialism. However, he was shrewd enough to know that his government needed popular support. During the 1880's, therefore, Bismarck gave Germany the world's first large-scale welfare program. His laws included insurance to help workers in case of accident or sickness. Soon he added old-age pensions for every German worker.

By passing these laws, Bismarck hoped to take support away from his enemies, the socialists. "Anybody who has before him the prospect of a pension, be it ever so small," Bismarck noted, "is much happier and more content with his lot, much more tractable and easy to manage, than he whose future is absolutely uncertain." Bismarck's goal was not so much to help the workers as to prevent revolution, and he succeeded.

Bismarck's political career ended abruptly. In 1888, Kaiser William II came to the throne. The young kaiser was headstrong, quarrelsome, and determined to rule Germany himself. Accordingly, he forced Bismarck to resign in 1890. However, Bismarck's system of state socialism, as he called his social programs, remained in effect. So did his military and nationalist policies. With their economic needs met, most Germans supported these policies even though Germany's government was basically undemocratic.

Britain faced two political crises.

Germany had half a dozen political parties, as did France and Italy. In Britain, two major parties dominated politics—the Liberals and the Conservatives. In the late 1800's, both parties produced prime ministers who were enormously popular, the Conservatives' Benjamin Disraeli and the Liberals' William Gladstone.

The Irish question The two parties differed little on questions of imperialism or reform. The issue on which the two parties were most seriously split was the Irish question. Ireland had been controlled by the British government for nearly 300 years. It had been ruled directly from London since 1801.

During the 1870's, nationalists in Ireland organized an Irish Home Rule Party. Its members sought a measure of independence for Ireland. In general, Conservatives opposed Irish Home Rule, while Liberals favored it. Liberal prime minister William Gladstone brought forward two home rule bills in parliament, but both were defeated.

Meanwhile, in Ireland, a drop in the prices for farm products made it impossible for thousands of people to pay their rents. In just one year, landlords forced more than 2,000 families out of their homes. Some angry farmers and other nationalists turned to violence, burning barns and beating landlords' agents.

Footnote to History

As a peaceful form of protest, the Irish decided to shun anyone who bought a farm after its tenant had been unfairly evicted. No neighbor would speak to or do business with the new owner. The first person to be treated this way was Charles Boycott. His name came to stand for breaking off all day-to-day dealings with a person or group.

Discussion question: Were Bismarck's policies comparable to those of the ancient Romans with their "bread and circuses?"

During the 1870's and 1880's, both Protestants and Catholics in Ireland worked for home rule. By the 1900's, however, many Irish Protestants had turned against it. Most Irish Protestants lived in the northern part of Ireland, known as Ulster. They feared being a minority in a country dominated by Catholics.

In 1914, Parliament finally approved a home rule bill. By then, Irish Protestants were gathering weapons and holding military drills to fight against home rule.

Just one month before home rule was to take effect, World War I broke out in Europe. The problem of Irish independence was left to wait and to fester.

The issue of the House of Lords In 1909, Britain's Liberal finance minister was David Lloyd George. Orphaned as a child, he had been raised by his uncle, a shoemaker. Lloyd George became the champion of social welfare programs. Under his leadership, the Liberals put forward a program to provide old-age pensions, accident and illness insurance for workers, and even some unemployment benefits. To pay for these benefits, Lloyd George called for an income tax that would hit hardest at the wealthy. He called his program the "People's Budget."

The People's Budget easily passed in the House of Commons, but the House of Lords vetoed it. The House of Lords seldom opposed the Commons, but many lords were wealthy landowners who stood to lose money from Lloyd George's new taxes.

Lloyd George and the Liberals turned the budget issue into a question on the place of the House of Lords in British government. The Liberal party wanted to limit the powers of the House of Lords. Liberals won the next two elections, but still the lords refused to accept reforms. Finally, the king threatened to name enough new, reform-minded lords to pass the changes that the Commons demanded. The threat was enough. Rather than accept dozens of new members, the House of Lords voted to limit its own powers.

Henceforth, the House of Lords could only *delay* bills passed by the House of Commons. After two years, such bills became law whether or not the Lords approved of them. Britain had taken one more step toward a fully democratic form of government.

Queen Victoria (center front) was called "the grandmother of Europe." Her many children married into royal families all over the continent. Here she is surrounded by her royal relatives. At left are her grandson, Kaiser William II (seated), Britain's future George V (in black hat), and Victoria's son, soon to be Edward VII (in light coat).

Discussion question: How did Lloyd George's program of social improvement differ from Bismarck's?

573

In Vienna at the turn of the century, all the most fashionable people could be seen walking or driving along the Ringstrasse ("ring street").

Social divisions marked life in "the beautiful era."

Despite the growth of democracy in some countries, by 1900, both Europe and the United States had a tiny but fabulously wealthy upper class. Its members seemed, in the words of one French writer, "to live upon a golden cloud, spending their riches as indolently [lazily] and naturally as the leaves grow green."

For the wealthy, the years around 1900 were *la belle epoque* (the beautiful era). Ladies and gentlemen of the upper class lived surrounded by servants. They maintained several homes, some in town and some in the country. All of Europe was their playground. In March, the wealthy went to the French seaside resort of Biarritz. In April, they visited the yearly exhibition of the French art society in Paris. In June, they flocked to the English Derby at Epsom Downs. The summer months found them at mountain spas such as Germany's Marienbad. In the fall, they went hunting at splendid country estates.

Only 1 or 2 percent of the European population belonged to the upper class. About 25 to 35 percent were members of the middle class. The middle class, as we have seen, had been growing since the Middle Ages and included a wide range of people—merchants, shopkeepers, doctors, lawyers, teachers, and government employees. Industrialization created new middle-class positions—factory supervisors, sales representatives, and thousands of office workers. Middle-class families had enough money to buy such labor-saving gadgets as washing and sewing machines and to take summer vacations. Many middle-class families built comfortable houses in the fast-growing neighborhoods just outside the city. With the coming of electric streetcars, middle-class people began to live outside the city and commute to work each day. Some even bought Henry Ford's new Model T's.

The urban lower class, as well as the peasantry in eastern Europe, still lived on the edge of poverty. Despite major medical advances during the 1800's, tuberculosis and other deadly diseases were still a menace in slums and tenements from Moscow to Chicago.

As the representative of the workers, trade unions were growing stronger. Although strikes were not always successful, workers sometimes won higher wages and better working conditions. In 1889, for example, Ben Tillett led a walkout of 10,000 London dockworkers. For a month, no cargoes were loaded or unloaded. Then the shipowners agreed to pay the dockworkers higher wages and cut the work week from 55 to 48 hours.

574

In 1900, a person of the English upper class, for example, made 2,000 times as much money per year as an English coal miner. Help students understand this gap by having them research the average annual wage of a coal miner and multiply by 2,000.

Despite such gains, some radicals still believed that only a revolution would improve the lives of the working class. One group of revolutionaries called themselves **anarchists**. Anarchists believed that all governments were evil and should be overthrown. These radicals committed a number of assassinations around the turn of the century, including that of the czar of Russia in 1881, the French president in 1894, the king of Italy in 1900, and President William McKinley of the United States in 1901. However, the number of anarchists and revolutionary socialists remained very small in every country.

Crises shook Europe's fragile peace.

In different ways, Britain and Germany had both achieved stability by 1900. France too was fairly stable under the Third Republic (page 523). For the countries in the heartland of Europe, the age of nation building was over.

Around the edges of Europe, nationalism was still a deeply troubling issue. Ireland was one example. Norway was another. Norwegians finally won their independence from Sweden in 1905. The greatest conflicts over nationalism, however, were arising in eastern Europe.

Austria-Hungary, Russia, and the Ottoman empire were all multinational empires. All three lagged behind western Europe industrially and militarily. (The once powerful Ottoman empire was now so weak that it was known as "the sick man of Europe.") All three included peoples who wanted their own nations.

Ethnic minorities in these empires faced the risk of persecution. Bulgarians were massacred by their Ottoman rulers in the 1870's. In 1895, Ottoman ruler Abdul Hamid II turned on the Armenian minority in his empire, beginning a series of massacres that eventually took more than 1 million lives. Jews in Russia lived under the threat of *pogroms*, mob attacks in which many were killed and still more had their homes and businesses destroyed.

The most complex national conflicts arose on the Balkan Peninsula. There, Serbs, Bosnians, Montenegrins, Croats, Slovenes, Albanians, Bulgarians, and Romanians all hoped to build their own countries. Many of these groups spoke Slavic languages, but they maintained their separate identities.

Between 1900 and 1914, repeated uprisings and crises in the Balkans threatened both Austria-Hungary and the Ottoman empire. Russia saw itself as protector of all the Slavic peoples and often encouraged the nationalism of Slavic groups in the Balkans. In this role, Russia was a constant threat to Austria-Hungary.

Crises also arose in western Europe. France was still bitter about the loss of Alsace and Lorraine (page 523). In 1911, France and Germany came to the brink of war when a German gunboat threatened Morocco, a French colony in Africa.

War in the Balkans, hostility along the Rhine, saber rattling in North Africa—all made peace difficult to keep. Yet a strange optimism grew in Europe. As each crisis was solved without a general war, people began to think that war had been banished forever.

Section Review 5

Define: (a) upper house, (b) lower house, (c) pogrom, (d) anarchist
Identify: (a) Reichstag, (b) Bundesrat, (c) William II, (d) David Lloyd George
Answer:
1. How did wider voting rights affect political parties and their leaders?
2. Why was Germany not a true democracy?
3. (a) What programs did Bismarck enact as his policy of state socialism? (b) What were his reasons for doing so?
4. (a) What was "the Irish question"? (b) How did the political situation in Ireland change between 1870 and 1900?
5. How did Britain's House of Lords lose its last political powers?
6. (a) What European countries were still multinational empires? (b) What groups were still frustrated in hopes for nations of their own?
7. How did each of the following create crises in this era? (a) Slavic nationalism (b) hostility between France and Germany (c) anarchists

Critical Thinking
8. Both Bismarck and Lloyd George passed social welfare programs. Did their actions reflect the same political philosophies? Explain.
9. (a) How is the phrase *la belle epoque* a good description of this era in Europe? (b) In what ways is the phrase a poor description?

Summary

1. Inventions changed ways of life. Between 1870 and 1914, numerous practical inventions made people's lives more comfortable. Bessemer's blast furnace brought on the Age of Steel. Thomas Edison invented new uses for electricity. The telephone, radio, and combustion engine transformed transportation and communication. Ford's assembly line established the modern manufacturing process.

2. Science presented new ideas. New standards of cleanliness, the introduction of pasteurization, and the widespread use of inoculation decreased the number of deaths from disease. Darwin proposed the theory of evolution to explain the variety of living things. Later, a number of thinkers applied his ideas to economics and politics. The development of genetics and theories about the composition of elements led to advances in chemistry and physics.

3. Women sought rights and freedoms. Although by the late 1800's more women worked outside the home, they still faced economic and political restrictions. Many women in the United States and Britain believed that the right to vote would improve their status. Although women used a variety of tactics to call attention to their cause, they achieved only limited success by 1914.

4. Art and entertainment took new forms. The spread of public education, improved communications, and more leisure time helped create mass culture in the late 1800's. Sports and movies became especially popular. Painting styles shifted from realism to increasingly abstract forms, and composers experimented with new harmonies and rhythms.

5. Europe faced rising tensions. By 1900, the views of ordinary people were impacting society. Democratic rights expanded in Britain when the House of Lords lost its last political power. However, the controversy over Irish home rule divided British voters and produced rising tensions. In the early 1900's, democracy in Germany was severely limited, although Bismarck's state socialism recognized increasing public interests in politics. In eastern Europe, independence movements among persecuted minorities caused rising tensions.

Reviewing the Facts

1. Define the following terms:
   a. assembly line   b. anarchist
2. Explain the importance of each of the following names or terms:
   a. blast furnace   c. Bell
   b. Edison   d. Marconi

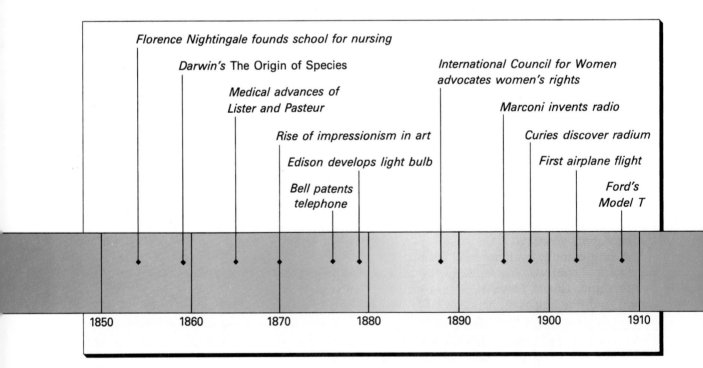

Florence Nightingale founds school for nursing

Darwin's The Origin of Species

International Council for Women advocates women's rights

Medical advances of Lister and Pasteur

Marconi invents radio

Rise of impressionism in art

Curies discover radium

Edison develops light bulb

First airplane flight

Bell patents telephone

Ford's Model T

1850   1860   1870   1880   1890   1900   1910

e. Wright brothers
f. anesthesia
g. pasteurization
h. impressionism
i. expressionism
j. Bismarck
k. Lloyd George
l. pogrom

3. (a) What metal largely replaced iron in the late 1800's? (b) What new source of energy came into use?
4. (a) How was Darwin's theory of evolution received? (b) Describe two ideas that were derived from it.
5. What contributions did each of the following scientists make? (a) Mendeleev (b) Dalton (c) Marie Curie (d) Rutherford
6. What steps did women take to win wider rights?
7. (a) What was the Irish question? (b) Describe the status of the Irish question in 1914.
8. How did the power of Britain's House of Lords decline?
9. (a) What issues threatened peace in eastern Europe? (b) What conflict threatened peace in western Europe?

Basic Skills

Reading and interpreting a table Study the table below. Then answer the questions that follow. (a) Which of the countries shown steadily increased their relative share of world manufacturing output? (b) Which countries suffered a steady decline in relative share? (c) Which countries met both increase and decline in their relative shares? (d) What reasons can you find for the changes in each group of countries?

Relative Shares of World Manufacturing Output, 1880–1938 (percent)

	1880	1900	1913
Britain	22.9	18.5	13.6
United States	14.7	23.6	32.0
Germany	8.5	13.2	14.8
France	7.8	6.8	6.1
Russia	7.6	8.8	8.2
Austria-Hungary	4.4	4.7	4.4

Source: P. Kennedy, *The Rise and Fall of the Great Powers*, page 202.

Researching and Reporting Skills
The Research Paper

1. **Making an oral presentation** In preparation for presenting your research paper orally to the class, review your paper and its outline. Use index cards to take notes on the main points and supporting ideas you wish to include. Assemble any visuals that may help your presentation. Practice making the presentation, using only the cards and visuals. Time yourself and trim your presentation to fit the time allotted. When you have made your presentation, invite discussion. Revise your paper to include suggestions from the discussion that may improve it.
2. **Giving feedback to others on their oral presentations** As others take turns presenting their papers, listen and make constructive suggestions about their presentation, arguments, and thesis.

Critical Thinking

1. **Evaluating** (a) Make two lists—one for the problems women faced at the turn of the century and another for the progress they made. (b) In terms of the problems, how much progress was actually made?
2. **Comparing and contrasting** Both Britain and Germany had famous prime ministers in the late 1800's. How did the position of prime minister differ in Britain and Germany? Give examples to illustrate your answer.
3. **Applying a concept** The 1900's saw the beginnings of mass culture. (a) Explain what this term means. (b) What technological and social changes favored it? (c) What effects did it have on social and political life?
4. **Inferring** (a) What social welfare programs did Bismarck introduce in Germany? (b) What was his objective? (c) What difference did Bismarck's programs make to the people of Germany?

Perspectives on Past and Present

1. (a) What broad political, economic, and social issues remained unresolved at the turn of the last century? (b) What great issues are likely to remain unresolved at the turn of this century?
2. Fellow scientists were greatly impressed by the Curies' discoveries. What applications of those discoveries affect the world today?

Investigating History

Reference is made on page 575 to the persecution and massacre of certain ethnic groups. Read about one of those groups and write several paragraphs discussing whether the incidents might have been cases of genocide.

Unit VII Review

Geographic Theme: Movement

When did a global economy begin?

The century after the voyages of Columbus and Da Gama brought enormous wealth to Spain and Portugal from their trade and colonies overseas. England lagged in exploration, although its development of the joint stock company provided an economic resource for the future.

Under the mercantilist policies of the 1600's and 1700's, European nations competed for lands and trade. Out of a series of wars that ended with the defeat of France in 1763, Britain emerged with the lion's share. Not only the lands of Canada and India but also the oceans became spheres of British power. Although the American Revolution caused a brief setback, it was offset for Britain by the voyages of Captain James Cook, which opened the Pacific to British enterprise. In 1787, the first British settlers reached Australia.

While Britain's political power was expanding around the globe, the Industrial Revolution was taking place at home. The first breakthroughs in manufacturing came in the cotton textile industry. Hungry spindles and looms in Britain devoured huge quantities of raw cotton bought from the United States. That same cotton was shipped to markets around the world as cloth. By 1840, a world economy was in a sense being woven together out of cotton thread.

Three graphs demonstrate the enormous growth of the cotton trade in the early nineteenth century. The graph on page 479 in your text shows the rise in British consumption of cotton to 1840. The two graphs shown below indicate how much raw cotton was produced in the United States and how many British-made cotton goods were sold overseas. A global economy, led by Britain, had begun.

1. How did the Industrial Revolution hasten the growth of a global economy?
2. What do you think accounts for the great increase in cotton production in the United States between 1800 and 1840?
3. What three regions of the world bought the greatest amount of British exports of cotton goods in 1840?
4. How does the cotton trade illustrate the geographic theme of movement?

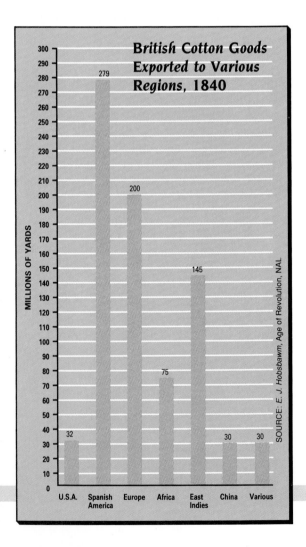

Raw Cotton Produced in the United States, 1800–1840

73 (1800), 178 (1810), 335 (1820), 732 (1830), 1,348 (1840)

IN THOUSAND BALES

SOURCE: *Historical Statistics of the United States*

British Cotton Goods Exported to Various Regions, 1840

MILLIONS OF YARDS

U.S.A. 32, Spanish America 279, Europe 200, Africa 75, East Indies 145, China 30, Various 30

SOURCE: *E. J. Hobsbawm, Age of Revolution, NAL*

Unit Perspectives

Understanding History

1. **Explaining** Describe the significance of the invention or discovery made by each of the following:

   a. Kay
   b. Whitney
   c. Watt
   d. Trevithick
   e. Morse
   f. Bell
   g. Marconi
   h. Ford
   i. Wright brothers
   j. Lister
   k. Pasteur
   l. Marie Curie

2. **Defining** Explain the relationship of the terms in each of the following groups:

   a. conservative; liberal; radical
   b. laissez-faire; industrialization
   c. industrialization; realism
   d. nationalism; romanticism; liberalism
   e. entrepreneur; stock; corporation; monopoly
   f. imperialism; social Darwinism

3. **Relating** With what artistic movement (romanticism, realism, impressionism) is each of the following people associated?

   a. Beethoven
   b. Courbet
   c. Delacroix
   d. Renoir
   e. Dickens
   f. Manet
   g. Monet

4. **Identifying** Describe the role that each of the following men played in nationalistic movements within their country:

   a. Mazzini
   b. Cavour
   c. Garibaldi
   d. Bolívar
   e. San Martín
   f. Dom Pedro
   g. Hidalgo
   h. L'Ouverture
   i. Bismarck

Critical Thinking

1. **Identifying outcomes** The Industrial Revolution had a tremendous impact on society. How did it change (a) the structure of social classes; (b) the distribution of wealth; and (c) representation in Parliament?

2. **Comparing** Explain how the following are both similar and different: (a) laissez-faire and social Darwinism; (b) the Monroe Doctrine and the Open-Door Policy in China; (c) imperialism in India and in Canada; and (d) utopian socialism and Marxist socialism.

3. **Inferring** What connection can be made between the following concepts? (a) imperialism and nationalism, (b) social Darwinism and colonialism, and (c) the ideas of the Enlightenment and the Industrial Revolution.

4. **Applying a concept** Imperialism was at times mainly political or mainly economic. (a) What are two examples of political imperialism? (b) Of economic imperialism? Explain your choice of examples.

5. **Comparing** (a) In what ways were Latin American revolutions of the early 1800's similar to the American Revolution? (b) How were they different?

6. **Analyzing** How did Japan's response to imperialism differ from China's? How did imperialism in Latin America differ from that in Africa and Southeast Asia?

7. **Evaluating** The growth of democracy was a major trend of the nineteenth century. (a) What were the democratic goals that people sought? (b) To what extent were those achieved by the end of the century?

Making Decisions

Discuss the following decisions in terms of the success of their outcome: (a) Congress of Vienna's decision to restore the Bourbons in France; (b) Bismarck's decision to set up welfare programs in Germany; (c) Napoleon III's decision to declare war on Prussia.

Continuity and Change

1. The Congress of Vienna sought to create an order that would preserve peace in Europe. (a) How successful was it in establishing and maintaining peace? (b) What new factors arose during that century to upset the balance in Europe?

2. Compare the Historical Atlas maps on pages 814–815 and 816–817 for the changes on each continent. How do those changes reflect both nationalism and imperialism?

Unit VIII

Years of Crisis

Chapters

	1880	1893	1906
Political and Governmental Life	**1880's–1914** Triple Alliance and Triple Entente divide Europe	**1890–1914** Kaiser Wilhelm II seeks to expand German power	**1914** World War I begins in Europe **1910** Revolution rages in Mexico
Economic and Technological Life	*Age of steam and steel*	**1898** Marie Curie discovers radioactivity	
Social and Cultural Life	**1882** Electricity lights New York streets **1880's** Women organize for legal and political rights	*Nijinsky of the Russian Ballet*	*Detail from mural by Siqueiros, Chapultepec Palace* **1914–1947** Gandhi protests against British rule in India

Although Europe dominated the globe at the start of the twentieth century, its worldwide empires were to crumble within 50 years. Several nations would undergo serious political changes. All endured a global depression that weakened industry and left people without work. Two terrible wars caused vast destruction and left millions of people dead. Among peoples of Asia, Africa, and the Middle East, the spread of nationalism brought a demand for freedom. Out of crisis, people discovered new hopes and aspirations.

1919　　　　　**1932**　　　　　**1945**

1917
Lenin leads Russian Revolution
▼

1929
Stock market crash begins depression

1928
Stalin launches Five-Year Plan

Flappers portray the 1920's

1933
Hitler comes to power

1936–1939
Civil war in Spain

Battle of Britain

1939
World War II begins in Europe

1935
Nuremberg Laws take citizenship away from German Jews

1945
The war is over ▶

1945
Atomic bombs destroy Hiroshima and Nagasaki

1945
United Nations is founded ▶

World War I

Soon after the assassination at Sarajevo, French newspaper readers saw this picture with a report of the event. The picture's tone would catch many an eye.

Read and Understand

1. Conflicts divided Europe.
2. Europe plunged into war.
3. The war dragged on for four years.
4. Peace stood on shaky foundations.

Key Terms

militarism
ultimatum
mobilize
rationing
propaganda
armistice
self-determination
mandate
reparation

June 28, 1914, was a hot, sultry day in Sarajevo (**SAHR**-uh-yeh-voh), capital of the Austrian province of Bosnia. Despite the heat, crowds had jammed the streets for hours. They were hoping to catch a glimpse of Archduke Franz Ferdinand, heir to the throne of Austria-Hungary. As nephew of the aged Emperor Franz Josef, Franz Ferdinand expected to rule Austria soon.

Not everyone in Sarajevo was pleased with this royal visit. Most Bosnians were Serbs, a Slavic people. Many wanted Bosnia to be part of Serbia, a neighboring Slavic country, instead of a province in the Austro-Hungarian empire. On this June morning, a handful of young

Emperor Franz Josef was admired throughout Austria-Hungary. Franz Ferdinand, however, was loved only by his wife and children. He was ill-tempered, miserly, and given to excess. For example, by the age of 46, he had shot 5,000 stags.

Serbian nationalists were scattered among the crowds awaiting the archduke's arrival. They were determined to give Franz Ferdinand their own terrible greeting.

The royal train arrived in Sarajevo shortly before 10 A.M. An honor guard of Austrian troops stood at attention while the archduke and his wife, Sophie, got into the open car that would take them to the official welcoming ceremonies at the town hall. A six-car motorcade left the station, led by the mayor of Sarajevo. Franz Ferdinand and Sophie rode in the second car. The royal couple smiled and waved while people cheered and threw flowers to them.

One of the Serbian nationalists, however, threw something else—a bomb. As it hurtled through the air, Franz Ferdinand threw up his arm to protect himself and his wife. The bomb struck his upraised arm and bounced off, exploding in the street. The blast injured a dozen people and sent a dark cloud of smoke into the sky.

After a brief pause, the motorcade continued at top speed toward the town hall. Although unhurt, Franz Ferdinand was furious. "Mr. Mayor," barked the archduke after the party had arrived safely at the hall, "we come to visit you, and we are greeted with bombs! This is outrageous!"

Before any further ceremonies, Franz Ferdinand wanted to go to the hospital to visit those who had been hurt by the bomb blast. Sophie insisted on going with him.

It was just after 11:00 A.M. when the motorcade resumed. Once again, the archduke and his wife were in the second car, riding behind the mayor. Unfortunately, no one had told the mayor's chauffeur about the visit to the hospital. Holding to the original plan, he turned down a side street. "You've gone the wrong way!" screamed the mayor. The driver braked and began to back up. So did the archduke's chauffeur.

It was too late. Standing at this intersection, no more than two steps from the archduke, was Gavrilo Princip (**PREEN**-tseep). The slightly built young Serb was a member of the Black Hand, a secret society of Slavic extremists. Princip drew a small pistol and from point-blank range fired two shots. The first struck Sophie, and the second hit the archduke. Both died within minutes.

News of the assassination spread quickly across Europe. People everywhere were horrified, yet not really surprised. After all, there had been

Comparing pictures *The tone of this photo, taken shortly before the assassination, contrasts with that of the painting on page 582. How might photography as a medium change the reporting of events in the news?*

more than 40 assassinations of political leaders between 1900 and 1914.

Yet the assassination in Sarajevo was different from the others. It started a chain of events that, within five weeks, dragged almost all the countries of Europe into war. Two people died that June morning in Bosnia, but the terrible conflict that followed claimed the lives of more than 8 million soldiers and 6 million civilians.

In this chapter, we will look at both the immediate and the underlying causes of the war. Then we will see why neither side was able to win the quick victory that all leaders expected. Finally, we will see how the war left a bitter legacy for victors and vanquished alike.

Conflicts divided Europe. 1

How did the assassination of Franz Ferdinand trigger a world war? The answers are not simple. By itself, the murder of Franz Ferdinand could never have started such a vast conflict. However, tensions had been building in Europe for more than 50 years. Rivalry among the Great Powers—

Photography resulted in more realistic representation of the news than that shown in the overly-sensational picture on page 582. Nonetheless, photography could be used to focus on relatively dramatic or sensational items in the news.

583

Kaiser William II liked nothing better than to review his troops. He is shown here dressed in his army greatcoat and spiked helmet.

Austria-Hungary, Great Britain, Germany, France, Italy, and Russia—had led to crisis after crisis. The assassination at Sarajevo was merely the last step on the long road to war, a road down which Europe had been drifting for decades.

Bismarck shaped European alliances.

The conflict grew in part from a network of alliances going back to the 1870's. Ironically, these alliances had been designed to keep peace.

Between 1865 and 1871, Prussia's blood-and-iron chancellor, Otto von Bismarck, freely used war to unify Germany (page 521). After 1871, however, Bismarck turned to a policy of peace. Germany, he said, was a "satisfied power." Bismarck's new goal was to prevent war because war might shatter his newly created German empire. From 1871 to 1890, Bismarck worked to keep peace in Europe.

Bismarck saw France as the greatest threat to peace, because the French wanted revenge for their defeat in the Franco-Prussian War (page 523). Bismarck's first goal, therefore, was to isolate France. "As long as it is without allies," Bismarck stressed, "France poses no danger to us."

In 1879, Bismarck succeeded in partially isolating France by forming the Dual Alliance between Germany and Austria-Hungary. Three years later, these two countries were joined by Italy, making the Triple Alliance. In 1887, Bismarck took yet another possible ally away from France by making a treaty with Russia.

Bismarck's alliances were a fragile network. Germany had ties to both Austria-Hungary and Russia. Yet those two empires were locked in a struggle over the Balkans. Could Germany hold both its allies? And what part would Britain play? For the moment, the British seemed content to stand proudly alone. However, it was clear that a shift in the diplomatic winds might blow apart the web of treaties.

Shifting alliances threatened peace.

In 1890, Germany's foreign policy changed abruptly. In that year, Kaiser William II forced Bismarck to resign. Unlike his grandfather, who had let Bismarck rule Germany for more than 20 years, the new kaiser was determined to be his own master. A proud and stubborn man, William II was eager to show the world just how mighty Germany had become. The army was his greatest pride. "I and the army were born for each other," said William II at his coronation in 1888.

William II set Germany on a new course. Shortly after coming to power, he let the treaty of friendship between Russia and Germany lapse. The French were delighted. For years, France had been loaning Russia money for industrial development, hoping to earn the goodwill of the Russian government. The French reaped their reward in 1894 when Russia made an alliance with France.

According to the terms of the treaty, France and Russia promised to come to each other's aid if either was attacked by a third country. Such a treaty had been Bismarck's greatest fear. A war with either Russia or France would make Germany the enemy of both. Germany would then be forced to fight on both its eastern and western borders.

The impulsive kaiser made an even greater mistake in his dealings with Great Britain. Britain and Germany were economic rivals, but they had remained on fairly friendly terms during much of the 1800's. The kaiser himself was half English, as his mother was Queen Victoria's eldest

Historians have speculated that Kaiser William II's militaristic qualities developed because he was born with a withered left arm. He became a warrior to prove himself equal to his respected grandfather, William I.

daughter. Nevertheless, he held a lifelong grudge against Britain. He envied its worldwide empire and its mighty navy. The kaiser decided that Germany should challenge Britain. During the 1890's, Germany built its own small colonial empire, threatening British and French dominance. At the same time, William II started a tremendous ship-building program, planning to make the German navy equal to Britain's.

Alarmed, Great Britain began to enlarge its own fleet, joining Germany in a naval arms race. Moreover, the British government ended its policy of isolation and sought allies.

In 1904, Britain signed a treaty of friendship with France. In 1907, it signed a second treaty, this time with France and Russia. These treaties were *ententes* (friendly understandings) rather than alliances. Although the Triple Entente did not bind Britain to fight alongside France and Russia, it did ensure that Britain would almost certainly not fight against them.

By 1907, two rival camps existed in Europe. On one side was the Triple Alliance—Germany, Austria-Hungary, and Italy. On the other side was the Triple Entente—Great Britain, France, and Russia. A dispute between any two powers could draw the entire continent into war.

The Balkans were a powder keg.

Nowhere was the situation more tense than on the Balkan Peninsula. With good reason, this area was called the powder keg of Europe. For nearly 100 years, many Balkan groups had been trying to free themselves from the Ottoman empire. As that empire weakened, several Balkan groups broke away. By the early 1900's, these breakaway groups had formed a half-dozen new nations—Albania, Bulgaria, Greece, Montenegro, Romania, and Serbia. Nationalism was a powerful force in all of these countries, each of which longed to extend its borders. For example, Serbia, which had a large Slavic population, hoped to absorb all the Slavs on the peninsula into its own nation.

Such nationalist movements threatened Austria-Hungary, which ruled many Slavic peoples. At the same time, Austria-Hungary saw the decline of the Ottoman empire as an opportunity to extend its own sphere of influence on the Balkan Peninsula.

Europe before World War I

KEY
- ▨ Triple Alliance
- ▢ Triple Entente

0 — 300 Miles

Map Study

To which alliance system did Italy belong? France? Belgium?

While Austria felt threatened by nationalism in the Balkans, Russia was delighted. The Russians were Slavs, part of the same large language family as the Serbs, Bulgarians, and many other Balkan peoples. Russia encouraged these Slavic groups in their struggles for independence. Russia had selfish reasons for supporting these countries. By gaining influence in the Balkans, Russia hoped to win access to the warm-water ports of the Mediterranean Sea.

Thus, Russia and Austria were on a collision course in the Balkans. The two countries almost went to war in 1908. In that year, Austria annexed Bosnia and Herzegovina, two Balkan areas with large Slavic populations. Serbian officials, who had hoped to take over the two provinces themselves, were outraged. Russia offered Serbia full support, but the Russian threat proved hollow. Russia was totally unprepared for war. When Germany stood firmly behind Austria, the Russians had no choice but to back down.

In the following years, one crisis after another broke out on the Balkan Peninsula. Each time, peace was maintained, but one nation or another felt humiliated. After 1913, no one was willing to yield again.

The German navy has been called William's toy. On every ship he had his own stateroom, decorated with pictures of his relatives and court favorites.

A warlike mood spread in Europe.

By the summer of 1914, many Europeans believed that war was inevitable. There were some leaders in every country who thought that war was the best way to settle international problems. As a result, all the Great Powers except Britain kept large standing armies. With such an army, every government now felt it had the muscle to back up its demands in a crisis.

Generals in each country tried to perfect their plans for war. Many military leaders yearned for a chance to put their plans into practice. Most believed that their weapons were so advanced that no war could last longer than six months. A number of generals feared that if war did not begin soon, other countries might grow stronger. They urged political leaders not to delay.

Militarism, the glorification of armed strength, won support from ordinary civilians too. To many people, war seemed the purest kind of patriotism. "Happy are those who have died in great battles, lying on the ground before the face of God," wrote a French poet in the summer of 1914. Millions of Europeans appeared to share such feelings. In the 100 years since the Napoleonic wars, Europeans had forgotten the horrors of war and remembered only its glories.

Section Review 1

Define: (a) entente, (b) militarism
Identify: (a) Sarajevo, (b) Franz Ferdinand, (c) Triple Alliance, (d) William II, (e) Triple Entente
Answer:
1. What factors led to the assassination of Archduke Franz Ferdinand?
2. (a) What were Bismarck's major goals after 1871? (b) What alliances did he make?
3. How was the Triple Entente formed?
4. How did Austria and Russia become rivals in the Balkans?
5. How did each of the following encourage the drift toward war in 1914? (a) political leaders (b) military leaders (c) popular opinion

Critical Thinking
6. Do you think World War I would have occurred if the archduke had not been assassinated? Explain your answer.

Europe plunged into war. 2

By 1914, rival alliances, nationalism, imperialism, and an arms race had brought Europe to the brink of war. All that was needed was a spark to light the fuse. The spark came with the killing of Franz Ferdinand on June 28, 1914, as you read at the beginning of this chapter.

Because the killer was a Serbian, Austria-Hungary decided to use the murder as an excuse to teach Serbia a lesson. "Serbia must learn to fear us again," one Austrian diplomat said bluntly.

Before acting, Austria consulted its main ally, Germany. Would the kaiser stand behind Austria if a war with Serbia involved other powers? Yes, came the kaiser's reply on July 5, and he set no limits on his support. The kaiser had given Austria-Hungary what amounted to a blank check. Germany would back its ally all the way.

Austria-Hungary made the first move.

On July 23, nearly a month after the assassination, Austria-Hungary sent Serbia an **ultimatum,** a set of demands that, if not met, would end negotiations and lead to war. The ultimatum was deliberately harsh. Serbia was to stop all anti-Austrian activity. In addition, the Serbian government would have to allow Austrian officials into Serbia to investigate the killing and judge those accused of the crime. Serbia had 48 hours to respond.

Serbian leaders hesitated. They knew that refusing the ultimatum would lead to a war with Austria-Hungary, a larger and more powerful country than Serbia. At the same time, they knew that they would be giving up their nation's independence if they allowed Austrian officials into Serbia. Serbia had no choice but to say no to this condition. Four days later, on July 28, Austria declared war on Serbia.

Russia mobilized for war.

Serbia, although weaker than Austria-Hungary, had a powerful friend of its own. As protector of the Slavic peoples in southeastern Europe, the Russian government announced that it would stand behind the Serbs. This time, Russia would make up for backing down in 1908.

At this point, railroad timetables played a crucial part in turning the conflict between Austria and Serbia into a full-scale European war. Because armies were larger than ever before, moving soldiers into battle took days of travel in thousands of railroad cars. Russia faced special difficulties because it had few railroads and a large army. Russia needed many weeks to **mobilize**—that is, to get its army into position for war. The Russians felt they could not afford to wait.

By July 30, the Russian government had begun moving its army toward the Russian-Austrian border. Expecting Germany to join Austria, Russia also mobilized along the German border. At the same time, Czar Nicholas II of Russia told the kaiser (who was his cousin) that the army moves were just a precaution. Yet to German eyes, Russia's mobilization amounted to a declaration of war. On August 1, the German government declared war on Russia.

Russia looked to its ally, France, for help. Germany did not wait for France to act. Two days after declaring war on Russia, Germany also declared war on France.

The Great Powers took sides.

Germany now faced Bismarck's nightmare— a two-front war. It would have to fight France on its western border and Russia in the east. However, Germany's generals had long had plans for such a war. During the 1890's, General Alfred von Schlieffen (SHLEE-fuhn) drew up a master plan that called for a lightning-quick attack against France while Russia slowly mobilized. Under the Schlieffen Plan, almost the entire German army would race west to knock France out of action before the Russian army was ready to fight in the east.

Speed was vital to the German plan. The French had troops and forts all along their border with Germany, and the Germans knew that breaking through this border would be slow work. There was another route, however. France's northern border with Belgium was unprotected.

Germany demanded that its troops be allowed to cross through Belgium on the way to France. Belgium, whose neutrality had been guaranteed by the Great Powers since 1839, refused. The Germans paid no attention to the refusal and marched into Belgium on August 4. Britain was

Posters were important in the war effort. Britain used Lord Kitchener, hero of the Sudan, on a recruiting poster (left). A poster with the medieval knight Siegfried urged Germans to buy war bonds (right).

saw fighting. Japan declared war against Germany within a few weeks after war had broken out in Europe. The Japanese quickly overran German possessions in China and captured most of Germany's Pacific island colonies. In Africa, the British and French conquered most of Germany's possessions. In German East Africa (modern Tanzania), however, Germany managed to hold out to the bitter end.

The Russian war effort weakened.

By 1917, Europe had lost more men in 3 years of fighting than in all the wars of the previous 300 years. Still there was no end in sight. Nowhere were the effects of war more sorely felt than in Russia. The Russians had poured all their resources into the war, but they were not enough. Russian soldiers faced the well-armed Germans with little more than their courage. They lacked guns, ammunition, warm clothes, and food. Badly led and lacking supplies, the Russian army felt betrayed by its leaders.

Discontent with the czar's government had been brewing for decades. In March 1917, Russian revolutionaries drove the czar from power and set up a provisional (temporary) government. (See Chapter 28.) Although the new government promised the Allies to go on fighting, few Russians were willing to fight any longer.

The United States entered the war.

Germany in 1917 also had its share of problems. Although the Central Powers had won important military successes in 1916, those efforts had nearly exhausted their resources and manpower. Food shortages were already critical because of the British blockade. Worse, Germany's potato crop failed in the summer of 1916.

Desperate to strike a decisive blow, Germany decided to take a new risk. On January 31, 1917, the Germans announced that their submarines would sink without warning any ship in the waters around Britain. This policy was called unrestricted submarine warfare.

The Germans had tried this policy earlier in the war. On May 7, 1915, a German U-boat had sunk the British passenger ship *Lusitania*, killing 1,198 people including 139 United States citizens. The attack had outraged people in the United States. President Woodrow Wilson had sent a strong protest to Germany. The Germans, fearing that the United States would declare war, backed down. They agreed to give warning to ships of a neutral country before firing.

When the Germans returned to unrestricted submarine warfare in 1917, they knew their decision would lead to war with the United States. However, they hoped to starve Britain into defeat before the United States could mobilize.

In fall 1916, Britain secretly shipped 47 of its fearsome new tanks to the Western Front for use in the Battle of the Somme.

Three days after Germany announced its plans, President Wilson warned Germany that the United States would take any action necessary to protect its citizens. Soon after, German U-boats sank three American ships bound for Great Britain.

In February 1917, another event added fuel to the fire. The British intercepted a telegram from Germany's foreign secretary, Arthur Zimmermann, to the German minister in Mexico. The message said that Germany would help Mexico get back its lost land in New Mexico, Texas, and Arizona if Mexico would side with Germany. The British quickly decoded the message and gave it to the United States government.

Many Americans demanded war against Germany. On April 2, 1917, President Wilson asked Congress to declare war. With this declaration, the United States entered the war on the side of the Allies.

The war came to an end.

At first, the German U-boat campaign went well. In April 1917 alone, German submarines sank over 800,000 tons of Allied shipping. However, the Allies quickly worked out a way to guard their ships. They organized convoys—large, specially equipped fleets designed to guard merchant ships. The convoy system dashed Germany's hopes for a quick defeat of Britain.

Yet the Germans were far from beaten. On the Eastern Front, they were making every effort to drive Russia out of the war. Although Russia was in chaos after the overthrow of the czar, its armies struggled on.

One party of Russian revolutionaries, the Bolsheviks, had pledged to make peace. The leader of the Bolsheviks, a man known as Lenin, was living as an exile in Switzerland. In March 1917, the Germans arranged for a special train to carry Lenin secretly back to Russia. Just as the Germans had hoped, Lenin quickly led his party to power. In November 1917, the Bolsheviks took control of Russia. In March 1918, Germany and Russia signed the Treaty of Brest Litovsk, which ended the war between those two countries.

Victory in the east allowed Germany to send nearly all its forces to the Western Front. For the first time since 1914, Germany now had more soldiers in northern France than did the Allies. Soon, however, the arrival of American troops would again tip the balance in the Allies' favor. Thus, Germany needed to act quickly.

The Germans prepared one final attack on the Western Front. They formed crack units of "shock troops" by putting veterans from the east alongside those who had fought in the west. In March 1918, 6,000 German cannons opened the attack with the largest artillery barrage of the entire war. The combination of artillery, skilled troops, and dense fog helped the Germans win victory after victory. By early June, they had once again reached the banks of the Marne. Paris was only 50 miles away.

Just as victory seemed within reach, the German drive stalled. The effort of reaching the Marne had exhausted supplies and men alike. Soldiers stopped advancing to loot shops for food. Germany had no more trained troops to replace those who had been killed or wounded. The only soldiers left were 15- and 16-year-old boys.

Meanwhile, American troops began arriving in France at a rate of about 250,000 a month. Marshal Ferdinand Foch (fawsh), the French general in command of the Allied forces, used the Americans to fill the gaps in his ranks. The "Yanks" were inexperienced but courageous and eager for action. With each passing day, the German army grew weaker while the Allied forces increased in strength.

In August 1918, the decisive battle of the war took place around Amiens. Leading the attack were some 300 Allied tanks that rumbled forward at a snail's pace, smashing through the German lines. The Germans continued to fight through September, but their resources were strained to the breaking point.

The other Central Powers were crumbling as well. First the Bulgarians and then the Ottoman Turks sued for peace. In November, a revolution in Austria-Hungary brought the empire to an end. Germany itself was on the very brink of revolution.

On November 9, 1918, Kaiser William II abdicated, and Germany became a republic. On the same day, a representative of the new government met with Marshal Foch. In a railway car in a forest not far from Paris, the two signed an **armistice,** an agreement to stop fighting. Two days later on November 11, World War I came to an end.

Trained airplane pilots were hard to find in World War I. After all, the Wright brothers first flew an airplane 120 feet in 1903. In fact, even experienced motor vehicle drivers were rare.

595

The cost of the war was staggering.

World War I had shaken the economic and social foundations of European society. A whole generation of young men had been struck down. France lost 20 percent of its men between the ages of 20 and 44, and Germany lost 15 percent. Almost every family in Europe had a son, a husband, or a brother who had been killed or maimed.

The war also left deep scars in the memories of those who survived. Among them were writers, painters, and composers who passed on their experiences to others through their works. Their bitterness and pessimism ran through much of the art and literature of the 1920's and 1930's. Disillusioned and disheartened, these young people became known as the Lost Generation.

Although the war had ended, it was foolish to speak of winners, said Winston Churchill, Britain's under-secretary of the navy. Victory, he said, had been "bought so dear as to be indistinguishable from defeat."

Section Review 3

Define: (a) no-man's-land, (b) U-boat, (c) rationing, (d) propaganda, (e) convoy, (f) armistice
Identify: (a) Woodrow Wilson, (b) *Lusitania*, (c) Treaty of Brest Litovsk
Answer:
1. What new weapons came into use in World War I?
2. Why is World War I called a total war?
3. How did the war affect the role of women in society?
4. What was the role of government during the war years?
5. (a) How did the war progress on the Western Front? (b) On the Eastern Front?
6. What part did each of the following countries play? (a) Ottoman empire (b) Italy (c) Japan (d) the United States
7. What factors led to Germany's defeat?

Critical Thinking
8. Restate Winston Churchill's evaluation of the Allies' victory in your own words. What evidence supports his statement?

Peace stood on shaky foundations. 4

The leaders of the victorious Allied Powers met at Versailles in January 1919 to hammer out the peace treaties that would officially end World War I. People hoped that these treaties would mark the beginning of a lasting era of peace. Yet even before the treaties were ready to sign, those hopes were dashed.

Wilson proposed a plan for peace.

It was largely because of one man that hopes had risen so high. That man was President Woodrow Wilson of the United States. Americans had fought this war, said Wilson, not for their own selfish ends but "to make the world safe for democracy."

In January 1918, while the war was still raging, Wilson had drawn up a series of proposals. Known as the Fourteen Points, they outlined his goals for a just and lasting peace.

Of the Fourteen Points, the first five set general goals for the postwar world. They were these:
1. Ending secret treaties
2. Agreeing to freedom of the seas
3. Removing economic barriers to trade
4. Reducing the size of national armies and navies
5. Adjusting colonial claims with fairness toward the colonial peoples

The sixth through the thirteenth points were specific suggestions on changing national borders and creating new nations. Wilson's guiding idea in these points was **self-determination**—allowing people to decide for themselves under what government they wished to live.

Finally, the fourteenth point proposed a "general association of nations" that would protect "great and small states alike." To Wilson, this was the most important point. He hoped for an organization that would keep peace by encouraging its members to solve problems through negotiation. This proposal eventually led to the formation of the League of Nations.

The world hailed Wilson's Fourteen Points as a landmark in the quest for world peace. Both the Allies and the Germans accepted Wilson's proposal as the basis for peace negotiations.

Wilson, a Democrat, angered members of the Republican party when he failed to name any of its most eminent members to the American delegation to the peace conference.

Conflicting demands dominated the conference.

When Wilson arrived in France for the peace conference in December 1918, people greeted him as an angel of peace. "Here and there along the way," wrote a reporter who traveled on Wilson's train, "peasant families were seen kneeling beside the track to pray for him and his mission."

The task facing Wilson at Versailles was not easy. Groups that had once been part of the Ottoman and Austro-Hungarian empires wanted the peacemakers to give them their own independent nations. However, many groups claimed the same lands. Not since Napoleon's defeat in 1815 had Europe faced such a task of rebuilding.

There were other problems as well. At first, both France and Britain had agreed with Wilson's ideas for a just peace. Now, however, both countries wanted to make the German people pay for the suffering the war had caused. Italy too had its own demands. In 1915, the Allies had lured Italy into the war by promising it parts of Austria-Hungary where many Italian-speaking people lived. Now Italy wanted its reward.

With so many conflicting ambitions, the peace talks at Versailles were stormy. Although more than two dozen countries were represented, the major decisions were hammered out in private by France, Britain, and the United States. Italy played only a minor part. Russia, which had suffered perhaps the greatest loss of life, was in the midst of a civil war and was not invited to attend the conference.

The Allies dictated peace terms.

Spring came late to northern France in 1919. April was dreary, cold, and damp. May at last brought sunshine and warmth. The finches and nightingales began to return to the gardens and parks at Versailles, the magnificent estate built by Louis XIV.

On the afternoon of May 7, about 4 months after the conference had begun, some 70 delegates representing 27 countries gathered in the ornate conference room. In the front, on a raised platform, sat the Big Three, the men whose views had dominated the peace conference. These were Georges Clemenceau (kleh-mahn-SOH) of France,

Wilson, Clemenceau, and Lloyd George (center three seated) look on as the treaty is signed.

David Lloyd George of Britain, and Woodrow Wilson of the United States. None of the defeated countries had been allowed to take part in the discussions. Their representatives were present now only to hear the verdict.

The verdict was indeed harsh. Back in Germany, officials were horrified as they studied the Versailles treaty. Several resigned in protest. In the end, however, they had no choice but to sign.

The final signing ceremony took place in the Hall of Mirrors at Versailles, the same room in which the Germans had forced the French to sign a humiliating treaty in 1871 (page 523). The date was June 28, 1919—five years to the day after Franz Ferdinand's assassination at Sarajevo.

The treaty fell far short of a just and lasting peace. These were its terms:

Territorial losses Germany lost 13 percent of its land, where nearly 10 percent of its people lived. France, Poland, Belgium, and Denmark all received some of the territory.

France regained Alsace-Lorraine, which Germany had taken in 1871. France also won the

After the war, American troops remained cooped up in camps in France waiting for ships to carry them home. Meanwhile, the nearly empty ship, *George Washington,* lay at anchor waiting for President Wilson. This soured the soldiers' attitude toward their commander in chief.

597

Europe after World War I

KEY

Territory lost by:

- Austria-Hungary
- Russia
- Germany
- Bulgaria

0 ——— 300 Miles

Map Study

Which of the Central Powers were forced to cede land to Poland? Which of the Allies?

Map Study answers: Germany, Austria; Russia

War guilt The most severe part of the Treaty, however, was Article 231, the "war-guilt" clause. This clause placed sole blame for World War I on Germany's shoulders. As a result, the Germans were obliged to pay **reparations** to the Allies— that is, money to compensate for the enormous costs of the war. The final reparations bill came to $31 billion, which Germany was to pay over the next 30 years.

The League of Nations Although the peace conference dashed many of Wilson's hopes for a just and lasting peace, he did win one major victory. The Allies agreed to create a League of Nations. Five large nations—the United States, Britain, France, Italy, and Japan—were to be permanent members of its Executive Council. The League would also have a general assembly at which representatives of 42 Allied and neutral nations would meet. Germany was deliberately left out. So was Russia, which was then in the midst of civil war and revolution.

Other treaties created new nations.

The treaty with Germany was just one of five signed in Paris during 1919 and 1920. The other Central Powers also suffered losses in territory. However, out of the ashes of these old empires, Wilson's idea of national self-determination guided the creation of several new nations.

The Turkish treaty The treaty with the Ottoman Turks forced them to give up almost all of their old empire. Their territory was limited to what is now the country of Turkey.

The lands that the Ottomans lost in Southwest Asia were formed into several new territories— Iraq, Lebanon, Palestine, Transjordan, and Syria. Like the former German colonies, these areas became mandates. The League of Nations assigned control of Palestine, Iraq, and Transjordan to Great

right to work the rich mines of the Saar basin for 15 years. After that time, the people of the Saar region were to have the right to rejoin Germany if they so wished.

Poland, which had not appeared on a map of Europe since it was partitioned in the 1790's, once again became an independent nation. The new Poland received a large strip of German land called the Polish corridor. This strip cut off East Prussia from the rest of Germany and gave Poland access to the Baltic Sea.

All of Germany's territories in Africa and the Pacific were given as **mandates** to Britain, France, and Japan. A mandate was a territory that was administered on behalf of the League of Nations. The Allies were to govern these lands until they were judged fit for independence.

Military restrictions The treaty had many clauses designed to keep Germany from ever again threatening the peace. The size of the German army was strictly limited. Germany could not manufacture war material. Submarines and airplanes were also banned. Furthermore, the Germans were forbidden to place any troops in the Rhineland, a strip of land in western Germany between the Rhine River and the French border.

Footnote to History

In 1918, one of the worst epidemics in history swept around the globe. It was a worldwide outbreak of influenza. In a year, it killed 10 million people—more than all the combat deaths of the war. The epidemic was partly a result of the war because troop movements carried the flu to every continent.

On May 7, delegates to the peace conference were greeted at the front gate by French soldiers, splendidly dressed in blue and red uniforms. The grim-faced Germans did not stop in front. Instead they drove around to the servants' entrance in back.

Britain. Syria and Lebanon went to France. Some Turkish territory went to Greece. The treaty also recognized the independence of Arabia.

The break-up of Austria-Hungary Several new countries were carved out of the Austro-Hungarian empire. Austria and Hungary were both recognized as independent nations. However, they lost some territory to the newly formed countries of Poland, Czechoslovakia, and Yugoslavia. Trieste and southern Tyrol went to Italy. Finally, Romania received a large area, thus doubling its size.

The Bulgarian treaty By this treaty, the defeated Bulgaria gave up land to Romania, Yugoslavia, and Greece. Bulgaria had to pay almost a half-billion dollars in reparations.

Russian losses Even before the peace treaty was signed, Germany had to cancel the severe Treaty of Brest Litovsk in which Germany had taken about a fourth of Russia's European territory. Even so, Russia ended by losing more land than Germany.

The Allies, fearful of Russia's new revolutionary government, wanted to protect Russia's neighbors on the west. As a result, Russia lost the province of Bessarabia in the southwest to Romania. Poland also gained much Russian territory. Finland, Estonia, Latvia, and Lithuania, which had all declared their independence from Russia in 1918, were recognized as nations.

In several of these other treaties, the Allies added clauses aimed at further limiting Germany's size and power. The new country of Czechoslovakia, for example, included a region called the Sudetenland (soo-**DAYT**-uhn-LAND). Some 3 million Germans lived in this border region. Furthermore, the treaties forbade any *anschluss* (union) between Germany and the now tiny state of Austria, whose 6 million people were nearly all German speaking.

The United States rejected the treaty.

Across the Atlantic, many Americans objected to the Treaty of Versailles, especially to the League of Nations. Some believed that the United States' best hope for peace was to stay out of European affairs. Other Americans feared the League might undermine the powers of Congress in foreign affairs. They wanted to be sure, for example, that no American soldiers could be ordered to fight without Congress's consent.

After a bitter debate, the United States Senate refused to join the League of Nations or accept the Treaty of Versailles. The United States worked out a separate treaty with Germany and its allies several years later.

In the end, the Treaty of Versailles did little to build a lasting peace. Instead, it left a legacy of bitterness and hatred in the hearts of the German people. Other countries felt cheated and betrayed by the peace settlements. Lacking the support of several world powers, the League of Nations was in no position to take action on these complaints. It was, as one observer described it, "a peace built on quicksand."

Section Review 4

Define: (a) self-determination, (b) mandate, (c) reparations
Identify: (a) Versailles, (b) Fourteen Points, (c) League of Nations, (d) Big Three
Answer:
1. What were the general goals of the Fourteen Points?
2. What attitudes did Britain, France, and Italy take at the peace conference?
3. (a) Whom did the Treaty of Versailles blame for the war? (b) What role did the Central Powers play in the negotiations?
4. (a) What territory did Germany lose to France? (b) What new countries were created in eastern Europe from lands lost by Austria-Hungary and Russia?
5. What changes took place in Southwest Asia as a result of the war?
6. (a) Describe the organization of the League of Nations. (b) What powerful nations did not become members?
7. Why did the United States reject the Treaty of Versailles?

Critical Thinking
8. Review the proposals of the Fourteen Points (page 596). Which of these points, if they had been accepted around 1900, might have prevented war from beginning in 1914? Explain your answer.

599

Chapter Review 27

Summary

1. Conflicts divided Europe. By 1913, nationalism and the race for empires had divided Europe into two opposing camps. On one side was the Triple Alliance—Germany, Austria-Hungary, and Italy. On the other side was the Triple Entente—Great Britain, France, and Russia. Many Europeans felt that the only answer to the conflicts lay in armed might.

2. Europe plunged into war.   The spark that set off the war was the assassination of Austrian Archduke Franz Ferdinand by a Serbian nationalist. When Serbia rejected Austria's ultimatum, Russia leaped to Serbia's defense. The mobilization of Russian forces led to a German declaration of war. Defeat at the Battle of Marne dashed German hopes for a quick victory.

3. The war dragged on for four years.   The war in the west turned into a stalemate that lasted for four years. During these years, new technologies of warfare and the total involvement of citizens and governments made World War I unlike any earlier war. In 1917, heavy Russian losses contributed to a revolution that overthrew the czar. The entrance into the war of the United States turned the tide for the Allies in 1917. On November 11, 1918, Germany surrendered.

4. Peace stood on shaky foundations.   Even before the war ended, President Wilson proposed Fourteen Points for a just and lasting peace. In the end, however, the Allies dictated harsh peace terms to the defeated powers, causing extreme bitterness, especially among the Germans. However, Wilson's proposal to form a League of Nations was accepted. Strong isolationist sentiment led the United States to reject both the treaty and the League.

Reviewing the Facts

1. Define the following terms:
   - a. militarism
   - b. ultimatum
   - c. mobilize
   - d. rationing
   - e. propaganda
   - f. armistice
   - g. self-determination
   - h. mandate
   - i. reparations

2. Explain the importance of each of the following names, events, or terms:
   - a. Franz Ferdinand
   - b. Bismarck
   - c. William II
   - d. Ottoman empire
   - e. Schlieffen Plan
   - f. Battle of the Marne
   - g. Zimmermann note
   - h. Woodrow Wilson
   - i. Versailles
   - j. war guilt

3. Briefly describe the chain of events that resulted in the outbreak of World War I.

4. (a) Describe war along the Western Front. (b) How did it differ from war in the east?

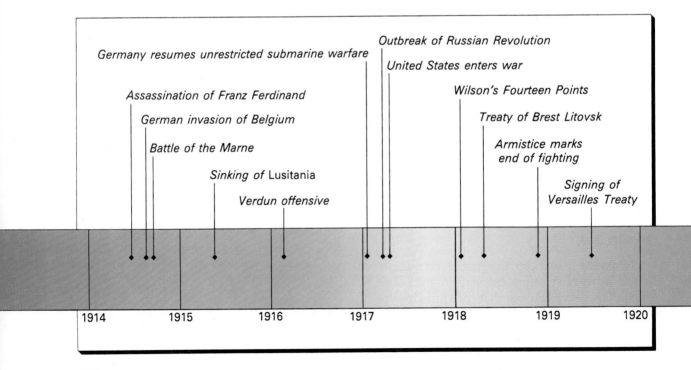

Germany resumes unrestricted submarine warfare

Outbreak of Russian Revolution

United States enters war

Assassination of Franz Ferdinand

Wilson's Fourteen Points

German invasion of Belgium

Treaty of Brest Litovsk

Battle of the Marne

Armistice marks end of fighting

Sinking of Lusitania

Verdun offensive

Signing of Versailles Treaty

1914   1915   1916   1917   1918   1919   1920

5. (a) What happened in Russia in 1917? (b) How had the war contributed to this event?
6. Why did the United States enter the war in 1917?
7. (a) What military restrictions were placed on Germany? (b) How did the Sudetenland and the prohibition of *anschluss* limit German power?
8. (a) Describe the League of Nations. (b) Which major powers did not belong? (c) Why?

Basic Skills

1. **Making a time line** Using information from pages 584 and 585, make a time line of events between 1875 and 1914 that led up to World War I.
2. **Making a Chart** Three major battles of World War I were the Marne (1914), Verdun (1916), and the Marne (1918). (a) Make a chart with the battles listed in a vertical column on the left. For the horizontal headings, use Objectives, Main Events, and Outcomes. (b) Which of these battles, if any, do you consider a turning point? Give reasons for your answer.

Researching and Reporting Skills

In this unit, you will be researching and reporting on history as viewed by contemporaries—the people who lived it and experienced it.

1. **Identifying primary sources** Using the subject catalog of your library, identify a number of primary sources, such as memoirs or contemporary accounts, about events during World War I. List the sources you find and select one to bring to class. Prepare a brief report on the book's content and point of view.
2. **Using biographies** Find a biography or biographical information about a political or military leader on either side in World War I. In what events did this person participate and what contribution did he or she make? Note that World War I marked the start of the air war, which had heroes such as Eddie Rickenbacker of the United States and Baron von Richthofen of Germany, as well as several famous squadrons.
3. **Using community resources** Find an individual in your community who remembers World War I or ask members of your family or friends for recollections of the war. Does your community have a memorial to those who died in the war?

Look for information on someone named on the memorial. What military units are represented and where did they see action?

Critical Thinking

1. **Applying a concept** Why is World War I considered a world war? Support your answer with evidence from two continents besides Europe.
2. **Comparing** Compare the membership and the objectives of the Triple Alliance and the Triple Entente.
3. **(a) Analyzing** To what extent had Bismarck's policies contributed to Kaiser William II's desire to strengthen Germany? (b) In what ways did the Kaiser's policies differ from those of Bismarck?
4. **Evaluating** (a) List five general goals proposed by Wilson in his Fourteen Points. (b) How were the objectives of France and Britain similar to Wilson's goals and how did they differ?
5. **Predicting trends** The era of the late 1800's and early 1900's was known as the beautiful era, *la belle epoque*. In view of the destruction and loss of life in World War I, how might that era be described?
6. **Evaluating** (a) Which terms of the Treaty of Versailles do you think resolved problems and thus contributed to lasting peace? (b) Which terms do you think failed to resolve problems or created new problems? Give examples and reasons to support your answer.

Perspectives Past and Present

The League of Nations was based on the idea of collective security—that nations would cooperate in maintaining peace. What examples exist today of international cooperation in keeping peace and resolving disputes?

Investigating History

1. The historian Barbara Tuchman has written two books about World War I, *The Guns of August* and *The Zimmerman Telegram*. Read selections from one of those books. How does the book help you to understand the war era?
2. Read or watch a film of the classic antiwar novel *All Quiet on the Western Front* by Erich Maria Remarque. What evidence does it use to support its viewpoint?

Russia in Revolution

This painting by a Russian artist shows the revolutionary leader Lenin speaking to a crowd of rebellious workers, soldiers, and sailors. In Russian art since 1917, Lenin always appears as a forceful, dynamic leader—the hero of the revolution.

Key Terms

abdicate
autocrat
nihilism
soviet
totalitarianism

Read and Understand

1. Russia struggled to reform.
2. Russia moved towards revolution.
3. The Bolsheviks led a second revolution.
4. Stalin became dictator.

It was cold, bitterly cold, in St. Petersburg on the morning of February 25, 1917. As the sun rose over the frozen Neva River, thousands of women huddled in the doorways of the city's bakeries, waiting, as they waited almost every morning, for bread. By the time sleepy-eyed workers began to trudge through the snow to factories and offices, the lines to some bakeries were several blocks long.

Then came the news: There was no bread. The bakers could not bake without flour, and there were no trains to bring flour to the city. Russia had been at war for nearly three years, and the country's railroads were under enormous strain. Nearly every boxcar was needed to carry food and supplies to the army.

With almost all of Russia's able-bodied men in the army, farming was done by women. They produced ample food, but the transportation system was unable to carry it both to the army and to the cities. As a result, the countryside had surplus food while the cities suffered shortages.

During past shortages, the women of St. Petersburg had quietly returned home without their bread. This time they refused to leave. Instead, they milled about the streets, shouting, "We want bread! We want bread!" They gathered on trolley tracks, stopping traffic. They forced passengers off streetcars and even turned over a few cars. Some women began throwing rocks through store windows.

The women did not consider themselves revolutionaries. They were just tired—tired of waiting for bread that never came, tired of watching their sons and husbands march off to die in war. They were tired of poverty—tired of seeing the carriages of the rich glide by while their own families huddled around grimy stoves in dark, crowded tenements.

Within hours, the women were joined by workers from several textile factories and the huge Putilov steelworks on the outskirts of the city. By early afternoon, great crowds had gathered along St. Petersburg's main street. The demonstrators shouted and sang. Many held up banners proclaiming "We want Bread!" or "End the War!" Others held a more menacing slogan—"Down with the Czar!"

Nicholas II, Russia's czar, did not pay much attention to the protesters. He was far more concerned with the war against Germany. On that same Thursday morning, Nicholas left St. Petersburg for his headquarters at the front. He felt certain that the police would easily handle the disturbances. Yet even as his train rumbled across the snowy Russian plains, unrest spread through the capital city.

By Monday, St. Petersburg was in the hands of rebellious workers and the many soldiers who had joined them. The czar soon realized that this was no ordinary disturbance, and he tried desperately to return to the capital. The uprising, however, had by then reached far beyond St. Petersburg. Railroad workers along the czar's route would not let his train pass. Meanwhile, at the front, soldiers refused to fight. Thousands deserted from the army daily. In this crisis, Nicholas called a meeting of his generals. They presented Nicholas with a bleak decision: He must **abdicate** (resign as ruler).

On March 2, 1917, Nicholas II gave up the throne that his family, the Romanovs, had held for more than three centuries. In this chapter, we will see that this revolution had been building for almost 100 years. We will also see why the czar's abdication did not bring peace or democracy to Russia.

Russia struggled to reform. 1

"Three centuries to build it up, and three days for it to vanish," wrote one observer in March 1917, speaking of the Russian monarchy. His comment was misleading. The old regime was not destroyed in a few days. The Russian Revolution was like a firecracker with a very long fuse. The explosion came in 1917, but the fuse had been burning for years.

To understand the revolution, it is necessary to go back in time at least to 1825. That year, Czar Alexander I, who had helped defeat Napoleon (page 464), died. With his death, Russia entered a period of turmoil that lasted nearly 100 years.

Most Russians lived as serfs.

In the early 1800's, while the Industrial Revolution was changing western Europe, Russia remained an agricultural country. More than 90 percent of all Russians depended on farming for their livelihood. A few owned large estates, but the vast majority—more than 80 percent of the people—were serfs. These men, women, and children worked for the owners of the large estates.

Serfdom had developed in Russia during the late Middle Ages (page 415). By the 1800's, serfs were permanently bound to the noble whose land they worked. Nobles had almost unlimited power over their serfs. They could buy and sell serfs in open markets like cattle. Landholders could beat their serfs or even exile them to Siberia. (Siberia is the bleak region of northeastern Russia that lies in Asia.)

By the 1820's, many Russians believed that serfdom must be ended. They argued that the system was morally wrong and also kept the empire economically backward. Serfs had no incentives to better themselves or learn new ways of farming. Why should they produce more food to fatten the landlords? Why should they learn

Discussion question: Why did serfdom continue in Russia long after its decline in western Europe?

603

Harnessed like oxen, Russian serfs haul a barge up the Volga River. In more industrialized countries, steam engines did such work.

new skills or start new businesses? Educated Russians were convinced that freeing the serfs was the first and most necessary step toward modernizing Russia.

In Russia, all it would have taken to end serfdom was the command of the czar. The czar was an absolute ruler. He had complete control over the lives and property of his subjects. He was the sole source of all laws. The czar was an **autocrat**, a ruler with unlimited power. (The word comes from Greek words meaning "rule by oneself.")

For a time, Czar Alexander I toyed with the idea of freeing the serfs. He even took a few slight steps in that direction. Yet he did not do so. When he died suddenly of a fever in 1825, an important chance for peaceful reform died with him.

The Decembrists revolted.

Alexander's death brought on a revolt in December 1825. The army officers who led it became known to history as the Decembrists, after the month in which their revolt took place.

The officers were all veterans of the long wars against Napoleon. While fighting in western Europe, they had come into contact with such ideas as bills of rights for citizens. When they returned to Russia, they found that the czar's government still ruled with unlimited powers. With no legal way to work for reform or even to express their ideas, a few young officers organized secret revolutionary societies. Their goal was to win a written constitution for Russia that allowed some of the rights of western Europe.

These secret groups were plotting an uprising when Alexander I died. No one was certain which of his several brothers would become the next czar. The oldest brother was Constantine, but he did not want to rule Russia.

Some young officers in St. Petersburg decided to take advantage of the confusion. They threw their support behind Constantine, even though he had already agreed to step aside for a younger brother, Nicholas. When it was time for the army to take the oath of loyalty to the new czar, the officers ordered their troops to shout "Constantine and Constitution." In their ignorance, many of the soldiers apparently believed that "Constitution" was Constantine's wife.

Troops loyal to Nicholas forcefully put down the Decembrists' revolt. Its leaders were executed or sent to forced labor in Siberia. Nicholas I never forgot the revolt. He ruled Russia with an iron hand for 30 years.

Nicholas I *resisted change.*

Nicholas I was determined to fight the "revolutionary spirit." He once said, "Revolution stands on the threshold of Russia, but I swear it will never enter Russia while my breath lasts."

When some educated Russians called for him to free the serfs, the czar refused. He agreed that serfdom was wrong, but he believed that he needed the support of the landlords to prevent peasant revolts. The czar explained, "The landlord is the most faithful, the unsleeping watchdog guarding the state; he is the natural police magistrate." Between 1825 and 1854, those faithful landlords and the czar crushed at least 500 peasant uprisings.

Nicholas also set out to combat any sign of political opposition among upper-class Russians. He did so by limiting education. After all, he argued, the government needed only a few educated officials. To end the demands for change, the czar's government strictly censored books, newspapers, and pamphlets. Nicholas also set up a secret police force to hunt out any person who dared to speak of change or reform.

Although Nicholas I succeeded in keeping revolution out of Russia, his foreign policy was less successful. In his efforts to take over parts of the Ottoman empire, he found himself at war not only with Turkey but also with Great Britain and France. The Crimean War (1853–1856) was a disaster for Russia. Russia's defeat on its own soil showed the weaknesses of the czar's autocratic government. The war also revealed that Russian technology was far behind that of Britain and France.

Alexander II *freed the serfs.*

In 1855, Nicholas I died, and his son Alexander II succeeded him. The new czar accepted the need for reforms. In fact, he commented that it was better to offer reforms from above than to have them forced on the government from below. Almost everyone agreed that the first step was the abolition of serfdom.

On March 3, 1861 (the day before Abraham Lincoln became president of the United States), Alexander issued a decree freeing the serfs. The new law left about half the farmable land in the hands of the nobles. The other half was parceled out to the serfs, who were required to pay the government for it. The government in turn paid the nobles for their lost lands.

The new law worked to the nobles' advantage. Most of them had heavily mortgaged their land. With the money the government gave them, they could pay off their debts. Moreover, they were also free of their old duties to feed, clothe, and house the serfs.

The newly freed peasants did not own their land outright as private property. Instead, the land became the property of the peasant community. Each peasant community was called a *mir* (meer). The mir as a whole owned the land, worked the land, and paid taxes to the government. It was almost impossible for a peasant to leave the mir, because then others would have to pay an extra share of taxes. Peasants remained tied to the mir much as serfs had been tied to their owners.

Freeing the serfs was only the first of Alexander's reforms. He also gave Russians a few more rights. For the first time, people charged with crimes could have public trials and a lawyer of their own choice. Alexander II also set up elected councils known as *zemstvos* to deal with local matters such as education and road maintenance. In addition, he expanded educational opportunities.

Reforms *encouraged unrest.*

Although some people were pleased with the reforms, many Russians believed that they fell far short of what was needed. In comparison with the people of western Europe, most Russians were still oppressed.

The peasants, for example, continued to bear many burdens. They alone paid a poll tax. They alone were subject to the death penalty if found guilty of a crime. They alone were bound to their mir by a system that kept them from moving freely from one place to another. To add to their discontent, few peasants had enough land to support their families. Russia's population was growing rapidly. Yet the amount of land available to peasants was limited. As a result, there were hundreds of peasant riots in the late 1800's.

Some educated Russians were also dissatisfied. Censorship still forced them to discuss their political ideas in secret. Their secret societies became

A total of 10 million serfs and their families were freed.

increasingly radical as the years went by. A few favored **nihilism** (from the Latin word *nihil* meaning "nothing"). Michael Bakunin, a nihilist leader, described their aims:

> Our first work must be destruction and annihilation of everything as it now exists. You must accustom yourself to destroying everything; the good with the bad; for if but an atom of this old world remains, the new will never be created.

Some idealistic students put their faith in the *narod*. (*Narod* means "people" in Russian.) Known as *narodniki*, these young students went among the peasants to teach them to read, to provide medical services, and to spread the idea of revolution. Hundreds of narodniki were arrested and shipped to Siberia. Those who remained grew more radical. Their goal soon became the assassination of the czar.

On March 13, 1881, as Alexander II rode in his carriage, a student threw a bomb at him. The bomb missed the czar but wounded several of his guards. As Alexander stepped down to help the injured, another radical threw a second bomb. His body shattered, Alexander could only whisper, "Home to the palace to die."

Alexander III upheld the autocracy.

Alexander III succeeded his father to the throne. Placing his faith in the "power and right of autocracy," he completely rejected reform. Alexander reduced the power of the zemstvos and put even stricter limits on what could be published. His secret police carefully watched both secondary schools and universities. Teachers were ordered to send detailed reports on every student.

Alexander set out to strengthen "autocracy, orthodoxy, and nationality." In other words, anyone who questioned the absolute power of the czar, who worshiped outside the Russian Orthodox Church, or who spoke a language other than Russian was regarded as dangerous. Finns, Poles, and other national groups within Russia were oppressed.

No group was treated more harshly than the Jews. They were forced to live in a special region in the southwestern part of the empire. Schools were closed to them. They were also subject to new laws that encouraged prejudice. As a result, pogroms (riots against Jews) broke out in many parts of Russia. Police and soldiers stood by and watched as Jewish homes, stores, and synagogues were looted and destroyed.

Nicholas II became czar.

When Alexander III died in 1894, most Russians breathed a sigh of relief. They hoped the new czar, Nicholas II, would lead a new era of reform. Once again, they were disappointed. When a number of zemstvos demanded a constitution, Nicholas told them to forget "such foolish dreams." "I shall maintain the principle of autocracy," he announced at his coronation, "just as firmly and unflinchingly as it was preserved by my unfortunate dead father."

Cultural changes Nonetheless, Russia was changing despite Nicholas's attempts to hold it back. In universities, students argued over the ideas of foreign thinkers such as Charles Darwin, Karl Marx, and Louis Pasteur. At the same time, Russian artists, thinkers, and scientists were making their own unique contributions. Novelists such as Leo Tolstoy and Fyodor Dostoevsky became great literary figures. For the first time, Russian authors were widely read in translation outside their own country. Sergei Diaghilev (dee-**AHG**-uh-lehf) helped give Russian ballet its reputation as the finest in the world. Composer Peter Ilyich Tchaikovsky (chy-**KAHF**-skee) wrote music for the ballet (*The Nutcracker Suite*), as well as for the concert hall. His *1812 Overture* celebrated Napoleon's defeat at Moscow.

Economic developments Russia moved closer to the European mainstream in other ways as well. Although more than 85 percent of the population still lived in rural areas, Russian cities were growing rapidly. Between 1861 and 1870, the population of cities and towns had increased 45 percent.

The czar's government encouraged the growth of industries by investing national funds directly or by loaning money to local businesses. The czar also ordered tariffs to protect Russian products from foreign competition. Most of the new industries were concentrated in such cities as St. Petersburg, Moscow, Lodz, Baku, and various Black Sea ports.

The czar also encouraged foreign investment. With the help of British and French investors,

Despite progress on many fronts, countless Russians still lived on the verge of starvation. Rural schoolteachers, for example, often lived in huts with the peasants' cattle, were housed in unheated sheds, or slept in the corner of a one-room schoolhouse.

One Fabergé egg held a working model of a
Trans-Siberian railroad locomotive and five cars.

*Inept as a ruler, Nicholas II
was devoted to his wife and five
children. Each Easter, the czar gave
his wife a gem-encrusted egg such
as the one above.*

work began in 1891 on the Trans-Siberian Railway
to connect European Russia with Russian ports
on the Pacific. When it was completed in 1904,
this railroad was the longest in the world.

Russia, however, was still far behind the West.
In 1914, even after decades of expansion, the
country's coal output was only one twentieth
that of the United States. At the same time, the
vast majority of the Russian people continued
to live much as their ancestors had, tending small
fields in the countryside. Those who did get jobs
in the cities were not much better off. Working
conditions in Russian factories were poor, and
wages were miserably low. Trade unions were
outlawed.

Russia was facing many of the same problems
that Britain and other countries had faced in the
early stages of the Industrial Revolution. The
gap between rich and poor was enormous. As
Leo Tolstoy wrote:

*All our palaces, all our theaters, all these
riches of ours, we owe to the effort of these
same hungry people who make these things
. . . The common people are hungry because
we [lucky ones] are too full.*

In the West, later stages of the Industrial Revolution brought a slow but steady improvement
in the standard of living for all. Perhaps the same
thing would have happened in Russia. We will
never know. Events moved too swiftly toward
a crisis.

Section Review 1

Define: (a) czar, (b) abdicate, (c) autocrat,
(d) mir, (e) zemstvo, (f) nihilism,
(g) narodniki
Identify: (a) St. Petersburg, (b) Nicholas II,
(c) Romanov, (d) Siberia, (e) Decembrists,
(f) Nicholas I, (g) Alexander II, (h) Alexander III
Answer:
1. (a) What group made up the largest share of
   Russia's population in the 1800's? (b) Describe
   their social and economic position.
2. What were the goals of the Decembrists?
3. (a) What attitude did Nicholas I take toward
   reform? (b) Toward freeing the serfs?
4. What reforms did Alexander II make?

5. (a) How did the position of the peasants change after they were freed? (b) How were their rights and freedom of movement still limited?
6. Describe Alexander III's policy of "autocracy, orthodoxy, and nationality."
7. (a) By 1900, how did Russia compare economically with western Europe? (b) What economic changes were taking place in Russia?

Critical Thinking

8. What opinion might each of the following people have expressed about Alexander II's reforms? (a) an old Decembrist (b) a serf in one of the new mirs (c) a nihilist (d) a narodnik

Russia moved toward revolution.

2

When the twentieth century began, Russia was still an autocracy. Yet a number of groups were trying to bring about change. Some were moderates, such as the Constitutional Democrats. This group hoped to limit the czar's power and create a constitutional monarchy like Britain's.

Other groups were interested not in reform but in revolution. Ever since the Decembrists of 1825, a handful of men and women in each generation had worked secretly for revolution. Only a few of these radicals were peasants or workers. Most were from middle-class backgrounds, sons and daughters of shopkeepers and teachers.

The revolutionaries were divided.

The radicals could be divided into two groups: those who appealed to the peasants and those who appealed to industrial workers. By the early 1900's, these two groups were known as the Social Revolutionaries (the SR's) and the Social Democrats (the SD's).

Social Revolutionaries The Social Revolutionaries believed the force to overthrow the czar's government would come from Russia's peasants. Unlike most European socialists, the SR's did not think that the revolution would begin with the urban working class. Instead, they considered Russia a special case because of its enormous peasant class. The SR's believed that Russia could develop its own special kind of rural socialism. Their goal was a government that would distribute the land fairly among the peasants. The SR's also wanted to replace the czar with a democratically elected government.

Social Democrats The Social Democrats were Marxists. Karl Marx (page 515) was a German philosopher who argued that the workers of the world would one day overthrow the ruling classes and share equally in society's wealth. Like Marxists in other countries, the Social Democrats were convinced that future revolutions would be led by an urban working class.

Among the leaders of the SD's was a short, balding man in his early 30's who called himself Lenin. Lenin (1870–1924) not only planned to overthrow the czar but also hoped to spark a worldwide Marxist revolution. The son of a prosperous school inspector, Lenin was born Vladimir Ilyich Ulyanov (ool-YAH-nof). He took the name Lenin for his underground activities. Lenin became a revolutionary after his older brother was executed in 1887 for plotting to assassinate Alexander III.

Lenin worked tirelessly for revolution. He was arrested, sent to Siberia, and eventually forced to live in exile outside Russia. Yet his faith in Marxism never wavered. Speaking of Lenin, an early colleague wrote:

There is no other man who is absorbed by the revolution 24 hours a day, who has no thoughts but thoughts of revolution, and even in his sleep dreams of nothing but revolution.

Bolsheviks and Mensheviks In 1903, Lenin's eagerness to act was the direct cause of a split in Social Democratic ranks. Most SD's thought that Russia would have to be industrialized before a Marxist revolution could take place.

Lenin believed the revolution could go forward at once. He admitted that Russia's working class was too small and too poorly educated to stage a revolution. Therefore, he argued, the workers needed a tiny, determined group of Marxists to show them the way. After overthrowing the czar, said Lenin, these radicals would establish a "dictatorship of the proletariat" until the people were able to take charge of society themselves.

Also prominent were the anarchists who believed in a society in which no person had control over another. However, to create such a society, they thought the existing system must first be completely destroyed.

Lenin presented these views at a stormy party conference in London, where many SD's gathered in exile. At that meeting, his policy was approved by a margin of one vote. From then on, Lenin and his followers called themselves Bolsheviks (BOHL-shuh-vihks), from the Russian word meaning "majority." Lenin's opponents who preferred to move more slowly were called Mensheviks (MEHN-shuh-vihks), from the word meaning "minority."

Actually, outside the convention the Mensheviks were by far the larger of the two groups within the Social Democrats. Most Russian SD's believed that Lenin's ideas contradicted those of Marx. Yet the names *Bolshevik* and *Menshevik* stuck with the two groups.

In 1903, such debates seemed academic—of interest to only a few political thinkers. None of the revolutionary parties posed a serious threat to the Russian government. Most of the radical leaders were either in prison or, like Lenin, in exile. None commanded wide popular support. These leaders were like officers in search of an army. They needed more than speeches and debates to enlist troops.

The czar made serious mistakes.

Between 1900 and 1914, Russia faced a series of crises that showed its weaknesses. Yet Czar Nicholas II still resisted change. Pressed by several moderate leaders, he grudgingly allowed some reforms. If World War I had not broken out, these changes might slowly have turned Russia into a constitutional monarchy. When the war came, however, time ran out for the Romanovs.

The Russo-Japanese War In 1904, Nicholas II decided that a victorious war would shift Russians' attention from problems within the country. Therefore, he declared war on Japan, Russia's neighbor in East Asia. Russia and Japan were both imperialist powers, and they were competing for control of Korea.

Russian soldiers and sailors marched off to war enthusiastically, but the result came as a complete surprise. They were soundly beaten. Defeat in war increased unrest at home and led to the revolution of 1905.

The revolution of 1905 On January 22, 1905, about 200,000 workers and their families approached the czar's Winter Palace with a petition.

They were asking for better working conditions, more personal freedom, and an elected national legislature. They were unarmed. Some carried pictures of the "Little Father," as they fondly called the czar. Nicholas was not at the palace, but his generals and police chiefs were. They ordered the soldiers to fire on the crowd. Between 500 and 1,000 people were killed. Russians called the day Bloody Sunday.

Bloody Sunday provoked a wave of strikes that spread across the country. By October 1905, the czar could no longer ignore the demands for change. He reluctantly promised more freedom. He also approved the creation of a Russian parliament, or *Duma* (DOO-muh).

The first Duma took office in May 1906. Its leaders were moderates who wanted Russia to become a constitutional monarchy more like Britain. The Constitutional Democrats, a middle-class party, held the largest number of seats. If Nicholas had chosen to work closely with the group, the history of Russia might have been different. The czar, however, hesitated to share his power with a parliament. Three months after the Duma opened, he dissolved it and sent its members home. There would be other Dumas, but none would have real power.

What were Nicholas's motives? He believed he was doing his duty to God and to the Russian

Russian troops leaving for the war with Japan knelt to the czar and the icon he displayed.

The first two Dumas were elected by universal male suffrage. The czar dissolved them as too liberal, suffrage was restricted, and a third Duma was elected. It supported imperial policies while the fourth Duma criticized the regime.

609

people by "being firm." In this opinion, he had the complete support of his closest adviser—his wife, the Czarina Alexandra. The czar was devoted to his "Alix." A German princess by birth, the czarina passionately loved her adopted country. She was determined to protect the Romanov dynasty's autocratic power and pass it on in full to her son, Alexis.

World War I ended Romanov rule.

In 1914, the assassination of Archduke Franz Ferdinand touched off a crisis (page 583). The long-standing feud between Russia and Austria-Hungary over the Balkans came to a head. Czar Nicholas made the fateful decision to go to war. It was this decision, more than any other single factor, that cost Nicholas his throne.

Few Russians understood why their country went to war with Austria and Germany in 1914. Nonetheless, they answered the call for volunteers with patriotic fervor. Millions of soldiers marched west, singing "God Save the Czar!"

Before the year was over, however, the dreams of glory had turned into a nightmare. Although they fought bravely, the poorly equipped Russians were no match for the German army. Germany's advanced artillery destroyed whole Russian battalions. German machine guns mowed down advancing Russians by the thousands. Defeat followed defeat. Before 1914 was over, more than 4 million Russian soldiers were killed, wounded, or taken prisoner.

The czarina and Rasputin's influence When more defeats followed in 1915, the czar made another mistake. Nicholas moved his headquarters to the front so that he could inspire his troops to victory. He left the government of Russia in Alexandra's hands. The czarina, unfortunately, was strongly influenced by her friend, the mysterious Rasputin (ra-SPYOOT-uhn).

Rasputin was a Siberian peasant who claimed to be a holy man. Burly, uncouth, and commanding, he won the confidence of Nicholas and Alexandra by seeming to cure their only son of a dangerous blood disease, hemophilia. For ten years, Rasputin wielded great influence at the court, nearly all of it bad. He obtained powerful positions for dozens of his friends, even though they were unqualified for the jobs. He urged the czarina to ignore demands for reform.

Most Russian nobles resented the influence of this upstart peasant. In December 1916, three young aristocrats decided he must be killed. They lured Rasputin to a mansion and fed him poisoned cakes. The poison seemed to have no effect on his bull-like strength, so the conspirators shot him a dozen times. Thinking he was finally dead, they then threw him in the Neva River. When his body was found three days later, he had died of drowning. The murderers confessed their crime, but they had such widespread support in the capital that they were never punished.

A nation in chaos By the winter of 1916–1917, conditions in Russia were desperate. Food and fuel were in short supply, and prices were wildly inflated. Most of the best soldiers had long since died, and the ranks of the army were filled with unwilling men gathered up by the draft. In St. Petersburg, the first strikes had begun.

With Rasputin out of the way, people began to grumble about Alexandra. Rumors spread that the German-born empress was spying for the enemy. At the palace, the czarina mourned Rasputin. She ignored those who advised her to withdraw from politics and allow the czar to choose ministers and advisers who better understood the public mood.

Nicholas himself seemed unable to make any decisions. "Is it possible," he wearily asked an adviser, "that for 22 years I have tried to act for the best, and that for 22 years I have been wrong?" Perhaps Nicholas already knew the answer. Back at his headquarters at the front, he spent hours playing dominoes, as if he knew that the real game was already over.

A provisional government tried to rule.

In February 1917 came the bread riots and strikes that forced Nicholas from his throne (pages 602–603). After he abdicated, no one was certain who ruled St. Petersburg, let alone Russia. The czar had delivered his abdication to members of the Duma. Accordingly, the Duma chose several leaders to act as a provisional, or temporary, government.

The members of the Duma were mostly conservative or moderate men. Their main goal was to create a constitution for Russia. They had taken no part in the demonstrations and strikes

Hemophilia is a disease transmitted by women to their sons. Alexandra's grandmother, Queen Victoria, was a carrier. Because her daughters married into most of the royal houses of Europe, hemophilia came to be called "the royal disease."

As in other countries, women in Russia held many crucial factory jobs during World War I. Women factory workers played a large part in the revolts of February 1917 that overthrew the czar's government.

that led to the downfall of the czar. As a result, radicals in the capital ignored both the Duma and the provisional government.

The power of the soviets Gradually, another political organization began to develop. Workers and soldiers in the capital gathered to form **soviets.** A soviet (SOHV-ee-EHT) was an elected workers' council. Many such councils had been formed during the 1905 revolution. Throughout the turbulent winter of 1916–1917, workers set up more councils to organize protests and plan demonstrations.

Every factory and military barracks in the city sent representatives to the St. Petersburg Soviet. Most of those representatives were socialists. Many were revolutionaries recently released from prison or just back from exile. They belonged to the major radical groups—the Social Revolutionaries, the Mensheviks, and the Bolsheviks.

Because most workers and soldiers obeyed its commands, the St. Petersburg Soviet was more powerful locally than the provisional government. Yet its members were seriously divided on many issues. For the time being, therefore, the soviet let the provisional government try to run the country.

Kerensky as leader The dominant figure in the provisional government was Alexander Kerensky (KEHR-uhn-skee), a young lawyer born in the same town as Lenin. Their fathers had been friends. Kerensky, however, became a Social Revolutionary rather than a Bolshevik. He was the only Duma deputy who was also a member of the St. Petersburg Soviet. Because he commanded the respect of both groups, he led the provisional government.

The provisional government failed.

Almost immediately, Kerensky and the provisional government made a fateful mistake. They chose to continue the war against Germany. Many Duma leaders felt honor-bound by treaties Russia had made with the Allies. Others feared that the Germans might seize St. Petersburg and restore the czar to his throne. Thus, they made the foolhardy decision to keep on fighting.

The Russian army was no more willing to fight and die for the provisional government than for the czar. Desertions continued. Peasants were eager to return home and obtain a share of the lands from the great estates, which were being divided. They ignored Kerensky's plea to forget land distribution until the war was over. "Let the officers do the fighting for themselves," a ragged soldier was heard to say on a train near Moscow. "I don't care who wins the war. It's only for a lot of capitalists anyhow. My house is far from the front, and the Germans will never get to my village."

While the Russian army was falling apart, the Germans launched their own "secret weapon."

On February 27, an estimated 1.5 million people flooded the streets of St. Petersburg to protest Nicholas's policies, yet the czar seemed more concerned about an outbreak of measles among his children.

611

They helped Lenin return to Russia. He traveled through Germany in a sealed passenger car. On April 3, 1917, he arrived at the Finland Station in St. Petersburg. A wild and happy crowd gathered to welcome the Bolshevik leader back to Russia. Lenin was home after 17 years in exile.

Section Review 2

Define: soviet
Identify: (a) Karl Marx, (b) Lenin, (c) Bolsheviks, (d) Mensheviks, (e) Bloody Sunday, (f) Duma, (g) Alexandra, (h) Rasputin, (i) Alexander Kerensky
Answer:
1. How did the ideas of the Social Revolutionaries differ from those of the Social Democrats?
2. (a) What course of action did Lenin support? (b) How did his proposal split the party?
3. (a) What was the czar's goal in the Russo-Japanese War? (b) What territory was in dispute? (c) What were the results of the war?
4. (a) Briefly describe the revolution of 1905. (b) What were its results?
5. How did World War I lead to the downfall of the czar?
6. After the czar's abdication, what part did the following play in government? (a) the Duma (b) St. Petersburg Soviet (c) Kerensky
7. Why was it a mistake for the provisional government to continue the war?

Critical Thinking
8. If Nicholas II had been a more competent ruler, could he have prevented the Russian Revolution? Or was it the result of events beyond his control? Present your viewpoint with evidence to support it.

The Bolsheviks led a second revolution.

3

Germany's strategy in helping Lenin return to Russia made sense. The Bolsheviks were strongly opposed to continuing the war. Lenin's return would certainly contribute to unrest in Russia, which in turn would help Germany's war effort.

Lenin, however, had bigger plans than simply pulling Russia out of the war. In a speech to the crowd that greeted him, he hurled abuse at the provisional government:

The people need peace, the people need bread . . . We must fight for the social revolution, fight to the end, till the complete victory of the proletariat. Long live the world social revolution!

The Bolsheviks gained support.

Later, Lenin met privately with his fellow Bolsheviks. The February revolution was only a modest beginning, he told them. It was now time to plan the Bolshevik takeover.

Lenin's plans seemed outrageous even to many of his followers. The Bolsheviks were not very popular. They had almost no support among the peasants. Even in St. Petersburg, most workers considered the Bolsheviks too narrow and undemocratic. There were only a few Bolsheviks among the St. Petersburg Soviet's deputies.

Revolutionaries soon toppled the statue of tyrannical Alexander III, the most hated czar.

The very narrowness of their party proved to be the Bolsheviks' greatest advantage. Among the dozens of parties that sprang up after the czar was overthrown, only the Bolsheviks were tightly organized and well disciplined. They were more like a tiny army than a political party. As a result, in the chaos of 1917, the Bolsheviks were able to exert more influence than larger but less organized groups.

During the summer and fall of 1917, events played into the hands of the Bolsheviks. First, the war went from bad to worse, and the provisional government still insisted on fighting it. Second, in September, General Lavr Kornilov (kawr-NEE-luhf) tried to seize power. As commander-in-chief of the army, he was much admired by the upper and middle classes, who felt that the revolution had gone too far. Some people even said that Kornilov would restore the czar. Gathering troops loyal to his cause, the general led an army toward St. Petersburg.

The revolutionaries stopped Kornilov in the same way that they had stopped Nicholas's attempt to return to St. Petersburg in February. Marshaled by the Bolsheviks, railroad workers tore up tracks and diverted trains, making it impossible for Kornilov's troops to advance. The Bolsheviks also organized Red Guard units to defend the capital. Meanwhile, groups of workers and soldiers met with the general's troops, urging them to join the revolution. Within a few days, Kornilov had no army left.

The Bolsheviks had saved St. Petersburg. Throughout September, popular support swung suddenly to the Bolsheviks. Party membership increased rapidly. Public opinion was clear on two things: Russians did not want the czar to return, and they did not want the war to continue.

Lenin's slogan of "Peace, Land, and Bread" captured the popular imagination. The Bolsheviks were the only party that seemed strong enough to protect the revolution against generals and czarists. They were the only party that seemed willing to end the war. They were the only party that promised land reform at once.

By late September, a majority of the deputies in the St. Petersburg Soviet supported the Bolsheviks. Leon Trotsky, second only to Lenin in popularity within the party, became the chairman of the soviet. Within days, soviets in Moscow and other cities also came under Bolshevik control.

Lenin took control.

Lenin decided that it was time to act. "History will not forgive us," he wrote, "if we do not seize power now." On the night of October 24, Bolshevik Red Guards took over government offices. The St. Petersburg Soviet ordered the arrest of the leaders of the provisional government.

The Bolshevik takeover was practically bloodless. The streetcars kept running, and the restaurants and theaters remained open. There were no loyal troops left to defend the provisional government. Kerensky and his colleagues disappeared as quickly and as completely as the czarist regime they had replaced.

The next evening, Lenin addressed the All-Russian Congress of Soviets, a group of representatives from soviets all over the country. They greeted him with thunderous cheers. After minutes of deafening applause, he told the crowd, "We shall now proceed to construct the socialist order!"

What was this new socialist order? The government ordered all farmland to be divided among the peasants. The Bolshevik government signed a truce with Germany, and peace talks began between the two countries. The new government also took over all major industries. From now on, workers' councils were to run the factories.

Lenin had long planned on a dictatorship of the proletariat, under which a small group would rule in the name of the people. He wanted Bolsheviks, and only Bolsheviks, to govern Russia. Yet other parties still had much popular support. When elections were held later in November 1917, the Social Revolutionary party won a majority in the new national assembly. In response, the Bolsheviks closed the assembly at once. The only democratically elected body in Russian history had a life span of a single day.

Footnote to History

Long before the rise of the Russian Bolsheviks, revolutionaries used the color red as their symbol. In one sense, it stood for the common blood of all people, regardless of social rank. In another sense, it stood for the bloodshed of violent revolution. The Bolsheviks' use of red has led many people to link it specifically with communism.

Artists, according to Harrison E. Salisbury, sensed that what was happening was "no orderly, conspiratorial movement but an elemental force . . . impossible to tame, as pervasive as a flood and as devastating as a forest fire."

613

Lenin was pleased. "The dissolution of the Constituent Assembly," he bluntly told Trotsky, "means a complete and frank liquidation of the idea of democracy by the idea of dictatorship. It will serve as a good lesson."

Many Russians objected to the Bolsheviks and their policies. There was widespread unrest. Discontent increased when Russians learned about the Treaty of Brest Litovsk, which the Bolshevik government signed with Germany in March 1918. In the treaty, the Bolsheviks surrendered one fourth of Russia's European territory to Germany. They also gave up many of the country's mines and factories. Many patriotic Russians were outraged.

Lenin was unconcerned about the lost lands. He was certain that the socialist revolution soon would spread to Germany and the treaty would be set aside. (He was half right. Russia got most of its territory back later in 1918. However, the land was returned because the Allies defeated Germany, not because of a revolution.)

Voice from the Past · *An Argument about Lenin*

A young American reporter, John Reed, arrived in St. Petersburg in August 1917. In his book, *Ten Days that Shook the World*, he wrote a vivid description of the Bolshevik rise to power. Soon after the Bolshevik coup, he heard the following argument between two Russians.

"Now brother," answered the soldier earnestly, "you don't understand. There are two classes, don't you see, the proletariat and the bourgeoisie. We—"

"Oh, I know that silly talk!" broke in the student rudely ... *"I'm a Marxian student. And I tell you that this isn't Socialism you are fighting for. It's just plain pro-German anarchy ... I suppose [the student went on] ... that you believe Lenin is a real friend of the proletariat?"*

"Yes, I do," answered the soldier ...

"Well, my friend, do you know that Lenin was sent through Germany in a closed car? Do you know that Lenin took money from the Germans?"

"Well, I don't know much about that," answered the soldier stubbornly, "but it seems to me that what he says is what I want to hear, and all simple men like me. Now there are two classes, the bourgeoisie and the proletariat—"

"You are a fool! Why, my friend, I spent two years in [the czar's prison] for revolutionary activity, when you were still ... singing 'God Save the Czar!' ... Didn't you ever hear of me?"

"I'm sorry to say I never did," answered the soldier with humility ... "You are probably a great hero."

"I am," said the student with conviction. "And I am opposed to the Bolsheviki, who are destroying our Russia, our free Revolution. Now how do you account for that?"

The soldier scratched his head. "I can't account for it at all," he said ... "but then, I'm not well educated. It seems to me that there are only two classes, the proletariat and the bourgeoisie—"

1. (a) What political group did the soldier support? (b) How can you tell what group the student probably supported?

2. What accusations did the student make against Lenin and the Bolsheviks?

3. What issue seemed to concern the soldier the most?

4. Toward which person was the reporter, John Reed, more sympathetic? Give evidence from the report for your answer.

Civil war divided Russia.

By summer, the Bolsheviks' opponents formed several "White" armies, so-called to distinguish them from the Bolshevik Red Army. Several Western nations, including the United States, sent small armies to Russia to help the Whites, a fact that the Bolsheviks later recalled bitterly.

Russia's civil war between the Whites and the Reds proved more deadly than any of the earlier revolutions. It lasted from 1918 to 1920, leaving an estimated 15 million Russians dead. Many died of hunger. Others were killed in the fighting. Still others fell victim to a worldwide flu epidemic that swept the globe beginning in 1918. Several thousand were shot by the Bolsheviks as suspected enemies of the new regime. Among the dead were the former czar, the czarina, and their five children. They were shot by the Bolsheviks in July 1918.

Victory eventually went to the Red Army, capably led and organized by Trotsky. The Whites might have won if they had not been deeply divided among themselves. They also lost support among peasants and workers because they threatened to restore farms and factories to their former owners.

In the aftermath of the civil war, Lenin and the Bolsheviks faced overwhelming problems. War and revolution had left the Russian economy in ruins. Trade was at a standstill. In the upheaval, factories had been destroyed. Many of the people who knew how to run those factories had been killed or imprisoned. Other skilled workers returned to farming just to survive.

Lenin restored order.

The socialist order of Lenin's plans seemed to be coming apart. Unrest spread. The Cheka, the Bolshevik secret police, became more and more ruthless toward "enemies of the revolution." Even some former Bolshevik supporters now turned against the new government.

The Kronstadt revolt For example, in March 1921, the sailors at Kronstadt, a major naval base on the outskirts of Petrograd, staged a revolt. In 1917, the sailors had been strong Bolshevik supporters. They had played a key role in overthrowing the czar. Now their list of complaints were almost the same as in 1917. They demanded free elections, freedom of speech, and the abolition of the secret police.

The Bolsheviks ignored the sailors' demands. Lenin and his colleagues brutally crushed the Kronstadt uprising. A former Lenin supporter was distressed. "What can I do now in this life?" he asked. "I cannot live outside this Russia of ours, and I cannot breathe within it."

The New Economic Policy Even Lenin realized that changes would have to be made if the Bolshevik regime were to survive. Late in 1921, he outlined what came to be known as the New Economic Policy (NEP). It called for a temporary compromise with capitalism.

Under the NEP, farmers were allowed to sell their surplus crops, livestock, and dairy goods on the free market. (Until this time, the Bolshevik government had simply taken whatever surpluses the peasants produced.) Individuals were permitted to buy and sell goods for profit. The government even allowed private ownership of some small businesses. At the same time, Lenin tried to encourage foreign investment.

A new name and a new party Lenin began some political reforms as well. Russia included many different national groups. Acknowledging these differences, Lenin created a number of autonomous (self-governing) republics within the country.

In 1922, the Bolsheviks gave Russia a new name. The country became the Union of Soviet Socialist Republics (USSR), a name sometimes shortened to the Soviet Union.

By 1922, the USSR had a new capital as well. During the civil war, Lenin had moved the capital from Petrograd (today called Leningrad) to Moscow, mainly because the inland city was safer from foreign invasion.

The Bolsheviks also gave their group a new name. It became the Communist party. The name came from the writings of Karl Marx. He used the word *communism* to describe the economic system that would exist after workers had seized power.

Thanks partly to the new policies and to the peace that followed the civil war, the USSR slowly recovered. By 1928, the country's farms and factories were producing as much as they had before World War I. After a decade of turmoil, life seemed to have returned to normal for most people in the Soviet Union.

The Soviets use the term *comrade* much as the French used the term *citizen* at the time of their revolution.

615

Two men struggled to succeed Lenin.

Lenin did not live to see this recovery. He died in 1924 after spending the last two years of his life as a semi-invalid owing to a series of strokes. In the year before Lenin's death, a quiet struggle took place within the Communist party to determine who would succeed Lenin.

Trotsky The most obvious candidate was Lev Davidovich Bronstein (1879–1940). He was better known as Leon Trotsky, the name he had used in the Bolshevik underground. Trotsky had been an important figure in the revolutionary movement since the revolution of 1905. He was the organizer of the 1917 takeover, founder of the Red Army, and a capable, popular leader.

Trotsky, however, had many enemies within the party. Some feared that he would become a dictator. They likened him to Napoleon in the French Revolution. Therefore, more and more party members gave their support to Joseph Stalin, secretary of the Communist party.

Stalin Stalin was a quiet man who rarely received much public notice. He had been born in 1879 in Georgia, the mountainous region on the southern border of the Russian empire. During his early days as a Bolshevik, he changed his name from Djugashvili (joo-guhsh-VEE-lee) to Stalin. It was an appropriate choice, since *Stalin* means "man of steel" in Russian. Joseph Djugashvili was certainly that: cold, hard, and impersonal. One Communist who worked with him during this period described him as "just a gray blur, looming up now and then darkly."

Stalin worked behind the scenes. As party secretary, he was responsible for hundreds of important appointments. By 1924, he had placed many of his supporters in key positions.

As he lay dying, Lenin realized that Stalin, not Trotsky, was the more dangerous man. "Comrade Stalin has concentrated enormous power in his hands," wrote Lenin in a secret document that was not published until long after his death, "and I am not sure that he always knows how to use that power with sufficient caution."

Other Communist leaders did not see the danger. After Lenin's death, most allied themselves with Stalin against Trotsky. Indeed, Trotsky was expelled and forced to leave the USSR in 1929.

Having disposed of Trotsky, Stalin turned against his recent allies. He used his enormous power within the party to isolate them one by one. By 1928, Stalin stood alone, as totally in command of the party—and therefore the government—as Lenin had been.

Section Review 3

Define: dictatorship of the proletariat
Identify: (a) Lavr Kornilov, (b) Treaty of Brest Litovsk, (c) White Army, (d) Red Army, (e) Kronstadt revolt, (f) New Economic Policy, (g) Union of Soviet Socialist Republics, (h) Communist party, (i) Leon Trotsky, (j) Joseph Stalin
Answer:
1. (a) What disadvantages did the Bolsheviks face in trying to take power in 1917? (b) What advantages did they have?
2. How did Kornilov's attempted coup help the Bolsheviks?
3. How did the Bolsheviks actually take control of the government?
4. What policies did the new government follow in each of these areas? (a) land (b) industry (c) democratic government (d) the war against Germany
5. What were the results of Russia's civil war?
6. (a) How did Lenin deal with political discontent after the civil war? (b) How did he deal with the country's economic problems?
7. How did Stalin rise to power between 1922 and 1928?

Critical Thinking
8. Why did Lenin's slogan of "Peace, Land, and Bread" win wide support? To what group or groups did each word appeal?

Stalin became dictator.   4

Although Trotsky and Stalin had much in common, their political views differed in one important way. Like Lenin, Trotsky was dedicated to the idea of *world* revolution. To him, the Russian Revolution was merely the first act in a worldwide uprising of the proletariat. Stalin, on the other hand, was not as concerned with developments outside the Soviet Union. He coined the phrase "socialism in one country" to describe his aims. To Stalin, the Soviet Union was the revolution, and it was up to the Soviet people to fashion a perfect Communist state. The rest of the world could wait.

Stalin blended Marxism with old-fashioned Russian nationalism. He was convinced that, sooner or later, foreign enemies would attack the Soviet Union. In the past, he observed, "Russia was ceaselessly beaten for her backwardness . . . She was beaten because to beat her was profitable and went unpunished." Stalin was determined to keep history from repeating itself. Thus, he set out to make his country powerful enough to withstand an attack. "We are 50 or 100 years behind the advanced countries," he said. "We must make good this lag in 10 years. Either we do it, or they crush us."

Stalin launched two new revolutions.

In 1928, Stalin broke with the policies of Lenin to create what were in effect two new Soviet revolutions. One revolution took place in industry and the other in agriculture.

An industrial revolution In 1928, Stalin outlined a Five-Year Plan for the development of the USSR's economy. The plan called for industrial growth in all parts of the country, especially in resource-rich eastern Siberia. He also set specific production targets for each industry.

The targets were deliberately set high. Many economists, including some in the USSR, were convinced that Stalin's goals were impossible to achieve. However, Stalin was determined to make the Soviet Union a great industrial power quickly.

From the start, the government decided who worked, where they worked, and for how long. It controlled every aspect of the worker's life. The secret police were ready to imprison or execute those who did not contribute.

Stalin's grim methods produced fantastic results. Although most of the targets of the first Five-Year Plan were not met, the Soviets made impressive gains. A second plan, launched in 1933, proved equally successful. Between 1928 and 1938, there was construction everywhere. The amount of electricity generated each year increased by nearly 800 percent. Over the same

Looking at economics *The rapid industrialization under Stalin's Five-Year Plans was achieved in part by limiting production of consumer goods. Instead, investment was made in state-owned mines, heavy industry, railroads, and energy resources.*

ten-year period, coal production jumped from 32 million tons per year to 115 million tons. Steel production increased from 4 million tons to 18 million tons annually. By 1938, the USSR was becoming a major industrial power.

An agricultural revolution Stalin's agricultural revolution was as complete and far more brutal than his industrial revolution. There were more than 25 million small farms in the USSR in 1928. That year, the government announced that these privately owned farms would be abolished.

In Siberia, with the help of icebreakers and aviation, vegetables and fruits were grown inside the Arctic Circle. Hitler envied Siberia's new-found mineral wealth and planned someday to make it his "new German living room."

617

They would be replaced by collective farms, large units worked by hundreds of families. The government expected that these large farms, equipped with modern machinery, would produce more food with fewer workers.

The peasants, many of whom had only recently won their own land, resisted fiercely. For centuries, they had struggled against the nobles. Now they were being forced to submit to yet another landlord, the Soviet government.

Stalin showed no mercy. Between 5 million and 10 million peasants died. Millions more were shipped to Siberia. Many farmers destroyed their crops and livestock in protest against collectivization. The government confiscated what remained of the harvest to feed city workers. Thus, for the peasants, the winters of 1931 and 1932 brought one of the greatest famines in the country's history.

Eventually, Stalin got his way. By 1938, more than 90 percent of all peasants lived on collective farms. Agricultural production was recovering. That year the country produced about as much wheat as it had in 1928, before collectivization.

The human cost of these forced changes was enormous. A British writer traveling in the country during this period met a secret-police colonel who had taken part in forcing peasants onto collective farms. The colonel told him:

I am an old Bolshevik. I worked in the underground against the czar, and then I fought in the civil war. Did I do all that in order that I should now surround villages with machine guns and order my men to fire indiscriminately into crowds of peasants? Oh, no, no!

The USSR *became a totalitarian state.*

If Stalin's government was this brutal, how did he stay in power? Why was there no rebellion? One answer is that people were afraid to speak out. The Soviet Union in the 1930's had become a **totalitarian** state—a country in which a dictator or a small group controls every part of the lives of its citizens. Not even the slightest dissent was tolerated by the government.

Joseph Stalin was an absolute dictator, more powerful than the most autocratic czar. He crushed his enemies and anyone who he thought might become an enemy. The secret police arrested and executed millions of suspected traitors.

One of Stalin's first targets was religion. The Bolsheviks had tried but failed to repress religion in 1921. In 1929, the government again struck at religion. Many churches, synagogues, and mosques were closed or put to other uses. Schools, which had been ordered to ignore religion, were now required to teach lessons presenting religion as backward and harmful. Yet many people in the Soviet Union remained devoutly religious.

In 1934, Stalin even turned against members of the Communist party itself. During the late 1930's, thousands of old Bolsheviks were brought to trial and executed for "crimes against the Soviet

Economics in Daily Life · *Tractors and Politics*

Tractors came to play both an economic and a political role in the USSR under Stalin. In 1928, there were only 7,000 tractors in the entire Soviet Union, even though most of the country's 150 million people were farmers. Tractors were far too expensive for individual peasant families. One of Stalin's goals in setting up large, state-run farms was to mechanize Soviet farming. By 1931, the need for tractors was even more serious. Angry peasants had killed about half the plow horses in the country as a desperate protest against Stalin's policy. During the 1930's, the government set up Machine-Tractor Stations throughout the countryside. They were more than equipment centers. They were also the rural political headquarters of the Communist party.

During Stalin's agricultural revolution, droves of peasants—sometimes entire villages—were packed off to the mines, timber camps, and construction projects of the Arctic north.

Many of those condemned during the purge were suspected of sympathy with Trotsky. Trotsky himself was murdered in exile by Stalin's agents in 1940.

Россійская соціалистическая федеративная Совѣтская республика   Пролетаріи всѣх страны, соединяйтесь!

РСФСР

**ОРУЖИЕМ МЫ ДОБИЛИ ВРАГА
ТРУДОМ МЫ ДОБУДЕМ ХЛЕБ
ВСЕ ЗА РАБОТУ, ТОВАРИЩИ!**

Much Soviet art in the Stalinist era celebrated the strength and importance of working men and women. This poster urges, "Let's all get to work, comrades."

state." Most of the accused had been longtime Communists who had fought in the revolution and the civil war. Indeed, many had helped Stalin become the party's leader. Among the accused were *all* the Bolsheviks who had held positions in Lenin's first government except Stalin himself.

People were arrested for having friends in foreign countries, for practicing their religion, for casual remarks overheard by police informers. Factory and farm managers who failed to meet their targets were in particular danger. Even the director of the Moscow Zoo was arrested because his monkeys got tuberculosis. The police themselves were not safe, especially if they didn't discover enough criminals.

Every family came to fear the knock on the door in the early hours of the morning. Such a visit might mean a son, father, mother, or daughter taken prisoner and not heard from again for months or years—or ever.

Only once during his long career did Stalin show any hesitancy. In 1932, after a bitter argument over the brutality of his campaign against the peasants, his wife Nadia killed herself. Grief-stricken, Stalin offered to resign. The party's leaders sat in shocked silence. No one wanted to be the first to agree that Stalin should step down. Finally, they asked him to stay in office. Never again did he offer to resign.

For almost 25 years, Joseph Stalin kept a firm grip on the USSR's destiny. More than any other individual, he was responsible for the Soviet Union's rise to a position as a great world power. Without his forced industrialization, the USSR might not have been able to stand up to Germany in World War II.

During Stalin's years in power, the Soviet Union became a modern state. Its people saw their standard of living rise. They became better educated and mastered the ever-changing world of science and technology.

The Soviet people paid a heavy price for the progress they made in the 1930's. In writing his autobiography, Soviet novelist Boris Pasternak refused to go any further than 1930. "To continue it would be immeasurably difficult," he said. "One would have to talk in a manner that would grip the heart and make the hair stand on end." In the end, the people of the USSR were less free in the 1930's than they had been in the days of the czars.

Section Review 4

Define: totalitarianism
Identify: Five-Year Plan
Answer:
1. How did Stalin's ideas on communism differ from Trotsky's?
2. (a) How did Stalin revolutionize Soviet industry? (b) What were his policies in agriculture?
3. What are the features of a totalitarian state?
4. What steps did Stalin take in the 1930's to stamp out all possible dissent?

Critical Thinking
5. What features of Stalin's government were similar to czarist government?

619

Chapter Review 28

Summary

1. Russia struggled to reform. While the Industrial Revolution was transforming western Europe, Russia remained largely agricultural. Most Russian peasants were bound to the land as serfs. A series of uprisings in the early 1800's caused Nicholas I to increase controls. The freeing of serfs in 1861 by Alexander II failed to end discontent. Alexander III tightened controls once again. Limited industrialization under Nicholas II brought some changes, but Russia still lagged far behind.

2. Russia moved toward revolution. In the early 1900's, Russian radicals worked secretly for revolution. Social revolutionaries favored a peasants' revolt, whereas Social Democrats, or Marxists, favored the revolt of urban workers. Lenin's call for a dictatorship of the proletariat split Marxists into Bolsheviks (Lenin's supporters) and Mensheviks (his opponents). Russia's defeat in the Russo-Japanese War, Bloody Sunday, and World War I all added fuel to the fire. Riots and strikes in March 1917 forced the abdication of the czar. When Kerensky's provisional government continued to fight in World War I, Germany helped Lenin return to Russia.

3. The Bolsheviks led a second revolution. In November 1917, Lenin's Bolsheviks came to power. The new government ended the war, divided land among the peasants, and took control of major industries. The following summer, civil war broke out as Reds (Bolsheviks) battled Whites, who were opposed to Lenin's reforms. After the Reds emerged victorious, Lenin instituted a New Economic Policy that offered a compromise with capitalism. The new government also changed the name of Russia to the USSR. Lenin's death provoked an internal struggle between Trotsky and Stalin, which Stalin won.

4. Stalin became a dictator. Determined to make the Soviet Union a world power, Stalin forced rapid industrialization and collectivization of agriculture. Millions of peasants were killed when they offered fierce resistance to Lenin's agricultural reforms. Stalin instituted a totalitarian state.

Reviewing the Facts

1. Define the following terms:
   a. abdicate   d. soviet
   b. autocrat   e. totalitarian
   c. nihilism
2. Explain the importance of each of the following names or terms:
   a. Decembrist revolt   c. Social Democrat
   b. Social Revolutionary   d. Marx

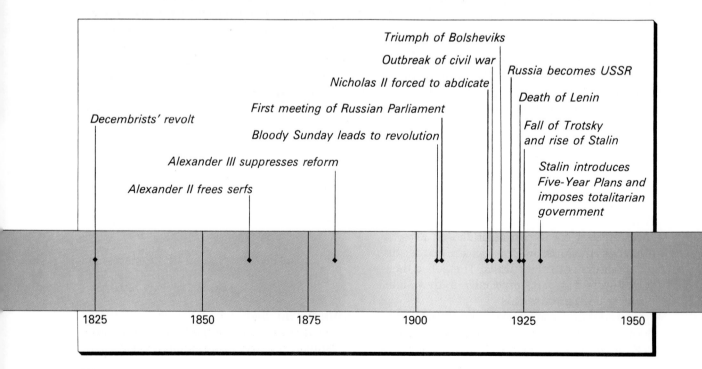

Triumph of Bolsheviks

Outbreak of civil war

Nicholas II forced to abdicate

Russia becomes USSR

First meeting of Russian Parliament

Death of Lenin

Decembrists' revolt

Bloody Sunday leads to revolution

Fall of Trotsky and rise of Stalin

Alexander III suppresses reform

Stalin introduces Five-Year Plans and imposes totalitarian government

Alexander II frees serfs

1825   1850   1875   1900   1925   1950

e. Lenin
f. Bolshevik
g. Menshevik
h. Nicholas II
i. Bloody Sunday
j. Duma

k. Rasputin
l. Kerensky
m. Trotsky
n. Kronstadt revolt
o. Communist party
p. Stalin

3. What was the attitude toward reform of each of the following czars? (a) Nicholas I (b) Alexander II (c) Alexander III (d) Nicholas II
4. (a) To what social class did Russia's radicals belong in the early 1900's? (b) Describe the goals of the two groups to which they belonged. (c) Into what two groups did the Social Democrats split?
5. Describe the role of each of the following in the provisional government of 1917. (a) Duma (b) Petrograd Soviet (c) Kerensky
6. (a) Briefly describe the Russian civil war that followed Lenin's takeover. (b) What was the result of the war?
7. (a) Describe the struggle between Trotsky and Stalin. (b) How did their views differ?

Basic Skills

1. **Sequencing** (a) List the following events in the order in which they happened: decree freeing the serfs, revolution of 1905, abdication of Nicholas II, Decembrist revolt, St. Petersburg bread riots, Russo-Japanese War. (b) Explain the importance of each event to the 1917 Russian Revolution.
2. **Reading a map** (a) Using the map on page 598, identify the European territories lost by Russia after World War I. (b) What was the effect of those losses?

Researching and Reporting Skills

1. **Using memoirs** Two memoirs from the time of the Russian Revolution provide first-hand accounts. During his exile in Mexico, Leon Trotsky wrote *A History of the Russian Revolution*. John Reed, a radical American journalist who traveled in Russia in 1917, wrote about his experiences in *Ten Days That Shook the World*. Read selections from one of these works. What impressions does it give of the times?
2. **Using literature** Find a book that discusses Russian literature. Identify some of the great Russian writers of the 1800's. Choose one and describe how that author's work anticipates the revolution.
3. **Using art or photographs** From history books,

encyclopedias, or art books, find three pictures that illustrate events leading up to or during the Russian Revolution. Explain what information these works provide about the revolution.

Critical Thinking

1. **Evaluating causes** Conditions within the country and the effects of the war both contributed to the breakdown of government in Russia. Which factor do you consider to be more important as a cause of that breakdown? Give reasons for your answer.
2. **Comparing** Lenin and Trotsky both emerged as powerful leaders during the Russian Revolution. (a) What contributions did each make to the revolution? (b) How essential was the work of each leader to the success of the revolution? Give evidence to support your answer.
3. **Analyzing** (a) List the original goals of the Russian Revolution. (b) To what extent did Stalin implement them or undermine them?
4. **Applying ideas** (a) What political and economic ideas introduced by Marx did Lenin adopt? (b) How did Lenin apply these ideas through the Russian Revolution?
5. **Analyzing economics** (a) Why did Stalin introduce the Five-Year Plans? (b) What were the objectives? (c) What were the economic results?
6. **Applying a concept** Identify five ways by which Stalin established totalitarian rule.

Perspectives on Past and Present

Terrible persecutions were known to have occurred in the Soviet Union during the Stalin era. The Gorbachev government has now permitted the release of information about some of these events. Use the *Readers' Guide* to locate news stories about the Stalin era. What events are mentioned and what is their significance?

Investigating History

1. Read selections from *Nicholas and Alexandra*, Robert K. Massie's history of the last czar and his family. Of special interest are the chapters "The Coronation," "Two Revolutionaries," "1905," and "Ekaterinberg." Write a brief report giving your impressions of the reading.
2. Watch one of the award-winning films of the Russian Revolution, *Dr. Zhivago* or *Reds*. What views about the revolution are expressed in each film?

Shifts in World Power

By 1930, massive demonstrations in support of independence were taking place all across India. This crowd carries a banner showing the wheel of Ashoka, a Buddhist symbol associated with the ancient ruler who had united much of India. India's flag carries the same symbol today.

Key Terms

shaykh
nationalized

Read and Understand

1. Indians organized for independence.
2. Nationalism spread to the Middle East.
3. Latin America faced difficult changes.
4. China overthrew its emperor.

On March 30, 1919, and again on April 6, Hindus and Muslims came to the ancient city of Amritsar to fast and pray in protest against British rule in India. Amritsar was the capital city of the Punjab, a province in north central India. The organizer of these protests was Mohandas Gandhi (GAHN-dee), leader of India's growing movement for *swaraj*, or self-rule.

Gandhi's appeal for self-rule won wide support in the Punjab. Most of the Indian soldiers who had fought for Great Britain in World War I had come from this province. Treated as valuable allies during the war, they had returned home only to find themselves once again second-class citizens.

Amritsar is an ancient city 200 miles north of New Delhi. In April 1919, its population of 160,000 swelled as peasants from the surrounding hills came to the Hindu festival.

The British were alarmed by the protests in Amritsar, especially by the cooperation between Hindus and Muslims. Often, the two groups had been hostile to each other. On April 10, the British deputy commissioner decided to take a stand against the protests. He arrested two leaders of the protest movement—one Hindu, the other Muslim—and had them jailed without a trial. When their supporters petitioned for their release, British troops opened fire on them. As word of the British action spread, an enraged Indian mob took revenge by burning British banks and killing several British people.

To restore order, British officials called for army troops under General Reginald Dyer. Dyer had been born in India and had spent much of his military career there. Like many Britons, he thought that Indian nationalists needed to be taught a lesson. He got his chance on April 13, 1919.

That day, Indian peasants, dressed in their best holiday clothes, poured into the city for a Hindu festival. About 10,000 celebrators gathered in a walled park called Jillianbagh near the center of the city. A small group of nationalists was also meeting there, defying Dyer's ban on public gatherings.

Late in the afternoon, General Dyer arrived at the park with about 90 Indian soldiers. Some were armed with rifles, others with knives. Without a word of warning, Dyer ordered his men to open fire on the unarmed men, women, and children in the park. The terror-stricken crowd had no way to escape because Dyer's soldiers blocked the only exit.

The shooting, which lasted for ten minutes, was a slaughter. Nearly 400 Indians were killed. More than 1,200 lay wounded. Dyer ordered his troops to withdraw, leaving the injured on the ground without medical care.

News of the massacre spread quickly throughout India and to Britain. The British government ordered an inquiry. When questioned, Dyer expressed no regrets for his actions. He admitted that his men could have scattered the crowd simply by firing into the air. Instead, he had ordered them to shoot to kill. "I was going to punish them," he said. "My idea from the military point of view was to make a wide impression."

In this sense, Dyer's murderous behavior was completely successful. Never had a single British action made such a "wide impression" on the people of India. Almost overnight, millions of Indians changed from loyal British subjects into revolutionaries who demanded independence.

India was not the only country that set out to rid itself of foreign rule in the years after World War I. In this chapter, we will study the growing importance of nationalism not only in India but in the Middle East and China as well. We will also examine developments in Latin America, where countries faced intervention from outsiders as well as internal struggles.

Indians organized for independence. 1

By the early 1900's, British merchants, soldiers, and officials had been in India for more than 200 years. During those years, the British had gradually gained more and more control of India. By 1858, Great Britain ruled most of the country (page 542).

The British government boasted of the many improvements it had brought to India—bridges, canals, irrigation projects, and railroads. Many Indians, however, were not impressed. Their tax money had paid for most of those improvements. At the same time, many upper-class Indians were educated in British schools. There they discovered such European political ideas as nationalism, socialism, and democracy. Soon Western-educated Indian leaders began to apply these ideas to their own country.

In 1885, a group of Indian nationalists formed the Indian National Congress. Most but not all of its members were Hindus. In 1906, Muslims formed their own nationalist group, the Muslim League. Muslims made up a quarter of the Indian population and lived side by side with Hindus in many places.

The Congress party wanted self-rule.

At first, the Indian National Congress—later called the Congress party—spoke of "unswerving loyalty to the British Crown." The party was concerned mainly with winning equal opportunities for Indians in the civil service. Gradually, however, the demands of the Congress party

Like the Congress party, the Muslim League remained an exclusive, upper-class group until well into the 1920's. It's founder, Muhammad Ali Jinnah, quit the Congress party because of the its overwhelmingly Hindu membership.

broadened. Its supporters wanted Indians to have greater control of their own government.

After 1900, radicals within the Congress party called for an end to cooperation with Britain. "Every Englishman knows they are a mere handful in this country," a party leader told his colleagues in 1906, "and it is the business of every one of them to befool you into believing that you are weak and they are strong. [You must] realize that the future rests entirely in your own hands."

Yet, while the British may have been a mere handful in India, the number of Congress party supporters was not much larger. The vast majority of Indians were uneducated and uninterested in politics. In a country of 325 million people, there were only 8,000 university graduates. These educated lawyers, doctors, teachers, and journalists formed the nucleus of the Congress party. Often, they were as out of touch with ordinary villagers as were the British.

Gandhi led the independence movement.

The person who breathed life into Indian nationalism and brought it to the common people was Mohandas Karamchand Gandhi (1869–1948). As a young man, Gandhi studied law in Britain. Then he went to South Africa, where Indians filled many positions in the British colonial government. Like black Africans, Indians in South Africa suffered from the country's harsh racial laws (page 540). His sense of injustice aroused, Gandhi took a stand against these laws. In South Africa, he developed the religious and political ideas that made him one of the most influential leaders of the twentieth century.

While very conscious of his Hindu roots, Gandhi belonged to no specific religious group. He borrowed freely from all of the major world religions, including Christianity and Islam. His philosophy of action was based upon these four general principles:

1. Live simply, never seeking material rewards.
2. Be tolerant of the religious beliefs of others.
3. Spend life in the service of others.
4. Battle injustice in all its forms but never by resorting to violence.

Gandhi practiced what he preached. He lived an almost monastic existence, fasting regularly and giving up all possessions. Yet he did not retreat from the world. In 1914, at the age of 45, Gandhi returned to India. There he was welcomed as a leader in the Indian movement for independence.

Gandhi did not limit his campaigns to fighting British injustice. He also worked to end the injustice of his fellow Indians toward the untouchables, the lowest group in Hindu society (page 72). Gandhi treated the untouchables as equals. He called them *harijans* (hahr-ih-JAHNS), meaning "people of God."

Gandhi built his philosophy around peace and love. Everywhere he went, "this great soul in a beggar's garb," as the poet Rabindranath Tagore called him, won the hearts of the Indian people. Soon they were calling him the *Mahatma* (muh-HAHT-muh), meaning "Great Soul."

When World War I broke out in 1914, Gandhi and millions of other Indians put aside their discontent with Britain. Indian soldiers helped Great Britain defeat Germany. Gandhi, in keeping with his principles of nonviolence, served as an ambulance driver and received a medal for bravery. In return for India's help, the British government promised to begin reforms in India that would eventually lead to self-government.

Tensions rose after World War I.

In 1918, Indian troops returned home from the war. They expected Britain to fulfill its promise. However, British reforms fell far short of Indian hopes. As a result, acts of anti-British terrorism erupted in parts of India. The British struck back with the Rowlatt Act, a law that gave the government the right to jail protesters without trial for as long as two years.

To protest the Rowlatt Act, Gandhi called for days of fasting and prayer in the spring of 1919, as you read at the beginning of this chapter. Then the Amritsar massacre took place, sparking an explosion of anger across India. After the massacre, Gandhi wrote, "Cooperation in any shape or form with this satanic government is sinful."

In December, Britain tried to soothe tensions by passing the Government of India Act. This law set up a dual system of administration in which the British governor-general shared power with an Indian legislature. Although the law gave Indians more voice in domestic affairs, the

British kept control over foreign policy and national security. Gandhi and many other nationalist leaders felt that the new law was a token offer. They rejected the British reforms.

Gandhi saw clearly that India could not defeat Britain by force of arms. Instead, he called on Indians to use nonviolent moral force. He called his policy *satyagraha*, meaning "hold fast to the truth." In English, it is called passive resistance or civil disobedience.

Gandhi argued that Indians did not need guns or weapons to bring the mighty British empire to its knees. He reasoned that Great Britain could not govern India if Indians peacefully refused to cooperate. Therefore, he urged Indians to boycott British goods and to refuse to pay British taxes, obey British laws, or attend British courts.

For example, Gandhi urged all Indians to boycott British cloth and make their own. Gandhi himself devoted two hours each day to spinning his own yarn on a simple handwheel. He wore nothing but *khadi* (homespun cloth) and urged millions of Indians to follow his example. The result was that the sale of British cloth in India fell sharply.

Civil disobedience took no money, no physical strength, no skill with weapons. It took only courage. Men and women, young and old, weak and strong—all could join in Gandhi's movement. Millions did so.

Throughout 1920, there were dozens of strikes, demonstrations, and protests. Thousands of Indians were arrested by the British, who struggled to keep trains running, factories open, and jails from bursting. Despite Gandhi's pleas to avoid violence, protests often led to riots. Sometimes, hundreds were killed or wounded. Alarmed by the violence, Gandhi called off civil disobedience in February, 1922. One month later, he was arrested and sentenced to six years in prison.

Hindus and Muslims drifted further apart.

Gandhi remained in prison for only two years. He was released in 1924 because his health was poor. What he found on his release horrified him. Unity between Hindus and Muslims, which he had worked so hard to achieve in 1920, had all but disappeared. Hatred between the two groups threatened to tear India apart.

Gandhi urged Indians to live simply. He spun cotton thread to make his own clothing and wore only a dhoti *in peasant style.*

Conflict between Hindus and Muslims was not new in India. The two groups differed sharply both in their religious ideas and in their social traditions. Muslims believed in one God. Hindus believed that God was manifest in many forms. Muslims believed that all followers of Islam were equal before God. Hinduism accepted the division of society into castes that were not considered equal.

Besides such basic beliefs, each group had a number of customs and traditions that antagonized the other. Muslims, for example, ate beef, and Hindus considered the cow sacred. Some Hindus drank alcoholic beverages, a practice that was forbidden among Muslims. In towns where Hindu temples and Muslim mosques were close together, Muslims sometimes complained that Hindu music and processions disturbed their prayers. Hindus complained of hearing the Muslim calls to prayer five times a day.

About 70 percent of the Indian population was Hindu. Within its rigid social structure existed more than 2,000 castes.

Tensions increased as India became more urbanized during the early 1900's. Hindus and Muslims competed for jobs and housing in cities such as Calcutta and Delhi.

Hatred and distrust between the two groups erupted in riots. During the 1920's, there were more than 90 such outbursts, in which hundreds of Indians were killed and thousands wounded.

As early as 1906, some Muslims formed the Muslim League to ensure that their interests would be considered in discussions about India's future. The British encouraged the leaders of the Muslim League. They saw the Muslims as important allies in the British struggle to keep control of India.

Gandhi worked hard to heal the rift between Muslims and Hindus. He often spoke of the need for Indian unity. "There is no force in the cry of driving out the English if the substitute is to be Hindu domination," he said. "That will be no swaraj." Despite his urgings, however, by 1930 the Muslim League was calling for a separate Muslim nation.

Indians called for full independence.

During the 1920's and 1930's, British and Indian leaders held numerous conferences and round-table meetings. Meanwhile, both violent and nonviolent protests continued. Finally, in 1935, Britain passed a new Government of India Act. It called for a democratically elected national legislature to govern India. Each province was also to have its own assembly for local government.

The new act allowed Indians home rule—that is, complete control over domestic affairs. In 1918, Indians might have welcomed such a law. By 1935, however, home rule was no longer enough for most Indian nationalists. The Congress party was committed to full independence. "Between Indian nationalism, Indian freedom, and British imperialism there can be no common ground," said Jawaharlal Nehru, the leading figure in the Congress party in the 1930's.

The British reforms were not popular with Muslims either. The 1935 law provided safeguards for Muslim interests. However, the Muslim

Voice from the Past · *Gandhi's Plan of Action*

In 1920, Gandhi and the Congress party set a goal of winning swaraj within a year. Here were the steps Gandhi asked of all Indians.

Firstly, we must acquire greater mastery over ourselves and secure an atmosphere of perfect calm, peace, and good will . . .

Secondly, we must still further cleanse our hearts, and we Hindus and Muslims must cease to suspect one another's motives, and we should believe ourselves incapable of wronging one another.

Thirdly, we Hindus must call no one unclean or mean or inferior to ourselves, and must therefore cease to regard the "Pariah" class to be untouchable. We must consider it sinful to regard a fellow-being as untouchable.

These three things are matters of inward transformation, and the result will be seen in our daily dealings.

The fourth is the curse of drink . . . A supreme effort should be made . . . [to lead] liquor-sellers to give up their licenses, and the habitual visitors to these shops to give up the habit . . .

The fifth thing is the introduction of the spinning wheel in every home, larger production and use of khadi, and complete giving up of foreign cloth.

1. What inner changes of mind and spirit did Gandhi ask of Indians?
2. What outward changes in habits did he want?
3. What major social divisions did he think Indians had to heal to achieve swaraj?
4. How was Gandhi's way of seeking swaraj different from a purely political approach?

Generally, the British Labour party was sympathetic to Indian demands for independence while the Conservatives were less so. In 1935, Conservative Winston Churchill declared, "We are there forever."

League had decided to settle for nothing less than a separate Muslim nation. They had already chosen a possible name for their country—Pakistan (Land of the Pure).

Members of the league wanted Pakistan to be carved out of the parts of India where most Muslims lived. "It is a dream that the Hindus and Muslims can ever evolve a common nationality," said Muhammad Jinnah, leader of the Muslim League. Muslims, he said, were "a nation according to any definition of a nation, and they must have their homelands, their territory, and their state."

Thus, there was no easy answer for the British. To give in to either side would mean almost certain civil war. Meanwhile, Hindu-Muslim tensions continued to build. Riots became increasingly common. "We neither govern nor misgovern," wrote one British observer in the 1930's. "We're just hanging on."

Section Review 1

Define: (a) swaraj, (b) harijan, (c) Mahatma, (d) satyagraha
Identify: (a) Amritsar massacre, (b) Indian National Congress, (c) Muslim League, (d) Mohandas Gandhi
Answer:
1. (a) How did the goals of the Congress party change from the time of its founding to 1935? (b) Why did the Congress party have little popular support in its early days?
2. What were Gandhi's four basic principles?
3. (a) How did World War I affect Indian nationalism? (b) What was the effect of the Amritsar massacre?
4. What course of action did Gandhi suggest against the British?
5. (a) What were some of the issues that divided Hindus and Muslims? (b) What course of action did Gandhi support? (c) What did the Muslims want?
6. (a) How did Britain try to solve the problem in 1935? (b) Why did their solution fail?

Critical Thinking
7. In your opinion, why was Gandhi able to win popular support for Indian independence when earlier nationalist leaders had not been able to do so?

Nationalism spread to the Middle East. 2

Nationalism was also on the rise in the region known today as the Middle East. The Middle East includes the part of Asia that stretches from Turkey to Afghanistan. When Europeans began trading with Asia, they called this region the Middle East because it lay between their homes and the more distant eastern lands of India, China, and Japan. Today, North Africa is also considered part of the Middle East because it has strong cultural ties to the Middle Eastern countries.

The Middle East is the birthplace of three great religions—Islam, Judaism, and Christianity. Islam is the youngest of the three and has by far the most followers in the region. During the 700's, warriors from the Arabian Peninsula turned much of the Middle East into a Muslim empire. Later, Seljuk Turks and then Ottoman Turks conquered the region and adopted the Muslim faith. By the 1400's, much of the Middle East was ruled by the Ottoman empire. Only Persia did not come under Ottoman control.

The Ottomans ruled the Middle East for about 500 years. After the 1500's, their empire began a long, slow decline that lasted into the twentieth century. The Scientific Revolution and the Industrial Revolution, which dramatically changed life in Europe, made little impact in Ottoman lands. The sultans, or rulers, of the empire were not interested in factories or new inventions. Thus, the Middle East fell behind Europe economically, but it preserved its traditional ways.

By the end of World War I, the Ottomans had lost control of all their lands outside present-day Turkey (page 598). Great Britain received the lands called Palestine, Transjordania, and Iraq as mandates (lands to be governed on behalf of the League of Nations). France received Syria and Lebanon as mandates.

Many people in the Middle East did not want to be ruled by France or Great Britain. Just as the people of India fought to have their own nation after World War I, the people of the Middle East also launched independence movements during this period. Each group in the Middle East chose a different path toward nation building.

During World War I, the Allies encouraged nationalist revolts within the Turkish empire. A number of British officers fought with Arab nationalist armies. Among them was T.E. Lawrence, "Lawrence of Arabia."

Several countries chose modernization.

At the end of World War I, two countries in the Middle East chose to break with many of their Islamic traditions. Those countries were Turkey and Persia.

The Republic of Turkey In 1918, Turkey was all that remained of the Ottoman empire. It included the old Turkish homeland of Anatolia and a small strip of land around Istanbul.

In 1919, Greek soldiers invaded Turkey and threatened to conquer it. The Turkish sultan, weak and corrupt, was powerless to stop them. Many Turks believed that their country's only hope for survival lay in the overthrow of the sultan. In 1922, a group of Turkish nationalists overthrew the last Ottoman emperor. The leader of the revolution was an able army officer named Mustafa Kemal (1881–1938).

In 1923, Kemal and other nationalists established the Republic of Turkey, the first republic in the Middle East. As its president, Kemal set out to make Turkey a modern nation.

As a first step in modernization, Kemal broke the close connection between church and state that had existed under the sultans. He wanted to separate the laws of Islam from the laws of the nation. Kemal replaced Islamic laws with laws from various European nations. He replaced Islamic religious courts with secular ones.

Kemal also gave Turkish women equal legal and political rights, including the right to vote and to be elected to office. He had nothing but scorn for the Islamic custom that required women to wear veils in public. "What is the sense in this behavior?" Kemal asked. "Do the mothers and daughters of a civilized nation assume this barbarian posture? It makes the nation look ridiculous." Kemal himself made a point of dressing in European style.

Kemal believed that the future of his country lay in the education of its young people. He closed traditional Islamic religious schools and set up secular public ones. Students in the new schools learned to read and write the Roman alphabet, not the Arabic script.

Despite the limited natural resources of Turkey, Kemal also pushed for economic growth. He built railroads and factories in many parts of the country.

Mustafa Kemal (Atatürk), founder of modern Turkey.

By the time of Kemal's death in 1938, Turkey had a firm sense of national identity. It was also committed to modernization in the pattern of Europe and the United States. Kemal's influence was so strong that the Turkish people gave him the name Atatürk, meaning "father of the Turks."

The change from Persia to Iran Unlike the rest of the Middle East, the ancient country of Persia never came under the control of the Ottoman Turks. However, both Great Britain and Russia established spheres of influence there in the 1800's. By the early 1900's, the two countries virtually controlled the Persian government.

In 1921, a Persian army officer named Reza Khan seized control of the weak Persian government. By 1925, he had deposed the ruling shah and taken the title for himself. He ruled as Reza Shah Pahlavi.

Reza Shah set out to modernize his country and free it from foreign rule. He was remarkably successful in both these goals. As Atatürk had done in Turkey, Reza Shah set up public schools, built roads and railroads, encouraged industrial growth, and gave women more rights. Unlike Atatürk, however, the shah kept all power in his own hands. In 1935, he changed the name of his country from Persia to Iran.

Because of its limited resources, Turkey remained primarily an agricultural country. Its ties to the West helped make Turkish culture considerably different from that of its neighbors.

Saudi Arabia kept Islamic traditions.

While Turkey and Iran broke with many Islamic traditions, another new country held strictly to Islamic law. Soon after World War I, much of the Arabian peninsula was united under a single ruler who ruled in traditional fashion.

Arabia is a harsh desert land where water can be as precious as gold. For thousands of years, the Arabian desert was home to groups of nomads who traveled from place to place in search of water and grazing for their herds. These nomads were known as Bedouin (page 174).

The Bedouin lived in family groups. Members were related through their fathers and grandfathers. At the head of each group was a **shaykh**— a man usually chosen from one leading family within the group. The shaykh commanded tremendous respect from those he led. They looked on him as both a father and a ruler.

In 1902, a shaykh named Abd al-Aziz Ibn Saud (sah-**OOD**) set out to extend his power. His early support came from a small sect of Islamic traditionalists. By military skill and well-planned marriages to the daughters of neighboring shaykhs, he gradually won control of eastern Arabia. After World War I, he began advancing westward. One by one, he overthrew the local ruling families.

In 1926, Ibn Saud proclaimed himself king of an Arab nation. Six years later, he renamed the country Saudi Arabia after his family.

Ibn Saud held firmly to Arab and Islamic traditions. He ran his country much like a Bedouin shaykhdom. Loyalty to the Saudi government was based on custom, religion, and family ties. Unlike Atatürk, who chose to separate church and state, Ibn Saud made the laws of Islam the laws of his kingdom. Women in Saudi Arabia had to wear veils in public as Islamic law required. Alcoholic drinks were banned. Legal penalties for crimes were set according to the Koran. For years, the Saudi government frowned on much modern technology, including telephones, automobiles, and even bicycles.

Jews and Arabs fought over Palestine.

After World War I, the British and the French held Lebanon, Syria, Transjordania, Iraq, and Palestine as mandates. The people of these lands faced a different problem from the people of Turkey or Saudi Arabia. Most people in the mandates were mainly concerned with breaking free from European control.

Worn out from World War I, France and Britain could not halt the force of Arab nationalism.

The banners of Ibn Saud's army proclaimed the basic beliefs of Islam: "There is no god but God, and Muhammad is his prophet."

Iraq became independent of Britain in 1922, Transjordania in 1923. France signed treaties accepting the independence of Syria and Lebanon in 1936. Only Palestine was not yet free.

Until about 2,000 years ago, Palestine was the homeland of the Jewish people. Around 1000 B.C., Jewish kings ruled the country from Jerusalem (page 37). Twice the Jewish kingdom was destroyed, once by the Babylonians in 586 B.C. and again by the Romans in A.D. 70. Each time, many Jews fled Palestine and settled in other countries. Only a few managed to remain in their ancient homeland. Jews continued to live in Palestine even after the country came under Arab and later Ottoman rule.

Jewish nationalists The exiled Jews faced centuries of persecution and anguish. Still, they held on to their beliefs and traditions. For many Jews, these traditions were not enough. They wanted a homeland, a place where Jewish laws and traditions would also be the laws and traditions of their nation.

During the 1800's, the desire for a homeland grew stronger among many Jews. Pogroms in eastern Europe and Russia forced thousands of Jews to escape to Great Britain, France, Germany, and the United States. Thousands also emigrated to Palestine. There they bought large parcels of land, which they organized into socialist farming communities, called *kibbutzim* (kih-boo-TSEEM).

At first, most of the new Jewish settlers in Palestine came from eastern Europe. In the 1890's, however, a scandal in the French army fanned the flames of Jewish nationalism in western Europe as well.

In 1894, Captain Alfred Dreyfus, one of the few Jewish officers in the French army, was accused of selling secrets to Germany. The evidence against him was flimsy, but some other officers disliked him because he was Jewish. The army found Dreyfus guilty and sentenced him to life in prison. For 12 years, his family and friends worked tirelessly to clear his name. The French army and its political supporters tried to hush up the issue. At last, another man was found to have been the spy, and Dreyfus was declared innocent.

The Dreyfus case showed the strength of anti-Jewish feeling in France and other parts of western Europe. In response, western European Jews too began to work for a Jewish homeland in Palestine.

Their leading spokesperson was Theodor Herzl (1860–1904), a writer and journalist in Vienna. These Jewish nationalists were known as Zionists. (Zion is another name for Israel, the Jewish homeland.)

The Balfour Declaration Chaim Weizmann (VYTES-mahn), a Russian-born university professor, was the leader of the Zionist movement in Britain. Weizmann succeeded in winning the support of Britain's foreign secretary, Sir Arthur Balfour. In 1917, at the height of World War I, the secretary issued a document known as the Balfour Declaration. It stated:

> *His Majesty's Government views with favor the establishment in Palestine of a national home for the Jewish people, and will use their best endeavors to facilitate the achievement of that object, it being clearly understood that nothing shall be done which may prejudice the civil and religious rights of existing non-Jewish communities in Palestine or the rights and political status enjoyed by Jews in any other country.*

Balfour worded his document carefully, fearing the loss of either Jewish or Arab support in the British war effort. According to the declaration, Britain favored a Jewish homeland but not at the expense of the Arabs in Palestine. The ambiguity of the Balfour Declaration laid the foundation for conflicts that would dominate the Middle East for the next 30 years.

British rule Britain took control of Palestine in 1920 as a mandate. Immediately, both Arab nationalists and Jewish nationalists asked the British to fulfill the promises of the Balfour Declaration. Each group wanted its own country in Palestine. Each side believed it had the support of the British government.

While the British looked for an answer to the problem, Jews continued to immigrate to Palestine. Weizmann often spoke of creating a Palestine "just as Jewish as England is English." This trend alarmed Palestinian Arabs, who feared that Jews might become a majority. In 1929, a riot broke out between Jews and Arabs in Jerusalem. Over 100 people on each side were killed.

Jewish immigration increased during the 1930's. In 1933, Hitler came to power in Germany and began persecuting Jews (Chapter 30). Thousands of Jews fled Germany and settled in Palestine.

In 1908, Jewish settlers in Palestine drew lots for land in the desert where they planned to build a new city. Today, that city is Tel-Aviv.

By 1939, Jewish settlers had founded 200 kibbutzim in Palestine. The number of Jews living in the region had increased from 85,000 in 1914 to 445,000. Jews now made up about one fourth of Palestine's population.

Palestinian Arabs, alarmed at the growing number of Jews, staged violent demonstrations against the British. Britain, fearful of alienating the Arab community, tightened restrictions on Jewish immigration into Palestine. Thousands of Jews were left stranded in Germany. Jewish terrorism against the British became increasingly common. By the outbreak of World War II in 1939, many despaired of ever finding an answer to the Palestinian conflict.

Oil brought outsiders to the Middle East.

While nationalism simmered in many Middle Eastern countries, the region's economy was also taking a new direction. Even while traditional Islamic kingdoms such as Saudi Arabia and Iraq frowned on modern machines, they were sitting on top of great deposits of oil to fuel those machines.

The knowledge that oil existed in the Middle East was not new. Since ancient times, people there had noticed places where petroleum seeped to the surface of the ground. In those days, however, people had little use for the sticky, foul-smelling liquid. That situation changed in the late 1800's and early 1900's when people found that oil could be used as fuel. Soon, oil was a valuable resource for industrialized countries.

The Middle Eastern countries themselves had little use for oil. They had few factories or machines to use it, nor did they have the technology to drill their own oil wells. Therefore, most Middle Eastern rulers were willing to rent drilling rights to foreign oil companies.

In the early 1900's, European and American companies began to drill for oil in the Middle East. In 1901, William Knox D'Arcy, a British speculator, made a deal with the shah of Persia, paying him a share of the profits in exchange for the right to drill oil wells in Persia. In 1908, D'Arcy made the first big oil strike in the Middle East. Soon his company, the Anglo-Iranian Oil Company, completely controlled the industry in that country.

During the 1920's and 1930's, European and American companies found huge deposits of oil in Iran, Iraq, Saudi Arabia, and Kuwait. Geologists later learned that the land around the Persian Gulf has nearly two thirds of the world's known supply of oil.

Although foreign companies paid some money to the leaders of each country where oil was found, most of the profits went to the companies. The discovery of oil in the Middle East intensified old quarrels over boundaries and spheres of influence. It also, as you will see in later chapters, created new pressures on Middle Eastern society.

By the late 1920's, the major oil companies in Iraq were American. Discussion question: Why did American companies go into the Middle East when there were rich oil reserves at home?

631

Section Review 2

Define: (a) mandate, (b) shaykh, (c) kibbutz
Identify: (a) Middle East, (b) Mustafa Kemal, (c) Reza Shah Pahlavi, (d) Abd al-Aziz Ibn Saud, (e) Zionism, (f) Balfour Declaration
Answer:
1. (a) Why did the Middle East lag behind Europe economically? (b) What were the political results of World War I in the Middle East?
2. (a) How did Turkey become a republic? (b) Describe Atatürk's general policy for Turkey and give two specific examples.
3. (a) How were Reza Shah Pahlavi's policies like Atatürk's? (b) How were they different?
4. (a) Describe the Bedouin way of life. (b) How did Ibn Saud combine nationalism and Islamic tradition?
5. (a) What was the goal of the Zionist movement? (b) How did the movement begin?
6. What problems did the Balfour Declaration create?
7. Why did the discovery of oil lead to the growth of foreign influence in the Middle East?

Critical Thinking
8. Evaluate the leaders described in this section. (a) Which probably was considered most successful by Europeans? Explain. (b) Which probably was the most admired by traditional Muslims? Explain.

Latin America faced difficult changes. 3

By 1900, most of Latin America had been free of foreign rule for about 80 years. Although free, Latin American countries still faced problems that hindered their efforts at nation building.

Politically, Latin American countries remained isolated. None of them played a large part in World War I. Economically, on the other hand, Latin America had many ties to other lands. Latin American resources and products were sold worldwide: beef from Argentina, coffee from Brazil and Colombia, oil from Venezuela and Mexico, tin from Bolivia, nitrates and copper from Chile, and sugar from Cuba.

Few countries had democratic governments.

In many Latin American countries, political strongmen called caudillos ruled as dictators (page 504). These men did little to help the common people. Together with a small group of wealthy aristocrats, they alone enjoyed the benefits of independence.

To further their own interests, many caudillos and their supporters encouraged foreigners to invest in Latin American mines, plantations, and other businesses. The money from these investments lined the pockets of the caudillos and the outsiders. The common people of Latin America gained nothing.

There were, of course, exceptions. Reform-minded presidents such as Uruguay's Lorenzo Batlle (BAHT-yay) and Hipólito Irigoyen (EE-reh-GOH-yane) in Argentina tried to improve education and welfare in their countries. Benito Juarez brought an era of reform to Mexico in the 1860's.

However, such reformers made few lasting changes. Sooner or later, the caudillos returned to power. Usually, they had the support of the upper classes, who felt threatened by programs to give more power to ordinary people. One typical caudillo was Juan Vicente Gómez, a ruthless man who ruled Venezuela for nearly 30 years after seizing power in 1908. "All Venezuela is my cattle ranch," he once boasted.

Mexicans revolted in 1910.

Mexico suffered from the same problems as other Latin American countries. In 1910, 800 wealthy aristocrats (in a country of 15 million people) owned more than 90 percent of the rural land. Peasants in rural villages lived at the mercy of the landowners. Conditions in the cities were not much better. Factory workers labored 12 to 15 hours a day for very low wages. No laws protected their rights.

The rule of Díaz Mexico's ruler at the turn of the century was Porfirio Díaz (1830–1915). Díaz was an army officer who came to power in 1876. Although he called for elections regularly between 1876 and 1910, they were not free elections. Díaz controlled who could run, who could vote, and how the votes were counted. He was reelected seven times.

The caudillos were usually military men. On a continent where there were few international conflicts, these generals used their armies to get and keep power at home.

The Mexican Constitution resembled the United States Constitution in some ways. It provided for election of government officials, a legislature with two [continued below]

José Clemente Orozco, *Zapatistas.* (1931)

These Zapatistas (followers of Zapata) were peasant men and women who fought in the Mexican Revolution. Their strength and unity shows in this painting by one of Mexico's foremost artists, José Orozco. Orozco did many paintings in support of the revolution.

During his rule, Díaz brought Mexico economic progress. Under his leadership, railroads spread across the country and foreign business people set up new factories in the countryside. To many outsiders, Mexico seemed to be a stable, prospering country. They did not see the anger that seethed beneath the surface.

Revolution In 1910, that anger erupted as poor workers and farmers rose up against the government. Roving bands of fighters killed rich landowners and burned their houses.

The revolution had no single leader. In each part of Mexico, local leaders gathered their own armies. Often they fought with one another as well as with the government soldiers. One of the most famous fighters was Emiliano Zapata (sah-**PAH**-tah), a mestizo. "It is better to die on your feet than to live on your knees," Zapata told the peasants who joined him.

Revolution raged in the cities as well. There, protestors demanded better working conditions. Some leaders criticized foreign ownership of businesses in Mexico. Others attacked the wealth of the Catholic Church. Nearly all Mexicans were Catholics, but Church leaders were closely allied with the rich and powerful.

The government of Díaz toppled in 1911. Unfortunately, no single figure could command

enough support to unite the country. The result was a bitter civil war that dragged on for nearly a decade.

Reform In 1917, a revolutionary leader named Venustiano Carranza took control in Mexico. He called for a convention to draft a new constitution for the country.

The constitution of 1917 was a revolutionary document. It provided for the breakup of large estates. It set up a labor code to protect the rights of workers. It set rules for foreign investments but did not eliminate them. It also limited the Catholic Church's role in politics and education and forced the Church to give up some of its property.

Although he had called for the constitution, Carranza failed to carry out its measures. Instead, he ruled as a dictator. Peasant armies under Zapata and other rebel leaders continued their revolutionary struggle. In 1920, Carranza was overthrown.

In the fall of 1920, a moderate leader named Alvaro Obregón came to power. His presidency marked the end of civil war and the beginning of reform. Obregón put into effect many of the ideas of the 1917 constitution. Gradually, peasant villages took over lands from wealthy landlords. Public schools were established. Although poverty

houses, and a president who served one six-year term. It also contained more radical provisions: national ownership of mineral resources, restrictions on the Church's involvement in government, and guarantees of fair wages and working conditions.

and corruption continued to plague Mexico, the country remained stable politically. President succeeded president in an orderly way, without the coups that troubled other parts of Latin America.

The United States interfered in Latin America.

The Mexican revolution drew the interest of many countries in the Western Hemisphere. None was more interested than Mexico's powerful neighbor to the north, the United States.

The United States' interest in Latin American affairs was not new. As early as 1823, its government had issued the Monroe Doctrine, warning European countries to keep hands off the newly formed Latin American countries (page 504). Many Latin Americans did not welcome the Monroe Doctrine. They believed that the United States itself was interfering in their countries by issuing such a declaration.

In the early 1900's, President Theodore Roosevelt aroused further fears in Latin America by his Roosevelt Corollary (page 553). This policy gave the United States the role of international police officer in the Americas.

By 1900, the United States was replacing Great Britain, Germany, and France as the major foreign investor in Latin America. Anxious about its economic interests, the United States used the Roosevelt Corollary to intervene in Latin American affairs time and time again.

The small republics in Central America and the Caribbean bore the brunt of United States intervention. These countries were Panama, Nicaragua, Haiti, Cuba, and the Dominican Republic.

For example, in the early 1900's, United States businesses owned large farms for growing tobacco, sugar cane, cotton, coffee, and bananas in Nicaragua. When rebels in Nicaragua took up arms against the government in 1912, the United States government sent marines to protect American business interests. The United States also wanted its troops to stop the fighting from spreading to nearby Panama, where the canal was being built. The marines stayed in Nicaragua until 1933.

Investments by United States businesses in Latin America grew rapidly between 1914 and 1929. At the outbreak of World War I, United States businesses jumped at the chance to buy British and German property in the region. By 1929, these businesses had invested nearly $5.4 billion in Latin America. This figure amounted to 35 percent of all United States investments in foreign lands.

Much of this money was invested in the oil business. In the early 1900's, deposits of petroleum were found in Mexico, Venezuela, Peru, and Colombia. United States companies channeled millions of dollars into Latin America. Other United States investments went into Chilean copper and nitrate, Argentinian beef and Cuban sugar.

Latin American nationalists resented the way in which the United States protected its interests

Daily Life · Art on Walls

Mexico's democratic revolution brought a revolution in art as well. No longer was art mainly for the rich. Instead, Obregón brought art to the people by offering the walls of public buildings for murals of Mexico's past. Mexican artists such as Diego Rivera, David Alfaro Siqueiros, and José Clement Orozco took up the offer and won worldwide fame for their powerful murals. Not only was this art in new places, but it had new subjects as well. Under Porfirio Díaz, Mexican artists had imitated Spanish and French painters. The new revolutionary artists turned instead to Mexico's Indian heritage. Their murals glorified the long-ago battle of the Aztecs against Cortés and also the ongoing struggle of the Indian peasants against the landowners.

in the region. Time and time again, they pointed out that the profits from United States businesses helped keep dictators in power. In Venezuela, for example, United States oil companies were on friendly terms with dictator Juan Vicente Gómez. When Gómez died in 1935, millions of Venezuelans hoped that the United States businesses would go as well.

Roosevelt announced the Good Neighbor Policy.

By 1935, however, the United States was taking steps to improve its relations with Latin America. In 1933, Franklin D. Roosevelt took office as president of the United States. (He was a cousin of the earlier president, Theodore Roosevelt.) The newly elected president announced a change of policy toward Latin America. The new plan was called the Good Neighbor Policy. Under this policy, the United States promised to respect the rights of Latin American countries.

True to his word, Roosevelt withdrew United States troops from Latin American countries where they had been posted. The last marines left Haiti in 1936. For the first time in 30 years, there were no United States armed forces anywhere in Latin America.

The damage to relations between Latin America and the United States, however, lasted after the troops went home. Latin Americans did not forget how the United States had treated them. Moreover, United States businesses still controlled millions of dollars' worth of property in the region. People in Latin America remained uneasy over the enormous power the United States had in their countries.

Latin American economies were weak.

Foreign ownership of Latin American businesses was only one part of a larger economic problem. In many Latin American countries, the entire national economy depended on a single export. For example, oil was the key to Venezuela's prosperity. Brazil and Colombia depended on coffee.

Countries that depend on a single resource have little control over their own economies. When the price of that resource falls on the world market, the economy of the country may collapse.

In the 1930's, many Latin American countries faced just such a crisis. During those years, the world economy slumped into a deep, long-lasting depression (Chapter 30). The crisis had widespread effects in Latin America.

Brazil is a good example. During the hard times of the 1930's, many people could no longer afford to drink coffee. World coffee consumption fell so sharply that more than 3 billion pounds of coffee sat in the warehouses of São Paulo, Brazil. Coffee workers lost their jobs. Unable to sell its coffee, Brazil had no money to buy the manufactured goods it needed from other countries.

Some Latin American governments reacted to the decline in foreign markets by encouraging the growth of national industries. Mexico went a step further. In 1938, it seized foreign oil properties and **nationalized** them—that is, it brought the oil industry under government control. Several other countries did the same. Later, Mexico compensated the foreign companies whose assets it had seized. Today, Mexicans celebrate March 18, the date of the oil takeover, as their declaration of economic independence.

Section Review 3

Define: (a) caudillo, (b) nationalize
Identify: (a) Porfirio Díaz, (b) Alvaro Obregón, (c) Monroe Doctrine, (d) Roosevelt Corollary, (e) Good Neighbor Policy
Answer:
1. (a) What political problems did most Latin American countries face in the early 1900's? (b) What economic problems?
2. (a) Describe Porfirio Díaz's rule in Mexico. (b) How did he fall from power?
3. What changes were called for by Mexico's constitution of 1917?
4. How did Mexico regain political stability?
5. How did economic interests lead the United States to intervene in Latin America?
6. How did United States policy toward Latin America change during the 1930's?
7. What problems did reliance on a single resource create for many Latin American economies?

Critical Thinking
8. How is political independence related to economic independence? Use examples from Latin America in your answer.

China overthrew its emperor. 4

In the early 1900's, China was independent in name only. Although the Chinese civilization was one of the oldest in the world, it had faced years of humiliation at the hands of outsiders (pages 544–547). Foreign countries had spheres of influence in China. Foreigners controlled China's trade and economic resources.

Many people in China believed that their country's only chance for survival lay in modernization and nationalism. They urged government officals to improve the army and navy, to build modern factories, and to reform education. Yet while some leaders wanted change, others feared it. They believed that China's greatness lay in its traditional ways.

Chinese nationalists overthrew the Ch'ing dynasty.

Among the groups pushing for modernization and nationalization was the Kuomintang, or Nationalist People's party. Its founder and leader was Sun Yat-sen. In 1911, the Nationalists succeeded in overthrowing the last emperor of the Ch'ing dynasty, which had ruled China since 1644. Sun Yat-sen became president of the new Republic of China.

Sun, a physician who had spent many years in the United States, hoped to establish a modern government based on what he called the Three Principles of the People. The three principles were (1) nationalism (meaning an end to foreign control); (2) people's rights (democracy); and (3) people's livelihood (meaning a form of non-Marxist socialism and land reform to benefit the peasant farmers).

Sun and his followers quickly discovered that it was easier to destroy an old government than to build a new one. The end of imperial rule, after 2,000 years, left China weak and disunited. Civil war broke out as one powerful group battled another. Provincial warlords ruled territories as large as their armies could conquer.

As always during times of unrest, the Chinese peasants suffered most. Warlord armies terrorized the countryside, pillaging and looting everywhere. Roads and bridges fell into disrepair, and crops were destroyed. Famine took the lives of millions. This was the situation in China when World War I broke out in 1914.

Sun Yat-sen's government, though practically powerless, sided with the Allies against Germany. Sun and other leaders hoped that the Allies, in gratitude, would return control of China to the Chinese.

On May 4, 1919, some 3,000 angry students—the first generation of young Chinese to receive a Western-style education—gathered in the center of Peking. They had just heard infuriating news from the peace conference at Versailles. The Allied leaders had refused to give up their territories and commercial interests in China. Even worse for China, Japan was to be allowed to keep the Chinese territory it had seized during the war. "Down with the European imperialists!" the students shouted. "Boycott Japan!"

The May Fourth protests spread to other cities and became a truly national movement. It was not a revolution as such—that would come later—but it showed how much China's young people wanted a strong, modern nation. "What should we fear?" asked Mao Tse-tung (MOW zuh-DUNG), a young schoolteacher from the countryside who supported the Peking students.

> We should not fear the militarists. We should not fear the capitalists. What is the greatest force? The greatest force is the union of the popular masses.

As you will read, Mao later turned the masses into a powerful revolutionary army.

A Communist party arose in China.

China's humiliation at the hands of the Allied powers left a deep scar on many young Chinese intellectuals. Many turned away from Sun's belief in Western-style democracy. They turned instead to the ideals and beliefs of a powerful new leader. That leader was Lenin of the Soviet Union (Chapter 28).

Lenin was willing to help China's Nationalist government. He believed that the Soviet Union and China had common enemies—the European powers and the United States. Early in 1920, Lenin began sending military advisers and equipment to the Nationalists. Several of

Young Chinese were especially angry at their weak government, whose delegation at Versailles they accused of "willingly and treacherously [selling] our country to the enemy."

the Chinese Nationalist leaders traveled to Moscow for military training.

In 1921, the Chinese set up their own Communist party. In the beginning, the Communist party was closely allied with the Nationalist (Kuomintang) party of Sun Yat-sen.

In 1925, Sun Yat-sen died, and leadership of the Nationalists passed to his brother-in-law, a Japanese-trained general named Chiang Kai-shek (jee-**AHNG** kye-shehk). Chiang set out to defeat the warlords and unite all of China under the Nationalists.

Although the Communists supported him, Chiang distrusted them. He believed that the Soviet Union was supporting the Nationalists only until the Communists grew strong enough to take over. Chiang, the son of a well-to-do landowner, did not agree with the Communists' goal of creating a socialist economy. Many of Chiang's supporters were bankers and business people in the coastal cities. They feared a revolution like the one that brought the Communists to power in the Soviet Union.

Together, Chiang's Nationalist forces and the Communists fought the warlords. Chiang led a successful march from Canton to Shanghai.

Then Chiang decided that time had come to strike at the Communists. At dawn on April 12, 1927, Nationalist troops and armed gangs moved into Shanghai. They killed many Communist leaders and trade union members in the streets of the city. Similar killings took place in other cities. The Chinese Communist party was nearly wiped out. Its few survivors went into hiding.

In 1928, Chiang became president of the Nationalist Republic of China. Great Britain and the United States both formally recognized the new government. The Soviet Union, as a result of the Shanghai massacre, did not.

Mao Tse-tung preached revolution.

The Nationalist government of Chiang promised democracy and political rights for all Chinese. As time went by, however, Chiang was not able to fulfill his promises. His government became less democratic and more corrupt. Those that disagreed with its policies were thrown into jail or killed.

In the cities, the Nationalist government set up new factories and businesses. It also built

Chiang Kai-shek (right) and Mao Tse-tung (left) were once allies but later became enemies.

railroads, updated China's laws, and opened new schools and hospitals. These improvements helped city people.

However, the Nationalists did nothing to improve life for China's rural peasants. Many peasants turned away from Chiang and the Nationalist government. They looked instead to the Chinese Communist party.

One of the leaders of the Communists in the late 1920's was Mao Tse-tung (1893–1976). Mao came from a prosperous peasant family. His father forced him to leave school to work when he was 13. Mao ran away and went to school whenever he could, finally finishing high school when he was 25. Afterward, he worked as a librarian and a teacher. He began his political activities in his student days and became a member of the Communist party.

When the Communists were nearly wiped out in 1927, Mao fled to the countryside. He had already begun to develop his own brand of communism. Karl Marx (pages 515–516) had written that the revolution would begin among urban workers. Lenin had already shown that a Marxist revolution could take place in a largely rural

Discussion question: Why has communism been more appealing in agricultural societies than in industrial ones, despite Marx's forecast that it would be factory workers who would rise in revolt against capitalism?

637

country, but he had based his organization in Russia's cities. Mao went one step further. He believed he could bring Marxist revolution to a rural country and the peasants could be the true revolutionaries. Mao predicted:

> In a very short time, several hundred million peasants will rise like a tornado or tempest, a force so swift and violent that no power, however great, will be able to suppress it. They will break all trammels [bonds] that now bind them and rush forward along the road to liberation. They will send all imperialists, warlords, corrupt officials, local bullies, and bad gentry to their graves.

Civil war broke out.

By 1930, civil war raged in China. The Communists set up strongholds in the southern Chingkang Mountains. The Nationalists attacked them repeatedly but failed to drive them out. From their mountain hideouts, the Communists waged a guerrilla war against Chiang's armies. Mao outlined his strategy:

1. Retreat when the enemy advances.
2. Harass when the enemy encamps.
3. Attack when the enemy hesitates.
4. Pursue when the enemy retreats.

Such tactics were only possible with the support of the peasants in the area where the guerrillas were fighting. "The people are the water, the soldiers are the fish," Mao observed. "The fish cannot live without water."

Mao ensured support for his army by dividing land the Communists won among local farmers. He also made sure that Communist soldiers respected peasant property by helping farmers with their harvest and protecting women and children. As a result, more and more Chinese farmers joined Mao's Red Army, as it came to be called.

The Red Army retreated.

In 1933, Chiang Kai-shek launched a huge campaign to destroy the Communists. He gathered an army of nearly a million men, surrounded the Communists' mountain stronghold, and began tightening the noose. Outnumbered nearly ten to one, Mao realized that battle was hopeless. In 1934, he and his followers fled the mountains.

This was the beginning of an epic journey called the Long March. Over the next year, the Communists covered about 6,000 miles, keeping one step ahead of Chiang's forces. They often traveled at night to escape being seen from Nationalist airplanes. The chase lasted more than a year. About 100,000 Communists began the march. No more than 30,000—perhaps as few as 10,000—reached safety in northwestern China. There they were beyond the reach of Chiang's forces.

Mao and the other Communists who survived the march settled in caves cut into hillsides of northwestern China. They quickly gained new followers. Meanwhile, as civil war between Nationalists and Communists continued, Japan invaded China.

Japan invaded Manchuria.

The Japanese had taken advantage of the fighting in China as early as 1931. In that year, Japanese forces invaded the northeast part of China, Manchuria. This attack marked the beginning of World War II in Asia.

In 1937, the Japanese attacked other parts of China. Thousands of Chinese lost their lives as cities and villages were bombed. Many more died of starvation because farms were destroyed. By 1938, Japan controlled a large part of China.

The Japanese invasion forced the Nationalists and the Communists to unite against this new enemy. Yet Chiang and Mao remained rivals with different goals for China. Although allied, they fought the Japanese in different ways.

Chiang was more concerned with fighting the Communists than with driving out the Japanese. He believed that the Communists were the greater threat. Although he received money and weapons

Footnote to History

In the course of the Long March, members of the Red Army crossed at least 24 rivers. They climbed over 18 mountain ranges, some of them deep in snow. They fought 15 major battles and faced minor skirmishes almost every day. They crossed miles of swampland where they had to sleep sitting up, leaning back to back in pairs, to keep from sinking into the mud and drowning.

Words of a Chinese peasant song: "Harvest every year; but yearly—nothing./Borrow money yearly; yearly still in debt./ Broken huts, small basins, crooked pots;/Half an acre of land; five graves."

With the Red Army, Mao (on horseback) and his wife, Chiang Ch'ing (in round hat), made the grueling Long March to safety in western China.

from the United States to fight Japan, Chiang saved those resources to use against Mao.

On the other hand, Mao and his Red Army fought the Japanese in every way they knew how. More and more Chinese peasants joined Mao's army to help his fight. They looked to the Communists as heroes who were defending China from foreigners. As we shall see in Chapter 32, the loyalty Mao won from the peasants was a powerful weapon against the Nationalists.

Section Review 4

Identify: (a) Sun Yat-sen, (b) Mao Tse-tung, (c) Nationalist party (Kuomintang), (d) Chiang Kai-shek, (e) Long March
Answer:
1. (a) What were the three principles of Sun Yat-sen's new government? (b) What problems did China face during his presidency?
2. Why were Chinese students angry over the terms of the Versailles settlement?
3. How did the Soviet Union gain influence in China?
4. (a) Why did Chiang turn against his Communist allies? (b) What did he do?
5. (a) What improvements did Chiang's government bring to China? (b) What were the weaknesses of his government?
6. How was Mao's form of communism different from Marx's and Lenin's?
7. (a) What military methods did Mao use to weaken the Nationalists? (b) What political methods did he use to win support from the people? (c) What events led to the Long March, and what were its results?
8. (a) How did the Japanese react to the civil war in China? (b) Contrast Chiang's and Mao's policies toward the Japanese.

Critical Thinking
9. What did Mao mean by his statement, "The people are the water, the soldiers are the fish"? What kinds of support does a guerrilla army need to fight successfully?

After Mao's death, Chiang Ch'ing (Jiang Qing) became a leader of the Gang of Four. When she fell from political power, her face was airbrushed out of this picture in Chinese books.

Summary

1. Indians organized for independence. Following World War I, Indian nationalists increased their demands for self-rule. When hundreds of Indians were killed at Amritsar, Gandhi led a program of civil disobedience and economic boycott. Although Gandhi hoped to unite Muslims and Hindus, Muslim leaders called for a separate state.

2. Nationalism spread to the Middle East. The collapse of the Ottoman empire in World War I led to independence movements in the Middle East. In 1923, Turkish nationalists, led by Kemal, established the Republic of Turkey. In 1921, Reza Khan seized control of what is now Iran and set out to modernize the country. Saudi Arabia, unified by Ibn Saud, was governed according to Islamic law. By 1936, only Palestine was not yet free of foreign rule. The Palestinian issue was complicated by conflict between Jews and Arabs, each of which wanted their own country.

3. Latin America faced difficult changes. Although politically independent, Latin American countries depended economically on foreign investors. Dictatorial governments did little to improve living conditions. In 1910, discontent led to a revolution in Mexico that turned into civil war. By 1920, Mexico had a stable government. Beginning in the early 1900's, the United States intervened in Latin American affairs to protect its investments. Although the Good Neighbor Policy of 1935 eased tensions, resentments remained.

4. China overthrew its emperor. In 1911, Chinese nationalists, led by Sun Yat-sen, overthrew the emperor and set up a republic. When the Nationalists were unable to maintain order, civil war broke out in the north. China's humiliation in the Treaty of Versailles convinced many Chinese to break with the West and embrace communism. In 1925, leadership of the Nationalists passed to Chiang Kai-shek, who came to mistrust the Communists. Led by Mao Tsetung, Communists won the suport of the people. In 1933, Chiang forced Mao's army into retreat. From their hiding places in the northern mountains, the Communists launched a campaign against invading Japanese, thus winning even more peasant support.

Reviewing the Facts

1. Define the following terms:
   a. shaykh
   b. nationalize
2. Explain the importance of each of the following names or terms:
   a. Indian National Congress
   b. Muslim League
   c. Kemal
   d. Reza Khan

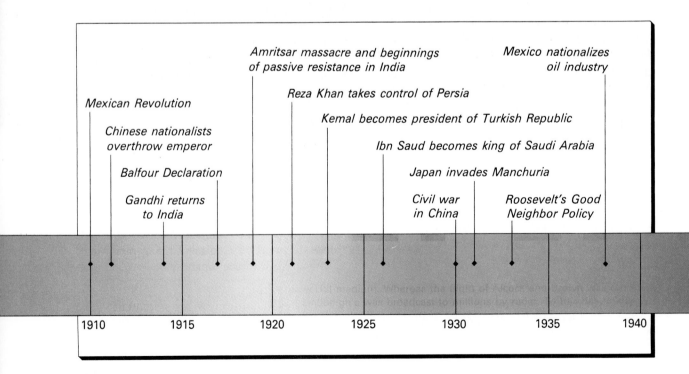

Amritsar massacre and beginnings of passive resistance in India

Mexico nationalizes oil industry

Reza Khan takes control of Persia

Mexican Revolution

Kemal becomes president of Turkish Republic

Chinese nationalists overthrow emperor

Ibn Saud becomes king of Saudi Arabia

Balfour Declaration

Japan invades Manchuria

Gandhi returns to India

Civil war in China

Roosevelt's Good Neighbor Policy

1910   1915   1920   1925   1930   1935   1940

e. Ibn Saud   k. Good Neighbor
f. Zionism   Policy
g. Balfour Declaration   l. Sun Yat-sen
h. caudillo   m. Mao Tse-tung
i. Díaz   n. Chiang Kai-shek
j. Obregón   o. Long March

3. (a) What were the goals of Hindu nationalists in 1930? (b) Of Muslim nationalists?
4. How did United States policy toward Latin America change between 1900 and 1935?
5. (a) What happened in China in 1911? (b) What problems did the new government face?
6. (a) How did the Treaty of Versailles contribute to the Communist movement in China? (b) Why did Chiang break from the Communists?

Basic Skills

1. **Reading and interpreting a table** (a) In the table on page 514, what trend exists in India and Pakistan's relative share of world manufacturing output between 1750 and 1900? (b) From what you know about British colonial policy, how can you account for this trend? (c) How is this trend related to Gandhi's focus on spinning and on wearing home-spun cloth?
2. **Summarizing** Summarize briefly the main points in Gandhi's action plan (page 626).

Researching and Reporting Skills

1. **Using biographies** Find biographical information about one of the nationalist leaders you have read about in this chapter. Choose an incident in the person's life that illustrates an important trait and report about it to the class.
2. **Identifying sources with opposing viewpoints** The history of Palestine between the two wars can be written from either a Jewish or an Arab point of view. Find two sources that will present these opposing viewpoints. Skim to find the arguments or interpretation of events on each side of the conflict.
3. **Using primary sources** Gandhi and Mao were both popular leaders who communicated their convictions to thousands of the uneducated poor. Find a source that quotes their sayings. List five important sayings of each person and explain how these sayings would appeal to the masses.

Critical Thinking

1. **Synthesizing** How did nationalist objectives in India and the Middle East differ from those in Latin America and China?
2. **Evaluating** Gandhi used a new method of resistance to British rule. (a) What were the main features of this method? (b) Was this the most effective method or should he have used a different approach?
3. **Applying a concept** Modernization as well as nationalism was an influence on many countries after World War I. (a) How did modernization affect countries in the Middle East? (b) What influences opposed modernization and where were they strongest?
4. **Analyzing** (a) For what reasons did Jews begin returning to Palestine? (b) What conflict in nationalist ambitions developed in Palestine?
5. **Summarizing** (a) List the various conditions that led to revolution in Mexico. (b) To what extent did the revolution change these conditions?
6. **Comparing** (a) How did Mao's brand of communism differ from that of Marx and Lenin? (b) How did Mao gain the support of Chinese peasants?

Perspectives on Past and Present

Many of the newly emerging countries after World War I had dynamic nationalist leaders. (a) Who have been some of the comparable leaders since World War II? (b) What kinds of changes have they sought?

Investigating History

1. The first issue of *Time* magazine appeared in 1925 and of *Newsweek* in 1933. Find out if your library has microfilm for these magazines in their early years. If so, read and report on events related to one country of Asia, the Middle East, or Latin America.
2. The films *Gandhi,* depicting the struggle for independence in India, and *The Last Emperor,* depicting two revolutions in China, provide background for Asian history in the twentieth century. Watch the videotape of one of these films and report on it to the class.

The Years between the Wars

The anger and discontent of German workers show in this picture of a Communist gathering of the 1920's by German artist George Grosz.

Key Terms

coalition
isolationism
fascism
appeasement

Read and Understand

1. Europe recovered from World War I.
2. Society faced rapid change.
3. Wall Street's crash opened the Depression.
4. Fascist leaders formed dictatorships.
5. The world drifted toward war.

In the summer of 1923, the printing presses at Germany's mints were rolling, and they were turning out money. Germans counted their currency in *marks,* and the presses printed 400 quadrillion (400,000,000,000,000,000) marks a day! Crushed by its huge war expenses and burdened with heavy payments to the Allies, Germany was in the midst of disastrous inflation. From 1918 to 1923, the value of the mark fell, slowly at first and then with terrifying speed.

What did inflation mean for the people of Germany? At the war's end, a loaf of bread cost two marks in Berlin. By December 1921, the price had risen to 40 marks, and just 1 year later a loaf cost more than 1,500 marks.

Bad as inflation already was, it went completely out of control in 1923. By that summer, a glass of beer cost 2 million marks and a loaf of bread 4 million. Workers collected their pay twice a day so

Before the war, the mark had been worth about 25 American cents. In June 1921, its value had fallen to about 14 cents. During 1923, the mark continued to fall until it was so low that it took millions of marks to equal a single penny.

that they could rush out to buy the things they needed before prices rose even higher. People took cartons and wheelbarrows full of money to buy food for supper. By autumn, the mark was worthless. Bank notes for billions of marks lay in street gutters.

Upper-class Germans suffered least from inflation because their lands and factories rose in value, keeping up with rising prices. Ordinary people faced harder times. Prices rose faster than wages, so people could not buy as much food or clothing as before. The inflation was a great shock to Germany's middle class. Civil servants, professionals, and people with fixed incomes or pensions saw their life savings become worthless. People discovered that the money they had saved to buy a house now barely covered the cost of a table.

What was the good of saving or planning for the future? Germans asked one another. What was the good of Germany's new democratic government, asked many, if people lost everything they had worked for? Germany eventually strengthened the mark, but the confidence of the German people was harder to rebuild.

In Germany and throughout Europe, the 1920's were a time of doubts and uncertainties. Embittered by the past war, people also feared the future. Some artists and writers expressed this bitterness in their work. Many people hid their fears by living for the pleasure of the moment. Thus, a thin shell of gaiety covered dark doubts and unanswered questions.

Europe recovered from World War I. 1

In human suffering, the cost of World War I had been staggering. The economic losses were also immense. The Allied and Central Powers had spent about $200 billion fighting the war. By 1918, every major European country was nearly bankrupt.

Only two world powers came out of the Great War in better financial shape than they entered it—Japan and the United States. Neither country had suffered fighting on its own soil. Both had expanded their international trade during the war.

These economic changes showed one of the major effects of World War I—the decline of European dominance in world affairs. Much wealth and power was still concentrated in Europe, of course, but the war had drained the continent's resources. The European Allies and the Central Powers were like two boxers who had battered each other in a long and brutal fight.

A second effect of the war was the sudden rise of new democracies. Between 1914 and 1918, Europe's last absolute rulers—the Hohenzollerns in Germany, the Hapsburgs in Austria-Hungary, and the Romanovs in Russia—were all overthrown. In Russia, the new democratic government soon fell to a Communist dictatorship. Even so, for the first time in history, most European countries were ruled by democratic governments.

New democracies were unstable.

Many citizens of the new democracies had little experience with parliamentary government. Germany and the new countries formed from Austria-Hungary, for example, had been ruled by kings and emperors for generations. There were problems even in France and Italy, whose parliaments pre-dated World War I. There, the large number of political parties made effective government difficult.

Democratic government is based on the principle of majority rule. In countries where there are only two or three major parties, it is fairly easy for one party to win a working majority. In countries with a dozen or more political groups, however, it is difficult for one party to win enough support to govern effectively.

In such countries, the largest party usually forms a **coalition** government. A coalition is a temporary alliance of several parties to form a parliamentary majority. Because the parties disagree on so many policies, coalitions seldom last long. In France, for example, there were some 40 changes of government in the 20 years between 1919 and 1939.

Coalition governments have other problems as well. Because they are in office for short times and because their members do not agree on important issues, such governments find it hard to provide leadership toward any long-term goals. People may accept this weak leadership as long

The United States lent more than $10 billion to its European allies. After the war, Britain and France were faced with loan repayment burdens that were almost as heavy as those of Germany.

643

as a country faces no major problems. When difficulties arise, however, the weaknesses of a coalition government are magnified. People may then be willing to sacrifice democracy in exchange for strong leadership. Such a course of events is exactly what happened in Italy, Germany, and several other countries in the 1920's and 1930's.

The German republic was weak.

The new democratic government set up in Germany in 1919 was known as the Weimar (VYE-mahr) Republic after the city where the national assembly met. The Weimar Republic had serious weaknesses from the start. Under Bismarck and William II, few democratic traditions had had a chance to take root. Furthermore, postwar Germany had seven major political parties and many minor ones.

Worst of all, the democratic government bore the burden of defeat. It was not the Hohenzollerns who had signed the Treaty of Versailles but representatives of the new republic. As a result, millions of Germans always viewed the Weimar government and its supporters as traitors.

Germany also faced enormous economic problems that had begun during the war. Unlike Britain and France, Germany did not increase taxes greatly during the war. Thus, while Germany spent $37 billion fighting World War I, its government collected only $1.5 billion in taxes. To make up the difference, the Germans simply printed money when they needed it. This paper money began to collapse after Germany's defeat in 1918. The result was a time of skyrocketing inflation (page 642).

Most Germans blamed the Weimar government and its weak leaders for Germany's problems. They failed to see that the war had caused most of their difficulties. As far as many Germans were concerned, Germany had made only one wartime mistake: It had lost. Next time, they swore, the result would be different.

The Dawes Plan brought stability.

Germany recovered swiftly from the 1923 inflation, thanks largely to the work of an international committee headed by Charles Dawes, an American banker and statesman. The committee worked out a financial plan to strengthen Germany's economy. The Dawes Plan provided for a $200 million loan from American banks to stabilize German currency. The plan also set a more realistic schedule for Germany's reparations payments.

Put into effect in 1924, the Dawes Plan worked extremely well. As the German economy began to recover, it attracted further loans and investments from the United States. By 1929, Germany's factories were producing as much as they had in 1913.

Treaties raised hopes for peace.

As prosperity returned, Germany began again to take an active part in European affairs. Germany's foreign minister, Gustav Stresemann (SHTRAY-zeh-mahn), tried to undo the worst features of the Versailles settlement through careful diplomacy. He was helped by France's foreign minister, Aristide Briand (bree-AHN), a moderate who favored better relations with Germany.

In 1925, Briand and Stresemann met in the Swiss town of Locarno, together with representatives from Belgium, Italy, and Great Britain. They signed a treaty promising that France and Germany would never again make war against each other. Germany also promised to respect the existing borders of France and Belgium. In return for this concession, Germany was admitted to the League of Nations.

In 1928, the "spirit of Locarno" led to the Kellogg-Briand peace pact. Frank Kellogg, the American secretary of state, arranged this agreement with France's Briand. Countries that signed the treaty pledged "to renounce war as an instrument of national policy." Almost every country in the world, including the Soviet Union, eventually signed.

Unfortunately, there was no realistic way to punish a country that broke its promise of peace. The League of Nations was the obvious choice to enforce the treaty, but it had no armed forces of its own.

Nonetheless, hopes were high in Europe in the late 1920's. Besides the peace treaties, Europeans were enjoying an economic boom. Industrial production rose to its pre–World War I level. However, much of the boom depended on massive American investment. As long as the American economy stayed healthy, the sun would shine on Europe.

One French woman described her reaction to the news of the Locarno pact this way. "I was literally drunk with joy. From now on, no more fears for the future! No more war!"

Section Review 1

Define: (a) inflation, (b) coalition
Identify: (a) Weimar Republic, (b) Dawes Plan, (c) Kellogg-Briand pact
Answer:
1. How did World War I change the balance of economic power in the world?
2. (a) How did the war change forms of government in Europe? (b) Why were many of the new governments weak?
3. (a) What political problems did the Weimar Republic face? (b) What economic problems? (c) How were the economic problems solved?
4. (a) How did relations improve between France and Germany in the 1920's? (b) Among nations worldwide?

Critical Thinking
5. Explain what leaders in the 1920's meant by "the spirit of Locarno." What policies would such a spirit have encouraged?

Society faced rapid change.   2

Fliers such as Katherine Stinson and Charles Lindbergh became celebrities in the 1920's.

Amid all the havoc World War I caused, it did have one positive result. It quickened the pace of invention. During the war, scientists developed new drugs and medical treatments that helped millions of people after the war. The principles of tank construction were put to use in building better automobiles, trucks, and tractors. The war's technological advances did not go to waste in the postwar years.

Technology made the world seem smaller.

During the war, millions of people communicated across battle zones and moved supplies thousands of miles. Therefore, many of the greatest improvements came in communication and transportation.

The spread of the automobile The automobile benefited from a host of wartime improvements—electric fuel pumps and starters, air-filled tires, and more powerful engines. "Check now what

the new, roomier Austin offers you! Dependability! Performance! Style! Comfort!" This British newspaper advertisement from the late 1920's showed how far the automobile industry had come since 1900. Cars no longer looked like buggies on wheels. They were sleek and brightly polished, complete with chrome-plated bumpers, headlights, and shock absorbers.

The beginnings of air travel The war also brought spectacular improvements in aircraft. By 1918, planes could fly several hundred miles.

During the 1920's, airplanes were put to many new uses. Daring pilots carried the first airmail letters. Wartime fliers became "barnstormers," visiting country fairs to perform aerial acrobatics and take people for their first airplane rides.

In 1919, two British pilots, John Alcock and Arthur Brown, made the first successful flight across the Atlantic Ocean, flying from Newfoundland to Ireland. The next major crossing came in 1927, when a young American pilot named Charles Lindbergh captured worldwide attention with his 33-hour solo flight from New York to Paris.

Most of the world's major passenger airlines were established during the 1930's, though air travel was too expensive for all but the rich. Still, everyone could enjoy the thrilling exploits of aviation pioneers such as Amelia Earhart, the first woman to fly across the Atlantic.

Section Review 4

Define: (a) fascism, (b) Il Duce, (c) führer
Identify: (a) Benito Mussolini, (b) Nazi party,
(c) Adolf Hitler, (d) *Mein Kampf*, (e) Gestapo,
(f) Third Reich
Answer:
1. (a) What ideas did most Fascists share?
   (b) How were fascism and communism alike?
   (c) How did they differ?
2. (a) What factors led to the rise of fascism
   in Italy? (b) How did Mussolini take control
   of the government?
3. What conditions led to the growth of extremist political groups in Germany?
4. What basic political ideas did Hitler develop during his stay in Vienna?
5. How did Hitler come to power in Germany?
6. (a) How did the Enabling Act increase Hitler's power? (b) What were the Nuremberg laws?
7. What plans did Hitler have for expansion of Germany?
8. (a) How did political power change hands in Japan during the Depression? (b) What policies did the new leaders advocate?

Critical Thinking
9. Compare the rise of Hitler with the rise of Mussolini. How did the following factors contribute to the each dictator's power? (a) economic conditions (b) political ideas (c) personal styles (d) private armies
10. (a) What "easy answers" did Hitler and Mussolini offer? (b) Why are such answers appealing in a time of crisis? (c) What steps can voters take to avoid being misled by such tactics?

The world drifted toward war. 5

By the mid-1930's, it was quite clear that the powerful countries of the world had split into two camps. On one side were dictatorships such as Germany and Italy whose leaders were bent on military conquest. On the other side were democracies such as Britain, France, and the United States whose leaders longed to keep peace.

One powerful nation—the Soviet Union—fit in neither category. During the 1930's, the Soviet Union took little part in world affairs while Stalin brutally forced the country through major economic changes (page 617). Nonetheless, the Soviet Union with its Communist government loomed large in the plans and fears of other countries.

The fear of a Communist revolution helped both Hitler and Mussolini in their rise to power. The Western democracies also deeply feared the Soviet Union. Indeed, many political leaders in Britain and the United States considered the Communist Soviet Union a greater threat than Nazi Germany. As the 1930's passed, however, it became obvious that fascism was a far more immediate danger. The democracies and the Soviet dictatorship temporarily set aside their differences to meet the Fascist threat.

The League of Nations was weak.

Many people pinned their hopes for world peace on the League of Nations. The League enjoyed high prestige in the 1920's. France and Germany signed the Locarno pact (page 644) in 1925. In 1926, Germany joined the League. For a brief period, it seemed that the League was indeed helping to create a more peaceful world. Unfortunately, these hopes collapsed as dictatorships encouraged militarism in the 1930's.

Ironically, the three countries that posed the greatest threats to peace—Germany, Japan, and Italy—were all members of the League of Nations in 1933. At the same time, the two countries that were strong enough to stand up to the dictators—the United States and the Soviet Union—were not members. (The Soviet Union joined in 1934.) Thus, the burden of supporting the League fell mainly on Great Britain and France.

Britain and France had been the two leading world powers of the 1800's. However, World War I had weakened them both severely. The French were still determined to uphold the terms of the Versailles treaty, but France was not strong enough to stand up to Germany alone. Many British people, on the other hand, believed that the Versailles treaty had been unfair and that Germany was entitled to some geographic and military expansion. Above all, Britain's leaders wanted to avoid a war that would further weaken their economy.

During the 1930's, therefore, Britain and France did not take a firm stand against Fascist aggression. Instead, they followed a policy of **appeasement**. That is, they made concessions to the Fascists in hopes of keeping peace.

Japan invaded China.

The first direct challenge to the League of Nations came in 1931 when the Japanese army invaded the Chinese province of Manchuria (page 657). The Japanese set up a *puppet government*— that is, a government controlled by an outside power—in Manchuria.

Japan's attack on Manchuria clearly violated the Kellogg-Briand peace pact, which Japan had signed. Other members of the League protested vigorously, as did the United States. However, the League had no armed forces of its own. Thus, it could do little. Japan ignored the protests and withdrew from the League in March 1933.

In 1937, a border incident touched off a full-scale war between Japan and China. On July 7, the Japanese and the Chinese exchanged shots at a railroad bridge 20 miles from Peking. One Japanese soldier was found dead near the bridge. Given this excuse, Japanese forces swept into northern China. These events marked the beginning of World War II in Asia.

China's leader, Chiang Kai-shek, had an army of more than 1 million soldiers, but it was no match for the superior equipment and training of the Japanese. Peking and other northern cities fell to the Japanese in less than a week. The capital, Nanking, fell by the end of 1937. Between 100,000 and 200,000 people in Nanking were executed within 6 weeks.

Yet the Chinese did not surrender. Forced to retreat westward, Chiang Kai-shek set up a new capital at Szechwan (sech-wahn). At the same time, Chinese guerrillas continued to fight within the area conquered by the Japanese. Many of the guerrilla fighters were organized by China's Communist leader, Mao Tse-tung (page 637).

Mussolini attacked Ethiopia.

Meanwhile, other dictators were also pursuing aggressive policies. Ever since coming to power in 1922, Mussolini had dreamed of building an Italian colonial empire in Africa. However, most of Africa had long ago been carved into British and French territories. Therefore, Mussolini decided to move against the independent African nation of Ethiopia.

In October 1935, Italy launched a massive invasion of Ethiopia. Mussolini used airplanes, tanks, guns, and poison gas against the Ethiopian army, many of whose soldiers still fought only with spears. The Ethiopians fought courageously, but their situation was hopeless. By the middle of 1936, Ethiopia was conquered.

Once again, the League was faced with a clear case of armed aggression. Once again, the League condemned the attack, but its members did nothing. The British government, for example, spoke out strongly against Italy's actions. Yet Britain continued to let Italian troops and supplies pass through the British-controlled Suez Canal on their way to Ethiopia.

No doubt the British and the French hoped that, by treating Mussolini gently, they could keep peace in Europe. Haile Selassie, the Ethiopian emperor, knew better. When he spoke at a League of Nations meeting in Switzerland, he said, "It is us today. It will be you tomorrow."

Hitler and Mussolini joined forces.

Even while Italy was conquering Ethiopia, Europeans faced the threat of war closer to home. Since becoming chancellor of Germany, Hitler had secretly strengthened the German army. In March 1935, he announced that Germany would no longer obey the military limits set by the Treaty of Versailles. France and Britain did nothing to stop this military buildup.

German troops in the Rhineland A year later, in March 1936, Hitler made his most daring move. The Nazi leader announced that he had sent German troops into the Rhineland. The Treaty of Versailles forbade Germany to place troops in this region along the French border.

The French might have challenged Hitler, but once again Britain's prime minister, Neville Chamberlain, urged appeasement. Why, asked Chamberlain, should Germany not station soldiers wherever it liked within its own borders?

Hitler later said that he would have been forced to back down if Britain or France had challenged his move into the Rhineland. "If the French had then marched into the Rhineland," he said, "we

The Ethiopians had successfully resisted an earlier Italian attempt at conquest during the 1890's. It was partly to avenge that defeat that Mussolini chose them as his victims now.

659

Pablo Picasso's Guernica *expressed his anguish at the wanton bombing of that village. The artist ordered that the painting should not go to Spain until democracy was restored there, as it was in the 1970's.*

would have had to withdraw with our tails between our legs." Whether that was true or not, the British and the French did nothing.

The Rome-Berlin Axis Hitler's growing strength convinced Mussolini that he should seek an alliance with Germany. In October 1936, Italy and Germany reached an agreement that became known as the Rome-Berlin Axis. An axis is a straight line around which an object rotates. Hitler and Mussolini expected their alliance to become the axis around which Europe would rotate. A month later, Germany also made an agreement with Japan. Thus, Germany, Italy, and Japan were called the Axis Powers.

Civil war broke out in Spain.

Hitler and Mussolini soon found another chance to test their strength against the democracies of Europe. In July 1936, civil war had broken out in Spain. The Fascist powers decided to support the Spanish general Francisco Franco.

Spain had been a monarchy until 1931. Between 1931 and 1936, a democratic government held office amid a series of crises. Many army leaders, however, favored a Fascist-style government. In July 1936, General Francisco Franco led a revolt against the elected government. Thus began a civil war that dragged on for three bloody years.

Hitler and Mussolini sent tanks, cannons, and airplanes to Franco's forces, called the Nationalists. German and Italian troops even fought alongside Nationalist troops.

The Republican army, as supporters of Spain's elected government were called, received little help from abroad. The Soviet Union sent some aid. The Western democracies remained neutral. An International Brigade of volunteers fought with gallantry on the Republican side, but it could do little against a professional army.

Early in 1939, the Republicans collapsed. Franco became Spain's Fascist dictator and remained in power for more than 30 years.

In many ways, the Spanish Civil War was a precursor of World War II. It showed what kind of war was soon to burst upon the world. In April 1937, a squadron of German planes appeared above the small village of Guernica (ger-NEE-kuh) in northern Spain. The planes dropped their load of bombs, killing hundreds of villagers, most of them women and children. There was no military reason for this attack. Several German pilots who took part later admitted that the bombing had been conducted as a "test." One of Franco's officers said of Guernica, "We bombed it, and bombed it, and bombed it, and *bueno*, why not?" Countless more bombs and immeasurably more agony lay in store for Europe and the world.

Hearing of the Munich agreement, Winston Churchill said that Chamberlain had had a choice between war and shame. "He has chosen shame. He will get war later."

Hitler demanded more lands.

By 1938, Hitler was ready for his next move. He planned to take over areas around Germany that had large German populations. His first target was his native Austria.

The takeover of Austria The Versailles treaty prohibited a union between Austria and Germany. Nevertheless, in March 1938, Hitler threatened to attack Austria. The Austrian chancellor was forced to resign, and an Austrian Nazi leader took his place. The new Nazi chancellor immediately asked Hitler to send troops into Austria to "keep order." On March 11, German troops crossed the border. On March 13, Austria became a German province. Again Britain and France did nothing.

The move into Czechoslovakia Hitler's next target was Czechoslovakia. Czechoslovakia had a large German minority, living mostly in the mountainous border area called the Sudetenland (SOO-**DAYT**-uhn-LAND). The Sudetenland was very heavily fortified. It was Czechoslovakia's main defense against German attack.

Hitler demanded that Czechoslovakia give up the Sudetenland and let Germany send in troops.

British Prime Minister Chamberlain (left) tried to appease Hitler (right) at Munich in 1938.

To settle the issue, four of Europe's Great Powers met in September 1938. The leaders of Germany, Great Britain, France, and Italy gathered at Munich in southern Germany. However, Czechoslovakia had no representative.

At the Munich conference, Britain and France agreed to allow Germany to take the Sudetenland. Hitler promised that the rest of Czechoslovakia would remain independent. The leader of appeasement, Prime Minister Neville Chamberlain, returned to Britain and announced that the Munich agreement ensured "peace in our time."

Six months later, in March 1939, Hitler broke the Munich agreement and took over the rest of Czechoslovakia. Clearly, the British and French policy of appeasement was a failure. Only war would stop Hitler.

Section Review 5

Define: (a) appeasement, (b) puppet government
Identify: (a) League of Nations, (b) Rhineland, (c) Neville Chamberlain, (d) Axis powers, (e) Francisco Franco, (f) Sudetenland, (g) Munich conference
Answer:
1. How did the attitude of the democracies toward the Soviet Union change during the 1930's?
2. What were some of the factors that weakened the League of Nations?
3. Why did France and Britain fail to take a strong stand against Hitler time after time?
4. How did World War II begin in Asia?
5. How did Mussolini try to create an Italian colonial empire?
6. (a) Why was the Spanish Civil War a test of strength between the Fascist powers and the democracies? (b) What was the outcome?
7. What part did each of the following play in Hitler's growing power? (a) the Rhineland (b) the Rome-Berlin Axis (c) Austria (d) the Munich conference

Critical Thinking

8. (a) What is the difference between appeasement and compromise? (b) What were the results of appeasement in Asia, Africa, and Europe? (c) Do you think a peaceful compromise was possible? Explain your answer.

661

Chapter Review 30

Summary

1. Europe recovered from World War I. World War I brought an end to European dominance and saw the rise of new democracies. One of these, the Weimar Republic in Germany, faced severe economic problems as a result of the war. These problems were resolved in part by loans offered by the Dawes Plan of 1924. As prosperity returned, Germany improved its relations with France.

2. Society faced rapid change. During the 1920's, automobiles, commercial air travel, and radios widened social contacts. Albert Einstein's theory of relativity caused a revolution in scientific thought, while Sigmund Freud provided insights into the workings of the human mind. A growing spirit of independence was reflected in the women's movement. American jazz and movies spread American culture, although politically the United States turned to isolationism.

3. Wall Street's crash opened the Depression. Stock prices in the United States soared in the 1920's, until a crash on Wall Street brought on the Great Depression. The effects of the Depression spread worldwide. In the United States, President Franklin Roosevelt introduced the New Deal. In Britain, the government raised tariffs and lowered interest rates. France passed temporary reforms to help workers.

4. Fascist leaders formed dictatorships. The crisis of the Depression brought on political upheavals in many countries. In Italy, Mussolini established a Fascist government in 1922. In Germany, Hitler came to power in 1933 and instituted a Nazi revolution. Japanese military leaders began empire building.

5. The world drifted toward war. During the 1930's, a weak League of Nations and Anglo-French appeasement opened the way for Fascist aggression. Japan invaded Manchuria in 1931 and China in 1937. Italy invaded Ethiopia in 1935. In 1936, Hitler moved into the Rhineland and made a formal alliance with Italy. Their combined forces helped Franco form a Fascist dictatorship in Spain. In 1938, Hitler claimed Austria and the Sudetenland.

Reviewing the Facts

1. Define the following terms:
   - a. coalition
   - b. isolationism
   - c. fascism
   - d. appeasement
2. Explain the importance of each of the following names, places, or terms:
   - a. inflation
   - b. Weimar Republic
   - c. Dawes Plan
   - d. Kellogg-Briand Pact
   - e. Einstein
   - f. Surrealists
   - g. Harlem Renaissance

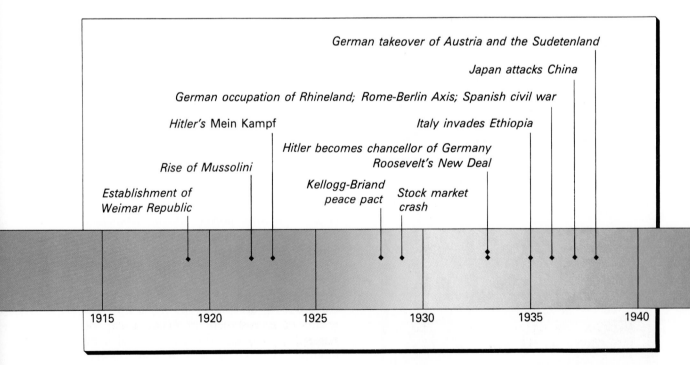

German takeover of Austria and the Sudetenland

Japan attacks China

German occupation of Rhineland; Rome-Berlin Axis; Spanish civil war

Hitler's Mein Kampf

Italy invades Ethiopia

Hitler becomes chancellor of Germany
Roosevelt's New Deal

Rise of Mussolini

Kellogg-Briand peace pact

Stock market crash

Establishment of Weimar Republic

1915   1920   1925   1930   1935   1940

h. Wall Street
i. Great Depression
j. New Deal
k. Mussolini
l. Nazi party
m. Hitler
n. *Mein Kampf*
o. Gestapo
p. Third Reich
q. Chamberlain
r. Rome-Berlin Axis
s. Franco
t. Munich conference

3. What steps were taken during the 1920's to assure future peace?
4. What changes occurred in the status of women in the postwar years?
5. Why did the economic crisis in the United States have a worldwide impact?
6. (a) What political changes did Mussolini institute? (b) What economic changes?
7. Describe the aggressions taken by each of the following countries between 1931 and 1938. (a) Italy (b) Japan
8. (a) How did Franco come to power in Spain? (b) In what way was the Spanish civil war a precursor of World War II?

Basic Skills

1. **Reading and interpreting a graph** (a) According to the graph on page 651, in what years was unemployment in Germany higher than in Britain? (b) How does the pattern of unemployment in Germany differ from that of Britain between 1936 and 1939?
2. **Sequencing** List the following events in the order in which they happened: Enabling Act, burning of the Reichstag, German troops in the Rhineland, Kristallnacht, the Munich agreement, Germany taking over Czechoslovakia, Germany taking over Austria, the establishment of the Weimar Republic.

Researching and Reporting Skills

1. **Interviewing** Find someone in your community who lived during the Depression. Make a list of questions you might ask about that person's experience. Tape or transcribe what is told you to share with the class.
2. **Using art and pictures** Divide your class into three groups to research (a) painting, (b) music, and (c) fashions and life styles of the 1920's. Have each group make a presentation to the class using audio tapes and pictures.

Critical Thinking

1. **Analyzing inconsistencies** In the 1920's, American cultural influences and economic interests in Europe were growing. Why might political isolationism develop at the same time?
2. **Applying concepts** According to your text, overproduction and underconsumption were weaknesses in the economy. (a) Explain what is meant by *overproduction* and *underconsumption*. (b) What direct effects did these have on the economy? (c) What indirect effects?
3. **Analyzing** (a) Review and list the terms of the Treaty of Versailles (pages 597–599) that affected Germany. (b) For each item, describe its effect on conditions in Germany during the 1920's. (c) What were the social, economic, and political consequences of these effects?
4. **Evaluating** The steps taken by Hitler in his rise to power were all within the law. At what points and by what democratic process could Hitler have been stopped?
5. **Interpreting** (a) What actions did the Nazis take against Jews in Germany? (b) What was the effect upon Jews as individuals and as a group?
6. **Forming a hypothesis** (a) Identify the reasons for the rise of fascism in the early 1930's. (b) From this list, develop a hypothesis about the rise of fascism, with major facts to support it.

Perspectives on Past and Present

The League of Nations failed to act when China invaded Manchuria, Italy invaded Ethiopia, and German troops moved into the Rhineland. To what extent has that situation changed under United Nations leadership?

Investigating History

1. William Shirer, a United States reporter in Nazi Germany, wrote two books about the Nazi era. Read a chapter from either *Berlin Diary* or *The Rise and Fall of the Third Reich*. What impressions does the chapter give of that time?
2. As a class or group project, draw up a list of movie titles from the 1930's—such as Chaplin's *Modern Times* and Welles's *Citizen Kane*—that are available as either films or videos. View one or two of the titles in class, evaluating it on style, quality, and historical significance.

World War II

In World War II, airplanes carried the war far from the battle front, bombing cities and towns and killing many civilians.

Key Term

genocide

Read and Understand

1. Germany overran much of Europe.
2. Japan conquered an Asian empire.
3. World War II was a total war.
4. The Allies launched a drive to victory.

Only 21 years after the end of World War I, a second world war broke out in Europe. A Pole named Martin Gray was 14 years old in September 1939 when he heard the shuddering screams of German dive-bombers over the Polish capital of Warsaw. Years later, Gray recorded his grim memories of the beginning of World War II:

> *The sirens wailed, the bombers skimmed the rooftops, their shadows glided across the road, and in the streets the people were running, clutching their heads . . . We went downstairs to the cellar, the walls were shaking and flakes of white plaster fell on our hair. My mother was deathly pale, my eyes stung, women screamed.*

Martin Gray was eventually captured by the Germans and taken to a concentration camp, but he escaped and joined the Russian resistance. After the war, he made his way to the United States. However, his family perished in the camps.

Day after day, Warsaw's buildings crumbled and burned from the merciless hammering of German tanks and planes. Martin Gray's family huddled around their radio to find out what was happening in their city and elsewhere in Poland. Germans had taken over some of the Polish radio stations. As a Polish Jew, Martin Gray was shocked by their broadcasts:

We listen to German broadcasts: they're announcing thousands of prisoners, to-morrow Hitler will be in Warsaw. "Poles," says the cheerful voice, "it's the Jews who are the cause of your troubles, the Jews who wanted the war, the Jews who are going to pay" . . . Then the bombers come back . . . the cellar shakes.

In two weeks, German tanks surrounded Warsaw and choked off all supplies. Civilians in the city could endure the bombing but not the lack of food. On September 27, 1939, the starving people of Warsaw surrendered to German troops. Martin Gray watched as the Germans took over the Polish capital:

They marched slowly, their heels ringing on the cobbles of the narrow streets. I was walking along the pavement, behind the rows of curious bystanders. Their planes were skimming the rooftops above Jerusalem Avenue. Patrols moved along the pavement; they didn't seem to notice the people, everyone drew aside. For a moment I followed three soldiers in ankle boots with long black bayonets. Yes, we were going to suffer.

The Poles suffered through six years of Nazi terror and oppression. Indeed, all of Europe suffered. Between 1939 and 1945, people in almost every major city of Europe heard what Martin Gray had heard—the sound of German bombers and tanks.

In Asia, the sounds were much the same. There the aggressor was not Germany but its ally in the east, Japan. Together the two countries hoped to dominate the world. They almost succeeded.

This chapter is the story of the drive by the so-called Axis countries—mainly Germany, Italy, and Japan—for world conquest. Opposing them were the Allies—Great Britain, France, the USSR, China, and the United States.

Germany overran much of Europe. 1

In the 1930's, the German dictator Adolf Hitler said over and over that Germany desired only peace and justice. Those who opposed Germany's reasonable desires, he said, were the enemies of peace. Yet all the while, he was preparing for war.

All during the 1930's, Britain and France followed a policy of appeasement. That is, they made concessions to Hitler in hopes of keeping peace. As a result, Hitler took the Sudetenland in 1938. One year later, German troops marched into western Czechoslovakia and seized it as well (page 661). The Italian dictator Mussolini, striving to keep up with his German ally, moved into the Balkans and took over Albania. Encouraged by these victories, Hitler abandoned his talk of peace. He talked instead of war and conquest.

Hitler prepared for war.

On April 28, 1939, Hitler stood before the Reichstag (Germany's parliament) and announced his newest plan. This time, he wanted the Polish Corridor. This strip of land had been cut from Germany after World War I to give Poland access to the sea (page 598). Hitler demanded that the seaport of Danzig within the Polish Corridor be returned to Germany. Furthermore, he wanted a German railway and highway route through the corridor.

Hitler's demands convinced Britain and France that appeasement was no longer possible. The governments of both countries pledged to defend Poland if Hitler threatened its independence. At the same time, they asked the Soviet Union to join them in stopping Hitler's aggression.

The Soviets were still smarting from their exclusion at the Munich conference (page 661). Soviet dictator Joseph Stalin was not eager to ally himself with the West. Furthermore, Hitler too was secretly seeking an agreement with Stalin.

In August 1939, Germany and the Soviet Union announced a ten-year nonaggression pact. In public, Hitler and Stalin pledged never to attack each other. In private, they agreed to divide eastern Europe. The Soviet Union was to have the Baltic

It has been written that out of the First World War came the seeds of the second. Ask students to review Chapter 30 to find examples to support this theory.

665

German artillery pounded Dunkirk's docks and beaches while British rescue ships steered through the smoke to save Allied soldiers.

the Danes had been. Even so, Norway's major seaports and its capital city, Oslo, fell to the Germans within two days.

German troops blitzed the west.

As war moved closer to Britain, a new leader came to power in Parliament. In May 1940, Neville Chamberlain, the leader of appeasement, was forced to resign as prime minister. His successor was Winston Churchill (1874–1965), who had long warned that Britain must make a stand against Hitler. In his first speech as prime minister, Churchill told the nation that there was no quick road to victory. "I have nothing to offer," he said, "but blood, toil, tears, and sweat." The next five years would prove how right he was.

In May 1940, a month after the Scandinavian attacks, Hitler prepared to strike at France. Along their border with Germany, the French had built an elaborate set of fortifications known as the Maginot (mah-jih-NOH) Line. The French expected this war to be a defensive one, as World War I had been, and the French army was well prepared for trench warfare. It was totally unprepared, however, for the German blitzkrieg.

France's 2 million soldiers stood ready to fight along the Maginot Line. Once more Hitler fooled them. As in World War I, the German army swung west around the French defenses and struck through Belgium.

On the morning of May 10, 1940, German parachutists dropped from the skies over the Low Countries—the Netherlands, Luxembourg, and Belgium. Luxembourg collapsed in only a few hours. On May 14, Germany threatened to destroy all Dutch cities if the Netherlands did not surrender. As proof, the Luftwaffe pounded Rotterdam to rubble even as talks about surrender were in progress. One day later, Belgium fell.

Columns of German tanks moved into northern France, driving Allied troops back toward the port of Dunkirk on the English Channel. There the Allied troops were trapped with their backs to the sea. The Germans closed in for the kill.

The seafaring people of Britain set out to rescue their trapped army. The fleet that sailed for Dunkirk from British ports on May 26, 1940, was perhaps the strangest naval expedition in history. Bobbing on the choppy sea were private yachts, ferries, lifeboats, motorboats, paddle steamers, fishing boats, and dockyard tugs. At the helm of these 850 craft were civilian volunteers. Their task was to help the British navy carry stranded soldiers across the Channel.

For eight days, from May 28 to June 4, this hodgepodge fleet sailed back and forth between

Discussion question: What does the building of the Maginot Line say about the lessons of history?

Britain and the burning, bombed-out docks of Dunkirk. When the operation ended on June 4, an incredible 338,000 battle-weary soldiers had been carried safely to Britain.

France fell to the Nazis.

Even as the Nazi blitzkrieg swept through France, Italian armies were also on the march. At first, Italy's Fascist dictator, Benito Mussolini, had hesitated to take part in the war. Now, with France about to fall, Mussolini decided to grab for conquest and glory. On June 10, he declared war against both Britain and France. Italy then attacked France from the south.

France seemed doomed. As German forces neared Paris, masses of people fled the city. Cars, bicycles, carts, and taxis jammed the roads leading south from Paris. German planes screamed overhead, firing into the snarled traffic.

As the end approached, the French government asked Marshall Henri Pétain (pay-TAN), an aged hero from World War I, to become prime minister. On June 16, 1940, he told the French army, "We must cease to fight."

Hitler demanded that the French leaders surrender at Compiègne in the same railroad car where Germans had been forced to sign the armistice ending World War I. On June 22, 1940, the meeting took place. Hitler walked from the railroad car giddy with triumph.

According to the terms of surrender, France was divided into two parts. The Germans were to occupy the northern two thirds of France and control the coastline. Pétain's government was to hold the southern part.

Pétain and his ministers moved to the city of Vichy (VISH-ee) in southern France. Their government became known as the Vichy Regime. Many French people regarded Pétain as a traitor. Others believed he had acted to save France from destruction. As time went on, however, the Vichy government cooperated more and more closely with the Nazis.

In time, French freedom fighters found their own way to combat the Nazis. Led by General Charles de Gaulle, they formed an underground movement known as the Free French. Although capture meant certain death, French resistance fighters made heroic efforts to sabotage the Nazis for the rest of the war.

Germany attacked Great Britain.

In all of Europe, only one country still held out against Hitler. That country was Great Britain. In a speech after Dunkirk, Churchill had already made clear that the British would never give in to the Nazis. Foreseeing the grim possibility of a German invasion, Churchill said:

> . . . [W]e shall fight in the seas and oceans, we shall fight with growing confidence and growing strength in the air; we shall defend our Island, whatever the cost may be. We shall fight on the beaches, we shall fight on the landing grounds, we shall fight in the fields and in the streets, we shall fight in the hills; we shall never surrender.

French resistance fighters used gadgets such as these to travel secretly behind German lines and communicate with others in the Free French. They hid a compass in a bootheel, a radio transmitter in a wine carrier, and news bulletins in a hollowed log.

Ignoring the advice of his generals, Hitler decided to invade Britain. During the summer of 1940, the Germans prepared for Operation Sea Lion, a seaborne attack on Britain that would begin in mid-September. First, however, Hitler sent the Luftwaffe bombers to knock out Britain's defenses, particularly its Royal Air Force (RAF).

To face the Germans' 900 fighter planes and 1,300 bombers, the British had only 650 fighters. The fate of Britain rested on the skill and raw courage of its 1,400 pilots.

Against these overwhelming odds, Britain had two secret weapons. One was an electronic tracking device known as radar. Blips on their radar screens warned the British as German planes approached. Britain's second secret weapon was the ability to crack German codes (page 680). Together, these warning systems gave RAF fliers the time they needed to scramble into their planes and rise to the attack.

The Battle of Britain began on August 8, 1940. Night and day, the RAF and the Luftwaffe battled for control of the skies. At first, the Germans concentrated their attacks on naval bases and airfields, although some bombing raids hit London. The RAF not only defended Britain but also struck back at Germany. In late August, British bombers flew over Germany, hitting Berlin and other cities.

Furious that Berlin had been bombed, Hitler ordered attacks against London and other British cities. The piercing wail of air-raid sirens filled the air as bomb after bomb exploded in city streets, setting buildings ablaze. The cost to British civilians was terrible—300 to 600 lives lost per day and from 1,000 to 3,000 injured daily.

Despite the fire-filled days and nights, the people of Britain fought on, more determined than ever not to give in. By the end of 1940, Hitler knew he could neither wipe out the RAF nor break the spirit of the British people. As a result, he abandoned Operation Sea Lion. Churchill expressed the gratitude of the British people to the RAF pilots when he said, "Never was so much owed by so many to so few."

Hitler invaded the Soviet Union.

The failure to take Britain stunned Hitler. It did not, however, defeat him. His next step was to break the pact he had made with Stalin less than two years earlier. Like Napoleon 150 years earlier, Hitler decided to strike eastward before finishing off Great Britain. Like Napoleon, Hitler was making a great mistake.

For Hitler, the Soviet Union was a tempting prize. There, he believed, his German master race would find the living space to prosper and expand. There too the Germans would win valuable mineral resources.

Hitler's first step was to take over the Balkans. In April 1941, Germany attacked both Greece

President Roosevelt and Prime Minister Churchill had both warned a disbelieving Stalin that Hitler would turn on his ally and invade Russia. When the invasion came, however, Stalin was not ashamed to ask for help from Britain.

and Yugoslavia on the same day. Yugoslavia fell in 11 days, Greece in 24. In Athens, the Nazis celebrated their victory by hanging swastikas on the Parthenon. By the end of the year, Bulgaria, Romania, and Hungary had all allied themselves with Germany.

With the Balkans in his power, Hitler was ready for war against the USSR. Early on Sunday morning, June 22, 1941, as the Soviet people slept, the roar of tanks and planes announced the beginning of the German blitzkrieg. In the first hours of the attack, Luftwaffe bombs destroyed 1,000 Soviet planes on the ground. Taken by surprise, the lines of the Red Army were smashed in a dozen places.

The invasion rolled on week after week. Like the pincers of a giant crab, two columns of the German army would crash through Russian defenses and surround whole divisions. In this way, the Germans moved steadily closer to their three goals—Leningrad in the north, Moscow in the center, and the rich grain and oil fields in the south.

By mid-November 1941 (five months after the assault began), Leningrad was surrounded by German armies. Hitler then tried to starve the 3 million inhabitants of the city into submission. More than 500,000 Leningraders died during the winter of 1941–1942. Yet the city refused to surrender.

Meanwhile, other German armies reached the outskirts of Moscow. There they met stiff resistance from Soviet troops. They also faced the brutal cold of a Soviet winter. The Germans, clad only in summer uniforms, were not ready for the cold. In his arrogance, Hitler had believed he would defeat the Soviet Union before winter set in. Hitler had underestimated the determination of Soviet troops.

Like Napoleon, Hitler faced a winter war near Moscow. Napoleon, however, had had the good sense to retreat when the snows started falling. Hitler instead sent a stunning order to his freezing generals: "No retreat!"

The German troops obeyed. They dug in to face the long winter. Indeed, even a retreat would have been difficult, as crankcases froze in their tanks and trucks. The Soviets, on the other hand, were well trained for winter warfare. For both sides, it now appeared the war would be a long one.

Section Review 1

Define: (a) appeasement, (b) blitzkrieg
Identify: (a) Polish Corridor, (b) Luftwaffe, (c) Winston Churchill, (d) Maginot Line, (e) Dunkirk, (f) Vichy Regime, (g) Free French, (h) Charles de Gaulle, (i) RAF
Answer:

1. (a) What new demands did Hitler make in the spring of 1939? (b) How did Britain and France end their policy of appeasement?
2. (a) Why was the Hitler-Stalin nonaggression pact unexpected? (b) Why was it important to Hitler?
3. How did World War II begin in Europe?
4. What territories did the USSR take in 1939?
5. Why did Hitler want control of Scandinavia?
6. (a) In what way was the German attack on France similar to the beginning of World War I? (b) What key difference between the two wars led to the French defeat?
7. How was France governed after its fall?
8. (a) How did Hitler plan to defeat Britain? (b) Why did he fail?
9. (a) What were Hitler's goals in attacking the Soviet Union? (b) What successes did the Germans achieve? (c) How did the campaign turn into a disaster for Germany?

Critical Thinking

10. Suppose you had been a news analyst in 1940. Write a short summary of the reasons why you expect Hitler to attack the USSR soon. Then take the opposite point of view and write a similar summary of the reasons why you would not expect him to do so.

Japan conquered an Asian empire. 2

While the German advance froze to a halt in the Soviet Union, the Japanese were making their plans in the east. Just as Hitler envisioned Europe ruled by the Aryan race, Japan had its own dreams of glory. Japan hoped to drive Western imperialists from Asian lands and establish its own broad sphere of influence. Japan called its planned empire the Greater East Asia Co-Prosperity Sphere.

Stretching from Manchuria in the north to Australia in the south, this new empire would be forced to serve the economic needs of its conqueror, Japan.

Japan's conquest of Asia began in 1931 when Japanese troops took over Manchuria, China's northeastern province. Six years later, in 1937, Japanese armies were once more on the march. This time they moved south into the ancient heartland of China.

The Japanese believed that the farmlands and rich resources of China would soon be theirs. They were wrong. As one Chinese general said, "China can exterminate the population of Japan while losing 105 million men. We shall still have 300 million left."

By 1939, the war between China and Japan had dragged on for three years. Japan's economy was strained to the breaking point. Japanese military leaders grew alarmed by their dwindling supplies of oil, iron, rubber, and tin. They began to eye the lands of Southeast Asia, where rich supplies of these resources lay.

The United States aided Great Britain.

In 1940, the only obstacle to Japanese expansion was the United States. Although thousands of miles away, Americans had been watching events in Asia and Europe with growing horror.

From the beginning, Hitler's aggression in Europe had sparked fierce debate in the United States. Many Americans reacted by vowing to keep their country out of war. Between 1935 and 1937, these isolationists succeeded in passing laws known as the neutrality acts. These laws made it illegal to sell arms to countries at war. They also made it illegal for Americans to lend money or sell on credit to such countries.

Franklin Roosevelt, then president of the United States, recognized the strong feelings of the isolationists. He also knew that the United States could not stand by helplessly as the Axis powers conquered country after country.

In 1939, Roosevelt persuaded Congress to allow the sale of weapons and other goods to fighting nations by a cash-and-carry policy. Thus, countries at war could buy such goods as long as they paid for them immediately and took them away on their ships. Because the British still controlled the sea routes, this act was a great help to them.

In September 1940, during the Battle of Britain, Roosevelt went a step further. He gave Britain 50 destroyers in return for 99-year leases on bases in Newfoundland, Bermuda, and Jamaica. That same year, Congress approved a Selective Service Act providing for the United States' first military draft during peacetime.

In the presidential election of 1940, Roosevelt tried to calm Americans' fears over the country's growing involvement in the war. He promised parents that their "boys were not going to be sent into any foreign wars." All he was doing, he argued, was helping the British defend themselves. Roosevelt stressed that the United States could serve as the "arsenal of democracy," supplying arms but not soldiers to the free countries of the world.

Soon after Roosevelt won reelection, Churchill told him that the British needed more help. By then, the entire northern coast of Europe was under Nazi control. Hitler's submarines were sinking British ships that carried food and war supplies to the island nation.

After a fierce debate, Congress passed Roosevelt's Lend-Lease Act in the spring of 1941. This act authorized the president to send war supplies to any country whose defenses he considered vital to the United States. Those countries could pay for the supplies after the war.

By the fall of 1941, the United States was arming merchant ships and using its navy to protect British ships across the Atlantic. In September, after a German submarine fired on an American ship, Roosevelt ordered navy commanders to shoot German submarines on sight. In effect, the United States was now engaged in an undeclared naval war against Hitler.

Japan threatened American interests in Asia.

Relations between the United States and Japan were also moving toward a crisis. Roosevelt was determined to keep Japan from taking over China. In addition, Japan threatened the American-controlled Philippine islands, the British colonies of Singapore and Malaya, and the oil-rich Dutch colonies in Indonesia.

Roosevelt justifying Lend-Lease: "Suppose my neighbor's house catches fire and I have a length of garden hose . . . I don't say to him, 'Neighbor, you have to pay me for the hose.' No, I say I want it back after the fire is out."

To put pressure on the Japanese, Roosevelt banned the shipment of American fuel, scrap iron, and steel to Japan. This loss of vital supplies made it difficult for Japan to continue its war in China. In effect, Japan's military rulers had two choices. One choice was to pull out of China and admit defeat. The other was to obtain more war materials by striking south against Indochina, Malaya, and the East Indies. The Japanese foresaw that the second choice would provoke war with the United States. In a fateful conference with Emperor Hirohito in September 1940, Japanese generals decided on the second choice—attack.

At the same time, Japan, Italy, and Germany signed the Tripartite (three-part) or Axis pact. Hitler now formally supported Japan's war plan.

The Japanese bombed Pearl Harbor.

War between Japan and the United States now seemed inevitable. To prepare for it, one of Japan's boldest leaders, Admiral Isoroku Yamamoto, made a daring plan. Yamamoto hoped to destroy American naval power in the Pacific by sinking the American fleet at Pearl Harbor, Hawaii.

On November 25, 1941, the Japanese First Air Fleet set sail. It included aircraft carriers, battleships, cruisers, and submarines. It moved secretly, sending no radio signals for anyone to trace.

American officials knew that a large Japanese fleet had gone to sea in late November. They braced themselves for an attack, perhaps on the Philippines or Malaya. Almost no one thought the Japanese could attack Hawaii, 3,000 miles distant from Japan.

By early Sunday morning, December 7, 1941, the Japanese fleet lay north of Hawaii. From the decks of its aircraft carriers, the first attack wave of 183 planes roared over the dark ocean as American sailors slept in their bunks. When the last planes returned to the carriers, Japan had blown up 200 American planes, sunk or damaged 8 American battleships, and killed more than 3,000 sailors and marines.

It was 2:30 P.M. in Washington, D.C., when stunned listeners on the United States mainland heard the first radio reports of the disaster at Pearl Harbor. For this "unprovoked and dastardly attack," as President Roosevelt called it, the

JUST WHAT THEY ACCOMPLISHED BY THE ATTACK ON PEARL HARBOR

BISHOP, *ST. LOUIS STAR-TIMES*

These cartoons present contrasting views of Japanese aggression. What does the Japanese warlord represent as a symbol? What is the message of the second cartoon in response?

673

At Pearl Harbor, a small boat picked up survivors from the burning USS West Virginia.

United States declared war against Japan on December 8, 1941. Soon after, Japan's allies, Germany and Italy, declared war on the United States.

Japan overran the Pacific.

Only ten hours after the attack on Pearl Harbor, planes from a second Japanese fleet pounded American military bases in the Philippines. The Japanese marched into the city of Manila in January 1942 and overwhelmed the American and Filipino defenders at Bataan (April 1942) and Corregidor (May 1942).

Meanwhile, the Japanese had been striking out in other directions. During December 1941, they took Hong Kong from the British and added the American islands of Guam and Wake to their empire. More important for their drive to the south, they also attacked the Malay Peninsula.

By February 1942, the Japanese had hacked their way through Malayan rain forests to Singapore and forced the surrender of some 70,000 British defenders. Possession of both Malaya and the Philippines gave the Japanese an ideal base from which to launch attacks against the Dutch East Indies to the south. By March 1942, Japan had conquered the oil-rich Dutch islands of Java, Borneo, Sumatra, and Celebes. By May 1942,

they had established full control of Burma, threatening both China and British India.

By mid-1942, Japan's red and white banner with its rising sun flew over most lands and islands of the western Pacific Ocean. Since the attack at Pearl Harbor, the Japanese had conquered a vast expanse of land and ocean. Their empire measured 5,000 miles from north to south and 6,000 miles from east to west. Now they hoped to push their conquests even farther, to Australia and perhaps Hawaii as well.

The Allies turned the tide in the Pacific.

The main Allied forces in the Pacific were the Americans and the Australians. In May 1942, they succeeded in stopping the Japanese drive toward Australia in the five-day Battle of the Coral Sea. During this battle, the fighting was done by airplanes that took off from enormous aircraft carriers. Not a single shot was fired by surface ships.

Japan's next thrust was toward Midway Island, which lies west of Hawaii. Here again, the Allies succeeded in stopping the Japanese. Americans had broken the Japanese code and learned that Midway was to be the target.

Admiral Chester W. Nimitz, the American commander in chief in the Pacific, moved to defend the island. On June 3, 1942, his scout planes found the Japanese fleet. The Americans sent torpedo planes and dive-bombers to the attack. The Japanese were caught with their planes still on the decks of their carriers. American fliers destroyed 322 Japanese planes, 4 aircraft carriers, and several other ships. Stripped of its air force, the Japanese fleet was forced to withdraw. Hawaii was never again seriously threatened.

The Allies went on the offensive.

The Battle of Midway was a turning point in the Pacific war. Soon the Allies began "island hopping." Island by island, they won back territory from the Japanese. With each island, Allied forces moved closer to Japan.

The first Allied offensive was at Gaudalcanal in the Solomon Islands. The savage struggle in the sweltering forests and tall grasses of Guadalcanal lasted from July 1942 to February 1943.

Americans considered the Battle of Midway revenge for Pearl Harbor since Admiral Nagumo, the commander of the Japanese fleet, had been Japan's hero in that battle.

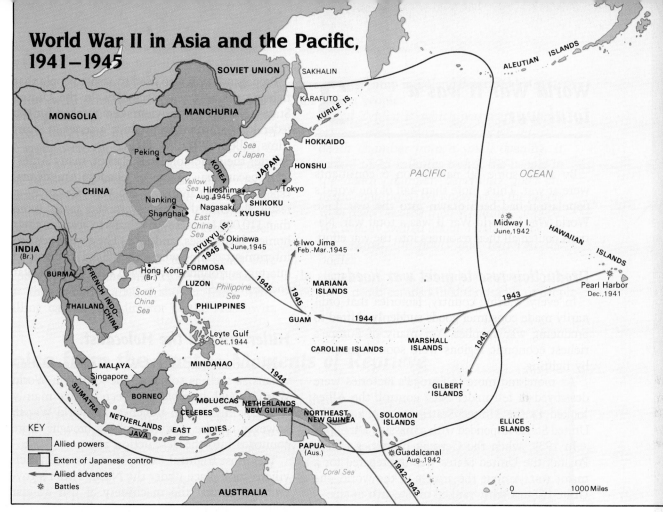

World War II in Asia and the Pacific, 1941–1945

KEY

- Allied powers
- Extent of Japanese control
- Allied advances
- Battles

0   1000 Miles

Map Study

What countries on mainland Southeast Asia did Japan rule at the height of its power? What two islands did the Allies attack after the Marianas?

Six times United States cruisers and battleships fought the Japanese navy to a stalemate. Finally, after losing thousands of men, Japan gave up the island.

The Japanese offensive in the Pacific had been halted. In the remaining years of the war, as we shall see, Japan was forced to yield all it had conquered to the relentless counterattack of the United States and other Allied powers.

Section Review 2

Define: isolationists
Identify: (a) Lend-Lease Act, (b) Isoroku Yamamoto, (c) December 7, 1941, (d) Chester W. Nimitz, (e) Battle of Midway
Answer:
1. How did World War II begin in Asia?
2. What steps did the United States take to help

the Allies before actually entering the war?
3. (a) What economic issues led to conflict between the United States and Japan? (b) How did Japan decide to solve its economic problems?
4. How did war break out between the United States and Japan?
5. Briefly describe the course of the war in the Pacific.
6. (a) What was the result of the Battle of the Coral Sea? (b) Of the Battle of Midway?

Critical Thinking

7. Admiral Yamamoto, who had visited the United States, warned Japanese leaders against provoking war with that country. If Pearl Harbor had not been attacked, do you think the United States would have remained the arsenal of democracy without actually entering the war? Explain your answer.

Map Study answers: Burma, Thailand, Malaya, French Indochina; Iwo Jima, Okinawa

On April 10, 1945, American troops reached Buchenwald, a concentration camp with 20,000 prisoners. Many were too near death to be saved.

Before World War II, there were about 11 million Jews living in Europe. By the end of the war, about 6 million had been deliberately and systematically murdered by the Nazis. Today, this horrible destruction is known as the Holocaust.

Jews were not the only victims of Nazi brutality. About 4 million other prisoners died in German concentration camps, including Poles, Russians, Czechs, and many Gypsies of southeastern Europe.

Squads of Nazi police rounded up Slavs by the thousands, packed them like cattle into boxcars, and hauled them to slave labor camps. Hundreds of thousands perished there from hunger, cold, exhaustion, and disease.

In Asia, civilians and prisoners of war also suffered terrible casualties. After the Battle of Bataan in the Philippines, 35,000 American and Filipino soldiers were taken prisoner by the Japanese in April 1942. Thousands of these prisoners died of hunger, thirst, torture, and disease on the "death marches" to Japanese prison camps. Likewise, hundreds of thousands of Chinese civilians died in bombing raids and zones under Japanese control.

Massive bombings and death-filled concentration camps took a high toll in civilian lives. By the war's end, more than 30 million civilians had died—twice the number of soldiers killed in battle.

Section Review 3

Define: (a) inflation, (b) propaganda, (c) genocide
Identify: (a) Selective Service Act, (b) Aryan, (c) Holocaust
Answer:
1. What steps did the United States take between 1939 and 1942 to prepare for war?
2. (a) How did the shift to a wartime economy change the work force? (b) How were prices and consumer goods affected?
3. What role did propaganda play in the war?
4. (a) What was Hitler's plan for the Aryan or Germanic peoples? (b) For the Slavs?
5. How did Hitler try to destroy the Jews of Europe?

678

German SS officers committed unimaginably brutal acts against individuals. The commander of a labor camp in Poland, for example, would stroll to his doorstep after breakfast and shoot a Jewish prisoner who was not working hard enough.

6. (a) How could a single leader such as Hitler be responsible for such a massive crime as the Holocaust? (b) Who else might bear part of the responsibility?

The Allies launched a drive to victory.

4

On December 8, 1941, in his war message to Congress, President Roosevelt described December 7—the day on which Pearl Harbor had been bombed—as "a date which will live in infamy." To Prime Minister Winston Churchill of Great Britain, however, the date represented something quite different. It marked the beginning of an alliance between Great Britain and the United States that would in time, he believed, ensure the very survival of Britain. Churchill knew that pain and agony lay in the years ahead, but he was now confident of an Allied victory.

Allied forces trapped the Desert Fox.

In October 1942, British and American forces began their first major campaign together, in North Africa. The stakes there were high. The Suez Canal, Britain's lifeline to India, would go to the victor.

Since 1939, control of North Africa had see-sawed back and forth between Germany and Great Britain. Then, early in 1942, German General Erwin Rommel had begun a massive offensive in the region. A genius in tank warfare, Rommel was known as the Desert Fox. He had slowly but surely pushed British forces east across Egypt. By summer, the British were holding on by a thread in the strategic city of El Alamein (el AHL-uh-MAYN), their backs to the Suez Canal.

In August 1942, General Bernard Montgomery arrived in the North African desert to command the British forces. Small, lean, and steely-eyed, Montgomery planned not to defend but to attack. He spent two months amassing artillery and tanks. Finally, in October, Montgomery was ready to strike. So swift and overwhelming was his attack that Rommel lost 60,000 men, 500 tanks, and 400 large artillery pieces in less than a week.

The Battle of El Alamein marked a turning point in North Africa and a major shift in the war as a whole. It was the beginning of the Allied drive to seize the North African coast.

American and British forces closed in on the staggering Axis army from two directions. From the west, American General Dwight D. Eisenhower led Allied troops through Morocco and Algeria. From the east, Montgomery continued to roll back the German army. In May 1943, the two pincers of the drive came together in Tunisia, trapping 250,000 Germans and Italians. The coast of North Africa was in Allied hands.

Soviet forces took the offensive.

For Hitler, the news from the North African desert was bad, but the news that had been coming from the Soviet Union was even worse. The Germans had been fighting in the Soviet Union for nearly two years, since June 1941. In November 1941, the bitter cold of winter had stopped them dead in their tracks outside Leningrad and Moscow (page 671). When spring came, the German tanks were ready to roll again.

In the spring of 1942, the Germans took the offensive in the southern Soviet Union. Hitler hoped to capture Soviet oil fields in the Caucasus. He also wanted to wipe out the city of Stalingrad, named in honor of the Soviet leader.

The Battle of Stalingrad began in August 1942. From Stalin came the order to defend his name-sake city at all costs. Soon the costs were appallingly high. Night after night and day after day, Soviet defenders holed up in bombed-out apartments and courtyards. From there, they fought the Germans with knives, guns, bayonets, and even clubs. Only death forced them to yield. Even so, after months of brutal house-to-house fighting, the Germans appeared to be in control. Then another winter set in.

Soviet commander Georgi Zhukov saw the cold as an opportunity to roll fresh tanks across the frozen landscape and begin a counterattack. Like a giant vise, Zhukov's army closed around Stalingrad, trapping the Germans in the city and cutting off their supplies. The Germans' situation was hopeless, but Hitler's order came: "Stay and fight! I am not leaving the Volga!"

The Germans did their best to follow the impossible order. When they finally surrendered on

The desert war in North Africa was such a seesaw kind of battle that citizens of the area were said to keep two flags handy. When the Germans were in control, locals raised the swastika, only to lower it and raise the Union Jack when the British took over.

On June 4, 1944, American troops triumphantly poured into Rome. The 33-mile push from their landing site at Anzio to the Eternal City had taken 4 months and thousands of lives.

January 31, 1943, defying Hitler's orders even then, there were only 91,000 Germans left out of an original army of 280,000. Dazed and frost-bitten, the German captives trudged through the snow to Soviet prison camps.

After Stalingrad, it was the Germans who were thrown on the defensive. Up and down the 1,800-mile front, Soviet tanks and artillery hammered Hitler's armies. By now, many German military leaders realized what Hitler refused to admit—that the Nazi empire was collapsing. The Third Reich's days were numbered.

Fascist rule crumbled in Italy.

By the spring of 1943, it was clear that the tide had turned in favor of the Allies. The question was where the Allied armies should attack next. Stalin urged the British and Americans to attack the Germans in western Europe, thus relieving pressure on the Soviet front. Churchill disagreed. Fearful of launching a full-scale invasion of western Europe too soon, he favored attacking Italy from the North African coast.

On July 9, 1943, an Allied invasion force of 160,000 soldiers and marines crossed the Mediterranean and approached the southern shore of Sicily. After a ferocious naval bombardment, they clambered into flat-bottomed landing craft, charged through knee-deep water, and won a beachhead on Sicily. Sicily fell to the Allies in August after a bloody but brief struggle lasting only 39 days.

Stunned by their army's collapse in Sicily, the Italian people forced the dictator Mussolini to resign. On July 25, 1943, he was placed under arrest. A new premier, Pietro Badoglio (bah-**DOHL**-yoh), took power. He renounced his country's pact with Hitler and urged the Italian people "to fight the Germans in every way, everywhere, and all the time."

Italy's sudden change of loyalties did not save it from invasion. Hitler was determined to stop the Allies in Italy rather than fight on German soil. For almost two years, German armies occupied much of Italy, fiercely opposing Allied landings on Italy's western coast. The effort to free Italy did not succeed until 1945, when Germany itself was close to collapse.

The Allies invaded France.

Even as the Allies were battling for Italy in 1943, they began work on a daring plan to invade France and free western Europe from the Nazis. The enormous task of commanding the invasion fell to American General Dwight D. Eisenhower. Under his direction, the Allies gathered a force of 2 million British, American, and Canadian troops together with mountains of military equipment and supplies. Another million stood ready to give sea and air support to the attack.

Hitler knew that such a force was being trained in Britain. The question was when the invasion would take place and where on the French coast it would strike.

Daily Life · *The Broken Code*

All during the war, hundreds of British men and women lived with a carefully guarded secret. They could read the coded radio messages that the German army beamed back and forth. The Germans generated their codes with a complex electrical device like the one at the right. They thought these codes were unbreakable. However, early in the war, a few daring Poles smuggled a copy of the machine to Britain. The British name for this secret source of information was "Ultra."

Ultra was vital to Montgomery in North Africa. From it, he learned that Rommel was ill and the German army was desperately short of fuel. Without Ultra, Montgomery might not have been the victor at El Alamein.

Germans bombed Stalingrad from the air but then could not move their tanks through the rubble-choked streets.

World War II in Europe and North Africa, 1939–1945

KEY
- Allies or under Allied control, Dec. 1941
- Major Axis powers
- Greatest extent of Axis control, Dec. 1941
- Neutral nations
- ← Allied advances
- ⏅⏅⏅⏅ Maginot line

Map Study

List the nations under Axis control in Europe in 1941. By what three major routes did the Allies close in on the Axis powers after 1943?

The Allies planned to attack Normandy in northern France. To keep their plans secret, the Allies set up a huge phantom army with its own headquarters and equipment. In radio messages they knew the Germans could read, Allied commanders sent orders to this make-believe army to attack the French port of Calais. Hitler was completely fooled and ordered his generals to keep a large army at Calais.

The Allied invasion began on June 6, 1944, code-named D day. In the dead of night, an immense fleet of 5,300 ships set sail for their target, the beaches of Normandy. Shortly after midnight, 13,000 airborne troops parachuted into France. They were followed in the early morning hours by thousands upon thousands of seaborne soldiers—history's largest amphibious attack. After 5 days of fighting, the Allies held a strip of France

80 miles long. Less than 3 weeks later, 1 million men were ashore and moving steadily inland.

By the beginning of August 1944, German troops were pulling out of Paris to escape the Allied onslaught. Several units of the Free French movement led by Charles de Gaulle joined the Allies in their race toward Paris. Finally, on August 24, 1945, the Allies entered the city in triumph. Parisians were delirious with joy.

Footnote to History

American paratroopers who landed in France on D day carried a simple signaling device to help them find one another in the dark. Each man had a metal "cricket" toy to click. No German radio operator could intercept these messages!

Map Study answers: France, Belgium, Netherlands, Luxemburg, Denmark, Norway, Finland, Estonia, Latvia, Lithuania, Poland, Czechoslovakia, Hungary, Romania, Bulgaria, Albania, Greece, Yugoslavia, part of USSR; from west through France, from south through Italy, and from east far USSR

The German Reich collapsed.

Hitler now faced the old German nightmare—war on two fronts. The Soviet army, 5 million strong, advanced against Germany from the east. To the west, British and American forces were sweeping across the Rhine River into Germany itself. The German armies retreated.

The end was near for Hitler's Reich, but Hitler refused to recognize it. Germany must fight on, he said. "We shall never capitulate—never. We may be destroyed, but if we are, we shall drag a world with us—a world in flames." Yet, when Soviet tanks stood at the very gates of Berlin, the thought of falling into Soviet hands proved too much for him. On April 30, 1945, Hitler killed himself.

Mussolini, the overthrown Fascist dictator of Italy, was dead too. He had been assassinated on April 25.

The Allies too lost a leader in the same month. Franklin Roosevelt had just begun his fourth term as president. On April 12, 1945, an artist was drawing the president's portrait. Suddenly Roosevelt said, "I have a terrific headache." He never spoke again. A few hours later, Americans were stunned to learn that Roosevelt had died from a cerebral hemorrhage. Across the United States, people wept at the news. Wartime allies from Britain to China mourned.

Roosevelt's successor, Harry Truman, was president when the German Reich finally collapsed. On May 2, 1945, Berlin formally surrendered to the Soviet army. On May 7, the commanders of the German army and navy signed papers declaring the unconditional surrender of their forces. The war in Europe was over.

A final horror ended the Pacific war.

Meanwhile, Allied forces in the Pacific were closing in on Japan. By 1945, the Allies had reclaimed much of the Pacific, including the Philippines. From strategic bases such as Saipan in the Mariana Islands, the Allies launched long-range bombing missions against Japan. Still, they wanted to get closer.

In February, American marines landed on Iwo Jima, an island only 750 miles from Tokyo. The marines took the island after a month of bitter fighting and heavy losses. Then they moved on to the Ryukyu Islands just south of Japan. They captured Okinawa on April 1. The ordeal cost 45,000 American lives.

The taking of Iwo Jima and Okinawa opened the way for an invasion of Japan. However, Allied leaders knew that such an invasion would be a desperate struggle. Japan still had a large army that would defend every inch of its homeland. Moreover, thousands of Japanese pilots volunteered for suicide missions. These *kamikazes*, as they were called, crashed their explosive-filled planes into Allied ships, killing themselves at the same time.

President Truman saw only one way to avoid an invasion of Japan. He decided to use a powerful new weapon called the atom bomb.

By the 1930's, nuclear physicists had shown that the splitting of uranium atoms let loose tremendous energy. During the war, American scientists had urged President Roosevelt to develop a bomb using the energy of the atom before the Germans did so. Among the international team of scientists who urged the building of such a bomb were a Jewish refugee from Nazi Germany named Albert Einstein and a refugee from Fascist Italy named Enrico Fermi.

The first test of the new bomb took place on July 16, 1945, at Alamogordo in the New Mexican desert. The blinding burst of light and awesome roar of the first explosion was described by one witness as "magnificent, beautiful, stupendous, and terrifying."

Truman was delighted that the testing of this secret weapon had been successful. From the German city of Potsdam, where he was meeting with Churchill and Stalin, Truman issued a declaration on July 26, 1945. He warned the Japanese that they faced "prompt and utter destruction" unless they surrendered at once. The Japanese government did not reply.

On the morning of August 6, 1945, an American B-52 bomber released an atom bomb nicknamed "Little Boy" over Japan. The bomb drifted by parachute toward its target, Hiroshima, a city of 343,000 people. Two thirds of Hiroshima was instantly destroyed by the blast. About 80,000 people perished in the searing heat. Three days later, on August 9, a second atom bomb destroyed the city of Nagasaki and killed 40,000 people.

Aghast at these horrors, Japan's Emperor Hirohito urged his generals to surrender. He told them,

In 1941, as General Douglas MacArthur, American commander in Asia, evacuated the Philippines he promised, "I shall return." Three years later, he stepped triumphantly onto Philippine soil and proclaimed, "People of the Philippines! I have returned."

Victims of the atom bomb at Hiroshima waited for help at a first-aid station. Many of the city's medical facilities had been destroyed.

"I cannot bear to see my innocent people suffer any longer." The formal surrender took place on September 2, 1945, on the wide deck of the American battleship *Missouri* in Tokyo Bay. Representatives of the Allied powers—China, Britain, Australia, France, the Soviet Union, and the United States—watched as the Japanese foreign minister signed the papers of surrender.

Section Review 4

Define: kamikaze
Identify: (a) Erwin Rommel, (b) Bernard Montgomery, (c) Dwight D. Eisenhower, (d) Georgi Zhukov, (e) D day, (f) Hiroshima
Answer:
1. (a) Why was North Africa vital to the British? (b) What did Rommel accomplish there? (c) Why was El Alamein a turning point?
2. How were the Germans defeated at Stalingrad?
3. What were the results of the Allied invasion of Sicily?
4. How was the invasion of France carried out?
5. How did the war in Europe draw to a close?
6. (a) How did the development of the atom bomb change Allied plans for the defeat of Japan? (b) When and where were the atom bombs used?

Critical Thinking
7. Evaluate Truman's decision to use the atomic bomb. How could it be justified as saving more lives than it cost? What alternatives might have been considered?
8. There is a saying that generals are always well prepared to fight the past war. Explain how this saying does or does not apply to each of the following countries in World War II. (a) Germany (b) France (c) Britain (d) USSR

Chapter Review 31

Summary

1. Germany overran much of Europe. In the spring of 1939, Hitler announced his intention to take over the Polish Corridor. Britain and France responded by ending appeasement. Soon after, Hitler signed a nonaggression pact with Stalin. World War II in Europe began when Germany overran Poland. The Soviets followed by taking over the Baltic nations. By June 1940, Germany had overwhelmed Scandinavia and moved into France. On June 10, Italy joined the war on the side of Germany. After the fall of France, Germany began an unsuccessful air attack on Britain. Germany next invaded the Soviet Union but was halted by the severe Russian winter.

2. Japan conquered an Asian empire. Japan's conquests in Asia began in 1931 with the takeover of Manchuria. Six years later, Japan moved into China proper. The war in China was slowed by dwindling Japanese resources even as the United States was aiding the Allies with war supplies. When the United States cut off shipments of resources to Japan, Japan prepared to move into Southeast Asia. On December 7, 1941, Japan bombed Pearl Harbor in Hawaii and brought the United States into the war. Soon Japan held most of the western Pacific, but Allied victories at Midway and in the Coral Sea halted Japan.

3. World War II was a total war. Production rose dramatically in the United States. The war effort provided jobs for the jobless and opened new opportunities for women. Both sides used propaganda to promote the war effort. In the United States, fear of the Japanese led to the internment of Japanese-American civilians. In Germany, Hitler waged a program of genocide against the Jewish people. Devastating air raids caused civilian deaths.

4. The Allies launched a drive to victory. After defeating German forces in North Africa, Allied troops successfully invaded southern Europe, thus causing the collapse of Mussolini's government. To the east, defeat at Stalingrad gave rise to the threat of invasion of Germany on two fronts. A major Allied offensive began on D day, resulting in German surrender. The Allies ended the war in the Pacific by dropping atomic bombs on Hiroshima and Nagasaki.

Reviewing the Facts

1. Define the following terms:
   a. blitzkrieg
   b. genocide
2. Explain the importance of each of the following names, dates, places, or terms:
   a. Polish Corridor
   b. Luftwaffe
   c. Churchill
   d. Maginot Line

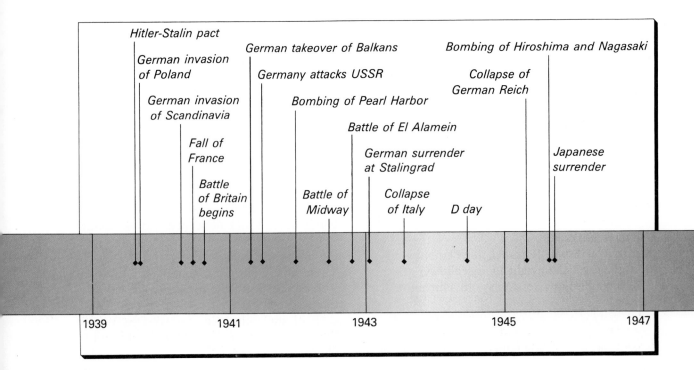

Hitler-Stalin pact

German invasion of Poland

German invasion of Scandinavia

Fall of France

Battle of Britain begins

German takeover of Balkans

Germany attacks USSR

Bombing of Pearl Harbor

Battle of Midway

Battle of El Alamein

German surrender at Stalingrad

Collapse of Italy

D day

Bombing of Hiroshima and Nagasaki

Collapse of German Reich

Japanese surrender

1939   1941   1943   1945   1947

e. Dunkirk
f. Vicky Regime
g. Free French
h. De Gaulle
i. RAF
j. Roosevelt
k. Lend-Lease Act

l. December 7, 1941
m. Battle of Midway
n. Holocaust
o. Rommel
p. Montgomery
q. Eisenhower
r. Truman

3. (a) What factors led to the fall of France? (b) How was France governed after its fall?
4. How did World War II in Asia begin?
5. (a) What did Roosevelt do to help the Allies between 1939 and 1941? (b) What brought the United States into the war?
6. (a) Why did the Allies look to the United States for supplies? (b) How did wartime propaganda harm Japanese-Americans?
7. (a) What was the significance of El Alamein? (b) Of the Battle of Stalingrad?
8. (a) What were the results of the Allied invasion of southern Europe? (b) How was the invasion of western Europe carried out?
9. (a) Describe the end of the war in Europe. (b) Describe the end of the war in the Pacific.

Basic Skills

1. **Reading and interpreting a time line** (a) On the time line on page 684, which events were victories for the allies? (b) For the Axis powers? (c) Why are the Battle of Britain and the Battle of Midway considered turning points in the war?
2. **Interpreting a map** (a) Judging from the map on page 681, why was victory in North Africa essential to an invasion of southern Europe? (b) How does this map explain why Hitler feared a two-front war?

Researching and Reporting Skills

1. **Interviewing an eyewitness** Interview someone in your community who experienced World War II. Prepare a list of questions about the person's experiences in the war. Ask if the person would mind if you taped the interview; otherwise, take brief notes. Report on the interview to the class.
2. **Using memoirs** In the memoirs of a key figure in World War II, such as Churchill or De Gaulle, read a chapter that deals with some critical moment of the war. How does this information add to your understanding of the time?
3. **Creating a museum of artifacts and souvenirs** As

a class, search your home and community for objects and memorabilia of World War II, such as old photographs, newspapers, letters, or other materials. Display these objects as a class exhibit, making labels for the different objects with a brief explanation.

Critical Thinking

1. **Analyzing** (a) What were the advantages and disadvantages of the Axis powers at the start of the war? (b) Of the Allies?
2. **Comparing** (a) Compare the kind of warfare introduced by the Germans in World War II with that of World War I. (b) What new weapons made this type of warfare possible?
3. **Analyzing** (a) Why did the Japanese government make the decision to attack Pearl Habor? (b) What did Japan expect the result to be? (c) What in fact was the outcome?
4. **Evaluating** (a) Evaluate three of Hitler's military decisions: the decisions to bomb Britain, to invade the Soviet Union, and not to retreat from the Soviet Union. (b) Which decision do you think was most important to Germany's defeat and why?
5. **Analyzing ideas** Through the Holocaust, Hitler directed a program of genocide against the Jewish people. (a) What measures were used to carry out this program? (b) Why is genocide considered a crime against humanity?

Perspectives on Past and Present

World War II was truly a worldwide war. How does it differ from local or regional wars, such as the Vietnam War, Iran-Iraq War, Falklands War, and other similar conflicts?

Investigating History

1. Watch the videotape of such movies as *The Sands of Iwo Jima, From Here to Eternity,* and *The Longest Day,* which are focused on aspects of World War II. What impressions do you gain about the war and the people in it?
2. Read selections from the writings or biography of one general of World War II, such as MacArthur, Eisenhower, Patton, Montgomery, or Rommel. Or read selections from Morison's *History of the United States Naval Operations in World War Two.* How do the impressions here differ from those in movies about the war?

Unit VIII Review

Geographic Theme: Location

How did Soviet territory expand in the course of World War II?

Every nation views the world from its own perspective. The view from Moscow is unique because of the vastness of the lands ruled from there. The Soviet Union occupies one third of Asia and nearly half of Europe. Only the waters of the Bering Strait separate Siberia from a third continent, North America.

Being the world's largest nation has its problems. In the 1930's, the Soviet Union shared a common border with more than a dozen nations. Along most of those borders, high mountains give natural protection. To the west, however, the North European Plain stretches unprotected. Thus, the military buildup of Nazi Germany during the 1930's was of great concern to Soviet leaders.

The map on page 666 of your text shows the Soviet position in Europe at the start of 1939. That situation lasted only briefly. In August of 1941, people in western Europe were stunned by word of a German-Soviet nonaggression pact. Each nation agreed to remain neutral if the other was at war. What people did not know was that a secret clause in the pact provided for the takeover of other countries by both nations. When German armies invaded Poland, Soviet armies took over the lands promised to them.

Almost two years after the start of World War II, the nonaggression pact ended abruptly when Hitler invaded the Soviet Union in June of 1941. German armies moved eastward, reaching as far as Moscow and Stalingrad (now Volvograd). Then invasion turned to retreat. Soviet armies surged west across the plain in pursuit of the retreating German army. At war's end, in 1945, they were at Berlin and the Elbe River, deep within Germany itself. The western Soviet Union and the lands it acquired as a result of the war are shown on the map below.

1. (a) What lands did the Soviets gain in the pact with Germany? (b) Compare the extent of Soviet territory in Europe in 1947 with that in January 1941.
2. What traditional policy of the czars did Stalin pursue in this seizure of territory?
3. (a) Describe the change in the Soviet role as a world power from 1941 to 1947. (b) How may the added territories have contributed to that change?

The Growth of the Soviet Union (Europe), 1939–1945

KEY
- Pre war boundaries, 1939
- Soviet aggressions, 1939-1940
- National boundaries, 1945
- Soviet territorrial gains since 1939

Unit Perspectives

Understanding History

1. **Explaining** Explain how each of the following contributed to the start of World War I: (a) rival alliances, (b) nationalism, (c) imperialism, (d) militarism.

2. **Relating** Explain the significance to World War I of each term listed below:
   a. Schlieffen Plan   f. Western Front
   b. Serbia   g. Eastern Front
   c. U-boat   h. Battle of the Marne
   d. Allied Powers   i. Treaty of Brest Litovsk
   e. Central Powers   j. Fourteen Points

3. **Relating** Explain the importance to World War II of each term listed below:
   a. blitzkrieg   f. Vichy Regime
   b. Polish Corridor   g. Lend Lease
   c. Luftwaffe   h. Battle of Stalingrad
   d. RAF   i. Battle of Midway
   e. Maginot Line   j. D-day

4. **Sequencing** Tell whether the following events happened before or after the Russian Revolution of 1917:
   a. Freeing of the serfs
   b. Civil war between the Reds and Whites
   c. Treaty of Brest Litovsk
   d. Decembrist revolt
   e. Bloody Sunday
   f. Russo-Japanese War
   g. Kronstadt revolt

5. **Explaining** How did each of the following people impact nationalistic movements in the early 1900's?
   a. Gandhi   g. Carranza
   b. Jinnah   h. Obregón
   c. Kemal   i. Sun Yat-sen
   d. Ibn Saud   j. Chiang Kai-shek
   e. Weizmann   k. Mao Tse-tung
   f. Zapata

Critical Thinking

1. **Evaluating** Before World War I, the great powers of Europe included Britain, France, Italy, Austria-Hungary, Germany, and Russia. (a) In terms of political and military power, what was the status of each country after the war? (b) Over the next two decades, what political systems emerged in Italy, Germany, and Russia that sought to regain national power?

2. **Analyzing** It has been said that revolutions tend to begin with moderate changes and move to more extreme changes that determine the outcome. To what extent was this true of the Russian Revolution? Give examples to support your answer.

3. **Comparing** (a) How were nationalist movements in India and the Middle East similar? (b) How did they differ?

4. **Identifying causes and effects** (a) What were the causes of the Mexican revolution and the overthrow of the emperor in China? (b) In each case, what were the short-term and long-term effects?

5. **Applying a concept** (a) What was the Great Depression? (b) How did it affect the rise of dictators?

6. **Comparing** (a) Compare the causes of World War I and World War II. (b) In what ways were conditions after World War II similar to those after World War I? (c) How did they differ?

Making Decisions

Hitler made a number of ill-advised decisions during the war. Of those decisions listed below, which one do you think was most important in Germany's defeat? What alternatives to each decision did Hitler have?
   a. the decision to bomb Great Britain
   d. the decision to invade the Soviet Union
   c. the decision not to retreat from the Soviet Union

Continuity and Change

1. Both world wars were enormously destructive. What new threats to humanity occurred in World War II that had not existed in World War I?

2. What political changes that occurred after World War I might you expect to have recurred after World War II?

Unit IX

The Modern World

Chapters

1946   **1954**   **1962**

| Political and Governmental Life | **1947** India and Pakistan become independent **1948** Israel becomes a nation | **1950's–1970's** African nations gain independence | **1964–1975** Vietnam War |

Kwame Nkrumah

Economic and Technological Life

Marshall Plan aid to Europe

1957 European Common Market is organized

1960 OPEC is founded

Social and Cultural Life

1948 South Africa adopts apartheid

1949 China becomes communist

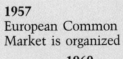

▲ **1966–1976** Mao leads China in Cultural Revolution

Detail of painting by Haitian artist Joseph Jean-Gilles

While many countries were recovering from the devastation of war, the United States and the Soviet Union became rivals for power, even engaging in regional conflicts. Meanwhile, newly independent nations in Asia and Africa began the long quest for stability, economic growth, and a greater role in world affairs. People around the world found their lives changed by a revolution in science and technology that yielded benefits but also created a problem of pollution on a global scale. The growing dispersal of power and prosperity among many countries brought sober recognition that a new era was at hand.

1970   **1978**   **1986**

1970's–1980's
Latin American nations make social and economic reforms

1979
Margaret Thatcher becomes British prime minister

1988
Carlos Salinas de Cortari elected president of Mexico

1985
Mikhail Gorbachev leads Soviet Union

Tokyo stock exchange

1969
United States astronauts land on moon

◀ **1980's**
Japan becomes world economic power

1986
Nuclear disaster occurs at Chernobyl

1988
United States and Canada make trade agreement

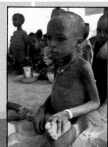

◀ **1970's–1980's**
Drought brings famine to African Sahel

1984
Archbishop Desmond Tutu receives Nobel Peace Prize

◀ **1988**
Benazir Bhutto leads Pakistan

The Cold War

Winston Churchill (left), Franklin Roosevelt (center), and Joseph Stalin (right) met at Yalta in the Soviet Union as World War II was drawing to a close.

Key terms

buffer zone
satellite
ideology

Read and Understand

1. Two superpowers arose after the war.
2. The war left Europe divided.
3. China became a Communist country

Traces of pink were lighting the predawn sky when hundreds of Soviet soldiers heard the roar of planes approaching the airfield. During the next hour, about 25 aircraft landed at Saki airfield on the Crimean Peninsula along the northern shores of the Black Sea.

The planes bore the insignias of the Soviet Union's two major wartime allies, Great Britain and the United States. They carried about 700 passengers, including Winston Churchill, the British prime minister, and Franklin D. Roosevelt, the American president. The date was February 3, 1945.

At the airport, a Red Army band greeted the leaders, playing each country's national anthem. Soviet officials led their visitors to three nearby tents where they dined on smoked salmon and caviar. Then

The conference at Yalta marked the first time an American president had visited the Soviet Union during his term of office.

they set out on a six-hour automobile ride over winding mountain roads to the small Black Sea resort city of Yalta.

Roosevelt, Churchill, and Stalin represented the Big Three among the Allied countries fighting Nazi Germany. Germany's defeat was now certain. At their first meeting at Yalta, Churchill toasted "the broad sunlight of victorious peace."

However, "victorious peace" meant different things to each of the three leaders. For Churchill, it meant a free and democratic Europe that Britain would lead, thanks to its centuries-old parliamentary traditions and its mighty empire. For Stalin, victorious peace meant increased Soviet power and a chance to safeguard the USSR against any further invasions from the West. For Roosevelt, victorious peace meant a world in which democracy could thrive under the leadership of the United States.

The discussions and debates at Yalta reflected these different viewpoints. For example, the three leaders disagreed sharply over Poland. Churchill wanted the Polish government-in-exile, which had operated in London during the war, to take power. Stalin had other ideas. The Soviet army already controlled most of Poland and had set up a pro-Soviet government there. Stalin wanted recognition for this Communist government. "Throughout history, Poland has always been a corridor for attacks on Russia," Stalin said at Yalta, explaining his point of view. "It is not only a question of honor for Russia, but one of life and death."

Roosevelt played the part of mediator. While he agreed in principle with Churchill that Poland should have a free, democratic government, he was prepared to make concessions to Stalin for two reasons. First, he hoped that the Soviet Union would quickly join the war against Japan in the Pacific. He expected that struggle to be long and difficult. Soviet help could shorten the war and save American lives. (The first test of the atom bomb was still five months away, and Roosevelt could not foresee how soon Japan would surrender.) Second, Roosevelt wanted Stalin's support for a new world peace organization, the United Nations.

Yalta was the last face-to-face meeting of the Big Three. About two months later, on April 12, 1945, Roosevelt died suddenly. Vice President Harry S. Truman succeeded him as president.

In later years, the Yalta conference became the subject of heated controversy. Should the United States have treated the USSR as a wartime ally or as a future rival?

The United States and the USSR are alike in many ways. Both are large countries, covering much of their continents. Size has given both countries many natural resources that have helped them to build strong economies. Both countries have citizens of many ethnic groups, so that each national government must deal with variety in language and culture among its citizens.

Finally, each country has a powerful **ideology**— a system of beliefs—that influences its political, social, and economic actions. The Soviet ideology is based on the writings of Marx and Lenin. This ideology calls for government control of the economy, political control by the Communist party, and support for worldwide Communist revolution. The American ideology includes democratic government with free elections, private enterprise in the economy, and support for the worldwide spread of democracy. Neither country has been completely consistent in following its ideology, either at home or abroad.

In this chapter, we will see how the United States and the USSR changed from wartime allies to unfriendly rivals. Their rivalry, which was neither true peace nor outright war, was called the Cold War.

Two superpowers arose after the war. 1

In spring of 1945, American troops rolled eastward across Germany. Soviet troops marched westward. On April 25, 1945, American and Soviet forces met at Torgau on the Elbe River in Germany. Nazi Germany had been crushed between the two great powers.

After months of fighting, the two armies were ready to celebrate. They saluted each other, drank toasts, danced jigs, sang, and shouted. "Today is the happiest day in all our lives," proclaimed a Soviet major to the Americans. "Long live your great leader! Long live our great leader!"

The United States and the Soviet Union now stood forth as the most powerful nations in the world. Unfortunately, all too soon the good feelings between Americans and Soviets came to an end. Almost before the last Nazi guns were silenced, a great rift began to develop between the United States and the Soviet Union.

The United States disarmed quickly.

At the war's end, the United States was both the most powerful and the most prosperous of all the countries that had taken part in the war. Many Americans had suffered during the war. About 400,000 had died in battle, and many more were injured. However, no bombs had fallen on American cities. American factories were unscathed. Few other industrialized countries were as lucky.

In 1945, the United States had the biggest navy and the best-equipped army and air force in the world. The United States was also the only country to possess the war's most formidable weapon, the atom bomb. Militarily, the United States was the unchallenged leader of the world.

However, Americans were eager to return to peace. Families wanted their sons, husbands, or fathers home from the army. Therefore, the United States demobilized as soon as the war was over. Between 1945 and 1947, the number of Americans in the armed forces dropped from 12 million to 1.5 million.

"No nation in history," President Truman wrote in his memoirs, "had ever won so great a victory and asked for so little in return." It was also true that no country had ever emerged from a war so prosperous. In 1947, the United States produced half of the world's manufactured goods, 57 percent of its steel, 43 percent of its electricity, and 62 percent of its oil. Never before in history had so large a percentage of the world's wealth been concentrated in a single country.

After World War I, as we saw in Chapter 30, the United States had turned to political isolationism (page 648). After World War II, however, the American attitude was different. The United States even offered to make New York City the permanent headquarters of the new United Nations. Shortly before his death, Franklin Roosevelt had said, "We have learned that we cannot live alone, at peace; that our own well-being is dependent on the well-being of other nations."

American soldiers (left) met their Soviet allies (right) on a ruined bridge over the Elbe River at Torgau in defeated Germany.

Voice from Our Time · *Stalin's Declaration of the Cold War*

On February 9, 1946, Joseph Stalin delivered a radio address to the Soviet people. His threatening message alarmed American leaders.

The catastrophe of war might be avoided if it were possible to make periodic redistribution of raw materials ... But this is impossible under present conditions of capitalistic development ... I have no doubt that if we render the necessary assistance to our scientists, they will be able not only to overtake but also in the very near future to surpass the achievements of science outside the boundaries of our country. The party intends to organize a new mighty upsurge of national economy, which will enable us to increase the level of our production ... Only [then] will our country be insured against any eventuality.

1. Does Stalin believe that another war can be avoided?
2. Which American achievement do you think Stalin wants to surpass?
3. Supreme Court Justice William Douglas called Stalin's speech "the declaration of World War III." Do you agree with his evaluation?

The USSR demanded a buffer zone.

Like the United States, the Soviet Union emerged from the war as a nation of enormous economic and military strength. In fact, it was second in power only to the United States.

Unlike the United States, however, the USSR had suffered heavy fighting on its own soil. Large areas of the Soviet Union had been occupied by brutal Nazi armies. Many Soviet cities were destroyed. Fields around the cities were filled with mass graves. Soviet war losses have been estimated at 20 million, of whom half were civilians. For every American killed in World War II, 50 Soviets died.

These losses help to explain why the United States and the Soviet Union acted differently after the war. While American leaders were most concerned about building a peaceful world, Soviet leaders were most concerned about protecting their country against future wars.

The best protection the USSR could have, Stalin reasoned, was a **buffer zone** along its western border. A buffer zone is a region that lies between two rivals, cutting down the threat of conflict. The area Stalin wanted as a buffer zone was eastern Europe. By dominating this region, Stalin hoped to ensure that the Soviets could stop any future invasion before the Soviet Union itself was hurt. Moreover, Soviet control of eastern Europe would bring about 100 million more people into the Communist system.

Stalin's plans ignored the wishes of the people who lived in eastern Europe. Like the USSR, most countries in eastern Europe lacked strong democratic traditions. Thus, the Soviet Union could hope to push Communist governments into power without effective opposition.

The United Nations was founded.

One of Roosevelt's chief goals at Yalta had been to win Soviet support for a worldwide peacekeeping organization. Even before the war was over, plans for such an organization began.

An international conference in San Francisco between April and June 1945 drew up a charter (constitution) for the United Nations. In signing this charter, 51 countries pledged to work together "to save succeeding generations from the scourge of war, which twice in our lifetime has brought untold sorrow to mankind."

The charter provided the United Nations (or UN) with a main representative body known as the General Assembly. Every member nation could cast a vote in the General Assembly. The General Assembly approved new members, discussed a broad range of issues, and made recommendations and agreements.

A second group, the Security Council, was in charge of investigating disputes, peacekeeping, and emergency action. Five countries—Britain, China, France, the United States, and the Soviet Union—were permanent members of the council.

Discussion questions: Is an organization of the world's nations necessary? Realistic?
Could the United Nations be reorganized to increase its effectiveness?

693

In the UN General Assembly, each member country has one vote. Votes are tallied on the electric voting boards at the front of the room with different colors standing for yes, no, or abstain.

Six other members were chosen from the UN membership at large. These members served two-year terms on the council. (Later, the number of other members was increased to 10, so that the Security Council now has 15 members.)

Both the United States and the Soviet Union insisted on being permanent council members when the UN charter was written. The two countries also agreed that each permanent member would have veto power. In other words, the Security Council could take no action unless all five permanent members agreed.

Besides the General Assembly and the Security Council, the UN included many other organizations and agencies. For example, an International Court of Justice dealt with questions of international law. The Secretariat, headed by the Secretary-General, organized the daily business of the United Nations.

From the start, the United Nations enjoyed at least two advantages over the old League of Nations. First, no major powers refused to join. Second, the charter provided for a UN peace-keeping force, an armed group that could be drawn from the troops of member countries. The UN could use these troops to enforce its decisions or to separate warring groups.

Despite these advantages, the UN also faced a major stumbling block. Unless all five permanent members of the Security Council agreed on a course of action, the UN could do nothing. Time and again, one permanent member or another used its veto power to paralyze the United Nations.

The United Nations proved more effective on social and economic issues than in solving political crises. Agencies such as UNESCO (United Nations Education, Scientific, and Cultural Organization), FAO (Food and Agriculture Organization), and WHO (World Health Organization) helped to coordinate worldwide efforts to battle disease, feed the hungry, and improve literacy.

Overall, the United Nations had a mixed record of successes and failures. However, the UN proved powerless to deal with one great threat that hung over the entire world after 1945—the threat of nuclear war.

Nuclear weapons spread.

Of all the new weapons of World War II, one stood out for its overwhelming power—the atom bomb. At Hiroshima and Nagasaki, just two of these murderous weapons killed 120,000 people. "The primary reaction of the populace to the bomb," as the official American report on its use noted, "was fear, uncontrolled terror, strengthened by the sheer horror of the destruction and suffering witnessed and experienced by the survivors."

The destructive power of the atom bomb was not limited to its tremendous blast. First came a heat flash that could burn, blind, and kill. Later, in the days and weeks after the blast, came radioactive fallout that spread sickness and slow death across a much broader area.

Once the United States had such a bomb, the Soviet Union was determined not to be left with

The hydrogen bomb was based on nuclear fusion, the joining of two hydrogen atoms under intense heat to form a heavier atom. The fusion process released even more energy than nuclear fission, the splitting of uranium atoms.

weaker weapons. The Soviets began a crash program to develop their own atom bomb immediately after World War II. In 1949, they tested their first atom bomb in a remote part of Siberia. That test marked the end of the American monopoly on such bombs.

Now that both superpowers possessed such weapons, the world faced a new situation. Winston Churchill called it "a balance of terror." He meant that both countries would be so terrified of destruction that they would avoid war.

The atom bomb was the first example of a *nuclear* weapon. Weapons of this type get their power from reactions involving the center or *nucleus* of an atom.

In 1952, American scientists produced an even more destructive nuclear weapon, the hydrogen bomb. Soviet scientists quickly followed suit, testing their country's first hydrogen bomb in 1953. In a contest that came to be called the arms race, the two superpowers continued to compete in making more and larger nuclear weapons. Knowing that such a race might end in worldwide disaster, leaders in both countries also searched from time to time for ways to limit or slow this arms race.

Section Review 1

Define: (a) demobilize, (b) buffer zone, (c) veto, (d) nuclear weapon
Identify: (a) Yalta conference, (b) Cold War, (c) Harry S. Truman, (d) United Nations, (e) General Assembly, (f) Security Council, (g) arms race
Answer:
1. (a) Why was the United States in a stronger economic position than other countries at the end of World War II? (b) Why was it in the strongest military position?
2. How was the United States' attitude in 1945 different from its attitude after World War I?
3. (a) What was the major Soviet goal in 1945? (b) Why was that goal important to Soviet leaders?
4. (a) What features made the UN stronger than the League of Nations had been? (b) What weakness sometimes kept the UN from taking effective action?
5. How did the arms race develop?

Critical Thinking
6. Compare and contrast the situations of the United States and the Soviet Union in 1945. What factors help to explain why they became rivals instead of allies?

The war left Europe divided.   2

In 1945, Europe, which had once dominated the globe, was struggling to survive. "What is Europe now?" Winston Churchill asked at the end of World War II. "It is a rubble-heap, a charnel house, a breeding ground of pestilence and hate."

Europe faced dark days indeed. Hunger and want stalked the land from Bulgaria to Belgium. Tens of millions of Europeans were homeless, classified by bureaucrats as "displaced persons." To make matters worse, the winter of 1946–1947 was the coldest in living memory, and fuel supplies were disastrously low.

Germany was defeated and divided.

Hitler's policies of destruction had, like a boomerang, come back to destroy Germany. Some 4 million Germans had died in the war. Cities lay in ruins. Transportation was at a standstill. Every bridge across such major rivers as the Rhine and the Main had been destroyed in Allied bombing raids. So too had most of the country's businesses. In the Ruhr valley, only one factory in ten was still operating at the war's end.

East-West split Germany's postwar fate was decided in part at Yalta. There Stalin argued that Germany should be permanently divided to prevent its ever again making war. Roosevelt and Churchill agreed to divide Germany into four occupation zones, expecting that the division would be temporary. The United States, Great Britain, France, and the USSR were each to control a zone.

The western Allies encouraged the growth of democratic government in their three occupation zones. In 1949, Britain, France, and the United States allowed their zones to join. The three zones became the Federal Republic of Germany.

Residential areas also suffered from the air war. Dresden and Essen had been almost completely demolished, while 75 percent of all the houses in Berlin had been destroyed or severely damaged.

Chapter Review 32

Summary

1. Two superpowers arose after the war. After the war, the western Allies hoped to spread democracy, whereas Stalin sought to increase Soviet power. The United States and the Soviet Union emerged from the war as rival superpowers engaged in a nuclear arms race. Although the founding of the United Nations symbolized a desire for peace, its efforts were hampered by the veto powers of the Security Council.

2. The war left Europe divided. World War II left Europe in ruins. A defeated Germany was divided into four occupied zones. In time, the zones occupied by the western Allies became a democratic state known as the Federal Republic of Germany, or West Germany. East Germany remained under Communist control, and much of Eastern Europe also fell to the Soviets. The United States instituted a course of containment to block the further spread of communism, set up the Marshall Plan to aid economic recovery in Western Europe, and joined NATO, a mutual defense pact. The Soviet Union responded with the Warsaw Pact and the Berlin blockade to starve West Berlin into submission. Although the Soviets loosened controls after Stalin's death, they quickly suppressed a revolution in Hungary. A final outcome of the war was the loss of overseas empires for Europe.

3. China became a Communist country. At the end of World War II, civil war once again broke out in China between Nationalists and Communists. Defeated Nationalists fled to Taiwan in 1949. Led by Mao Tse-tung, Communists set up the People's Republic of China, which the United States refused to recognize. After the war, Korea was occupied by Soviets in the north and United States troops in the South. In 1950, North Koreans, aided by Chinese Communists, swept into South Korea. The United Nations sent a peacekeeping force to stop the invasion. The war ended in a stalemate in 1953.

Reviewing the Facts

1. Define the following terms:
   - a. buffer zone
   - b. satellite

2. Explain the importance of each of the following names, places, or terms:
   - a. Yalta conference
   - b. Cold War
   - c. Truman
   - d. Nuremberg trials
   - e. Tito
   - f. iron curtain
   - g. Truman Doctrine
   - h. Marshall Plan
   - i. NATO
   - j. Warsaw Pact
   - k. West Berlin
   - l. Khrushchev
   - m. Imre Nagy
   - n. Mao Tse-tung
   - o. Chiang Kai-shek
   - p. Taiwan

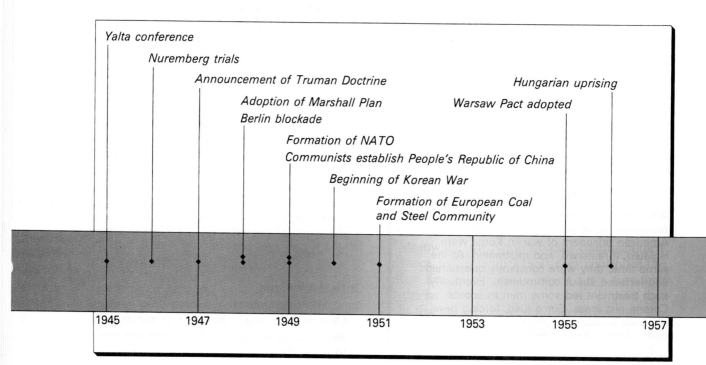

Yalta conference
Nuremberg trials
Announcement of Truman Doctrine
Adoption of Marshall Plan
Berlin blockade
Formation of NATO
Communists establish People's Republic of China
Beginning of Korean War
Formation of European Coal and Steel Community
Hungarian uprising
Warsaw Pact adopted

1945 | 1947 | 1949 | 1951 | 1953 | 1955 | 1957

Basic Skills

1. **Interpreting a map** (a) Judging from the map on page 699, what geographic advantages helped Yugoslavia avoid domination by the Soviets? (b) What geographic disadvantages faced countries such as Romania, Hungary, and Czechoslovakia?
2. **Making a chart** (a) Make a chart comparing the ideologies of the United States and the Soviet Union. For the vertical columns, use the headings Role of Government, Political Parties, Economic System, Role of Individuals, and International Objectives. (b) Both governments call themselves democratic. In terms of the information in your chart, how accurate is that description?

Researching and Reporting Skills

1. **Using biographical indexes** Biographical articles on leaders in all fields may be found in a multi-volume source, *Current Biography.* Use the cumulative index in the volume for 1950 to find articles about one of the following leaders or some other prominent leader of the time: George Marshall, Josip Broz (Tito), Joseph Stalin, Winston Churchill, Clement Attlee, Chiang Kai-shek, or Mao Tse-tung.
2. **Using microfilm** Choose a date (year, month, and day) between 1947 and 1960. Look up on microfilm the text of *The New York Times* for that date. Make a list of the major events discussed in that day's paper. Report on these to your class.
3. **Using television** From current news broadcasts, obtain information about a topic (such as one pertaining to divided Germany or to satellite countries) that dates from the postwar period. How have the issues pertaining to that topic changed since the postwar era? To what extent have they remained the same?

Critical Thinking

1. **Applying a concept** President Truman's policy of containment sought to limit Soviet expansion after World War II. Explain how each of the following served to implement that policy: (a) Truman Doctrine, (b) NATO, (c) Marshall Plan.
2. **Analyzing** Which of the postwar changes in Eastern Europe provided the security sought by the Soviet Union? Give examples to support your answer.
3. **Comparing** Compare the international role of the United States after World War II with its role after World War I.
4. **Analyzing economics** (a) What factors enabled the countries of Western Europe to recover economically after the war? (b) What were the economic outcomes of the recovery? (c) The political outcomes?
5. **Comparing** Compare the United Nations and the League of Nations in terms of (a) membership, (b) potential for peace-keeping, and (c) role of the great powers.
6. **Analyzing** (a) What factors and events accounted for the start of the Cold War? (b) What alternatives, if any, were there to the Cold War?
7. **Inferring** (a) What factors enabled the Communists to take over China? (b) What problems might the Communist government have faced after it came into power?
8. **Evaluating** Although the United Nations sent forces to Korea in 1950, it did not send forces to Hungary in 1956. (a) In what ways were the situations alike? (b) How did they differ?

Perspectives on Past and Present

Notice that in the chapters of this unit, the "Voice from the Past" feature is retitled "Voice from Our Time." Why might the years after 1945 be called "our time"? Do you agree that 1945 marks the beginning of the era in which you live? Why or why not?

Investigating History

1. Read about the Cold War as recalled in Merle Muller's *Plain Speaking: An Oral Biography of Harry S. Truman.* The most relevant chapters are these: 21, "General Marshall and the Marshall Plan"; 23, "The Korean Decision"; and 24, "Firing the General".
2. Make a study of one of the Eastern European countries that came under communist control after World War II. What were the forces for resistance? Why did the Communists gain control? What was life like for people under communist rule? Share the results of your findings with the class.
3. Investigate one agency of the United Nations. What was its purpose? In what places has it operated? What have been some of its achievements? What problems has it faced?

Cooperation and Division in Europe

Economic cooperation has brought prosperity to much of Western Europe. Here, shops line a pedestrian mall in the West German city of Aachen, which was Charlemagne's capital nearly 1,200 years ago.

Key terms

import quota
welfare state
productivity
martial law
dissident

Read and Understand

1. Western Europe moved toward cooperation
2. Eastern Europe was linked to the USSR.
3. Policies changed within the USSR.

In Europe's long and war-torn history, few cities have seen more of war than Strasbourg on the eastern edge of France. In the days of the Roman empire, it was an army outpost guarding the Rhine River. When the Roman empire crumbled, the Franks took over Strasbourg. During much of the Middle Ages, it was a free city in the Holy Roman Empire. Then France's Louis XIV seized the city in 1681.

Strasbourg remained part of France until the Prussian army besieged the city for seven weeks and captured it in 1870. Strasbourg and all of Alsace and Lorraine then passed into German hands for nearly 50 years. The French triumphantly retook Strasbourg after World War I, only to lose it again to Germany at the outbreak of World War II. After the war, Strasbourg became part of France once again.

Strasbourg changed hands many times because it stood near the Rhine, an important boundary in European geography. For centuries,

In 1988, Strasbourg celebrated its 2,000th anniversary. It had begun as a Roman army camp in 12 B.C.

Europe has been a continent of boundaries. Boundaries between countries were often battle zones. Even in times of peace, borders were often heavily fortified. Travelers had to show their documents—passports, visas, or other permits—to cross from one country into another.

Arrival at a border also signaled price changes. The same item might cost the equivalent of $5.00 in Britain, $5.60 in France, and $6.00 in Italy. The differences arose because each country had different tariff laws. Doing business across European frontiers involved much paperwork.

Then, in 1957, something happened to change this situation. Several countries in Western Europe formed a *Common Market* to encourage trade by reducing tariffs among members. The Common Market countries also agreed to charge the same import duties on goods brought from other countries. This made prices more uniform.

The Common Market has made a difference in Strasbourg. "For centuries," explained the city's mayor, "we in the border areas have known nothing but fear and insecurity. Now that nightmare has ended. The Common Market and the concept of Europe have made a basic and fundamental change in our lives."

Before the Common Market, the people of Strasbourg could not work in neighboring German towns even though there were plenty of jobs there. The Common Market agreement allowed workers to travel freely among member countries.

By the early 1970's, some 26,000 French workers were making daily trips across the Rhine to German factories. On returning home, they could shop at supermarkets and department stores that offered a selection of food, clothing, and appliances from all over Western Europe. Before the Common Market, only about 1 percent of the goods in French department stores had been imported. Every day, about 10,000 Germans drove into Alsace, where many loaded their cars with food, which was cheaper in France than in West Germany. The Common Market was an economic success. It also fostered a spirit of international cooperation in Western Europe.

The Eastern European countries formed an economic organization of their own called Comecon. However, it was not as successful as the Common Market. After years of hardship, Eastern Europe began after the mid-1970's to enjoy a rising standard of living. The reforms of

Gorbachev in the Soviet Union brought a new political climate. They also introduced the possibility of more economic freedom. Thus, the easing of controls under Gorbachev's leadership brought new hope. Nonetheless, many uncertainties remained.

Western Europe moved toward cooperation. 1

Over the course of European history, conquerors from Charlemagne to Hitler tried unsuccessfully to unite Europe. After World War II, a French statesman began a peaceful revolution to unite Europe economically. Jean Monnet (zhahn moh-NEH) saw economic cooperation as a first step toward a politically united Europe. He prophesied in the 1950's, "Once a common market has been created, then political union will come naturally." Most European leaders, however, were more interested in the immediate practical benefits of economic cooperation than in long-range plans for political unity.

Western Europe formed a Common Market.

In 1950, Monnet and French Foreign Minister Robert Schumann suggested a tariff-free market in coal and steel. These were the key products Europe needed for rebuilding after the war. Six countries—West Germany, France, Italy, Belgium, the Netherlands, and Luxembourg—agreed to form such a market. The European Coal and Steel Community (ECSC) proved a great success. By 1960, steel production in its member nations had doubled.

In 1957, the six nations took a further step toward economic cooperation. By the Treaty of Rome, they created the European Economic Community (EEC), usually called the Common Market. Member nations pledged to remove trade barriers among themselves by gradually ending tariffs and **import quotas.** An import quota is a limit that one country sets on the amount of goods that may be brought in from another country.

While encouraging trade among themselves, the Common Market countries continued to trade with nonmembers as well. Goods coming into the Common Market from outside were subject to a common tariff.

The Common Market quickly became one of the most important economic units in the world. The rising prosperity of its members led other countries to apply for membership. In 1973, the Common Market expanded, admitting Great Britain, Denmark, and Ireland. The group continued to grow in the 1980's. Greece became a member in 1981, and Spain and Portugal joined in 1986.

The 12 members of the Common Market are preparing for the next step in their region's development. On December 31, 1992, all trade barriers within the Common Market are due to be removed. Goods will move as freely as they now do in the United States. The effects of this change are not clear. Yet, as one Dutch observer said, "If we can get as far in 30 years as the U.S. has in 200 years of interstate trade, then we're doing quite well."

West Germany prospered in peace.

The most dramatic political and economic transformation in postwar Europe took place in West Germany. Within a few years of the war, the West Germans had built a stable democratic government. Soon they also enjoyed the most prosperous economy in Europe.

West Germany's political rebirth began in 1949. The German Federal Republic (or West Germany) was formed when Britain, France, and the United States combined the parts of Germany that their troops occupied (pages 695–696). The new German republic was headed by a chancellor who was responsible to a democratically elected legislature.

West Germany's first chancellor was Konrad Adenauer, a former mayor of Cologne who had been jailed several times by the Nazis. Adenauer took office in 1949 at the age of 73. The "Old Man," as he was known, dominated West German politics until he retired in 1963.

The most pressing problem that Adenauer faced was rebuilding West Germany's ruined economy. More than $3 billion of economic aid from the Marshall Plan helped to get the wheels of industry

turning again. German business leaders rebuilt their bombed-out factories, installing new, efficient equipment. Germany soon had some of the most up-to-date factories in the world. By 1958, West German industry was producing nearly twice as much as the German factories of 1938, even though West Germany was only about half the size of prewar Germany. West Germany became the foremost industrial nation in Europe.

Between West and East Another major problem facing Adenauer was West Germany's place in the Cold War. "Our country," he noted, "is the point of tension between two world blocs . . . Long ago I made a great decision: we belong to the West, and not the East." Adenauer used his long term of office to steer his country into a close alliance with the United States and the countries of Western Europe. West Germany joined NATO in 1955 and the Common Market in 1957. In 1963, the West Germans signed a Treaty of Cooperation with France. Under Adenauer's leadership, West Germany rose from shame and defeat to a new position of respect.

Ostpolitik While West Germany enjoyed close ties with the West, it remained isolated from Eastern Europe and the Soviet Union for 20 years. Neither Adenauer nor his immediate successors recognized East Germany. In 1969, however, a new chancellor, Willy Brandt, decided to improve relations with the Soviet Union and Eastern Europe. His program was called *Ostpolitik* (eastern policy).

Brandt visited both Moscow and Warsaw in 1970. With the Soviet Union, he negotiated a treaty calling for normal relations between the two countries. In a similar agreement with Poland, West Germany formally accepted the loss of once-German lands. Ostpolitik led to a diplomatic breakthrough in 1973: East and West Germany formally recognized each other as sovereign states.

Economic development Helmut Schmidt and Helmut Kohl, the successors to Brandt, continued many of his policies. Under their leadership, West Germany has enjoyed prosperity. It is a major exporting nation, selling autos and electronic goods around the world. Within the last few years, a high-technology area employing about 300,000 people has developed around Munich.

The people of West Germany enjoy a high standard of living. German autoworkers are among the highest paid in the world. Many people

In Germany, a nation often characterized as warlike, pacifist sentiment is now stronger than in any other nation of Western Europe.

What Europe Buys	
Petroleum products	$55.7
Office equipment	19.0
Apparel and accessories	16.7
Road vehicles, including cars	16.5
Electrical machinery and parts	16.1
Telecommunications equipment	12.8
Textiles, yarn, and fabrics	10.6
Paper and paperboard	10.5
Fruits and vegetables	9.5
Plastics and artificial resins	9.3
IN BILLIONS OF DOLLARS	

SOURCE: European Commission of the European Community

Who Sells to Europe	
United States	$66.4
Japan	41.9
Soviet Union	15.0
Brazil	8.3
Canada	8.0
Taiwan	7.9
Hong Kong	7.4
South Korea	7.1
Saudi Arabia	6.6
Algeria	6.1
Yugoslavia	6.1
China	5.9
Libya	5.8
South Africa	5.6
Australia	4.8
IN BILLIONS OF U.S. DOLLARS	

SOURCE: Organization for Economic Cooperation and Development

Reading a table *This table shows the top 10 imports of the European Community (Common Market) in 1987. Which import is largest, and why?*

Reading a table *Imports from abroad by members of the European Community in 1987 totaled almost $400 billion. What two nations provided most of those imports?*

now work a 37 1/2-hour week. Germans believe that their advanced technology will be an advantage in trade with the Common Market after 1992. High wages and relatively high taxes, however, may make some products less competitive than those of other Market members.

The spread of industry in West Germany has taken a toll on the environment. Western Europe has long suffered from air and water pollution. In spite of efforts to protect the environment, problems remain. In 1986, pesticides were accidentally poured into the Rhine River during a fire at a Swiss chemical plant. The effect was to poison the river from Switzerland all the way to the North Sea.

New directions Both Schmidt and Kohl have continued Brandt's policies of Ostpolitik. In 1987, Erich Honecker became the first East German Communist Party chief to visit Bonn. Although the two countries agreed to more scientific cooperation and environmental protection, relations between their countries remain cool.

West Germany remains a pivotal member of the NATO alliance and has increased its military cooperation with France. Many West Germans are concerned about the thousands of tactical nuclear warheads stationed there.

West Germany celebrated its 40th anniversary of democratic government in 1989. Its leaders could look back on four decades of important achievements. They also recognized that their successes brought new responsibilities and that the time had come for West Germany to become more involved in issues of worldwide concern.

Great Britain faced difficulties.

Great Britain's postwar economic plight stood in sharp contrast to West Germany's vigorous growth. World War II left Britain victorious on the battlefield but with a weak economy and a restless empire.

A planned economy The Labour party, which came to power as the war was ending in 1945, responded to the crisis with a sweeping program of economic and social change. Within two years, the government had nationalized railroads, coal mines, airlines, the Bank of England, and the electric and gas utilities. At the same time, new laws extended unemployment and old-age insurance and gave the public a broad program of free medical services. As a result of these far-reaching changes, Great Britain became a **welfare state**—that is, a country in which government

Winston Churchill was returned as prime minister in 1951. The next year, Elizabeth II became queen, 30 generations after her ancestor William the Conqueror landed in England.

Map Study

Compare this map with the one on page 666. How have Germany and Poland changed? (Note that the German Danzig has become the Polish Gdansk.)

assumes basic responsibility for people's social and economic well-being.

During the 1950's and 1960's, government changed hands between the Labour and Conservative parties. The Conservatives accepted most of the Labour party's changes, although they did end the nationalization program.

Economic changes During the 1950's, Britain's economy slowly improved. The unemployment rate dropped. At the same time, the average worker's income nearly doubled, bringing a rise in the standard of living.

In the 1960's, however, Britain's economy again ran into difficulties, and the decline lasted well into the 1980's. Many of Britain's factories were old, and factory equipment was outdated. British business was also plagued by low **productivity**. Productivity is a worker's hourly output of goods and services. Britain had one of the lowest levels of productivity in the industrialized world. Britain's exports fell, but the cost of its imports remained high.

Economic growth was also hampered because thousands of highly trained scientists and engineers left Great Britain for more promising opportunities in the United States, Canada, and Australia. This migration was sometimes called the "brain drain."

712

The Thatcher Revolution After a long period of Labour dominance, the Conservatives took control of Parliament in 1979. Their leader, Margaret Thatcher, became prime minister. Thatcher was the first woman to head a modern British government or a modern Western nation.

Thatcher warned Britons that tough measures were needed to revive their economy. The "Iron Lady," as Britons called her, promised to cut government spending, reduce income taxes, and curb the power of labor unions. In addition, she wanted to turn nationalized businesses into private companies.

Thatcher recognized that these changes would not be easy. She warned that things would get worse before they got better. Her prediction proved to be accurate. During the early 1980's, Britain suffered its worst economic decline since the Great Depression. Unemployment rates climbed to more than 10 percent, and inflation reached as high as 22 percent.

Despite these setbacks, Thatcher remained confident that her economic program would work. Her optimism proved to be justified. The development of rich deposits of oil and natural gas discovered under the North Sea has brought increased income from exports. Efficient new companies have replaced aging industries. Tough new laws have helped to reduce the number of days lost to labor disputes and thus to increase productivity.

The Thatcher revolution has helped to transform Britain into the fastest-growing economic power in Europe. Thatcher proudly boasted, "We have put the Great back into Britain." British voters agreed. Thatcher and the Conservatives won impressive victories in the 1983 and 1987 elections. The Iron Lady thus became the first prime minister in modern British history to win three successive general elections.

Thatcher's policies have helped to strengthen Britain's middle class. Under a program called people's capitalism, many state-owned companies have been sold to the public. As a result, almost 20 percent of the adults in Britain now own stock. Since Thatcher came to office, the middle class has expanded from 30 percent to 50 percent of the population.

The prime minister's critics point out that much remains to be done. Although unemployment has begun to decline, it remains high. Industrial cities such as Manchester still contain aging factories and discouraged workers. Britain's two million blacks and other minorities continue to experience discrimination and low wages. But Thatcher remains optimistic. "Capitalism and enterprise," she says, "are a system which only works by spreading ever more widely to more and more of the population what used to be the privileges of the few."

Northern Ireland One of Britain's thorniest problems was on its neighboring island. There was ongoing unrest in Northern Ireland. This region, sometimes called Ulster, had remained part of Great Britain when Ireland became an independent republic in 1921.

Most people in Northern Ireland were Protestants, but Catholics made up a large minority. Protestants dominated the government. During the late 1960's and 1970's, Catholics demanded more political power. Demonstrations and violence increased. In 1969, Britain sent soldiers to keep order, but violence continued in Northern Ireland and spread to England as well. Bombs exploded in London shopping districts and hotels. Between 1969 and 1986, more than 2,500 people were killed.

In November 1985, the prime ministers of Britain and Ireland signed an agreement that gave the Irish Republic a say in the way Northern Ireland was governed. Radical Protestants in Northern Ireland reacted with rage. Extremists on both sides continued their terrorist acts.

Margaret Thatcher began her third term as prime minister in June 1987.

After wild sprees of "Paki-bashing" by gangs of British youth, Parliament passed laws, based on American civil rights legislation, aimed at improving race relations.

713

France took an independent route.

World War II dealt France a devastating blow. Many homes, factories, and towns lay in ruins at the war's end. About 600,000 French people had been killed. The survivors were bitterly divided between those who had cooperated with their German conquerors and those who had resisted. The war left wounds that would have challenged any government.

The Fourth Republic In the fall of 1946, French voters approved a new constitution. The government it set up was known as the Fourth Republic. Unfortunately, this new system had a built-in weakness. It lacked strong executive leadership. The president of the republic was mainly a ceremonial figure. Nearly all power lay in the hands of a legislative body called the National Assembly.

In the Assembly, many small political parties continually struggled for control. No one party was strong enough to form a stable government. Between 1946 and 1958, 21 different administrations tried to govern the country.

Despite such political problems, the Fourth Republic did succeed in restoring economic prosperity. By 1952, French industry was producing half again as much as it had just before the war.

Colonial wars Like Britain, France faced the breakup of its colonial empire. Unlike the British, however, the French chose to resist independence movements in several of their colonies.

France fought bitterly to hold on to its colonies in Southeast Asia. The French withdrew from Indochina only after a disastrous defeat at Dien Bien Phu in 1954.

That same year, Algerian nationalists launched a widespread rebellion against French rule. As a colony, Algeria was particularly important to France. The French government regarded Algeria as an overseas part of France itself. There were 1 million French settlers in Algeria, far more than in any other French colony. These settlers made up about 10 percent of the total population there. They enjoyed a privileged life that they were determined to protect. Moreover, the French army vowed to avenge its defeat in Indochina by destroying the Algerian rebels.

By 1958, more than 400,000 French soldiers were engaged in a bloody and seemingly endless war in Algeria. The Algerians fought as guerrillas, striking and then withdrawing before the French army could respond.

As the war lost support in France, the French government began to discuss making peace with the rebel forces. This idea infuriated the army, and in May 1958, the French army seized control of the government in Algeria.

Faced with an open revolt that might lead to a civil war, the National Assembly turned to the one man who could unite the country—General Charles de Gaulle. On June 2, 1958, the National Assembly granted De Gaulle full powers of government for six months. They asked him to end

Daily Life · The English Channel Tunnel

On January 21, 1986, French President François Mitterand and British Prime Minister Margaret Thatcher announced that their governments had approved construction of a 31-mile rail tunnel linking their two countries. The $10 billion project calls for the construction of three tunnels 131 feet below the English Channel. Two tubes will carry rail traffic, while a smaller tube will handle ventilation, maintenance, and safety needs. Completion is set for 1993.

Both countries expect great benefits from the project. Reducing the travel time from 5 to 3 1/4 hours will encourage travel and trade. Easier contact between the people of France and Britain will increase communication and strengthen the close ties that already bind their nations together.

General DeGaulle had few doubts about his place in history.

the crisis and supervise the writing of a new constitution.

De Gaulle and the Fifth Republic De Gaulle was virtually a living legend. During World War II, he had led the French government-in-exile and championed resistance to the Nazis. To the French, he stood for courage, determination, and patriotism. In 1944, De Gaulle had become head of the provisional government. However, in 1946, he had resigned in protest over the weak executive branch of the new Fourth Republic.

When he returned to power in 1958, De Gaulle's first priority was to replace the Fourth Republic. Under his guidance, a new constitution was written. The Fifth Republic, as the new government was called, gave more power to the executive. In late 1958, French voters approved the new constitution and elected De Gaulle president for a seven-year term.

De Gaulle's great prestige as a military leader won back the loyalty of the French army. He brought the army revolt in Algeria to a peaceful end. Then he began peace talks with the Algerian nationalists. After lengthy negotiations, Algeria finally received its independence in 1962.

De Gaulle wanted France to play a powerful and independent role in world politics. In particular, he did not want France to seem tied to the United States. To show its independence, France developed its own atom bomb, joining the "nuclear club" of the United States, the Soviet Union, and Great Britain in 1960. France also became the first Western European country to recognize the People's Republic of China. As a

further show of independence, France withdrew from NATO in 1966.

De Gaulle's nationalist policies won the support of many French people. His economic policies were also successful. France remained the leading agricultural producer of Western Europe, and its industries prospered as well.

With these many successes, De Gaulle was taken by surprise in 1968 when rioting students called for his resignation. They took over parts of Paris around the university, blocking streets with barricades and fighting with police. The number of college students had tripled in France between 1958 and 1968. Yet the universities had not expanded or changed their programs to meet the needs of a new generation. Workers joined the protests in widespread strikes. They wanted a shorter work week and higher wages.

The specific demands of the protesters were less important than the general mood of discontent. Many people were simply tired of leaders whose ideas came from the 1930's and 1940's.

De Gaulle won reelection after promising raises for workers and reforms in the universities. However, he soon lost an important vote in the Assembly. He resigned in 1969 and died a year later.

After De Gaulle De Gaulle's influence on France's government survived through the 1970's. The next two presidents, Georges Pompidou and Valéry Giscard d'Estaing, followed most of the same foreign policies as De Gaulle.

In 1981, the French elected the first Socialist president of the Fifth Republic, François Mitterand. Mitterand's sympathies were with the unemployed workers, but his plans to create jobs were less successful than he had hoped. Nonetheless, the French voters reelected Mitterand to a new seven-year term in 1988. The victorious Mitterand aimed to make France the leader of Europe. He hoped to accomplish this goal by working closely with West Germany and by encouraging Western Europe to play a more independent role in world affairs.

Prosperity grew in Southern Europe.

The 1970's were a time of transition for the nations of Southern Europe. Three countries—Spain, Portugal, and Greece—had spent long periods of time under the rule of dictators. In the

Student rebels in Paris hurled cobblestones from the streets at the police. Parisian authorities later paved over all the city's cobblestone streets to eliminate those weapons from future arsenals.

715

1970's, all three countries gained democratic governments. When Francisco Franco, dictator of Spain since the 1930's, died in 1975, King Juan Carlos turned Spain toward democracy. In Portugal, elections in 1975 brought a democratic government to power. Greece, in elections held in 1975, replaced its former monarchy and military leaders with a republic. Italy too survived a crisis caused by a group of terrorists.

The more stable political conditions of Southern Europe provided a favorable environment for economic growth. Since the time of the Industrial Revolution, the nations of Southern Europe had lagged behind their northern neighbors in economic development. Lacking the rich resources, trade, and high level of development that had brought wealth to northwestern Europe, the southern region remained a backwater. Certain special activities such as Greek shipping and Italian auto production had grown in importance. Yet major advances in technology and production had eluded Europe's Mediterranean lands.

This situation changed in the 1980's. One reason was the favorable climate as Europeans rediscovered the Mediterranean sun belt. Innovation too was a factor as businesses launched new enterprises. Soon domestic businesses were expanding and foreign ones moving in. The result was a surge in economic growth that brought new prosperity to many areas.

Development has increased most quickly in Italy and Spain. Northern Italy's Po Valley has become highly industrialized, turning out sports cars, electronic equipment, textiles, and designer fashions. Spain is benefiting from a rush of foreign investment in its industries, real estate, and businesses related to tourism. Although unemployment remains high, the prospect of new jobs provides hope for the future. Tourism is certain to increase in the 1990's. In 1992, Barcelona will host the summer Olympic Games. That same year, all Spain will celebrate the 500th anniversary of the voyage of Columbus.

Development in Greece and Portugal has moved more slowly, but there too conditions are changing. For Greece, the rules of the 1992 Common Market will limit the regulation of business by the present Socialist government. Portugal, the least developed country in Western Europe, is seeing a rise in industry. That will help to balance its dependence on agriculture and tourism.

Section Review 1

Define: (a) tariff, (b) import quota, (c) welfare state, (d) productivity, (e) guerrillas
Identify: (a) Common Market, (b) Comecon, (c) Jean Monnet, (d) Konrad Adenauer, (e) Ostpolitik, (f) Margaret Thatcher, (g) Charles de Gaulle, (h) Francisco Franco, (i) Juan Carlos
Answer:
1. Describe some of the changes that the Common Market brought to Strasbourg.
2. (a) What was the first postwar effort at economic cooperation in Europe? (b) How was the Common Market formed?
3. (a) What were Adenauer's major accomplishments? (b) How did German foreign policy change under Willy Brandt? (c) What political issues arose in West Germany in the 1980's?
4. (a) What changes did the Labour party make? (b) What economic problems did Britain face beginning in the 1960's? (c) How did Thatcher's government try to solve them?
5. Describe the issues that led to violence in Northern Ireland.
6. (a) What serious weakness undermined France's Fourth Republic? (b) What problems did France face abroad?
7. (a) How did De Gaulle come to power? (b) What stand did he take in foreign policy?
8. What economic changes are taking place in Southern Europe?

Critical Thinking
9. Why has it proved much harder to unite Europe politically than economically? Briefly suggest three reasons. Compare your ideas with those of others in your class.

Eastern Europe was linked to the USSR.   2

After World War II, the countries of Eastern Europe were dominated by the Soviet Union (page 696). The USSR did not allow them to accept aid from the Marshall Plan. However, the aid that the Soviets offered through Comecon (the Council for Mutual Economic Assistance) was

Before East Germany built the Berlin Wall in 1961, only a barbed-wire barricade separated East and West Berlin. This East German soldier was one of many people who fled to the West simply by jumping across the barricade.

far too little to repair the war's damages. Moreover, the USSR did not allow Eastern Europeans to choose their own economic priorities. Instead, the USSR insisted that they concentrate on developing industries that fit Soviet needs.

Such obstacles made Eastern Europe's economic recovery slower than Western Europe's. Gradually, however, industrialization spread more widely in Eastern Europe. East Germany and Czechoslovakia took the lead, with Albania remaining the least developed. By the 1970's, the standard of living in Eastern Europe had improved.

Most Eastern Europeans were loyal to their Communist governments. Yet there was a constant undercurrent of discontent with Soviet control. Sometimes these feelings erupted in protests.

Footnote to History

Humor can be a form of protest, and Eastern Europeans often make jokes about their economic shortages. One joke tells of an East German who sees a coffin being delivered to her neighbor's house. "Oh," she says, "I didn't realize that there was a death in your family." "There wasn't," replies her friend, "but you have to buy what you can when you can."

East Germany led in industry.

Life in East Germany, as the German Democratic Republic is known, was bleak for many years after World War II. In East Berlin, whole blocks of bombed-out buildings stood as grim reminders of the war. East German stores and markets had few consumer goods. Meat and fresh vegetables were often in short supply. Meanwhile, in nearby West Berlin, new construction had replaced the ruins, and the standard of living was steadily rising.

Faced with this contrast, more than 3 million East Germans fled to West Germany between 1949 and 1961. Most of these refugees escaped by going from East Berlin to West Berlin. Suddenly, on August 13, 1961, the Communists built a barrier between the two halves of Berlin. Known as the Berlin Wall, the barrier eventually became a 28-mile wall of concrete and barbed wire. Escape to the West became much more difficult, although a few East Berliners still try it each year.

In the meantime, life in East Germany has improved. Its economy is the strongest in Eastern Europe and continues to expand. East German leaders have begun to make some economic contacts with the West.

The Berlin Wall was the first barrier ever built to keep a population *in* rather than to keep enemies out.

Like parts of Western Europe, East Germans have paid a price for their industrial growth. East Germany suffers from the highest levels of water, air, and ground pollution of any European country. Chemicals such as DDT that have been banned in the United States and Western Europe are still used in Eastern Europe. East German citizens have little information on pollution levels because the government-controlled press carries few reports on environmental issues.

Reforms were stamped out in Czechoslovakia.

In 1968, students staged protests in many parts of Europe, both East and West. In Czechoslovakia, a new Communist leader, Alexander Dubcek (DOOB-chek), responded with a program of reforms.

He loosened controls on writings and discussions. Dubcek said he wanted to create "socialism with a human face" but without giving up the basic ideas of communism. The time of Dubcek's reforms is often called "Prague Spring," when new ideas bloomed in Czechoslovakia's capital.

Dubcek's new policies alarmed the Soviets. They called on the other Warsaw Pact countries to take action with them against Czechoslovakia. On August 20, armed forces from the USSR, Poland, East Germany, Hungary, and Bulgaria invaded Czechoslovakia over four frontiers. Dubcek remained in power briefly but was soon replaced by a leader more in tune with the USSR.

Since its Prague Spring, Czechoslovakia has had one of the strictest governments in Eastern Europe. Its leaders even resisted orders from Moscow to reform in 1986.

Voice from Our Time · A Czechoslovak Protest

During the occupation of Czechoslovakia in 1968, a group of Czechoslovakian scientists and writers living in Austria issued this *Manifesto against Aggression*.

. . . In the fateful hours of the occupation of . . . Czechoslovakia, we consider it necessary to proclaim certain basic convictions which we hold in common as intellectuals, as Czechs and Slovaks, as citizens of the Czechoslovak Socialist Republic.

1. We believe that as intellectuals we have one basic duty to our nation: to speak the truth . . .

2. We trust the strength of ideas, and we distrust power . . . We have no weapons but words and ideas, yet we are convinced that no force of oppression can withstand the thrust of thought. Today more than ever, we realize that an attack on ideas is an attack on man himself.

3. People may be deprived of all their civil rights, but they cannot be deprived of their freedom to think. Totalitarian dictatorships may rob people of everything except their will to resist. Tanks can occupy territory but not the minds of men . . .

7. The violent acts of recent days have demonstrated again that totalitarian dictatorship represents the greatest danger to mankind. It is a matter of indifference under what ideology the dictators send their tanks into peaceful countries and for what ostensible motives soldiers shoot unarmed citizens.

1. Why was this document not issued in Czechoslovakia?
2. What do the authors say is the basic duty of intellectuals to their country?
3. Why do the authors claim that dictatorships cannot totally defeat a people?

Today, many Czechs hope for another and longer Prague Spring under the new Soviet policies of Mikhail Gorbachev.

Polish workers formed Solidarity.

Poles rebelled in 1956 to protest harsh working conditions and plans to form collective farms. At that time, the Soviets installed Wladyslaw Gomulka (goh-**MOOL**-kuh) as head of Poland's government. He stopped the move to collectivization, gave more freedom to the Roman Catholic Church, and loosened government control of industry. Discontent among the Poles quieted but did not disappear.

Over the years, Gomulka's regime became more restrictive. Poles resented his government because it had been forced on them by the Soviets. His economic policies did not bring prosperity to Poland. Food prices were high, and meat was scarce. One Polish consumer complained,

Products appear and disappear, reappear . . . And then sometimes they just disappear for good. It used to be that our stores were stocked with many different kinds of cheese. I haven't seen cheese in six months.

The Poles continued to hope for change. Their national spirit soared in 1979 when the Roman Catholic Church selected a Pole, John Paul II, as the new pope. In June 1979, when the popular pope visited his homeland, millions of Poles turned out to greet him and receive his blessing.

National pride soon led the Poles to defy Soviet dominance again. When the Polish Communist government announced another increase in meat prices, protests broke out in several cities.

Workers at the shipyard in Gdansk (guh-**DAHNSK**) took the lead. They declared a strike in August 1980. The workers shut themselves inside the shipyard and refused to work until the government recognized their union, called Solidarity. Both the union and the strike were illegal under Poland's Communist regime. Nonetheless, Solidarity and its leader, Lech Walesa (vah-**WEHN**-suh), received the fervent support of millions of Poles.

Eventually, the government agreed to the most important of Walesa's demands. Solidarity won the right to exist as an independent trade union, and Polish workers won the right to strike. These were astonishing concessions for an Eastern European government.

For several months in 1981, Solidarity's workers moved aggressively to win even more reforms. Watching and waiting from abroad, the Western democracies feared that Soviet tanks might crush

The impact of perestroika *and* glasnost *on Eastern European nations (above) remains unclear. Hungary appears to welcome economic change; the government of Czechoslovakia resists it.*

Lech Walesa (left) continued to lead resistance to actions of the Communist government.

In 1984, a Catholic priest, Father Jerzy Popieluszko, was brutally assassinated by three members of the Polish security police. Now each parish provides round-the-clock bodyguards for its priests.

the union. Instead, the Soviets urged Polish authorities to crack down on the protesters.

In 1981, the Polish government declared **martial law,** setting up military rule. Walesa and other Solidarity leaders were arrested and the union was declared illegal. In secret, however, Solidarity continued to oppose the government. In 1983, after two years in prison, Walesa was released. In the same year, he received the Nobel Peace Prize. That award brought worldwide attention to the plight of Polish workers.

The year 1988 brought a new round of strikes in Poland. In an effort to end the stoppage, government officials met with Walesa. After receiving their promise to consider legalizing Solidarity, Walesa encouraged workers to end the strike. Conditions in Poland remained tense as the government sought ways to deal with growing economic problems.

Some countries weakened ties with the Soviet Union.

Although all the countries of Eastern Europe have Communist governments, not all have equally close ties with the Soviet Union. Romania, for example, shares a long border with the Soviet Union. Nonetheless, Romanians have tried to avoid complete Soviet dominance. They have remained neutral in a quarrel between the Soviet Union and China. However, Romania allows its citizens little personal freedom.

Albania broke with the Soviet Union by siding with China in a split between the Soviet Union and China. In spite of aid from China, Albania chose to become isolated.

Yugoslavia has succeeded in maintaining ties with both Communist and non-Communist countries. Yugoslavia's postwar Communist leader, Josip Broz (known as Tito), broke with the Soviet Union in 1949 to avoid outside control in Yugoslavia. Since the death of Tito in 1980, no one strong leader has emerged. Unrest has grown between ethnic groups, and protests have grown over inflation and unemployment.

Eastern Europe faces changes.

After years of repression under Soviet domination, the people of Europe are wary of the new policy of openness announced by Mikhail Gorbachev for the Soviet Union and Eastern Europe. Memories of the Prague Spring of 20 years ago arouse new hope but also caution. A generation raised under the repression of the old regime questions the depth and sincerity of the new policies. Many of the younger generation, however, are willing to risk protest in the hope that change is possible.

The need for economic changes in Eastern Europe is clear. Obsolete equipment and lowered productivity threaten to depress the already-low standard of living. New ideas and incentives are needed to improve output. These, however, operate best in an atmosphere of individual freedom. Are Communist leaders willing to ease their political control in order to obtain their economic objectives? That dilemma faces the governments of Eastern Europe at a time when Western Europe is entering a new period of growth.

Section Review 2

Define: martial law
Identify: (a) Berlin Wall, (b) Alexander Dubcek, (c) Prague Spring, (d) Wladyslaw Gomulka, (e) Solidarity, (f) Lech Walesa, (g) Tito, (h) Mikhail Gorbachev
Answer:
1. (a) How were conditions in East Germany different from those in West Germany in the 1950's? (b) How has East Germany changed since 1961?
2. (a) What changes did Dubcek try to make in Czechoslovakia? (b) How did the Soviets react?
3. (a) What factors led to protests in Poland in 1980? (b) How successful were reforms in Poland? (c) Why were Polish leaders willing to meet with Walesa?
4. (a) In what ways have three Eastern European countries weakened their ties with the USSR? (b) What dilemma faces Communist leaders in Eastern Europe?

Critical Thinking
5. How have the following issues contributed to uneasy relations between Eastern Europe and the Soviet Union? (a) economic policies (b) nationalism

The Soviet Union

KEY
★ National capital

0   600 Miles

Map Study

Which is the largest of the Soviet Republics? Which border the Caspian Sea?

Policies changed within the USSR.

3

On March 5, 1953, Joseph Stalin died. His death marked the end of an era in Soviet history. During Stalin's 29 years of leadership, he had transformed the Soviet Union into a global power. The Soviet people, however, had paid a high price for this success. They not only endured constant shortages of consumer goods and food but also lived in almost constant fear of the secret police. His death raised hopes that new leaders would improve the Soviet standard of living and reduce the powers of the secret police.

Since Stalin's death, the Soviet Union has had a number of leaders. Yet certain issues that faced Stalin, Lenin, and in some cases even the czars have remained the same. The questions of po-

litical leadership, economic development, the right to dissent, religious freedom, and ethnic variety have long been crucial and remain major questions in the Soviet Union today.

Khrushchev rose to power.

Stalin's death made clear a basic problem in the Soviet system. There is no legal, well-defined way for one leader to succeed another. No public election identifies winners or losers in the struggle for power. Instead, party leaders compete with one another, maneuvering for important posts within the party and trying to win supporters.

For the first few years after Stalin's death, a group of Soviet leaders shared power. As time went by, however, one man was able to gain more and more power. That man was Nikita Khruschev (1894–1971). Few people would have predicted Khrushchev's rise. The son of a coal

721

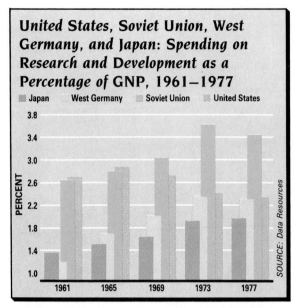

United States, Soviet Union, West Germany, and Japan: Spending on Research and Development as a Percentage of GNP, 1961–1977

SOURCE: Data Resources

Reading a graph How did spending on research and development change in each country between 1961 and 1979? What factors might account for the increases? Why is such spending important?

miner, he first worked as a metalworker and mechanic. He had little formal education before he joined the Communist party in 1918 when he was 24. During the next 20 years, Khrushchev rose in the party. In 1939, he became a full member of the Politburo, the political bureau of the Communist party's central committee. This elite group of about 20 leaders makes policy decisions for the party.

Although his bluff, earthy manners led some Soviet leaders to underestimate him, Khrushchev was shrewd, tough, and at times ruthless. By 1956, he had pushed aside his rivals. By 1958, he was both first secretary of the Communist party and premier of the Soviet Union, the two most powerful positions in the country. Once more, a single leader was in control.

De-Stalinization Khrushchev boldly demonstrated his power at a secret session of the Twentieth Communist Party Congress in Moscow in February 1956. Before an astounded audience, he attacked Stalin and his policies. He accused the late dictator of jailing and killing loyal Soviet citizens.

Khrushchev's speech signaled the beginning of a policy called "de-Stalinization." Party workers destroyed pictures and monuments of the former dictator. Stalin's body was moved from its place of honor next to Lenin and buried outside the Kremlin wall. The city of Stalingrad was renamed Volgograd.

Khrushchev's overthrow Khrushchev called for a number of economic and political reforms that eventually led to his undoing. Many party leaders disliked the changes he was making in party organization, which threatened to reduce their power. They were worried by the greater intellectual freedom he allowed. Khrushchev also faced crises abroad. Several times, he confronted the United States and then was forced to back down, as happened in the Cuban missile crisis (page 770). Such problems in foreign policy weakened his power at home.

In 1964, party leaders voted to remove Khrushchev from his powerful position as first secretary of the party. Later, Khrushchev noted with some pride that a simple vote had ended his power. He was not arrested or put on trial. The USSR had indeed changed since Stalin's time.

The "old guard" held power until 1985.

Again, party leaders maneuvered for power. Again, there was a period in which several leaders shared power.

Brezhnev By the late 1960's, however, Leonid Brezhnev (1906–1982) had established himself as the top Soviet leader, the first among equals. He was a less colorful leader than Khrushchev and aroused less controversy within the party. Brezhnev reversed many of Khrushchev's policies. For example, he clamped down on dissent within the Soviet Union. Brezhnev held power until his death in 1982.

Many Soviets thought that their country suffered from a general lack of direction during Brezhnev's last years. The economy was stagnant. Soviet troops were bogged down in a war in Afghanistan (page 788). When Brezhnev died at the age of 76, many people were ready for a leader from a younger generation. Yet most members of the Politburo came from Brezhnev's generation. This "old guard" managed to delay changes in policy for several years.

Andropov and Chernenko Brezhnev's successor was Yuri Andropov (1914–1984). Andropov did replace some aging leaders in the government

Some have speculated that Khrushchev took a hard line against the United States in the 1960's because he felt that the young President Kennedy, with far less foreign policy experience than Eisenhower, would be a pushover.

and party with younger people. However, Andropov himself did not hold office long. In poor health, he stopped appearing in public in August 1983. Rumors circulated that he was seriously ill. He died in February 1984.

Konstantin Chernenko (1911–1985), a member of the "old guard" in the party, was chosen to replace Andropov. He held office for less than a year. His death was announced in March 1985.

A *new generation* On March 11, 1985, Mikhail Gorbachev succeeded Chernenko as general secretary of the Communist party. His rise to power marked a new era in the Soviet Union. At 54, he was the youngest member of the Politburo and the first top Soviet leader who had not been born under czarist rule. Many of Gorbachev's most pressing problems, however, were the same ones that had confronted earlier leaders. Chief among those problems was the economy.

The USSR *has a planned economy.*

Even before the revolution of 1917, Russian leaders were trying to catch up with the West economically. All Soviet leaders since that time have faced the same problem.

The role of planning The Soviet system calls for the government to make most economic decisions. Officials make plans and set goals for both agriculture and industry. In theory, such a plan tells managers at every factory and farm how much to produce. The plan also sets the price that farms and factories will receive for their output.

In practice, the Soviet government has changed its attitude toward plans from time to time. Under Lenin's New Economic Policy (page 615), for example, farmers and factory managers had more freedom to make their own decisions. Stalin's Five-Year Plans, on the other hand, were rigid, and their goals were often unrealistically high.

In his last year in power, Khrushchev supported the idea of allowing factory managers to make more decisions on their own. From 1965 to 1970, the Soviets experimented with such a system. Factory efficiency improved, and wages rose as well. However, some party leaders objected because the new system gave them less control. Brezhnev returned to strict central plans in 1970.

In the mid-1980's, Gorbachev seemed to be trying to make the central plans more flexible again. He clearly favored economic reforms. However, many party conservatives feared reforms would conflict with the Communist party's centralized control.

Priorities in industry Since 1917, the USSR has almost always given top priority to "heavy" industries—basic industries that produce metals, farm machinery, trucks, and weapons. Soviet economic planners have given much lower priority to consumer goods—clothing, refrigerators, washing machines, and wristwatches.

By putting its efforts into heavy industry, the USSR became a world leader in the production

Mikhail Gorbachev and Andrei Gromyko stood in front of Lenin's tomb to review a parade in Moscow's Red Square. Gromyko was the Soviet foreign minister.

Red Square lies just outside the walls of the Kremlin, the center of Soviet government. The Square is the scene of parades and occasions of national importance.

723

of coal, steel, cement, and in many types of mining. Such progress came with a price, however. Consumers grew more and more discontent with shortages of such items as toothpaste, towels, rugs, and shoes. People who had enough money to buy a refrigerator or television waited months until the appliances were available. When shoppers did find goods to purchase, their quality was generally poor. Gorbachev promised to raise the amount and quality of consumer goods.

Environmental issues   In their drive for rapid economic growth, Soviet planners paid little attention to environmental issues such as pollution in air and water. Long after Western Europe and the United States had begun to work toward cleaner air and water, the Soviet Union continued to ignore the issue.

In 1986, however, a disastrous event forced the USSR to take a new look at environmental concerns. In April 1986, the most serious accident in the history of nuclear power occurred at the Chernobyl nuclear plant 60 miles north of Kiev. A reactor caught fire, spewing radioactive smoke into the air. About 30 people were killed, and thousands faced the risk of developing cancer later. Winds carried the radiation across Europe and beyond. Some observers expected that this event would strengthen the influence of Soviet groups concerned about the environment.

Dissent has gone in cycles.

Since Stalin's time, freedom of expression has risen and fallen in cycles. Such shifts affect people in many fields—poets, moviemakers, reporters, artists, scientists, religious leaders, and ordinary people who wish to discuss issues freely.

During de-Stalinization, Khrushchev loosened the ties of censorship. For example, in 1962, Alexander Solzhenitsyn (SOHL-zuh-NEET-suhn) published a novel titled *One Day in the Life of Ivan Denisovich*. The book exposed the brutality of Stalin's labor camps, where workers had to scheme and struggle to get a crust of bread.

Under Brezhnev, government censors severely limited what could be published. When Solzhenitsyn won the Nobel Prize for literature in 1970, he was not allowed to go to Sweden to accept it. He was also expelled from the writers' union, which meant that his works could no longer be published in the USSR.

Dissident Andrei Sakharov and his wife Yelena Bonner were allowed to return to their Moscow apartment in 1986 after years of internal exile to the distant city of Gorky.

In response to such censorship, some writers passed around their works secretly. This system was called *samizdat*, or "self-publishing." Some writers smuggled their works out of the Soviet Union to be published abroad. Such actions were risky. When Solzhenitsyn's detailed account of life in Soviet prison camps, *The Gulag Archipelago*, was published in Europe, the author was forced to leave the Soviet Union.

Several leading **dissidents**—those who protest government policy—came from among Soviet scientists. One of these was the famous physicist Andrei Sakharov, who helped build the Soviet's first hydrogen bomb. Because he criticized the Brezhnev government, he and his wife, Yelena Bonner, were sent to live in the remote city of Gorky.

After many years, Sakharov was allowed to return to his home in Moscow in December 1986. His return marked the first stage of *glasnost* (openness), the Gorbachev government's new policy of toleration. In 1988, Sakharov was allowed to visit the United States.

Gorbachev was determined to streamline both the Soviet political system and the economy. In June 1988, he shocked observers at the Communist Party's annual congress by calling for freely contested elections, with non-Communist candidates taking part. At a meeting in September, he took the title of President, thus increasing his power to make reforms.

Students can find out more about Gorbachev's attitude toward dissidents and can decide whether his actions represented a fundamental change in attitude or were merely a public relations ploy.

Like Lenin in the 1920's, Gorbachev believed that the Soviet Union needed to compromise with capitalism in order to reach full development. "There is no state that has nothing to learn from others," he said in 1987. "We are all teachers and pupils in one way or another."

Glasnost allowed Soviet citizens to speak openly about the cruelty and repression that had been a tragic part of their recent history. It also provided an opportunity for review of Soviet history and the role of leaders such as Lenin and Stalin. This review of the past became the basis for opening new directions for development. Only time will tell whether the Gorbachev reforms will bring real progress toward liberty and freedom for the people of the Soviet Union.

Religion is controversial in the USSR.

Although Soviet authorities frown on organized religion, many religions still flourish in the USSR. Foreign observers estimate that about 40 percent of the Soviet people believe in some religion, although many never attend services.

The Russian Orthodox Church has about 50 million members, and it is the best treated of the organized religions in the country. Islam is also strong, especially in the Central Asian republics of the USSR, and Muslims are generally free to practice their religion. Baptists and Jews, on the other hand, face many difficulties in practicing their religions, and hold their services secretly.

Jews are viewed not only as a religious group but also as a national minority. Thousands of Jews have left the USSR for Israel and other countries. However, the USSR has denied exit permits to thousands more who wish to leave.

The USSR has many nationalities.

Another challenge to the Soviet government arises from the many different groups that live within its borders. Like the United States, the USSR has a variety of ethnic groups. In the United States, the great variety of ethnic groups is the result of years of immigration. The situation is different in the USSR. There, most groups still live in their traditional homelands. Beginning in czarist times, Russia's borders expanded to take

in these lands. Altogether, the USSR today includes more than 100 ethnic groups.

For the country as a whole, Russians were the dominant ethnic group under the czars and remained so under the Communist regime. Several czars followed a policy of "russification." That is, they tried to force other ethnic groups to accept the Russian language and culture. The Bolsheviks promised to end that policy. However, they continued to favor the Russian language for use in schools and government.

The ethnic issue is a growing problem for the USSR. Birthrates are higher among the Muslim groups of Central Asia than they are among Russians. In the most recent census, Russians made up a little more than half the Soviet Union's population. By the year 2000, Russians may be outnumbered by other nationalities.

Section Review 3

Define: (a) de-Stalinization, (b) heavy industry, (c) samizdat, (d) dissident, (e) russification
Identify: (a) Nikita Khrushchev, (b) Politburo, (c) Leonid Brezhnev, (d) Mikhail Gorbachev, (e) Chernobyl, (f) Alexander Solzhenitsyn
Answer:
1. (a) What basic problem in the Soviet political system did Stalin's death reveal? (b) Why did it take three years for Khrushchev to emerge as the new leader?
2. What events led to Khrushchev's loss of power?
3. What changes in policy did Brezhnev make?
4. What new policies did Gorbachev seem to support?
5. (a) How has Soviet policy on economic planning shifted from time to time? (b) What problems has the country faced in industry?
6. (a) During what periods has a greater measure of dissent been allowed in the USSR? (b) What are some of the risks dissidents face?
7. (a) How does the USSR regard its various religious groups? (b) Its ethnic groups?

Critical Thinking
8. Suppose a Soviet citizen and an American citizen were discussing the Soviet way of choosing leaders. What advantages might the Soviet see in the USSR's way? What disadvantages might the American point out?

The terrible earthquake of December 8, 1988, in the Armenian SSR was an added disaster for the Armenian people. They were already in conflict with the people of neighboring Azerbaijan.

725

Summary

1. Western Europe moved toward cooperation. After World War II, many countries in Western Europe joined the Common Market, which achieved economic unity by abolishing tariffs and import quotas. Postwar West Germany became a prosperous industrialized nation with a democratic form of government and strong ties to the West. Postwar Britain suffered major economic problems, which the Labour government tried to solve with a massive welfare program. In the 1980's, Prime Minister Margaret Thatcher introduced reforms to strengthen the economy. Like Britain, France also faced political and economic problems after the war. Charles de Gaulle and succeeding presidents restored stability. Most countries in Southern Europe became more democratic and economically more prosperous.

2. Eastern Europe was linked to the USSR. Eastern Europe, which was dominated by the Soviet Union, experienced slow economic growth after the war. East Germany industrialized and made economic progress. In 1968, Dubcek's reforms in Czechoslovakia led to tightening of Soviet controls. In Poland, a severe economic crisis led to strikes and a labor union called Solidarity, which was banned by Poland's Communist government.

3. Policies changed within the USSR. In 1958, five years after Stalin's death, Nikita Khrushchev emerged as the leader of the Soviet Union. Failures in his internal program and a loss of prestige abroad led to his fall in 1964. For the next 20 years, a succession of Soviet leaders reversed many of Khrushchev's policies. In 1985, Mikhail Gorbachev took power. Gorbachev has seemed to favor flexible central plans and a relaxation of censorship.

Reviewing the Facts

1. Define the following terms:
   a. import quota
   b. welfare state
   c. productivity
   d. martial law

2. Explain the importance of each of the following names, places, or terms:

   a. Common Market
   b. Adenauer
   c. Comecon
   d. Ostpolitik
   e. Brandt
   f. Schmidt
   g. Thatcher
   h. Northern Ireland
   i. De Gaulle
   j. Mitterand
   k. Juan Carlos
   l. Berlin Wall
   m. Dubcek
   n. Solidarity

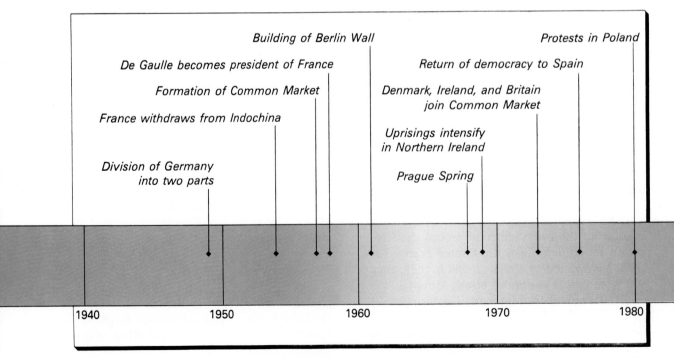

Building of Berlin Wall

De Gaulle becomes president of France

Formation of Common Market

France withdraws from Indochina

Division of Germany into two parts

Protests in Poland

Return of democracy to Spain

Denmark, Ireland, and Britain join Common Market

Uprisings intensify in Northern Ireland

Prague Spring

1940   1950   1960   1970   1980

The death of Emperor Hirohito on January 7, 1989, marked the end of an era. The emphasis on both tradition and modernization is likely to continue under the new emperor, Akihito.

Basic Skills

1. **Supporting the main idea**   Give two supporting details for each of the following generalizations: (a) "The most dramatic political and economic transformation took place in West Germany" (page 710) and (b) "Life in East Germany . . . was bleak for many years after World War II" (page 718).
2. **Comparing maps**   Compare the maps of European nations today, on page 712, with the map of European kingdoms in 1160, on page 222. (a) What nations were formed out of the Holy Roman Empire and the Byzantine empire? (b) To what extent do the boundaries of modern Poland and Hungary resemble those of the medieval kingdoms?

Researching and Reporting Skills

In research teams of three to five students, choose one of the following projects to do.

1. **Analyzing television news**   For one week, watch the evening news on a selected television station. Determine (a) the percentage of time devoted to news events outside the United States and (b) the percentage of the news that deals with Europe. Take notes on the European events to report on to your class.
2. **Analyzing newspapers**   For seven consecutive days, copy or clip articles from a daily newspaper that pertain to Europe. Classify the clippings into categories. Summarize the week's developments in a team report.
3. **Using an almanac**   From an almanac for the current year, find information on the government and economy of every country in Europe. Divide the work fairly, with each team member responsible for researching certain countries. Use charts, diagrams, or written descriptions to present the information. Assemble the information into a large chart for display in class.

Critical Thinking

1. **Analyzing a quotation**   "Once a common market has been created, then political union will come naturally." (a) To what extent has Jean Monnet's prediction come true? (b) What are possible barriers to a politically united Europe?
2. **Comparing**   (a) Compare conditions in Germany 20 years after World War II with those 20 years after World War I. (b) What might be some reasons for the differences?
3. **Applying a concept**   What programs introduced in Britain by the Labour Party led to the term *welfare state?* (b) Compare the measures introduced in Britain with those introduced by Bismarck in Germany in the 1880's (page 572).
4. **Identifying viewpoints**   (a) If you were a Soviet policymaker in 1961, what positive outcomes would you expect from the building of the Berlin Wall? (b) What negative outcomes? (c) Would you favor or oppose the building of the wall? Why?
5. **Inferring**   (a) From current economic conditions in Eastern Europe, what can you infer about the success of communist economic policies there? (b) What problems are highlighted by present economic conditions?
6. **Interpreting**   What was the significance of the Prague Spring and the organizing of Solidarity in Eastern Europe?
7. **Identifying reasons**   What might be three reasons for Gorbachev's launching the policy of *glasnost?*
8. **Predicting**   If you were Gorbachev, what are three measures you would use to strengthen the Soviet economy?

Perspectives on Past and Present

Like Monnet, Napoleon (page 461) and Metternich (page 491) dreamed of unifying Europe. (a) What was Napoleon's approach? (b) What was Metternich's? (c) Evaluate Monnet's plan in the light of past experience and present circumstances.

Investigating History

The extent of social welfare programs is an issue in many countries. (a) Research the status of such programs in ten major industrial nations. Make a chart of your findings, using the horizontal headings of Old-Age Pensions, Sickness/Accident Insurance, Disability/Survivor's Insurance, Unemployment Insurance, Workmen's Compensation, and Aid to Families. (b) What do your findings indicate about the extent of such programs?

Chapter 34

1945 - Present

Change and Conflict in Asia

At Expo 70 in Japan, pedestrians strolled amid futuristic architecture while a gondola car (far left) offered others an aerial view of the fair.

Read and Understand

1. Japan became an industrial giant.
2. China changed under a Communist government.
3. India and Pakistan became independent.
4. Southeast Asia faced revolution and war.

Key term

gross national product

For the people of Japan, March 14, 1970, was a long-awaited day of national pride. That day, Emperor Hirohito opened Expo 70 on the outskirts of the city of Osaka. It was the first World's Fair ever held in Asia.

For the emperor, the occasion marked a triumph in a reign that had seen both triumphs and tragedies. He had been his country's ruler for almost half a century, since 1926. He had reigned during Japan's expansion in East Asia in the 1930's, its early military successes during World War II, and its final defeat.

Now Japan had risen again to take its place among the world's richest and most powerful nations. This time, its power was based on economic, not military, strength. As Expo 70 showed the world,

The death of Emperor Hirohito on January 7, 1989, marked the end of an era. The emphasis on both tradition and modernization is likely to continue under the new emperor, Akihito.

Japan had become an industrial powerhouse. Out of the ashes of defeat, the Japanese had created an economic miracle. The results of this miracle were on display at Expo 70. During the six months of the exhibition, more than 50 million visitors marveled at its sights.

At the steel pavilion, 1,300 loudspeakers stunned visitors with a "Song of Steel." In 1970, Japan produced more steel than any other country except the United States and the USSR—despite having almost no iron ore deposits. In steel and many other industries, Japan had become the new "workshop of the world," as Britain had once been. The Japanese imported raw materials and exported quality finished goods.

The millions of Japanese who visited Expo 70 showed at least as much interest in what the rest of the world had to offer as in their own exhibits. Perhaps the favorite display of all was the United States' pavilion. It included not only some moon rocks brought back to Earth by the *Apollo* astronauts in 1969 but also Babe Ruth's baseball uniform.

The Japanese had achieved a workable blend between their own culture and the ways of the Western nations. Economically, Japan seemed poised to challenge the two great superpowers. One American futurologist (a specialist who estimates future developments) believed that this dream would become a reality. "It would not be surprising," he said, "if the twenty-first century turned out to be the Japanese century."

In this chapter we will see how Japan and China changed after World War II. We will also see how a third major Asian nation, India, faced independence. Finally, we will examine events in Southeast Asia, where almost constant warfare posed threats not only to that region but also to the whole world.

Japan became an industrial giant.   1

In August 1945, Hirohito became the first Japanese emperor in centuries to speak publicly to his subjects. Atom bombs had just destroyed the cities of Hiroshima and Nagasaki. The whole country was on the brink of ruin. Over the radio, Hirohito asked all loyal Japanese to "bear the unbearable"—defeat. On September 2, his country formally surrendered to the Allies.

The once prosperous Japanese economy was in ruins. Moreover, Japan itself was soon occupied by foreign forces. Most Japanese felt that their world had been turned upside down.

The United States occupied Japan.

From 1945 to 1952, about 30,000 American soldiers and civilians were based in Japan. General Douglas MacArthur, hero of the war in the Pacific, was in charge. MacArthur ran his army with an iron hand, and during the occupation he ran Japan the same way. The Japanese, devastated by the war, accepted the occupation as the price of defeat. In fact, many were pleased that the changes MacArthur ordered were not as harsh as those that had been forced on the losing countries after World War I.

The leaders of the United States had three goals for Japan. First, they planned to *demilitarize* the country (that is, to disband its armed forces and remove its military equipment). Second, they wanted to give Japan a stable, democratic government. Third, they hoped to revive the Japanese economy and make Japan a vital part of the capitalist world.

All three efforts succeeded. The armed forces were disbanded except for a small police force. In 1947, the Japanese adopted a new constitution that significantly changed the government. The emperor became a constitutional monarch in a role similar to that of the monarch in Britain. Real political power now rested with the Diet (the Japanese parliament), led by a prime minister chosen by a majority of the Diet. All Japanese men and women over age twenty gained the right to vote.

One further change helped to strengthen the new government. Partly because of the pressures of the Korean War (pages 703–705), a new status became essential for Japan. In September 1951, the United States and 47 other nations signed a formal peace treaty with Japan, officially restoring the independence of that nation. Six months later the last occupation troops were withdrawn. The two former enemies—the United States and Japan—now became allies. A new era had begun.

To get around the prohibition of military forces, Japan has established "Self-Defense Forces." About 2 percent of the nation's GNP is spent on the military.

Many Japanese companies offer daily exercise classes to help employees stay fit and alert.

The revival of the Japanese economy after World War II was truly remarkable. Factories were rebuilt, new industries were launched, and agriculture flourished. Japan's factories could now benefit from having the latest equipment. Many of the new industries were oriented toward electronics, the growing technology that would lead to television, computers, automation, and a host of new consumer products. Land reform measures giving ordinary farmers title to the lands they worked proved an incentive to increase production. By 1953, the Japanese economy was performing at prewar levels.

Japan's economy boomed.

The progress made during the occupation period, however, was only the beginning. Through the 1950's and 1960's, Japan's economy expanded at the almost unheard-of rate of 10 percent a year. Japanese businessmen began to enter world markets in one new industry after another. Soon Japanese steel, ships, automobiles, cameras, bicycles, and even pianos were being sold around the world.

The rapid rise in exports brought prosperity at home. Between 1950 and 1970, for example,

Japan's **gross national product**—the value of goods and services produced by the country—soared from $10 billion to $200 billion a year. By the time of Expo 70, Japan had roared past Britain, France, and West Germany to become the world's third leading industrial nation. By 1990, Japan's GNP will approach $2 trillion, or 20 times what it had been in 1950.

What accounts for the remarkable success of Japanese industry and trade? At least four key factors were involved.

Effective use of imported technology In the Meiji Era (page 548), the Japanese began adopting the technology of Europe and the United States. After the war, they continued to borrow the best of Western technology. For example, the Sony Corporation bought the rights to manufacture transistors from an American company. Within 20 years, Sony had built a business empire based on the transistor. Sony sold radios, stereo equipment, and television sets worldwide.

A productive labor force Company loyalty was a key ingredient in Japan's economic success. In factories and offices across Japan, employees began their workday with songs such as this one:

> *For building a new Japan,*
> *Let's put our strength and minds together,*
> *Sending our goods to the people of the world,*
> *Endlessly and continuously*
> *Like water from a fountain.*
> *Grow, industry, grow, grow!*
> *Harmony and Sincerity!*
> *Matsushita Electric!*

Because workers felt a part of their company, they took pride in their work. Japanese companies set high standards for their products, and the workers tried hard to meet those standards.

Job security was one key to this strong loyalty. Japan's largest companies often guaranteed their most important workers lifetime jobs. Strikes were rare, and absentee rates were among the lowest in the world. With their jobs secure, Japanese workers also proved willing to change with the times. They eagerly adopted new technology.

High rates of saving and investment People in Japan saved a large part of their wages. In 1986 for example, Japanese workers saved 16.5 percent of their yearly incomes. (By contrast, American workers saved less than 6 percent.) Japanese banks

In the late 1980's, production in Japan's steel industry began to falter owing to competition from countries such as Korea, where production costs were lower. Workers in these industries began to lose their so-called "lifetime" jobs.

Because Japan is heavily dependent on imported oil, price fluctuations on the world oil market have a profound effect on the Japanese economy.

used these deposits to lend businesses money for new equipment and projects.

The role of government The Japanese government has actively supported business since the 1950's. The government does not control industries, which are owned privately. However, the success of Japanese businesses is a major government goal. To encourage investments, the government sets few regulations and keeps taxes on business low.

Economic growth brought changes.

The tremendous expansion of the Japanese economy after 1950 brought dramatic changes in the way people lived.

Urban growth Between 1950 and 1970, the percentage of the Japanese population living in rural areas dropped from 60 percent to just 8 percent. Millions of people moved into already overcrowded cities. Other people found that the sprawling cities spread out to absorb their homes and farms.

By 1970, more than half of Japan's 100 million people lived in the Tokaido Corridor. This is a narrow, 350-mile-long strip that stretches along the Pacific coast of the island of Honshu from Tokyo to Kobe. It includes Japan's six largest cities.

Pollution Thousands of factories and millions of automobiles gave the Tokaido Corridor smog levels worse than those of any other urban area in the world. Sometimes Japanese schoolchildren had to wear face masks simply to play outdoors.

Water pollution was also a severe problem. In the 1960's, a number of people in the city of Minamata died of mercury poisoning. The poison came from the fish that make up a large part of the Japanese diet. Fish in Minamata Bay had absorbed high levels of mercury from chemical pollution. Since that time, Japan's government and industry have made great strides in reducing pollution.

Roles for women Economic expansion brought new opportunities for Japanese women. Besides winning the right to vote in 1947, women gained the right to own property in their own name. During the 1970's, Japanese women became increasingly active in the work force. By 1990, more than 50 percent of them will hold jobs outside the home. Most top positions in Japanese government and business, however, remained in the hands of men. This was but one sign of the continuing strength of custom and tradition in Japanese society.

Tokyo became a megacity

As Japan grew and prospered, so too did Tokyo, the nation's capital. More than 97 square miles of the central city had been destroyed by Allied fire bombing in 1945. Rising from the ashes, Tokyo was rebuilt and soon growing rapidly. By 1988, the Tokyo metropolitan area was home to more than 11 million people.

Modern Tokyo remains a place of contrasts, where fast-food restaurants like those in the United States stand beside ancient Buddhist

Daily Life · *Preparing for Exams*

February has a special meaning for high school seniors across Japan. At that time, they take a comprehensive college entrance exam. The tests are difficult. Only one third of those taking them get into college on their first try.

Everything in Japanese education is focused on preparing for the exams. Students attend school 240 days a year, with half days on Saturday. Homework assignments often keep students busy for five hours a night. The pressure to succeed is so great that many students also attend afternoon "cram" schools. Both parents and students know that top scores will open the way to good colleges and high-paying jobs.

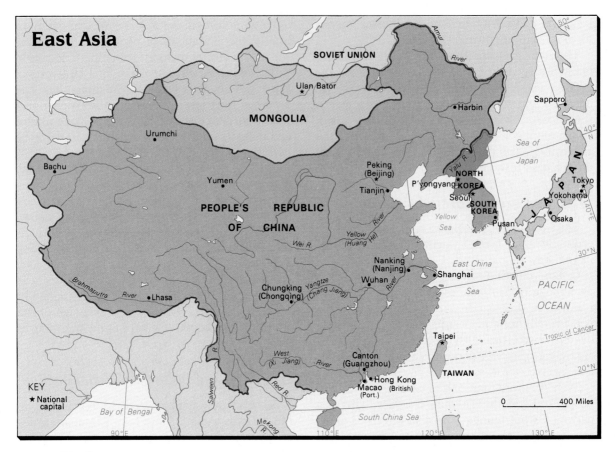

East Asia

Map Study

What are the two ways of spelling the name of China's capital city? Of what country is Taipei the capital?

temples. Visitors to Tokyo can attend both the most popular new Broadway shows and the traditional Kabuki drama.

The heart of Tokyo is the city's financial district. During the 1980's, Tokyo wrested away from New York the honor of having the world's busiest stock exchange. Nearby is the Akihabara district, a shopping area that bills itself as the electronics capital of the world. There shoppers can find cameras, stereos, computers, and other electronic gadgets—all made in Japan, of course.

Despite the hustle and bustle, tradition remains strong in Tokyo. By Western standards, crime scarcely exists. And while the Japanese enjoy imports such as baseball and Mickey Mouse, they still flock to traditional sumo wrestling matches. In cobblestoned side streets, away from the traffic jams, delicate wooden teahouses still serve customers in the age-old tea ceremony—while jumbo jets roar overhead.

Section Review 1

Define: (a) demilitarize, (b) gross national product
Identify: (a) Hirohito, (b) Douglas MacArthur, (c) Diet
Answer:
1. Why was Expo 70 significant for Japan?
2. (a) What goals did the United States set for Japan in 1945? (b) How was each achieved?
3. What factors help to account for Japan's economic miracle?
4. Briefly describe some of the changes rapid growth has brought to Japan.
5. How have the changes since 1945 affected the lives of women in Japan?

Critical Thinking

6. Some historians have called the 1800's the British century and the 1900's the American

732

The Japanese enjoy European and American music and dance as well as traditional entertainment such as the Kabuki dancers. Country-western music sung in Japanese is very popular.

century. The futurologist quoted on page 729 said that the next century might be the Japanese century. What factors make a century "belong" to any given power? To what extent can such a statement be accurate?

China changed under a Communist government. 2

The triumph of the Red Army and Mao's Communist party in 1949 ended nearly half a century of revolution, civil war, and chaos for China. Their victory also marked the beginning of a new era in Chinese history. Over the next 20 years, Mao and his colleagues strove to change China into both a Communist society and a modern industrial nation. To reach these goals, China's leaders experimented with a number of different—and often conflicting—policies.

Communist leaders made reforms.

In its early years of power, the Chinese Communist party was quite small. Its 4.5 million members were only about 1 percent of China's whole population. However, party members were dedicated and highly disciplined.

Government organization As a first step after taking power in 1949, Communist leaders set out to solidify their hold on the country. They set up new governments for all of China's provinces, cities, towns, and villages.

The Chinese Communists closely modeled their new system on that of the Soviet Union. As the Soviets had done, the Chinese set up two parallel organizations, the Communist party and the national government. There was considerable overlap between the two. This system remains in force today. The party sets policy, and the government carries it out. The party is the more powerful institution, and government officials do nothing without the party's approval.

Until 1959, Mao Tse-tung was both head of state and chairman of the Communist party's Central Committee. His rule was authoritarian, but it also provided stability after years of turmoil.

Land reform The new government's most pressing task was to improve China's economy.

Half a century of wars and general chaos had left the country in ruins. Inflation was so bad that Chinese money was almost worthless.

Mao was determined to reshape the economy along socialist lines. Party leaders made economic plans for the whole country. At first, they followed the model of the Soviet Union but tried to adapt it to Chinese needs. In later years, they tried other systems.

In a country where more than 80 percent of the population still lived in rural areas, farming was the obvious place to start. Most farmers owned no land. Just 10 percent of the rural population owned 70 percent of the country's farmland. The poorer farmers rented land from these wealthy landlords. One of the new government's first acts was an Agrarian Reform Law (1950). Under this law, the government took the holdings of landlords and divided them among the peasants.

The process of redividing the land often turned bloody. Peasants had long suffered at the hands of the landlords, and now the poor took the law into their own hands. Many landlords and others accused of exploiting the poor were stoned to death in town squares or condemned to forced labor. Altogether, about 2 million people were killed during the first 5 years of Communist control.

Mao never intended that peasant families keep the farmland as private property. He had a vision of a new rural China based on peasants owning and working the land in groups, or collectively.

Between 1953 and 1957, the government tried to increase food production by combining many small farms into larger, more efficient ones. These large collective farms were usually several thousand acres in size. Several hundred peasant families lived on each of them. The state controlled the use of equipment, labor, and the land itself, but families still worked their own small plots.

Industry The Communists were also concerned with industry and business. They wanted to set up centralized planning for the whole economy. Gradually, the government took over, or nationalized, all private industries and businesses.

In 1953, Mao launched a Soviet-style Five-Year Plan, which set production targets for industry and stressed rapid growth. The plan was a striking success. By 1957, steel production had quadrupled, and the output of coal, cement, and electricity had doubled.

The Great Leap Forward The success of the first Five-Year Plan encouraged Chinese leaders to plan an even more ambitious program. Mao thought that China could make "great leaps" toward both a truly socialist society and a stronger economy. He hoped to harness the energy of millions of peasants and workers to make great progress.

Early in 1958, Mao proclaimed what he called "the Great Leap Forward." The plan called for still larger collective farms called communes. These communes were expected to increase efficiency. By pooling labor and land, peasants on communes could buy equipment and set up local industries.

By the end of 1958, some 26,000 of these self-sufficient *people's communes* had been set up. The average commune was more than 15,000 acres in size and had a work force of more than 25,000 people. Each commune had small factories as well as farmlands. Local groups even tried to produce their own iron and steel with backyard blast furnaces.

All workers on a commune earned nearly the same amount of money, no matter how much or how little work they did. Workers ate in communal dining rooms, slept in communal dormitories, and raised their children in communal nurseries. The peasants hated living this way and eventually gave up most of the communal arrangements.

During the Great Leap Forward, China tried to make steel with small blast furnaces such as these.

Cities too formed collective groups. In urban areas, each neighborhood formed a street association. These street associations assigned people to jobs and housing, ran health programs, and enforced laws.

The Great Leap Forward was a failure. Poor planning slowed industrial growth. The local blast furnaces, for example, could not produce usable steel. Productivity dropped. Crops failed in 1958, in 1959, and again in 1960, causing famine all across China. Vast numbers of people starved to death. Faced with such disaster, the government officially gave up the Great Leap Forward in 1961.

China and the USSR split.

Between 1949 and 1960, the USSR was the only nation to send aid to China. The Soviets sent workers and money to help the Chinese meet their goals. The leaders of the USSR assumed that the Chinese would follow the Soviet model of communism. Mao, however, wanted China to develop its own form of communism. His experiments in policy angered the Soviets.

In 1960, the growing rift between the countries reached a climax. The Soviet government suddenly called home all its workers and advisers in China. In some cases, they took with them the blueprints for factories that were only half-built. All Soviet aid stopped.

After 1960, relations between the two countries remained tense. China and the USSR share the longest border in the world, and troops from the two countries began to threaten and harass each other along that border. In 1969, fighting broke out in Manchuria. Although peace was quickly restored, the conflict showed how wide the split had become.

A Cultural Revolution swept China.

After the failure of the Great Leap Forward and the split with the USSR, Mao took a less active part in leadership for a while. Other leaders tried to modernize China in less drastic ways.

The new leaders modified the communal system. For example, farm families were allowed to live in their own homes and to keep or sell crops they grew on their small private plots. Factory workers could earn wage increases, bonuses, and promotions if they exceeded production

Review China's role in the Korean War (pages 703–704).

goals. China also modernized its army. In 1964, China exploded its first atom bomb, a dramatic sign of modern technology.

While such policies brought steady progress, Mao disapproved of them. He believed that rewards such as higher wages weakened workers' revolutionary spirit. Such policies, he claimed, also created a new privileged class, undercutting the Communist goal of social equality.

Though Mao was now more than 70 years old, he still held the powerful position of chairman of the Communist party. He was still extremely popular as the hero of the revolution throughout China. Mao decided to use his standing and go directly to the people. He called on them to restore the purity of the revolution.

In 1966, Mao launched a "great revolution to establish proletarian culture." He appealed directly to the country's youth, calling on them "to learn revolution by making revolution." Mao told students to destroy all "feudal" elements in Chinese culture—that is, all the remaining traces of the old upper classes. Young people left their classrooms by the thousands to form revolutionary units called Red Guards.

Over the next 18 months, the Cultural Revolution swept through every part of Chinese society. The Red Guards shut down colleges and schools. They lashed out at professors, government officials, factory managers, even their own parents—anyone who seemed to have special privileges. Some of the people accused by the Red Guards were beaten to death. Others died in jail. Scientists and doctors were sent to the countryside to do farm work. Meanwhile, other young fanatics destroyed Buddhist temples, books, and other reminders of pre-1949 China.

The result of this outbreak was that the Chinese economy headed for collapse. Factories were shut down, and farm production stopped almost completely in some places.

By 1967, even Mao had to admit that matters had gone too far. He tried to use the army to restore order. Soldiers disbanded Red Guard units and reopened schools and colleges. Zhou Enlai*

*In 1958, the Chinese adopted a new method of spelling Chinese words in the roman alphabet. Under the new system, called Pinyin, *Mao Tse-tung* became *Mao Zedong*. *Peking* became *Beijing*. Because many newspapers in the United States have now adopted the new form, Pinyin spellings are used hereafter for the names of contemporary leaders.

Red Guards devotedly studied Mao's sayings, collected in a small red book. (Masks were protection from the dusty winds of the winter monsoon.)

(joh ehn-lye), one of the founders of the Chinese Communist party and a veteran of the Long March, played a key role in these events. During the early 1970's, Zhou worked to restore order in China. However, turmoil continued until 1976. The effect on the country and on the Communist party was devastating.

China made broader world contacts.

During the Cultural Revolution, China's borders were closed to most foreigners, and China played little part in world affairs. Zhou Enlai ended this isolationist policy.

One major part of Zhou's foreign policy after 1969 was better relations with the United States. The United States and China had had almost no contact since the Korean War. Throughout the 1950's and 1960's, the Chinese had called the United States their most dangerous enemy. However, as relations between China and the Soviet Union grew colder, Zhou saw the advantage of closer ties with the United States. The United States was also eager to take advantage of the split between China and the USSR.

Mao considered Stalin's successor, Nikita Khrushchev, a young upstart, while Khrushchev thought of the aging Chinese leader as a relic of the past.

The first American group to pay an official visit to China was a table-tennis team in 1971. Its tour was such a success that it was called "ping-pong diplomacy." In the same year, the United States allowed the People's Republic of China to join the United Nations. (Since 1949, the United States had used its veto in the Security Council to keep out the Communist government.)

Chinese-American relations warmed greatly in February 1972, when President Richard Nixon paid a visit to China. Politically, of course, the two countries remained far apart. However, they were now at least on speaking terms. Some trade agreements also came from the official visit.

A new leader emerged after Mao.

Both Mao and Zhou Enlai died in 1976. In their place, Deng Xiaoping (dung shah-oh-ping)—like Mao and Zhou a veteran of the Long March—emerged as the most powerful figure in the Chinese government. Deng continued Zhou's policy of improving relations with the West.

Unlike Mao and Zhou, however, Deng believed that progress could come only if China—following the example of Japan—borrowed heavily from the West to develop its economy. Deng was willing to compromise with capitalism if that could benefit China. In particular, he sought the "Four Modernizations,"—in agriculture, industry, technology, and national defense. Deng hoped to make China a world economic superpower by the year 2000.

In January 1980, China adopted a new constitution and many new laws. Their purpose, in part, was to keep anything like the Cultural Revolution from happening again. In 1981, four leaders of the Cultural Revolution, including Mao's widow Jiang Qing, were brought to trial. Called the Gang of Four, they were accused of "defaming, torturing, and killing thousands of opponents in an attempt to usurp party power and state leadership." Found guilty, the four were imprisoned.

The Chinese economy was transformed.

During the 1980's, China embarked on what Deng himself proudly called the Second Revolution—a change designed to raise the living

Voice from Our Time · China's New Revolution

China's new leaders have undertaken a vast program to modernize their country. In the following excerpt, Winston Lord, United States ambassador to China, describes some of the changes since Mao's death.

There is a different mood here compared with ten years ago . . . You see this in the influx of foreign people and goods and in China's efforts to join international organizations. There is somewhat greater freedom of expression in the political and cultural realms . . . You can also see the improvements in living standards . . . There is . . . more extensive coverage of international news . . . There are still, of course, many guarded elements in the society. This is far from being a democracy or market economy.

The relationship [with the United States] has broadened greatly . . . Now there are growing economic links as well as cultural, educational, scientific, and technological exchanges. Trade has gone from nothing to $8 billion a year. U.S. investment here has gone from zero to more than $1.5 billion . . . For the first time in a century, the U.S., China, and Japan have a mutually cooperative relationship.

1. In what ways does China's new mood show more openness to the outside world?
2. How has the standard of living changed in China?
3. How have the economic links between the United States and China changed?
4. Why is the current relationship among the United States, China, and Japan important in terms of history?

The greater acceptance of free markets became an important stimulus to economic and technological development in China.

standards of China's one billion people. Peasants, for example, were encouraged to sell their surpluses at free markets. Scientists who had spent years plowing fields during the Cultural Revolution were now encouraged to resume their research. The government negotiated new trade agreements with the United States, Japan, and the countries of Western Europe. It also sent its engineers and factory managers abroad to learn about the latest changes in technology.

Deng's policies were successful. Food production increased by 50 percent. Industrial production increased at a rate faster than that of any other country in the world. Companies from Europe, the United States, and Japan set up offices and factories in many cities in China. The province of Guangdong, where hundreds of new companies were set up to produce goods for export, was the center for much of this development.

In time, Deng's program encountered problems. Inflation—unknown in China under Mao—became a major concern for consumers in the late 1980's. Actual opposition arose from many who felt that the country had strayed too far away from socialism. There was no question, however, that living standards had improved and that the country would play an important role in the world of the twenty-first century.

Other East Asian nations enjoyed prosperity.

Other East Asian nations followed the example of Japanese economic development in the years after World War II. Foremost among them was South Korea. After the Korean War, it rebuilt its economy so successfully that by 1970 it was a major competitor in foreign trade. The nation's huge corporations enjoyed special success in the export of electronics and autos. In 1988, South Korea was host for the summer Olympic Games.

Footnote to History

A very popular result of President Nixon's visit to China was the arrival of two special immigrants to the National Zoological Park in Washington, D.C. China sent the United States two giant pandas, Ling-ling and Hsing-hsing, in exchange for two rare musk oxen. The pandas soon became the zoo's most popular residents.

Farther south, on the island of Taiwan, another capitalist economy took hold during the 1950's. Led by Chiang Kai-shek, who had fled from China after his defeat by Mao's Red Army, Taiwan entered a period of prosperity and economic growth. Relations between the Taiwanese and Chinese governments remained tense until the 1980's. Then, after the deaths of both Chiang and Mao, both countries began to seek closer economic ties.

Under Deng, China also drew closer to two East Asian city-states, Singapore and Hong Kong. Their varied free-enterprise activities gained for them a significant role in the international economy. With British control of Hong Kong due to end in 1997, Britain and China have reached agreement on the transfer of political authority. Hong Kong will keep its capitalist economy within the socialist economy of China for at least 50 years.

Section Review 2

Identify: (a) Mao Tse-tung, (b) Five-Year Plan, (c) Great Leap Forward, (d) Cultural Revolution, (e) Zhou Enlai, (f) Pinyin, (g) Deng Xiaoping

Answer:
1. (a) How is the Communist party related to the government in China? (b) What powerful positions did Mao hold?
2. (a) Why was land reform an important issue for China? (b) How did the ownership of land change under communism?
3. (a) What were the results of Mao's Five-Year Plan? (b) Of the Great Leap Forward?
4. (a) Why did Mao call for a Cultural Revolution? (b) Briefly describe what followed.
5. (a) What changes did Deng Xiaoping introduce? (b) What were their effects?
6. What changes in economic development have occurred in other areas of East Asia?

Critical Thinking
7. Chinese Communist leaders have sought both economic modernization and total social equality. (a) Which of Mao's policies stressed economic progress? (b) Which stressed total social equality? (c) Which goal seemed more important to Deng Xiaoping? Explain.

India and Pakistan became independent. 3

The people of India had been working since the early 1900's to win their independence from Great Britain (pages 622–627). Under their great leader, Mohandas Gandhi, many Indians had waged a peaceful struggle of marches, boycotts, and noncooperation against their British rulers. At the end of World War II, British public opinion turned against imperialism. It was clear that India would soon be free. It was not clear, however, whether independence could be achieved without bloodshed among Indians themselves.

Independence brought partition.

In February 1947, British Prime Minister Clement Attlee announced that Britain would turn over the government of India "into responsible Indian hands" no later than June 1948.

Attlee later explained why he had set this deadline:

I had come to the conclusion that it was useless to try to get agreement by discussion between leaders of rival [Indian] communities. Unless these men were faced with the urgency of a time limit, there would always be procrastination.

The Indian leaders who had been negotiating with Attlee included Jawaharlal Nehru of the Congress party and Muhammad Ali Jinnah of the Muslim League. As you have read in Chapter 29, India's Hindus and Muslims were bitterly divided. The Muslim League stated that it would never accept Indian independence if it meant rule by the Hindu-dominated Congress party. Jinnah said, "The only thing the Muslim has in common with the Hindu is his slavery to the British."

The Muslim League demanded *partition*, the division of British India into two countries, one Hindu and one Muslim. Muslims planned for an independent country to be called Pakistan.

At first, the British disagreed, insisting that a single Indian government take over when they withdrew. However, Hindus and Muslims were already clashing with each other. In August 1946, four days of rioting in Calcutta left more than 5,000 people dead and more than 15,000 hurt.

British leaders decided that partition was the best way to limit bloodshed. A boundary commission hastily drew the borders of the two new countries. Pakistan consisted of two Muslim regions 1,000 miles apart. One lay to the northeast of India, the other to the northwest. In the words of one historian, Pakistan "hung like elephant's ears from the body of India."

The new borders made little economic sense. East Pakistan included many jute-growing regions, for example. The jute mills were in Calcutta, which remained in India. Moreover, the boundaries left millions of Hindus in Pakistan and millions of Muslims in India.

On August 15, 1947, India and Pakistan became independent. Nehru became prime minister of India, and Jinnah became prime minister of Pakistan.

As Gandhi and others had feared, a bloodbath followed. Millions of people struggled to cross from one side of the India-Pakistan border to the other. Trainloads of refugees were massacred on both sides of the border. In all, more than 500,000 Hindus and Muslims died.

Gandhi himself fell victim to the violence of Hindu against Hindu. In January 1948, he was shot to death by a young Hindu who opposed Gandhi's efforts to win equal treatment for Harijans (untouchables). His death deprived India of its most honored leader.

Nehru sought to modernize India.

For the first 17 years after independence, India had one prime minister—Jawaharlal Nehru, who had been one of Gandhi's most devoted followers. Educated in Britain, Nehru described himself as a "mixture of East and West, out of place everywhere, at home nowhere." Nehru was a brilliant and skillful politician who won great popularity among all groups in India. He emphasized democracy, unity, and economic modernization.

In foreign affairs, Nehru took a strong stand against colonialism. He also tried to follow a policy of nonalignment—that is, taking neither side in the Cold War. India and other countries that chose to remain nonaligned came to be known as the Third World. Distinct from the First World—that of the democracies—and the Second World—that of communism—they would become a new influence in world politics.

India moved quickly to industrialize as a basis for economic development. Rapid population growth, however, limited the benefits from industrialization.

Economic difficulties One major problem facing India was the lack of industry. Because Britain discouraged the growth of industry, India still depended heavily on agriculture. Almost 80 percent of the population lived in some 550,000 rural villages. The result was that most Indians lived in poverty, with average family income less than $1,000 a year.

Nehru and later leaders strove to modernize the country's economy. India began to adopt modern farming techniques in the 1960's. New strains of seed, for example, greatly increased crop yields. Likewise, India's industries grew slowly but steadily.

Despite great progress, major obstacles remained. One problem was the unequal distribution of land. More than 35 percent of India's farmland was owned by the wealthiest 5 percent of the rural population, while half the people owned no land at all.

Another obstacle was India's constantly growing population. The government set up birth control clinics around the country. Posters urged couples to have no more than two children. Such programs, however, had little success. Large families were a tradition in India, and poor couples counted on children for care in their old age. By 1985, India was home to about 768 million people—120 percent more than in 1947. That number was growing by 40,000 *every day!* "It's like a flood," one government official declared. "Every year we need an additional 2.5 million tons of grain—just to stay even."

Conflict with China and Pakistan Trouble on its borders distracted India from its domestic issues. India and China share a 1500-mile border. In 1962, the two countries went to war briefly over a disputed area. China's forces surprised and overpowered those of India and occupied most of the land in question.

India's relations with neighboring Pakistan were almost always hostile. Indian leaders thought that partition had mutilated their country. The Pakistanis, for their part, were dismayed that their country did not include Kashmir, a large province in northern India where 75 percent of the people were Muslims. Clashes in Kashmir and other spots along the border led to full-scale war in 1965. After three weeks of fighting, India and Pakistan signed a truce that established an uneasy peace.

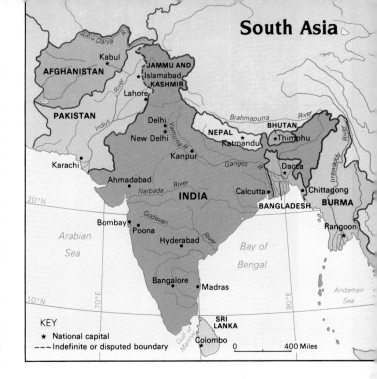

What nations have a border disagreement? Which South Asian nations are landlocked?

Indira Gandhi governed India.

Nehru's death in 1964 left the Congress party with no leader strong enough to hold together its many factions. Then in 1966, Nehru's daughter Indira Gandhi (no relation to the Mahatma) was chosen prime minister. Over the next ten years, she proved a forceful leader in her own right.

Under Indira Gandhi, India made economic progress. Both industrial and agricultural production grew during the 1970's. India became one of the world's top ten industrial nations. However, only some of this progress trickled down to the poor. Meanwhile, India's birthrate dropped slightly but remained among the highest in the world. By 1990, more than 15 percent of the total world population lived in India. That population was increasing rapidly.

Like Nehru, Indira Gandhi often pointed out that her country was the world's largest democracy. India also sought the status of a world power by exploding its first nuclear device in 1974.

Indira Gandhi was a controversial figure. In 1975, she was found guilty of illegal campaign practices, but she refused to step down as prime minister. Instead, she declared a state of emergency, arrested political opponents, and clamped

The diversity of religious, cultural, and language groups in India contributes to political unrest in the country. State boundaries within the country are redrawn almost annually to accommodate one group or another.

Nationalism in Africa and the Middle East

Ghana's independence ceremony in 1957 was attended by representatives from many countries. Britain's Duchess of Kent and Ghana's new president, Kwame Nkrumah, were at the forefront of the ceremony. The white wigs worn by some officials are a tradition from British courtrooms.

Key terms

apartheid
fundamentalism

Read and Understand

1. The age of imperialism ended in Africa.
2. Africans built new nations.
3. Nationalism sparked Mideast conflicts.

Church bells pealed joyously through the night air in the African city of Accra. It was midnight, March 6, 1957. The bells marked the end of the British colony of Gold Coast and the birth of the new nation of Ghana, named in honor of the ninth-century African kingdom. As the red, green, and yellow flag of Ghana was hoisted atop the parliament building in Accra, 50,000 people cheered. The new country's president, Kwame Nkrumah (KWAHM-ee en-KROO-muh), wept for joy.

The next day, a week-long celebration began. Accra was host to 2,000 foreign visitors. Among them was a Soviet delegation that presented Ghana with a jet plane and several automobiles. Vice President Richard Nixon headed the United States' delegation. With him were UN representative Ralph Bunche and the Reverend Martin Luther King, Jr. They gave the new country a library of technical books.

(opposite) Libya, which had come under the control of Italy in 1912, became independent in 1951. The established monarchy was overthrown in 1969 by a military group led by the radical leader Colonel Muammar al-Qadhafi, who continues to rule. Libya is a member of OPEC and a major oil-producing nation.

Ghana was one of the first African nations to gain independence. That independence was an important symbol for all Africans. In the 500 years since the ship captains sent by Prince Henry had explored Africa's west coast, the people of Africa had lived under European domination. The terrors of the slave trade had been followed by the unending burdens that came with colonialism. Now, at last, freedom was within reach.

In this chapter, you will see how the nations of Africa and the Middle East won their independence and sought to develop as nations. You will also see how nationalism led to conflicts throughout Africa and the Middle East.

The age of imperialism ended in Africa. 1

In 1950, the political map of Africa showed only 4 independent countries—Egypt, Ethiopia, Liberia, and white-controlled South Africa. Two decades later this number had risen to 38. Another two decades brought the total to more than 46. Behind this vast change lay a new spirit of nationalism among the peoples of Africa.

British Prime Minister Harold Macmillan recognized that spirit in a speech in South Africa in 1960. "The wind of change is blowing through this continent," he said, "and whether we like it or not, this growth of national consciousness is a political fact."

Nationalism led to independence in Africa.

The years following World War II marked a turning point for Africa. Signs of this change had appeared earlier. Between World War I and World War II, an educated and westernized African middle class had appeared in cities throughout the continent. Those Africans had studied at schools run by missionaries and colonial governments. Often these Africans had attended college in Europe or the United States. From this educated elite came the first nationalist leaders who worked to end colonial rule.

After World War II, these leaders gained new support. About 200,000 African soldiers fought alongside British and French soldiers in North Africa, Asia, and Europe. They helped to free France, Burma, and Ethiopia. Fighting for the freedom of others made them determined to gain their own. The examples of new nations such as India and Pakistan inspired them to begin.

North African nations gained independence.

The first of the countries to win their freedom were in North Africa. That region had a strong Islamic tradition and close ties to the Middle East. When the Ottoman empire collapsed after World War I, Muslims in the Middle East began to build their own nations. Muslim nationalists in North Africa watched with growing determination to do the same.

Soon after World War II, a new and more nationalistic government came into power in the land of the Nile. Egypt had become an unofficial British protectorate in the late 1800's, and Britain had recognized its independence in 1922. Egypt's king continued to cooperate closely with Britain— too closely, some Egyptians thought. In 1952, a group of young army officers overthrew the king and declared a republic. Their leader, Colonel Gamal Abdel Nasser, became its president.

One action taken by Nasser symbolized the new nationalism. In 1956, he moved to take over the Suez Canal. Built by an Anglo-French company and still controlled by British and French interests, the Suez Canal was Egypt's most valuable resource. Although not immediately successful, Nasser's policy in time brought the Canal under Egyptian control.

In its colonies of Morocco, Tunisia, and Algeria, France tried to resist demands for independence. Soon, however, Muslim nationalists in all three countries revolted. The French gave up quickly in Morocco and Tunisia but turned all their energies to keeping Algeria. A bitter war between Algerians and French troops raged from 1954 to 1961. The peace settlement with Algeria left all Africa north of the Sahara independent.

Nationalism spread in sub-Saharan Africa.

In the late 1950's, the focus for independence shifted south of the Sahara. There too Britain and France were the greatest colonial powers, although Belgium and Portugal also had large holdings. European rulers did not welcome the independence movement in sub-Saharan Africa any more than they had in North Africa or southern Asia. Weakened by World War II, however, they were unable to keep strong control.

In Britain, Labour Party policies supported the idea of giving up African colonies. Britain was more ready to grant independence to West African lands where Africans made up most of the population than to areas with many white settlers—for example, in Kenya and Southern Rhodesia. Unlike Britain, France was determined to keep its colonial empire. The result was prolonged war in several colonies.

As African independence movements gained in strength, European governments sought to contain them. They arrested and imprisoned nationalist leaders and executed extreme nationalists. But in most parts of Africa, Europeans were simply too few in number and too widely scattered to control the tide of African nationalism. European leaders soon realized that the

Africans, who outnumbered European settlers 800 to 1 throughout sub-Saharan Africa, would have to be given the reins of power.

South of the Sahara the first African nation to gain independence was Ghana, under the leadership of Kwame Nkrumah. Nkrumah represented a new generation of black leaders who emerged to guide the movements for independence. Educated in the United States, Nkrumah had founded the Convention People's Party to work toward independence from Britain. Now, after spending most of the previous five years in British prisons, he became prime minister of Ghana.

Leaders recognized that once independence was won, establishing new nations would not be easy. The price of independence would be hardship and sacrifice. Yet, as Nkrumah said, "There is a new African in the world, and that new African is ready to fight his own battles ... We prefer self-government with danger to servitude in tranquillity."

Colonialism left a legacy of problems.

The joy that Africans felt over independence was soon overshadowed by the reality of the enormous problems facing them. Nationalist leaders had promised that independence would bring great benefits. In reality, that promise raised hopes that could not be fulfilled. Years of colonial rule had left most African countries without either their traditional forms of government or the institutions for truly representative government. Britain and France had done little to prepare their colonies for independence, and Belgium and Portugal had made no effort at all. So repressive had been the regime in the Belgian Congo that only 16 educated leaders could be found in that vast country. Thus, when independence came, many former colonies lacked organized systems for governing and were unprepared to deal with problems that arose.

In many countries, the practices of colonialism had undermined social stability. Thousands of men had been forced to work in the gold and copper mines of the Congo, Rhodesia, and South Africa. Often they were away from home for months or years at a time. Elsewhere forced migrations disrupted communities and weakened traditional ties and the customs of everyday life.

This copy of a bronze head and the crowned head in bronze are from Ife, a Yoruba city, and are dated between the twelfth and fifteenth centuries. African nations are seeking to recover their cultural heritage.

Inspired by independence, African writers began a literary tradition originating from their unique cultural heritage and historical experience.

Unity within colonies had not been a priority for colonial rulers. Thus, boundaries had been drawn without regard for the African ethnic groups living within them. Some borders divided groups that shared the same language and culture. Other borders joined groups whose cultures clashed or who were traditional enemies. Creating a sense of national unity under these conditions would be difficult.

Economic problems also faced the new nations. Africa has great potential wealth. Its many valuable minerals include gold, copper, platinum, uranium, and diamonds. Its hydroelectric resources, when developed, will be enormous. Yet, under colonialism, the wealth from Africa's resources had gone to the ruling nations.

Poverty was not new to people in the African colonies. Traditional ways of living—whether by herding or farming—in precolonial times were often at a subsistence level, with scarcely enough means to survive.

Colonial rulers introduced commercial agriculture, intended to yield a surplus that could be exported. Plantations were developed to produce coffee, rice, sugar, and cocoa, while rubber and palm oil were obtained from tropical forests. Income from agriculture and forests, like that from mining, went to the ruler and to companies overseas rather than being invested in developing the colony. Thus, the new nations lacked both the benefits of development and the money to carry out the development themselves. The new nations would have to continue to sell plantation crops and minerals abroad to obtain money for development. Meanwhile poverty became even more acute.

Transportation too presented problems. In order to export products and resources, colonial rulers had built railroads from mines or market towns to the coast. Internal transportation, however, was not developed. For effective government and economic development to take place, networks of transportation and communication were essential. Building them would be a major cost for new nations.

Because rulers had little or no interest in the education of their colonial subjects, the new nations lacked people trained as teachers, doctors, lawyers, officials, and technicians. They also lacked people trained in the methods of modern technology—technology that was essential to

Famine victims in Ethiopia search for grain after sacks broke on being dropped from relief planes.

economic development. In many countries, only a small percent of the population was even literate. Yet these people were now the citizens of new nations, and they expected to participate in self-government and economic growth.

The African environment caused problems.

Certain conditions in the geography and environment of Africa also influenced the prospects for the new nations. The huge size of the continent means that distances are great. In some areas, such as the vast Sudd swamp of the upper Nile or the rain forests of the Congo Basin, the terrain is impassable. A number of interior countries are landlocked, with access to the sea only through other countries.

Most of Africa is a vast plateau, broken by five great rivers. These rivers leave the plateau in falls that prevent navigation inland from the sea. The lack of navigable rivers and the regular coastline—with few natural harbors—limited shipping and trade both within Africa and overseas. Air travel has enabled Africans to conquer

751

distance, cross natural barriers, and establish regular communication.

The climate of Africa presents its own set of problems. One third of the continent is desert. Of all the continents, Africa has the largest area—about 90 percent of its land—within the tropics. The altitude of the vast African plateau helps to offset the high temperatures and make it habitable. However, it does not prevent the spread of tropical diseases or the insects that carry many of them. Sleeping sickness, carried by the tsetse fly, and malaria, carried by mosquitoes, are only two of many hazards to human health.

South of the Sahara, a wide strip of semiarid grassland, the Sahel, extends across Africa. This is an area of nomadic herding and light farming. Rainfall here is uncertain, providing adequate moisture for grass and crops in some years and little rainfall in others. Since the 1960's, the Sahel has suffered serious droughts, which have been made worse by overgrazing. The result has been starvation for millions of people. In the 1980's, drought has spread to Ethiopia and parts of the Sudan with the same terrible result.

Drought affects not only people, herds, and vegetation but also the land itself. Once the grass that holds the soil is gone, the land of the Sahel begins to turn to desert. The southward spread of the Sahara has become a threat to the whole region of the Sahel.

Section Review 1

Define: (a) subsistence, (b) drought
Identify: (a) Ghana, (b) Kwame Nkrumah, (c) Gamal Abdel Nasser, (d) Sahel
Answer:
1. What groups of Africans took the lead in nationalism?
2. (a) What countries were first to gain independence? (b) Why did nationalism develop there?
3. What was the attitude of colonial rulers toward independence in Africa?
4. What problems remained from colonial rule?
5. What problems did the African environment cause?

Critical Thinking
6. How might the problems resulting from colonialism and the environment affect the development of nations in Africa?

Africans built new nations. 2

The granting of independence to Ghana began a wave of nation building. New nations appeared almost regularly as the British and French governments made an orderly but rapid withdrawal. Following their departure, the real challenge of independence began. Could the new nations develop unified and responsible governments? And could their economies grow enough to assure at least a minimum standard of living for their people?

In creating new governments, most African nations—like India and Pakistan earlier—chose to be politically nonaligned as part of the Third World. Nonetheless, both democratic and communist countries sought to establish spheres of influence. Often this was done through outright aid, support for education, and assistance in industrial development.

New nations sought political stability.

When they became independent, most African countries patterned their new governments and economic systems after those of Western Europe and the United States. Most of them set up representative democracies with capitalist economies. Some countries, such as Gabon, succeeded in following the Western model. They were successful because they had fairly solid economic bases and a growing middle class. Those countries also relied on their former rulers for support. Gabon, for instance, kept close ties with France.

The Western model, however, was not fully implemented in many countries. In some, an elite upper class ran the country for their own benefit. Other countries experienced periods of unstable rule with coups and uprisings. A few became ruthless dictatorships. Thus, a variety of governments came to power in Africa.

Côte d'Ivoire Côte d'Ivoire (Ivory Coast) is an example of a country that made the transition to independence in a peaceful fashion. Felix Houphouet-Boigny (HOO-fway-BWAH-nyee) provided that country with stable leadership for more than three decades. Although there was only one political party, it represented all major groups. Such stability, however, was the exception rather than the rule.

Ivory Coast was Africa's largest producer of coffee, cocoa, and timber.

Tanzania In Tanzania too, the move to independence was peaceful. Julius Nyerere led the new nation and its one-party government. Nyerere adopted some socialist methods. His objective was to obtain greater economic efficiency, unite the ethnic groups, and provide social services.

Kenya In Kenya, conflict preceded independence. People of the Kikuyu had once been driven from their land by white settlers. From 1952 to 1956, the Mau Mau, a secret Kikuyu society, tried to retake their lands by force. Kenya became a republic in 1963, with Jomo Kenyatta, a Kikuyu leader, as president.

Zaire and Uganda Zaire experienced a series of problems, from civil war to the secession of one province. Those upheavals gave way to a highly authoritarian government under General Joseph Mobutu. The most extreme problems following independence occurred in Uganda. There the dictator Idi Amin seized power and launched

Map Study

Name the nations through which the Nile River flows from its sources.

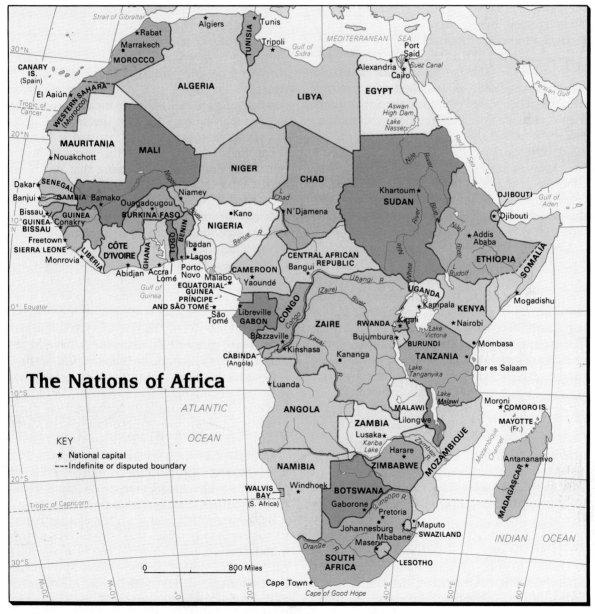

The Nations of Africa

KEY
★ National capital
--- Indefinite or disputed boundary

Map Study answers: Ethiopia, Sudan, Uganda, Egypt

753

a seven-year reign of terror. An estimated 300,000 Ugandans perished under Amin's rule. Whole ethnic groups were wiped out, while suspected political opponents were simply murdered at will. The aftermath of chaos left that nation torn apart.

Nigeria One of the richest and most advanced of the new nations, Nigeria, became independent from Britain in 1960. The most populous of African countries, it is also the most fragmented. It is home to more than 250 ethnic groups who speak dozens of different languages and dialects. The three dominant groups—the Hausa in the North, the Yoruba in the west, and the Ibo in the east—had been mortal enemies for generations. Forging these groups into a national unit seemed an almost impossible task.

Conflict over political control led in time to civil war—after the Ibo leaders had sought to form a separate state, Biafra. More than two million Ibo perished before a final surrender. Since then, an uneasy truce has prevailed, with military leaders heading the government. During the 1970's, enormous wealth poured into Nigeria from the export of the nation's rich oil resources. Distribution of that wealth, however, is highly unequal. Nigeria has used some of the income from the sale of oil to develop industries that in time will strengthen its economy.

Zimbabwe Zimbabwe was one of the later nations to come under the control of its African peoples. Known as Southern Rhodesia, it was home to many British settlers, who lived on farms in the highlands. Those settlers, led by Ian Smith, declared independence from Britain in 1965. However, they refused to grant any power to black political parties. Pressure by Britain and the United Nations to grant Africans a greater voice in the government was unsuccessful. In 1979, an agreement was finally reached to give the black majority control of the government. Under President Robert Mugabe, whites and Africans have tried to set aside their differences and live in peace.

Namibia and Angola The last country of Africa to gain its independence is Namibia. A former German colony, Namibia has for the past three quarters of a century been controlled by South Africa. Its fate has in recent years been linked to that of Angola, a former Portuguese colony. After becoming independent, Angola received support from Soviet-bloc countries, including thousands of troops from Cuba. After years of civil war between the government and non-communist guerrillas, negotiations have ended the fighting. South Africa has agreed that when Cuban troops are withdrawn from Angola, it will recognize the independence of Namibia. This agreement is still being implemented.

Nations faced problems in economic development.

European colonial policy had sought to keep colonies as suppliers of food, raw materials, and resources—but without the industry that was the monopoly of the ruling nation. Nowhere was this policy more successful than in Africa. African workers produced plantation crops and mineral resources for export and provided a market for goods manufactured abroad. Africans hoped that with independence, some of the income from plantations and mines could be used at home.

Experience quickly showed that many problems remained. Countries like Ghana that depended on the export of a single crop such as cocoa found that a fall in world prices could greatly reduce national income. Many African countries had a similar experience: Zambia with copper, Uganda with coffee, Chad with cotton.

The long-term solution was to develop a wider range of economic activities, based upon each nation's resources, and to produce for world markets. But modernizing was slow in a continent where soil is generally poor and farmers followed subsistence methods. In many areas, drought reduced crop production far below earlier levels.

Another possibility was the development of industry. The problem there was capital. Money was needed to build roads for transportation, dams for energy, and factories for producing goods. Many African leaders attempted to develop their country's economies by borrowing from abroad. Yet even when new industries were built, they rarely produced enough wealth to repay the loans. Thus, most countries remained continuously in debt.

By the late 1980's, some bright spots had begun to appear in economic development. The huge Kariba Dam on the Zambezi River now provided electricity to Zambia and Zimbabwe. By changing from subsistence to commercial methods, farmers in Zimbabwe made that nation self-sufficient in

Namibia, a former German colony, was made a mandate of South Africa in 1918. Until 1988, South Africa had refused to consider independence for Namibia.

food, and Zimbabwe even began to export food to neighboring countries.

With income from oil exports, Nigeria has been able to fund some of its own industrialization. Building a petrochemical industry has enabled the nation to refine its own oil before selling it abroad. Nigeria also plans to begin selling liquefied natural gas to Europe by 1995. The plant for producing the gas will be black Africa's largest construction project of the early 1990's.

A different kind of economic change is taking place in Tanzania. There, socialism had had the effect of limiting economic growth. Today Tanzania is returning to some capitalist methods, including focus on the market to adjust prices and provide incentives for production. Letting prices rise encourages farmers to produce more food. Some benefits of Nyerere's early policies remain, however. A model education system, based on the use of Swahili (the language of East Africa), has raised Tanzania's literacy rate to a remarkable 80 percent.

Social changes affected development.

Probably the greatest threat to Africa's future development is the current explosion in population. In 1950, Africa's population was estimated at 215 million. Today it is 600 million or more. It may even double by some time in the first decade of the next century. Africa's population is the fastest growing in the world.

Several factors make such rapid population growth an acute problem. The continent is already so short of food that many countries have to import food to help people survive. Shortages are increased by the drought in the Sahel, which is taking land out of cultivation and thus reducing the amount of food produced. Also, as India discovered, a large and growing population cannot live from the land alone. Industry is needed to provide employment, but the amount of industry—and therefore the number of jobs—is limited. Nonetheless, governments that provide food do so at the cost of industrial growth.

Increasing population is a special problem for cities because of the migration of people from rural to urban areas. Hundreds of thousands of families are living in slum areas that have grown up around major cities. Among the largest are those of Kinshasa in Zaire. There, many people live without a stable food supply, jobs, education, or medical care. The overcrowding also leads to crime and disease. A related problem is that of refugees. War, ethnic differences, hunger, and political strife have forced millions of people to leave their homes.

Among the seemingly insurmountable social problems, some progress is being made. Because most countries have established educational systems, literacy is increasing and future leaders are being educated. Also, the traditionally important role of women in African society—as traders, producers of food, and keepers of the home—is expanding in many areas. New educational opportunities for women are a key to improving their position in society. One example of the changing status of women is Angie Brooks of Liberia, the first woman to become president of the United Nations General Assembly.

In many countries, the transition to independence has brought rapid modernization. Television and radio are playing an enormous role in bringing the outside world to even the most remote corners of the continent. The result is a culture in transition—with ox-drawn carts and motorcycles jostling for position on dusty village roads, soft-drink cans littering refugee camps in the drought-stricken Sahel, and farmers listening to radios while harvesting millet by hand, just as their great-grandfathers had done a century earlier.

South Africa's peoples remained divided.

Of the sub-Saharan nations, South Africa is the most advanced in economic and technological development and has the greatest wealth. South Africa in 1910 became a self-governing country within the British empire and in 1931 gained full independence within the Commonwealth of Nations. In 1961, South Africa left the Commonwealth and became a republic.

The population of South Africa is composed of four groups: blacks, people of mixed race, Asians, and whites. Most of the Asians are of Indian descent. The white population is made up of two groups—Dutch and English. The Dutch, known as Boers or Afrikaners, are descendents of settlers who came to South Africa several hundred years ago. Most English settlers have come within the past hundred years. Blacks, people of mixed race, and Asians together make up about 87 percent of the population, with blacks—at 73 percent—the majority.

Apartheid Although South Africa has been independent since 1931, the vast majority of its people have never had self-government. Afrikaners—the larger white group—have always dominated the government. Their vision of independence was based on white control. Black South Africans could not vote or hold seats in parliament and were denied opportunity in all spheres of political life.

In 1948, the government established an even more extreme policy called **apartheid,** which called for the complete separation of the races. New laws banned all social contacts between whites and blacks. Schools, hospitals, and neighborhoods were to be separate. Parks, playgrounds, and beaches were also segregated. Even certain jobs and higher education were closed to blacks.

In 1959, new laws extended racial segregation by creating separate homelands for South Africa's major ethnic groups. Afrikaners hoped that all blacks would in time be resettled on these homelands, which would have semi-independent status.

The homelands policy was highly unfair. About 13 percent of the nation's land was set aside for blacks, who made up 73 percent of the population. The remaining 87 percent of the country—including its best farmland and its fabulously rich gold and diamond mines—remained in the hands of whites, who represented just 15 percent of the population. Many blacks were forced to return to homelands that they had never seen. Other blacks remained in the areas reserved for whites because they had jobs on farms, in the mines, or as laborers in the cities.

During the 1960's and 1970's, huge slums, or townships—the urban homes of blacks—grew up around the major cities. Soweto, on the outskirts of Johannesburg, was one such township. Blacks living in those areas were required to carry registration passes. Because cards were available only to those with jobs, families were often separated. To be together, families had to live in the shanty towns illegally. Without these workers, South Africa's economy would have collapsed. Yet the government made no real provisions for them in the community. Instead, a strong army stood ready to enforce control.

Black resistance Blacks in South Africa had long resisted the government's repressive treatment. In 1912, they founded the African National

Comparing pictures Johannesburg, South Africa (left), is a center of wealth. Outside it lie black townships such as Crossroads (right). What factors might account for the economic differences?

Voice from Our Time · The Effects of Banning

Bakone Moloto, a young South African black, was active in a movement to increase literacy among blacks. One day, without warning, the police seized him and sent him to a distant town. He was placed under a banning order. Here his mother describes what banning means.

My son was banned to [the town of] Mafekeng. I hardly knew any person I could request to . . . give him moral support . . . Word had already reached me that my son had been dumped in an empty house somewhere in Mafekeng . . . [Later] he described in detail the restrictions of his banning order and some of its limitations. He highlighted the following points:

That he was allowed only one visitor at a time. If he spoke to more than one person at a time, it was an offence for which he could be charged, convicted, and imprisoned.

That he might not enter any school, church, or publishing office.

That he must remain within Montshioa township, except on his way to work, when he must not stop anywhere.

All of these restrictions had far-reaching implications. Mafekeng being such a small town . . . he was compelled to take the first [job] offer he received. He was never quite certain of whether he could use a shared taxi.

1. What is the purpose of the banning rules?
2. Why was Bakone never sure if he could use a shared taxi?
3. How would banning restrict a normal family life?

Congress to work for equality. In the 1950's, the ANC and other groups sought reform of segregation laws. In 1960, a group protesting the use of passes was fired upon at Sharpeville, and 69 people were killed. The nation's foremost black leader, Nelson Mandela, was jailed. He was still in prison in 1988.

A new wave of protest began in 1976. The immediate cause was a new government policy that required some classes for black students to be taught in the Afrikaners' language. Blacks protested strongly. Because that language was foreign to them, their children would be further disadvantaged in education. In the course of the conflict, more than 600 people were killed. Protests, arrests, and detentions continue to the present.

In recent years, the South African government under President P. W. Botha has relaxed somewhat its strict segregation laws. Segregation continued, however, in education and residence. In 1984, a new constitution that gave limited representation to Asians and people of mixed race still excluded blacks from participation in government. Protest against this exclusion resulted in the government's declaring a state of emergency that allowed arrest without charges and censorship of the press.

Foreign pressures against apartheid Many countries have urged the South African government to change its policies. Some countries, including the United States, have limited trade with South Africa, and a number of foreign businesses have left. The United Nations has voted sanctions against South Africa. Archbishop Desmond Tutu, a leader of nonviolent protest against the policies of the South African government, received the Nobel Peace Prize in recognition of his work. The situation in South Africa remains tense, with little prospect for positive change.

In South Africa, any protest against government policy or actions may be considered treason, punishable by imprisonment or death.

757

Define: (a) authoritarian, (b) apartheid
Identify: (a) Felix Houphouet-Boigny, (b) Julius Nyerere, (c) Jomo Kenyatta, (d) Joseph Mobutu, (e) Idi Amin, (f) Ian Smith, (g) Robert Mugabe, (h) Nelson Mandela, (i) P. W. Botha, (j) Desmond Tutu
Answer:
1. (a) Describe the transition to independence for three African countries. (b) What problems did various nations meet? (c) How did they solve the problems?
2. In what ways did the new governments differ from those of Western democracies?
3. (a) What economic problems did the new nations face? (b) In what ways might those problems be solved?
4. Why were economic development and technology important to African nations?
5. Why was rapid population growth such a great threat to stability in Africa?
6. (a) What policies of the South African government caused protests by blacks? (b) In what various ways did blacks resist those policies?

Critical Thinking
7. (a) In what ways were most African nations like other Third World nations? (b) In what ways did they differ?

Nationalism sparked Mideast conflicts.

3

The Middle East has been a crossroads since antiquity. Located at the meeting place of three continents, it has been swept by conquests and often dominated by foreign powers. Nationalism thus had a special meaning for the countries of that region. They felt that the time had come for them to establish their own nations and govern themselves.

Within the Middle East, sharp differences exist. That region is the source of three great religions: Judaism, Christianity, and Islam. The majority of the people are Muslim. Yet even within that religion there are differences, such as those be-

tween Sunni and Shi'ite Muslims. Some differences, such as those between Arabs and Turks, are based on ethnic and cultural differences. When nations began to form in this area, these many conflicting loyalties of religion and ethnic identity met with explosive effect.

Nationalism arose after World War I.

A number of Mideast nations were formed after World War I. As you read in Chapter 29 (pages 627–631), the collapse of the Ottoman empire provided an opportunity for national groups to organize and secure power. By the start of World War II, all Mideast countries except Palestine were independent.

Like the new nations of Asia and Africa, the Mideast countries became nonaligned members of the Third World. Like other Third World nations, they lacked economic development and modern technology. In some countries, the strength of religious custom and cultural tradition caused resistance to modernization.

The factor that led to economic change in the Middle East was oil. Although oil had long been known to exist there, it took on a new importance

Reading a graph The rise in oil prices caused a worldwide energy crisis. What prices in the past decade were highest and lowest?

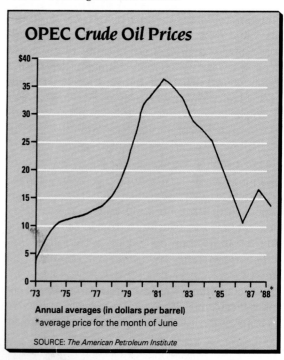

OPEC Crude Oil Prices

Annual averages (in dollars per barrel)
*average price for the month of June

SOURCE: *The American Petroleum Institute*

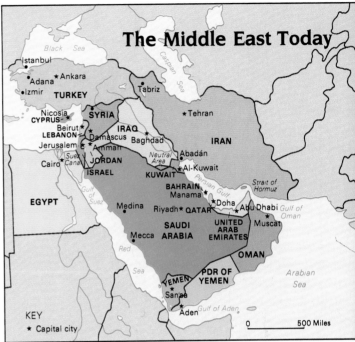

The Middle East Today

KEY
★ Capital city

Map Study

Oil and oil refineries (left) have brought sudden wealth to much of the Middle East, especially to countries along the Persian Gulf. What countries border the gulf? What strait controls entrance into the Persian Gulf?

as the demand for it increased in the 1920's. At first, oil development was in the hands of foreign companies. In the decades after World War II, however, most Mideast countries began to nationalize their oil industry.

In order to strengthen their control further, five Mideast nations formed in 1960 the Organization of Petroleum Exporting Countries (OPEC). Since then, a number of other oil-producing countries have become members of OPEC. A major purpose of the organization was to set levels for oil production. If the supply of oil could be limited, demand would increase and the price—and profits—would go up.

The 1970's made clear the importance of OPEC to the rest of the world. In the 1960's and early 1970's, OPEC supplied more than 60 percent of the world's oil. In 1973, OPEC raised its prices fourfold in protest against the support from the United States and Europe for Israel in a short but intense war. The result was an energy crisis that inflicted great damage on the world economy.

Another price rise in 1979 had a similar effect. Oil had become a weapon of worldwide influence—one that brought vast and sudden wealth to OPEC nations.

In the long run, OPEC did not achieve its goal of controlling oil prices. People learned to conserve energy, and nations began to seek out non-OPEC sources of oil. Today OPEC supplies only about one third of the world's oil. Divisions have arisen within OPEC, as some members no longer abide by the production levels set. Oil actually fell in price after 1986. Nonetheless, nations around the world had become aware of their dependence on oil and the need for alternate sources of energy.

Israel became a nation.

The one Mideast country not yet independent at the end of World War II was Palestine. There religious and ethnic loyalties were to collide. Although in ancient times the location of the kingdom of Israel, Palestine had for centuries

The flow of oil from the Middle East is critical to the economies of many industrialized nations. The geography of the region, however, creates bottlenecks at the Suez Canal, Bab el Mandeb, and Strait of Hormuz, where the movement of oil can be halted.

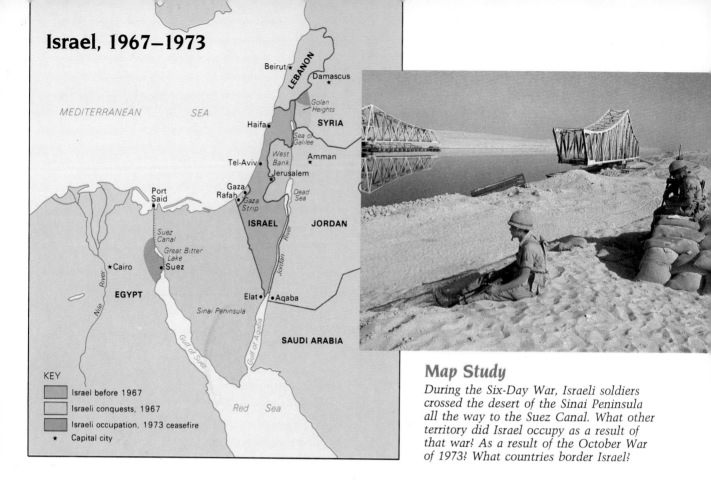

Israel, 1967–1973

KEY
- Israel before 1967
- Israeli conquests, 1967
- Israeli occupation, 1973 ceasefire
- ★ Capital city

Labels on map: MEDITERRANEAN SEA, Beirut, LEBANON, Damascus, Golan Heights, SYRIA, Haifa, Sea of Galilee, West Bank, Amman, Tel-Aviv, Jerusalem, Gaza, Rafah, Gaza Strip, Dead Sea, ISRAEL, JORDAN, Jordan River, Port Said, Suez Canal, Great Bitter Lake, Suez, Cairo, EGYPT, Nile River, Elat, Aqaba, Sinai Peninsula, Gulf of Suez, Gulf of Aqaba, SAUDI ARABIA, Red Sea

Map Study

During the Six-Day War, Israeli soldiers crossed the desert of the Sinai Peninsula all the way to the Suez Canal. What other territory did Israel occupy as a result of that war? As a result of the October War of 1973? What countries border Israel?

been Arab. As you read in Chapter 29, Jews had begun to migrate to Palestine in the late 1800's. Britain's Balfour Declaration in 1918 had recognized the interest of Jews in Palestine. Many Jews had hoped for a homeland there. Arabs, however, still made up 70 percent of Palestine's population. They wanted Palestine to be an Arab nation.

Birth of a nation The end of World War II, when knowledge of the Holocaust reached the world, brought a tremendous outpouring of sympathy for the Jewish people and their desire for a homeland in Palestine. In 1948, Britain turned over to the United Nations the responsibility for Palestine. A special UN committee recommended the creation of not one but two Palestines, one Jewish and the other Arab. The UN General Assembly accepted the compromise plan. In May 1948, David Ben-Gurion, longtime leader of the Jews in Palestine, announced the creation of an independent Israel, the fulfillment of his people's 2,000-year-old dream.

Arab-Israeli conflict Arabs in the Middle East were dissatisfied with the decision of the UN. They felt that Israel had been created at their expense and that Israel had been given by far the more valuable lands and cities of Palestine. Within hours of Ben-Gurion's announcement, six Arab states attacked Israel. The war quickly became a victory for the Israelis. By the end of 1948, they controlled nearly three fourths of Palestine. When the fighting stopped, Egypt and Jordan divided what remained of Palestine. The Jews had a homeland, but the Palestinian Arabs were left without a country.

Even as the war was raging, thousands of Palestinian and Arab families began fleeing from areas under Jewish control. By 1949, more than half a million Arabs had left the country. Most were settled in UN-sponsored refugee camps that ringed the borders of their former homeland.

Economic progress More than a million Jews, many of them highly educated or skilled, flocked to Israel from around the world. With their help, Israel made remarkable economic progress. Using the most modern agricultural methods, kibbutz farmers were able to turn some desert areas into thriving farmland. Industry also prospered—so well, in fact, that Israel rapidly became a highly industrialized nation.

Map Study answers: Gaza Strip, Sinai Peninsula, Golan Heights, West Bank; areas west of Suez Canal and north of Golan Heights; Egypt, Jordan, Syria, Lebanon

Israel and its neighbors remained in conflict.

No peace treaty ended the war between Arabs and Israelis because the Arabs refused to recognize Israel as a nation. Instead, an uneasy cease-fire prevailed, frequently broken by raids. In 1967, actual war broke out again. It began when Egypt closed off the Gulf of Aqaba, Israel's outlet to the Red Sea. Israel responded by attacking Egypt. In six days, the Israelis defeated the armies of Egypt, Syria, and Jordan. Israel also occupied much new territory.

Five years of fragile peace followed the Six-Day War. Then, in October 1973, while Israelis observed Yom Kippur, the holiest day of the year for Jews, Egypt and Syria attacked. Taken by surprise, the Israeli army lost ground at first but quickly recovered. In the south, it surrounded the Egyptians in the Sinai Peninsula; and in the north, it forced the Syrians back across the border.

By an agreement made between Israel and Egypt in 1974, Israel withdrew east of the Suez Canal and returned part of the Sinai Peninsula to Egypt. Egypt, in turn, agreed not to put troops there. In 1977, Egyptian President Anwar el-Sadat went to Israel to meet with the newly elected Israeli prime minister, Menachim Begin. Sadat's action was a shock to the Arab world, which had refused to recognize Israel. Sadat, however, had realized that his nation could never support economic development unless it ceased fighting with Israel.

The Camp David Accords When Sadat and Begin could not reach an agreement, President Jimmy Carter of the United States invited both men to meet at Camp David, the presidential retreat outside Washington. For 13 days, the three men talked, argued, and jogged along the paths of a pine forest. At last, Carter announced that Sadat and Begin had agreed to sign a peace treaty.

Under the final terms of the treaty, Egypt recognized Israel's right to exist. Leaders in other Arab countries called Sadat a traitor and broke ties with Egypt. Sadat himself was assassinated in 1981 by Egyptians who opposed recognition of Israel. Not until the mid-1980's did several Arab nations again seek ties with Egypt.

The Palestinian struggle Israeli expansion as a result of the October War brought another million Palestinian Arabs under Israel's rule. Some remained in Israel, but others fled to the refugee camps outside Israel's borders. They continued to hope for a return to their homes. The chief organization that represented their nationalistic goals was the Palestinian Liberation Organization (PLO), a radical Arab group.

During the 1970's and 1980's, PLO guerrillas conducted a terrorist campaign against Israel that included attacks on citizens of many countries. Israel answered PLO attacks with bombing raids on Palestinian refugee camps and strongholds. From 1982 to 1985, the Israeli army invaded neighboring Lebanon in an attempt to drive the PLO out of that country.

Daily Life · Veiled Faces

In many Muslim nations, women wear veils called *chadors* in public. The strictness of rules about veiling varies greatly from country to country. In Turkey, for example, veils are rare. In Iran, however, women who leave home without veils risk severe penalties. Most women in Saudi Arabia do not wear veils in public. In Qatar, women are not photographed even for passports. The wife of the ruler of Abu Dhabi has never been seen by a man outside her immediate family. Yet she is president of the Abu Dhabi women's association, whose members try to improve the lives of desert women. The organization publishes a magazine for women and runs a bank that is managed, staffed, and patronized entirely by women.

In December 1987, a new kind of protest began among the Palestinian people. In the occupied areas of the Left Bank and Golan Heights, a new and younger group of leaders gained mass support for a campaign of civil disobedience. Although the uprising was forcefully put down by the Israeli army, it gave new urgency to the issue of Palestinian rights. It was clear that the Palestinian situation had entered a new stage. In 1988, in an effort to reach a solution, Jordan withdrew its support from the Palestinians. It was widely believed that this action would force Palestinians and Israelis to reach some decision about the fate of Arab refugees and those living in Israeli-occupied territory. Elections in Israel in November 1988, however, supported a conservative government that would be reluctant to accept any change.

Palestinians, in turn, declared themselves a nation and indicated some willingness to consider recognizing Israel. Their hope for an eventual Palestinian state remained. The possibility of negotiation as a means to solving problems brought new hope for peace in the region.

The Islamic world underwent transition.

The postwar era was a time of change for many Mideast nations. Tradition remained strong in most countries of the region. Several nations—Saudi Arabia and Kuwait, for example—remained monarchies, where kings continued to rule with almost absolute power, aided by wealth from oil. Countries with little or no oil—such as Egypt and Syria—faced many of the same problems that limited development in other Third World countries. Nonetheless, nations such as Saudi Arabia and Egypt provided some political stability in the turbulent Middle East.

In the course of the twentieth century, modernization had brought the Islamic world into direct contact with Western ideas and values. Some countries welcomed this interchange, but others strongly opposed it. One movement that resisted Western influence was Islamic **fundamentalism,** or obedience to the basic laws of that religion. In no country was the clash between modern and traditional values more dramatic than in Iran.

The presence of a UN peacekeeping force helped to prevent outbreaks of fighting on the Iran-Iraq border. UN troops help to contain conflict in many areas around the world.

Iran's Islamic revolution In 1925, Reza Khan, an army officer, became the shah, or ruler, of Iran (page 628). He took the name Reza Shah Pahlavi. He tried to modernize his country in the European style. He built Iran's first railroad and gave women more rights. His son, Muhammad Reza Shah Pahlavi, became shah in 1941 and ruled until 1979.

The reign of Muhammad Reza Pahlavi was a mixture of tyranny and enlightenment. On the one hand, he used secret police to silence his opponents with arrest, torture, and execution. On the other, he set up schools, reformed land ownership, and gave more freedom—including the right to vote—to women. A highly educated man, the shah wanted to westernize his country. The money for modernization came from the sale of more than 6 million barrels of oil that flowed daily from Iran's wells. Wealth from oil made Tehran, Iran's capital, a city of gleaming skyscrapers, modern factories, and international

To impress the world with the changes the country had undergone, the shah changed his nation's name from Persia to Iran.

banks. Outside the city, however, many Iranians lived in mud huts. Poor Iranians bitterly resented the wealthy foreigners and their Western influence and values.

The actions of the shah were also viewed with concern by conservative Muslim leaders. They wanted Iran to become an Islamic republic, ruled in strict accordance with the teachings of the Koran. The leader of this group was the elderly Ayatollah Ruhollah Khomeini (koh-MAY-nee), who lived in exile in Paris. At his urging, oil workers in 1978 went on strike, and riots broke out in the cities. Early in 1979, the shah fled and the ayatollah returned from France to set up a government.

The new government proved even more repressive than that of the shah. Arrests, torture, and executions increased. The new legal code, based on the Koran, sought to apply traditional Islamic laws to all aspects of life. Advances in women's rights were reversed, and inhumane punishments were set even for minor offenses.

One cornerstone of Khomeini's policies was hatred for the United States, which had strongly supported the shah. In 1979, with Khomeini's support, a group of Islamic radicals seized the United States embassy in Tehran. They took more than 50 United States citizens hostage and held them captive for over a year.

The Iran-Iraq War The Iranian revolution was part of a broader Islamic religious revival that swept across the Middle East during the 1970's and 1980's. The new rulers of Iran belonged to the Shi'ite branch of Islam. They encouraged Shi'ites elsewhere—in Iraq, in particular—to rise up and overthrow their Sunni governments. Angered by this and hoping to take advantage of the turmoil in Iran to gain territory, Iraqi leaders attacked Iran in 1980. Iran responded with a holy war against Iraq.

The Iran-Iraq War proved to be one of the most terrible of modern times. For eight years, Muslim killed Muslim in the name of religion. In 1988, both Iran and Iraq agreed to a cease-fire arranged by the United Nations. The UN also set up an international peacekeeping force to prevent further warfare around the Persian Gulf. In a region torn by war, the prospect of peace had a stabilizing influence.

Lebanon One of the most tragic examples of conflicting loyalties and of the link between Mideast and world politics has been Lebanon. Conflicts between Muslims and Christians, Sunnis and Shi'ites, and Israelis and Palestinians all became intertwined within a single country.

Civil war has occurred a number of times among the various groups. Great power politics became involved in 1975 as the United States supported the Christians and Syria, seeking control, obtained Soviet weapons. In the early 1980's, fighting continued almost daily. Terrorists blew up the United States embassy in April 1983. Later that year 250 United States marines and 58 French soldiers died in a bomb attack by Muslim terrorists. United States and European teachers, doctors, and reporters were kidnapped by terrorist groups.

Lebanon had become a battleground where each small faction looked out for its own interests. No leader could speak with authority for any group or for the government. As a nation, Lebanon stood on the brink of destruction.

Section Review 3

Define: (a) recession, (b) fundamentalism, (c) ayatollah, (d) hostage
Identify: (a) OPEC, (b) Palestine, (c) Israel, (d) PLO, (e) Shi'ite
Answer
1. (a) What was the purpose for the founding of OPEC? (b) How did oil become a weapon for OPEC nations?
2. (a) Why was there widespread support for the creation of Israel? (b) Why did some groups oppose Israel?
3. Why was the treaty between Egypt and Israel a major diplomatic achievement?
4. (a) What were the shah's goals for Iran? (b) The ayatollah's?
5. (a) Why did war break out between Iran and Iraq? (b) What was the outcome of the war?
6. What were the causes of the continuing war in Lebanon?

Critical Thinking
7. (a) How are nationalism and religion linked in the conflict over Palestine? (b) How are they linked in the conflict between Iran and Iraq? (c) How does such a link make it difficult to reach agreements?

In 1986, the United States, using Israel as an intermediary, secretly sold arms to Iran in return for that country's help in securing the release of American hostages held by Lebanese factions.

763

Chapter Review 35

Summary

1. Africans resumed the fight for independence. In the 1920's, a westernized African middle class took the lead in independence movements. The struggle for independence began in North Africa, where it took many forms and spread south. African countries faced economic and political crises brought on by colonial rule.

2. African nations took diverse paths. After independence, African nations patterned their new countries after Western democracies. When the Western model failed, Africans experimented with a variety of political and economic systems, including one-party democracy in Ivory Coast, one-man rule in Zaire, and a federal republic in Nigeria. In Nigeria, a military coup in 1985 brought democracy to an end. Tanzania was led by Julius Nyerere, who worked hard to bring economic stability. South Africa remained under white rule after independence in 1931. In 1948, South Africa set up apartheid to segregate the black majority and keep power in the hands of the whites. In 1959, South Africa forced the black majority to settle in homelands. The white government uses brute force to crush resistance.

3. Nationalism sparked Mideast conflicts. Although the partition of Israel in 1948 provided Jews with a homeland, it led to the loss of a homeland for Palestinian Arabs and sparked several Arab-Israeli wars. In 1979, Egypt and Israel signed a peace accord, but relations in the region remain tense. In Iran, a revolution ended modernization and brought Shi'ite Muslim religious leaders to power. Iran has tried to spread a Shi'ite revolution to neighboring Iraq. Division in Lebanon led to civil war in 1958. Fighting has intensified because of the presence of the PLO, which has launched attacks against Israel.

Reviewing the Facts

1. Define the following terms:
   - a. jihad
   - b. ethnic group
   - c. apartheid
   - d. homeland
   - e. Middle East
   - f. ayatollah
2. Explain the importance of each of the following names, places, or terms:
   - a. Ghana
   - b. Nkrumah
   - c. Nasser
   - d. Ivory Coast
   - e. Houphouet-Boigny
   - f. Mobutu
   - g. Nigeria
   - h. Nyerere
   - i. Soweto
   - j. PLO
   - k. Shi'ite
   - l. Lebanon
3. (a) How did the effects of colonial rule weaken African countries economically? (b) What problems

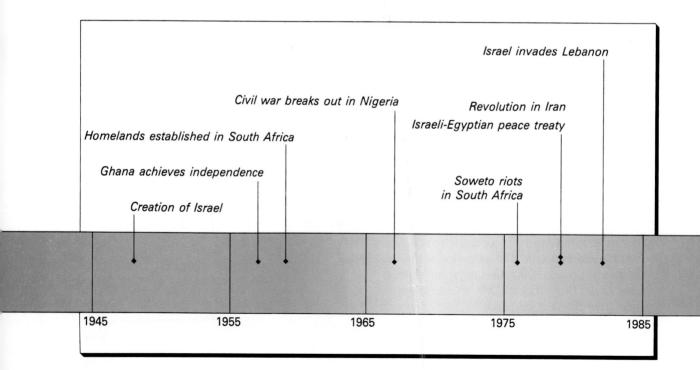

Israel invades Lebanon

Civil war breaks out in Nigeria

Revolution in Iran
Israeli-Egyptian peace treaty

Homelands established in South Africa

Ghana achieves independence

Soweto riots
in South Africa

Creation of Israel

1945   1955   1965   1975   1985

did they face in nation building?

4. (a) Who controls South Africa today? (b) What methods has the South African government used to keep control?

5. (a) How was the state of Israel created? (b) What was the result for Palestinian Arabs?

Basic Skills

1. **Reading and interpreting a map** (a) The five great rivers of Africa are the Nile, Niger, Congo, Zambezi, and Limpopo. Using the map on page 753, list the countries that touch each river. (b) Compare the continental position of these rivers with that of the Mississippi River system in North America. What differences do you find?

2. **Classifying** Section 1 describes a number of problems caused by colonialism and the African environment. (a) List the problems described in each group. (b) For each problem, find examples of countries in the chapter that illustrate it.

3. **Locating** The water routes of the African-Middle East crossroads are important to world trade. Certain parts of these routes are critical because they are bottlenecks for shipping. (a) Using the maps on pages 759 and 760, identify the waterway between the Mediterranean and Red seas and between the Persian Gulf and the Arabian Sea. (b) There is also a third bottleneck. Where is it located?

Researching and Reporting Skills

1. **Using a newspaper index** *The New York Times Index* is a major resource for finding current information. Use a recent volume to locate articles about some aspect of life in one African or Mideast country.

2. **Using regional or national magazines** Using periodicals such as *Africa Report* or *Asia,* find information about cultural events in or pertaining to Africa or the Middle East. What similarities and contrasts are shown between traditional and modern aspects of that culture?

Critical Thinking

1. **Synthesizing** What various influences contributed to the growth of nationalism in North Africa?

2. **Solving problems** (a) Make a list of major problems related to the geography and environments of Africa. (b) What possible solutions exist for each problem?

3. **Analyzing** (a) What conditions made it difficult for the new nations in sub-Saharan Africa to organize and launch new governments? (b) Which of these do you think was most important? Why?

4. **Resolving conflicts** One reason why conflict continues between Israel and the Palestinians is that the basic interests of both groups have been in opposition. (a) Identify the various basic interests of both groups. (b) In what ways are these opposed? (c) What range of alternatives exists for resolving these differences? (d) Which basic interests are vital to each group, as a start for negotiations?

5. **Analyzing** The tension between tradition and modernization continues in the Middle East. (a) What are several current examples of this tension? (b) How has wealth from oil affected the balance in the OPEC nations of the Middle East?

Perspectives on Past and Present

Review the content in your text about nineteenth-century Western attitudes concerning imperialism (pages 534 and 562–563). To what extent have these attitudes changed at the end of the twentieth century? What factors account for that change, as well as any lack of change?

Investigating History

The lack of protection for basic political rights in South Africa contrasts with the progress made in most countries of the world. As a class or group project, read about current political and social conditions in South Africa. Then, using the first eight amendments to the United States Constitution as criteria, evaluate the status of political rights among the different population groups in South Africa.

Chapter **36**

1945 - Present

The Americas in the Modern World

The Pan-American Highway crosses rugged terrain ranging from the rain forests of Brazil and Guatemala to the tundra of Canada. Here it descends from the Andes Mountains of Peru to a river valley.

Key terms

multinational corporation
separatism

Read and Understand

1. Two nations prospered in northern North America.
2. Latin America searched for stability.
3. Caribbean nations took different paths.

In August 1929, the Brazilian capital of Rio de Janeiro buzzed with excitement. The first International Highways Exposition ever held in the Americas had captured the imagination of the city. Featured in the exposition was the highway that would link the Americas from northern Alaska to the Straits of Magellan.

Thousands of Brazilians waited in long lines for hours to see exhibits highlighting the proposed Pan-American Highway. Displays showed the latest construction techniques and equipment, and films dramatized the efforts of workers carving roads through dense jungles and over lofty mountains. As part of the exposition, 200 delegates from countries all over the Western Hemisphere met in a spirit of international friendship to establish a timetable and raise funds for building the highway.

Neither the United States nor Canada has officially designated a roadway as part of the Pan-American highway.

The launching of the highway project was delayed by the Great Depression. Finally, in 1936, construction began. Over the next three decades, road builders in two dozen countries overcame obstacles of all kinds to complete 17,000 miles of highway. From Alaska, the road ran into Canada and through the United States, Mexico, and Central America. It ran the entire length of South America, with several east-west links across the continent. By the late 1980's, only two short stretches of the highway remained incomplete.

The Pan-American Highway has more than fulfilled the hopes of its founders. It has helped to foster trade, tourism, and communication among all the countries along its route. It has proved a fitting symbol of the countless ways in which the countries of the Western Hemisphere are linked. In this chapter, you will see how the countries of North and South America have developed in recent times.

Two nations prospered in northern North America. 1

Northern North America is a region with two of the world's largest nations, the United States and Canada. In southern North America, Mexico is linked culturally with Central and South America in the region known as Latin America.

The United States and Canada are mainly English in language and heritage, although French too is an official language in Canada. Both countries are democracies, and both have highly developed economies. In the decades after World War II, these two neighbors prospered and grew in influence.

The United States enjoyed two decades of prosperity.

The United States emerged from World War II as the richest and most powerful nation in the world. The average income and standard of living in the United States was significantly higher than that in other countries. One measure of the wealth of the United States was its gross national product (GNP). That GNP rose from $200 billion in 1945 to $500 billion in 1960.

United States Investment Abroad/ Foreign Investment in United States

(in billions of dollars)

■ U.S. investment abroad

■ Foreign investment in U.S.

1970 · 1980 · 1983 · 1984 · 1985

13.3 · 75.5 · 83.0 · 215.4 · 137.1 · 207.2 · 164.6 · 213.0 · 183.0 · 232.7

SOURCE: U.S. Statistical Abstracts, 1987

Reading a graph *Which investment was greater for the years 1970 to 1980? Which was greater from 1980 to 1985?*

The United States had escaped the devastation that World War II had brought to Great Britain, France, the Soviet Union, Germany, Japan, and other countries. The economy of the United States thus emerged from the war intact. By supplying goods to countries rebuilding after the war, the United States developed a huge foreign trade. The nation also entered an era of technological change, based on electronics.

These factors combined to make the United States a leader in the postwar global economy. This situation provided an opportunity for United States businesses to expand overseas. Companies that set up branches and operated overseas as well as at home became known as **multinational corporations.** Some of these companies became worldwide businesses with thousands of workers in countries around the world. One giant multinational company might have more resources and influence in international affairs than many small countries.

Social issues became a major concern.

Prosperity brought dramatic changes in society during the postwar era. One sign of this was the housing boom that began after the war and continued for two decades. Whole new suburbs appeared, complete with shopping centers, schools, and parks.

Not all people in the United States shared in the new prosperity. One of the poorest areas was the mountain region of Appalachia. There the coal mines that had provided jobs for thousands

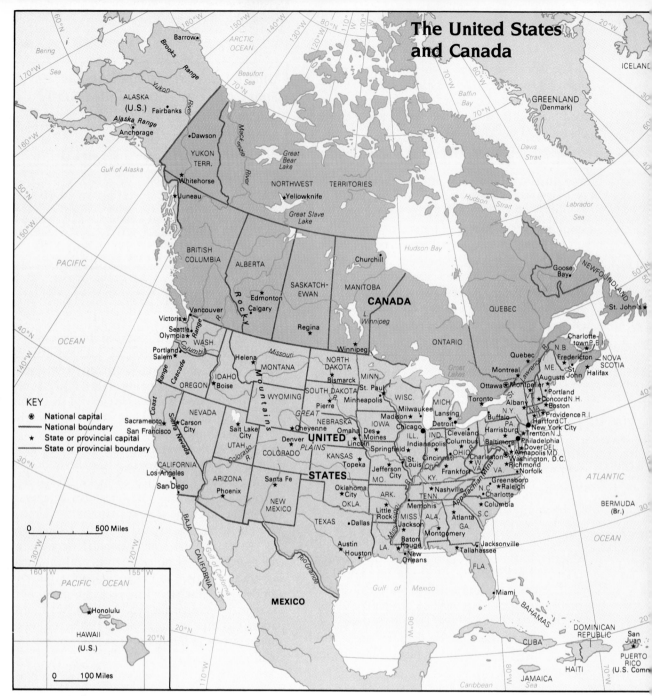

The United States and Canada

KEY

⊛ National capital

— National boundary

★ State or provincial capital

— State or provincial boundary

0   500 Miles

0   100 Miles

Map Study

What states of the United States share a land border with Canada? What Canadian provinces or territories do not border the United States?

of workers gave out. With no new jobs available, the people there lived in extreme poverty. People in the inner cities also faced hardship as businesses and jobs moved to the suburbs.

The civil rights movement Among those who did not share in the new prosperity were most black Americans. For them, progress was difficult to achieve because prejudice limited the opportunities for education and jobs. In many parts of the country, they were treated as social inferiors and even denied the full rights of citizens.

A major change came in 1954, when the Supreme Court, in the case *Brown v. Board of Education of Topeka,* ruled that educating blacks and whites in separate schools was illegal. Change was slow, however, and often there was resistance to it. The real pressure for change came from blacks themselves, under the leadership of Dr. Martin Luther King, Jr., an Atlanta minister. Dr. King followed the pattern used by Gandhi in India, which was based on nonviolent protest.

That method slowly became effective. "Nonviolent resistance paralyzed and confused the power structures against which it was directed," noted Dr. King in 1964. By outlawing racial discrimination and by supporting equal opportunity, the Civil Rights Act of 1964 ended the old system of racial segregation.

Sometimes violence did occur. Dr. King himself was assassinated in April 1968. The passage of civil rights laws did not completely end prejudice and racism. Nonetheless, by 1970, blacks and other minorities had taken significant steps toward full equality as citizens of the United States.

The movement for women's rights Closely related to the civil rights movement was the quest for equal rights for women. During the 1960's and 1970's, many women sought to enter the work force. There they often encountered discrimination in employment and salary. In 1963, the average female worker earned only 63 percent as much as the average male worker.

By the end of the 1980's, women could point to significant changes in law and the attitudes of society. Sandra Day O'Connor had become the first woman justice on the Supreme Court of the United States, and several states had had

The Vietnam War Memorial lists all the soldiers who died in combat. At its dedication, people searched for the names of friends and relatives.

women governors. Setbacks too had occurred. The Equal Rights Amendment (ERA), a proposed amendment to the Constitution banning discrimination against women, was not approved by enough states to become law. Custom and tradition made society slow to recognize the changes taking place in the role of women.

The Vietnam War Another issue of public concern during the 1960's was the Vietnam War. As you read in Chapter 34, the United States supported an anticommunist government in South Vietnam between 1957 and 1973. In 1965, when the buildup of United States troops began, about 82 percent of the people in the United States approved of the nation's role in helping South Vietnam to survive. By 1971, public opinion had reversed itself. A poll showed that 65 percent of the people thought the United States should not be involved in the war.

Opposition to the war came to a head in 1969 when 200,000 protesters marched on Washington. At the same time, many other people considered the protesters unpatriotic. The nation remained divided on the question even after President Nixon had withdrawn the last troops in 1973. The raising of the Vietnam Memorial in Washington in 1982 symbolized the end of differences over the war.

Dr. King emphasized traditional civic values to create a moral force against segregation.

Despite many gains, the average woman's wage remained far below that of the average man. In 1981, for example, wives who worked full-time averaged $13,700 per year while their husbands averaged $23,800.

The Nations of Latin America

UNITED STATES

Monterrey

Puerto Vallarta

Mexico City ★
• Veracruz

Acapulco •

MEXICO

Gulf of Mexico

Havana •   ★ Nassau

CUBA

THE BAHAMAS

Belmopan ★
BELIZE
HONDURAS

GUATEMALA
Guatemala ★
San Salvador ★
EL SALVADOR

Tegucigalpa ★

JAMAICA   **HAITI**
Kingston ★   Port-
au-Prince ★

Caribbean Sea

DOMINICAN
REPUBLIC
• Santo Domingo
★ San Juan
PUERTO
RICO
(U.S.)

NICARAGUA
Managua ★

COSTA   **PANAMA**
RICA
San José ★   Panama
Canal

Maracaibo •

Caracas   **GRENADA**
★
Lake
Maracaibo   **VENEZUELA**   **TRINIDAD**
AND TOBAGO

Panama
City

Medellín •
★ Bogotá
• Cali
COLOMBIA

Orinoco River

Georgetown ★
SURINAME
Paramaribo
Cayenne •
FRENCH
GUIANA
(Fr.)

GUYANA

GALÁPAGOS
ISLANDS
(Ecuador)

Quito ★
ECUADOR
Guayaquil •

Negro

Amazon   River

ATLANTIC   OCEAN

Tropic of Cancer

30°N

20°N

10°N

Equator   0°

PACIFIC

Andes

PERU
Lima ★   • Cuzco
La Paz •
L. Titicaca
• Arequipa

BRAZIL   São Francisco River   Recife •

10°S

Brasília ★

Belo
Horizonte •

OCEAN

Mountains

BOLIVIA
★ Sucre

PARAGUAY

Paraguay R.

Rio de Janeiro •
São Paulo •

20°S

Tropic of Capricorn

CHILE

Tucumán •
Asunción ★

Paraná River

Uruguay R.

Valparaíso •
Santiago ★

ARGENTINA

URUGUAY
★ Montevideo

Buenos Aires ★

Concepción •

Bahía
Blanca •

Río de la
Plata

ATLANTIC   OCEAN

30°S

KEY
★ Capital city

0   1000 Miles

40°S

FALKLAND ISLANDS
(United Kingdom)

Strait of
Magellan
Cape
Horn

120°W   110°W   100°W   90°W   80°W   70°W   60°W   50°W   40°W   30°W   20°W

Map Study

What countries border Mexico? What is the largest island in the Caribbean?
What country's capital lies almost directly on the equator? What is the largest
country in Latin America?

772

Mexico City prospered during the oil boom of the late 1970's but faced hard times in the 1980's.

Population growth outstripped economic development.

The twentieth century has been a time of enormous population growth in Latin America. Population there has gone from 60 million in 1900 to more than 300 million in 1980. This explosion in population has been accompanied by migration within countries. Millions of people have left farms and villages for the teeming streets of cities such as Buenos Aires, Caracas, and Lima. By 1980, more than 60 percent of Latin Americans lived in urban areas, compared to less than 40 percent in 1950. Mexico City, with more than 15 million inhabitants, is the third largest metropolitan area in the world.

Significant economic growth has taken place in Latin America in the past 30 years. Mexico, Argentina, and Brazil have all become developing nations with rapid industrial growth. Economic development should enable those countries to support a higher standard of living for their people. The rate of economic growth, however, has not kept pace with the rate of population increase. Thus, people leaving the land exchange poverty in the countryside for even greater poverty in the cities.

The worst urban poverty is found in the growing slums that have appeared on the outskirts of most Latin American cities. Different terms are used to identify such areas. In Mexico, they are *barrios;* in Brazil, they are called *favellas;* in Argentina, they are known as *villas miserias.* Here, hundreds of thousands of people huddle together in tin shacks and wooden lean-tos without water or electricity and with only open drains for sewers. Lack of education tends to keep people in poverty, which in turn leads to poor nutrition, disease, and often early death. Even today, in the cities of northeastern Brazil, one out of every two children dies before the age of two.

Prosperity proved hard to attain in Latin America.

Economic development in Latin America has faced many problems besides population growth. Even in the postwar era, many countries still relied upon a single major export. Coffee accounted for 54 percent of Colombia's exports in 1980. Other examples included such exports as Venezuela's petroleum (90 percent), Chile's copper (48 percent), and Cuba's sugar (80 percent). Reliance upon a single major export meant risk. Loss of a coffee crop or a decline in the price of sugar or oil could cause disaster.

After World War II, many Latin American countries tried to reduce their dependence on single exports. Some sought more varied agricultural products. Others nationalized key industries, hoping that such control would enable them to keep a larger share of the profits. Nonetheless, worldwide price changes could still cause problems.

Some countries tried to strengthen their economies by encouraging the growth of industry. To obtain capital for building industries, they borrowed heavily from banks in foreign countries. They also protected new industries by putting high tariffs on imported goods. These countries hoped that income from the domestic sale and the export of new products would cover the cost of borrowing. That hope was seldom realized.

Economic development in Brazil Brazil is an example of achievements and problems in economic growth. From the 1930's to the 1960's, Brazil's economy grew at a rapid pace. During this time, the government began building a new capital, Brasília, in the wilderness some 600 miles northwest of Rio de Janeiro. Brasília symbolized both the drive to develop the nation's interior and the dream of raising the nation's standard of living.

With capital borrowed from foreign investors, the government encouraged the growth of industry and trade. For a time, the outlook was bright. The need to repay loans and the interest on loans, however, became a serious burden. By the early 1980's, Brazil's foreign debts approached $100 billion, and the government had to delay payments to lenders.

Some observers still saw hope for Brazil. Its industry now produces everything from steel to electronic goods and from clothing to cars. Agricultural products include not only coffee and cocoa but also soybeans, maize, rice, and cassava. In spite of the nation's debt problems, major nations are still eager to trade with Brazil. Whether foreign trade can grow enough to help Brazil to recover remains to be seen. Meanwhile, the population continues to increase.

Economic changes in Mexico Like Brazil, Mexico experienced rapid economic growth in the postwar years, only to become mired in debt by the 1970's. Then, in 1976, the discovery of huge petroleum deposits both inland and offshore offered the nation a second chance for prosperity. As oil production increased, earnings from exports grew from $500 million in 1976 to $16 billion in the early 1980's.

Instead of repaying its debts, however, the government continued to borrow. Large sums went toward social programs to help the ever-growing ranks of the urban poor. Some went into the pockets of government officials.

In 1981, Mexico faced a crisis as the world price for oil began to fall. The result was that in 1982, the government announced that it could not make payments on its debts. Although emergency loans were made, the effects of this default were felt in the world economy. The economy of Mexico remains in crisis.

Democracy remained elusive in Latin America.

Many Latin American nations have acquired great wealth from resources, industry, and trade.

Looking at economics *This Japanese-owned plantation shows foreign investment in Brazil.*

That wealth, however, is distributed very unevenly among the region's people. In most countries, a handful of wealthy families own huge estates or businesses, while the majority of people struggle to survive as tenants, poor workers, or the unemployed. This uneven distribution has been little affected by gains from the growth of industry. Instead, poverty increases as population growth forces more people to share the limited financial means available to the poor.

Most Latin American nations consider themselves democracies, but in only a few do citizens enjoy free elections and real civil rights. Even in the more democratic countries, the right to vote is limited to those who can read and who own a certain amount of property.

Two different factors continued to limit democracy. One was caudillo rule (page 504), which still prevailed in some countries in the postwar period. The second factor was frequent change in leadership as rulers in some countries came and went. Bolivia, for example, experienced 180 revolutions during the first 150 years of its existence.

The major reason for political instability rested with the armies maintained by Latin American

Some economists fear that huge loans made to Mexico and other nearly bankrupt countries by United States banks threaten the stability of the United States banking system. Economists think that Brazil's economic troubles can be traced, at least in part, to the unequal distribution of wealth. Why would this be so?

rulers. "We have no reason for fighting one another," a former president of Colombia remarked. "Each country is being occupied by its own army." The real purpose of such an army was to maintain the power of the rulers and at times to seize power itself. At best, the armies served to resist major reform or a broader sharing of political power.

The 1980's brought changes.

The 1980's were a time of movement away from military to greater civilian rule, particularly in Argentina, Peru, and Brazil. With civilian rule came an increasing respect for human rights.

Argentina The 1980's were a critical time for Argentina. During the decade from the mid-1940's to the mid-1950's, Argentina was ruled by the dictator Juan Perón. The next two decades were a period of military rule, with no clear or responsible leadership. The years from 1976 to 1982 were a time of despair as military leaders launched a campaign of terror against all who might oppose their rule. Torture and murder became everyday events as more than 20,000 Argentines simply vanished.

In 1982, the generals attempted to increase public support and national unity by seizing the Falkland Islands in the stormy South Atlantic. This action led to war with Britain, which had controlled the islands for more than two centuries. Instead of backing down, the British government reacted strongly and defeated Argentina.

That defeat brought an end to military rule in Argentina. In 1983, the first free election in more than 40 years chose Raul Alfonsin president. He worked to reestablish democratic institutions, control inflation, and punish the generals who had caused their nation so much grief.

Mexico In the 80 years following the revolution of 1910, Mexico enjoyed a political stability rare in Latin America. Since World War II, all of Mexico's presidents have been civilians, chosen in democratic elections held every six years. The army has not been a factor in the politics of modern Mexico. Instead, one political party—the Partido Revolucionario Institucional (PRI)—has dominated elections and the government.

Control by the PRI was not always in the nation's interest. Over time, members of the political party became a privileged elite. Corruption too became a problem as wealth from oil

Voice from Our Time · *Literature Is Fire*

Many Latin American writers are actively involved in social reform and revolutionary politics. The Peruvian writer Mario Vargas Llosa explained his view of literature.

[I]t is necessary to remind our societies what awaits them [if they encourage writers]. To warn them that literature is fire, that it signifies non-conformism and rebellion, that the writer's very reason for being is protest, contradiction, and criticism . . . Literature is a form of permanent [rebellion] and recognizes no straitjackets . . . Literature may perish but it will never conform.

Only if this condition is fulfilled is literature useful to society . . . Its mission is to agitate, disturb, alarm, keep men constantly dissatisfied with themselves: its function is to unconditionally stimulate the will to change and improve, even though in order to achieve this the most deadly and poisonous weapons must be employed. It must be understood once and for all that the more terrible and cruel an author's writings against his country, the more intense the passion that binds him to it.

1. Why does the author compare literature to fire?
2. According to Llosa, what is the purpose of literature?
3. What might he mean by "deadly and poisonous weapons" in literature?
4. With what groups might such a writer come into conflict?
5. Do you agree or disagree with this evaluation of literature? Explain.

In 1985, inflation in Argentina reached an annual rate of 850 percent.

775

increased. The first real opposition to the PRI came in the presidential elections held in July 1988. Although the PRI candidate, Carlos Salinas de Cortari, won by a narrow margin, it was clear that the PRI's political monopoly had been broken.

Chile As the 1980's drew to a close, the world watched to see if the military government in power in Chile since 1973 would yield peacefully to democracy. A constitution adopted in 1980 had called for a national vote in 1988 on a major political question. Should General Augusto Pinochet, who had seized power in 1973, remain in office, or should he step aside to allow open presidential elections in 1989? When the votes were counted, Pinochet had lost. The way was now clear for a return to democracy—provided that Pinochet abided by the constitution.

Section Review 2

Identify: (a) Brasília, (b) Juan Perón, (c) Falkland Islands, (d) Raul Alfonsin, (e) Carlos Salinas de Cortari, (f) General Augusto Pinochet
Answer:
1. What changes has rapid population growth caused in Latin America?
2. (a) What did Brazil and Mexico hope to accomplish by borrowing money from other countries? (b) How successful was their plan?
3. In what ways is democracy limited in Latin America?
4. (a) What progress toward greater democracy occurred in Argentina? (b) In Mexico? (c) In Chile?

Critical Thinking
5. (a) In what ways are the Latin American nations similar to other Third World countries you have studied? (b) In what ways do they differ?

Caribbean nations took different paths. 3

The postwar period was a time of change in the Caribbean Basin. That region includes the nations of Central America and island countries

Puerto Rico honors Columbus, who landed there in 1493. The 500th anniversary of Columbus' first voyage will be celebrated in 1992.

such as Jamaica, Cuba, Haiti, the Dominican Republic, and many smaller islands.

Central American nations, Haiti, and Cuba had gained independence much earlier (pages 504, 500, and 552). For most other islands, however, this was the time when nationalists launched movements for independence. Independence was achieved in the two decades after World War II. As members of the Third World, the new nations sought to be nonaligned and to increase their economic development.

Ever since proclaiming the Monroe Doctrine in 1823 (page 504), the United States had had a strong interest in Latin America. As Spanish influence in the Caribbean waned with the Spanish-American War, United States influence increased. Cuba became independent after the War, and Puerto Rico became a territory of the United States. The Roosevelt Corollary to the Monroe Doctrine, announced in 1904, extended United States influence. It asserted the right of the United States to intervene in countries to preserve order.

Intervention occurred in several countries. Most often it was to protect United States businesses and investments. Although intervention helped to keep order, it at times led to support for caudillo regimes and caused resentment among the people of the country. Nonetheless, businesses brought economic development that was important to the region. That development was very extensive. In 1960, investments in Latin America accounted for fully one third of all United States investments overseas.

Puerto Rico became a commonwealth.

Under United States rule, Puerto Rico underwent new economic development. The first changes focused on agriculture—in particular, on raising sugar for export. Since World War II, many new industries have come to the island. These have helped to raise the average level of income. Although opportunities for work have increased at home, many Puerto Ricans have migrated to the United States. As citizens, they can enter and leave without restrictions.

Puerto Rico today is a commonwealth of the United States. It has broad powers of self-government, although Congress holds final authority. A commissioner represents Puerto Rico in Congress but has no vote in final legislation. Residents of Puerto Rico cannot vote in presidential elections.

Cuba became aligned with communism.

Independence came to Cuba in 1898 after the Spanish-American War. As with Puerto Rico, the Cuban economy became closely linked to that of the United States. Investments in sugar plantations, public utilities, railways, banks, hotels, and stores reflected a direct interest by United States businesses. Here too wealth from development went to a small group of Cubans and to foreign companies. The millions of workers remained poor, benefiting little from the development of their country.

Political power in Cuba lay with wealthy Cubans and a series of caudillo leaders. The last of these was Fulgencio Batista, a corrupt and cruel ruler. Although hated by many Cubans, he had strong support from the United States government. Batista ruled as a virtual dictator.

Resentment against Batista grew in Cuba during the 1950's. Among the opponents to Batista was a young lawyer named Fidel Castro. A Cuban nationalist, Castro wanted the wealth of Cuba to be divided more evenly and the influence of the United States in Cuba reduced. His message won wide support among the rural and urban poor. In 1959, Castro and his supporters overthrew Batista.

For a time, Castro was praised for bringing democracy to Cuba. That attitude changed when he suspended elections and named himself president. People who opposed him were jailed or executed. Newspapers and radio stations that criticized his policies were suspended.

One of Castro's main objectives was to gain control of the economy. He nationalized the United States-owned oil refineries, as well as sugar plantations and other businesses owned by citizens of the United States. When the United States objected and stopped all its trade with Cuba, Castro turned to the Soviet Union for trade.

Daily Life · Pottery Old and New

Pieces of pre-Columbian pottery from Central America are prized for their beauty and rarity. Throughout rural Central America, however, potters still make fine jars, bowls, pitchers, and bottles using some of the same methods and designs used by pre-Columbian artisans. The Spanish conquerors introduced the use of glazes and the potter's wheel. Some of the styles and methods of production used today in remote villages are unique. However, as roads are built and villagers have more contact with outsiders, folk-art pottery will probably become more uniform and may even be replaced by manufactured items.

Many supporters of Batista fled to Miami after the revolution. There they built a prosperous community.

777

Soviet trade with Cuba was accompanied by political influence. Cuba thus became aligned with the Soviet Union. To the United States, this connection seemed a threat. The nation could ill afford to have a major foreign rival 90 miles off its coast.

The Bay of Pigs Concerned by the Cuban-Soviet agreements, President John Kennedy supported groups opposed to Castro's government. Anti-Castro refugees were trained and armed in preparation for an invasion of Cuba. When these forces landed 2,000 men at the Bay of Pigs in April 1961, however, they got no help from the Cuban people and were soon captured. After this incident, Soviet military equipment began to flow into Cuba, along with military advisers.

The missile crisis In October 1962, a United States spy plane brought back photographs of Soviet missiles being installed in Cuba. President Kennedy feared that the Soviets would use these weapons to launch nuclear attacks on cities in the United States. Backing up his demand with a naval blockade of Cuba, Kennedy insisted that the Soviets remove the missiles. Finally the Soviets agreed to remove the missiles from Cuba if the United States would promise not to invade Cuba again.

Cuba today Fidel Castro has now ruled Cuba for three decades. During this time, the country has seen sweeping political and economic changes. All major industries and large land holdings have been nationalized, including those of both Cubans and foreigners. Supporters of the revolution in Cuba point to its many successes. Improved medical care has reduced birth rates and infant death rates. Life expectancy for the average Cuban is greater now than it was in 1959. Public education has raised the literacy rate greatly.

The economic and human costs of the changes in Cuba have been high. Without the Soviet economic aid that averages one million dollars per day, the Cuban economy would collapse. Because the economy still relies on one crop—sugar— it remains threatened by crop failures, falling prices, and declining demand.

Revolution has not brought liberty to the people of Cuba. Instead, the Communist Party dominates political life. There have been no free elections in the 30 years of Castro's rule. During one brief opportunity in 1980, more than 125,000 people left Cuba for refuge in the United States.

War brought turmoil to Nicaragua.

In the decades since the Communist revolution in Cuba, the United States has sought to check the spread of communist influence in the Caribbean region. In 1965, Marines occupied the capital of the Dominican Republic to forestall a possible turn to socialism. A government dominated by friends of former dictator Rafael Trujillo proved acceptable to the United States.

Latin Americans wondered why some dictators were acceptable but others were not. "Why did you support Trujillo for 30 years?" asked Mexican novelist Carlos Fuentes in 1964. The question highlighted the dilemma for United States policy toward the Caribbean region. On the one hand, it was essential to prevent the kind of revolutions that brought communist governments to power. On the other hand, the existing governments in Central America, except in Costa Rica, were corrupt and undemocratic. This dilemma was reflected in the internal affairs of three nations— El Salvador, Guatemala, and Nicaragua. All were torn by civil war.

The Nicaraguan conflict Despite efforts by the United States to contain communism, the largest Central American country, Nicaragua, became an ally of the Soviet Union. Nicaragua too had been occupied by Marines—from 1912 to 1933. They trained a national guard to maintain order. After they left, the leader of the guard, Anastasio Somoza, gained political power. Somoza and other members of his family ruled Nicaragua for more

At the Guatemala Conference of May 1986, leaders of Central American nations shared ideas.

The Soviet Union continues to be Cuba's largest trading partner, accounting for more than 60 percent of both imports and exports.

than 40 years. To keep hold of its financial empire, the family controlled elections and assassinated political rivals.

Civil war During the 1970's, various dissident groups joined to form the Sandinista National Liberation Front. It was named for Augusto Cesar Sandino, an early victim of Somoza. The Sandinista movement drew wide support among peasants and the urban poor. From 1977 to 1979, Nicaragua was engulfed in a civil war in which 50,000 people perished. The corrupt Somoza fled the country in 1979.

Once in control of the government, the Sandinistas launched a program that included land distribution, nationalizing of key industries, and increased spending on schools and hospitals. Even though the Soviet Union and Cuba provided financial aid, the economy was burdened with an enormous debt.

As criticism of the new government grew, the Sandinistas suspended newspapers and radio broadcasts. Rebel groups calling themselves Contras (from the Spanish word for *against*) began to fight the Sandinistas. Among the Contras were middle- and upper-class Nicaraguans who had opposed Somoza but did not want him replaced with a new dictator. The United States government sent millions of dollars in aid to the Contras.

An uncertain peace In August 1987, the five Central American nations signed a peace plan for their region. One of the leaders in the search for peace was Costa Rican President Oscar Arias Sánchez. Under the terms of the peace plan, fighting between the Nicaraguan government and the Contras ended in 1988 with an uneasy truce. The outcome of the plan would mean the difference between war and peace in Nicaragua in the 1990's.

United States policy toward Latin America began to change.

Besides seeking to limit communist expansion in Latin America, the United States has acted in other ways to benefit the region. In 1961, President Kennedy launched the Alliance for Progress, a program intended to help Latin America just as the Marshall Plan had aided Europe after World War II. Another Kennedy program, the Peace Corps, also had a significant impact in Latin America. Thousands of young

volunteers from the United States worked to improve the quality of life for people in rural villages. In 1983, President Ronald Reagan began the Caribbean Basin Initiative to help the economies of the new Caribbean nations.

The United States also began to show less tolerance for oppressive regimes. The governments of Bolivia and Colombia were a particular concern in the 1980's because of the illegal export of drugs from those countries to the United States.

More immediate problems arose with the government of Panama. In 1988, after years of support for Panama's leader, General Manuel Noriega, the United States accused him of trafficking in drugs and tried to end his rule. The people of Panama worried that the United States might use Noriega as an excuse to end the Panama Canal Treaty of 1978. That treaty provided for returning control of the Panama Canal (page 552) to Panama by the year 2000. Then, a stable government would be essential.

Section Review 3

Identify: (a) Roosevelt Corollary, (b) Fulgencio Batista, (c) Fidel Castro, (d) Bay of Pigs, (e) Anastasio Somoza, (f) Sandinistas, (g) Contras, (h) Oscar Arias Sánchez, (i) General Manuel Noriega

Answer:
1. Describe the political relationship between Puerto Rico and the United States.
2. (a) What kinds of investments did the United States make in the Caribbean? (b) How did it protect those investments?
3. How did Castro come to power in Cuba?
4. (a) What political policies did Castro follow? (b) What economic policies?
5. How did a confrontation develop between the United States and the Soviet Union in Cuba?
6. (a) What policies did the Sandinistas follow in Nicaragua? (b) What did the Contras seek?
7. Why did the United States turn against Noriega in Panama?

Critical Thinking
8. Suppose you were a journalist trying to write an objective evaluation of life in Cuba under Castro. (a) What groups of people should you interview? (b) Why might it be difficult to reach a fair conclusion?

harsh rule. The United States supported the rebels and loaned them money on the condition that the United States control Nicaragua's finances. When, in 1912, Nicaraguans rose up in opposition to that control, the United States sent in the marines.

779

Chapter Review 36

Summary

1. Canada confronts a changing world. Canada's prestige and economic strength after World War II led the country to assume an active role in world affairs. Although conflicts developed between the United States and Canada over NORAD, the two countries were able to resolve their differences in the early 1960's. Demands for more economic and political power among French Canadians led to a separatist movement. The issue was resolved in a general election when the people of Quebec voted to remain a part of Canada.

2. South American nations seek solutions. In 1964, Brazilian military officers overthrew the republic and set up a dictatorship, which achieved an economic miracle in the cities but left extreme poverty in the countryside. In 1985, democratic government returned to Brazil. In the early 1970's, President Allende of Chile experimented with socialism. Military leaders, supported by the upper class, overthrew Allende in 1973 and set up a harsh dictatorship. Abuses of human rights continue in Chile. Argentina was controlled by Juan Perón from 1946 to 1955 and again between 1973 and 1974. In 1976, the military took over but was not able to unite the country. In 1983, Argentines elected a new president who has attempted to stabilize the economy.

3. Caribbean nations take different paths. In the early 1900's, United States sugarcane plantations imposed a single-resource economy on Puerto Rico. After World War II, Operation Bootstrap improved the Puerto Rican economy, although problems still remained. In 1959, Fidel Castro set up a Communist government in Cuba. Today, Cuba remains tied to the Soviet Union.

Reviewing the Facts

1. Define the following terms:
   a. multinational corporation
   b. separatism
2. Explain the importance of each of the following names, places, or terms:
   a. Dr. Martin Luther King, Jr.
   b. George Bush
   c. Brian Mulroney
   d. Juan Perón
   e. Falkland Islands

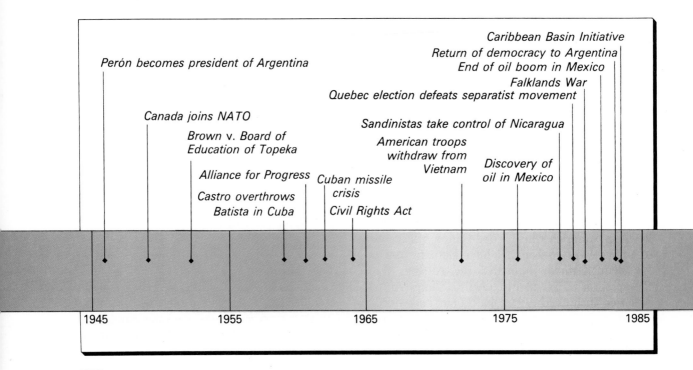

Caribbean Basin Initiative
Return of democracy to Argentina
End of oil boom in Mexico
Falklands War
Quebec election defeats separatist movement

Perón becomes president of Argentina

Sandinistas take control of Nicaragua

Canada joins NATO

American troops withdraw from Vietnam

Brown v. Board of Education of Topeka

Discovery of oil in Mexico

Alliance for Progress

Cuban missile crisis

Castro overthrows Batista in Cuba

Civil Rights Act

1945   1955   1965   1975   1985

f. Raul Alfonsin
g. Carlos Salinas de Cortari
h. General Augusto Pinochet
i. Fulgencio Batista
j. Fidel Castro
k. Anastasio Somoza
l. Sandinistas
m. Contras
n. Oscar Arias Sánchez
o. Peace Corps
p. General Manuel Noriega

3. (a) After World War II, how did the economic role of the United States change? (b) How did society change?
4. (a) What problems persisted in Mexico despite the economic miracle? (b) What happened when oil prices plummeted in 1981?
5. How has rural poverty in Mexico affected relations with the United States?
6. (a) How did the Sandinistas come to power in Nicaragua? (b) What changes did they make? (c) Why did the United States support their opponents?

Basic Skills

1. **Reading a map** (a) Using the map of Latin America on page 772, list the countries located mainly within the tropics and those located mainly outside the tropics. (b) What does this information tell you about the kinds of foods, crops, and raw materials produced in Latin America?
2. **Making a chart** (a) From the 1950's through the 1970's, three issues stirred controversy in United States society: the civil rights movement, the women's movement, and the Vietnam War. Make a chart, using those topics for the horizontal headings. For the vertical column, use the headings Issue, Arguments Pro, Arguments Con, and Outcomes. (b) How did the outcomes of each issue affect the society?

Researching and Reporting Skills

1. **Identifying sources with opposing viewpoints** Choose a current controversial issue relating to Central America and read about it in two different newspapers. If possible, also consult a magazine likely to present a Latin American viewpoint. To what extent do these three sources agree or disagree concerning the issue?
2. **Using regional publications** Skim several issues of *Americas,* the magazine about Latin America published by the Organization of American States. This publication often features information on Latin American writers or artists and their works. Note what different countries and ethnic groups are represented.

Critical Thinking

1. **Analyzing economics** (a) What were the main reasons for the United States' becoming a global economic power after World War II? (b) What were the economic effects for the United States at home and abroad?
2. **Interpreting a concept** (a) What are the reasons for the deficit in the United States balance of payments? (b) What is the significance of the deficit in terms of United States foreign trade?
3. **Analyzing** Since World War II, Canada has assumed a more active and independent role in world affairs. What factors may have contributed to this new role?
4. **Inferring** (a) Why did the United States and Canada make such a strong trade agreement? (b) What changes may result?
5. **Solving problems** Lack of representative and democratic governments has remained a problem in Latin America. (a) What have been major reasons for this situation? (b) What recent progress have several countries made in solving this problem?
6. **Synthesizing** One of the advantages of industrialization is that it provides employment. Why then is the growth of industry so important to Latin America?
7. **Analyzing** (a) What factors have contributed to instability in some countries of the Caribbean and Central America? (b) In what different ways has United States policy responded to that instability?

Perspectives on Past and Present

The Monroe Doctrine marked the start of United States involvement in Latin America. What stages have occurred in that involvement? What are the current trends in United States policy toward that region?

Investigating History

In the past 50 years, Latin American writers have made a significant contribution to world literature. Among these writers are Gabriela Mistral, Pablo Neruda, Gabriel Marquez, Miguel Asturias, Carlos Fuentes, Octavio Paz, Mario Vargas Llosa, and Jorge Luis Borges. Read selections from the works of one or more of these authors. What viewpoints are expressed?

The World in Change

In 1969, Astronaut Edwin Aldrin became the second person to walk on the moon. The Lunar Expedition Module is reflected in his face mask. Astronaut Neil Armstrong took the photograph.

Key term

superconductor

Read and Understand

1. Technology led in new directions.
2. Technology affected the quality of life.
3. Dangers to the global environment developed.
4. A new era of economic and political change began.

Neil Armstrong sounded relaxed—just another traveler, it seemed, strolling about a strange new land and gathering his impressions to tell to those at home. "It has a stark beauty all its own," he said of the empty gray landscape before his eyes. "It's different, but it's very pretty out here."

Armstrong, of course, was no ordinary tourist. He and his traveling companion, Buzz Aldrin, were farther from home than anyone had ever been—some 240,000 miles. The date was July 20, 1969, and these two American astronauts had just become the first people to set foot on the moon.

For generations beyond count, men and women had looked up at the moon, the brightest object in the night sky, and dreamed of the fantastic voyage that might someday take them there. Now that voyage had just been completed, while almost a billion people watched on television. The first moonwalk seemed to mark one of the ultimate goals of technological progress. As Neil Armstrong put it, stepping off the ladder of his spacecraft and planting the first human footstep on the dusty surface of the moon, "That's one small step for a man, one giant leap for mankind."

That giant leap was just the first of many. Over the years, from the mid-1960's to 1990 and beyond, the pace of technological change increased with each new discovery. Change affected nearly every aspect of human life and knowledge.

As if mirroring the new technologies, great shifts took place in the economy and political structure of the world as well. New nations began to make their efforts and energies felt, and long-established nations began to rethink their traditional roles in the changing world.

This chapter is about the remarkable advances in technology either made or predicted between 1965 and the year 2000. It is also about the new trends in economics and international politics that are making this era one of continuing and astonishing change.

Technology led in new directions. 1

The postwar era brought a revolution in technology. A swift succession of inventions and scientific discoveries created a wide range of new capabilities with unforeseen uses. These changes profoundly influenced people's lives.

Space programs opened new goals.

After Armstrong and Aldrin, another 6 missions of the *Apollo* space program with 12 more astronauts explored the moon. Then, in 1975, the *Apollo* program came to an end with the *Apollo-Soyuz* Test Project. That was a joint United States-Soviet venture in which the *Apollo* docked with the *Soyuz* spacecraft in orbit around the earth.

Following their launching of *Sputnik* in 1957, the Soviets placed space stations in orbit on a regular basis after 1971. The United States followed in 1973 with *Skylab*, a scientific research station that remained aloft until 1979. During the 1970's, both nations also sent space probes to explore other planets in the solar system.

While the Soviets continued their space activities by using well-tested technology over and over again, the United States took a new direction. Efforts went to developing a less expensive, reusable space vehicle.

The space shuttle The first space shuttle, as this craft was called, was launched in 1981. Twenty-four missions followed, most of them successful in their objectives. Shuttle astronauts put satellites into orbit, retrieved and repaired damaged satellites, and ferried research teams such as the European Space Agency scientists who operated *Spacelab*, another orbiting experiment station. The United States seemed well on its way toward perfecting a reliable, efficient, and reusable space vehicle.

Then, in January 1986, disaster struck the space program. Seven astronauts were killed when the *Challenger* exploded less than two minutes after takeoff. In the shock and grief that followed, many people questioned the shuttle program, wondering if it was worth the risk of human lives. They also pointed out that launching satellites was less expensive than putting the huge shuttles into orbit. European nations had been successful in their more limited satellite programs.

As the redesigned shuttle rose again in 1988, however, confidence returned. The space program began to look to new goals for the 1990's and the next century: a new space station, a colony on the moon, even a manned voyage to Mars—perhaps in cooperation with the Soviets.

Military technology Another aspect of space technology was its military uses. The 1950's had seen the development of long-range intercontinental ballistic missiles (ICBM's). These weapons were capable of carrying nuclear warheads. Although operating in the stratosphere, these missiles led to space-oriented antimissile systems. Other space applications of military technology included reconnaissance and warning satellites and antisatellite systems. Both the United States and the Soviet Union have promised not to place any offensive weapons in space.

In 1975, United States astronauts and Soviet cosmonauts (top) took part in a joint space venture. Tragedy struck the American program in 1986 when the space shuttle Challenger exploded, killing all its crew (left). The successful flight of Discovery in 1988 gave new impetus to the space program (top left). In December 1986, test pilots Jeana Yeager and Dick Rutan (above) set a new aviation record by flying nonstop around the world. "What kind of world would there be," asked Rutan, "if there were no daring!"

Space technology and exploration provided a wealth of scientific information and new applications of technology. Among these were telecommunications, guidance and navigation systems, computer applications, the findings of space medicine, and new knowledge of the solar system.

Defending against ICBM's remained a major military problem. In the late 1980's, the United States undertook the military research project known as the Strategic Defense Initiative (SDI), or Star Wars. Its purpose was to provide a defense against ICBM attack. This defense would be based in space and would include much new technology, such as orbiting satellites, laser beams, and airborne sensors.

Worldwide communications increased.

Techniques and knowledge gained from the space program found many other uses. Among these were weather, navigation, and scientific satellites. The first communications satellite, Telstar, was lofted in 1962. Beaming television, radio, and telephone signals around the world in seconds, Telstar and its more advanced versions, such as INTELSAT (1967) and Comstar (1981), seemed to bring the peoples of the earth closer together.

Other advances also aided communication. Fiber-optic cables carried data underseas on cables of piped light. Facsimile (fax) machines rapidly transmitted copies of every type of data. New telephone links allowed conferences between offices in different cities and countries as if time and distance had ceased to exist.

The effect of these advances was to encourage new types of businesses on a global scale. Manufacturing industries had long since produced components in factories around the world. Until the 1980's, however, the service industries (such as insurance and data processing) had not duplicated this use of the global economy. The new global communications links enabled service companies in developed nations to carry on their work in the developing countries, where it was eagerly sought.

Computers continued to evolve.

Supporting this new sharing of worldwide communications and work flow was the microcomputer. So widespread is the computer today that it is hard to believe that its basic component—the transistor—did not even exist until 1950. Although the transistor was a major advance in technology, it was only the beginning of even greater changes.

The real impact of computers upon society came in the 1980's. In that decade, dramatic improvements in the production of transistors and silicone chips made possible the production of inexpensive but powerful personal computers. These small computers took on great importance as a majority of businesses began to use them to organize the information necessary to their work.

By 1988, more than ten million people in the United States alone were using computerized word processors. Computer-aided design (CAD) and computer-aided manufacturing (CAM) simplified the complex processes by which industries transformed ideas into useful products. Meanwhile, scientists in the United States and Japan raced to develop generation after generation of supercomputers. As the number of these supercomputers increased, more scientists and designers had access to them, with resulting innovations in every field.

In the future, computers will become an even more efficient tool. Increasingly, computer design will focus on making these machines easier for everyone to use. Someday computers will readily understand human speech. Storing information on optical disks—already common for music, video, and some data recordings—will permit whole libraries to be copied onto just a few pieces of metallized plastic. This vast amount of material can not only be readily stored but also instantly searched and retrieved. This in turn will mean greater access to information, and ready information will further multiply the rate and the effects of technological growth.

Changes occurred in materials technology.

Scientists in the twentieth century had produced an avalanche of new materials. Plastics and synthetics were examples of materials for everyday use. Others, however, were intended for scientific and industrial use. Thus, scientific and industrial laboratories in various countries often competed in creating new materials.

Superconductors Continuing research and development sought to solve problems that had long baffled scientists. One such problem had been to find a material that could conduct electricity more cheaply and effectively. Materials

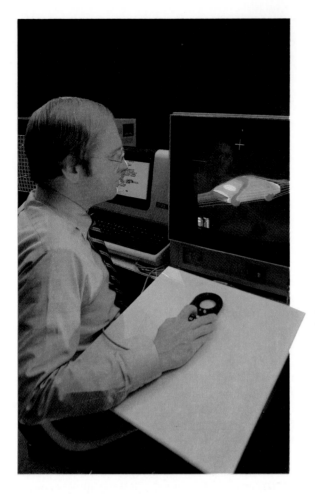

Computer-aided design and manufacturing became important new tools for industry. Human-computer interaction gave work a new dimension.

of this kind had been known but were impractical because they could be used only at or near temperatures of absolute zero.

A race to develop improved current-carrying materials, or superconductors, began in the late 1980's. Scientists in several countries rushed to complete projects that would enable industries to produce and use the new materials.

Thin film technology Another advance of the 1970's and 1980's may have an effect even greater than that of superconductors. New techniques were developed to apply a substance in a very thin film on another material, thus combining the advantages of each. Synthetic diamonds were made in the form of films that could give almost anything a hard, durable coating. Superior microcircuit chips could be built up out of these films, allowing designers to pack more computing power into a circuit than ever before. A metallic compound used in a similar way in supercomputers was sure to gain much wider use.

Section Review 1

Define: (a) satellite, (b) transistor, (c) superconductor

Identify: (a) Neil Armstrong, (b) *Apollo* program, (c) space shuttle, (d) Strategic Defense Initiative, (e) microcomputer

Answer:

1. Why are the technological changes of the postwar era referred to as a revolution?
2. (a) Describe three scientific projects carried out in space. (b) What was the purpose of each project?
3. Why was space science and technology important to everyday life?
4. (a) What was the purpose of satellites such as Telstar? (b) How did those satellites affect global communication?
5. (a) What role did computers have in relation to information? (b) To industry?
6. (a) What are some of the future uses of computers? (b) How may these affect your life?
7. Why are superconductors important to both science and society?

Critical Thinking

8. Why does one new advance in technology often lead to others and to advances in other related fields?

786

Technology affected the quality of life. 2

Technology increasingly affected not only ways of living and working but also people's appreciation of life—their sense of the quality of their lives. Some of these changes, such as worldwide communication and improved medical treatment, were positive. Others, such as industrial pollution, were negative.

Worldwide cultural patterns began to emerge.

The communications technology that revolutionized business had a profound effect on culture as well. Satellite transmission and recording technology encouraged the people of different cultures and continents to share their music, literature, and art.

Music The most striking effect of the new technology was in the field of music. Performers of classical music had always traveled widely around the world. Except for a few international stars, however, popular music artists had been successful mainly in their own countries. Perhaps the first sign that this was changing appeared in the early 1960's when an English rock-and-roll group, the Beatles, won large followings on several continents. Soon innumerable pop groups followed the Beatles' example. Successful records or tapes led to world tours, which in turn meant television coverage, radio interviews, concert films, new recordings, and videos. The result was a publicity blitz that made millionaires out of once-impoverished musicians. A worldwide mass culture had arrived.

New worldwide communications systems made possible the mingling of musical traditions from different nations at a faster pace than ever before. The rhythms of Latin America, Africa, and the United States could now become blended into a new style in a matter of weeks or months instead of decades. People also became more aware of different cultures. After appearing in a film about a Chicano rock-and-roll star, for example, a Mexican-influenced band from Los Angeles became popular throughout the United States and Britain. Without the high-tech exchange of music, this kind of cross-cultural exchange would have been less possible.

Technology also brought classical music to more people. Operas and concerts in Berlin or the Netherlands could be heard in the United States by instant satellite transmission. Compact disc (CD) development dramatically improved the quality and durability of musical recordings. It resulted in an upsurge of rereleases and new recordings of classical masterpieces. Computers assisted in preserving sound quality by digitalizing music for recordings or breaking it down into information easily stored and recalled from the compact disc read by laser light. Electronics also became a part of music itself, either built into new instruments or programmed for a musician to play.

Literature Although the new technology of recent decades was applied immediately to printing and book production, these new technical processes did not create a mass-cultural phenomenon in literature similar to that in the popular music field. Only where literature could merge with another form of art did it touch the lives of many millions around the world. Novels were made into films, and artists who once might have been poets achieved success as popular musicians.

Literature was, however, affected indirectly as people around the world developed more common interests. Writers from the Third World gained a wider readership in the developed world after the 1960's. Of the 57 Nobel Prizes for Literature awarded before 1964, only 2 were given to citizens of Third World countries. Of the first 20 prize-winners after 1964, however, 4 were citizens of Third World countries: Miguel Angel Asturais of Guatemala, Pablo Neruda of Chile, Gabriel Garcia Marquez of Colombia, and Wole Soyinka of Nigeria. Through the diffusion of culture, these writers—already established in the Third World—now received worldwide attention.

Art The global community created by technology found an interest in the art of all nations. Art exhibits from many countries toured the world: Chinese sculpture appeared in Philadelphia, Israeli art was exhibited in Los Angeles and Houston, and French Impressionist paintings from the Soviet Union were shown in Switzerland and other countries. Another sign of the trend toward a truly global art culture was the number of foreign purchasers of art at auctions. In 1987, for example, a painting by Van Gogh was sold in London for more than $50 million to a Japanese insurance company.

Technology aided surgical and medical care.

Technology affected not only the quality of people's cultural life but also their physical well-being. The result was improved health and greater life expectancy for most people.

New surgical methods The years after 1965 saw continuous advances in medical techniques, especially those of surgery. Dr. Christiaan Barnard of South Africa transplanted the first human heart in 1967. By the mid-1980's, heart bypass operations—once difficult and dangerous—had become almost routine. This complex procedure allowed millions of people who would otherwise have died of heart disease to enjoy longer and more normal lives. Surgeons also learned how to rebuild and repair damaged members such as fingers and skin. Lasers healed damaged eyes, microsurgery joined severed nerves, and protons were used to destroy cancers. Through the long operations required for delicate surgery, artificial hearts, lungs, and kidneys kept patients alive.

New diagnostic tools As an improved means to diagnose illnesses, scientists developed new ways to view internal areas of the human body. Starting in the 1970's, Computerized Axial Tomography, or CAT scans, gave doctors video X-ray pictures that allowed them to diagnose diseases better than they could with ordinary X-ray machines. Computers were also used to interpret data and assemble it into an image. Equally useful was a similar diagnostic tool called magnetic resonance imaging (MRI), which used superconductors to read the magnetic field of the body's individual atoms. Superconductors were also used in another medical machine that allowed doctors to see the electrical impulses given off by the living, working brain.

One aspect of global mass culture was the staging of events dedicated to causes such as famine relief and the plight of farmers. The Live Aid concert, held in July 1985, raised about $70 million for famine relief in Africa.

The disease AIDS became a major threat to the lives of people around the world. In spite of massive research programs, the disease continued to ravage many centers of population.

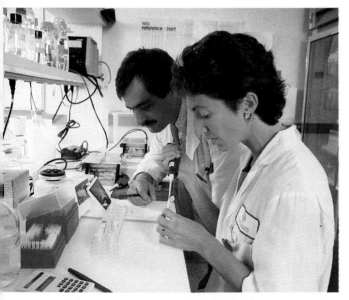

Research scientists are seeking a cure or ways to limit the effects of the terrible disease AIDS (Acquired Immune Deficiency Syndrome).

Genetic research caused controversy.

Many of this century's scientific advances came from a better understanding of processes that occurred in the smallest units of life. Each cell of a living organism contains genes that determine the characteristics of the organism. By manipulating genes—the chemical codes that control cell growth—scientists learned to insert new characteristics into nearly any cell.

New techniques with genes found many applications. Biologists discovered that adding genes from other plants could make certain food plants more productive or resistant to disease. Entirely new types of food crops were developed using this technique. Genetically altered bacteria were devised that prevented frost damage to plants when sprayed on crops. The new technique found medical uses as well. When researchers put an insulin-producing gene into bacteria, they created a new source of pure, inexpensive medicine for diabetics.

An even greater advance occurred when scientists began to identify the points on the human chromosomes—the gene carriers—where missing or damaged genes transmitted certain diseases from one generation to another. In the hope of finding cures for genetically caused diseases, the United States government in 1986 began to organize a project to map the human genome, or gene system. This meant nothing less than identifying the function of every single one of the 3 billion units in the 100,000 genes that make up the human chromosomes. In 1988, James Watson, who with Francis Crick had received a Nobel Prize for work on the structure of genes, was asked to head this effort. It was expected to cost $3 billion and to take 15 years.

Genetic research and its applications found many critics, however. Some people wondered whether releasing genetically altered bacteria and plants into the environment might have unforeseen consequences. Would these new forms of life overrun their bounds or mutate (change genetically) into a form dangerous to the environment? Other people questioned whether it was right to alter genes that determine the basic nature of human beings.

A few people saw genome mapping as the first step toward engineering a superhuman person. They pointed out that it would be far easier to damage and deform a gene accidentally than it would be to repair some long-standing defect. Others feared that the genome project might divert money from other equally worthy projects. As the new science gathered momentum, the debate between researchers and critics continued.

Section Review 2

Define: (a) gene, (b) chromosome
Identify: (a) CAT scan, (b) James Watson
Answer:
1. Explain the meaning of the term *quality of life.*
2. How did changes in communications technology affect the field of music?
3. How did technology encourage the growth of a global mass culture?
4. Why were Third World writers important to their countries?
5. Describe the new methods and diagnostic tools that improved health care.

Critical Thinking
6. What is the significance of the emergence of worldwide cultural patterns?

789

Dangers to the global environment developed. 3

One of the things that astronauts brought back from space was a new view of the earth. Astronaut William Anders described what he saw. "From the moon, Earth appeared as a small, blue-green sphere, like a beautiful, fragile Christmas tree ornament . . . very delicate and limited, the only color in the universe, the only friendly place we could see." Just how fragile that sphere was became apparent in the years following the Apollo flights.

New factors affected the environment.

Two factors in the twentieth century were of special importance to the earth's environment. One was a tremendous surge in world population growth. World population in 1900 was about 1.6 billion people. By 1987, it had passed 5 billion and was predicted to grow to at least 10 billion in the next century.

This huge increase directly affected the earth itself. More food and resources were needed for human consumption. One by-product of consumption, however, was waste—garbage and trash. The higher the level of consumption, the greater the amount of waste produced. Throughout the 1970's and 1980's, evidence mounted that the earth could no longer absorb the waste produced. To keep the earth habitable, rapid and effective changes were needed in the way people used the earth's resources and dealt with waste.

The other factor that presented a threat to the environment was in part technology itself. That threat was an indirect one, caused by the fact that modern technology and standards of living consume huge quantities of energy. Coal had long been known to give off polluting by-products such as sulfur. After the 1960's, developed nations began to pay the price for the cheap coal they had burned since the start of the Industrial Revolution. Acid rain, caused by sulfur in coal, fell over large areas of North America and Europe, destroying forests and killing life in lakes and ponds.

The greenhouse effect Fossil fuels caused further problems by giving off large amounts of carbon dioxide to a total of five billion tons a year. In the years between 1958 and 1988, the amount of carbon dioxide in the earth's atmosphere rose by 25 percent. By trapping heat that would otherwise have escaped from the lower part of the atmosphere, carbon dioxide and other gases began a worldwide warming trend.

Called the greenhouse effect, this unwanted heat threatened to raise temperatures worldwide by three to eight degrees Fahrenheit by the year 2050. Some scientists predicted that so great a rise in temperature would melt once-permanent ice and snow, causing the seas to rise one to four feet and flood coastal areas. In fact, the world's seas had already risen four inches since 1900. If the trend continued, heavily populated low-lying areas such as Bangledesh and the Chang Jiang (Yangtze) Valley would be permanently flooded. Furthermore, weather patterns would change unpredictably. Some of the world's best food-producing areas might become wastelands, while rain might fall unused on the thirsty sands of the Sahara and other deserts.

Shrinking forests, polluted oceans The greenhouse effect became even more serious as major forest areas, which absorb carbon dioxide and convert it to oxygen, were being destroyed at increasing rates. Estimates indicated that in the tropics alone more than 26 million acres of forest were destroyed every year. Another place where carbon dioxide could be converted to oxygen was the oceans. However, the microscopic life-forms that performed this task were being poisoned by pollution.

The ozone layer In 1974, scientists discovered another danger to the earth's environment. Chemicals called chlorofluorocarbons (CFC's) that are used in refrigerating systems, aerosol sprays, and some foam plastics were destroying the ozone layer in the earth's upper atmosphere. Without this thin layer, ultraviolent radiation would flood the earth, destroying plants and causing cancer in people and animals. A hole in the ozone layer over the Antarctic region was discovered in 1985, and another was detected over the Arctic in 1988. The layer over the entire globe was estimated to have decreased by 3 percent between 1969 and 1986.

Steps have already been taken to end the use of CFC's. An international conference held in Montreal in 1987 called for a 50 percent reduction

The world's rain forests are part of the hydrologic cycle that regulates rainfall and, to some extent, climate. Their destruction, besides contributing to the greenhouse effect, could have disastrous effects on weather and climate patterns.

Vast areas of Brazil's rain forests are being cut to provide land for settlement. The need for living space by Brazil's expanding population conflicts with conserving the rain forest because of its role in climate.

in CFC's by the year 2000. Much damage, however, was already done. CFC's can linger in the atmosphere for a century. Continued ozone loss was certain to present the world with new problems for decades to come.

New sources of energy were developed.

To limit the polluting effects from using fossil fuels for energy, new inventions seemed the best hope. The 1980's saw development of solar cells that used thin-film technology to produce electricity more cheaply and efficiently from sunlight. The new superconductors promised to help a new kind of nuclear energy—fusion power—become practical sometime in the new century.

New and safer types of power plants using fission, the old type of nuclear power, were designed in the late 1980's. For the time being, however, few nations were interested in them. After the accident at the Chernobyl nuclear power station in the Soviet Union in 1985 had spread a radioactive cloud over much of Europe, public confidence in nuclear power declined. Even if a

safe fission plant could be built, there remained the problem of disposing of nuclear waste.

Another effort to use traditional sources of energy in new ways was the invention of a cleaner way to burn coal. The new method promised to put an end to sulfur emissions that cause acid rain and to eliminate the nitrogen oxides that contribute to smog. Like all technology, however, it was expensive. Most Third World nations could not afford such sophisticated power plants.

Attitudes about the environment changed.

A few scientists, groups, and individuals had for many years been concerned about the effects of pollution on the environment. By the 1980's, those effects were becoming obvious to all. Public attitudes, however, were slow to change. One reason was that the connection between pollution and damage to the environment was often not clear. Who would have thought that the dying of whole forests in West Germany was caused by rain carried from industrial regions? That sparkling Canadian lakes would be unable to

Discuss with students why there has been so much resistance to protecting the environment.

791

support aquatic life? Or that shellfish from traditional ocean fishing grounds could cause sickness and even death?

The industrialized world Recognition of the dangers from environmental pollution came slowly in the industrialized world. For nations there, industry was the basis of economic life. They feared that environmental protection would limit development and add to the costs of production. Why take such steps when proof was lacking that they were necessary?

Only over time did the patterns showing the dangers of pollution become clear. Air, soil, and water—as well as plant, animal, and human life—were indeed vulnerable to those dangers. Toxic chemical wastes—from fertilizers, insect sprays, and a number of industrial processes, as well as household chemicals—and nuclear wastes were a special threat because of their direct effect on living things. Finally, the emerging environmental problems of the 1980's began to convince scientists and governments that protecting the global environment had become essential.

The Third World Destruction of the environment posed an especially difficult problem in the Third World. Leaders there too were reluctant to recognize the need for environmental protection. Eventually, however, they too began to experience the increase in waste materials and the dangers from toxic waste. They also faced the need to protect their lands from the dumping of trash and contaminated wastes by industrialized nations. A further problem lay in the need to protect the environment from floods, soil erosion, and the loss of farmland to spreading deserts. (By the end of the 1980's, some 14.8 million acres a year were turning to wasteland in the less developed countries.) When these nations saw the seriousness of the disaster facing them, their attitudes began to change.

Nonetheless, many Third World countries still had to exploit their environments in order to buy food and new technology and to pay their huge debts. In the late 1980's, some Western groups concerned about the environment began to suggest that the developed nations should forgive the debts of Third World nations in exchange for better environmental policies. One example suggested was Brazil, where the great rain forest of the Amazon Basin was being destroyed at an alarming rate.

Section Review 3

Define: (a) fossil fuels, (b) greenhouse effect, (c) ozone layer, (d) acid rain

Answer:

1. (a) How did population growth affect the environment? (b) How did technology pose a threat to the environment?
2. What environmental problems were caused by the burning of fossil fuels?
3. (a) What were possible new sources of energy? (b) What were their benefits and limitations?
4. (a) How did attitudes toward the environment change in the industrialized world? (b) The Third World?

Critical Thinking

5. (a) List four major types of pollution that threaten the global environment. (b) What are possible solutions to each problem?

A new era of change began. 4

The economic dominance of the United States after World War II had given way by the 1970's to the new role of a nation sharing economic leadership. New centers of growth in Europe and Asia challenged the United States in industrial output, exports, and research and development.

Pacific nations began economic expansion.

By the late 1980's, one of the emerging economic regions was the Pacific Rim. It was made up of the nations bordering the Pacific Ocean, particularly those in East and Southeast Asia. Japan was the first of these nations to achieve spectacular economic growth. Soon South Korea, Taiwan, Hong Kong, and Singapore followed. Other nations, such as Thailand and Indonesia, were not far behind. Looming over them all was the vast and undeveloped power of China.

The Asian Pacific Rim, together with the West Coast area of the United States and Canada, was quickly becoming one of the most important economic regions in the world. In the closing decade of the century, it was certain to compete strongly with other expanding economies, such as those of the European Common Market after 1992 or the wealthy oil-producing states of the Middle East.

Japan You have read in Chapter 34 how Japan, as it recovered from World War II, entered into economic competition with the United States. During the 1970's and 1980's, its economy continued to expand at an average rate of 10 percent annually, or three times that of the United States economy. With foreign investments of more than $240 billion and ownership of eight of the ten largest banks in the world, Japan also came to dominate international finance.

There were many reasons for Japan's phenomenal growth. One was efficiency. Japan's government, society, and industry were all highly centralized. Japanese companies were like huge, well-disciplined families, where loyalties were strong and productivity high. The Japanese had also learned an important lesson: nothing sells as well as quality. Planning too was a factor. The government of Japan targeted certain industries

for development and then poured in funds. Much of this money was available because Japan was prohibited from developing its military forces. The import tariffs that had long closed Japan's domestic markets to foreign competition also served to protect Japanese industry. Finally the people of Japan were accustomed to putting the needs of the country above those of the individual and to working together for the common good.

South Korea The achievements in economic growth in South Korea were also remarkable, coming after years of uncertainty. In 1984, South Korea imported almost 1 billion dollars' worth of goods more than it exported, leaving the nation $46 billion in debt. Then its exports took off, rising to an estimated $9 billion or more in 1988. Korea paid off $12 billion of its debt and became the only major debtor nation in the world to be paying off its loans ahead of time.

What factors contributed to this turnabout? First of all, wages in South Korea were low. South Korean workers also toiled long hours—54 hours a week, or 40 percent more than their American competition. South Korean companies were skillful at focusing on established markets such

Reading a graph Which nation imports the most merchandise? What are some reasons for that? Which three nations export the most merchandise? Which nations export less than they import, with an unfavorable balance of trade?

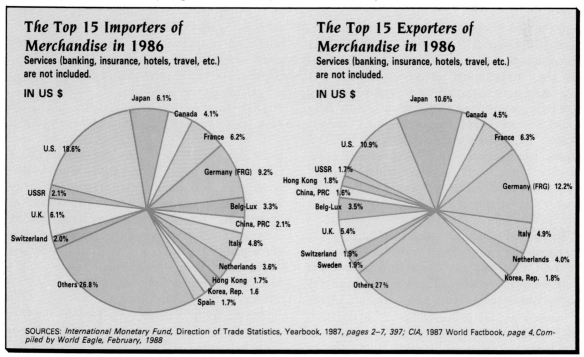

The Top 15 Importers of Merchandise in 1986
Services (banking, insurance, hotels, travel, etc.) are not included.

IN US $

Japan 6.1%
Canada 4.1%
France 6.2%
U.S. 18.6%
Germany (FRG) 9.2%
USSR 2.1%
U.K. 6.1%
Belg-Lux 3.3%
Switzerland 2.0%
China, PRC 2.1%
Italy 4.8%
Others 26.8%
Netherlands 3.6%
Hong Kong 1.7%
Korea, Rep. 1.6
Spain 1.7%

The Top 15 Exporters of Merchandise in 1986
Services (banking, insurance, hotels, travel, etc.) are not included.

IN US $

Japan 10.6%
Canada 4.5%
France 6.3%
U.S. 10.9%
USSR 1.7%
Hong Kong 1.8%
China, PRC 1.6%
Germany (FRG) 12.2%
Belg-Lux 3.5%
U.K. 5.4%
Italy 4.9%
Switzerland 1.9%
Netherlands 4.0%
Sweden 1.9%
Korea, Rep. 1.8%
Others 27%

SOURCES: *International Monetary Fund,* Direction of Trade Statistics, Yearbook, 1987, *pages 2–7, 397; CIA,* 1987 World Factbook, *page 4. Compiled by World Eagle, February, 1988*

The Geographic Theme on page 800 provides a chart showing the population and economic growth of the nations of the Pacific Rim.

as the electronics market and then investing huge sums in developing industries to produce for those markets. As true multinational corporations, those industries were quick to set up factories around the world in order to compete better with local industries everywhere.

Once far poorer than North Korea, South Korea by the end of the 1980's outranked North Korea by every measure of economic strength. Its Gross National Product (GNP) was more than 6 times that of North Korea, and its total foreign trade was 22 times greater. Even its millions of inhabitants were an asset, since nearly all of them were employed—most at very low wages.

China Communist China's contribution to the miracle of the Pacific Rim was centered on the coast of the China Sea, from Hong Kong north. As China began to use free market tactics to encourage growth, the enormous population of this coastal area—estimated to be in excess of 100 million people—responded by developing a wide variety of industries in just a few years. Although the Chinese government ordered a slowing of the shift to free market practices in 1988, it stood to gain too much economically for it to clamp down on industry in the coastal provinces.

The superpowers faced challenges.

By the mid-1960's, the recovery of most nations from World War II was almost complete. This was a significant change for the two nations— the United States and the Soviet Union—that had emerged from the war as superpowers. Now economic recovery in the nations of East Asia and of Western Europe, especially the Common Market group, also meant increased political power. The rise of the Third World created other new centers of influence, particularly in the United Nations. Political power was thus more widely shared around the world. This, in turn, affected the role of the two greatest powers.

The United States Although the United States remained the world's most powerful country as the century neared its close, new realities led it to reassess its position. The Vietnam War was one of these realities, as was a change in the political and economic policies of population giants like Communist China. The growing trade deficit was another reality—one that left the United States in debt to other countries and opened its economy to foreign investment.

The Soviet Union The Soviet Union too faced new realities. On March 11, 1985, Mikhail Gorbachev succeeded Konstantin Chernenko as general secretary of the Soviet Communist Party. His rise to power marked a new era in the history of the Soviet Union. At fifty-four, he was the youngest member of the Politburo and the first top Soviet leader who had not been born under czarist rule. Although many of Gorbachev's most pressing problems were the same ones that had confronted earlier leaders, they now took on new urgency. Chief among these problems was the Soviet economy.

Ever since Stalin's first Five Year Plan, the Soviets had concentrated on building up heavy industry—the basic industries that enable a nation to build its own machines. Progress had been made in producing such things as industrial equipment, farm machinery, and weapons systems. The focus on heavy industry, however, led to serious neglect of consumer needs. Consumer goods such as food, appliances, and clothing had to wait until Soviet heavy industry could compete with that of the West.

Without many basic comforts to show for their labors, Soviet workers had little incentive to work efficiently or to produce quality goods. Gorbachev and other party leaders realized that the Soviet economy would stagnate unless incentives were offered to workers. To the West, this new program—called *perestroika*, or restructuring— seemed to contain elements of capitalism.

Perestroika was a bold move, challenging almost 70 years of Communist planning. Gorbachev gave local units of the economy more control over what they would produce. Farmers were allowed to sell produce in free marketplaces. Gorbachev spoke of firing those who worked poorly. This was an unheard-of practice in a nation where unemployment is not supposed to exist. By removing price controls on materials used by factories, Gorbachev hoped that prices would become realistic. In order to hasten the production of consumer goods, the Soviet government sought loans from Western nations.

Soon after the new program was underway, however, Soviet planners realized that ending restrictions on consumer prices was causing inflation. To ease the complaints of consumers, the

The Soviet withdrawal from Afghanistan, like the United States withdrawal from Korea, was a sobering reminder of the costs of war and of military commitments.

Economics in Daily Life · *Blue Jeans*

The denim pants called blue jeans are an example of a product sold around the world. Blue jeans were first worn by miners in the days of the 1849 California Gold Rush. Over the years, they became the uniform of American farmers and blue-collar workers. Then, in the 1960's, young Americans began to wear blue jeans almost everywhere. Blue jeans even caught on with noted fashion designers.

Love of blue jeans spread to Europe and to the USSR, where jeans were linked to rock-and-roll music and other Western styles. In the Soviet Union, jeans are scarce, and American jeans are smuggled in for sale on the black market. Whether viewed as a status symbol or a sign of dissent, blue jeans illustrate cultural diffusion. They also mean good business. The original maker is the world's largest manufacturer of clothing.

government raised wages and printed more money, thus causing prices to rise even higher. In 1988, as part of its policy of *glasnost*—or openness about Soviet society, politics, and the economy—officials admitted to an inflation rate of 1.5 percent. (Western analysts suggested it might be as high as 7 percent.) Because Soviet economists had few tools for dealing with such inflation, the economy clearly faced difficulties in the years ahead.

The new policy of *glasnost* had remarkable effects on Soviet society. In 1988, for the first time in more than 50 years, several opposition votes were cast in the Supreme Soviet, the legislature that traditionally approved all Communist party decisions. On some ballots at the local levels, voters were even offered a choice between candidates instead of the usual one-party slate of candidates. Gorbachev made at least a token show of ending some of the repressive measures that had characterized Soviet government since Stalin's time. Dissidents found they had more freedom, and some opposition publications began to circulate more openly.

Reform was unlikely to move very fast. Gorbachev's proposal to provide for multiparty candidates and the use of the secret ballot in national elections was linked to measures that would give new and dictatorial powers to the president, or chairman of the Supreme Soviet—that is, to Gorbachev.

Although Gorbachev was an easy mark for Western criticism, he seemed to be doing well at a difficult task. Any effort to reform a huge bureaucracy like that of the Soviet Union was certain to cause many stresses and strains. The best reason for believing in Gorbachev's sincerity was his confession that the Soviet economy was in trouble. Thus, the Soviet Union began to reassess its present situation and plan for the future, particularly its economic survival.

East-West dialogue began again.

The world in general viewed Gorbachev's liberalizing policies with relief. It seemed that at last the Soviet Union might develop a concern for the rights of its own citizens and become a more responsible member of the world community. The Soviet pullback in Afghanistan was an important step in that direction. Even President Ronald Reagan, who had characterized the Soviet Union as an "evil empire," was willing to discuss issues with Gorbachev face-to-face. The first item on the summit agenda in 1988 was reducing the number of nuclear weapons in United States and Soviet stockpiles.

Nuclear danger One reason Reagan and Gorbachev took up the nuclear issue was that each of the two superpowers had hundreds of times more weapons than it needed to annihilate the other. Two kinds of missiles in particular, the medium- and shorter-range types, were a special concern to the people of Europe, where these weapons were designed to be used. The danger of accidental or intentional use of nuclear weapons had become far more frightening to most people than problems such as pollution. Even a limited nuclear war—one involving less than 1 percent of the world's nuclear weapons—would create enough radioactive debris in the atmosphere to alter world weather patterns drastically. It might even cause a nuclear winter that would turn the world into a frozen desert.

The nuclear club Another influence on the two leaders was the growing number of members of the nuclear club—the nations of the world that possessed nuclear weapons. Besides the United States and the Soviet Union, Britain, France, and China openly admitted that they had such weapons. Pakistan, India, Israel, and South Africa would neither confirm nor deny their nuclear capabilities. Nonetheless, it was well known that each of these countries had some kind of nuclear device it could use against other nations. By reducing their own stockpiles, the United States and the Soviet Union could argue that it was unnecessary for other nations to build nuclear weapons.

The INF treaty On December 8, 1987, Gorbachev and Reagan signed the Intermediate Nuclear Forces (INF) Treaty that called for the destruction of 1,752 Soviet and 859 United States missiles. Over a period of three years, almost a

Voice from Our Time · *One Leader Speaks*

President Mikhail Gorbachev of the Soviet Union spoke on December 7, 1988, to the United Nations General Assembly in New York. His speech received attention around the world.

The world in which we live today is radically different from what it was at the beginning or even in the middle of this century. And it continues to change . . . The advent of nuclear weapons was just another tragic reminder of the fundamental nature of that change . . . The problem of mankind's survival and self-preservation came to the fore . . . The new phase also requires de-ideologizing relations among states. We are not abandoning our convictions, our philosophy or traditions, nor do we urge anyone to abandon theirs.

But neither do we have any intention to be hemmed in by our values. That would . . . mean rejecting a powerful source of development—the exchange of everything original that each nation has independently created.

In the course of such exchange, let everyone show the advantages of their social system, way of life or values— and not just by words or propaganda, but by real deeds . . . We have concluded that it is on those lines that we should jointly seek the way leading to the supremacy of the universal human idea . . . the way to preserve the vitality of this civilization . . . I am convinced that our time and the realities of today's world call for internationalizing dialogue and the negotiating process. This is the main . . . conclusion that we have come to in studying global trends that have been gaining momentun in recent years, and in participating in world politics.

1. What does Gorbachev say is the effect of having nuclear weapons?
2. What does he mean by "hemmed in by our values"?
3. What procedure is he proposing for relations between nations and between different political systems?
4. What are two possible but contrasting ways of interpreting this speech?

Progress in the reduction of nuclear arms was one step toward cooperation in such undertakings as space exploration, medical research, and environmental protection.

Three leaders—Ronald Reagan and George Bush of the United States and Mikhail Gorbachev of the Soviet Union—toured New York City on December 8, 1988.

tenth of the world's nuclear stockpile was to be dismantled. Elaborate precautions ensured that each side would abide by the treaty.

The INF Treaty was a significant sign of change. It not only began a new dialogue between East and West but also symbolized the hope that cooperation might prevail into the coming century.

The world is interdependent.

As the twentieth century draws to a close, Planet Earth is more than ever a small and fragile place. The key to the future lies in an awareness of that fragility and the common interests of what some people refer to as "Spaceship Earth."

While Armstrong and Aldrin were exploring the moon on that July day in 1969, another astronaut, Michael Collins, piloted the command module that orbited overhead, awaiting their return. As the spacecraft drifted silently over the scarred surface of the moon, he watched the gleaming sphere of the earth from his narrow window. Like Armstrong, his thoughts turned to the meaning of his mission.

"I really believe," Collins later wrote, "that if the political leaders of the world could see their planet from a distance of 100,000 or 200,000 miles, their outlook could be fundamentally changed. Those all-important borders and their noisy arguments would be suddenly silenced. The tiny globe would continue to turn, serenely ignoring its subdivisions, presenting a united front that would cry out for united understanding."

Section Review 4

Identify: (a) Pacific Rim, (b) *perestroika*, (c) *glasnost*, (d) nuclear club, (e) INF Treaty
Answer:
1. What various kinds of economic changes are currently taking place in nations of the Asian Pacific Rim?
2. What are four reasons for the economic success of the Asian Pacific Rim?
3. (a) What economic problems does Gorbachev face? (b) How do *perestroika* and *glasnost* seek to deal with them?
4. Why is the growth of the nuclear club a concern to both the United States and the Soviet Union?
5. What are the objectives of the INF Treaty?

Critical Thinking
6. What events in the past 25 years have made nations more interdependent?

Summary

1. Technology led in new directions. The postwar era brought a revolution in technology. The foremost example of this was the space program. The *Apollo* program and the space shuttle were major successes, although the *Challenger* disaster brought a temporary setback. Other areas of change included worldwide communication networks and expanded use of computers. Changes in materials technology brought the possibility of superconductors in the years ahead.

2. Technology affected the quality of life. The new communications technology led to worldwide cultural exchange in music, literature, and art. Surgical and medical care improved through the help of technology. Genetic research opened new possibilities but remained controversial.

3. Dangers to the global environment developed. The growth of world population and the increasing use of energy resources contributed to environmental problems on a worldwide scale. Of particular concern were the increasingly serious greenhouse effect and the reduction in the earth's ozone layer. By the late 1980's, people in both industrialized and Third World countries were becoming more aware of the need to protect the environment.

4. A new era of economic and political change began. The Pacific Rim emerged as a major new nation in international trade, with Japan a major power in the global economy. Both the United States and the Soviet Union entered a period of transition. In the Soviet Union, Gorbachev's policies of *perestroika* and *glasnost* sought to deal with growing weaknesses in the Soviet system. Out of this period of transition came new dialogue between East and West, recognition of the danger from nuclear catastrophe, and greater willingness to accept some disarmament.

Reviewing the Facts

1. Define the following terms:

a. satellite f. fossil fuel
b. transistor g. greenhouse effect
c. superconductor h. ozone layer
d. gene i. *perestroika*
e. chromosome j. *glasnost*

2. Explain the importance or meaning of each of the following names, places, or terms:

a. Neil Armstrong d. space shuttle
b. *Apollo* e. SDI
c. *Sputnik* f. Telstar

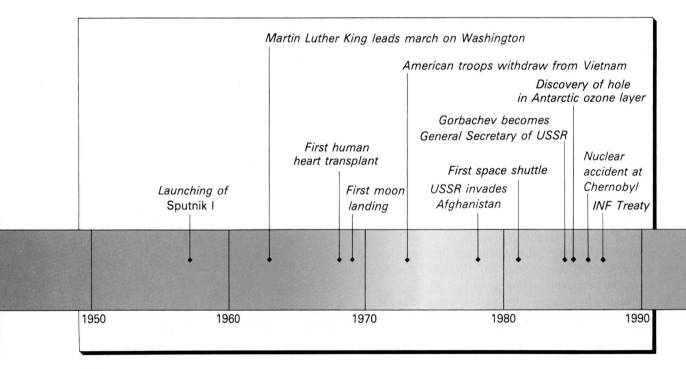

Martin Luther King leads march on Washington

American troops withdraw from Vietnam

Discovery of hole in Antarctic ozone layer

Gorbachev becomes General Secretary of USSR

First human heart transplant

Nuclear accident at Chernobyl

First space shuttle

Launching of Sputnik I

First moon landing

USSR invades Afghanistan

INF Treaty

1950　1960　1970　1980　1990

g. microcomputer
h. CAT scan
i. genetic research
j. CFC's

k. Chernobyl
l. Pacific Rim
m. nuclear club
n. INF Treaty

Basic Skills

1. **Reading graphs** Study the two circle graphs on page 793. (a) List the top importers of 1986 and the top exporters. Do each list in sequence, starting with the largest and including the percentages of total imports and exports. (b) Which nations import more than they export? (c) Which export more than they import? (d) What is the status of each nation's balance of trade?

2. **Interpreting graphs** (a) What is the significance of having an unfavorable (negative) balance of trade? (b) What are some ways that a country with a negative balance could gain a favorable balance?

Researching and Reporting Skills

1. **Using community resources** As a class, identify an expert in your community on one of the following subjects: recent changes in medical technology, global environmental protection, or new sources of energy. Invite this person to talk to your class. Conclude the presentation with a question and answer period. What new ideas have you gained?

2. **Using a newspaper index** Using *The New York Times Index* or that of another major newspaper, look up, read about, and report on the major achievements in space flight and exploration. What future exploration is planned for the rest of this century?

3. **Doing field research** As a class project to investigate the extent of the sale of foreign goods, go to a department store or some other kind of store and check the labels of various items for the country of origin. Take notes on the findings and summarize them to share with the class. What conclusions emerge from this research?

Critical Thinking

1. **Inferring** (a) What has been the military importance of space travel and exploration? (b) The nonmilitary importance?

2. **Predicting trends** (a) How is the growth of the global office likely to affect business? (b) What is its importance in terms of multinational companies?

3. **Synthesizing** How does worldwide cultural exchange improve the quality of people's lives?

4. **Relating** The continuous improvement in medical care is extending life expectancy. (a) How may this affect trends in world population growth? (b) What are some recent negative influences on life expectancy?

5. **Analyzing** Many of the emerging environmental problems are global in scope. (a) Why does that make it difficult to deal with them? (b) What are some possible means for doing that?

6. **Evaluating** Evaluate the factors involved in arms control. (a) Why has it been difficult for the superpowers to reach agreement on it? (b) What kinds of provisions would be needed in an agreement?

7. **Solving problems** (a) List the problems in the Soviet economy that Gorbachev is trying to solve. (b) How are *perestroika* and *glasnost* intended to accomplish this?

Perspectives on Past and Present

Compare the ideas in Gorbachev's speech (page 796) with those of Stalin (page 693). How do the circumstances for the speeches differ? What similarities and differences in ideas can you find? What factors might account for any differences?

Investigating History

1. One of the pioneers in environmental protection was Rachel Carson, whose book *Silent Spring* alerted people to the dangers of toxic chemicals in the environment. Read selections from some of her writings. What new concepts do you find? What steps have been taken to correct conditions she described?

2. One of the major achievements of the United Nations was the Universal Declaration of Human Rights. Obtain a copy of this document and read it as a class project. What conditions is it intended to prevent? Why is it so valuable?

Unit IX Review

Geographic Theme: Region

What dynamic new region is emerging in the world economy?

The Pacific Rim—the nations that border the Pacific Ocean—is today becoming a major new trading area. Just as the Mediterranean once united the ancient world, so today the Pacific links the lands around it. Unlike the Mediterranean, however, no one nation or empire controls this region. Instead, a number of powerful and less-powerful nations interact across the vast Pacific.

Today that interaction is heavily based on economic development and trade. Both of those are in a period of rapid change. The economic powers—such as Japan, China, the United States, and Canada—are finding new opportunities in the region's growth. The small nations, though lacking political power, are industrialized and capable of advanced technology. They are thus able to produce and export goods that bring a high return. That income, in turn, can be invested to produce more wealth. Not only trade but also banking and finance are becoming important activities throughout the region.

The chart below shows the economic growth of Pacific Rim nations. Note the relative amount of growth in GNP and per capita income in the various countries. Clearly, this is a time of rapid change for the smaller countries. It is also a period of transition for long-industrialized countries. They are facing competition in special areas of industry and technology where they have previously held the lead. Thus, they must seek to develop new specialties and take greater advantage of their resources in order to maintain their own economic growth.

1. (a) Which three nations had the highest rate of population growth? (b) Which three had the least?
2. (a) Which three countries had the highest rate of increase in GNP? (b) Which three had the lowest? (c) Which three had the highest rate of growth in per capita GNP? (d) Which three had the lowest?
3. What conclusions about the Pacific Rim can you draw on the basis of this chart?

Nations of the Pacific Rim: Population and Economic Growth

NATION	POPULATION		GROSS NATIONAL PRODUCT (Billions of US Dollars)		PER CAPITA INCOME (US Dollars)	
	1970	1987 (est.)	1969*	mid-1980's	1969*	mid-1980's
Australia	12,522,400	16,200,000	30.4	166.2 (1983)	1,861	9,960 (1983)
Canada	21,400,000	25,900,000	78.5	335 (1985)	2,313	13,541 (1985)
China	759,600,000	1,062,000,000	80.0 (1966)	343 (1985)	100 (1966)	330 (1985)
Japan	103,500,000	122,200,000	168.0	1,233 (1984)	1,300	10,200 (1984)
Singapore	2,100,000	2,600,000	1.3 (1968)	18.4 (1984)	672 (1968)	7,270 (1984)
South Korea	32,100,000	42,100,000	8.0	90.6 (1986)	170 (1968)	2,180 (1986)
Taiwan	14,000,000	19,600,000	4.8	60 (1985)	373	3,142 (1983)
United States	207,678,247	243,800,000	931.4	4,206.1 (1986)	3,687	14,461 (1986)
U.S.S.R.	241,748,000	284,000,000	400.0 (1968)	2,062 (1985)	1,678 (1968)	7,896 (1985)

SOURCE: D. Phillips and S. Levi, The Pacific Rim Region, Enslow Publishers, Inc., 1988.

*Except as noted

Unit Perspectives

Understanding History

1. **Explaining** Explain the origin and purpose of each of the following agreements or policies:
   a. Truman Doctrine   e. Common Market
   b. Marshall Plan   f. Comecon
   c. NATO   g. Solidarity
   d. Warsaw Pact   h. Brezhnev Doctrine

2. **Locating** Each of the following countries has experienced unrest since World War II. Match each country with the correct geographic location: (a) Eastern Europe (b) Middle East (c) Africa (d) East Asia (e) South Asia (f) Southeast Asia (g) Latin America.
   a. Bangladesh   g. Poland
   b. Cuba   h. Nigeria
   c. Iran   i. Nicaragua
   d. Israel   j. Chile
   e. Korea   k. Lebanon
   f. Vietnam   l. Zaire

3. **Relating** With what country is each of the following people associated? What role did that person play in the country after independence?
   a. Nehru   d. Nasser
   b. Gandhi   e. Houphouet-Boigny
   c. Nkrumah   f. Nyerere

4. **Matching** Match the name or term in the left column with the correct country in the right.
   1. economic miracle   a. Indonesia
   2. Cultural Revolution   b. Kampuchea
   3. conflict with Pakistan   c. Philippines
   4. Sukarno   d. South Vietnam
   5. Aquino   e. China
   6. Diem   f. Japan
   7. Khmer Rouge   g. India

5. With what country is each of the following people associated? What stand against oppression or inequality has each person taken?
   a. Dubcek   d. Solzhenitsyn
   b. Walesa   e. Martin Luther
   c. Tito   King, Jr.

Critical Thinking

1. **Analyzing** (a) What was the impact of the Cold War in Europe? (b) What alliances reflected that impact?

2. **Solving Problems** After its defeat in World War II, Japan faced the need to rebuild its economy. What steps did Japan take to do that? What was the result?

3. **Comparing** (a) Compare China's role in the world today with that in 1900. (b) What does this change suggest about China's role in the next century?

4. **Analyzing** (a) What factors explain the difficulty in building stable governments in Africa? (b) How stable do you consider the South African government? Why?

5. **Solving problems** Israel has not felt secure as a nation among its Arab neighbors. If you were a consultant to the government of Israel, what advice would you give for dealing with the problem of security? Give reasons for your answer.

6. **Synthesizing** (a) How has the role of the world's two superpowers changed since the years just after World War II? (b) What are the major reasons for those changes?

7. **Applying a concept** In countries with very rapid population growth, such as those of Latin America, why is that growth often referred to as a time bomb?

8. **Evaluating** Why is environmental pollution now seen as a global problem?

Making Decisions

Three important presidential decisions or actions were Truman's decision to aid South Korea (page 704), Johnson's report to Congress on the Tonkin Gulf attack (page 739), and Kennedy's demand for the removal of Soviet missiles from Cuba (page 770). Evaluate one of these situations in terms of the reasons for it, the outcome, and possible alternatives and their advantages.

Continuity and Change

Only 21 years passed between the end of World War I and the start of World War II, but four and a half decades have passed since the end of World War II without a major world war. What factors may account for that long period of relative peace? What other conditions may contribute to that peace?

The World about 1700 B.C.

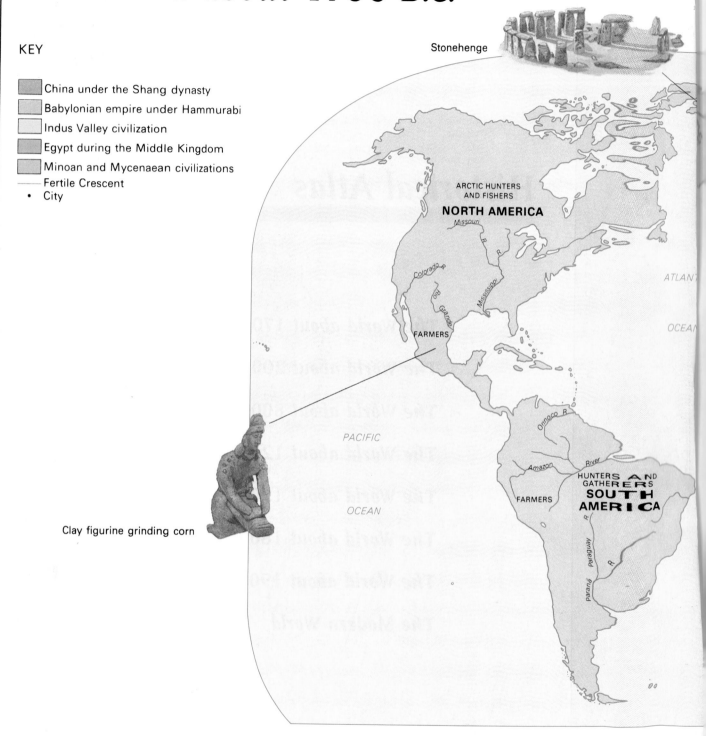

KEY

China under the Shang dynasty
Babylonian empire under Hammurabi
Indus Valley civilization
Egypt during the Middle Kingdom
Minoan and Mycenaean civilizations
— Fertile Crescent
• City

Stonehenge

ARCTIC HUNTERS AND FISHERS

NORTH AMERICA

Missouri

Colorado R.

Rio Grande

Mississippi R.

FARMERS

ATLANTIC OCEAN

PACIFIC OCEAN

Clay figurine grinding corn

Orinoco R.

Amazon River

FARMERS

SOUTH AMERICA
HUNTERS AND GATHERERS

Paraguay R.

Paraná R.

Historical Atlas

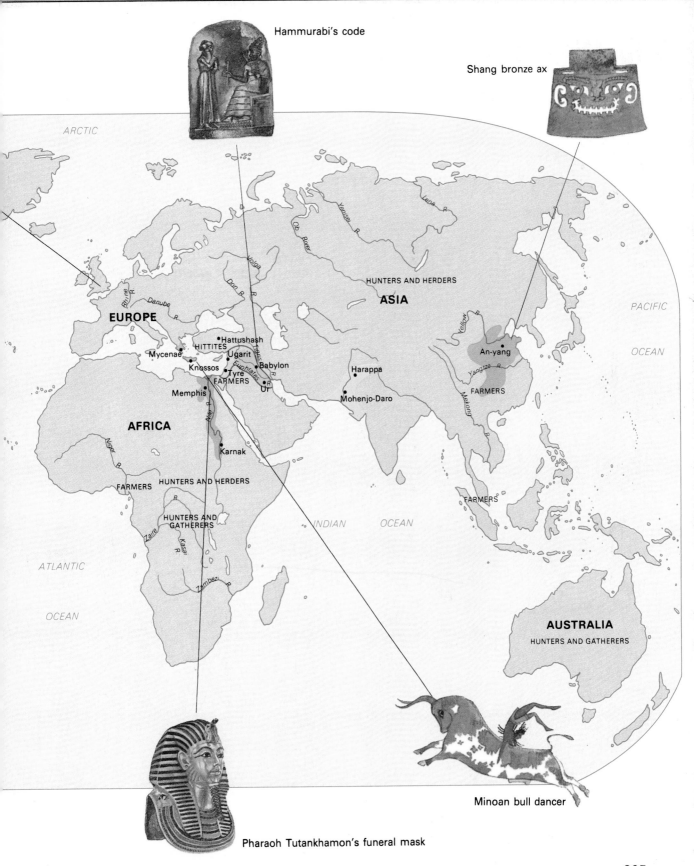

Hammurabi's code

Shang bronze ax

ARCTIC

EUROPE

ASIA

HUNTERS AND HERDERS

PACIFIC

OCEAN

Rhine R

Danube R

Don R

Volga

Ob River

Yenisei R

Lena R

Yellow

Yangtze R

Mekong

An-yang

FARMERS

Mycenae

HITTITES

Hattushash

Ugarit

Knossos

Tyre

FARMERS

Babylon

Ur

Harappa

Mohenjo-Daro

Euphrates

Tigris

Memphis

AFRICA

Nile R

Niger R

Karnak

FARMERS

HUNTERS AND HERDERS

HUNTERS AND GATHERERS

Zaire R

Kasai R

Zambezi R

INDIAN

OCEAN

FARMERS

ATLANTIC

OCEAN

AUSTRALIA

HUNTERS AND GATHERERS

Minoan bull dancer

Pharaoh Tutankhamon's funeral mask

The World about 200 B.C.

KEY

- China under the Han dynasty
- Mauryan empire under Ashoka
- Roman republic
- Hopewell farming villages
- Olmec farming villages
- Kingdom of Kush
- • City

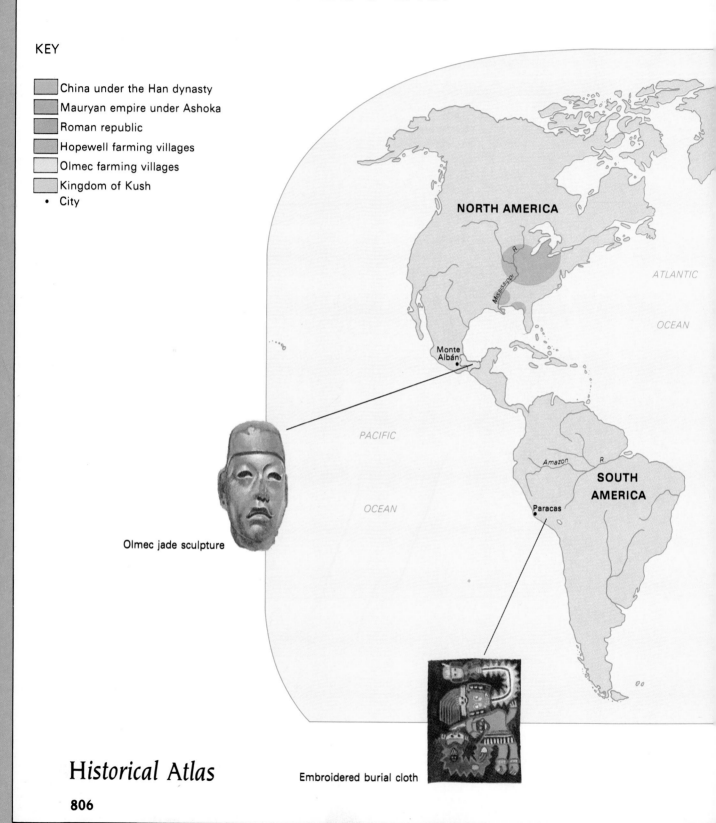

NORTH AMERICA

ATLANTIC

OCEAN

Mississippi

Monte
Albán

PACIFIC

OCEAN

Amazon

R

SOUTH
AMERICA

Paracas

Olmec jade sculpture

Embroidered burial cloth

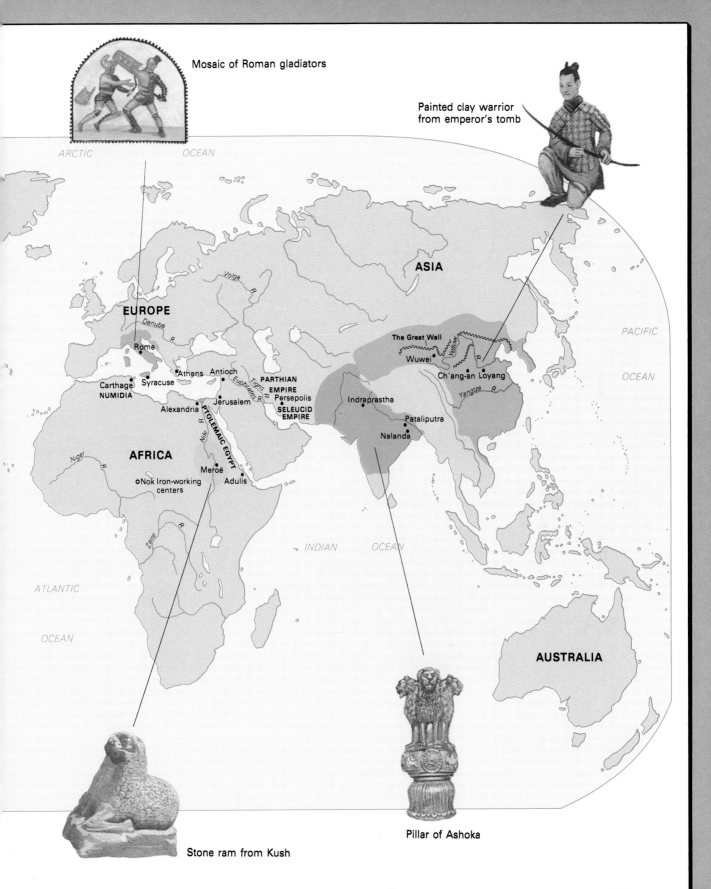

Mosaic of Roman gladiators

Painted clay warrior
from emperor's tomb

ARCTIC   OCEAN

ASIA

PACIFIC

Volga R

EUROPE

OCEAN

Danube R

The Great Wall

Rome

Wuwei

Yellow R

Athens Antioch

Ch'ang-an Loyang

Carthage Syracuse

PARTHIAN
EMPIRE

Yangtze R

NUMIDIA

Euphrates R

Tigris R

Persepolis

Indraprastha

Jerusalem

SELEUCID
EMPIRE

Pataliputra

Alexandria

PTOLEMAIC EGYPT

Nalanda

Niger R

AFRICA

Nile R

Meroë

Nok Iron-working
centers

Adulis

INDIAN   OCEAN

Zaire R

ATLANTIC

AUSTRALIA

OCEAN

Pillar of Ashoka

Stone ram from Kush

807

The World about 800

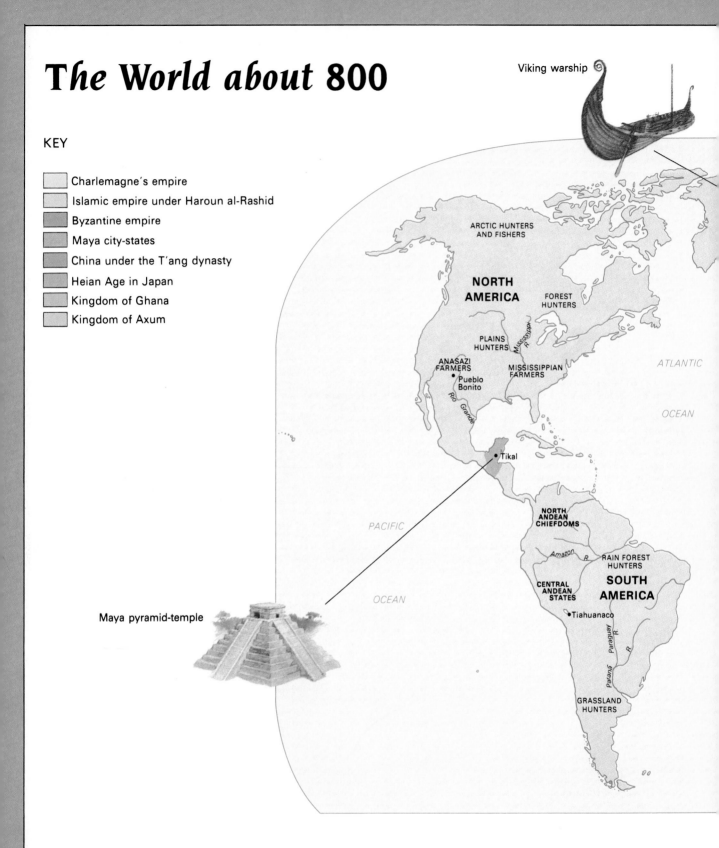

Viking warship

KEY

- Charlemagne's empire
- Islamic empire under Haroun al-Rashid
- Byzantine empire
- Maya city-states
- China under the T'ang dynasty
- Heian Age in Japan
- Kingdom of Ghana
- Kingdom of Axum

Maya pyramid-temple

ARCTIC HUNTERS AND FISHERS

NORTH AMERICA

FOREST HUNTERS

PLAINS HUNTERS

ANASAZI FARMERS
- Pueblo Bonito

MISSISSIPPIAN FARMERS

Mississippi R.

Rio Grande

- Tikal

ATLANTIC

OCEAN

PACIFIC

OCEAN

NORTH ANDEAN CHIEFDOMS

Amazon R.

RAIN FOREST HUNTERS

CENTRAL ANDEAN STATES

SOUTH AMERICA

- Tiahuanaco

Paraguay R.

Paraná R.

GRASSLAND HUNTERS

Historical Atlas

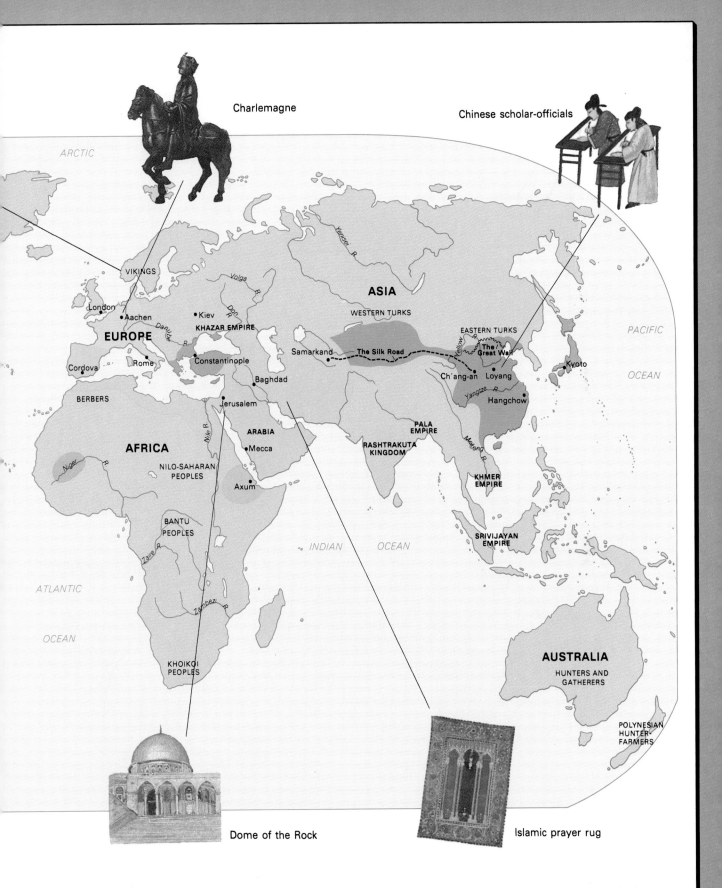

Charlemagne

Chinese scholar-officials

ARCTIC

VIKINGS

London

Aachen

EUROPE

Kiev

Volga R.

Don R.

Danube R.

KHAZAR EMPIRE

Cordova

Rome

Constantinople

Baghdad

Jerusalem

BERBERS

Nile R.

AFRICA

ARABIA

Mecca

NILO-SAHARAN PEOPLES

Niger R.

Axum

BANTU PEOPLES

Zaire R.

KHOIKOI PEOPLES

Zambezi R.

ATLANTIC

OCEAN

ASIA

Yenisei R.

WESTERN TURKS

EASTERN TURKS

Samarkand

The Silk Road

Yellow R.

The Great Wall

Ch'ang-an

Loyang

Kyoto

PACIFIC

OCEAN

Yangtze R.

Hangchow

Mekong R.

PALA EMPIRE

RASHTRAKUTA KINGDOM

KHMER EMPIRE

SRIVIJAYAN EMPIRE

INDIAN

OCEAN

AUSTRALIA

HUNTERS AND GATHERERS

POLYNESIAN HUNTER-FARMERS

Dome of the Rock

Islamic prayer rug

The World about 1250

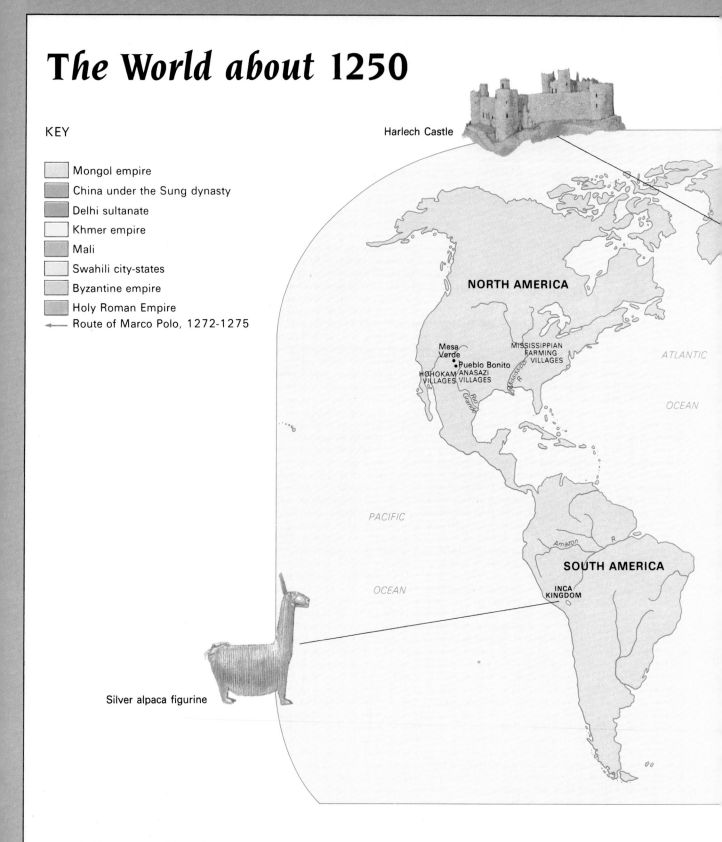

KEY

- Mongol empire
- China under the Sung dynasty
- Delhi sultanate
- Khmer empire
- Mali
- Swahili city-states
- Byzantine empire
- Holy Roman Empire
- ← Route of Marco Polo, 1272-1275

Harlech Castle

NORTH AMERICA

Mesa Verde

Pueblo Bonito

HOHOKAM VILLAGES ANASAZI VILLAGES

MISSISSIPPIAN FARMING VILLAGES

MISSISSIPPI R.

Rio Grande

ATLANTIC

OCEAN

PACIFIC

OCEAN

Amazon R.

SOUTH AMERICA

INCA KINGDOM

Silver alpaca figurine

Historical Atlas

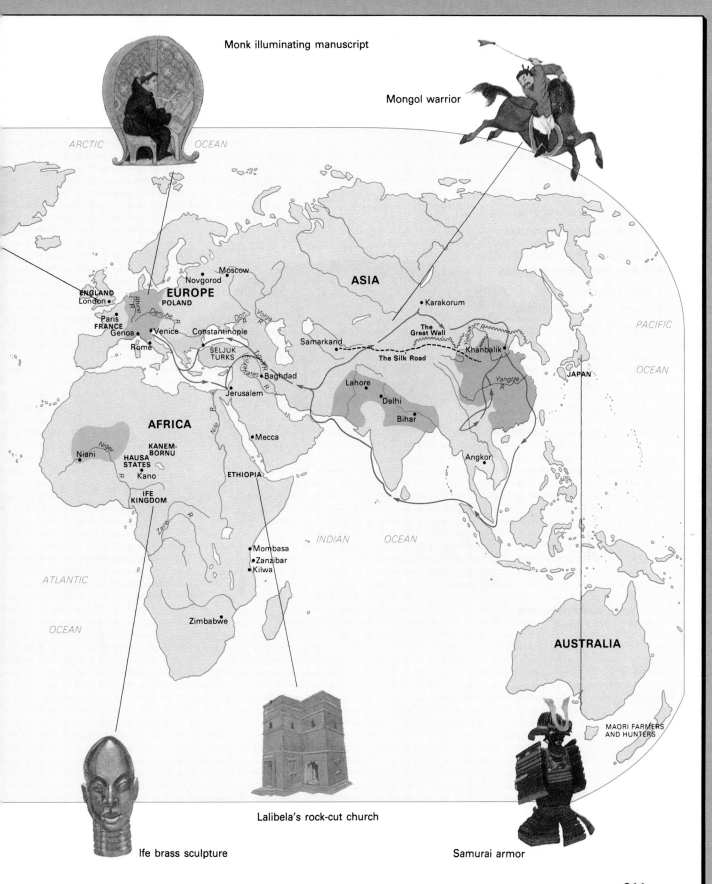

Monk illuminating manuscript

Mongol warrior

ARCTIC   OCEAN

Moscow
Novgorod

ASIA

ENGLAND
London
EUROPE
POLAND

• Karakorum

PACIFIC

Paris
FRANCE
Rhine R.
Danube R.
Don R.
Volga R.

The
Great Wall

Genoa
Venice
Rome
Constantinople

Samarkand

The Silk Road

Khanbalik

OCEAN

SELJUK
TURKS
Tigris R.
Euphrates R.
• Baghdad

Lahore

Yangtze R.

JAPAN

Jerusalem

• Delhi

Nile R.

Bihar

AFRICA

KANEM-
BORNU

• Mecca

Angkor

Niani
Niger R.
HAUSA
STATES
Kano

ETHIOPIA

IFE
KINGDOM
Zaire R.

• Mombasa
• Zanzibar
• Kilwa

INDIAN   OCEAN

ATLANTIC

Zimbabwe

OCEAN

AUSTRALIA

MAORI FARMERS
AND HUNTERS

Ife brass sculpture

Lalibela's rock-cut church

Samurai armor

811

The World about 1500

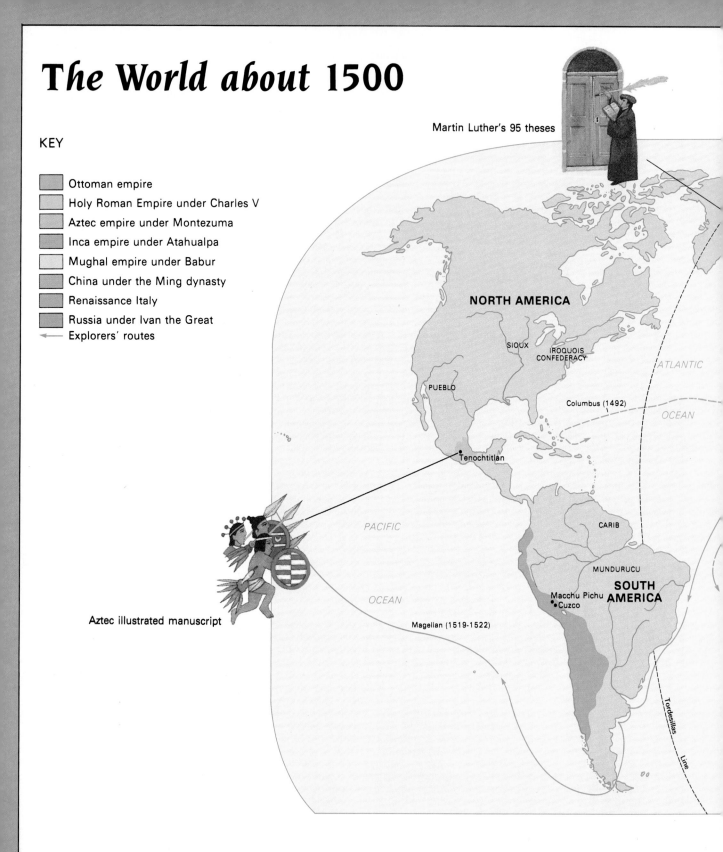

Martin Luther's 95 theses

KEY

- Ottoman empire
- Holy Roman Empire under Charles V
- Aztec empire under Montezuma
- Inca empire under Atahualpa
- Mughal empire under Babur
- China under the Ming dynasty
- Renaissance Italy
- Russia under Ivan the Great
- ← Explorers' routes

NORTH AMERICA

SIOUX

IROQUOIS
CONFEDERACY

PUEBLO

ATLANTIC

Columbus (1492)

OCEAN

Tenochtitlan

PACIFIC

CARIB

MUNDURUCU

SOUTH
AMERICA

Macchu Pichu
Cuzco

OCEAN

Magellan (1519-1522)

Tordesillas Line

Aztec illustrated manuscript

Historical Atlas

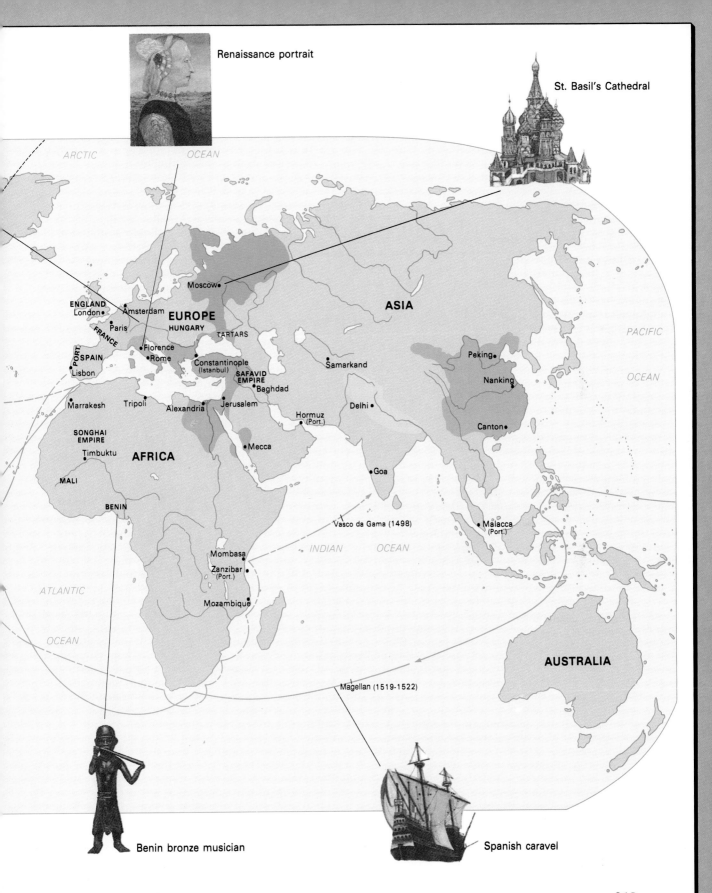

Renaissance portrait

St. Basil's Cathedral

ARCTIC   OCEAN

EUROPE
ENGLAND
London •
• Amsterdam
• Paris
HUNGARY
FRANCE
PORT.
SPAIN
Lisbon •
Florence •
• Rome
TARTARS
Constantinople
(Istanbul)
SAFAVID
EMPIRE
• Baghdad

Moscow •

ASIA

PACIFIC

OCEAN

Peking •
Nanking •

Samarkand •

Marrakesh •   Tripoli •   Alexandria •   Jerusalem •
• Mecca
Hormuz
(Port.)
Delhi •

Canton •

SONGHAI
EMPIRE
Timbuktu •
AFRICA

MALI

BENIN

• Goa

Vasco da Gama (1498)

Malacca
(Port.)

ATLANTIC

Mombasa •
Zanzibar
(Port.)
Mozambique •

INDIAN   OCEAN

OCEAN

AUSTRALIA

Magellan (1519-1522)

Benin bronze musician

Spanish caravel

The World about 1800

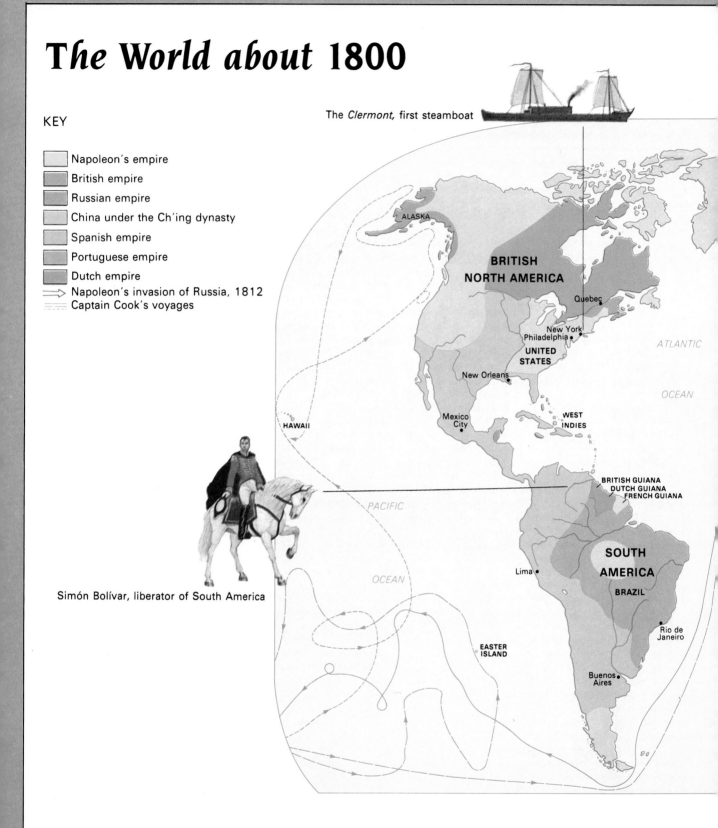

KEY

- Napoleon's empire
- British empire
- Russian empire
- China under the Ch'ing dynasty
- Spanish empire
- Portuguese empire
- Dutch empire
- ⟹ Napoleon's invasion of Russia, 1812
- Captain Cook's voyages

The *Clermont,* first steamboat

ALASKA

BRITISH NORTH AMERICA

Quebec

New York
Philadelphia

UNITED STATES

ATLANTIC

New Orleans

OCEAN

Mexico City

HAWAII

WEST INDIES

Simón Bolívar, liberator of South America

BRITISH GUIANA
DUTCH GUIANA
FRENCH GUIANA

PACIFIC

SOUTH AMERICA

Lima

BRAZIL

OCEAN

Rio de Janeiro

EASTER ISLAND

Buenos Aires

Historical Atlas

814

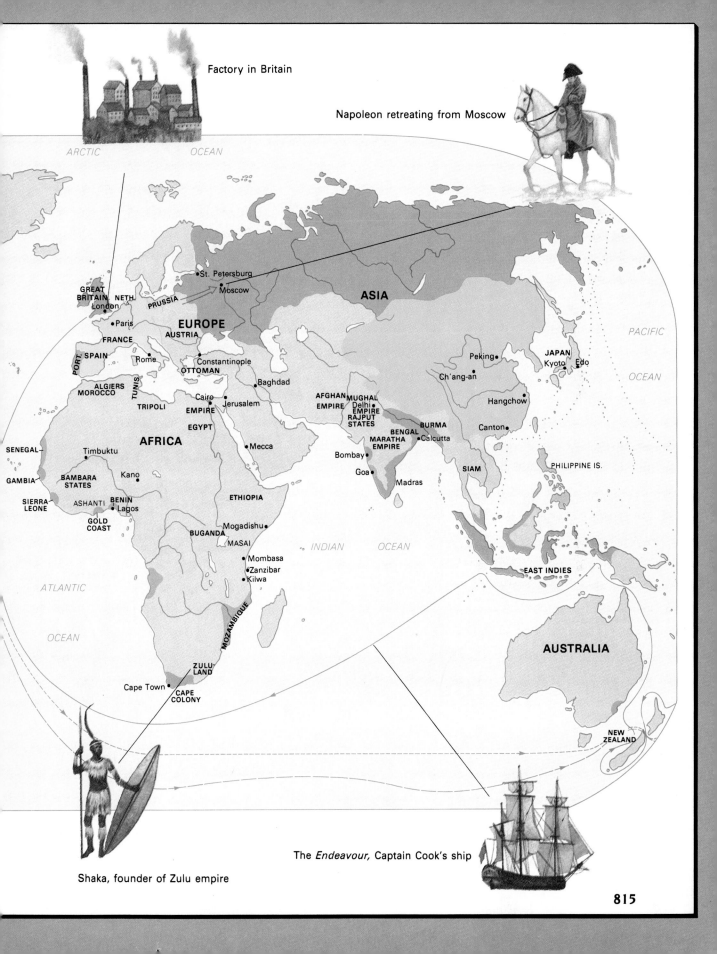

Factory in Britain

Napoleon retreating from Moscow

ARCTIC OCEAN

GREAT BRITAIN
NETH.
London
PRUSSIA
St. Petersburg
Moscow

ASIA

PACIFIC OCEAN

EUROPE
AUSTRIA
Paris
FRANCE
PORT.
SPAIN
Rome
Constantinople
OTTOMAN

JAPAN
Peking
Kyoto Edo
Ch'ang-an

ALGIERS
MOROCCO
TUNIS
TRIPOLI
EMPIRE
Cairo
Jerusalem

AFGHAN
EMPIRE
Delhi
MUGHAL
EMPIRE
RAJPUT
STATES

Hangchow

EGYPT

BENGAL
MARATHA
EMPIRE
Calcutta
BURMA
Canton

SENEGAL
Timbuktu
AFRICA
Mecca
Bombay
Goa
Madras
SIAM

GAMBIA
BAMBARA
STATES
Kano

SIERRA
LEONE
ASHANTI
BENIN
ETHIOPIA

GOLD
COAST
Lagos
BUGANDA
Mogadishu
MASAI

PHILIPPINE IS.

INDIAN OCEAN

Mombasa
Zanzibar
Kilwa

EAST INDIES

ATLANTIC

OCEAN

MOZAMBIQUE

AUSTRALIA

ZULU-
LAND
Cape Town
CAPE
COLONY

NEW
ZEALAND

The *Endeavour,* Captain Cook's ship

Shaka, founder of Zulu empire

The World about 1900

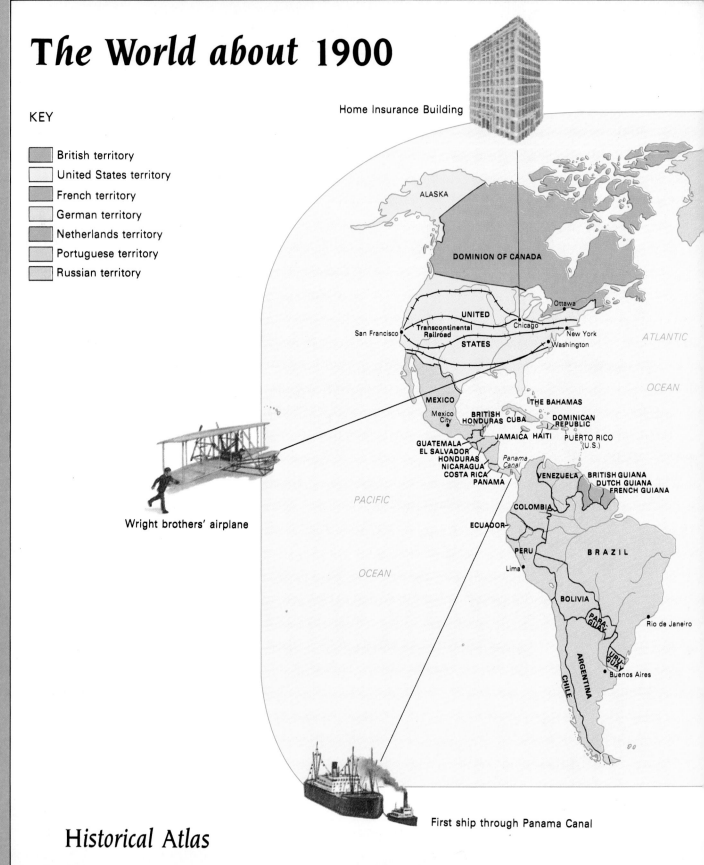

Home Insurance Building

KEY

- British territory
- United States territory
- French territory
- German territory
- Netherlands territory
- Portuguese territory
- Russian territory

ALASKA

DOMINION OF CANADA

UNITED
STATES

Transcontinental
Railroad

San Francisco
Chicago
Ottawa
New York
Washington

ATLANTIC

OCEAN

Wright brothers' airplane

MEXICO

Mexico
City

BRITISH
HONDURAS CUBA

THE BAHAMAS

DOMINICAN
REPUBLIC

GUATEMALA
EL SALVADOR
HONDURAS
NICARAGUA
COSTA RICA
PANAMA

JAMAICA HAITI

PUERTO RICO
(U.S.)

Panama
Canal

VENEZUELA

BRITISH GUIANA
DUTCH GUIANA
FRENCH GUIANA

COLOMBIA

ECUADOR

PACIFIC

PERU

Lima

BRAZIL

OCEAN

BOLIVIA

PARA-
GUAY

Rio de Janeiro

CHILE

ARGENTINA

URU-
GUAY

Buenos Aires

First ship through Panama Canal

Historical Atlas

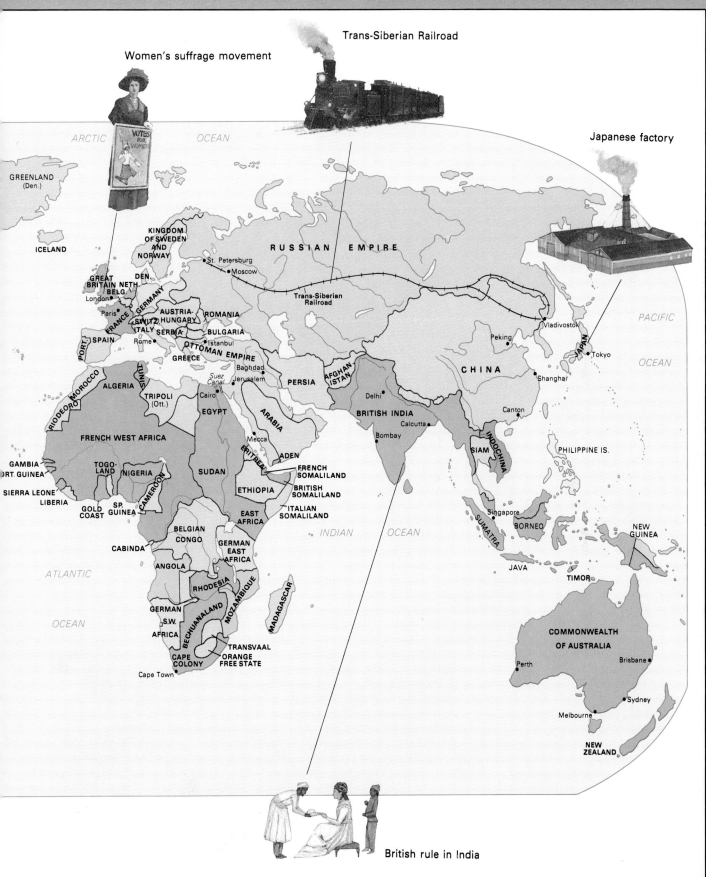

Women's suffrage movement

Trans-Siberian Railroad

Japanese factory

GREENLAND
(Den.)

ICELAND

ARCTIC   OCEAN

KINGDOM
OF SWEDEN
AND
NORWAY

RUSSIAN   EMPIRE

St. Petersburg

Moscow

GREAT
BRITAIN NETH.
BELG.

DEN.

London

GERMANY

Paris

FRANCE

SWITZ.

AUSTRIA-
HUNGARY

ROMANIA

ITALY

SERBIA

BULGARIA

PORT.

SPAIN

Rome

Istanbul

OTTOMAN EMPIRE

GREECE

Baghdad

Trans-Siberian
Railroad

Vladivostok

Peking

PACIFIC

Shanghai

JAPAN

Tokyo

OCEAN

CHINA

RIO DE ORO

MOROCCO

ALGERIA

TUNIS

TRIPOLI
(Ott.)

Cairo

Suez
Canal

Jerusalem

PERSIA

AFGHAN-
ISTAN

Delhi

EGYPT

ARABIA

BRITISH INDIA

Canton

FRENCH WEST AFRICA

Mecca

ERITREA

ADEN

Calcutta

Bombay

SIAM

INDOCHINA

PHILIPPINE IS.

GAMBIA

PORT. GUINEA

TOGO-
LAND

NIGERIA

SUDAN

FRENCH
SOMALILAND

SIERRA LEONE

LIBERIA

GOLD
COAST

SP.
GUINEA

CAMEROON

ETHIOPIA

BRITISH
SOMALILAND

Singapore

SUMATRA

BORNEO

NEW
GUINEA

EAST
AFRICA

ITALIAN
SOMALILAND

BELGIAN
CONGO

CABINDA

INDIAN   OCEAN

JAVA

TIMOR

GERMAN
EAST
AFRICA

ANGOLA

ATLANTIC

RHODESIA

MADAGASCAR

MOZAMBIQUE

COMMONWEALTH
OF AUSTRALIA

OCEAN

GERMAN
S.W.
AFRICA

BECHUANALAND

Perth

Brisbane

TRANSVAAL

CAPE
COLONY

ORANGE
FREE STATE

Cape Town

Sydney

Melbourne

NEW
ZEALAND

British rule in India

The Modern World

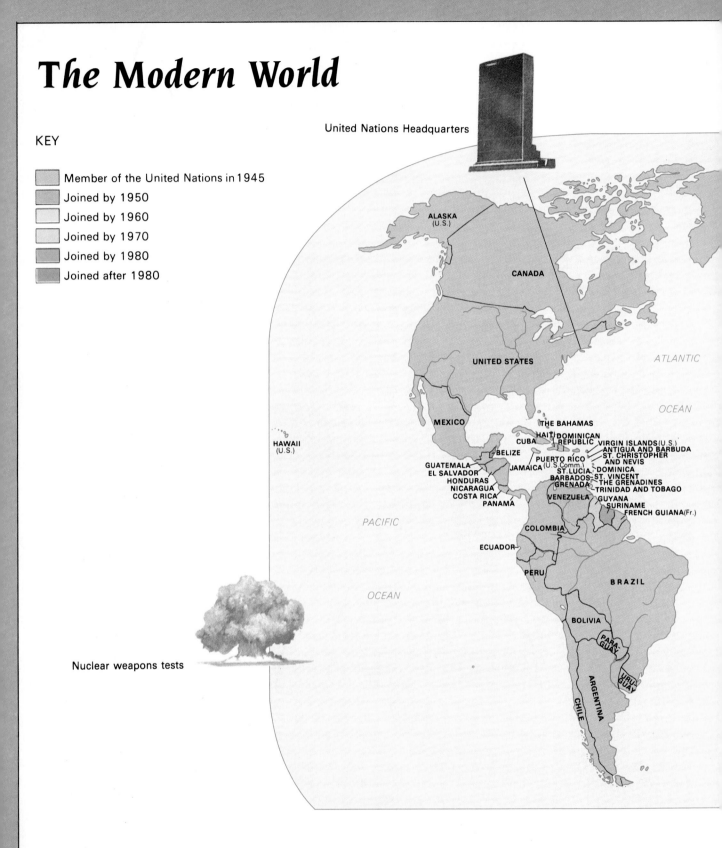

KEY

- Member of the United Nations in 1945
- Joined by 1950
- Joined by 1960
- Joined by 1970
- Joined by 1980
- Joined after 1980

United Nations Headquarters

Nuclear weapons tests

ALASKA (U.S.)

CANADA

UNITED STATES

ATLANTIC

OCEAN

MEXICO

HAWAII (U.S.)

THE BAHAMAS

HAITI
DOMINICAN
REPUBLIC

CUBA

VIRGIN ISLANDS (U.S.)
ANTIGUA AND BARBUDA
ST. CHRISTOPHER
AND NEVIS

BELIZE

PUERTO RICO
(U.S. Comm.)

GUATEMALA
EL SALVADOR
HONDURAS
NICARAGUA
COSTA RICA
PANAMA

JAMAICA

ST. LUCIA
BARBADOS
GRENADA

DOMINICA
ST. VINCENT
THE GRENADINES
TRINIDAD AND TOBAGO

VENEZUELA

GUYANA
SURINAME
FRENCH GUIANA (Fr.)

COLOMBIA

ECUADOR

PERU

BRAZIL

BOLIVIA

PARA-
GUAY

URU-
GUAY

ARGENTINA

CHILE

PACIFIC

OCEAN

Historical Atlas

818

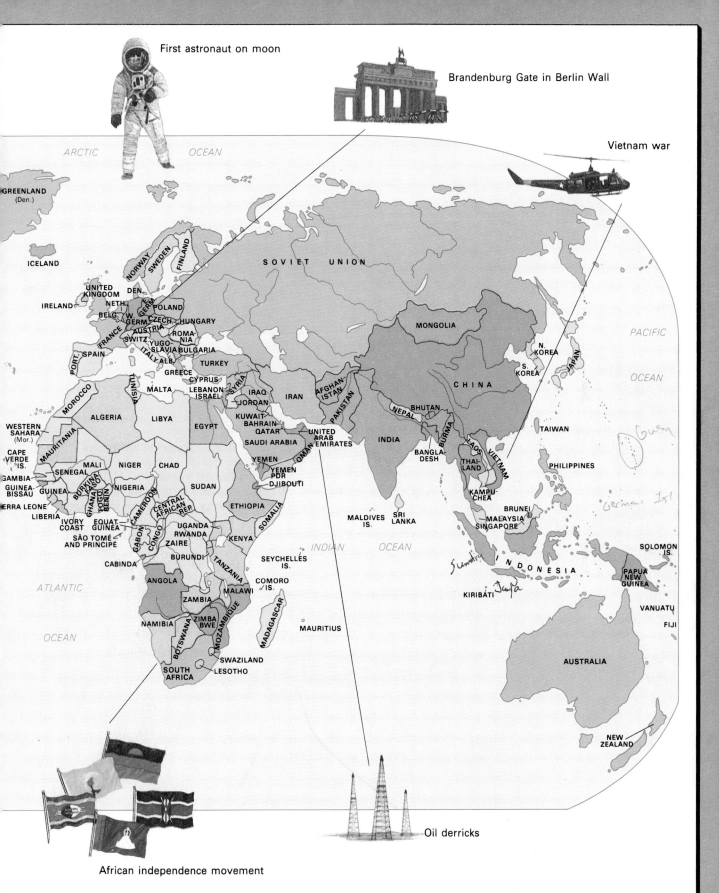

First astronaut on moon

Brandenburg Gate in Berlin Wall

Vietnam war

GREENLAND
(Den.)

ARCTIC   OCEAN

ICELAND

NORWAY   SWEDEN   FINLAND

SOVIET   UNION

UNITED
KINGDOM   DEN.

IRELAND   NETH.

BELG.   E.
GERM   POLAND

FRANCE   W.
GERM   CZECH.   HUNGARY

SWITZ.   AUSTRIA

ITALY   YUGO-
SLAVIA   ROMA-
NIA

ALB.   BULGARIA

PORT.   SPAIN

MONGOLIA

PACIFIC

N.
KOREA

S.
KOREA   JAPAN

OCEAN

GREECE

CYPRUS

TURKEY

MALTA

TUNISIA

MOROCCO

LEBANON
ISRAEL   SYRIA

IRAQ

JORDAN

IRAN

AFGHAN-
ISTAN

PAKISTAN

CHINA

TAIWAN

WESTERN
SAHARA
(Mor.)

ALGERIA

LIBYA

EGYPT

KUWAIT
BAHRAIN
QATAR

UNITED
ARAB
EMIRATES

OMAN

NEPAL   BHUTAN

BURMA

INDIA

BANGLA-
DESH

LAOS   VIETNAM

THAI-
LAND

PHILIPPINES

MAURITANIA

CAPE
VERDE
IS.

SAUDI ARABIA

YEMEN

YEMEN
PDR

DJIBOUTI

MALI

NIGER

CHAD

SUDAN

ETHIOPIA

SENEGAL

GAMBIA

GUINEA-
BISSAU

GUINEA

ERRA LEONE

LIBERIA

IVORY
COAST

BURKINA
FASO

GHANA   TOGO
BENIN

NIGERIA

EQUAT.
GUINEA

CAMEROON

CENTRAL
AFRICAN
REP.

UGANDA
RWANDA

SOMALIA

KAMPU-
CHEA

BRUNEI

MALAYSIA

SINGAPORE

MALDIVES
IS.

SRI
LANKA

INDIAN   OCEAN

SÃO TOMÉ
AND PRINCIPÉ

GABON   CONGO   ZAIRE

KENYA

BURUNDI

TANZANIA

CABINDA

ANGOLA

ZAMBIA

MALAWI

COMORO
IS.

SEYCHELLES
IS.

INDONESIA

SOLOMON
IS.

PAPUA
NEW
GUINEA

KIRIBATI

ATLANTIC

NAMIBIA

BOTSWANA   ZIMBA-
BWE

MOZAMBIQUE

MADAGASCAR

MAURITIUS

VANUATU

FIJI

OCEAN

SOUTH
AFRICA

SWAZILAND

LESOTHO

AUSTRALIA

NEW
ZEALAND

African independence movement

Oil derricks

819

a

abdicate: To resign as ruler. (p. 603)

absolute monarch: A ruler with unlimited power. (p. 409)

aid: A grant of money that a vassal gives to a lord. (p. 203)

anarchist: A person who believes that all governments are evil and therefore should be overthrown. (p. 575)

apartheid: South Africa's legal system of rigid separation between blacks and whites. (p. 756)

appeasement: The policy of making concessions in the hope of avoiding war. (p. 659)

apprentice: A person who is learning a trade or craft from a master and who works without pay except for room and board. (p. 213)

archaeologist: A person who studies the remains of ancient societies to learn about past ways of life. (p. 12)

arete: The ideal of striving for excellence, showing courage, and winning fame and honor. (p. 99)

aristocracy: A government dominated by a small group of noble families. (p. 101)

armistice: An agreement to stop fighting. (p. 595)

artisan: A skilled worker who makes goods by hand. (p. 28)

assembly line: A line of factory workers and machinery along which a product passes with each worker doing a specialized task until the product is complete. (p. 560)

autocrat: A ruler with unlimited power; an absolute ruler. (p. 604)

b

balance of power: A defensive strategy in which weak countries join together to match or exceed the power of a stronger country. (p. 413)

balance of trade: The difference in value between a country's imports and its exports. (p. 410)

barter: A form of trade in which people exchange goods without the use of money. (p. 31)

bishop: A church official who sets moral standards and supervises the finances of several local churches. (p. 153)

bourgeoisie: In medieval France, people who live in burghs or towns rather than in rural areas (p. 211); according to Marx, the factory-owning middle class. (p. 516)

boyar: A Russian noble who owns a large estate. (p. 253)

buffer zone: A region that lies between two rivals, cutting down the threat of conflict. (p. 693)

burgher: A person who lives in a walled town, or a burgh. (p. 211)

c

cabinet: An executive committee chosen by the head of a country to help make government decisions. (p. 439)

caliph: An Islamic leader who holds both political and religious power. (p. 178)

canon law: The law of the Roman Catholic Church. (p. 216)

capitalism: An economic system characterized by the investment of money in business ventures with the goal of making a profit. (p. 373)

caravel: A ship developed in the 1400's with triangular sails for tacking into the wind and square sails for running before the wind. (p. 335)

cardinal: A leading bishop in the Roman Catholic Church. (p. 215)

caste: A rigid social group, membership in which is determined at birth and never changes during a person's life; in Hinduism, caste is linked to religious purity. (p. 72)

cataract: A set of rapids in a river, blocking the passage of boats. (p. 48)

caudillo: A dictator, usually an army officer, of a Latin American country. (p. 504)

chivalry: A code of ideals demanding that a knight aid the poor, defend the weak, and fight bravely for his three masters—his earthly feudal lord, his heavenly Lord, and his chosen lady. (p. 226)

city-state: A political unit made up of a city and the surrounding countryside that is under the control of the city. (p. 30)

civilization: A form of culture that includes cities, specialized workers, writing, advanced technology, and complex institutions. (p. 27)

civil service: Workers employed by a government to carry out its daily functions such as repairing roads, delivering mail, collecting taxes, and so on. (p. 142)

clan: A group of people who are descended from the same ancestor. (p. 275)

coalition: A temporary alliance between groups who are usually on different sides. (p. 455)

colony: A settlement in a new territory by a group of people who keep their ties to their home government; a region governed by a foreign power. (p. 101)

common law: The unified body of law that developed, case by case, from the rulings of England's royal judges and became common to the whole kingdom. (p. 221)

condominium: A country ruled jointly by two other countries. (p. 536)

conquistador: A Spanish soldier and fortune hunter who took part in the conquest of the Americas. (p. 364)

constitutional monarchy: A government led by a ruler whose power is limited by law. (p. 439)

consul: A powerful official in the Roman republic who commanded the army and directed the government. (p. 126)

corporation: A business owned by stockholders who share in its profits but are not personally responsible for its debts. (p. 513)

count: A powerful landowner who ruled a county in a king's name, administered justice, and raised armies. (p. 196)

coup: A sudden takeover of a country's government. (p. 458)

crop rotation: The system of growing a different crop in a field each year to preserve the fertility of the land. (p. 473)

crusader: A person who fights on behalf of a religious or moral cause. (p. 228)

culture: The way of life that a group of people develops and passes on to its children; culture includes language, tools, skills, beliefs, and traditions. Every human group has a culture. Civilization is one form of culture. (p. 14)

cuneiform: An ancient form of writing that used wedge-shaped symbols. (p. 28)

czar: The Russian emperor. (p. 252)

d

daimyo: A feudal lord in Japan who commanded a private army of samurai. (p. 278)

delta: A broad, triangular, marshy region at the mouth of a river. (p. 48)

democracy: A government in which the citizens hold the final power. (p. 103)

dictator: In Rome, a political leader elected for a limited time and given absolute power to make laws and command the army; later any political leader who takes on such powers, usually without legal basis. (p. 126)

dissident: A person who expresses an opinion that differs from those held by the general society. (p. 724)

divine right: The idea that rulers receive their authority from God and are answerable only to God. (p. 398)

dynasty: A series of rulers from a single family. (p. 52)

e

edict: A public announcement of a policy. (p. 75)

emigration: The departure from a country to live elsewhere. (p. 514)

empire: A state that conquers other lands and then rules them. (p. 34)

enclosure: The process by which wealthy landowners buy the open fields in a village, fence them, and then rent them to tenant farmers who work the land. (p. 473)

enlightened despot: An absolute ruler who uses his or her power for the good of the people he or she rules. (p. 436)

entrepreneur: A person who organizes, manages, and takes on the risks of running a business. (p. 477)

epic: A long poem that tells the story of a historical or legendary hero. (p. 98)

excommunicate: To cut off from the church. (p. 173)

executive: Having to do with the branch of government that carries out the laws. (p. 434)

f

factory: A building where goods are manufactured. (p. 476)

fascism: A political movement that believes in an extreme form of nationalism—denying individual rights, insisting upon the supremacy of the state, and advocating dictatorial one-party rule. (p. 653)

federal: A form of government in which power is shared between the national government and the governments of the separate states. (p. 445)

feudalism: A political and military system based on the holding of land, with an emphasis on local protection, local government, and local self-sufficiency. (p. 201)

fief: The piece of land given to a vassal by a lord. (p. 202)

friar: A member of a Roman Catholic religious order who takes the same vows as a monk but travels about preaching instead of living in a monastery. (p. 217)

fundamentalism: religion emphasizing obedience to basic laws (762)

g

genocide: The intentional killing of an entire people. (p. 677)

gentry: A social class ranking below nobles but above common people; in Chinese society, the class of scholar-officials. (p. 263)

gravitas: The Roman virtue of weightiness or seriousness, related to the qualities of discipline, strength, and loyalty. (p. 123)

gross national product: The total value of goods and services produced by a country in a year. (p. 730)

guerrillas: Bands of fighters who are not part of a formal army and who usually attack by surprise and withdraw swiftly. (p. 463)

guild: An association of people who work at the same occupation. (p. 213)

h

heretic: A person whose ideas are incorrect in the opinion of the Church. (p. 173)

hieroglyphics: A form of writing based on pictorial characters that developed in Egypt. (p. 62)

hoplite: A soldier of ancient Greece who fought on foot with a shield and a spear. (p. 101)

humanist: One who studies classical texts. (p. 326)

i

ideology: A system of beliefs that influences political, social, and economic actions. (p. 691)

immigration: The act of entering and settling in a country other than one's native country. (p. 514)

imperialism: The policy of extending one country's rule over many lands. (p. 533)

import quota: A limit that one country sets on the amount of goods that may be brought in from another country. (p. 709)

inflation: An overall rise in the prices of goods and services. (p. 155)

institution: A long-lasting pattern of organization in a society. Governments, families, education systems, and organized religions are examples of institutions. (p. 29)

interdict: An order from the pope prohibiting Church ceremonies in the lands of a ruler who is disobedient to the pope. (p. 216)

investiture: A feudal ceremony in which a vassal receives land or a bishop takes office; an act that symbolically confirms an agreement through the exchange of objects. (p. 202)

isolationism: The idea that a country should avoid political or military alliances with other countries. (p. 648)

j

jihad: In Islam, a holy war. (p. 177)

joint-stock company: A business arrangement in which many investors together raise money for a venture too large for any of them to undertake alone. They share the profits in proportion to the amount they invested. (p. 392)

journeyman: A person who, after completing an apprenticeship, works at a craft for wages under the supervision of a master. (p. 213)

judicial: Having to do with the branch of government that interprets the laws. (p. 434)

jury: A group of people sworn to give a verdict based on evidence in a court of law; in medieval England, usually 12 neighbors who answered questions about the facts of a case for a royal judge. (p. 221)

k

khan: The leader of a group of Mongols. (p. 268)

knight: An armored warrior who fought on horseback. (p. 193)

l

legislative: Having to do with the branch of government that makes the laws. (p. 434)

lineage: A group of families—including past generations, living members, and future generations—descended from a common ancestor. (p. 300)

literacy: The ability to read and write. (p. 36)

lord: In the feudal system, the person who makes a grant of land to another person (the vassal). (p. 202)

m

maat: In ancient Egypt, the idea of goodness that included justice, right, truth, and order. (p. 60)

mandate: A territory that was administered on behalf of the League of Nations until it was judged ready for independence. (p. 598)

manor: A small estate from which a lord's family gained its livelihood. (p. 204)

martial law: Law that is enforced by military authorities over the civilian population of a country as if the country were in a state of war. (p. 720)

mercantilism: An economic theory under which a country increases its wealth by exporting more goods than it imports. (p. 410)

mercenary: A soldier who fights in any country's army for pay. (p. 128)

militarism: Glorification of armed strength. (p. 586)

mobilize: To position an army for war. (p. 587)

monastery: A religious community of men or women who give up all their possessions and devote their lives to worship and prayer. (p. 191)

monopoly: The situation in which a single company controls an entire industry. (p. 513)

monotheist: A person who believes in one God. (p. 36)

monsoon: A seasonal wind that blows dry air part of the year and then shifts directions, bringing heavy rainfall the other part of the year. (p. 67)

multinational corporation: A company that has branches in many countries. (p. 767).

n

nationalism: A feeling of loyalty to one's own land and people (p. 245); the belief that one's greatest loyalty should be to a nation-state. (p. 495)

nationalize: To bring under government control. (p. 635)

nation-state: A group of people who share similar traditions, history, and language, who occupy a definite territory, and who are united under one government. (p. 240)

nihilism: A belief that the existing society and government must be destroyed so that a better society can be created. (p. 606)

nomad: A person who has no permanent home and moves from place to place. (p. 16)

o

oasis: A place in a desert where underground water comes to the surface in a spring or well. (p. 299)

p

patriarch: The bishop of Constantinople, head of the Eastern Orthodox Church. (p. 173)

patrician: In ancient Rome, a member of the privileged upper class. (p. 123)

phalanx: A Greek army unit made up of soldiers standing side by side, their shields forming a solid wall. (p. 101)

pharaoh: A king of Egypt, considered a god. (p. 52)

philosophes: A group of thinkers in the early 1700's who believed in reason, liberty, natural law, progress, and human happiness. (p. 429)

plebeian: A common farmer, artisan, or merchant in ancient Rome; a plebeian was a free citizen with the right to vote. (p. 124)

plebiscite: An election in which all citizens vote yes or no on an issue. (p. 459)

polis: A Greek city-state. (p. 100)

polytheist: A person who believes in more than one god. (p. 32)

pope: The bishop of Rome, head of the Roman Catholic Church. (p. 154)

predestination: The doctrine that God has known since the beginning of time who will be saved. (p. 354)

prehistory: The period of time before the beginning of written records. (p. 13)

prime minister: The leader of the majority party in a country's parliament. The prime minister heads the cabinet. (p. 440)

productivity: A worker's hourly output of goods and services. (p. 712)

proletariat: The poorest class in ancient Rome (p. 131); according to Marx, the urban working class. (p. 516)

propaganda: One-sided information designed to convince people of a certain point of view. (p. 591)

prophet: A messenger sent to reveal God's will. (p. 38)

protectorate: A country whose foreign policy is controlled by an outside government. (p. 536)

purdah: The practice of keeping women in seclusion. (p. 291)

pyramid: An immense structure used as a tomb by the pharaohs. (p. 52)

r

rationing: A system limiting the amount of goods people can buy during a time of shortage. (p. 590)

reincarnation: The idea that the inner self is reborn in another form. (p. 71)

reparations: Compensation paid after a war by a defeated nation for the damages it caused other nations. (p. 598)

republic: A government under which citizens with the right to vote choose their leaders. (p. 123)

s

samurai: A Japanese warrior who fought for his lord and lived according to the code of bushido. (p. 277)

satellite: A country whose policies are dictated or heavily influenced by another country. (p. 696)

satire: Literature that mocks society for its foolishness and wickedness. (p. 147)

savanna: A grassy plain with a few scattered trees. (p. 299)

self-determination: Free choice of people in a territory to decide under what government they wish to live. (p. 596)

senate: In ancient Rome, the aristocratic branch of government. (p. 126)

separation of powers: The idea that governmental power should be divided among three branches—executive, legislative, and judicial—so that no single branch can become a threat to liberty. (p. 434)

separatism: A movement for the creation of an independent state (p. 771)

serf: A peasant who was bound to a manor and owed duties to the lord of the manor. (p. 204)

shaykh: The leader of a group of Bedouin. (p. 629)

shogun: The supreme general of Japan's army, having the powers of a military dictator. (p. 277)

socialism: The belief that the wealth of a country should be shared equally among all its citizens. (p. 515)

society: A lasting group of people who have a network of relationships with one another. (p. 14)

soviet: A workers' council that has political powers and organizes political activities. (p. 611)

sphere of influence: A region dominated but not directly ruled by a foreign nation. (p. 543)

steppe: A vast stretch of dry grassland in Asia and eastern Europe. (p. 267)

stock: A share in the ownership of a business. (p. 513)

subcontinent: A large region that is part of a continent, yet separated from the rest of the continent in some way. (p. 67)

suffrage: The right to vote. (p. 517)

sultan: An Islamic ruler who has political power but not religious authority. (p. 183)

superconductor: a material with little or no resistance to the transmitting of electricity (p. 785)

t

tariff: A tax on goods imported from another country. (p. 410)

technology: The part of a culture that includes tools and the skills to make and use them. (p. 16)

theocracy: A government controlled by church leaders. (p. 354)

totalitarianism: A political system in which the government has total control over the lives of individual citizens. (p. 618)

tragedy: A play that portrays men and women of heroic character whose very strength leads to their downfall. (p. 109)

tribune: A Roman official elected by the assembly to speak on behalf of the plebeians. (p. 132)

triumvirate: A group of three political leaders who ruled Rome. (p. 135)

tyrant: In ancient Greece, a man who took over the government by force but usually supported the interest of the common people against the nobles. (p. 101)

u

ultimatum: A final demand that, if not met, will end negotiations and lead to war. (p. 586)

union: A group of workers in a trade or industry who join together to bargain for better working conditions and higher wages. (p. 487)

v

vassal: A person who receives land from a lord and pledges military service in return. (p. 202)

vernacular: The everyday language of a region or country. (p. 325)

veto: To overrule another's decision. (p. 126)

viceroy: A person who governs on behalf of a king; in Spain's empire, a noble who governed a part of Spain's territory in the Americas. (p. 367)

villa: A country estate. (p. 150)

w

welfare state: A country in which the government assumes responsibility for people's welfare in terms of employment, retirement, and medical care. (p. 711)

North Africa (continued)
War II, 749. *See also* Africa
North America: geography of, 309,
*m*309, 767; Indians of, 310–312,
*m*311
**North Atlantic Treaty Organization
(NATO),** 699, 710, 716
Northern Ireland, 713. *See also*
Ireland
North Korea, 703–705, 794. *See
also* Korea
North Sea, 713
Norway, 354, 575, 667–668, 699
Nova Scotia, 413
Novgorod, 182
Nubian slaves, 55, 60
Nuclear power, 791
Nuclear war, threat of, 694, 794,
796
Nuclear weapons. *See* Weapons
Numidia, 128, 130
Nuremberg trials, 696
Nursing, 565–566
Nyerere, Julius, 753

Obregón, Alvaro, 633
O'Connell, Daniel, 505
O'Connor, Sandra Day, 769
Octavian. *See* Augustus (Octavian),
Roman Emperor
October War, 761
Odoacer, 159
Odyssey **(Homer),** 98–99
Oedipus **(Sophocles),** 109
Oil: U.S. industry, 513; in Middle
East, 631, 759, 762, 793; in Latin
America, U.S. interests in, 632,
634, 635, 774, 775–776; under
North Sea, 713; in Indonesia,
741–742; in Africa, 754, 755
Okinawa, 682
Old Stone Age. *See* Paleolithic Age
Olga, Russian princess, 182
Olmecs, 313
Olympia, 95
Olympic games, 95, 99–100, 570,
716, 737
Olympus, Mount, 95, 100
Omar, caliph, 178
*One Day in the Life of Ivan Deni-
sovich* **(Solzhenitsyn),** 724
*On the Revolutions of the Heav-
enly Bodies* **(Copernicus),** 358
On the Spirit of Laws **(Montes-
quieu),** 434
**OPEC (Organization of Petroleum
Exporting Countries),** *g*258, 259
Open-Door Policy, 547
Opera, 412, 433, 569, 787
Opium War, 544–545
Oral history, 301
Orange Free State, 540
Oregon Territory, 547
Origin of Species, The **(Darwin),**
562, 563
Orleans, 235, 246, 247
Osiris (god), 60–61, 62
Oslo, 668

Ostpolitik, 710, 711
Ostrogoths, 157, 158, 159, 168–169,
188, 192; religion of, 190
Otto I (the Great), German ruler,
223
Ottoman empire: Constantinople
falls to, 183–184, 201; defeated
by Spanish, 369; wars with Russia, 417, 437, 524, 605; decline of,
419, 524, 536, 575, 585, 627, 758;
Greek revolt against, 495–496;
and World War I, 593, 595, 598,
628
Owen, Robert, 515
Ozone layer, 790–791

Pacific Islands: explorations of, 431;
U.S. interests in, 552, 553; Euro-
pean interests in, 552, 553, 578;
and World War I, 594; and World
War II, 674–675, 682–683
Pacific Ocean, 338, 339, 431
Pacific Rim, 792, 800; economic
growth in, *c*800
Padua, 324
Pahlavi. *See* Muhammad Reza Shah
Pahlavi; Reza Shah Pahlavi
Pakistan, 67, 627, 738, 739, 740,
749
Palatine Hill, 121
Paleolithic Age, *p*12, *c*15, 15–19
Palestine, 36, 40, 56, 598; under
Romans, 151, 152; under Byzan-
tium, 174; Muslims in, 177; after
World War I, 627; Jews and Arabs
fight over, 629–631, 758, 759;
British rule in, 630–631, 701,
760; Israeli rule in, 759
Palestine Liberation Army (PLO),
761
Palestinians, 760, 762
Panama, 338, 552, 634, 779
Panama Canal, *p*551, 552–553, 634,
779
Pan-American Highway, 766–767
Pankhurst, Emmeline, 567
Pantheon, 148
Papal States, 194, 520
Paper, 63, 347
Paper money, 265
Papyrus, 63
Paradise Lost **(Milton),** 402
Paris, *m*468; in Middle Ages, 183,
211, 468; treaties of, 423–424,
445; in French Revolution, 452,
455; in revolution of 1848; 506–
507; workers' revolts, 516; and
Franco-Prussian War, 523; Com-
munards in, 524; and World War
I, 588; and World War II, 669,
681; student riots in, 715
Paris Commune, 455
Park, Mungo, 536
Parliament, English: established,
237–238; Model, 237–238; Henry
VIII and, 352; Reformation, 352;
Elizabeth I and, 393; James I
clashes with, 398; Charles I and

Petition of Right, 399, 400;
Cromwell and, 400, 401; Habeas
Corpus Act, 402–403; and Resto-
ration, 402, 404; and Glorious
Revolution, 404; Bill of Rights,
404–405; Corn Laws, 486; and In-
dustrial Revolution, 486–487;
powers in, 494, 505, 573; and
People's budget, 573
Parma, 519
Parr, Catherine, 353
Parthenon, *p*94, 107
**Partido Revolucionario Institucional
(PRI),** 775, 776
Pasternak, Boris, 619
Pasteur, Louis, 562, 563, 606
Pasteurization, 562
Pastoral Care **(Gregory),** 192
Pater familias, 123, 147
Pathet Lao, 745
Patriarch, 173
Patricians, 123–124, 125, 131
Patrick, missionary, 190
Patriotism, 497, 586
Paul, apostle, 152, 153
Paul III, pope, 356
Paul IV, pope, 356, 357
Pax Romana, 141–144, 146, 152,
153, 154, 256
Peace Corps, 779
Pearl Harbor, 673–674
Peasants: in Egypt, 59; in Greece,
102; in Rome, 150; of Middle
Ages, 204–205
Pease, Joseph, 472
Pedro I, of Brazil, 503
Peking: under Kublai Khan, 269,
272; under Mongols, 269, 270–
274; Marco Polo in, 270
Peloponnesian War, 111–112
Peloponnesus, 102
Pendulum, 360
Pennine Hills, 483, 484
People's Budget, 573
Peoples of the Sea, 56, 98
Pepin the Short, 193–194
Perestroika, 794
Pericles, 107, 109, 111, 112, 329;
funeral oration of, 111
Perón, Juan, 775
Perry, Matthew, 548
Persia: empire of, 42–44, *m*43, 57,
74, 86, 94–95, 115–117, 129, 151,
155, 173; government of, 43–44;
Royal Road of, 44; conquered by
Muslims, 177, 178, 179, 183; at-
tacked by Mongols, 268; in
1400's, 627; becomes Iran, 628,
631
Persian Gulf, 292, 763
Persian Wars, 94–95, 104–106,
*m*105, 107
Peru, 501, 634, 775; early civiliza-
tion in, 315, 339, 340, 366
Pétain, Henri, 669
Peter, apostle, 152, 153, 154
Peter I (the Great), czar, 414–419,
436, 438

Pyramids (continued)
the Mayas, 298, 299, 313; of the Toltecs, 314
Pyrrhus, Greek king, 127

Quebec, 771
Quetzalcoatl, 363, 364, 365

Rabelais, François, 379
Racine, Jean Baptiste, 412, 413
Radicalism, 493–494, 505, 506
Radio, 559–660, 646, 652, 693
Radioactivity, 564
Railroads, 751; and industrial growth, 478–480, 482, 511–512, 529; in Europe, 542–543; Trans-Siberian, 607; English Channel tunnel, 714
Raj, 542, 543–544
Rajputs, 286, 287, 288, 289, 290
Ramses II, Egyptian pharoah, 56
Raphael Santi, p326, 332, 334
Rasputin, 610
Rationing, 589, 590, 676
Ravel, Maurice, 569–570
Reagan, Ronald, 721, 779, 795
Realism, 517–518, 519
Realpolitik, 519, 521
Reason: versus faith, 225; philosophy of, 428, 429, 433–435; versus romanticism, 497–498
Reconquista, 249
Red Army, 638, 639, 671
Red Guards, 613, 735
Red Sea, 174, 761
Red Shirts, 520
Reed, John, 614
Reformation, 242, 348–356, m355
Reformation Parliament, 352
Reform bill, 505, 517
Refugees: in Africa, 755; in Middle East, 762; Cuban, 778
Region, geographic theme, 9, 162, 800
Reichstag, 572, 655, 665
Reign of Terror, 456–457, 493
Reincarnation, 71
Relativity, theory of, 646–647
Religion: in Neolithic Age, 21; organized, 30; in Sumer, 30, 31, 32, 36, 44; monotheism, 36–38; Judaism, 37–38; in Persia, 44; in ancient Egypt, 52–53, 54, 60–62; in ancient India, 66–67, 70–74, 76; in ancient China, 81–82, 86, 87; in ancient Greece, 100; in early Rome, 122; in Roman Empire, 145, 151–154, 156; effect on peoples of, 167; in Byzantine times, 172–181; monotheism, 174–175; in Russia, 182, 252, 415, 417, 618, 724–725; in the Middle Ages, 191, 214–218, 240–242; against Islam, 228–231; Crusades and trade, 241; in Germany, 242, 380–381; in Japan, 275, 279, 280; in Southeast Asia, 295; in early Africa, 300–301, 306; of the

Mayas, 313; of the Aztecs, 314–315; in Europe of 1400's, 345–351; Reformation, 348–356; in England, 352, 370, 390, 393, 398, 399, 403, 404; Counter-Reformation, 356–357; and division of Europe, 357–358, 364, 368–369, 372–376, 380–381; in Spain and Netherlands, 364, 369–370, 372–373; and Thirty Years' War, 364, 379–381, 409, 422; in France, 377–379, 411, 459; in Ireland, 573, 713; in the Middle East, 627–631, 758, 762; in North Africa, 758. *See also names of religions*
Religious persecution: in Rome, 153, 157; in England, 399; in France, 411, 428; in Germany, 656
Remarque, Erich Maria, 592
Rembrandt van Rijn, 375
Renaissance: time line of, 320–321; in northern Italy, 322–334, m324, 345; art and architecture of, 324, 327, 328–330, 332–334; compared to Middle Ages, 325, 326, 345; in northern Europe, 346
Renoir, Auguste, 568
Reparations, 598
Republic, 123, 373
Republic, The **(Plato),** 113
Revolutions of 1848, 505–506
Reza Shah Pahlavi, 628
Rhazes, 180
Rhineland, 598; Hitler's invasion of, 659–660
Rhine River, 158, 505, 708, 711
Rhodes, Cecil, 534, 536, 540
Ricci, Mateo, 273–274
Richard I (the Lionheart), king of England, 227, 230, 235
Richard III, king of England, 248
Richelieu, Cardinal, 378–379, 381, 409
Rig-Veda, 71, 72
Rio de Janeiro, 766, 774
Rio Grande River, 771
Roads: Roman, 142; during the Industrial Revolution, 478, 479; Pan-American Highway, 766–767
Robespierre, Maximilien, 456, 457
Rockefeller, John D., 513
Rocky Mountains, 309
Roland, 225–226
Rollo, Viking leader, 201, 202, 203, 220
Roman Catholic Church: pope as head of, 154, 173, 191, 228; Byzantine emperor as head of, 168, 173; Eastern Orthodox Church formed, 172–173, 231; in the Middle Ages, 190, 191, 194, 197, 215–216, 228, 231; role of monasteries, 190–191, 196, 215, 217–218, 352; popes and monarchs, 194, 197, 215–216, 351; abuses in, 215, 345, 348, 356; reform in, 215, 356; laws of, 216; Inquisi-

tion, 217; and the Crusades, 228; and feudalism, 235, 240–242; Great Schism, popes move to Avignon, 241–242, 324; Luther's challenge to, 345, 348–349; and Scientific Revolution, 345, 360; Reformation and, 348–356; Henry VIII breaks with, 351–353, 390; Jesuits, 356, 360; Council of Trent, 356–357; reforming popes, 356–357; Counter-Reformation, 357; Elizabeth I excommunicated, 390; wealth of, 449; French Revolution and, 449, 453; Napoleon and, 459. *See also* Catholicism
Romance languages, 189, 220, 499
Roman Empire, 137, m162; life in, 140–141, 150; Augustus' rule, 141–144; Christianity in, 141, 151–154, m153, 156–157; Pax Romana, 141–144, 146, 256; Greek culture in, 142, 145–150; Five Good Emperors, 142, 146; Julian emperors, 142–146; culture of, 142, 145–147, p148, 150, 189; citizenship in, 143; extent of, m144, 145, 146, m153, 158; religion in, 145, 151–153; government and law in, 149; society in, 149–150; fall of, 149, 154–159, 164, 256, 708; Jews in, 151–154; barbarian invasion of, 154, 155–156, 157–159, m158, 169, 188–189; trade in, m155, 256; division of 156, 157
Roman Forum, p148
Romania, 575, 585, 599, 671; after World War II, 696, 699, 720
Romanovs, 253, 414, 415, 603, 610, 643
Roman Republic, 120–137; army and warfare of, p120, 124, 125, 128, 133–134; established, 123; class structure in, 123–124, 125, 131–133; culture in, 123–124, p126, 136; daily life in, 124; government of, 125–127, 132–133, 135, 137; dictators of, 126–127, 134, 135; war with Greece, 127, 129–130; Punic Wars with Carthage, 127–131, 132; Hannibal's invasion of, 128; expansion to East, 129–130, m130, 137; end of, 130, 137; slavery in, 132; the Triumvirates, 134–135, 136; under Caesar, 134–136, 137; conquest of Gaul, 135; civil war in, 136–137
Romanticism, 495, 497–499, 517; and nationalism, 497, 499, 505, 519
Rome, 93, 117, 162; founding of, 120–124; invasion of the Gauls, 127; invasion of Germanic tribes, 133, 149, 159, 169, 192; in Roman Empire, 141, 147–148, m162; tax reform in, 150; Catholic Church in, 159, 191, 194, 241;

Text Credits

p. 50 From James B. Pritchard, ed., *The Ancient Near East: An Anthology of Texts and Pictures.* Copyright © 1958 by Princeton University Press. Excerpts reprinted with permission of Princeton University Press. p. 75 From *The Teachings of the Compassionate Buddha*, edited by E. A. Burtt, © 1955, published by Mentor. p. 214 From *English Historical Documents*, II, edited by D.C. Douglas and G.E. Greenaway, © 1961, published by Eyre and Spottiswoode, London, pages 969–970. p. 239 From *Memoirs of the Crusades*, Geoffrion de Villehardouin and Jean de Joinville, translated by Sir Frank T. Marziolo, © 1958, published by Dutton. p. 365 From *The Broken Spears* by Miguel Leon-Portilla, copyright © 1962 by the Beacon Press. Reprinted by permission of Beacon Press. p. 592 From *All Quiet on the Western Front*, Erich Maria Remarque, copyright 1929, 1930 by Little, Brown, and Company, copyright renewed 1957, 1958 by Erich Maria Remarque. p. 614 From *Ten Days that Shook the World* by John Reed, © 1960, published by Random House. p. 647 From "The Waste Land" by T.S. Eliot from *Collected Poems 1900–1935*, © 1963 by T.S. Eliot, published by Faber and Faber, Ltd. p. 656 From article by Francis H. Schott in *The New York Times*, November 9, 1988. pp. 664, 665 From *For Those I Loved*, Martin Gray, translated from the French by Anthony White, © 1972 by Little, Brown, and Company and the Bodley Head. p. 677 From *New Voices* by Primo Levi, translated from the Italian by Ruth Feldman, © 1986, Summit Books, a division of Simon and Schuster, Inc. p. 693 From speech by Joseph Stalin, quoted in *Vital Speeches*, March 1, 1946. p. 736 From *U.S. News and World Report*, article by Winston Lord, September 8, 1986, page 33. p. 796 From speech by Mikhail Gorbachev, quoted in *The New York Times*, December 8, 1988.

Maps

p. 256 From *A History of Western Society*, Third Edition, by McKay, Hill, Buckler, © 1987, published by Houghton Mifflin Company, page 334. p. 468 From *The French Kings* by Frederic V. Greenfeld, © 1982, published by Stonehenge Press, Inc., pages 8–9. p. 318 From *Lost Empires, Living Tribes* and *Peoples of the Past: The Aztecs*

Tables and Graphs

p. 711 From *The New York Times*, Oct. 23, 1988. p. 758 From *The New York Times*, Oct. 2, 1988.

Art Credits:

Photo Research: Carole Frohlich
Art Editor: Penny Peters
Maps: Charthouse/Dick Pusey
Illustrations: pp. 31, 53, 101, 108, 148, 202, 205, 211, 219, 272, 804–818, 318, 397, Tony Smith, Virgil Pomfret Agency
Graphs and charts: pp. 36, 62r, 330, 479, 483, James R. Hamilton; Graph p. 464, after Charles Joseph Minard, 1861; Graphs and charts pp. 475, 514, 578, 651, 711, 722, 758, 767, 793, 800, Fern Sandhouse
Unit opener silhouettes: Pamela R. Levy
Time line illustrations: pp. 92tl, 93tr, 164r, 321l, 387r, 580l, Leslie Evans
Chapter review time lines: James R. Hamilton

Cover: Robert Frerck/Odyssey Productions

Title page: R. Vroom/Miller Services/Photo Researchers

Contents: v Hirmer Verlag München. vi Metropolitan Museum of Art (**MMA**), Rogers Fund, 1917 (17.230.14a,b). vii C.M. Dixon Colour Photo Library. viii Gemini Smith Inc. La Jolla © Bradley Smith. ix Independence National Historical Park Collection. xt (detail) Historisches Museen der Stadt Wien. xb Science Museum, London/Michael Holford. xi ET Archive Ltd. xii Bill Strode/Woodfin Camp & Associates. xiii National Aeronautics and Space Administration (**NASA**).

Introduction: 1 © 1988 Dallas & Heaton/TSW-CLICK/Chicago. 2l Michael Holford; m Courtesy, Audemars Piguet, N.Y.; r Science Museum, London/A.C. Cooper Ltd. photographer. 4 Michael Holford. 5 GEOPIC™, Earth Satellite Corporation. 7 Robert Frerck/Odyssey Productions. 8t, bl Robert Frerck/Odyssey Productions; r Anne Bolt.

Unit I: 10l Scala/Art Resource; m Cultural Relics Bureau, Beijing, and MMA; tr Jehangir Gazdar/Woodfin Camp & Associates. 11bl, t Michael Holford; br © 1988 Dallas & Heaton/TSW-CLICK/Chicago. 12 Amplicaciones y Reproducciones "MAS." 14 Peter Menzel. 16tl Courtesy, Institut Royal des Sciences Naturelles de Belgique, Brussels; bl Michael Holford; tr Courtesy, Wiltshire Archaeological & Natural History Society, Devizes, England; br Lee Boltin Picture Library. 17 Michael Holford. 18 Irven DeVore/Anthro-Photo. 19 © Alexander Marshack 1972. 21 Elizabeth Zeschin. 22l Courtesy of The Oriental Institute of the University of Chicago; r By Courtesy of the Board of Trustees of the Victoria and Albert Museum, London. 23 Reproduced by Courtesy of the Trustees of the British Museum (**BM**). 26 Standard of Ur, peace panel. BM. 29t Michael Holford; b Hirmer Verlag München. 32 Scala/Art Resource (**AR**). 33 Courtesy of The Oriental Institute of the University of Chicago. 35 Hirmer Verlag München. 37 Jewish Museum/Art Resource. 38 A. Louis Goldman/Photo Researchers. 40 BM. 41 Erich Lessing/Magnum. 47 Lee Boltin Picture Library. 51t (detail) Egyptian Expedition of MMA, Rogers Fund, 1930 (30.4.44); b Jean Vertut. 53 Michael Holford. 55 John G. Ross/Mediterranean Archives. 56 George Holton/Photo Researchers. 58 BM/Michael Holford. 59t BM; b Reproduced by permission of the Syndics of the Fitzwilliam Museum, Cambridge. 60 Egyptian Museum, Cairo. 61l Ny Carlsberg Glyptotek, Copenhagen; m Staatliche Museen, Berlin/Hirmer Verlag München; r John G. Ross/Newsweek Books Picture Collection/Laurie Platt Winfrey, Inc. 62 BM. 66 Roland & Sabrina Michaud/Woodfin Camp & Associates. 69tl Paolo Koch/Photo Researchers; tr, b Jehangir Gazdar/Woodfin Camp & Associates. 71 The British Library (**BL**)/Michael Holford. 73 C.M. Dixon Colour Photo Library. 76 © Raghubir Singh 1972. 79l Michael Holford; r Cultural Relics Bureau, Beijing, and MMA. 80 The Seattle Art Museum, Eugene Fuller Memorial Collection. 82 Collection of The National Palace Museum, Taipei, Taiwan, Republic of China. 84 © 1988 Dallas & Heaton/TSW-CLICK/Chicago. 85 Pang Wei-liang/Xinhua News Agency. 87 Robert Harding Picture Library.

Unit II: 92 Michael Holford. 93l Giraudon/AR; r Wall painting from the Villa of the Mysteries. Scala/AR. 94 R. Manley/Shostal Associates. 97 Fresco, Palace of Knossos. Archaeologisches Museum Stierspringer/Hirmer Verlag München. 99l MMA, Dodge Fund, 1907 (07.96); m, r BM. 104 MMA, Rogers Fund, 1917 (17.230.14a, b). 107 BM. 109l Robert Frerck/Odyssey Productions; r Archaeological Museum, Piraeus/Ekdotike Athenon S.A. 110l © Caecilia H. Moessner; m BM; r Museo Nazionale, Taranto. Giraudon/AR. 113 MMA, Catharine Lorillard Wolfe Fund, 1931 (31.45). 115 (detail) "La Battaglia di Alessandro." Museo Nazionale, Naples. Scala/AR. 120 Josephine Powell. 122 Emmett Bright/Photo Researchers. 124 Giraudon/AR. 126l Courtesy, Soprintendenza Archeologica di Ostia; r Stela of Lucius Erennius Praesens. Musée Calvet, Avignon. 132 (detail) Mosaic of Dar Bue Ammera, from Aliten. Musée des Antiquities, Tripoli. Pierre Belzeaux/Rapho Agence/Photo Researchers. 134 © M. Grimoldi. 137 BM. 140 Josephine Powell. 142 Robert Frerck/Odyssey Productions. 144b Thomas B. Hollyman/Photo Researchers. 149l MMA, Rogers Fund, 1903 (03.14.13); m, r Museo Nazionale, Naples/Fotografia Foglia, photographer. 150 Michael Holford. 157 Claus Hansmann, München.

Unit III: 164l MS. Canon. Misc. 378, f. 84. Bodleian Library, Oxford; b Foto Biblioteca Vaticana. 165bl Sonia Halliday; m Ms Royal 14 E IV fol. 59. BL; br Robert Frerck/Odyssey Productions. 166 Alon Reininger/Contact Press Images. 168 Constantinople, *Notitia Dignitatum*, 1436. MS. Canon. Misc. 378, f. 84. Bodleian Library, Oxford. 170l, r (details) Scala/AR. 172 K. Scholz/Shostal

Associates. 175 Camerapix, Nairobi. 176 Page from a Qur'an, late 11th c. Courtesy of The Harvard University Art Museums (Arthur M. Sackler Museum). Private collection. 178 MMA, The James F. Ballard Collection, Gift of James F. Ballard, 1922. Otto Nelson, photographer. 180*l* From an Ottoman illuminated manuscript, late 16th c. The Granger Collection, NY; *r* Astrolabe, 1291. MMA, Bequest of Edward C. Moore, 1891. The Edward C. Moore Collection (91.1.535 a-h). 187 C.M. Dixon Colour Photo Library. 191 Foto Biblioteca Vaticana. 192 Lindisfarne Gospels, Northumbria, c. 1700. Initial page at the beginning of the Gospel according to Saint John. Cotton MS. Nero D, IV. BL. 193 BM. 195*r* Metz Cathedral. Giraudon/AR. 199*l* Statens Historiska Museet, Stockholm/Werner Forman Archive; *m* Viking Ship Museum, Bygdøy, Oslo/Werner Forman Archive; *r* © University Museum of National Antiquities, Oslo. Eirik Irgens Johnsen, photographer. 206 Luttrell Psalter, AD 1335-40. Add. MS 42130, f. 171. BM. 209 (detail) #E 2432-c, Cod 2549, fol. 164. Österreichische Nationalbibliothek, Vienna. 210 *Hours of the Virgin*, MS 399 (September). Pierpont Morgan Library, NY. 212 (detail) *Ethiques politiques et économiques d'Aristote*. Ms. 927, fol. 145 R. Musée Municipal, Rouen. Giraudon/AR. 217 *Livre de la vie active des réligieuses de l'Hôtel-Dieu*, 15th c. Musée de l'Assistance Publique, Paris. 219*bl* Sonia Halliday; *br* Michael Holford. 221 (detail) Michael Holford. 225 Pietro di Pavia illuminating an initial. *Naturalis historia*, Pliny, 1389. MS E. 24 inf., f. 332. Biblioteca Ambrosiana, Milan. 226 MS 5073, fol. 140 v Bibliothèque Arsenal, Paris. Giraudon/AR. 227 *Heures de la Bienheureuse Vierge Marie* (November). Dutuit B. 37, fol. 15r. Petit Palais, Paris/Bulloz. 230*l* Bildarchiv Foto Marburg/AR; *r* R. Manley/Shostal Associates. 234 Painting by Antoine Dufour, c. 1505. Musée Dobree, Nantes. Giraudon/AR. 237 Add. MS 4838, The Article of Barons, 1215. BL. 238 Reproduced by gracious permission of Her Majesty Queen Elizabeth II. 241 Sonia Halliday. 243 MS 13076-77, FOL 24verso. © Bibliothèque royale Albert 1er, Brussels. 245 *Chronique d'Angleterre*, Jean de Wavrin. Royal 14 E IV fol. 59. Flemish, late 15th c. BL. 249 Portrait by M. Sittow, National Portrait Gallery, London. 253 TASS/Sovfoto.

Unit IV: 258*l, t* Lee Boltin Picture Library; *r* (detail) *The Tale of Genji*. Scroll, 12th c. Artist unknown. Tokugawa Art Museum, Nagoya. Bradley Smith Collection from Laurie Platt Winfrey, Inc. 259*bl, m* Lee Boltin Picture Library; *tl* The Board of Trustees of the Royal Armouries, London; *r* Courtesy Museum of New Mexico. Neg. No. 143771. 260 (detail) Edimedia. 263 From a Ch'ing album. OE 5 a fol. p. 31/RcC 1486. Bibliothèque Nationale, Paris. 264 Wan-go H.C. Weng. 266*l* "Pine and Mountains in Spring," Mi Fei. National Palace Museum, Taipei, Taiwan, Republic of China; *r* Courtesy of The Harvard University Art Museums (The Arthur M. Sackler Museum). Gift of Ernest B. Dane, 1892 and Helen P. Dane. 268 By courtesy of the Board of Trustees of the Victoria and Albert Museum, London. 272*b* Wan-go H.C. Weng/Collection of the National Palace Museum, Taipei, Taiwan, Republic of China. 276 Benrido Company, Ltd., Kyoto. 278 The Board of Trustees of the Royal Armouries, London. 280 Courtesy of the Freer Gallery of Art, Smithsonian Institution, Washington, D.C. (67.20). 281 © 1988 Bob Brudd/TSW-CLICK/Chicago. 284 Ric Ergenbright. 287 Robert Ivey/Ric Ergenbright Photography. 291 Reproduced by permission of The India Office Library (BL). 292 (detail) India, Golconda or northern Madras. Painting on cotton, 1630–1640 A.D. The Brooklyn Museum (14.719.2), Museum Collection Fund. 295 Shostal Associates. 298 Norman Prince. 301 MMA, The Michael C. Rockefeller Memorial Collection, Gift of Nelson A. Rockefeller, 1972 (1978.412.310). 303*r* Kal Muller/Woodfin Camp & Associates. 307*l* Lee Boltin Picture Library; *r* Bibliothèque Nationale, Paris. 310 Gemini Smith Inc. La Jolla © Bradley Smith. 312 Courtesy of Museum of the American Indian, Heye Foundation, NY. 313 Gemini Smith Inc. La Jolla © Bradley Smith. 315 MS. Arch. Seldon A.1, f. 2. Bodleian Library, Oxford.

Unit V: 320*bl* (detail) "Crucifixion," Giotto, Padua, Capella Scrovegni. Scala/AR; *t* (detail) "Porto del Paradiso," Ghiberti. Florence. Scala/AR; *br* Giraudon/AR. 321*m* John R. Freeman & Co., Ltd.; *r* (detail) "Flowers and Baluser, Motifs," 17th c. CAT #77. Philadelphia Museum of Art. Gift of Mrs. Frances P. Garvan. Eric Mitchell, photographer. 322 "Copy of Map of Catena," Florence 1490, S. Buonsignori. Museum of Florence. Scala/AR. 323 Bibliothèque de l'Institut de France. 326 "The School of Athens,"

1509–11, Raphael. Stanza della Segnatura, Vatican. Scala/AR. 327*l* "Battista Sforza," Piero della Francesca. Uffizi. Scala/AR; *r* "Federico da Montefeltro, Duke of Urbino," Piero della Francesca. Uffizi. Scala/AR. 330 "Story of St. Peter: Resurrection of Tabitha, and Healing of the Cripple," c. 1425, Masaccio. Brancacci Chapel, S. Maria del Carmine, Florence. Scala/AR. 332 "Pieta," 1497–9, Michelangelo. St. Peter's Rome. Scala/AR. 333*l* "David," 1501–4, Michelangelo. Accademia, Florence. Scala/AR; *r* Scala/AR. 334 "Mona Lisa," 1503, Leonardo da Vinci. Musée de Louvre. Scala/AR. 337*t* Painting by Ridolfo Ghirlandaio (attr.). Museo Navale, Pegli. Scala/AR; *b* Michael Holford. 338 "Treatise of Piero de Cresienzi," end 15th c. *Le Livre de Rustican des Proiffiz rurals*. BL. 340 The Granger Collection, NY. 344 Courtesy, Dr. Henning Schleifenbaum, Siegen, Germany. 347 Giraudon/AR. 348 *Martin Luther*, 1526, Lucas Cranach the Elder. Nationalmuseum, Stockholm. 352 Painting from studio of Hans Holbein. By kind permission of Warwick Castle, England. 353 Musée Condé, Chantilly. Giraudon/AR. 357*l* Bibliothèque publique et universitaire, Geneva; *r* Papal Coronation of Pius II, 3 Sept., 1458, Siena. Duomo, Libreria Piccolomini. Scala/AR. 359*l* Museo della Scienza, Florence. Scala/AR; *r* Gal. 48 c. 29v. Biblioteca Nazionale Centrale, Florence/Guido Sansoni, photographer. 360 Courtesy, Museum of Our National Heritage, Lexington. 363 Cat. #2183, Anon. Government Art Collection, London. 366 R. Manley/Shostal Associates. 369*l* Reproduced by permission of Patrimonio Nacional. Amplicaciones y Reproducciones "MAS"; *r* Portrait by Alonson Sanchez. © Museo del Prado, Madrid. 370 Museo-Casa Greco. Amplicaciones y Reproducciones "MAS." 373 "The Little Street," Johannes Vermeer. Rijksmuseum-Stichting, Amsterdam. 374 (detail) "Flowers and Baluser, Motifs," 17th c. CAT #77. Philadelphia Museum of Art. Gift of Mrs. Francis P. Garvan. Eric Mitchell, photographer. 375 "The Nightwatch," Rembrandt. Rijksmuseum-Stichting, Amsterdam. 376 "Young Woman with a Water Jug," Johannes Vermeer. MMA, Gift of Henry G. Marquand, 1889. Marquand Collection (89.15.21). 378 Painting by Philippe de Campaigne. Musée de Louvre. Giraudon/AR.

Unit VI: 386*tl* By kind permission of the Marquess of Tavistock, and the Trustees of the Bedford Estates; *b* "Self-portrait with first wife Isabella Brandt," Peter Paul Rubens. Alte Pinakothek Munchen; *tr* Painting by H. Rigaud. Musée de Louvre. Scala/AR. 387*l* New York Public Library, Slavonic Division; *m* (detail) "Die Tafelrunde," J. Tietze. Bildarchiv Preussischer Kulturbesitz; *r* Musée Carnavalet, Paris/Jean-Loup Charmet. 388 "Armada Portrait," George Gower (attr.), c. 1588. By kind permission of the Marquess of Tavistock, and the Trustees of the Bedford Estates. 391 Reproduced by permission of The India Office Library (BL). 392 "Monteverdi," Hendrik Vroom. Tiroler Landesmuseum Ferdinandeum. 394–5 Visscher's View of London, MAP L85c no. 7 c.l. By permission of the Folger Shakespeare Library. 396 Portrait by Chardos. National Portrait Gallery, London. 399 Courtesy, Massachusetts State Archives. 401 Historical Pictures Service, Chicago. 404 S. Vidler/Leo de Wys Inc. 408 Giraudon/AR. 411 Painting by H. Rigaud. Musée de Louvre. Scala/AR. 412 Scala/AR. 415 "Peter the Great," Russian School. Rijksmuseum-Stichting, Amsterdam. 416 New York Public Library, Slavonic Division. 418 Bibliothèque Nationale, Paris/Bulloz. 421 Painting by Möller. Kunsthistorisches Museum, Vienna. 423 "Die Wachtparade," Daniel Chodowiecki. Staatliche Museen, Berlin/Bildarchiv Preussischer Kulturbesitz. Jörg P. Anders, photographer. 427 "Die Tafelrunde," J. Tietze. Bildarchiv Preussischer Kulturbesitz. 430 "First Reading of L'Orphelin de Chine at the home of Mme Geoffrin." Musée des Beaux-Arts, Rouen. Giraudon/AR. 432 Courtesy, Wellcome Institute, London. 433 "Mozart as a Child with his Father and his Sister," Louis Carmotelle. Musée Condé, Chantilly. Giraudon/AR. 434 From a medallion by Tassiel; engraved by W. Hott. The Bettmann Archive. 437 Painting by Groot, 1745. Leningrad Russian Museum/Novosti Press Agency. 444*l* Independence National Historical Park Collection; *tr, br* Robert Llewellyn. 448 "Pillage des Invalides," J.-B. Lallemand fils. Musée Carnavalet, Paris/Bulloz. 451 "Le Serment du Jeu de Paume," d'après Jacques-Louis David. Musée Carnavalet, Paris/Bulloz. 452*l* "La Maraichère," Jacques-Louis David. Musée des Beaux-Arts, Lyon; *r* Painting by Gautier d'Agoty. Bulloz. 456 "Execution of Louis XVI, January 21, 1793," anon. Musée Carnavalet/Gemini Smith Inc. La Jolla © Bradley Smith. 459 "Napoleon in His Study," Jacques-Louis David. National Gallery of Art, Washington, D.C. Samuel H. Kress Collection. 462 Bibliothèque Nationale, Paris/Jean-Loup Charmet. 463 © Museo del Prado, Madrid.

Unit VII: 470*tl* Kunsthistorisches Museum, Vienna; *bl* Michael Holford; *tr* Organization of American States; *br* (detail) Historisches Museen der Stadt Wien. 471*tl* © Don Hamilton Photographer; *bl* Culver Pictures; *tr* The Bettmann Archive; *br* 48.593 "Lady with a Parasol and a Small Child on a Sunlit Hillside," Pierre Auguste Renoir. French, 1841–1919. Oil on canvas, 47.0 × 56.2 cm. (18½ × 22 in.). Bequest of John R. Spaulding. Courtesy, Museum of Fine Arts, Boston. 472 Ann Ronan Picture Library, Somerset, England. 474 Henlow Enclosure, from a map by John Goodman Maxwell, 1798. Bedfordshire County Record Office, England. 477*l, r* Mansell Collection. 480 Ann Ronan Picture Library, Somerset, England. 485 Illustration appended to British Parliamentary Commission's report on work in mines, 1844. 486 Mansell Collection. 490 "Redoute paree am 10. November 1814," J.N. Hochle. Österreichische Nationalbibliothek, Vienna. 491 Copyright reserved to Her Majesty Queen Elizabeth II. 494 (detail) "Court Ball in the Ceremonial Ballroom, New Year," Wilhelm Gauss. Historisches Museen der Stadt Wien. 496 National Portrait Gallery, London. 498*l* Bodleian Library, Oxford; *mt* Portrait by Eugène Delacroix. Jean-Loup Charmet; *mb* Mansell Collection; *r* "Wanderer über dem Nebelmeer," Caspar David Friedrich. Hamburger Kunsthalle. 500 The Granger Collection, NY. 501 Organization of American States, Washington, D.C. 506 "Am 13. Marz 1848 vor dem Landhause," J. Albert. Historiches Museen der Stadt Wien. 510 The Bridgeman Art Library/AR. 512 "Inauguration of the Suez Canal," 1869, Edouard Riou. Compiègne Chateau/Bulloz. 516 The Bettmann Archive. 517 "The Third-Class Carriage," Honoré Daumier. MMA, Bequest of Mrs. H.O. Havemeyer, 1929. The H.O. Havemeyer Collection (29.100.129). 520*r* Portrait by Francesco Hayez. Giraudon/AR. 522*b* The Bettmann Archive. 524 The Granger Collection, NY. 527 Historical Pictures Service, Chicago. 528 Library of Congress. Alexander Gardner, photographer. 532 "Celebrations in India 1897," M.E. Caddy. The Bridgeman Art Library. 538 "Battle of Omdurman, 6:30 A.M., Sept. 2, 1898." ET Archive Ltd. 541 Lawrence Impey, Hampshire, England. 542 (detail) "Scots Guards, attached to Guards Camel Corps, Nile Expedition, 1885"; painting by Lt. Frank Baden-Powell. National Army Museum, London. 545 Peabody Museum of Salem. 547 Jean-Loup Charmet. 548 "Commodore Perry Landing in Japan," Tsukioki Yoshitoshi. BM. 549 Exterior of the Tomioka silk reeling factory, c. 1870. Tsuneo Tamba Collection, Yokahama, Japan. Japan Information Bureau, London. 551 The Granger Collection, NY. 556 Musée Toulouse-Lautrec, Albi. 557*l, r* Association des Amis de Jacques Henri Lartigue, Paris. 559 Science Museum, London/Michael Holford. 561 From *Milestones of History* (George Weidenfeld and Nicolson Ltd., publishers). Reproduced with permission. 564 Brown Brothers. 565 Mary Evans Picture Library/Photo Researchers. 566 Museum of London. 569*l* (detail) "Gladioli," 1893, Claude Monet. French 1840–1926. Oil on canvas. 22" × 32½". The Detroit Institute of Arts, City of Detroit (21.71); *r* "The Starry Night," Vincent van Gogh 1889. Oil on canvas, 29" × 36¼". Collection, The Museum of Modern Art, NY. Acquired through the Lillie P. Bliss Bequest. 570 National Baseball Hall of Fame and Museum, Inc. 573 Mary Evans Picture Library/Photo Researchers. 574 "Sirk-Ecke," Maximilian Lenz, 1900. Historisches Museen der Stadt Wien.

Unit VIII: 580*b* "L'Après-midi d'un Faune: Portrait of Nijinsky as the Faun, 1912," Leon Bakst. Wadsworth Atheneum, Hartford. From the Serge Lifar Collection. The Ella Gallup Sumner and Mary Catlin Sumner Collection; *r* Robert Frerck/Odyssey Productions. 581*tl* (detail) TASS/Sovfoto; *bl* Jean-Loup Charmet; *m* Courtesy, Royal Air Force Museum, England; *tr* Copyright 1945 Time Inc. Reprinted by permission; *br* United Nations Photo, J. Isaac. 583 *Le Petit Journal*, July 19. Jean-Loup Charmet. 583 © Librairie Larousse. 584 Culver Pictures. 587*l, m* ET Archive Ltd. 587*r*, 589 Trustees of the Imperial War Museum (IWM). 590 "Over the Top," John Nash. IWM. 591 "Gassed," John Singer Sargent. IWM. 594 IWM. 597 "Peace Conference," Orpen. IWM. 602 Painting by Axenov. TASS/Sovfoto. 604 "Volga's Barge Haulers," 1870–73, I. Repin. Novosti Press Agency. 607*l* Brown Brothers; *r* © The Forbes Magazine Collection, NY. Larry Stein, photographer. 609 Popperfoto. 611 H. Roger-Viollet. 612 New York Public Library Collection. 617, 618 TASS/Sovfoto. 619 From *Art of the October Revolution*, Mikhail Guerman (Aurora Publishers, Leningrad). Re-

produced with permission. 622 The Bettmann Archive. 625 "The Spinner," 1946, Margaret Bourke-White, Life Magazine © Time Inc. 628 The Bettmann Archive. 629 Royal Geographical Society Picture Library, London. 631 Zionist Archives and Library, NY. 633 "Zapatistas," José Clemente Orozco, 1931. Oil on canvas, 45" × 55". Collection, The Museum of Modern Art, NY. Given anonymously. 634 Peter Menzel. 637 Jack Wilkes, Life Magazine © Time Inc. 639 PRC/Sovfoto. 642 "KPA Versammlung, 1932," Hans Grundig. Staatliche Museen zu Berlin (DDR), Nationalgalerie. 645*t* © Heritage Press/Underwood, Collinge & Associates; *b* Hake's Americana & Collectibles, York, PA. 646 "Wassily" Chair, Marcel Breuer, 1902–1981. Courtesy of The Harvard University Art Museums (Busch-Reisinger). Anonymous Gift. 647 UPI/Bettmann Newsphotos. 648 Courtesy of the William Ransom Hogan Jazz Archives, Tulane University. 651 Courtesy, Conservative Research Department, London. 652 Brown Brothers. 654 Wide World Photos. 660 "Guernica," Pablo Picasso, 1937. © Museo del Prado, Madrid. © ARS, New York/SPADEM, Paris 1987. 661 The Bettmann Archive. 664 Painting by Junghaus. U.S. Air Force Art Collection. 667 Courtesy, *Richmond Times-Dispatch*. 668 "The Withdrawal from Dunkirk," Charles Cundall. IWM. 669 © 1987 Erich Lessing-Culture and Fine Arts Archives/Magnum. 670 Mansell Collection. 673*l* Reprinted with permission; *r* C. Golding. 674 National Archives. 678 "Buchenwald, 1945," Margaret Bourke-White, Life Magazine © Time Inc. 680 Polish Institute and Sikorski Museum/A.C. Cooper Ltd. photographer. 683 Wide World Photos.

Unit IX: 688*l* Bundesarchiv, Koblenz; *t* UPI/Bettmann Newsphotos; *b* "Haitian landscape," Joseph-Jean Gilles. Museum of Modern Art of Latin America; *r* Harry Redl/Black Star. 689*l* Thierry Rannou/Gamma-Liaison; *r* A. Suau/Black Star. 690 Franklin D. Roosevelt Library, Hyde Park, NY. 692 Wide World Photos. 693 Bundesarchiv, Koblenz. 694 Owen Franken/Sygma. 697, 700*l, r*, 703 Wide World Photos. 704*r* Suzanne Engelmann/Shostal Associates. 708 Milt & Joan Mann/Cameramann International. 713 Peter Jordan/Gamma-Liaison. 714 Bouvet/Gamma-Liaison. 715 Rothco Cartoons. 717 Wide World Photos. 719*l* Chris Niedenthal/Black Star; *r* By permission of the Colorado Springs *Gazette Telegraph*. 723 N. Rhyzhkov/Gamma-Liaison. 728 Milt & Joan Mann/Cameramann International. 730 Diego Goldberg/Sygma. 731 H. Yamagushi/Gamma-Liaison. 734 Henri Cartier-Bresson/Magnum. 735 Harry Redl/Black Star. 740 Santosh Basak/Gamma-Liaison. 742 A. Hernandez/Sygma. 744 Gamma-Liaison. 745*l* Wide World Photos; *r* Tom Lubin/Sygma. 748 Mark Kauffman, Life Magazine © Time Inc. 750 Eliot Elisofon Archives/Museum of African Art (Smithsonian Institution). 751 Camerapix/Gamma-Liaison. 756*l* Abbas/Magnum. *r* A. Tannenbaum/Sygma. 759*l* Alain Nogues/Sygma. 760*r* Wide World Photos. 761 Bill Strode/Woodfin Camp & Associates. 762 Al-Rabas/Gamma-Liaison. 766 Betty Crowell. *tr* Medford Taylor/Black Star. 770 Dan Ford Connolly/Picture Group. 771 Jim Merrithew/Picture Group. 773 Peter Menzel. 774 Tony Linck/Shostal Associates. 776 Bill Wassman/The Stock Market. 777 Girard Foundation Collection, Museum of International Folk Art, a unit of the Museum of New Mexico, Santa Fe. © Cradoc Bagshaw. 778 Jerry Bigwood/Gamma-Liaison. 782 NASA. 784*bl* Sygma; *tl* Greenwood/Gamma Liaison; *tr* NASA; *br* Ron Siddle/Sygma. 786*l* Hank Morgan/Rainbow; *r* Rothco Cartoons. 788 Benson/Gamma-Liaison. 789 Hemsey/Gamma-Liaison. 791 Kevin Horan/Picture Group. 795 TASS/Sovfoto. 797 J.L. Atlan/Sygma. 769 *bl* Copyright Time Inc. Reprinted by permission.

Lesson Planner Credits

p. T72 From *History of Rome* by Michael Grant, © 1978, published by Scribner. p. T270 From "When Yale was given to SUMNEROLOGY" by William Lyon Phelps, © 1925, published by Literary Digest International Book Review, Vol. III, page 661. p. T346 From *Communist China: The Politics of Student Opposition* by Dennis J. Doolin, © 1964, published by Stanford (Hoover Institution). p. T353 Quoted in *Africa* by Fred Burke, © 1970, published by Houghton Mifflin Company.

Lesson Planner edited and produced by Book Production Systems, Inc., San Diego, California.